standard catalog of
BUICK

1903-1990

Edited by Mary Sieber & Ken Buttolph

FIRST EDITION

© 1995 by Krause Publications, Inc.

Published by

 **krause publications**

700 E. State Street • Iola, WI 54990-0001
Telephone: 715/445-2214

Please call or write for our free catalog of automotive publications. Our toll-free number to place an order or obtain a free catalog is 800-258-0929 or please use our regular business telephone 715-445-2214 for editorial comment and further information.

Library of Congress Catalog Number: 91-61302
ISBN: 0-87341-173-0

Printed in the United States of America

First Printing September 1991
Second Printing April 1995

Reprinted with Updated Prices 1998

CATALOG STAFF

PUBLISHER:	John A. Gunnell
EDITORS:	Mary Sieber & Ken Buttolph
DATA PROCESSING:	Bruce Denny
COVER DESIGN:	Paul Tofte
BOOKS MANAGER:	Patricia Klug

CONTENTS

FOREWORD

Traditionally, the concept behind Krause Publications' Standard Catalogs is to compile massive amounts of information about motor vehicles and present it in a standard format which the hobbyist, collector or professional dealer can use to answer some commonly asked questions.

Those questions include: What year, make and model is the vehicle? What did it sell for new? How rare is it? What is special about it? Some answers are provided by photos and others by the fact-filled text.

Chester L. Krause of Krause Publications is responsible for the overall concept of creating the Standard Catalog series covering American automobiles. David V. Brownell, editor of *Special-Interest Autos*, undertook preliminary work on the concept while serving as editor of *Old Cars Weekly* in the 1970s. Then editor John A. Gunnell assumed the project in 1978. The first Standard Catalog, covering postwar models (1946-1975) was published in 1982, while Beverly Rae Kimes continued writing and researching *The Standard Catalog of American Cars (1805-1942)*, which was published in 1985. In 1987 *The Standard Catalog of Light-Duty American Trucks (1900-1986)*, was published by John Gunnell, while the second edition of the 1946-1975 volume was printed. In 1988, the 1805-1942 volume by Kimes appeared in second edition form. Also in 1988, James M. Flammang authored *The Standard Catalog of American Cars (1976-1986)*, which went into its second edition in 1990. Currently the four-volume set of Standard Catalogs enjoys good sales in the automotive/truck collector hobby, and provides a wealth of detailed information that car and truck collectors, hobbyists, restorers and investors will not find from any other publishing house.

The scope of these catalogs has been to cover the major manufacturers, which have survived into the 1990s: Chrysler, Ford and General Motors as well as companies they have absorbed and companies no longer with us today, independent companies such as Checker, Hudson, Kaiser-Frazer, Nash, Packard, Studebaker and Willys are included in the earlier catalogs, as well as some 200 producers of low-volume nameplates from Airscoot to Yenko. In each case, the data compiled encompasses a physical description; list of known equipment and original specifications; technical data; historical footnotes and appraisal of the car's current "ballpark value."

In each catalog, all compilations were made by an experienced editorial team consisting of the automotive staff of Krause Publications and numerous contributors who are recognized experts on a certain marque or specific area of automotive history. A major benefit of combining teamwork with expertise has been the gathering of many significant facts about each model.

No claims are made about the catalogs being history textbooks or encyclopedias. Nor are they repair manuals or "bibles" for motor vehicle enthusiasts. They are, rather, intended as a contribution to the pursuit of greater knowledge about the many wonderful automobiles and trucks built in the United States since 1805. They are much larger in size, broader in scope and more deluxe in format than any previously published collector's guides, buyers' digests or pricing guides.

The long-range goal of Krause Publications is to make all of these catalogs as nearly perfect as possible. At the same time, we expect such catalogs will always raise new questions and bring forth new facts that were not previously unearthed in the countless hours of research by our team. All contributors are requested to maintain an ongoing file of new research, corrections and additional photos which can be used to refine and expand future editions.

We thank the editors and contributors to the three volume *Standard Catalog of American Cars* for providing much of the material herein. For it is through their research and editing effort that we produce this *Catalog of Buick*, with an assurance that most of the information which we've combined herewith from those three catalogs is accurate and well-researched. Additionally, we have included some of the best Buick articles from past issues of *Old Cars Weekly*, authored by experts in the field. Should you have access to expanded information that you wish to share, please don't hestitate to contact the editors, in care of Krause Publications, *Standard Catalog of Buick*, 700 East State Street, Iola, WI 54990.

Other catalogs currently available are: *Standard Catalog of American Cars 1805-1942; Standard Catalog of American Cars 1946-1975; Standard Catalog of American Cars 1976-1986; Standard Catalog of Light-Duty American Trucks 1900-1986; Standard Catalog of Chevrolet, Standard Catalog of Chrysler* and *Standard Catalog of Ford*. For ordering information and current prices write: Krause Publications, 700 East State Street, Iola, WI 54990.

ABBREVIATIONS

A/C	Air conditioning
A.L.A.M.	Assoc. of Licensed Automobile Mfgs.
Adj.	Adjustable
Aero.	Fastback
AM, FM, AM/FM	Radio types
Amp.	Amperes
Approx.	Approximate
Auto.	Automatic
Auxil.	Auxiliary
Avail.	Available
Avg.	Average
BxS	Bore x Stroke
Base	Base (usually lowest-priced) model
Bbl.	Barrel (carburetor)
B.H.P.	Brake horsepower
BSW	Black sidewall (tire)
Brk/Brkwd/Brkwood	Brookwood
Brdcl.	Broadcloth
Bus.	Business (i.e. Business Coupe)
C-A	Carryall
C.C.	Close-coupled
Cabr.	Cabrielet
Carb.	Carburetor
Capr.	Caprice
Cass.	Cassette (tape player)
Cav.	Cavalier
CB	Citizens Band (radio)
Celeb.	Celebrity
CEO	Chief Executive Officer
CFI	Cross Fire (fuel) Injection
Chvt.	Chevette
C.I.D.	Cubic inch displacement
Cit.	Citation
Clb	Club (Club Coupe)
Clth.	Cloth-covered roof
Col.	Colonnade (coupe body style)
Col.	Column (shift)
Conv/Conv.	Convertible
Conv. Sed.	Convertible Sedan
Corp Limo	Corporate Limousine
Cpe	Coupe
Cpe P.U.	Coupe Pickup
C.R.	Compression ratio
Crsr.	Cruiser
Cu. In.	Cubic Inch (displacement)
Cust.	Custom
Cyl.	Cylinder
DeL.	DeLuxe
DFRS	Dual facing rear seats
Dia.	Diameter
Disp.	Displacement
Dr.	Door
Ea.	Each
E.D.	Enclosed Drive
E.F.I.	Electronic Fuel Injection
E.W.B.	Extended Wheelbase
Eight	Eight-cylinder engine
8-tr.	Eight-track
Encl.	Enclosed
EPA	Environmental Protection Agency
Equip.	Equipment
Est. Wag.	Estate Wagon
Exc.	Except
Exec.	Executive
F.	Forward (3F - 3 forward speeds)
F.W.D.	Four-wheel drive

Fam.	Family
Fml.	Formal
"Four"	Four-cylinder engine
4WD	Four-wheel drive
4-dr.	Four-door
4-spd.	Four-speed (transmission)
4V	Four-barrel carburetor
FP	Factory Price
Frsm.	Foursome
Frt.	Front
FsBk	Fastback
Ft.	Foot/feet
FWD	Front wheel drive
G.B.	Greenbrier
GBR	Glass-belted radial (tire)
Gal.	Gallon
GM	General Motors (Corporation)
GT	Gran Turismo
G.R.	Gear Ratio
H	Height
H.B.	Hatchback
H.D.	Heavy Duty
HEI	High Energy Ignition
H.O.	High-output
H.P.	Horsepower
HT/HT Hdtp.	Hardtop
Hr.	Hour
Hwg.	Highway
I.	Inline
I.D.	Identification
Imp	Impala
In.	Inches
Incl.	Included or Including
Int.	Interior
King/Kingwd.	Kingswood
Lan	Landau (coupe body style)
Lb. or Lbs.	Pound-feet (torque)
LH	Left hand
Lift.	Liftback (body style)
Limo	Limousine
LPO	Limited production option
Ltd.	Limited
Lthr. Trm.	Leather Trim
L.W.B.	Long Wheelbase
Mag.	Wheel style
Mast.	Master
Max.	Maximum
MFI	Multi-port Fuel Injection
M.M.	Millimeters
Monte.	Monte Carlo
MPG	Miles per gallon
MPH	Miles per hour
Mstr.	Master
N/A	Not available (or not applicable)
NC	No charge
N.H.P.	Net horsepower
No.	Number
Notch or N.B.	Notchback
OHC	Overhead cam (engine)
OHV	Overhead valve (engine)
O.L.	Overall length
OPEC	Organization of Petroleum Exporting Countries
Opt.	Optional
OSRV	Outside rear view
O.W. or O/W	Opera window
OWL	Outline White Letter (tire)

Oz.	Ounce
P	Passenger
Park/Parkwd	Parkwood
PFI	Port fuel injection
Phae.	Phaeton
Pkg.	Package (e.g. option pkg)
Prod.	Production
Pwr.	Power
R	Reverse
RBL	Raised black letter (tire)
Rbt.	Runabout
Rds.	Roadster
Reg.	Regular
Remote	Remote control
Req.	Requires
RH	Right-hand drive
Roch.	Rochester (carburetor)
R.P.M.	Revolutions per minute
RPO	Regular production option
R.S. or R/S	Rumbleseat
RV	Recreational vehicle
RVL	Raised white letter (tire)
S	Gm lowtrim model designation
S.A.E.	Society of Automotive Engineers
SBR	Steel-belted radials
Sed.	Sedan
SFI	Sequential fuel injection
"Six"	Six-cylinder engine
S.M.	Side Mount
Spd.	Speed
Spec.	Special
Spt.	Sport
Sq. In.	Square inch
SR	Sunroof
SS	Super Sport
Sta. Wag.	Station wagon
Std.	Standard
Sub.	Suburban
S.W.B.	Short Wheelbase
Tach.	Tachometer
Tax.	Taxable (horsepower)
TBI	Throttle body (fuel) injection
Temp.	Temperature
THM	Turbo Hydramatic (transmission)
3S	Three-seat
Trans.	Transmission
Trk.	Trunk
2-Dr.	Two-door
2 V	Two-barrel (carburetor)
2WD	Two-wheel drive
Univ.	Universal
Utl.	Utility
V.	Venturi (carburetor)
V-6, V-8	Vee-type engine
VIN	Vehicle Identification Number
W	With
W/O	Without
Wag.	Wagon
w (2w)	Window (two window)
W.B.	Wheelbase
Woodie	Wood-bodied car
WLT	White-lettered tire
WSW	White sidewall (tire)
W.W.	Whitewalls
W. Whl.	Wire wheel

PHOTO CREDITS

Whenever possible, throughout the Catalog, we have strived to picture all cars with photographs that show them in their most original form. All photos gathered from reliable outside sources have an alphabetical code following the caption which indicates the photo source. An explanation of these codes is given below. Additional photos from Krause Publications file are marked accordingly. With special thanks to the editors of the previous *Standard Catalogs of American Cars* for their original research and obtaining many of these photos of Chevrolet over the years.

(AA)	Applegate & Applegate
(CH)	Chevrolet
(CP)	Crestline Publishing
(GM)	General Motors
(HAC)	Henry Austin Clark, Jr.
(HFM)	Henry Ford Museum
(IMSC)	Indianapolis Motor Speedway Corporation

(JAC)	John A. Conde
(JG)	John Gunnell
(NAHC)	National Automotive History Collection
(OCW)	Old Cars Weekly
(PH)	Phil Hall
(WLB)	William L. Bailey

INTRODUCTION

This new standard catalog, focusing on the Buick Motor Division of General Motors, is a compilation of photos, articles, specifications tables and current value listings for all Buick models. As such, the introduction to this book should recognize the valued contributions of writers and historians whose work is included in its pages.

Realizing that many automotive hobbyists have a preference for a specific brand (marque) of cars or various marques built by a single corporation, it seemed logical that a catalog formatted along those lines whould be appealing. Therefore, the editors were asked to handle the organization of such a catalog from material existing at Krause Publications.

The primary source of photos showing the styling and features of Buick Motor Divsion automobiles was the *Old Cars* photo archives, a vast collection containing over 14,000 pictures, advertisements and illustrations of automobiles.

This archives includes automakers' publicity stills, photos obtained from specialized vendors such as Applegate & Applegate, pictures taken at hobby shows by the *Old Cars* staff and news photos snapped at thousands of hobby events. Photos were also obtained through the Buick Motor Division of GM. In addition, where photographs were unavailable, illustrations from sales and technical literature and advertisements were used to show what the cars looked like when they were new.

This catalog begins with a selection of informative histories and articles which have appeared in *Old Cars* since the launch of the weekly tabloid in 1971, as well as selected articles and photos reprinted from the Buick Club of America's official publication, *The Buick Bugle*. The stories were organized in a manner which provide a look at the background histories and product developments of Buick Motor Division.

Inside the catalog, you'll find almost 60 articles, some of which were first published so many years ago that they are now, themselves, considered "classics." They highlight Buick milestones from the times of the first Buick runabout to the resurrection of the Roadmaster name in 1990.

The second section of this catalog is the lengthy and detailed specifications tables which present, in standardized format, styling and engineering features of virtually all of Buick's models. You'll find engine sizes, horsepower ratings, wheelbases, measurements and tire sizes — just to name a few things.

Thanks for the gathering of these facts and figures go to the authors of three other catalogs previously published by Krause Publications: *Standard Catalog of American Cars 1805-1942* by Beverly Rae Kimes and Henry Austin Clark Jr.; *Standard Catalog of American Cars 1946-1975* by John A. Gunnell; and *Standard Catalog of American Cars 1976-1986* by James Flammang. Thanks also go to Robert Ackerson for his work in organizing the 1987-1990 specifications section.

The final element that comes into use in this catalog is the presentation of current "ballpark prices" for all Buick models from 1903 to 1984. The source for these values came from the *Old Cars Price Guide*, which is compiled as a bimonthly magazine edited by Ken Buttolph and James T. Lenzke. The prices are formatted according to Krause Publications' time-tested 1-6 condition scale, so that Buick fans who use the catalog can determine their cars' values in a variety of conditions.

MEET THE EDITORS

Ken Buttolph can't remember when he wasn't interested in old cars. From the purchase of his first car, a 1927 Nash bought in 1957 for $50, through the purchase of some 350-plus vehicles since then, he has never owned a new car. He thinks that old cars are more fun.

His present, 60-vehicle collection runs the gamut from a 1940 Buick Century convertible to a Nash Metropolitan. He currently owns six Buicks.

Ken's superior knowledge of the hobby market is reflected in the value section in this catalog. He also spent many hours locating photos and verifying model designations.

Well-known in the collector car hobby, Ken has traveled extensively in fulfillment of his duties as editor of *Old Cars Price Guide* and research editor of *Old Cars New & Marketplace*.

Ken and his 60 old cars reside north of Iola, Wis.

After spending more than five years on the editorial staff of *Old Cars News & Marketplace*, Mary Sieber moved to the driver's seat as editor of that publication in 1989. In 1991 she left *Old Cars* to pursue a different outlet for her talents as managing editor of the books division of Krause Publications.

She's still involved in the old car hobby, though, as two of her new duties included co-editing this *Standard Catalog of Buick* as well as the *Standard Catalog of Cadillac*.

Mary used her journalism experience to organize the vast amounts of material presented in this catalog as well as to edit and lay out the different sections of articles and photographs.

Mary and her husband, Arlyn, live in Iola, Wis.

INDEX TO ARTICLES

Baby Boom Era, 1946-1960

Wouldn't You Really Rather Have a Buick? 1961-1990 141

BODY STYLES

Body style designations describe the shape and character of an automobile. In earlier years automakers exhibited great imagination in coining words to name their products. This led to names that were not totally accurate. Many of those **'car words'** were taken from other fields: mythology, carriage building, architecture, railroading, and so on. Therefore, there was no 'correct' automotive meaning other than that brought about through actual use. Inconsistences have persisted into the recent period, though some of the imaginative terms of past eras have faded away. One manufacturer's 'sedan' might resemble another's 'coupe.' Some automakers have persisted in describing a model by a word different from common usage, such as Ford's label for Mustang as a 'sedan.' Following the demise of the true pillarless hardtop (two- and four-door) in the mid-1970s, various manufacturers continued to use the term 'hardtop' to describe their offerings, even though a 'B' pillar was part of the newer car's structure and the front door glass may not always have been frameless. Some took on the description 'pillared hardtop' or 'thin pillar hardtop' to define what observers might otherwise consider, essentially, a sedan. Descriptions in this catalog generally follow the manufacturers' choice of words, except when they conflict strongly with accepted usage.

One specific example of inconsistency is worth noting: the description of many hatchback models as 'three-door' and 'five-door,' even though that extra 'door' is not an entryway for people. While the 1976-1986 domestic era offered no real phaetons or roadsters in the earlier senses of the words, those designations continue to turn up now and then, too.

TWO-DOOR (CLUB) COUPE: The Club Coupe designation seems to come from club car, describing the lounge (or parlor car) in a railroad train. The early postwar club coupe combined a shorter-than-sedan body structure with the convenience of a full back seat, unlike the single-seat business coupe. That name has been used less frequently in the 1976-86 period, as most notchback two-door models (with trunk rather than hatch) have been referred to as just 'coupes.' Moreover, the distinction between two-door coupes and two-door sedans has grown fuzzy.

TWO-DOOR SEDAN: The term sedan originally described a conveyance seen only in movies today: a wheelless vehicle for one person, borne on poles by two men, one ahead and one behind. Automakers pirated the word and applied it to cars with a permanent top, seating four to seven (including driver) in a single compartment. The two-door sedan of recent times has sometimes been called a pillared coupe, or plain coupe, depending on the manufacturer's whim. On the other hand, some cars commonly referred to as coupes carry the sedan designation on factory documents.

TWO-DOOR (THREE-DOOR) HATCHBACK COUPE: Originally a small opening in the deck of a sailing ship, the term 'hatch' was later applied to airplane doors and to passenger cars with rear liftgates. Various models appeared in the early 1950s, but weather-tightness was a problem. The concept emerged again in the early 1970s, when fuel economy factors began to signal the trend toward compact cars. Technology had remedied the sealing difficulties. By the 1980s, most manufacturers produced one or more hatchback models, though the question of whether to call them 'two-door' or 'three-door' never was resolved. Their main common feature was the lack of a separate trunk. 'Liftback' coupes may have had a different rear-end shape, but the two terms often described essentially the same vehicle.

TWO-DOOR FASTBACK: By definition, a fastback is any automobile with a long, moderately curving, downward slope to the rear of the roof. This body style relates to an interest in streamlining and aerodynamics and has gone in and out of fashion at various times. Some (Mustangs for one) have grown quite popular. Others have tended to turn customers off. Certain fastbacks are, technically, two-door sedans or pillared coupes. Four-door fastbacks have also been produced. Many of these (such as Buick's late 1970s four-door Century sedan) lacked sales appeal. Fastbacks may or may not have a rear-opening hatch.

TWO-DOOR HARDTOP: The term hardtop, as used for postwar cars up to the mid-1970s, describes an automobile styled to resemble a convertible, but with a rigid metal (or fiberglass) top. In a production sense, this body style evolved after World War II, first called 'hardtop convertible.' Other generic names have included sports coupe, hardtop coupe or pillarless coupe. In the face of proposed rollover standards, nearly all automakers turned away from the pillarless design to a pillared version by 1976-77.

COLONNADE HARDTOP: In architecture, the term colonnade describes a series of columns, set at regular intervals, usually supporting an entablature, roof or series of arches. To meet Federal rollover standards in 1974 (standards that never emerged), General Motors introduced two- and four-door pillared body types with arch-like quarter windows and sandwich type roof construction. They looked like a cross between true hardtops and miniature limousines. Both styles proved popular (especially the coupe with louvered coach windows and canopy top) and the term colonnade was applied. As their 'true' hardtops disappeared, other manufacturers produced similar bodies with a variety of quarter-window shapes and sizes. These were known by such terms as hardtop coupe, pillared hardtop or opera-window coupe.

FORMAL HARDTOP: The hardtop roofline was a long-lasting fashion hit of the postwar car era. The word 'formal' can be applied to things that are stiffly conservative and follow the established rule. The limousine, being the popular choice of conservative buyers who belonged to the Establishment, was looked upon as a formal motorcar. So when designers combined the lines of these two body styles, the result was the Formal Hardtop. This style has been marketed with two or four doors, canopy and vinyl roofs (full or partial) and conventional or opera-type windows, under various trade names. The distinction between a formal hardtop and plain pillared-hardtop coupe (see above) hasn't always followed a strict rule.

CONVERTIBLE: To Depression-era buyers, a convertible was a car with a fixed-position windshield and folding top that, when raised, displayed the lines of a coupe. Buyers in the postwar period expected a convertible to have roll-up windows, too. Yet the definition of the word includes no such qualifications. It states only that such a car should have a lowerable or removable top. American convertibles became extinct by 1976, except for Cadillac's Eldorado, then in its final season. In 1982, though, Chrysler brought out a LeBaron ragtop; Dodge a 400; and several other companies followed it a year or two later.

ROADSTER: This term derives from equestrian vocabulary where it was applied to a horse used for riding on the roads. Old dictionaries define the roadster as an open-type car designed for use on *ordinary* roads, with a single seat for two persons and, often, a rumbleseat as well. Hobbyists associate folding windshields and side curtains (rather than roll-up windows) with roadsters, although such qualifications stem from usage, not definition of term. Most recent roadsters are either sports cars, small alternative-type vehicles or replicas of early models.

RUNABOUT: By definition, a runabout is the equivalent of a roadster. The term was used by carriage makers and has been applied in the past to light, open cars on which a top is unavailable or totally an add-on option. None of this explains its use by Ford on certain Pinto models. Other than this inaccurate usage, recent runabouts are found mainly in the alternative vehicle field, including certain electric-powered models.

FOUR-DOOR SEDAN: If you took the wheels off a car, mounted it on poles and hired two weightlifters (one in front and one in back) to carry you around in it, you'd have a true sedan. Since this idea isn't very practical, it's better to use the term for an automobile with a permanent top (affixed by solid pillars) that seats four or more persons, including the driver, on two full-width seats.

FOUR-DOOR HARDTOP: This is a four-door car styled to resemble a convertible, but having a rigid top of metal or fiberglass. Buick introduced a totally pillarless design in 1955. A year later most automakers offered equivalent bodies. Four-door hardtops have also been labeled sports sedans and hardtop sedans. By 1976, potential rollover standards and waning popularity had taken their toll. Only a few makes still produced a four-door hardtop and those disappeared soon thereafter.

FOUR-DOOR PILLARED HARDTOP: Once the 'true' four-door hardtop began to fade away, manufacturers needed another name for their luxury four-doors. Many were styled to look almost like the former pillarless models, with thin or unobtrusive pillars between the doors. Some, in fact, were called 'thin-pillar hardtops.' The distinction between certain pillared hardtops and ordinary (presumably humdrum) sedans occasionally grew hazy.

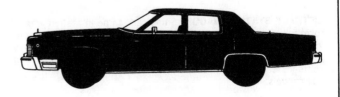

11

FOUR-DOOR (FIVE-DOOR) HATCHBACK: Essentially unknown among domestic models in the mid-1970s, the four-door hatchback became a popular model as cars grew smaller and front-wheel-drive versions appeared. Styling was similar to the orignal two-door hatchback, except for — obviously — two more doors. Luggage was carried in the back of the car itself, loaded through the hatch opening, not in a separate trunk.

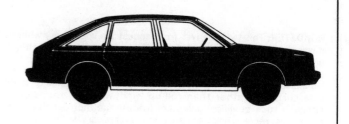

LIMOUSINE: This word's literal meaning is 'a cloak.' In France, Limousine means any passenger vehicle. An early dictionary defined limousine as an auto with a permanently enclosed compartment for 3-5, with a roof projecting over a front driver's seat. However, modern dictionaries drop the separate compartment idea and refer to limousines as large luxury autos, often chauffeur-driven. Some have a movable division window between the driver and passenger compartments, but that isn't a requirement.

TWO-DOOR STATION WAGON: Originally defined as a car with an enclosed wooden body of paneled design (with several rows of folding or removable seats behind the driver), the station wagon became a different and much more popular type of vehicle in the postwar years. A recent dictionary states that such models have a larger interior than sedans of the line and seats that can be readily lifted out, or folded down, to facilitate light trucking. In addition, there's usually a tailgate, but no separate luggage compartment. The two-door wagon often has sliding or flip-out rear side windows.

FOUR-DOOR STATION WAGON: Since functionality and adaptability are advantages of station wagons, four-door versions have traditionally been sales leaders. At least they were until cars began to grow smaller. This style usually has lowerable windows in all four doors and fixed rear side glass. The term 'suburban' was almost synonymous with station wagon at one time, but is now more commonly applied to light trucks with similar styling. Station wagons have had many trade names, such as Country Squire (Ford) and Sport Suburban (Plymouth). Quite a few have retained simulated wood paneling, keeping alive the wagon's origin as a wood-bodied vehicle.

LIFTBACK STATION WAGON: Small cars came in station wagon form too. The idea was the same as bigger versions, but the conventional tailgate was replaced by a single lift-up hatch. For obvious reasons, compact and subcompact wagons had only two seats instead of the three that had been available in many full-size models.

DIMENSIONS

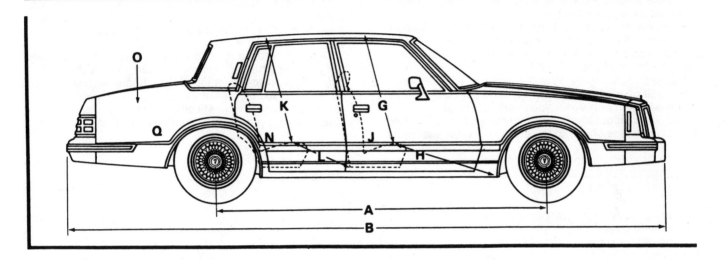

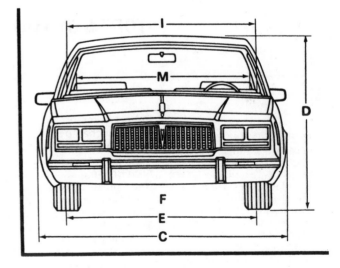

DIMENSIONS

Exterior:
A Wheelbase
B Overall length
C Width
D Overall height
E Tread, front
F Tread, rear

Interior—front:
G Headroom
H Legroom
I Shoulder room
J Hip room

Interior—rear:
K Headroom
L Legroom
M Shoulder room
N Hip room
O Trunk capacity (liters/cu. ft.)
P Cargo index volume (liters/cu. ft.)
Q Fuel tank capacity (liters/gallons)

INTRODUCTION TO THE BEST OF OLD CARS WEEKLY CONTRIBUTIONS

Over the years, contributors to *Old Cars* have written numerous stories and articles about the Buick Motor Division. Their subjects ranged from histories of David Dunbar Buick, Harlow Curtice and others who made Buick a reality to the resurrection of Buick's famous ''Roadmaster'' name, which occurred in 1990.

In the words of many experts and analysts, from Robert Ackerson to Keith Marvin, the history of the Buick Motor Division has been looked at, dissected, analyzed, criticized, poked fun at and praised.

By carefully selecting from the works of these writers, we wound up with a wonderful collection of Buick stories gathered together here for your reading pleasure.

You'll read about the Buick's humble beginnings, its rise to a cornerstone status of General Motors, the marque's innovations, and individual stories about various models from 1903 all the way to 1990.

More than 60 stories will take you through 85-plus years of Buick history and product development.

The articles included in the front portion of this catalog tell about historic cars and men who built them. Buick's good times and bad times are both covered, since both played a role in Flint, Mich. lore and legend.

Originally written for *Old Cars Weekly*, the stories we present here have been contributed from a variety of experts — professional journalists, hobby writers, members of the Society of Automotive Historians, specialized technical advisors from specific marque clubs and columnists who regularly cover the automotive beat.

STORIES BY YOUR FAVORITE WRITER

Buick...

Building Better Cars Since 1903

(An Overview)

The history of Buick

By Robert C. Ackerson

Curtice WAS Buick

For much of Buicks modern history two events overshadow all other developments as the prime forces of its remarkable success. Ranking as the number one factor is the career of Harlow Curtice as its general manager. From Oct. 23, 1933, when he assumed the top position at Buick until late 1948 when he left Buick to become a GM executive vice president, Curtice was Buick and vice versa. Undoubtedly one of his greatest achievements was the successful launching of the Series 40 Buick in 1934. The introduction of this low-priced Buick was not perhaps as dramatic a development as was the creation of the Packard 120, but the Series 40 certainly played an important role in Buick's survival of the Depression years. The Series 40, which weighed over 500 pounds less than any other contemporary Buick model was powered by a 233 cid straight eight developing 93 hp at 3,200 rpm. This was a fine little engine, capable of propelling the Buick to a top speed of 85 mph.

Four years later it grew to 248 cubic inches and as late as 1950 was to be found under the hood of a Buick automobile. In truth, however, the original Series 40 wasn't quite all Buick, after all it did use a Pontiac frame and some Chevrolet body components. But Curtice was determined not to allow the Series 40 to diminish in the least Buick's prestige among American automobiles and thus while the Series 40 gave Buick a source of badly needed income, he went on to produce the Series 90 Limited Buicks that, from Cadillac's viewpoint, were just a bit too good for comfort. This type of juxaposition was automotive marketing at its best. Packard's decline, at least in part, was due to the ramifications of placing its name on inexpensive models and Cadillac was so nervous about the whole affair that it decided to call its comparison car a La Salle.

Even decades later, in 1982 the Cimarron initially debuted not as a Cadillac but a Cimarron *by* Cadillac. But Buick prospered as no other comparable type of American automobile ever did. It became a viable challenger for the third place in sales behind Chevrolet and Ford with a line of cars priced from just above the traditional domain of Ford, Chevrolet and Plymouth to a position of near parity with Cadillac. Buick's leadership hasn't always been as outstanding as was provided by Harlow Curtice but as we'll eventually detail, the man currently at its helm, Lloyd Reuss possesses a vision and enthusiasm that would make Curtice mighty proud.

During the mid and late '30s Curtice saw to it that Buick not only kept a pace of change within the industry but was also a change-maker. Examples of the former was the blending in 1940 of the Special (in 1936 all Buick lines received name as well as number identifications) engine and chassis with the Roadmaster body to create the Super series. The same year Buick also introduced the first of its famous Estate Wagons. A multitude of developments could be cited as manifestations of Curtice's forward thinking, but for sheer drama none could compare with the introduction of Compound Carburetion in 1941. This was, of course, a twin carb setup provided as standard equipment on that year's Century Roadmaster and Limited model and optional on the Specials. With only slightly disguised pride (Cadillac's maximum horsepower in 1941 was 150) Buick told the American public: "The mighty straight-eight that propels the 1941 Buick Century, Roadmaster and Limited, is, we believe, America's most powerful standard-production automobile engine." Although these Buicks were extremely fast (a pre-compound carburetion, 1938 Century with 141 horsepower was clocked by Buick engineers at 103 mph) Buick explained that high speed wasn't the prime reason for the use of twin carburetors. Essentially said Buick, the goal was a more efficient use of fuel. The result it claimed, was that "this husky 165 horsepower giant actually gives more gasoline economy than our 107 horsepower engine of a year ago." Although it didn't survive the production hiatus of the war years, the power and economy of Compound Carburetion were to be reincarnated respectively many years later in the guise of GS Rivieras, GS 400s, and Buicks powered by V-6 and diesel engines.

Somehow it's hard to believe that all of these developments plus countless others would have become reality if Harlow Curtice hadn't served as Buick's boss. In the same sense the form and personality of the production model Buicks of the 1940s bear the indelible influence of General Motor's first dream car, the Y-Job. In another age this two-seater would have been graced with a far more dramatic name, but no matter, all that business about a rose by any other name is still a rose, applies equally well to automobiles. The Y-Job is no less a great car because of it title, history has proven that.

Construction of the Y-Job began in 1938, although Buick didn't provide a press release until April 1940. In terms of its mechanical elements the Y-Job was pure Buick. Its' chassis was that of a Buick Super which for the occasion was stretched to provide a 123 inch wheelbase. Its' powerplant was a standard Buick straight eight. As has been often noted the Buick engine was quite tall, which necessitated a relatively high hoodline. This "built-in" design factor was used by GM styling chief Harley Earl in combination with 13-inch wheels to provide an image of power via a hood that loomed well over the front fenders along with a relatively low silhouette. Not until 1954 did this styling format finally disappear from the General Motors lineup. Although the news media labeled the Y-Job as "The Car of the Future," it would also have been appropriate to regard it as "The Buick of the Future" since the general form of its grille later appeared on the 1942

1934 Model 41 four-door.

1938 Special 48 two-door sedan.

Buicks. Furthermore, Buicks from the first postwar versions through the 1958 models were destined to carry its gunsight hood ornament.

In profile, the Y-Job's boattail rear deck was a carry-over from the classic years of the 1930s but its front fenders which extended into the door region were harbingers of future styling from GM. Cadillac's 60 Special was in 1941 the first General Motor's production car with this feature but the rest of the pack wasn't far behind and in 1942 Buicks not only were available with "fade-away" fenders but were the only GM cars to offer full-length front fenders that extended to the rear fenders.

The Y-Job was also the inspiration for the dash and instrumentation layout used from 1946 through 1948 on the Buick Super and Roadmaster models. Their high-mounted speedometer, flanked by two smaller circular faces containing additional instrumentation, centrally located radio controls mounted high on the dash plus a chromed cover for the radio speaker were all first seen on the Y-Job.

One feature of the Y-Job that was not to be seen on any GM automobile for many years was its enclosed headlights. During World War II the Y-Job served as Harley Earl's daily transportation and in 1947 when it was restyled a conventional fender-headlight arrangement was installed.

In 1941 many of Buick's mechanical components (excepting Compound Carburetors) were well-proved veterans of many production years. Its big, 320 cubic inch straight-eight had been introduced in 1936 and the following year as we've noted the smaller, 248 cubic inch engine had debuted. Buick had narrowly averted a major disaster in 1939 when early production models of the Series 40 and 60 appeared with bob-tailed frames. But this gloomy episode was the exception to Buick's consistently high engineering standards and with an all-coil suspension system plus modern and potent straight-eights the 1941 Buicks were both well tested and contemporary automobiles. Indeed few critics could dispute the division's claim that the 1941 version was the "Best Buick Yet." The Series 40 (Special) 60 (Century) and 90 (Limited) models all received new bodies and the Series 50 (Super) and Series 70 (Roadmaster) models which had received GM's new C-body a year earlier were given new outer body panels.

To say the least, the Buick lineup was extremely competitive. The sales appeal of the 320 cid straight-eight with 165hp was obvious and if Buick styling was not revolutionary, it was extremely progressive. There was a certain degree of unpleasantness revolving around the fouling problems resulting from the use of ten millimeter spark plugs but overall Buick's solid reputation as the "Exeplar of General Motors Value" remained intact.

Early in February 1941 Buick introduced four new models to the Special series. These automobiles with a Series 40-A designation allowed Buick to advertise a starting price of $915, instead of $935 for its lowest priced Business Coupe. But more importantly, at least in retrospect, was 40-A's trail blazing role as a Buick heralding the Skylarks and Skyhawks of the future. "Ever wish," asked Buick, "someone would build a trimmer, *more compact* car with all the sturdiness, comfort and hug-the-road-ability that only really a BIG car can have?" If so, the car (Buick hoped) for you was one the the new Specials. Buick touted their six inches shorter length as a real plus that made them "agile travelers" . . . easier to park, easier to handle." However, prospective owners were encouraged to "make no mistake — there's nothing *little* about Buick's new models." As proof of the latter claim Buick pointed to the Special's coil springs, wide front seat and quality. But, continued Buick "Best of all, their cost is lower — putting within your reach a car with the suave style first introduced by the Buick Super." Production of these Buicks fell just short of 27,000, but when all the totals were added up, Buick had a record breaking sales year with 370,299 units sold.

From this high point, production of 1942 model Buicks plummeted to 94,442 and ended on Feb. 2, 1942. But while production lasted Buick advertised the 1942 models with a mixture of traditional salesmanship, patriotism and a growing degree of sober overtures best exemplified by the dual interpretation of the "Better Buy Buick" slogan. Before a squadron of military aircraft a Buick Super was, in one advertisement, shown speeding by with its occupants apparently oblivious to the nation's growing war time status. But the ads' text made it clear that rapid change was afoot. Buick, in clear, no nonsense language reported that two ideas had dominated the planning of its 1942 models. The first was that "in their materials these cars must not trespass on the current needs of national defense." The second mandate was that "in their quality and performance they must not be an 'ersatz' product." But those words were published in October 1941 and by mid-Jan. 1942, an awful lot had changed.

Thus beginning on Jan. 14, Buick began production of its Series H models. These automobiles lost much of their chrome trim, which was now limited to bumpers and exterior door handles. However, some of the last prewar Buicks left the factory with painted bumpers. Other changes included use of plastic for some interior trim components and the dropping of several models from the Buick line. In this regard, the most historically significant move was the decision to drop the Series 90 models altogether. Not until 1958 would a Buick again carry the Limited label. Among the mechanical changes found on Series H Buicks was the deletion of the engine oil filter and a compression ratio reduction fo 6.3:1 (from 6.7:1) on the 320 cid engines.

The premature end of output in early 1942 obviously put the brakes on Buick's rapid styling evolution but at the same time it extended the life-cycle of the '42 models by several years. Although all Buick models had either new sheet metal or new body shells that gave them Y-Job type front fenders, the really exciting news was found on the Super and Roadmaster two-door sedans and convertibles.

Much has been written and rightly so about the contribution to American automotive styling history of the postwar Studebaker, Hudson and Kaiser-Frazer models. But when Buick touted the new Super (and Roadmaster) as the styling leader of a line of no less than twenty-three "sparkling new models" it was being far too modest. The Buick's Airfoil fenders not only accentuated the flowing lines of the Sedanet and convertible bodies but repre-

17

sented the final transition step away from the styling themes of the late '30s that lead to the postwar look. We're not suggesting that everyone was taking their lead from Buick, but it's certainly worth noting that Hudson regarded the 1942 Super two-door as the car to surpass when it designed its 1948 model. Even in the 1950s it was difficult to look at the fender line of a Triumph TR-3 and not see it as an abridged version of the 1942 Buick Roadmaster convertible's. In a classic ad released when the war in Europe ended, Buick spotlighted a 1942 Roadmaster convertible as the car "... so nice to come home to!" And with only slightly subdued pride it added the comment that it was "the 1942 Buick which sets the high standards to be surpassed in new models now being made ready."

Postwar expansion

Several weeks before the end of hostilities in the Pacific in August 1945, Harlow Curtice outlined his plans for Buick's initial postwar expansion. They included new factories with 1.3 million square feet of operating space where over 20,000 workers could produce well over ½ million Buicks annually. When production did resume, in early October 1945, Curtice announced that output would be initially restricted to the Series 50 Super models with a 124 inch wheelbase and that as manufacturing got under way and materials became more abundant the Series 70 Roadmaster and Series 40 Special would be built.

Buick's early postwar ads didn't have as we'll note shortly, a great deal of new styling and engineering devel-

opments to boast of but that hardly mattered, What was important was the availability of cars to sell and Buick wasted no time in getting that message across. One particularly interesting ad appearing in the December 1945 *National Geographic*, touted the power of Buick's Fireball straight-eight, and advised drivers to "Put foot to treadle, and in the leaping response of weight-thrifty Fliteweight pistons you find still more lift and life than in the last Buicks to come your way." This was an obvious reference to the use of Domite, cast iron pistons in the 1942 Special and Super engines which developed 110 hp with a single carburetor and 118 hp with dual carbs. However in 1946, Compound Carburetion was not offered and the Buick's horsepower remained at 110. Indirectly reacting to the many articles published during the war years about the radical automobiles of the future that were sure to be, Buick headlined this ad with the statement, "Yes, its Engine is still out front . . . Probably it is no real surprise to you that the new cars for '46 have their engines out front where good engineering sense puts them."

Although Buick did claim that "numerous major changes in design and refinements have been achieved throughout the body, chassis and engine of the 1946 model, actually changes were minimal. The most notable mechanical developments were a new method of precision finishing of the cylinder walls, revised carburetion and rear axle sets plus a new noiseless method of operating the windshield wipers; in light of what was to come, not the most earth shaking of developments. In a similar fashion styling changes were decidedly modest. However, that generation's age of car-wise kids had no trouble distinguishing a '42 from a '46. The new models carried thin

1942 Model 41 Special four-door.

1947 Super Series 50 convertible.

chrome bars mounted between the front and rear bumper uprights with a circular centerpiece providing series identification. The outline of the grille was little changed from 1942 but its 21 vertical sections were far more prominent and the upper portion of the grille bearing the "Buick Eight" inscription assumed an identity of its own. Although it was part of the droll commentary of automotive critics, who were conditioned to say nothing good about postwar automobiles, to criticize them for their excessive use of chrome trim, the 1946 Buick was, if anything, a cleaner, more attractive automobile than the 1942 version. The new grille provided a more appealing front end appearance and the removal of the chrome spears emanating from the front parking lights plus the use of less side body trim gave the Buick Super a subdued, pleasing form. In the years to come Buick wouldn't be accused of being conservative when it came to using chrome as styling technique but there were precious few occasions when Buick's appearance was out of step with the styling preferences of its customers.

Curtice had hoped to produce some 300,000 Buicks during the 1946 model run but on Nov. 21, 1945 a strike by the UAW that effectively shut General Motors down for 119 days made that goal unattainable. Instead, only 158,728 were produced. Prior to this work stoppage however, there were plenty of obstacles that would have made the production goal of 300,000 cars extremely difficult to achieve. Although total production by August 1946 totaled 43,667 and Curtice had reported, "We are doing everything possible to meet the demand for new automobiles" he had bad news for those Americans eager to purchase a new Buick. "Production currently is restricted" he explained "by a critical shortage of certain parts due to current supplier's strikes and to previous strikes among our suppliers and in the basic industries. In addition, abnormal absenteeism and turnover among workers in our plants, as well as in the plants of our suppliers, are contributing to the present low rate of output. We are hopeful, however, that these conditions can be corrected so that our production may reach the heavy volume for which we have facilities."

There were however, some bright spots. Buick's labor force stood at a peacetime high of 20,128 and on August 10, 1946 the car that was "so nice to come to!" the Buick

convertible both in Super (124 inch wheelbase) and Roadmaster (129 inch wheelbase) went into production. Among its "important changes in appearance, design and performance" were pushbutton controls for the top, windows and front seat.

In November 1946 when production of the Special series began Buick's first postwar lineup was completed. It wasn't as expensive as offered in prewar days with nine models in three series and, with either 110 hp (Special and Super models) or 144 hp (Roadmaster) Buick's engines weren't quite the powerhouses they once were, but with an unprecedented demand for new cars greeting every automobile as it rolled off the assembly line there were no tears shed for a few lost horsepower. When the new Buicks were displayed in New York's Glidden Buick showroom a crowd estimated at 60,000 came forth with orders that Buick's Eastern Zone Sales Manager H. J. Miller reported was a new record for any comparable time span.

In 1947 Buick did very well, moving into fourth place in production output with a model year run of 277,134. Once again it wasn't a year of great engineering or design developments. The most notable and obvious styling change took place in the Buick's front end where the hood medallion was lowered and given chrome side accents. At the same time the grille was reshaped into a lower, oblong form and its vertical bars assumed a separate identity instead of being completely integrated into the grille work. The result was more graceful and pleasing. But not even Buick's ad agency could turn out an entire year's ad copy about a new grille! Instead Buick was depicted as the only car to offer such "Star Features" as Airfoil Fenders, Fireball Power, Accurite Cylinder Boring, Silent Zone Body Mounting, Fliteweight Pistons and PermiFirm Steering."

During the model year Buick added an Estate Wagon to the Roadmaster series but only a mere handful (300) were produced. Considerably more impressive were the 11,959 Roadmaster and 26,297 Super Convertibles that were acquired by lucky new car buyers.

Buick helped out the curbside car watching crowd sort out its '48 models from the rest of the new car crop by placing (when appropriate) either Super or Roadmaster script in the front fenders. Specials were easy to pick out

19

thanks to a new upper body chrome spear. But appearance changes of this miniscule nature weren't what made the 1948 Buick the newsworthy and historic car it was. Nor for that matter was it due to most of the "30 odd new advances" claimed for this "New Fashion Plate" Buick although some of them such as new piston rings with "Flex-Fit" steel oil control rings and a new oil filter were worthwhile advances. Instead the big excitement came from Buick's offering of its first Dynaflow automatic transmission. This writer's memory of Buicks with the first generation Dynaflow consists almost entirely of the sound of a very frustrated straight eight that couldn't understand why it had to work so hard to achieve so little. Buick had a slightly different perspective. It regarded Dynaflow as providing "smooth fast starts, silken speedups . . . something close to driving magic." But if Dynaflow was less than perfect, it was also badly needed as a sales weapon. With the exception of Lincoln and Chrysler all of Buick's upper price class competition was available with automatic transmissions in 1948 and although Buick had offered a semi-automatic gearbox for the 1938 Specials, it was lagging badly behind Oldsmobile and Cadillac that had respectively been available with HydraMatic since the 1940 and 1941 model years. Thus if perfection initially eluded Buick's torque converter, it at the very least kept Buick from being perceived as old fashioned and behind the times. For 1948 only the Roadmaster models were available with Dynaflow. When so equipped the Roadmaster, thanks to a higher (6.9:1 instead of 6.6:1) compression ratio was rated at 150 hp. Other features separating this engine from the 144 hp straight eight used in manual transmission Roadmasters were a different crankshaft, flywheel plus hydraulic valve lifters. For the first time since its introduction in 1940 the Buick Super had an engine more powerful than that used in the Specials. For 1948 the Super engine was rated 115 horsepower, up five from the Special's output.

Although it wasn't nearly the news maker that Dynaflow was, Buick's use of synthetic rubber engine mounts was given equal rank with Dynaflow as one of Buick's "two major advances that no other car offers." Buick described the resulting "Vibra-Shielded" ride as "the first ride in which car occupants are fully shielded against vibration buildup against the harmonizing of little tremors into big ones."

Buick was once again America's fourth best selling automobile in 1948, having produced 219,718 cars during the model year. But 1949 loomed just ahead, a year of excitement by any measure anyone cared to conjure up. It would be a year of all-new bodies, the first since 1942; a year when a revamped but very attractive Buick Special would appear as would the first Buick Riviera hardtop.

Styling innovations

Buick's move into the first round of the postwar styling years was just a bit untidy. While both the Oldsmobile 98 and the Series 60, 61 and 62 Cadillacs received GM's new C-body for the 1948 model year, Buick didn't get the chance to use it for the Super and Roadmaster series until the 1949 production run. The debut of the 1949 Special which shared a new B-body with the Oldsmobile 88 was even more confused. It wasn't available until August 1949, thus also serving as a styling forerunner of the entire 1950 Buick lineup. But the Buick story for 1949 was far more than merely a tale of shared bodies and awkwardly timed models' introductions; it was also a grand and glorious year of sweepspears, VentiPorts and Riviera hardtops.

In the 1950s there were dramatic image turnabouts at Chevrolet and Pontiac that made automotive history, but seldom had any automobile introduced three styling innovations that almost instantly captured the new car buyer's fancy. The concept of a steel-topped automobile without center or B-posts wasn't a new one but Buick not only was the first manufacturer to adopt it for mass-production and thus establish one of the decades' key styling themes but it did so with class. They could have picked some dull old name for their creation but that wasn't the Buick way. Instead they selected "Riviera" and for all time that silky, sultry label, through thick and thin, good times and bad, always would stand for something extra-nice (or controversial) from Buick.

Buick's chief stylist, Ned Nickels, who had worked up a scale model of what became the Riviera back in 1945, also was the originator of Buick's VentiPorts. By installing a "prototype" system on his 1948 Roadmaster convertible complete with a distributor-activated set of flashing lights he attracted plenty of attention. But the aroused interest that really counted was Harlow Curtice's and thus the 1949 Super and Roadmaster Buicks sported slightly toned down (no flashing lights) versions. Then there was that lusciously thick expanse of chrome voluptuously sprawling across the Riviera's flank. Sure, the self-proclaimed arbiters of good taste complained that except for some function as a rear fender gravel shield the sweep-spear as pure excess but so what? It looked great, gave the Riviera even more distinction and class and much to the chagrin of those nay-sayers was greeted with joy by multitudes of new car buyers.

Both the 1949 Super and Roadmaster Buicks were slightly shorter overall than their 1948 counterparts yet, with respective wheelbases of 121 and 126 inches they were never mistaken for someone's early attempt at downsizing. Instead they carried their bulk in style. Besides the design features we've already mentioned, they boasted of (on sedan models) over 25 square feet of glass area which represented a 22 percent increase over 1948. The elimination of a separate identity for the rear fender would wait until 1950. GM's decision to keep this link with the past was hardly noticed since Buick featured both a beautifully rounded rear fender line extending several inches beyond its high bustle trunk deck and an extremely graceful taillight form.

For sheer class the Super and Roadmaster Sedanet, two-door fastback models gave the Riviera a close run for top honors but in the hands of the *Consumer Reports* test crew the Super version with optional Dynaflow (it was standard on Roadmasters) came in for some harsh words. Among the features singled out for criticism was the Buick's high noise level, poorly positioned battery, and oil dipstick and ashtrays. *Consumer Reports* also complained of trunk leaks, loose interior trim screws and an inaccurate speedometer. But on the positive side of the ledger *Consumer Reports* praised Dynaflow's acceleration as a "powerful and prompt response," regarded its roadability as "in general extremely good" and judged visibility from the driver's seat as "much better than average."

With new styling as their main attraction the 1949 Buicks didn't possess any earth shaking technical features but there were a number of worthwhile improvements. A three-point synthetic rubber engine mounted system reduced the transferral of engine vibration to the chassis and new hydraulic lifters for the Roadmaster's 150 hp, 320 cid straight eight, provided a lower noise level. Other improvements whose virtues surely found their way into many a Buick salesman's repertoire included stiffer frame and softer front and rear coil springs.

The Buick dash was arranged to place all essential instrumentation directly in front of the driver for his perusal. The Buick's parking brake was now foot-operated. Small but worthwhile changes included the use of more insulation behind the dash to keep engine heat

out of the interior and the gathering together of all electrical fuses on a single panel behind the dash.

Since they were prestige automobiles all of the 4,314 Rivieras produced during the 1949 model year sported standard power windows and seats plus a choice of leather or leather-cloth interiors. The Riviera had been first shown in January 1949 at the Waldorf Astoria. The title of this GM extravaganza, ''Transportation Unlimited'' aptly described Buick's first two-door hardtop.

Back in 1947 *Fortune* published an extensive study of Buick, ''The Ubiquitous Buick'' in which it detailed the means by which Buick intended to overtake Plymouth and move into third place in auto sales. Buick didn't achieve that goal until 1954 and then after just two years as ''Number Three'' it fell into a serious downward sales spiral whose direction wasn't reversed until 1973. But in its drive to become the nations' third best selling automobile, the years from 1949 through 1952 were important ones. Although many of the developments such as its V-8 engine, reintroduction of the Century series and Dynaflow's redesign didn't come until later, those years represented a time of solid accomplishments for Buick. For example after a 1949 production run of 327,321 Buick's 1950 model output not only exceeeded the 670,000 mark but in December the six millionth Buick was assembled. Although the Korean War plus the end of the long post World War II buyer's market acted as sales impediments, Buick still managed to turn out over 700,000 automobiles in the 1951 and 1952 model years.

Although it had more than a fair share of bad press one of the best examples of Buick's marketing expertise was the extensively revamped Special that debuted in early August 1949.

Initially these Buicks were available in only three models, two and four door sedans plus a 3-passenger business coupe. This in itself was hardly very interesting. But the fact that all three were fastbacks certainly was. Buick called these Specials ''Jetbacks'' and although this type of body style admittedly had plenty of drawbacks they were visually exciting automobiles. No one needs

1949 56C Super convertible.

reminding that the combination of a long wheelbase and a sloping roofline can spell real trouble in terms of both interior accommodations and external appearance. In regard to the latter consider the original Dodge Charger and Rambler Marlin. We're not casting disparaging barbs in their direction but it's certainly hard to get excited about either car as a monument to good taste. Yet the Jetback Buick Specials were extremely handsome automobiles. With very little bright work they relied upon their flowing fenders and accent lines for visual impact and although they were far less expensive than the Roadmaster Rivieras, the Jetback Specials were every bit as sleek and smooth appearing. Moreover, with a $1,925 price tag the four-door version was a formidable competitor for sales to virtually every full-sized, low-priced automobile produced in the U.S. This isn't to say the Jetback Special was immune to criticism. *Consumer Reports* (February 1950) noted that in comparison to the Pontiac fastback which with its standard 108 hp flathead eight was about $100 less expensive, the Buick had three inches less rear shoulder room. Matched against the competing models from Dodge and DeSoto the Buick was inferior in 20 of 24 interior measurements that *Consumer Reports* considered

1951 Model 76 Roadmaster two-door hardtop.

significant. Moreover, due to the extreme slope of the roofline the Buick's rear seat had to be positioned just 12⅛ inches from floor level to provide sufficient headroom for rear seat passengers.

Yet the Buick not only had just 32 inches of rear head room compared to Pontiac's 35 inches but was also the Pontiac's inferior in front headroom by 1.5 inches. When it came to evaluating the Special's trunk room, *Consumer Reports* said, "the reactions of motorists checked by CU when the miserable 'Jetback' Buick trunk was opened for them were predictable and graphic; they either laughed at it or commented in disgust." But no one could laugh or issue a disgusting comment about the Special's sales. After all, the production of nearly 82,000 new model Specials during 1949 was impressive regardless of the size of their trunk. There's little doubt that the Special's appearance, which accurately foretold the styling of all the 1950 Buicks was a key factor of its success. Although its waterfall grille of vertical bars flooding over the old bumper-dam was destined for an early exit, the rest of the Special's design was appealing. Its new front to rear fender line replaced the slightly pinched in at the center look of the 1949's with a far more modern and sleek arrangement which included the very practical feature of bolt-on fenders. Buick was still experimenting with the proper positioning of its VentiPorts and for 1950 all Buicks had these marks of status placed on their hoodline.

Although it was far from a rapid accelerator the Special's performance was respectable. With the same 248 cid straight eight used by the 1949 Super but rated at 122 hp instead of 120 hp the Special was more powerful than any of its competitors except of course for the Oldsmobiles. Buick took several measures to insure the Special conveyed the impression of being a more refined, quieter automobile than other cars in its price class. Thus its engine noise was muffled by under-hood insulation and a 4.1:1 instead of the 4.454:1 axle used on 1949 Supers was supplied with manual shift Specials. Those with Dynaflow also had 4.1:1 axles. Although Dynaflow was far from the last word in automatic transmissions it compared quite favorably with Chrysler's semi-automatic which was essentially a four-speed transmission operating through a fluid flywheel. The Chrysler setup had the edge over Dynaflow in providing superior engine braking and certainly was less obtrusive than the high revving Buick in normal operation. But the combination of a strong straight eight and Dynaflow was too much for any semi-automatic Chrysler product either in terms of standing start performance or accelerating from highway speeds.

Although Buick was often symbolized by American car critics as the arch-type of the poor handling Detroit product, *Consumer Reports* regarded the Special's roadability as "downright excellent." It also found the Buick's ride neither soft nor floating. We hasten to add that the Special with its 121.5 inch wheelbase, 204 inches of overall length, heavy and slow steering was far from a nimble road machine ready to challenge a Mark VII Jaguar on a back country road. Instead it was tailored in classic Alfred Sloan mode; an appealing automobile for upwardly mobile folks ready to make a move from the lower price market for a taste of upper-middle class motoring.

When the rest of the 1950 Buicks debuted on Dec. 28, 1949 the Jetback Special models were joined both by slightly more expensive deluxe versions and conventional notchbacks or as they were officially identified, Tourback models. During 1949 and 1950 all Buick two-door sedans were fastbacks while 4-door models were available in either Jetback or Tourback form. With the Riviera name already ingrained in the public's view as representing the best from Buick, no time was lost in exploiting prestige by applying it to both Super and Roadmaster four-door

130.25 inch wheelbase notchback sedans as well as a super version of its original two-door hardtop form. This mini-proliferation hasn't always been hailed by Buick historians as the best of ideas but judging from the popularity of these spin-offs plus the use of the Riviera name for Buick's 1963 entry into the personal car field its impact had little if any negative effect.

Although development of a new V-8 engine was well along, a new version of the old straight eight design was prepared for use in Super models. Known as the F-263 by virtue of its 263 cubic inch displacement this 128 hp engine weighed no more than its predecessor. Among its salient features were a bigger 3 3/16 inch bore (up 3/32 inch) shorter but larger diameter connecting rods plus main bearings increased in size to 2 9/16 inches. With Dynaflow its compression ratio was 7.2:1. With standard transmission a 6.9:1 compression ratio was specified.

The 1951 Buick Super, with its 128 hp and 225 lb/ft of torque was capable of quick acceleration. Tom McCahill (*Mechanix Illustrated,* April 1951) reported his Dynaflow-equipped test car could reach 60 mph in 13.9 seconds using both low and high range. McCahill who regarded the Super as "the best Buick I have ever driven" also found his two-door Riviera a good-handling and stable automobile. "This is" remarked McCahill, "an excellently balanced car for general use on American highways."

Buick broadened the base of the Special's sales appeal by offering both convertible and two-door hardtop versions for the first time. In addition Custom versions fitted with some Super body panels to extend their overall length to 206.2 instead of the normal Special's 204.8 inches were offered. All 1951 Specials were powered by a 120 hp version of the 263 cid Super engine. A more important development was Buick's decision to standardize sweepspear side trim for all its models. This move obviously had no intrinsic value but its role in providing Buicks with instant identity was substantial. Regardless of its basic logic, the annual new model introduction was a major part of our automotive life-cycle back in the fifties and by embracing this unique trim shape Buick had the means on hand to create an unusual new car look while at the same time retaining styling continuity with older models. In a similar fashion Buick decided that moving the VentiPorts onto the hood wasn't such a great idea after all. Not until 1959 would they disappear from their front fender location and even then it was only a one-year hiatus. It wouldn't be until 1972 that a production model Buick would again appear with hood positioned VentiPorts.

Buick's solid and confidence image was further solidified with its 1952 models. It was the end of the road for the big, 320 cubic inch Roadmaster straight eight but it went out in a blaze of glory with the highest horsepower rating in Buick history (170) and a new, four-barrel "Airpower" carburetor that, said Buick, "needs less fuel at 40 mph than was formerly used at 30 — but lets loose a mighty reserve of power when needed." All 1952 Buicks were also fitted with larger brakes, and power steering was introduced as an option for Super and Roadmaster models. The fastback models were no longer available.

Nineteen fifty two was a difficult year as both the Korean War and a steel strike hampered the entire industry. Nonetheless Buick managed to turn out 320,000 cars, of which one had the distinction of being the seven millionth Buick.

When Buick sales nosedived in 1957 some critics pointed to the poor quality of the 1955 and 1956 models as a partial explanation. We'll be looking into this matter more closely in an upcoming segment but for now it's worth pointing out that in the early '50s Buick quality wasn't all that it could have been. For example, the

1953 Super Riviera two-door hardtop.

November 1950 issue of *Consumer Reports* contains a photo of a Buick Super with a very poor fit between its front door and hood. Tom McCahill (*Mechanix Illustrated*, April 1951) also had some harsh words about Buick's finish; "The paint job in some new Buicks is not the best by a long shot. Some I have examined looked as though somebody took aboard a mouthful of paint and sprayed it on through his teeth."

Nonetheless Buick was poised on the eve of its fiftieth anniversary to begin its final assault on the industry's number three sales position. A new V-8 was ready for introduction, great new styling was to follow just a year later and with the revival of the Century series Buick was to become one of America's great performing automobiles.

Buick's 50th anniversary in 1953

1953 is an automotive year probably best remembered for the stunning new Studebaker coupes, the sales failure of Chrysler Corp.'s "biggest on the inside, shorter on the outside" automobiles and the opening salvos of the Ford Blitz upon General Motor's dominant position in the industry. But viewed from Buick's perspective, the year's highlights really were a new V-8 engine, a revamped Dynaflow transmission, the exciting Skylark convertible and the best sales performances since the great year of 1950. It wasn't all wine and roses for Buick in 1953 since, as we'll shortly detail, early examples of its new V-8 demonstrated a healthy thirst for oil during their break-in period thus offending some Buick owners who regarded such behavior as unbecoming a Buick. More serious was a braking problem that had far-reaching ramifications both positive and negative upon Buick and the entire industry.

1953 was Buick's 50th anniversary and with V-8s rapidly gaining popularity it was quite natural that Buick would celebrate its Golden Anniversary by breaking with its straight-eight tradition and introduce a modern, over-

head valve V-8. Buick, on the surface at least, had lagged well behind both Oldsmobile and Cadillac in V-8 engine development. Buick had been researching V-type engines since 1931 when it had developed a Twin-Six. In 1944 this project took on a more modern tone when the era of high compression V-8 engine research and development began at Buick. In the years that followed, Buick gave consideration to ten different V-type engines and constructed more than 100 experimental engines. As were its competitors both in and out of General Motors, Buick was compiling volumes of data concerning cylinder arrangements, "V" angles and combustion chamber design that would later be put to good use.

One engine that resulted from this project was a 30° V that Buick described as having "many desirable characteristics." However, it was rejected because of its height which was not consistent with the then radical styling proposals being considered by GM for its future automobiles.

The impact of styling considerations upon engineering was demonstrated by the comments of Buicks engine designers V.P. Mathews and Joe Turlay in a paper presented to the Society of Automotive Engineers in January 1953. "The proportions of the 'V' engine" they noted, "are more suitable for installation in cars with newer styling and particularly in cars with the styling which General Motors believes will be standard several years from now. The "cars of the future", the XP-300 and LeSabre have extremely low lines and the 90°. "V" type engine was chosen for these cars because it was the only design which we could fit within the allotted space under the hood." As a result, they continued, "space requirements as dictated by the body stylist, are one of the most important, if not the most important factor, in determining the future trend of engine design."

Despite Buick's backlog of experience and interest in both engine design and advanced styling the actual program leading to the Fireball V-8 of 1953 did not get underway until March 1950. But it's also worth noting that since the basic tooling of the Roadmaster engine had been

unchanged since 1936, the emphasis would be upon creation of an engine that would represent a dramatic step forward in both performance and design. Towards this goal Buick established six basic areas of excellence for the Fireball V-8. These include smoothness, quietness, durability and ease of service. In addition, they were to be enclosed within "the lightest and most compact package which" said Mathews and Turlay "we could produce, consistent with minimum manufacturing cost."

Early fruits of this effort were impressive. The Fireball V-8 was tested 10,000 hours on dynamometers, and was operated in excess of one million road-test miles in cars at the General Motors Proving Ground. As we mentioned earlier some of the early production Buick V-8s demonstrated an inordinately high level of oil consumption. In regard to a specific query from *Popular Mechanics* about this matter, Buick noted that "in early production models of its new V-8 engine, Buick used a slow-seating ring and during the break-in period the oil consumption in some cars was higher than normal. In many instances, this fault had corrected itself by the time the engine was broken in and the rings had seated themselves properly. Now Buick is using a faster-seating ring in order to avoid excessive oil consumption during the break-in stage." But this relatively minor problem was far over-shadowed by the Fireball's impressive durability. For example, the second experimental V-8, assembled in the fall of 1950, survived a full-throttle endurance test at 4,200-4,500 rpm "several hours longer" Buick reported, "than any of the notably rugged straight-eight Roadmaster engines have ever run in the same standard test." The new V-8 also compared very favorably with the veteran straight-eight in terms of weight and exterior dimensions. Whereas the 1952 Roadmaster engine weighed just over 794 pounds, its successor was at slightly less than 624 pounds, over 170 pounds lighter. Buick also claimed that its V-8 weighed less than any production V-8 of over 300 cubic inches. In terms of sheer bulk the new Buick engine was four inches lower than the old eight and a startling 13½ inches shorter. However as expected, the new V-8 was considerably wider. In order to keep width at a minimum, Buick adopted a very short 3.2 inch stroke, which with a 4.0 inch bore, provided a displacement of 322 cubic inches. This excellent stroke/bore ratio of 0.8 plus the use of vertically-positioned valves made it possible to install the modern V-8 into Buick's five-year old body-chassis with just a one-inch increase in its front tread.

Over the years Buick received plenty of flak about the small "nailhead" exhaust valves this arrangement required. But Buick was unimpressed. It advertised the Roadmaster as powered by the "first V-8 engine to function with vertical valves" and both Mathews and Turlay justified the Buick's small valves before the S.A.E. They expressed the view that a smaller valve opening earlier opens to when the piston reaches a little past bottom dead center. Furthermore, they argued, "The use of this relatively small exhaust valve made a more compact combustion chamber possible, improved valve cooling, and reduced cost, without entailing any loss in power."

Buick also defended the use of 1.250 inch exhaust and 1.750 inch intake valves by referring to the Buick-Bug of 1910 which it noted had exceeded 105 mph with exhaust valves much smaller than the intakes. Another strong argument provided by Buick originated in its mid-30's research into the impact of manifold, port and valve design upon gas flow. While pointing out that the "inline valve arrangement was retained in the 1953 Buick engine chiefly to make the engine more compact, to save weight, and to facilitate manufacture," Buick also credited the small exhaust valve with maintaining a more efficient gas flow since it avoided the negative affect of the gases suddenly expanding into a larger port. Perhaps the most impressive argument on behalf of the Fireball V-8's valve arrangement came from a comparison with the XP-300 and LeSabre engine. As explained by Mathews and Turlay in their S.A.E. paper, "the flow restriction of the Buick V-8 inlet port and valve was no greater than that of the experimental engine used in the XP-300 and LeSabre cars, under the same conditions with the same size valve and valve openings." After noting that "this experimental

1954 Century Estate Wagon.

1955 Roadmaster four-door sedan.

engine was designed for high output'' they also reported that ''upon investigation, the curving inlet port of the Buick V-8...was shown to have a slight advantage over the straight-in port of the XP-300.''

But regardless of the virtues of shortcomings of the Buick's valves there were plenty of other features worthy of praise. No one was complaining about its compact, semi-hemi shaped combusion chamber of centrally-located spark plugs that provided both a minimum flame travel and excellent ignition characteristics when the throttle was only partially opened.

A major portion of the weight advantage enjoyed by the V-8 over the old straight-eight came from the V-8's five-bearing crankshaft which weighed just 56 pounds. This was an impressive drop from the 114 pounds crank used in 1952. Buick spoke with pride of the ''outstanding rigidity'' of the new crankshaft which it reported was ''from our tests...greater than that of any other American automobile engine now in production.''

Other noteworthy attributes of the Fireball V-8 included its fuel economy which was claimed to be eight percent better than the older straight-eight and its lower by seven percent production costs.

But with horsepower becoming more and more a prime selling point for most American cars, Buick could hardly avoid touting the Fireball V-8's performance. For 1953 only the Super and Roadmaster series were available with V-8s differing only in their carburetion. The 188 hp Roadmaster engine used a four-barrel version while the Super, rated at 170 hp (164 hp with manual transmission) was fitted with a two-barrel unit. Except for the carburetor flange the intake manifolds used on these engines were identical. Buick also was a pathblazer, along with Cadillac, Oldsmobile and the Chrysler Imperial with its 12 volt electrical system (on Roadmasters and Supers) and 8.5:1 compression ratio (on Roadmasters). This latter feature represented the highest compression ratio then available on any production automobile.

Surprisingly none of the major automotive publications tested the more powerful Roadmasters. Instead *Motor Trend, Auto Age* and *Popular Mechanics* put the 170 hp

Super through its paces. The results indicated it was capable of zero to 60 mph runs of 15.5 seconds and a top speed of just over 102 mph. Floyd Clymer *(Popular Mechanics,* June 1953) rated his Super test car as ''one of the three fastest United States stock cars.'' But the record shows otherwise since a survey of contemporary road tests indicates the Cadillac 62, Chrysler New Yorker, Olds 88 and Lincoln were all capable of a higher maximum speed. But Clymer's misstatement really wasn't of consequences since Buick, in 1953, hadn't yet really begun its post-war emphasis in performance. The opening salvo in that compaign would come in 1954 with the introduction of the Century.

Avoiding staleness

You really had to have a lot of pity for Buick in 1955. After all, its competitors, Ford and Chrysler, were debuting with all new styling and poor Buick had to make do with a face lifted version of its 1954 model. But before we get too emotional and start shedding tears for Buick's fate in 1955, a few specifics are in order. Buick did very well that year. It set a new model year production record of 738,814, produced its eight-millionth car in April, held on to third position in sales, and along with Oldsmobile, introduced the four-door hardtop body style to the American market. Buick thus had the honor of producing General Motors' one millionth hardtop in August.

Buick's combination of model and broad price range mix plus potent engines and effective styling was probably unequalled in the industry. There were more attractive and more powerful automobiles available in 1955 yet none of them, except for Chevrolet and Ford, were more popular sellers. *Motor Trend* (March 1955), finding much in the Buick's revamped appearance to praise, noted that the ''industry could learn from Buick's '55 face lift, which gives new freshness without pointless, too-frequent investments in entirely new dies for all parts.'' In just a few years Buick would be doing just that but in 1955, by altering key elements such as the rear fenders, taillights and

grille work Buick was offering an automobile that continued the basic themes of 1954 but with enough of a new look to avoid any impression of staleness. A stamped grille with a center crossbar replaced the 1954 version which had closely followed the toothy look introduced back in 1947. Replacing the small twin taillights of 1954 was a heavily chromed, semi-fender fin arrangement which contained both the taillights and back-up lights. The result was pleasing by 1955 standards but less handsome than the simple arrangement of the 1953-54.

Although Chevrolet's spectacular V-8 engine and Chrysler's new C-300 seemed to steal the performance show from Buick, it remained one of the fastest accelerating American passenger cars.

While displacement remained unchanged at 322 cubic inches, the engine for the Century, Super and Roadmaster series was boosted to 236 hp for 1955. The 36 extra horses for 1955 were accounted for by the use of larger (1⅜ inch instead of 1¼ inch) exhaust valves, a higher lift cam, more efficient intake and exhaust manifolds plus higher domed pistons providing a 9.0:1 compression ratio. Also revised for 1955 was Buick's four-barrel carburetor which had slightly larger throats. Making excellent use of Buick's 236 horsepower was a revamped Dynaflow fitted with variable pitch stator vanes.

Buick claimed that "Thanks to constant improvement in Dynaflow Drive and in engine design, the 1955 Buicks give far better gas mileage. Even the new Roadmaster averages 4.8 more miles per gallon than Buicks of six years ago, yet delivers 57 percent more power." That this was not a mere boast that could not be substantiated was made obvious by the Roadmaster's Class D victory in the 1955 Mobilgas Economy Run with a 19.7 mpg average. As Buick noted, "You save gas when these blades are set for cruising. Since the vanes were controlled by the accelerator, its sudden depression provided," said Buick, "a safety-surge, when you need it out on the highway, such as you've never had in any earth-bound vehicle." This was a slight exageration but since Dynaflow could easily run well above 60 mph on Low the result was spectacular.

For example, *Auto Age* (January 1956) reported, "The Buick is undoubtedly the fastest American production sedan when it comes to initial acceleration, say up to 30, 40 or 50 mph." In this respect even the heavy Super and Roadmaster were quick off the line. A Roadmaster tested by *Motor Trend* (July 1955) ran from zero to 30 mph in just 3.5 seconds and *Auto Age's* July 1955 test of a Super netted a time of 3.3 seconds from zero to 30 mph. Surprisingly, the results of contemporary road tests of the Century show slower zero to 30 mph times. However it had the fastest zero to 60 mph (9.8 seconds) and quarter-mile times (17.5 seconds) of any American sedan tested by *Motor Trend* during 1955. Perhaps that's why Buick decided to equip it with four portholes for 1955!

Although Buick recalibrated the valving of the front shock absorbers on all its 1955 models there was little change of any consequence in their handling characteristics. There was slightly more resistance to roll in turns and *Motor Trend* (April 1955) described Buick's understeering characteristic as "almost sportscar like."

With its smaller 264 cubic inch, 188 hp V-8 the 1955 Buick Special couldn't keep pace with the Centurys but its performance (zero to 60 in under 14 seconds) with Dynaflow was certainly acceptable. Special V-8 engines matched with three-speed manual transmission had a lower 7.5:1 compression ratio. In similar fashion the few Centurys and Supers delivered with manual transmissions also had lower (8.5:1 instead of 9.0:1) compression ratios.

In contrast to more recent assertions that Buick's quality control crumbled under the pressure of its record output in 1955, most contemporary results spoke favorably of Buick's workmanship. *Motor Trend* (July 1955) after testing both a Special and a Roadmaster reported: "Basic components in each car were generally above par...Neither car had body rattles. Finishes were excellent, fit of panels good." Buick did run into difficulty with rear axle failures during 1955 and the following year a heavier design with larger bearings, and stronger ring and pinion gears was adopted.

In a move away from the overt sports car nature of the 1954 Wildcat II show car, Buick's 1955 dream car, the Wildcat III brought back memories of the original 1953 Skylark. With a 110 inch wheelbase it provided bucket seats for each of its four passengers. In profile, the Wildcat III was extra clean. Although there were no portholes in sight, a graceful sweepspear reminded everyone it was a Buick. Although Buick did not release any specific performance details, the Wildcat's 280 hp engine equipped with four carburetors was undoubtedly capable of providing excellent acceleration.

While Buick general manager Ivan Wiles issued an optimistic forecast of a 900,000 sales year for 1956, the signs all pointed to a downturn. This decline was not restricted to Buick, since the entire industry had in general been oversold during 1955. Many people who would normally have purchased automobiles in 1956 or 1957 had succumbed to the razzle-dazzle of the 1955 models thus thinning the ranks of the 1956 crop of car buyers. For Buick these factors would translate into a model year output of 572,024 automobiles. This still placed Buick third in the industry, but it represented the beginning of a time of difficulty for Buick.

Although Buick's sales in 1956 fell sharply from the 1955 level of 738,814 to 572,024, there's little evidence to indicate that the 1956 Buicks were the culprits.

As in previous years, the Buick lineup covered the market range from just above Chevrolet's bastion to a point just below Cadillac's rarified position of unquestioned dominance of the American prestige car market. In terms of styling, Buick changed its obviously successful formula only modestly. The finer mesh grille work, instead of having a flat surface as in 1955 was given a slight V-ed effect vaguely related to the style of the early '30s. The shape of the large bumper guards that had been part and parcel of Buick's postwar styling resembled those last used in 1953 and as in 1953, enclosed the front directional lights. Buick, it seems, liked to experiment with a variety of locations, sizes and shapes of the parking lights and for 1956 moved them further out on the fender extremities where they were molded into a streamlined cowling. Also unique to the 1956 models was a functional hood scoop that directed air to the air cleaner and, on Roadmasters a less deeply cut side spear with a flat rather than the contoured surface used on the side trim of lesser Buicks. 1956 was also the first year the four-door hardtop body style was available in the Super and Roadmaster series. Some critics panned Buick's decision to include a "1956" indentification both in the grille center and on the rear deck as evidence tht Buick styling had been ineffectual in setting the new model apart from the 1955 version. But this charge didn't really hold water. Buick's front end, if not a great styling triumph, was attractive and the form of its taillights made the 1956 Buick very easy to identify on the road.

Buick's suspension system was altered through the use of a longer radius arm and Delco direct-acting tubular shocks in place of the older lever types at the rear and a realignment of the front kingpins that were now included at seven degrees from vertical. The result, Buick claimed, was "the year's most luxurious ride" plus, thanks to the new radius rod, less "side motion on turns, curves, and uneven roads." Reaction to the changes made in Buick's suspension by road testers was mixed. *Motor Trend*

(December 1955) which considered Buick a car with a very smooth ride, reported that "as far as directional stability is concerned, the changes are definitely for the better." Tom McCahill (*Mechanix Illustrated*, July 1956) concluded, after his test of a four-door Century hardtop that "on my test corners I failed to find any improvement over the '54 Century." *Auto Age* (August 1956) after including a Buick in a three car comparison test with Chrysler and Packard, wasn't too pleased with the Buick's tendency to lean in the turns. "At any rate," its readers were told, "we wouldn't want to race this car over ultra-winding roads."

However, Sam Hanks took quite a different position. "I say," Hanks declared in *Speed Age*, June 1956, "the 1956 Buick Century has great potential as a competition auto in any stock car race today. In addition, I consider the Buick as one of the finest highway cars on the road." As part of his test, Hanks took the Century around the winding Willow Springs track and turned a best lap of two minutes, 10 seconds.

Another area where Buick was improving an already excellent design was its Dynaflow transmission. Roger Huntington (*Motor Life*, 1956) claimed "Buick is two years ahead of the industry with this fine 1956 Dynaflow torque converter." Buick revamped Dynaflow by adding a stator between the first and second turbine wheels. When the car was accelerating from a standard start to approximately 39 mph, the new stator pitched the transmission oil into the second turbine at an angle that raised the initial torque multiplication from 2.44:1 to 3.4:1. In addition, the overall weight of the Dynaflow transmission was reduced 20 pounds by use of an aluminum torque converter housing.

Along with these developments, Buick had improved its 322 cid V-8 (which was installed in all models for 1956) to yield 255 hp at 4,400 rpm and 341 lb/ft of torque at 3,200 rpm when installed in the Century, Super or Roadmaster series. Primary changes included a reshaped combustion chamber providing better valve breathing a new 9.5:1 compression ratio piston design with a smaller raised section. Also used was a somewhat hotter cam and tulip-shaped, lighter weight exhaust valves heads that presented less gas flow restriction. Dual exhausts were standard on Roadmasters and optional for all other series.

As expected, these changes kept the Centurys among the leaders in the American performance derby.

Power steering which was standard in Supers and Roadmasters and a $108 option for Specials and Centurys, was a totally new Saginaw unit for 1956. Of a more compact size with fewer parts and less weight this system required a minimum force of under three pounds to commence operation. Buick also took another step towards producing the industry's best brakes in 1956. Total lining area (219 square inches) on Centurys, Supers and Roadmasters remained unchanged but with wider, 2¼ inch instead of 1¾ inch as in 1955 linings; the Specials's total lining area was 207.5 square inches. An interesting feature common to all Buicks was a three-eighths-inch center groove in the brake shoes that was intended to more equally distribute the braking load across the entire lining area and provide better brake cooling with less fade. *Motor Trend*, (June 1956) reported that its Special and Century test cars stopped in shorter distances than their 1955 counterparts. Although *Auto Age* (August 1956) rated the Buick Century's brakes as above average in terms of fade and recovery it regarded them as not the

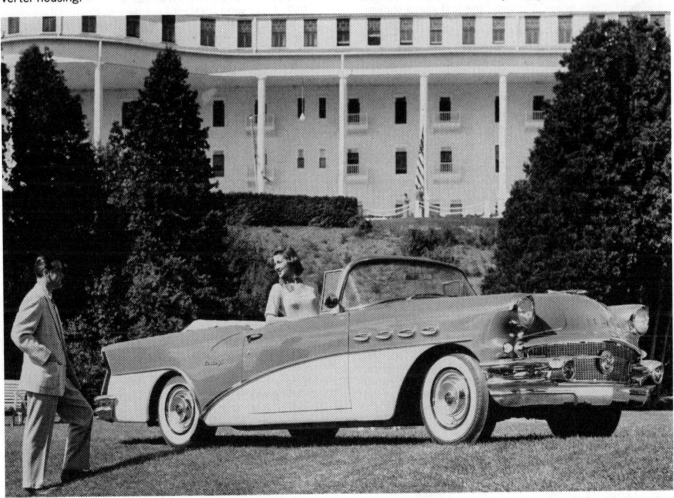

1956 Century convertible.

The 1957 Buick Model 49 four-door Estate Wagon.

equal of those used by Chrysler and Packard.

Unlike previous years, all 1956 Buicks shared the same basic instrument panel although the padded section, standard on the Roadmaster was part of a $38, "Safety Group" option for the other series. Aside from the horizontally read, "Redliner" speedometer the Buick panel was noteworthy for its dual gauge-warning light arrangement for engine temperature, oil pressure and fuel tank level. If the temperature and oil pressure were in the danger zone, a small window glowed red, while under normal conditions it was green. Similarly, the fuel gauge showed green until the fuel tank level fell below the quarter full point. As a result of these changes *Motor Trend* (January 1956) concluded, "legibility of all gauges has jumped from bad to excellent." Another change for the better found inside the 1956 Buicks was a new suspended brake pedal that substantially improved overall body sealing.

Buick, at least in the view of contemporary road testers, was a well-made 1956 automobile.

Buick also acquitted itself well in a poll taken by *Tide Magazine*, an advertising trade journal, of several thousand business executives about their preference among 1956 automobiles. In this survey Buick placed second behind Chrysler but above Cadillac, Lincoln, Oldsmobile, Mercury and Pontiac.

Thus it seemed that Buick's basic sales strength was intact as 1957 approached. Although sales had declined in 1956 it appeared that with new bodies scheduled for 1957 Buick's momentum in the market place would quickly be regained. But that would not be the case. Buick (and General Motors for that matter) was about to learn a harsh lesson from Chrysler Corp. about the role styling played in selling automobiles in the United States.

New body dies in 1957

Measured against the standards that had made Buick the nation's third best selling automobile, its 1957 models had all the ingredients needed to turn in another great sales performance. The lineup of Special, Super, Century and Roadmaster models was given added strength at the top end by the introduction of the Roadmaster 75 (available either as a two or four door hardtop) that Buick claimed was "the most luxurious automobile our stylists and skilled craftsmen could create." Although the lowly Rambler had offered a four-door hardtop station wagon a year earlier, the 1957 Century Caballero wagon took this body style to a height of opulence that seemed right in tune with the times.

More importantly Buick was entering 1957 with its first

set of new body dies in three years. Since 1954 Buick has sharpened and refined a certain "look" whose popularity has effectively muted the comments of its critics. There seemed no reason to tamper with success and thus the 1957 version was readily identifiable as a Buick. The side spear, derived from the 1956 Centurion showcar was now a flat, stainless steel stamping whose center section was slightly depressed to allow space for an enameled tangerine colored strip. Its sleeker form was reflected in Buick's venti-ports that assumed a streamlined teardrop form for 1957. This "wind splitting" theme was further developed by twin parallel ribs that ran down the roof and onto the trunklid. There was certainly no difficulty in determining the 1957 Buick's identity by an examination of its front grille. Constructed of chromed die-cast zinc, it included no less than 121 vertical bars that easily linked the 1957 model with a look shared by every other postwar Buick.

But tradition, custom and business as usual didn't play very well in 1957. No one really expected industry production to nudge 1955 with its nearly eight million car output from the record book, but chances appeared good for a healthy move up from 1956. This did take place as output moved from the 5.8 million level to just over 6.1 million cars produced in 1957. But Buick didn't share in this swing upward. Instead, its production fell from 572,024 in 1956 to 405,098 for the 1957 model run.

What happened to Buick, which lost that coveted third place in sales to Plymouth, was, in retrospect, simple. Like a nation expecting that a future conflict will be fought on the same type of battleground as the previous war, Buick had adopted a Maginot Line type of mentality. Its new cars for example were lower by as much as three inches, but said *Motor Life* (December 1956) retained a "stronge resemblance to 1956 models." In more ominous tones *Motor Trend* (February 1957) summed up its evaluation of the 1957 Buicks by noting "Bodies throughout the line, though entirely redesigned, keep Buick's traditionally substantial look, and you'll have no trouble recognizing a '57 of any series as a relative of earlier models. This is great news for those who want to keep their older version, even if it means less excitement for this year's buyers."

In other words, Buick could do well in 1957 if there was no dramatic change in the market's environment. As we'll be detailing shortly, the new Buicks had some interesting technical changes in 1957, but if any competitor matched radically new styling of its own with engineering changes that were perceived by the public as major advances, Buick's seemingly impervious sales position could rapidly

erode away.

In essence that is what happened in 1957. Although Buick's status and prestige was based upon its image as a medium to upper price class automobile, its sales strength was founded upon the popularity of the Special series. For example, during 1956 nearly 55 percent of Buick output had carried the Special's three portholes on their front fenders. Thus anything that cut into the Special's popularity would profoundly affect Buick's economic health. In 1957 that is exactly what Plymouth accomplished. As Chrysler Corp.'s number one sales division, Plymouth carried Chrysler's Forward Look to the forefront of the public's attention. Whatever sins of omission and neglect Chrysler committed that year in terms of workmanship and quality control, the impact of its new corporate image was profound. Thus when the Buick Special and the top of the line Plymouth series were compared, the results were often, for Buick, unfavorable. While Buick styling adhered to tradition, Plymouth had left its past far behind. Although the 1957 Buick did have a larger panoramic windshield than in 1956, its rear window with its three panels contrasted very unfavorably with Plymouth's huge expanse of glass area that gave its hardtop model a light and lithe look. Even the Buick Super which had one-piece windows (this feature was also a no-cost option for Roadmaster) paled in comparison. Buick also suffered in an analysis of its interior space, since the Plymouth body shell, which was shared with the other Chrysler auto divisions, offered more leg, head and hip room for its occupants. Unfortunately for Buick, the longer this Special-Plymouth confrontation continued, the more it became a Buick debacle. Buick could boast of a new ball-joint front suspension but Plymouth pulverized that more with front torsion bars that lead *Motor Life* (June 1957) to claim "Plymouth is outstanding in roadability, in fact it's tops among all current models of standard passenger cars."

While Plymouth was receiving such plaudits, Buick was on the receiving end of far less complimentary remarks about its roadability. *Motor Trend* (February 1957) reported, "Buick's highway handling, greatly favored by some, is too mushy for us. On bad dips it loses its head, coming out with a great bounding and wallowing that could mean trouble." *Motor Life* (June 1957) was a bit more sympathetic but not by much: "The current model, although improved somewhat from last year, is not outstanding. Lower center of gravity and chassis changes helped, but Buick roadability has not bettered as much as some of its competitors."

Plymouth also scored points with push button Torqueflite and center-plane brakes that regardless of their specific merits conveyed the message that it, not Buick offered more for the customer's dollars. Although Buick Specials had never been the division's performance leader, they hadn't been sloughs either and for 1957 their standard 250 hp, 364 cid, V-8 seemed capable of dominating Plymouth's 215 hp 301 cid V-8.

However Plymouth also offered the Fury's 290 hp engine as an option, which once again suggested it and not Buick was surging ahead in performance.

Yet, the Buick Century remained one of the best accelerating American sedans in 1957. All Buick engines were boosted to 364 cubic inches due to a larger 3.4 inch stroke and 4.125 inch bore. As had been the case, since its introduction back in 1953 the Buick V-8 drove critics slightly crazy by performing far better than they claimed it had a right to. Even Max Balchowsky, who used Buick V-8s in his competition sports cars, found fault with its large intake ports that he claimed seriously reduced fuel-air turbulence. But none the less the Buick V-8 came into 1957 with significant increases in intake and exhaust valve and manifold area plus a big 30 percent boost in the

dimensions of its carburetor venturi. With stronger valve springs and a higher lift, longer duration cam, the Buick V-8 had a 6000+ rpm capability plus the ability to pump out, even in Special tune, 384 lb/ft of torque at 2400 rpm. The 300 hp Century version with 400 lb/ft was especially strong in the 50 mph to 80 mph range where it was 3.2 seconds quicker than the 1956 model. Buick's top speed claims (Special-110 mph, Century-116 mph, Super-112 mph, Roadmaster-115 mph) were in line with contemporary road test results and the only cars tested by *Motor Life* during 1957 that could improve upon the Century's zero to 60 mph time of 8.7 seconds were the 283 hp Corvette, 270 hp Chevrolet Bel Air and Chrysler 300-C. Although it's not known how many Buicks were so equipped, an optional high performance kit rated at 330 hp at 4800 rmp and consisting of 11.0:1 domed pistons, hotter cam, solid lifters and blocked heat risers was also offered by Buick.

Since Buick resisted the move towards smaller wheels and instead chose to retain 15-inch rims for 1957, the main source of its lower height was a new frame. Its side rails were wider apart between the axle kickups and the front cross member was reshaped to allow the use of new ball joints and engine mounts that Buick claimed transmitted less vibration to the frame. The lowering of the floorpan necessitated the slanting downward of the torque tube and the installation of a second universal joint at the rear end of the drive shaft.

Among the more interesting Buick options was a clock that automatically compensated for fast or slow running after being manually corrected. Also of interest was a "Safety-Minder" feature which allowed the driver or a passenger to activate an annoying buzzer that would come alive whenever a predetermined speed was exceeded.

In essence, therefore, Buick's problem in 1957 wasn't that its cars were lacking new styling, performance, or their share of gimmicks. The real source of its sales decline was that its key rivals had moved further ahead at a faster pace. Robert P. Matthews, who subjected the Buick Special to a severe point by point comparison in the June 1957 issue of *Speed Age*, concluded by noting "As to whether the '57 Buick is a lemon we can say very emphatically that it is not. It is certainly ever bit as good as last year's car. But there's the problem: It isn't very much better either."

Ironically, Buick had stumbled over one of the key elements of Alfred Sloan's formula for success, the need to keep the customer dissatisfied. Customers were dissatisfied to be sure but the source of their unhappiness wasn't the old car they were driving, but the new Buicks they saw in the showroom. It made little sense to produce an automobile with a newly designed body that was very similar in appearance to its immediate predecessor.

"Gaudy and big"

Whatever faults the 1958 Buick possessed, no one could criticize it for resembling the 1957 model. Seldom had an automotive face lift been so dramatic, and seldom had restyling been as controversial.

Motor Life (April 1958) described the 1958 Buick as "Gaudy, big and complex." *Speed Age* (July 1958) reported that "they have turned out a car so loaded with chromium bric-a-brac and styling twists that it is difficult to see what is underneath. The new Buick looks as though it has just been driven at high speed through a flatware sale."

Although he had plenty of negative comments for other elements of the 1958 Buick's design, *Motor Trend* magazine's Don Francisco regarded them as "handsome cars,"

yet he quickly explained that they were handsome "in a sedate, conservative fashion that has little appeal to the young in heart."

A strong case can be made for 1958 as a particularly poor year for American automotive styling. Chrysler ineptly revamped its sleek 1957 line into less graceful 1958 models, Ford had considerable difficulty in matching the grace of its 1957s, and the effort of Studebaker-Packard and American Motors to keep their dated automobiles alive were ineffective.

A tour of Buick's new styling format began with its "FashionAire Dynastar grille" where 160 three-quarter-inch square chrome pieces were arrayed. This really was a reasonably attractive setup, but it was only a stepping stone for the Buick's designers to go on a styling rampage. Everywhere, it seemed, was some sort of chromed shape or form. Huge chromed pods placed almost in out-

confusing, to be good," was the consensus of a group of stylists who evaluated the 1958 models for *Motor Life* (April 1958). Strange as it seems, the Buick's hood lacked any sort of ornamentation except for a narrow trough running down its center. Although there were no port holes to be found on the '58 Buicks, there was a huge bulletshaped form on their rear flanks that, on all but the top of the line Limited series, served as a carrier case for what appeared to be a shovel! The Limited models, instead of bearing such a proletarian symbol, were bedecked with three sets of false louvers, a Limited identification, plus a bevy of chrome chevrons.

The 1958 Buick was fitted with neither taillights or tail fins. Instead it introduced "tail towers" to the automotive world. Of course a rose by any other name is still a rose and Buick's "tail towers" were finny, bright and gaudy. Joined by what Buick claimed was the industry's largest

1958 Special convertible.

rigger fashion at the extreme ends of the grille encased the parking lights while "Vista Vision" dual headlights were recessed within chromed ridges that also served as the starting point for 1958's rendition of the Buick sidespear.

Judging from the modest dimensions of the front bumper it seems as if the Buick's stylists for a moment at least had regained their sense of taste and proportion, but if so, it was very short lived. Centrally located on the lower hood surface was a large V positioned within four chromed rings. Of course, someone apparently reasoned it needed a pair of chrome bars on each side to give it balance. Thus the Buick sported a couple of cat whiskers. But if one ringed V is fine, why not three? And where but the front fenders is a better place to put a pair?

"This front end is much too busy, too cluttered, too

bumpers, they gave the 1958 an appearance unlike that of any other automobile. In a strange turnabout of thinking, the Limited models actually had less chrome on their "tail towers" than the less expensive Buicks. Instead it was fitted with special lenses with chrome accents. The Limited had been last produced in 1942 and its revival for 1958 in three body styles (two- or four-door Riviera hardtops or convertible) tended to rekindle the old Buick-Cadillac rivalry of the prewar years.

The general lack of direction and overall confusion that characterized Buick's styling in 1958 had its counterpart in Buick's Air Poise suspension and Flight-Pitch Dynaflow. We hasten to point out that Buick was far from alone in squandering time and talent both on styling that was excessive instead of functional and engineering programs that yielded novelties rather than positive innovations.

Yet in Buick's case, these misdirected efforts tended to obscure more praiseworthy features.

Air Poise, which was optional on all 1958 Buicks, was initially praised by *Motor Trend* (December 1957), which commented, "Most surprising quality of the new air-suspended Buick is its ability to better previous Buicks in overall handling and roadability. The air installation, here, is one of the best." However, after testing an air suspended Buick, Don Francisco (*Motor Trend*, May 1958) presented a devastating report on Air Poise. Although he found no fault with its behavior on "glass-smooth" roads, Francisco reported the Air Poise Buick leaned badly on turns and rocked its passengers back in their seats whenever it started from rest. On irregular road surfaces, the Buick's wheels "would hop up and down in an uncontrolled manner." As a result there was a considerable amount of frame and body vibration.

In fairness to Buick, Air Poise was a corporate, not divisional, development. Along with the rest of the industry, Buick got the air out of its suspension system in fairly short order. Before the year was out, Air Poise was both downplayed and renamed (Air Ride) and after spending a year (1959) with a rear height levelizer variation, the entire system was eliminated for the 1960 model year. On the small number of 1958 Buicks equipped with Air Poise, the conventional springs were replaced with bellows fed by air supplied at 100 psi from a reservoir tank mounted forward of the engine. In turn, a two-cylinder compressor driven off the engine maintained tank pressure at 290 psi. These high pressure requirements were a tip off that leaks would be common Air Poise problems. Since the spring rate of the air bellows was just 60 percent that of the conventional coil springs, an Air Poise Buick had an extremely soft ride.

To limit lean in turns, larger shock absorbers and radius rods were installed along with a transverse stabilizer bar behind the rear axle. Operating with a one-second time delay, the car's leveling system would alter air pressure in the bellows to maintain normal road clearance. The driver could also manually operate this sytem via a control mounted beneath the dash to the right side of the steering column. The driver could thus raise the Buick as much as 5.5 inches. However, while Buick said the frame should be raised when the car was either jacked up or placed on a hoist to avoid damage to the self-leveling system, it strongly advised against driving the car any distance in its elevated position.

Joining Air Poise as a source of unhappiness for Buick during 1958 was its new Flight Pitch Dynaflow. This was an expensive transmission to produce. Its triple turbines created a sensation of slippage and power response that suggested poor performance. Buick had pretty much lost its hot car image by 1958, but a Roadmaster 75 with Flight Pitch (it was standard on Roadmaster and Limited models, optional on other Buicks) achieved a very quick zero to 30 mph time of 3.0 seconds in a *Speed Age* (July 1958) road test. Instead of a low range, the Flight Pitch quadrant contained a G (grade retarding) position that was to be used only under a 40 mph speed for braking purposes, which obviously wasn't what performance fans were lining up for.

Yet in the midst of these technical missteps, Buick offered as standard equipment on all models, except the Special series, air-cooled aluminum front brakes that received kudos as the best in the industry. *Sports Cars Illustrated*, which along with NASCAR, citied Buick for this achievement, regarded their use "as significant today as Oldsmobile's V-8 was in 1949." *Motor Life* (March 1958) reported Buick's braking system "definitely rates as one of the more important technical advances for 1958." Historically, *Sports Cars Illustrated* was slightly off the mark since these brakes had been part of the Roadmaster 75

Another '58 Special, this time a two-door hardtop.

package in 1957.

The essential features of these brakes included use of a special Pearlite, desulphurized iron alloy for the drum liner. During a casting process an aluminum outer surface with 45 fins was applied and the 120 holes drilled in the circumference of the iron portion was fitted with aluminum. Thanks to the greater surface and air turbulance provided by fins, plus aluminum's superior heat conducting ability, these brakes had excellent anti-fade characteristics.

Buick had proclaimed its 1958 models as representing "a decisive breakthrough into a new era of transportation by land." But at model year's end, only 241,908 Buicks had been produced.

It's doubtful if the problems Francisco experienced with his test cars really were representative of Buick's efforts for 1958. Its problems which were shared with most of the industry were being manifested in the increasing sales of Ramblers and imported cars plus steadily mounting criticism of the excessive bulk and ornamentation common to many American automobiles. Customers expectations and preferences were changing direction more rapidly than most industry leaders had anticipated. The Edsel would, as a result, die in infancy, DeSoto would fade away, but Buick would not only survive but go on to enjoy one of the greatest comebacks of modern automobile history.

Dramatic face lift

Buick began preliminary design work on its 1959 models in 1956, a year when it sold 529,371 automobiles, had a firm grip on the number three sales slot and an image for performance, styling and prestige that was the envy of its medium price field competitors. But what a difference three years made! By September 1958 on the eve of its 1959 model introduction, Buick had suffered two consecutive downslide years.

The uninspired, dated-when-new look of the 1957 Buicks had clearly been out of synch with the buyer's tastes and although drastically restyled in the 1958 models had failed to turn the tide, in retrospect Buick's Chief Engineer Olive Kelley conceded (*Business Week*; Sept. 20, 1958) its 1958 models "simply weren't the bombshells' of styling...needed to make customers 'want so much to buy that they can taste it.'" To produce an automobile that could achieve Buick's general manager Edward Ragsdale's announced goal of a 10 percent slide of the 1959 new car market was only part of the challenge facing Buick as the model year began.

1959 Invicta convertible.

For many years it had been the dominant automobile in the medium price class, using this base to send out the Special series on very successful forays into the lucrative low-priced field. But Buick's problems (for most of the 1958 model year Buick sold only half as many cars as it had in 1957) were due not only to a recession and unpopular styling. Perhaps even more crucial was the changed market environment in which Buick was doing business.

In a tremendously successful response to the Buick Special's intrusion into what had long been their domain, the "low priced three," Ford, Chevrolet and Plymouth had created their own brand of "Special" models. These were of course Fairlanes, Impalas and Belvederes and their impact upon the old-line members of the medium price field was severe. By 1958 Chevrolet was selling 32.2 percent of all two- and four-door sedans in the Buick Special's price range and the traditional medium priced cars had had their market share trimmed by the intruders from 39 percent in 1955 to 27 percent in 1958.

Rather than preside over the dismemberment of the Buick empire without a struggle, Ragsdale and his lieutenants came out fighting hard for that earlier mentioned 10 percent market share. That goal was probably intentionally inflated but you couldn't tell that from the rhetoric surrounding the 1959 Buick's debut. Buick was ready to tackle the "upper low-priced cars" said Ragsdale, "with a new sales theme: A car for two out of three new car buyers." That really didn't have much of a ring to it but at a preview showing of the '59 models for Buick dealers the LeSabre was displayed with a sign reading "Competition — Dodge, DeSoto, Firesweep, Mercury Monterey, Pontiac, Plymouth Belvedere, Chevrolet Impala, Ford Fairlane." Buick's general sales manager, Edward C. Kennard

underscored this aggressive stand by telling his audience at the 1959 models' official introduction that "One look at the car, one look at the year, and you just know Buick's going places in 1959."

For nearly a quarter-century Buick advertising (which by 1958 represented a hefty $25 million annual expenditure) had been handled by Kudner, Inc. which also had responsiblity for several other GM auto division accounts. But with Buick recharting its direction, Ragsdale decided it was time for a change. Thus after a two month sojourn into the Madison Avenue heartland of America's advertising agencies Mr. Ragsdale selected McCann-Erickson to be the purveyor of Buick's bright new image. At this time McCann-Erickson was the nation's second largest advertising agency and for fifteen years had managed a lucrative Chrysler Corporation account. No doubt Ed Ragsdale had images of a "Forward Look" type of ad campaign that would do for Buick what it had done for Chrsyler. However, as *Fortune* (May 1958) reported, "Ed Ragsdale...is under no illusion that some nostrum of McCann's concoction will cure Buick's ills. The first imperative is to build a better Buick for 1959."

It's fair to say that Buick worked mighty hard to do just that. It's also no secret that GM was cut to the core of its corporate self confidenced by the success of the 1957 Chrysler products and came soaring into view two years later with five lines of automobiles that in terms of length, width, height (low) and sweeping, soaring and swooping fins took second place to no other American automobile. But never let it be said that the '59 Buick was little more than a carbon copy Chrysler. Its concave windshield, canted rear fender fins and similarly shaped "gull wing" front end were all directly traceable to the 1956 Centu-

rion Motorama show car. *Popular Science* (October 1958) brought Harlow Curtice in as a key factor behind the 1959 Buick look by quoting him as remarking: "If we haven't got anywhere else to start — I've got an idea...one of the prettiest cars we've ever designed was the Centurion."

The result was a radical departure from what had been a predictable styling pattern. In the past, whenever a new Buick body style had been introduced it had retained key appearance elements thus maintaining a continuity with previous models. The only such feature to be found on the 1959 Buick was its grille and even then its link to the 1958 model was very tenuous. This close to revolutionary change, had at least one Buick dealer a bit worried since he was overheard remarking at an early preview, "It certainly doesn't look like a Buick." This didn't apparently bother Buick since it later printed this comment in a press release.

Buick also decided 1959 was the year for dumping overboard those vintage Special, Century, Super, Roadmaster and Limited labels in favor of LeSabre, Invicta, Electra and Electra 225. To some old-time Buick types this bordered on heresy but it was a clear signal that Buick was ready to jellison just about every link with its past if it would help its dealers sell more cars. However, *Motor Life* (November 1958) pondering the obvious, remarked, "Just how the public will react to departure of the traditional 'Buick look' remains to be seen." However, initial sales reports were extremely encouraging. *Speed Age* (February 1959) reported "The dramatically restyled Buick not only set early-weeks sales records but whetted the public interest in all the new cars." But this early momentum was not sustained and for the model year Buick fell from fith to seventh position with a final production figure of just over 285,000 cars.

Buick had hoped that not only would its new styling appeal to younger buyers but that a goodly number of the 740,000 Americans who had purchased Buicks in 1955 would decide it was time to trade in for a new '59. Why this didn't happen remains a mystery to the present. It's true that a steel strike early in the sales year hurt Buick's sales offensive but it wasn't alone in suffering its consequences. It's possible that the new models were just a bit too advanced for owners of older Buicks to accept. But the other GM cars were also radically changed and their market didn't turn sour.

It is possible however that Buick's poor sales, reflected the continuing success of its competition's relentless expansion of their sales spheres. Thus Buick not only had to build a better Buick but Buick designed-to-a-different-beat if it was ever to regain its former sales strength. It would not be only due to an expanding national economy that Buick would begin its long road back in the early sixties. Closely tied to the renaissance of a great American automobile were the introduction of some of the most interesting models yet to bear the Buick name.

Where then does all this leave the 1959 Buick? By any measure they deserved a warmer response from new car buyers. While Buick wisely reduced its available color and trim options from over 3,000 in 1958 to just 25 in 1959 as a means to (reported *Business Week*, Sept. 20, 1958) "put only tasteful looking cars on the raod" it was also building automobiles whose performance required no apologies. The LeSabre used the same 364 cid V-8 of 1958 with ratings of 250 hp at 3,300 rpm and 384 lb/ft of torque at 2,400 rpm. In the interest of improved fuel economy a 3.7:1 axle ratio was standard with Twin Turbine Dynaflow. The venturi of the LeSabre two-barrel carburetor were also slightly reduced in size from the 1958 version. With a larger, 4.1875 inch bore and 3.640 inch stroke, the engine for the Invicta and Electra series displaced 401 cubic inches. Equipped with a four-barrel carburetor and 10.5:1 compression ratio this was good for

325 hp at 4,400 rpm and 445 pound/foot at 2,800 rpm. Buick offered a variety of performance and economy packages that allowed for example, a LaSabre to be fitted with Twin Turbine, four barrel carburetor dual exhausts and a 3.23 axle for optimum acceleration.

At the other extreme, all three series could be ordered with Triple-Turbine Dynaflow, the four barrel carb and dual exhaust set up plus a 2.78:1 axle. Invictas, and Electras could have the same package but with the 3.23 axle. The result were some pretty quick automobiles since even with the ecomony, 2.78:1 axle a Triple Turbine Invicta needed only 8.8 seconds to run from zero to 60 mph. In this form its top speed exceeded 126 mph.

The typical 1959 Buick weighed well over two tons and with a 123 inch (Le Sabre and Invicta) or 126.3 inch (all Electras) wheelbase plus an intimidating 80.7 inch width it was well up in standing as one of America's largest automobiles. This bulk obviously didn't forecast nimble handling and two-seater-like roadability. On the other hand, the Buick's engineers had managed to improve the ride and drive characteristics. Significantly higher front and rear roll centers, a wider (by three inches) tread, an additional 0.5 inch of front coil spring travel, use of all-weather shock absorbers and a larger front stabilizer bar made the 1959 models the best handling Buicks yet.

Chief Buick engineer Oliver Kelley never tired of touting them as far superior in this regard to the 1958s. Yet the traditional Buick soft and smooth ride remained intact. An improved Saginaw power steering with only four turns lock to lock, close attention to sound proofing plus the use of thicker and softer rubber body mounts all contributed to Buick's good reputation in this category.

Unfortunately, much of this competent road behavior went by the boards when rough surfaces were encountered. Buick prolonged the life of its torque tube rear end a bit too long with the '59's and this "ponderous mass of unsprung weight" (in the words of *Speed Age* (January 1959) caused any ambitious maneuvers over a bumpy road to "set the car," continued *Speed Age* "to shaking and shuddering like a sailing ship in a typhoon."

On the other hand, Buick's brakes continued to be first class. For 1959 the aluminum front brakes were refined to become, except perhaps for the Corvette's cerametallic-lined drums, the best in the business. The process by which the aluminum outer surface was bonded to its cast iron liner was both novel and effective. The first stage involved the immersing of the liner into molten aluminum whose temperature was 1,375 degrees F. This caused the aluminum to combine chemically with the raw iron to form an iron aluminum alloy surface coating. With no temperature reduction, the liner was placed in a mold where the aluminum drum was cast around it. The result was a brake with improved heat transfer, superior internal dimensional stability and since there were no holes as on the 1958 version, a smoother and stronger braking surface. Buick retained conventional cast iron drums for the rear wheels but their performance was improved, thanks to the 60 fins cast into their outer diameters. Even its harshest critics had to approve of Buick's decision to equip all its 1959 models with this braking system as standard equipment.

It's easy to dismiss the 1959 Buicks as failures because of their dismal sales, yet they were cars that were just too good in too many ways for that. Everyone knows about the lowest ebb being the turning of the tide and although Buick sales would fall a bit further in 1960, it was on the way back. Within two years, production would be back above the 400,000 level and just a bit further down the road was a new model whose existence would symbolize Buick's climb back up to the top.

1906 Buick Model G runabout.

Buicks's innovations

By Walter O. MacIlvain

It seems that the valve-in-head engine was not the invention of David Buick, in spite of rumors to the contrary. His stationary engines, produced by the Auto Vim and Power Co., Detroit, at the turn of the century, were of the side-valve type. While his associate, Walter Marr, claimed to have invented the OHV engine, it was engineer Eugene C. Richard who saw it in his native France and patented it in 1902, assigning the patent to Buick Manufacturing Co. Richard did likewise with his patents on a carburetor and a muffler in 1904.

A selective type of lever shift controlled the planetary transmission in the 1907 Model F, with a master clutch to disconnect the entire system. The same features were found in the Model 10 four-cylinder Buick made from 1908 to 1911, and planetary-geared small Buicks as late as 1912.

The 1912 models were unique in having the brake and gearshift levers positioned just inside the right front door with only the handles showing.

A unique bulb horn mount beneath the valance, or filler board, above the running board in 1912 alone showed only the mouth of the horn protruding.

Buick was along in positioning the brake bedal about two inches higher than the clutch pedal from 1924 through 1930.

Buick engines featured an oil cooling radiator beneath the car's regular radiator in 1931. Its place was later taken by an oil temperature control device mounted on the engine.

The bulging side, or "pregnant cow" look, was unique to Buick in 1929, somewhat modified in 1930 and '31.

In 1932 the Buick "Wizard Control" was a small button placed beneath the clutch pedal to control the clutch by vacuum, releasing it at closed throttle for a free-wheeling effect, one of the gimmicks offered by the manufacturers during the Depression in an attempt to sell cars.

"Anolite," anodized aluminum pistons, in 1936 solved the scuffing and fast wear problems inherent in the light material.

A runningboard antenna for the radio was a novelty for 1937, using the runningboard itself for this function, insulated from the car.

An automatic transmission in late 1937 was first with hydraulic control, optional on series 40. Called the Self-Shifter, it was offered through 1938 only, although Buick sold these transmissions to Oldsmobile for use on some 1937 Olds eights.

Domed pistons in 1938 permitted a higher compression ratio to be used without detonation.

Coil springs at all four corners were first used by Buick

in 1938 if we overlook the Brush runabout, which had them from 1907 through 1912.

Another Buick innovation was the first U.S. use of directional signals. The flashing lights were applied at the rear in 1939 and both front and rear in 1940.

Two changes were made in 1941, one a mistake and the other a success. The mistake was the adoption of 10 mm metric spark plugs; and the good news was compound carburetion on the big eights. Those having 10 mm plugs were soon recalled and the threads opened up to 14 mm to overcome excessive fouling.

"Venti-ports" (port holes) on the sides of the front fenders/hood were a distinguishing Buick feature from 1949-'57, and again from 1961-'75 in modified form.

Ribbed aluminum brake drums in 1957-'58 gave superior heat dissipation. They were lined with steel to take the wear.

A styling innovation was the gunsight hood ornament, 1948 through 1957, as was the "Sweepspear" feature along the sides, starting with the 1949 Riviera and running for 10 years. The toothed grille was unique with Buick from 1942 until copied by DeSoto in 1953. It lasted until 1955.

Dynaflow Drive came along in 1948, a hydraulic torque converter in connection with a two-speed planetary gearset, providing two ranges. There was no shifting of speeds, but it operated with a churning action, sometimes called a "slush pump," providing a torque multiplication of 2.25:1. This system turned into Twin Dynaflow in 1953 and Variable Pitch Dynaflow in '55. A fixed blade stator was added between the first and second turbines for 1956. This seemed the ultimate until 1958 when the Triple Action Flight Pitch Dynaflow was applied to the big Buicks, option on others. For 1961, Buick went to the Dual Path Turbine Drive in conjunction with a three-speed planetary step shift in the Special. This was superseded in '64 by the Super Turbine 300. For 1969 the THM 300 (Turbo-Hydra-Matic 300) was used in cooperation with Chevrolet, and thus the Dynaflow was laid to rest.

Buick's version of the station wagon, the "Estate Wagon," had a smaller, more compact body than most, being based on a sedan rather than a truck.

In 1954 Buick's speedometer registered the mph by means of a horizontal red bar progressing from left to right. This continued through 1961.

The wraparound windshield with its knee-knocking "dog legs" was shared with Oldsmobile, beginning in 1954 and continuing through 1960.

Aluminum alloy connecting rod bearings were reputedly a Buick first in 1955.

1907 Buick Model G roadster.

A "Twilight Sentinel" (an extra cost option) turned the lights off and on automatically in 1960.

The aluminum block V-8 was a Buick innovation in the 1961-'62 Special, replaced in '63 by a V-6 cast iron block.

The first 90-degree V-6 was pioneered by Buick in 1961, designed to be machined on the same production line as the small V-8. When Buick finished with this engine in 1967, the production facilities were sold to American Motors. During the oil crisis of 1974, AMC sold this machinery back to GM. In a 60-degree V-6 there are inherent unbalanced forces, i.e., it fires in an off-beat manner.

In the 1966 Riviera, the vent windows adjoining the windshield were eliminated in the interest of better ventilation flow.

The controversial boar-rail design of the 1971 Riviera was the first example of this style feature since the Hudson-Essex roadsters of 1927-'31. It did not gain universal approval. You either loved it or hated it. In 1974 it was superseded by a more conventional rear deck design.

An extra-cost item in 1971 was "Max-Trac," a device that electronically interrupted the ignition circuit in case of wheelspin. It was soon discontinued.

The V-6 was made into an even firing engine for 1978 by the clever engineering expedient of splitting the crank throws and rotating the two halves in relation to one another.

Sequential fuel injection is a novelty in the 1984 Buick Turbo-V-6.

Unusual Features

Three-quarter elliptic springs in front and semi-elliptic rear in the 1904-'11 two-cylinder models (usually the other way around).

Tilting steering columns for easier entrance and egress, 1905-'10 two-cylinder models.

Unit power plant with flywheel at the front, 1906 four cylinder Model D, a feature shared with the Maxwell. This was not a valve-in-head engine.

Single coil, distributor ignition, 1908 Model 10 and onward.

Self-contained crankcase oiling system, 1908-on.

Hub-type friction spark and throttle levers on steering wheel, 1908 Model 10.

High-wheel type motor buggy with low pneumatic tired wheels, 1910-'11 Model 14.

Fenders curved at juncture with running boards, front, and on roadster and coupe models rear, 1913 through 1919 (shared with other GM cars).

Nickel plated steering column, 1913-'24; brass, 1904-'13 (shared with other GM cars).

Packard-shaped radiator shell, 1924 through 1928, shared with Studebaker, Paterson, Star and Gray.

Radiator shell like Leon-Bolee (France) 1929-'32.

Muffler cut-out furnished through 1918, removable exhaust plug through 1922.

Multiple-disc clutch, 1918 through 1930.

Fisher "No-Draft" ventilation, 1933 through 1968 (a GM feature).

Automatic Ride Control, 1933.

Touch-screen electronic control, 1985 Riviera.

Buick trivia

Non-standard gearshift pattern, pre-1909 to 1928. First: right and back; second: left and forward; high: left and back; reverse: right and forward.

Cantilever rear spring suspension, 1915 to 1930, sixes, only.

Integral cylinder head with valves in cages, 1904 through 1923, sixes only.

Two-cylinder engine, 1903 to 1913, certain models; to 1914 as a truck.

Torque-tube drive, 1908 through 1961 (except certain models).

Low, rounded radiator shell and hood lines, 1914 through 1920.

High-mounted brake pedal (see innovations) 1924 through 1931.

Pedal shift starter, 1914 through 1932.

Single-unit starting-lighting-ignition, 1914-1931.

Mechanical four-wheel brakes, 1924 through 1935.

Straight-eight engine, 1931 through 1953.

More Buick Trivia

If "Chevrolet is as American as apple pie," then by the same token, Buick might be likened to blueberry pie, corn bread, or the hot dog in our society. Buick history has been written over and over again. Most everyone knows that W. C. Durant built the great General Motors empire around his company in 1908. Most people know that David Dunbar Buick, to whom we owe the porcelainized bathroom fixtures, sold his plumbing business at the turn of the century. He started building stationary engines, but ran into financial difficulties when he tried to build a car. He was assisted first by the brothers Briscoe who ran a sheet metal shop in Detroit; when Benjamin Briscoe, who really wanted to build John Maxwell's car, gave up on Buick, J. H. Whiting, a successful wagon manufacturer in Flint, took over what by mid-1903 had become the Buick Motor Co., moving it from Detroit to Flint, the "Vehicle City" early in 1904.

By this time, Buick, assisted by able engineers Walter L. Marr and Eugene C. Richard, had evolved an excellent engine with the valves in the head, forming the nucleus of their business. Around a two-cylinder version a workable vehicle had been built. It had the features that would launch the Buick car into the business world: radiator in front, engine beneath the seat, planetary two-speed and reverse transmission, and a single chain taking the drive to the center of a live rear axle in the typical American fashion. A dummy hood in front concealed not only the engine, but fuel and oil tanks.

Not so well known is that the Buick Motor Co. purchased the Pope-Robinson Co. of Hyde Park, Mass. in 1904 to obtain a Selden Patent license to avoid being sued for infringement.

William C. Durant came upon the scene in 1904. With J. Dallas Dort, Durant also made horsedrawn vehicles in

1912 Buick touring.

Flint. Overcoming the natural antipathy that horse people felt toward motor vehicles, he took a ride in a Buick and admired it for its hill climbing ability. In fact, he liked it so well that he bought the company.

It is also common knowledge that the man who founded and gave his name to this popular vehicle died in poverty in 1929, having unwisely disposed of his stock in the company at an early date. He left in 1908.

The first four-cylinder Buick was the 1906 Model D, which had not a valve-in-head, but a T-head motor with the flywheel in front and unit power plant configuration. This model was built in the J. H. Whiting plant in Jackson, Mich.; Whiting was president of Buick. The breadwinner of the Buick family was still the two-cylinder car that remained in the line until 1909 in single chain drive form.

A Buick won the Dead Horse Hill Climb in Worcester, Mass. in 1907. The year 1908 was Buick's best, for in that year Durant organized GM as a holding company, and with Buick profits purchased control of Olds Motor Works and Cadillac Motor Car Co. (1909). The year 1908 saw Buick's rise to first place, with 8,820 units produced. The little white Model 10 runabouts accounted for most of these sales. It used a valve-in-head 3¾-inch "square" bi-block engine, was shaft driven through a planetary gear-set operated by a side lever, had an 88-inch wheelbase, and sold for $850. With wheelbase increased to 92 inches in 1909, touring bodies were added. Model 10 was replaced in 1911 by Model 32 with the same engine, but with improved appearance.

A luxury Model 5 continued the T-head engine at $2,500, becoming Model 7 in 1909. Later big Buicks used valve-in-head engines, giving rise to the slogan in later years: "Valve-in-head means Buick."

Buick lost first place in 1909 to Henry Ford, who held it for many years thereafter.

During 1910 the single chain Model F was laid to rest, and a double chain driven, double opposed motored Model 14 was brought out. It sold for the low price of $550. This was the year in which Durant lost control of General Motors.

At this time, Buick was making racing history. Driven by Bob Burman, a Buick "Bug" went 105 mph on the Indianapolis track in 1910, the fastest time recorded for an American car. Burman also won the Lowell Cup, a 318-mile road race, in 1909.

Enclosed bodies from 1910 on were supplied by the Fisher brothers. In the shake-up of GM's top management, W. C. Durant was succeeded as general manager by Charles W. Nash. Nash in turn was succeeded in 1912 by Walter P. Chrysler. Meanwhile, the Buick car was devel-

oping and achieving a fine reputation for dependability. Some of the engines were made by GM's newly acquired Northway Motor and Manufacturing Co. All passenger cars had four cylinders in 1912 and 1913. GM's Welch-Detroit cars were built by Buick in 1911 pending the completion of their own factory in Saginaw. These were practically Model 7 Buicks under the Welch name. Buick also turned out several Marquette-Buick racing cars in 1912 having six-inch diameter cylinders (593.8 cubic inches). In 1912 the shape of the Buick nameplate was changed from round to rectangular, the blue and white style which was recognized for many years.

All but the smallest Buicks in 1914 had new rounded hood and radiator lines blended with a smooth cowl and body, ushering the new "streamline" era. Left drive and self-starters also appeared. A six-cylinder model was added with a third block of 3¾ inch by five inch cylinders, (displacing 268.3 cid), Delco single unit electrics and torque tube drive. The five-passenger touring on a 130-inch wheelbase sold for $1,985. It was modified for 1915 with a seven-passenger body and cantilever rear suspension at a price reduced to $1,650. Fours were continued that year, but the only four produced in 1916 was the three-quarter ton truck.

Series letters were B in 1914, C in 1915, and D in 1916-1917, E in 1918, H for 1919, and K in 1920.

More Buick Trivia

For 1916 the light six Model 44-45 appeared, destined for a long run, with modifications until 1924. Like its big brother, the 6-45 had cantilever rear springs and torque tube drive to a full floating rear axle. The later big sixes had one-piece type paneling fenders of artistic design. These were picked up again for models in 1923. The fenders of the 1916 light six were of flat, beaded design, changed to crown style in 1917 except for the four.

A small four-35 of advanced design appeared in August 1916, with detachable cylinder head and semi-elliptic rear springs. Priced at $635, it had the full Delco system and a 106-inch wheelbase.

The president of Buick at this time was W. P. Chrysler. He succeeded C. W. Nash who left General Motors to purchase the Thomas B. Jeffery Co. Walter L. Marr, chief engineer, left in mid-'16; he was succeeded by Arthur E. Chase, body designer.

In the World War I period, Buick's contribution included tanks, Liberty engines, and ambulances.

The first choice of space at the national automobile shows was awarded to Buick from 1919 through 1923. It was based on dollar volume of sales by the N.A.C.C. (Ford was not a member of the National Automobile Chamber of Commerce, so his profits, though higher, didn't count.)

The big six had been dropped in 1917, but to satisfy the demand for a seven-passenger car, a longer wheelbase (124 inch) chassis was added in August for the 1918 season. Series E had a one-eighth inch larger bore and three-inch longer wheelbase (118 inches) in the shorter chassis. Open cars were distinguished by slanting windshields. Sixes only were offered in the 1919, 1920, and 1921 years, and the light delivery car was discontinued. The four was revived from 1922 through 1924, with a 109-inch wheelbase, underslung rear springs, and valve covers. The last mentioned were applied to six-cylinder engines in 1919. Chrysler was succeeded as president in 1920 by H. H. Bassett.

It seems that an improvement in car design was not accepted as official until it had been adopted by Buick. For example, four-wheel braking was not new prior to 1924, but it remained for Buick to popularize it. Buick also popularized the sport open-type car with maroon finish and khaki top, plus a wealth of extra equipment, red leather upholstery, and so on. These very desirable models in roadster and four-passenger touring form were offered on the longer chassis from 1922 and 1923, respectively, and for several years thereafter.

Radiators were taller in 1921, with straight hood and cowl lines. The tops had gypsy-type rear curtains. For 1923, chassis were lowered, with smaller tires and better riding qualities. Car number 1,000,000 was produced in 1923. Two-door touring sedans were added that year.

The famous copy of the Packard radiator and other

1916 Buick five-passenger touring.

THE loyalty to quality which prevails in Buick design and manufacture is revealed by the sincerity and charm of Buick style. Every Buick model is an accomplishment in good taste—an achievement in luxurious living.

THE GREATEST **BUICK** EVER BUILT

When Better Automobiles are Built Buick will Build Them

1927 Buick — "The greatest Buick ever built."

1932 Buick five-passenger coupe.

external design features occurred in the 1924 models. These also introduced standard mechanical four-wheel brakes and a larger engine with a detachable head and pressure lubrication to the bearings. A proliferation of models included a brougham-sedan with provision for a trunk at the rear on the long chassis.

Balloon tires were standard in 1925, along with Duco pyroxylin lacquer sprayed-on finishes. A lighter Standard Six replaced the four, based on the design of the continued Master Six. "Triple Sealing" in 1926 marked the addition of oil filter, air cleaner, and gasoline filters. General refinement in 1927 showed harmonic crankshaft balancers, new colors and longer tail pipes. Standard shift was adopted for 1928, and double-drop frames made the cars much lower. Fenders were a plain full-crown design without paneling. This was the final year of the "Packard radiator."

The 1929s had the famous "pregnant cow" look with new radiator and hood lines. The lack of mouldings were designed to catch the highlights by the use of horizontal curved surfaces.

Engines were larger, wheelbases were longer, fuel pumps replaced vacuum tanks, and chromium replaced nickel plating.

A smaller companion car, the Marquette, was marketed by Buick dealers in 1929-1930. Mechanically, it resembled the Oldsmobile rather than Buick, having the L-head engine, open prop-shaft with semi-elliptic springs and hotchkiss drive.

From 1928 on, a purchaser could have the spares in fender wells. Beginning in 1929, wire wheels became available with painted or natural wood wheels as options. E. A. DeWaters, chief engineer, retired after 25 years of service with Buick. He was succeeded by F. A. ("Dutch") Bowers.

For 1930, body lines were modified. A semi-elliptic underslung rear spring replaced the time-honored cantilever, and brakes were placed inside the drums, still mechanically operated. These were the last of the straight-sixes; for 1931 all models were straight-eights. New five-bearing engines in three sizes were dropped into the same space formerly occupied by the former sixes. Along with the new engines came the synchromesh gearboxes, an improvement badly needed by this maker. The smallest, Series 50, was actually a continuation of the Marquette chassis, with open driveshaft and Hotchkiss drive. Series 60, 80, and 90 continued the torque-tube drive. New were intake silencer and regrouped dials on the dashboard. New plate clutches replaced the old multiple disc used since 1918.

Now into the Great Depression, Buicks for 1932 were replete with innovations in an effort to stimulate sales. Cars were lower with long, sweeping fenders, lower sills, bullet instead of clamshell lamps, single bar bumpers, and slanting windshields with inside visors. Larger models had ride control, but all had "Wizard Control" (a small button under the clutch pedal providing vacuum clutch action plus free-wheeling when desired.) As appealing as were the 1932 Buicks, sales (47,664) were less than one-half those of the previous year, and much lower than the 121,333 figure of 1930. Again revamped for 1933, the streamlined era was manifested in the use of V-radiator, vent windows, new rearward sloping bodies and skirted fenders. Wheelbases were longer, treads wider, and X-frames came in. Safety glass became standard equipment, and one had his choice of steel spoked or wire wheels.

On the retirement of Ed Strong, Harlow H. Curtice became president in October 1933, and Charles Chayne was made assistant to chief engineer Bower.

Even More Buick Trivia

Improvements came along thick and fast during the Depression years; engineering departments throughout the industry were striving to justify their existence by

creating new models for which there would be a demand, and Buick was no exception.

At Buick, "Knee Action" was the big development for 1934, independent front suspension with unequal "A" arms, greatly improving the riding qualities. A stabilizer bar was provided at the rear to combat side sway; handling was further assisted by center point steering, and a vacuum booster was provided to assist the mechanical brake system. Also new was accelerator pedal starting. Styling alterations included more complete enclosure at the front, and the substitution of horizontal louvres for the door type vents in the sides of the hood.

A new "40" introduced several engine features new to Buick, such as chain timing drive, generator and water pump belt-driven, on the fan shaft, eliminating the accessories shaft. Announced in May 1934, the "40" showed brilliant performance characteristics at reasonable prices.

Minor improvements for 1935 included Stromberg dual downdraft carburetion with automatic choke, a ball clutch release bearing, and improved handling.

Harlow H. Curtice's hand was seen in an entirely new line of Buicks for 1936, characterized by a high, narrow radiator and hood line, "Turret Tops," V-windshields, and a repositioning forward of the entire car with respect to the wheels. New also was hydraulic, internal braking. Model nomenclature now included names in addition to the number "Special" (40), "Century" (60), "Roadmaster" (80), and "Limited" (90). A new 320-cubic inch engine utilized the new features found in the 40, developing 120 bhp at 3,200 rpm. This engine powered the Century, Roadmaster and Limited. Wheelbases were adjusted to 118 inches, 122 inches, 131 inches, and 138 inches, and prices ranged from $885 to $1,695, f.o.b. Flint.

The three millionth Buick was built May 24, 1936. Charles Chayne was promoted to chief engineer succeeding Bower, who went to Opel in Germany. Despite the Depression, Buick launched a $15 million rehabilitation program of the factories. In 1936, production rose from 109,724 to 179,533, and the work force was increased from 11,167 to 13,899.

Hypoid gearing on the 40 and 60 marked the 1937 lines, of which there were four series in 21 body types. Century and Special series featured Unisteel bodies. All but the 40 had the larger straight-eight engine. Radiator grilles now had horizontal instead of vertical fins, and bodies were roomier. The wheelbase of the 40 increased to match the 60 at 122 inches.

Buick opened its new transmission factory in '37 and began to supply the new self shifting gearset, the first with hydraulic controls as extra equipment on the 40 and also on Oldsmobiles.

In 1938, Buick pioneered the use of coil springing at all chassis points (if we overlook their use on the 1907-1913 Brush runabout). In appearance, this year's output resembled the 1937's except for a new die-cast grille with horizontal bars instead of fins, new hood hinges, and new rear license plate treatment. The so-called "Dynaflash" engine introduced domed pistons to raise the compression, and batteries were placed under the hood. The sales figure of 173,905 was fourth highest in the industry. All models now used hypoid gearing in the rear axle, and the wheelbase of the 90 was increased to 140 inches.

The 1939 Buicks featured "Speed Styling," "Unisteel Bodies," higher windshields, and concealed running

1940 Buick Model 41 Special four-door.

boards. The gearshift lever was placed on the steering column, and the selfshifter formerly offered on the 40 was discontinued. Glass area was greatly increased all around, and an industry first was the use of flashing directional signals at the rear. Instrument boards were of a new convex design, and push-button radios were a novelty. Charles Chayne paced the Indianapolis 500 in a Buick that year.

The Buick "Estate Wagon" was introduced with the 1940 line, also two new series, the 50 "Super" and the '70 "Roadmaster." Headlights with the new sealed beam feature now blended into the fenders, and Foamtex rubber padding was built into the seats. Directional signals, now standard front and rear, were wired into the parking lamps. Other mechanical points included A. C. oil filter, pressure cooling, vacuum starter control, and terne plated mufflers. Buick number four million came off the line Nov. 18, 1940. Several hundred Buick 41-T taxicabs were sold.

A sensational streamlined roadster was seen in May 1940 on a Series 50 chassis, conceived by stylist Harley Earl. It had 13 inch tires, special airplane brakes, scirocco air cooled, retractable headlights, and inbuilt running boards concealed by the doors.

All doors opened from the rear in the 1941 Buicks, as in previous year's Super 51 sedan, following a trend started by Cadillac's "60 Special" sedan (1938). The upper sections of the front fenders were flared into the body, stopping just forward of the doors, and the headlights were now fully imbedded into the fenders. The "Fireball" engine featured "Compound Dual Carburetion" (two dual carburetors) for improved power and fuel economy. One unit functioned at partial throttle, the second coming in at full throttle. Ten millimeter spark plugs resulted in a recall whereby the holes were rebored and rethreaded to take 14 millimeter plugs. There was an oil bath air cleaner and recirculating ball type. Saginaw steering gear. A few Limited chassis were custom fitted to bodies by Brunn & Co., respected old coach builders.

The 1942 Buicks carried the front fender lines further back into the bodies, even intersecting with the rear fenders in some cases. Wrap-around bumpers were introduced, also broad-base safety rims and a foot-operated parking brake. only 16,601 Buicks were produced during the 1942 calendar year, to the time when, by government edict, all production passenger car lines were down early in February.

We've carried Buick up to World War II. For a continuation and for further reading, we refer you to the excellent accounts appearing in two catalogs, titled *The Standard Catalog of American Cars, 1805 to 1942* and *The Standard Catalog of American Cars, 1946 to 1975*. Another good reference work, *Buick, the Complete History*, by Dunham and Gustin, will take you up to 1985. Much of the foregoing was taken from various magazine articles in such as *The Horseless Age, Motor, Automotive Industries*, and from personal experiences.

The writer's experience with Buick started when his father purchased a little four-cylinder 1917 Buick, his first car. The ruggedness of this car was put to the test on a blueberry expedition in the remote Adirondacks area in northern New York. There was one place where the road had deteriorated to a sharp incline of rocks and sand. The car simply ground to a halt.

My dad restarted the motor and let in the clutch, only to have the wheels spin a few times, then stall. This routine was repeated several times and finally my dad gave up. Imagine our consternation to find that he had been trying to start the car not in first, but in third gear!

With any lesser car we would have had a 25-mile hike back to civilization.

Later, when I arrived at the age when a boy had to have a car, we found a fairly good used 1919 Buick three-

passenger roadster. We learned the facts of life as a backyard mechanic with this car: how to take up the bearings, grind the valves, and general maintenance. To grind the valves on these non-detachable head engines, one would simply remove a valve cage, one at a time. A self-contained valve and seat in a cylindrical casting had openings that would match up with the gas or exhaust passages in the cylinder block. You could take out this cage by means of a pry-bar after lifing the push rod out of the way, then compress the spring in a vise, remove the key, and sit down in a rocking chair and grind the valve into the seat. Then we would test our work by filling the cage with gasoline, holding it vertically by the valve stem. No drip would mean that it was okay. When we adjusted the bearings, it was a mater of taking out shims or filing the face of the cap until one could just feel the drag on the crank. After taking up the six connecting rod bearings and the four mains, that shaft would be stiff! The procedure of starting the newly overhauled engine would involve two men, one on the starter and the other on the crank. We were not above making alterations. Substituting a Stromberg OE-2 for the original Marvel carburetor made a tremendous difference in smooth running, and swapping mufflers with my father's Oldsmobile, together with a flexible metal tube tailpipe, produced a really nice exhaust note—still better when we rammed a crow-bar into the back of the muffler for a straight through effect. The Buick muffler also made the Olds run more quietly. Some young fellows had girls . . . we had cars!

1942 Buick Roadmaster four-door.

Buick — GM's financial pillar

Buick Motor Division, which claims one of the most dramatic and important chapters in the history of the American automobile, celebrated its 85th anniversary in 1988.

The division's founder, David Dunbar Buick, was building gasoline engines by 1899, and his engineer, Walter L. Marr, apparently built the first automobile to be called a Buick in 1900. But Buick traditionally dates its true beginnings to 1903. That was the year the company was reorganized, refinanced and moved from Detroit to Flint.

The division's history has been exciting from the beginning. Buick recovered from near-bankruptcy in 1904 to become the No. 1 producer of automobiles in 1908 — surpassing the combined production of Ford and Cadillac, its two closest competitors.

Buick was the financial pillar on which General Motors was created.

Buick was where such automotive giants as Billy Durant, GM's founder; Charles W. Nash, a founder of what later became American Motors; Walter P. Chrysler, founder of Chrysler Corp.; and Harlow H. Curtice, a GM president in the postwar era, first headed an auto-building company. Louis Chevrolet, co-founder of the Chevrolet automobile, had earlier achieved fame as a Buick race driver.

And Buick has been a product innovator from Day 1— from its creation of the valve-in-head engine, which earned an unsurpassed early reputation in competition around the world, to the high-tech engines and electronics of the 1980s.

Buick made news around the globe in the '20s. The company even opened a sales office in Shanghai, China. Shown above is a 1929 Buick Master Six Model 58.

In 1940, Chris Sinsabaugh, who as a newspaperman had covered the automobile industry from its inception, reflected that "barring the initial success of Olds, which had begun to bog down toward the end of the first decade of the century, Buick was the first real success of the automobile industry and did more to promote the industry's well-being in terms of public education, engineering advancement, and manufacturing progress than perhaps any other company."

Yet in 1903, the Buick Motor Co., then headquartered in Detroit, was one of the least promising of the hundreds of tiny automobile companies across the country.

Its founder had produced only two cars in three years of trying. David Buick, though an inventor of merit, generally was considered a dreamer. The company was in debt, its chief engineer had just left, and the firm's financial backer wanted to bail out.

David Buick, born in Scotland Sept. 17, 1854, and brought to the United States at age two, had been a successful plumbing inventor and manufacturer in Detroit when he turned his attention to gasoline engines in the late 1890s. He started a succession of companies: Buick Auto-Vim and Power Co. (1899), Buick Manufacturing Co. (1902) and Buick Motor Co. (1903), all in Detroit.

These companies produced some engines for power boats and stationary farm use. And by 1901 a horseless carriage, referred to in letters as "The Buick Automobile," was in existence. David Buick tried to sell it that year to his former chief engineer, Walter Marr, for $300. Marr held out and got it for $225. Marr had probably built the car for Buick.

Buick and his engineers argued often. Marr said he worked for David Buick three times, and each time the company had a different name. But between Buick, Marr and another engineer, Eugene Richard, a sensational powerplant was developed — the "valve-in-head" engine. It was light, powerful and reliable, and eventually the entire industry would make use of the principle. But in 1903, David Buick had neither the manpower nor financial backing to fully develop it.

That year, Buick's financial backer, Benjamin Briscoe Jr., sold his interest in Buick to a group of wagon makers in Flint, Mich., 60 miles north of Detroit. Eighteen years later, Brisco was sufficiently struck by Buick's success that he called the chain of events "so fraught with romance that it made the Arabian Nights tales look commonplace."

Buick traditionally dates its history to Sept. 11, 1903, when James H. Whiting, manager of the Flint Wagon Works, announced that the wagon works directors had bought the Buick company from Briscoe and moved it — bag, baggage and David Buick — from Detroit to Flint.

Flint, an old lumbering center, was already known as the "Vehicle City" — but not for automobiles. It had been the center of horse-drawn carriage production for several decades.

In the summer of 1904, the company built the first Flint Buick. Walter Marr, the chief engineer (he had returned after patching up an old quarrel with David Buick), and Thomas Buick, David's son, took it on a test run to Detroit and back July 9-12. The test was so successful that Whiting's group ordered production to start. When the company ran into financial problems a few months later, Whiting turned to one of Flint's other carriage builders for help.

The man was William Crapo (Billy) Durant, Flint's carriage "king." Grandson of a Michigan governor, Durant had gotten into the vehicle business almost on a whim. One evening in 1886, he saw an attractive horse-drawn road cart on the streets of Flint. The next night, he went to Coldwater, Mich., where the cart was manufactured,

and bought the rights to build it. That year he started the Flint Road Cart Co. By 1900, the firm, renamed the Durant-Dort Carriage Co., was the largest producer of horse-drawn vehicles in the country.

Durant didn't particularly like automobiles — he was no different from most carriage men — but he was a strong supporter of Flint, and he knew a "self-seller" when he saw one. The Buick, he observed, drew plenty of attention because it could climb hills and run through mud like no other car he had ever seen. If automobiles could be this good, he thought, then mabye it was time to get out of the horse-and-buggy business.

Once Durant made the decision, Buick's success was assured. No one could raise money, sell products and plan big organizations like Billy Druant. He went to the 1905 New York Auto Show and took orders for 1,000 Buicks before the company had built 40.

He moved Buick assembly briefly to Jackson, Mich. in 1905 while he gathered money from Flint banks and businessmen to build the largest assembly facility in the country on Flint's north side. He persuaded Charles Stewart Mott (later a GM director for 60 years) to move his axle business from Utica, N.Y., to Flint to build axles for Buick. He promoted Buicks across the country, using Durant-Dort carriage outlets and salespeople as the nucleus of a giant distribution system.

He created a racing team — with stars such as Louis Chevrolet and Wild Bob Burman — that won 500 racing trophies in 1909 and 1910.

The success of Buick engines was visible not only on the race tracks (including 1909 successes at Indianapolis two years before the Indy 500 started), but in endurance tests across the country and around the world. Buick was the only car to complete a 1,000-mile Chicago-to-New York relay race in 1906; a Buick was the first car to travel across South America, driven from Buenos Aires, Argentina, over the Andes to Santiago, Chile, in 1914. Buicks won hillclimbs across the country — including one in 1904 with one of the first 40 Buicks ever built.

In 1908, with production totaling a little more than 8,000, Buick led the country in production. Durant had made the transition from the biggest seller of buggies to the biggest seller of automobiles. And, on Buick's success, Durant created a holding company that year. He called it General Motors.

The story of Durant's development of GM is too complex to detail here. Briefly, he pulled first Buick, then Oldsmobile, into the GM organization. Then he added Cadillac and Oakland (forerunner of Pontiac) and dozens of truck and supplier businesses — including AC Spark Plug, which he helped create with Albert Champion (whose initials form the division's name).

Durant became financially over-extended as he pulled more than 30 companies under the GM umbrella in 1908-'10. He lost control of GM to a financial group in 1910. He and Louis Chevrolet developed the Chevrolet company the following year, and Durant used Chevrolet to regain control of GM in 1915-'16. Ironically he succeeded, as GM president, Charles W. Nash — whom Durant had hired into his carriage business and later helped make president of Buick.

Nash had brought Walter Chrysler to Buick as works manager. Durant retained Chrysler and made him Buick president, though Chrylser later resigned in a dispute with Durant. In 1920, Durant resigned as GM president in a short depression during which he was again over-extended in the stock market. According to Alfred P. Sloan Jr., who in 1923 became GM president, Buick's strong reputation and financial position was a major factor in pulling the corporation through that period.

Buick's star climbed steadily during the roaring '20s, with production reaching more than 260,000 units in

Buick had a record sales year in 1973. Above: Three Buick Apollos — four-door sedan, hatchback coupe and thin-pillar coupe.

1926. The car's reliability was world famous. In 1923, the famous writer-traveler Lowell Thomas used a Buick in his first automotive expedition into Afghanistan. Two years later, a Buick won trophies in a series of Leningrad-to-Moscow endurance and reliability runs, beating more than 40 cars from throughout the world.

Also, in 1925, a Buick was taken around the world without a driver to show the reliability of Buick's and GM Export's service operations worldwide. The car, driven by dealer representatives in the various countries, went to England, the Netherlands, Belgium, France, Egypt, by trans-desert convoy to Damascus, Baghdad and Basra, through India and Ceylon, across Australia, and then from San Francisco to New York.

A Buick magazine of the '20s routinely reported such events as a hill-climb victory in Africa, winning a tug-of-war with an elephant, a trek through New Zealand, and the Sultan of Johore with his Buick in the Far East. In addition to U.S. production, Buicks were built in Canada (a result of an early agreement with the McLaughlin family) and, in those decades before World War II, Buick chassis were shipped to such countries as Spain, Belgium, England, Australia — even Java — where assembly was completed. In 1929, Buick opened a sales office in Shanghai, China.

Being a maker of premier automobiles, Buick was harder hit by the Great Depression than most of its competitors. In 1933, production plummeted to a little more than 40,000 units. But late that year, Harlow H. Curtice, the 39-year-old president of AC Spark Plug, was tapped by GM to bring Buick back to its former greatness.

A supersalesman in the Durant mold, Curtice brought power and speed back to Buick. In 1934, the small Series 40 (later called Special) was launched. It gave exceptional performance for its price of $865. Production that year topped 78,000.

Next he issued a simple challenge to Harley Earl, GM's design chief, who always drove Cadillacs. Curtice's challenge: "Design me a Buick you would like to own." The result was the 1936 line which added Roadmaster and other successful names to the Buick stable: Special, Super, Century, Limited. That year production was close to 200,000. Buick, said a GM executive, was "off relief."

Buick continued to break ground in styling and engineering until it turned to World War II military production Feb. 2, 1942. During World War I, Buick had built Libery aircraft engines, as well as Red Cross ambulances so successful that one was awarded the Croix de Guerre by the French government. In World War II Buick helped make Flint an "arsenal of democracy" by building aircraft engines, Hellcat tank destroyers and other military hardware. Buick was awarded more than 30 separate military contacts, and Buick-built material could be found at virtually every fighting front.

After the war, Buick expanded its facilites under Curtice, who in late 1948 became a GM executive vice president, a job that led to the GM presidency four years later. But despite the fact his responsibilities now included all the car and truck divisions, he never really left Buick or Flint. He maintained his home in that city and never owned any other make of car but a Buick.

Curtice was succeeded by Ivan L. Wiles, his comptroller at Buick. The postwar period was a great era for Buick in styling, engineering and sales. Sales rose rapidly, to 550,000 in 1950, to 745,000 in 1955. The torque converter automatic transmission, Dynaflow, was introduced on the 1948 Roadmaster; a high-compression V-8 was introduced in 1953. Buick's famous vertical-pillar

"toothy" grille, introduced in 1942, became more massive in the postwar era. "Hardtop convertible" styling was introduced on the 1949 Roadmaster, along with Buick's famous "portholes."

These styling innovations are attributed to Buick designer Ned Nickles, though Edward T. Ragsdale, Buick manufacturing manager and later general manager, helped inspire the hardtop convertible styling. Ragsdale noticed that his wife, Sarah, always ordered convertibles, but never put the top down. She said she liked the styling but didn't want to muss her hair. The basic styling innovation was to eliminate the center side pillar. Buick built 4,000 hardtop convertibles in 1949, the first of hundreds of thousands it would produce over the next few years.

But in the late 1950s, Buick went into another tailspin because of a combination of unpopular styling, product problems, and an economic recession that helped make small cars popular. From a high of nearly three-quarters of a million cars in 1955, sales plunged to fewer than a quarter of a million units in 1959.

In '59, Buick changed the names of its entire product line, discarding Special, Century, Limited and Roadmaster in favor of LeSabre, Invicta and Electra. The Special name returned on a compact car with an aluminum V-8 engine in 1961. The following year, Buick offered the first production V-6 in the Special, which was named *Motor Trend* magazine's "Car of the Year." Its upper-series cars were also new that year and sales climbed to more than 450,000. In 1963, the Riviera, today considered a modern classic, was introduced.

Buick sales continued to rise through the 1960s and hit a record 821,165 in the 1973 model year. But the bottom fell out again with the oil embargo late that year, and sales totaled fewer than 500,000 in both 1974 and '75.

Buick rebounded. The division re-introduced the V-6 and continued to develop economical engines and attractively designed cars that became ever lighter and more innovative. And when the U.S. auto industry as a whole became severely hurt by the high gasoline prices in the early 1980s, Buick actually increased its market penetration significantly. Among its most heralded models during this period was the first front-wheel drive Buick, the 1979 Riviera S Type with turbocharged V-6 engine, named *Motor Trend*'s "Car of the Year."

Buick broke sales records in both 1983 and 1984 — with more than one million Buicks sold worldwide in '84 — and had its second-best sales year in history in 1985. Also in 1985, Buick-powered cars won the pole position and second spot in qualifying for the Indianapolis 500 — the first time since 1931 that an American-production based car had won the Indy 500 pole. Although those cars did not finish the race itself, the qualifying success was a strong indication that Buick's high-tech engines were highly competitive on the race tracks of America.

Buick's 1986 and 1987 Regal Grand National, and a limited-edition 1987 GNX, were widely acclaimed as the quickest American-built cars. They were powered by intercooled and turbocharged versions of the 3.8-liter V-6.

One featured car for '86 was the front-wheel drive LeSabre, built at "Buick City" in Flint. Buick City, built inside walls of old buildings in Buick's former Flint complex which formed the cornerstone of General Motors, is a state-of-the-art assembly facility with more than 200 robots and other high-tech equipment, completed at a cost of more than $350 million in the fall of 1985.

Buick continued to innovate. General Manager Edward H. Mertz announced a two-place luxury car, Reatta, in January 1988. A front-wheel drive Regal, first of a new generation of GM mid-sized coupes, was also introduced as a 1988 model.

Defining Buick's future direction, Mertz said Buick would provide automobiles with the qualities that made it famous — "premium American motorcars" that would be substantial, powerful, distinctive and mature. Buick would emphasize its position of providing upscale cars — the most American of all GM cars— and would continue to emphasize smooth power and high performance along with rich detail and comfortable accommodation.

Mertz said Buick would unveil at least one new major model each year, a strong indication that Buick intends to continue its reputation for product leadership. For the most part, that has been true for 85 years, since the days when David Buick, Eugene Richard and Walter Marr experimented with the valve-in-head engine, even before Billy Druant used Buick to build what became General Motors.

Buick had its second-best sales year in history in 1985. The Buick above is a 1985 Grand National coupe.

Buicks made headlines around the world

A widely respected early auto reporter, Hugh Dolnar, writing in this case for *Cycle and Automobile Trade Journal,* was the first writer to drive a Buick. He wrote his impressions in September 1904, after driving the first Flint Buick sold, a car owned by Flint physician Herbert Hills.

Noted Dolnar: "Dr. Hills has driven this car almost the whole time, day and night, over the very hilly and sandy country about Flint, and has had no repairs, except a split gasoline pipe, this day, Sept. 16, and believes he has the best car in the world."

Dolnar (real name Horace Arnold) was fairly ecstatic about the Buick. The factory, he wrote, "is equipped with the best machinery made by the best American tool builders." And on Sept. 17, 1904, he was given a ride by Tom Buick, son of the firm's founder, David Dunbar Buick. Dolnar found the car "thoroughly responsive; had more power everywhere than could be used. . . this was a ride to be remembered."

He continued: "At first, (Tom) Buick drove with some decent regard for law and prudence, but the road was hard, the clear air was intoxicating, and after one request to 'push her' up one steep hill, which the car mounted at 25 miles speed, Buick began to be proud of his mount and drive for fun. Later in the day he was fined $12 for fast driving. The Beak considerably informing him it would be more next time. The car simply ran to perfection, and is extremely easy, especially in sharp side crooks of road wheel ruts, and has very little bounce over short road depressions.

"The writer never went so fast on a rough, hilly road. The car flew down the hills and flew up the hills, all the same rate, and the engine purred and the wind whistled past and the soft September sun smiled benignly on the fine farms we went by, and it was all delightful."

* * *

For decades, Buick was often referred to as the "doctor's car." The reference apparently first appeared in 1907, after a Buick Model F in 1906 was the only car to complete a 1,000-mile run from Chicago to New York sponsored by the *Chicago American and Examiner* newspaper.

As a result of that success, Buick began calling the Model F "Old Faithful," a title it used on a booklet of specifications for that model in 1907.

"As a doctor's car, there is no automobile manufactured that will prove anywhere near its equal," the booklet said. The tag stuck.

* * *

Right from the beginning — when Buick set a record in a major hill climb in 1904 with one of the first 37 Buicks built — Buick was making headlines in hill climbs, on the race tracks, on cross-country runs and even around the world. The firm's patented high-performance valve-in-head engine quickly won converts.

In 1906, for example, H.J. Koehler won a 100-mile race at Yonkers, N.Y., and another Buick won a 100-mile free-for-all at the Empire City Track in New York City.

Also in 1906, a Model F Buick was the only car to complete a 1,000-mile relay run from Chicago to New York, sponsored by the *Chicago American and Examiner.* According to one published report: "The only drawbacks in the entire trip were the stretches of bad road . . . rendered well nigh impassable by rainstorms . . . In the few places where the roads were good the Buick was run at its highest speed . . . from 35 to 40 miles per hour. Even

when the roads were full of chuckholes and the car hit only the high places, half the time off the ground, the speed registered 20 to 25 miles . . . Yet through all this struggle of a thousand miles, the Buick never failed to move forward."

* * *

Buick built trucks for a few years and even a Buick truck won a race — winning the commercial class in a hill climb at Fort Lee, N.J., late in 1910.

Although Buick officially got out of racing for many years after 1910, its cars still made a lot of news. The *Buick Bulletin,* which began in 1912, routinely published photographs and reports of the cars around the world: a victory in a hill climb in South Africa, winning a tug-of-war with an elephant, a trek through New Zealand, the Sultan of Johore and his Buick in the Far East, General John J. Pershing and his flag-bedecked official staff car.

In 1914, a Buick dealer in Argentina claimed to be the first person to drive a car across South America, taking a 1912 Model 28 Buick from Buenos Aires over the Andes to Santiago, Chile.

* * *

When Walter Chrysler was president of Buick, during World War I, Chrysler and his master mechanic, K.T. Keller, negotiated a contract with the War Department to build 3,000 Liberty engines for World War I fighter planes. (Later, after Chrysler left Buick to form Chrysler Corp., he made Keller head of Chrysler.) Buick also produced mortar shells, cartridge containers, trucks and ambulances for the war effort.

Partly because of Buicks' military production, GM received a congratulatory note from Winston Churchill, then Great Britain's minister of munitions. One Buick ambulance had such an outstanding war record it was awarded the Croix de Guerre by the French government. A 1923 Buick bought by writer/traveler Lowell Thomas was driven on a widely reported trip to Afghanistan that year. He claimed he and his entourage were the first outsiders to penetrate that country in an automobile.

* * *

On April 17, 1923, racing driver Joe Nikrent stormed across a dry lake near Muroc, Calif., in a mildly tweaked example of a Buick Special 6-54 and hit 108.25 mph. Buick officially commented: "Buick does not intend to again enter the racing game . . . this performance was just another little demonstration to call attention to the fact that the 1923 Buick is the greatest Buick ever built."

* * *

In 1925, a Buick Standard Six touring car traveled around the world — without a specific driver. The idea of Buick Motor Division and GM Export Co. was to show that Buick and GM had such a strong service organization it could support sending a Buick around the world without a specific driver or mechanic. It went to England, the Netherlands, Belgium, France, Egypt, by trans-desert convoy to Damascus, Baghdad and Basra, through India and Ceylon, across Australia, and then from San Francisco to New York, with the car being handed to drivers for various GM and affiliated organizations along the route.

Buicks were smash hits in endurance competition sponsored by the Soviet Union in 1925 that drew 78 cars from a dozen countries (including 42 American entries). Five

Buicks were entered in the events that ended in Moscow's Red Square. One Buick won the first prize of the State Trade Committee, a silver bowl with cups covered with enamel, "for the totality of abilities," apparently the top overall winner. Another received the Organizing Committee prize "for endurance and strong construction." And yet another took the Soviet Ministry of Communication Means prize "for dynamic."

At about the same time, the Buick four-cylinder was winning honors in Japan as the lowest gasoline consumer (18.08 mpg) among a dozen American entries undergoing tests conducted by the military there. Only three cars in the entire competition used less fuel than the Buick, all of them of much less horsepower, one of them a little two-cylinder "Jinrickashawette."

* * *

In 1928, Buick used the new medium of radio to introduce its cars. The hook-up to dealers across the country was the largest network ever used commercially — in fact the largest ever used anywhere except for a broadcast of the Dempsey-Sharkey fight that had been arranged by a newspaper syndicate.

Dealers installed radio receivers in their dealerhips and invited the public to come in for the double purpose of looking over the new line and enjoying music. The music was performed by Arthur Pryor's band and the orchestra of the St. Francis Hotel in San Francisco.

In the decades between the two World Wars, Buick chassis were being shipped to such countries as Spain, Belgium, Australia — even Java — where assembly was completed. And in 1929, Buick opened a sales office in Shanghai, China.

More fun facts...

In 1931, Buick claimed to be the first large producer of automobiles to adopt eight-cylinder engines exclusively.

In 1936, England's King Edward VIII bought a 1936 Buick Limited limousine with special coachwork, along with a 1936 Roadmaster, for Mrs. Wallace Warfield Simpson, the woman for whom he would give up his throne to marry.

In 1939, an industry first was Buick's introduction of turn signals as standard equipment. The signal was on the rear of the car only, using a red plastic lens in the emblem mounted in the center of the trunk and operated by a switch on the gearshift lever.

During World War II, Buick was assigned more than 30 separate war production operations. Among them 424,000 steel cartridge cases, 19,428 tank power trains, 9.7 million 20 mm shell bodies, 2,507 Hellcat tank destroyers, 2,952 mounts for anti-aircraft guns, plus parts for the Pratt & Whitney aircraft engine.

General Motors' first "dream car," called the Buick Y Job, was completed in 1939 and was modified after World War II. In addition to its futuristic oblong shape, it featured disappearing headlamps, flush-type door handles, a convertible top completely concealed automatically by a metal deck, electrically operated windows and small wheels with airplane-type air-cooled brake drums.

In 1948, with the introduction of Dynaflow, Buick became the first American-built car to use a torque converter automatic transmission. By 1954, fully 85 percent of Buick cars were being sold with Dynaflow.

Above: 1912 Buick Model 28 roadster. Below: 1936 Buick Roadmaster Model 80C convertible sedan. (Photo courtesy Buick Motor Division.)

Starting a Tradition

1903–1930

1908 Buick.

Buick's humble beginnings

By Roger Mease

It is indeed a paradox that the world's largest automobile manufacturer was founded on the failure of one man to do just that. David Dunbar Buick, along with his partner William Sherwood, enjoyed a high degree of success in their Detroit-based plumbing and supply business. Their success was partially attributed to David Buick's patented process for bonding porcelain to cast iron, enabling the firm to produce white bathtubs and fixtures for the first time. But David's tinkering mind was not satisfied with the world's prettiest bathtub. No, he was enraptured with the gasoline engine and the automobile.

If success is measured by accomplishment, then David Dunbar Buick should have stayed in the plumbing business. In 1899 Buick solely established the Auto Vim and Power Co. to produce gasoline engines for farm and sta-

tionary use. But, David was infatuated with automobiles and he soon began to tinker with the idea of connecting his gasoline engines to a four wheeled vehicle. To aid in this project he enlisted the services of Walter Marr, a self styled free lance machinist with a will of his own. Prior to his accepting Buick's invitation, Walter had established a bicycle company in Detroit. Prior to the turn of the century, he had created a gasoline engine and successfully mated it to a three wheeled vehicle.

Armed with $100,000 supplied by Buick as a result of selling his profitable plumbing supply business, David and Walter set about to the business of producing an automobile. The Buick-Marr association was hardly a marriage made in heaven. Marr, a loner who actually refused to share any of his accomplishments could hardly get along with the cranky Buick, who had an amazing propensity for losing complete financial control. They used their capital

1904 Buick.

1905 Buick.

at an alarming rate. Finally Marr washed his hands of the entire matter and left. David Buick immediately hired Eugene Richard, an engineer from the Olds plant. Continuing on the basic designs developed by Buick and Marr, Mssrs. Richard and Buick built their first auto in 1902 using their new value-in head engine design. This design would be the hallmark for all Buicks for generations to come.

But, as was David's penchant, he had practically bankrupted the company to produce a single automobile. He enlisted the aid of the Briscoe brothers whom he already owed for parts they had supplied. A continuing supply of capital followed with the result of reorganizing of David's company in 1903. The Buick Motor Co. was capitalized at $100,000. Three hundred dollars was supplied by David and $99,700 supplied by the Briscoes! David still could not produce a profit and the Briscoes took over entirely with the object of unloading it as quickly as possible.

Now the good businessmen of Flint, Mich. were starting to get nervous. You see, Flint was a center for production of horse drawn vehicles and the farsighted men were looking at the fledgling motorcar industry as a possible future threat to their well being. Through the efforts of Dwight Stone, a successful Flint real estate dealer, Ben Briscoe was introduced to James Whiting of The Flint Wagon Works. A deal was made and for the sum of $10,000, the Buick Motor Co. was moved to a newly constructed building at the Flint Wagon Works. Along with the deal came David Buick, along with none other than Walter Marr. Marr had decided to rejoin the firm after some unsuccessful bouts with Detroit industry. Another year of tinkering by Marr, spending by Buick, and fighting by both produced the Buick Model B. In July of 1904, Water Marr and David's son Tom climbed aboard and drove to Detroit and back without incident. The successful Buick motorcar was born at the Flint Wagon Works.

This successful trip created quite a stir in automotive circles. Buick's claim that their two-cylinder engine produced 22 horsepower was viewed skeptically by knowledgeable automobilemen until a H.L. Arnold went to Flint and conducted tests. The three tests produced horsepower readings of 29.07 bhp, 31.53 bhp, and 32.52. The Buick was getting national publicity and the first car was sold in August of 1904, with backorders for 17 more.

But, as was David's nemesis, the company was deep in debt. And debt was the concern of Whiting, and his circle of Flint investors. They began to look for a buyer of the unprofitable Buick and they finally set their sights on William C. Durant. Billy Durant at age 40, had already done wonders for the city of Flint. W.C. Durant and J.D. Dort had established the Flint Road Cart Co. in 1886. By 1901 under the banner "The Durant Carriage Co." they were operating 14 plants. Billy had done his share to produce employment and wealth to the men of Flint. As he languished in New York, occupied with the manipulations of the moguls of Wall Street, Billy was persuaded to return to Flint. Durant was introduced to the Buick motorcar in the fall of 1904. W.C. drove that Buick under all possible conditions. After two months of torturous testing and learning, Billy Durant was ready to throw in his expertise. Billy had a new challenge and it was Buick's good fortune, as the good men of Flint put W.C. Durant in complete control. They let him do it in the past and Billy made them a lot of money, and they were willing and eager to do it again.

On the first Durant day, the capitalization of the company was raised from $75,000 to $300,000. Fifteen days later it was raised to $500,000. Mr. Durant possessed that three-fold thrust necessary for success. One, he was not afraid to take risks; two, he knew that salesmanship must

always successfully precede production; and thirdly, a well thought out plan for production must keep pace with growth. Billy sold the good men of Flint on the idea of investing in an unsuccessful automobile company. He then went to the automobile show in New York just six weeks after he took over the company and returned with orders for 1,108 Buicks!

Billy immediately leased a vacant factory from his own Durant Dort Company. The vacant Imperial Wheel Co. plant in Jackson, Mich., would suit his purposes for the production of the Buick automobile. But, the good entrepreneurs of Flint wanted Billy and his auto company to stay in Flint. Billy agreed after securing another $100,000 from three Flint banks! And so it was that Buick assembly would be located in Flint in new buildings financed and conceded by the good leaders of the city. Was the Jackson announcement a Durant ploy to raise additional funds? One cannot say for sure, but such was the brilliance of William C.

With so many orders to be filled, Durant realized that subsidiary manufacturing facilities must locate near Flint. By the end of 1905, 750 Buicks were built. In 1906 1,400 cars were produced and this marked the beginning of the end of assembly at the old Jackson plant. By 1907 practically all manufacturing operations were moved to Flint and the company produced 4,641 cars that year. It was during these years that other companies were cajoled into locating at Flint. Billy enticed Charles Stewart Mott of New York to build a factory adjacent to the Buick works in Flint. To sweeten the pot for the skeptical Weston-Mott group, the good bankers of Flint came up with another $100,000 and Billy promised a contract for axles. This deal was hardly complete when the W.F. Stewart Co. moved its largest body building plant in Flint. The old Flint wagon and carriage companies and suppliers soon took to the task of building automobile components.

Along with adjacent manufacturing, Billy needed distribution. He enlisted the aid of his Durant Dort carriage showrooms throughout the country to display the new Buick automobile. He then capitalized on Buick's fantastic auto racing accomplishments as good advertising copy. And it was here that the Buick slogan was born. As the story goes, Bob Burman of the Buick racing team of Louis and Gaston Chevrolet, Bob Burman, and Louis Strang visited the factory and was touring the facility with Mr. Durant as Durant explained that he wanted any parts that failed in a race sent back to the factory so they could improve on them." The next time we build it we'll build it better. When better cars are built, Buick will build them."

By the close of 1908 Buick produced 8,820 cars coming second only to Ford with 10,202 vehicles. W.C. Durant had taken a floundering company from obscurity to number two in three years. Meanwhile David Dunbar Buick faded into obscurity unable to cope with the success of Durant and envious, David resigned in 1906, received a cash settlement from Durant and spent the remaining 15 years of his life as a wanderer.

It was spring of 1908 that the first moves toward a merger of auto producers on a large scale took place. Benjamin Briscoe now of the firm Maxwell-Briscoe met with W.C. Durant in Flint for the purpose of combining several companies. Briscoe had received the go ahead from the gigantic financial firm, The House of Morgan, in New York City. They agreed to underwrite the idea if it looked feasible. Durant suggested a possible merger of Buick, Maxwell-Briscoe, Ford, and Reo. The principals of these companies met a short time later in Detroit. A second meeting was arranged and took place in New York, but negotiations stopped abruptly when Henry Ford demanded cash rather than stock transfers. The meeting was adjourned with no accomplishments.

But Billy Durant liked the idea, so with typical Durant fashion decided to go it alone. In September 1908 he incorporated General Motors in New Jersey with a total capitalization of $2,000. By the end of the month the new GM Board increased the company's assets to $12,500,000 and purchased Buick with stock. Six weeks later General Motors acquired the Olds Corp. of Lansing, Mich. for $3 million worth of GM stock plus $17,279 in cash. GM also agreed to take on one million dollars in debts owed by the Olds Corp. to Samuel L. Smith. Shortly after the acquisition of Olds, Billy completed a deal with the financially floundering Oakland Co. acquiring his third car producer. The Oakland was manufactured in Pontiac, Mich. and would later become the Pontiac. With companies now in Lansing, Flint, and Pontiac, Billy turned to Detroit. He set his sights on none other than the prestigious Cadillac Motor Car Co. owned by the father and son team of Henry H. Leland and Wilfred Leland. They drove a hard bargain and they were not interested in any stock exchanges. They requested cold hard cash, $4.5 million worth. GM was unable to raise the necessary amount, but Buick, GM's backbone, could. So W.C. purchased Cadillac with Buick funds, thereby making Cadillac a subsidiary of Buick. GM eventually purchased Cadillac from its own holding — Buick. Durant continued on a path of acquisition, but these early participants formed the nucleus and their names exist to this day as divisions of General Motors — Pontiac, Olds, Buick, Cadillac. The remaining division, Chevrolet is a story unto itself, and once again demonstrates the ability of one Billy Durant.

And so from the tinkerings of the financially inept David Dunbar Buick rose a mighty motor empire. The Buick was the start of it all and through the years stood as the leader of the corporation it started. The valve in head idea stayed in the Buick division to this day. The overhead valve straight eight was synonymous with Buick and it had its origins with David Dunbar. The Buick division of later years stood on its own, refusing to yield to the demands of the corporate offices. The Buick division always produced their own brand of vehicle with little or no help from the other divisions.

In 1938 the Olds-developed auto transmission was forced on the Buick division. They had so much trouble with it that the Buicks execs refused to offer an automatic until 1948, even though the Buick was a luxury car. And even in 1948 they only offered automatic on the Roadmaster and the brand of automatic was their own design. Perhaps some of old Billy C.'s tenacity stayed with this division all these years. And all you proud owners of early and collectible Buicks can attest to that.

1911 Buick model 38 roadster.

Engine boosted Buick at beginning

A major factor separating the fledgling Buick Motor Co. from hundreds of other tiny auto companies in the first decade of the 20th century was Buick's valve-in-head engine — developed for David Buick by two of his engineers, Eugene Richard and Walter Marr.

With its valves positioned directly over the pistons (unlike the L-head engine in general use at that time), the Buick powerplant had a more compact combustion chamber and a faster fuel-burn rate than the competition. It was, in essence, a more efficient machine. And because it was so efficient, it developed more horsepower than other engines its size.

Eventually the entire industry would make use of its principle, but not before the Buick engine developed a reputation for power and performance which helped the company survive in those desperate early years. Eugene Richard probably developed the principle for Buick. Marr gets credit for perfecting it.

The tiny Buick company produced one experimental automobile in 1900 and another in 1902-'03, both in Detroit, and got into "mass" production in Flint, Mich., in 1904 — by producing 37 cars. But even that small number made an impact. When Buick opened an agency in Cleveland in November 1904, *Motor Age* magazine, in announcing this, described Buick as "a little machine that has attracted an immense amount of attention in the past few weeks owing to its high power and low price."

Competition proved the point. On Thanksgiving Day, 1904, one of the several dozen Buicks in existence was entered by H.J. Koehler in a major hill climbing contest against stiff foreign and American competition at Eagle Rock, near Newark, N.J. *Motor World* magazine reported: "In the class for cars between $850 and $1,250, the new Buick car made its initial appearance and in a twinkling stamped itself a wonder. It easily carried off first honors in its class by a wide margin, cutting the record .... The clean-cut and businesslike appearance of the car and its quiet running caused much favorable comment."

Before the year was out, another Buick, this one stripped to the chassis, won its class in the first Race to the Clouds up Mount Washington in New Hampshire.

It was only the beginning of a period in which Buick racing teams would gather trophies — and headlines — across the country.

Billy Durant, the promoter who made Buick the No. 1-selling car in America in 1908 and then founded General Motors on Buick's success, had this to say about those early days in his memoirs: "Power . . . became synonymous with Buick. We played on that one item: Power! Power to outclimb, power to outspeed anything on wheels in your class. With Buick we sold the assurance that the power to perform was there. Power sold Buick and made it what it is today."

In the fall of 1903, the Buick Motor Co. of Detroit was

Buick's chief engineer, Walter L. Marr (left), and Thomas D. Buick, son of founder David Dunbar Buick, in the first Flint Buick as it ended its successful Flint-Detroit round trip in July 1904. (Photo courtesy Buick Motor Division.)

moved — bag, baggage and David Buick — from Detroit to Flint, 60 miles to the north. But the Flint Wagon Works directors, who had bought the company, claimed they were first interested in producing engines for farm use.

David Buick wanted to build automobiles. James Whiting, the wagon works manager who had spearheaded the purchase, was interested in cars, too — but he had to persuade his more cautious business associates. So Dave Buick hired back his former chief engineer, Walter Marr, and together they started work on a horseless carriage. By July 1904, it was ready. To demonstrate, Buick decided to send the car on a weekend trip to Detroit and back. Marr would be the driver; Buick's son, Thomas, went along for the ride.

They started out Saturday, July 9, 1904, at 1:15 p.m. from Flint's Sherman House hotel on a 90-mile route to Detroit via Lapeer. A rear-bearing failure caused them to spend the night in Lapeer. They arrived in Detroit Sunday, the Flint *Journal* reporting, "the distance from Pontiac to Birmingham being covered in 10 minutes." They bought car license No. 1024 Monday and headed back to Flint Tuesday.

Marr decided to see how fast he could go. Driving in a steady rain through the small towns of Pontiac, Oxford and Lapeer, Marr was able to average more than 30 miles an hour. "The roads were deep in mud every mile of the way," Marr said. "I did the driving and (Tom) Buick was kept busy wiping the mud off my goggles."

In one town they were challenged to a race by an electric car but the Buick "showed them the way," Marr said. He continued: "We went so fast at another time that we could not see the village six-miles-an-hour sign." He did not explain whether a local constable had pointed this out to him. He said: "At one place, going down a hill, I saw a bump at a bridge too late to slow up. When I hit it, I threw on all the power and landed over it safely on the road. Buick was just taking a chew of tobacco, and a lump of mud as large as a baseball hit him square in the face, filling his mouth completely. We were plastered with mud from head to foot when we rached Flint."

Marr was so excited about the first test of the first Flint Buick that he drove it directly to the office of the Flint *Journal* on his return. "The machine made the run without a skip," he boasted. "It reached here in the best of condition. We took the hills handily with our high-speed gear and the machine sounded like a locomotive. It simply climbed."

Here's the lead on the reporter's news story: "Bespattered with flying real estate from every county they had touched, but with the knowledge that they had made a 'record,' Tom Buick and W. L. Marr of the Buick Motor Works, who left for Detroit on Saturday to give the first automobile turned out by that concern a trial on the road, returned to the city late yesterday afternoon. The test of the machine was eminently satisfactory and, in fact, exceeded expectations."

When Marr arrived back at the plant, and told the Flint Wagon Works directors, "Well, we are here," they replied, "So are we." And they found the money to begin production of the Buick automobile. It was July 12, 1904.

David Dunbar Buick, founder of Buick. (Photo courtesy Buick Motor Division.)

William C. "Billy" Durant made Buick No. 1 and then founded General Motors. (Photo courtesy Buick Motor Division.)

When there were no roads and no maps

By Leigh J. Longfellow, age 86
as told to Marjorie Smith

The year was 1908, I was 10 and I had stopped in at the hardware store my dad co-owned with Frank Stover. I needed 15 cents to get a haircut.

Dad was busy with a customer and, as I waited, in came Will Lower, president of the Republic State Bank of Republic, Kansas, across the street.

He paced impatiently until father was free and then said, right out of the blue, "Charlie, what would you think of driving to the mountains this summer?"

I knew at once that father would be in favor of it. The two families owned the only two automobiles in town, identical red Buicks purchased in the fall of 1907.

A great deal of talk prefaced the preparations, which began in April 1908.

The car had a chain drive with the engine under the front seat. It was cranked on the side. The muffler was a cylinder-like affair, about six inches in diameter, just underneath the back seat and visible from the rear. It extended the full width of the car.

The car had no windshield, but at 15 miles an hour there was no blast of air in one's face. Straps about an inch and a half in width fastened the top to the frame with buckles. The top had bows just like a buggy top and could be folded down. The straps extended from the front edge of the top, to the front of the frame.

The steering wheel was an upright shaft and, by pushing a button with the foot near the brake, the wheel could be pushed forward so the driver could get in and out of the car.

The tires were all 34 inches by 3½ inches and of very poor construction. The gasoline tank was under the hood and there was no water pump, but a thermosiphon water system was used. Incidentally, this later was used on the Ford Model T.

Father and Lower had boxes built to fit on the right running board of each car to hold cooking utensils, since we would be camping along the way.

We left at 6 a.m., June 25. A number of the villagers were on hand to watch. There was considerable speculation about the time it would take us to get to Colorado Springs.

The end of the first day found us at Guide Rock, Nebraska where we camped for the night on the prairie. We had gone 40 miles. I can't figure out why we went north to Guide Rock, except that was a direct route out of the Republican River Valley and we tried to follow the Burlington Railroad tracks.

We stopped early that first day, evidently feeling that putting up our tents and making camp might take a little doing. It did!

Our rubber mattresses were inflated with a bicycle pump. Collapsible canvas buckets and tubs for washing were untied from the car. Each family had a gasoline stove, and they also had to be "pumped" to be used for cooking.

Everyone was up with the sun the next morning. We followed the Burlington to Red Cloud, on to Franklin and Alma and then struck off southwest until we came to the Rock Island Railroad. The railroad was our only guide between towns. Then on to Norton, Colby, Goodland and Limon Junction, Colorado. It wasn't all uninterrupted driving.

June is a rainy month and 1908 was no exception. Weston, Kan. was full of dry washes.

Taking the Buick on a family vacation was an adventure in 1908.

This group seated in a 1908 Buick Model 5 touring looks ready for a ride.

1908 Buick Model 5 was built for luxury touring

Buick called itself the largest auto-maker in the world in 1908, although it's still not clear if the claim could be substantiated in fact. Some historical sources back this point of view, while others give the honor to Ford Motor Co.

Despite the confusion, it's clear that one 1908 Buick *wasn't* a very hot seller. This was the Model 5 touring car, which was built just the one year. Only 402 copies of this large, powerful luxury automobile were ever made and few have survived through the years.

The Model 5 was the company's largest and most expensive offering. it was over 10 feet long and sold for $800 more than the next lowest priced Buick and over two and one-half times as much as the famous — and much more popular — Model 10.

A large four-cylinder T-head engine powered the Model 5. A three-speed selective transmission and leather-faced cone clutch were used. A stripped down Model 5 competed in the Savannah Road Races to prove the capabilities of the new car, but did little to boost up its sales.

Production versions of the Model 5 were impressive to behold. They featured full tonneau body styling with doors providing entry to the rear passenger compartment. There was plenty of brass plated trim to set off the radiator, acetylene headlights, sidelamps and folding windscreen. A large fabric top was provided, with side curtains used for added weather protection.

Following the standard practice of the day, right-hand steering was featured with gear selector and brake controls mounted outboard, on the right side of the car.

Although production was low, there were several variations in the appearance characteristics of Model 5s. Some had curved front lower body sills, while others had a more angular type. Rear fenders could be of at least two types, straight-back or turned up at the rear. Several different rear door treatments were also used.

Standard factory colors were red or blue for bodies and ivory for running gear and spoke wheels. Buyers, however, could have their cars custom finished in accordance with personal tastes.

Our feature car, from the Helgesen Antique and Classic Car Collection in Janesville, Wis., seems to have been restored accordingly. The white tires and ivory paint add a lot to the appearance of the fabulous brass-era Buick.

1908 Buick Specifications

Manufacturer	Buick Motor Car Co.
Model	Model 5
Body Type	5-pass. Tonneau Touring
Original Price	$2500
Wheelbase	108 in.
Tires	43x4 in.
Weight	3700 lbs.
Engine	T-head, cast en block
BxS	4⅝x5 in.
Disp.	336 cu. in.
Horsepower	34-40
Trans.	3-speed; selective
Clutch	Cone type
Top Speed	45-49 mph

Two hobbyists researched the historical details behind this old photo of the popular Model 10 Buick.

Story behind an old photograph

By Peter Winnewisser

The photo that illustrates this article was taken more than 80 years ago in Potsdam, N.Y. It offers a tantalizing glimpse into the early era of automotive history when those who owned and drove cars were pioneers in every sense of the term.

As researched by Glenn and Donna Seymour of Potsdam, the car is a 1909 Buick Model 10; either a tourabout or surrey. The Seymours identified the driver, passengers and the location in the photo. They found it was taken at the Potsdam Auto Garage, which featured an underground fuel storage tank.

The Model 10 was the most popular Buick between 1908-1910. More than 23,000 were produced; 8,100 in 1909. It had a 92 inch wheelbase (88 inches for 1908), 30 x 3½ clincher tires and weighed 1,500-1,600 pounds. The engine was a 165 cid, four-cylinder block, rated at 22.5 hp. It was attached to a two-speed planetary transmission.

Body styles included a three-passenger runabout, a four-passenger surrey with a straight back rear seat, a four-passenger tourabout with bucket seats both front and rear, and a four-passenger Toy Tonneau with a single-unit body and full rear doors.

According to Automobile Quarterly's *The Buick A Complete History*, the Model 10's popularity stemmed from its ease of control, smooth engine, eventual racing success and its price tag ($900 in 1908 and $1,000 in 1910).

On the back of this old photo there is a brief notation. "Taken at Potsdam Aug. 7, 1910. Trip from Massena to Potsdam, Madrid, Chases Mills, State road and home." A look at a New York State road map tells us that this was about 50 miles, a mere hour's drive or less in today's terms. But in 1910, what an exciting trip it must have been.

57

Buick, with Wild Bob Burman driving, won this race against an airplane at a Daytona Beach, Fla. "Speed Festival" in 1910. (Photo courtesy Buick Motor Division.)

Buick was the cornerstone for the creation of General Motors

Buick was the financial pillar on which General Motors — today the world's largest automaker — was created. And both Buick and GM can trace their initial successes to one man — William C. "Billy" Durant.

Grandson of a Michigan governor, Henry Howland Crapo (CRAY-po), Durant had gotten into the vehicle business almost on a whim. One evening in 1886, he saw an

attractive horse-drawn road cart on the streets of Flint. The next night, he took a train to Coldwater, Mich., where the cart was manufactured, and bought the rights to build it. That year he started the Flint Road Cart Co. By 1900 the firm, renamed the Durant-Dort Carriage Co., was the largest producer of horse-drawn vehicles in the country.

Durant didn't particularly like automobiles — he was no different from most carriage men in that opinion — but he was a strong supporter of Flint, and he knew a "self-seller" when he saw one. The Buick, he observed, drew plenty of attention because it could climb hills and run through mud like no other car he had ever seen. If automobiles could be this good, he thought, then maybe it was time to get out of the horse-and-buggy business.

James Whiting of the Flint Wagon Works had engineered the move of the fledgling Buick Motor Co. from Detroit to Flint in 1903. But in late 1904, the firm was in financial trouble after building only 37 cars. Whiting asked the effervescent Durant — despite the fact he headed a competing local carriage firm — if he would consider taking control.

Once Durant made that decision — by November 1904 — Buick's success was assured. No one could raise money, sell products and plan big organizations like Billy Durant. He went to the 1905 New York Auto Show and took orders for 1,000 Buicks before the company had built 40.

He moved Buick assembly briefly to Jackson, Mich., in 1905 while he gathered money from Flint banks and businessmen to build the largest assembly facility in the country on Flint's north side. He persuaded Charles Stewart Mott (later a GM director for 60 years) to move his axle business from New York State to Flint to build axles for Buick. He promoted Buicks across the country, using his

Durant-Dort carriage outlets and salespeople as the nucleus of a giant distribution system.

He created a racing team — with stars such as Louis Chevrolet and Wild Bob Burman — that won 500 racing trophies in 1909 and 1910, including major victories at the new Indianapolis Motor Speedway in its inaugural 1909 season, two years before the first Indy 500.

In 1908, with a total of more than 8,000 cars, Buick led the country in production. Durant had made the transition from the biggest builder of buggies to the biggest producer of automobiles. And on Buick's success, Durant created a holding company that year. He called it General Motors.

Durant's career was like a roller-coaster. He pulled 30 companies under the GM umbrella in a whirlwind period between 1908 and 1910. Among them were Oldsmobile, Cadillac, Oakland (forerunner of Pontiac) and AC Spark Plug, which he helped create with Albert Champion (whose initials form the AC name). He helped develop and bring into the GM fold such auto pioneers as Louis Chevrolet, Charles W. Nash, Walter P. Chrysler, Charles Stewart Mott, Charles F. Kettering and Alfred P. Sloan Jr.

In 1910 Durant, judged by his creditors as being overextended, lost control of GM to banking syndicates. Starting over, he created the Chevrolet Motor Co. with Louis Chevrolet and regained control of GM in 1916. He lost control again during a financial crisis in 1920, then started a new career, forming Durant Motors and becoming a bull on Wall Street. Durant went broke during the Depression, and in his last years operated a bowling establishment in Flint — almost in the shadow of the Buick complex he had created.

But his legacy is remembered. In 1988, the city of Flint, Mich. erected a statue of its industrial wizard — the legendary Billy Durant.

Louis Chevrolet at the wheel of a Buick Model 10 racer in 1910. (Photo courtesy Buick Motor Division.)

The Buick I never cared for

By Gerald Perschbacher

The brilliant beams of sunlight cut through the early morning sky on that crisp spring morning I remember so well. It was the morning of our antique car club's car show, and I had been pressed into service in a half-dozen roles. I was no different from any of the other 20 or so helpers that day who got things on track and rolling down the pike by noon.

I remember that new pickup truck pulling a closed trailer behind, how it found a place to park and unload its cargo, and how a small crowd milled around in anticipation as the trailer's rear doors opened. What caught my eye at the moment of that grand opening was a golden reflection of unmatched brilliance as the sun's rays caressed the gold-colored brass radiator and headlights.

In a few seconds, I found myself over by the trailer, helping to keep back onlookers as the owner cranked up the engine and put down the ramps.

"What is it?" asked a bystander.

"A Buick—says so right on the radiator," answered a gruff sounding man standing on the other side of the ramps.

Heads craned as pairs of eyes studied the blue touring car from front wheels to rear axle, hinged windshield to running boards. As the Buick idled with a slight jitter, one little boy piped, "Mommy, I think the car's getting too chilly."

Few of us noticed the owner as he slid across the black leather seat and eased behind the righthand steering wheel. With a smile, the owner glided the Buick forward onto the show field as each of the car's four cylinders

This 1911 Buick Model 33 touring car was one of 2,000 made and was powered by a four-cylinder engine.

marched in perfect timing to the whispered beat of the car's exhaust.

All day long the owner would pet and polish that brass Buick, frequently pausing to provide an off-the-cuff lecture on one of its virtues to the crowd which always lingered. My curiosity got the better of me, and when I had an hour to myself, I made a beeline to the Buick.

"It's a 1911 Model 33 touring car," said the owner as he watched me squint to read the show registration card on the windshield. "I've had the car about 30 years, and it's like one of the family," he added.

He told me how the car carried a 100-inch wheelbase and had a capacity of five passengers. Someone asked the inevitable question, "How much is it worth?"

"About $950," he said in a matter-of-fact way. "Not in today's dollars, mind you, but back in 1911. To find out how the purchasing power of one dollar back then matches today's dollar bill, multiply that figure by 12 or 15. That's what the car was worth when it was new, but to me it's priceless. Because every time I look at the car, I remember by father," said the owner.

"My father had this 1911 Buick when it was new, and I can remember touring around in the brass beauty when I was a youngster," the owner said to me as he finished polishing a rear fender. "Daddy had his own little business then, a printing shop, and did pretty well. That Buick was a sign that he had reached financial security, that he had reached independence. At least, that's what he would say when mama wasn't around," he added with a grin.

"He went with Buick because we lived near Flint, Michigan, and he had heard a lot about the Buicks that were built there. Buick was number two in sales that year behind Ford, although the company slipped to about 13,000 cars for 1911. But that didn't bother my father. He was convinced that Buick was the car for him.

"He kept the car in nice shape, polishing it every Sunday afternoon that the weather would permit, even when it got pretty cold. He kept the car covered inside a small carriage house behind our home, and he seldom drove the car in snow or rain. But daddy's business went sour in the early 1920s when some type of recession set in after World War I. He spent less time with the car, and it started showing wear, first on the leather upholstery which started to crack, then the brass which traded its gold-colored armour for a dingy brown. The paint soon popped off the wooden spokes, tears developed in the top, and somehow the windshield started to crack. I can remember my father having trouble with the car overheating and then leaking oil, big puddles at a time.

"Daddy didn't take care of that car; it wasn't because he didn't love it any less, but because he was getting tired and sick as his health ran down with his business. We didn't know it at the time, but he was coming down with tuberculosis, a real killer back in the 1920s. He spent several months recuperating in a hospital. When he got out, one of the first things he did was to slowly walk to the carriage house and take a look at the Buick.

"He cried when he saw it. Neglected, cats had gotten to the upholstery and mice had eaten at the wiring. The tires were flat and the radiator had frozen and burst. The car was quite sad, and father bemoaned the car's fallen state.

1911 Buick.

"I never cared for that car like I should have," father said to me, 'But I can't let the car go. It's been too good a friend,' father said with downcast eyes. He held on to that car through the Depression, through World War II, and up until the early 1950s.

"The antique car hobby was budding then, and I got bit by the bug. I remembered what that Buick had looked like in its glory days, and dad and I would talk about it frequently when I would pay my weekly visit. I remember in 1953, the first day of spring, I stopped to see dad. He had a surprise for me.

"I never cared for that Buick like I should have son, but I can see by the twinkle in your eyes every time we talk about that car that you look past all its weak points and see the car as it used to be. I think you really would take care of the car, give it the love and attention it needs, much more than I am doing. Here's the title, signed and everything. The car is yours!'

"I told my father he wouldn't regret it, and I started to work on that car at once. He truly didn't care for that car because I've had to have so many things done to it from recoring the radiator to fixing a crack in the engine, to replacing the differential. One of the headlights was mangled beyond repair, so I had to scrounge for years to find a replacement. It was a long slow process, but the car was pieced back together to what you see today.

"I would never be able to sell the car, since it reminds me of my father each time I see it. It's like a time machine, whisking me back to a bygone day when horses still plodded down main street and life marched to a different beat. And it takes me back to those days when dad would sit tall and proud behind the steering wheel, touring across town with that shiny brass radiator sparkling in the sun. He may not have cared for the car, but I always have!"

The strange story of David Dunbar Buick

DAVID DUNBAR BUICK

By A. Stanley Kramer

The 1929 Buick was a bulgy travesty on what was generally accepted as good automotive design. Among other uncomplimentary things said about it, it was claimed with some justification that it looked like a bathtub. Curiously enough it was the bathtub that years earlier had given David Dunbar Buick the nest egg with which to go into the fledgling automobile business, first as a maker of engines for other manufacturers and then as a producer of complete cars of his own.

For it was Buick, a plumber, born in Scotland in 1854, who invented the process that permanently bonded enamel to cast iron, making the white bathtub possible. His invention brought him a small fortune because it was perfectly timed; coming in the 1880s when the plumbing fixtures industry was booming. Hot and cold running water, tubs and indoor flush toilets were obsoleting the privy, and bathrooms were considered a civilized necessity.

Buick, sterotype caricature of the unworldly tinkerer/inventor, had little commercial savvy and was happy only in his workshop. In today's parlance he was a "born loser" destined to be exploited by others.

In 1900, when he was 46, he grew tired of his profitable enameling business and sold it outright. He began working on gasoline engines and in 1902 organized the Buick Manufacturing Company, making engines for various automobile manufacturers.

Supposedly it was Buick who invented the "valve-in-head" or overhead valve engine used by practically every automobile in the world today. However, both of his original partners, Walter Marr, and Eugene C. Richards, also claimed (in their later years) to have invented it. Which of the three actually conceived the basic idea, and which developed and refined it, is still a matter of dispute. More-

over, the actual overhead valve patent was filed by Richards in 1902 and issued and assigned to the Buick Company in 1904. To further confuse the issue, "Improvements" were invented (but not patented) by Walter Marr and the sale of these negotiated with the company in 1905.

On Nov. 1, 1904, William Crapo Durant, the organizer of the soon-to-be-assembled General Motors, refinanced and took over the Buick Motor Company. In the reorganization, David Buick was largely lost in the shuffle but didn't seem to mind. Durant was Chief Executive Officer and Charles M. Begole was President. Buick went into the engineering department where his continuous tinkering served to slow down production. However, he was well-paid and a member of the Board of Directors, although he seldom bothered to attend their meetings.

In 1908 he left the company still bearing his name, Durant had previously given him $100,000 to invest, which he lost. Now he needed money and went to California where he organized an oil company which went bankrupt.

He returned to Michigan and, with his son, Tom, he organized a company to manufacture carburetors. They failed. In the early 1920's he acquired a controlling interest in Grand Rapids' Lorraine Motors, which failed. He then became a partner in a Florida real estate company that went bust. After that David Dunbar Buick dropped out of sight for several years.

In 1927, at the age of 72, with his name on the radiator emblems of well over a million cars, Buick returned to Detroit as an instructor/clerk in the Detroit School of Trades. None of his former associates knew he was there. He was too poor to have a telephone. One day in April 1928, now famous author, Bruce Catton (then a Detroit newspaper reporter) discovered Buick and interviewed

him in his office. Buick wanted neither pity nor charity, just a job and security. He told Catton: "It's kind of hard for a man of my age to be uncertain about the future."

He died, practically unnoticed in the Detroit Harper hospital on March 3, 1929. A former business associate, early auto pioneer, Benjamin Briscoe, said, "David Dunbar Buick made a hundred men millionaires and himself died in poverty."

The 1911 Buick "Bug"

While Buick's personal fortunes were a disaster, his car, pushed by Durant's ferocious energy, flourished. A terrific saleman as well as an organizer, Durant took complete control of Buick in January 1905, when total production was only 50 cars. He went east to the New York Auto Show and sold 1,108 cars. Buick's sales increased year after year from then on. Stimulated by the road-racing success of the famous Model 10 or "White Streak", 8,400 Buicks were sold in 1908. Selling for only $850 (the same price as Ford's Model T) the White Streak was enticingly advertised for "Men with real red blood, who don't like to eat dust."

The 1911 Model 14 Roadster, known as the "Bug" was the low end of a range of models offered that year. It was the only 2 cylinder car in the lineup and a poor performer, even by 1911 standards. The "Bug" was dropped after only one year of production. Actually it was an old design, originally developed in 1908.

Very early Durant embraced the modern concept of blanketing a range of prices so as to exclude competition — a merchandising practice still followed by General Motors.

Despite the profusion of models, 1911 sales were just over 13,000. By the end of that year Buick boasted that its Flint factory was the largest auto plant in the world, making nearly all its own parts, from ignition to hubcaps. Boss of Buick in 1911 was an ex-Kansas farm boy and former superintendent of the American Locomotive Works, Walter Percival Chrysler, only 37 at the time. By 1912 sales increased by nearly 20,000 cars.

The "Bug" had a 14 hp, horizontal opposed, water-cooled two cylinder engine with a Shebler carburetor. Dual ignition was provided by jump spark. Top speed was only 30 miles an hour. Wheelbase was 79 inches. Three forward speeds and reverse were applied through a disc clutch. Power to the rear wheels was through double chains. Braking from internal expanding brakes was effective.

Recently a man in Ohio advertised a model 14 for sale but called it a 1910. The only other "Bug" I have ever encountered in addition to my own mint specimen, was in the Long Island Auto Museum when I was there a few years ago. Aside from my car's fancy striped spokes and red upholstery they are identifcal. If any Old Cars Weekly readers know of another "Bug" in existence, I would be grateful for the information.

1911 Buick "Bug."

63

The First Dunbar Car is Shown Here This Week

The New Dunbar Car, Roadster Model.

Sketch of the Dunbar Buick.

Dunbar Buick — forgotten car

By Keith Marvin

David Dunbar Buick was actively associated with three different makes of car and of this trio, one is so obscure that it has eluded the attention of the rank and file of automotive historians.

Of course the Buick car itself and its reputation over the years goes without saying. It is known from Tierra del Fuego to Timbuktu. Even the Lorraine with whom Buick had a brief love affair in the early 1920s is occasionally encountered, especially among old timers of Grand Rapids, Mich., where it was built. But the Dunbar. Ah, now that's a different kettle of fish. It never even made the automotive rosters of its own time, but just bring the subject up with the senior citizens of Walden or Wallkill, NY, and you get the same reaction as had you tossed kerosene on a bonfire. They remember. Many of them invested in the Dunbar automobile. All of them lost.

The day that David Buick decided to get out of the bathroom furniture business to concentrate his attention on the valve-in-head motor, what had been a potentially successful career on his part started grinding to a halt. True, the valve-in-head engine would revolutionize the automobile industry and so would the car that he started building in which to promote it. The trouble is that having invented the process of affixing enamel to cast iron, Buick had stumbled onto a remarkably good thing, for with that process, bathroom necessities became respectful overnight and to this day, not every one refers to 'going to the john.'

Had Buick stuck with his plumbing pursuits, it is not at all unlikely that today, instead of saying, "You got me out of the tub", one might have remarked instead, "Sorry, Liz, but I was in the buick." Note that lower case 'b'. When a proper name is absorbed as a word in the vernacular,

the move from capital to small letter is the supreme compliment.

Yet, with his engine and subsequent Buick car, he was not successful as a businessman and severed his connection with the company. As William C. Durant took over the reins of management and turned the Buick company into an industrial giant, Buick struck out for himself. Alas, unlike the late King Midas, he didn't do well in any of his subsequent attempts at business and although dabbling in the oil business, carburetor manufacturing, the brief fling with the Lorraine automobile and real estate, the trek toward oblivion continued over the years culminating with his death on March 3, 1929. At the time, Buick was serving as an instructor in a trade school.

It may be said that of the rank and file of automotive giants — those who pioneered and otherwise moulded the automobile business, as well as those who tried, David Buick is one of the most obscure. Despite an auspicious beginning, the shimmer of the name dulled after his divorce from the motor company he had formed and there are lapses in time as to exactly what he was engaged in. What is still needed is a comprehensive biography of the man and his accomplishments.

In simple language, when he left the bathroom busines in which he was a success to strike out in a new field of endeavor, Buick took the wrong fork in the road of life.

One of the obscure periods in David Buick's tragic but nonetheless interesting career was that immediately following the demise of the Lorraine car. Buick had assumed the post of company president in 1920 and after a year or so in that post and a production of an estimated 350 to 400 cars, like so many concerns in that depression year of 1921, Lorraine gave up the ghost. Buick was high and dry and looking around for something to do when the Dunbar car came into the picture.

The origins of the enterprise are obscure but it appears that the motivating power of the Dunbar was one Harry C. Hoeft, who would occupy the position as corporation secretary. Mr. Buick was named president and general manager. J. L. Dornbos was appointed vice president and treasurer.

But why Dunbar? Simple. It appears to me that David Buick, whose name was David Dunbar Buick, was probably added to the company for the commercial value of his last name which, for obvious reasons, couldn't be used for the proposed new car. Dunbar was something else again so Dunbar it would be.

Incorporating in the State of Delaware, Hoeft and his group used the means of news items in the local newspaper, the Citizen-Herald. The citizenry was intrigued by the prospect of a new industry and lots of stock was subscribed for the pie-in-the-sky venture.

Now, one might ask how the David Dunbar Buick Corporation could have met with such instantaneous success and the answer is readily available. It was a psychological ploy which banked on three magic words — "backed by Buick."

And this is probably exactly why David D. Buick had turned up as the corporation's president in the first place. His name was Buick. His signature was on every stock certificate. It also probably explains the group's apparent reluctance to shun printed literature as without it, no written text appeared explaining HOW it was backed by Buick.

And of course it was backed by Buick — David D. Buick, that is, and not by the Buick Motor Company which is what the term really implied. Had the natives checked out the business history of David Buick, that stock might have gone begging.

Adam Ulrich of nearby Wallkill recalls the operation and started searching for a satisfactory location and incidentally, sell stock, and they didn't search for long.

The village of Walden, N.Y., in Orange County, about 80 miles northwest of New York City, seemed to offer the ideal answer. A modern plant which had been used for cream separation was available and a large hat factory had just closed down. These two items presented dual advantages — a site for automobile manufacturing and readily available employment.

So Mr. Hoeft and company arrived in Walden and the big sell started in earnest.

What made the operation unusual was the lack of published material on the proposed car itself. There were no flyers or catalogues — just stock certificates and free promotion as both he and his father bought stock. "We never questioned it," he explained. "The promoters told us that the car would be built by Buick and that was good enough for us." The new car was the talk of the town, he recalls, and that stock was sold just about anywhere and everywhere — in the barber shop, drug store, the hotel — all over.

Eventually, the plans for securing the cream separating plant became a reality and the time came for the formal acquisition. Mr Buick came in from Detroit and was present for the ceremonies. As yet, no Dunbar prototype cars had been seen although a small item in *Automotive Industries* for April 26th, 1923, stated that the production was about to begin and the cars would sell for $1,100 for open models and $1,400 for closed ones. Listing corporation headquarters at 25 West 43rd St., it added that one car had been built and that three more were under construction.

Part of this was true. One car had been completed, a maroon roadster sporting disc wheels and a general sporty appearance, and not long afterward the car arrived in Walden where it was pictured and described in the local press. Whether it was actually put together in the new factory or, more likely, elsewhere, isn't known nor is much

A stock certificate for the David Dunbar Buick Co., was soon a worthless document.

else known excepting that the Dunbar had a Continental "8R" engine and other standard components, based on a chassis of 112 inches. The car did have visual appeal aplenty and, from contemporary accounts in the *Citizen-Herald*, performed extremely well.

Came August and up to then, nothing had really been going on out at the former cream separating plant. The officers decided to throw a bash there to show the car, serve refreshments and sell more stock to anyone they could. It was all very nice, Mr. Ulrich recalled, and guests were told that the plant would then close down for a bit of "retooling" prior to the commencement of manufacturing activity.

It all seemed logical and that was that. For a time, that is, and then all of a sudden it began to appear that the whole thing had been too pat. The plant was checked and, sure enough, nobody home! The remains of the gala of August hadn't even been cleaned up!

According to Mr. Ulrich, some of the speculators cried foul and consulted their attorneys. Those worthies advised the clients to forget it. They'd been had.

And so, the saga of the David Dunbar Buick Corporation ground to an inglorious halt. Or almost.

Early in 1924, an undated letter bearing the letterhead of the corporation — now located at Suite 1306, 165 Broadway, New York City, was sent to the stockholders pointing out that the company was in good shape and that it was contemplating the further production of Dunbar automobiles. It spoke of the "readjustment of our affairs", whatever they were, discussed new designs, and referred to "a disturbing element" which had been associated with the corporation but which, happily, had now been eliminated. Then came the whammy:

"The Management wishes to go into a large production of Dunbars starting early this year and to do so will require a substantial amount of additional capital." No beating around the bush here. The letter was signed by one William Dick, chairman of the Stockholders Administration Committee.

Where David Buick was by this time or whether he was even still associated with the corporation I don't know. But the letter was probably the final attempt to keep the company above water. I'd assume that the stockholders receiving the message, with their past experience with Dunbar, reacted predictably.

What became of the pretty little roadster, lone repesentative of a defunct concern is unknown and as for the Dunbar name itself, it was quickly forgotten.

And one can't say that about the Buick.

Louis Rickbiel checks over the 1912 Buick truck owned by the Cavalier Bottling Works. Owner O.A. Krippner and his daughters, Gertrude Krippner Bechtel and Inez Krippner Page, look on.

Buick built trucks, too

By Jim Benjaminson

Like most of the early manufacturers, Buick production also included a truck line — but like most of the major manufacturers, Buick chose to concentrate its production and advertising on its passenger car lines.

Buick's first truck was the M-2A offered in 1907; it came equipped with a body called "the plumber's body." Whether this had anything to do with the fact that David Dunbar Buick had made his initial fortunes in the plumbing supply business has to remain purely as conjecture.

The next Buick truck was the Model F, which was in all ways identical to the Model F passenger car. By 1910 Buick saw fit to re-open the old Jackson, Mich. plant where the first Buick cars had been built, and devote it solely to truck production. This new truck, the Model 2, was powered by a 22 hp two-cylinder opposed engine and sold for $950. Built on a 92-inch wheelbase, the Model 2 used the same engine and transmission as the Model F, but there the similarities ended. The Model 2 moved the engine farther forward in the chassis and used a double set of chains to transmit power to the rear wheels. A second version of the Model 2, this on a 110-inch wheelbase, sold for $1,065.

For 1911 the Buick truck became the Model 2A, although it was basically unchanged from the previous Model 2. It was still powered by a two-cylinder engine, while the rest of the Buick lines were switching to four-cylinder power.

For 1912 Buick continued the Model 2A although it was phased out of production by year's end. In fact, the old Buick plant in Jackson was sold by the end of the year. When Buick production of trucks began elsewhere in 1913, the old two-cylinder engine was gone for good — somewhere around 2,700 two-cylinder trucks had been built over the years at the Jackson plant.

The 1912 Buick truck pictured here belonged to O.A. Krippner of Cavalier, N.D. Krippner was the owner of the Cavalier Bottling Works, the makers of a locally popular brand of soda water. As demand for soda water declined, the bottling works began making ice cream. Probably no man was better liked by the children of the community than Louis Rickbiel, who was hired to drive the truck. Over the years the bottling works and creamery business was sold, although the building stands to this day.

What became of the Buick truck is unknown. We do know from early motor vehicle records that the Buick truck was a 1912 model bearing serial number 24874.

Buick continued producing a line of trucks through the 1923 model year under its own name, and in later years provided chassis to other builders. The sight of a Buick truck is a rare one today.

Around the world by Buick

Transporation has played its most vital part in the history of man, and every phase of its development is of tremendous interest and importance.

Of all the forms of present-day transportation, the motorcar is the most personal. By its means one can go anywhere, at any time, without the restriction of a timetable. Proper facilities have made the automobile as reliable as the railway train, while having far more flexibility of schedule and riding comfort.

Demonstrating that the time has arrived when the motorcar owner can confidently travel anywhere, even around the world, a Buick touring car has recently completely encircled the globe, unaccompanied by either a fixed driver or mechanic, the car being driven the entire distance by Buick distributors and dealers in relay.

It is on Dec. 20, 1924, that the trip officially starts. On that date, the "Around the World" Buick, in its export box, is swung aboard the *S.S. Aurania* in New York, bound for Liverpool. From that point on, the future of the intrepid car depends solely upon its sturdy mechanism and the Buick sales and service organization.

Landing at the port of Liverpool, the world traveler becomes temporarily the charge of the local Buick dealer, and under his guidance sets out immediately for London.

Between tidy English fields and hedges it speeds, through Litchfield — hesitating a moment at Stratford-on-Avon to pay its respects to William Shakespeare — through Warwick, Swindon, Nottingham, and into the fog and grime of London. A quick panorama of historic England, and then the boat for Amsterdam. Over rough brick highways, across the flat lowlands of Holland to Haarlem, the Hague and Rotterdam flies the Buick. Along the road, in the cities, people are enthusiastic. Crowds collect — questions are asked. "What do you say?" asks a curious one. "A car without a driver? How is it possible? Does it have special mechanism?" "Why no," a guard informs him. "Why no. In every country there is a different driver." And the boys: "Around the world, sir? Why, I would like to come along. Can I? If you say yes I will stop right in dressed as I am now. May I?"

"Hurrah, around the world!" shouts another urchin, who has climbed up on the spare tires on the rear, and who, with his profane hobnailed shoes, gives the car the first souvenir of its long trip around the world.

Southward, toward the Belgian border, and the car crosses small rivers and canals, their banks lined with willows drooping in the chill winter air. Into Belgium, and through busy industrial towns. The schedule is not elastic, and the Belgian Buick distributor wastes no time in touring. Straight to Paris he drives, where the venturous car again changes hands. Through the crowded streets of Paris, then south again, past Fontainebleau and castled towns reminiscent of the days of monarchical and imperial France. Towards Lyons, where the ubiquitous vineyards give way to mulberry trees, a heavy fog impedes progress not at all. Through Avignon, on roads over which Napoleon thundered in his swaying coach, and the Buick reaches Marseilles, 875 kilometers from Paris, in 15 hours. Almost a record!

Boarding ship at Marseilles, the car has a few days of salt air on the Mediterranean before taking to the road again. Then the busy clangor of Port Said, the gateway of the East, where the bustle and rush of commerce never end.

From Port Said, under the guidance of the Egyptian Buick distributor, towards Cairo, over miles of dreary, dusty roads. Suddenly the desert gives way to fertility, and the car is passing through the ancient "Land of Goshen."

Then Cairo, the indescribable. Here East and West meet as nowhere else on earth. Reeking bazaars within a stone's throw of magnificent buildings and broad streets. An overflowing tide of changing, restless people — a strange mingling of the Orient with Western civilization.

Crossing the Nile, the Buick, like any world tourist, visits the Sphinx and the Great Pyramid at Gaza. Then back, eastward again, across the Isthmus of Suez and into Palestine. At Gaza on Feb. 4, 1925, the distributor for Syria takes charge of the Buick, and the most colorful part of the trip commences. From Gaza the way leads to Jerusalem, the Holy City, with its teeming, odorous streets. Ancient brick-walled houses that witnessed the birth of Christianity stare uncomprehendingly at the irreverent piece of steel and human ingenuity that dares to stir up the dust about them.

Undaunted, the car continues, coming before long to Nazareth — a mere village in the time of Christ, now covering the bowl-shaped valley in which it is built to the tops of the surrounding hills. From Nazareth across the bleak hills to Haifa — a white city perched on the nose of recumbent Mount Carmel. Then Beirut.

Beirut welcomes the Buick as an old friend. The desert route from Beirut to Baghdad was opened for the first time, a few years ago, by Buick, and Buick cars are running regularly as part of the passenger and mail service operated by the Nairn Transport Co. over the 600 miles of the Syrian Desert. For political and geographic reasons, the desert crossing is not safe for a single car, and the "Around-the-World" Buick joins one of the Nairn convoys for the trans-desert trip.

East from Beirut, for miles the road ascends sharply over the Lebanon Mountains, elbowing its way through narrow gorges. Few corners of the globe offer more utter solitude than Syria and Palestine. Soon in the distance Damascus, "Pearl of the Desert," gleams in the sun on its green oasis. Straight east the car flies, maintaining a speed of 65 miles an hour over the flat floor of the desert, across the Tigris and Euphrates by primitive bridges of boats into the Labyrinthian bazaars of the "City of Caliphs," Baghdad.

The road now leads to Basra, on the Persian Gulf. All goes well until just after leaving Kut, the town where Townshend's army was penned in by the Turks near the end of the Great War. Here the Buick breaks through an ancient culvert, and the pulling cable and bridging boards are brought into action. There is some delay but no damage, and soon the car is on its way again. But before long new difficulties present themselves. For the next 70 miles the road is intersected by irrigation ditches at frequent intervals — ditches six feet deep and from 15 to 20 feet broad, most of them unbridged.

It now becomes a matter of crawling down and crawling out again, and making the best of it. Four-wheel brakes prove, as usual, a blessing, and largely as a result of accelerating and decelerating efficiency, the Buick arrives in Basra a little in advance of schedule time.

Thence by steamer down the shallow Persian Gulf to Bombay, lying in the curve of the shore and backed by its straight hills. All roads in India lead to Bombay, and in its busy streets can be seen all types and nationalities. The Bombay distributor encounters little of incident on the road from Bombay to Agra, aside from one mishap, when the Buick has to be pulled out of the ever-present Indian mud by bullocks, in trying to board a native ferry boat.

The speedometer now reads 3,828 miles. Agra and the Taj Mahal, set among palms and spacious lawns, and mirrors in its often pictured waterway. Dazzling whiteness of masonry against the rich, radiantly tropical sky. Here the Calcutta distributor takes the driver's seat.

Then the open road again to Delhi — the inscrutable heart of India — and the Buick enters the great "city within a city" through the magnificent Lahore Gate, towering high above the entrance to the fort. The car's splendid appearance excites comment everywhere, as the damp climate of India works particular havoc with the average automobile paint work. "When was it last painted?" inquire casual bystanders, marveling at the lustre of the Duco finish.

From Delhi through Cawnpore — city of sad memories — and the stately grandeur of Lucknow the car speeds. On to Calcutta, by the Ganges delta, where the symbols of Western civilization stand aside with the thoroughly Oriental. From Calcutta to Colombo, Ceylon, by steamer, and another distributor takes the wheel of the indefatigable Buick.

Seven thousand feet through the verdant tropical vegetation of Ceylon the car climbs, past tea estates and cinammon fields and occasionally a rambling village of bamboo houses. The weather changes suddenly, and the return journey is made through pouring rains and over flooded roads. Then Colombo again — highways flanked by thick forests of towering palm trees. Before leaving by steamer for Premantle, the landing port of Perth, Australia, the Buick's average petrol consumption in Ceylon is worked out at 25.2 miles to the gallon.

From Perth to Adelaide, across the trackless transcontinental wastes to Australia, is an arduous journey at best. It represents, in this case, the supreme test, and means the success or failure of the whole trip. Leaving Perth, the car follows the dreary reaches of the Goldfields as far as Coolgardie — the center of the gold rush in 1892 — then branches off for the mining town of Norseman, 480 miles from Fremantle and the coast. As settlements and roads are left behind, troubles commence. For the first 30 miles the track is exceedingly rough and stony, after which without warning, comes a mile of heavy sand, followed by a stretch of boggy ground in the zone of a recent thunderstorm. In a little while down goes the Buick to the running-boards. Out comes spades, and the car is laboriously dug loose. Then with infinite patience, a corduroy road is built of small trees and branches. For 160 miles these intolerable conditions persist, the car sinking in 15 or more times. But the worst of the ordeal is over. The character of the country changes as the South Australian border is passed, and for 135 miles the car travels the Nullabar Plains where the salt bush and blue bush are the only forms of vegetation and where the going is at least level.

The beautiful city of Adelaide at last, after eight days of constant strain during which the car has traveled 1,826 miles. It is weather-stained and muddy but still running as smoothly as ever. Leaving Adelaide on Easter Sunday, April 13, the Buick speeds to Melbourne and thence to Sydney, in New South Wales, over the southern road which almost impassable in places, is famous for its stretches of sand, mud and loose stones.

From Sydney to Auckland by boat, and the Buick faces the mountains and gorgeous scenery of New Zealand. From Auckland, spread out over its seven hills, the car tours through Rotorua, which besides being the center of the thermal spring region, is the heart of the Maori territory through Gisborne and Napier to Wellington, seat of the New Zealand government, whence it is shipped to Christchurch in the South Island. Christchurch is in the center of Canterbury Plain, a great sheep-raising territory stretching 150 miles from north to south. Here the car skirts the coast, passing through the prosperous seaside towns of Ashburton, Timaru and Oamaru, arriving in due course at Dunedin, the center of trade and port of the district of Otago. This was originally a Scotch settlement, and Dunedin City is planned and the streets named after Edinburgh. Then to Invercargill, the southernmost town in New Zealand and incidentally the point farthest south reached by the Buick on its world tour.

The return journey from Invercargill to Dunedin is perhaps the most delightful part of the whole trip. The Buick performs to perfection, even taking the most fearsome Kilmog Hill without difficulty. Up one, two, three miles with never a falter. There is no need to change gears; silkily and without effort the car reaches the top, then coasts down to Waitati. Mount Cargill is the next climb, reached towards nightfall. The Buick slips easily over the top and Port Chalmers glitters below, while far away at the end of the bay, the myriad lights of Dunedin twinkle a welcome. From Dunedin the itinerary leads back to Auckland and the car is shipped to Honolulu, Hawaii after covering a total of 2,281 miles in New Zealand.

Tropical Hawaii accords the world traveler an enthusiastic reception. Then the boat for San Francisco, and the Buick, relayed from dealer to dealer, starts from the Pacific Coast across the United States. At Flint, Mich., its birthplace, the Buick receives a royal welcome from the 16,000 members of the Buick family at the factory. Speeding on to Detroit, the car crosses over into Canada, coming back into the United States at Niagara Falls.

The last lap of the "Around-the-World" Buick tour is completed in New York on June 23, when the car is driven through the streets to City Hall where the mayor of New York adds the final signature to the "log" which has been signed by various drivers and officials throughout the entire trip. When the car reaches New York, it has been handled by 94 different drivers. The speedometer reads 16,499 miles.

From New York to New York, completely around the world, and the Buick has accomplished its aim. Another milestone has been reached in the records of pioneer automotive achievement. Before the trip started, the whole itinerary was timed. Steamers were booked far in advance to transport the car between countries separated by water. Distributors were informed as to just when they would receive the car and to whom and when they would deliver it.

The successful completion of the trip attests both to the faultless performance of the car itself, and to the efficient manner in which it was handled in the many different countries. The "Around-the-World" Buick tour is a true demonstration of the extent to which the Buick car and the Buick organization can be relied upon by Buick owners wherever they may be or go. It is a great satisfaction for each of the 900,000 Buick owners to know that "the sun never sets on Buick service."

(Reprinted with permission from the October 1969 issue of *The Buick Bugle*.)

Buick cheered in Red Square after winning "For Dynamic" trophy.

Letter from Moscow reveals Russian adventure

Why is the Buick in the old photo above being cheered by a crowd in Moscow's Red Square?

The quick answer is because it won. But nobody seemed to know what it won, or other details — until a thick registered-mail package from the Soviet Union, marked "Urgent," arrived in *Inside Buick*'s office.

The photos on these pages had been found in a file drawer at Buick headquarters in Flint early this year. Based on brief information written on the back of the 60-year-old prints, we knew only that a Buick had won some sort of a Leningrad-to-Moscow endurance run in 1925.

The yellowing photos were a tantalizing tip of some forgotten adventure, and a reminder that Buick had had a long and exciting history, which goes far beyond its best-remembered role as the financial rock on which General Motors was founded.

But a search for the story behind the photos published here seemed to reach a dead end. The usual historical sources had no record of Buicks racing in the Soviet Union. We called the Soviet Embassy in Washington. The press office there suggested an address in Moscow. A short letter was sent, with copies of the photos. It seemed a long shot, and for months there was no reply.

Then, one day, the package arrived, covered with 33 postage stamps. It included a two-page letter in Russian, an English translation, a map of the race route, and clippings from several Soviet publications circa 1925. The letter was signed by S. Ushakov, secretary responsible of an organization, which, freely translated, is called Federation of Automobile Sports of the Soviet Union.

It is clear that Ushakov went to considerable trouble to respond to *Inside Buick*'s request, and it is also clear that Buicks did quite well in a competition in the Soviet Union in 1925.

Ushakov wrote that his organization had "carefully examined the photographs...and have come to the unanimous conclusion that they show some fragments of the

1925 National Test Motor Run in which Buick automobiles participated."

He credited Lev Shugurov, chairman of the Speed Contests Committee of the FAS USSR and chairman of the Vintage Automoto Section, for researching information on the run, which Ushakov said could also be referred to as Reliability Trial or Endurance Rally.

Soviet mountains didn't faze Buicks.

"Its aim was to test foreign automobiles in hard national road conditions in order to reveal their operational capabilities," Ushakov wrote. "On the basis of the run's results, the conclusions and recommendations were made on importing foreign cars to the USSR."

The Russian Run was 3,090 miles, 48 percent on "earth" roads, 44 percent on macadam, eight percent on mountain roads, on a route (see map) from Leningrad to Moscow. There were 78 cars entered from such countries as the United States, Germany, England, France, Italy, Austria and Czechoslovakia. The 42 U.S. cars included Buick, Cadillac, Chrysler, Dodge, Hudson, Lincoln, Moon, Nash, Packard, Pierce-Arrow, Studebaker and Ford.

The Russians were particularly interested in the U.S. cars, Ushakov said, because "they were very strongly constructed, simple and reliable, with big clearance and margin of torsion movement."

Five Buicks, probably Model 55 with "touring type" bodies, entered the run. One, driven by an American driver named Levstrem, "left the run for some reasons and there is no information about it." Another was a judge's car. But other Buicks did extremely well.

One Buick (No. 37 driven by a Russian, Solomatin) won the first prize of the State Trade Committee, a silver bowl with cups covered with enamel, "for the totality of abilities," which would appear to be the top overall reward. Another (No. 40, driven by an American named Fatter) received the Organizing Committee prize, a notebook with silver board, "for endurance and strong construction." Only 10 of the 78 entries matched its total number of points — 200.

And Car 38 (the Buick shown in the big picture in Red Square) won the prize of the Ministry of Communication Means, a silver tea set, "for dynamic." This car, driven by a Russian, Kuznetsov, on a one-kilometer (0.62 of a mile) course on the Vladimirskoe motor road near Moscow, was clocked in 71.85 km/h (44.5 mph) from a standing start and 99.8 km/h (61.8 mph) from a running start. Kuznetsov also received a watch as a prize for good driving, and Fatter, in Car 40, received a cigarette case for participation.

This Buick won for "totality of abilities."

Ushakov wrote that after the run, 41 cars including Buick No. 38 "were exposed at the large automobile exhibition in Moscow." And he noted he had included some pages, in Russian, from publications of the time. "Wishing you every success we remain sincerely yours," he concluded.

The Russian experience is only one example of Buick adventures in this country and around the world in the early days.

(Reprinted with permission from the winter 1985-'86 issue of *Inside Buick* and the July 1986 issue of the *Buick Bugle*.)

Last-minute check in Leningrad.

Dreamboats

1931–1942

Great, big, beautiful Buicks!

By Ned Comstock

If you were wheeling a Buick 90 in 1931 you had a fast powerful car under you; a great big beautiful car and one of the most reliable road machines on earth. If your Buick 90 in 1931 carried the Seven Passenger Phaeton body, with its superbly tailored Burbank top, deep dish wire wheels and soft real leather seats, you were riding in a style that was fast disappearing then and now is not seen any more.

Long-time old car man Lowell Gypsum who lives in Albany, NY now, found for me my 1931 Buick 90 Phaeton. I do not remember the transaction well except that I went to the railroad station in Utica, N.Y. to take delivery. Two good humored men in mechanics' garb met me, took my $600 and pointed to the curb. The long black 1931 Buick 90 was standing there in the rain, the deep gloss of it shining, every side curtain buttoned without any crack in the isinglass.

It had been a flower car for an undertaker in New Paltz, N.Y., delivered there new for $1,895. It is hard to translate 1931 dollars now but taking the price of gold as a standard, $1,895 then would mean almost $15,000 today. The speedometer showed 29,000 and a few more miles. It would need tires, the men said. The original Silvertowns, big fat 7.00 x 19s still showed tread but should be replaced. They thought I'd find everything else in order. We shook hands and I drove home. When I got there my wife said she had never seen me look so happy.

Four years and another 30,000 miles later I was parked in front of the Post Office in Rome, N.Y. reading the mail. It was drizzling then, too. A stranger approached and asked me how much I wanted for the Buick. I hadn't considered selling, but startled out of whatever I was thinking about, I said $600. I had too many cars then, or too many children, I forget which; anyway I was hard up. The man produced some impressive credentials and wrote me a check on a Detroit bank. I handed him the keys and walked home in the rain. I had a bad three days until my check cleared. Then I forgot about my 1931 Buick 90 seven passenger phaeton.

But for four years and 30,000 miles I had some of the best 1931 motoring this world ever saw.

It was a whale of a car, that Buick, a great big brute of a car. With its five inch stroke it would pull away from a walking pace on high and never buck. Its massive 364 inch engine would build speed like a steam locomotive until you ran out of road to hold it. All through the speed range that mighty Buick surged with power as long as you held the pedal down.

Looking at the yellowing old tables of 1931 engine specifications you can see why. At 2,800 RPM the Buick was pushing out 104 horses, competing head on with the great and famous American luxury liners. Even Cadillac,

1931 Buick 90 seven-passenger phaeton.

priced half again as high could work up only 95 horsepower and took 3,000 revs to do it. That Buick had the heart of a lion.

Then there was the glory of it. The fresh painted jonquil yellow wire wheels with their clean whitewall tires flashed bright in the sun, a vivid contrast to the long black body, Side mounted spares covered skin tight with best quality material matched the tailored top. Instead of old covered wagon style, the low flat top looked lean as a starved horse. The deep chrome glinted blue like ice. Huge headlamps were individually mounted on chrome stanchions. Decoration was in faultless taste. Varnished wood top bows hinted luxury. The long sweep of the body was clean and uncluttered, without meaningless embellishments. There was no radiator ornament, just the flat chrome cap as big as the palm of your hand. Quality showed through everything.

Everything looked businesslike too, The long bank of vertical hood louvres cooled the engine. Windshield wings protected the driver and his front seat passenger. A strong steady windshield wiper cleared the view for the driver only. For and aft heavy spring steel frame mounted bumpers warded off danger. No nonsense anywhere on the 1931 Buick 90.

Perhaps because so few big cars of any make were sold in 1931 we had no appreciation of the bountiful bargain Buick 90 offered that year. At a base price of $1,785, weighing in at 4,340 pounds Buick sold for 41¢ a pound when Cadillacs were going at 60¢, big Packards for 76¢ and Lincolns no less than 88¢ a pound. Of course nobody figured it that way, but these statistics hid the reason this 1931 Buick 90 phaeton was a Milestone model that marked the end of an era, the last of the old generation.

The touring car body sold in minuscule numbers was never again a real factor in American motor car production after 1931 except for Ford. Buick built its last phaetons in 1932, only a very few were produced. Probably Ford was the last volume producer of touring, continuing through Model A and into 1938. We were told at the time the Ford V8 touring production was to satisfy New York State Trooper requirements, but that may be apocryphal. The last Packard advertisement of a touring car that I ever saw was 1936 and significantly featured the U.S. capital building in the background since most of their market was ceremonial use. Pierce Arrow and Lincoln continued token production of touring cars through the 1930s and there was some export trade in lower priced touring cars.

But as a regular bread-and-butter offering, except for Ford, 1931 Buick was among the very last American touring cars.

Probably the end of touring cars began when the role of automobiles in our lives changed from a some-time sporting partner to a daily necessity. Then the need for protection from weather drove us to demand closed bodies.

Roy Chapin, Hudson founder and father of the American Motors Chairman whose been riding that roller coaster all these years, made it price-possible. In 1921 he had introduced an Essex coach at $1,495 reducing the price premium for the closed body at $300, a small difference in those days.

By 1931, Buick 90 seven passenger phaeton carried on the old open car tradition almost alone. With the size of the sedan without the bulk, it had an up-to-date look of speed and power. Yet the romantic aura of the early days still lingered. The straight through styling that we now call classic was there. All the components still spoke their separate functions. The strong big wheels, the high massive hood and the fleet fenders swept back as if in the wind combined to project the image of a high quality carriage in the old tradition. 1931 Buick 90 phaeton was a final expression of old-style at its very best. But underneath, this mighty Buick hid the cutting edge of newest technology. *Automobile Quarterly* points out that the 1931 Buick straight eight, new that year was continued for 20 years until the V8 replaced it, and that 1931 Buick overhead valve arrangement set standards for auto generations after.

But boxed in the middle market from the beginning Buick had built an image of conservative respectability, and had left performance records to cars costing double and more Buick prices. But now, with this giant killer Buick squeezed hard on the performance gap. Higher priced American cars were still more refined, finished more luxuriously and conferred more prestige. But out on the road the difference between them and 1931 Buick 90 narrowed and nearly disappeared. And in 1931 the dollar difference bulked very big indeed.

1931 Buick 90 did mark the introduction of top technology of the day into the middle market and permanently revised the relationship between performance and price in the American market.

1931 Buick 90 seven-passenger phaeton was a crossing point between tradition and innovation. It should live forever.

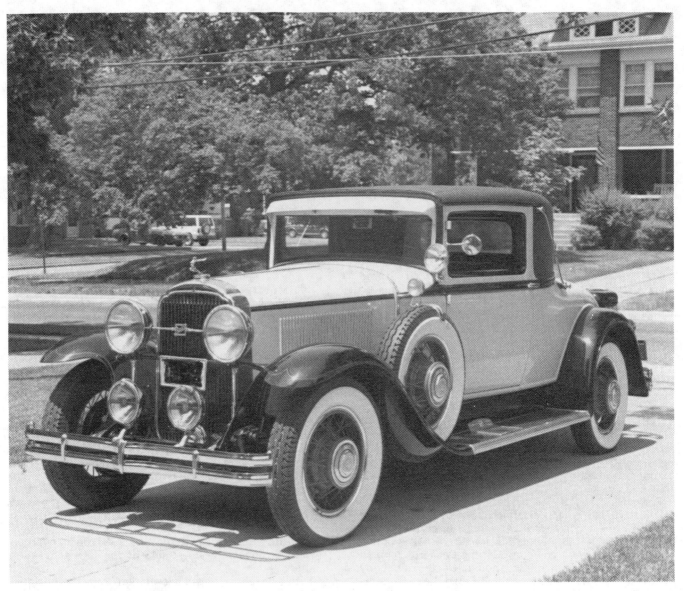

1931 Buick. Was this the last old-fashioned car?

1931 Buick: Last old-fashioned car?

In 1931 Buick was bringing first class personal transportation to the middle price range of American automobiles. It used proved technology (we didn't know that word then) the best quality materials and plenty of pounds and inches. The result was 8-90, a refined car, a wonderfully capable car and at $1,620 for Model 95 seven- passenger phaeton a rare bargain. The Depression did it in, of course, but it may have been the last best expression of traditional American road machinery. In 1932 came Ford V-8 and the hot car revolution, but at Buick in 1931 for a little while things were the way they always had been, almost from the beginning.

In one way only did 1931 8-90 concede something to fashion. A straight eight replaced the six cylinder engine of previous years without any evident advantage. The 1931 Buick "*Reference Book*" and impressive 70-page slick paper manual that came with my 8-90 Model 95 is silent on the subject, although it was Buick's new departure for the year. But since the seeping success of 1924 Packard Single Eight which had been building since, it simply was

not realistic in 1931 to market a mid-price car without eight cylinders, and Buick proposed to be practical. This engine was hugely successful—it moved Buick without major modification for the next 22 years.

Practical didn't mean cheap. Translated into 1982 dollars, the delivered purchase price would push $24,000. When you filled her up, it meant 9 quarts of oil and 22 gallons of gasoline. Things were dirt cheap then, but they had their price even in 1931. Buick 8-90 was looking for prosperous buyers.

Particularly Model 95 Seven Passenger Phaeton needed an affluent owner, one with other cars. That's why only 392 were built, and after 1932, no more. It would seem in the south there might be a pace for an open car, or as a sometime car anywhere, and it still seems so, but that did not come to pass. Perhaps higher road speeds killed the graceful old touring car, because they demanded protection from the hard air steam. Station wagons filled the place, led by Ford in 1934. But in 1931 8-90 Seven Passenger Phaeton with its two jump seats

74

and long Burbank top still rolled free as all outdoors.

With the price of gasoline and the state of the art the way it was in 1931, inches and pounds were the way to go to performance and comfort, and that's the way Buick went, exactly opposite of todays stampede to high-tech design. Eight-ninety was set on 132 inch wheelbase, weighed in at 4,320 pounds. The engine filled the underhood space completely, and no wonder. It was a long engine, eight-in-line, a tall engine with overhead valves on top of a five inch stroke, and it displaced 344 inches.

Low speed capability was highly prized then, and Buick performed superbly there. Once moved from rest there was little need for the gears although they were the new Syncor-mesh design and changed positively effortlessly, and 104 horses at only 2800 revs combined with a five inch stroke made them almost unnecessary. Buick 8-90 moved with the ease of steam power, and up to 80 miles an hour was there if you could find the road to hold it.

Tire trouble which had plagued early day motorist had been almost eliminated. Here-too dimensions helped — 6.50 inch tires on 19 inch wheels were lightly stressed.

One thing didn't work. In contradiction to their 1931 policy of traditional methods, Buick included a "heat control" of the engine which was best left in "off" position. It was intended to heat the intake manifold to "insure minimum consumption of gasoline." Why this was thought necessary in a car that could never be coaxed to do 10 miles to the gallon, I do not know. It was attempted by directing hot exhaust fumes through a double walled riser along the intake manifold. The trouble came when the exhaust ate through the intake riser and got sucked into the engine, at which time you got no miles per gallon at all because the Buick died in a paroxysm of coughing.

No special styling characterized 1931. It just looked like an automble. The 1929 bulge was gone, of course, but the vestige of the Packard inspired radiator lingered. Wheels were emphasized, and nothing dresses a car more effectively. You could get lovely deep dish wire wheels on demand, or thick spoke artillery wheels, both types mountable, painted a contrasting color. But overall 1931 looked just like 1930.

Which is where we started. The 1931 Buick was probably the last old-fashioned car, or nearly, and maybe the best of the breed. But the next year it was honked and passed by a $500 Ford.

It was the end of an era.

1931 Buick Model 3-96 five-passenger coupe. Inset: 1931 Model 90 opera coupe.

McLaughlin built better Buicks

By R. Perry Zavitz

Long before the Studebakers made wheelbarrows, Robert McLaughlin was carving axe handles.

Later, this young Canadian lad was impressed by a catalog of horsedrawn wagons, carriages and cutters, so he decided to build himself a cutter. Someone saw his work and ordered one like it.

That was the simple start of what became the McLaughlin Carriage Co. of Oshawa, Ontario. The company grew as its line of products included carriages, and McLaughlin quality was recognized.

McLaughlin had three sons, John, George, and Samuel. After studying pharmacy, John discovered a ginger extract, then founded the company that became Canada Dry.

His brothers worked with their father. George apprenticed in the factory, but young Sam couldn't decide whether to be a hardware merchant, lawyer, draftsman or champion cyclist. But by the age 16, he was persuaded to join the family firm, and began apprenticing in the upholstery department.

Sam loved his work, which later included designing carriages. Eventually, he saw the automobile threatening the carriage business. His father disagreed, but did grant him the chance to visit the U.S. manufacturers and test their cars. Sam returned with an agreement from William Durant to build Buicks.

"The Governor," as the boys called their father, reluctantly agreed to the new undertaking, and immediately preparations began. When the chief engineer was taken seriously ill, work halted. Sam frantically called Durant for the loan of an engineer. Instead, Durant came, quickly resolving the matter. Buick would supply motors while McLaughlins would build the rest of the car. A 15-year contract was signed in 1907.

Their first car was a two-cylinder 1908 Model F. The 154 made that year included the four-cylinder 10 and G models, as well as the D, S and 5, which duplicated Buick's models.

The pattern of isinglass in the rear windows was like that used on McLaughlin buggies, which Canadians recognized. That established McLaughlin's identity. Reputation was established by maintaining high quality, which Canadians expected from McLaughlin. "One grade only, and that the best" was a longtime McLaughlin motto.

Second year production totaled 423, which was just 63 short of Ford of Canada's output. McLaughlin built 10 models, including Models 4, 25 and 26, which had no Buick equivalent. This illustrates McLaughlin's independence, despite close association and excellent relationship with Buick.

McLaughlin's Model 7 was continued in 1911, even though it was a 1910 Buick dropout. McLaughlin used a T-head engine of Welch design in it. Total disgression from

1931 McLaughlin-Buick Series 8-90 seven-passenger touring in front of Parkwood, Sam McLaughlin's home in Oshawa, Ontario, Canada.

Buick was the 1911 McLaughlin Rauch & Lang electric. But the Model 7 was McLaughlin's pride and joy.

"From bumper to tip of rear fender, as fine a piece of work as could be desired, a truly elegant design, in style and finish," was McLaughlin's unusually immodest description of their Model 7. It was available in any color the buyer desired.

Sam McLaughlin recalled: "I imported black material from England for the tops, East African mahogany for the instrument panels, fine wood for the bodies. We brought in beautiful wool upholstery from England, and leather and cords. Always the best."

The McLaughlin B-55 of 1914, which introduced six-cylinder power simultaneously with Buick, was "much sleeker than its Buick counterpart," stated one observer. Recessed mahogany dashboards with clocks and locking glove boxes, extra nickel trim, and power-driven tire pumps were thoughtful McLaughlin extras.

Exhibited in New York at General Motors' invitation, a McLaughlin attracted much attention. When Alfred Sloan saw it, he ordered it right away, complaining, "It's no more like our Buicks than a St. Bernard is like a dachshund!"

As the 15-year agreement with Buick was expiring, a reorganization was necessary. Other considerations included George's poor health and the fact that Sam had no sons to take over. Forming an all-Canadian company was unthinkable. Sam knew that would fail because of the examples around him.

The complete sale of their company to General Motors was negotiated. But first, some housecleaning was done. The carriage business was sold. The Chevrolet division, in production since 1915, was merged with McLaughlin before the American purchase in late 1918.

Sam was president of General Motors of Canada Limited, and George was vice president. Sam also joined the General Motors board holding that position until 1967.

There is uncertainty as to whether the cars were McLaughlin or McLaughlin-Buicks, but after 1922 the McLaughlin-Buick name seems consistent.

Regarding models, post-1922 production was simplified considerably. For 1923 and '24, there were two lines — Master Four and Master Six. No fours were built after 1924, so the 1925 series were called Special Six and Master Six. The Master Six name was adopted by Buick that year and kept through 1928.

McLaughlin-Buick Sixes were faster than their American mates. An enterprising Canadian sold McLaughlin-Buick sixes to certain American clients requiring superior performance during the Prohibition. Such McLaughlin-Buicks were nick-named "Whisky Sixes."

A change in Canadian model names occurred in 1927 when they were dubbed Series 115, 120 and 128, indicating respective wheelbases. After 1927, it was back to Buick nomenclature. During the 1930s, all Buick series were matched in Canada. From 1938 to 1941, GM operated an assembly plant in Regina, Saskatchewan, from which McLaughlin-Buicks flowed.

As mass production increased, and more steel was used in bodies, there was less difference between McLaughlin-Buicks and Buicks. Although there was more attention to details in Canada. By 1939, the name McLaughlin-Buick appeared only as a decal on the valve covers.

Still, specially built models came from Oshawa. A 1930 two-passenger tear-drop shaped experimental model, Silver Flash, was sensational. As well as its racy appearance, speed was a remarkable 118 m.p.h.

McLaughlin-Buick provided several Royal Tour cars in Canada. For the Prince of Wales' 1927 tour, two 1928 McLaughlin-Buicks were provided. Lizard upholstery inside and beige finish with green wire wheels were special

McLaughlin-Buick display at the Canadian National Exhibition in Toronto.

features of these phaetons. Until recently one was owned by Bernice Marshall of Toronto. The other is owned by a Prince of India, who has done an amazing job of restoration.

McLaughlin-Buick developed a good export business in Britain, and some cars were custom-made for royalty. One was a 1936 Limited with closed rear quarters and a sumptuous interior. It was ordered by the Prince of Wales, who became King Edward VIII before delivery. He also ordered a McLaughlin-Buick Roadmaster for Wally Simpson.

In 1939, two McLaughlin-Buicks were customized for the King George V and Queen Elizabeth Canadian tour. These Limited four-door convertibles were stretched 15 inches, and had tops seven inches higher than normal so not to cramp their Royal Highnesses. One of these cars is at the National Museum of Science & Technology in Ottawa. The other, owned by Vern Bethel of Vancouver, was reused last May when Prince Charles and Lady Diana opened Expo 86.

The final McLaughlin-Buicks were 211 Special and Century models of 1942. Many were devoid of chrome and painted khaki for army use.

Buick production didn't resume at Oshawa until 1951. Alas, they were not McLaughlin-Buicks, but 1951 Buick Custom models. GM of Canada did not use the Special name, even though that was what these really were.

Almost 52,000 McLaughlins were made until 1922, then 133,000 McLaughlin-Buicks after that. It is a remarkable sum considering Canada's population is roughly one-tenth that of the United States.

Also remarkable is Sam McLaughlin. "Col. Sam," as he was affectionately known, being honorary colonel of the Ontario Regiment R.C.A.C., was the spark plug that drove a family venture into one of Canada's largest corporations. Samuel McLaughlin died at age 100.

One of two 1939 McLaughlin-Buicks custom-built for the 1939 Royal Tour, parked at the front door of Sam McLaughlin's home in Oshawa, Ontario, Canada.

Royal Tour McLaughlin-Buicks

By R. Perry Zavitz

"Cars for king's use in Canada dwarf everything on the road . . .Magnificence of beauty and proportions in feature of official vehicles built by General Motors at Oshawa, Ontario," proclaimed an April 1939 GM press release on the Royal Tour cars. What may have seemed exaggerated was totally accurate.

General Motors of Canada was commissioned to build two cars for the 1939 tour of King George VI and Queen Elizabeth. The cars were extensively modified 1939 McLaughlin-Buick Series 90 Limited sedans. The tops were cut off, then the bodies were cut in two and stretched 15 inches. They were made into maxi convertibles with beige, superfine duck, powered tops. Headroom was raised seven inches. Shatter-proof side windows extended farther back than normal.

The interiors were finished in the finest materials. Maroon broadcloth upholstery in car no. 1, beige in no. 2 were used. Folding arm rests had built-in sterling silver vanity pieces selected by the queen's wardrobe designer. An electrically powered glass partition separated the front and rear compartments. This division had two built-in walnut-faced cabinets and an electric clock. Two rear facing auxiliary seats accommodated other royal party members. The front compartment was upholstered in top quality leather. The chauffeur had contact with the rear by "an electric communication system."

Both cars were painted Royal maroon. Aside from the 20 foot length, their lower exteriors differed from production models by the addition of two special driving lights and Cadillac V-16 taillights. The "McLaughlin-Buick" name appeared on the hubcaps and step-plates. (These

were the last cars to physically carry the McLaughlin-Buick name, though production continued until 1942.) The royal crest and a blue light were mounted atop the windshield. When on, the light signaled royalty aboard.

The alterations were done by select craftsmen at the Oshawa factory. They were instructed to "work at your own pace and redo any of the work you feel could be done better." Each car was said to cost $15,000, but $25,000 was more realistic.

After the tour, these cars were returned to GM in Oshawa. A year later, the maroon car was sold to Mrs. Helen Ross Palmer of Victoria by a Windsor GM dealer. She and a friend went to Oshawa to get the car. They were chauffeured to Windsor, where the next day Mrs. Palmer was officially given the keys. The women took a leisurely trip home.

Nearing home, they encountered a rear axle problem. Mrs. Palmer received a telegram from the Windsor dealer advising her of arrangements to ship a replacement to Victoria GM dealer. She was to get temporary repairs, then send the bills to the Windsor dealer.

About the same time Sam McLaughlin received a letter that the government approved one of the Royal Tour cars be supplied to the Governor-General, the Earl of Athlone. So the beige McLaughlin-Buick saw several years of official service in Ottawa; and some unofficial service, too. Prime Minister Mackenzie King, who had a liking for luxury cars, used it, maybe more than the governor-general.

This car was returned in 1946 to Oshawa, where it stayed until 1955. GM sold it to the Oshawa Pontiac-Buick dealer. Larry and Cal Norton of Oshawa spied it, but before they could do anything, it was resold to a GM dealer in remote Larder Lake, Ontario. By 1962, Nortons

The two almost identical Royal Tour McLaughlin-Buicks were custom-built by General Motors of Canada. The Roadmaster chassis was used but lengthened.

relocated the car and arranged its purchase. Their uncle and nephew helped build these extraordinary McLaughlin-Buicks.

Registering only 19,000 miles on the odometer, it was repatriated to Oshawa. In 1971, it was in a parade by Parkwood, Col. Sam McLaughlin's mansion, celebrating the venerable gentleman's 100th birthday. McLaughlin-Buicks of every age passed in review. This car is now in the National Museum of Science and Technology in Ottawa.

Persistant rumors had the other car destroyed in a Vancouver warehouse fire. But evidence of its continued existence reached Vern Bethel, a 1939 Buick collector in Ottawa. By 1972, he traced it to a Victoria address, so immediately flew there. He found the no. 1 Royal Tour McLaughlin-Buick owned by Mrs. Helen Margaret Martay, who inherited it from her mother, Mrs. Palmer.

After Vern negotiated the purchase, several amazing events followed. On his return to Ottawa, he pulled into a Vancouver service station to check the overheating radiator. Suddenly there was a screech of tires as a car made a U-turn into the service station. It was a local McLaughlin-Buick Club member who saw Vern's new acquisition, and offered him secure storage for it.

Vern told a woman in his Ottawa office about his car. She also had a part-time job at a car dealer, and relayed the story to the manager. He had two of the flag staffs used on the Royal Tour cars. Now one of those rides proudly above the windshield on Vern's car.

A hubcap was missing. As mentioned before, these cars had special McLaughlin-Buick caps. Another McLaughlin-Buick club member found one at Hershey, Pa. which had to be the actual missing hubcap. It was in better condition than the others.

The maroon Royal Tour McLaughlin-Buick led a much busier life than its mate. Mrs. Palmer placed the car at the disposal of the Duke of Kent in 1941 during his Canadian visit. In 1946 and 1947, she loaned it to the Royal Canadian Army Service Corps., which used it for visiting dignitaries including the next Governor-General Viscount Alexander and Viscount Lord Montgomery. Normally the latter preferred Jeeps, but newspapers reported his "boyish" pleasure at the McLaughlin-Buick's performance. For a

time this car was used by a taxi company for sight-seeing tours in Victoria. The odometer read 65,000 miles when Vern got the car. Indications are that mileage was actually 265,000.

These McLaughlin-Buicks that took the royal guests on their 9,150-mile, month-long Canadian tour helped make it a memorable occasion. In 1974, Vern received a letter from the personal secretary of Queen Elizabeth, now the Queen Mother. She fondly recalled "the magnificent appearance and splendid performance of the McLaughlin-Buick automobiles." Prince Charles and Princess Diana arrived at the opening ceremonies of Vancouver's Expo '86 in Vern's car.

The two McLaughlin-Buicks were truly cars fit for a king. How fortunate these recognized Classics are both still around.

Specifications

Engine Type	Straight-eight
Bore	3-7/16 in.
Stroke	4-5/16 in.
Displacement	320.2 cu. in.
Maximum hp @ r.p.m.	141 3600
Maximum torque (ft/lbs)	@ r.p.m. 269 @ 2000
Overall length	243 in.
Overall height	78-5/8 in.
Wheelbase	155 in.
Weight	5800 lbs.
Fuel consumption: city	7 mpg (Imperial)
Fuel consumption: highway	11 mpg (Imperial)
Zero to 60 time	18.5 sec.
Top speed	85 mph (approx.)
Original price	$15,000 (wholesale)

(Research information courtesy of Buick Club of America *Bugle*.)

One of the McLaughlin-Buick Royal Tour cars is owned by a collector and restorer in Vancouver. He lent the 47-year-old car to Prince Charles and Princess Diana to tour the city when they visited Vancouver to open Expo '86.

1934 Buick 61 — middle class car

Despite the negative affects of the Great Depression, Buick Motor Division was able to increase its business by almost 100 percent in the 1934 model year. Part of the company's successful sales program was based upon offering three different eight-cylinder lines, one of which could please almost any type of buyer. The company's "middle" price range offering was the Series 34-60, which included six body styles selling in the $1,400-1,700 range.

Priced at $1,465, the Model 61 5-passenger Club Sedan drew a total of 5,395 assemblies for the U.S. market, plus 234 additional builds for customers overseas. This model

past. In fact, by 1935, Rolls-Royce obtained a license from General Motors to adopt this system to its V-12 Phantom III line.

Another technical innovation for Buick in 1934 was the combination starter and accelerator, a feature that remained in production through the 1960 model year. Pushing the accelerator fully to the floor or pulling the hand-operated throttle completely out automatically engaged the starter.

Standard equipment on the Model 61 Club Sedan included built-in trunk, rich interior appointments, steel

1934 Buick Series 60 Model 61 Club Sedan.

was, technically, a "touring sedan" with four doors and a built-in trunk. It was constructed on the mid-sized, 128 in. wheelbase and used 7.50 x 16 size tires.

Styling attributes included new "wind stream" body contours, horizontal louvered hood and a slightly redesigned radiator grille. Improved Fisher No-Draft ventilation was featured.

Under the hood was Buick's mid-sized powerplant, an inline eight of overhead valve design. It had a bore and stroke of 3-3/32 x 4-58 in. and displaced 278.1 cu. in. Brake horsepower was rated 100 at 3,200 r.p.m. A Marvel carburetor and Delco Remy ignition was used. Overall gear ratio was given as 4.7:1.

A new type of front suspension system was introduced on all 1934 Buick models. It was of the "Knee-Action" type and combined Delco-Lovejoy shock absorber with a rear stabilizer bar. This setup gave a much smoother, easy handling ride and was a vast improvement over the

spoke wheels, dual horns and twin windshield wipers. Bumper guards, trunk rack and steel-covered sidemount spares were options available at slight extra cost.

The Buick 34-60 Series models entered production on January 1, 1934. Serial Numbers 2706453 and up were used on these cars. This number will be found under the right or left front fender on the frame in back of the front axle. Motor Numbers used in production were 2861223 and up. The Motor Number will be stamped on either the right or left side of the upper crankcase.

Buick's ability to boost sales during the Depression was a major factor in helping the division to become the 8th ranked automaker in the United States for 1934. Although much of the credit for strong sales goes to the smaller, Series 40 models which Harlow H. Curtice had the foresight to market, the mid-priced class Sixty models were also a significant factor in the firm's success of the time.

Retired North Dakota Highway Patrol officer Maurice Arves models a 1935 uniform with a 1935 Buick Series 40 coupe in front of the state capitol building in Bismarck.

North Dakota Highway Patrol's Buick squad car

By Jim Benjaminson

Prior to 1935, the only traffic enforcement on North Dakota highways came from county sheriff departments, with local enforcement handled by various city police departments. As the number of fatal traffic accidents began to increase it became apparent there was need for a state level agency.

At its December 1934 annual meeting, the North Dakota Peace Officers Association passed a resolution calling for the creation of a state highway patrol. The resolution instructed the Peace Officers Association, through its various committees, to actively promote the new idea with legislators, county-level state attorneys, judges and other influential citizens of the state.

The 1935 legislative assembly passed a law giving authority to appoint a highway patrol superintendent and assistant superintendent to the state's highway commissioner. With the consent of the governor, he was authorized to appoint not more than 10 officers to an organization that would constitue the state highway patrol.

On July 3, 1935, Gov. Walter Welford announced the appointment of State Assistant Adjustant General Herman A. Brocopp to a position as a patrol superintendent while Frank L. Putnam was named as deputy superintendent. Brocopp soon stepped aside, leaving Putnam to full control. Putnam, a Carrington police officer and four other recruits — George A. Swenson, of Walcott; George Robin-

son, of Hillsboro; Curtis Sill, of Beach, and Emil Lundquist, of Parshall were sent to the Minnesota Highway Patrol training program in St. Paul. In their uniforms of light blue coats and dark blue trousers their first act as a team was to travel to Duluth, Minn. to take delivery of five 1935 Buick Series 40 business coupes that had been shipped from Michigan via a Geat Lakes freighter and drive the cars back home. Actual field operations began Aug. 22, 1935.

An oversight in the original legislation that created the patrol had failed to appropriate any money to fund the patrols operations — the intent had been to start operations with $5,000. The patrol's first assignment was to deliver 100,000 drivers licenses to clerks of court in the state's 53 counties — revenue generated by the sale of these drivers licenses was to be directed into a fund for the patrol's operations; the program proved so successful that it was continued througgh 1938!

Each car was equipped with a "long-wave" radio system. Radio stations throughout the state were used to dispatch messages to the officers while on the road. It wasn't until 1941, in fact, that two-way radio communications equipment was installed in the state patrol vehicles.

The five Buicks saw service with the patrol for several years — four of the cars were traded in 1938, being replaced by a 1938 DeSoto coupe, a 1938 Ford coupe and two 1939 Ford coupes. The last Buick disappeared from the roster by 1939 (by which time the patrol now had

12 vehicles) but its replacement vehicle was not noted in patrol records.

Prior to the patrol's 40th anniversary in 1975 an effort was made to locate one of the original North Dakota Highway Patrol Buicks and have it restored. After intensive searching, no original cars were found. A nationwide search resulted in the purchase of a restored 1935 Buick coupe found in Paw Paw, W.V. This Buick was transported back to North Dakota where it underwent reconditioning to create a replica of a 1935 patrol car. Col. Ralph Wood (then NDHP superintendent), presented the keys of the Buick to ex-governor Arthur Link on behalf of the men in the contemporary patrol who had paid for the purchase and restoration out of their own pockets.

As part of the patrol's 50th anniversary celebration, the 1935 Buick patrol car was put in a special display at the State Heritage Center in Bismarck, along with other artifacts of the patrol's history. The patrol later presented the car to the State Historical Society for permanent display at the Heritage Center.

Over the years the North Dakota Highway patrol's use of Buicks as pursuit sedans had dwindled. In 1950, only two Buicks — a '48 and a '50 — were in use. 1951 saw a record number of Buicks in use as 15 cars — four 1950 models purchased late in '50 and 11 '51s — patroled the state's highways. By 1953 these cars had been replaced by a half dozen '52 and '53 models respectively but by the following year only carryover Buicks were in use. For 1957 just one new Buick was added to the fleet and by the mid-'60s, Buicks were missing from the vehicle roster entirely.

The five original 1935 Buick patrol cars used by the North Dakota Highway Patrol are, left to right: Unit 461 assigned to Frank Putnam, serial number 2829350, engine number 42993928; Unit 462 assigned to George Robinson, serial number 2830682, engine number 42994949; Unit 463 assigned to George Swenson, serial number 2829567, engine number 42994184; Unit 464 assigned to Emil Lundquist, serial number 2829568, engine number 42994190; and Unit 465 assigned to Curtis Sill, serial number 2829601, engine number 42994189.

1936 Century: Buick's new image

By Arch Brown

1936 Buick Century Model 68 five-passenger Victoria trunk coupe.

1936 Buick Century Model 66-C convertible.

1936 Buick Century Sport Coupe participated in the Great American Race.

For years, Buick was America's favorite family car; a dominant factor in the medium price field. In 1926, it was comfortably in third place, behind Ford and Chevrolet in U.S. sales. Then things began to turn sour. Buick's ranking fell to fourth in 1927, sixth in 1928 and eighth in 1933. Production fell 85 percent in seven years. The division was in big trouble.

It was then that Harlow "Red" Curtice took charge. He saw Buick's problems as twofold: First, the market segment in which Buick competed had all but evaporated. Speaking later to a group of dealers, Curtice noted that "in 1927, the price brackets within which Buick worked represented 28 percent of the total car market. We got the lion's share of that percentage, and it gave us a good business. But by 1933 that picture had radically changed. Those same price brackets embraced only four percent of the market."

Curtice's answer to that problem was, of course, the Series 40, later dubbed the Buick Special. Slowly, Buick began to climb out of the hole.

The other problem had to do with Buick's image. In terms of both styling and performance, the car was widely perceived as stodgy and out-of-date. The Series 60 Buick was a good example. In sedan form, this 1935 model tipped the scales at a hefty 4,303 pounds. This meant that for each of its 100 hp, there were 43 pounds to be moved along. The brakes were still mechanical and Buick was clinging stubbornly to heavy cast iron pistons. Even the one-piece steel "turret" top, featured by most other General Motors divisions, was conspicuously absent from the Buick.

By way of contrast, the 1935 Oldsmobile Eight also developed 100 hp, but its weight-to-power ratio was only 35.3:1. It employed Lockheed hydraulic brakes, had the popular turret top and rode on a wheelbase two inches longer than that of the much heavier Buick. Worse, from Buick's perspective, it undercut the price of the Series 60 by $485 — enough money for the buyer to supplement his Olds with a Chevrolet Standard coach!

Predictably then, Oldsmobile sold 72 percent more cars than Buick did that year.

But Red Curtice and his staff were hard at work developing the car that would change Buick's image, literally overnight. Displayed to the dealer body in August 1935, along with the rest of the 1936 Buick line, was the new Series 60 Century. It was aptly named, for this 120 hp beauty — more than 500 pounds lighter and $335 cheaper than its 1935 counterpart — was the first Buick to be capable of reaching 100 miles an hour! Hydraulic brakes gave it stopping power to match its speed. And the brand new 320.2-cubic inch engine, employing aluminum alloy pistons, was substantially higher than the power plant it replaced.

Buick was on the comeback trail. Model year production came to 161,180 cars, up from 49,961 the previous season. And even better days were to follow.

Shown here is the top model of Buick's 1936 Century line: a convertible coupe that belonged, at the time these photographs were taken, to Dr. Donald Mangus of Chico, Calif. Only 766 of these lovely cars were built, 49 of them being export models. The figure is a modest one, yet it represents nearly seven times as many Series 60 convertibles as the factory produced for 1935.

Standard equipment on this model included a single sidemounted spare tire nestled in the left front fender. But like most 1936 Buick convertibles, Dr. Mangus' car is equipped with the optional dual sidemounts.

"Buick's the Buy" was the advertising theme for 1936. And at $1,135 for this fast, powerful, smartly styled convertible, Buick really was a buy.

Buick...

"Our neighbor's '37 Buick sedan was five years old and still as smart as anything on the street. Today you would say too bad it wasn't a '38. But not then." Car pictured is a 1937 Century four-door.

Detroit's ultimate dreamboat

By Tim Howley

Of all the cars offered by GM, Buick was the ultimate. Even an old Buick had more prestige than a new Ford. If you owned a Buick you had definitely moved into the upper end of the upper middle class, and you were probably soon due to move out of the neighborhood. It seemed that half the cars on the street of the Twin Cities of Minneapolis/St Paul, Minn. were Buicks, and half the Buicks were Centurys or Specials.

There was a very wealthy family across the street from us named Rosacker. They owned the Hans Rosacker Floral Company. Hans Jr., our neighbor, had a bright, metallic green 1937 Buick sedan with banjo steering wheel and side mounted tires. Now, that was the ultimate. Five years old, and still as smart as anything on the streets. Today you would say, too bad it wasn't a '38. But in 1941 the distinctions were not being made by collectors.

In the summers of 1940 and 1941 I sat on the curb at the corner of 22nd Avenue and Stinson Boulevard with

about five little friends. We would carefully observe the passing motorcade and play car identification games. The idea was to see who could first name the correct make and year of any car coming down the boulevard. That's how I remember that GM cars dominated, and so many of them were very late models. I've since heard that people in those days felt that war might be inevitable, that new cars might not always be available. So, anybody could afford a new car bought one. You did see a fair number of new Fords, but not like the Chevrolets and Pontiacs. So many of the Fords were older ones, especially Model As, truly a "blight" on Stinson Boulevard.

Now Mercurys were something else. They were quite rare and very "spiffy." Lincoln Zephyrs were even rarer. You never saw a Lincoln Continental except in the advertisements. Packards were pretty commonplace, especially the 110s and 120s. The problems with Packards were they could be several years old and still look a lot like the new ones. Packard had really lost a lot of its prestige

84

Just look what you're missing, Mister!

THIS year's crop of misses knows what travel bliss is—so if you want to play leading man you'll set the stage with Buick's spry and sparkling style.

You'll put yourself out front with power that flows from a valve-in-head straight-eight engine silent and smooth and easy as water from a bubbling spring.

You'll give yourself a car that rides serene as the evening star—a level, steady, upright car, with neither wander on the straightaway nor sidesway on the curves.

You'll put foot to brakes soft and velvety as moonlight, and just about as sure as sunrise in their action.

In this year's glorious Buick you'll find controls manageable as your fingers—you'll ride in deep and cushioned comfort that leaves you ready for fun whether your journey measures five miles or fifty.

You'll travel in style—the smart, stand-out, stunning style of the bellwether car of the year —you'll travel safe and secure in a road-wise automobile built low and staunch and fortified with bodies of steel-plus-style.

GET OFF THE BEATEN TRACK — this Buick is stout of heart and you can't make it whimper!

You'll travel as a smart man should—in the frugal, faultless, far-ranging manner that makes Buick now so clearly the master of them all.

For the astonishing thing about this marvel car is the fact that it's so easily within your financial reach—it's actually priced lower than some smaller sixes!

★　★　★　★

LOWEST PRICE EVER ON A BUICK 4-DOOR SEDAN! GENERAL MOTORS TERMS TO SUIT YOUR LIKING

WHEN BETTER AUTOMOBILES ARE BUILT BUICK WILL BUILD THEM

DRIVE IT FAR— drive it hard—Buick can take all you can give it — and come uncomplainingly back for more!

USA 1937

"It's Buick again!"

YOUR MONEY GOES FARTHER IN A GENERAL MOTORS CAR

1937 Buick convertible advertisement proclaims ''It's Buick again!''

by 1941. My father said that Packard was the car to own, and my answer was, "He would say that." Anybody who was "with it" in 1941 knew that nothing even began to compare with a Cadillac.

Chrysler products were in a class all by themselves. They were cars driven by bankers, engineers and college professors. Men who wore wide brim hats, had little moustaches and smoked pipes. A Plymouth always seemed to have a little more status than a Ford, but a Chrysler was never quite as elegant as a Cadillac. You could never be sure whether the Chrysler owner was rich or just smart.

After Pearl Harbor the car scene changed very fast. The 1942 crop of cars simply never got out on the streets. Later on during the war years you would see a few of them, their chrome and stainless painted over, and even their bodies were in the dullest, drabbest wartime colors. Nobody ever got very excited about the '42s. By late summer of '42 the traffic along Stinson Boulevard had dwindled down to almost nothing. You could play baseball all day long on any of the nearby streets like 22nd or McKinley. The cars sat at the curbs or in their garages for lack of gasoline or to save on tires.

In the summer of '43 my parents bought a small cottage on Martin Lake, some 30 miles north of Minneapolis. I can very well recall driving north on Highway 65 that summer, and maybe meeting only one or two other cars coming the opposite direction. This along a 20 mile stretch of highway! The way my dad kept his '37 Ford going was that he would mix up a concoction of 50/50 gasoline and kerosene. The Ford was the little 60 model which probably got around 20 mph. He never worried too much about gas rationing.

By the summer of 1944 the allies were clearly winning, and at a tremendous cost. I remember air raid alerts, victory gardens, tin can drives, paper drives, scrapped car drives. It was at that time unpatriotic to keep an old Marmon or Franklin up on blocks in your backyard, and in some places downright illegal. I can remember more and more of the blue stars hanging in living room windows being exchanged for gold stars. Driving a fancy car was pretty unimportant to most Americans. You kept your old car patched up and used it as little as possible. I remember our trips to Martin Lake were fewer and fewer.

Then, there was 1945, V-E Day, and finally V-J Day. The newspapers in Minneapolis played the effects of the A-bomb way down. It wasn't long after Dad traded in the old '37 Ford and we patiently waited nine months for the arrival of our new 1946 Ford club coupe. I doubt that any new car introduction in the future will ever have the impact of those first postwar models. They were nothing more than 1942 models with new grilles, but who cared. The 1942s had hardly been seen anyway. These 1946 cars were actually being put into production, and for a few hundred dollars or your old car down they would happily take your order.

The excitement surrounding the first really postwar designs in 1948 was just as great. They stood in elegant '20s showrooms on Harmon Place, surrounded by potted palms and big silk banners. The Germans had been kicked, the Japanese had been licked. We now looked forward to a prosperous postwar era with two slab-sided sedans in every driveway and a 12-inch TV in every living room. Yesterday, the '40s. An eternity away for those too young to have experienced it. Yet a very real time to the older half of today's American population. Any car that survived that era to fall into collector hands now must have a real history. Once upon a time it belonged to somebody who gave it tender loving care through a period when all cars were scarce and highly prized simply for transportation purposes. If it is a prewar car, somebody must have put it up on blocks, and for some reason never returned it to service. If it is an early postwar car that fact that it has survived is pretty amazing. Those cars of the 1946-1950 era were really driven, and often passed very quickly through the hands of several owners.

One thing puzzling to me about the cars at shows today is that they do not represent the cars I remember. I remember a lot of sedans, a few coupes, but very few convertibles and woodies. I don't ever recall seeing a four-door convertible. But, then, I was just a little squirt growing up in northeast Minneapolis. What did we kids know about anything beyond the end of Stinson Boulevard.

A new Buick was GM's ultimate dreamboat. This is a 1941 Super four-door at auction.

These advertisements of the 1938 Buick advised, "Better buy Buick!"

For a great 1938 — better buy Buick

By Robert C. Ackerson

Buick production for the 1938 model year fell 23 percent from the level of 1937. At first glance this seemed to be the type of performance for which the word "dismal" had been coined. But 1938 was also a year when the economy slipped into a major recession and unemployment increased from 14.3 percent in 1937 to 19.1 percent in 1938.

The President and Congress, after cutting back on government projects in early 1937, had no choice but to increase expenditures for such programs as the WPA and the CCC. When viewed in this perspective, Buick's position in the automobile industry loomed far healthier as a comparison of Buick production from 1936 through 1938 indicates:

Calendar Year	Buick Production	Buick's Market Share
1936	179,533	4.9%
1937	227,038	5.8%
1938	173,905	8.8%

The view of numerous Buick historians regarding the 1938 models as the most desirous of the prewar Buicks was foreseen by a writer in the October 1937 issue of *The Buick Magazine*, who depicted the 1938 model as possessing two of the most remarkable engineering advances of the century. This bold assertion referred to the use of new "Tubulator" pistons in the "Dynaflash engines plus the introduction of rear coil springs on all Buicks."

As in the past, the Buick's pistons were constructed of an aluminum alloy. But a new crown contour provided an increase of the compression ratio that in turn allowed for an eight percent increase in horsepower without any loss of fuel economy.

Buick's president and general manager, Harlow H. Curtice, put the new pistons in recent historical perspective. Understandably proud of the Buick engine, he noted that "long ago, Buick settled on the valve-in-head principle," even though "costlier to make, it is nevertheless basically better." With 30 years of experience producing these engines, Curtis added: "To see just how fine the process of development has been drawn, just consider what has happened in the past two years.

"Two years ago we gave you the Anolite piston, to sup-

ply more of that brilliance and nimbleness you so desire.

"Last year, the principle change in the engine consisted of streamlining the intake valves, though we also redesigned the tail pipe and developed a new carburetor patterned after airplane practice."

With the introduction of the turbulator piston, Curtis promised his audience that "when you drive the 1938 Buick with the Dynaflash engine, you command a powerplant unlike any other on the highway." It was "livelier, faster, more brilliant, more responsive," an engine that "covers familiar distances with definitely increased economy of fuel."

Relative to their immediate predecessors, the latest Dynaflash engines were significantly more powerful. The 248 cid version used in the Series 40 models now had 107 (instead of 100) hp. Its compression ratio was increased from 5.7:1 to 6.15:1. The larger, 320.2 cid straight-eight for the Series 60, 80 and 90 models now with a 6.35:1 instead of 5.9:1 compression ratio moved up to 141 from 130 hp.

The use of rear coil springs by Buick was a true modern automotive milestone. This concept had been used before, but only on one American car, the 1907 Brush. The use of rear coil springs in conjunction with Buick's almost traditional torque tube gave Curtice the opportunity to portray Buick as a manufacturer that combined the best of the past with the newest of the new. "Buick has clung to the torque tube drive," he noted, "because we thoroughly believe this method of propulsion is fundamentally better. But for 1938, the old-fashioned leaf spring is gone.... This new springing not only adds to safety by reducing skidding dangers by about one-third, but also provides a greatly improved ride."

"The car doesn't bounce, doesn't throw, and doesn't roll on curves; it flows over bumps with an almost fluid smoothness."

Less successful than the use of crowned pistons and rear coil springs was Buick's venture into the murky nether world of primitive semi-automatic transmissions. Buick's version, appealingly called the "self-shifting" transmission, was available only on the lowest priced Series 40. But it was dropped after the 1938 model year in which less than 3,000 units were installed. The Self-Shifter was essentially a semi-automatic, four-speed planetary transmission with a clutch pedal used to select low gear to set the car in motion. Subsequent shifts were made automatically as the selector lever (mounted on the steering column) was moved into the high range. When the car moved away from a stop with the selector still in the high range, the transmission started in first gear before shifting to third (bypassing second gear) and finally to high gear.

More often in conflict rather than in concert with the Buick's torque tube drive, Select-Shift was not offered for 1939. Not until 1948 when Dynaflow was introduced was a Buick offered with a truly automatic transmission.

In terms of styling, the 1938 Buicks closely resemble the 1937 models. Primary differences consist of a new grille and front fenders. This close proximity to an older model marked the 1938 Buicks as cars that brought a styling cycle dominated by massive grille work with bold vertical bars and hood-mounted headlights to a close.

The 1939 models, in contrast, moved the grille lower and outward, while positioning the headlights into the flow-line of the front fenders. The age of streamlining had arrived at Buick, but the 1938 models were not impediments to progress. Rather, they were the beneficiaries of a tradition of solid engineering that made "better buy Buick" advice well worth heeding.

1938 Buick Model 41 Special four-door.

'38 Century 61

touring sedan

The 1938 Century is treasured by Buick collectors as a driver's car.

By Terry Boyce

The doctor, lawyer, and even the Indian chief who needed to get to his destination quickly and with minimal bother usually chose a medium-sized eight-cylinder car for transportation in the late '30s. A favored choice among upper middle-class professionals with families was the Buick Century Model 61 touring sedan. Not too large by standards of the era, the 126-inch wheelbase Century was an outstanding performer. Its ability to peg the speedometer needle at the "century mark" had given the car its series name. Under the long, narrow hood was overhead valve straight eight displacing 320 cubic inches and developing 141 hp. Only Hudson's eight gave a more favorable power-to-weight ratio. The big Buick eight was designed to power the larger, heavier Roadmaster and Limited series. But, the Century body, from the cowl back, was the light all-steel design used on the smallest Buick, the Special. The Century, then, was simply born to run!

Only a bolder grille design, new hub caps and some trim detailing set the 1938 Century apart visually from its 1937 predecessor. But, under the stream-lined sheet metal was a more powerful engine and a new suspension system.

Buick introduced its full-coil suspension system for 1938. "Bui-Coil" springing meant the 1937 car's semi-elliptic leaf springs were replaced with coils. The technology was new, and a pair of giant shock absorbers — four times bigger than later units — were designed for the 1938 rear suspension. Helping the Century's suspension keep up with the big eight cylinder engine were that line's 7.50 x 15 tires; all other 1938 Buicks had 16 inch wheels and corresponding tire sizes.

Though the displacement of the Century engine was unchanged from when it was introduced in 1936, the horsepower rating was up eleven over the previous year, and the actual increase in response was quite evident. Best of all, it was obtained through a bit of engineering wizardry that, if any thing, improved fuel economy. "Turbulator" pistons were the answer. Buick engineers had discovered that adding dished domes to piston tops altered the combustion flame travel in a positive manner, increasing performance at least 10 percent without using more gasoline.

The Century series consisted of a two-door sedan, convertible coupe and phaeton, a handsome sport coupe and two sedan styles. Model 67 was a fully-streamlined, fastback sedan style with a small storage area behind the passenger compartment. Most Century buyers ignored this model and chose instead the Model 61, named the touring sedan because it had a built-in trunk at the rear with more luggage space. Total U.S. production of the Model 61 was 12,364 cars, compared to 1,515 of the fastbacks.

The Model 61 Century listed for $1,297, and at that price came with a durable brown-tone mohair interior. Buick's plusher broadcloths and even leather could be specified by special order. All Centurys had a beautiful large, bone-colored Tenite plastic tri-spoked steering wheel with a full horn ring similar to that of the contemporary Teutonic Mercedes Benz. In full view of the driver was a larger 120 mph speedometer with four informational gauges around it in a half-circle.

For the last time, a long, curved shift lever rose from the Buick's floor. Slightly stiff in operation, its postive throws were nonetheless a delight to the enthusiastic driver.

Many Century owners shopped liberally among the options offerd by Buick. Two of the most popular were the firewall-mounted heater/defroster system and the Centerline radio set. Many customers also specified side-mounted spare wheels, which included handsome covers. The sidemounts increased trunk space and gave the 1938 Buick a rich, purposeful look. A rare option was a large Buick 8 center bumper plaque.

Buick added 200 dealers to its sales network in 1938, and an aggressive ad campaign helped push sales into the territory held by Plymouth — one of the "low priced three." Even with the recession of that year cutting into the industry's recovery from the Depression, Buick sold 168,689 1938 models.

General Motors cars for 1939 would have a new look, with broader grilles and larger window openings. Buicks would have a column-mounted gearshift for the first time — the linkage putting yet another bit of distance between driver and machine.

Today the 1938 Century is among the most treasured of prewar Buicks. Not because it is a good looking car, though it is; not because it is a fast road car, though it still is; but most of all, because it is a driver's automobile.

A General Motors masterpiece:

Y-Job Buick featured sleek styling and hidden head lights.

Buick's beautiful Y-Job

They called this car the Y-Job because Y follows X, and "X" or "X-Jobs" in that day meant "experimental." The Y-Job, then, went one step beyond. Or actually several steps beyond.

The Y-Job's original purpose was to test advanced ideas, among them electric windows and a hydro-electric convertible top that stowed beneath a hinged metal boot. The car also had hydraulic power steering, which Buick had hoped to introduce for 1942. It mounted 7.00 x 13 tires at a time when standard wheel size was still 16-inches, incorporated hidden headlamps, and carried an odd braking system that substituted bladders for wheel

cylinders. Toward the end of World War II, Buick fitted it with an early version of the Dynaflow transmission.

But the car's greatest influence was stylistic, not mechanical. The Y-Job was very long and low — only 58 inches high at the windshield. Its "harp" grille, inspired by the 1938 Mercedes W-154 Grand Prix car, emphasized horizontal rather than vertical lines, and that alone had great impact on future GM (and other) cars. Such details as flush door handles (later replaced by electric buttons with a mechanical override), hidden headlamps, a pop-out decklid handle, and the bombsight hood ornament all eventually found their way into production cars — mostly

90

Buick production cars.

The Buick connection is significant. Soon after Harlow Curtice became Buick's president in 1933, he mentioned to GM styling director Harley J. Earl that he'd like Earl to design Buicks as though he were designing them for himself. In effect, Curtice was giving Earl a lot more styling latitude than Earl was getting from other GM divisions, and Earl took Curtice at his word. Earl gave Buick the attention he and his staff had formerly lavished on Cadillac when Cadillac was still being run by his good friend, Lawrence P. Fisher. After Fisher left Cadillac, Earl became as close to Curtice as he'd been with Larry Fisher.

Auto historian David R. Holls, who's now GM's director of advanced design, feels that Earl came to regard the Y-Job as his own personal automobile. It served not only GM and Buick but also Earl himself as an answer to a series of boattail custom speedsters created for Ed Macauley, who was Earl's counterpart at Packard. Ed Macauley's father, Alvan Macauley, resigned as Packard's president, and Earl and the Macauleys were neighbors in Grosse Pointe. So for Earl the Y-Job represented stylistic oneupmanship. Fact is, Earl drove the Y-Job as his personal car from sometime in 1939 all through the war and well into 1948.

Mechanically, the Y-Job was built on a coil-suspended 1938 Buick Century chassis, using a 320-cid Straight 8 Buick valve-in-head engine. This engine put out 141 hp at 3,600 rpm in stock form, but modifications over the years boosted that into the neighborhood of 200 hp so the car must have been great fun to drive; certainly to be seen in.

The man in charge of the Y-Job's technical side was Buick's newly arrived chief engineer, Charles A. Chayne. Chayne went on to become GM's corporate vice president in charge of engineering, just as Curtice would become GM's president and Earl himself a GM vice president (in 1940, the first "stylist" in any auto company to win that title). The Y-Job's body engineer was Vince Kaptur Sr., who worked for 28 years on Earl's staff.

And in charge of keeping the car serviced, running, and painted black (it needed repainting constantly) was Leonard McLay, who became, in effect, Harley Earl's personal mechanic. As head of the Buick studio, chief designer George Snyder oversaw the Y-Job's styling development, but always under the watchful eye and meticulous guidance of the master himself.

The Y-Job was not, as several writers have said, GM's first "idea" or show car. That honor probably goes to the 1933 Cadillac V-16 Aerodynamic coupe.

General Motors still owns the Y-Job, and it's on display — along with its Buick descendants, the Motorama LeSabre and Charles Chayne's XP-300 — at the Sloan Museum in Flint, Mich. If you get a chance to visit this most significant and interesting car, by all means do.

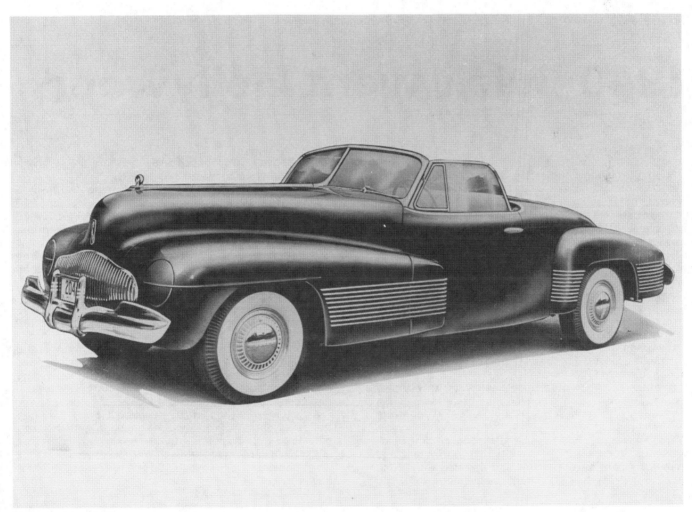

Y-Job's original design.

Clark Gable with the 1940 Buick Estate Wagon he took on a two-week hunting and fishing expedition in Mexico.

1940 Buick went Hollywood

By Tom LaMarre

When the National Automobile Show opened in October 1939, spectators flocked around the 1940 model station wagons that were on display. And one of the handsomest of these cars was Buick's offering the Estate Wagon.

Available only in the new Super series, Buicks wagon was featured in many magazine ads. One such ad pictured Clark Gable with his new Buick and stated, "This is a case of one good actor liking another. When the star of *Gone With the Wind* had finished his work in another picture, *Strange Cargo*, he left the MGM studios for a two-week hunting and fishing expedition in Mexico, going along easy street, all the way, in a new Buick estate wagon. As shown in this photo, a luggage rack and the spare tire were installed on the roof, making all the spacious rear compartment available for the film star's camping and out-door equipment."

Another ad spotlighted Ruby Keeler Jolson with her Estate Wagaon "...smart, comfortable, useful in no end of ways, and a bargain at $1,242, plus $19.50 for white sidewall tires."

Wood has always had a special attraction, and the Buick wagon made excellent use of it. Its rich ash framing and mahogany panels were "glued and doweled with lavish care." For strength and quietness, steel braces were used

as reinforcements. The Estate Wagon had 56 cubic feet of luggage space. Two locks secured the spare tire compartment. Overall weight was 3,870 pounds.

Like all Supers, The Estate Wagon was powered by a 107 hp Dynaflash straight-eight of 248 cubic inches. 1940 was the year that the auto industry generally adopted sealed beam headlights, and Buick was no exception. Instead of ordinary springing, Buick used coil springs all around—knee-action in front and BuiCoil behind. The Super chassis had a 121-inch wheelbase, 19 inches shorter than the massive Limited 90 Buicks.

Although the natural wood was the highlight of the Estate Wagon, it was complemented by the updated styling of the 1940 Buicks. The horizontal grille bars gave the car a wider appearance, while the blending of the head-lights into the fenders made it seem lower. On top of the headlight pods were mounted the directional signals, something that would still be an option on some cars many years later. And Buick's "Fore-n-Aft Flashaway" directional signal shut off automatically.

As it turned out, not many people could say they had the same car as Clark Gable. Production amounted to only 459 Estate Wagon for domestic sale and another six units special ordered for export. With the attrition rate for wood-bodied wagons so high, it's safe to say that very few have survived.

What might have been for Buick

By Ned Comstock

Rumor has it that General Motors will abandon its tradition of fielding a fleet of automobiles under different names through separate sales channels, and consolidate them in one system. Probably there isn't a snowball's chance of this, but it's easy to see that great economies could result. And now, with mounting Japanese pressure and owner loyalties confused, would be an ideal time. It could be done. Buick could have taken over General Motors in 1941.

In 1940 Buick introduced Super, a new style car that offended no tradition, a performance car without sacrificing simplicity, a car that made best use of its dimensions with a price as sharp as the product. Buyers agreed, and in 1941 swept Buick to fourth place in production totals, pressing low priced Plymouth hard. Of particular significance, Buick sold more convertibles than anybody else but Ford. This appeal to the young bode well for Buick's future.

In early times, when automobiles didn't work very well, each maker needed a special feature to lift his car above the competition. Thus Packard touted Straight Eight, Willys the Knight engine, and Cord Front Drive. For Buick it was Valve-in-Head. Now I never saw a flat headed Buick and I never hope to see one, but by 1941 it didn't make any difference. After 40 years of evolution all American cars were sound mechanically. Buyers were looking for performance and high style — they didn't care what caused it. Buick gave them both, packed down and flowing over. General Motors had no need in 1941 for alternate auto technology.

Price was important in 1941 too, but in a different way. All through the Depression there were no extra dollars, they simply didn't exist. On $25 a week, a good salary then, there was a quick limit to a family's money for cars.

No matter when Buick had offered, for 10 years few people could afford it. In 1941 things were different.

Based on full employment, with wages nearly double Depression levels, easy credit expanded Buick's market until virtually any new car buyer could afford a Buick. The $200 step-up from Chevrolet became $5 a week, enabling Buick to compete effectively at the low end of the market where it had been effectively barred before.

At the same time Buick threatened Chevrolet, it planted a flag deep in Cadillac territory. Cadillac dominion over the "fine car" field had not been fully established in 1941. Buick Limited was shorter by only two inches than the largest Cadillac, lighter by less than 100 pounds. And it ran 15 more horses to perform on. Actually Buick Limited did better at the top of the prestige market than most of us remember. Production of Limited in 1941 substantially exceeded Cadillac 75, although it was never emphasized. Limited was featured in the motion picture *Ghandi* alongside Rolls-Royce as transportation for the Viceroy of India.

So, Buick was poised at the top and bottom of the 1941 price scale. But it was in the middle market that Buick stole the show.

I didn't know I was looking at a post-war car when I first came upon 1940 Super four-door Sedan parked in a city street. It was late Fall (Buick used to introduced its new models in August) and Pearl Harbor hadn't happened yet. I didn't even know there was going to be a war. But I knew I was looking at something new and different, different in a way I liked.

Since the docile days of 1935 when conservative doctors bought them for their reliability, Buick had gradually built the power in and the performance up until just before World War II Buicks were virtually unbeatable on the road. This was accomplished without forsaking balanced design. Super for 1941 came with new dual carbs, and when you

1941 Buick Super four-door.

poured the power to them, they understood. But gentle drivers could still trundle along—like 75 mph—on one, if they wished. By 1940, Buick was a going machine, and everybody knew it. But in 1940 Buick style caught up with Buick performance, and the result was stunning.

Not that there was anything wrong with the previous style cycle. The 39's had a crisp, lean look in the best of taste. But 1940 was something else.

When you first laid eyes on 1940 Super, you were immediately aware of a new style concept. It was as though you were looking for the first time at a package of cigarettes laid on its flat side, instead of set up on its edge. It was the same package, but now instead of tall it looked wide, close to the ground. That made everything different.

This became the basis of postwar styling—full width bodies (no running boards) and lower roof lines. Everything looked better on this new basis, and passengers were better treated. Buick quickly exploited its massive success. Sales soared. Now Buick had everything—Price, Performance and Style Leadership.

In retrospect, one wonders why GM didn't drive Buick to the head of the line and gradually absorb the other divisions. Two good reasons probably prevailed.

In 1941, owner loyalty was sacrosanct. Now, of course, Cadillac builds cars you can't tell from Chevrolets, but in 1941, things were different. Owner allegiance was like religion. But something else made an all-Buick GM impossible—fear of success.

If GM had done the unthinkable, and dropped the other lines, concentrating on Buick it would have quickly monopolized the industry. Then, the Government would have broken GM up into little pieces. That's why it didn't happen.

Buick's sleek Specials for 1941

The year 1941 was an outstanding one for Buick. The company offered the largest model selection in its history that season and also sold more cars than ever before. One very popular and good-looking model that helped ensure such success was the Buick Special B-Bodied two-door sedanette.

Because the Special Series had recently become a hot selling Buick line, the company offered two such choices for '41. The Series 40-A included a variety of different body styles on a 118 inch wheelbase, while Series 40-B models were built on a 122 inch wheelbase. With two-door fastbacks a way to separate the cars visually was to check the window molding treatment. The longer wheelbase sedanettes, like our feature car, had one thin loop of bright metal trim encircling *all* of the side windows.

This car was designated the Model 46-S and it accounted for a total of 87,687 domestic sales and 461 additional deliveries overseas. Its factory list price was $1,006 and it weighed 3,700 pounds. In addition, there was also a "Super" trim version which cost $1,063 and reached 9,614 buyers here and abroad. Known as the Model 46-SSE, it had the same exterior styling, but featured special interior trimmings and compound carburetion.

The basic powerplant for all 1941 Buick Specials was the company's famous overhead valve straight eight. This was the "small" straight eight, with piston displacement of 248 cid. With a single carburetor the brake horsepower was rated 115 at 3500 rpm. With the compound carburetor setup, this changed to 125 bhp at 3800 rpm.

The compound carburetion system was new for Buick in 1941 and was actually the forerunner of the modern four-barrel carburetor. At idle or low speed, only one of the carburetors was functional. During acceleration or high-speed operation, the progressive linkage system kicked-in the second carb. In its day, this "Buick, valve-in-head, fireball, Dynaflash eight" was recognized as a true high-performance powerplant.

Like other '41 Buicks, the fastback sedanette had a number of new styling characteristics. They included a slightly restyled grille, a sleek new fender line, the total elimination of running boards, fully concealed door hinges and the total integration of the headlights into the front sheetmetal.

Additional technical features included 6.50 x 16 size tires, 18-gallon fuel tank and an overall length of 209 inches for all B-Series Specials. Two-tone paint finish was a no-cost option that many 1941 car buyers preferred. All models came with directional signals and radio wiring.

1941 Buick Special Model 46-S.

Buick's big Limited ...

1941 Buick Limited Series 90 six-passenger formal sedan.

A classic candidate?

By Earl D. Beauchamp Jr.

Did you know there is a car which is perhaps the largest, fastest, smoothest, most powerful, advanced and unique of its time, while carrying appointments equal to the best — yet no club considers it a classic? We think the car is all these things, but in addition, we know it is rare and beautiful, even a bit awesome.

What is this proud beast, you say? How could the chronologists of automotive history have missed it? Would you believe we are talking about a Buick? Sounds heretical, doesn't it? Well, read on.

This hobby policy has long been an enigma to the author, dating back through 20 years of activity. Just what is the knock on Buick?

In this piece we'll discuss what is, in our own opinion, the finest Buick of them all. We have chosen this "grandest" Buick carefully, with the idea being to try and pierce the armour of disbelief with the point of an arrow. The fact that a 1941 Buick Roadmaster four-door convertible shares basically the same body as the 1941 Cadillac 62 four-door convertible, or the 1940 Buick Limited four-door convertible is larger than the 1940 Cadillac 62 four-door convertible will become palatable to you after serious, objective thought: These are exquisite examples of the Buick to be sure, but they are not, in our opinion, the ultimate in fine luxury machines produced under the mar-

que's name. That title is reserved for the one and only "parlor car that flies," the 1941 Buick Limited.

Perhaps you've heard of the Brunn-bodied 1941 Buick Limiteds. These were Buick's greatest (though tentative) effort at custom-bodied cars. We will touch on them, but we will speak mainly about the Fisher-bodied Limited.

The Limited for 1941 was a new concept to the luxury car market. Buick was not alone in offering the first truly good-looking, streamlined limousines, for the Cadillac 67 was also introduced in 1941, and shared the same body. They were both real eye-openers, spread the length of a massive, new 139-inch wheelbase. Their chassis was longer than Cadillac's top-line Series 75 limousine, and the Buick was slightly less than an inch greater in overall length than the Cadillac 67.

The new Buick frame was a deep-silled, rigidly cross-braced "X" design. Independent coil spring suspension on all four corners had been introduced on Buick cars back in 1938, and of course, as we know, this design eventually became pretty-much universally used throughout the auto industry. In speaking here of riding comfort, we hasten to mention we are talking about new cars, not worn out cars. We've heard Buicks take a justified rap in the past about their "bounciness" after many years and miles, but when they were in good condition, with good, fluid-filled shock absorbers, the Buick coil-spring, torque-tube chassis gave a ride which was just about unequaled

95

at the time. With the huge Limited and its massive weight, a level, floating ride was improved still further over other Buick models. The comfort-ride suspension was enhanced by quiet-producing, weather-resisting rock wool insulation in the body, and seats were designed for arm-chair comfort. Across the line in 1941, Buick made its first use of Foamtex rubber cushioning and this was used in conjunction with stoutly constructed Marshall springs covered with white wool on the Limited.

There were four models of Buick Limited cars built in 1941: the Series 90; 90-L; 91; and 91-F. The Series 90 was a straight 4-door sedan with no jump-seats or divider window. It had limited appeal for those who had money, liked a big, roomy car with power; yet liked to drive themselves. In 1941 the Series 90 found 885 such souls who paid their money and got behind the wheel. The model designed for those who really had a limousine in mind was the Series 90-L, an eight-passenger car equipped with jump seats and an electrically-powered divider window. Most of these were equipped with genuine cowhide leather front compartments and deluxe broadcloth or Bedford Cord rear compartments, but some were ordered with cloth in the chauffeur's compartment as well. Almost exclusively a car of the wealthy, there were 605 of the 90-L cars built.

The most popular of the 1941 Limiteds was the Series 91, six-passenger model with jump seats, but no divider window. As on all the Limiteds, there were choices of rich Bedfords and other cloths on these cars. Some were equipped with brown, some gray, some a startling beautiful navy blue and so on — a car with warmth and comfort for Sunday touring with the family — if you were the local banker! There were 1,223 of these Limiteds built. The fourth and least popular model, was the Series 91-F, or formal sedan, a six-passenger model with a divider window. Perhaps designed for wealthy introverts, not accustomed to companions and wishing seclusion from the chauffeur also, the "F" models had never sold well in the Limited and Roadmaster models of the past. In 1941

there were only 293 of these cars built, so they are the rarest today with the exception of the custom Brunns or export models.

Coachwork on the interior of the '41 Limited was as commodious as it was well done, exuding quality and style. When looking at the interior of a Limited there is more than a family resemblance to a Cadillac 67 of the same vintage. For style and class there is little to separate the two cars, except for the dash. We've seen engine turning on dashes of Duesenbergs and Cords, and Ford V-8s as well, but one thing they have in common is to make the heart throb. The engine turning on the Buick dash was, only a couple of years ago, thought to have been merely a decal, but the fact is: the engine turning is real, just as real as on a Cord 810. As more 1940-'42 Buicks have been restored, collectors have found this out to their chagrin, of course, because it is very difficult for restoration. Nevertheless, with the grey oak woodgraining on the dashtop and window sills, and the white bone plastic steering wheel and knobs, the effect of sitting behind the wheel of any 1941 Buick was thrilling.

On the Limited, however, you were treated to a little extra class. Window sills were broad, showing more woodgraining, and there was the Buick crest mounted in just the right spot. You were treated to still more woodgraining across the back of the front seat, so the rear passenger could get the warm feel of wood as well. Notepads and vanities were provided to the passenger, large, sturdy hand-straps hung in the rear, identical to those used in the Cadillac 67. Rear compartment radios, and four speaker phones to the driver were available to those with the ultimate in mind. If you were a short wave radio nut, you could buy a factory short wave Sonematic set with five bands in your Buick. Courtesy lights flooded the passenger compartment with illumination when doors were opened, and floor registers were in the rear to distribute heat as if passengers were at home.

Speaking of the Buick heater, it was the underseat variety. Standard equipment on the Limited, it was the "fresh

1941 Buick Limited Series 90 eight-passenger sedan.

air" type, which means outside air was mixed and heated to provide interior warmth on cold days, or simply not heated on warm days and allowed to provide fresh air in the car. Buick had introduced this type of heater in 1940 and they like to claim a first for its design. Be that as it may, we lived to see the day when all auto heaters were some variation of the "fresh air" design. Unfortunately, the trunk-mounted air conditioning unit offered in Chrysler, Cadillac and Packard was not available on Buick. As this was a big gimmick in 1941, we must assume Buick did not use it because they were pushing speed and power that year, and the air conditioner would possibly have adversely affected this — but more on speed and power later.

There were a few Limiteds built for export, and collectors traveling overseas may still run across one and ship it back. It is entirely possible some of these may have foreign custom bodies, by builders like Carlton of London for example. These included the Model 90-X with 21 units; the 90-XL with 64 units; the 90-X with 8 units, and the 91-FX with 3 units. The rarest and most desirable 1941 Limited would be, however, a Brunn custom-bodied job.

Efforts were begun in 1939 by Buick President, Harlow Curtice, to build a prestige custom-bodied car. Assistant Chief Engineer Ed Ragsdale was placed in charge of the project and the Buffalo, N.Y. custom body builder, Hermann Brunn, was retained to come up with an adaptation on a Buick chassis. One or two show cars were built in 1940, and plans were for a car on the Limited chassis in 1941. There were four styles of Brunn-bodied cars presented in the 1941 introductory folder — the cabriolet sedan; three-window town car; landau sedan; and four-door convertible. Brunn built several of these fantastic cars, yet none are known to survive. Hermann Brunn had indicated there were five, maybe six of these cars built. Unless one turns up, there should be little conjecturing on their merits as a would-be classic. If Brunn used a chassis as the beginning of his car, we know there were three Model 900 and one Model 900-X produced — a model designation we think was assigned to running chassis', but these could just as easily have been used by Hercules to build ambulances or hearses. If Brunn used Fisher bodies and modified them to produce his creations, which is more likely, then it is unknown exactly how many Brunn town cars were built. The man who turns one up should be able to name his own price.

We have detailed to you a beautiful new idea in a luxury car, a limousine which personified speed and power, yet still had luxury, beauty and class. Therefore, the mechanical points of the car needed to produce what styling promised. This was accomplished on the 1941 Buick with engineering which was unique and thrilling, as well as being advanced beyond its time.

The basic component of power for the 1941 Buick was called the "Fireball 8" engine. It was so christened by the Buick publicity and advertising genius of the period, Arthur Kudner, who had a way with names. The engine was an extension of the "Dynaflash 8" engine of 1938, an engine which had first introduced Buick's new, unique piston design. The engine for 1941 carried the concept of "domed" pistons a step further, in that the piston top was raised on one edge, about two-thirds the circumference of the piston top, but dished, or hollowed in the middle. The effect forced the combustion, or fire as it were, into sort of a concentrated ball, thus increasing the intensity of the combustion.

One of the chief designers of the engine was an immigrant who had formerly worked for Hispano-Suiza in their engine design department. The Buick engineers took pains to beef up the bottom end of the engine with more and better babbitt bearing material, and then set to work on another extension of the engine design. The result was

an engine employing one of the first production designs where increased power was centered around increased compression. A very thin, all-metal head gasket was used, and this truly high-compression straight eight came off the assembly line with a compression ratio of 7.0-1. Numbers of people in the spark plug industry were preaching the benefits of 10mm spark plugs at the time. These appeared to have advantages, and the first 1941 Buicks used them for that reason — more on that in a minute.

In another section of the engineering department, Adolph Brunn — no relation to Hermann — had been experimenting with dual carburetor setups since 1939. Brunn, who had come over to Buick from Marvel Carburetor, was a carburetor expert of considerable stature. These dual setups were evolutionary, and their experimentation was designed toward the end of developing the four barrel carburetor. Brunn eventually designed the first workable four barrel carburetor for GM. He had it on display at the Flint Factory Meet of the Buick Club this past August, and he also was the father of the first production four barrel carburetors used by GM. Back in 1941, however, he was experimenting with Compound Carburetion, whereby a pair of two barrel jobs were connected by progressive linkage, and worked in the manner of a four barrel carburetor. He had developed some working carburetors and placed them on some experimental cars. They performed well, and management was quick to note the possibilities available to thrill prospective buyers, as the carburetors added a lot of punch to the already hot straight eight.

The engine in the Limited was a big seven main bearing, overhead valve straight 8 which is shared with the Century, and Roadmaster in 1941. Having 320.2 cubic inches of displacement, with a bore and stroke of 3-7/16 x 4-5/16, it drove a semi-floating Hypoid rear axle through a 10½-inch clutch. The power it developed through one of the first uses of high compression and advanced carburetion was a whopping 165 horsepower, greater even than GM's top of the line Cadillac at 150 hp. Yet, the story of innovation for 1941 is not quite over. In these days of pollution controls and pollution worries, it is hard to imagine that way back in 1941 Buick utilized the concept of positive crankcase ventilation. A tube was run over from the rocker arm cover to the air cleaner, where exhaust gasses were reburned as in modern systems. Adolph Brunn told this author he thought the system could pass most restrictions placed on engines today.

The 1941 Limited was and is capable of loafing along effortlessly at 75-80 mph. The car is so large and long it evens out the bumps, and seems to be barely moving at those speeds. Although neither automatic transmission or overdrive was available, there is little shifting once the car is moving. Torque and power are such that it cruises at high speed, and lugs at low speed, and top speed is well over 100 mph.

The kick in driving one of these brutes is nearly indescribable, and put that engineering into the '41 Century which could scream from a stop, and then you're really talking about a man's car. Like the supercharged Auburn or the record-breaking speed of the Cord, these 165 hp, dual carburetored babies thrilled buyers and car lovers of the time, and perhaps this is best brought to light by the fact the 1941 Buick is the most collected Buick in the Buick Club of America, and the most collected car in all of CHVA.

Yes, there were problems with the 1941 Buick — there are problems with all unique and advanced designs. Cord had problems with the front drive and electric transmission linkage and the Lincoln Continental V-12 displeased some owners. This is perhaps the price a manufacturer pays for producing an exceptional car. When reports came back to Buick about spark plug fouling, Adolph

Brunn had to face accusations it was his carburetors. Soon, however, he could point to the single carburetor Series 40 jobs which were also fouling plugs. It was found the average fuels of the day, when combined with the average driver and his driving conditions, caused the 10mm spark plugs to fail under the high compression load. Cars were called back and the heads retapped for 14mm plugs. Just to be safe, it was recommended the high compression head gaskets be replaced with 1940-style gaskets. As for the carburetors themselves, their only field problem laid in the inability of the average mechanic to fathom the complexity of progressive linkage and adjustment.

But despite the recall we have a few 1941 Buick big-engined cars still around in restored condition with the original dual carburetors, high compression head gaskets and 10mm spark plugs. Bill Ningard of Baltimore had a Roadmaster which performed flawlessly on several trips to Bluffton, Ohio, and in local tours for several years — and this can be attributed to the high quality of modern fuel, which, had it been available in 1941 would, we believe, have negated the spark plug problem.

So we present the case of the 1941 Buick Limited to you. It was mechanically advanced, powerful and unique, graceful and lithe in styling, comfortable and sumptious in appointment.

Before closing, we should also mention the last Buicks to carry the Limited name for 16 years were built in the 1942 model year, using the same power plant and body, with revised sheet metal.

1941 Buick Limited Model 90-L eight-passenger limousine.

By Tim Howley

The year was 1940. Hitler's conquests, unequaled since the days of Napoleon, were beginning to shock America out of her isolationism. But most Americans preferred laughing along with Jack Benny and Edgar Bergan and Charlie McCarthy on Sunday night radio to reading about the horror in Europe. In the sky, the Pan American "Yankee Clippers" were setting flight records around the world. Color television was first demonstrated in New York. "Gone With The Wind" opened at movie theaters across the country. An obscure singer with the Benny Goodman Band made an unsuccessful attempt at recording the song "All or Nothing At All." His name was Frank Sinatra.

The car of the year was the 1940 Buick, which for the third year straight held fourth place in sales, right behind Chevrolet, Ford and Plymouth. Buick sold 283,204 units for the 1940 model year. The GM quartet of Bill Hufstader, Harlow Curtice, Charlie Chayne and Ed Ragsdale was unbeatable. What they offered the public for just a little more money than a low priced car was just a lot more automobile. For a few dollars more than a Ford or Chevrolet, the Buick buyer could get quality equal to that of the Cadillac.

The Buick success story in the prewar era was based on very contemporary styling, excellent engineering and a very small but dedicated dealer organization. Earl Beauchamp had called the Buick of that era the "now" car. It was certainly the ultimate middle-class status symbol of the day. In fact, Buicks of that era were so common that they were slow to become collectibles. But anybody who has tried to find a nice, original 1936-41 Buick today knows how scarce they are becoming. Even good sedans and coupes are getting hard to find, but convertibles and convertible sedans, of course, are the rarest and most desirable.

The car of the year

One of the most successful show cars in the San Francisco Bay area is a 1940 Buick model 41C (Special) convertible sedan. It is owned by Bob Coates of Pleasant Hill, in the San Francisco East Bay area. Everywhere the car goes, it generates as much excitement as those shiny new Buicks did in showrooms years ago. Buick offered convertible sedans from 1932 through 1941. But 1940 was the only year that the model was offered in every series. In 1940, Buick built 1,740 convertible sedans, 552 of them Specials. In 1941, the convertible sedan was again offered throughout the line, except for the Limited,

For a few dollars more, Americans could step up to Buick, the ultimate middle-class status symbol of its time. This prize-winning model 41C (Special) convertible sedan is owned by Bob Coates of Pleasant Hill, Calif.

which was built on special order only. If any do exist, they are the rarest of their breed.

Bob's Special was truly the car that belonged to a "little old lady from Pasadena." Emma Bouvier Childs Peterson Rumsey of Pasedena, Calif., purchased the car new in September 1939. Completely equipped with sidemount spare wheels, Sonomatic radio, clock, wheel beauty rings, deluxe steering and license frames, the car priced out at $1,499 plus $200 delivery on the West Coast. Rumsey's pretty Bandelier blue Buick was a familiar sight around the Pasedena area until her death in 1952. The car was always chauffeur driven, and at the time of her death, was still in meticulous original condition.

Rumsey's great niece inherited the car and brought it up to Stinson Beach, a secluded coastal community a few miles north of San Francisco. By 1966, the car's soft trim had badly deteriorated in the salt air. The body was still sound, but the engine now had 200,000 tired miles. The Buick eventually wound up on an Oakland used car lot, where Coates found it in 1967. By California standards, the car was rough, but Bob had been looking for a Buick convertible sedan for a long time. He felt he was not likely to find another, so he bought the car, and committed himself to a four-year restoration.

He was lucky with the body; there was no rust. The only dents of any consequence were on the fenders. Bob insisted on pounding every dent out to the original contours of the car. He used no body putty, and only a minimum of lead. He steam cleaned the undercarriage, then scrubbed it by hand. The undercarriage was amazingly good, considering the mileage, and most of the original paint was still there, but Bob repainted the entire frame by hand. He did not remove the body from the frame for fear of getting it out of alignment.

The engine still ran well, considering its deplorable condition, but there wasn't much left to save. The cylinders had .030 taper, one piston had been replaced, and most of the others had broken lands and rings. All of the bearing shims had been removed; the head was cracked, and so were the manifolds. Bob found a badly worn rocker shaft assembly and the wrong carburetor. He had hoped to save the engine in the interests of authenticity, but ended up salvaging only the block and the bell housing. He used later model connecting rods with insert bearings, a later type oil pump, thin head gaskets and shorter pushrods, all to improve oil pressure and increase compression. All rotating parts were dynamically balanced to assure smoothness and quietness. These engines were balanced at the factory when new.

"I think any restorer is foolish if he doesn't balance the engine," says Coates. "After you go all the way through an engine, you might as well finish it up right. It makes so much difference in how the engine runs."

Many restorers contend that sedans are the most difficult and costly to restore because of the upholstery. Coates wouldn't agree. He found the convertible sedan restoration to be a nightmare due to all the adjustments of the windows, doors and the convertible top. In addition, the badly deteriorated top bows had to be replated. Chrome plated top bows were a nice little extra in all GM convertibles when new, but they are a pain to replate now.

All that chromed pot metal made Buicks flashy cars in their day. "But try and replate it all now," says Coates. "Or just try to find those trim parts." This Buick had badly deteriorated trim, very little of which would take replating. So Bob combed the junkyards and small Buick dealers in little out-of-the-way towns. Now and then, he'd find one or two good pieces off an old sedan. Sometimes he'd find new old stock at some obscure Buick dealership, but it was a slow go.

100

The biggest frustration was restoring the badly deteriorated dashboard. Bob finally decided it would be easiest to remove the dashboard from a 1940 sedan. It would have been near impossible to reproduce the unusual wood grain finish on the upper part of the dash. This was produced, no doubt, by a lithographic process, and even the best old timers would have a difficult time duplicating it. The dash panel and glove box trim are two other items which defy restorers, as both are machine turned.

Originally, these pieces were stamped out on flat steel, then cut and formed to the compound curves of the dashboard. But after all this effort, the factory protected their fine workmanship with only one thin coat of clear lacquer. As soon as it wears off, the fine "tooling" quickly rusts away. Bob was very fortunate in finding an original, mint dashboard.

Coates salvaged a lot of small plastic trim parts from sedans. Now, Buick restorers are beginning to manufacture many of these plastic parts. However, a deluxe 1940 Buick steering wheel is still a near impossible item to find. Coates advertised for two years for such a wheel, finally locating a new, old stock wheel in Joliet, Ill. The $80 price seemed high, but where do you find one of these? Those elegant Buick steering wheels cracked easily. Of course, they can be repaired with epoxy and painted. "But you will never have the beautiful ivory luminescence of the original," says Coates.

What has made this car a prize winner is not just perfect paint, chrome and upholstery, but a lot of attention to detail in all little places. Bob even took the trouble to fabricate new sun visors. Rather than restore the car to be something that would impress the judges, he put the car back into precisely the same condition as it was the day Mrs. Ramsey bought it in 1939. He even found an original and perfect 1940 Buick owner's manual. This kind of attention to detail does impress the judges more than a lot of glitter.

Bob's pretty blue "Bu" now holds the best record of winnings of any Buick on the West Coast. In 1972, it won first in class at six major shows in the San Francisco Bay area. In 1973, it won first in class at Silverado, and was named second SCCA concours car of the year. It won a second in class at Harrah's, was named best of show at the Northern California CHVA national at Los Gatos, and the final triumph was best of show at the Buick Club of America national meet at Morro Bay. What's so amazing is that this car is always driven, never trailered. Bob even drives the car regularly on Buick Club and CHVA tours.

Buicks from this period are real sleepers. A lot of collectors are still passing them up for more exotic cars. But once you inspect a restoration like Bob's, you will appreciate the prewar Buick for the fine car it really was.

The dependable Buick straight-eight engine became more powerful every year. Coates' 1940 Special has a 248 cid engine rated at 107 hp. If you went up to the Century, you got the 320 cid 141 hp Roadmaster engine. A Roadmaster will give you about 13 mpg. Bob reports averaging 15 mpg. with his Special. It would be unfair to compare his car with the smooth riding 1940 Roadmaster. The 1939 GM "B" body is a little stiffer, but it is a body that collectors seem to prefer "Those torpedo Buicks just aren't the same cars," says Coates.

No doubt, every Buick owner has his own favorite. We find all the older Buicks highly interesting cars. Now, when we see significant collectors like Owen Owens of Orinda, Calif., choosing Buicks over more exotic cars, we can only conclude that Buicks must be coming up in the hobby, and very, very fast. Back in the days when better automobiles were built, Buick certainly built their share of them.

1912 Buick by jazz stand.

1941 Buick Roadmaster convertible owned by Otto Oswald.

When better cars are collected...

By Tim Howley

Some years ago I visited the Merrill, Wis., home town of my old automobile idol, Ned Jordan, and met with Norman Chilsen, a schoolmate of the little advertising wizard behind the Jordan automobile. Chilsen had been a publisher, an early Buick dealer, and still remembered all the skeletons in the Jordan family closet. One story he told left far more of an impression on me than the yarn about Ned's sister, Ella, who fell down the cellar steps, or the scandal of sister Blanche, who ran off with a San Francisco lumberman.

Chilsen said that along about 1909 he got the idea of a slogan, "When better automobiles are built...Buick will build them." It wasn't in quite the same words then. But that was the general idea. Anyway, Chilsen had the slogan painted on his Buick establishment. At the next meeting of Wisconsin area Buick dealers in Milwaukee, the dealer organization voted to accept the slogan. The factory copied it, and a year later copywrited it. Chilsen claimed he could prove that his story was factual. At the time I was more interested in Jordan trivia than in Buick history, and I'm sorry to say that I never followed up on it.

But I do know now that "When better automobiles are built," not "Somewhere west of Laramie," was the greater of the two ad lines. That is if you're measuring advertising by its effectiveness. Laramie sold a concept, selling the sizzle instead of the steak. "When better automobiles are built" went on selling Buicks for decades. And the better automobiles it promised have been delivered by Buick now for three-quarters of a century. The poor Jordan never made it past the great Depression. 1978 marked Buick's 75th Anniversary. Never has there been so much emphasis on the marque's history as there is today.

We attended the Buick Club of America's '77 West Coast Meet in Los Gatos, Calif.,a sunny south bay suburb nestled at the foot of the Santa Cruz Mountains some 50 miles south of San Francisco. The Los Gatos Lodge has

been a popular national show site here in the past. They're very accommodating to car clubs, and they're located right next to the Los Gatos High School athletic field, an ideal display area. But this time the high school was cool about having another car meet on their field. Possibly they were afraid of more damage to the grass and the problems they're having maintaining it during the water shortage.

For whatever reason, the swap and show ended up in the south parking lot of the lodge, and nearly 100 Buicks were packed in like Model A Fords on the last ferryboat to Berkeley. Nobody bothered to think of removing a large garbage container at the back of the lot. As a result, some of the best cars on display were placed right next to the trash, and the stench down at the end of the lot was simply unbearable. I suppose that Buick's detractors might say they always knew that a Buick was an "ick." But we didn't hear one single complaint about this meet, only the highest praise for the organizational job done by Tim Cox and Dick Stechelin. Only about 50 cars were registered before the meet. 84 were entered and another 15 or 20 came just to park.

This was the first time we had ever attended a "for Buicks only" event, and we wanted to search out some of the reasons for Buick's relatively recent rise in popularity as a collector car. The Buick Club of America started in Southern California in 1966. Its main event is the bi-annual Flint, Mich. meet held in cooperation with the Buick Division of General Motors. While the Los Gatos meet was a national regional, it drew most of its cars from within a 100 mile radius. We were a little amazed at how many Buicks, and rare Buicks, are hidden in the Northern California coastal hills and out in the barns up and down the Great Valley. There were at least a dozen open 1937 and 1938 models. There was a '42 Buick Super convertible, a '49 Roadmaster Riviera hardtop and at least three Buick estate wagons. We saw a '31 Buick convertible, the first direct descendant of more modern Buick convertibles, and a '53 Skylark, the grandest Buick convertible.

One member brought out a fully restored 1930 Marquette. The meet was one magnificent panorama of most of Buick's 75 years, from a 1912 touring right on up to some very recent models. The Buicks have always been around. They've just taken a little longer than some cars in staging a strong comeback. Only a few weeks earlier 378 of them showed up at Cleveland, which, to date, is a record turnout.

We asked Terry Dunham, well known Buick historian, just what special magic is making Buicks grow so rapidly in popularity these days? Dunham assured us that it's nothing that's CHVA tours in Northern California. The Monterey Bay Classic Jazz Band drove up in their '26 Buick seven passenger sedan and provided the afternoon's entertainment. About the only tune they didn't play was, "How I Love to Drive My Buick."

The success of the Buick Club is as ubiquitous as the appeal of the car itself. Buick collectors are drawn from every segment of the hobby from the Cadillac, Packard or Lincoln collector to the Ford, Plymouth or Chevrolet enthusiast. Most Buick Club members got into the hobby with some other make, and came to appreciate the many satisfactions of Buick ownership, and have added a big Buick to their stable. There are very few speculators in Buicks. The club tolerates them but doesn't really want them. It's a family oriented club. At all of the national meets members are encouraged to bring their wives and children. Meet sites are picked to accommodate the family. All of the chapter activities are geared towards family participation.

One car of particular interest at the meet was Lee Greer's 1938 Buick Century pickup, originally owned by famous San Francisco and East Bay Buick dealer, Charlie Howard. Howard owned a number of race horses including the famous Sea Biscuit and War Wagon. The Century pickup was specially built to haul happened overnight. "There has always been an aura and a sex appeal that Buick has gathered," Terry told us. "It started in the Teens and Twenties, and it came back again in 1934 when Harlow Curtice came with the firm. He just had a handle on the automobile business and on his product that's just about impossible to duplicate. That's one of the reasons why so many people are interested in the marque now, and why what you see here are mostly the cars that Cur-

tice built from about 1934 to 1948 or '49."

Dunham revealed that he was not on a Buick nostalgia trip. His family never owned Buicks. The marque had won him over. Back when he was in high school he was into drag racing. He owned a highly modified '37 Dodge coupe. "Then one night this guy came out with a stock '37 Buick Century sedan that he'd hauled out of some famer's chicken coupe," said Terry. "He just completely blew me off the road. That was the beginning of my interest in Buicks."

John Gerstkemper, one of the club's founding members, had more observations on the rise of Buick in the hobby. "Buicks are getting to be a scarce breed," Gerstkemper pointed out. "There were a lot of them made, but they were driven and driven, and finally scrapped out. But a Buick properly restored is a wonderful driving car. You can put one on Sea Biscuit's trailer. The great horse died tragically in a fire which destroyed Sea Biscuit Farms, but the Century pickup managed to escape. Greer found it in a Carson City, Nevada, junkyard, where it had been rotting away for 12 years, brought it back to California, and gave it a ground up restoration.

Time was in Northern California, when real status was a new Buick license plate frame reading "C. S. Howard Buick."

Once Buick was more a part of the American scene than just about any other automobile. In 1942, when General MacArthur met with President Franklin Roosevelt at Pearl Harbor to finalize strategy for the Pacific theater, he wanted to drive up in a car that FDR wouldn't forget. MacArthur chose a red 1941 Buick Roadmaster four-door convertible. When World War II was over, America came home to those enormous Buick convertibles. They were the driveway dreams of every GI Joe.

Not so long ago Buick stood for something as safe as Fort Knox, as dependable as interest from the Bank of America, and as stylish as a fashion window on Park Avenue. I thought it was a sad time in American history, when, near the close of the Vietnam War, Buick had to resort to the slogan, "Something to believe in."

Maybe that's the whole mystique of Buick as a collectible. Something to believe in again. And maybe it's the final answer to our question, why do people collect Buicks?

1942 Buick Super convertible brought by John Plough. Note missing upper strip on fender skirt.

New Boulevard Ride – even on the byways

Along a city street, it rides with sweeping grace—and from the envying eyes that follow you in a long linger, you know you're traveling in the freshest fashion on wheels.

At a light, along a turnpike, climbing a hill —it moves like pure performance—with silent might and flash-fast response—the zest, highest-compression horsepower in Buick history—and with the instant take-hold take-off of a terrific new Variable Pitch Dynaflow.*

That you know from merely pressing the gas pedal a small fraction of its full travel.

But not till you guide this great new Buick to the off-beat roads and the high-crowned black-top will you fully know what wonderful new magnificence has been brought to the Buick ride for 1956.

Consider this:

There's more here than just the constant buoy-ancy of coil springs on all four wheels—and the on-target track of a full-length torque-tube —and the solid substance of a massive X-member frame.

There's a new deep-oil cushioning of jars and jolts that brings a boulevard smoothness to every road you travel.

There's a whole new front-end geometry that gives a brand-new "sweetness" to the feel of the car—that holds this broad Buick to a level plane on full-turn curves—eases steering to a new deftness—lends a new and more positive "sense of direction" to the car's every inch of travel.

We're ready now to offer you a sampling of what ride-engineering at its Buick best can mean.

Drop in on us soon—and take your own measure of the automobile that just had to be called the best Buick yet.

Baby Boom Era

1946–1960

NEW Precision-Balanced Chassis, engineered all new from front to rear for extra-rugged roadability

NEW V8 Power Peaks In Every Buick

NEW Variable Pitch Dynaflow*—with double-action take-off

NEW Coil-Cushioned Luxury Ride—with swinging and true torque-tube drive

NEW Sweep-Ahead Styling—with Fashion Color Harmony inside and out

NEW Smoother-Action Brakes with Suspended Pedal

NEW Stepped-Up Gas Mileage in All Buicks

NEW Safety Power Steering! for instant and constant response

Best Buick yet

SEE YOUR BUICK DEALER

SEE JACKIE GLEASON ON TV

Airfoil-styled '48 Super convertible

By Tom LaMarre

During World War II, Buick claimed that its postwar models would be "...all that returning warriors have dreamed about — cars that from go-treadle to stop light will fit the stirring pattern of the lively, exciting, forward-moving new world so many millions have fought for."

Pictured in the ad was a 1942 Roadmaster convertible, a good indication of what car buyers could look forward to. The "airfoil" styling of the '42 Roadmaster and Super made them the most modern cars on the road. As a result, Buick had the jump on other manufacturers when the war ended.

As exemplified by the model 56C Super convertible, the flowing fender design still looked good in 1948. Only a few small changes were made to set the '48 Super apart from the '47 model. "Super" nameplates were mounted on the front fenders and the new tire size was 7.60 x 15 inches. New interior features included a black Tenite steering wheel and silver tone instruments on a two-tone grey panel.

At $2,518, the Super convertible was $319 less than the Roadmaster ragtop. Yet it offered such standard luxury items as a power top, power seat and power front windows. Buick's new Dynaflow automatic transmission was available only on the Roadmaster, though.

Powering the Super was a 248 cubic-inch straight eight with a 6.6:1 compression ratio; it produced 115 horsepower at 3600 rpm.

Evidently many veterans did find Buick convertibles "so nice to come home to." With an 18.9 percent market share, Buick led the industry in the production of convertibles for 1948. A total 19,217 Super convertibles were made.

Specifications:

1948 Buick Super Convertible

Series	Super
Factory Price	$2,158
Weight Engine	248 cubic-inch straight eight
BHP	115 at 3600 rpm
CR	6.6:1
Tires	7.60x15
Wheelbase	124 in.
Overall Length	212½ in.
No. 1 Value	$17,000
Production	19,217

'48 Super convertible was a lot of car for the money. Styling was little changed from the '42 version.

See the Canadian Rockies by Buick

Canadian Rockies provide a beautiful backdrop for Ivor Nixon's 1948 Buick Super convertible.

By Ivor Nixon

The story starts in April 1982. We had reservations on a flight to London leaving Toronto, Canada at 9:30 a.m. on Sunday, April 19. But on Saturday the 18th there was a no-reserve auction of Fred Miller's entire car inventory in Exeter, N.H. — an irresistible temptation featuring an original 1932 DeSoto roadster with 16,000 miles.

But how to solve a logistics problem which at first glance would appear both difficult and foolhardy to tackle? Fortunately, old car buffs are rarely deterred by that which is difficult, and generally only slowed down slightly by the impossible. In consequence, both trips were completed on schedule.

After my wife assured me that our packing for England would be done competently (she didn't actually say more competently than if I were underfoot), a flight to Boston on Friday afternoon and a rental car to Exeter enabled me to be at the Miller showroom bright and early on Saturday morning. The DeSoto was even better-looking than I had hoped. Unfortunately this reaction was shared by quite a number of the several hundred others present, some from as far away as Florida, many of whom appeared to have resources considerably in excess of mine. The yellow DeSoto went for $29,000 and at that point I nearly went as well. However, earlier I had seen several other cars of the 75 total which appeared to be in better than average condition, and since I still had more than enough time to catch my flight home from Logan, why not stay around

and see how the rest of the auction went just out of curiosity? That seemingly innocent decision was my undoing.

After a '49 Ford convertible went for $20,000 and two gorgeous open '37 Fords went for similarly unaffordable amounts, there was left only the black '48 Buick Super 56C convertible, car no. 25. It was immediately preceded

View through the windshield of Nixon's Buick Super.

by a 1953 Skylark which attracted intense competition, but which seemed to me to be in poorer shape. A few minutes later I heard a hoarse voice, which turned out to be mine, topping the initial bid on the '48, and then raising it once again at which point I was fingered as the proud owner. Did I really want a Buick? Did I pay too much? Should I have crawled underneath to see what I was really getting? Should I catch a flight from Boston to Buenos Aires rather than explain to my wife that we now owned a 35-year-old convertible? Did I have any idea how I was going to get it home and when? What would Canadian customs tap me for? These and other questions went through my mind as I bade farewell to beautiful downtown Exeter, and for the next 30 days as well (free storage was courtesy of Fred Miller).

Fortunately, none of the bleak consequences came to pass, and obviously I did want a Buick without knowing it — if the subsequent satisfaction and enjoyment mean anything. Of course, I did find out that most of the wiring had no insulation, and that the motor consumed 38 liters of oil on the first 1,200-mile trip, but these and similar deficiencies were overcome by rewiring, rechroming, reupholstering, retopping, repainting and reboring, with almost no regretting. Having spent the first 30 years of its life in California, the body and frame were immaculate under the dirt — no evidence of as much as a ding. For good measure, it had once been undercoated. For safety, I added seat belts and seat back latches.

In June 1984, the Electrical & Electronic Manufacturers Association of Canada, of which I am a member, held its annual electronics conference at Jasper Lodge in Jasper National Park, Alberta. At some point in the restoration process, a crazy thought began to emerge: Wouldn't it be fun to drive the Buick out? Or would it indeed be crazy? Was I indeed becoming senile at the same time as I was becoming poor? Did it really matter? The answers turned out to be yes, yes, probably and no in that order. We went.

The route took us via Port Huron, Marquette, Duluth, Grand Forks and Minot to Weyburn, Saskatchewan, then to Calgary, Banff, Lake Louise and the Columbia Icefields Parkway to Jasper. He or she who has never traveled through the Canadian Rockies in a convertible has yet to experience scenery that competes with the best of the Alps or New Zealand. When it's a 1948 Buick convertible which attracts crowds at every stop, the thrill is enhanced beyond measure.

After four days in heaven, we returned through Edmonton, Saskatoon, Yorkton, Winnipeg and across the Trans-Canada Highway north of Lake Superior. Spares carried consisted largely of a windshield wiper motor and fuel/vacuum pump (both of which were used) and an assortment of bulbs and fuses (which were not). Although there were frequent picnics and rest stops in the course of the 4,800-mile trip, none were forced, and my Yaesu twp-meter handheld was needed only to rag-chew with other hams along the way. And of course there were several hundred tiny stone chips, and the rock in the windshield which also (no connection) leaked in every rainstorm, and the radio lead-in which developed an intermittent short to ground, and the wind and thunderstorms in Saskatchewan, and the several thousand 18-wheelers all going 10 mph faster than I wanted to, but then when is life ever easy? Ultimately all these petty annoyances were fixed up, and in August of '84 the car won best of class at the Buick Club of America Great Lakes Regional at Canandaigua, N.Y., and in September was accorded 94.7 points at the Antique & Classic Car Club of Canada's annual concours. So who says you can't drive and enjoy your handiwork? I recommend it, especially if it's a Buick and you're heading West. They may have built better cars since, but you couldn't prove it by me.

(Reprinted with permission from the February 1986 issue of *The Buick Bugle*.)

Another view of Nixon's Buick and the Canadian Rockies.

1949 Buick Roadmaster Riviera hardtop coupe, model 76-R.

Buick's instant success story

By Tim Howley

Hardtops scarcely turn your head today. They've become about as romantic as washing machines or the latest model grocery carts at Safeway. But years ago, when all my world was young, the almost convertible was just about the most exciting thing to come down the pike since the Stutz Bearcat. Post-World War II America loved convertibles. Only increasing city congestion and smog were making them impractical. Buick designers got the message.

In July 1949, they introduced America's first mass-produced hardtop. It was a car for wandering roads of the west. It was a highway machine for the man who liked to take to the open road with the top down, but had lost a bit of his boyhood courage. It was the spirit of adventure, as interpreted by Detroit for the masses — and they called it the Buick Roadmaster Riviera.

Now, hardtops were nothing new in that year of "Bib-bidi-Bobbidi-Boo" and "Bali Hai." The earliest ones go back to about 1918. Franklin had one in the early Twenties. "California tops" were quite common by the middle of that decade. Chrysler demonstrated the first postwar hardtop in its Town & Country line as early as 1946. But these were only prototypes, and the all steel top was bolted right on the standard T&C convertible body.

It took GM to finally weld the top to the convertible body. They did this in 1949, coming up with three totally desirable mutants. These were the buick Roadmaster Riviera, the Cadillac coupe deVille and the Oldsmobile Holiday 98. Buick got the jump on the other two by a matter of weeks and promoted the car heavily in magazine advertising. GM has never disclosed MTC hardtop production figures for that very limited model year. It is believed that the Buick Rivieras were the most plentiful, but more of the Cadillac coupe deVilles have survived. The Oldsmobile Holiday 98s are probably the rarest, but are less

desirable than the other two makes — maybe because very few collectors are aware that Oldsmobile did, indeed, build a hardtop at a very early date.

The Buick Riviera was the first production hardtop with the frame actually an integral part of the body. The car was announced in December 1948, previewed at the Waldorf Astoria in January 1949, but never made available until six months later. Buick never offered an explanation for the delay. Then, less than a month after the car hit the showrooms, Buick reintroduced the "Special," and entirely new 1950 body styling. For 1950, Buick had a whole new line of hardtops, and the lovely '49 Riviera was completely obsolete. It was a shame. For my money, the short lived '49 Buick body was the most attractive one of the decade, and in the Riviera it reached its finest development. By the same token, the orginal Riviera's short life only makes it more desirable as a collector's item now. When did you last see a '49 Buick Riviera?

Buick had cut out a big share of the market beginning with the 1936 model. By 1941, Buick was in fourth place in sales. The '46 Buick was a "warmed over" version of the '42, and this same styling was carried through the 1948 model. The Sedanette is considered one of its most attractive versions. Remember Buick's "bombsight" hood ornament? It dates back to an experimental model of 1938, was introduced in '42, and was one of several Buick trademarks through the Fifties.

In 1948, Buick built its five millionth car. Dynaflow was offered for the first time that year. Dynaflow really came into its own in 1949 when it became standard equipment on the Roadmaster series. It was a simple, rugged and reliable torque-converter transmission, the only real drawbacks being performance and economy. A Dynaflow would wind up like a jet aircraft engine before the car ever left the curb. At city speeds it felt like a standard shift with a slipping clutch, but at highway speeds the direct drive took over, and it was smooth sailing all the way up to a top

speed of 100 mph. With the possible exception of Cadillac, I don't think there was a better car in the 70-90 mph range than the '49 Buick. It was a veritable locomotive.

For 1949, Buick offered a 150 hp 320.2 cid Fireball straight eight engine. (Buick wouldn't get an overhead V-8 until 1953.) The '49 Buicks have been severely criticized for their "Beautyrest mattress" ride and "suspension by jello." Those who loved them called them "Beaus"; those who didn't called them "Icks." They just reeked upper middle-class class. They had a special opulence all their own which made them the most impressive mode of transportation to visit your Aunt Minnie back in Iowa or to take that big family vacation way out west. But Mexican Road racers they weren't.

Styling was clean and simple. Buick designers hadn't yet come up with their answer to the monster movies — the 1950 Buick "buck tooth" grille. A '49 Buick coming down the road rather reminds me of a small town church on wheels. Come to think of it. I did see most of those '49 Buicks in church parking lots.

Buick's "mousehole" portholes made their appearance in 1949. According to the often repeated story, Buick's chief designer, Ned Nickles, put them on his own car, rigging them with flashing lights to indicate cylinder firing order. As soon as Buick President Harlow Curtice saw the car, he insisted on boring holes in the entire 1949 line, sans the flashers. The promotion department labeled them "Ventri ports." The Super got three ports on each side; the Roadmaster got four. They did serve a purpose; they were connected to the engine compartment by conduits to aid cooling. Funny, Buick got along for decades without them, but from '49 on, they were the crowning status symbols of moving up to a Buick.

The '49 "Beau" had a lot of other niceties. That dashboard was the neatest ever. It was absolutely huge, and might have done service in the cockpit of a Stratocruiser. The Dynaflow gear selector read PNDLR. I think Buick scored a first with that slight bit of auto-trivia. To start your '49 "Ick" you simply floored the gas pedal. This activated a starter switch on the carburetor. The hood could be opened from either side for easy service, or it could be removed entirely in seconds. Mechanics loved it. Another nice '49 Buick feature was the "step-on" parking brake a Buick first in 1942 which is commonplace today. The turn signal lever was on the right side instead of the left, but you got used to it.

The crown of the line — the Riviera — came only in the Roadmaster series and was sold as a completely equipped car. You could have an all-leather interior or a leather-and-gray-cloth interior. The interior was designed to simulate the convertible, and designers even went so far as to put thin stainless steel strips across the roof to look like top bows. Curved glass technology had not yet developed to the point of one-piece wraparound rear windows. The rear window was a three-piece affair and was quite attractive.

Some say the Riviera came about at the suggestion of Sarah Ragsdale, wife of Buick general manager Ed Ragsdale. That story doesn't hold much credence. The hardtop was an idea whose time had come. Convertibles were very popular in the West in the fifties. They were desirable but highly impractical in the winter regions. Now, America could have its convertible styling and snug top, too. Within a few years, the hardtop became the most popular body style in the nation — and it still is. The hardtop succeeded because it was what America wanted when we wanted it. It made no sense. It cost more than a standard coupe and in the early years it was full of rattles and leaks, but it was "the right car."

I remember the first time I set eyes on a '49 Buick Riviera. It was a beautiful pearl blue job with a white top. I discovered it parked in front of the Yellowstone Falls hotel in Yellowstone Park. Being born and raised in Minneapolis, this was my first journey into the west. As a starry-eyed lad of 14, I was completely taken away with the car. When I returned to Minneapolis, there were none to be found, which was odd, because Minneapolis was Buick territory.

The next time I found a '49 Riviera was in 1972, and it was here in Oakland, Calif. The car belonged to Oakland collector Bud Juneau, who said it took him two cars to build up this one. It is a show restoration finished up in a beautiful pale yellow which Buick called "Sequoia cream." According to Juneau, there are only a few of them in California and probably not more than half a dozen in the East.

Buick brought back the Riviera in 1963, but it's not the same car. The latter is simply a modern touring car with a grand old name. To me, the name Buick Riviera means that grand old machine I saw in Yellowstone Park years ago.

Buick's 1949 Super was a popular ragtop

The '49 Super convertible was a popular postwar car when it was new and makes an outstanding show car today. Its sales of 22,110 units originally set an all-time record for Buick ragtop deliveries up to that point in time.

Like other cars in the '49 Super lineup, the convertible shared a new General Motors "C" body with the upscale Roadmasters, but had a five-inch smaller wheelbase (121 inches for Super vs. 126 inches for Roadmaster). Trim distinctions included three chrome ventiports on each front fender and a "Super" script above the fender molding.

New fender-edge taillamps were used on all Supers to give a modernized appearance. Customizers of the day frequently replaced them with '49 Cadillac taillights "frenched" into modified fender openings. A toothylooking grille was seen up front, along with fender-top parking lamps and a "bombsight" hood ornament.

Regular equipment on Supers included cigar lighter, ash tray, automatic choke, full wheel trim discs and rear fender skirts. The convertible also had leather upholstery with leatherette trim, power top, power seat and power windows standard.

Buick's power team for Supers included a 248 cid overhead valve straight eight engine with bore and stroke of 3-3/32x4-⅛ inches. It had 6.6:1 compression and developed 115 bhp at 3,600 rpm (30.6 A.M.A. horsepower). Advertised torque was 212 pounds-foot, at 2,000 rpm. This engine had solid valve lifters and five main bearings. A Carter WCD type, two-barrel, Model 663S carburetor was used. (Repair kit No. 1,391; gasket set No. 189.)

A three-speed manual transmission was standard in all Supers and Dynaflow Drive was available at extra cost. Cars equipped with the automatic transmission option had a higher 6.9:1 compression ratio, which raised the power output to 120 bhp at 3,600 rpm.

All 1949 Buicks had a 59 inch front tread and 62 inch rear tread. Supers used 7.60 x 15 tires as factory equipment. A negative ground, Delco Group Number 2E, six-volt battery was employed.

Buick Serial Numbers were located underneath the hood of the car on a plate attached to the upper right side of the shroud. The Fisher Body Style Number 49-4567 appeared on the Super convertible and provides a very good way to positively determine model year (49=1949), series code (45=Buick 50 Super) and body style (67=convertible).

The Super convertible carried an original factory suggested price of $2,583. It was considered a six-passenger automobile and tipped the scales in the Buick shipping department at 3,985 lbs.

Our feature car is a restored example with just 32,000 original miles, owned by Jack Bucholtz, of Roscommon, Mich. Finished in Sequora Cream, it features the standard transmission, a black top and black leather interior. The more than a dozen First Place honors this car has attained since restoration include awards at the Buick National Meet, in Columbus, Ohio; the Carnival of Cars, in Detroit, Mich. and the Red Farm Meet, in Kalamazoo, Mich. It also captured First in Class and "Best Buick" ratings at the 1983 Sloan Museum Festival.

1949 Buick Super convertible.

1949 Buick Roadmaster with three styling features — hardtop "convertible," massive grille and portholes. (Photo courtesy Buick Motor Division.)

Ned Nickles: famous postwar Buick designer

Buick developed a number of well-remembered design themes in the years immediately following World War II, including hardtop convertible styling (eliminating the center side pillar), massive "carnivorous" grilles, VentiPorts (portholes) and the sweepspear side decoration.

Most can be attributed to GM designer Ned Nickles, but partial credit for one of them goes to Edward T. Ragsdale, then Buick's manufacturing manager, and his wife, Sarah.

Recalled Nickles: "It was about 1945. Ragsdale looked at my model of the hardtop and said his wife always wanted convertibles because she liked the styling, but never put the top down because it made her hair blow around."

This observation by Ragsdale, later a Buick general manager, was credited with helping "sell" the idea as a production feature in 1949.

Although historians credit Chrysler's 1947 Town & Country cars with being the first "hardtop convertibles," only seven were built. Buick popularized the idea with more than 4,000 hardtop convertibles in 1949, the first of hundreds of thousands it would produce over the next few years.

A few of the 1949 Roadmaster Rivieras (the Riviera name at that time referring to hardtop convertible) included the sweepspear, described as a bright metal side decoration that began in the front fender as a slim horizontal molding and became wider as it swept in a downward curve along the doors, dipping to the base of the leading edge of the rear fender, and then kicking up over the rear wheel openings. It would become another long-lived Buick identity feature from Nickles (now deceased), changing in detail though not in concept.

While Ragsdale supported the hardtop convertible idea, he didn't think much of Nickles' portholes. Nickles had cut holes in the sides of the hood of his own 1948 Roadmaster convertible and behind them installed amber lights attached to the distributor. The lights, flashing on and off, suggested an unusually powerful engine with flaming exhaust. Nickles said he got the idea from World War II fighter planes.

Ragsdale saw the custom work one day and complained to Buick General Manager Harlow Curtice that Nickles had "ruined" his convertible. Curtice, however, was so intrigued he immediately ordered the portholes into production for 1949 — but without the lights.

(Curiously, Nickles soon afterward designed two Buicks now considered "modern classics" — the 1953 and 1954 Skylark — and in both cases he eliminated portholes, which were on all other models in those years. He also created the first design of a later Buick classic — the 1963 Riviera — under the direction of GM styling chief Bill Mitchell.)

The vertical-bar grille theme was started on 1942 Buicks (an abbreviated run before Buick turned to war production) and the grilles became ever more massive after the war.

On styling in general during this period, Nickles said: "I have heard criticism of the amount of chrome we used on those postwar Buicks, but I come from a different perspective than some of these writers. You have to judge things in the context of their times. We had just come through a war, and you couldn't get chrome during the war. So in the postwar years, we were entertaining people with chrome on cars. I think the cars fit in well with the times."

By Ned Comstock

Exactly like the American himself, the American automobile is an European invention. In the very beginning the best cars came from Europe — Delauney-Beleville, Isota-Frachini, Renault. Later on, state side models followed European leaders. Moon copies Rolls-Royce, and the original LaSalle stole its style from Hispano-Suiza. Five years ago, Cadillac pasted the rear end of a 1956 Daimler on Seville. But Buick was all American from the beginning.

Some European makes owed their success in America to the counter-culture. Beetle was a protest against price, and Mercedes-Benz owed much of its post-war vogue to a reaction from the Cadillac cult. But these lucky strikes were not repeated, and Buick just kept on rolling.

We still adapt European auto innovations. The trans-axle front drive is English and the box body General Motors touts today came from Italy long ago.

But like the European man, transplanted to America the automobile becomes something different. It's this difference that won the world for America, in War and Peace and in auto design. Of all our automobiles, 1950 Buick was the most American. That's why we loved it so.

Buick sales in 1950 jumped almost off the chart, a whopping 38 percent over the previous year, pressed low-priced Plymouth hard for third place, a record not to my knowledge seen again. Perhaps 1950 Buick was the most successful single model in US auto history. For the next 25 years, every car that came out of Detroit owed it something.

Americans love big cars, and 1950 Buick was big. Roadmaster 72R measured 130¼ inches hub to hub, four inches longer than Cadillac 62, the Standard of the World. At 213 inches overall, with seat wide enough for four

When better 1950s cars were built, Buick usually made them!

1950 Buick Super four-door.

1950 Buick 76C Roadmaster convertible.

abreast, Buick was so big that many a new Buick owner had to remodel his garage. But he didn't mind. In the days before technology refined itself, size was the accepted way to performance and comfort. The bigger the better, and Buick was enormous.

And it was a bargain. New Buick owners that year were fond of remarking that you got a lot of car for the money. You did, too. Roadmaster 72 weighed in at 4,220 pounds, heavier than Cadillac 62 by 200 pounds and $700 cheaper. Figured by the pound, Buick came out to 60¢ a pound against Cadillac's 80¢, a 25 percent advantage. And compare that to the $10,000-2,500 pounders they sell today.

If the 1950 Buick buyer needed a logical reason to love his outsize sweetheart, he could figure it out on the back of an envelope. Buick was a beautiful buy.

Performance is as performance does; and 152 horses took care of that. With 1950 Buick, Dynaflow gave it special meaning, so special that the word was lifted by the French and applied in France to anything with extra impact. Slipped into Drive, there was a tiny jolt when Dynaflow took hold, then a muffled roar as the engine leaped to 3,000 revs and held it until the car caught up. Then at cruising loads the silent direct fluid coupling made you feel you were floating. Various self-shifters were vying for the market in those days, but none gave the engine the freedom of Dynaflow and the silky delivery of its power.

Style is how you like it, and in 1950 people liked the looks of Buick. It looked heavy because it was heavy, and bulky for the same reason. The agressive bumper-grille gave it the face of a charging bull. A great big beautiful brute, you might sum up contemporary opinion.

There was a wide choice that year. Studebaker looked light and fleeting, Chrysler sensible and comfortable. Ford crisp and clean. All three designs were trampled in a buyer stampede to Buick, and that's what style is for. Then with a touch of genius, Buick asserted itself with a unique touch — you could tell it was a Buick as far as you could see it. The "ventiports" (carried forward from 1949) became Buick's international trademark, shouting its identity, a key note equal to Cadillac tail fins. In case you missed the four holes, Roadmaster 72R dazzled you with a chromium "sweepspear" running along side the entire length of the car.

Inside those portholes everything was working. Since 1930 the "Micro-poise Dynaflash" OHV Straight Eight, now 320 inches, had come a long way. Domed aluminum "turbulator" pistons improved combustion hydraulic tappets smoothed the valve system, the crankshaft had been finely balanced, ran on nine main bearings. The compound two barrel dual carburetor opened wide with a lovely roar-when you floored the gas pedal, at idle the engine was dead silent. It could move the whole show with six aboard the 60 MPH from a standing start in 15 seconds or less.

New then adapted from WW II aircraft practice, push-buttons were everywhere. At a touch these buttons rolled the windows up and down, the drivers seat back and forth, on convertibles lowered the top. Buick owners loved the novelty of this.

There was one little fly in all this ointment. This Buick gulped gas as if it didn't make any difference. The answer is of course, in 1950, it didn't. And today, if you own one of these magnificent machines, do what the English owner reported in *Autocar* does — run it only on Sundays, and on the Fourth of July, because it's a Yankee Doodle Dandy.

1950 Buick Special four-door sedan owned by James J. Holzschuh of Wausau, Wis.

By Ned Comstock

The designers at Buick must have been touched with genius in 1950 — they knew what we wanted in a post-war automobile. We were looking for a big car, a going machine, and a car that looked the part. Sensible cars were for other people, we got no kick from economy cars, and now that we could travel without wartime restrictions we wanted a car that could keep up with our dreams of distant places. And it had to fit in the monthly pay check. Buick understood this better than anybody. Better, perhaps than we ourselves did.

Buick was brave. In 1950, there were more customers than there were new cars, and it would have been easy and natural for long established Buick to market a follow-the-leader, and cash in on the panting demand. Buick didn't. In a daring adventure, Buick invaded the lower price mass market with a bomb that exploded with such resonance that it echoed for 20 years. That was 1950 Special.

All the more remarkable, in an industry that demands conformity Buick dared to be different, different from other makes, different from its cousins at General Motors, different even from Buicks past.

Special was an almost unbelieveable bargain in 1950. Base list squeezed under $2,000, and if *World Almanac* has figured right, the dollar then was worth about three-and-a-half times as much as it is now. Today, lowest priced Buick lists about $7,000 which sounds about right in constant dollars until you see what you get. Instead of the hefty (3,715 pounds) Special of 1950 with a 248 inch straight eight OHV engine to boot it along, you get a little machine that barely tops a ton (2,365 pounds) pulled by a docile 1.8 litre four-banger. Put it another way, Buick prices per pound have gone up from around 50¢ in 1950 to over $3 today, an increase of some 600 percent. We'll never see another new car bargain like 1950 Buick Special. And to those who say price per pound is no way to measure auto value, I say that's the way we did it in 1950.

Buick stylists knew we wanted a big car. In his book *Chrome Dreams* Paul Wilson points out that 1950 Buick Special style was intended to make the car look even bigger and heavier than it really was. The front end was built like a battering ram, everywhere large curves instead of square corners suggested mass, maximum width and low cut fenders partially shrouding the wheels confirmed it.

Consumer Reports (May 1950) didn't understand all this, and faulted Special 1950 for its low profile and squat seating, mentioning only in passing "a heavy, solid car with powerful performance, good riding qualities and excellent roadability." *CR* simply didn't know what we were looking for: If we wanted chair-high seats we'd have stayed home.

The men at Buick were marketeers, too. Harking back perhaps to the Ford/Chevrolet battle of 1927, they made no effort to meet the mass market price head on. Instead, they gently lowered Special down onto the Big Three, offering lots more car for a little more money. In the prosperous, confident atmosphere of 1950 this worked like a charm. The number of Big Three owners who traded up to Special in 1950 was limited more by the supply of new cars than by the demand for them.

No wonder. The price difference between Special and the top-of-the-line Chevrolet Deluxe in 1950 was whittled down to $253, and that didn't mean a thing in the 1950 land of dreams. The customer who could buy one could as easily buy the other. If he chose Special instead of Chevrolet Deluxe, his car was six inches longer, five inches wider, its wheelbase was seven inches greater, it weighed 430 pounds more. The tires were fatter, the engine was bigger and it boasted eight cylinders instead of six, and there were lots more horses in there.

We didn't stop to think how Buick did it, but if we had we'd understood the old principle that it doesn't cost very much more to build a big can than a small one, the axiom that Chevrolet had used to defeat Model T a generation before.

What we saw when we looked at 1950 Special was more of everything at a price we could afford. And we loved it.

Tune in HENRY J. TAYLOR, ABC Network, every Monday evening.
Time for some Readin', Ridin' and 'Rithmetic
The readin' part sort of starts things . . . You look at this brawny beauty and find it mighty handsome.
Then you read it's a Buick SPECIAL—
That a romping big Fireball straight-eight waits under its bonnet. That gentle coil springs cushion all four of its wheels. That Dynaflow Drive* is available as optional equipment.
*Standard on ROADMASTER, optional at extra cost on SUPER and SPECIAL models.
That makes you ready for the ridin' part, so you drop in on a Buick dealer, arrange a trial drive and put this lively stepper to the acid test of firsthand experience.
When you find it stepping away at the lights like a greyhound unleashed—when you see for yourself that Dynaflow really is a wholly new sensation in driving smoothness—when you find how much room, outlook and restful comfort the family has in Buick's spacious interior — you're ready for the 'rithmetic.
That is where you run into the clincher.
For this big straight-eight, with its matchless ride and the easy handling of far lesser cars, actually delivers for less than some sixes.
Worked out on a per-day basis, the difference in price between this and some of the lowest-priced automobiles comes down to mere pocket change.
Which suggests, since your readin' has carried you this far, it might be smart to arrange for the ridin' right away by getting in touch with your dealer. He'll be delighted to go into the 'rithmetic with you!
FOUR-WAY FOREFRONT—This rugged front end (1) sets the style note, (2) saves on repair costs—vertical bars are individually replaceable, (3) avoids "locking horns," (4) makes parking and garaging easier.
WHATEVER YOUR PRICE RANGE
"Better buy Buick"
When better automobiles are built BUICK will build them
Your Key to Greater Value
ONLY BUICK HAS Dynaflow— AND WITH IT GOES:
HIGHER-COMPRESSION Fireball valve-in-head power in three engines. (New F-263 engine in SUPER models.) • NEW-PATTERN STYLING, with MULTI-GUARD forefront, taper-through fenders, "double bubble" taillights • WIDE-ANGLE VISIBILITY, close-up road view both forward and back • TRAFFIC-HANDY SIZE, less over-all length for easier parking and garaging, short turning radius • EXTRA-WIDE SEATS cradled between the axles • SOFT BUICK RIDE, from all-coil springing, Safety-Ride rims, low-pressure tires, ride-steadying torque-tube • WIDE ARRAY OF MODELS with Body by Fisher.
SEE YOUR NEAREST BUICK DEALER
MAGAZINE. OCTOBER 22, 1950.
21

This advertisement showcases the 1950 Buick Special.

Buick's

1951 Roadmaster Estate Wagon

Side view of '51 Roadmaster Estate Wagon shows "Sweepspear" body trim piece.

By Robert C. Ackerson

Much has been written about the reason for Packard's inability to successfully compete with Cadillac in the postwar luxury car market. One of the most widely accepted views maintains that Packard, rather than competing head-on with Cadillac continued to offer less-expensive products that ultimately "cheapened" the Packard name with predictable results.

As plausible as this viewpoint is, it seems to fly in the face of the tremendous success Buick enjoyed for so many years by offering automobiles that at one of its price spectrum came very close to competing with the "Low-Priced Three" while at the other extreme were priced in close proximity to Cadillac.

With a strong base of popularity in the medium-priced field, Buick was thus a formidable sales opponent to virtually any other American car producer. Indeed, it was almost impossible for any producer not to avoid facing competition from an attractively priced Buick model.

In 1947 *Fortune* magazine aptly titled an article analyzing Buick's success, "The Ubiquitous Buick." Not only was Buick the undisputed leader in the medium-priced field but, as *Fortune* noted: "The versatility of its line makes it. . .a terror in the luxury market, where Buick offers almost as much automobile for a lot less money, and in the so-called low-priced field, where Buick tempts the trade with what looks like a lot more car for the money."

With only Chevrolet, Ford and Plymouth outselling Buick in 1951, the long sought-after goal of displacing Plymouth from its position as the nation's third most popular car remained a possibility. Although this battle has been waging since the start up of postwar production, it was one that Plymouth had also fought with a good deal of

determination. Not until 1954, when Buick's spectacular lineup overwhelmed the languid sales appeal of Plymouth's warmed-over 1953 models did the tide swing in Buick's favor.

Until the arrival of the Skylark in 1953, the most expensive model Buick offered was its Roadmaster Estate Wagon. It also was produced in extremely low numbers. Out of the three-plus million postwar Buicks built up to 1955, just 4,591 were Roadmaster wagons. Even in 1953 more Skylarks (1,690 to 670) were built than were Roadmaster Estate Wagons.

Typical of their design was the 1951 version. Built on a long 126¼-inch wheelbase, its overall length of 208¾ inches was exceeded only by that of the Model 72 Roadmaster Tourback sedan whose 130¼-inch wheelbase gave it an overall length of 212¾ inches.

Buick styling for 1951 was little changed from the format of 1950. With the verticle elements of the grille pulled back inside the bumper from their rather vulnerable 1950 location, the overall arrangement closely resembled that used by Buick since 1942. As a "Deluxe" Buick model, the Roadmaster wagon had what was to become, along with its ventiports, one of Buick's most memorable styling themes; the "Sweepspear" side body trim.

Powering all Roadmasters was the penultimate version of Buick's big 320-cid ohv straight-eight engine. When first introduced in 1936 it had developed 120 horsepower. For 1951 its output (unchanged from 1950) stood at 152 horsepower. Standard on all Roadmasters, as it had been since 1949, was Dynaflow automatic transmission.

Only 679 Roadmaster Estate Wagons were built for the 1951 model year. Most have not been as fortunate as the example shown here. It is the prized possession of its original owner.

115

The unusual Kurtis Buick

Motor Trend called him "a man who is no diploma-packing engineer, but who knows his machines with the intimacy that only 35 years of trial-and-error experimentation can give." Frank Kurtis used the same trial-and-error experimentation to develop the production autos bearing his name.

Kurtis began building race cars on the West coast in the 1930s. In the '40s, the direction of his efforts shifted from midget racers to Indy machines, and his creations influenced the direction of Indy racing for many years.

Three Kurtis-built cars were among the finishers at Indianapolis in 1946. In 1952 the first 11 finishers were Kurtis cars. The Indy winner from 1950 through 1955 originated at the Kurtis factory, which Frank Kurtis called the world's largest builder of racing cars (a claim which the Cooper Car Co. of Surrey, England probably disputed).

Frank Kurtis also claimed to have produced the first postwar American sports car. For many years he had contemplated manufacturing production autos. A Kurtis-Kar planned for 1948 never materialized. But in 1949, Kurtis-Kraft Inc., racing car manufacturer, finally entered the passenger car field with the announcement of a low-slung convertible sports car. Only 36 Kurtis autos were built at the small Glendale, Calif. factory in 1949-'50.

The prototype of the production model was Frank Kurtis' personal car, custom-built on the 126-inch wheelbase chassis of a wrecked Buick Century. Kurtis began building the car in 1941, but the war delayed its completion until 1946. Happily, its debut took place the same year the Kurtis racers became a factor at Indy.

The smooth, bulbous styling that characterized the prototype was a Kurtis hallmark. So was the fluted chrome spear on the hood. Its shape was mirrored by a single grille guard embossed with the Kurtis name. Fender skirts contributed to the sleek lines of the aluminum body, and tubular bumpers wrapped around the fenders. Buick taillights were used.

Perhaps the Kurtis Buick's most innovative feature was its canvas-covered aluminum top, which folded in three places for storage in a well behind the rear seat. The removable hardtop concept would later be used for the Corvette and Thunderbird, among others, and the Kurtis Buick's folding top foreshadowed the Ford retractable.

Long before safety became fashionable, the Kurtis Buick's instruments were set in a padded dash.

Road & Track said that the production Kurtis handled better than a Jaguar XK-120; and veteran road-tester Tom McCahill pushed the first Kurtis to more than 104 mph. The prototype, powered by a modified engine and fitted with dual exhausts, was also a high-performance model.

The production Kurtis was transformed into a 100-inch wheelbase two-seater, but its resemblance to the Kurtis Buick was unmistakable. Earl "Mad-man" Muntz bought the prototype for $5,000 to use as his personal transportation, and in 1950 he purchased Kurtis-Kraft for $200,000. The Kurtis evolved into the two-passenger Muntz Jet.

Frank Kurtis had one more fling at sports car production when he organized the Kurtis Sports Car Corp. in 1954. After its closing in 1955, Kurtis turned to other projects, including the construction of airport servicing vehicles for jets and rocket sleds for Cook Electric Research Labs.

Kurtis Buick. Note unique grille.

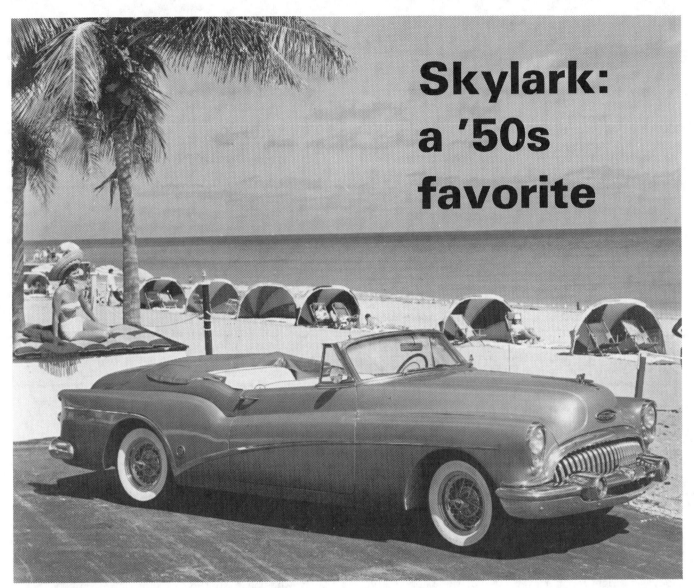

The 1953 Skylark was fittingly described as being like the world of flight on wheels.

By John Gunnell

Somewhere, deep inside any designer who creates a new automobile, lies the soul of an artist. It is the type of soul that won't accept compromise and yearns to create something that's not only beautiful, but truly ahead of its time. A soul that's given over to the boundless flight of the human spirit and imagination.

That the realities of automotive production have a way of limiting the free-flight of creativity cannot be denied. The young artists who flock to Detroit with sketchbooks full of dreams soon enough learn of corporate contingencies and the compromising factors that will dictate the character of their ultimate work. "Dream cars, Hell! You'll do door handle designs and like it!"

And yet, there are those — call them artists or stylists — who, somehow, stand apart. Those who can temper their dreams with a touch of reality and functionality and still bring to life a car that smacks of the future.

Ned F. Nickles was such a man. Enough of a realist to raise to a position of Chief Designer in Buick's postwar styling studios, but still the kind of dreamer who would rig up back-lighted portholes on the hood of his own Buick that flashed in unison with spark plug impulses. Part busi-

nessman and part artist, super-sane and slightly wacky — Nickle's complex personal make-up was one destined to weave a crazy flight pattern over Flint and straight into dreamland.

While Detroit was busy cranking out oversized gunboats in the years following World War II, this tall, long legged lad from Wisconsin was involved in a love affair with imported automobiles like the MG TC and TD and a unique creation known as the Siata. His experience with these cars left Nickles with two distinct impressions; foreign cars looked great, but they left a lot to be desired in terms of comfort. Yet, Nickles was convinced that he could adapt their sports car looks to Detroit made gunboats and transform a Buick into an automotive dreamboat that would incorporate the best features found on both sides of the Atlantic. The idea gave impetus to the flight of the Skylark.

Most automotive historians trace the evolution of the '53 Skylark to Buick's XF-300 dream car, or even back as far as the spectacular Y-Job of 1939. But, if one man had to get credit for each design, it would be Harley Earl for the '39 dream car; Charles A. Chayne (Buick's Chief Engineer in 1950) for the motorama prototype and Ned Nickles for the Skylark. Nickles had a knack for making

117

the type of changes that could easily be incorporated into his own personal cars and therefore economically adapted to production models. His Skylark design exhibited this type of modifications.

The original sketch for the Skylark convertible was made by Nickles on May 3, 1951, and the '53 production version varied very little from that sketch. The story behind the transformation goes as follows: Late in the spring of 1951 Ned had acquired a Roadmaster convertible for his own use. He wanted to make some actual changes in the car's sheetmetal that would personalize it to his own sports car tastes, without costing him a fortune. He sketched a series of pictures tht slightly modified the contours of the car and gave it a continental flavor. He planned to have a body shop alter his car to the lines of his favorite drawing, at his own expense.

The sketch that Nickles favored showed a grey car with red upholstery, featuring a lowered beltline with tapered doors and a cut-down seat. The front and rear wheel openings were enlarged in size and the rear panel was entirely smooth and flush with the body at the bottom. Chrome side trim was slenderized and reworked at the rear to curve up over the enlarged wheel opening and straight to the back of the car. A Buick shield emblem was positioned above the trim in front of the rear wheel well. The design included a chrome fin on the rear fender top, a leather strap on the hood sides, mirrors mounted in the middle of the front fenders and chrome wirewheels. Overall, this sketch had a true sports car look.

Skylark legend has it that the day after the drawings were done, Ivan Wiles, Buick's general manager at the time, happened to see Nickle's work and decided to transfer Ned's ideas to an actual pilot model based on a 1952 Roadmaster drop-top. Work on this car carried out over the next few months.

The pilot model was introduced to the automotive press in the late summer and fall of 1952. At this time, Wiles announced that the Skylark would probably be produced in limited quantities during the coming model year as a premium Buick model. The fact that Ned Nickles tailored the design to fit his own pocketbook was the reason such a decision could be made. This pilot model had a white body with bright red, narrow-pleated cowhide upholstery. The rear deck had a "faster" slope than production Roadmaster convertibles with a smaller trunk emblem mounted at the bottom edge of the trunk. The chrome fins, hood strap and front fender-mounted mirrors were not used on this prototype. Otherwise, it nearly duplicated Ned's original sketch. It was powered by Buick's stock 170 h.p. OHV straight eight, but Wiles hinted that the production model might have a powerful, lighweight, V-8, such as that which motivated the XP-300. This prototype looked more like a "Kalifornia Kustom" of the day, than an imported sports car, but it was sleek, clean and very attractive, and an immediate hit with all who viewed it.

1953 was Buick's Golden Anniversary year and that seemed a perfect reason to bring Nickle's special design into production. To enhance the offering, '53 Skylarks were fitted with many custom features as standard equipment. The engine used was Buick's new 322 cubic inch Fireball V-8 that produced 188 horsepower. It was the third most powerful engine available in any car that year and the highest compression V-8 (8.5:1) offered by the industry. The Skylark's transmission was a new Dynaflow design that had a four-element torque converter and twin turbines. The windshield was "chopped" a full four inches, to make the production car even more racy-looking than Ned's sketches. The Italian-made Borrani wirewheels that the pilot model used were replaced with 40-spoke Kelsey-Hayes versions that looked as good, but were a bit less costly. The price of a '53 Skylark being $4,596 Buick wanted to avoid tagging on some $600 for the imported spokes. But that was the one concession to economy. Other standard equipment included E-Z eye tinted glass, a Delco signal-seeking radio, the two-tone leather upholstery, power steering and power brakes and a clear lucite horn button bearing the owner's signature.

To judge the Skylark's performance, it's necessary to take into consideration two viewpoints, one offered by Wilbur Shaw, who road tested the pilot model for *Popular Science* magazine in Oct. 1952 and one offered in retrospect, by Kyle Given in *Motor Trend*'s September issue twenty years later. Shaw liked the handling of the straight-eight powered prototype and said, "This is no old matron's automobile. There's continental crispness in the ride it gives you. That's what the sports car boys love." He hoped that the addition of a V-8 would improve performance and ultimately lead to a shorter, lower Skylark. In part, his feelings were carried out in the less-admired '54 Skylark, but even the larger appearing '53 was a good handling car for its day and Shaw's comments on the pilot model make this clear. When Givens drove a Skylark in '72, he criticized the handling in light of advances over 20 years in Detroit. He spoke of the huge 211.6" length, the high roll center and narrow track, the 8.00 x 5 4-ply tires and suspension system, typical of the early fifties, that didn't do much for handling. "You can figure it handled about as well as you can figure it did" was what he wrote, while calling the zero to 60 time of 12.1 seconds "adequate." I'm sure it would have seemed even more so to Wilbur Shaw.

In '54, the Skylark became a hot rod as well as a custom car. The Skylark "sports car" designation was transferred to a new place in the revived Century series (last seen in 1942). The 1954 Century models were built on a 122 inch wheelbase shared with the lowest-priced Special series, but used the 322 cubic inch V-8 that powered Supers and Roadmasters. Horsepower on the Dyna-flow Skylark was better, the styling suffered a bit. The wheel openings were enlarged even further to the point where it looked strange. The rear deck sloped drastically downward to match the curve of the rear wheel cut out and globs of chrome were added to the rear, including two shiny, high, grooved fins with a "stuck-on" look. Though prices for the model were cut to $4,100 only 836 '54 models were sold, less than half of the 1,690 total for the cleaner '53.

With the 1955 model year, the Skylark was dropped from Buick's offerings. The model designation later returned, but it never meant quite the same thing again. Nevertheless, the '53 Skylark has become a prized collector's item and a classic of modern automotive artistry. And the artist who created this car, which in its own time was compared to the "world of flight...on wheels!" was a slightly "spacey" sports car pilot named Ned F. Nickles who had the ability to create a state of "dreams come true."

Yesteryear's Reatta — the Skylark

By Robert C. Ackerson

Thirty-eight years ago, Buick celebrated its 50th anniversary by introducing its first production model overhead valve V-8, offering an improved "Twin Turbine" version of its Dynaflow transmission, and for the first time providing air conditioning and power steering as options. But the real attention-grabber was the limited production Buick Skylark convertible.

Buick's error is rather pointedly suggesting the Skylark was a sports car overshadowed the innate attractiveness of the Skylark design. The Skylark was based upon the 125.5 inch wheelbase Roadmaster chassis, which gave it an overall length of 211.6 inches — obviously not in the same class as a 94 inch wheelbase MG TD! The Skylark's underpinning also failed to impress the tweed cap crowd, which spoke in reverent terms of such delight as a DeDion rear suspension. The Skylark's tube drive and rear coil springs were almost, from their viewpoint, laughable.

But the Skylark, regardless of Buick's brash words about it being an "American-built sports car," wasn't intended to attract those drivers who worshipped Lord Nuffield and others of his ilk amidst the leaders of the British automotive industry. Instead it was geared towards American motorists whose automotive jargon was sprinkled with platitudes about cars that "rode like a cloud" and who firmly believed that a "heavy car holds the road better than a light one."

Of course even traditionalists such as these had been affected by the sports car movement then underway in the United States, and thus the Skylark was fitted with the sine qua non of sports cars, wire wheels. Moreover, those found on the Skylark were visual delights.

Provided by Kelsey-Hayes, they were chrome-plated beauties whose 40 spokes were undoubtedly lovingly caressed each Sunday morning as part of the weekend American ritual called "washing the car."

With a base price of $4,596, the Skylark ranked as one of America's most expensive automobiles in 1953. In the Buick lineup, only the Roadmaster Estate Wagon at $4,031 came close. Obviously Buick didn't cut corners when it came to outfitting the Skylark with standard equipment. Found on each of the 1,690 1953 Skylarks built was power steering, windows, seats and radio antenna. Also, Twin Turbine Dynaflow, air conditioning, Selectronic radio, tinted glass and leather upholstery were also installed.

But yesteryear's adolescent car nut didn't have to wait to get a close look inside the Skylark to get excited about this Buick. Granted, the basic Buick body which had last received a sprucing up way back in 1950 was showing its age by 1953. Even in 1950 it had been hard to describe it as particularly exciting. But in Skylark's form, this body took on a surprisingly fresh look.

The changes made to attain this mini-miracle were not extensive. Most apparent was a reduced height windshield (by four inches), giving the Skylark an overall height of less than five feet. Unlike other Buicks with their semi-skirted rear wheels, the Skylark had circular front and rear wheel cutouts that showed off the wire wheels and its wide whitewall 8.00 x 15 tires. Also apparent was the Skylark's notched beltline and slimmed down bodyside chrome spear.

In 1954, Buick once again offered the Skylark but on the shorter 122 inch Century body/chassis. Like the first edition, it was a distinctive automobile but somehow it didn't quite jar the sensations of the beholder as did the 1954 model. Perhaps we were just getting accustomed to special models from Detroit.

1953 Buick Skylark

1953 Buick 72R four-door.

Buick's image changed in 1953

By Robert C. Ackerson

Although the 1953 Buick Roadmaster was touted as a car with "panther-like performance," Buick also described it as possessing power "that pours like a silken Niagara."

In this regard, Buick had revamped its Dynaflow transmission, which for 1953 was promoted as Twin-Turbine Dynaflow. By adding a second turbine and a planetary gearset to Dynaflow, Buick engineering made possible a torque multiplication increase (from 2.25:1 to 2.45:1) of nearly 10 percent as well as an even smoother delivery of power. When starting from a full stop, the first turbine delivered the driving torque, which was multiplied by the planetary gearing. As speed rose and the torque from the first turbine fell, that from the second increased fairly rapidly until at highway cruising speed the second turbine was delivering all the torque to the rear wheels while the second one was free-wheeling with no distinct upshift. Twin-Turbine Dynaflow power delivery was, said Buick "utterly smooth." *Consumer Reports* (May 1953) concurred, explaining that Dynaflow "is very smooth and quiet-much better than it was last year." Although Twin-Turbine-Dynaflow (standard on Roadmaster, optioned at $192 on Specials and Supers) did have a low range that Buick regarded as an emergency low, its greatest shortcoming was the lack of a suitable intermediate driving range. Motor Trend (June 1953) praised Dynaflow's low range for providing "plenty of power under severe driving conditions" but concluded, "it is geared entirely too low for practical use as in mountains." This also made a Twin Turbine Buick inferior to its competition in high-speed acceleration.

The sole example of Buick's straight-eight heritage available in 1953 was found in the lowest-priced Special series. As it had for many years, the Buick Special offered

Buick prestige and features at a very competitive price. The two-door sedan was Buick's price leader at $2,196.88. Other Special models were priced at $2,255.32 (four-door sedan), $2,295.43 (hardtop coupe) and $2,553.17 (convertible). Its engine, which had debuted back in 1950 as the Super's F-263 engine, displaced 263.6 cubic inches and was rated at 125 h.p. (7:1 compression ratio) when linked to a manual transmission or 130 h.p. (7.5:1 compression ratio) when Dynaflow was installed. With a road weight of 4,000 pounds, the Special's power to weight ratio of 32:1 promised leisurely performance that was born out by its zero to 60 m.p.h. time of 19 plus seconds.

Buick's torque tube and four-wheel coil springs were intended to provide (in Buick's words) a "suave and gentle ride." Nonetheless, Floyd Clymer reported *(Popular Mechanics*, June 1953), "For a large American car, the Super handles well on corners." As had earlier been the case, there were plenty of gripes about Buick's power steering. No one was complaining about the ease it brought to wheeling a two-ton Buick down Main Street but, said *Motor Trend* (June 1953) it "gave the impression of having no physical connection between the steering wheel and the front wheels."

Since the 1953 models represented the tail-end of the Buick styling cycle that had begun in 1949, there were no dramatic changes awaiting their buyers. However the '53s were easily identified by their XP-300-derived headlight/parking light arrangement and twin bullet shaped taillights. Buick's familiar bombsight hood ornament was lowered into a chromed (on Super and Roadmaster models) valley, and on V-8-engined models was joined by a chrome "V." Less obvious was the replacement of Buick's "open from either side" hood with a convention rear-hinged unit. Far more serious, however, was the

120

1953 Buick Model 59 station wagon.

problem that befell some Roadmasters equipped with power brakes when the rubber O-ring sealing the master cylinders from the vacuum cylinder failed. In a very short period of time, the brake fluid was pumped out of the brake lines and into the engine!

Buick quickly developed an improved O-ring and notified its dealers to replace the O-rings on all 1953 Buick Roadmasters brought into their shops. With wider 2¼-inch (up from 1¾-inch) brake drums, on Special and Super models, Buick's overall braking performance was improved from 1952's level. For example, whereas a 1952 Roadmaster tested by *Motor Trend* needed 239 feet to stop from 60 m.p.h., a 1953 Super stopped from the same speed in just under 191 feet. Not all of this improved braking performance could be credited to the Buick's larger brakes however, since the older model at 4,530 pounds outweighed the 1953 Super by approximately 230 pounds.

General Motors described the Wildcat, Buick's contribution to its 1953 Motorama Dream Car collection, as "a single-seat sports convertible of futuristic design." The Wildcat wasn't, unlike the Corvette, destined for production, but its name was recycled not only for use on future GM dream cars, but nearly 20 years later would be applied to a sharp performing, good looking full-sized Buick. In its original dream car form, the Wildcat had a 114-inch wheelbase and an overall length of 192 inches. Critics who were quick to point out the foibles of American design and styling efforts had a field day with the Wildcat's "Roto-Static" front wheel discs that remained stationary as the wheels turned. But the Wildcat also reflected to those observers with somewhat greater objectivity Buick's growing interest in building automobiles with improved roadability and overall performance. For example, its front suspension had zero-degree caster, vertical kingpins and direct-action shocks. At the rear, Buick's familiar coil springs featured new radius rods. The Wildcat's engine-transmission power train was pure stock 188 h.p. V-8 and Twin Turbine Dynaflow, but its power steering operated through a fairly quick 15:1 over ratio instead of the normal 23:1.

Although honors as Buick's 7,000,000th production automobile went to a Roadmaster sedan in June 1953, the Buick that really stood out as the flagship of its 50th anniversary fleet was the Skylark convertible. Like Wild-

cat, this was a name that would return to play a major role in Buick's modern history, but in 1953 it was applied to a low-production (1690) convertible that Buick said was "like the world of flight...on wheels." Buick was off base in referring to the Skylark as "a six-passenger sports car" since its basic mechanics and suspension were pure stock Roadmaster components. In other words, a 121.5 inch wheelbase and 4,300 pound road weight were not compatable with road performance usually associated with small European sports cars. But if regarded more realistically as a low volume (and at $4,596 expensive) Buick, which combined sporty styling with the luxury features common to American convertibles, the Skylark was an extremely interesting automobile. Its interior was offered with leather upholstery (available in four colors) and such features as Selectric radio with foot control, electric antenna, Twin-Turbine Dynaflow, power steering and brakes were standard equipment for the Skylark. The Skylark's steering wheel center proclaimed 1953 as Buick's 50th anniversary by depicting in silhouette an antique Buick that was soon indentified as a 1904 model by Buick historians. But, no doubt more satisfying to the ego of the Skylark's proud owner was the inscription encircling the old Buick that filled the blank in the inscription: "Skylark customized for ——————" with his or her signature. But no one had to peer into the Skylark's interior to get the message that it was a very special Buick. That was very nicely conveyed by a profile four inches lower than a standard Roadmaster convertible, the elimination of the fender portholes, and a very graceful side spear that nicely harmonized with the Skylark's fender and door lines. Although critics were quick to remind us that "wire wheels do not a sports car make," those on the Skylark were absolutely stunning. When the prototype Skylark appeared in July 1952, it was fitted with Borrani wire wheels, but production models used a 40-spoke chrome-plated version by Kelsey-Hayes.

Buick promoted the Skylark as an automobile "especially styled for those who want exclusiveness plus the complete modernity of Buick's Golden Anniversary automobiles," and beyond any doubt it handsomely delivered on that claim. But just ahead was a whole new generation of Buicks with trim sharp styling, a name returning in glory from the past and an exciting new performance image.

Its beauty is just the beginning

THIS joyous thing of exquisite grace is the Skylark — Buick's stunning new luxury sports car.

Yet the gorgeous beauty of this motorcar is just the beginning of the deep excitement.

For it's a Buick. And in any Buick, the real heart-lift you get is from the manner of its going — impeccably smooth, gentle of ride, superbly easy to handle, trigger-quick in response.

Upon the Skylark, we have lavished practically every modern automotive advance — including the world's newest V8 Engine, Twin-Turbine Dynaflow, Power Steering, Power Brakes, hydraulic control of the radio antenna, windows, top, and front-seat adjustment.

In other Buicks — SPECIAL, SUPER and ROADMASTER — many of these advances are yours either as standard equipment, or as options at moderate extra cost.

But in all Buicks — even the low-priced SPECIAL — you get the Buick Million Dollar Ride, Buick room, Buick comfort, Buick Fireball power—the highest horsepowers and compression ratios, Series for Series, in all Buick history.

Your Buick dealer is waiting to seat you at the wheel of the car that will do fullest justice to your dreams and your purse. See him this week.

BUICK *Division of* GENERAL MOTORS

When better automobiles are built Buick will build them

The greatest
BUICK
in 50 great years

This ad shows off the 1953 Buick Skylark.

1954 Buick 76R Roadmaster.

Buick Roadmaster had it all in the '50s

By Tom LaMarre

"Roadmaster"—in the 1950s this one word said it all. It evoked an image of pure comfort, effortless power, and posh luxury, four-holer style. And no car was more deserving of the name than the 1954 model.

Its styling was all new, but the design was definitely in the Buick tradition. For starters, the Roadmaster was much bigger than its 1953 counterpart. Its overall length was 216.8 inches, compared to 207.6 inches for the 1953 Roadmaster, and its wheelbase grew 5½ inches to 127 inches. But the Roadmaster was impressive for more reasons than size alone.

Contributing to its good looks was a "Panoramic" wrap-around windshield, which blended in very nicely with the Riviera hardtop. In addition, the Roadmaster convertible (model 76-C) and Riviera coupe (model 76-R) featured full rear wheel openings similar to those of the '53 Skylark. And the sweepspear moldings accented them perfectly.

The smaller openings on the Roadmaster Riviera sedan (model 72-R) gave it a more formal appearance.

All Roadmasters used a 322 cubic inch engine that produced automatic transmission, it gave the 4,214 pound Riviera coupe one s-m-o-o-t-h ride. With new steering linkage and a redesigned power steering unit, the Buick also had easier handling.

Inside, the most noticeable aspect of the Roadmaster was its chrome trim. The bands on the front seat were a focal point for anyone entering the car, but from that point on the new dashboard was the center of attention. The center band of the dash was engine-turned stainless steel, with the upper and lower areas of the dashboard finished in the body color. Even the headliner was not neglected, having chrome bands.

1954 turned out to be one of Buick's best years ever; model year production reached 444,609 units. The Roadmaster production figures by model were: coupe, 20,404 units; sedan, 26,862 units; and convertible, 3,305 units.

1951 Buick 76 Roadmaster Riviera, probably a prototype. Note parking lights.

Buick's romantic Riviera

By R. Perry Zavitz

Buick's first Riviera appeared in 1949, as GM's first hardtop. Based on the Roadmaster, it featured a non-removable steel roof on a convertible type body, and this model is a certified Milestone car.

The Riviera name has been in use by Buick ever since, though it almost faded completely from the scene in the early 1960s. As a distinct model, the Riviera lasted only during the 1949 model year. For 1950, the Riviera was restyled and offered in both the Super and Roadmaster series—hardtops, of course.

A Special Riviera was introduced in the 1951 line, but the name was also applied to the Super and Roadmaster four-door sedans. All these Rivieras continued through 1954, and in that year a Riviera was offered in the revived Century series.

The Riviera title was given only to the hardtops of 1955. The same was true for 1956, but in that year it also included the newly introduced four-door hardtops. Ditto for 1957, with the addition of the four-door hardtop Estate Wagon in the Special line. The similar model in the Century series was not called Riviera, but Caballero. Riviera was applied to the same 1958 models, as well as the two and four-door hardtops of the top luxury Limited line. That totalled 11 Riviera models, a record number for one year.

Completely new styling with completely new nomenclature marked the 1959 Buicks. The Riviera name was almost swept out with the old model names, but did manage to remain on one model, an Electra 225 four-door. Identifiable by its different roof style, this Riviera continued on through 1962.

After 1962 the Electra 225 model was called the four-

The 4-Door Riviera

It's what America wanted
—and it's going great guns

You see pictured here an automobile long awaited and long expected by the nation's car buyers.

It is a Riviera — the "hardtop" that Buick pioneered for the entire industry six years ago.

But it is a Riviera with separate doors for the rear-seat passengers — and that's the combination now taking the country by storm.

It's easy to see why.

Folks wanted the sleek and racy "convertible look" styling of the hardtop—but they wanted it with the room, comfort and convenience of a true 4-door sedan. *And here they have it all* . . .

The full and open airiness of the Riviera . . .

A completely unobstructed view to both sides, with no center doorposts above the window line . . .

The extra-generous legroom, headroom and hiproom of a full-sized Buick Sedan . . .

Front doors *and* rear doors — and all four of them hinged at their front edges for greater safety, and to assure easy entrance and exit.

But not by a long shot is that all.

This new kind of automobile is coming off the production line in the two lowest-priced Buick Series—the budget-tagged SPECIAL and the supremely-powered CENTURY.

So you get the last word in automobiles with the sizzling might of a V8 engine of 188-hp or 236-hp. You get it with the spectacular performance and better gas mileage of the new Variable Pitch Dynaflow.* *And you get it with the easy-to-take prices that have helped sweep Buick into the top circle of America's best sellers.*

Why not take a firsthand look at the newest idea in new cars? With demand for the 4-Door Riviera pushing production capacity to the limit, the sooner you see it—and place your order—the sooner you can have one for your very own.

*Dynaflow Drive is standard on Roadmaster, optional at extra cost on other Series.

MILTON BERLE STARS FOR BUICK—See the Buick-Berle Show
Alternate Tuesday Evenings

Thrill of the year is Buick

See Your Buick Dealer

1955 Buick ad features the four-door Riviera.

1965 Buick Riviera. Inset: 1961 LeSabre four-door hardtop.

door six-window hardtop. This released the Riviera name so it could be used on a unique new Buick model. It was "America's bid for a new international classic car," a brochure hopefully stated.

The new Riviera was offered only as a two-door hardtop. Its styling—identifiably GM— was very neat and conservative, yet contemporary. In size, the Riviera fit between the small Special and the full size Buicks. It had a 117 inch wheelbase and was 208 inches long overall.

The engine was the 401 cid V-8 used in all full size Buicks of that year. However, the Riviera's was the four-barrel caburetor, 10.25:1 compression version, standard in the Wildcat and Electra 225 models.

Standard equipment in the Riviera included Turbine Drive automatic transmission, power brakes, power steering, and distinctive wire type wheel covers. The Riviera price was $4,333, topped only by the Electra convertible of the 1963 Buicks. Options included power windows for $107.50, radio and antenna $90.30, and air-conditioning at $430. An even 40,000 Rivieras were built for 1963.

Except for the Riviera "R" symbol added to the hood ornament, hubs and taillights, virtually no changes were made in the appearance of the 1964 model. There were a number of other changes, however. The engine displacement was increased to 425 cubic inches, and horsepower

was accordingly rated at 340. For $139.75, a dual carb version with dual exhausts was offered, having 360 advertised horsepower. That was the industry's most powerful '64 engine rating, except for one or two Corvette options. Buick's new Super Turbine 400 automatic transmission was standard.

The interior was changed a bit, with a few controls relocated. Some people feel that the 1964 model was cheapened somewhat. For this reason the '64 Riviera failed to receive Milestone status, while the '63 edition did. The '64 Riviera will no doubt be renominated, and perhaps yet become a certified Milestone. The difference between the two models hardly seems extensive enough to allow one the Milestone designation, but not the other.

Two new options were offered on the '64 models. For $70.95, power seats could be had, and for $43 a tilting steering wheel was available. Base price of the Riviera was raised a bit to $4,374 and production slipped slightly to 37,658.

Noticeable exterior changes were made to the 1965 model. The body was basically unchanged, but headlights were hidden behind the shields in leading edges of front fenders. This allowed for a cleaner looking grille of similar criss-cross pattern as previously. The simulated air intake indentations just ahead of the rear wheels were removed,

Split personality

Two Rivieras illustrate a point—that the Riviera is a car with two distinct personalities.
For some people it's the most beautiful car around. Then there's another group, equally audible, who insist
it's not so much how the Riviera looks but what it does. And they have quite a case. The
whole idea behind the Riviera was to put some adventure back in driving. We knew we'd succeeded
with at least one man when he told us, "I felt like I was driving a car for the first time." Which group is
right? Which is the real Riviera? You decide. Get in touch with your Buick dealer
and decide in the comfort of a Riviera's left front bucket seat. If you
decide to take the car home with you, the price he quotes will come as a happy surprise.

THE RIVIERA BY BUICK  AMERICA'S BID FOR A GREAT NEW INTERNATIONAL CLASSIC CAR

1963 Riviera advertisement.

which cleaned the side appearance. New wheel covers were fitted, and 8.45 x 15 tires replaced the former 7.10 x 15's. The '65 Riviera grew one inch in length to 209 inches.

Three engines were available on the '65 models. The 325 hp engine (returned from '63) was standard. At $48.38 extra, the 340 hp motor (standard in the '64s) was offered. The optional 360 hp engine of '64 was offered in the 65s for a $219.30 premium.

Actually, that $219.30 bought more than the Super Wildcat engine. Rivieras so equipped were called Gran Sport, or GS. The Riviera GS had a Gran Sport nameplate below the Riviera script on the front fenders; ribbed chrome trim covered the sills and bottoms of the doors. Instead of the new wheel covers, the former wire wheel covers or chromed steel wheels were GS option. A 3.42 ratio limited-slip rear axle was standard, instead of the 3.23 on the regular model. A 3.58 ratio was optional on the GS. A slightly more sumptuous interior was a Gran Sport feature.

The standard Riviera price edged up to $4,408, but that included a tilting steering wheel, formerly an option. Production again dropped, but 34.586 Rivieras for 1965 was a respectable quantity.

Riviera's first completely restyled body appeard on the 1966 model. (Actually the body was shared with Oldsmobile's new front-wheel-drive Toronado.) Riviera retained rear wheel drive, but each division made numerous changes to the common body and avoided a sameness. Riviera wheelbase and overall length were increased 2 and 2¼ inches respectively.

Engine choices were reduced to one—the 340 hp mill. The Riviera GS had the same engine, but with chrome plated air cleaner, cast aluminum rocker arm covers, heavy duty suspension, model identification, etc. for $176.82 more.

The slightly roomier interior was redesigned as well, with a choice of bench or bucket front seats, the passenger side reclining in either case. The basic price inched upward, as might be expected, to $4,424. Despite the less distinctive styling of the 1966 Riviera, a new production record of 45,348 units was set.

After a completely new body for 1966, the 1967 Riviera emerged virtually unchanged. A thicker horizontal middle bar in the grille was one of the more evident differences. Under the hood, the engine displacement was increased to 430 cubic inches and horsepower upped to 360. No engine options were available.

The Gran Sport was available, but as in '66 it was really a trim option rather than a higher performance model. With a basic list price of $4,469, Riviera sales dropped slightly. Production was 42,799 for its second best year up to then.

The 1968 Riviera featured a redesigned front bumper, completely surrounding the revamped grille. The grillework was of a squared pattern, more like the earlier years, and headlights remained hidden. Large retangular parking lights in the ends of the bumper lent a look of mystery to the car. It would seem that the new front bumper is what added four inches, making the Riviera 215.2 inches overall.

The engine remained basically unchanged. Front disc brakes were available at $78.94. The Gran Sport, at $131.57 extra was offered with the usual superficial goodies. The biggest interior change for '68 was the redesign and more easily read instrument panel. Riviera's base price was $4,589, and a new production record of 49,284 was set.

Very little change took place for the 1969 model. Different grille pattern on the exterior and better quality trim on the interior just about sum up the changes. The same engine powered the car, and usual GS items were featured in that optional package.

The price changed more than the car — up to $4,683. Surprisingly, the combination of ever increasing prices and three years of minimal change brought about an all time production high. A total of 52,872 Rivieras were built for the '69 model year.

The last year for the Riviera's second body was 1970. Once more the front end was restyled, headlights were brought out into the open, and the wide rectangular grille had many thin vertical bars, some of which extended down into the bumper. It looked like it could have been inspired by the buck-tooth Buick of 1950, though much more refined.

On the sides, the greatest change was the addition of rear fender skirts, which made the car look rather tail heavy. Two very thin strips of chrome formed a subtle Buick spear sweep.

A different engine powered the 1970 Rivieras. It was a 455 cid motor of 370 hp. The Riviera GS continued as a trim option. List price of the basic model was up (again) — to $4,854. However, production took an almost 30 percent plunge to 37,336.

New and much more distinctive Riviera styling followed the 1970 model. We will not deal with the most recent models, except to say that, all have brought a new degree of distinction and personality to the whole Buick line, and they have been consistent with the luxury and pleasure associated with that area of France called the Riviera. Perhaps the Rivieras have been the better automobiles Buick has promised us for so many years.

1955 Century...

1955 Buick Century Riviera.

...it could top 100 mph

By Tom LaMarre

For 1955, Buick boasted the highest horsepower, series for series, in its history. And the fastest Buick series of all was the Century.

Standard equipment on the Century included a trip meter, redliner speedometer, electric clock, automatic trunk light, and rear license plate frame. Like all '55 Buicks, it had a new widescreen grille and rakish taillights. In addition to leather upholstery, the Century convertible came with power windows and seat.

But it was the Century's preformance that appealed to many people. Packed under its hood was the same 322-cubic inch V-8 used in the Roadmaster, with a 9:1 compression ratio, it produced 236 hp at 4600 rpm. Yet the Century was built on the short 122-inch Special wheelbase instead of the 127-inch Roadmaster and Super wheelbase. At 207 inches, the overall length of the Century was nine inches shorter than its big brothers. The combination of the big Buick engine and the Century's light weight resulted in a top speed of 110 mph.

Century prices ranged from $2,548 to $3,175, contributing to Buick's claim that it offered more horsepower per dollar than any other American car. The line included a four-door sedan, Riviera hardtop sedan, convertible, Riviera hardtop coupe, two-door sedan, and four-door wagon. The hardtop sedan, a new body style, had a production run of 55,088, a figure that was surpassed in the

Century series only by the hardtop coupe. The Riviera coupe weighed 3,805 pounds and sold for $2,601; 80,338 were built.

"It's instantaneous response on getaway. It's absolute smoothness through every single speed range. It's far greater gas mileage in all normal cruising and driving. It's electrifying safety-surge for sudden acceleration to get out of a tight spot on the highway. It's a supreme thrill, and a joy, and a blessing." Perhaps Buick ads did go a bit overboard. But 1955 turned out to be a record year for the division, with model year production of 738,814 units. Of that total, 158,796 were Centurys.

Specifications:
1955 Buick Century Riviera

Series	Century
Factory Price	$2,601
Weight	3,805 pounds
Wheelbase	122 inch
Overall length	207 inch
Engine	322 cubic inch V-8
BHP	236 at 4600 rpm
Bor and Stroke	4 x 3.2 inch bore
C.R.	9:1
Carburetor	Carter 4-barrel
Tires	7.60 x 15
Production Total	80,338
No. 1 Value	$4,500

It's the Hardtop with 4 Doors!

Another big reason for Buick's soaring sales is the 4-Door Riviera — the new hit in hardtops that's taking the country by storm. The "Convertible" look — but with separate doors for rear-seat passengers. Shown here in the high-powered CENTURY model — also available in the low-price SPECIAL Series. Both now in volume production to insure prompt deliveries.

When it's your will – you're away!

(*Variable Pitch Dynaflow** is taking the country by storm!*)

It happens that quick!

The need comes up, your foot goes down — and you get full power go-ahead in the split of a second.

That's what people by the hundreds of thousands are discovering about Buick's spectacular Variable Pitch Dynaflow . . .

That it's a great new kind of thrill never known before in an automobile . . .

That it's really a leaf taken right from the modern plane's variable pitch propeller . . .

That you drive and cruise with far better gas mileage — like a pilot does aloft . . .

And that just by pressing the pedal way down, you switch the pitch of Dynaflow's propeller-like blades for instant getaway response or safety-surge acceleration when the need arises — as a pilot does for take-off and climb.

Surely, you ought to try this sensational transmission that *Motor Life* Magazine says is "three blocks ahead of the rest of the industry."

You ought to try what goes with it, too — brilliant new V8 power raised to record highs — the soft and solid steadiness of Buick's all-coil-spring ride — the lift and sparkle and comfort that come of Buick styling, Buick luxury, Buick size and structure and handling ease.

And most certainly you ought to look into the "great buy" prices that are helping Buick sales soar to all-time best-seller highs.

Drop in for a visit with us this week to check things for yourself — and to see how Buick's biggest year permits the biggest trade-in allowances ever.

* *Variable Pitch Dynaflow is the only Dynaflow Buick builds today. It is standard on ROADMASTER, optional at modest extra cost on other Series.*

When better automobiles are built Buick will build them

Thrill of the year is Buick

S E E   Y O U R   B U I C K   D E A L E R

Thrilling 1955 Buick Century Riviera four-door ad.

1956 Buick 46-C convertible.

The 1956 Buick 46-C

By Ned Comstock

In 1956 in the barn behind the Old House where I lived in Upstate New York there were two new cars. They were both convertibles, each had cost $2,995 give or take a $100. Both would see you to 60 in 10 seconds and hold 100 miles an hour on the straight. They were both painted bright red. The Buick had scarlet vinyl upholstery, too; and I remember thinking that a little flamboyant but maybe good in an accident, it wouldn't show the blood. The Porsche Continental 1500 Speedster was the reddest red I ever saw, a deep glowing cherry red, but inside everything was black. Everything else was different from Buick, too.

Now, I am a great Buick believer. The roadways of this country are worn deep with Buick wheel tracks. Buick is the rock on which General Motors was founded. Nothing on wheels has a better record of service over the years than Buick. But I'm also prepared to defend the proposition that no two automobiles ever loose on the road at the same time were as different from each other as 1956 Porsche Speedster and 1956 Buick Special 46-C convertible.

Buick 46-C was called small. You could tell right away it was the small Buick because it flaunted only three imitation exhaust ports on each side of the hood. It was not a Four Holer. They were Roadmasters, and cost another $750, weighed another 750 pounds. But inside the 121 inch Special wheelbase there was lounging room for four, and you could if you wanted carry six in comfort. And 46-C boasted the big 322 inch engine block, was prepared to deliver 220 horses on demand. Through the new, tight Dynaflow its response was prompt and sharp. Pulling 3,880 pounds only, a little over 17 per horsepower, Buick 46-C convertible was packed with power. When you pushed the pedal down, power would gush out in torrents up the speed range until three figures stood plain on the bar-style speedometer.

Porsche Speedster was really small. Fifty-five DIN horsepower was carefully tucked into an 83 inch wheelbase package that weighed in at 1,610 pounds dry — one quarter the horsepower, one third less in inches and 40 percent of the pounds of 1956 "small" Buick 46-C. There were bucket seats for two, and a rear emergency seat "which has no back rest" the driver's manual warned. It stood 48 inches high, stark in its skin without embellishment. And in 1956, it could get anywhere quicker than anything else on wheels.

Which brings an interesting question: How could the German Porsche and the American Buick seek solutions so different to the same problem of high performance personal transportation? Probably there's three answers: The special genius of Ferdinand Porsche to which Buick had no answer, the vast bank of natural resources in America to which Porsche had no answer, and the way Germans think differently about their cars than Americans do.

From the beginning Germans thought of a sports car driver as rugged, like Nietzsche's Superman and as daring as Baron Von Richthofen. This hero rode all alone — he would no more take his family when he went prowling than General Rommel would have tucked the kids in his Kubelwagen. Germans left their families home and that's why their sports cars never got big and fat.

But most of all, Porsche Speedster's top show what kind of drivers Germans were. The top was something thrown over the car like a blanket, on a horse to protect the horse from the weather. It was not for driving. There was really no room underneath it for a driver. If you put it up, it was as though someone had grabbed your cap by the visor and pulled it down over your eyes. Underneath you couldn't see much in the daytime, less at night and in the frost your breath in that tiny airspace promptly condensed and froze on the glass, and you could see nothing. It flapped viciously at speed, and made entrance to the

car a feat of contortion. If you were "too tall" your Porsche dealer would tell you that support rails under the seat could be removed, leaving you two inches "more headroom", and sitting flat on the floor, legs straight out and acutely uncomfortable. Clearly when Dr. Porsche put a top on his Continental Speedster he did it to protect the car in case it were left out in the rain. But it was not for driving. You drove with the top down.

In the years between the wars, German high politicians thundered over the autobans in leather helmets and flight jackets, always with the top on the Mercedes folded flat. There were no concession to creature comforts then and there was none in Porsche Speedster in 1956, either. In Germany, sports cars were not for sissies.

Instead of comfort Porsche Speedster seduced you with mechanical excellence that the 1956 generation had not seen before in this country. Maybe the 1949 Cadillac engine was of Porsche design quality. But you had to go back to Leland-built Lincoln to find an American automobile like Porsche. Of course, the Leland's concept did not last in America. Devoted so single-mindedly to superlative engineering Leland-Lincolns came out ugly ducklings, no survivors in the market place. When Henry Ford took over, he tired of the losses. He bred Lincoln with Detroit style to sell it. But for a while, in 1920-1925 maybe Leland-Lincolns were so refined, the machinery so tuned and the design so perfect that the car seemed at certain speeds to float weightless, like a glider. Porsche Speedster was like that. It ran so light.

They sell Speedster replicas somewhere, in California I think. They get $6,500 for them, a fine bargain now, but they are not Porsche-Porsche. God knows what it would cost to build Speedsters the way Ferdinand Porsche did, on a bench, one engine at a time. And fit everything so superbly that a Porsche driver in 1956 could almost believe the car was part of him.

Steering was like pointing your finger, 14 to one, actually 1:14.15 the manual said; two point three turns lock to lock. By contrast you wound 1956 Buick over twice as far for direction change, which came slowly as in an old motor boat.

Shifting came naturally in a Porsche Speedster. The tach was right up in front of your face, and you drove by that, really. Driving turned into an exercise in maintaining steady revs where freest. Second was best for traffic, you could sweep out and around anything on the highway ahead of you in third, anything up to 80 anyway; and settle down to cruise at any speed in overdrive, always with the engine happy and the tachometer steady. You played

on those gears like a musical instrument. *Automobile Quarterly* has said somewhere that the shift was so light you felt as though it had disconnected itself. But it hadn't. In the six years I drove two lovely Porsches 100,000 miles nothing ever went wrong. Until at last my then son-in-law at Harvard under ran the rear end of a truck; but that is another story.

Ferdinand Porsche's mind was on his car, not on his customers. He knew the best design would speak for itself. But also in central Europe after the war, he knew he was limited. His market was limited, his access to raw materials was limited and so was his capital.

So when Ferdinand Porsche looked for a market for a quality design he knew there was no market for super cars, and he didn't have wherewithall to build them. Instead he decided to do the best he could with what he had. What came out was Porsche. And Porsche Continental 1500 Speedster, perhaps the purest Porsche of all. Just automobile. No gimmick, no gadgets not even any comforts. Just the best Ferdinand Porsche could do with what he had, in 1956.

But Buick, Buick was different. Buick was dealing from strength. Because the middle class is strongest here, Buick wasn't cheap and it wasn't high priced. Because America is rich in raw materials Buick was oversized everywhere, including its appetite for fuel. And because General Motors knows what it is doing, Buick 46-C delivered what Americans wanted most. At Buick they thought of customers first.

Performance was there. George Dammon says (*Seventy Years of Buick*) Buick was the quickest car that year, either from the stop light or cruising the prairies. The heaviest Buicks could reach 60 mph in under 12 seconds, pass from 50 to 70 in under seven. All 1946's could top 110 mph, Dammon claims.

Americans wanted room for the whole family and Buick had that, too. There were no two seater Buicks after World War II. All would carry six and their luggage. Styling was added like frosting. Gone was the mailed fist motif of 1950, but the massive locomotive look was still there.

Buick 46-C convertible had its shortcomings. All that engine dumped out on the front axle put it down by the bow, and without power steering you never forgot it. You missed traction sometimes, too; like a light loaded pickup. But that Buick was built like a battle cruiser and asked no quarter from anybody, ever.

And Porsche Speedster? She was a lady. Some people like ladies best.

The Special four-door sedan cost $2,660 and weighed 4,012 pounds. A total of 59,739 were made.

By Tom LaMarre

There was no danger of anyone mistaking the 1957 Buick; an ornament with the date was at the center of the car's grille. However, this detail wasn't really necessary, for the '57 was a one-year only design.

Perhaps the date on the grille was just a matter of pride — for Buick itself and the purchaser. A more practical touch was the safety-buzzer, standard on the Roadmaster and optional in all other series. Buick advertising explained, ''Just dial the number you wish to stay under — 35, 40, 50 — and the Safety-Buzzer buzzes when you get there!'' A new advanced variable pitch Dynaflow transmission was also standard on the Roadmaster, Super and Century.

Buick's new models for '57 were the Caballero wagons with hardtop styling and the luxurious Roadmaster 75, available in Riviera coupe and sedan form. Powering all Buicks was a new 364-cubic inch engine. But in Special models it had a 9.5 to 1 compression ratio and developed 250 hp at 4400 rpm, while the other Buick series featured a 10 to 1 compression ratio and 300 hp.

It was the Special that proved to be the most popular series. Of the total model year production of 405,086 cars, 220,700 were Specials. The range included a four-door sedan, Riviera hardtop sedan, convertible coupe, two-door sedan, four-door wagon and Caballero wagon. Prices ranged from $2,596 for the two-door sedan to $3,167 for the Caballero wagon. The Special shared the 122 inch wheelbase of the Century, compared to the 127.5 inch wheelbase of the Super and Roadmaster. Buick retained 15 inch wheels, bucking the trend toward 14 inch wheels.

It is estimated that Buick spent several hundred million dollars retooling for the '57 models. Nevertheless, calendar year production was down 24 percent from the previous year.

1957 Buick: dated for posterity

Buick SUPER 4-Door Riviera

When better automobiles are built Buick will build them

Roomiest hit in the Style Parade

(Step in and s-t-r-e-t-c-h

—it's the Buick SUPER—and what a dream car <u>to</u> <u>drive</u>!)

WE COULD give you facts and figures, chapter and verse, about the '57 Buick as the *roomiest* of America's best-selling cars.

And that's doubly true of the Buick SUPER pictured here.

Just step into a Buick SUPER—move your arms, relax your shoulders, cross your legs.

Then you'll know comfort that gets sweeter the longer you're there—and

styling that looks smarter the longer you stare.

But that's only the start of the thrills you'll find in this most completely changed Buick in history. The real excitement comes from performance that makes this the dream car *to drive.*

Power? You have it, in abundance— for you boss more might than ever gave vigor to a Buick before.

Response? Like nothing in an earth-

bound vehicle. For you have the instant action of today's new Dynaflow.*

Ride? Handling? Roadability? Braking? Try 'em and see!

Ask your Buick dealer for a demonstration—and for figures that make Buick your best buy today.

BUICK *Division of* GENERAL MOTORS

*New Advanced Variable Pitch Dynaflow is the only Dynaflow Buick builds today. It is standard on Roadmaster, Super and Century — optional at modest extra cost on the Special

Only Buick brings you this built-in "conscience"
SAFETY-BUZZER

—a simple device that's a great boon to your safety. You merely preset the miles-per-hour you want. When you reach that pace, a warning buzzer sounds. Drop below that pace and the buzzer stops. Standard on ROADMASTER, optional at extra cost on other Series.

Big Thrill's Buick

SPECIAL · CENTURY · SUPER · ROADMASTER · and ROADMASTER 75

1957 Buick Super Riviera four-door is spotlighted in this old advertisement.

By Tom LaMarre

When Buick brought out its super luxury line for 1958, it was only fitting that the Limited name be revived. This was to be the ultimate Buick, an auto that infringed on the turf of Cadillac and Lincoln.

The Limited line was comprised of three models; the Riviera coupe (Model 755), the Riviera sedan (Model 750) and the convertible (Model 756). All three were built on the 127.5 inches wheelbase Roadmaster chassis. However, the overall length of the Limited was stretched out to 227 inches. No wonder the Buick's advertising proclaimed, "Even in the matter of its extra length the Limited goes beyond the call of familiar dimensions."

According to many critcs, the extensive use of chrome and stainless trim went beyond the call of good taste. Buick Limited owners today, however, pay no atention to the assertion that the '58 Limited was one of the least attractive Buicks of all time. They know better.

In an age when plastic grilles are the rule, who cannot admire or as least be amazed by the 160 individual chrome plated metal squares used in the 1958 Limited's grille? There was no danger of stone chips behind the rear wheels; massive chrome gravel shields extended from the wheel openings to the bumper. Adorning the quarter panels were three groupings of angled chrome strips, with four ribs in each section. The Limited also featured chrome ribs over the taillights. Instead of a customary Buick bombsight hood ornament, fender-mounted bombsights were used. Gone were the traditional portholes, but the familiar sweepspear molding was retained.

If the name "Limited" brought to mind a locomotive, the image was consistent with the car's weight. The sedan tipped the scales at 4,710 pounds. Power was provided by a 364 cubic inch V-8 with a 10:1 compression radio and 300 hp. Dynaflow was standard and an air suspension system could be ordered.

With prices ranging from $5,002 for the Limited Riviera coupe to $5,125 for the Limited convertible, Buick's top of the line series was priced higher than the Lincoln Capri line and the Series 62 Cadillac hardtop coupe and hardtop sedan.

With only 839 units built, the convertible is the rarest of the Limiteds. A total of 1,026 coupes and 5,571 sedans were made.

Buick's Limited meant super-luxury motoring

1958 Buick Limited two-door hardtop.

135

1958 Buick Limited four-door hardtop.

'58 Limited — a big postwar Buick

By Bill Siuru

In the chrome era of the later '50s cars grew bigger and bigger. General Motors' products reached huge proportions in both bulk and in the mass of chrome ornamentation. However, probably no car stereotypes the era better than the 1958 Buick Limited series.

The 1958 Buick Limited was one of the largest postwar Buicks. At an overall length of 227.2 inches, it was about four inches longer than the equally huge 1958 Cadillac (except for limousines). The Limited rode on the same 127-½ inch wheelbase as the Super and Roadmaster models, but was eight inches longer.

The added inches went into trunk and tail. In 1958, the Roadmaster had been reduced one notch in the Buick pecking order. For 1958, Buick resurrected the Limited nameplate. It hadn't been used on Buicks since 1942. The next year, when Buick completely revised its model nomenclature, the Roadmaster and Limited were replaced, respectively, by the Electra and Electra 225.

In the glitter department, the Limited not only had the gobs of chrome adornment found on all the 1958 Buicks, but also its own distinguishing ornamentation. Like all 1958 Buicks, there were the 160 chrome "drawer pulls" that made up the grille and the chrome side spears. The Limited had its unique massive louvered taillamps and twelve simulated louvers within the rocket-like rear quarter panel. There were the words "Limited" written in script on the quarter panel or rear doors. About the only trim missing was the familiar ventaports that had been a Buick trademark since 1949. This was the first year they weren't used, but they would return in 1960. The year 1958 was also the first for quad headlights on Buicks.

Under the Limited's hood was a 300 hp, 364 cid V-8. The engine used a 10:1 compression ratio. It took lots of power to move the Limiteds. They weighed in at over 4,600 pounds. Buick's Variable-Pitch Dynaflow was standard, as was power steering and brakes. The standard creature comforts included power windows, six-way power seat and air conditioning.

Mark Faulkner, a professor at the Air Force Academy, has been a car collector since he restored a 1940 Chrysler Windsor convertible while in high school. Incidently, Mark teaches English; with a name like Faulkner, what else! He and his wife, Gayle, found their baby blue with white Buick Limited in Colorado Springs, where the salt free winters were kind to it. Under many years grime, he found an excellent paint job and upholstery in great shape. His four-door hardtop is one of the 5,571 made. In 1958, 1,026 two-door hardtops and 839 convertibles were also produced.

The engine only required a tune-up, but the Dynaflow required a complete rebuild. In 1958, an air suspension system was available as an option on GM products. Mark's car came equipped with this option. However, like most cars so equipped, his has been changed to conventional coil springs. The compressor for the suspension system is still under the hood. Air suspension was not well accepted by 1958 auto buyers.

As on the exterior, there is an equal abundance of chrome inside. The dash is well chromed and there is chrome trim everywhere else. The Faulkner's car has ultra-plush cloth upholstery. Cloth with leather trim was also available and the convertible came in leather. On the dash is an Autronic Eye automatic headlight dimmer.

What's it like to drive this large car. It's definitely not a sports car. The ride is what you would expect from a large '50s car and a Buick at that. The engine, while thirsty, has more than adequate power. The Dynaflow is smooth as silk and the power steering leads to effortless driving. It also absorbs a lot of road feel. The seats are extremely wide and it is fortunate that the car is so quiet. An obvious change that has taken place over the years is a switch to more modern, narrow band whitewall tires.

The Limited four door hardtop listed for $5,112; only a couple of hundred dollars less than a comparable 1958 Cadillac. The 1958 Buick Limited epitomizes the typical and extreme characteristics of motoring tastes and automobile design that evolved in the 1950s and 1960s.

136

1959 Buick Model 4867 Electra 225 convertible.

New names, new styles for '59

By Tony Hossain

The 1959 Buicks really looked new. And they didn't look like Buicks. Even the names were changed. The division's new general manager, Edward Ragsdale, insisted on that. Ever since the thirties, the cheapest Buick had been called Special. Now it was the LeSabre. The mid-series was no longer Century. It was the Invicta. At the top of the heap were the Electra and Electra 225, replacing the Super and Roadmaster.

All the GM cars (except Corvette) were new in '59 and they were overwhelmingly finny. And every one of them was longer, lower and wider. The feeling was that Chrysler had out-finned GM in '57 and that it wasn't going to happen again.

The Buick was a real standout, even in that unusual bunch. Dual headlamps were carried over from '58 but they weren't placed horizontally. And they weren't stacked vertically. They were placed on an angle. This theme was repeated around back where the tail fins were also placed on an angle. Below the fins were simple round tail lights.

Overall length was 217 inches (220 inches in the Electra/225 series) and the wheelbase was 123 or 126, depending on series. There was lots of glass and the huge wraparound windshield was a sight to behold.

Underneath a new chassis featured coil springs all around. Air suspension, 1958's failed experiment, was still available but the public continued to shun it.

The LeSabre was designed to compete with the new Pontiac Catalina, Olds Dynamic 88, Mercurys, Chevy Impalas and all the other entries in the highly competitive medium price class. Everyone wanted volume and in the fragile auto market of the late '50s, something had to give. In fact, DeSoto and the new Edsel were both rushing headfirst towards the executioner.

A complete line unto itself, the LeSabre was available as a four-door sedan, four-door hardtop, two-door sedan, two-door hardtop, convertible and station wagon.

A surprisingly spartan cloth and vinyl interior, all vinyl on wagons and convertibles, was included in the base price of $2,804 (four-door sedan). Standard equipment included a glove box light, dual horns, electric wipers, horizontal red-liner speedometer and a trip mileage odometer. Also standard was a 364 cid 250 hp V-8.

Replacing the Century series was the Invicta, available as a four-door sedan, four-door hardtop, two-door hardtop, convertible and station wagon. Exterior trim distinguishing the Invicta from the lower priced LeSabre included a rocker panel molding and Invicta nameplates. Fancier interior trim was available in four colors. Other features offered at no extra cost on all Invicta models were "Foamtex" seat cushions, electric clock, "Deluxe" steering wheel, full wheel covers and a padded instrument panel.

Carrying on the Century tradition, the Invicta was equipped with a hot 401 cid version of the Buick V-8 with an advertised horsepower rating of 325.

A Roadmaster by another name, the Electra featured fancier yet trim; a three-inch longer wheelbase and plusher interior appointments than the LeSabre or Invicta. The Electra was offered in four-door sedan, four-door hardtop and convertible body styles.

Standard equipment included two-speed electric wipers, dual exhaust and rich cloth/vinyl interiors.

The top-of-the-line Buick for 1959 was the Electra 225, available as a four-door sedan, four-door hardtop and convertible. Distinguishing this car from lesser Buicks was easy, with its wide rocker panel mouldings and a large Electra emblem on the front fenders. Leather interiors, power windows and top were standard in convertibles.

For all that was new, and in light of an improving car market, one would suspect that the 1959 Buicks helped carry the division out of its four-year slump. That did not happen. Buick sales dropped to a postwar low. The new names and new styling may have been too much for conservative Buick buyers. Buick advertised that the '59s didn't even look like Buicks. Maybe they should have.

Those '59s sure look great today though.

WHEN BETTER AUTOMOBILES ARE BUILT BUICK WILL BUILD THEM

Hundreds of thousands of families have already made the magnificent change to the

MOST TALKED-ABOUT STYLE OF TODAY

Right from the start there was talk about this '59 Buick's style. Clean, fresh, totally new, designed to stay new for years to come . . . and as the year rolls on, more and more we hear enthusiasm from owners for the pleasures beneath the eye-stopping style.

Owners tell of 15 to 18 miles per gallon from

the ablest engines and transmissions Buick ever built. They talk of the amazing quietness of these cars and of their superb riding comfort and roadability. They like the extra safety of brakes found only on Buick in America today . . . big, fast-acting, sure-feeling brakes with aluminum front drums, fin-cooled both front and rear. Take

it from these hundreds of thousands of owners . . . more that's new will happen to you in Buick '59 than in any other car. Let your Quality Buick Dealer show you The Car . . . today!

LeSABRE · INVICTA · ELECTRA

BUICK MOTOR DIVISION, GENERAL MOTORS CORPORATION

THE CAR: BUICK '59

This advertisement for the 1959 Buick LeSabre, Invicta and Electra talks about style, of which all three had plenty.

FINS GALORE!

1959 Buick Model 4719 Electra four-door sedan.

1960 Buick LeSabre four-door.

The 1959 and 1960 Buicks

By Bill Siuru

Much has been written about the rear fin treatment on the distinctive 1959 Chevys. Most have been less than rave reviews. Often it is forgotten that Chevrolet's sister divisions had some rather flamboyant fins on their 1959 and 1960 models.

Buick's were as wild as any of them; and 1959 ushered in several other changes for the marque as well. But first let's look at the fin issue.

The Buick's fins started at the front of the body, reaching a climax at the rear corner then abruptly descending to meet the lower edge of the rear deck lid. Most of the fin line was accented by heavy chrome trim.

Although photos may make it appear that the fins rose in height as they approached the tail, it is really an optical illusion. When viewed from the side, the entire sweeping fin feature is essentially level. Even though the '59 Buick's fins are every bit as wild as those on the Chevy, the Buick version appears to be better executed.

Buick went through a complete nameplate revision for its 1959 models. Gone were familiar names like Special, Century, Super and Roadmaster, which had been around for decades. Now the lowest priced Buicks were LeSabres, the mid-priced cars, Invictas, and the top-of-line models were Electras.

The plushest models were the Electra 225s. This huge car's designation came from its overall length, a whopping 225 inches. The LeSabres and Invictas were a "mere" 217.4 inches in length and the regular Electras measured 220.6 inches.

In overall styling, the '59s were totally redesigned from 1958. About the only thing retained was the grille treatment with its individual chrome squares, and for '59 there were fewer squares.

139

One distinctive model offered in all series except the Electra 225, was the four-door hardtop with its essentially flat roof and large wrap around rear windows. While providing excellent visibility, it tended to bake the car's inhabitants on sunny days; also there was some rearward distortion. All five GM marques offered this "greenhouse" design in 1959 and 1960.

In 1959 and '60 Buick shared the A body with several of its sisters in the GM family, but is those years badge-engineering resulted in much better disguising of common-body components. By 1962 the greenhouse hardtop design was gone from all GM marques. In counting the side windows, you can see why this model is sometimes referred to as a four-window hardtop.

The Electra 225 used a more conventional four-door hardtop with "six windows," a body style it shared with Cadillac. One thing missing on 1959 Buicks was the traditional portholes or ventiports. They had not been used in 1958 either.

In the engine department, the LeSabre was powered by the same 364 cid, 250 hp engine used on all Buicks in 1958, but the compression ratio was raised a bit to 10.5:1. The rest of the '59 Buicks were powered by a new 401 cid V-8 that produced 325 horses, a worthwhile feature for cars that tipped the scales at weights ranging from 4,300 to 4,700 pounds.

A 1959 Buick Electra 225 convertible was given the honor of pacing the Indianapolis 500 that year. Sam Hanks, the 1957 race winner, was behind the wheel.

Because the 1959 fin treatment didn't bring heavy floor traffic or sales to dealers, for 1960 Buick toned down the wild fin treatment, clipping and rounding them off. The side and front sculpturing was more severe. Indeed, while the same body was used one more year, the 1960 restyling was more than a typical Detroit face-lift.

Most Buick fans think the '59 is a better integrated design. Ventiports returned in 1960 and would stay through 1968. However, sales did not improve. In fact they declined from over 284,000 cars in 1959 to not quite 254,000 in 1960. But this was still better than the approximately 240,000 Buicks sold in model year 1958.

1959 Buick fins, up close and personal

Something to believe in.

Something great.
Just for you.
The Buick LeSabre Custom. Something to believe in.
Quality.
Craftsmanship.
Integrity.

Wouldn't You Really Rather Have a Buick?

you've want...

Engine? A 350 cubic-inch V8 with 260 horsepower that runs on regular gas. Premium
performance...

Wide tread bias belted tires for added traction and longer wear.
AccuDrive. Buick's exclusive suspension system that gives almost unheard of handling
and cornering ease.
Radio antenna hidden in the windshield.
Comfort-Flo ventilating system...passenger comfort.

1961–1990

Famous Magic-Mirror finish baked on a strong, silent Body by Fisher.
And many more things to believe in.
All standard.
Plus a long list of performance options, should you want to order them.
It's something to believe in.
Believe.
Wouldn't you really rather have a Buick.

Buick's V-6 —

First production V-6 American car was the 1962 Buick Special.

An oddity's odyssey

Along with the arrival of smaller cars in the early 1960s came the need for smaller engines.

The whole purpose of compact cars, at least at the beginning, was to lower costs — both initial price and operating costs. So big V-8 engines were frowned upon. The Falcon and Valiant used scaled-down versions of their big brothers' six-cylinder motors. Corvair was a one-of-a-kind car and required a totally new engine. But the new crop of compacts, such as the Buick Special and Pontiac Tempest, created the need for something in the power range between the little sixes and the big V-8s.

Pontiac met this challenge by amputating one bank of its V-8 to make a slanted four-cylinder engine. Buick did something similar. But it made the cut crosswise, instead of along one side. In other words, Buick made a V-6. That sounds simple enough, but there were a lot of problems to overcome. The greatest was the fact that the V-8 engine has a 90° angle between the banks. That works out fine for balancing firing cylinders of a V-8. But take away two cylinders and the remaining six cylinders are thrown way out of balance, causing serious vibration.

Normally V-6 engines used a 60° angle between the cylinder banks to bring the firing back into balance. This is what the Italian Lancia had been doing with their V-6s since about 1950. Actually, the V-6 had already made its American debut in the 1960 model year. Certain GMC trucks were available with V-6 engines. They were offered in 305, 351 and 401 cubic inch displacements. Each had a 60° angle between the cylinder banks. So there was little

help Buick engineers could get in this regard from the GMC counterparts.

Buick designed a new crankshaft, and a firing order of 1-6-5-4-3-2 was used. That firing order is not very complicated. If you start counting with cylinder #6, the firing order is simply backwards. Anyway, this eliminated much of the chopped-off engine's vibration. Because the remaining vibration was lateral, much of it was absorbed up by special rubber engine mounts at each side. Interestingly, Pontiac's half V-8 had vertical vibration, which was much more difficult to overcome.

Many of Buick's V-8 components were used on the V-6, items such as generator, starter flywheel (with automatic transmission), valves, fuel pump, and flywheel housing (with manual transmission). But the bore and stroke of Buick's V-8 was altered. With a 3.625 inch bore and 3.2 inch stroke, the V-6 had a displacement of 198 cubic inches. That was about four cubic inches larger than the Tempest's four-cylinder engine or the Chevy II's six.

The V-6 is a very compact configuration. It is half the length of an inline six, of course. It is shorter than either a V-8 or a four. Amazingly, Buick's V-6 weighed just 362 pounds — about the same as the Chevy II's little four-cylinder motor. Debuting concurrently with the V-6, Ford's new thin-wall 221 cid V-8 was 80 pounds heavier.

Buick's V-6 developed 135 h.p. and 205 ft./lbs. of torque. That was significantly more power and torque than any of the other 1962 engines in its displacement class. The V-6 was standard in the Standard line of 1962

Buick Specials but not available in the Deluxe line or Skylark. However, the next year it did become available in the 1963 Deluxe Specials.

From management decision to actual production, this engine was developed in the amazingly short time of six months. When it appeared, it was greeted by an enthusiastic press. Performance was excellent. Zero to 60 acceleration took as little as 12.4 seconds. Top speed was 100 mph. *Popular Mechanics* magazine took a V-6 automatic on a 1,100-mile test run and compared it with a manual V-6 and five other competitive cars. The V-6 automatic averaged 19.3 miles per gallon. In shorter runs the manual V-6 reached 23.25 miles a gallon, which was better than any of the other cars.

Improvements were made to the V-6 as they were developed, and for 1964 the bore and stroke were increased to match Buick's 300 cid V-8. With 225 cubic inches, the enlarged V-6 produced 155 hp. That was practically three-quarters of the output of the V-8, so there appeared to be equal efficiency in the eight and the sawed-off six.

V-6 availability was extended to the Skylark for 1964, except the sports wagons. The enlarged V-6 gave excellent fuel economy. In the 3,244-mile Mobilgas Economy Run from Los Angeles to the New York World's Fair, Buick led its class of intermediate six-cylinder cars with a 25.2986 mpg average. In fact, it was fourth best overall. Only the Rambler American, Dodge Dart and Plymouth Valiant were able to better it.

But economy was not a serious goal for most people in the mid '60s. Many more buyers were looking for power instead. Blockbusting V-8s were squeezed into cars like Buick's Special and Skylark. As interest shifted to the musclecars, Buick's interest in its V-6 faded. For its 1968 models, Buick dropped its V-6 in favor of Chevrolet's larger inline six for the few who abhorred eight cylinders.

From 1962 through 1967 — six model years — Buick installed over 302,000 V-6 engines in their cars. Some 66,100 of them were built for the 1964 model year alone. That was the peak, but 1963 marked the biggest percentage of V-6 powered Specials and Skylarks. Two out of every five Buick Specials and Skylarks had V-6 power. But the ratio fell to one in 10 by 1967.

However, the V-6 did not disappear. Jeep found that Buick's compact engine would fit nicely in some of their models. So, an arrangement was negotiated with Buick to buy their V-6 engines. The Kaiser-Jeep people liked this engine so much that eventually they bought the rights and tooling from Buick. Jeep's V-6 was virtually unchanged from Buick's specifications, except that developed horsepower was rated at 160 — up five.

Jeep used this engine as an option in their Jeepster Commando and related models, as well as in the Universal Jeep. It was not available in the larger Wagoneer type models. Jeep offered its V-6, with little or no change, in the 1967 through 1971 model years.

In February 1970, American Motors purchased Jeep from the Kaiser-Jeep Corp. Probably that takeover was a factor in dropping the V-6 because it was replaced by AMC's inline six. But something else much more important was taking place. The fuel crisis of the '70s renewed Buick's interest in the economical V-6, so history repeated itself but in reverse. Buick negotiated with Jeep, and bought its V-6 engine back.

After further vibration dampening and a slight enlargement to 231 cubic inches, Buick was back in the V-6 business with a 110 hp motor. That rating is down from before, but by this time net horsepower figures were published instead of gross horsepower.

The V-6 made its comeback in the 1975 model of the Skylark, where it had its home before. The Apollo, which was really a four-door version of the Skylark, could not be ordered with a V-6 until midway in the model year. The reason was probably a matter of building production volume to a level to meet the demand.

And there certainly was a demand. In all, there were 113,000 V-6 powered 1975 Buicks. The new Skyhawk used the V-6 exclusively instead of Chevrolet's questionable four. The V-6 was also offered in the mid-size Century. The 45,174 V-6 Centurys actually accounted for more than any of the other Buick lines. The quantity of 1976 V-6s rose 110 percent to 238,300. Of that number, 9,651 were installed in full-size LeSabres.

V-6 popularity leveled off for the 1977 models but took another sharp rise to 342,059 installations in the 1978 Buicks. That was far more than the entire Buick V-6 total during the '60s. Several different versions were made available for the first time in 1978 models.

There was a mini V-6 of only 196 cubic inches — smaller even than the original 1962 engine. This 90 hp motor was not for the Skyhawk or Skylark, as one might expect. Instead, it was the standard engine for the Century. The regular 231 V-6 was a Century option.

An option in the Regal sport coupe was a turbocharged edition of the 231 engine rated at 150 hp with two-barrel carburetor, or 165 hp with four-barrel carburetion. The restyled Riviera for 1979 could also be ordered with a turbocharged V-6. It was rated at 185 hp. There were 36,038 V-6 turbo Buicks built during the 1979 season.

In the 1980s, the V-6 took off — becoming the most popular new type of engine since the high-compression shortstroke V-8s of the '50s. It has been embraced by many other car makers. Buick supplied Oldsmobile and Pontiac with V-6 engines beginning with the 1977 models, and Chevrolet starting with 1980 models, even though they were getting their own V-6 programs rolling.

The V-6 has come a long, long way since its shaky beginning 25 years ago. It has grown from a dubious novelty to a forgotten oddity to an inevitable necessity.

The premier Riviera

Dramatic shot of 1963 Buick Riviera.

By R. Perry Zavitz

It was amid eager anticipation that the first Buick Riviera greeted the public.

We don't mean the very first Buick Riviera: We are referring to the 1963 model, which was the first of the present series of Rivieras. Buick built a lot of Rivieras before 1963. Most of them were hardtops, but they are not cars we want to focus on at this time.

Ford's four-passenger Thunderbird of 1958 uncorked a whole new segment of the market, which, until then, no one really knew existed. It was a growing group of buyers who were comfortably well off. They wanted an agile car — not the monstrous sedans most manufacturers offered in this price range. The cars were to be about mid-size.

Compact cars were too cramped and lacked the performance these people were used to. They also had a cheap aura about them, which, of course, these buyers would not consider for a moment. Sports cars were too extreme. They certainly had agility and performance, but were short on the comfort these people were accustomed to and unwilling to give up.

The four-seater Thunderbird was put together with the right combination of these desired characteristics. It had this lucrative market all to itself; that is, until the 1963

Buick Riviera appeared in showrooms all across the land.

Riviera styling was totally new and bore no resemblance to existing or previous Buicks. That can be a very risky move, but it was a resounding success in this case. No doubt the Riviera's great appeal was due in no small way to its pure and simple body lines. It came close to the simple elegance of such great designs as the 1936-'37 Cord and the Continental Mark II.

The unfamiliar new body covered a mixture of old and new Buick components. The 117 inch wheelbase came from Buick's X-type frame, which was a shortened version of the full size X frame. Wheelbase was about five inches longer than the contemporary Buick Skylark, but overall length was almost 1¼ feet more. Both front and rear tread were two inches narrower than the full-size Buicks, but three to four inches wider than the mid-size models. So Riviera had a totally different stance than its fellow Buicks.

Mechanically, the Riviera borrowed heavily from the senior Buicks. The engine was the 325 hp 401 cid V-8 that powered the Invicta and the Electra. The transmission was Buick's Turbine Drive automatic.

The transmission lever was located on the console between the bucket seats. The Riviera's interior was sumptuous, befitting a car bearing the Buick name. Elegant looking all-vinyl upholstery was standard. But buyers

Here's where man and Riviera get to know each other

You slide behind the wheel and reach for the stick. It's a bit like sitting in a small plane. In two miles you're aware that before this driving has been pretty uninteresting. We planned it that way. Buick built the Riviera to put some adventure back in driving. You know it first time you corner (the Riviera takes them tight and level, tracking like a Gran Turismo racer). You could guess it just from the way the Riviera looks (the look of a great new international classic car). You and the Riviera should make friends. Get your Buick dealer to let you drive one. He'll let you take it home with you for a lot less than you'd guess.

Buick Motor Division—General Motors Corporation

ADVENTURE IS A CAR CALLED RIVIERA —— AND IT'S A BUICK

The Buick Riviera was featured in this 1963 advertisement.

had fabric and vinyl or leather and vinyl interiors to select from the option list if they wished.

Other creature comforts, not on the option list but standard equipment, included: electric clock, trip mileage odometer, two-speed wipers with windshield washer, courtesy lights, deep pile carpeting, front and rear bucket seats, foam rubber seat padding, deluxe wheel covers, power steering, power brakes and many more items too numerous to mention.

Despite the long list of standard equipment, there was an option list, too. Items such as cruise control, air conditioning and wire wheel covers could be ordered at extra cost. There was an optional engine as well. It was a variation of the standard engine, but with a one-eighth inch larger bore. That increased the displacement to 425 cubic inches. Consequently, the horsepower was boosted to 340.

Although it was smaller than the Electra and LeSabre, the Riviera tipped the scales at just about the same amount as the LeSabre two-door hardtop — a hair under two tons. But its price was aout $170 more than the Electra two-door hardtop. For a smaller car, its equal weight and higher cost is an indication that the Riviera was a better equipped and more luxurious car. Its base price was $4,333.

Surprisingly, that was more than $100 under the lowest priced 1963 Thunderbird model. That states quite clearly who Buick was trying to lure into their sales offices.

As for performance, the new Riviera could do zero to 60 mph in 8.1 seconds, and a quarter mile in 16.01 seconds at 85.71 mph. John Bond reported in *Car Life* a zero to 60 time of 7.7 seconds with the 340 hp engine. Either engine gave the Riviera performance that was superior to the contemporary Thunderbird. These test results also substantiate the subtle look of performance the Riviera had.

Sales of Buick's new car were so good that an even 40,000 were produced for 1963. Meanwhile, Thunderbird sales dropped just over 13 percent during 1963.

Only a few minor details altered the 1964 Riviera's exterior appearance. The same 325 hp engine remained standard. The 340 hp engine was joined on the option list by a 360 hp motor. It used two four-barrel carburetors instead of just one. Production was down slightly to 37,958 for the '64 model.

The first noticeable styling change for the Riviera came on the 1965 model. Most obvious were the hidden headlights. They were located behind the grilles on the front end of the fenders. This change was an improvement, making the Riviera look even cleaner than before. Many people think the 1965 edition was the best looking Riviera, at least until 1979.

Probably the most significant mechanical change made to the 1965 Riviera was the Gran Sport option. The GS package included the 360 hp engine as well as dual exhausts and Positraction rear axle with a 3.42 ratio (3.23 was standard). Heavy-duty suspension was not part of the GS option, but was available with or without it.

A totally new Riviera appeared for 1966, using a variation of the new front-wheel-drive Oldsmobile Toronado body. The Riviera stayed with rear-wheel-drive. Indeed, this Riviera has stayed with its 1963 basic concept of providing personal transportation for those wishing comfort, luxury and performance, and who have no worries about meeting the payments. Riviera has frequently been Buick's best selling model during the last century.

1963 Buick Riviera
Specifications:

Engine type	V-8
Bore:	4.1875 in.
Stroke:	3.64 in.
Displacement:	401 cu. in.
Compression:	10.25:1
Horsepower @ rpm:	325 @ 4400
Horsepower per cu. in.	0.81
Torque (lb/ft): @ rpm	445 @ 2800
Rear Axle ratio:	3.23:1
Overall length:	208 ins.
Overall width:	76.6 ins.
Overall height:	53.2 ins.
Wheelbase:	117 ins.
Tread (front):	60 ins
(rear)	59 ins.
Weight:	3998 lbs.
Tire Size:	7.50 x 15
Body type:	two-door hardtop
Original Base Price:	$4,333
Current #1 Value:	$8,000

1963 Buick Riviera on the road.

Sail panels, Buick's term to describe the extensions of the roof beyond the rear window, were new for 1966, as was the Coke bottle treatment on the quarter panels.

1966 Buick Gran Sports were mid-sized treats

By Tom LaMarre

The top performer in the Skylark line for 1966 was the Gran Sport model. Visually, the GS was distinguished from the standard Skylark by the use of Gran Sport ornamentation on the grille, rear quarter, rear end panel, and instrument panel. Also featured were simulated hood scoops and black out paint treatment beneath the side trim. The buyer was offered his choice of whitewall or red line tires measuring 7.75 x 14.

But there was more to the Skylark GS than a few name tags and fake scoops. Power was provided by a mighty 325 hp Wildcat 445 V-8. Standard equipment included dual exhaust, heavy duty springs and shocks, and a floor-mounted 3-speed transmission. A four-speed was optional, as was a tachometer.

The GS Sport coupe, model 44617, was priced at $3,019 and weighed 3,428 pounds. Production of this model was 9.934 units. In contrast, the scarcest GS model has to be the thin pillar coupe, often listed simply as the coupe. With the windows raised, it had the appearance of a hardtop, but with the windows lowered the narrow posts could be seen. Only 1,835 thin pillar GS coupes were produced. At $2,956, the price was just too close to the sport coupe. The model designation for the thin pillar GS was number 44607.

Rounding out the Skylark GS range was the convertible coupe, model 44667, which was priced at $3,167 and weighed 3,532 pounds. Production of the ragtop version reached 2,047 units.

A '67 Buick GS for every budget

Some of the most important changes were under the hood of the 1967 Buick GS-400. This is the convertible model.

By Tom LaMarre

Buick's Gran Sport was no longer a Skylark in 1967. "Probably feeling that the 'Skylark' tag might be too much for the birds, Buick folks 'officially divorced' what is now the GS-400 from the Skylark series," said *Popular Mechanics*. "They're probably right — a ruddy young male would much prefer a masculine GS-400 to a fine-feathered bird."

The "400" in the model designation meant cubic inches. To clear up the confusion created by the "Wildcat 445" engine name (the "445" stood for torque), the rocker arm covers were decaled with the displacement and number of barrels.

The engine was a masterpiece. Bigger manifold branches, larger valves and improved exhaust headers assured minimum gas flow restriction. The intake valves were 18 percent larger than those used in 1966, and the exhaust valves were 56 percent larger. The intake manifold branches were 17 percent larger. In addition, the manifold had a more efficient heat-rise section for warm-up.

There were other innovations. The water jackets in the cylinder head were carried around the spark plug holes. Conical spark plug seats eliminated the need for plug washers. Topping off the engine was a plastic-covered, dual-induction air cleaner.

The Gran Sport chassis had stronger side rails and bracing than the Skylark, and the GS-400 differed from the Skylark visually, too. Instead of fender skirts, it had open wheels, which Buick said were in the "grand touring tradition." The wheel openings showed off F70 x 14 wide oval

red or white stripe tires. Front disc brakes were available, and when ordered required special wheels, hubcaps and beauty rings.

As impressive as the GS-400 was, the big news was the low-bucks GS-340, the hit of the Chicago Auto Show. A Buick ad explained, "Our now-famous GS-400 doesn't come for peanuts. It's a great car — but just a little rich for some people. So we set to work and designed the Buick GS-340. It has a smaller engine (but it weighs a lot less.) Its interior isn't quite as sumptuous (but it's clean and simple and tasteful)...We ended up with a car that does cost less than the GS-400. But one with its own brand of excitement."

Although the GS-340 lacked the guts of the GS-400, it had all of the eye-appeal. There was only one body style, a two-door hardtop coupe (model 43417) priced at $2,845 — only $174 less than the GS-400 hardtop and $111 less than the GS-400 thin-pillar coupe. Contrasting with broad red rally stripes, red rally wheels and matching fake hood scoops was the white or platinum body, the only GS-340 colors. Tires were 7.75 x 14 rayon cord.

The GS-340 was not exactly a sheep in wolf's clothing, but it wasn't a GS-400 either. Its engine was the same one used in the Skylark four-door sedan and Sportwagon, a 220 h.p. 340-cubic inch V-8 with a 9.0:1 compression ratio and two-barrel carb. As with the GS-400, a four-speed transmission was available for $184 extra. Cars with bucket seats and automatic transmission could be fitted with a full-length console.

The GS-340 was a lot of car for the money. Today, like all Gran Sports, it seems to ask, "Wouldn't you really rather have a Buick?"

1968–'72 Buick Gran Sports

1968 Buick GS 400 two-door hardtop.

Above: Side view of another '68 Buick GS 400 two-door hardtop. Below: 1970 Buick GS 455 two-door hardtop.

Buick intermediates with two doors shrank in 1968. The new 112-inch Skylark wheelbase matched that of the original Gran Sport. Big news for musclecar lovers was the release of a Stage I engine option, available through dealers, which was unusual for Buick. It included improved breathing for the 400 cid engine and increased power so much that *Car life* magazine found the GS 400 its fastest test vehicle the second year in a row.

The GS 400 was down to two models, a hardtop base-priced at $3,528 and a ragtop with prices starting at $3,672. The GS 350 was available as a hardtop only, from $3,295 up. A special edition of the "junior" musclecar was the California GS, which was made for sale in that state. Its equipment list included a vinyl top, special emblems and styled wheels. The 350 V-8, replacing the 340, featured 10.25:1 compression, a four-barrel and 280 hp at 4600 rpm.

In 1969, Buick's premium performance machine was the Stage I, a specially modified GS 400. Functional ram-air hood scoops, a high-lift cam, low restriction dual exhausts, a modified Quadrajet carb and 3.64:1 positraction axle were included in the Stage I, along with a special TH-400 automatic transmission (optional) that provided higher shift points and firmer engagement, plus heavy-duty Rallye suspension and power disc brakes.

Other models offered included the GS 350 hardtop ($2,980) and the GS 400 hardtop ($3,578) and convertible ($3,722).

According to musclecar expert Phil Hall, the 1970 Buick GS 455 and GSX were the wildest of all Buicks on paper. The 455 cid engine was derived from the "430" and produced 350 hp. With Stage I modification, this climbed to 360 hp and meant zero to 60 mph in 5.5 seconds and 13.4 second quarter-miles.

The GSX was a mid-year option introduced at the Chicago Auto Show. It cost $880 and included front and rear spoilers, striping, a hood tach and four-speed transmission, but used the same engines as the GS 455.

A hardtop ($3,685) and convertible ($3,871) were available as GS 455s. Also still offered by Buick was the 350 V-8 powered "cosmetic" musclecar, now called simply the GS. Though not as hot as the big blocks, this engine retained 10.25:1 compression and went to 315 hp at 4800 rpm.

For 1971, the Skylark-based musclecar line combined the GS/GS 455 models in one series. The GS came with a 260 hp Stage I big-block. All engines were detuned to run on regular gas. The GSX option package was available, too. Prices for the hardtop began at $3,666 and at $3,857 for the ragtop. The engines were extra-cost options, as was the GSX.

In 1972, the GS 350/GS 455 models continued. The hardtop dropped in price to $3,641 and the convertible was down to $3,822. Horsepower was now expressed in net ratings of 175 nhp for the GS 350 and 225 nhp for the GS 455. The latter engine had a 275 nhp option which was still good for snappy performance of zero to 60 mph in 5.8 seconds and a 14.1 second quarter-mile.

150

1983 Riviera paced the Indy 500.

Buick paced Indianapolis 500 in 1983

A Buick Riviera convertible, powered by a sophisticated twin turbo charged 4.1 liter (252 CID) Buick V-6 engine, paced the 67th running of the Indianapolis 500 on May 29, 1983.

The 1983 pace car was the third to use a V-6 engine, and the first two also were Buicks — in 1976 (a turbocharged 3.8 liter Century Coupe), and in 1981 (a naturally aspirated 4.1 liter Regal Coupe).

Buicks also paced the race in 1939, 1959 and 1975.

In ceremonies to unveil the pace car, Buick General manager Lloyd E. Reuss, said "Although the Riviera might not fit at some racing events, it is a natural for the Indianapolis 500. Both the Riviera and the race are classics — American traditions.

But while the car has a nostalgic air, the engine is a leap into the future.

"The 1983 Buick pace car engine — developing 350-plus horsepower — may well be the most technically sophisticated powerplant ever to appear at the Indianapolis Motor Speedway, in a pace car or in a race," Reuss said.

A digital onboard computer provided by GM's Delco Electronics Division, controled all major engine functions, including sequential port fuel injection, and water/methanol injection.

Twin 80mm mass air flow sensors built by GM's AC Spark Plug Division, are linked to the computer to control the air/fuel mixture, and AC high pressure in-tank pumps deliver the fuel.

The computer also controls the coil ignition system, idle and speed and turbo wastegate.

The basic pace car engine is made up of many standard Buick heavy duty engine components, available for the Buick 4.1 liter engine, including Stage II block and cylinder heads, forged steel crankshaft and connecting rods and forged aluminum pistons. Bore and stroke are the same as on the stock 4.1 liter.

The twin turbochargers are modified production units of the type that are standard on Buick's 1983 Riviera and Regal T Types.

Like the standard Riviera, the 1983 pace car has longitudinal front-wheel drive, with four-wheel independent suspension, and four-wheel disc brakes (a regular Riviera option).

Specially made 15 x 7 inch wire wheels and Goodyear P225/70HR15 blackwall tires will be used.

The pace car decor is understated, with a main body color of cream, with a light chocolate brown on the sides. The interior is of saddle cowhide leather, with dark chocolate pigskin seat inserts. Real wood trim and a real wood steering wheel are featured.

The Riviera convertible was introduced as a limited edition version of the Riviera, first produced in 1963.

Roadmaster returns

Roadmaster, one of the great names in Buick history, is back.

Buick expects to quickly build name recognition for its new family of rear-wheel-drive, V-8 powered vehicles — its completely redesigned 1991 Estate Wagon and its all-new 1991 full-size sedans.

In the fall of 1990, Buick introduced its completely redesigned 1991 Roadmaster Estate Wagon. Then, in the spring of 1991, the all-new 1992 Roadmaster and Roadmaster Limited sedans made their debuts. Both wagon and sedans carry the name "Roadmaster" — and that name has instant recognition.

Even though more than three decades have passed since the Roadmaster name last adorned a new Buick, Roadmasters are widely remembered as premium Buicks with powerful eight-cylinder engines, smooth rides and distinctive styling.

The Roadmaster name first appeared in 1936 on premium Buick sedans. During the boom years following World War II, Roadmasters were famous for their power, ride and distinctive design.

Even though the first Roadmasters were 1936 models, many people particularly remember the Roadmasters of the postwar era — large cars with enormous "carnivorous" vertical-bar grilles, sweepspear side moldings, four portholes — officially called ventiports — and "hardtop convertible" (no center side pillar) styling on some models.

The Roadmaster name was discontinued at the end of the 1958 model year as Buick shifted to new names across its lineup. Limited, Roadmaster, Super, Century and Special were replaced by Electra, LeSabre and Invicta.

Eventually, some of the other names came back. Roadmaster, perhaps the strongest name of them all, for some reason stayed on the shelf.

"When we needed a name for our '92 rear-drive sedan, we considered a lot of candidates," said Darwin E. Clark, Buick's general marketing manager. "But always, Roadmaster was in our minds. It's a very powerful name — and not just with people old enough to remember the Roadmasters of the '50s.

"It's interesting how that name affects people. We received suggestions from all sources. Our dealers wanted Roadmaster. Some of our own employees wrote memos urging us to bring it back. Even some of the auto writers, when they asked us about rumors that we were considering Roadmaster, said they would like to see the name return.

"Ultimately, we selected this historic Buick name because we wanted to create a new classic in a traditional vein."

Coincidentally, the 1988 Academy Award-winning film, "Rain Man," prominently featured a 1949 Roadmaster convertible, which was described in the film as a classic. In the film, brothers Charlie Babbitt (Tom Cruise), a smooth-talking businessman, and Raymond Babbitt (Dustin Hoffman), his autistic savant sibling, embark on a cross-country drive in the Roadmaster.

The 1991 Roadmaster Estate Wagon is an aerodynamic eight-passenger vehicle powered by a fuel-injected five-liter V-8 engine delivering 170 hp. This is the first major redesign since 1978 of the most luxurious wagon offered by General Motors.

The 1992 Roadmaster and Roadmaster Limited six-pas-

The Buick Roadmaster name returned for the first time in more than three decades on the 1991 Roadmaster Estate Wagon and 1992 Roadmaster sedan. Representing the previous Roadmasters, which were produced from 1936 to 1958, is a '49 Roadmaster (background) with its characteristic grille and portholes.

senger sedans will feature a 180-hp fuel-injected 5.7-liter V-8.

The sedans will be Buick's first rear-drive automobiles, except Estate Wagon, since the 1987 Regal. They will be the first Buicks except Estate Wagon with a standard V-8 engine since the 1985 Riviera.

Buick General Manager Edward H. Mertz said Roadmaster was "a great name for premium Buicks" in the past and that the new Roadmaster Estate Wagon and the '92 Roadmaster and Roadmaster Limited sedans "are perfect models to wear that proud name."

"For those who prefer full-frame vehicles with rear-wheel drive, these models perfectly define Buick's mission of providing contemporary cars that are substantial, distinctive, powerful and mature — premium American motorcars."

Although the new Roadmaster will be the largest Buicks, in keeping with the heritage of the name, they will also be both responsive and fuel efficient — the result of a combination of aerodynamics and engine sophistication.

Roadmaster Estate Wagon's overall length is 217.7 inches and the wheelbase is 115.9 inches. Roadmaster sedans will have an overall length of 215.8 inches and wheelbase of 115.9. (By comparison, the 1991 Park Avenue's overall length is 205.2 inches and its wheelbase is 110.8 inches; the last Roadmaster, in 1958, had an overall length of 219.1 inches and a wheelbase of 127.5 inches. It was not the biggest Buick in 1958. That year only, there was a Buick Limited with an overall length of 227.1 inches on the same 127.5-inch wheelbase.)

Both the Estate Wagon and the sedans have standard anti-lock brakes, standard driver's side supplemental inflatable restraints (air bags) and 5,000-pound towing capacities. A new variable effort steering system will be standard on Limited.

1991 Roadmaster Estate Wagon

In addition to a newly designed aerodynamic body, the new Roadmaster Estate Wagon has flush-mounted tinted glass and flush door handles to increase efficiency.

"Vista roof," a dark-tinted glass panel positioned midway in the roof, provides an open-air look.

The two-way tailgate provides instant access to the rear cargo or seating area. A rear-compartment convenience net and rear-window wiper are standard. A standard roof luggage rack provides additional carrying capability.

A long list of other standard equipment includes air conditioning, power windows with a driver's-side "express down" feature, power steering, tilt steering wheel, heavy-duty suspension, reclining 55/45 split bench front seats, side window defoggers, visor vanity mirrors for driver and front passenger, third seat, child security latches on rear doors, 15-inch aluminum wheels and an electronically tuned AM/FM stereo radio with seek, scan and extended-range rear speakers.

The five-liter V-8 with electronic fuel injection delivers 170 hp at 4200 rpm, with 255 pound/feet of torque available at 2400 rpm. The engine is coupled to a four-speed automatic transmission with overdrive.

A special effort has been made to maximize storage space with a large glove box, a pull-out instrument panel storage tray with two cup holders, front and rear door storage compartments, front seat back pockets and an optional folding center arm rest with a hidden storage area and dual cup holders.

Both the second and third bench seats fold down easily to create a large cargo area. Interior volume is an ample 170.1 cubic feet.

A trailering package includes automatic rear load leveling, additional radiator and engine oil cooling and a 3.23:1 axle ratio. A limited slip differential is also available.

Estate Wagon's exterior sheet metal is double galvanized for additional rust protection and has base coat/clear coat paint. Simulated woodgrain exterior paneling is standard.

1992 Roadmaster sedans

The 1992 Buick Roadmaster and Roadmaster Limited sedans are Buick's answer to those who want, in a contemporary package, a full-size, full-frame sedan with V-8 power.

Mertz said the new Roadmaster sedans reflect Buick's responsiveness to the marketplace. All other Buicks (except Roadmaster Estate Wagon) have front-wheel drive, which many customers prefer. Roadmaster is a response to a significant number of buyers who either prefer the ride and handling characteristics of rear drive or who want even more towing capacity, he said.

"We also found that the combination of sophisticated electronic engine management and aerodynamic design has enabled us to provide traditional big-car attributes in an efficient package," Mertz said.

Contributing to fuel economy is the exterior shape. The understated sedan has a formal roof line, yet employs subtle wind-cheating details such as flush-mounted glass and door handles and aerodynamic bumpers and mirrors for a drag co-efficient of 0.34.

Exterior sheet metal panels are galvanized on both sides for additional protection against rust and base coat/clear coat paint is standard.

A new Buick feature debuting as standard on Roadmaster Limited is a variable effort steering system, designed to make steering easier in parking and low-speed maneuvers while providing more "road feel" at highway speeds.

The system reduces the flow rate from the power steering pump as the speed of the car increases. The reduction in flow rate to the steering gear produces a higher steering effort. This provides a more firm on-center steering effort for improved road feel at highway speeds.

Roadmaster sedans offer more interior room than any other car (except Roadmaster Estate Wagon) in the Buick lineup: More than 134 cubic feet for passengers and 20.6 cubic feet in the trunk.

Among a long list of Roadmaster sedan standard features are anti-lock brakes, driver's side supplemental inflatable restraint (air bag), analog instrument panel with gauges including tachometer, visor vanity mirrors for driver and front passenger, built-in front and rear door storage, split-bench front seat and large storage armrest with two cupholders, truck convenience net, child security latch on rear doors, side front window defoggers, instrument panel pull-out tray, power windows with driver-side express-down feature, dual manual seat recliners, chrome covers for the 15-inch wheels, four assist handles, four-way manual headrests and AM/FM stereo radio.

HOW TO USE THIS CATALOG

APPEARANCE AND EQUIPMENT: Word descriptions identify cars by styling features, trim and (to a lesser extent) interior appointments. Most standard equipment lists begin with the lowest-priced model, then enumerate items added by upgrade models and option packages. Most lists reflect equipment available at model introductions.

I.D. DATA: Information is given about the Vehicle Identification Number (VIN) found on the dashboard. VIN codes show model or series, body style, engine size, model year and place built. Beginning in 1981, a standardized 17 symbol VIN is used. Earlier VINs are shorter. Locations of other coded information on the body and/or engine block may be supplied. Deciphering those codes is beyond the scope of this catalog.

SPECIFICATIONS CHART: The first column gives series or model numbers. The second gives body style numbers revealing body type and trim. Not all cars use two separate numbers. Some sources combine the two. Column three tells number of doors, body style and passenger capacity ('4-dr Sed-6P' means four-door sedan, six-passenger). Passenger capacity is normally the maximum. Cars with bucket seats hold fewer. Column four gives suggested retail price of the car when new, on or near its introduction date, not including freight or other charges. Column five gives the original shipping weight. The sixth column provides model year production totals or refers to notes below the chart. In cases where the same car came with different engines, a slash is used to separate factory prices and shipping weights for each version. Unless noted, the amount on the left of the slash is for the smallest, least expensive engine. The amount on the right is for the least costly engine with additional cylinders. 'N/A' means data not available.

ENGINE DATA: Engines are normally listed in size order with smallest displacement first. A 'base' engine is the basic one offered in each model at the lowest price. 'Optional' describes all alternate engines, including those that have a price listed in the specifications chart. (Cars that came with either a six or V-8, for instance, list the six as 'base' and V-8 'optional'). Introductory specifications are used, where possible.

CHASSIS DATA: Major dimensions (wheelbase, overall length, height, width and front/rear tread) are given for each model, along with standard tire size. Dimensions sometimes varied and could change during a model year.

TECHNICAL DATA: This section indicates transmissions standard on each model, usually including gear ratios; the standard final drive axle ratio (which may differ by engine or transmission); steering and brake system type; front and rear suspension description; body construction; and fuel tank capacity.

OPTIONAL EQUIPMENT LISTS: Most listings begin with drive-train options (engines, transmissions, steering/suspension and mechanical components) applying to all models. Convenience/appearance items are listed separately for each model, except where several related models are combined into a single listing. Option packages are listed first, followed by individual items in categories: comfort/convenience, lighting/mirrors, entertainment, exterior, interior, then wheels/tires. Contents of some option packages are listed prior to the price; others are described in the Appearance/Equipment text. Prices are suggested retail, usually effective early in the model year. ('N/A' indicates prices are unavailable.) Most items are Regular Production Options (RPO), rather than limited-production (LPO), special-order or dealer-installed equipment. Many options were available only on certain series or body types or in conjunction with other items. Space does not permit including every detail.

HISTORY: This block lists introduction dates, total sales and production amounts for the model year and calendar year. Production totals supplied by auto-makers do not always coincide with those from other sources. Some reflect shipments from the factories rather than actual production or define the model year a different way.

HISTORICAL FOOTNOTES: In addition to notes on the rise and fall of sales and production, this block includes significant statistics, performance milestones, major personnel changes, important dates and places and facts that add flavor to this segment of America's automotive heritage.

ELECTRA 225/ELECTRA 225 CUSTOM SERIES — (V-8) — Styling changes for the big Buicks paralleled those seen on LeSabres with individual head lamp bezels and slot style front gravel pans. A wide, chrome header bar was added to the grille and had the word Buick lettered at the center. Notch style cornering lamps were set into the front corners of the body. Standard equipment was the same as on LeSabre Luxus models, plus accessory lamp group (less sunshade light); foam padded seats; remote control OSRV mirror; Super DeLuxe wheel covers; seat belt restrainers; Custom safety belts; evaporative emissions control system; integral voltage regulator and Delcotron; Turbo-Hydramatic 400 transmission; J78-15 blackwall tires and the four-barrel '455' V-8. Custom trimmed Electra 225s had carpeted lower door panels and Custom exterior and interior trim. The Limited was now a separate series identified by wide rocker panel moldings, plus all other Custom features.

BUICK I.D. NUMBERS: All Buicks continued to use the same type of serial numbers as in 1973. The sixth symbol was changed to a '4' to indicate 1974 model year.

ELECTRA 222/ELECTRA 225 CUSTOM SERIES

Model Number	Body/Style Number	Body Type & Seating	Factory Price	Shipping Weight	Production Total
ELECTRA 225					
4CT	T39	4-dr HT Sed-6P	5373	4682	5,750
4CT	T37	2-dr HT Cpe-6P	5260	4607	3,339
ELECTRA 225 CUSTOM					
4CV	V39	4-dr HT Sed-6P	5550	4702	29,089
4CV	V37	2-dr HT Cpe-6P	5438	4682	15,099
ELECTRA LIMITED					
4CX	X39	4-dr HT Sed-6P	5921	4732	30,051
4CX	X37	2-dr HT Cpe-6P	5886	4682	16,086

ELECTRA ENGINE
V-8. Overhead valves. Cast iron block. Displacement: 455 cubic inches. Bore and stroke: 4.31 x 3.9. Compression ratio: 8.0:1. SAE net horsepower: 210. Hydraulic valve lifters. Carburetor: four-barrel.

CHASSIS FEATURES: Wheelbase: (Apollo) 111 inches; (Century four-door) 116 inches; (Century two-door) 112 inches; (LeSabre) 123.5 inches; (Estate Wagon and Electra) 127 inches; (Riviera) 122 inches. Overall lengths: (Apollo) 200.2 inches; (Century four-door) 212 inches; (Sport Wagons) 218.2 inches; (Century two-door) 209.5 inches; (LeSabre) 225.9 inches; (Estate Wagon) 231.1 inches; (Electra) 231.5 inches; (Riviera) 226.4 inches. Tires: (Apollo) E78-14; (Century) G78-14; (Sport Wagon) H78-14; (LeSabre) H78-15; (Estate Wagon) L78-14; (Electra) J78-15; (Riviera) J78-15.

CONVENIENCE OPTIONS: Air-conditioning ($396-446). Air cushion restraint system ($181-225). Station wagon air deflector ($21). Automatic climate control ($488-522). Custom safety belts ($11-37). Apollo bumper impact strips ($13). Riviera bumper reinforcement ($12). Electra rear bumper reinforcement ($6). Cargo area carpeting in Sport Wagons ($19); in Estate Wagons ($51). Trunk carpet in Electras and Riviera ($41). Electric clock, Apollo ($16); Century ($18). Full-length console for Century and Riviera two-doors ($61). Mini console in Century two-doors ($36). Convenience center console ($26). Customline convertible cover ($36). Cruise control in Century ($65). Rear window defogger ($33). Electric rear window defogger ($64). Tinted glass ($30-50). Tinted windshield ($30-35). Front and rear bumper guards ($31-35). Automatic level control ($77). Buick cornering lights ($36). Front monitors ($22). Front and rear monitors ($48). Station wagon luggage rack ($64-84). Sports mirrors, right and left ($22-44). Special order paint ($113). Apollo body striping ($21). Riviera body striping ($31). Wide rocker moldings for LeSabre Luxus and Electra 225s, except Limited ($28). Custom body side trim ($24-46). Custom door/window trim ($21-27). Two-tone paint ($27-43). Wide rocker panel group for LeSabre and Estate, including lower rear quarter, front and rear wheel well moldings ($69). Six-way right hand and left hand power seats of 60/40 design or 40/40 design ($211). Other six-way seat options ($80-106). Electric sunroof in Century ($325); in all Sports Coupes ($589). Manual sunroof in Century ($275); in Sport Coupes ($539). Vinyl trim with Custom bucket seats ($124); with lumbar-support reclining bucket seats ($236); vinyl bucket seats ($119), all in Century two-doors only. Vinyl roofs, Custom Apollo ($82); Custom Century ($99); Custom padded Electra ($385); Custom Landau Riviera ($385); Custom Landau Electra Sport Coupe ($525); Custom with moldings on Estate ($138); Custom Regal Landau ($310); Custom padded with moldings on Electra/LeSabre/Riviera ($123-138). DeLuxe wheel covers ($26); wire wheel covers ($56-82). Super DeLuxe wheel covers ($34-56). DeLuxe wire wheel covers ($60-108). Chrome wheels ($66-118). Wood grain exterior station wagon panelling on Estate ($177); Luxus ($136); Century ($168). Code V4 accessory group ($26-36). Code V1 convenience group ($12-27). Ride and handling package ($15). LeSabre Luxus ride and performance package ($423-575). (Note: Prices for certain options and accessories varied by Series or body style. In such cases, the low-to-high range is reflected above.)

Historical footnotes: Model year introductions took place on September 27, 1974. Calendar year production peaked at 400,262 cars or 5.49 percent of industry output. Model year production hit 495,063 units. Buick dealers also marketed Opels this year. George R. Elges remained Buick's general manager in 1974 and P.C. Bowser was chief engineer.

BUICK
1904-1942

BUICK — Detroit, Michigan — (1903)/Flint, Michigan — (1904-1942) — That the man behind the first Buick was also the man who developed a method of affixing porcelain to cast iron and thus gave the world the white bathtub is a piece of historical trivia that has become part of the popular saga of the automobile. Beyond that, however, little is known about David Dunbar Buick.

An inveterate tinkerer, he was a consummately poor businessman. In 1899, finding the mechanical age more challenging than bathtubs, Buick sold off his plumbing business to the Standard Sanitary Manufacturing Company and organized the Buick Auto-Vim and Power Company to produce gasoline engines for farm and marine use, this venture reorganized in 1902 to Buick Manufacturing Company. Joining Buick's venture were Walter Marr (beginning an on-again, off-again relationship with Buick) and Eugene Richard (who worked for Olds prior to its historic fire).

Among these three men, the famous Buick valve-in-head engine was developed, and the first Buick car was built and tested in 1903. Putting up the money was Detroit sheet-metal manufacturer Benjamin Briscoe, who soon tired of doing only that. Despite Briscoe's yet-again reorganization of the Buick venture into the Buick Motor Company in the spring of 1903, all he had to show thus far for his continuing infusions of cash was a factory facility, one Buick car and no sign that production was about to commence.

Meanwhile, he had met another Olds veteran named Jonathan D. Maxwell who did not seem quite so tentative about the production side of the automobile industry. Divesting himself of David Dunbar Buick was next on Briscoe's agenda, and he did this neatly by unloading the whole Buick business to James H. Whiting of Flint Wagon Works during the late summer of 1903. In Flint the Buick pace did not pick up appreciably, the production prototype arriving only during the summer of 1904, the first sale of a Buick following in August.

Within two months sixteen Buicks had been ordered, but Whiting's capital investment had been entirely expended, and David Buick's procrastination at the factory did not hold promise that the business would ever be a particularly profitable one. Thus the Buick business was again unloaded, Whiting turning over the company and its future on Nov. 1, 1904 to a fellow Flint resident, the co-owner of the Durant-Dort Carriage Company, one William Crapo Durant.

Durant was a dynamo. Within a year he increased the capital stock of the Buick Motor Company from $75,000 to $1,500,000, reportedly selling a half million dollars of it in a single day to neighbors in Flint. Joining the company engineering staff in 1905 was Enos DeWaters, who had previously worked at Thomas and Cadillac and who would take over as chief engineer upon Walter Marr's retirement during World War I.

Being lost in the shuffle somehow was David Dunbar Buick. By the end of 1908 he would leave the company, his series of financial misadventures thereafter to include carburetor manufacture and two automobiles (the Lorraine and the Dunbar); in 1928 he would be found working at the information desk at the Detroit School of Trades; in 1929 he would die impoverished at age seventy-four. That

responsibility for David Buick's tragic career largely lay with David Buick himself is unassailable; unassailable too is the astonishing success Billy Durant made of Buick's company.

Aside from their overhead-valve design, the early two-cylinder Buicks were conventional, with two-speed planetary transmissions and single chain final drive. But with Durant as super salesman, Buick production rose to 750 cars in 1905, 1400 in 1906, 4641 in 1907. For the 1907 model year, a four had joined the twin, this a T-head design featuring shaft drive and, depending upon model, either three-speed sliding gear or two-speed planetary transmission.

In 1908, as production was practically doubling (to 8820 units), Billy Durant used Buick as his base for founding another company: General Motors, in mid-September. The most popular Buick that year was the four-cylinder Model 10 which was priced in the $1000 range and which was a close competitor of Henry Ford's new Model T. Ford's monolithic vision of the auto industry was not Durant's, however, and though the latter's multi-dimensional approach to setting up his new corporation would ultimately bear incredible fruit, Durant's idea of a bargain in companies to buy up for General Motors during these first years very frequently brought real lemons. Nineteen ten found Durant desperately in need of money, which the banks agreed to provide only if he gave up effective control of General Motors. He had no choice but to accept, and left GM to join forces with Louis Chevrolet in the establishment of another automobile company with which he ultimately planned to get GM back.

Meanwhile, among his last suggestions before relinquishing control of GM was for his Durant-Dort superintendent to take over Buick. To this the banking interests agreed, and Charles W. Nash moved into Buick's presidential chair until November 1912, when he was promoted to the same one for General Motors itself. Taking over from Nash as Buick president at that time was Walter P. Chrysler. That both Nash and Chrysler were superb managers for Buick is undeniable, but the car Durant had left them was already a success: in the marketplace and in competition.

Though Durant's interest in the latter was not overwhelming, he was aware that racing could sell cars. This was of paramount importance. It was Durant who recruited Bob Burman and Louis Chevrolet as the stars of the Buick racing team, and it was Burman and Chevrolet who made the Buick stock automobile a racing star.

Though the factory seldom contested the major international events of the day, its record in middle-echelon contests was unsurpassed. In 1909 alone, Buick won 166 events, over ninety percent of those entered, and by 1913, when Buick racing ended, the company held a flurry of AAA speed records, thirty of which would still stand in the record books a decade later.

In 1914 Buick's first six arrived. Like the first Buicks, the new 48 hp unit was an overhead valve, with the cylinders cast in pairs. Unlike earlier Buicks, it was a big car, set in a 130-inch wheelbase chassis more than a foot longer than most models which had preceded. Production for 1915 of 43,946 cars practically sextupled to 124,834 in 1916. Part of the reason for this astounding increase was the

salesmanship of Richard H. Collins, who earned the nickname "Trainload" (which was how he sold Buicks) before moving over to the presidency of Cadillac in 1917 following the Lelands' departure.

The Lelands' departure from Cadillac had followed Durant's triumphant return to the helm of General Motors which soon resulted in the departure from GM and Buick of Charles Nash and Walter Chrysler. Most people liked Billy Durant; few found it possible to work for him for long. Of brief duration, too, was Durant's second incumbency at GM. Getting himself into financial trouble again, he was forced out of the company for the last time in November 1920.

As Alfred Sloan began to pick up the pieces of Durant's GM empire, he recognized Buick as its vital link. "It is far better that the rest of General Motors be scrapped than any chances taken with Buick's earning power," he wrote Pierre du Pont. But no chances would be taken at Buick.

In charge since Chrysler's departure was Harry H. Bassett, the likeable, careful former Weston-Mott executive who would remain with Buick until his sudden death in 1926. Unlike sister GM companies, Buick had neither a long love affair nor even a brief flirtation with a V-8. Fours and sixes satisfied Buick just fine, with detachable cylinder heads and four-wheel brakes being the biggest engineering news from the company for '24, though the new styling caused some additional comment because it looked rather like a Packard.

Packard, exercising noblesse oblige, did not take legal steps, but did rather cleverly plagiarize the famous Buick slogan in a few ads that year — "When prettier cars are built, Packard will build them" — with the result that Buick redefined its radiator configuration somewhat away from the Packard's for '25. In 1925, too, after vacillating for years as to whether fours or sixes were preferred, Buick opted for sixes across the board.

Thereafter, Buick did very little, except gloat. The company was riding high, with one of America's most popular cars, routinely placing in the top five of the industry and, except for the 1921 recession year, with annual production in six figures (and usually over 200,000) throughout the Twenties.

Buick's Silver Anniversary was in 1929, and the company chose to celebrate it with bigger and better Buicks featuring sloping non-glare windshields (which was fine) and new styling with side panels that bulged perceptibly (which was not). The infamous pregnant Buick had arrived.

Compared to the good years of the Twenties, not many of these cars were delivered. Buick also conceived a cheaper companion car that year called the Marquette, which didn't deliver well either. The early Depression years were awful at Buick. In mid-1932, Edward T. Strong, the former Buick sales manager who had been elevated to Buick's presidency after Bassett's death, retired — and former Olds man Irving Reuter took over briefly.

Still heading engineering was the conservative Ferdinand A. ("Dutch") Bower, who had taken over from DeWaters who had retired in ill health in '29. For 1931 the company had remained overhead valve, but went straight-eight across the board. Synchromesh came for '32, together with Wizard Control, a combined freewheeling and automatic clutch. But Buick's real wizard entered late in '33, when Harlow H. ("Red") Curtice, the former spark of the AC plug division, came onboard as Buick's president.

Recognizing that the cars had become literally heavy with the success of the Twenties and that complacency had resulted in a Buick look that was by now old-fashioned, Curtice first attacked the remedial, making Buicks overall lighter in both weight and price tag, and introducing the Series 40, a smaller, less expensive car that could be counted upon for volume sales while Curtice geared up for the all-new Buick line for '36. These were the cars for which names joined designations: the Special (Series 40), Century (Series 60), Roadmaster (Series 80) and Limited (Series 90).

Harley Earl at GM Art and Colour had contributed in great measure to their styling; Buick engineering had introduced aluminum pistons and, following the earlier lead of other GM cars, hydraulic brakes and turret tops. (Independent front suspension had been a feature since '34.) It was in a 1936 Roadmaster that Wallis Warfield Simpson made her celebrated escape to the Continent — and to worldwide headlines — during the British Abdication crisis which followed her romance with the Prince of Wales, briefly Edward VIII. Roadmasters, too, were driven for fine exposure by Joan Crawford and Bette Davis in vintage films of this period.

The Curtice-era Buicks found considerable favor among movie folk; indeed the Estate Wagon of 1940 was conceived in Hollywood. But a *cause celebre* or cinema celebrity wasn't necessary to sell Buicks now. In 1937, for the first time since 1928, Buick surpassed the 200,000 mark. And in 1938, the Buick company, having been relegated to the bottom half of the top ten for a half-decade, returned to a solid number four spot it would enjoy until the war brought a halt to all automobile production.

By now Charles A. Chayne was Buick's chief engineer and Chayne's handiwork for the '38 Buicks included all-around coil springs. Also new for '38 were domed high-compression pistons for the Buick engine which was now designated "Dynaflash"; a Century model was clocked by Buick at 103 mph, which was admittedly a flashy performance. Dynaflow would follow postwar, but Buick did have a tentative go with a semi-automatic Self-Shifting Transmission in '39.

A genuine industry first were the Buick's turn signals as standard equipment in '39, and though Harlow Curtice's attempts to go custom with Brunn and the Limited — to the consternation of Cadillac — produced only a few cars at decade's turn, he had to be pleased with what the Buick had become since he took over. Once again, it was one of America's most popular cars.

Buick's record year production of 310,955 cars in 1940 was followed in 1941 by another new record: 316,251. Soon there were Hellcats on the Buick assembly line, but with the arrival of peace in '45, Curtice and Buick would be ready to take up where they had left off.

Buick Data Compilation
by Robert C. Ackerson

1904 BUICK

1904 Buick, model B, touring, JAC

BUICK — MODEL B — TWO: The Model B Buick was a four-passenger touring car with an indigo blue body and bright yellow wheels. Typical of most early designs, right hand drive was installed and simple curved fenders were used. Doors were provided for the rear seat compartment but none were provided for the front passengers. Weather protection was nonexistent since neither a windshield or top were provided as standard equipment.

I.D. DATA: Serial numbers on plate on left side of frame.

Model No.	Body Type & Seating	Price	Weight	Prod. Total
B	Tr.-4P	950	1850	37

ENGINE: Inline. Valve in head. Two. Cast iron block. B & S: 4.5 x 5. Disp.: 159 cu. in. Brake H.P.: 21 @ 1230 R.P.M./N.A.C.C. H.P.: 16.2. Valve lifters: mechanical. Carb.: float feed.

CHASSIS: [Model B] W.B.: 87 in. Frt/Rear Tread: 56 in. Tires: 30 x 3.5.

TECHNICAL: Planetary transmission. Speeds: 2F/1R. Floor shift controls. Cone clutch. Chain drive. Mechanical brakes on two wheels. Wood spoke wheels.

OPTIONS: Top (100.00). Windshield (20.00). Acetylene headlamps and oil side lights (75.00).

HISTORICAL: Introduced August 13, 1904 (date of first Buick sold). Calendar year production: 37. Model year production: 37. The president of Buick was James Whiting to November 1, succeeded by Charles L. Begole. A Model B won its class in hill climb held at Eagle Rock, NJ on Thanksgiving Day 1904. Another Model B sans body and nonessential features won its class in the first "Race to the Clouds" up Mt. Washington, New Hampshire.

1905 BUICK

1905 Buick, model C, touring, HAC

BUICK — MODEL C — TWO: The Model C was virtually identical to the Model B, however, a new royal blue body, ivory wheels color combination was used. In addition room was provided for 5 passengers and the service brake was now foot-operated.

I.D. DATA: Serial numbers on plate on left side of frame. Body and engine were made in Flint and final assembly took place in Jackson.

Model No.	Body Type & Seating	Price	Weight	Prod. Total
C	Tr.-5P	1200	1850	750

ENGINE: Inline. Two. Cast iron block. B & S: 4.5 x 5 in. Disp.: 159 cu. in. Brake H.P.: 22 @ 1200 R.P.M./N.A.C.C. H.P.: 16.2. Valve lifters: mechanical. Carb.: float feed, Kingston adjustable.

CHASSIS: [Model C] W.B.: 87 in. Frt/Rear Tread: 56 in. Tires: 30 x 3.5.

TECHNICAL: Planetary transmission. Speeds: 2F/1R. Floor and steering column controls. Cone clutch. Chain drive. Mechanical brakes on two wheels. Wood spoke wheels.

OPTIONS: Cape Cart Top.

HISTORICAL: Buick claimed 3 major performance records in 1905. In Boston at the Readville track a world's record for two cylinder cars for the five mile distance was established. The Buick's time was 6 minutes, 19-3/5 seconds. At a one mile Newark, NJ track a Buick set a new track record of 62 seconds. In a six mile event held at the same location a Buick also was the overall winner. Calendar year production: 750. Model year production: 750. The president of Buick was Charles L. Begole.

1906 BUICK

1906 Buick, model G, runabout, HAC

BUICK — MODEL G — TWO: The Model G was a 2-seat roadster version of the Model F. Its running gear was identical to the Model F. All Buicks had as standard equipment acetylene headlight and oil side and tail lamps. Also included in the base price was a storage battery and vibrator horn.

BUICK — MODEL F — TWO: The Model F was a revised version of the Model C. A new radiator design ran the full height of the hood and provided easy identification. The paint scheme for 1906 consisted of a purple lake body with ivory wheels and running gear.

I.D. DATA: Serial numbers on plate on left side of frame. Starting: 1 to 1207 Model F.

Model No.	Body Type & Seating	Price	Weight	Prod. Total
F	Tr.-5P	1250	1850	1207
G	Rds.-2P	1150	—	193

Note 1: Model G Price reduced to $1000.

ENGINE: Inline. Two. Cast iron block. B & S: 4.5 x 5. Disp. 159 cu. in. Brake H.P.: 22 @ 1200 R.P.M./N.A.C.C. H.P.: 16.2. Valve lifters: mechanical. Carb.: float feed, Kingston adjustable.

CHASSIS: [Model G] W.B.: 87 in. Frt/Rear Tread: 56 in. Tires: 30 x 3.5. [Model F] W.B.: 87 in. Frt/Rear Tread: 56 in. Tires: 30 x 3.5

TECHNICAL: Planetary transmission. Speeds: 2F/1R. Floor and steering column controls. Cone clutch. Chain drive. Mechanical brakes on two wheels. Wood spoke wheels.

OPTIONS: Cape Cart top (100.00).

HISTORICAL: Introduced January, 1906. Calendar year production: 1,400. Model year production: 1,400. The president of Buick was Charles L. Begole. Buicks set new overall records at the Eagle Rock, NJ and Mt. Washington, NH hill climbs. Race victories were attained at Yonkers, NY and the New York City Empire City track in events of 100 mile duration. In addition a Model F Buick was the only car to complete a 1,000 mile, New York to Chicago Relay run.

1907 BUICK

BUICK — MODELS F TR & G RDS — TWO: These two Buick models were given a longer, 89" wheelbase and a belly pan which enclosed the engine and transmission. A smaller 15 instead of 16 gallon fuel tank was installed.

BUICK — MODELS D TR & S RDS — FOUR: These two new Buick models were powered by Buick's first 4-cylinder engine linked to a 3-speed, sliding gear transmission. The Model D was introduced in May 1906 as a 1907 model and featured a royal blue body with ivory wheels. The sporty Model S had a French gray body accentuated by green striping.

BUICK — MODELS H TR & K RDS — FOUR: These two Buicks had the same finishes as the Model D and Model S models and were identical in all other areas except they used the 2-speed planetary transmission.

I.D. DATA: Serial numbers on plate on left side of frame. Starting: 101 (Models D and S). Ending: 523. During 1906 construction of a new Buick plant began in Flint and thus Buicks were constructed both in Jackson and Flint, Michigan. Engine No. Starting: 101 (Models D and S). Ending: 523.

Model No.	Body Type & Seating	Price	Weight	Prod. Total
F	Tr.-5P	1250	1850	3365
G	Rds.-2P	1150	1800	535
D	Tr.-5P	2000	2250	523
S	Rds.-2P	2500	2000	69
H	Tr.-5P	1750	2250	36
K	Rds.-2P	2500	NA	13

1907 Buick, model G, roadster, OCW

ENGINE: [Models F and G] Inline. Two. Cast iron block. B & S: 4.5 x 5. Disp.: 159 cu. in. Brake H.P.: 22 @ 1200 R.P.M./N.A.C.C. H.P.: 16.2. Valve lifters: mechanical. Carb.: float feed. [Models D, S, H and K] Inline. T-head. Four. Cast iron block. B & S: 4.25 x 4.5. Disp.: 255 cu. in. Brake H.P.: 30. Main bearings: 5. Valve lifters: mechanical.

CHASSIS: [Model F] W.B.: 89 in. Frt/Rear Tread: 59 in. Tires: 30 x 3.5. [Model G] W.B.: 89 in. Frt/Rear Tread: 59 in. Tires: 30 x 3.5. [Model D] W.B.: 102.5 in. Tires: 32 x 4. [Model S] W.B.: 106.5 in. Tires: 32 x 4. [Model H] W.B.: 102.5 in. Tires: 32 x 4. [Model K] W.B.: 106.5 in. Tires: 32 x 4.

TECHNICAL: Models F and G Planetary transmission. Speeds: 2F/1R. Floor and steering column controls. Cone clutch. Chain drive. Mechanical brakes on two wheels. Wooden spoke wheels. Models D and S Sliding gear transmission. Speeds: 3F/1R. Floor shift. Multiple disc in oil bath. Shaft drive. Mechanical brakes on two wheels. Wooden spoke wheels. Models K and H Planetary transmission. Speeds: 2F/1R. Floor and steering column controls. Cone clutch. Chain drive. Mechanical brakes on two wheels. Wooden spoke wheels.

OPTIONS: Top - Model G (70.00).

HISTORICAL: Introduced May 1906 Model D. The Model D was Buick's first 4-cylinder engine. Calendar year production: 4,641. Model year production: 4,641. The president of Buick was Charles L. Begole. The only automobile company to out produce the Buick in 1907 was Ford. Buick introduced torque tube drive on the Model D and Model S in 1907 and continued its use until 1962.

1908 BUICK

BUICK — MODELS F & G — TWO: The Model F and Model G Buicks were extensively restyled with a longer wheelbase plus reshaped hoods, fenders and grille form. Both cars had wine-colored bodies with red wheels.

BUICK — MODELS D & S — FOUR: Body styles for the Model S were extended to include a rumble seat version and a 4-place tourabout as well as the original roadster. The Model D was virtually unchanged but a $100 price drop helped maintain its popularity. Even more dramatic was the Model S price reduction of $750.

1908 Buick, model 10, touring, JAC

BUICK — MODEL 10 — FOUR: This new Buick was its most popular model in 1908 and for good reason. With brass trim, an off-white Buick Gray finish and an attractive $900 price (which included acetylene headlights, oil-fired side and taillights and a bulb horn) it was bound to be a success.

1908 Buick, model 5, touring, HAC

BUICK — MODEL 5 — FOUR: Replacing the Model K was this big touring car available in either red or blue bodies with ivory wheels and appointments. Its engine was a new 4-cylinder with its cylinders cast in pairs and fitted with an aluminum crank case.

I.D. DATA: Serial numbers on plate on left side of frame. Starting: Models D & S 524, Model 10 1, Model 5 101. Ending: Models D & S 1692, Model 10 4002, Model 5 501. Starting: Models F & G 6301, Models D & S 524, Model 10 1, Model 5 1. Ending: Models F & G 15,010, Models D & S 1699, Model 10 4002, Model 5 405.

Model No.	Body Type & Seating	Price	Weight	Prod. Total
F	Tr.-5P	1250	1850	3281
G	Rds.-2P	1150	1800	219
D	Tr.-5P	1750	2250	543
S	Rds.-2P	1750	2000	373
10	Tr.-3P	900	NA	4002
5	Tr.-5P	2500	3700	402

Note 1: Model S, 4P Tourabout body available for 1800.

ENGINE: [Models F and G] Inline. Two. Cast iron block. B & S: 4.5 x 5. Disp.: 159 cu. in. Brake H.P. 22 @ 1200 R.P.M. SAE H.P.: 16.2 Valve lifters: mechanical. Carb.: float feed Schebler. [Models D and S] Inline. T-head. Four. Cast iron block. B & S: 4.25 x 4.5. Disp.: 255 cu. in. Brake H.P.: 30. Main bearings: 5. Valve lifters: mechanical. Carb.: Schebler. [Model 10] Inline. Valve in head. Four. Cast iron block. B & S: 3-3/4 x 3-3/4. Disp.: 165 cu. in. Brake H.P.: 22.5. Valve lifters: mechanical. Carb.: Schebler. Model 5 Inline. T-head, cast in pairs. Four. Cast iron block. B & S: 4-5/8 x 5. Disp.: 336 cu. in. Brake H.P.: 40. SAE H.P.: 34.2.

CHASSIS: [Model F] W.B.: 92 in. Frt/Rear Tread: 59 in. Tires: 30 x 3.5. [Model G] W.B.: 92 in. Frt/Rear Tread: 59 in. Tires: 30 x 3.5. [Model D] W.B.: 102.5 in. Tires: 32 x 4. [Model S] W.B.: 106.5 in. Tires: 32 x 4. [Model 10] W.B.: 88 in. Tires: 30 x 3. [Model 5] W.B.: 108 in. Tires: 34 x 4.

TECHNICAL: Models F & G Planetary transmission. Speeds: 2F/1R. Floor and steering column controls. Cone clutch. Chain drive. Mechanical brakes on two wheels. Wooden spoke wheels. Models D & S Sliding gear transmission. Speeds: 3F/1R. Floor shift. Multiple disc in oil. Shaft drive. Mechanical brakes on two wheels. Wooden spoke wheels. Model 10 Planetary transmission. Speeds: 2F/1R. Floor and steering column controls. Cone clutch. Shaft drive. Divided rear axle. Mechanical brakes on two wheels. Wooden spoke wheels. Model 5 Sliding gear transmission. Speeds: 3F/1R. Floor shift. Cone clutch. Shaft drive. Mechanical brakes on two wheels. Wooden spoke wheels.

OPTIONS: Model F — gas headlights, horn, tool kit (90.00). Model 10 — top (50.00).

HISTORICAL: Introduced November, 1907. Calendar year production: 8,820. Model year production: 8,820. The president of Buick was Charles L. Begole. Both the Model D and Model 5 Buicks served as the basis for racing ventures during 1908 that included victories in the light car class at the Vanderbilt Cup Races. Buicks also participated in the Savannah, GA races as well as in a Montreal 2-day affair where they won 11 of 14 races.

159

1909 BUICK

1909 Buick, model 10, roadster, OCW

BUICK MODELS 10 & 15: Buick remained the nation's number two auto producer with a model lineup that retained its most popular models and replaced the poor sellers with improved offerings. No longer produced were the Model D, Model S and Model 5 styles. The Model 10 was offered in 4 body types all of which had a longer, 92 inch wheelbase and the new and racy Model 16 Buicks took on a modern appearance by virtue of their rounded front and rear fenders.

BUICK MODEL 6 — FOUR: Replacing the Model 5 was the Model 6A Rds with a 113'' wheelbase.

BUICK MODELS F & G — TWO: The 2-cylinder Model F and G Buick continued unchanged but remained strong sellers. Their exterior color schemes retained the same wine body finish with red wheels and running gear.

Overshadowing Buick's tremendous sales success which enabled it to hold onto second place in the industry were the machinations of William Durant which brought Buick into the fold of his newly created General Motors.

I.D. DATA: Serial numbers on plate on left side of frame. Starting: Models F and S 9950, Model 10 4003, Models 16 and 17 1, Model 6A 1. Ending: Models F and S 13900, Model 10 12152, Models 16 and 17 2500, Model 6A 6. Engine No. Starting: Models F and S 15011, Model 10 4003, Models 16 and 17 1, Model 6A 1. Ending: Models F and S 19050, Model 10 12111, Models 16 and 17 2517, Model 6A 6.

1909 Buick, model 17, touring, HAC

Model No.	Body Type & Seating	Price	Weight	Prod. Total
F	Tr.-5P	1250	1850	3856
G	Rbt.-2P	1150	1800	144
6A	Rds.-2P	2750	3700	6
10	Rds.-3P	1000	—	Note 2
10	Tourabout-4P	1050	—	Note 2
10	Toy Tonneau-4P	—	—	Note 2
16	Rds.-2P	1750	2620	Note 3
16	Tourabout-4P	1750	2620	Note 3
17	Tr.-5P	1750	2790	2003

Note 1: There was a mid-year price reduction on the Model F touring to $1000.
Note 2: Total production of all Model 10 styles were 8100.
Note 3: Total production of all Model 16 styles was 497.

ENGINE: [Models F and G] Inline. Two. Cast iron block. B & S: 4.5 x 5. Disp.: 159 cu. in. Brake H.P.: 22 @ 1200 R.P.M. SAE H.P.: 16.2. Valve lifters: mechanical. Carb.: float feed Schebler. [Model 6A] Inline, T-head, cast in pairs. Four. Cast iron block. B & S: 4-5/8 x 5. Disp.: 336 cu. in. Brake H.P.: 40. N.A.C.C. H.P.: 34.2. Valve lifters: mechanical. [Model 10] Inline, valve in head. Four. Cast iron block. B & S: 3-3/4 x 3-3/4. Disp.: 165 cu. in. Brake H.P.: 22.5. Valve lifters: mechanical. Carb.: Schebler. [Models 16 and 17] Inline. Four. Cast iron block. B & S: 4.5 x 5. Disp.: 318 cu. in. SAE H.P.: 32.4. Carb.: Schebler.

CHASSIS: [Model F] W.B.: 92 in. Frt/Rear Tread: 59 in. Tires: 30 x3.5. [Model G] W.B.: 92 in. Frt/Rear Tread: 59 in. Tires: 30 x 3.5. [Model 6A] W.B.: 113 in. [Model 10] W.B.: 92 in. Frt/Rear Tread: 56 in. Tires: 30 x 3. [Model 16] W.B.: 112 in. Tires: 34 x 4. [Model 17] W.B.: 112.5 in. Tires: 34 x 4.

TECHNICAL: Models 16 and 17 Sliding gear transmission. Speeds: 3F/1R. Floor shift controls. Shaft drive. Bevel gear, torque tube. Mechanical brakes on two wheels. Wooden spoke wheels. Models F and G Planetary transmission. Speeds: 2F/1R. Floor and steering column controls. Cone clutch. Chain drive. Mechanical brakes on two wheels. Wooden spoke wheels. Model 6A Sliding gear transmission. Speeds: 3F/1R. Floor shift controls. Cone clutch. Shaft drive. Mechanical brakes on two wheels. Wooden spoke wheels. Model 10 Planetary transmission. Speeds: 2F/1R. Floor and steering column controls. Cone clutch. Shaft drive. Divided rear axle. Mechanical brakes on two wheels. Wooden spoke wheels.

OPTIONS: Rumble Seat (Model 10) (100). Hood straps. Windshield. Side mounted spare.

HISTORICAL: Calendar year production: 14,606. Model year production: 14,606. The president of Buick was Charles L. Begole. Buick was an active, enthusiastic competitor in racing events during 1909. Modified Model 17's competed at the old Indianapolis raceway and at the Atlanta, GA race. At both locations the Buicks set track records with ease. Louis Chevrolet drove a Model 16 to a victory in the 200 race in Atlanta and a win in a 393 mile race, the Cobe Trophy Stock Car Road Race at Coren Point, IN. Other Buick successes took place at Daytona Beach and Giant's Despair hill climb at Wilkes-Barre, PA.

1910 BUICK

1910 Buick, touring, OCW

BUICK — MODEL 10 — FOUR: The Model 10 was essentially unchanged for 1910 but its basic appeal and 13 different body styles boosted output to nearly 11,000 cars.

BUICK — MODEL F — TWO: No changes for 1910 except for a new vertical tube radiator.

BUICK — MODELS 16 & 17: No changes for 1910 except for a new vertical tube radiator.

BUICK — MODEL 7 — FOUR: This new model with a big 392.6 cid engine was Buick's prestige open vehicle for 1910.

BUICK — MODEL 19 — FOUR: The Model 19 touring car was a new model with a Buick green body and ivory wheels. Its engine was based on the Model D unit from 1907. However its wheelbase was increased from 102 to 105 inches.

BUICK — MODEL 41 — FOUR: With this limousine model Buick made its first venture into the closed car market. Among its prestige features was imported goatskin upholstery and a rear compartment speaking tube.

I.D. DATA: Serial numbers on plate on left side of frame. Starting: Model 10 12152, Model F 13951, Models 16 & 17 2501, Model 7 1, Model 19 1, Model 41 1. Ending: Model 10 23150, Model F 17901, Models 16 & 17 10754, Model 7 85, Model 19 4012, Model 41 41. Engine No. Starting: Model 10 12251, Model F 19051, Models 16 & 17 2518, Model 7 1, Model 19 1, Model 41 1. Ending: Model 10 23267, Model F 25203, Models 16 & 17 10878, Model 7 96, Model 19 4023, Model 41 40.

1910 Buick, model 41, limousine, JAC

Model No.	Body Type & Seating	Price	Weight	Prod. Total
10	Rbt.-3P	1000	NA	Note 1
10	Tourabout-4P	1050	NA	Note 1
10	Toy Tonneau-4P	1150	1730	Note 1
F	Tr.-5P	1000	2300	4000
16	Rds.-2P	1750	2620	Note 2
16	Surrey-4P	1750	2620	Note 2
16	Toy Tonneau-4P	1750	2620	Note 2
7	Tr.-7P	2750	3700	85
17	Tr.-5P	1750	2790	6002
19	Tr.-5P	1400	2500	4000
41	Limo.-5P	2750	3400	40

Note 1: Total production of all Model 10 styles was 10,998.
Note 2: Total production of all Model 16 styles was 2252.

ENGINE: [Model 19] Inline. T-head. Four. Cast iron block. B & S: 4.25 x 4.5. Disp.: 255 cu. in. Brake H.P.: 28.9. Main bearings: 5. Valve lifters: mechanical. Carb.: Schebler. Model 7 Inline. T-head, cast in pairs. Four. Cast iron block. B & S: 4-5/8 x 5. Disp.: 336 cu. in. Brake H.P.: 40. SAE H.P.: 34.2. Valve lifters: mechanical. [Model 10] Inline. Valve in head. Four. Cast iron block. B & S: 3-3/4 x 3-3/4. Disp.: 165 cu. in. Brake H.P.: 22.5. Valve lifters: mechanical. Carb.: Marvel 10-501. [Model F] Inline. Two. Cast iron block. B & S: 4.5 x 5. Disp.: 159 cu. in. Brake H.P.: 22. SAE H.P.: 16.2. Valve lifters: mechanical. Carb.: float feed Schebler. [Models 16, 17 and 41] Inline. Four. Cast iron block. B & S: 4.5 x 5. Disp.: 318 cu. in. SAE H.P.: 32.4. Valve lifters: mechanical. Carb.: Marvel 10-508.

CHASSIS: [Model 10] W.B.: 92 in. Frt/Rear Tread: 56 in. Tires: 30 x 3. [Model 16] W.B.: 112 in. Tires: 34 x 4. [Model 17] W.B.: 112.5 in. Tires: 34 x 4. [Model 7] W.B.: 122 in. Tires: 36 x 4. [Model 19] W.B.: 105 in. Tires: 32 x 4. [Model 41] Tires: 34 x 4.

TECHNICAL: Model 10 Planetary transmission. Speeds: 2F/1R. Floor and steering column controls. Cone clutch. Shaft drive. Divided rear axle. Mechanical brakes on two wheels. Wooden spoke wheels. Model F Planetary transmission. Speeds: 2F/1R. Floor and steering column controls. Cone clutch. Chain drive. Mechanical brakes on two wheels. Wooden spoke wheels. Models 16 & 17 Sliding gear transmission. Speeds: 3F/1R. Floor shift controls. Shaft clutch. Bevel gear, torque tube. Mechanical brakes on two wheels. Wooden spoke wheels. Model 7 Sliding gear transmission. Speeds: 3F/1R. Floor shift controls. Leather faced cone clutch. Shaft drive. Mechanical brakes on two wheels. Wooden spoke wheels. Model 19 Sliding gear transmission. Speeds: 3F/1R. Floor shift controls. Cone clutch. Shaft drive. Mechanical brakes on two wheels. Wooden spoke wheels. Model 41 Sliding gear transmission. Speeds: 3F/1R. Floor shift controls. Cone clutch. Shaft drive. Mechanical brakes on two wheels. Wooden spoke wheels.

OPTIONS: Model 7 — top, side curtains. Model 17 — spare tire. Model 10 — windshield, wicker picnic basket.

HISTORICAL: Calendar year sales: 29,425 (includes 2048 Model 14 Buicks generally regarded as 1911 models). Model year production: 27,377. The president of Buick was Thomas Neal. The famous Buick Bugs appeared in 1910 and in July 1910 they were driven by Bob Burman and Louis Chevrolet to an impressive array of records at the Grand Circuit Speedway Meet in Indianapolis. A total of 5 firsts, and 3 second place marks were set including a time trial record of 105.87 mph. Other victories were achieved in races ranging from 10 to 100 miles held at Indianapolis. At a 3 day meet held at Lowell, MA Buick won 7 of 10 races in the stock chassis division as well as the Vesper Trophy for cars in the 301 - 450 cid engine class. Marquette Buicks competed in the Vanderbilt Cup Race and one such racer driven by Burman finished 3rd in the 1910 Savannah, GA Grand Prize race behind two Benz racers.

1911 BUICK

BUICK — MODELS 14 & 14B — TWO: The Model 14 or Buggyabout (also available as the 14B with the fuel tank moved from under the seat to the rear) was a tiny, 79 inch wheelbase 2-seater. It was the last Buick to be equipped with a 2 cylinder engine and chain drive. It's possible that if it had been produced in 1908 when it was first developed that the Model 14 could have provided the base for a Buick challenge to Ford's supremacy in the low priced field.

BUICK — MODELS 32 & 33 — FOUR: These two new Buicks used the 165cid engine of the discontinued Model 10 and were respectively a roadster and tourer. Both cars were equipped with an automatic high speed clutch release.

BUICK — MODEL 21 — FOUR: This touring model was one of the most attractive Buicks with its angular body particularly pleasing in its Buick green finish and available cream-colored wheels.

BUICK — MODELS 26 & 27 — FOUR: Both of these Buicks in roadster and touring bodies were powered by a new 210cid 4-cylinder engine. The standard color for the Model 26 was battleship gray. The Model 27 was given a dark blue body with white wheels.

1911 Buick, model 38, roadster, JAC

BUICK — MODELS 38 & 39 — FOUR: In effect these two Buicks were larger versions of the Model 26 and Model 27 Buicks. The Model 38 roadster with its large, 27 gallon, rear mounted fuel tank was finished in a dark blue body and gray wheels. The Model 39 tourer attracted attention with its four door body. However the driver's door was inoperative. The standard color for the Model 39 was dark blue. Its wooden wheels were painted gray.

BUICK — MODEL 41 — FOUR: The Model 41 limousine was powered by a 4-cylinder engine of 318 cubic inch displacement.

I.D. DATA: Serial numbers on plate on left side of frame. Starting: Model 21 1, Model 26 & 27 1, Model 32 & 33 1, Model 38 & 39 1, Model 41 41. Ending: Model 21 300, Model 26 & 27 400, Model 32 & 33 3150, Model 38 & 39 1050, Model 41 67. Engine Nos. Starting: Model 21 1, Model 26 & 27 1, Model 32 & 33 1, Model 38 & 39 1, Model 41 41. Ending: Model 21 300, Model 26 & 27 405, Model 32 & 33 3153, Model 38 & 39 1059, Model 41 67.

Model No.	Body Type & Seating	Price	Weight	Prod. Total
14	Rds.-2P	550	1500	Note 1
21	Tr.-5P	1500	2610	Note 2
21	Tr. CIC.-5P	1500	2610	Note 2
21	Rds. R./S.-3P	1550	2610	Note 2
26	Rds.-2P	1050	2100	1000
27	Tr.-5P	1150	2280	3000
32	Rds.-2P	800	1695	1150
33	Tr.-5P	950	1855	2000
38	Rds.-2P	1850	2650	153
39	Tr.-5P	1850	3225	905
41	Limo.-5P	2750	3400	27

Note 1: Total production of 3300, includes 2048 built in late 1910.
Note 2: Total production of all Model 21 styles was 3000.

ENGINE: [Model 14] Inline. Two. Cast iron block. B & S: 4.5 x 40. Disp. 127 cu. in. SAE H.P.: 14.2. Valve lifters: mechanical. [Model 21] Inline. Four. Cast iron block. B & S: 4.25 x 4.5. Disp.: 255 cu. in. Brake H.P.: 40. SAE H.P.: 28.9. Main bearings: 5. Valve lifters: mechanical. Carb. Schebler. [Models 32 & 33] Inline. Valve in head. Four. Cast iron block. B & S: 3-3/4 x 3-3/4. Disp.: 165 cu. in. SAE H.P.: 22.5. Valve lifters: mechanical. Carb.: Schebler. [Models 26 & 27] Inline. Four. Cast iron block. B & S: 4 x 4. Disp.: 201 cu. in. SAE H.P.: 25.6. Valve lifters: mechanical. Carb.: Marvel E 10-501. [Models 38 and 39] Inline. Four. Cast iron block. B & S: 4.5 x 5. Disp.: 318 cu. in. Brake H.P.: 48. SAE H.P. 32.4. Valve lifters: mechanical. Carb.: Marvel E 10-502. [Model 41] Inline. Four. Cast iron block. B & S: 4.5 x 5. Disp.: 318 cu. in. (some sources credit Model 41 with a 338cid engine). SAE H.P.: 32.4. Valve lifters: mechanical.

CHASSIS: [Model 14] W.B.: 79 in. Tires: 30 x 3. [Model 21] W.B.: 110 in. Tires: 34 x 4. [Model 26] W.B.: 100 in. Tires: 32 x 3.5. [Model 27] W.B.: 106 in. Tires: 32 x 3.5. [Model 32] W.B.: 89 in. Tires: 30 x 3.5. [Model 33] W.B.: 100 in. Tires: 30 x 3.5. [Models 38 & 39] W.B.: 116 in. Tires: 36 x 4. [Model 41] W.B.: 112.5 in. Tires: 36 x 4.5.

TECHNICAL: Model 14 Selective sliding gear transmission. Speeds: 2F/1R. Floor & steering column controls. Disc clutch. Chain drive. Mechanical brakes on two wheels. Wooden wheels. Model 21 Sliding gear transmission. Speeds: 3F/1R. Floor shift controls. Cone clutch. Shaft drive. Mechanical brakes on two wheels. Wooden wheels. Models 26 & 27 Sliding gear transmission. Speeds: 3F/1R. Floor shift controls. Multiple disc clutch. Shaft drive. Mechanical brakes on two wheels. Wooden wheels. Models 32 & 33 Planetary transmission. Speeds: 2F/1R. Floor and steering column controls. Cone clutch. Shaft drive. Mechanical brakes on two wheels. Wooden rim wheels. Models 38 & 39 & 41 Sliding gear transmission. Speeds: 3F/1R. Floor shift controls. Multiple disc clutch. Shaft drive. Mechanical brakes on two wheels. Wooden rim wheels.

OPTIONS: Windshield. Top.

HISTORICAL: Calendar year production: 13,389. Model year production: 13,389. The president of Buick was Thomas Neal. Two Marquette-Buicks were entered in the first Indianapolis 500. However they retired after 30 and 46 laps respectively. Similarly two Marquette-Buicks competed in the Savannah, GA Grand Prize race but neither car finished.

1912 BUICK

1912 Buick, touring, OCW

1912 BUICK — OVERVIEW: Improvements common to all 1912 Buicks included improved lubrication arrangements for the pushrods and the addition of grease cups to the spring shackles, steering knuckles and clutch. All models were fitted with three-speed sliding-gear transmission.

Buick eliminated a number of Models for 1912 including Model 14, Model 21, Model 38 and Model 41.

BUICK — MODEL 28 — FOUR: This roadster as all Buicks for 1912 was fitted with true doors, thus acquiring a more modern appearance. A number of color combinations were available including a two-tone wine and black body and blue-black fenders as well as a body finish of Buick gray and black body with blue-black fenders, hood and tank.

BUICK — MODEL 29 — FOUR: Customers could also order this touring model in either of two color combinations. Its hood, fenders and wheels were finished in blue-black while body color could be gray or wine.

BUICK — MODEL 34: This roadster was fitted on a trim, 90.7'' wheelbase and was delivered with a gray body, matching wheels and blue hood and fenders.

BUICK — MODEL 35 — FOUR: This most popular Buick for 1912 was updated with a three-speed selective sliding gear transmission replacing the planetary transmission used previously. Also sharing in this change over was the Model 34. The driver's door on the Model 35 was inoperative. Standard body color was dark blue with the wheels finished in gray.

BUICK — MODEL 36 — FOUR: This model was one of three roadsters offered by Buick in 1912. It shared its 201cid engine with both the Model 28 and Model 29 Buicks and was available in two color schemes. A blue and gray body with blue-black hood, fenders and fuel tank was standard. A second choice was a Buick-brown body with blue-black fenders.

BUICK — MODEL 43 — FOUR: This was the largest Buick offered in 1912. The Model 43 318cid engine like all 1912 Buick engines had its spark plugs positioned in the cylinder head at a 45° angle instead of the older, horizontal location.

I.D. DATA: Serial numbers on plate on left side of frame. Starting: Model 29 1, Models 34, 35, 36 1, Model 43 1. Ending: Model 29 8,500, Models 34, 35, 36 9051, Model 43 1501. Engine No. Starting: Model 29 1, Models 34, 35, 36 1, Model 43, 1. Ending: Model 29 8500, Models 34, 35, 36 9059, Model 43 1506.

Model No.	Body Type & Seating	Price	Weight	Prod. Total
28	2-dr. Rds.-2/4P	1025	2375	2500
29	3-dr. Tr.-5P	1180	2600	6000
34	2-dr. Rds.-2P	900	1875	1400
35	3-dr. Tr.-5P	1000	2100	6050
36	2-dr. Rds.-2P	900	1950	1600
43	3-dr. Tr.-5P	1725	3360	1501

ENGINE: [Models 28 and 29] Inline. Four. Cast iron block. B & S: 4 x 4. Disp.: 201 cu. in. SAE H.P.: 25.5. Valve lifters: mechanical. Carb.: Marvel E 10-543. [Models 34, 35 and 36] Inline. Four. Cast iron block. B & S: 3.75 x 3.75. Disp.: 165 cu. in. SAE H.P.: 22.5. Valve lifters: mechanical. Carb.: Schebler. [Model 43] Inline. Four. Cast iron block. B & S: 4.5 x 5. Disp.: 318 cu. in. Brake H.P.: 48. SAE H.P.: 32.4. Valve lifters: mechanical. Carb.: Schebler.

CHASSIS: [Model 28] W.B.: 108 in. Tires: 34 x 3.5. [Model 29] W.B.: 108 in. Tires: 34 x 3.5. [Model 34] W.B.: 90.75 in. Tires: 30 x 3.5. [Model 35] W.B.: 101.75 in. Tires: 32 x 3.5. [Model 36] W.B.: 101.75 in. Tires: 32 x 3.5. [Model 43] W.B.: 116 in. Tires: 36 x 4.

TECHNICAL: All models Sliding gear transmission. Speeds: 3F/1R. Floor shift controls. Leather faced, aluminum cone clutch. Shaft drive. Mechanical brakes on two wheels. Wooden wheels.

OPTIONS: Top. Windshield.

HISTORICAL: Innovations: Buick enclosed the selective type shift lever and emerging brake in a panel attached to the non-operating front right hand door on all models. Calendar year production: 19,051. Model year production: 19,051. The president of Buick was Walter P. Chrysler. A Marquette-Buick was entered in the 1912 Indianapolis 500 but retired after 72 laps.

1913 BUICK

1913 Buick, touring, OCW

1913 Buick, touring (Louis Chevrolet at wheel), JAC

BUICK — MODEL 24 & 25 — FOUR: These two Buicks with roadster and touring bodies replaced the Models 34, 35 and 36 of 1912. Both were offered in maroon or Buick gray bodies with blue-black fenders and wheels.

BUICK — MODEL 30 & 31 — FOUR: These roadsters and touring Buicks were offered in blue-black or gray finished bodies.

BUICK — MODEL 40 — FOUR: The prestige Buick for 1913 was this touring model. An interesting design feature was the extension of its leather upholstery over the upper door surfaces.

I.D. DATA: Serial numbers on plate on left side of frame. Starting: Model 24 & 25 1, Model 30 6250 and 12751, Model 31 1 and 8000, Model 40 1. Ending: Models 24 & 25 11000, Model 30 7999 and 13501, Model 31 6250 and 12749, Model 40 1508. Engine No. Starting: Models 24 & 25 1, Model 30 & 31 1, Model 40 1. Ending: Models 24 & 25 11005, Models 30 & 31 13504, Model 40 1510.

Model No.	Body Type & Seating	Price	Weight	Prod. Total
24	2-dr. Rds.-2P	950	2130	2850
25	3-dr. Tr.-5P	1050	2335	8150
30	2-dr. Rds.-2P	1125	2480	3500
31	3-dr. Tr.-5P	1285	2750	10,000
40	3-dr. Tr.-5P	1650	—	1506

ENGINE: [Models 24 and 25] Inline. Ohv. Four. Cast iron block. B & S: 3.75 x 3.75. Disp.: 165 cu. in. N.A.C.C. H.P.: 22.5. Valve lifters: mechanical. Carb.: Schebler. [Models 30 and 31] Inline. Ohv. Four. Cast iron block. B & S: 4 x 4. Disp. 201 cu. in. N.A.C.C. H.P.: 25.6. Valve lifters: mechanical. Carb.: Marvel E 10-501. [Model 40] Inline. Ohv. Four. Cast iron block. B & S: 4.25 x 4.5. Disp.: 255 cu. in. Brake H.P.: 40. N.A.C.C. H.P.: 28.9. Main bearings: 5. Valve lifters: mechanical. Carb.: Schebler.

CHASSIS: [Model 24] W.B.: 105 in. Frt/Rear Tread: 56 or 60 in. Tires: 32 x 3.5. [Model 25] W.B.: 105 in. Frt/Rear Tread: 56 or 60 in. Tires: 32 x 3.5. [Model 30] W.B.: 108 in. Tires: 34 x 3.5. [Model 31] W.B.: 108 in. Tires: 34 x 3.5. [Model 40] W.B.: 115 in. Tires: 36 x 4.

TECHNICAL: Sliding gear transmission. Speeds: 3F/1R. Floor shift control. Cone clutch. Shaft drive. Mechanical brakes on two wheels. Wooden wheels.

OPTIONS: Electric head, tail and side lights.

HISTORICAL: Calendar year production: 26,006. Model year production: 26,006. The president of Buick was Walter P. Chrysler. A Buick won a 102 mile "Corona Race" on the West coast in 1913. In addition, on July 17, 1913 a Model 10 Buick of 1910 vintage became the first car to climb Pike's Peak unassisted. 1913 was the last year for right hand drive in a Buick. Nickel plating instead of brass was also introduced.

1914 BUICK

1914 Buick, model B-25, touring, HAC

1914 BUICK: Highlighting the 1914 Buicks was a new 6-cylinder engine, the use of a Delco electric starter and lighting system and a switch to left hand drive with center mounted gear shift and emergency brake.

1914 Buick, model B-24, roadster, JAC

BUICK — SERIES B — MODELS B-24 & B-25 — FOUR: These roadster and touring models retained Buick's familiar front end design with angular forms for the hood and radiator. Adding to their sales appeal were a standard top and windshield.

BUICK — SERIES B — MODELS B-36 & B-37 — FOUR: With their rounded hoods and grille outlines, these roadster and touring Buicks took on a more modern appearance which was accompanied by running boards free from supporting the battery boxes.

BUICK — SERIES B — MODEL B-38 — FOUR: In a year of major styling and engineering changes the B-38 was a benchmark Buick since it was the first production Buick with a fully enclosed coupe body.

BUICK — SERIES B — MODEL B-55 — SIX: This touring model was the first Buick available with a 6-cylinder, overhead valve engine. With the rounded hood and nose of the B-24 and B-25 models plus fenders set lower then previously, the B-55 represented a break from the styling confines of Buick's early years.

I.D. DATA: Serial numbers on plate on left side of frame. Starting: B-24 101, B-25 101, B-55 101. Ending: B-24 3226, B-25 13521, B-55 2137. Engine No. Starting: B-24 101, B-25 101, B-55 104. Ending: B-24 16674, B-25 16774, B-55 2103.

Model No.	Body Type & Seating	Price	Weight	Prod. Total
B-24	2-dr. Rds.-2P	950	2200	3126 (A)
B-25	4-dr. Tr.-5P	1050	2400	13446 (B)
B-36	2-dr. Rds.-2P	1375	2726	2550
B-37	4-dr. Trer.-5P	1485	2930	9050
B-38	2-dr. Cpe.-2P	1800	2930	50
B-55	4-dr. Tr.-5P	1985	3664	2045

Note 1: (A) — 239 built for export (chassis only).
Note 2: (B) — 1544 were built for export (chassis only).

ENGINE: [Models B-24 and B-25] Inline Ohv. Four. Cast iron block. B & S: 3.75 x 3.75. Disp.: 165 cu. in. SAE H.P.: 22. Main bearings: 3. Valve lifters: mechanical. Carb.: Marvel E 10-501. [Models B-36, B-37 and B-38] Inline Ohv. Four. Cast iron block. B & S: 3.75 x 5. Disp.: 221 cu. in. Brake H.P.: 35. Main bearings: 3. Valve lifters: mechanical. Carb.: Marvel E 10-502. [Model B-55] Inline Ohv. Six-cast in pairs. Cast iron block. B & S: 3.75 x 5. Disp.: 331 cu. in. Brake H.P.: 48. SAE H.P.: 33.75. Main bearings: 4. Valve lifters: mechanical. Carb.: Marvel.

CHASSIS: [Series B-24] W.B.: 105 in. Frt/Rear Tread: 56 in. or 60 in. Tires: 32 x 3.5. [Series B-25] W.B.: 105 in. Frt/Rear Tread: 56 in. or 60 in. Tires: 32 x 3.5. [Series B-36] W.B.: 112 in. Frt/Rear Tread: 56 in. or 60 in. Tires: 34 x 4. [Series B-37] W.B.: 112 in. Frt/Rear Tread: 56 in. or 60 in. Tires: 34 x 4. [Series B-38] W.B.: 112 in. Frt/Rear Tread: 56 in. or 60 in. Tires: 34 x 4. [Series B-55] W.B.: 130 in. Frt/Rear Tread: 56 in. Tires: 36 x 4.5.

TECHNICAL: Sliding gear transmission. Speeds: 3F/1R. Floor shift controls. Cone clutch. Shaft drive. 3/4 floating rear axle. Mechanical brakes on two wheels. Wooden wheels.

OPTIONS: Front bumper. Rear bumper. Spotlight.

HISTORICAL: Calendar year production: 21,217. Model year production: 21,217. The president of Buick was Walter P. Chrysler.

1915 BUICK

1915 Buick, model C-55, touring, HAC

1915 Buick, model C-36, roadster, HAC

1915 BUICK: This was a record production year for Buick. Lower prices and improvements such as cantilevered rear springs on 6-cylinder models, an improved electric starter on 4-cylinder Buicks and the use of concealed door hinges on all models were the most important revisions.

163

BUICK — SERIES C — MODELS C-24 & C-25 — FOUR: The roadster body of the C-24 with its exposed gas tank was definitely dated. However the rounded front end of this Buick and the C-25 tourer helped maintain their popularity with Buick customers.

BUICK — SERIES C — MODELS C-36 & C-37 — FOUR: These Buicks were visually nearly identical to their 1914 counterparts. Both models were offered with an all-black finish or a combination of blue-black hood and body with black fenders and wheels.

BUICK — SERIES C — MODELS C-54 & C-55 — SIX: Joining the C-55 Buick which now had a 7-passenger capacity was the C-54 roadster model.

I.D. DATA: Serial numbers on plate on left side of frame. Starting: C-24 and C-25 100000, C-36 and C-37 106000, C-54 and C-55 105000. Ending: C-24 and C-25 144713, C-36 and C-37 143913, C-54 and C-55 144715. Engine No. Starting: C-24 and C-25 100000, C-36 and C-37 100000, C-54 and C-55 100000. Ending: C-24 and C-25 144723, C-36 and C-37 144723, C-54 and C-55 144723.

Model No.	Body Type & Seating	Price	Weight	Prod. Total
C-24	2-dr. Rds.-2P	900	2200	3256 (A)
C-25	4-dr. Trer.-5P	950	2334	19080 (B)
C-36	2-dr. Rds.-2P	1185	2795	2849
C-37	4-dr. Trer.-5P	1235	2980	12450
C-54	2-dr. Rds.-2P	1635	3400	352
C-55	4-dr. Trer.-7P	1650	3680	3449

Note 1: (A) — 186 CX-24 export models were also produced.
Note 2: (B) — 931 CX-25 export models were also produced.

ENGINE: [Models C-24 and C-25] Inline. Ohv. Four. Cast iron block. B & S: 3.75 x 3.75. Disp.: 165 cu. in. N.A.C.C. H.P.: 22.5. Main bearings: 3. Valve lifters: mechanical. Carb.: Marvel E 10-501. [Models C-36 and C-37] Inline Ohv. Four. Cast iron block. B & S: 3.75 x 5. Disp.: 221 cu. in. Brake H.P.: 37. N.A.C.C. H.P.: 22.5. Main bearings: 3. Valve lifters: mechanical. Carb.: Marvel 10-502. [Models C-54 and C-55] Inline Ohv. Six. Cast iron block. B & S: 3.75 x 5. Disp.: 331 cu. in. Brake H.P.: 55. N.A.C.C. H.P.: 33.75. Main bearings: 4. Valve lifters: mechanical. Carb.: Marvel.

CHASSIS: [Model C-24] W.B.: 106 in. Frt/Rear Tread: 56 or 60 in. Tires: 32 x 3.5. [Model C-25] W.B.: 106 in. Frt/Rear Tread: 56 or 60 in. Tires: 32 x 3.5. [Model C-36] W.B.: 112 in. Frt/Rear Tread: 56 or 60 in. Tires: 34 x 4. [Model C-37] W.B.: 112 in. Frt/Rear Tread: 56 or 60 in. Tires: 34 x 4. [Model C-54] W.B.: 130 in. Frt/Rear Tread: 56 in. Tires: 36 x 4.5. [Model C-55] W.B.: 130 in. Frt/Rear Tread: 56 in. Tires: 36 x 4.5.

TECHNICAL: All models sliding gear transmission. Speeds: 3F/1R. Floor shift controls. Cone clutch. Shaft drive. 3/4 floating rear axle. Mechanical brakes on two wheels. Wooden wheels.

OPTIONS: Speedometer (C-24, C-25). Bumpers. Spot lighter.

HISTORICAL: The C-36 was the first Buick to carry its spare tire enclosed in the body. Calendar year production: 42,553. Model year production: 42,553. The president of Buick was Walter P. Chrysler.

1916 BUICK

1916 Buick, funeral car, JAC

BUICK — SERIES D — MODELS D44 & D45 — SIX: These Buicks were powered by a new 6-cylinder engine with a single block casting and a displacement of 224 cubic inches. The D-44 roadster had trim new lines including a squared off rear deck while the D-45 was to become the most popular Buick of 1916.

BUICK — SERIES D — MODELS D46 & D47 — SIX: The D-46 Coupe was the first true Buick convertible and was equipped with plate glass windows. The D-47 was the first Buick with a sedan body style.

BUICK — SERIES D — MODELS D-54 & D-55: Both of these Buicks, unchanged from 1915, were discontinued at the end of the 1916 model year.
    This was Buick's greatest production year to date with an output of 124,834 cars.

I.D. DATA: Serial numbers on plate on left side of frame. Starting: D-44 & D-45 144717, D-54 59217, D-55 156717. Ending: D-44 & D-45 254501, D-54 213022, D-55 214822. Engine No. Starting: All models — 144729 & up.

Model No.	Body Type & Seating	Price	Weight	Prod. Total
D-44	2-dr. Rds.-2P	985	2660	12,978 (A)
D-45	4-dr. Trer.-5P	1020	2760	73,827 (B)
D-46	2-dr. Cpe.-2P	1425	2900	1443
D-47	2-dr. Sed.-5P	1800	3130	881
D-54	2-dr. Rds.-2P	1450	3400	1194
D-55	4-dr. Trer.-5P	1485	3670	9866

Note 1: (A) — 541 were produced for export.
Note 2: (B) — 4741 were produced for export.

ENGINE: [Models D-44, D-45, D-46 and D-47] Inline. Ohv. Six. Cast iron block. B & S: 3.25 x 4.5. Disp.: 225 cu. in. Brake H.P.: 45. N.A.C.C. H.P.: 25.35. Main bearings: 4. Valve lifters: mechanical. Carb.: Marvel 10-543. [Models D-54 and D-55] Inline. Ohv. Six. Cast iron block. B & S: 3.75 x 5. Disp.: 331 cu. in. Bearings: 4. Valve lifters: mechanical. Carb.: Marvel.

CHASSIS: [Model D-44] W.B.: 115 in. Frt/Rear Tread: 56 in. Tires: 34 x 4. [Model D-45] W.B.: 115 in. Frt/Rear Tread: 56 in. Tires: 34 x 4. [Model D-46] W.B.: 115 in. Frt/Rear Tread: 56. Tires: 34 x 4. [Model D-47] W.B.: 115 in. Frt/Rear Tread: 56. Tires: 34 x 4. [Model D-54] W.B.: 130 in. Frt/Rear Tread: 56 in. Tires: 36 x 4-1/2. [Model D-55] W.B.: 130 in. Frt/Rear Tread: 56 in. Tires: 36 x 4-1/2.

TECHNICAL: Sliding gear transmission. Speeds: 3F/1R. Floor shift controls. Cone clutch. Shaft drive. Full floating rear axle. Mechanical brakes on two wheels. Wooden spoke wheels.

OPTIONS: Front bumper. Cowl spot lights.

HISTORICAL: Introduced August, 1916. Calendar year production: 122,315. Model year production: 105,471. The president of Buick was Walter P. Chrysler. Calendar year production included Model D-34 and D-35 4-cylinder models which, while most Buick histories regard as 1916 models, Buick tended to almost totally ignore. Because of this inconsistency they will be examined in the 1917 model year section.

1917 BUICK

1917 Buick, roadster, OCW

BUICK — SERIES D — D-34 & D-35 — FOUR: Buick production, due to limited supplies of strategic materials, fell to 115,267 in 1917. The large Model D-54 and D-55 Buicks were dropped while the D-34 and D-35 models were given considerable publicity. Their 4-cylinder engine developed an impressive 35hp and displaced 170 cubic inches. A detachable cylinder head was incorporated and the chassis used semi-elliptic springs rather than cantilever units.
    The remaining cars in the Buick lineup remained unchanged.

I.D. DATA: Serial numbers on plate on left side of frame. Starting: Model D-34, D-35 — 215,823, D-44 154717. Ending: Model D-34, D-35 — 331774, D-44 289851.* Engine No. Starting: all models 144729 & up.
Note 1: Includes some D-54, D-55 models built in 1916.

Model No.	Body Type & Seating	Price	Weight	Prod. Total
D-34	2-dr. Rds.-2P	660	1900	2292 (A)
D-35	4-dr. Tr.-5P	675	2100	20,126 (B)
D-44	2-dr. Rds.-2P	1040	2660	4366 (C)
D-45	4-dr. Tr.-5P	1070	—	25,371 (D)
D-46	2-dr. Cpe.-3P	1440	2900	485
D-47	2-dr. Sed.-5P	1835	3130	132

Note 1: (A) — 238 more were built for export.
Note 2: (B) — 1097 more were built for export.
Note 3: (C) — 100 more were built for export.
Note 4: (D) — 1371 more were built for export.

ENGINE: [Model D-34 and D-35] Inline. Ohv. Four. Cast iron block. B & S: 3-3/8 x 4-3/4. Disp.: 170 cu. in. Brake H.P.: 35. N.A.C.C. H.P.: 18.2. Main bearings: 3. Valve lifters: mechanical. Carb.: Marvel 14. [Model D-44, D-45, D-46, D-47] Inline. Ohv. Six. Cast iron block. B & S: 3-1/4 x 4-1/2. Disp.: 225 cu. in. Brake H.P.: 45. N.A.C.C. H.P.: 25.3. Main bearings: 4. Valve lifters: mechanical. Carb.: Marvel.

CHASSIS: [Model D-34] W.B.: 106 in. Frt/Rear Tread: 56 in. Tires: 31 x 4. [Model D-35] W.B.: 106 in. Frt/Rear Tread: 56 in. Tires: 31 x 4. [Model D-44] W.B.: 115 in. Frt/Rear Tread: 56 in. Tires: 34 x 4. [Model D-45] W.B.: 115 in. Frt/Rear Tread: 56 in. Tires: 34 x 4. [Model D-46] W.B.: 115 in. Frt/Rear Tread: 56 in. Tires: 34 x 4. [Model D-47] W.B.: 115 in. Frt/Rear Tread: 56 in. Tires: 35 x 4-1/2.

TECHNICAL: Sliding gear transmission. Speeds: 3F/1R. Floor shift controls. Cone clutch. Shaft drive. Full floating rear axle. Mechanical brakes on two wheels. Wooden spoke wheels.

OPTIONS: Front bumper. Rear bumper. Solid top — D-34.

HISTORICAL: Introduced Aug. 1916. Calendar year production: 115,267. Model year production: 55,578. The president of Buick was Walter P. Chrysler.

1918 BUICK

1918 Buick, roadster, JAC

1918 Buick E-6-49, touring, HAC

BUICK — SERIES E — FOUR & SIX: Buick dropped the 225 cid six in favor of a larger 242 cid version. The 4-cylinder models continued with a new gear-driven oil pump and new oil and ammeter gauges were installed on the dash. Other changes included a trimmer instrument panel, revised seats with higher backs and the substitution of linoleum in place of rubber for the floor covering.

With windshields given a slight rearward slant the open Buick models took on a racier appearance. An interesting feature of the Model E-50 sedan was its removable rear door post. This early example of "hard top styling" was featured only in 1918.

I.D. DATA: Serial numbers on plate on left side of frame. Starting: 343,783. Ending: 480,995.

Model No.	Body Type & Seating	Price	Weight	Prod. Total
E-34	2-dr. Rds.-2P	795	1900	3800 (A)
E-35	4-dr. Tr.-5P	795	2100	27,125 (B)
E-37	2-dr. Sed.-5P	1185	2420	700
E-44	2-dr. Rds.-2P	1265	2750	10,391 (C)
E-45	4-dr. Tr.-5P	1265	2850	58,971 (D)
E-46	2-dr. Cpe.-2P	1695	2965	2965
E-47	4-dr. Sed.-5P	1845	3230	463
E-49	4-dr. Tr.-7P	1385	3075	16,148
E-50	4-dr. Sed.-7P	2175	3620	987

Note 1: (A) — 172 were built for export.
Note 2: (B) — 1190 were built for export.
Note 3: (C) — 275 were built for export.
Note 4: (D) — 3035 were built for export.

ENGINE: [Models E-34, E-35, E-37] Inline Ohv. Four. Cast iron block. B & S: 3-3/8 x 4-3/4. Disp.: 170 cu. in. Brake H.P.: 35. N.A.C.C. H.P.: 18.2. Valve lifters: mechanical. Carb.: Marvel E 10-517. [Models E-44, E-45, E-46, E-47, E-49, E-50] Inline Ohv. Six. Cast iron block. B & S: 3-3/8 x 4-1/2. Disp.: 242 cu. in. Brake H.P.: 60. N.A.C.C. H.P.: 27.3. Valve lifters: mechanical. Carb.: Marvel 10-520.

CHASSIS: [Models E-34, E-35, E-37] W.B.: 106 in. Tires: 31 x 4 (E-37 — 23 x 3.5). [Models E-44, E-45, E-46, E-47] W.B.: 118 in. Tires: 34 x 4. [Models E-49, E-50] W.B.: 124 in. Tires: 34 x 4.5.

TECHNICAL: Sliding gear transmission. Speeds: 3F/1R. Floor shift controls. Multiple disc clutch. Shaft drive. Full floating rear axle. Mechanical brakes on two wheels. Wooden rim wheels.

OPTIONS: Front bumper. Spotlight. Dual spare tire carrier.

HISTORICAL: Introduced Aug. 1917. Calendar year production: 77,691. Model year production: 126,222. The president of Buick was Walter P. Chrysler.

1919 BUICK

BUICK — SERIES H — SIX: Only cosmetic changes were made in the appearance of the 1919 Buick. Thinner and more numerous hood louvers were used and the six cylinder engine which was common to all Buicks had new valve, push rod and spark plug covers.

The instrument panel was not illuminated and the pull-type switches for the ignition and lights gave way to a lever-action Delco combined ignition and light switch.

I.D. DATA: Serial numbers on left side of frame by gas tank and again behind left front wheel. Starting: 480996. Ending: 547523.

1919 Buick H-6-46, coupe, HAC

Model No.	Body Type & Seating	Price	Weight	Prod. Total
H-44	2-dr. Rds.-2P	1595	2813	7839 (A)
H-45	4-dr. Tr.-5P	1595	2950	44,589 (B)
H-46	2-dr. Cpe.-4P	2085	3100	3971
H-47	4-dr. Sed.-5P	2195	3296	501
H-49	4-dr. Tr.-7P	1985	3175	6795
H-50	4-dr. Sed.-7P	2585	3736	531

Note 1: (A) — 176 were also exported.
Note 2: (B) — 2595 were also exported.

ENGINE: Inline. Ohv. Six. Cast iron block. B & S: 3-3/8 x 4-1/2. Disp.: 242 cu. in. Brake H.P.: 60. N.A.C.C. H.P.: 27.3. Valve lifters: mechanical. Carb.: Marvel E 10-526.

CHASSIS: [Models H-44, H-45, H-46, H-47] W.B.: 118 in. Tires: 33 x 4. [Models H-49, H-50] W.B.: 124 in. Frt/Rear Tread: 56 in. Tires: 34 x 4.5.

TECHNICAL: Sliding gear transmission. Speeds: 3F/1R. Floor shift controls. Multiple disc clutch. Shaft drive. Full floating rear axle. Mechanical brakes on two wheels. Wooden spoke wheels.

OPTIONS: Front bumper. Spot light.

HISTORICAL: Calendar year production: 119,310. Model year production: 65,997. The president of Buick was Walter P. Chrysler.

1920 BUICK

BUICK — SERIES K — SIX: The Series K Buicks were unchanged from the 1919 Series H versions.

I.D. DATA: Serial numbers on left side of frame by gas tank and repeated behind left front wheel. Starting: 547524. Ending: 687794. Engine numbers on crankcase on left side near front of oil filler tube.

Model No.	Body Type & Seating	Price	Weight	Prod. Total
K-44	2-dr. Rds.-3P	1495	2813	19,000 (A)
K-45	2-dr. Tr.-5P	1495	2950	85,245 (B)
K-46	2-dr. Cpe.-4P	2085	3100	6503
K-47	4-dr. Sed.-5P	2255	3296	2252
K-49	4-dr. Tr.-7P	1785	3175	16,801 (C)
K-50	4-dr. Sed.-7P	2695	3736	1499

Note 1: (A) — 200 built for export.
Note 2: (B) — 7400 built for export.
Note 3: (C) — 1100 built for export.

ENGINE: Inline Ohv. Six. Cast iron block. B & S: 3-3/8 x 4-1/2. Disp.: 242 cu. in. Brake H.P.: 60. N.A.C.C. H.P.: 27.3. Main bearings: 4. Valve lifters: mechanical. Carb.: Marvel E 10-526.

CHASSIS: [Models K-44, 45, 46] W.B.: 118 in. Frt/Rear Tread: 56 in. Tires: 33 x 4. [Model K-47] W.B.: 118 in. Frt/Rear Tread: 56 in. Tires: 34 x 4.5. [Models K-49, 50] W.B.: 124 in. Frt/Rear Tread: 56 in. Tires: 34 x 4.5.

1920 Buick K-6-44, roadster, HAC

TECHNICAL: Sliding gear transmission. Speeds: 3F/1R. Floor shift controls. Multiple disc clutch. Shaft drive. Full floating rear axle. Mechanical brakes on two wheels. Wooden spoke wheels with detachable rims.

OPTIONS: Front bumper. Spotlight.

HISTORICAL: Calendar year production: 115,176. Model year production: 140,000. The president of Buick was Harry H. Bassett.

1921 BUICK

1921 Buick, model 48, coupe, HAC

1921 Buick, model 50, sedan, JAC

BUICK — SERIES 21 — SIX: Buick's styling was moderately changed for 1921 with its higher hood and radiator now forming a straight horizontal line to the windshield base. Technical improvements included cord tires on all models produced after Jan. 1, 1921.

I.D. DATA: Serial numbers on brass plate left side of frame by gas tank and repeated behind left front wheel. Starting: 687795. Ending: 760555. Engine numbers on brass-plate next to timing gear inspection hole. Starting: 687795. Ending: 760555.

Model No.	Body Type & Seating	Price	Weight	Prod. Total
44	2-dr. Rds.-3P	1795	2845	7236 (A)
45	2-dr. Tr.-5P	1795	2972	31,877 (B)
46	2-dr. Cpe.-4P	2585	3137	4063
47	4-dr. Sed.-5P	2895	3397	2252
48	2-dr. Cpe.-4P	2985	3397	2606
49	4-dr. Tr.-7P	2060	3272	6424 (C)
50	4-dr. Sed.-7P	3295	3612	1460

Note 1: (A) — 56 produced for export
Note 2: (B) — 1192 produced for export
Note 3: (C) — 366 produced for export
Note 4: All models carry a 21 prefix i.e. 21-44.

ENGINE: Inline. Ohv. Six. Cast iron block. B & S: 3-3/8 x 4-1/2. Disp.: 242 cu. in. Brake H.P.: 60. N.A.C.C. H.P.: 27.3. Main bearings: 4. Valve lifters: mechanical. Carb.: Marvel E 10-526.

CHASSIS: [Models 44, 45, 46 and 47] W.B.: 118 in. Frt/Rear Tread: 56 in. Tires: 34 x 4.5. [Models 48, 49 and 50] W.B.: 124 in. Frt/Rear Tread: 56 in. Tires: 34 x 4.5.

TECHNICAL: Sliding gear transmission. Speeds: 3F/1R. Floor shift controls. Multiple disc clutch. Shaft drive. Full floating rear axle. Mechanical brakes on two wheels. Wooden spoke wheels with detachable rims.

OPTIONS: Tool box. Bumper. Spotlight. Step plates. 2 tops (Tr. Car)

HISTORICAL: A Buick Model 46 completed the 750 mile route between San Francisco and Portland in 29 hours which was 44 minutes less than the Southern Pacific's crack Shasta Limited train. Calendar year production: 82,930. Model year production: 55,337. The president of Buick was Harry H. Bassett.

1922 BUICK

1922 Buick, model 22-44, roadster, OCW

BUICK — SERIES 22-FOUR — FOUR: Buick's big news for 1922 was the reintroduction of a 4-cylinder model in August 1921. Retained from 1921 were the smoother and higher radiators and hoods.

BUICK — SERIES 22-SIX — SIX: Highlighting the 6-cylinder Buick line were new Sport Roadster and Sport Touring models with standard Houk wire wheels, red interior and dash-installed clock and speedometer manufactured by Van Sicklen.

I.D. DATA: Serial numbers on left side of frame by gas tank and repeated behind left front wheel. Starting: Models 34, 35, 36, 37 — 688795 & up. Models 44, 45, 46, 47, 48, 49, 50 — 753000 & up. Model 55 — 852537. Ending: Model 55 — 857599. Engine numbers on crank case.

Model No.	Body Type & Seating	Price	Weight	Prod. Total
34	2-dr. Rds.-2P	935	2310	5583 (A)
35	4-dr. Tr.-5P	975	2380	22,521 (B)
36	2-dr. Cpe.-3P	1475	2560	2225
37	4-dr. Sed.-5P	1650	2780	3118
44	2-dr. Rds.-3P	1495	2285	7666 (C)
45	4-dr. Tr.-5P	1525	3005	34,433 (D)
46	2-dr. Cpe.-4P	2135	3235	2293
47	4-dr. Sed.-5P	2435	3425	4878
48	2-dr. Cpe.-4P	2325	3430	8903
49	4-dr. Tr.-7P	1735	3280	6714 (E)
50	4-dr. Sed.-7P	2635	3615	4201
50L	4-dr. Limo.7P	2735	—	178
54	2-dr. Spt. Rds.-3P	1785	3180	2562
55	2-dr. Spt. Tr.-4P	1785	3270	900

Note 1: (A) — 5 built for export.
Note 2: (B) — 29 built for export.
Note 3: (C) — 9 built for export.
Note 4: (D) — 499 built for export.
Note 5: (E) — 71 built for export.
Note 6: All models carry a 22 prefix i.e. 22-34.

1922 Buick, model 22-36, coupe, JAC

ENGINE: [Models 34, 35, 36, 37 Series 22-4] Inline. Ohv. Four. Cast iron block. B & S: 3-3/8 x 4-3/4. Disp.: 170 cu. in. Brake H.P.: 35-40. N.A.C.C. H.P.: 18.23. Main bearings: 3. Valve lifters: mechanical. Carb.: Marvel H 10-502. [Models 44, 45, 46, 47, 48, 49, 50, 50L, 54, 55 Series 22-Six] Inline. Ohv. Six. Cast iron block. B & S: 3-3/8 x 4-1/2. Disp.: 242 cu. in. Brake H.P.: 60. N.A.C.C. H.P.: 27.3. Main bearings: 4. Valve lifters: mechanical. Carb.: Marvel H 10-54.

CHASSIS: [Models 34, 35, 36, 37] W.B.: 109 in. Tires: 31 x 4. [Models 44, 45, 46, 47] W.B.: 118 in. Frt/Rear Tread: 56 in. Tires: 33 x 4. [Models 48, 49, 50, 50L] W.B.: 124 in. Frt/Rear Tread: 56 in. Tires: 34 x 4.5. [Models 54, 55] W.B.: 124 in. Frt/Rear Tread: 56 in. Tires: 32 x 4.5.

TECHNICAL: Sliding gear transmission. Speeds: 3F/1R. Floor shift controls. Multiple disc clutch. Shaft drive. Full floating rear axle. Mechanical brakes on two wheels. Wooden spoke wheels with detachable rims. (Models 54, 55 have Houk wire wheels).

OPTIONS: Dual Sidemount (124" wheelbase cars only). Cowl lamps (open models).

HISTORICAL: Introduced Aug. 1921. Calendar year production: 123,152 (including truck models). Model year production: 106,788. The president of Buick was Harry H. Bassett.

1923 BUICK

1923 Buick, coupe, OCW

BUICK — SERIES 23-FOUR — FOUR: Buick styling was substantially improved with crowned fenders, cowl lights, new drum-shaped headlights and rounded window edges. Also providing the Buick with a fresh appearance was its new grille form which would remain virtually unchanged through 1927. Technical improvements included repositioned rear spring hangers, a lower suspension system and a transmission lock. Increased engine life was achieved through a harder cylinder casting, a larger crankshaft and stronger connecting rods, pistons and main bearings.

BUICK — SERIES 23-SIX — SIX: The 6-cylinder Buicks although sharing the styling of the Series 23-Four were identified by their longer 188 and 124" wheelbases. In addition open bodied 6-cylinder Buicks had rectangular rear windows while those of the 4-cylinder models were oval-shaped.

I.D. DATA: Serial numbers on left side of frame by gas tank and repeated behind left front wheel. Starting: 4-cylinder models 34, 35, 36, 37, 38, 39 — 832673, 6-cylinder models 44, 45, 47, 48, 49, 50, 54, 55 — 871321. Ending: 4-cylinder models — 1051558, 6-cylinder models — 1060176. Engine numbers on left side of crankcase near front of oil filler tube.

Model No.	Body Type & Seating	Price	Weight	Prod. Total
34	2-dr. Rds.-2P	865	2415	5768 (A)
35	4-dr. Tr.-5P	885	2520	36,935 (B)
36	2-dr. Cpe.-3P	1175	2745	7004
37	4-dr. Sed.-5P	1395	2875	8885 (C)
38	2-dr. Tr. Sed.-5P	1325	2750	6025
39	2-dr. Spt. Rds.-2P	1025	2445	1971
41	2-dr. Tr. Sed.-5P	1935	3380	8719
44	2-dr. Rds.-3P	1175	2940	6488 (D)
45	4-dr. Tr.-5P	1195	3085	45,227 (E)
47	4-dr. Sed.-5P	1985	3475	7358
48	2-dr. Cpe.-4P	1895	3440	10,847
49	4-dr. Tr.-7P	1435	3290	5906 (F)
50	4-dr. Sed.-7P	2195	3670	10,279 (G)
54	2-dr. Spt. Rds.-3P	1625	—	4501
55	4-dr. Spt. Tr.-4P	1675	3330	12,857

Note 1: (A) — 8 built for export.
Note 2: (B) — 7004 built for export.
Note 3: (C) — 1 built for export.
Note 4: (D) — 3 built for export.
Note 5: (E) — 47 built for export.
Note 6: (F) — 25 built for export.
Note 7: (G) — 1 built for export.
Note 8: All models carry a 23 prefix i.e. 23-34.

ENGINE: [Series 23-Four] Inline. Ohv. Four. Cast iron block. B & S: 3-3/8 x 4-3/4. Disp.: 170 cu. in. Brake H.P.: 35. N.A.C.C. H.P.: 18.23. Main bearings: 3. Valve lifters: mechanical. Carb.: Marvel K 10-514. [Series 23-Six] Inline Ohv. Six. Cast iron block. B & S: 3-3/8 x 4-1/2. Disp.: 242 cu. in. Brake H.P.: 60. N.A.C.C. H.P.: 27.3. Main bearings: 4. Valve lifters: mechanical. Carb.: Marvel K 10-511.

CHASSIS: [Models 34-39] W.B.: 109 in. Tires: 31 x 4. [Models 44, 45] W.B.: 118 in. Frt/Rear Tread: 56 in. Tires: 32 x 4. [Models 48, 49, 50] W.B.: 124 in. Tires: 33 x 4.5. [Models 54, 55] W.B.: 124 in. Tires: 32 x 4.5.

TECHNICAL: Sliding gear transmission. Speeds: 3F/1R. Floor shift controls. Multiple disc clutch. Shaft drive. Full floating rear axle. Mechanical brakes on two wheels. Wooden spoke wheels with detachable rims.

Note 1: Models 39 & 50 Spt. Rds. and Model 55 Spt. Tr. were offered with either Houk wire or Tuare steel disc wheels as well as wooden.

OPTIONS: Disc wheels. Front bumper. Spotlight. Wind wings. White sidewall tires. Taillights (diamond-shaped). Spare tire cover. Heater (Perfection types AB, GB).

HISTORICAL: Introduced Jan. 1923. Calendar year production: 210,572. Model year production: 181,657. The president of Buick was Harry H. Bassett. A modified Model 54 Series 23-Six was timed at 108.24mph in a run at the Muroc dry lake in California. Buick built its one-millionth car on March 21, 1923.

1924 BUICK

1924 Buick 24-Six-55, sport touring, HAC

BUICK — SERIES 24-FOUR — FOUR: The Buicks for 1924 were with the exception of the engine in its 4-cylinder line, new automobiles. With a gently sloping hood and smoothly molded fenders the Buick attracted plenty of attention. With a radiator shell that was extremely close to Packard's familiar pattern it also became the center of controversy that Packard responded to with its "When prettier automobiles are built, Packard will build them."

BUICK — SERIES 24-SIX — SIX: Giving the 6-cylinder models added distinction was their nickel-plated trim and longer 128" wheelbase for some models.
Mechanically, Buick's 1924 models were noted for their 4-wheel mechanical brakes, stronger frames and axles. The 6 cylinder engine had a larger displacement and was equipped with a removable cylinder head and aluminum crankcase. 1924 was the last year for Buick's closed cars to have horizontally divided windshields.

I.D. DATA: Serial numbers on left side of frame by gas tank and repeated behind left front wheel. Starting: Series 24-Four 1060178 & up, Series 24-Six 1064324. Ending: Series 24-Six 1239258. Engine numbers on left side of crank case near front of oil filler tube.

1924 Buick, model 24-Four-33, 4-pass. coupe, HAC

Model No.	Body Type & Seating	Price	Weight	Prod. Total
33	2-dr. Cpe.-4P	1395	2845	5479 (A)
34	2-dr. Rds.-2P	935	2576	4296
35	4-dr. Tr.-5P	965	2680	21,857
37	4-dr. Sed.-5P	1495	2955	6563
41	4-dr. Dbl. Service Sed.-5P	1695	3675	14,094
44	2-dr. Rds.-2P	1275	3300	9700
45	4-dr. Tr.-5P	1295	3455	48,912
47	4-dr. Sed.-5P	2095	3845	10,377
48	2-dr. Cpe.-4P	1995	3770	13,009
49	4-dr. Tr.-7P	1565	3645	7224
50	4-dr. Sed.-7P	2285	4020	9561
50L	4-dr. Limo. Sed.-7P	2385	—	713
51	4-dr. Brgm. Tr. Sed.-5P	2235	3940	4991
54	2-dr. Spt. Rds.-3P	1675	3470	1938
54C	2-dr. Ctry. Clb. Cpe.-3P	1945	3765	1107
55	4-dr. Spt. Tr.-4P	1725	3605	4111
57	4-dr. Twn. Car-7P	2795	3860	25

Note 1: (A) A total of 6087 Buicks of various models and body styles were built for export.
Note 2: All models carry a 24 prefix i.e.: 24-33.

ENGINE: [Models 24-Four] Inline. Ohv. Four. Cast iron block. B & S: 3-3/8 x 4-3/4. Disp.: 170 cu. in. Brake H.P.: 35. N.A.C.C. H.P.: 18.23. Main bearings: 3. Valve lifters: mechanical. Carb.: Marvel K 10-514. [Models 24-Six] Inline. Ohv. Four. Cast iron block. B & S: 3-3/8 x 4-3/4. Disp.: 255 cu. in. Brake H.P.: 70. N.A.C.C. H.P.: 27.3. Main bearings: 4. Valve lifters: mechanical. Carb.: Marvel R 10-578.

CHASSIS: [24-Four] W.B.: 109 in. Tires: 31 x 4. [24-Six Models 41, 44, 45, 46, 47] W.B.: 120 in. Tires: 32 x4. [24-Six Models 48, 49, 50, 51, 54, 55] W.B.: 128 in. Tires: 32 x 4-1/2.

TECHNICAL: Series 24-Four. Sliding gear transmission. Speeds: 3F/1R. Floor shift controls. Multiple disc clutch. Shaft drive. 3/4 floating rear axle. Mechanical brakes on four wheels. Wooden spoke wheels with detachable rim. Series 24-Six. Sliding gear transmission. Speeds: 3F/1R. Floor shift controls. Multiple disc clutch. Shaft drive. Full floating rear axle. Mechanical brakes on four wheels. Wooden spoke wheels with detachable rims.

OPTIONS: Front bumper. Rear bumper. Wind wings. Motometer.

HISTORICAL: Introduced Aug. 1, 1923. Four wheel mechanical brakes. Calendar year production: 160,411. Model year production: 171,561. The president of Buick was Harry H. Bassett.

1925 BUICK

1925 Buick, model 25-Six-51, brougham sedan, HAC

1925 Buick, roadster, OCW

BUICK — STANDARD SIX — SIX: Buick adopted a new series designation for 1925 and Standard Six models replaced the 24-Four's as the lower priced Buicks. A new six cylinder engine powered the 9 models of this series all of which were higher priced than their predecessors. A longer, 114.3'' wheelbase was used.

BUICK — MASTER SIX — SIX: The Master Six was powered by the same engine used in 1924 by the 24-Six of 1924. Styling changes were extremely modest but several new body styles kept public interest in Buick high. The age of the open tourer as the dominant product of any manufacturer was passing and for the first time Buick's best selling body styles were closed models. An interesting response to the tourer's decline was Buick's introduction of ''Enclosed Touring'' models in both the Standard and Master series. These cars used normal Touring bodies fitted with permanently fixed tops.

I.D. DATA: Serial numbers on left side of frame by gas tank and repeated behind left front wheel. Starting: Std.-1239259 & up, Master — 1211720 & up. Engine numbers on crankcase on left side near front of oil filler tube.

Standard Six Series

Model No.	Body Type & Seating	Price	Weight	Prod. Total
20	4-dr. C'ch.-5P	1295	3050	21,900
21	4-dr. Dbl. Serivce Sed.-5P	1475	3185	9252
24	2-dr. Rds.-2P	1150	2750	3315
24A	2-dr. Encl. Rds.-2P	1190	2800	1725
24S	2-dr. Spt. Rds.-5P	1250	—	501
25	4-dr. Tr.-5P	1175	2920	16,040
25A	4-dr. Encl. Tr.-5P	1250	2970	4450
25S	4-dr. Spt. Tr.-5P	—	—	651
26	2-dr. Cpe.-2P	1375	2960	4398
26S	2-dr. Spt. Cpe.-4P	—	—	550
27	4-dr. Sed.-5P	1665	3245	10,772
28	2-dr. Cpe.-4P	1565	3075	7743

Master Six Series

Model No.	Body Type & Seating	Price	Weight	Prod. Total
40	2-dr. C'ch.-5P	1495	3560	30,600
44	2-dr. Rds.-2P	1365	3285	2975
44A	2-dr. Encl. Rds.-2P	1400	3335	850
45	4-dr. Tr.-5P	1395	3465	5203
45A	4-dr. Encl. Tr.-5P	1475	3540	1900
47	4-dr. Sed.-5P	2225	3850	4200
47A	4-dr. Encl. Tr.-7P	1475	3540	500
50	4-dr. Sed.-7P	2425	3995	4606
50L	4-dr. Limo.-7P	2525	4030	768
51	4-dr. Brgm. Sed.-5P	2350	3905	6850
54	2-dr. Spt. Rds.-3P	1750	3485	1917
54C	2-dr. Ctry. Clb. Cpe.-3P	2075	3745	2751
55S	2-dr. Spt. Tr.-4P	1800	3550	2774
57	4-dr. Twn. Car-7P	2925	3850	92

Note 1: All models had a 25 prefix i.e.: 25-20.
In addition a total of 9412 Buicks of all models were exported.

ENGINE: [Standard Six] Inline. Ohv. Six. Cast iron block. B & S: 3 x 4-1/2. Disp.: 191 cu. in. Brake H.P.: 50 at 2800 R.P.M. N.A.C.C. H.P.: 21.6. Main bearings: 4. Valve lifters: mechanical. Carb.: Marvel T38. Torque: 120 lbs.-ft. at 1600 R.P.M. [Master Six] Inline. Ohv. Four. Cast iron block. B & S: 3-3/8 x 4-3/4. Disp.: 255 cu. in. Brake H.P.: 70. N.A.C.C. H.P.: 27.3. Main bearings: 4. Valve lifters: mechanical. Carb.: Marvel T4S.

CHASSIS: [Standard Six] W.B.: 114.3 in. Tires: 5.00 x 22. [Master Six] W.B.: 120/128 in. Tires: 32 x 5.77 (6.00 x 22 opt.)

TECHNICAL: Sliding gear transmission. Speeds: 3F/1R. Floor shift controls. Multiple disc clutch. Shaft drive. 3/4 floating-Std. Six, full floating-Master Six. Mechanical brakes on four wheels. Wooden spoke wheels with detachable rims.

OPTIONS: White sidewall tires. Bumpers. Spotlight. Wind wings. Motometer.

HISTORICAL: Introduced Aug. 1924. Vacuum operated windshield wipers replaced hand-powered versions. 1925 was the first model year Buick equipped its car with balloon tires. Calendar year production: 192,100. Model year production: 157,071 plus 9412 for export. The president of Buick was Harry H. Bassett. Buick sent a touring model around the world via a dealer-to-dealer route. Each dealer was responsible for driving the car to the next and having its log book signed. 1925 was the first year Buick used a nitrocellulose lacquer in place of a varnish-color finish process.

1926 BUICK

1926 Buick, Master Six, sedan, JAC

1926 Buick, Standard Six, 2-dr. coupe, HAC

BUICK STANDARD SIX, MASTER SIX — SIX: Both Buick series were restyled for 1926 with smoother radiator edges and on those cars with Fisher bodies, double belt moldings. Hubcaps and the gas filler caps were now constructed of aluminum and a straight tie rod running vertically across the grille supported the headlights.

Technical improvements included new air, oil and gas filters, a stronger clutch and one-piece brake linings. The Buick's new dual-beam headlights were mounted in interchangeable shells. The dimming switch for these lights was mounted in the steering wheel center. Components such as the chassis, drive shaft and rear axle were now of a heavier construction. In addition the Buick chassis had Zerk lubrication fittings.

BUICK MASTER SIX — SIX: Engine displacement and power was increased in both series. In addition to their longer wheelbase the Master series models were distinguished from their Standard running mates by such features as a Motometer, scuff plates, clock, cigarette lighter and heater that were included in their base price.

I.D. DATA: Serial numbers on right side of frame behind front wheel position. Starting: Std — 1398244, Master — 1426599. Ending: Std — 1638576, Master — 1638773. Engine numbers on left side of crankcase near front of oil filler tube.

Model No	Body Type & Seating	Price	Weight	Prod. Total
Standard Six Series				
20	2-dr. Sed.-5P	1195	3140	40,113
24	2-dr. Rds.-2P	1125	2865	1891
25	4-dr. Tr.-5P	1150	2920	4859
26	2-dr. Cpe.-2P	1195	3030	10,531
27	4-dr. Sed.-5P	1295	3210	43,375
28	2-dr. Cpe.-4P	1275	3110	8271
Master Six Series				
40	2-dr. Sed.-5P	1395	3655	21,861
44	2-dr. Rds.-2P	1250	3380	2654
45	4-dr. Tr.-5P	1295	3535	2630
47	4-dr. Sed.-5P	1495	3790	53,490
48	2-dr. Cpe.-4P	1795	3845	10,028
49	4-dr. Sed.-7P	1995	—	1
50	4-dr. Sed.-7P	1995	4040	12,690
50T	4-dr. Taxi Cab-7P	—	4040	220
51	4-dr. Brgm. Tr. Sed.-5P	1925	3945	10,873
54	2-dr. Spt. Rds.-3P	1495	3580	2501
54C	2-dr. C.C. Spt. Cpe.-3P	1765	3820	4436
55	4-dr. Spt. Tr.-4P	1525	3650	2051
58	2-dr. Cpe.-4P	1275	—	1

Note 1: All models carry a 26 prefix i.e. 26-20.

ENGINE: [Standard Six] Inline. Ohv. Six. Cast iron block. B & S: 3-1/8 x 4-1/2. Disp.: 207 cu. in. Brake H.P.: 60. N.A.C.C. H.P.: 23.4. Main bearings: 4. Valve lifters: mechanical. Carb.: Marvel T3. Torque: 140. [Master Six] Inline. Ohv. Six. Cast iron block. B & S: 3-1/2 x 4-3/4. Disp.: 274 cu. in. Brake H.P.: 75. N.A.C.C. H.P.: 29.4. Main bearings: 4. Valve lifters: mechanical. Carb.: Marvel T-4. Torque: 178.

CHASSIS: [Standard Six] W.B.: 114.5 in. Tires: 6.00 x 21. [Master Six] W.B.: 120/128 in. Tires: 6.00 x 21.

TECHNICAL: Sliding gear transmission. Speeds: 3F/1R. Floor shift controls. Multiple disc clutch. Shaft drive. 3/4 floating-Std Six, full floating-Master Six. Mechanical brakes on four wheels. Wooden spoke wheels with detachable rims.

OPTIONS: Bumpers. Fog lights. Motometer (Std Six). Running board step plates (Std Six). Instrument panel light. Cadmium rims. White side wall tires.

HISTORICAL: Introduced Aug. 1, 1925. The old combination starter-generator was replaced by separate Delco starter and generator units. Calendar year production: 266,753. Model year production: 240,533 (including 7480 for export and 1 experimental model). On Oct. 17, 1926 Harry Bassett (president of Buick) died of pneumonia. His successor was Edward Thomas Strong.

1927 BUICK

1927 Buick, 4-dr. sedan, OCW

1927 Buick, Standard Six, sport roadster, HAC

BUICK — STANDARD SIX — SIX: The appearance of both Buick lines was left almost unaltered for 1927. All open models in both series had one piece windshields and a reorganized dash which placed the speedometer directly before the driver and provided dashboard lighting on all models.

Technical advancements were headlined by new motor mounts, a counter balanced crankshaft, a "vacuum ventilation" for the crankcase, and a torsional balancer which enabled Buick to describe its engines as "Vibrationless Beyond Belief". The Standard Six models continued to have gas tank mounted fuel gauges.

BUICK MASTER SIX — SIX: Master Six Models on the 128" wheelbase chassis had a Gothic Goddess radiator cap replete with wings. This ornament was also fitted to Models 24 and 25 of the Standard Six series. Master Six closed car interiors were finished in walnut, satin and broadcloth. With the exception of the 3 lowest priced Models 40, 47 and 48, the Master Six Buicks featured new dash-mounted fuel gauges.

I.D. DATA: Serial numbers on right side of frame behind front wheel position. Starting: Std. Six Ser.-1638800, Master Six Ser.-1661435. Engine numbers on crankcase on left side near front of oil filler tube.

169

Model No.	Body Type & Seating	Price	Weight	Prod. Total
Standard Six Series				
20	2-dr. Sed.-5P	1195	3215	33,190
24	2-dr. Spt. Rds.-4P	1195	2990	4985
25	4-dr. DeL. Spt. Tr.-5P	1225	3040	3272
26	2-dr. Cpe.-2P	1195	3110	10,512
26S	2-dr. Ctry. Clb. Cpe.-4P	1275	3190	11,688
26CC	2-dr. Clp. Top. Cpe.-4P	—	—	1
27	4-dr. Sed.-5P	1295	3300	40,272
28	2-dr. Cpe.-4P	1275	3190	7178
29	4-dr. Twn. Brgm. Sed.-5P	1375	3305	11,032
Master Six Series				
40	2-dr. Sed.-5P	1395	3750	12,130
47	2-dr. Sed.-5P	1495	3870	49,105
48	2-dr. Cpe.-4P	1465	3800	9350
50	4-dr. Sed.-7P	1995	4115	11,259
50T	4-dr. Taxi Cab.-7P	—	—	60
51	4-dr. Brgm. Sed.-5P	1925	4050	13,862
54	2-dr. DeL. Spt. Rds.-4P	1495	3655	4310
54C	2-dr. Ctry. Clb. Cpe.-4P	1765	3905	7095
54CC	2-dr. Conv. Cpe.-4P	1925	3915	2354
55	4-dr. DeL. Spt. Tr.-4P	1525	3735	2092
58	2-dr. Cpe.-5P	1850	3940	7655

ENGINE: [Standard Six] Inline. Ohv. Six. Cast iron block. B & S: 3-1/8 x 4-1/2. Disp.: 207 cu. in. Brake H.P.: 63 @ 2800 R.P.M. N.A.C.C. H.P.: 23.4. Main bearings: 4. Valve lifters: mechanical. Carb.: Marvel T3. Torque: 140. [Master Six] Inline. Ohv. Six. Cast iron block. B & S: 3-1/2 x 4-3/4. Disp.: 274 cu. in. Brake H.P.: 75. N.A.C.C. H.P.: 29.4. Main bearings: 4. Valve lifters: mechanical. Carb.: Marvel T4. Torque: 178.

CHASSIS: [Standard Six] W.B.: 114.5 in. Tires: 33 x 6. [Master Six] W.B.: 120/128 in. Tires: 33 x 6.

TECHNICAL: Sliding gear transmission. Speeds: 3F/1R. Floor shift controls. Multiple disc clutch. Shaft drive. 3/4 floating rear axle - Std Six, full floating rear axle - Master Six. Mechanical brakes on four wheels. Wooden spoke wheels with detachable rims.

OPTIONS: Bumpers. Trunk.

HISTORICAL: Introduced August 1926. Calendar year production: 255,160. Model year production: 250,116 (includes 8109 for export). The president of Buick was Edward Thomas Strong. The two-millionth Buick was produced on November 1, 1927.

1928 BUICK

1928 Buick, opera coupe, DM

BUICK STANDARD SIX — SERIES 115 — SIX: Buick's styling for 1928 featured thinner windshield and corner posts (on closed models) standard hood emblems and smooth-surfaced fenders. The older, barrel-shaped headlight cases gave way to bullet-shaped versions which along with the radiator, windshield molding and hood fasteners, were nickel-plated. Giving the Buick a new face was a smoother radiator shell which shed almost all that had remained of its Packard-look.

A new stronger, double-drop frame with deeper side channels allowed body height to be reduced by 3 inches. A noteworthy improvement in handling and roadability was attained by the use of 4-wheel Lovejoy hydraulic shock absorbers on all models. Engine changes for 1928 were highlighted by reshaped hemispherical combustion chambers.

Interior improvements were lead by Buick's adoption of the standard H-shift pattern, an adjustable steering column and dash-mounted engine temperature and fuel level gauges. Plush mohair was used for the upholstery.

Also added to the Buick's standard equipment list for 1928 were Wolverine bumpers. All Standard Six models had dash-mounted gas gauges and painted headlight shells. The exceptions to the latter were Models 24 and 25 which had chromed shells.

BUICK MASTER SIX — SERIES 120 — SIX: A new DeLuxe 4-door Sedan was added to the Master Six line while Models 54CC (Convertible Coupe) and 40 (2 door Sedan) were eliminated. The 4-door Sport Touring Master Six was the only Buick offered with standard side mounts. All Master Six models had chromed headlight shells. A new model on the 120'' wheelbase chassis was the 47S, 5-passenger DeLuxe Sedan. Its back was leather trimmed and was fitted with side landau hinges. Interiors were finished in Taupe and Green figured-design mohair plush. All closed models in both series had wide doors, new outside door handles and rear compartment carpets. The Master Six Buicks on the 128'' wheelbase has a 128 Series designation.

I.D. DATA: Serial numbers on right side of frame behind front wheel opening. Starting: Std. Six — 1901476, Master Six — 1911026. Ending: Std. Six — 2137872, Master Six — 2169650. Engine numbers on crankcase.

1928 Buick, roadster, OCW

Model No.	Body Type & Seating	Price	Weight	Prod. Total
Std Six Series				
20	2-dr. Sed.-5P	1195	3310	32,481
24	2-dr. Spt. Rds.-4P	1195	3090	4513
25	4-dr. Spt. Tr.-5P	1225	3140	3134
26	2-dr. Cpe.-2P	1195	3215	12,417
26S	2-dr. Ctry. Clb. Cpe.-4P	1275	3300	13,211
27	4-dr. Sed.-5P	1295	3370	50,224
29	4-dr. Twn. Brgm.-5P	1375	3400	10,840
Master Six Series				
47	4-dr. Sed.-5P	1495	3920	34,197
47S	4-dr. DeL. Sed.-5P	1575	3930	16,398
48	2-dr. Cpe.-4P	1465	3835	9002
49	4-dr. Tr.-7P	NA	NA	2
50	4-dr. Sed.-7P	1995	4085	10,827
51	4-dr. Brgm. Sed.-5P	1925	3980	10,258
54	2-dr. Spt. Rds.-4P	1495	3655	3853
54C	2-dr. Ctry. Clb. Cpe.-4P	1765	3890	6555
55	4-dr. Spt. Tr.-5P	1525	3735	1333
58	2-dr. Cpe.-5P	1850	3925	9984

Note 1: All models carry a 28 prefix, i.e. 28-20.

ENGINE: [Standard Six] Inline. Ohv. Six. Cast iron block. B & S: 3-1/8 x 4-1/2. Disp.: 207 cu. in. Brake H.P.: 63 @ 2800 R.P.M. N.A.C.C. H.P.: 23.44. Main bearings: 4. Valve lifters: mechanical. Carb.: Marvel T3. Torque: 140. [Master Six] Inline. Ohv. Six. Cast iron block. B & S: 3-1/2 x 4-3/4. Disp.: 274 cu. in. Brake H.P.: 77 @ 2800 R.P.M. N.A.C.C. H.P.: 29.4. Main bearings: 4. Valve lifters: mechanical. Carb.: Marvel T4. Torque: 178.

CHASSIS: [Standard Six] W.B.: 114.5 in. Tires: 31 x 5.25. [Master Six] W.B.: 120 in. (Models 47 and 47S only). Tires: 33 x 6.00. [Master Six] (Models 50, 51, 54, 54C, 55 and 58): W.B.: 128 in. Tires: 33 x 6.

TECHNICAL: Sliding gear transmission. Speeds: 3F/1R. Floor shift controls. Multiple disc clutch. Shaft drive. 3/4 floating rear axle — (Std Six) full floating rear axle — (Master Six). Overall Drive Ratio: Models 20, 27, 29 — 5.1:1. Models 48, 54, 54C, 55, 58 — 4.72:1. Models 24, 25, 26, 26S, 47, 47S, 50, 51 — 4.9:1. Mechanical brakes on four wheels. Wooden spoke wheels with detachable rims.

OPTIONS: Buffalo wire wheels (Std Six Models 24 & 25 and 128'' wheelbase Master Six models only). Dual tire carrier. Motometer.

HISTORICAL: Introduced July 28, 1927. Calendar year production: 221,758. Model year production: 235,009 (including 5194 for export). The president of Buick was Edward Thomas Strong. A 1928 model coupe produced in November 1927 was the two-millionth Buick built.

1929 BUICK

1929 Buick, series 129, model 58, coupe, JAC

BUICK — SERIES 116 — SIX: The 1929 Buicks were the first cars styled in their entirety by General Motors Art and Colour department. Three new series the 116, 121 and 129 (which represented wheelbase measurements) replaced the older Standard and Master Six designations and all were fitted with the body form that earned them the label of Pregnant Buicks. This non-complimentary label was due to the 1-1/2'' body bulge below the beltline.

Aside from this feature which lasted only for one year the 1929 Buicks had slightly slanted windshields on closed body models and a radiator bearing the Buick nameplate in its center rather than on the shell. Major technical improvements included (on closed models) dual electric windshield wipers and side cowl ventilators.

Buick was also celebrating its silver anniversary with a total of 43 exterior color options. Standard in all models was a mechanical fuel pump in place of the vacuum tank.

The chassis' design of all three series was, with the exception of the external mechanical brakes, virtually all new. The frame was constructed of thicker steel with deeper cross sections and key suspension components were strengthened. Lovejoy shock absorbers were also installed. All engines were increased both in terms of displacement and power and steel-backed main bearings were also used by Buick for the first time.

The 116" wheelbase chassis Buick now featured interiors with ashtrays and cigarette lighters as standard equipment.

1929 Buick, series 129, model 57, sedan, JAC

1929 Buick, series 121, model 44, sport roadster, JAC

BUICK — SERIES 121 — SIX: Offered in 6 styles, the 121 Series Buick shared its walnut interior trim with all 1929 Buicks. Also common to all Buicks was a new molded rubber steering wheel.

1929 Buick, series 129, model 51, sport sedan, JAC

BUICK — SERIES 129 — SIX: Eight body styles all on the 129" wheelbase were available in this series. The optional bumpers now consisted of 3 rather than 2 horizontal bars.

I.D. DATA: Serial numbers on right side of frame behind front fender opening. Starting: 2123926. Ending: 2313805. Engine numbers on crankcase. Starting: Ser. 116-22225361, Ser. 121,129-2340300.

Model No.	Body Type & Seating	Price	Weight	Prod. Total
Series 116				
20	2-dr. Sed.-5P	1220	3525	17,783
25	4-dr. Tr.-5P	1225	3330	2938
26	2-dr. Bus. Cpe.-2P	1195	3465	8745
26S	2-dr. Spt. Cpe. R/S-4P	1250	3520	10,308
27	4-dr. Sed.-5P	1320	3630	44,345
Series 121				
41	4-dr. Cl. C. Sed.-5P	1450	4180	10,110
44	4-dr. Spt. Rds.-4P	1325	3795	6195
46	2-dr. Bus. Cpe.-2P	1395	3990	4339
46S	2-dr. Spt. Cpe. R./S.-4P	1450	4055	6638
47	4-dr. Sed.-5P	1520	4175	30,356
48	2-dr. Cpe.-4P	1445	4010	4255
Series 129				
49	4-dr. Tr.-7P	1550	3990	1530
50	4-dr. Sed.-7P	2045	4360	8058
50L	4-dr. Imp. Sed. Limo.-7P	2145	4405	736
51	4-dr. Spt. Sed.	1875	4230	7014
54CC	2-dr. DeL. Conv. Cpe.-4P	1875	4085	2021
55	4-dr. Spt. Tr.-5P	1525	3905	1122
57	4-dr. Sed.-5P	1935	4260	5175
58	2-dr. Cpe.-5P	1865	4145	734

Note 1: All models carry a 29 prefix, i.e.: 29-20

ENGINE: [Series 116] Inline. Ohv. Six. Cast iron block. B & S: 3-5/16 x 4-5/8. Disp.: 239.1 cu. in. C.R.: 4.3:1. Brake H.P.: 94 at 2800 R.P.M. Taxable H.P.: 26.3. Main bearings: 4. Valve lifters: mechanical. Carb.: Marvel 3-jet, updraft T3-10-704. Torque: 172 lbs.-ft. at 1200 R.P.M. [Series 121, 129] Inline. Ohv. Six. Cast iron block. B & S: 3-5/8 x 5. Disp.: 309.6 cu. in. C.R.: 4.3:1. Brake H.P.: 91. N.A.C.C. H.P.: 31.5. Main bearings: 4. Valve lifters: mechanical. Carb.: Marvel 3-jet updraft T4-10-706.

CHASSIS: [Series 116] W.B.: 116 in. O.L.: 167-3/4 in. Height: 74-7/8 in. Frt/Rear Tread: 56-7/16 in./58 in. Tires: 30 x 5.50. [Series 121] W.B.: 121 in. Frt/Rear Tread: 56-7/16 in./58 in. Tires: 30 x 6.5. [Series 129] W.B.: 129 in. Frt/Rear Tread: 56-7/16 in./58 in. Tires: 32 x 6.50.

TECHNICAL: Sliding gear transmission. Speeds: 3F/1R. Floor shift controls. Multiple disc clutch. Shaft drive. Ser. 116-3/4 floating rear axle — all others — full floating rear axle. Overall Drive Ratio: 4.9:1. Mechanical external contracting brakes on four wheels. Wooden spoke wheels with detachable rims. Rim size: 20 in.

OPTIONS: Front bumper. Rear bumper. Clock. Welled fenders, side mounts. Wide-spoke artillery. Wire wheels. Step plates. Spare tire, tube. Spare tire cover. Spare tire lock. Disc wheels.

HISTORICAL: Introduced July 29, 1928. Calendar year production: 196,104. Model year production: 187,861 (includes 8932 cars built for export). The president of Buick was Edward Thomas Strong.

1930 BUICK

1930 Buick, series 40, model 46S, sport coupe, JAC

BUICK — SERIES 40 — SIX: The Buicks for 1930 appeared as handsome and graceful as the 1929 models had been bulbous. As one observer noted, "the cars retain the Buick individuality without . . . the bulge." A new vertically mounted, thermostatically controlled shutter system gave the Buick's radiator a long racy appearance. More importantly a height reduction of 2" and a new around the body belt line worked visual wonders in the Buick's appearance. Also contributing to the Buick's more modern styling were flatter hubcaps for the increasingly popular wire wheel option.

The Series 40 Buicks replaced the Series 116 and were mounted on a longer 118" wheelbase. Interiors carried rubber floor mats.

BUICK — SERIES 50 — SIX: Series 50 models which replaced the Series 121 all had wheelbases of 124" plus fully carpeted interiors as did the Series 60 Buicks.

BUICK — SERIES 60 — SIX: Both the 132" wheelbase Series 60 and the Series 50 shared a 331.5 cid engine for 1931. All Buicks had a new dash panel with the instruments both directly and indirectly lighted. Beginning on Jan 1, 1930 a new sport roadster with rumble seat, model 30-64 was added to Series 60.

171

1931 BUICK

1931 Buick, series 90, model 96, coupe, OCW

1930 Buick, series 50, model 57, sedan, JAC

1930 Buick, series 60, model 64, sport roadster, JAC

BUICK — SERIES 50 —- EIGHT: Buick's styling was all but unchanged (the only observable difference was a radiator cap bearing a figure 8) but that hardly mattered since three new straight-eight engines were introduced for 1931. None of these engines shared any interchangeable parts and the smallest, displacing 220 cubic inches was used for the Series 40 which had the same 114'' wheelbase of the discontinued Marquette.

The Series 50 interior was equipped with either mohair or cloth upholstery, carpeting for the rear seat floor area, dome lights and arm rests. A rear foot rail was provided as was an adjustable driver's seat. Midway through the model year the Series 50 received the synchromesh transmission previously available only on the more costly Buicks. Also appearing as a mid-season offering was a new convertible coupe model.

BUICK — SERIES 60 — EIGHT: In Buick's new lineup the Series 60 corresponded to the old Series 40 models with a 118'' wheelbase and a 272 cid engine. Their interior of either mohair plush or cloth was of higher quality than that of the Series 50. Open models were finished in a leather interior. All Series 60, 80 and 90 Buicks closed cars had a standard equipment passenger-side windshield wiper.

BUICK — SERIES 80 — EIGHT: Only 2 models were offered in this series with a 124'' wheelbase and 344 cid engine. As were all 1930 Buicks, the Series 80's had a revamped instrument panel, lower front seats with deeper cushions and a new cooling system with thermostatically controlled shutters.

I.D. DATA:
Serial numbers on right side of frame behind front fender opening. Starting: Series 40 — 2313806, Series 50, 60 — 2334956. Ending: Series 40 — 2459715, Series 50, 60 — 2460543. Engine numbers on crankcase. Starting: Series 40 — 2439593, Series 50, 60 — 2489593. Ending: Series 40 — 2568138, Series 50, 60 — 2613337.

Model No.	Body Type & Seating	Price	Weight	Prod. Total
Series 40				
40	2-dr. Sed.-5P	1270	3600	6101
44	2-dr. Spt. Rds.-4P	1310	3420	3476
45	4-dr. Phae.-5P	1310	3410	972
46	2-dr. Bus. Cpe.-2P	1260	3540	5695
46S	2-dr. Sp. Cpe.-4P	1300	3600	10,719
47	4-dr. Sed.-5P	1330	3700	47,294
Series 50				
57	4-dr. Sed.-5P	1540	4235	22,929
58	2-dr. Cpe.-4P	1510	4120	5275
Series 60				
60	4-dr. Sed.-7P	1910	4415	6583
60L	4-dr. Limo.-7P	2070	4475	690
61	4-dr. Sp. Sed.-5P	1760	4330	12,508
64	2-dr. Spt. Rds.-4P	1585	4015	2006
64C	2-dr. DeL. Cpe.-4P	1695	4225	5370
68	2-dr. Cpe.-4P	1740	4200	10,216
69	4-dr. Phae.-7P	1595	4100	807

Note 1: All models carry a 30 prefix, i.e. 30-40.

ENGINE:
[Series 40] Inline. Ohv. Six. Cast iron block. B & S: 3-7/16 x 4-5/8. Disp.: 257.5 cu. in. Brake H.P.: 80.5 @ 2800 R.P.M. N.A.C.C. H.P.: 28.39. Main bearings: 4. Valve lifters: mechanical. Carb.: Marvel T3S-10-758. [Series 50, 60] Inline. Ohv. Six. Cast iron block. B & S: 3-3/4 x 5. Disp.: 331.4 cu. in. Brake H.P.: 99 @ 2800 R.P.M. N.A.C.C. H.P.: 33.75. Main bearings: 4. Valve lifters: mechanical. Carb.: Marvel T4-10-754.

CHASSIS:
[Series 40] W.B.: 118 in. Tires: 29 x 5.50. [Series 50] W.B.: 124 in. Frt/Rear Tread: 56-7/8 in. / 58 in. Tires: 31 x 6.50. [Series 60] W.B.: 132 in. Frt/Rear Tread: 56-7/8 in. / 58 in. Tires: 19 x 6.50.

TECHNICAL:
Sliding gear transmission. Speeds: 3F/1R. Floor shift controls. Multiple disc clutch. Shaft drive. 3/4 floating rear axle. Mechanical, internal expanding brakes on four wheels. Wooden spoke wheels with detachable rims.

OPTIONS:
Wire wheels. Chrome grille guard. Side mounts. White sidewall tires. Luggage rack. Fog lights. Wind wings.

HISTORICAL:
Introduced July 28, 1929. Calendar year production: 119,265. Model year production: 181,743 (including 6098 stripped chassis and cars for export.) The president of Buick was Edward Thomas Strong. Entered at Indianapolis was a Buick 6 powered car, The Butchers Brothers Special, which was credited with a 14th place finish.

1931 Buick, series 90, model 94, sport roadster, JAC

BUICK — SERIES 90 — EIGHT: The Series 90 Buick was powered by the 344 cid engine and had a wheelbase of 132''. Closed car interiors had mohair plush interiors with silk roller shades for the rear side and back windows; full floor carpeting was provided. The convertible coupe which had a mid-season introduction had a leather interior as did the other open-model Series 90 Buicks.

I.D. DATA:
Serial numbers on right side of frame behind front fender opening. Starting: 2460544. Ending: 2602731. Engine numbers on crank case. Starting: 2624638. Ending: 2751921.

Model No.	Body Type & Seating	Price	Weight	Prod. Total
Series 50				
50	2-dr. Sed.-5P	1035	3145	3616
54	2-dr. Spt. Rds.-4P	1055	2935	907
55	4-dr. Phae.-5P	1055	2970	358
56	2-dr. Bus. Cpe.	1025	3055	2782
56C	2-dr. Conv. Cpe.-4P	1095	3095	1531
56S	2-dr. Sp. Cpe.-4P	1055	3155	5733
57	4-dr. Sed.-5P	1095	3265	33,184
Series 60				
64	2-dr. Spt. Rds.-4P	1335	3465	1050
65	4-dr. Phae.-5P	1335	3525	463
66	2-dr. Bus. Cpe.-2P	1285	3615	2732
66S	2-dr. Sp. Cpe.-4P	1325	3695	6489
67	4-dr. Sed.-5P	1355	3795	30.665

172

Model No.	Body Type & Seating	Price	Weight	Prod. Total
Series 80				
86	2-dr. Cpe.-4P	1535	4120	3579
87	4-dr. Sed.-5P	1565	4255	14,731
Series 90				
90	4-dr. Sed.-7P	1935	4435	4159
90L	4-dr. Limo.-7P	2035	4505	514
91	4-dr. Sp. Sed.-5P	1785	4340	7853
94	2-dr. Spt. Rds.-4P	1610	4010	824
95	4-dr. Phae.-4P	1620	4125	392
96	2-dr. Cpe.-5P	1765	4260	7705
96C	2-dr. Conv. Cpe.-4P	1785	4195	1066
96S	2-dr. Ctry. Club. Cpe.-4P	1720	4250	2990

ENGINE: [Series 50] Inline. Ohv. Eight. Cast iron block. B & S: 2-7/8 x 4-1/4. Disp.: 220.7 cu. in. C.R.: 4.75:1. Brake H.P.: 77 at 3200 R.P.M. N.A.C.C. H.P.: 26.45. Main bearings: 5. Valve lifters: mechanical. Carb.: 2 barrel Marvel updraft T-3-10-894. Torque (Compression): 156 lbs.-ft. at 1600 R.P.M. [Series 60] Inline. Ohv. Eight. Cast iron block. B & S: 3-1/16 x 5. Disp.: 272.6 cu. in. C.R.: 4.63:1. Brake H.P.: 90 at 3000 R.P.M. N.A.C.C. H.P.: 30.02. Main bearings: 5. Valve lifters: mechanical. Carb.: Marvel TD25-10-795, late 1931 TD-25-10-983. Torque: 200 lbs.-ft. 43.5 @ 1600 R.P.M. [Series 80, 90] Inline. Ohv. Eight. Cast iron block. B & S: 3-5/16 x 5. Disp.: 344.8 cu. in. C.R.: 4.5:1. Brake H.P.: 104 at 2800 R.P.M. N.A.C.C. H.P.: 35.12. Main bearings: 5. Valve lifters: mechanical. Carb.: Marvel TD-3 10-796, late 1931 TD-3 10-984. Torque: 250 lbs.-ft. at 1400 R.P.M.

CHASSIS: [Series 50] W.B.: 114 in. Frt/Rear Tread: 56-1/2 in./57 in. Tires: 18 x 5.25. [Series 60] W.B.: 118 in. Length: 175. Height: 72. Frt/Rear Tread: 56-3/4 in./58 in. Tires: 19 x 6.50. [Series 80] W.B.: 124 in. Frt/Rear Tread: 56-7/8 in./58 in. Tires: 19 x 6.50. [Series 90] W.B.: 132 in. Frt/Rear Tread: 56-7/8 in./58 in. Tires: 19 x 6.50.

TECHNICAL: Sliding gear, synchromesh transmission (Series 60, 80, 90). Speeds: 3F/1R. Floor shift controls. Ser. 50, 60 — single dry plate, Ser. 80, 90 — double dry plate clutch. Shaft drive. 3/4 floating rear axle. Ser. 50 — semi-floating rear axle. Overall Drive Ratio: Ser. 60-4.5:1, Ser. 80, 90 — 4.5:1, 4.18:1. Mechanical brakes on four wheels. Wooden spoke wheels on demountable rims. Ser. 50 — 18 x 4, Ser. 60, 19 x 4, Ser. 80, 90 — 19 x 4-1/2.

OPTIONS: Front bumper. Rear Bumper. Dual sidemount. Heater (two types, hot water and exhaust pipe types). Clock. Side mounts. Side mount covers (metal and wood). Trunk cover. Demountable wire wheels. Grille guard. Luggage rack. White side walls. Wind wings. Gravel deflectors.

HISTORICAL: Introduced July 26, 1930. The Buick 8-cylinder engines were equipped with an oil temperature regulator that cooled the oil at high speeds and warmed it in cold weather. Calendar year production: 88,417. Model year production: 138,965 (including 5642 stripped chassis and cars for export). President of Buick was Edward Thomas Strong. The Butcher Brothers Special with a Buick 8 crashed at Indianapolis after 6 laps of racing. The Shafer 8 powered by a 272 cid Buick engine qualified for the 500 at a speed of 105.103 mph and finished in 12th place.

1932 BUICK

1932 Buick, series 90, model 96, victoria coupe, JAC

1932 Buick, club sedan & convertible coupe, JAC

BUICK — SERIES 50 — EIGHT: The 1932 Buicks were easily identified by their new hood doors which replaced the long-used louvers, the elimination of external sun visors and a more pronounced 10° rearward windshield slope. The radiator grille was given a new tapered shape with a narrower base. All Buicks also were equipped with dual taillights and longer and more streamlined fenders. The Series 60 and 80 models were available with a thinner head gasket and different spark plugs at no extra cost which raised their compression ratio and boosted top speed by 3mph.

The Series 50 Buick which continued to use the 114'' wheelbase chassis was available, along with the rest of the Buick line, with Wizard Control which provided owners with both free wheeling and no clutch shifting between second and third gears. New styles for the Series 50 consisted of a 2-door 5-passenger Victoria Coupe, and an attractive 5-passenger Convertible Phaeton with a choice of either leather or whipcord upholstery. Setting the Series 50 from other Buicks was their lack of chrome beaded radiator shutters and chrome plated hood handles. Their headlight shells were painted rather than chromed. Only a single taillight was fitted.

BUICK — SERIES 60 — EIGHT: The larger 118'' wheelbase Series 60 line also added the Victoria Coupe and Convertible Phaeton models to its offerings. The interior of the latter model featured leather upholstery and dual rear ashtrays.

BUICK — SERIES 80 — EIGHT: Only 2 models were offered in this series on a new 126'' wheelbase. The Victoria Coupe version had a unit-type rear trunk.

BUICK — SERIES 90 — EIGHT: The top of the line Series 90 Buick used a new 134'' wheelbase chassis and among its various models were two new body styles, the 4-door Club Sedan and 2-door Victoria Coupe. Standard on all Series 90 Buicks were wire wheels and dual side mounts.

I.D. DATA: Serial numbers right side of frame behind front fender opening. Starting: 2602732. Ending: 2659522. Engine numbers on crankcase. Starting: 2751922.

Model No.	Body Type & Seating	Price	Weight	Prod. Total
Series 50				
55	4-dr. Spt. Phae.-5P	1155	3270	69
56	2-dr. Bus. Cpe.-2P	935	3275	1726
56C	2-dr. Conv. Cpe.-4P	1080	3335	630
56S	2-dr. Spe. Cpe.-4P	1040	3395	1905
57	4-dr. Sed.-5P	995	3450	10,803
57S	4-dr. Spe. Sed.-5P	1080	3510	9766
58	2-dr. Vic. Cpe.	1060	3420	2194
58C	2-dr. Conv. Phae.-5P	1080	3425	380
Series 60				
65	4-dr. Spt. Phae.-5P	1390	3795	79
66	2-dr. Bus. Cpe.-2P	1250	3796	636
66C	2-dr. Conv. Cpe.-4P	1310	3795	450
66S	2-dr. Spe. Cpe.-4P	1270	3860	1678
67	4-dr. Sed.-5P	1310	3980	9013
68	2-dr. Vic. Cpe.-5P	1290	3875	1514
68C	2-dr. Conv. Cpe.-4P	1310	3880	366
Series 80				
86	2-dr. Vic. Trav. Cpe.-5P	1540	4335	1800
87	4-dr. Sed.-5P	1570	4450	4089
Series 90				
90	4-dr. Sed.-7P	1955	4695	1368
90L	4-dr. Limo.-7P	2055	4810	164
91	2-dr. Clb. Sed.-5P	1820	4620	2237
95	4-dr. Spt. Phae.-7P	1675	4470	131
96	2-dr. Vic. Cpe.-5P	1785	4460	1460
96C	2-dr. Conv. Cpe.-4P	1805	4460	289
96S	2-dr. Ctry. Clb. Cpe.-4P	1740	4470	586
97	4-dr. Sed.-5P	1805	4565	1485
98	2-dr. Conv. Phae.-5P	1830	4550	268

ENGINE: [Series 50] Inline. Ohv. Eight. Cast iron block. B & S: 2-15/16 x 4-1/4. Disp.: 230.4 cu. in. C.R.: 4.75. Brake H.P.: 82.5 @ 3200 R.P.M. N.A.C.C. H.P.: 27.61. Main bearings: 5. Valve lifters: mechanical. Carb.: 2 barrel Marvel updraft TD-15 10 982. Torque: 200 lbs.-ft. @ 1600 R.P.M. [Series 60] Inline. Ohv. Eight. Cast iron block. B & S: 3-1/16 x 5. Disp.: 272.6 cu. in. C.R.: 4.63:1. Brake H.P.: 90 (high compression 96) @ 3000 R.P.M. N.A.C.C. H.P.: 30.02. Main bearings: 5. Valve lifters: mechanical. Carb.: 2 barrel Marvel updraft TD-25 10-1501. Torque: 200 lbs.-ft. @ 1600 R.P.M. [Series 80, 90] Inline. Ohv. Eight. Cast iron block. B & S: 3-5/16 x 5. Disp.: 344.8 cu. in. C.R.: 4.5. Brake H.P.: High compression 113, 104 @ 2800 R.P.M. N.A.C.C. H.P.: 35.12. Main bearings: 5. Valve lifters: mechanical. Carb.: 2 barrel Marvel updraft TD-3 10-1503. Torque: 250 lbs.-ft. @ 1400 R.P.M.

CHASSIS: [Series 50] W.B.: 114 in. Frt/Rear Tread: 56-1/2 in. / 57 in. Tires: 18 x 5.50. [Series 60] W.B.: 118 in. Frt/Rear Tread: 56-3/4 in. / 58 in. Tires: 18 x 6.00. [Series 80] W.B.: 126 in. Tires: 18 x 7.00. [Series 90] W.B.: 134 in. Tires: 18 x 7.00.

TECHNICAL: Sliding gear, synchromesh transmission. Speeds: 3F/1R. Floor shift controls. Ser. 50, 60 — single dry plate, Ser. 80, 90 — double dry plate. Shaft drive. 3/4 floating rear axle. Ser. 50 — 4.6:1, Ser. 60 — 4.27, 4.545:1, Ser. 80 — 4.27:1, Ser. 90 — 4.18, 4.27:1. Mechanical brakes on four wheels. Painted wire wheels or 12 wooden spoke wheels with demountable rims. Wizard Control. Automatic clutch (series 80, 90).

OPTIONS: Heater. Clock. Chrome grille guard. Dual side mounts. Single bar bumpers. Tire locks. Tire covers. Cigarette lighter. Wheel trim rings. Trunk. Trunk rack. Vacuum windshield pump (Ser. 50 only, std on all others). 12 spoke wood wheel (Ser. 50, DeLuxe models).

HISTORICAL: Introduced Nov. 14, 1931. A Buick powered racer entered and driven by Phil Shafer finished 11th in the Indy. Shafer also won an Elgin, Ill. race with the same car. Innovations: Adjustable shock absorbers, Wizard Control free wheeling and automatic clutch. Calendar year production: 41,522. Model year production: 55,086 (another 1,704 stripped chassis and cars for export were produced). The president of Buick was Irving J. Reuter. Buick discontinued the use of wooden spoke wheels at the end of the 1932 model year.

1933 BUICK

BUICK — SERIES 50 — EIGHT: This was a year of major styling changes for Buick. New front and rear fenders with deeper valances and more sweeping curves plus a 2¼'' height reduction, gave all models a fresh appearance. Adding to this sense of newness was the Buick's new V-shaped grille and the discontinuation of wooden spoke wheels throughout all series. Customers could now select either wire or steel spoke artillery wheels.

Technical improvements were headlined by a new x-crossmember frame and the Fisher No-Draft ventilation. In addition the free-wheeling unit now allowed the driver to switch back and forth from direct drive to free wheeling as desired. The adjustable shock absorber system wasn't offered in 1933. A new type of headlight whose passing beam brightly illuminated the pavement edge while shedding a far dimmer light on the traffic side was common to all Buicks.

The Series 50 Buicks continued to use a 114'' wheelbase chassis. Body styles were trimmed to 5 from the 1932 level of 8 as the Sport Phaeton, Special Sedan and Convertible Phaeton were dropped. Twin taillights were fitted to all models.

1933 Buick, series 50, model 57, sedan, JAC

1933 Buick, series 60, model 66C, convertible coupe, OCW

BUICK — SERIES 60 — EIGHT: A 127'' wheelbase was used for the Series 60 which also consisted of 5 models for 1933. Eliminated for the 1933 model year were the Sport Phaeton and Business Coupe models.

BUICK — SERIES 80 — EIGHT: The Series 80 wheelbase for 1933 was an impressive 130''. Whereas only 2 models were offered in this series in 1932, 3 new models, the Convertible Coupe, Sport Coupe and Convertible Phaeton were added for the new model year.

BUICK — SERIES 90 — EIGHT: 1933 was the poorest sales year for Buick since 1915 but in terms of prestige the Series 90 models with an ultra-long 138'' wheelbase took Buick to a new status level. However only 5 body styles were offered as Buick eliminated the Sport Phaeton, Country Club Coupe, 5-passenger Sedan, Convertible Coupe Roadster and Convertible Phaeton from the Series 90 line. Closed car interiors were available in mohair plush, whipcord or cloth.

I.D. DATA: Serial numbers on right side of frame behind front fender opening, on plate on firewall. Starting: 2659523. Ending: 2706452. Engine numbers on right side of crankcase. Starting: 2751922.

Model No.	Body Type & Seating	Price	Weight	Prod. Total
Series 50				
56	2-dr. Bus. Cpe.-2P	995	3520	1321
56C	2-dr. Conv. Cpe.-2P	1115	3525	346
56S	2-dr. Spt. Cpe.-2P	1030	3585	1643
57	4-dr. Sed.-5P	1045	3705	19,109
58	2-dr. Vic. Cpe.-5P	1065	3605	4118
Series 60				
66C	2-dr. Conv. Cpe.-2P	1365	3940	152
66S	2-dr. Spt. Cpe.	1270	3975	1000
67	4-dr. Sed.-5P	1310	4115	7450
68	2-dr. Vic. Cpe.-5P	1310	4005	2887
68C	4-dr. Conv. Phae.-5P	1585	4110	183
Series 80				
86	2-dr. Vic. Cpe.-5P	1540	4420	758
86C	2-dr. Conv. Cpe.-2P	1575	4325	90
86S	2-dr. Spt. Cpe.-2P	1495	4355	401
87	4-dr. Sed.-5P	1570	4505	1545
88C	4-dr. Conv. Phae.-5P	1845	4525	124
Series 90				
90	4-dr. Sed.-7P	1955	4705	890
90L	4-dr. Limo.-7P	2055	4780	299
91	2-dr. Clb. Sed.-5P	1820	4520	1637
96	2-dr. Vic. Cpe.-5P	1785	4520	556
97	4-dr. Sed.-5P	1805	4595	641

174

ENGINE: [Series 50] Inline. Ohv. Eight. Cast iron block. B & S: 2-15/16 x 4-1/4. Disp.: 230.4 cu. in. C.R.: 4.63. Brake H.P.: 86 @ 3200 R.P.M. N.A.C.C. H.P.: 27.61. Main bearings: 5. Valve lifters: mechanical. Carb.: 2 barrel Marvel updraft ED-18 10-1515. [Series 60] Inline. Ohv. Eight. Cast iron block. B & S: 3-1/16 x 5. Disp.: 272.6 cu in. C.R.: 4.63:1. Brake H.P.: 97 @ 3200 R.P.M. N.A.C.C. H.P.: 30.02. Main bearings: 5. Valve lifters: mechanical. Carb.: 2 barrel Marvel updraft ED-28 10-1518. [Series 80, 90] Inline. Ohv. Eight. Cast iron block. B & S: 3-5/16 x 5. Disp.: 344.8 cu. in. C.R.: 4.63:1. Brake H.P.: 104 @ 2800 R.P.M. Main bearings: 5. Valve lifters: mechanical. Carb.: 2 barrel Marvel updraft ED-3 10-1514.

CHASSIS: [Series 50] W.B.: 119 in. Frt/Rear Tread: 59/60-1/2 in. Tires: 17 x 6. [Series 60] W.B.: 127 in. Frt/Rear Tread: 59/60-1/2 in. Tires: 17 x 6.50. [Series 80] W.B.: 130 in. Frt/Rear Tread: 58-1/2 in. / 60-1/2 in. Tires: 17 x 7. [Series 90] W.B.: 138 in. Frt/Rear Tread: 58-1/2 in. / 60-1/2 in. Tires: 17 x 7.

TECHNICAL: Sliding gear, synchromesh transmission. Speeds: 3F/1R. Floor shift controls. Single dry plate clutch — Ser. 50, 60. Double dry plate clutch — Ser. 80, 90. Shaft drive. 3/4 floating rear axle. Overall ratio: Ser. 50 - 4.7:1, Ser. 60 - 4.6:1, Ser. 80 - 4.273:1, Ser. 90 - 4.27, 4.36:1. Mechanical brakes on four wheels. Wire on steel spoke artillery wheels. Wizard control.

OPTIONS: Side mounts. Luggage rack. Trunk. Fog lights. Wire wheels. Artillery-type all steel wheels.

HISTORICAL: Introduced Dec. 3, 1932. The Shafer 8 Special powered by a 284 cid Buick engine was driven by H. W. ''Stubby'' Stubblefield to a 5th place finish at an average speed of 100.762 mph. The top 4 cars were powered by Miller racing engines. Dash mounted starter button. Calendar year production: 40,620. Model year sales: 43,247. Model year production: 45,150 (1774 stripped chassis and cars for export were also produced). Harlow Herbert Curtice became Buick President on Oct. 23, 1933.

1934 BUICK

1934 Buick, series 40, model 41, sedan, AA

1934 BUICK: Buick's year old synchromesh transmission was improved by the adoption of helical gears. The actual gear shifting procedure was made more convenient by the shift lever's shorter movement. Also noteworthy was the mid-year revision made in the automatic starting mechanism that prevented the starter from being used to move the car when the ignition was locked.

An interesting feature of the Buick instrument panel was its octane selector handle which altered the spark timing to allow the use of either standard or premium fuel.

The headlights used on the 1934 models produced 20% more illumination and provided four different light patterns: city and country driving beams, a passing beam and a parking light. Series 40 Buicks had 3 horizontal hood louvers while models in the remaining series had 4. Also not included as standard equipment on the Series 40 were the dual chrome horns of the Series 50 through 90.

BUICK — SERIES 40 — EIGHT: In terms of Buick's recent past the introduction of this low priced series on May 12, 1934 was nothing short of revolutionary. But it came at a time when business as usual patterns could spell disaster. Although its wheelbase of 117'' was longer than the 1933 Series 50 Buick it was both considerably lighter in weight and less expensive. Series 40 models were the only Buicks not equipped with dual exterior mounted horns. Closed models in the Series 40 had either whipcord or mohair velvet upholstery with leather used for open models. All models in all series had their radiator filler cap placed under the hood.

1934 Buick, series 50, model 56S, sport coupe, JAC

BUICK — SERIES 50 — EIGHT: Body choices in this Buick line remained unchanged but a longer 119'' wheelbase was used. As was the case with all Buicks, the new Series 50 had narrow horizontal hood louvers and safety glass in their windshields and vent windows. Interiors featured (on closed models) wide walnut grained metal window trim.

BUICK — SERIES 60 — EIGHT: Series 60 Buicks had a longer, by one inch, wheelbase for 1934. A new Club Sedan model was added to its lineup. A more powerful 100 hp, 278 cid engine was also introduced. Common to all Buicks for 1934 was General Motors ''Knee Action'' independent front suspension and a ''Ride Stabilizer'' rear anti-roll bar.

1934 Buick, series 90, model 91, club sedan, JAC

BUICK — SERIES 90 — EIGHT: With the Series 80 dropped for 1934, the Series 90 received new Convertible Coupe, Sport Coupe and Convertible Phaeton models. The Series 90 was equipped both with safety glass in all windows and a Bendix vacuum power brake booster. The Series 90 models shared their combination accelerator-starter with the rest of the 1934 Buicks. Interiors of closed models featured mohair velvet plush upholstery.

I.D. DATA: Serial numbers on right side of frame, behind front fender opening. Starting: 2706453. Ending: 2777649. Engine numbers on crankcase. Starting. Ser. 40 — 2984900, Ser. 50, 60, 90 — 2861223.

Model No.	Body Type & Seating	Price	Weight	Prod. Total
Series 40				
41	4-dr. Sed. Built-in trunk-5P	925	3175	10,953
46	2-dr. Bus. Cpe.-2P	795	2995	1806
46S	2-dr. Spt. Cpe. R/S-4P	855	3085	1232
47	4-dr. Sed.-5P	895	3155	7425
48	4-dr. Tr. Sed. Built-in Trunk-5P	865	3120	4779
Series 50				
56	2-dr. Bus. Cpe.-2P	1110	3682	1078
56C	2-dr. Conv. Cpe.-2P	1230	3692	506
56S	2-dr. Sp. Cpe. R/S-4P	1145	3712	1150
57	4-dr. Sed.-5P	1190	3852	12,094
58	2-dr. Vic. Cpe. Built-in Trunk-5P	1160	4316	4405
Series 60				
61	2-dr. Clb. Sed. Built-in Trunk-5P	1465	4318	5395
66C	2-dr. Conv. Cpe. R/S-4P	1495	NA	253
66S	2-dr. Sp. Cpe.-2P	1375	4193	816
67	4-dr. Sed.-5P	1425	4303	5171
68	2-dr. Vic. Cpe. Built-in Trunk-5P	1395	4213	1935
68C	4-dr. Conv. Phae. Built-in Trunk-5P	1675	4353	444
Series 90				
90	4-dr. Sed.-7P	2055	4906	1151
90L	4-dr. Limo.-7P	2175	4876	262
91	2-dr. Clb. Sed. Built-in trunk-5P	1965	4696	1477
96C	2-dr. Conv. Cpe. R/S-4P	1945	4511	68
96S	2-dr. Spt. Cpe. R/S-4P	1875	4546	137
97	4-dr. Sed.-4P	1945	4691	635
98	2-dr. Vic. Cpe.-5P	1895	4571	347
98C	4-dr. Conv. Phae. Built-in trunk-5P	2145	4691	119

1934 Buick, series 90, model 96C, convertible coupe, OCW

ENGINE: [Series 40] Inline. Ohv. Eight. Cast iron block. B & S: 3-3/32 x 3-7/8. Disp.: 233 cu. in. Brake H.P.: 93 @ 3200 R.P.M. N.A.C.C. H.P.: 30.63. Main bearings: 5. Valve lifters: mechanical. Carb.: 2 barrel Marvel downdraft BB-1, 10-1633. [Series 50] Inline. Ohv. Eight. Cast iron block. B & S: 2-31/32 x 4-1/4. Disp.: 235 cu. in. Brake H.P.: 88 @ 3200 R.P.M. N.A.C.C. H.P.: 28.2. Main bearings: 5. Valve lifters: mechanical. Carb.: 2 barrel Marvel updraft ED-1S, 10-1577. [Series 60] Inline. Ohv. Eight. Cast iron block. B & S: 3-3/32 x 3-7/8. Disp.: 278 cu. in. Brake H.P.: 100 @ 3200 R.P.M. N.A.C.C. H.P.: 30.63. Main bearings: 5. Valve lifters: mechanical. Carb.: 2 barrel Marvel ED-2S, 10-1579. [Series 90] Inline. Ohv. Eight. Cast iron block. B & S: 3-5/16 x 5. Disp.: 344.8 cu. in. Brake H.P.: 116 @ 3200 R.P.M. N.A.C.C. H.P.: 35.12. Main bearings: 5. Valve lifters: mechanical. Carb.: Marvel ED3S 10-1581.

CHASSIS: [Series 40] W.B.: 117 in. Tires: 16 x 6.25. [Series 50] W.B.: 119 in. Frt/Rear Tread: 59/60-1/2 in. Tires: 16 x 7.00. [Series 60] W.B.: 128 in. Tires: 16 x 7.50. [Series 90] W.B.: 136 in. Tires: 16 x 7.50.

TECHNICAL: Sliding gear, synchromesh transmission. Speeds: 3F/1R. Floor shift controls. Single dry plate clutch. Shaft drive. 3/4 floating rear axle. Overall Ratio: Ser. 40 — 4.33:1, Ser. 50 — 4.89:1, Ser. 60 — 4.7:1, Ser. 90 — 4.36:1. Mechanical brakes on four wheels. Steel spoke artillery wheels.

OPTIONS: White side walls. Two-tone paint. Safety glass (Ser 50 & 60) ($9.75 — $20.00). Radio (dealer installed). Metal spare tire cover. Luggage rack. Side mounts. Passenger side windshield wipers — Series 40.

HISTORICAL: Introduced Dec. 27, 1933. Calendar year production: 78,757. Model year production: 63,647 (plus 7362 stripped chassis and cars for export). The president of Buick was Harlow Curtice. Two Buick-powered Rigling cars were qualified in 6th and 8th places starting position in the Indy. One car retired with a broken cam drive after 130 laps. The second entry, the ''Shafer Special'' with a 286 cid Buick 8 finished in 6th position with an average speed of 98.26mph. The cars in front at the race's end were powered by either Duesenberg or Miller engines.

1935 BUICK

1935 Buick, convertible coupe, OCW

1935 Buick, series 60, model 61, club sedan, JAC

BUICK — SERIES 40 — EIGHT: Visual changes in the Buick's appearance for 1935 were extremely modest consisting mainly of new colors and exterior trim revisions. The Series 40 models received a glove box lock and dual windshield wipers along with numerous design improvements intended to remedy complaints of poor clutch and timing chain durability. A Convertible Coupe was also added to the Series 40 model

line. Whereas the more costly Buicks were fitted with chrome headlight shells, those on the Series 40 were painted. All models received automatic chokes and a girder-type frame was used on all Buick convertibles.

1935 Buick, series 50, model 57, 4-dr. sedan, OCW

BUICK — SERIES 50 — EIGHT: Changes to the Series 50 were limited to the installation of center rear arm rests on closed models.

BUICK — SERIES 60 — EIGHT: All body styles were continued unchanged for 1935. Series 60 sedans shared the folding center rear seat arm rest with Series 90 models.

1935 Buick series 90, model 98C, convertible phaeton, JAC

BUICK — SERIES 90 — EIGHT: Series 90 models were equipped with shatter proof glass in all windows.

I.D. DATA: Serial numbers on right side of frame, behind front fender opening. Starting: 2777650. Ending: 2830898. Engine numbers on crankcase. Starting: Ser. 40-42937408, Ser. 50, 60, 90 — 2922072. Ending: Ser. 40-42995237, Ser. 50, 60, 90 — 2984413.

Model No.	Body Type & Seating	Price	Weight	Prod. Total
Series 40				
41	4-dr. Sed.-5P	925	3210	18,638
46	2-dr. Bus. Cpe.-2P	795	3020	2850
46C	2-dr. Conv. Cpe.-4P	925	3140	933
46S	2-dr. Spt. Cpe.-4P	855	NA	1136
47	4-dr. Sed.-5P	895	3180	6250
48	2-dr. Tr. Sed.-5P	865	3160	4957
Series 50				
56	2-dr. Bus. Cpe.-2P	1110	3652	257
56C	2-dr. Conv. Cpe.-2P	1230	3662	170
56S	2-dr. Sp. Cpe.-4P	1145	3682	268
57	4-dr. Sed.-5P	1190	3822	3778
58	2-dr. Vic. Cpe.	1160	3737	1589
Series 60				
61	2-dr. Clb. Sed.-5P	1462	4288	2762
66C	2-dr. Conv. Cpe.-4P	1375	4163	111
66S	2-dr. Sp. Cpe.-4P	NA	NA	257
67	4-dr. Sed.-5P	1425	4273	1716
68	2-dr. Vic. Cpe.-5P	1395	4183	597
68C	4-dr. Conv. Phae.-5P	1675	4323	256
Series 90				
90	4-dr. Sed.-7P	2055	4766	609
90L	4-dr. Limo.-7P	2175	4846	191
91	4-dr. Clb. Sed.-5P	1965	4606	573
96C	2-dr. Conv. Cpe.-4P	1945	4481	10
96S	2-dr. Spt. Cpe.-4P	1875	4516	41
97	4-dr. Sed.-5P	1945	4661	117
98	2-dr. Vic. Cpe.-5P	1895	4541	32
98C	4-dr. Conv. Phae.-5P	2145	4661	38

ENGINE: [Series 40] Inline. Ohv. Eight. Cast iron block. B & S: 3-3/12 x 3-7/8. Disp.: 233 cu. in. Brake H.P.: 93 @ 3200 R.P.M. N.A.C.C. H.P.: 30.63. Main bearings: 5. Valve lifters: mechanical. Carb.: 2 barrel, Stromberg downdraft EE-1 or Marvel ED-15. [Series 50] Inline. Ohv. Eight. Cast iron block. B & S: 2-31/32 x 4-1/4. Disp.: 235 cu. in. Brake H.P.: 88 @ 3200 R.P.M. N.A.C.C. H.P.: 28.2. Main bearings: 5. Valve lifters: mechanical. Carb.: Marvel ED-15, 10-157. [Series 60] Inline. Ohv. Eight. Cast iron block. B & S: 3-3/32 x 4-5/8. Disp. 278.1 cu. in. Brake H.P.: 100 @ 3200 R.P.M. N.A.C.C. H.P.: 30.63. Main bearings: 5. Valve lifters: mechanical. Carb. Marvel ED-25, 10-1579. [Series 90] Inline. Ohv. Eight. Cast iron block. B & S: 3-5/16 x 5. Disp.: 344.8. C.R.: 4.63. Brake H.P.: 116 @ 3200 R.P.M. N.A.C.C. H.P.: 35.12. Main bearings: 5. Valve lifters: mechanical. Carb. Marvel ED-3, 10-1581.

CHASSIS: [Series 40] W.B.: 117 in. Tires: 16 x 6.25. [Series 50] W.B.: 119 in. Frt/Rear Tread: 59/60-1/2 in. Tires: 16 x 7.00. [Series 60] W.B.: 128 in. Tires: 16 x 7.50. [Series 90] W.B.: 136 in. Tires: 16 x 7.50.

TECHNICAL: Sliding gear, synchromesh transmission. Speeds: 3F/1R. Floor shift controls. Single dry plate clutch. Shaft drive. 3/4 floating rear axle. Overall Ratio: Ser. 40-4.33:1, Ser. 50 4.88:1, Ser. 60 4.7:1, Ser. 90 4.36:1. Mechanical brakes on four wheels. Steel spoke artillery wheels.

OPTIONS: Sidemount (standard on Model 98C). Wire wheels. Luggage rack. Steel side mount tire covers. 2-tone paint.

HISTORICAL: Introduced Oct. 18, 1934. Calendar year production: 107,611. Model year production: 48,256 (4993 stripped chassis and cars for export were also produced). The president of Buick was Harlow Curtice. A Shafer Special with a Buick 8 cylinder engine was qualified by Cliff Bergers at 114.1 mph at Indy. After starting in 16th position it ran out of gas just 4 laps from the finish.

1936 BUICK

1936 Buick, Special, model 46C, convertible coupe, JAC

BUICK SPECIAL — SERIES 40 — EIGHT: Buick historians are unanimous in regarding the 1936 models as the cars that marked the start of the Buick renaissance. Across the board were Turret-Top bodies, hydraulic brakes and dramatic new styling with sharply slanted V-type windshields, high, wedged-shaped radiators, twin taillamps and bullet-shaped headlights. Technical advancements included an improved independent front suspension, new alloy pistons and an improved water temperature control. To celebrate the occasion Buick also assigned names to its traditional Series designations. Buick wasn't the least bit bashful about touting the top speed ability of these new cars. The Special was capable of 85 mph, the Limited, 87 mph and the Roadmaster, 90 mph. The hot new Century could achieve a sizzling 95 mph.

The Series 40 Special retained the 233 cid engine, which now featured Anolite aluminum pistons, as did the 320 cid Buick engine.

BUICK CENTURY — SERIES 60 — EIGHT: The first of the great Century Buicks shared a new 320.2 cid straight eight with the Series 80 (Roadmaster) and Series 90 (Limited) models that was destined to remain in production through 1952. On a relatively short, 118 inch wheelbase the Century's styling with its rearward sweeping lines and rounded grille with vertical bars was particularly appealing.

1936 Buick, Roadmaster, model 80C, convertible phaeton, AA

BUICK ROADMASTER — SERIES 80 — EIGHT: Only 2 body styles, a 4-door Trunk Sedan, and an elegant Convertible Phaeton were offered in this Roadmaster Series. Standard on the latter was a single side mount.

BUICK LIMITED — SERIES 90 — EIGHT: The 4 Limited models all used the same 4-door body style with glass partitions provided for the Limousine and Formal Sedan versions. Standard on all Buick Limited models was a left side external tire mount.

I.D. DATA: Serial numbers on right side of frame, behind front fender opening. Starting: 2830899. Ending: 2999496. Engine numbers on crankcase. Starting: Ser. 40-42995239, Ser. 60, 80, 90 — 63001000. Ending: Ser. 40 — 43166224, Ser. 60, 80, 90 — 93166224.

1936 Buick, Limited, model 91, sedan, JAC

Model No.	Body Type & Seating	Price	Weight	Prod. Total
Series 40 (Special)				
41	4-dr. Sed.-5P	885	3360	77,007
46	2-dr. Bus. Cpe.-2P	765	3150	10,912
46C	2-dr. Conv. Cpe.-4P	820	3190	1488
46S	2-dr. Spt. Cpe.-4P	820	3190	1086
46Sr	2-dr. Spt. Cpe.-4P	820	3190	1390
48	2-dr. Vic. Cpe.-5P	835	3305	21,214
Series 60 (Century)				
61	4-dr. Sed.-5P	1090	—	17,806
66C	2-dr. Conv. Cpe.-4P	1135	3775	717
66So	2-dr. Spt. Cpe.-4P	1035	3625	1078
66Sr	2-dr. Spt. Cpe.-4P	1035	3635	1001
68	2-dr. Vic. Cpe.-5P	1055	3730	3762
Series 80 (Roadmaster)				
80C	4-dr. Conv. Phae.-6P	1565	4228	1064
81	4-dr. Sed.-6P	1255	4098	14,985
Series 90 (Limited)				
90	4-dr. Sed.-8P	1845	4517	1590
90	4-dr. Limo.-8P	1945	4577	709
91	4-dr. Sed.-6P	1695	4477	1713
91F	4-dr. Formal Sed.-6P	1795	4487	74

1936 Buick, Special, model 46, coupe, OCW

ENGINE: [Series 40] Inline. Ohv. Eight. Cast iron block. B & S: 3-3/32 x 3-7/8. Disp.: 233 cu. in. Brake H.P.: 93 @ 3200 R.P.M. N.A.C.C. H.P.: 30.63. Main bearings: 5. Valve lifters: mechanical. Carb.: 2 barrel Stromberg downdraft EE1. [Series 60, 80, 90] Inline. Ohv. Eight. Cast iron block. B & S: 3-7/16 x 4-5/16. Disp. 320.2 cu. in. C.R.: Brake H.P.: 120 @ 3200 R.P.M. N.A.C.C. H.P.: 37.81. Main bearings: 5. Valve lifters: mechanical. Carb.: 2 barrel Stromberg downdraft EE22. Torque: 238 lbs.-ft. @ 1600 R.P.M.

CHASSIS: [Series 40] W.B.: 118 in. Tires: 16 x 6.50. [Series 60] W.B. 122 in. O.L.: 197 in. Height: 68 in. Frt/Rear Tread: 58.1 in. / 57.5 in. Tires: 15 x 7.00. [Series 80] W.B.: 131 in. Tires: 16 x 7.00. [Series 90] W.B.: 138 in. Tires: 16 x 7.50.

TECHNICAL: Sliding gear transmission. Speeds: 3F/1R. Floor shift control. Single dry plate clutch. Shaft drive. Semi-floating rear axle. Overall Ratio: Ser. 40-4.44:1, Ser. 60-3.90:1, Ser. 80-4.22:1, Ser. 90-4.55:1. Hydraulic brakes on four wheels. Pressed steel wheels. 16 in. (Series 60-15'').

OPTIONS: Heater Master and DeLuxe. Dual side mounts. Fog lights. White side walls. Grille guard. Electric watch. Buick Master 5-tube radio. Buick Ranger 6-tube radio. Trim rings.

HISTORICAL: Introduced Sept. 28, 1935. Hydraulic brake, Turret top. Calendar year sales: 164,861. Calendar year production: 179,533. Model year production: 157,623 (in addition 10,973 stripped chassis and cars for export were produced). The president of Buick was Harlow Curtice. The 3 millionth Buick, a Series 40 Special 4-door sedan was built on May 28, 1936.

1937 BUICK

1937 Buick, Special, model 46C, convertible coupe, AA

BUICK SPECIAL — SERIES 40 — EIGHT: Buick's art deco styling of 1937 was substantially revised with a divided grille with horizontal bars, fenders with squared-off ends and extremely graceful streamlined head light shells. The center section of the die cast grille was painted to match the body color. While overall height was reduced by 1½ inches the floors were lowered 2½'' to maintain interior head room.

Among Buick's technical improvements for 1937 was a quieter overhead valve mechanism, ''streamlined'' intake valves, a new oil pump and a cooling system with 7% greater capacity.

The Buick Special received both a longer 122'' wheelbase chassis and a new 248 cid engine. Particularly attractive was the 4-door Model 47 with its swept-back rear deck. Another addition to the Special line was the 5 passenger Convertible Phaeton. Buick claimed the Series 40 Sedan could accelerate from 10 to 60 mph in 19.2 seconds.

1937 Buick, Century, model 66C, convertible coupe, JAC

BUICK CENTURY — SERIES 60 — EIGHT: The Century series with a 126'' wheelbase was highlighted by 2 swept-back body styles, the Model 64 2-door Sedan and Model 67 4-door Sedan. With an official top speed of 101 mph the Century was one of the most impressive automobiles of 1937. The coupe bodies in both the Series 40 and Series 60 Buicks were lengthened to provide space for two passengers behind the front seat. These ''opera'' seats could also be folded flush into the body when not in use.

BUICK ROADMASTER — SERIES 80 — EIGHT: The Roadmaster, on the same 131'' wheelbase of 1936 were available in 3 body styles, including a new 6 passenger Formal Sedan.

BUICK LIMITED — SERIES 90 — EIGHT: The 7 Limited models along with all other Buicks were available with a windshield defroster and a radio antenna installed in the running board. Unlike the Special and Century models which used all-steel body construction, the Limited and Roadmaster Buick retained composite wood and steel bodies.

I.D. DATA: Serial numbers on right side of frame, behind front fender opening. Starting: 2999497. Ending: 3219847. Engine numbers on crankcase. Starting: Ser. 40 - 43166225, all others - 63176225. Ending: Ser. 40 - 43396936, all others - 43388399.

Model No.	Body Type & Seating	Price	Weight	Prod. Total
Series 40 (Special)				
40C	4-dr. Conv. Phae.-5P	1302	3630	1689
41	4-dr. Trunk Back Sed.-5P	1021	3490	82,440
44	2-dr. Tr. Sed.-5P	959	3490	9330
46	2-dr. Bus. Cpe.-2P	913	3380	13,742
46C	2-dr. Conv. Cpe.-4P	1056	3480	2265
46S	2-dr. Spt. Cpe.-4P	975	3445	5059
47	4-dr. Tr. Sed.	995	3510	22,312
48	2-dr. Trunk Back Sed.-5P	895	3480	15,936

Model No.	Body Type & Seating	Price	Weight	Prod. Total
Series 60 (Century)				
60C	4-dr. Conv. Phae.-5P	1524	3840	410
61	4-dr. Trunk Back Sed.-5P	1233	3720	20,679
64	2-dr. Tr. Sed.-5P	1172	3720	1117
66C	2-dr. Conv. Cpe.-4P	1269	3715	787
66S	2-dr. Spt. Cpe.-4P	1187	3660	2840
67	4-dr. Tr. Sed.-5P	1207	3750	4750
68	2-dr. Trunk Back Sed.-5P	1197	3750	2874
Series 80 (Roadmaster)				
80C	4-dr. Phae.-6P	1856	4214	1040
81	4-dr. Trunk Back Sed.-6P	1518	4159	14,637
81C	4-dr. Formal Sed.-6P	1641	4299	452
Series 90 (Limited)				
90	4-dr. Trunk Back Sed.-8P	2240	4549	1592
90L	4-dr. Limo.-8P	2342	4599	720
91	4-dr. Trunk Back Sed.-6P	2066	4469	1229
91F	4-dr. Formal Sed.-6P	2240	4409	156

ENGINE: [Series 40] Inline. Ohv. Eight. Cast iron block. B & S: 3-3/32 x 11-1/8. Disp.: 248 cu. in. C.R.: 5.7:1. Brake H.P.: 100 @ 3200 R.P.M. N.A.C.C. H.P.: 30.6. Main bearings: 5. Valve lifters: mechanical. Carb.: Stromberg AA1. [Series 60, 80, 90] Inline. Ohv. Eight. Cast iron block. B & S: 3-7/16 x 4-5/16. Disp.: 320.2 cu. in. C.R.: 5.9:1. Brake H.P.: 130 @ 3400 R.P.M. N.A.C.C. H.P.: 37.81. Main bearings: 5. Valve lifters: mechanical. Carb.: Stromberg AA2.

CHASSIS: [Series 40] W.B.: 122 in. O.L.: 200-1/16 in. Frt/Rear Tread: 58-7/16 in. / 59-5/32 in. Tires: 16 x 6.50. [Series 60] W.B.: 126 in. O.L.: 203-9/16 in. Frt/Rear Tread: 58-5/16 in. / 59-1/4 in. Tires: 16 x 7.00. [Series 80] W.B.: 131 in. O.L.: 210-1/4 in. Frt/Rear Tread: 59-19/32 in. / 62-1/2 in. Tires: 16 x 7.00. [Series 90] W.B.: 138 in. O.L.: 216-1/2 in. Frt/Rear Tread: 59-7/16 in. / 62-1/2 in. Tires: 16 x 7.50.

TECHNICAL: Sliding gear transmission. Speeds: 3F/1R. Floor shift controls. Single dry plate clutch. Shaft drive. Semi-floating rear axle. (Ser. 40 & 60 - hypoid gears. Ser. 80 & 90 continues to use spiral bevel gears.) Overall ratio: Ser. 40 - 4.44:1, Ser. 60 - 3.90:1, Ser. 80 - 4.22:1, Ser. 90 - 4.55:1.) Hydraulic brakes on four wheels. Pressed steel wheels. Rim: 16 in. (Ser. 60 - 15 in.)

OPTIONS: Heater. Dual side mounts. Fog lights. White side wall tires. Grille Guard. Defroster in combination with heater. Heater. Dash installed radio with built-in speaker grille.

HISTORICAL: Introduced Oct. 18, 1936. Cowl-mounted windshield wipers on all models. Calendar year sales: 203,739. Calendar year production: 227,038. Model year production: 220,346 (including 14,290 stripped chassis and cars for export). The president of Buick was Harlow Curtice. The 3,000,000th Buick, a 1937 Model 81 Roadmaster 6 passenger sedan was presented to Arthur L. Newton on Oct. 25, 1936. Mr. Newton was president of Glidden Buick Corporation of New York City which had been Buick's largest dealer for 20 years.

1938 BUICK

1938 BUICK: The major changes in the Buick line for 1938 consisted of the adoption of coil springs for its rear suspension and the availability of a semi-automatic transmission for the Series 40 models.

Styling changes were minor. The front line of the grille was now nearly vertical which enabled a longer hood to be used. The graceful form of the headlights was mirrored in the shape of the front fender-mounted parking lights and the front bumper guards were taller than previously.

Other engineering changes included a redesigned frame X-member of channel section rather than I-beam construction. Although it wasn't the first to move its battery to a location under the hood, this Buick feature for 1938 was a welcomed development.

BUICK SPECIAL — SERIES 40 — EIGHT: The Automatic Safety Transmission semi-automatic transmission option (which Oldsmobile had introduced in June 1937) required use of the clutch only when the car was started or stopped. A steering column-mounted lever with reverse, neutral, low-range and high range Forward position controlled the operation of the transmission. Low range provided first and second gears with an automatic upshift. High range encompassed first, third and fourth gears. Above 20 mph in High range the car was in fourth gear with a downshift to third possible by fully depressing the accelerator. The use of crowned head pistons raised the Series 40 engine's compression ratio to 6.15:1 and increased maximum horsepower to 107 at 3400 rpm.

BUICK CENTURY — SERIES 60 — EIGHT: The wheelbase of the Buick Century remained unchanged at 126''. The two-door Touring Sedan was dropped for 1938. Its engine, identical to that used in the Series 80 and 90 developed 141hp.

1938 Buick, Roadmaster, model 81, 4-dr. sedan, JAC

1938 Buick, Special, model 41, trunkback sedan, OCW

BUICK ROADMASTER & LIMITED — SERIES 80 & 90 — EIGHT: Wheelbases of the 80 and 90 Buick were increased 2'' to 133 and 140 inches respectively. The use of the crowned ''turbulator'' pistons raised their engine's compression ratio to 6.5:1. Horsepower was boosted to 141 at 3600rpm. The Series 90 Formal Sedan was not offered while the Four-door Sedan was added to the Series 80 line.

I.D. DATA: Serial numbers on riveted plate on right side cowling under hood, right frame rail at cowl. Starting: 13219848 (Flint), 23238767 (South Gate), 33245765 (Linden). Ending: 13388546 (Flint), 23386843 (South Gate), 33376283 (Linden). Identification of different numbers used at other factories: Prefix 1 — Flint Michigan assembly. Prefix 2 — South Gate, California assembly. Prefix 3 — Linden, New Jersey assembly. Engine numbers on low right rear side of crankcase adjacent to dipstick. Starting: 43396937 — Ser. 40, 63396937 — Ser. 60, 83396937 — Ser. 80, 93396937 — Ser. 90. Ending: 93544292 — Ser. 90.

Model No.	Body Type & Seating	Price	Weight	Prod. Total
Series 40 (Special)				
40C	2-dr. Conv. Phae.-5P	1406	3705	776
41	4-dr. Tr. Sed.-5P	1047	3560	79,510
44	2-dr. Spt. Sed.-5P	981	3515	5943
46	2-dr. Bus. Cpe.-2P	945	3385	11,337
46C	2-dr. Conv. Cpe.-4P	1103	3575	2473
46S	2-dr. Spt. Cpe.-4P	1001	3425	5381
47	4-dr. Spt. Sed.-5P	1022	3535	11,265
48	2-dr. Tr. Sed.	1006	3520	14,153
Series 60 (Century)				
60C	4-dr. Conv. Phae.-5P	1713	3950	208
61	4-dr. Tr. Sed.-5P	1297	3780	12,364
66C	2-dr. Conv. Cpe.-4P	1359	3815	642
66S	2-dr. Spt. Cpe.-4P	1226	3690	1991
67	4-dr. Spt. Sed.-5P	1272	3785	1515
68	2-dr. Tr. Sed.-5P	1256	3760	1380
Series 80 (Roadmaster)				
80C	4-dr. Spt. Phae.-6P	1983	4325	350
81	4-dr. Tr. Sed.-6P	1645	4245	4505
81F	4-dr. Fml. Sed.-6P	1759	4305	247
87	4-dr. Spt. Sed.-6P	1645	4245	466
Series 90 (Limited)				
90	4-dr. Tr. Sed.-8P	2350	4608	644
90L	4-dr. Limo.-8P	2453	4653	410
91	4-dr. Tr. Sed.-6P	2077	4568	437

1938 Buick, Century, model 68, 2-dr. sedan, OCW

ENGINE: [Series 40] Inline. Ohv. Eight. Cast iron block. B & S: 3-3/32 x 4-1/8. Disp.: 248 cu. in. C.R.: 6.15:1. Brake H.P.: 107 @ 3400 R.P.M. Taxable H.P.: 30.63. Main bearings: 5. Valve lifters: mechanical. Carb.: Marvel CD1 or Stromberg AAV-1 dual downdraft. Torque: 203 lbs.-ft. @ 2000 R.P.M. [Series 60, 80, 90] Inline. Ohv. Eight. Cast iron block. B & S: 3-7/16 x 4-5/16. Disp.: 320.2 cu. in. C.R.: 6.35:1. Brake H.P.: 141 @ 3600 R.P.M. Taxable H.P.: 37.81. Main bearings: 5. Valve lifters: mechanical. Carb.: Marvel CD-2 or Stromberg AAV-2 dual downdraft (1-1/4 inch). Torque: 269 lbs.-ft. @ 2000 R.P.M.

1938 Buick, Limited, model 91, 4-dr. sedan, AA

CHASSIS: [Series 40] W.B.: 122 in. O.L.: 200-1/16 in. Frt/Rear Tread: 58-7/16 in. / 59-5/32 in. Tires: 15 x 6.50. [Series 60] W.B.: 126 in. O.L.: 203-9/16 in. Frt/Rear Tread: 58-5/16 in. / 59-1/4 in. Tires: 15 x 7.00. [Series 80] W.B.: 133 in. O.L.: 213-1/4 in. Frt/Rear Tread: 59-19/32 in. / 62-1/2 in. Tires: 16 x 7.00. [Series 90] W.B.: 140 in. O.L.: 219-1/2 in. Frt/Rear Tread: 59-7/16 in. / 62-1/2 in. Tires: 16 x 7.50.

TECHNICAL: Sliding gear transmission. Speeds: 3F/1R. Floor shift controls. Single dry plate clutch. Shaft drive. Semi-floating rear axle. Overall Ratio: 4.40:1 — Ser. 40, 3.90:1 — Ser. 60, 4.18:1 — Ser. 80, 4.56:1 — Ser. 90. Hydraulic brakes on four wheels. Pressed steel wheels. Automatic Safety transmission ($80.00). No Rol Hill-Holder (Series 60, 80, 90).

OPTIONS: Single sidemount. Dual sidemount. Electric clock (Special only). DeLuxe modern seat covers (6.55 — 9.35). Master heater ($13.95). DeLuxe heater (18.95). Grille guard (1.85). Ivory plastic steering wheel with full horn ring (Special Model 48 only). Fog lamps (5.50). Grille covers (1.35). Centerline radio (59.75). Centerline dual radio (67.50). Electric windshield defroster (3.00). Dual heater defroster (8.85).

HISTORICAL: Introduced Oct. 1937. A Shafer Special powered by a Buick engine was bumped from the starting line up after initially qualifying at 112.7 mph at Indy. The 1938 Series 80 and 90 models were the last Buicks using wood in the construction of their bodies. Innovations: Although Buick offered the Automatic Safety Transmission only for the 1938 model year it still represented an important step in the development of the modern automatic transmission. The use of coil springs at the rear was also an industry first. Calendar year production: 173,905. Model year production: 168,689 (including 12,692 stripped chassis and cars for export). The president of Buick was Harlow Curtice.

1939 BUICK

1939 BUICK: Buick's styling for 1939 was highlighted by a new two-piece "waterfall" grille with thin vertical bars and a substantial increase in window area. On the Series 40 and 60 bodies the windshield area was 26% larger, their front door windows were 16% larger and a 21% increase in area was claimed for their rear windows, which were on all models of a one-piece design. Other key design changes included a narrower hood, thinner front door pillars and larger hubcaps.

A new dash arrangement and "Handi-shift" column-mounted gearshifts were key interior changes. All major gauges except for the clock which was mounted on the passenger's side were positioned directly in front of the driver.

1939 Buick, Special, model 41, 4-dr. sedan, OCW

BUICK SPECIAL — SERIES 40 — EIGHT: The Series 40 wheelbase was reduced 2" to 120". Both a new clutch with only 9 parts as compared to 41 in 1938 and a new lighter and stronger transmission were introduced. In place of the normal running boards, optional narrow trim strips could be installed. The Series 40 interior was finished in walnut finish garnish moldings.

The Sport Sedan, Model 47 was dropped from the Special and Century lines and the Convertible Coupe now was fitted with rear opera seats rather than the rumble seat which was no longer offered for any Buick. The Convertible Phaeton model was also dropped for 1939. Its successor was the Convertible Sport Phaeton with a trunk-back body style in both the Special and Century lines.

BUICK CENTURY — SERIES 60 — EIGHT: The Series 60 shared the new clutch assembly with the Series 40 and was also available with the optional rocker panel trim strip. Its interior garnish molding was mahogany.

BUICK ROADMASTER — SERIES 80 — EIGHT: The Roadmaster shared stainless steel windshield and rear window trim plus mahogany interior trim panels with the Limited models. The Series 80 Sport Phaeton could be ordered with either the fastback or rear trunk style.

BUICK LIMITED — SERIES 90 — EIGHT: The 3 Series 90 Buicks continued to use a 140" wheelbase and the Limousine model featured a movable glass partition in back of the chauffeur's compartment. Standard equipment for Models 90 and 90L included rear compartment cigarette lighter and vanity case.

I.D. DATA: Serial numbers on riveted plate on right side cowling under hood. Starting: 13388547 (Flint), 23395088 (South Gate), 33405088 (Linden). Ending: 13596806 (Flint), 23592131 (South Gate), 33593652 (Linden). Same factory build identification as 1938. Engine numbers on low right rear side of crankcase adjacent to dipstick. Starting: 43572652 (Ser. 40), 63576652 (Ser. 60, 80, 90). Ending: 43786213 (Ser. 40), 93755912 (Ser. 60, 80, 90).

Note 1: Some cars were fitted with 0.010" overside pistons. These engines are identified by a dash (-) following the engine number.

1939 Buick, Century, model 61, 4-dr. sedan, AA

Model No.	Body Type & Seating	Price	Weight	Prod. Total
Series 40				
41	4-dr. Tr. Sed.-5P	996	3547	109,213
41C	4-dr. Spt. Phae.-5P	1406	3707	724
46	2-dr. Bus. Cpe.-2P	849	3387	14,582
46C	2-dr. Conv. Cpe.-4P	1077	3517	4569
46S	2-dr. Spt. Cpe.-4P	950	3437	10,043
48	2-dr. Tr. Sed.-5P	955	3482	27,218
Series 60				
61	4-dr. Tr. Sed.-5P	1246	3832	18,462
61C	4-dr. Spt. Phae.-5P	1713	3967	249
66C	2-dr. Conv. Cpe.-4P	1343	3762	790
66S	2-dr. Spt. Cpe.-4P	1175	3687	3408
68	2-dr. Tr. Sed.-5P	1205	3557	521
Series 80				
80C	4-dr. Spt. Phae.-6P	1938	4932	3
81	4-dr. Tr. Sed.-6P	1543	4247	5460
81C	4-dr. Phae.-6P	1983	4362	311
81F	4-dr. Fml. Sed.-6P	1758	4312	303
87	4-dr. Spt. Sed.-6P	1543	4247	20
Series 90				
90	4-dr. Tr. Sed.-8P	2350	4608	650
90L	4-dr. Limo.-8P	2453	4653	423
91	4-dr. Tr. Sed.-6P	2074	4568	378

ENGINE: [Series 40] Inline. Ohv. Eight. Cast iron block. B & S: 3-3/32 x 4-1/8. Disp.: 248 cu. in. C.R.: 6.15:1. Brake H.P.: 107 @ 3400 R.P.M. Taxable H.P.: 30.63. Main bearings: 5. Valve lifters: mechanical. Carb.: Carter 4195. Torque: 126 lbs.-ft. @ 1000 R.P.M. [Series 60, 80, 90] Inline. Ohv. Eight. Cast iron block. B & S: 3-7/16 x 4-5/16. Disp.: 320.2 cu. in. C.R.: 635:1. Brake H.P. 141 @ 3600 R.P.M. Taxable H.P.: 37.81. Main bearings: 5. Valve lifters: mechanical. Carb.: Stromberg AAV26. Torque: 130 lbs.-ft. @ 1000 R.P.M.

CHASSIS: [Series 40] W.B.: 120 in. O.L.: 198-1/16 in. Frt/Rear Tread: 58-1/4- in. / 59-3/32 in. Tires: 15 x 6.50 4 ply. [Series 60] W.B.: 126 in. O.L.: 203-9/16 in. Frt/Rear Tread: 58-23/32 in. / 59-21/32 in. Tires: 15 x 7.00 4 ply. [Series 80] W.B.: 133 in. O.L.: 213-1/4 in. Frt/Rear Tread: 59-19/32 in. / 62-1/2 in. Tires: 16 x 7.00 4 ply. [Series 90] W.B.: 140 in. O.L.: 219-1/2 in. Frt/Rear Tread: 59-7/16 in. / 62-1/2 in. Tires: 16 x 7.50 6 ply.

TECHNICAL: Sliding gear transmission. Speeds: 3F/1R. Column controls. Single dry plate clutch. Shaft drive. Semi-floating rear axle. Overall Ratio: 4.40, 3.9, 3.6-Ser. 40, 3.9, 3.6, 3.4 — Ser. 60 4.18-Ser. 80 4.56 — Ser. 90. Hydraulic brakes on four wheels. Pressed steel wheels. No Rol Hill-Holder (Series 60, 80, 90).

OPTIONS: Dual sidemounts. Fender skirts. Push button radio. Leather interior. Sonomatic push button radio. White side walls. Sunshine turret roof. Fender-mounted parking lights.

HISTORICAL: Introduced Oct. 9, 1938. Standard equipment directional signals (rear only), push-button "Sonomatic" radio, "Sunshine Turret-Roof" (sun roof) optional for Series 40 and 60 2-door and 4-door. Calendar year production: 231,219. Model year production: 208,256 (including 10,932 stripped chassis and cars for export). The president of Buick was Harlow Curtice.

1940 BUICK

1940 BUICK: The 1940 Buicks received a major facelift that eliminated the external running boards on the new Torpedo-bodied models in the Super and Roadmaster series, incorporated the headlights into the front fender form and provided a grille fitted with horizontal bars that extended further into the catwalk region.

1940 Buick, Special, model 41, 4-dr. sedan, OCW

1940 Buick Special, model 46S, sport coupe, JAC

Model No.	Body Type & Seating	Price	Weight	Prod. Total
Series 40				
41	4-dr. Tr. Sed.-5P	996	3660	67,308
41C	4-dr. Conv. Phae.	1355	3755	552
41T	4-dr. Taxi-5P	NA	NA	48
46	2-dr. Bus. Cpe.-2P	895	3505	12,372
46C	2-dr. Conv. Cpe.-4P	1077	3665	3664
46S	2-dr. Spt. Cpe.-4P	950	3540	8291
48	2-dr. Tr. Sed.-5P	955	3605	20,739
Series 50				
51	4-dr. Tr. Sed.-6P	1109	3790	95,875
51C	4-dr. Conv. Phae.-6P	1549	3895	1351
56C	2-dr. Conv. Cpe.-6P	1211	3785	4764
56S	2-dr. Spt. Cpe.-5P	1058	3735	26,251
59	4-dr. Est. Wag.-6P	1242	3870	495
Series 60				
61	4-dr. Tr. Sed.-6P	1211	3935	8597
61C	4-dr. Conv. Phae.-5P	1620	4050	194
66	2-dr. Bus. Cpe.-2P	1128	3800	44
66C	2-dr. Conv. Cpe.-4P	1343	3915	542
66S	2-dr. Spt. Cpe.-5P	1175	3765	96
Series 70				
71	4-dr. Tr. Sed.-6P	1359	4045	13,583
71C	4-dr. Conv. Phae.-6P	1768	4195	235
76C	4-dr. Conv. Cpe.6P	1431	4055	606
76S	2-dr. Spt. Cpe.-5P	1277	3990	3921
Series 80				
80C	4-dr. Conv. Phae.-6P	1952	4550	7
81	4-dr. Tr. Sed.-6P	1553	4400	3810
81C	4-dr. Fsbk. Conv. Phae.-6P	1952	4540	230
81F	4-dr. Fml. Sed.-6P	1727	4455	248
87	4-dr. Spt. Sed.-6P	1553	4380	14
87F	4-dr. Fml. Spt. Sed.-6P	1727	4435	7
Series 90				
90	4-dr. Tr. Sed.-8P	2096	4645	796
90L	4-dr. Limo.-8P	2199	4705	526
91	4-dr. Tr. Sed.-6P	1942	4590	417

BUICK SPECIAL — SERIES 40 — EIGHT: A 1 inch wheelbase increase to 121" enabled the side mount option and front doors that fully opened to coexist. A full-width rear seat was installed in the Sport Coupe model and a dual diaphragm fuel pump was used to improve windshield wiper operation. Interior features included white trim panels and combination Bedford cloth and mohair upholstery.

BUICK SUPER — SERIES 50 — EIGHT: The new Series 50 Buick shared the 121" wheelbase chassis with the Specials. Five body styles were offered, all of which were devoid of running boards. Bedford cord upholstery in a two-tone tan was standard. A mid-year Estate wagon model was exclusive to the Super Series.

BUICK CENTURY — SERIES 60 — EIGHT: Five body styles were offered in the Century line.

BUICK ROADMASTER — SERIES 70 — EIGHT: To make room for the new Series 80 Limited models the Roadmaster was given a new Series 70 designation. It shared its body shell with the new Super line and was available in 4 body styles. Interiors of either gray or tan Bedford cord were offered.

BUICK LIMITED — SERIES 80 — EIGHT: These Limited models, mounted on 133 inch wheelbase chassis previously used for the Roadmasters had standard equipment heaters and defrosters. All body styles were of a 6 passenger capacity. Interior appointments included a choice of Bedford cloth (either tan or grey), broadcloth or cloth (tan or grey) or leather.

BUICK LIMITED — SERIES 90 — EIGHT: Although all Buicks had the same front end design the 140" wheelbase and 8 passenger capacity set the Series 90 models apart. Three body styles were offered.

I.D. DATA: Serial numbers on riveted plate on right side cowling under hood, right side of frame top near cowling. Starting: 13596807 (Flint), 23601856 (South Gate), 33611856 (Linden). Ending: 13880011 (Flint), 23871217 (South Gate), 33874783 (Linden). Same factory built identification was 1939. Engine numbers on right side of crankcase below pushrod cover toward front (Ser 40-50) same location except near rear of engine (Ser 60, 70, 80). Starting: 43786214 (Ser 40), 53786214 (50, 60, 70, 80, 90). Ending: 44074857 (Ser 40), 94074858 (Ser 50, 60 70, 80, 90).

ENGINE: [Series 40, 50] Inline. Ohv. Eight. Cast iron block. B & S: 3-3/32 x 4-1/8. Disp.: 248 cu. in. C.R.: 6.15:1. Brake H.P.: 107 @ 3400 R.P.M. Taxable H.P.: 30.63. Main bearings: 5. Valve lifters: mechanical. Carb.: Carter Model 440S, 474S or Stromberg AAV-16, A-19181. Torque: 126 lbs.-ft. @ 1000 R.P.M. [Series 60, 70, 80, 90] Inline. Ohv. Eight. Cast iron block. B & S: 3-7/16 x 4-5/16. Disp.: 320.2 cu. in. C.R.: 6.35:1. Brake H.P.: 141 @ 3600 R.P.M. Taxable H.P.: 37.81. Main bearings: 5. Valve lifters: mechanical. Carb.: Carter No 4485 or Stromberg AAV-25 A-19182. Torque: 130 lbs.-ft. @ 1000 R.P.M.

CHASSIS: [Series 40] W.B.: 121 in. O.L.: 204 in. Frt/Rear Tread: 58-7/16 in. / 59-5/32 in. Tires: 16 x 6.50. [Series 50] W.B.: 121 in. O.L.: 204 in. Frt/Rear Tread: 58-7/16 in. / 59-5/32 in. Tires: 16 x 6.50. [Series 60] W.B.: 126 in. O.L.: 209 in. Frt/Rear Tread: 58-5/16 in. / 59-1/4 in. Tires: 15 x 7.00. [Series 70] W.B.: 126 in. O.L.: 214 in. Frt/Rear Tread: 58-5/16 in. / 59-1/4 in. Tires: 15 x 7.00. [Series 80] W.B.: 133 in. O.L.: 213-1/4 in. Frt/Rear Tread: 59-19/32 in. / 62-1/2 in. Tires: 16 x 7.50. [Series 90] W.B.: 140 in. O.L.: 219-1/2 in. Frt/Rear Tread: 59-7/16 in. / 62-1/2 in. Tires: 16 x 7.50.

TECHNICAL: Sliding gear transmission. Speeds: 3F/1R. Column controls. Single dry plate clutch. Shaft drive. Semi-floating rear axle. Overall Ratio: 3.9 (Ser. 40). Hydraulic brakes on four wheels. Pressed steel wheels. No Rol Hill-Holder.

OPTIONS: Seat covers. Front bumper guard. Fog lights. Roof mounted radio antenna (closed cars). Telescoping vacuum-powered mounted on left front fender (open cars). Sonomatic radio (63.00). Fender skirts. Dual white sidewall tires. Fresh Aire underseat heater/defroster. DeLuxe steering wheel (12.50). Rear seat radio (Model 90-L). Outside mirrors. Grille guard. Electric clock (Std Series 60, 70, 80, 90). Folding rear center guard. Winter grille cover. Radiator insect screen. Twin comfort cushions. Front door scuff pads. Visor vanity mirrors.

HISTORICAL: Introduced Sept. 22, 1939. Innovations: All Buick engines were equipped with oil filters and sealed beam headlights were used on all models. A new feature was Fore-N-Aft Flash-Way directionals. Calendar year production: 310,995. Model year production: 283,404 (including 8288 stripped chassis and cars for export). The president of Buick was Harlow Curtice. Buick had its best production year in history in 1940. On Nov. 18, 1940 the 4 millionth Buick was produced. 1940 was the last year Buicks were available with side mounts.

1940 Buick, Super, model 59, estate wagon, JAC

1940 Buick, Super, model 56C, convertible coupe, OCW

1940 Buick, Century, model 61C, convertible phaeton, OCW

1940 Buick, Roadmaster, model 76S, sport coupe, OCW

1941 BUICK

1941 BUICK: For the 1941 model year which was destined to set new records Buick introduced twin carburation, new bodies and on a very limited (5 cars in all) basis custom body work by Brunn on Roadmaster and Limited Series chassis. Buick's ''Fireball'' engine for 1941 was fitted with dome-shaped pistons and combustion chambers. All series were available with a choice of rear axle ratios at no extra cost. All cars were offered in two-tone color combinations with 19 selections at no extra charge.

1941 Buick, Special, model 44C, convertible coupe, OCW

BUICK SPECIAL — SERIES 40 — EIGHT: Both the Special and Century lines received new bodies for 1941. As with all 1941 Buicks they featured front fenders that extended nearly to the front door, headlights that were almost totally integrated into the front fender line and a broader front grille. The Estate model moved into the Series 40 line for 1941. On Feb. 3, 1941 four new Special series 40A models were introduced with a 118'' wheelbase. These carried a 40-A designation which brought a new 40-B identification for the original Series 40.

BUICK SUPER — SERIES 50 — EIGHT: The Super Buicks as all other Buicks above Series 40 were equipped with standard compound carburetion. Bodies were carried over from 1940 but all Buicks had overall heights lowered from 9/10 to 2-3/4''.

BUICK CENTURY — SERIES 60 — EIGHT: With its new body and 165 hp the Century Buick ranked both as America's most powerful automobile and one of its most attractive. It shared thin chrome strips on the front fenders with all production Buicks except the 40-B Specials. Introduced into both the Century and Special lines was the new Sedanet body style.

BUICK ROADMASTER — SERIES 70 — EIGHT: Four Roadmaster body styles were available, all with the 165 hp carburetion engine.

BUICK LIMITED — SERIES 90 — EIGHT: The 133'' wheelbase Limited Series was not offered in 1941. Standard equipment on the 139'' Limited included rear fender skirts.

I.D. DATA: Serial numbers underhood, on right side of firewall. Starting: Ser. 40A-14034052 (Flint), 23994170 (South Gate), 34007924 (Linden). All others — 13880012 (Flint), 23892008 (South Gate), 33897008 (Linden). Ending: Ser. 40A — 14257441 (Flint). Engine numbers on crankcase as in 1940. Starting: Ser. 40 — 44074859, Ser. 40-A - A4074859, Ser. 50, 60, 70, 90 — 54074859. Ending: Ser. 40-A — A4457940, Ser. 50, 60, 70, 80, 90 — 94453893.

Model No.	Body Type & Seating	Price	Weight	Prod. Total
Series 40-A				
44	2-dr. Bus. Cpe.-3P	915	3530	3258
44C	2-dr. Conv. Cpe.-6P	1138	3780	4282
44S	2-dr. Spt. Cpe.-6P	980	3590	5269
47	4-dr. Tr. Sed.-6P	1021	3670	13,992
Series 40-B				
41	4-dr. Tr. Sed.-6P	1052	3730	91,138
44SE	4-dr. Sed. Sup. Equipment	NA	NA	13,378
46	2-dr. Bus. Cpe.-3P	735	3630	9185
46S	2-dr. S'net.	1006	3700	87,687
46SSE	2-dr. S'net. Sup. Equip.-6P	1063	NA	9591
49	4-dr. Est. Wag.-6P	1463	3980	838
Series 50				
51	4-dr. Tr. Sed.-6P	1185	3770	57,367
51C	2-dr. Conv. Phae.-6P	1555	4015	467
56	2-dr. Bus. Cpe.-3P	1031	3620	2449
56C	2-dr. Conv. Cpe.-6P	1267	3810	12,181
56S	2-dr. Spt. Cpe.-6P	1113	3670	19,603
Series 60				
61	4-dr. Tr. Sed.-6P	1288	4239	15,027
66	2-dr. Bus. Cpe.-3P	1195	4093	220
66S	2-dr. S'net.-6P	1241	4157	5521
Series 70				
71	4-dr. Tr. Sed.-6P	1364	4204	10,431
71C	4-dr. Conv. Phae.-6P	1457	4285	312
76C	2-dr. Conv. Cpe.-6P	1775	4451	1845
76S	2-dr. Spt. Cpe.-6P	1282	4109	2784
Series 90				
90	4-dr. Tr. Sed.-8P	2360	4680	885
90L	4-dr. Limo.-8P	2465	4760	605
91	4-dr. Tr. Sed.-6P	2155	4575	1223
90F	Fml. Sed.-6P	2310	4665	293

ENGINE: [Series 40A, 40B] Inline. Ohv. Eight. Cast iron block. B & S: 3-3/32 x 4-1/8. Disp.: 248 cu. in. C.R.: 6.15:1. Brake H.P.: 115 @ 3500 R.P.M. opt compound carburetion for Series 40A & 40B boosts H.P. to 125 at 3800 R.P.M. Main bearings: 5. Valve lifters: mechanical. Carb.: Carter 487-S or Stromberg AAV-16. Torque: 210 lbs.-ft. @ 2000 R.P.M. [Series 50] Inline. Ohv. Eight. Cast iron block. B & S: 3-3/32 x 4-1/8. Disp.: 248 cu. in. C.R.: 7:0. Brake H.P. 125 @ 3800 R.P.M. Main bearings: 5. Valve lifters: mechanical. Carb.: Carter 509S, 510S or Stromberg AAV-16, AA-1. Torque: 278 lbs.-ft. @ 2200 R.P.M. [Series 60, 70, 90] Inline. Ohv. Eight. Cast iron block. B & S: 3-7/16 x 4-5/16. Disp.: 320.2 cu. in. C.R.: 7.0:1. Brake H.P.: 165 @ 3800 R.P.M. Main bearings: 5. Valve lifters: mechanical. Carb.: Carter 509S, 510S or Stromberg AAV-16, AA1. Torque: 278 lbs.-ft. @ 2200 R.P.M.

CHASSIS: [Series 40-A] W.B.: 118 in. O.L.: 202-17/32 W-75-15/16 in. Height: 67-13/32 in. Frt/Rear Tread: 59-1/8 in. / 62-3/16 in. Tires: 15 x 6.50. [Series 40B] W.B.: 121 in. O.L.: 208-3/4 in. Height 66-11/16 in. Frt/Rear Tread: 58-7/16 in. / 59-5/32 in. Tires: 16 x 6.50. [Series 50] W.B.: 121 in. O.L.: 210-3/8 in. Height: 66 in. Frt/Rear Tread: 58-7/16 in. / 59-5/32 in. Tires: 16 x 6.50. [Series 60] W.B.: 126 in. O.L.: 213-1/2 in. Height: 66-13/16 in. Frt/Rear Tread: 58-5/16 in. / 59-1/4 in. Tires: 15 x 7.00. [Series 70] W.B.: 126 in. O.L.: 215 in. Height: 66-1/8 in. Frt/Rear Tread: 59-1/8 in. / 62-1/4 in. Tires: 15 x 7.00. [Series 90] W.B.: 139 in. O.L.: 228-5/8 in. Height: 68-7/8 in. Frt/Rear Tread: 58-11/32 in. / 62-1/2 in. Tires: 16 x 7.50.

TECHNICAL: Sliding gear transmission. Speeds: 3F/1R. Column controls. Single dry plate clutch. Shaft drive. Semi floating rear axle. Overall Ratio: Ser. 40 — single carburetor, 4.4:1, compound carburetor 4.1:1. Ser. 50, 4.4:1. Ser. 60, 70 — 3.9:1. Ser. 90 4.2:1. Hydraulic brakes on four wheels. Pressed steel wheels. Drivetrain Options: Hill-Holder No Rol (9.00). Compound carburetion (Ser. 40 except Models 41SE & 46SSE) (15.39).

OPTIONS: Clock electric (special only). Super Sonomatic (shortwave & regular band). Underseat heater & defroster (standard on models 51C, 71C, & Ser. 90) (33.00). Rear stainless steel footrest molding (Sed.). Vacuum pump windshield washer (std. Ser. 90) (3.85). EZI, no glare mirrors. Fender skirts (std. on Ser. 90) (10.00). Fog lights (10.75). Sonomatic pushbutton radio & antenna (65.00). Special paint (41.05). DeLuxe Dash Heater (15.50). Dual Defroster (7.50).

HISTORICAL: Introduced Oct. 13, 1940. Buick introduced its 2-way hood which could be opened from either side for 1941. Calendar year sales: 297,381. Calendar year production: 316,251. Model year production: 377,428 (including 7597 stripped chassis & cars for export.) The president of Buick was Harlow Curtis.

1941 Buick, Super, model 51C, convertible phaeton, OCW

1942 BUICK

1942 BUICK: The 1942 Buicks offered the very appealing Sedanet fastback style which had been the sensation of 1941 in all series except the Limited line. New wider and lower bodies were offered for the Series 50 and Series 70 and "Airfoil" front fenders that flowed into the lines of the rear fenders were introduced on Convertibles and Sedanet models in Series 50 and Series 70. All models had new front fender trim featuring parallel chrome strips. Also featured for 1942 was a handsome new grille with a lower outline and thin vertical bars.

After the government prohibited the use of chrome trim on Jan. 1, 1942 Buick began production of the H models. A number of body styles were dropped and most trim was now painted. Cast iron pistons were used in the 248 cid engine and the Series 90 cars were dropped. The last of the 1942 Buicks was completed on Feb. 4, 1942.

1942 Buick, Special model 41, 4-dr. sedan, AA

BUICK SPECIAL — SERIES 40-A, 40-B — EIGHT: All Series 40 Buicks had new front fenders that extended well into the front door region. Models 41SE and 46SSE were fitted with Century interiors.

BUICK SUPER — SERIES 50 — EIGHT: The swept-back fenders of the Convertible and Sedanet Supers made them styling leaders. A feature the Supers shared with other Buicks was a new interior air intake positioned near the front grille which eliminated the old cowl-level ventilator.

BUICK CENTURY — SERIES 60 — EIGHT: The Century 4-door models along with those in the Special and Limited series had 6 side windows. All Century models had, prior to Jan. 1942, added side trim in their rear fenders. This feature was also common to all Buicks except the Series 40A and the Series 50 and Series 70 models with "Airfoil" front fenders. Those cars had twin side bars that ran unbroken the full length of the body.

1942 Buick, Roadmaster, model 71, 4-dr. sedan, JAC

BUICK ROADMASTER — SERIES 70 — EIGHT: The new Roadmaster bodies were lower and wider than in 1941 and along with the Series 50 models featured small reflector lenses on their rear fenders.

BUICK LIMITED — SERIES 90 — EIGHT: The 3 Series 90 models combined the older notch back styling with the extended length front fender format of the Series 40, 50 and 60 Buicks. With standard rear fender skirts the Limited also carried twin chrome trim strips on their front and rear fenders.

I.D. DATA: Serial numbers under hood, on right side of firewall. Starting: 14257442 - Flint, 24273684 - South Gate, 3426384 - Linden. The same factory-built identification of 1941 was continued. Engine numbers on crankcase as in 1941. Starting: Series 40A 4457941A, Ser 40B 4457971-4, Ser 50 4457941-5, Ser 60 4457941-6, Ser 70 4457941-7, Ser 90 4457941-9. Ending: Series 40A 4556599A, Ser 40B 4556599-4.

Model No.	Body Type & Seating	Price	Weight	Prod. Total
Series 40A				
44	2-dr. Util. Cpe.-3P	990	3510	461
44C	2-dr. Conv. Cpe.-6P	1260	3790	1776
47	4-dr. Tr. Sed.	1080	3650	1611
48	2-dr. Bus. S'dnt.-3P	1010	3555	559
48S	4-dr. Family S'dnt.-6P	1045	3610	5981
Special 40-B				
41	4-dr. Tr. Sed.-6P	1203	NA	17,187
41SE	Sed. Sup. Equipment-4P	1287	NA	2286
46	2-dr. Bus. S'dnt.-3P	1020	3650	1406
46S	2-dr. Sup. S'dnt.-6P	1075	3705	11,856
46SSE	8-dr. S'dnt. Sup. Equipment	NA	NA	1809
49	4-dr. Est. Wag.	1450	3925	326
Series 50				
51	4-dr. Tr. Sed.-6P	1280	3890	16,001
56C	2-dr. Conv. Cpe.-6P	1450	4025	2454
56S	4-dr. S'dnt.-6P	1230	3800	14,579
Series 60				
61	4-dr. Sed.-6P	1350	4065	3342
66S	2-dr. S'dnt.-6P	1300	3985	1229
Series 70				
71	4-dr. Tr. Sed.-6P	1465	4150	5418
76C	2-dr. Conv. Cpe.-6P	1675	4300	509
76S	2-dr. S'dnt.-6P	1365	4075	2471
Series 90				
90	4-dr. Tr. Sed.-8P	2455	4710	144
90L	4-dr. Limo.-8P	2716	NA	192
91	4-dr. Tr. Sed.-6P	2245	4665	215
90F	Formal Sed.-6P	2395	4695	85

ENGINE: [Series 40A, 40B] Inline. Ohv. Eight. Cast iron block. B & S: 3-3/32 x 4-1/8. Disp.: 248 cu. in. Brake H.P.: 110* @ 3400 R.P.M. * 118hp @ 3600 with compound combustion. Main bearings: 5. Valve lifters: mechanical. Carb.: Carter 487-S or Stromberg AAV-16. [Series 50] Inline. Ohv. Eight. Cast iron block. B & S: 3-3/32 x 4-1/8. Disp.: 2118 cu. in. Brake H.P.: 118 @ 3600 R.P.M. Main bearings: 5. Valve lifters: mechanical. Carb.: Carter 509S, 510S or Stromberg AAV-16, AA1. [Series 60, 70, 90] Inline. Ohv. Eight. Cast iron block. B & S: 3-7/16 x 4-5/16. Disp.: 320.2 cu. in. C.R.: 6.7:1. Brake H.P.: 165 @ 3800 R.P.M. Main bearings: 5. Valve lifters: mechanical. Carb.: Carter 509S, 510S or Stromberg AAV-16, AA-1. Torque: 278 lbs.-ft. @ 2200 R.P.M.

CHASSIS: [Series 40A; 40B] W.B.: 118 in. O.L.: 202-17/32 in. Height: 67-13/32 in. Frt/Rear Tread: 59-1/8 in. / 62-3/16 in. Tires: 15 x 6.50. [Series 50] W.B.: 124 in. O.L.: 210 in. Height: 66-11/16 in. Frt/Rear Tread: 58-7/16 in. / 59-5/32 in. Tires: 15 x 6.5. [Series 60] W.B.: 126 in. O.L.: 213-1/2 in. Height: 66-13/16 in. [Series 70] W.B.: 129 in. O.L.: 217 in. Height: 66-1/8 in. Frt/Rear Tread: 59-1/8 in. / 62-1/4 in. Tires: 15 x 7.00. [Series 90] W.B.: 139 in. O.L.: 228-5/8 in. Height: 68-7/8 in. Tires: 15 x7.00. [Series 40B] W.B.: 121 in. O.L.: 208-3/4 in.

TECHNICAL: Sliding gear transmission. Speeds: 3F/1R. Column controls. Single dry plate clutch. Shaft drive. Semi-floating rear axle. Overall ratio: 3.90 - Ser 70, 3.6 or 3.9 - Ser 60. Hydraulic brakes on four wheels. Pressed steel wheels. Hill-holder: No Rol.

OPTIONS: Fender skirts on Series 40 & 50. Electric clock (special only). Super sonomatic radio. Under seat heater & defroster. Windshield washer. EZI mirrors. Fender skirts. Fog lamps. Sonomatic radio.

HISTORICAL: Introduced Oct. 3, 1941. Calendar year production: 16,601. Model year production: 94,442 (including 2575 stripped chassis and cars for export). The president of Buick was Harlow Curtice.

Production of 1942 model Buicks ended on Feb. 2, 1942.

MARQUETTE

1930 Marquette, rumble-seat coupe, OCW

MARQUETTE — Flint, Michigan — (1930) — The Marquette was introduced by Buick in the wake of the success that Oakland had discovered with its Pontiac and Cadillac with its LaSalle.

It was a companion car, a distinct marque of its own, but produced and marketed under the aegis of the Buick Motor Company. A smaller car on a 114-inch wheelbase, the Marquette was powered by an L-head six, unlike the Buick's famous valve-in-head engine. It was offered in six body styles in the $1000 price range, and was rushed into production on June 1st, 1929, nearly two months before the introduction of Buick's 1930 model line. Promotion was vigorous, and press reaction was favorable.

Although the car looked Oldsmobile-like, one admiring reporter saw it as "a small edition of the Cadillac." Its herringbone-pattern radiator core set it apart from other GM cars. If it shone in neither styling nor engineering, the Marquette acquitted itself admirably in performance.

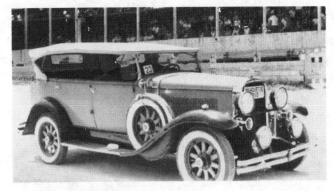
1930 Marquette, touring, OCW

Maximum speed approached 70 mph, and a Marquette was driven from Death Valley to the top of Pikes Peak with no problem at all. The Marquette's biggest problem appears to have been the stock market crash, and the Buick Motor Company's impatience with its initial lackluster sales.

After 35,007 Marquettes were built (all of them designated 1930 models), the car was abruptly dropped. Just a few months earlier, 4000 Marquette service signs had been dispatched to Buick dealer/service stations. (See Buick section for further details.)

I.D. DATA: Serial numbers on frame beneath left front fender. Starting: 10000. Ending: 52998. Engine numbers on crankcase. Starting: 10000. Ending: 48450.

Model No.	Body Type & Seating	Price	Weight	Prod. Total
30	2-dr. Sed.-5P	1000	2850	4630
34	2-dr. Spt. Rds.-4P	1020	2640	2397
35	4-dr. Phae.-5P	1020	2670	889
36	2-dr. Bus. Cpe.-2P	990	2760	2475
36S	2-dr. Sp. Cpe.-4P	1020	2760	4384
37	4-dr. Sed.-5P	1060	2925	15,795

Note 1: All models carried a 30 prefix i.e.: 30-30

ENGINE: Inline. L-head. Six. Cast iron block. B & S: 3-1/8 x 4-5/8. Disp.: 212.8 cu. in. Brake H.P.: 67.5 at 3000 R.P.M. N.A.C.C. H.P.: 23.4. Main bearings: 4. Valve lifters: mechanical. Carb.: Marvel.

CHASSIS: W.B. 114 in. Tires: 28 x 5.25.

TECHNICAL: Sliding gear transmission. Speeds: 3F/1R. Floor shift controls. Single plate clutch. Shaft drive. Semi-floating rear axle. Overall Ratio: 4.5:1. Mechanical brakes on four wheels. Wooden spoke wheels.

OPTIONS: Wire wheels. Side mounts. Demountable wood wheels. Trunk rack.

HISTORICAL: Calendar year production: 35,007. Model year production: 35,007 (including 4,437 stripped chassis and cars for export). The president of Buick was Edward Thomas Strong. The Marquette took part in a number of performance trials including a 778 mile run from Death Valley to Pikes Peak in 40 hours, 45 minutes.

BUICK
1946-1975

Buick entered the post-World War II market with a product for which there was enormous pent-up demand. During the years just prior to the war, Buick had become one of America's favorite cars. Large, but fast, and with sporting lines, the pre-war Buick symbolized upward mobility. In 1946, many veterans came home with a dream of a family, a home in suburbia — and a Buick in the driveway. ''So nice to come home to,'' a 1943 ad had proclaimed — using a yellow 1942 Roadmaster convertible for the illustration.

The Buick's role as part of the postwar dream was more than an ad man's pitch. This was born out by public acceptance of Buick's 1946-1948 models, although they were little more than warmed-over 1942s. Indeed, Buick's convertible styles, in Roadmaster and Super trim, were extremely popular. They are, today, treasured collector cars.

By Terry V. Boyce

Though the styling hadn't changed for 1948, there was an important innovation — Dynaflow automatic drive. Optional on the 1948 Roadmaster, it would soon power all Roadmasters and become a very popular option for other series.

New styling, still drawing on traditional design elements, appeared in 1949. Ventiports made their initial appearance on Buick front fenders. Mid-1949 saw the unveiling of a new Riviera hardtop which led the way towards acceptance of this design. The two-door hardtop coupe was destined to be one of the most popular models of the Fifties.

Then came 1950. According to many marque enthusiasts, Buick went a step too far. It was the year of the ''bucktooth Buick,'' with a grille cavity full of large bumper guards. Actually, this new design had appeared during mid-calendar 1949, in a new ''1950'' Special line. There had been Specials from 1946 on, but they had been largely ignored by Buick's sales staff, which concentrated on the more expensive Supers and Roadmasters. As late as the beginning of 1949, the Buick Special had been almost identical to 1942 models. The time had come for a new push into the lower-priced field, so the Special got the new styling first.

The 1950-1952 Buicks were solidly built and heavily trimmed. Yet, they were somehow a bit lacking in excitement and, even today, are not ranked among the most popular models. The straight eight era ended for the larger cars in 1952, when a four-barrel carbureted, 170-hp Roadmaster version made a fitting farewell.

Whatever excitement had been missing from Buick was back in 1953. The big news was under the hood — a 322 cubic inch overhead valve V-8 for Super and Roadmaster models. For the first time ever, all Buicks shared a common wheelbase. Celebrating their 50th anniversary, the Buick Division of General Motors offered an Anniversary Convertible, also known as the Skylark, for a cool $5,000. Just 1,690 were sold. Today, many still survive and are in great demand by collectors.

Buick chassis engineering began to catch up with the new V-8 in 1954. The updated cars were lower and wider, with greatly improved handling. Even the Special now had V-8 power. The Skylark returned for an unsuccessful encore, but the year was otherwise a smashing performance sales-wise. The next year, 1955, was even better. Buick broke all the old records. A popular model line was the Century, which had returned in 1954. A new four-door Riviera pillarless hardtop debuted mid-year.

By 1957, Buick styling had began to lag. Sales started to slump. An over-chromed, over-weight 1958 edition proved even less palatable to consumer tastes. It was a time of rapid change. The year 1959 brought new Buicks, with new series designations replacing those used since 1936. Wildly finned, and lacking almost any sort of continuity with Buick's past, the 1959 Buicks continued to get a cool reception in the showrooms. Buick was committed to the same basic body for 1960, but completely changed its look by blunting edges everywhere.

For 1961, Buicks looked lighter and cleaner. A new compact, the Special, was introduced and would soon be joined by a fancier Skylark Sport Coupe version. There was little real news for 1962, but the season's offerings were attractive and well-executed. A Buick highpoint, in

the Sixties, came the next year with the introduction of the 1963 Riviera. It was a four-passenger sporting car that was immediately, and correctly, termed a classic design.

By 1965, the Special/Skylark had grown to intermediate proportions and was wrapped in a very handsome package. The larger Buicks, too, were restyled. Increasingly distinctive was the mid-range, Buick performance line — offering the Wildcat. Continuing through 1970, the Wildcat series, provided extra performance and style. Beginning in 1963, the largest Buicks, (Electras and Electra 225s) were given styling touches of their own, including unique rear fenders with skirts, distinctive bright trim and even specific grille work. They obtained a following that lasted for two decades.

A new Riviera, with some of the smoothest lines ever rendered by GM stylists, came in 1966. A GS or 'Gran Sport' equipment option was continued, from 1965, and would be a rare option for the rest of the decade. The GS badge also appeared on a high-performance Skylark late in 1965, and evolved into a series designation by 1966.

By the end of the Sixties, Buick had strong followings in many segments of the market. Never a large part of the

sales picture, but still catered to with great care, were Buick's performance buyers. A 1970-1971 GSX option for

the GS 455 coupe featured special paint colors, wild stripes and performance touches. The GSX may become the most sought after Buick of the Seventies. Buick lovers also said goodbye to the prestige Buick convertible in 1970, with discontinuation of the Electra 225 edition marked that year.

Buick Division shocked the automotive world, in 1971, with a new tapered-deck 'boattail' Riviera. This design, built through 1973, will always standout on the road. A new Centurion line also replaced the Wildcat, as Buick's full-size luxury performance line. The Centurion convertible became Buick's plushest, most expensive open car and is sure to be increasingly appreciated by collectors.

Skylark/GS models continued with little change from 1970 to 1972, although the potent GS 455s, with their Stage I engine option topping most performance cars in sheer acceleration, were detuned for 1971 to run on regular gas and decrease emissions. The Skylark/GS Sport Coupes and Convertibles, when optioned with desirable accessories, are sure bets for enthusiast attention.

An interesting series of Buick station wagons were issued throughout the post-World War II era. The Roadmaster Estates of 1947-1953 are among the most sought-after of all wooden-bodied cars. The 1953 model's combination of V-8 power and traditional wood sportiness presents a stunning combination. The all-steel wagons of 1954-1956 are rare. A four-door hardtop Caballero version followed in 1957. Innovative styling continued on Buick wagons into the Sixties. The famous Skyroof Sport Wagons, featured raised, glass-paneled roof sections, making them true specialty cars.

Buicks from any post-war year abound with the fine touches that make the cars interesting and collectible. From the 'Showboats' of the late Forties to the compact, but well-trimmed and gutsy Skylarks of the early Sixties, to the "boattail" Riviera of the Seventies, plenty of appreciation for restoration, or conservator's efforts are assured. For thousands of collector car enthusiasts, the question, "Wouldn't you really rather have a Buick?" is still answered with a resounding, "Yes."

1946 BUICK

NOTE: Through 1950 Buick provided separate production totals for cars built for export. These are given in brackets on the charts below.

SPECIAL — SERIES 40 — The Special was Buick's lowest priced line. It was the only Buick line continuing the Fisher "B-body" fastback styles from 1941-42 into the postwar era. Standard equipment included an automatic choke, ash receiver and turn signals. Exterior bright trim echoed 1942 models with twin strips of stainless steel flowing from the front wheelhouse to the rear edge of the standard rear wheelhouse skirts. Bright rocker moldings were also standard. Interiors featured rubber floor mats and painted instrument panels with round gauges. Series identification was found between the bumper guards, front and rear, on the cross bar. A cloisonne emblem carried the "Special" signature.

SPECIAL I.D. NUMBERS: The serial numbers for the 1946 Special series were the same as for other 1946 Buick series, which were mixed in production. They were: (Flint) 1436445 to 14524130, (Calif.) 24380001 to 24511494, (N.J.) 34390001 to 34429256, (Kans.) 44415001 to 44419786. Motor numbers began at 4558037-4 and up, the suffix '4' denoting a Series 40 motor.

Model Number	Body/Style Number	Body Type & Seating	Factory Price	Shipping Weight	Production Total
41	46-4409	4-dr. Sedan-6P	1580	3720	1649 (1)
46S	46-4407	2 dr. Sedanette-6P	1522	3670	1350

SPECIAL ENGINE
Eight-cylinder: Overhead valve. Cast iron block. Displacement: 248.0 cubic inches. Bore and stroke: 3-3/32 x 4-1/8 inches. Compression ratio: 6.3:1. Brake horsepower: 110 at 3600 R.P.M. Five main bearings. Mechanical valve lifters. Carburetor: Stromberg AAV-16 number 380106 two-barrel or Carter 608 or 663 two-barrel.

SUPER — SERIES 50 — Buick combined the large Series 70 body with the economical Series 40 powerplant to create the Super Series 50 line. Basic styling was continued from 1942, but now sedans had the front fender sweep across the doors to the rear fenders as did sedanettes and convertible styles. A stamped grille with vertical bars dominated the frontal ensemble. Single stainless body trim lines began on the front fenders and ended at the rear edge of the standard rear wheelhouse shields. Standard equipment was the same as the Series 40, but Series 50 Buicks had two-tone, woodgrained, instrument panels. Exterior series identification was found on the crossbar between the bumper guards, front and rear. Cloisonne emblems carried the super signature.

SUPER I.D. NUMBERS: The serial number sequence was the same for all series (see Special — Series 40). Motor numbers began at 4558037-5 and up. The suffix '5' denoting a Series 50 motor.

Model Number	Body/Style Number	Body Type & Seating	Factory Price	Shipping Weight	Production Total
51	46-4569	4-dr. Sedan-6P	1822	3935	74,045 (3679)
56S	46-4507	2-dr. Sedanette-6P	1741	3795	34,235 (190)
56C	46-4567	Convertible Cpe.-6P	2046	4050	5,931 (456)
59	(Ionia)	Station Wagon-6P	2594	4170	786 (12)

SUPER ENGINE
Specifications were the same as previously listed for the 1946 Special — Series 40.

ROADMASTER — SERIES 70 — The Roadmaster was Buick's biggest and fastest car. It's larger and longer straight eight required five inches more wheelbase and longer front fenders and hood. Exterior trim was identical to the Super, except for the longer stainless moldings on the frontal sheetmetal. Standard equipment was the same as for the Super, but richer interior fabrics were used. The instrument panel was two-toned with wood grains except on convertibles, which used body-colored panels. Series identification was found on cloisonne emblems centered in the bumper guard crossbars front and rear.

ROADMASTER I.D. NUMBERS: The serial number sequence was the same for all series (see Special — Series 40). Motor numbers began at 455829-7 and up.

Model Number	Body/Style Number	Body Type & Seating	Factory Price	Shipping Weight	Production Total
71	46-4769	4-dr. Sedan-6P	2110	4165	20,597 (267)
76S	46-4707	2-dr. Sedanette-6P	2014	4095	8,226 (66)
76C	46-4767	Convertible Cpe.-6P	2347	4345	2,576 (11)

ROADMASTER ENGINE
Eight-cylinder: Overhead valve. Cast iron block. Displacement: 320.2 cubic inches. Bore and stroke: 3-7/16 x 4-5/16 inches. Compression ratio: 6.6:1. Brake horsepower: 144 at 3600 R.P.M. Five main bearings. Mechanical valve lifters. Carburetor: Stromberg AAV-26 number 380097 two-barrel or Carter 609 or 664 two-barrel.

CHASSIS FEATURES: Wheelbase: Series 40-121 inches; Series 50 — 124 inches; Series 70 — 129 inches. Overall length: Series 40 — 207-1/2 inches; Series 50 — 212-3/8 inches; Series 70 — 217-1/8 inches. Front tread: Series 40 — 58-7/8 inches; Series 50 and 70 — 59-1/8 inches. Rear tread: Series 40 — 61-15/16 inches; Series 50 and 70 — 62-3/16 inches. Tires: Series 40 and 50, 6.50 x 16; Series 70, 7.00 x 15.

POWERTRAIN OPTIONS: A three-speed manual transmission with steering column-mounted shift lever was standard on all series. There were no optional gear boxes.

CONVENIENCE OPTIONS: Spotlite. Sonomatic radio. Weather-Warden heater/defroster. Side view mirror. E-Z-I non-glare rear view mirror. Prismatic inside rear-view mirror. Vanity visor mirror. Seat covers. Auxillary driving lights. Multi-purpose trouble lamp. "Breeze-Ease" draft deflectors.

Historical footnotes: Model 59 was the Estate Wagon, with wooden upper body, by Ionia.

186

1947 BUICK

SPECIAL — SERIES 40 — Buick's lowest-priced line continued to use the Fisher "B-body" design from before World War II this year. A new stamped grille with separate upper bar distinguished 1947 Buick's from their 1946 predecessors. Standard equipment included an automatic choke, ash receiver and turn signals. Front and rear bumper guards were standard and the series designation was found, filled in red, on the chrome buttons centered in the guards' crossbars. Twin stainless moldings continued to be a Special hallmark, along the body and onto the standard rear fender wheelhouse skirts. Interiors featured round gauges with control switches flanking a center grille on the instrument panel. Rubber floor mats were standard.

SPECIAL I.D. NUMBERS: The serial numbers for the 1947 Special Series 40 were the same as for other 1947 Buick series, which were mixed in production. They were: Flint — 14524131 to 14801264, Calif. — 24530001 to 24775798, N.J. — 3454001 to 34776843, and Kans. 44536001 to 44774870. Special Series 40 motor numbers were continued from 1946, ending at 4999880-4, the suffix 4 denoting a Series 40 motor.

Model Number	Body/Style Number	Body Type & Seating	Factory Price	Shipping Weight	Production Total
41	47-4409	4-dr. Sedan 6P	1673	3720	17,136 (1,295)
46	47-4407	2-dr. S'dn't 6P	1611	3670	14,278 (325)

SPECIAL ENGINE
Eight-cylinder: overhead valve. Cast iron block. Displacement: 248.0 cubic inches. Bore and stroke: 3-3/32 x 4-1/8 inches. Compression ration: 6.3:1. Brake horsepower: 110 at 3600 R.P.M. Five main bearings. Mechanical valve lifters. Carburetor: Stromberg AAV-16 number 380106 two-barrel or Carter 608 or 663 two-barrel.

1947 Buick, Super 2-door convertible coupe, 8-cyl(AA)

SUPER I.D. NUMBERS: The serial number sequence was the same for all series (see Special — Series 40). Motor numbers continued from 1946, ending at 4999880-5 and up, the suffix 5 denoting a Series 50 motor.

SUPER — SERIES 50 — Combining big Buick room and ride with an economical Special engine continued to make an American favorite. The 1947 Super was little changed from its 1946 counterpart, except for a new stamped grille that had a separate upper bar and a new emblem. Stainless lower body moldings made a single line along the body and continued onto the standard rear wheelhouse shields. A white Tenite steering wheel was standard, while the instruments were round and set in a two-toned dash panel. Exterior series identification was found on the crossbars between the standard bumper guards. A chrome emblem with the series script embossed and filled with red was used.

Model Number	Body/Style Number	Body Type & Seating	Factory Price	Shipping Weight	Production Total
51	47-4569	4-dr. Sedan 6P	1929	3920	76,866 (6710)
56S	47-4507	2-dr. S'dn't 6P	1843	3795	46,311 (606)
56C	47-4567	Conv. Coupe 6P	2333	4050	27,796 (501)
59	Ionia	Station Wgn 6P	2594	4170	786 (12)

SUPER ENGINE
Specifications were the same as previously listed for the 1947 Special Series 40.

1947 Buick, Roadmaster 2-dr sedanette, 8-cyl

ROADMASTER — SERIES 70 — Buick's master of the road was a large car which continued basically unchanged from 1946. A new grille, shared with other series, was used. Exterior trim continued to be the same as used on the Super, except that the Roadmaster's longer wheelbase and front dog house required longer moldings ahead of the doors. Standard equipment was the same as found on the Super, but richer interior fabrics were used. Two-tone, neutral colored, instrument panels were employed, except on convertibles, which had body-colored panels. The Roadmaster name appeared in red-filled script on a chrome button within the bumper guard crossbars, front and rear.

ROADMASTER I.D. NUMBERS: The serial number sequence was the same for all series (see Special — Series 40). Motor numbers continued from 1946, ending at 499980-7, the suffix 7 denoting a Series 70 motor.

Model Number	Body/Style Number	Body Type & Seating	Factory Price	Shipping Weight	Production Total
71	47-4769	4-dr. Sedan 6P	2232	4190	46,531 (621)
76S	47-4707	2-dr S'dn't 6P	2131	4095	18,983 (229)
76C	47-4767	Conv. Coupe 6P	2651	4345	11,947 (127)
79	(Ionia)	Station Wgn 6P	3249	4445	300

ROADMASTER ENGINE
Eight-cylinder: Overhead valve. Cast iron block. Displacement: 320.2 cubic inches. Bore and stroke: 3-7/16 x 4-5/16. Compression ratio: 6.6:1. Brake horsepower: 144 at 3600 R.P.M. Five main bearings. Mechanical valve lifters. Carburetor: Stromberg AAV-26 number 380097 or Carter 609 or 664 two-barrel.

CHASSIS FEATURES: Wheelbase: Series 40 — 121 inches, Series 50 — 124 inches, Series 70 — 129 inches. Overall length: Series 40 — 207 1/2 inches; Series 50 — 212 3/8 inches; Series 70 — 217 1/8 inches. Front tread: Series 40 — 58 7/8 inches; Series 50 and 70 — 59 1/8 inches. Rear tread: Series 40 — 61 15/16 inches; Series 50 and 70 — 63 3/16 inches. Tires: Series 40 and 50, 6.50 x 16; Series 70, 7.00 x 15.

POWERTRAIN OPTIONS: A three-speed manual transmission with steering column-mounted shift lever was standard on all series. There were no optional gearboxes.

CONVENIENCE OPTIONS: Spotlite. Sonomatic radio. Weather-Warden heater/defroster. Side view mirror. E-Z-I non-glare rear view mirror. Prismatic inside rear-view mirror. Vanity visor mirror. Seat covers. Auxillary driving lights. Multi-purpose trouble lamp. "Breeze-Ease" draft deflectors.

Historial footnotes: Models 59 and 79 were Estate Wagons, with wooden upper bodies by Ionia.

1948 BUICK

SPECIAL — SERIES 40 — Even more bright metal trim adorned the 1948 Special, as a full-length upper body molding was added. Dual stainless bands along the lower body, fenders and rear skirts were continued. Inside, new nickle grey garnish moldings and a black Tenite steering wheel were featured. Sedans were carpeted in the rear, while front compartment mats had a simulated carpet insert. Leatherette seat risers and scuff pads were standard. Equipment included an automatic choke, turn signals and an ash receiver. Series identification was found within a round emblem in the bumper guard crossbars.

SPECIAL I.D. NUMBERS: The serial numbers for the 1948 Special Series 40 were the same as for other 1948 Buick series, which were mixed in production. They were: (Flint) 14801266 to 15020983, (Calif.) 2482001 to 25003031, (N.J.) 34824001 to 5004975, (Kans.) 4483001 to 64834001, (Ga.) 64834001 to 64987817. Series 40 motor numbers were 4999881-4 to 52220971-4, the suffix 4 denoting a Series 40 motor.

1948 Buick, Special 2-door sedanette, 8-cyl(AA)

Model Number	Body/Style Number	Body Type & Seating	Factory Price	Shipping Weight	Production Total
41	48-4409	4-dr. Sedan 6P	1809	3705	13,326 (815)
46S	48-4407	2-dr. S'dn't 6P	1735	3635	10,775 (401)

SPECIAL ENGINE
Eight-cylinder: overhead valve. Cast iron block. Displacement: 248.0 cubic inches. Bore and stroke: 3-3/32 x 4-1/8 inches. Compression ratio: 6.3:1. Brake horsepower: 110 at 3600 R.P.M. Five main bearings. Mechanical valve lifters. Carburetor: Stromberg AAV-167 number 380225 or Carter 608 or 663 two-barrel.

1948 Buick, Super 4-dr sedan, 8-cyl

SUPER—SERIES 50—The main external change to the 1948 Super from its 1947 counterpart was the (Super) script on each front fender. Other series identification continued to be carried on the bumper guard cross bar. The car was a bit lower than in 1947, rolling on new 7.60 x 15 tires mounted on wheels with trim rings and small hubcaps. Super identification was also found on the center crest of the new black Tenite steering wheel. New cloth interiors featured leatherette scuff pads and trim risers. The instrument panel was redone, using silver-tone instruments on a two-tone grey panel. The sedan was carpeted in the rear, with a carpet insert also found in the front rubber mat. The Model 56C featured cloth and leather interior trim, with power top, seat and front windows standard.

SUPER I.D. NUMBERS: The serial number sequence was the same for all series (see Special—Series 40). Motor numbers continued from 1947, running from 4999881-5 to 5220971-5, the suffix (5) denoting a Series 50 motor.

Model Number	Body/Style Number	Body Type & Seating	Factory Price	Shipping Weight	Production Total
51	48-4569	4-dr. Sedan-6P	2087	3855	47,991 (5456)
56S	48-4507	2-dr. S'dn't-6P	1987	3770	32,860 (959)
56C	48-4567	Conv. Coupe-6P	2518	4020	18,311 (906)
59	(Ionia)	Station Wgn-6P	3124	4170	1,955 (63)

SUPER ENGINE
Specifications were the same as prevously listed for the 1948 Special Series 40, except that compression ratio was 6.6:1, brake horsepower was 115 at 3600 RP.M.

1948 Buick, Roadmaster 2-door convertible, 8-cyl(AA)

ROADMASTER — SERIES 70 — Exterior appearance of the 1948 Roadmaster was changed only by the addition of series script to the front fenders. Other series identification continued to be found on the bumper guards' crossbars and within the steering wheel center medallion. The wheel was now black Tenite, coordinated with the new two-tone grey intrument panel with silver tone instruments. Chrome full wheel discs were standard, along with features found on lesser Buicks. Interiors were cloth, with plusher grades of material available. A new optional Custom Trim was offered, consisting of cloth upholstery with leather bolsters; the robe cord cover, and lower door panels were done in leatherette. The Model 76C convertible coupe included power windows, seat and top in its standard equipment.

ROADMASTER I.D. NUMBERS: The serial number sequence was the same for all 1948 series (see Special-Series 40). Series 70 motor numbers were 4999881-7 to 5220971-7, the suffix (7) denoting a Series 70 motor.

Model Number	Body/Style Number	Body Type & Seating	Factory Price	Shipping Weight	Production Total
71	48-4769	4-dr. Sedan-6P	2418	4160	47,042 (527)
76S	48-4707	2-dr. S'dn't-6P	2297	4065	20,542 (107)
76C	48-4767	Conv. Cpe-6P	2837	4315	11,367 (136)
79	(Ionia)	Station Wgn-6P	3433	4460	344 (6)

ROADMASTER ENGINE
Eight-cylinder: Overhead valve. Cast iron block. Displacement: 320.2 cubic inches. Bore and stroke: 3-7/16 x 4-5/16 inches. Compression ratio: 6.6:1. Brake horsepower: 144 at 3600 R.P.M. Five main bearings. Mechanical valve lifters. Carburetor: Stromberg AAV-267 #380226 or Carter 609 or 664 two-barrel.

CHASSIS FEATUES: Wheelbase: Series 40—121 inches; Series 50—124 inches; Series 70—129 inches. Overall length: Series 40— 207½ inches; Series 50—212½ inches; Series 70—217½ inches. Front tread: Series 40—58⅞ inches; Series 50&70—59⅛ inches. Rear tread: Series 40—61-15/16 inches, Series 50&70—62-3/16 inches. Tires: Series 40—6.50 x 16; Series 50—7.60 x 15; Series 70—8.20 x 15.

POWERTRAIN OPTIONS: A three-speed manual transmission with column-mounted shift lever was standard on all series. Dynaflow automatic transmission was optional on Series 70. Cars so equipped also had 6.9:1 compression ratio, 150 brake horsepower motors.

CONVENIENCE OPTIONS: Spotlite. Sonomatic radio. Weathe-Warden heater/defroster. Side-view mirror. Tissue dispenser. Vanity visor mirror. E-Z-I non-glare rear view mirror. Prismatic inside rear-view mirror. Seat covers. Auxillary driving lights. Multi-purpose trouble lamp. "Breeze-Ease" draft deflectors. NoRol assembly. Automatic windshield washer. Back-up lights. Polaroid visor. Rear window wiper. Power Pak fire extinguisher/tire inflator.

Historical footnotes: Models 59 and 79 were Estate Wagons, with wooden upper bodies by Ionia.

1949 BUICK

SPECIAL — SERIES 40 — continued from 1948 production without change until mid-year. Data plates, however, have '49' prefix. The second series 1949 Special was continued into 1950 and its specifications may be found under that year.

SPECIAL I.D. NUMBERS: The serial numbers for the 1949 Special Series 40 were mixed in production with other 1949 series. They were: (Flint) 15020984 to 15348304, (Calif.) 25030001 to 25332419, (N.J.) 35036001 to 35333911, (Kans.) 45043001 to 45335606, (Del.) 55050001 to 5517948 and 55417001 to 55417948, (Mass.) 75057001 to 75338786, (Ga.) 65054001 to 65337687. Series 40 motor numbers were 5220972-4 to 5259136-4, the suffix 4 denoting a Series 40 motor.

Model Number	Body/Style Number	Body Type & Seating	Factory Price	Shipping Weight	Production Total
41	49-4409	4-dr. Sedan6P	1861	3695	5,777 (163)
46S	49-4407	2-dr. S'dn't 6P	1787	3625	4,631 (56)

SPECIAL ENGINE
Eight-cylinder: overhead valve. Cast iron block. Displacement: 248.0 cubic inches. Bore and stroke: 3-3/32 x 4-1/8 inches. Compression ratio: 6.3:1. Brake horsepower: 110 at 3600 R.P.M. Five main bearings. Mechanical valve lifters. Carburetor: Stromberg AAV-167 number 380225 or Carter 608 or 663 two-barrel.

SUPER — SERIES 50 — Shared a new GM "C-body" with the Roadmaster, but on a shorter wheelbase. Featured three chromed Ventiports on each front fender. Super script was found just above the full-length body/fender molding on the front fenders. New fender-edge taillamps were featured, while rear fender skirts remained a Buick standard. New fender-top parking lamps, harking back to 1941 styling, appeared. Full wheel trim discs were standard, along with such features as a cigar lighter, ashtray and automatic choke. Cloth interiors were standard, except for the Model 56C which was trimmed in leather and leatherette and had a power top, seat and windows as standard equipment.

1949 Buick, Super 4-door Estate Wagon, 8-cyl(AA)

SUPER I.D. NUMBERS: The serial number sequence was the same for all series (see Special — Series 40). Motor numbers were 5220972-5 to 5659598-5, the suffix '5' denoting a Series 50 motor.

Model Number	Body/Style Number	Body Type & Seating	Factory Price	Shipping Weight	Production Total
51	49-4569	4-dr. Sedan 6P6P	2157	3835	131,514 (4909)
56S	49-4507	2-dr. S'dn't 6P6P	2059	3735	65,395 (865)
56C	49-4567	Conv. Cpe 6P6P	2583	3985	21,426 (684)
59	(Ionia)	Station Wgn 6P6P	3178	4100	1,830 (17)

SUPER ENGINE
Specifications were the same as listed for the 1949 Special Series 40, except the compression ratio was 6.6:1 and brake horsepower was 115 at 3600 R.P.M.

ROADMASTER — SERIES 70 — Shared the new GM "C-body", which used closed quarters in sedan roofs and fastback sedanette styling for coupes. Roadmasters had longer front fenders and four Ventiports per side, with series script below and also within bumper guard crossbar centers. Skirted rear wheelhouse openings were standard, as were all features found on the Super Series 50. Interior fabrics were plusher, with a Custom trim option again offered. A new instrument panel was used that continued Buick's centered radio grille flanked by operational switches. Windshield panels were curved but still had a division bar. The Model 79R Estate Wagon had mahogany veneer panels inside, with leather upholstery and carpeted floors and cargo area, while the Model 76C was upholstered in leather and had standard power windows, seat and top. The mid-year Model 76R Riviera was upholstered in leather and cloth and also had standard power windows.

1949 Buick, Roadmaster Riviera 2-door hardtop coupe, 8-cyl(AA)

ROADMASTER I.D. NUMBERS: The serial number sequence was the same for all 1949 series (see Special — Series 40). Series 70 motor numbers were 5220972-7 to 5548366-7, the suffix '7' denoting a Series 70 motor.

Model Number	Body/Style Number	Body Type & Seating	Factory Price	Shipping Weight	Production Total
71	49-4769	4 dr. Sedan 6P	2735	4205	54,674 (568)
76S	49-4707	2 dr. S'dn't 6P	2618	4115	18,415 (122)
76R	49-4737	2 dr. h'dtop 6P	3203	4420	4,314 (29)
76C	49-4767	Conv. cpe 6P	3150	4370	8,095 (149)
79	(Ionia)	Station Wgn. 6P	3734	4490	632 (21)

ROADMASTER ENGINE
Eight cylinder: Overhead valve. Cast iron block. Displacement: 320.2 cubic inches. Bore and stroke: 3-7/16 x 4-4/16. Compression ratio: 6.9:1. Brake horsepower: 150 at 3600 R.P.M. Five main bearings. Mechanical valve lifters. Carburetor: Stromberg AAV-267 #380226 and Carter 609 or 664.

CHASSIS FEATURES: Wheelbase: Series 40 & 50 — 121 inches; Series 70 — 126 inches. Overall length: Series 40 — 207-1/2 inches; Series 50 — 209-1/2 inches; Series 70 — 214-1/8 inches. Front tread: Series 40 — 58-7/8 inches; Series 50 & 70 — 59-1/8 inches. Rear Tread: Series 40 — 61-15/16 inches; Series 50 & 70 — 62-3/16 inches. Tires: Series 40 — 6.50 x 15; Series 50 — 7.60 x 15; Series 70 — 8.20 x 15.

POWERTRAIN OPTIONS: Three-speed manual transmission standard on Series 40 & 50. Dynaflow drive standard on Series 70. Column-mounted shift levers. Dynaflow drive optional on Series 50; cars so equipped have 6.9:1 compression ratio, 120 brake horsepower motors.

CONVENIENCE OPTIONS: Spotlite (Series 40). Spotlamp with mirror. Sonomatic radio. Weather Warden heater/defroster. Seat covers. NoRo1 assembly. Windshield washer. E-Z-I or Prismatic rear view mirrors. Vanity visor mirror. Tissue dispenser. Auxiliary driving lamps. multi-purpose trouble lamp. All-rubber floor mats.

Historical footnotes: Models 59 and 79 were Estate Wagons. Model 76R was the Riviera, a mid-year model.

1950 BUICK

SPECIAL — SERIES 40 — Introduced as late 1949 style. The first Special with postwar styling previewed the basic styling for 1950. Most prominent and memorable was the car's 'bucktooth' grille, consisting of bumper guards. Specials had three rectangular Ventiports on each hood side. A unique feature of the late 1949 cars was that the hood was opened through a Ventiport key and slot system; 1950 production cars had inside hood releases. Specials had no side body moldings. Special Deluxe models had plusher interiors, a full-length body side molding, bright window outlines and 'Special' script on the front fenders. They were indicated by the code 'D' in the model number.

SPECIAL I.D. NUMBERS: The serial numbers for the 1950 Special Series 40 were mixed in production with other 1950 series. They were: Flint 15360001-up, N.J. 35374001-up, Kans. 45380001-up, Del. 55388001-up (except 55417001 to 55417948), Mass. 65393001-up. Series 40 motor numbers were 5568000-4 up, the suffix 4 denoting a Series 40 motor.

Model Number	Body/Style Number	Body Type & Seating	Factory Price	Shipping Weight	Production Total
43	50-4408	4-dr. Sedan-6P	1909	3715	58,700
41	50-4469	4-dr. Sedan-6P	1941	3710	1,141
46S	50-4407	2-dr. S'dn't-6P	1856	3655	42,935
46	50-4407B	Bus. Cpe-6P	1803	3615	2,500
43D	50-4408D	4-dr. Sedan-6P	1952	3720	14,335
41D	50-4469D	4-dr. Sedan-6P	1983	3735	141,396
46D	50-4407D	2-dr. S'dn't-6P	1899	3665	76,902

SPECIAL ENGINE
Eight-cylinder: Overhead valve. Cast iron block. Displacement: 248.0 cubic inches. Bore and stroke: 3-3/32 x 3-1/8 inches. Compression ratio: 6.3:1. Brake horsepower: 110 at 3600 R.P.M. Five main bearings. Mechanical valve lifters. Carburetor: Stromberg AA UVB 267 #380309 or Carter 725 and 782.

SUPER — SERIES 50 — shared other series' totally new, all-bumper guard grille, more rounded styling. Super script appeared on front fenders, just above the full-length lower body side molding. A new, long wheelbase sedan featured a plusher interior than most Supers, which normally had cloth interiors of finer material than the Special. Supers had three Ventiports on each hood side. The Model 56C convertible had leather power seats plus power windows and top.

1950 Buick, Super 4-door sedan, 8-cyl(AA)

SUPER I.D. NUMBERS: The serial number sequence was the same for all 1950 series (see Special — Series 40). Motor numbers began at 5628758-**5** (manual transmission) and 5624743-**5** (Dynaflow), the suffix '5' denoting a Series 50 motor.

Model Number	Body/Style Number	Body Type & Seating	Factory Price	Shipping Weight	Production Total
51	50-4569	4-dr. Sedan-6P	2139	3745	55,672
56S	50-4507	2-dr. S'dn't-6P	2041	3645	10,697
56R	50-4537	H.T. Cpe-6P	2139	3790	56,030
56C	50-4567	Conv Cpe	2476	3965	12,259
59	(Ionia)	Station Wag-6P	2844	4115	2,480
52	50-4519	4-dr. Sedan-6P	2212	3870	114,745

SUPER ENGINE
Eight cylinder: Overhead valve. Cast iron block. Displacement: 263.3 cubic inches. Bore and stroke: 3-3/16 x 4-1/8 inches. Compression ratio: 6.6:1. Brake horsepower: 124 at 3600 R.P.M. Five main bearings. Carburetor: Stromberg AA UVB #380309 or Carter 725 and 782.

1950 Buick, Roadmaster 2-door convertible, 8-cyl(AA)

ROADMASTER — SERIES 70 — Buick's finest cars with larger engines and plusher interior trims than comparable Super models, were readily identified by the four Ventiports on the hood sides. Roadmaster script was found above the full-length body side molding on cars so equipped; cars with 'Sweepspear' moldings had Roadmaster script engraved in the upper body trim strip behind the door trim (except on the Model 79 and 72R which received the Sweepspear mid-year). Deluxe models had plusher interiors and hydraulic window and seat controls. They were identified by an 'X' suffix in their style numbers.

ROADMASTER I.D. NUMBERS: The serial numbers sequence was the same for all 1950 series (see Special — Series 40). Series 70 motor numbers began at 5635021-up.

Model Number	Body/Style Number	Body Type & Seating	Factory Price	Shipping Weight	Production Total
71	50-4769	4-dr. Sedan-6P	2633	4135	6,738
76S	50-4707	2-dr. S'dn't-6P	2528	4025	2,968
75R	50-4737	H.T. Cpe-6P	2633	4135	2,300
76C	50-4767	Conv. Cpe-6P	2981	4345	2,964
79	(Ionia)	Station Wag-6P	3407	4470	420
72	50-4719	4-dr. Sedan-6P	2738	4220	51,212 (incl. 72R)
72R	50-4737X	4-dr. Sedan-6P	2854	4245	
76R	50-4737X	H.T. Cpe-6P	2764	4215	8,432

ROADMASTER ENGINE
Eight cylinder: Overhead valve. Cast iron block. Displacement: 320.2 cubic inches. Bore and stroke: 3-7/16 x 4-5/16. Compression ratio: 6.9:1. Brake horsepower: 152 at 3600 R.P.M. Hydraulic valve lifters. Carburetor: Stromberg AAVG-267 #380258 or Carter 726.

CHASSIS FEATURES: Wheelbase: Series 40 — 121-1/2 inches; Series 50 — 121-1/2 inches (except Model 52, which was 125.5 inches); Series 70 — 126-1/4 inches (except Models 72 and 72R which were 130-1/4 inches). Overall length: Series 40 — 204 inches, Series 50 — 209-1/2 inches (except Model 52, 213-1/2 inches); Series 70 — 214-7/8 inches (except Models 72 and 72R 217-1/2 inches). Front tread: Series 40 — 59.1 inches; Series 50 & 70 — 59-1/8 inches. Rear tread: Series 40 — 62.2 inches; Series 50 & 70 — 62-2/3 inches. Tires: Series 40 & 50 — 7.60 x 15; Series 70 — 8.00 x 15.

POWERTRAIN OPTIONS: Three-speed manual transmission standard on Series 40 and 50. Dynaflow drive standard on Series 70, optional on Series 40 and 50. Series 40 cars so equipped had 6.9:1 compression ratio, 120 brake horsepower motors. Series 50 cars with Dynaflow had 6.9:1 compression ratio and 124 brake horsepower.

CONVENIENCE OPTIONS: Parking brake release warning light. Cushion toppers. License frames. Handy-Mats. Visor vanity mirror. Took kit. Full wheel covers (standard on Series 70). "Breeze-Ease" draft deflectors. Outside rear view mirror. Safety Spotlite with mirror. Multi-purpose trouble lamp. Tissue dispenser. Glare-proof inside rear view mirror. Seat covers. All-rubber floor mat. Auxiliary driving lamps. Exhaust pipe trim. Polish cloth kit.

Historical footnotes:: Body Styles 50-4408 and 50-4408D were Jetback sedans. Body styles 50-4537 and 50-4737 were Riviera hardtops. Body styles 50-4519, 50-4719 and 50-4719X were Riviera sedans. Models 59 and 79 were Estate Wagons.

1951 BUICK

1951 Buick, Special DeLuxe 4-door sedan, 8-cyl(AA)

SPECIAL — SERIES 40 — Standard and DeLuxe trims were offered on the Special Series. The low-priced models had only bright rear fender trim moldings and three Ventiports on each fender. DeLuxe models had a full-length sweepspear molding leading into the rear fender trim. A new, vertical bar grille with a more conventional bumper was used on all 1951 Buicks. Interiors were cloth, with a plusher grade used on DeLuxe models. Specials had a unique instrument panel, with speedometer and gauges housed in two large, round units flanking the steering column notch. Controls were centered vertically, flanking the radio speaker grille. The standard Specials were the only 1951 Buicks to have a two-piece windshield, DeLuxe and other lines had a new one-piece type.

SPECIAL I.D. NUMBERS: Serial numbers were mixed in production with other 1951 series. Numbers were Flint 16740001 to 17214100, (Calif.) 26765001 to 27214776; (N.J.) 36774001 to 37217064; (Kans.) 46783001 to 47224950; (Del.) 56799001 to 57222180; (Ga.) 66808001 to 67228458; (Mass.) 76815001 to 77228805. All 1951 motor numbers start at 62400100, Series 40 motors have suffix -**4**.

Model Number	Body/Style Number	Body Type & Seating	Factory Price	Shipping Weight	Production Total
41	51-4367	4-dr. Sedan-6P	2139	3605	999
46S	51-4327	Sport Cpe-6P	2046	3600	2700
DeLuxe Models:					
41D	51-4369	4-dr. Sedan-6P	2185	3680	87,848
48D	51-4311D	2-dr. Sedan-6P	2127	3615	54,311
45R	51-4337	H.T. Cpe-6P	2225	3645	16,491
46C	51-4367X	Conv. Cpe-6P	2561	3830	2,099

SPECIAL FEATURE: Eight cylinder: Overhead valve. Cast iron block. Displacement: 263.3 inches. Bore and stroke: 3-3/16 x 4-1/8 inches. Compression ratio: 6.6:1. Brake horsepower 120 at 3600 R.P.M. Five main bearings. Hydraulic valve lifters. Carburetor: Stromberg AAUVB 267 or Carter two-barrel 725, 882 two-barrel.

1951 Buick, Super 4-door Estate Wagon, 8-cyl(AA)

SUPER — SERIES 50 — Supers had larger bodies than Specials, but looked very similar with three round Ventiports per front fender and full-length "Sweepspear" molding and broad bright rear fender shield. Series script was found on the deck lid and within the steering wheel center. Supers were trimmed in materials similar to Special DeLuxes, except for in the plush Model 52 Super Riviera sedan. Front turn signals were within the bumper guard "bombs", while rear signals shared the stop lamps' housing on the rear fender edges. The Model 56C and Model 59 were trimmed in leather.

SUPER I.D. NUMBERS: Serial numbers were mixed with other 1951 series (see 1951 Special — Series 40). Motor numbers were mixed in production, but Super motors have suffix **5**.

Model Number	Body/Style Number	Body Type & Seating	Factory Price	Shipping Weight	Production Total
51	51-4569	4-dr. Sedan-6P	2356	3755	10,000
56S	51-4507	2-dr. S'dn't-6P	2248	2685	1,500
56R	51-4537	H.T. Cpe-6P	2356	3765	54,512
56C	51-4567X	Conv Cpe-6P	2728	3965	8,116
59	(Ionia)	Station Wag-6P	3133	4100	2,212
52	51-4519	4-dr. Sedan	2563	3825	92,886

SUPER ENGINE
Specifications were the same as those listed for the 1951 Special — Series 40, except manual transmission cars had 6.9:1 compression ratio and 124 brake horse power.

1951 Buick, Roadmaster Riviera 2-door hardtop coupe, 8-cyl(AA)

ROADMASTER — SERIES 70 - Buick's longest and most DeLuxe models featured a new grille ensemble for 1951. Roadmasters had the series designation script on the rear deck, with additional identification coming from four Ventiports on each front fender. Full-length, wide rocker panel moldings were used with the 'Sweepspear' molding found on cheaper models. Cloth interiors in closed models were plusher than lower-priced Series, with carpeting used on the floors. The Model 56C and Model 59 used leather seats. Standard equipment on the Model 56C convertible included power top, windows and seat. A Custom interior option for the Roadmaster included leatherette door panel trim. Full wheel covers were standard.

ROADMASTER I.D. NUMBERS: Serial numbers were mixed with other 1951 series (see 1951 Special — Series 40). Motor numbers were mixed in production, but Roadmaster motors have suffix 7.

Model Number	Body/Style Number	Body Type & Seating	Factory Price	Shipping Weight	Production Total
76R	51-4737X	H.T. Cpe-6P	3143	4235	12,901
76MR	51-4737	H.T. Cpe-6P	3051	4185	809
76C	51-4767X	Conv. Cpe-6P	3453	4395	2,911
79R	(Ionia)	Station Wag-6P	3977	4505	679
72R	51-4719X	4-dr. Sedan-6P	3200	4285	48,758

ROADMASTER ENGINE
Eight cylinder: Overhead valve. Cast iron Block. Displacement: 320.2 cubic inches. Bore and stroke: 3-7/16 x 4-5/16 inches. Compression ratio: 7.2:1. Brake horse-power: 152 at 3600 R.P.M. Five main bearings. Hydraulic valve lifters. Carburetor: Stromberg AAVB267, Carter two-barrel 726 two barrel.

CHASSIS FEATURES: Wheelbase: Series 40 & 50 — 121-1/2 inches which was 125-1/2 inches.) Series 70 — 126-1/4 inches (except Model 72R which was 130-1/4 inches.) Overall length: Series 40 & 50 — 206.2 inches (except Model 52 which was 210.2 inches.) Series 70 — 211 inches (except Model 72R which was 215 inches.) Front tread: Series 40 — 59 inches; Series 50 & 70 — 59 inches. Rear tread: Series 40 — 59 inches; Series 50 & 70 — 62 inches. Tires: Series 40 & 50 — 7.60 x 15; Series 70 — 8.00 x 15.

POWERTRAIN OPTIONS: A three-speed manual transmission was standard on Series 40 and 50. Dynaflow drive was standard on Series 70, optional on Series 40 and 50. Cars equipped with optional Dynaflow had 7.2:1 compression ratio and 128 horse-power engines.

CONVENIENCE OPTIONS: Parking brake release signal light. Took kit. Cushion topper. Electric clock (Series 50 and 70). License frames. Remote control outside rear view mirror. Visor vanity mirror. Handy mats. Full wheel covers (standard on Series 70).

Historical footnotes: Body Styles 51-4337, 51-4537, 51-4737 and 51-4737 are Riviera hardtops. Styles 51-4519 and 51-4719X are Riviera 4-dr. sedans (pillared). An X in the style number indicates hydraulic control of the seat, windows and (convertibles) top. Models 59 and 79R are Estate Wagons.

1952 BUICK

SPECIAL — SERIES 40 — Buick Special styling changed little from 1951. A new 'Sweepspear' molding, now incorporated the rear fender gravel guard, was used. Three round chrome Ventiports on each front fender continued to be Series 40 hallmark and were also found on Series 50 models. Specials were again divided into standard and Deluxe categories. The standard models (41 and 46S) had a windshield center division bar and lacked the bright rocker panel molding of Deluxe models. Interiors were spartan on the standard models, while Deluxe models were trimmed in a plusher cloth. The Special continued to use a distinctive instrument panel with two large dials containing the indicators. Special script was now found on rear fenders and Deluxe models had bright fender fins.

SPECIAL I.D. NUMBERS: Serial numbers were mixed in production with other 1952 series. Numbers were: (Flint) 1643001 to 16739745, (Calif.) 26456001 to 26714109, (N.J.) 36464001 to 36717383, (Kans.) 46471001 to 46722742, (Del.) 56483001 to 56726449, (Ga.) 66490001 to 66729512, (Mass.) 76496001 to 76730564. All 1952 motor numbers start at 6646230, Series 40 motor numbers have suffix 4.

Model Number	Body/Style Number	Body Type & Seating	Factory Price	Shipping Weight	Production Total
41	52-4369	4-dr. Sedan-6P	2209	3650	317
46S	52-4327	Sport Cpe-6P	2115	3605	2,206
Deluxe Models:					
41D	52-4369D	4-dr. Sedan-6P	2255	3665	63,346
48D	52-4311D	2-dr. Sedan-6P	2197	3620	32,684
45R	52-4337	H.T. Cpe-6P	2295	3665	21,180
46C	52-4367X	Conv Cpe-6P	2634	3850	600

SPECIAL ENGINE
Eight cylinder: Overhead valve. Cast iron block. Displacement: 263.3 inches. Bore and stroke: 3-3/16 x 4-1/8 inches. Compression ratio: 6.6:1. Brake horsepower: 120 at 3600 R.P.M. Five main bearings. Hydraulic valve lifters. Carburetor: Stromberg AAUBV267 or Carter 882.

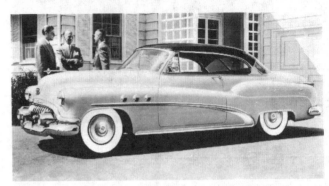

1952 Buick, Super Riviera 2-door hardtop, 8-cyl(AA)

SUPER — SERIES 50 — Buick's mid-sized line resembled the Series 40 with three Ventiports per fender and new 'Sweepspear' rocker panel trim. Super script on the rear fenders aided identification. The Super was built with the larger GM "C-body", however. The full-flowing fenderline dipped deeper on this body and rear fenders had a crease line absent on the "B-body" Specials. A new deck lid gave a more squared-off appearance. Like other Buick series, it was a near carbon copy year for 1952. Chromed rear fender fins gave distinction to 1952 Supers. Interiors were cloth, except on the Models 56C and 59, which were trimmed with leather. The Super used a differ-ent instrument panel than the Special. It was distinguished by a large center speedometer housing flanked by smaller gauge housings. Series identification was found within the steering wheel center.

SUPER I.D. NUMBERS: Serial numbers were mixed with other 1952 series (see 1952 Special — Series 40). Motor numbers were mixed in production, but Super motors have suffix 5.

Model Number	Body/Style Number	Body Type & Seating	Factory Price	Shipping Weight	Production Total
56R	52-4537	H.T. Cpe-6P	2478	3775	55,400
56C	52-4567X	Conv Cpe-6P	2869	3970	6,904
59	(Ionia)	Estate Wag-6P	3296	4105	1,641
52	52-4519	4-dr. Sedan-6P	2563	3825	71,387

SUPER ENGINE:
Specifications were the same as those listed for the 1952 Special, except manual transmission cars had 6.9:1 compression ratio with 124 brake horsepower.

1952 Buick, Roadmaster 4-door sedan, 8-cyl (AA)

ROADMASTER — SERIES 70 — Roadmasters are easy to spot by their longer front fenders and hood, and four Ventiports on each side. A rehash of 1951 styling, new 'Sweepspear' moldings and bright rocker trim provided distinction. Series identification appeared on the rear fenders. New deck lids gave a higher, more substantial rear-end appearance, while the frontal view was unchanged from 1951. Roadmasters continued to be the plushest Buicks. Custom trim options were available for even more richness. Quality cloth was used in sedans, while the Models 76C and 79R were trimmed in leather. The specially-lengthened, extra-posh Model 72R Riviera sedan continued to be the most popular Roadmaster style. All Roadmasters had the popular 1952 Buick "sombrero" wheel disc as standard equipment.

ROADMASTER E.D. NUMBERS: Serial numbers were mixed with the other 1952 series (see 1952 Special — Series 40). Motor numbers were mixed in production, but Road-master motors have suffix 7.

Model Number	Body/Style Number	Body Type & Seating	Factory Price	Shipping Weight	Production Total
76R	52-4737X	H.T. Cpe-6P	3306	4235	11,387
76C	52-4767X	Conv Cpe-6P	3453	4395	2,402
79R	(Ionia)	Estate Wag-6P	3977	4505	359
72R	52-4719X	4-dr. Sedan-6P	3200	4285	32,069

ROADMASTER ENGINE

Eight cylinder: Overhead valve. Cast iron block. Displacement: 320.2 cubic inches. Bore and stroke: 3-7/16 x 4-5/16 inches. Compression ratio: 7.5:1. Brake horsepower: 170 at 3800 R.P.M. Five main bearings. Hydraulic valve lifters. Carburetor: Stromberg 4AUV267 or Carter 894S-5A four-barrel.

POWERTRAIN OPTIONS: A three-speed manual tranmission was standard on Series 40 and 50. Dynaflow drive was standard on Series 70. Series 40 and 50 cars equipped with the $193 Dynaflow option had 7.2:1 compression ratio and 128 brake horsepower engines.

CONVENIENCE OPTIONS: Power steering, Series 70, ($199). Parking brake release signal light. Cushion toppers. Electric clock (Series 50-70). License plate frames. Remote control rear view mirror. Visor vanity mirror. Full wheel covers (standard on Series 70). Handy-Spot. Seat covers. Auto-Jack case.

Historical footnotes: Body Styles 52-4337, 52-4537 and 52-4737X are Riviera hardtop coupes. Styles 52-4519 and 52-4719 are Riviera four-door sedans (pillared). An 'X' suffix to the style number indicates hydraulic control of the seat, windows and (convertible) top. Models 59 and 79R are Estate Wagons.

1953 BUICK

1953 Buick, Special 2-door convertible, 8-cyl (AA)

SPECIAL — SERIES 40 — The Series 40 was Buick's only line carrying a straight eight in 1953. The small series Buick had its own version of the 1953 frontal look: since it was a narrower car, the grilles, bumpers and sheet metal parts did not interchange with larger models. On the fenders were new teardrop-shaped Ventiports, three to a side. The hood bombsight ornament had no Vee on the Special. All 1953 Specials were Deluxe models, with bright 'Sweepspears' and rocker panel moldings. Interiors were cloth, with the unique Special instrument panel continuing for another year. Model 46C, the convertible, was trimmed in leather. Series I.D. was found on the rear deck emblem.

SPECIAL I.D. NUMBERS: Serial numbers were mixed in production with other 1953 series. Numbers were: (Flint) 1674001 to 17214106; (Calif.) 26765001 to 27214776; (N.J.) 36774001 to 37127064; (Kans.) 46783001 to 47224950; (Del.) 56799001 to 57226180; (Ga.) 66808001 to 67228458; (Mass.) 76815001 to 77228805. All **1953** motors start at 6950620, Series 40 motor numbers have suffix **4**.

Model Number	Body/Style Number	Body Type & Seating	Factory Price	Shipping Weight	Production Total
41D	53-4369D	4-door Sedan-6P	2255	3710	100,312
48D	53-4311D	2-dr. Sedan-6P	2197	3675	53,796
45R	53-4337	H.T. Cpe-6P	2295	3705	58,780
46C	53-4367X	Conv Cpe-6P	2553	3815	4,282

SPECIAL ENGINE

Eight cylinder: Overhead valve. Cast iron block. Displacement: 263.3 cubic inches. Bore and stroke: 3-3/16 x 4-1/8 inches. Compression ratio: 6.6:1. Brake horsepower: 120 at 3600 R.P.M. Five main bearings. Hydraulic valve lifters. Carburetor: Stromberg AAUVB267 or Carter 882S.

SUPER — SERIES 50 — Buick's middle-priced line shared the Roadmaster's new V-8 and for this year, the Roadmaster shared the Super and Special's 121.5 inch wheelbase. The Super carried a horizontal trim bar on its rear fenders that distinguished it from Series 70 Roadmasters. Otherwise its side trim was identical, although the Super had only three Ventiports on each front fender. Series I.D was found on the deck emblem. Full wheelcovers were now standard. The Vee in the bombsight ornament signified the V-8 power under the hood. Interiors of most models were in nylon and silky broadcloth. The Model 56C and Model 59 were trimmed in leather. Model 56C, the convertible, had power windows, seat and top as standard equipment.

SUPER I.D. NUMBERS: Serial numbers were mixed with other 1953 series (see 1953 Special — Series 40). Motor numbers began with V-2415-5.

Model Number	Body/Style Number	Body Type & Seating	Factory Price	Shipping Weight	Production Total
56R	53-4567	H.T. Cpe-6P	2611	3845	91,298
56C	53-4567X	Conv Cpe-6P	3002	4035	6,701
59	(Ionia)	Estate Wag-6P	3430	4150	1,830
52	53-4519	4-dr. Sedan-6P	2696	3905	90,685

SUPER ENGINE

V-8: Overhead valve. Cast iron block. Displacement: 322 cubic inches. Bore and stroke: 4.0 x 3.2 inches. Compression ratio: 8.0:1. Brake horsepower: 164 at 4,000 R.P.M. Five main bearings. Hydraulic valve lifters. Carburetor: Stromberg AAVB267 or Carter 2017S two-barrel.

1953 Buick Roadmaster 4-door sedan (AA)

ROADMASTER — SERIES 70 — Buick's finest had a fore-shortened nose in 1953, to emphasize the compact power of the new V-8 under the hood. Roadmasters had chrome rear fender gravel shields between the rear wheelhouse and the bumper in addition to the same 'Sweepspear' used on the Super. However, the upper horizontal trim strip on Super rear fenders was absent. Series I.D. was found within the deck emblem and on the steering wheel hub. Full wheelcovers were standard. Interiors were nylon, broadcloth or leather, depending on the model. Foam-backed Roxpoint nylon carpeting was standard, as were power steering, power brakes and Dynaflow drive. Color-keyed instrument panels with damscene-patterned lower panels were used. A very special 1953 Roadmaster model was the Model 76X Skylark Anniversary Convertible. It was on the Roadmaster chassis, but had its own fenders with open wheelhouses, painted white or red, and it did not have any Ventiports. A lowered top, 40-spoke Kelsey-Hayes wire wheels and a full complement of luxury accessories were included. The Skylark had its own slim, cast Sweepspear moldings and special body side emblems on the rear quarters. Interiors were in leather.

ROADMASTER I.D. NUMBERS: Serial numbers were mixed with other 1953 series (see 1953 Buick Special-Series 40). Motor numbers began with V-2001-7.

1953 Buick, Roadmaster Skylark sport convertible, V-8 (AA)

Model Number	Body/Style Number	Body Type & Seating	Factory Price	Shipping Weight	Production Total
76R	53-4737	H.T. Cpe-6P	3358	4125	22,927
76C	53-4767X	Conv Cpe-6P	3506	4250	3,318
79R	(Ionia)	Estate Wag-6P	3254	4100	670
72R	53-4719	4-dr. Sedan-6P	4031	4315	50,523
76X	53-4767SX	Conv Cpe-6P	5000	4315	1,690

ROADMASTER ENGINE

Specifications were the same as those listed for the 1953 Super, except compression ratio was 8.5:1 and brake horsepower was 188 at 4,000 R.P.M. Carburetors were Stromberg 4AUV267 or Carter 996 or 2082 S 4-barrel.

CHASSIS FEATURES: Wheelbase: Series 40, 50 and 70: 121-1/2 inches (except Models 52 and 72R which were 125-1/2 inches). Overall length: Series 40 — 205.8 inches. Series 50 and 70 — 207.6 inches (except Model 52 and 72R — 211.6 inches). Front tread: Series 40 — 59 inches; Series 50 and 70 — 60 inches. Rear tread: Series 40 — 59 inches, Series 50 and 70 — 62 inches. Tires: Series 40 and 50 — 6.70 x 15; Series 70 — 8.00 x 15.

POWERTRAIN OPTIONS: Three-speed manual transmission was standard on Series 40 Specials and Series 50 Supers. Dynaflow drive was an option on Specials and Supers at $193 extra, but was standard in the Roadmaster Series. Specials equipped with Dynaflow had 7.2:1 compression powerplants with 128 brake horsepower. Supers equipped with Dynaflow had 8.1:1 compression powerplant with 170 brake horsepower.

CONVENIENCE OPTIONS: Power steering ($177) (standard on Series 70). Power brakes (standard on Series 70). Simulated wire wheel covers (Buick shield center type on Series 40; bright Vee with black background type on Series 50 and 70). Full wheelcovers (standard on Series 50 and 70). 8-inch rear seat speaker. Tool kit. Handy spot. Dor-Gard. Cushion toppers. Selectronic radio (optional Series 50 and 70 and standard Model 76X). Electric clock. License frames. Righthand outside rear view mirror. Lefthand remote control outside mirror. Handy mats. Air conditioning (Series 50 and 70). Fold-down tissue dispenser.

Historical footnotes: Styles 53-4337, 53-4537 and 53-4737X wre Riviera hardtop coupes. Style 53-4767SX was the Skylark Anniversary convertible. Models 59 and 79R were Estate Wagons. An X suffix to the style number indicates hydraulic control of the seat, windows and (convertible) top.

1954 BUICK

1954 Buick, Special 4-door Estate Wagon, V-8 (AA)

SPECIAL — SERIES 40 — The Special had a new body for 1954, lower and wider, on a new V-8-powered chassis. Series I.D. was found on the rear quarters and within the deck ornament. Three oval Ventiports adorned each front fender. Stainless (Sweepspears) on the body sides arched over the rectangular rear wheelhouses of the sedans or station wagons and the rounded rear wheel opening of the Riviera hardtop and convertible. Rear fenders had a blunted fin at their rear edge, with dual 'bullet' taillamps below. A new Panoramic windshield, with slanting side pillars was used. Specials were upholstered in Nylon (two-tones in the Riviera hardtop), except for the Model 46C, which had leather trim and an outside rear view mirror as standard equipment, along with a power top, windows and front seat.

SERIES 40 I.D. NUMBERS: Buick Special serial numbers were mixed in production with other 1954 Series. Numbers used at the beginning of the season were as follows: (Flint)-A-1001001-up; (Calif.)-A-2001001-up; (N.J.)-A-3001001-up; (Kans.)-A-4001001-up; (Del.)-A-5001001-up; (Ga.)-A-6001001-up; (Mass.)-A-7001001-up and Texas (Tex.)-A-8001001-up. Effective April 1, 1954 beginning numbers changed as follows: (Flint)-4A1-056800-up; (Calif.)-4A2-014905-up; (N.J.)-6A3-020700-up; (Kan.)-7A4-021783-up; (Del.)-7A5-013983-up; (Ga.)-7A6-012742-up; (Mass.)-6A7-010471-up and (Tex.)-7A8-002765-up. Motor numbers were also mixed in production, beginning with number Y-273956.

Model Number	Body/Style Number	Body Type & Seating	Factory Price	Shipping Weight	Production Total
41D	54-4469D	4-dr. Sedan-6P	2265	3735	70,356
48D	54-4411D	2-dr. Sedan-6P	2207	3690	41,557
46R	54-4437	H.T. Cpe-6	2305	3740	71,186
46C	54-4467X	Conv. Cpe-6P	2563	3810	6,135
49	54-4481	Estate Wag.-6	3163	3905	1,650

SPECIAL ENGINE:
V-8 Overhead valve. Cast iron block. Displacement: 264 cubic inches. Bore and stroke: 3.625 x 3.2 inches. Compression ratio: 7.2:1. Brake horsepower: 143 at 4200 R.P.M. (150 w/automatic transmission). Five main bearings. Hydraulic valve lifters. Carburetor: Stromberg AAVB267 or Carter 2081 or 2179 two-barrel.

CENTURY — SERIES 60 — Revived for the first time since 1942, the new Century shared the Series 40 Special body and basic chassis, but carried the Roadmaster engine. The new performance car carried three Ventiports per fender and was identical to the Special in most other exterior trim, except for the Century scripts on the quarter panels and the series designation within the deck ornament. It shared the Special's instrument panel, with gages set into twin round housings. Nylon cloth upholstery, with foam cushions (two-tones in Riviera hardtops), were standard. The Model 66C convertible was trimmed in leather and had an outside rearview mirror and power-operated windows, seat and top as part of its base equipment.

1954 Buick, Century 2-dr hardtop coupe, V-8

CENTURY I.D. NUMBERS: Serial numbers were mixed with other 1954 series (see 1954 Special—Series 40). Motor numbers were mixed in production.

192

Model Number	Body/Style Number	Body Type & Seating	Factory Price	Weight Weight	Total Total
61	54-4669	4-dr. Sedan-6P	2520	3805	31,919
66R	54-4637	H.T. Cpe-6P	2534	3795	45,710
66C	54-4667X	Conv. Cpe-6P	2963	3950	2,790
69	54-4681	Estate Wag-6P	3470	3975	1,563

CENTURY ENGINE: Overhead valve. Cast iron block. Displacement: 322 cubic inches. Bore and stroke: 4.0 x 3.2 inches. Compression ratio: 7.2:1. Brake horsepower: 195 at 4100 R.P.M. Five main bearings. Hydraulic valve lifters. Carburetor: Stromberg 4AUV267 or Carter 2082S four-barrel.

1954 Buick, Super 4-dr sedan, V-8

SUPER — SERIES 50 — Using the new, larger GM "C-body", with vertical windshield pillars and the new Panoramic windshild, the Super for 1954 was a big Buick for the budget minded. Identified by its three Ventiports per fender, the (Super) script on quarters and the series designation within the deck ornament, the Super shared other bright work with the Roadmaster. Interiors were Nylon and were plainer than in the Roadmasters. The Super did have the expensive car's horizontal speedometer instrument panel. Model 56C, the line's convertible, was upholstered in leather and had power-operated windows, seat and top, along with an outside rearview mirror on the left, as standard equipment.

SUPER I.D. NUMBERS: Serial numbers were mixed in 1954 production (see 1954 Special—Series 40). Motor numbers were also mixed in production.

Model Number	Body/Style Number	Body Type & Seating	Factory Price	Shipping Weight	Production Total
52	54-4519	4-dr. Sedan-6P	2711	4105	41,756
56R	54-4567	H.T. Cpe-6P	2626	4035	73,531
56C	54-4537X	Conv Cpe-6P	2964	4145	3,343

SUPER ENGINE:
Specifications were the same as listed for the 1954 Century except a 7.2:1 compression ratio was used. Brake horsepower was 177 at 4100 R.P.M. carburetors: Stromberg AAVB267 or Carter 2081 or 2179 two-barrel.

ROADMASTER — SERIES 70 — The top-of-the line Buick looked like the cheaper Super from the outside, with the exception of a fourth Ventiport on each front fender, (Roadmaster) script on the rear quarters and series I.D. within the deck ornament. Inside, though, the upholstery was much posher, with various Nylon, broadcloth and leather combinations available depending on the model. Seats had chrome bands on the two-door models and all cars were fully carpeted. Power steering, brakes and Dynaflow were standard features, as was a rear seat armrest on the Sedan. All had the new instrument panel with horizontal speedometer. Models 76C and 76R had an outside rearview mirror on the left and the 76C convertible was additionally equipped with power-operated windows, (vertical) seat adjustment and top.

ROADMASTER I.D. NUMBERS: Serial and motor numbers were mixed with other 1954 series (see 1954 Special—Series 40).

Model Number	Body/Style Number	Body Type & Seating	Factory Price	Shipping Weight	Production Total
72R	54-4719	4-dr. Sedan-6P	3269	4250	26,862
76RX	54-4737X	H.T. Cpe-6P	3373	4215	20,404
76CX	54-4767X	Conv Cpe-6P	3521	4355	3,305

ROADMASTER ENGINE
Specifications were the same as those listed for the 1954 Century, except compression ratio was 8.0:1 and brake horsepower was 200 at 4100 R.P.M.

1954 Buick, Skylark Sport 2-door convertible, V-8 (AA)

SKYLARK — SERIES 100 — Buick's wild prestige convertible was the only model in this series. A new tapered deck with big chrome fins was grafted onto the 1954 Century body to create the 1954 Skylark. Specific front fenders with wide-open wheelhouse, echoed at the rear wheel house, had no Ventiports. Forty-spoke Kelsey-Hayes wire wheels were standard, along with leather trim, special emblems, power brakes, power steering, Dynaflow, 4-way powered seat, power top, power windows, Selectronic radio with power antenna, Easy-Eye glass, heater-defroster and whitewall tires.

Model Number	Body/Style Number	Body Type & Seating	Factory Price	Shipping Weight	Production Total
100	54-4667SX	Sport Conv	4355	4260	836

SKYLARK ENGINE
Specifications were the same as those listed for the 1954 Century, except compression ratio was 8.0:1 and brake horsepower was 200 at 4100 R.PM.

CHASSIS FEATURES: Wheelbase: Series 40, 60 and 100 — 122 inches; Series 50 and 70 — 127 inches. Overall length: Series 40, 60 and 100 — 206.3 inches; Series 50 and 70 — 216-4/5 inches. Front tread: Series 40, 60 and 100 — 59 inches; Series 50 and 70 — 59 inches. Rear tread: Series 40, 60 and 100 — 59 inches; Series 50 and 70 — 62-1/5 inches. Tires: Series 40, 60, 50 and 100 — 6.70 x 15; Series 70 — 8.00 x 15.

POWERTRAIN OPTIONS: Three-speed manual transmission standard on Series 40, 50 and 60. Dynaflow drive standard on Series 70 and 100. Series 40 cars equipped with Dynaflow option had 8.0:1 compression ratio and 150 brake horsepower. Series 50 cars equipped with Dynaflow option had 8.0:1 compression ratio and 182 brake horsepower. Series 60 cars equipped with Dynaflow option had 8.0:1 compression ratio and 200 brake horsepower.

CONVENIENCE OPTIONS: Full wheel covers (standard Series 70). Set of five genuine 40 spoke wire wheels for Series 50, 60 and 70 (standard for Model 100). Power brakes (standard Series 70 and Model 100). Power steering (standard Series 70 and Model 100). Dor-Gard. Rear fender gas door guard. Windshield washer. Tool kit. Handy-Spot. Cushion toppers. Electric radio antenna (standard Model 100). Sonomatic radio. Selectronic radio (standard Model 100). Rear seat speaker (except convertibles, station wagons). Vent shades. Electric clock. License frames. Inside optional rear view mirror. Glare-proof outside rearview mirrors, right and lefthand. Visor vanity mirror. Handy mats. Air conditioning (except convertibles, Model 48). Hydraulic-electric windows (standard on Models 76RX, 76CX, 100). Horizontal front seat adjustment (standard, Model 100).

Historical footnotes: Styles number 54-4437, 54-4537, 54-4637, 54-4737X are Riviera hardtop coupes. Styles number 54-4481 and 55-4681 are all-steel Estate Wagons. An (X) suffix to the Style Number indicates hydraulic control of the seat, windows, and (convertible) top.

1955 BUICK

1955 Buick, Special Riviera 2-door hardtop coupe, V-8 (AA)

SPECIAL — SERIES 40 — A major facelift, with new rear fenders, housing 'tower' taillights, new front fenders and a new oval grille opening (housing a textured grille panel and a large horizontal emblem bar) distinguished the 1955 Buicks. 'Sweepspear' moldings on the Special were the same as in 1954, but new round Ventiports were grouped by threes on each front fender. Series script was found on the rear quarters and within the grille emblem. Cordaveen upholstery was used. The distinctive Series 40 and 60 instrument panel, with twin round gauge pods was continued. Tubeless tires were now standard, as were directional signals, front and rear side armrests, sliding sunshades, Step On parking brake and heavy insulation.

SPECIAL I.D. NUMBERS: Serial numbers were mixed in production with other 1955 series. Beginning numbers were: (Flint) 5B1001001-up; (Cal.) 5B2001001-up; (N.J.) 4B3001001-up; (Kans.) 4B4001001-up; (Del.) 4B5001001-up; (Ga.) 5B6001001-up; (Mass.) 5B7001001-up; and (Texas) 4B8001001-up. Motor numbers were mixed in production.

Model Number	Body/Style Number	Body Type & Seating	Factory Price	Shipping Weight	Production Total
41	55-4469	4-dr. Sedan-6P	2291	3745	84,182
43	55-4439	4-dr. H.T.-6P	2409	3820	66,409
48	55-4411	2-dr. Sedan-6P	2233	3715	61,879
46R	55-4437	H.T. Cpe-6P	2332	3720	155,818
46C	55-4467	Conv Cpe-6P	2590	3825	10,009
49	55-4481	Estate Wag-6P	2974	3940	2,952

SPECIAL ENGINE
V-8: Overhead valve. Cast iron block. Displacement: 264 cubic inches. Bore and stroke: 3.625 x 3.2 inches. Compression ratio: 8.4:1. Brake horsepower: 188 at 4800 R.P.M. Five main bearings. Hydraulic valve lifters. Carburetor: Stromberg AAVB267, AA7-102 or Carter 2179 or 2292 two-barrel.

1955 Buick, Century 4-door Riviera hardtop, V-8 (AA)

CENTURY — SERIES 60 — Buick's new performance car, combining Roadmaster power and the Special's lighter, more agile body, shared in the facelift given other 1955 Buicks. Century models were easily identified by their four Ventiports per fender, the 'Century' script on rear quarters and the series designation within the deck emblem. Inside, damascene panels were inset on the instrument panel and a quilted metallic door panel section was featured. The Century had a round 'Red Liner' speedometer with a trip mileage indicator. An electric clock was also standard, along with features found on the Special. Interiors were cloth and Cordaveen except for the Model 66C convertible, which was trimmed in leather and had power windows and a power horizontal seat adjuster as standard equipment.

CENTURY I.D. NUMBERS: Serial numbers were mixed with other 1955 series (see 1955 Special — Series 40). Motor numbers were mixed in production.

Model Number	Body/Style Number	Body Type & Seating	Factory Price	Shipping Weight	Production Total
61	55-4669	4-dr. Sedan-6P	2548	3825	13,629
63D	55-4639	4-dr. H.T.-6P	2733	3900	55,088
66R	55-4637	H.T.-Cpe-6P	2601	3805	80,338
66C	55-4667X	Conv Cpe-6P	2991	3950	5,588
69	55-4681	Estate Wag-6P	3175	3995	4,243
68	55-4611	2-dr. Sedan-6P	—	—	268

CENTURY ENGINE:
V8: Overhead valve. Cast iron block. Displacement: 322 cubic inches. Bore and stroke: 4 x 3.2 inches. Compression ratio: 9.1:1. Brake horsepower: 236 at 4600 R.P.M. Five main bearings. Hydraulic valve lifters. Carburetor: Carter 2197 or 2358 four-barrel.

SUPER — SERIES 50 — Buick's popular Super combined the large "C-body" interior expanse with medium-bracket interiors and performance. Supers had four of the new round Ventiports per fender this year, with additional series script found on rear quarters and within the deck emblem. The side 'Sweepspear' was unchanged from 1954. The larger bodied Buicks were readily identifiable by their more rounded contours, straight up windshield pillars and sedan rear quarter windows. Series 50 and 70 headlamp bezels also housed park lights. Inside, a new 'Red Liner' speedometer lay horizontally across the instrument panel. Interiors were trimmed in Nylon/Cordaveen combinations, except for the Model 56C convertible that featured leather seats. Standard Super equipment included trip mileage indicator, electric clock and, on the Model 56C convertible, a power horizontal seat adjuster.

SUPER I.D. NUMBERS: Serial numbers were mixed in 1955 production (see 1955 Special — Series 40). Motor numbers were also mixed in production.

Model Number	Body/Style Number	Body Type & Seating	Factory Price	Shipping Weight	Production Total
52	55-4569	4-dr. Sedan-6P	2876	4140	43,280
56R	55-4537	H.T. Cpe-6P	2831	4075	85,656
56C	55-4567X	Conv Cpe-6P	3225	4280	3,527

SUPER ENGINE:
Specifications were the same as listed for the 1955 Century.

1955 Buick, Roadmaster 4-door sedan, V-8 (AA)

ROADMASTER — SERIES 70 — Buick's prestige car was given more distinction for 1955. Broad bright lower rear fender bands, gold-colored 'Roadmaster' deck script and hood ornament, bars on the wheelcovers and a gold-accented grille set the car apart. Four round Ventiports were found on each front fender of the "C-bodied" Buicks, which were distinguished by vertical windshield posts and headlamp rims containing the parking lamp units as well. Interiors were plusher, with ten choices, including brocaded fabrics. The Model 76C convertible had a standard leather interior. Standard features of all Roadmasters included Variable-pitch Dynaflow, power steering, back-up lights, brake warning signal light, electric clock, windshield washer, Custom wheel covers, double-depth foam seat cushions, plus features found on other Buick series.

ROADMASTER I.D. NUMBERS: Serial numbers were mixed with other 1955 Series (see 1955 Special — Series 40). Motor numbers were mixed in production.

Model Number	Body/Style Number	Body Type & Seating	Factory Price	Shipping Weight	Production Total
72	55-4769	4-dr. Sedan-6P	3349	4300	31,717
76R	55-4737	H.T. Cpe-6P	3453	4270	28,071
76C	55-4767X	Conv Cpe-6P	3552	4415	4,730

ROADMASTER ENGINE:
Specifications are the same as listed for the 1955 Century.

CHASSIS FEATURES: Wheelbase: Series 40 and 60 — 122 inches; Series 50 and 70 — 127 inches. Overall length: Series 40 and 60 — 206.7 inches; Series 50 and 70 — 216 inches. Front tread: Series 40 and 60 — 59 inches; Series 50 and 70 — 59 inches. Read tread: Series 40 and 60 — 59 inches; Series 50 and 70 — 62.2 inches. Tires: Series 40 — 7.10 x 15; Series 60 and 50 — 7.60 x 15; Series 70 — 8.00 x 15.

POWERTRAIN OPTIONS: A three-speed manual transmission was standard on the Special, Series 40; Century, Series 60; and Super, Series 50. Dynaflow drive was standard on the Roadmaster, Series 70, optional on other series ($193).

CONVENIENCE OPTIONS: Two-tone and tri-tone paint. Windshield washer. Whitewall tubeless tires. Easy-Eye glass. Outside rearview mirrors. Deluxe Handy mats. Sonomatic radio. Selectronic radio. Electric antenna. Full wheel covers (standard on 70). Genuine 40-spoke wire wheels (except Series 40). Spotlite. Tissue dispenser. Dor-Gard. Gas door guard. Visor vanity mirror. 'Red Liner' speedometer with trip mileage indicator (for Series 40 — standard other Series). Power steering ($108 — standard Series 50 and 70). Air conditioning. Safety group (back-up lights, brake warning light, windshield washer — standard Series 70). Accessory group (for Series 40 — electric clock, rear license frame, full wheelcovers, trunk light.

Historical footnotes: Body styles 55-4437, 55-4637, 55-4537 and 55-4737 are Riviera hardtop coupes. Styles 55-4439 and 55-4639 are Riviera hardtop sedans (pillarless) introduced mid-year. Body styles 55-4481 and 55-4681 are Estate Wagons with all-steel bodies. An 'X' suffix to the Style Number indicates power-operated windows.

1956 BUICK

1956 Buick, Special 4-door Estate Wagon, V-8 (AA)

SPECIAL — SERIES 40 — The Special continued to use the popular Sweepspear side motif in 1956, but now all models, including sedans and wagons, had round rear wheel house cutouts. Facelifting included new taillights, and a new, slightly forward thrust grille. Series script continued to appear on rear quarters and within the deck and grille emblems. Specials had three oval Ventiports per front fender this year, as was traditional. Closed car interiors were vinyl/Cordaveen combinations, while the Model 46C convertible was upholstered in all-Cordaveen. Standard Special equipment included directional signals, front and rear armrests, sliding sunshades, cigarette lighter, glove compartment light, map light, dual horns, Step-on parking brake, a new horizontal red line speedometer and a trip mileage indicator.

SPECIAL I.D. NUMBERS: Serial numbers were mixed in production with other 1959 series. Numbers were: (Flint) 4C1001001 to 4C12444927; (Calif.) 4C2001001 to 4C2087498; (N.J.) 4C3001001 to 4C3093179; (Kans.) 4C4001001 to 4C4094934; (Del.) 4C5001001 to 4C5070979; (Mass.) 4C7001001 to 4C7037771; (Texas) 4C8001001 to 4C8049469.

Model Number	Body/Style Number	Body Type & Seating	Factory Price	Shipping Weight	Production Total
41	56-4469	4-dr Sedan-6P	2416	3790	66,977
43	56-4439	4-dr H.T.-6P	2528	3860	91,025
48	56-4411	2-dr Sedan-6P	2537	2750	38,672
46R	56-4437	H.D. Cpe-6P	2457	3775	113,861
46C	56-4467	Conv Cpe-6P	2740	3880	9,712
49	56-4481	Station Wag-6P	2775	3945	13,770

SPECIAL ENGINE
V-8: overhead valve. Cast iron block. Displacement: 322 cubic inches. Bore and stroke: 4 x 3.2 inches. Compression ratio: 8.9:1. Brake horsepower: 220 at 4400 R.P.M. Five main bearings. Hydraulic valve lifters. Carburetor: Stromberg 7-104 (manual trans), 7-105 (Dynaflow); Carter 2378 (manual trans), 2400 (Dynaflow).

1956 Buick, Century 2-door convertible, V-8

CENTURY — SERIES 60 — The Century relied chiefly on a fourth oval Ventiport on each front fender, its series script on the rear quarters and the series designations within the deck and grille emblems for its exterior identity. It shared the GM "B-Body", recognizable by its reverse slanting windshield pillars, with the Series 40 Special. All bright moldings interchanged. Colorful Nylon/Cordaveen interior combinations were used in duo and tri-tones. The convertible, Model 66C, was once more trimmed in leather. Standard features, in addition to those found on the Special, included foam seat cushions, a trunk light, electric clock and rear license frame. Model 66C, the convertible, had a power top, windows and horizontal seat adjuster included in its equipment.

CENTURY I.D. NUMBERS: Serial numbers were mixed with other 1956 Series (see 1956 Special — Series 40). Motor numbers were mixed in production.

Model Number	Body/Style Number	Body Type & Seating	Factory Price	Shipping Weight	Production Total
63	56-4639	4-dr H.T.-6P	3025	4000	20,891
63D	56-4639D	4-dr H.T.-6P	3041	4000	35,082
66R	56-4637	H.T. Cpe-6P	2963	3890	33,334
66C	56-4667X	Conv Cpe-6P	3306	4045	4,721
69	56-4681	Station Wag-6P	3256	4080	8,160

CENTURY ENGINE
Specifications were the same as listed for the 1956 Special except compression ratio was 9.5:1, brake horsepower was 255 at 4400 R.P.M. and carburetor was a Carter 2347 or Rochester 7009200-9900 four-barrel.

1956 Buick, Super Riviera 4-door hardtop, V-8 (AA)

SUPER - SERIES 50 — Although the Super was a larger Buick, with vertical windshield posts and four Ventiports per fender, it had a deep Sweepspear similar to the smaller Series 40 and 60 cars. Series script was found on rear quarters and within the deck and grille emblems. Interiors were Cordaveen and patterned Nylon, except the Model 56C which was all-Cordaveen trimmed and had power windows, horizontal seat adjustment, and top up in its standard form. Dynaflow was now standard on all Supers, along with foam seat cushions, a trunk light and electric clock, plus features found on the lower-priced Special.

SUPER I.D. NUMBERS: Serial numbers were mixed in 1956 production (see 1956 Special — Series 40). Motor numbers were also mixed in production.

SUPER SERIES 50

Model Number	Body/Style Number	Body Type & Seating	Factory Price	Shipping Weight	Production Total
52	56-4569	4-dr Sedan-6P	3250	4200	14,940
53	56-4539	4-dr H.T.-6P	3340	4265	34,029
56R	56-4537	H.T. Cpe-6p	3204	4140	29,540
56C	56-4567	Conv Cpe-6P	3544	4340	2,489

SUPER ENGINE
Specifications are the same as listed for the 1956 Century.

ROADMASTER — SERIES 70 — An effort was made to further distinguish the first class Buick for 1956. Roadmasters had a shallow Sweepspear that didn't dip to the rocker panel as on other series. Twin chrome strips graced the deck lid, with Roadmaster spelled out in block letters between. Roadmaster script was found on the front doors, beneath the vent windows. Fender-top dual bombsights were standard and the grille emblem carried futher series identification. Standard Roadmaster equipment included a perimeter heating system, Variable-Pitch Dynaflow, power steering, power brakes, back-up lights, windshield washers, glare-proof rear view mirror, parking brake signal release light, electric clock, DeLuxe wheelcovers, foam-cushioned seats, foam-backed carpets and dash pad. Interiors included Custom Nylon and cord combinations and leather in the convertible, Model 76C. Two-door models had bright front seat cushion bands and Models 76R and 76C had power windows and seat adjuster as standard equipment.

1956 Buick, Roadmaster 4-door sedan, V-8 (AA)

ROADMASTER I.D. NUMBERS:
Serial numbers were mixed in production with other 1956 series (see 1956 Special — Series 40). Motor numbers were mixed in production.

Model Number	Body/Style Number	Body Type & Seating	Factory Price	Shipping Weight	Production Total
72	56-4769	4-dr Sedan-6P	3503	4280	11,804
73	56-4739	4-dr H.T.-6P	3692	4355	24,770
76R	56-4737	H.T. Cpe-6P	3591	4235	12,490
76C	56-4767	Conv Cpe-6P	3704	4395	4,354

ROADMASTER ENGINE
Specifications were the same as listed for the 1956 Century.

CHASSIS FEATURES: Wheelbase: (Series 40 and 60) 122 inches; (Series 50 and 70) 127 inches. Overall length: (Series 40 and 60) 205 inches; (Series 50 and 70) 213.6 inches. Front tread: (All) 59 inches. Rear tread: (All) 59 inches. Tires: (Series 40) 7.10 x 15; (Series 60 and 50) 7.60 x 15; (Series 70) 8.00 x 15.

POWERTRAIN OPTIONS: Three-speed manual transmission standard on Series 40 and 60. Dynaflow drive standard on Series 50 and 70, optional ($204) on Series 40 and 60.

CONVENIENCE OPTIONS: Power steering ($108 — standard on Series 50 and 70). Air conditioning ($403). Spotlite. Carpet cover. Cushion topper. Exhaust pipe trim. Dor-Gard. Gas door guard. Rear seat speaker. Tissue dispenser. Visor Vanity mirror. License frame (open top). Seat belts. Custom Cordaveen interior on Series 40, 60 and 50. Power windows (standard on Models 66C, 56C, 76C, 76R, available all other except Model 48). Wire wheels (set of five) on Series 60-50-70. Padded instrument panel (standard Series 50, available for Series 50). 6-way power seat. Sonomatic radio. Selectronic radio. Electric antenna. 1/3 — 2/3 rear seat (Model 49 and 69 wagons.)

Historical footnotes: Body styles 56-4437, 56-4537, 56-4637 and 56-4737X are Riviera hardtop coupes. Styles 56-4439, 56-4539, 56-4639 and 56-4739 are Riviera hardtop sedans (Pillarless). Body styles 56-4481 and 56-4681 are Estate wagons. The symbol 'X' after Body Style Number indicates power windows.

1957 BUICK

SPECIAL — SERIES 40 — A new, wider and lower body graced the 1957 Special. A red-filled bright Sweepspear lined the body sides and a chromed rear fender lower panel filled the area between wheelhouse and bumper end. A new centered fuel filler door was found in the rear bumper, the ends of which the single or optional dual exhausts passed through. Three ventiports were found on each front fender. Series script was found within the deck and grille emblems. Closed models were upholstered in nylon/Cordaveen combinations except for the Model 49D Estate Wagon which had cloth and Cordaveen upholstery. The Model 46C convertible was trimmed in two-tone Cordaveen. Standard Special equipment included a red-line speedometer, glovebox lamp, dual horns, trip mileage indicator, directional signals, dual sunshades, color-coordinated dash panel and, on Model 46C only, an outside left-hand rear view mirror.

SPECIAL I.D. NUMBERS: Serial numbers were mixed in production with other 1957 Series. Numbers were: (Flint) 4D1000989 to 4D1149460; (Calif.) 4D2001001 to 4D2038462; (N.J.) 4D3001001 to 4D3047645, (Kans.) 4D4001001 to 4D4046155, (Del.) 4D5001001 to 4D5039991, (Ga.) 4D6001001 to 4D6042248, (Mass.) 4D7001001 to 4D7018900 (Tex.) 4D8001001 to 4D8030225.

SPECIAL SERIES 40

Model Number	Body/Style Number	Body Type & Seating	Factory Price	Shipping Weight	Production Total
41	57-4469	4-dr Sedan-6P	2660	4012	59,739
43	57-4439	4-dr H.T.-6P	2780	4041	50,563
48	57-4411	2-dr Sedan-6P	2596	3955	23,180
46R	57-4437	H.T. Cpe-6P	2704	3956	64,425
46C	57-4467	Conv Cpe-6P	2987	4082	8,505
49D	57-4481	4-dr Riv Sta Wag-6P	3167	4309	6,817
49	57-4482	Sta Wag-6P	3047	4292	7,013

SPECIAL ENGINE
V8: Overhead valve. Cast iron block. Displacement: 364 cubic inches. Bore and stroke: 4.125 x 3.4 inches. Compression ratio: 9.5:1. Brake horsepower: 250 at 4400 R.P.M. Five main bearings. Hydraulic valve lifters. Carburetor: Stromberg two-barrel, model 7-106 or Carter 2529 or 2536.

1957 Buick, Century Riviera 2-door hardtop, V-8 (AA)

CENTURY — SERIES 60 — Buick's performance star was very similar to the Special in exterior trim, except for an identifying fourth Ventiport on each front fender. Series designation was also found on the rear quarters or doors and within front and rear emblems. Interiors were plusher, with Rivieras upholstered in Nylon/Cordaveen combinations and the Model 66C convertible being trimmed in Cordaveen and leather (Power windows and seats were standard on this model). Regular features, in addition to those found on the Special, included foam rubber seat cushions and an automatic trunk lamp.

CENTURY I.D. NUMBERS: Serial numbers were mixed with other 1957 Series (See 1957 Special — Series 40). Motor numbers were mixed in production.

CENTURY SERIES 60

Model Number	Body/Style Number	Body Type & Seating	Factory Price	Shipping Weight	Production Total
61	57-4669	4-dr Sedan-6P	3234	4137	8,075
63	57-4639	4-dr H.T.-6P	3354	4163	26,589
66R	57-4637	H.T. Cpe-6P	3270	4081	17,029
66C	57-4667X	Conv Cpe-6P	3598	4234	4,085
69	57-4682	Sta Wag-6P	3706	4423	10,186

CENTURY ENGINE
Specifications were the same as listed for the 1957 Special, except compression ratio was 10.0:1, brake horsepower was 300 at 4600 R.P.M. (330 h.p. with high performance kit) and the four-barrel carburetor was a Carter 2507 or Rochester 7010070 (late — 7011570).

SUPER — SERIES 50 — The Super used a new C-Body treatment for 1957. Larger than the Series 40-60 bodies, the Riviera styles had different roof treatments as well. Supers had a group of three Chevrons on each rear quarter or door for series identification, in addition to the normal wording within the grille and deck emblems. Four Ventiports were used on each front fender. Closed models were upholstered in Nylon/Cordaveen combinations, while the Model 56C convertible had an all-Cordaveen interior and featured power windows and seat controls as part of its equipment. Standard Super equipment approximated that of the Century.

SUPER I.D. NUMBERS: Serial numbers were mixed in 1957 production (see 1957 Special — Series 40). Motor numbers were also mixed in production.

SUPER SERIES 50

Model Number	Body/Style Number	Body Type & Seating	Factory Price	Shipping Weight	Production Total
53	57-4539	4-dr H.T.-6P	3681	4356	41,665
56R	57-4537	H.T. Cpe-6P	3536	4271	26,529
56C	57-4567	Convertible-6P	3981	4414	2,056

SUPER ENGINE:
Specifications are the same as listed for the 1957 Century.

1957 Buick, Roadmaster 2-door convertible, V-8 (AA)

ROADMASTER — SERIES 70 — The Roadmaster Rivieras featured a new body and revised rooflines, with chrome bands sweeping over the top and down division bars on the three-piece rear windows. Consumer resistance led to the optional deletion of these bars and substitution of a one-piece rear window (Models 73A and 76A). Roadmasters had four Ventiports per fender. Two-door models had the trio of Chevrons on the rear quarters like the Super, but the four-door styles had a Roadmaster emblem nestled within the Sweepspear's dip. Interiors were broadcloth and Nylon in the four-door, Nylon in the Rivieras and leather in the Model 76C convertible. A padded instrument panel was among the extra touches of luxury found in the Roadmaster.

ROADMASTER I.D. NUMBERS: Serial numbers were mixed in production with other 1957 series (see 1957 Special — Series 40). Motor numbers were mixed in production.

195

ROADMASTER SERIES 70

Model Number	Body/Style Number	Body Type & Seating	Factory Price	Shipping Weight	Production Total
73	57-4739	4-dr H.T.-6P	4053	4469	11,401
73A	57-4739A	4-dr H.T.-6P	4053	4455	10,526
76A	57-4737A	H.T. Cpe-6P	3944	4370	2,812
76R	57-4737	H.T. Cpe-6P	3944	4374	3,826
76C	57-4767X	Convertible-6P	4066	4500	4,364

ROADMASTER ENGINE
Specifications were the same as listed for the 1957 Century.

ROADMASTER 75 — SERIES 75 — A new line for 1957, introduced to cap the prestigious Roadmaster line. Both models used one-piece rear windows and differed from the Roadmaster only by the use of Roadmaster 75 script on the rear quarters or doors on the exterior. Inside, a plusher custom design interior was found. Roadmaster 75s included almost every power assist in their standard price, except for air conditioning.

ROADMASTER 75 I.D. NUMBERS: Serial numbers were mixed in production (see 1957 Special — Series 40). Motor numbers were mixed in production.

Model Number	Body/Style Number	Body Type & Seating	Factory Price	Shipping Weight	Production Total
75	57-4839	4-dr H.T. Sed	4483	4539	12,250
75R	57-4847	2-dr H.T. Cpe-6P	4373	4427	2,404

ROADMASTER 75 ENGINE
Specifications were the same as listed for the 1957 Century.

CHASSIS FEATURES: Wheelbase: (Series 40 and 60) 122 inches; (Series 50, 70 and 75) 127.5 inches. Overall length: (Series 40 and 60) 208.4 inches; (Series 50, 70 and 75) 215.3 inches. Front tread: (All) 59.5 inches. Rear tread: (Series 40 and 60) 59.5 inches; (Series 50, 70 and 75) 61.0 inches. Tires: (Series 40) 7.10 x 15; (Series 60 and 50 7.60 x 15; (Series 70 and 75) 8.00 x 15.

POWERTRAIN OPTIONS: Three-speed manual standard on Series 40, Dynaflow optional at $220. Dynaflow standard on Series 50, 60, 70 and 75.

CONVENIENCE OPTIONS: Included Power steering ($107 — standard on Series 50 and 70). Air conditioning ($430). Spotlite, Carpet cover. Cushion topper. Dor-Gard. Rear seat speaker. Front bumper guards. Rear seat speaker. Sonomatic radio. Selectronic radio. Electric antenna. Seat belts. Tissue dispenser. Visor Vanity mirror. License frames. Padded instrument panel (standard Series 70). Six-way power seat.

Historical footnotes: Body Styles 57-4437, 57-4637, 57-4537 and 57-4737 are Riviera hardtop coupes. Styles 57-4439, 57-4539, 57-4639 and 57-4739 are Riviera hardtop sedans. Styles 57-4481 and 57-4482 are Estate wagons. Style 57-4681 is the Caballero station wagon.

1958 BUICK

1958 Buick, Special 2-dr convertible, V-8 (AA)

SPECIAL — SERIES 40 — Bulkier, more heavily chromed styling adorned the 1958 Special chassis. New "Lucite" paints were used in many colors. For the first time since 1948 there were no distinguishing Ventiports on Buick's front fenders. At the front a new "drawer pull" grille, made up of rectangular chrome squares, was used. The Special name was spelled out across the deck lid, while a bright sweepspear and a large rear fender bright flash was similar to other models. All 1958 Buicks had four headlamps. Standard features on the Special included an ignition key light, glove box, cigar lighter, trip mileage indicator, geared vent panes, bumper guards, variable-speed wipers, Step-On parking brake and on the Model 46C convertible an outside left-hand rear view mirror. Special interiors were trimmed with grey cloth and vinyl or Cordaveen and vinyl, or all Cordaveen in the convertible. A plusher "Custom" interior was available at extra cost.

SPECIAL I.D. NUMBERS: Serial numbers were mixed in production with other 1958 series. Numbers were: (Flint) 4E1000985 to 4E1091650, (Calif.) 4E2001001 to 4E2020239, (N.J.) 4E3001001 to 4E3026555, (Kans.) 4E4001001 to 4E4031146, (Del.) 4E5001001 to 4E5022304, (Ga.) 4E6001001 to 4E6027283, (Mass.) 4E7001001 to 4E7011105 and (Tex.) 4E8001001 to 4E8019510.

SPECIAL SERIES

Model Number	Body/Style Number	Body Type & Seating	Factory Price	Shipping Weight	Production Total
41	584469	4-dr Sedan-6P	2700	4115	48,238
43	584439	4-dr H.T.-6P	2820	4180	31,921
48	584411	2-dr Sedan-6P	2636	4063	11,566
46R	584437	H.T. Cpe-6P	2744	4058	34,903
46C	584467	Convertible-6P	3041	4165	5,502
49D	584482	Station Wag-6P	3261	4408	3,420
49	584481	Station Wag-6P	3145	4396	3,663

SPECIAL ENGINE
V-8: Overhead valve. Cast iron block. Displacement: 364 cubic inches. Bore and stroke: 4.25 x 3.4 inches. Compression ratio: 9.5:1. Brake horsepower: 250 at 4400 R.P.M. Five main bearings. Hydraulic valve lifters. Carburetors: Stromberg two-barrel Model WW7-109B — also — Carter two-barrel (with Synchro) Model 2674; (with Dynaflow) Model 2675.

1958 Buick, Century Caballero hardtop station wagon, V-8 (AA)

CENTURY — SERIES 60 — The Century shared the Special's bulky new sheetmetal and had as much plated bright work. In addition to the Century name spelled out in block lettering on the deck lid, the 60 Series had Century script within the rear fender flashes. Standard equipment in addition to features found on the Special included Variable-Pitch Dynaflow, full wheelcovers, carpeting, padded dash, foam rubber cushions, electric clock, dual horns. Custom-interiors were trimmed in Nylon except for the Model 69 Estate Wagon, which was upholstered in Cordaveen. The Model 46C convertible had electric windows and 2-way seat controls.

CENTURY I.D. NUMBERS: Serial numbers were mixed with other 1958 Series (see 1958 Special — Series 40). Motor numbers were mixed in production.

CENTURY SERIES

Model Number	Body/Style Number	Body Type & Seating	Factory Price	Shipping Weight	Production Total
61	584669	4-dr Sedan-6P	3224	4137	7,421
63	584639	4-dr H.T.-6P	3354	4163	15,171
66R	584637	2-dr H.T.-6P	3270	4081	8,110
66C	584667X	Convertible-6P	3598	4234	2,588
69	584682	Station Wag-6P	3706	4423	4,456

CENTURY ENGINE:
Specifications were the same as listed for the 1958 Special, except compression ratio was 10.0:1, Brake horsepower was 300 at 4600 R.P.M. and the four-barrel carburetor was a Carter model 2800 or Rochester models 7011600 or (late) 7013100.

SUPER — SERIES 50 — The once most popular Buick line was reduced to two models for 1958. Side trim was similar to lesser series, except for the Super lettering on the rear fender flashes, but Supers were longer than the Series 40 and 60 models. The Super name was also lettered across the deck lid. Standard equipment included Variable-Pitch Dynaflow, power steering, power brakes, a safety-cushion instrument panel, fully carpeted floor, courtesy lights and other items found on lesser models.

SUPER I.D. NUMBERS: Serial numbers were mixed in 1958 production (see 1958 Special — Series 40). Motor numbers were also mixed in production.

SUPER SERIES

Model Number	Body/Style Number	Body Type & Seating	Factory Price	Shipping Weight	Production Total
53	584539	4-dr H.T.-6P	3789	4500	28,460
56R	584537	2-dr-H.T.-6P	3644	4392	13,928

SUPER ENGINE
Specifications were the same as listed for the 1958 Century.

ROADMASTER — SERIES 75 — The Roadmaster carried all the bright work of the Super and added bright wheelhouse moldings, a ribbed rocker panel molding and ribbed inserts to the rear fender flashes. All 1958 Roadmasters were in the 75 series as attested by the script and numerals on the fender flashes. On the rear deck, Roadmaster was spelled out in block lettering beneath a Buick emblem housing the trunk lock keyway. Standard Roadmaster features in addition to those found on lesser Buicks included power windows, a power six-way front seat, safety cushion dash, carpeted floors and lower doors, Glare-proof rear view mirror, safety buzzer, brake warning light and DeLuxe wheel covers. Interiors were cloth or cloth and leather except for the convertible, trimmed in all leather.

ROADMASTER I.D. NUMBERS: Serial numbers were mixed in production with other 1958 Series (see 1958 Special — Series 40). Motor numbers were mixed in production.

ROADMASTER SERIES

Model Number	Body/Style Number	Body Type & Seating	Factory Price	Shipping Weight	Production Total
75	584739X	4-dr H.T.-6P	4667	4668	10,505
75R	584737X	2-dr H.T.-6P	4557	4568	2,368
75C	584767X	Convertible-6P	4680	4676	1,181

ROADMASTER ENGINE
Specifications were the same as listed for the 1958 Century.

LIMITED — SERIES 700 — Buick resurrected a grand old nameplate for a new extra-long luxury line in 1958. Twelve vertical louvers, set within the rear fender's rocket-like trim motif, distinguished the Limited. All the chrome associated with other 1958 Buicks was present as well. The Limited had its own massive louvered taillamps. Limited script was found on the rear doors or quarters, and a Buick badge flanked by four chrome bars was found on the Limited which featured ultra-plush cloth, cloth and leather and in the case of the Model 756 Convertible, all-leather upholstry.

LIMITED I.D. NUMBERS: Serial numbers were mixed in production with other 1958 series (see 1958 Special — Series 40). Motor numbers were mixed in production.

1958 Buick, Limited 4-door hardtop sedan, V-8 (AA)

LIMITED SERIES

Model Number	Body/Style Number	Body Type & Seating	Factory Price	Shipping Weight	Production Total
750	584839X	4-dr H.T.-6P	5112	4710	5,571
755	584837X	2-dr H.T.-6P	5002	4691	1,026
756	584867X	Convertible-6P	5125	4603	839

LIMITED ENGINE
Specifications were the same as listed for the 1958 Century.

CHASSIS FEATURES: Wheelbase: (Series 40 and 60) 122 inches; (Series 50, 75 and 700) 127.5 inches. Overall length: (Series 40 and 60) 211.8 inches; (Series 50 and 75) 219.1 inches; (Series 700) 227.1 inches. Front tread: (Series 40, 60 and 50) 59.5 inches; (Series 75 and 700) 60 inches. Rear tread: (Series 40, 60 and 50) 59 inches; (Series 75 and 700) 61 inches. Tires: (Series 40) 7.10 x 15 (Models 46C and 49) 7.60 x 15; (Series 60 and 50) 7.60 x 15; (Series 75 and 700) 8.00 x 15.

POWERTRAIN OPTIONS: Three-speed manual standard on Series 40. Variable Pitch Dynaflow optional at $220. Variable Pitch Dynaflow standard on Series 60 and 50. Flight Pitch Dynaflow standard on Series 75 and 700, optional on other series ($296 — Series 40, $75 — Series 60 and 50). Dual exhausts optional.

CONVENIENCE OPTIONS: Power steering ($108 — standard Series 50, 75, 700). Power brakes (standard Series 50, 75, 700). 'Air Poise' air suspension. In-dash or under-dash air conditioning. Sonomatic radio. Wonder Bar signal-seeking radio. Power windows (standard Model 66C, all Series 75 and 700). Perimeter heater/defroster. Autronic Eye. Electric radio antenna. Windshield washer (standard Series 75 and 700). E-Z Eye glass. Safety group — back-up lights, lower instrument panel pad, parking brake warning light, glare-proof insider rear view mirror (standard on Series 75 and 700). Upper instrument panel pad (for Series 40, standard other series). Six-way power seat (standard Series 75, 700). Series 40 accessory group-electric clock, full wheel covers, automatic trunk light, rear license frame.

Historical footnotes: Body styles 584437, 584637, 584537, 584737 and 584837X are Riviera coupes. Styles 584439, 584639, 584539, 584739, 584839X are Riviera sedans. Styles 584482 and 584682 are Riviera Estate Wagons. An X in the style designation indicates electric controls of the windows, front seat, and in convertibles, top.

1959 BUICK

LESABRE — SERIES 4400 — New series names and totally new styling greeted the 1959 Buick buyer. These were the wildest Buicks yet, with blade fins sweeping from the front of the body rearward. One of the few continued hallmarks from 1958 was the grille made up of rectangular squares. On the sides, bright trim strips ran the length of the LeSabre body. Taillights were low and round. Interiors were trimmed in 'Barbary cloth' and Cordaveen except on Models 4467 and 4435 which were all-Cordaveen. An optional 'Balfour Cloth' and Cordaveen Custom combination was offered on all except the Convertible and Station wagon. Standard LeSabre equipment included a glove box light, dual horns, electric wipers, horizontal red-liner speedometer, trip mileage indicator and an outside rear veiw mirror on the Model 4467 Convertible.

LESABRE I.D. NUMBERS: Serial numbers began with 4F1001001, the first digit identifying the series (4400), the second symbol, the letter F representing the code for the 1959 model year, the 3rd symbol the number '1' representing the assembly plant code for Flint (2 - California, 3 - New Jersey, 4 - Kansas City, Kansas, 5 - Delaware, 6 - Atlanta, 7 - Masschusetts and 8 - Texas).

LESABRE SERIES

Series Number	Model Number	Body Type & Seating	Factory Price	Shipping Weight	Production Total
4400	4419	4-dr Sedan-6P	2804	4229	51,379
4400	4439	4-dr H.T.-6P	2925	4266	46,069
4400	4411	2-dr Sedan-6P	2740	4159	13,492
4400	4437	2-dr H.T.-6P	2849	4188	35,189
4400	4467	Convertible-6P	3129	4216	10,489
4400	4435	Station Wag-6P	3320	4565	8,286

LESABRE ENGINE
V-8: Overhead valve. Cast iron block. Displacement: 364 cubic inches. Bore and stroke: 4.25 x 3.4 inches. Compression ratio: 10.5:1. Brake horsepower: 250 at 4400 R.P.M. Five main bearings. Hydraulic lifters. Carburetor: Stromberg two-barrel Model WW7-112A or Carter two-barrels (with Synchromesh) model 2847; (with Dynaflow) Model 2838 or Rochester two-barrel model 7019042.

INVICTA — SERIES 4600 — Replacing the Century Series 60 for 1959 was this new performance line. The exterior was distinguished by a bright rocker panel molding and Invicta scripts on the front fenders. Inside, standard trim was 'Balfour' cloth in a more intricate weave than the LeSabre and in four color combinations. The Estate Wagon was trimmed in Saran 'Balfour' and Cordaveen, and the Convertible was upholstered in all-Cordaveen. Standard equipment on the Invicta, in addition to features found on the LeSabre, included Foamtex seat cushions, electric clock, DeLuxe steering wheel, full wheel covers, and an instrument panel cover.

INVICTA I.D. NUMBERS: Serial numbers were distinguished by the use of the numeral '6' as the first symbol of the number. The rest of the number was coded as explained under the 1959 LeSabre Series 4400 listing.

1959 Buick, Invicta 4-door hardtop sedan, V-8 (AA)

INVICTA SERIES

Series Number	Model Number	Body Type & Seating	Factory Price	Shipping Weight	Production Total
4600	4619	4-dr Sedan-6P	3357	4331	10,566
4600	4639	4-dr H.T.-6P	3515	4373	20,156
4600	4637	2-dr H.T.-6P	3447	4274	11,451
4600	4667	Convertible-6P	3620	4317	5,447
4600	4635	Station Wag-6P	3841	4660	5,231

INVICTA ENGINE
V-8: Overhead valve. Cast iron block. Displacement: 401 cubic inches. Bore and stroke: 4.1875 x 3.64 inches. Compression ratio: 10.5:1. Brake horsepower: 325 at 4400 R.P.M. Five main bearings. Hydraulic lifters. Carburetor: Carter four-barrel model 2840 or Rochester four-barrel model 7013044-15900.

ELECTRA — SERIES 4700 — A Roadmaster by another name, the Electra was trimmed with bright rocker moldings, wheel house moldings and Electra script on the front fenders in addition to the bright work found on other Buicks. Standard features in addition to those found on lower-priced Buicks included a Safety Pad dash, power steering, power brakes, two-speed electric wipers, and dual exhausts. Interiors were plusher, being trimmed in Nylon Mojave cloth or Broadcloth combinations with Cordaveen.

ELECTRA I.D. NUMBERS: Serial numbers were distinguished by the use of the numeral '7' as the first symbol of the number. The rest of the number was coded as explained under the 1959 LeSabre Series 4400 listing.

ELECTRA SERIES

Series Number	Model Number	Body Type & Seating	Factory Price	Shipping Weight	Production Total
4700	4719	4-dr Sedan-6P	3856	4557	12,357
4700	4739	4-dr H.T.-6P	3963	4573	20,612
4700	4737	Convertible-6P	3818	4465	11,216

ELECTRA ENGINE
Specifications are the same as those listed for the 1959 Invicta.

1959 Buick, Electra 225 2-door convertible, V-8 (AA)

ELECTRA 225 — SERIES 4800 — The First Electra-225, with the 225 coming from the overall length of this stretched-body luxury car. Exterior distinction came from extra-wide moldings with a massive Electra emblem on the front fender extension. Electra 225 script was found on the front fenders ahead of the wheelhouse. The four-door models had a lower bright rear fender molding as well. Standard features in addition to those found on lesser Buicks included plusher interiors (leather in the Convertible), power windows and top for the Convertible, Safety group, Super DeLuxe wheelcovers and an outside rear view mirror.

ELECTRA 225 I.D. NUMBERS: Serial numbers were distinguished by the use of the number '8' as the first symbol of the number. The rest of the number was coded as explained under the 1959 LeSabre series 4400 listing.

ELECTRA 225 SERIES

Series Number	Model Number	Body Type & Seating	Factory Price	Shipping Weight	Production Total
4800	4829	4-dr Sedan-6P	4300	4632	6,324
4800	4839	4-dr H.T.-6P	4300	4641	10,491
4800	4867	Convertible-6P	4192	4562	5,493

ELECTRA ENGINE
Specifications are the same as those listed for the 1959 Invicta.

CHASSIS FEATURES: Wheelbase: (Series 4400 and 4600) 123 inches; (Series 4700 and 4800) 126.3 inches. Overall length: (Series 4400 and 4600) 217.4 inches; (Series 4700) 220.6 inches; (Series 4800 225.4 inches). Front tread: (All series) 62 inches. Rear tread: (All series) 60 inches. Tires: (Series 4400 and 4600) 7.60 x 15; (Series 4700 and 4800) 8.00 x 15 tubeless.

POWERTRAIN OPTIONS: A three-speed manual transmission was standard on Series 4400, Twin Turbine Dynaflow (standard on Series 4600, 4700, 4800) was optional at $220. Triple Turbine Dynaflow was optional on all Series at $296 on Series 4400 and $75 on all others. A Positive Traction differential was offered.

CONVENIENCE OPTIONS: Power steering and power brakes were optional on Series 4400 models (with automatic transmission only) and on Series 4600 models. Both features were standard on Series 4700 and 4800 models. Air conditioning. Power seat (except Style 4411). Safety Pad dash on Series 4400. Heater/Defroster. Automatic heat fresh air control. Wonderbar signal-seeking radio. Transistor portable radio. Sonomatic radio. Electric antenna. Rear seat speaker. Speed control safety buzzer. DeLuxe steering wheel on Series 4400. DeLuxe wheel covers on Series 4400. Super DeLuxe wheel covers on Series 4400, 4600, 4700. Two-speed electric wipers on Series 4400 and 4600. E-Z-Eye glass (windshield only or all glass). Bucket seats (Electric 225 convertible only). Power windows. Power vents. Autronic Eye. Electric rear window for Estate Wagon. Junior third seat for Estate Wagon. Safety Group — safety buzzer, back-up lights, glare-proof insider rear view mirror, parking brake warning light, map light (standard Series 4800). Accessory group for Series 4400 — electric clock, trunk light, license frame.

Historical footnotes: Models 4435 and 4635 are Estate Wagons. Model 4829 is the Riviera sedan.

1960 BUICK

1960 Buick, LeSabre 4-door sedan, V-8 (AA)

LESABRE — SERIES 4400 — Buick rounded and softened the lines of its 1960 models. Clipping the wild fins of 1959 gave the car a shortened, heavier appearance. Ventiports returned for 1960, with a trio of the highly stylized ornaments on each LeSabre front fender. Series identification was further enhanced by LeSabre name bars on each front fender ahead of the wheelhouse. A bright lower body molding accented the car's other bright metal. Interiors were of Cordaveen and cloth (all-Cordaveen on the station wagon). A plusher 'Custom' interior featuring deep-pile carpeting, padded instrument panel, DeLuxe door handles, window cranks and armrests, was optional. Standard features of all Specials included Mirromatic adjustable speedometer, electric windshield wipers, trip mileage indicator, cigar lighter, dual sunshades, Step-On parking brake, dual horns and a single-key locking system.

LESABRE I.D. NUMBERS: Serial numbers began with 4G( )001001, the first digit identifying the series (4400), the second symbol, the letter G, representing the code for the 1960 model year, the third symbol, a numeral ( ), representing the plant code. The last six symbols are the numerical sequence of the assembly at the coded plant, with series mixed in production. Plant codes were 1 - Flint, 2 - California, 3 - New Jersey, 4 - Kans., 5 - Delaware, 6 - Atlanta, 7 - Massachusetts and 8 - Texas.

LESABRE SERIES

Series Number	Model Number	Body Type & Seating	Factory Price	Shipping Weight	Production Total
4400	4419	4-dr Sedan-6P	2870	4219	54,033
4400	4439	4-dr H.T.-6P	2991	4269	35,999
4400	4411	2-dr Sedan-6P	2756	4139	14,388
4400	4437	2-dr H.T.-6P	2915	4163	26,521
4400	4467	Convertible-6P	3145	4233	13,588
4400	4445	Sta Wagon-8P	3493	4574	2,222
4400	4435	Sta Wagon-6P	3386	4568	5,331

LESABRE ENGINE

V-8: Overhead valve. Cast iron block. Displacement: 364 cubic inches. Bore and stroke: 4.125 x 3.4 inches. Compression ratio: 10.25:1. Brake horsepower: 250 at 4400 R.P.M. Five main bearings. Hydraulic lifters. Carburetor: two-barrels, Stromberg model WW7-11A; Carter model 2979 (syncromesh) or model 2980 (automatic); or Rochester model 7019042.

INVICTA — SERIES 4600 — "The most spirited Buick," said the sales catalog of the Invicta. Wearing three ventiports per front fender, the Invicta had all of the LeSabre's bright work plus bright metal wheelhouse moldings. The front fender plaques carried Invicta lettering, of course. Interiors were cloth and Cordaveen with all-Cordaveen color-coordinated trim optional (standard in the convertible). Station wagon styles were trimmed in Saran cloth and Cordaveen. Standard Invicta features in addition to those found on the LeSabre included Twin Turbine automatic transmission, Foamtex seat cushions, electric clock, trunk light, DeLuxe steering wheel, DeLuxe wheel covers, license plate frames and a glove box light.

1960 Buick, Invicta 4-door station wagon, V-8

INVICTA I.D. NUMBERS: Serial numbers were distinguished by the use of the numeral '6' as the first symbol of the number. The rest of the number was coded as explained under the 1960 LeSabre Series 4400 listing.

INVICTA SERIES

Series Number	Model Number	Body Type & Seating	Factory Price	Shipping Weight	Production Total
4600	4619	4-dr Sedan-6P	3357	4324	10,839
4600	4639	4-dr H.T.-6P	3515	4365	15,300
4600	4637	2-dr H.T.-6P	3447	4255	8,960
4600	4667	Convertible-6P	3620	4347	5,236
4600	4645	Sta Wagon-8P	3948	4679	1,605
4600	4635	Sta Wagon-6P	3841	4644	3,471

INVICTA ENGINE:

V-8: Overhead valve. Cast iron block. Displacement: 401 cubic inches. Bore and stroke: 4.1875 x 3.640 inches. Compression ratio: 10.25:1. Brake horsepower: 325 at 4400 R.P.M. Five main bearings. Hydraulic lifters. Carburetor: four-barrel Carter model 29825 or Rochester 7015040.

ELECTRA — SERIES 4700 — A larger Buick, identified by its four ventiports per front fender, wider rocker panel bright moldings and the Electra script on the front fenders ahead of the wheelhouse. Electras had plusher cloth and Cordaveen interiors and featured power steering, power brakes and all the features found on the Invicta and LeSabre models as standard.

ELECTRA I.D. NUMBERS: Serial numbers were distinguished by the use of the numeral '7' as the first symbol of the number. The rest of the number was coded as explained under the 1960 LeSabre 4400 listing.

ELECTRA SERIES

Series Number	Model Number	Body Type & Seating	Factory Price	Shipping Weight	Production Total
4700	4719	4-dr Sedan-6P	3856	4544	13,794
4700	4739	4-dr H.T.-6P	3963	4554	14,488
4700	4737	2-dr H.T.-6P	3818	4453	7,416

ELECTRA ENGINE

Specifications were the same as those listed for the 1960 Invicta.

ELECTRA 225 — SERIES 4800 — Buick's plushest, fanciest model was outstanding this year with its broad, ribbed, lower body bright trim panels. An Electra 225 badge was circled on the deck lid. The Electra 225 name was found on front fenders. Brisbane cloth interiors graced closed models while the convertible was trimmed in leather, with bucket seats for front passenger optional. All of Buick's standard features were found on the Electra plus back-up lights, a glare proof rear view mirror, parking brake signal light, safety buzzer, map light, Super DeLuxe wheelcovers and a two-way power seat adjuster and power windows for the Convertible.

ELECTRA 225 I.D. NUMBERS: Serial numbers were distinguished by the use of the numeral '8' as the first symbol of the number. The rest of the number was coded as explained under the 1960 LeSabre Series 4400 listing.

1960 Buick, Electra 225, 4-door hardtop sedan, V-8 (AA)

ELECTRA 225 SERIES

Series Number	Model Number	Body Type & Seating	Factory Price	Shipping Weight	Production Total
4800	4829	4-dr Sedan-6P	4300	4653	8,029
4800	4839	4-dr H.T.-6P	4300	4650	4,841
4800	4867	Convertible-6P	4192	4571	6,746

ELECTRA ENGINE

Specifications were the same as those listed for the 1960 Invicta.

POWER TRAIN OPTIONS: A regular fuel Wildcat 375E V-8 was optional on Series 4400 models. This engine featured a 9.1:1 compression ratio and produced 235 brake horsepower at 4400 R.P.M. and cost $52 extra. A high-performance Wildcat 405 four-barrel V-8 was also optional on Series 4400 models with three-speed manual transmission. This combination featured 300 horsepower at 4400 R.P.M. and cost $220 additional.

CONVENIENCE OPTIONS: Power steering was standard on Series 4700 and 4800 models and optional on Series 4400 and 4600 models ($108). Power brakes were standard on Series 4700 and 4800 models, optional on others. ($43). Air conditioning $430). Twilight Sentinel automatic headlamp dimmer ($29). Tissue dispenser. Compass. Visor vanity mirror. Trunk mat (plastic foam-backed). DeLuxe handy mats. Litter basket. Six-Way power seat ($52-103). Six/Two-Way Power seat ($69). Four-Way power seat ($65). Four/Two-Way power seat ($37). Bucket seats ($108). Power vent windows ($54). Power windows ($108). Sonotone radio with manual antenna ($99); with electric antenna ($121). Wonder Bar radio with manual antenna ($135); with electric antenna ($158). Rear seat speaker ($17). Guidematic ($43). DeLuxe steering wheel on LeSabre ($16). DeLuxe wheel covers on LeSabre ($19). Super DeLuxe wheel covers ($17-37). White sidewall tires. Custom exterior moldings ($13-41). Station wagon electric rear window ($27). Station wagon luggage rack ($100). Standard two-tone finish ($16-43). Special order two-toning ($97). Dual exhausts ($31). Turbine Drive transmission ($220). Dual-speed windshield washers/wipers ($19). Accessory group including trunk compartment light, electric clock and license plate frame for LeSabre ($22). Safety accessory group including Glare-Proof mirror, backup lights, parking brake warning signal and safety buzzer light for 4400-4600-4700 Series ($34).

Historical footnotes: Models 4435, 4445, 4635 and 4645 are Estate Wagons. Model 4829 is the Riviera sedan.

1961 BUICK

1961 Buick, Special 4-door sedan, V-8 (AA)

SPECIAL — SERIES 4000 STANDARD 4100 AND 4300 DELUXE — Buick's new quality car in a small package immediately found an enthusiastic following. Styling was related to the larger 1961 Buicks. Specials had three ventiport appliques per front fender. Trim was minimal on the Special. Standard features of the Special included dual sun visors, dual armrests, cigar lighter and electric windshield wipers. The base Special was trimmed in cloth and vinyl. DeLuxe models had richer Custom interiors of cloth and vinyl (all-vinyl in the Station Wagon), plush carpeting, rear arm rests, rear ash trays and DeLuxe steering wheel. They were distinguished by Custom exterior moldings which included a highlight bright strip on the upper body. A mid-year Skylark Sport Coupe was added (Model 4317) that featured unique emblems, an even plusher all-vinyl interior with optional bucket front seats and unique taillamp housings, additional lower body bright moldings and Turbine wheel covers. A vinyl top was standard.

SPECIAL I.D. NUMBERS: Serial numbers began with OH(   )501001-Up. The first symbol indicated the series (4000, 4100 or 4300). The second symbol, the letter H is the code for the 1961 model year. The third symbol is a numeral (   ) representing the plant code. The last six symbols are the numerical sequence of assembly at the coded plant, with series mixed in production.

Series Number	Model Number	Body Type & Seating	Factory Price	Shipping Weight	Production Total
SPECIAL STANDARD MODELS					
4000	4019	4-dr Sedan-6P	2384	2610	18,339
4000	4027	Sport Cpe-6P	2330	2579	4,232
4000	4035	Station Wag-6P	2681	2775	6,101
4000	4045	Station Wag-8P	2762	2844	798
SPECIAL DELUXE MODELS					
4100	4119	4-dr Sedan-6P	2519	2632	32,986
4100	4135	Station Wag-6P	2816	2794	11,729
4300	4317	Sport Cpe-5P	2621	2687	12,683

SPECIAL ENGINE
V-8: Overhead valve. Cast aluminum block. Displacement: 215 cubic inches. Bore and stroke: 3.50 x 2.80 inches. Compression ratio: 8.8:1. Brake horsepower 155 at 4600 R.P.M. Five main bearings. Hydraulic lifters. Carburetor: two-barrel Rochester model 7019090 (automatic) or model 7019093 (manual). Note: Skylark was equipped with four-barrel Rochester model 7020043 (automatic) or model 7020045 (manual) and had 10.25:1 compression ratio, 185 brake horsepower.

LESABRE — SERIES 4400 — A new slimmer and trimmer image was presented by Buick's sales leading series for 1961. Body sculpturing allowed for a relatively light application of exterior bright work, with a single narrow bright molding along the upper body. LeSabre script was found on the front fenders, along with three ventiports. Turbine drive automatic transmission was standard on the 1961 LeSabre along with a revised Mirromagic instrument panel, direction signals, full-flo oil filter, electric windshield wipers, a DeLuxe steering wheel, trip mileage indicator, cigar lighter, Step-On brake, dual arm rests, cloth and vinyl trim combinations and carpeting on some models. Estate wagons had a standard all-vinyl interior, with cloth and vinyl optional. A power rear window was standard on the three-seat Estate Wagon.

1961 Buick, LeSabre 4-door hardtop sedan, V-8 (AA)

LESABRE I.D. NUMBERS: Serial numbers were distinguished by the use of the numeral '4' as the first symbol of the number. The rest of the number was coded as explained under the 1961 Special Series 4000, 4100 and 4300 listing.

Series Number	Model Number	Body Type & Seating	Factory Price	Shipping Weight	Production Total
LESABRE SERIES					
4400	4469	4-dr Sedan-6P	3107	4102	35,005
4400	4439	4-dr H.T.-6P	3228	4129	37,790
4400	4411	2-dr Sedan-6P	2993	4033	5,959
4400	4437	2-dr H.T.-6P	3152	4054	14,474
4400	4467	Convertible-6P	3382	4186	11,971
4400	4435	Station Wag-6P	3623	4450	5,628
4400	4445	Station Wag-9P	3730	4483	2,423

LESABRE ENGINE
V-8: Overhead valve. Cast iron block. Displacement: 364 cubic inches. Bore and stroke: 4.25 x 3.4 inches. Compression ratio: 10.25:1. Brake horsepower: 250 at 4400 R.P.M. Five main bearings. Hydraulic lifters. Carburetor: Carter model 3089 four-barrel.

INVICTA — SERIES 4600 — Buick's slightly sportier performance line was graced with double belt moldings in 1961 to set it apart from the LeSabre, with which it shared three ventiports per front fender. Invicta nameplates were used on each front fender as well as the rear deck. Full wheel covers, an electric clock, automatic trunk light and license frame were additional standard features of the Invicta over lesser models. Standard trim was cloth and vinyl, except for the Convertible which was all-vinyl. An optional Custom interior featured leather trim while another featured vinyl with contrasting vertical stripes and front bucket seats with a storage consolex and power two-way seat adjustment.

INVICTA I.D. NUMBERS: Serial numbers were distinguished by the use of the numeral '6' as the first symbol of the number. The rest of the number was coded as explained under the 1961 Special Series 4000, 4100 and 4300 listing.

1961 Buick, Invicta 2-door hardtop coupe, V-8 (AA)

Series Number	Model Number	Body Type & Seating	Factory Price	Shipping Weight	Production Total
INVICTA SERIES					
4600	4639	4-dr H.T.-6P	3515	4179	18,398
4600	4637	2-dr H.T.-6P	3447	4090	6,382
4600	4667	Convertible-6P	3620	4206	3,953

INVICTA ENGINE
V-8: Overhead valve. Cast iron block. Displacement: 401 cubic inches. Bore and stroke: 4.1875 x 3.640 inches. Compression ratio: 10.25:1. Brake horsepower: 325 at 4400 R.P.M. Five main bearings. Hydraulic lifters. Carburetor: four-barrel Carter model 3088S.

ELECTRA — SERIES 4700 — Buick's first step up to the larger models featured bright rocker panel and wheelhouse moldings for 1961. Four ventiports per front fender were a hallmark, with identification spelled out on the front fender plaques. Interiors were trimmed in fabric. Standard Electra features included those of lower-priced Buicks, plus power steering, power brakes, a 2-speed windshield wiper/washer system, glove box light, Custom-padded seat cushions, and DeLuxe wheel covers. Two-tone Electras had a color accent on the rear cove.

ELECTRA I.D. NUMBERS: Serial numbers were distinguished by the use of the numeral 7 as the first symbol of the number. The rest of the number was coded as explained under the 1961 Special — Series 4000, 4100 and 4300 listing.

Series Number	Model Number	Body Type & Seating	Factory Price	Shipping Weight	Production Total
ELECTRA SERIES 4700					
4700	4719	4-dr Sedan-6P	3825	4298	13,818
4700	4739	4-dr H.T.-6P	3932	4333	8,978
4700	4737	2-dr H.T.-6P	3818	4260	4,250

ELECTRA ENGINE

Specifications were the same as those listed for the 1961 Invicta.

1961 Buick, Electra 225 2-door convertible, V-8 (AA)

ELECTRA 225 — SERIES 4800 — Buick's plushest model had a wide strip of bright trim along the lower body, with vertical "hash marks" interupting behind the wheelhouse of the rear fender. Electra 225 nameplates were found on the front fenders. Calais cloth or leather trim was found inside. Standard equipment was the same as the Electra except for the addition of back-up lights, Glare-proof rear view mirror, Parking brake signal light, safety buzzer, courtesy lights, 2-way power seat, Super DeLuxe wheel covers with gold accents and power windows.

ELECTRA 225 I.D. NUMBERS: Serial numbers were distinguished by the use of the numeral '8' as the first symbol of the number. The rest of the number was coded as explained under the 1961 Special Series 4000, 4100 and 4300 listing.

ELECTRA SERIES 4800

Model Number	Body/Style Number	Body Type & Seating	Factory Price	Shipping Weight	Production Total
4800	4829	H.T. Sedan-6P	4350	4417	13,719
4800	4867	Convertible-6P	4192	4441	7,158

ELECTRA 225 ENGINE

Specifications were the same as listed for the 1961 Invicta.

CHASSIS FEATURES: Wheelbase: (4000, 4100 and 4300) 112 inches; (4400 and 4600) 123 inches; (4700 and 4800) 126 inches. Overall length: (4000, 4100 and 4300) 188.4 inches; (4400 and 4600) 213.2 inches; (4700 and 4800) 219.2 inches. Tires: (400, 4100 and 4300) 6.50 x 13; (4400 and 4600) 7.60 x 15; (4700 and 4800 8.00 x 15.

POWER TRAIN OPTIONS: A three-speed manual transmission was standard on Series 4000, 4100 and 4300. Dual-path Turbine Drive was optional at $189. A four-speed manual was also an option for the Series 4300 Skylark. A regular fuel V-8 was optional for the Series 4400 and was the same basic 364 cubic inch engine with two-barrel carburetor, 9.0:1 compression and 235 brake horsepower at 4400 R.P.M. Dual exhausts were standard on the Series 4700 two-door hardtop and Series 4800 Convertible, optional on all other full-size models. Positive traction differential was offered.

CONVENIENCE OPTIONS included Power steering on 4000, 4100, 4300 ($86); and 4400-4600 ($108 — standard on 4700 and 4800). Power brakes ($43). (standard 4700 and 4800). Air conditioning ($378 on 4000-4100-4300; $430 on full-size models). Size 7.00 x 13 tires on 4300. Power windows ($108) (standard on 4800). Four-way power seat adjustment. ($65). Sonotone radio ($90). Wonderbar radio ($127). Twilight Sentinel ($29). Guide-matic dimmer ($43). Heater/Defroster ($99). DeLuxe Special wheelcovers ($15). Back-up lights (standard on 4800). Cool-Pak air conditioning on 4000, 4100 and 4300. Luggage rack on Estate Wagons ($100). Power rear window on 6-pass. Estate Wagon ($27).

Historical footnotes: Model 4829 was the Riviera sedan. Models 4435 and 4445 were Estate Wagons.

1962 BUICK

SPECIAL — SERIES 4000 — The second edition of Buick's compact Special was little changed from the 1961 version. Once again the basic Special had no bright side trim except for three ventiports per front fender and a Special script ahead of the front wheelhouses. Small hubcaps were standard, as were dual sun visors, dual arm rests, cigar lighter and electric windshield wipers, directional signals, heater and defroster and outside rear view mirror on convertible. Interiors were cloth and vinyl.

SPECIAL I.D. NUMBERS: Serial numbers for cars equipped with the V-6 began with AI( )501001-up. Serial numbers for cars equipped with the V-8 began with OI( )501001-up. The first digit denotes the series or engine equipment. The second symbol, the letter I, is the code for the 1962 model year. The third symbol ( ) is a numeral representing the plant code. The last six symbols are the numerical sequence of assembly at the coded plant, with series mixed in production.

Series Number	Model Number	Body Type & Seating	Factory Price	Shipping Weight	Production Total
4000	4019	4-dr Sedan-6P	2358	2666	23,249
4000	4027	Coupe-6P	2304	2638	19,135
4000	4067	Convertible-6P	2587	2858	7,918
4000	4045	Sta Wag-8P	2736	2896	2,814
4000	4035	Sta Wag-6P	2655	2876	7,382

SPECIAL 6-CYL ENGINE

V-6: Overhead valve. Cast-iron block. Displacement: 198 cubic inches. Bore and stroke: 3.625 x 3.2 inches. Compression ratio: 8.8:1. Brake horsepower: 135 at 4600 R.P.M. Four main bearings. Hydraulic lifters. Carburetor: two-barrel.

SPECIAL V-8 ENGINE

V-8: Overhead valve. Cast aluminum block. Displacement: 215 cubic inches. Bore and stroke: 3.50 x 2.80 inches. Compression ratio: 8.8:1. Brake horsepower: 155 at 4600 R.P.M. Five main bearings. Hydraulic lifters. Carburetor: two-barrel.

SPECIAL DELUXE — SERIES 4100 — A slightly plusher Special, with a bright strip along the body, nicer vinyls and fabrics inside and full carpeting. Rear arm rests, rear ash trays, a DeLuxe steering wheel, foam seat cushions, cigarette lighter, oil filter and dual horns and visors were addition features found on the DeLuxe.

SPECIAL DELUXE I.D. NUMBERS: Serial numbers were distinguished by the use of the numeral '1' as the first symbol of the number (as did the series 4000 V-8). The rest of the number was coded as explained under the 1962 Special Series 4000 listing.

SPECIAL DELUXE SERIES

Series Number	Model Number	Body Type & Seating	Factory Price	Shipping Weight	Production Total
4100	4119	4-dr Sedan-6P	2593	2648	31,660
4100	4167	Convertible-6P	2879	2820	8,332
4100	4135	Sta Wag-6P	2890	2845	10,300

SPECIAL DELUXE ENGINE

Specifications were the same as listed for the 1962 Special Series 4000 V-8.

1962 Buick, Skylark 2-door coupe, V-8 (AA)

SKYLARK — SERIES 4300 — Buick's most refined compact featured a new convertible model and slightly changed styling for 1962. The hardtop coupe was of true "hardtop" design this year, without a side window. The Skylark had a Buick emblem centered in the grille and a Skylark badge on each front fender along with the three ventiports. Taillamp housings wrapped around onto the rear fenders. Lower body bright rocker and wheelhouse moldings accented the Skylark which came with Turbine wheel covers. Interiors were all-vinyl, with front bucket seats. Standard features in addition to those found on the lesser Specials included a padded dash, Skylark steering wheel, heater and defroster, rear courtesy lamps and, on the convertible, a power top.

SKYLARK I.D. NUMBERS: Serial numbers were distinguished by the use of the numeral '3' as the first symbol of the number. The rest of the number was coded as explained under the 1962 Special Series 4000 listing.

SKYLARK SERIES

Series Number	Model Number	Body Type & Seating	Factory Price	Shipping Weight	Production Total
4300	4347	2-dr H.T.-6P	2787	2707	34,060
4300	4367	Convertible-5P	3012	2871	8,913

SKYLARK ENGINE

V-8: Specifications were the same as those listed for the 1962 Special — Series 4000 V-8 except compression ratio was 11.0:1, a four-barrel carburetor was used and brake horsepower was 190 at 4800 R.P.M.

1962 Buick, LeSabre 2-door hardtop sport coupe, V-8 (AA)

LESABRE — SERIES 4400 — Refreshing new lines graced the 1962 LeSabre, although its body structure was unchanged from 1961. Still sporting a trio of ventiports on each front fender, LeSabres were identified by script on the front fenders and emblems front and rear. The two-door Hardtop featured a new "landau" style top simulating an erected convertible top, but in steel. Standard features included directional signals, full-flo oil filter, electric windshield wipers, a DeLuxe steering wheel, cigar lighter, Step-On parking brake, dual arm rests, Turbine drive transmission, padded dashboard, heater and defroster and glove box light. Interiors were cloth and vinyl combinations.

LESABRE I.D. NUMBERS: Serial numbers were distinguished by the use of the numeral '4' as the first symbol of the number. The rest of the number was coded as explained under the 1962 Special Series 4000 listing.

LESABRE SERIES

Series Number	Model Number	Body Type & Seating	Factory Price	Shipping Weight	Production Total
4400	4469	4-dr Sedan-6P	3227	4104	56,783
4400	4439	4-dr H.T. Sed-6P	3369	4156	37,518
4400	4411	2-dr Sedan-6P	3091	4041	7,418
4400	4447	2-dr H.T.-6P	3293	4054	25,479

LESABRE ENGINE

V-8: Overhead valve. Cast-iron block. Displacement: 401 cubic inches. Bore and stroke: 4.1875 x 3.64 inches. Compression ratio: 10.25:1. Brake horsepower: 280 at 4400 R.P.M. Five main bearings. Hydraulic lifters. Carburetor: Rochester two-barrel model 2GC.

1962 Buick, Invicta 4-door Estate station wagon, V-8 (AA)

INVICTA — SERIES 4600 — The Invicta models had all LeSabre features plus DeLuxe wheel covers and the engine 'Power Pak' (four-barrel induction system). The four-door hardtop and two-door hardtop also had the Code 06 Accessory Group (trunk light, electric clock and license plate frames) as standard equipment, plus padded cushions. The distinctive Invicta nine-passenger station wagon offered a power tailgate as a regular feature and the convertible in the line came equipped with an outside rear view mirror. All models in this line were generally plusher than LeSabres, although both series shared the same body shell. Exterior distinction came from the use of Invicta front fender badges, with other trim items matching the LeSabre theme.

NOTE: The Wildcat sport coupe was part of the Invicta line, featuring Custom equipment like a DeLuxe steering wheel, all-vinyl front bucket seats with a center console housing the Turbine drive transmission lever, a tachometer, and rear floor lamp. An electric clock, chrome roof bows and license frames were other Wildcat equipment. The Wildcat sport coupe had a vinyl top covering, with Wildcat emblems on the roof quarter panels and special wheelcovers. Custom bright metal exterior moldings, including lower body rocker panel and wheelhouse bright trim, were used. Dual exhausts were standard. The Wildcat was included with the Invicta hardtop coupe's 13,471 production figure and shared its 4647 Model number. However, Wildcat listed for $3927 and weighed 4,150 pounds.

INVICTA SERIES

Series Number	Model Number	Body Type & Seating	Factory Price	Shipping Weight	Production Total
4600	4639	4-dr H.T. Sed-6P	3667	4159	16,443
4600	4547	2-dr H.T. Cpe-6P	3733	4077	12,355
4600	4667	Convertible-6P	3617	4217	13,471
4600	4645	Sta Wag-8P	3917	4505	4,617
4600	4635	Sta Wag-6P	3836	4471	9,131

INVICTA ENGINE

Specifications were the same as the LeSabre Series 4400 except brake horsepower was 325 and four-barrel carburetor was used.

1962 Buick, Electra 225 2-door hardtop sport coupe, V-8 (AA)

ELECTRA 225 — SERIES 4800 — The big Buick for 1962 carried four ventiports per front fender and featured a rakish, sculptured restyle of its 1961 guise. The hardtop coupe and new Model 4839 hardtop sedan featured convertible-inspired semi-formal roof lines, while the Model 4829 Riviera sedan continued to use a six-window pillarless configuration. Electra 225 rear fenders had a group of vertical 'hash marks' with Electra 225 spelled out in block letters just above. A full-length bright strip crowned the upper body ridge, while the lower rocker moldings and wheelhouses were accented with bright trim. Wheelcovers had a gold accent ring. Interiors were of the finest cloth and on the Convertible leather was used. Standard features, in addition to those found on the less expensive Buicks, included back-up lights, power steering, Glare-proof rear view mirror, power brakes, parking brake signal light, safety buzzer, courtesy lights, two-way power seats, power windows, dual speed wash/wipers, Super DeLuxe wheelcovers, Safety option group, custom padded cushions, Accessory Group options and custom moldings.

ELECTRA 225 I.D. NUMBERS: Serial numbers were distinguished by the use of the numeral '8' as the first symbol of the number. The rest of the number was coded as explained under the 1962 Special Series 4000 listing.

ELECTRA 225 SERIES

Series Number	Model Number	Body Type & Seating	Factory Price	Shipping Weight	Production Total
4800	4819	4-dr Sedan-6P	4051	4304	13,523
4800	4829	4-dr Riv Sed-6P	4448	4390	15,395
4800	4839	4-dr H.T. Sed-6P	4186	4309	16,734
4800	4847	2-dr H.T. Cpe-6P	4062	4235	8,922
4800	4867	Convertible-6P	4366	4396	7,894

ELECTRA ENGINE

Specifications were the same as those listed for the 1962 Invicta Series 4600.

CHASSIS FEATURES: Wheelbase: (Series 4000, 4100 and 4300) 112.1 inches; (Series 400 and 4600) 123 inches; (Series 4800) 126 inches. Overall length: (Series 4000, 4100 and 4300) 188.4 inches; (Series 4400 and 4600) 214.1 inches; (Series 4800) 220.1 inches; (Estate wagons) 213.6 inches. Front tread: (Series 4000, 4100 and 4300) 56 inches; (Series 4400, 4600 and 4800) 62.1 inches. Rear Tread: (Series 4000, 4100 and 4300) 56 inches; (Series 4400, 4600 and 4800) 61 inches. Tires: (Series 4000, 4100 and 4300) 6.50 x 13; (Series 4400 and 4600) 7.60 x 15; (Series 4800) 8.00 x 15.

POWERTRAIN OPTIONS: A three-speed manual transmission was standard on Series 4000, 4100 and 4300. Turbine drive was optional at $189. A four-speed was optional for V-8s at $200. The 190 horsepower Skylark V-8 was optional on the Special at $145 and on the Special DeLuxe at $39. A regular fuel V-8 was optional on the LeSabre Series 4400; it was the same basic 401 cubic inch engine with 9.0:1 compression ratio and 265 brake horsepower. The Wildcat 325 horsepower 401 cubic inch V-8 was optional on the LeSabre. Also available was a 280 horsepower 401 cubic inch engine. Turbine drive was standard on Series 4400, 4600 and 4800.

BUICK CONVENIENCE OPTIONS: Air conditioning ($430). Air conditioning modification ($24). PCV system ($5). Custom padded cushions as option ($23). Divided rear seat on station wagons ($38). Chrome door guards two-door/four-door ($5/9). Posi Traction ($48). Dual exhausts as option ($31). Tinted glass, all windows/windshield only ($43/29). Guide-Matic ($29). Luggage locker for station wagon ($22). Station wagon luggage rack ($100). Outside remote control rear view mirror ($12). Power brakes ($43). Power door locks ($70). Four-barrel Power-Pack ($22). Six-Way power seat ($97). Six/Two-Way power seat ($69). Four-Way power seat ($65) Four/Two-Way power seat ($37). Power steering ($108). Power trunk release ($10). Sonotone radio with manual/electric antennas ($90/116). Wonder Bar radio with manual/electric antennas ($127/153). Rear seat speaker ($17). Convertible buckets seats w/console ($229). Coupe bucket seats w/console ($296). Power bucket seat option ($129 extra). Twilight Sentinel ($29). Code 06 Accessory Group ($22). Safety Options Group (glare-proof mirror, backup lamps, parking brake warning signal, safety buzzer light, courtesy lights) $40.

BUICK SPECIAL CONVENIENCE OPTIONS: Air conditioning ($351). Code W1 185 horsepower engine — Series 4000 ($145)/Series 4100 ($39). Backup lights ($11). Padded dash ($13-26). Two-tone finish ($16). Power brakes ($43). Power steering ($86). Power windows ($102). Bucket seats Series 4000/4100 ($96/70). Turbine drive ($189). Four-speed manual transmission ($200). DeLuxe wheel covers ($15).

Historical footnotes: Not since 1956 had Buick built and sold as many cars as delivered in 1962. The company captured 6.1 percent of U.S. sales and the Special series gained 65 percent over the previous years. The new V-6 gave the Special a price edge in the growing domestic small car market. On standard cars the engines were moved four inches forward, decreasing the size of floor humps. Style Numbers 4645 and 4635 were called Estate Wagons. Style Number 4829 was known as the Riviera sedan.

1963 BUICK

1963 Buick, Special 2-door coupe, V-8 (AA)

SPECIAL — SERIES 4000 — An almost complete lack of brightwork on the body sides of a new, slightly larger and much more square-cut body shell was a 1963 Special hallmark. There were three bright metal ventiports on each front fender. A vertical bar grille was spread across the car's flat face. Special series script appeared high on the rear fender. Interiors were done in cloth and vinyl, except for the convertible, which had all vinyl upholstery.

SPECIAL I.D. NUMBERS: Serial numbers for cars equipped with the V-6 began with AJ( )501001. Serial numbers for cars equipped with the V-8 began with OJ( )501001. The first digit indicates the series and engine. The second symbol indicates the 1963 model year (J). The third symbol, indicated by ( ) is a numerical code indicating assembly plant. The last six symbols are the numerical sequence of assembly at the coded plant with series mixed in production.

SPECIAL SERIES 4000

Series Number	Model Number	Body Type & Seating	Factory Price	Shipping Weight	Production Total
4000	4019	4-dr Sedan-6P	2363	2696	21,733
4000	4027	2-dr Coupe-6P	2309	2661	21,866
4000	4067	Convertible-6P	2591	2768	8,082
4000	4045	4-dr Sta Wag-8P	2740	2903	2,415
4000	4035	4-dr Sta Wag-6P	2659	2866	5,867

SPECIAL SERIES 4000 ENGINES

V-6: Overhead valves. Cast iron block. Displacement: 198 cubic inches. Bore and stroke: 3.625 x 3.2 inches. Compression ratio: 8.8:1. Brake horsepower: 135 at 4600 R.P.M. Four main bearings. Hydraulic valve lifters. Two-barrel carburetor.
V-8: Overhead valves. Cast aluminum block. Displacement: 215 cubic inches. Bore and stroke: 3.5 x 2.8 inches. Compression ratio: 8.8:1. Brake horsepower: 155 at 4600 R.P.M. Five main bearings. Hydraulic lifters. Two-barrel carburetor.

SPECIAL DELUXE — SERIES 4100 — Exterior distinction for DeLuxe models came from a narrow, full-length body side molding. Otherwise the trim was identical to the base line, except on the interior where upholstery combinations were richer.

SPECIAL DELUXE SERIES 4100 I.D. NUMBERS: Serial numbers for cars equipped with the V-6 began with BJ( )501001. Serial numbers for cars equipped with the V-8 began with IJ( )501001. The number coded as explained under the 1963 Special Series 4000 listing.

SPECIAL DELUXE SERIES 4100

Series Number	Model Number	Body Type & Seating	Factory Price	Shipping Weight	Production Total
4100	4119	4-dr Sedan-6P	2592	2684	37,695
4100	4135	4-dr Sta Wag-6P	2889	2858	8,771

SPECIAL DELUXE SERIES 4100 ENGINES

See 1963 Buick Series 4000 engine data.

SKYLARK — SERIES 4300 — Full-length body side moldings graced the 1963 Skylark, which was further identified on the coupe by rear quarter roof pillar emblems. A Buick insignia was centered in the grille and another was found in the bright rear cove insert. All vinyl interior trim was standard in the convertible and optional in the coupe. Front bucket seats were optional.

SKYLARK SERIES 4300 I.D. NUMBERS: Serial numbers began with 3J(   )501001 and were otherwise coded as explained under the 1963 Special Series 4000 listing.

SKYLARK SERIES 4300

Series Number	Model Number	Body Type & Seating	Factory Price	Shipping Weight	Production Total
4300	4347	2-dr H.T. Cpe-5P	2757	2857	32,109
4300	4367	Convertible-5P	3011	2810	10,212

SKYLARK SERIES 4300 ENGINES
Powerplant specifications were the same as those listed for the 1963 Special Series 4000 V-8 except compression ratio was raised to 11:1 providing 200 horsepower at 5000 R.P.M. in combination with the use of a four-barrel carburetor.

LESABRE — SERIES 4400 — A revised styling theme was featured for 1963 with vertical taillights capping the rear fenders. A new stamped grille was seen up front. Side trim was minimal, with a narrow bright strip running horizontally along the rear body and triple ventiports on each front fender. The word LeSabre was spelled out in script on the rear fenders. Standard features included directional signals, electric windshield wipers, cigar lighter, Step-On parking brake and dual arm rests and carpeting. Bayonne cloth with vinyl bolsters was used for the interior, except for the convertible which was trimmed in all vinyl. LeSabre I.D. was found on the glovebox door. Station wagons had all vinyl trim and full carpeting.

LESABRE SERIES 4400 I.D. NUMBERS: Serial numbers began with 4J(   )001001. The number was coded as explained under the 1963 Special Series 4000 listing.

LESABRE SERIES 4400

Series Number	Model Number	Body Type & Seating	Factory Price	Shipping Weight	Production Total
4400	4469	4-dr Sedan-6P	3004	3970	64,995
4400	4439	2-dr H.T. Sed-6P	3146	4007	50,420
4400	4411	2-dr Sedan-6P	2869	3905	8,328
4400	4447	2-dr Spt Cpe-6P	3070	3924	27,977
4400	4467	Convertible-6P	3339	4052	9,975
4400	4445	4-dr Sta Wag-8P	3606	4340	3,922
4400	4435	4-dr Sta Wag-6P	3526	4320	5,566

LESABRE SERIES 4400 ENGINE
V-8: Overhead valves. Cast iron block. Displacement: 401 cubic inches. Bore and stroke: 4.1875 x 3.64 inches. Compression ratio: 10.25:1. Brake horsepower 280 at 4400 R.P.M. Five main bearings. Hydraulic valve lifters. Carburetor: Two-barrel.

WILDCAT — SERIES 4600 — A plusher, more sporting Buick line for 1963 grew from success of the 1962 Wildcat Sport Coupe. Standard Wildcat features for 1963 included an electric clock, DeLuxe steering wheel, trunk light, license frames, padded instrument panel, foam-rubber headliner, tachometer (except on hardtops with bench seats), bucket seats (optional on four-door hardtop, standard other models), and a center console. Wildcat script was found on rear fenders and within the rear cove, while the name was lettered across the hood. A brushed finish bright insert began on the front fenders and contained the three ventiports on each fender. Bright wheelhouse and rocker moldings were used. A special grille, with distinct horizontal heavy bars and a center emblem, further distinguished the Wildcat. Sport coupes had roof rear quarter emblems with the Wildcat logo, while the same badge was placed on the rear flanks of convertibles. Bucket-seat interiors were all-vinyl. Specific full wheel covers were used.
NOTE: Also in the 4600 series was the Invicta Estate Wagon, Model 4635. This station wagon had a plusher interior than the 4400 wagons and was available in two seat form only. A full-length narrow body side molding was used, along with bright wheelhouse and rocker moldings and chromed roof bars. All standard Wildcat features were included.

WILDCAT AND INVICTA — SERIES 4600 — I.D. NUMBERS: Serial numbers began with 6J(   )001001. The number was coded as explained under the 1963 Special Series 4000 listing.

WILDCAT/INVICTA SERIES 4600

Series Number	Model Number	Body Type & Seating	Factory Price	Shipping Weight	Production Total
4600	4639	4-dr H.T. Cpe-6P	3871	4222	17,519
4600	4647	2 dr Sport Cpe-6P	3849	4123	12,185
4600	4667	Convertible-6P	3961	4228	6,021
4600	4635	4-dr Sta Wag-6P	3969	3897	3,495

WILDCAT SERIES 4600 ENGINE
Specifications were the same as those listed for the 1963 LeSabre Series 4400, except compression ratio was 10.25:1. Brake horsepower was 325 at 4400 R.P.M. and a four-barrel carburetor was used.

1963 Buick, Electra 225 4-door hardtop sedan, V-8

ELECTRA 225 — SERIES 4800 — Buick's largest, plushest and most expensive models were redesigned for 1963, with distinctive rear fenders cumulating in a sharp vertical edge housing narrow backup lights. The taillights were horizontally placed in the vertical deck cove. A unique cast grille was used at the front. Bright wheelhouse and lower body moldings, with ribbed rear fender panels, were used. Red-filled Electra 225 badges were found on the rear fenders, while four Ventiports lent status to the front units. Interiors were cloth and vinyl combinations, while a Custom interior in vinyl and leather, with front bucket seats and a storage console, was available for the convertible and sport coupe. Standard equipment, in addition to items found on lower-priced Buicks, included power steering; power brakes; back-up lights; power brake signal light; map light; safety buzzer; Custom padded seat cushions; Super DeLuxe wheel covers; power windows and two-way seat adjustment on the convertibles (these two features were included with the Custom interior on closed models).

ELECTRA 225 SERIES I.D. NUMBERS: Serial numbers began with 8J(   )1001001. The number was coded as explained under the 1963 Special Series 4000 listings.

ELECTRA 225 SERIES 4800

Series Number	Model Number	Body Type & Seating	Factory Price	Shipping Weight	Production Total
4800	4819	4-dr Sedan-6P	4051	4241	14,628
4800	4829	4-dr H.T. Sed-6P	4254	4284	11,468
4800	4839	H.T. Sed-6P	4186	4272	19,714
4800	4847	2-dr Spt Cpe-6P	4062	4153	6,848
4800	4867	Convertible-6P	4365	4297	6,367

ELECTRA 225 SERIES 4800 ENGINE
Specifications were the same as those listed for the 1963 LeSabre Series 4400 except compression ratio was 10.25:1, brake horsepower was 325 at 4400 R.P.M. and a four-barrel carburetor was used.

RIVIERA — SERIES 4700 — A new sports/luxury model for 1963, issued only in a stunning sport coupe body style. From the front fenders, whose leading edges were vertical grilles, to the razor-edged rear contours, the Riviera looked both elegant and fast. A car for Buick's most affluent customers, the Riviera was delivered with a host of standard features, including two-speed wipers with washers; back-up lights; Glare-proof inside mirror; parking brake signal light; safety buzzer; Riviera wheel covers; electric clock; license frame; padded instrument panel; trip mileage odometer; smoking set; front and rear bucket seats; courtesy lamps; deep-pile carpet; foam-padded seat cushions: center console; heater and defroster; and frameless side windows.

RIVIERA SERIES 4700 I.D. NUMBERS: Serial numbers began with 7J(   )001001. The number was coded as explained under the 1963 Special — Series 4000 listing.

RIVIERA SERIES 4700

Series Number	Model Number	Body Type & Seating	Factory Price	Shipping Weight	Production Total
4700	4747	Sport Cpe-4P	4333	3998	40,000

RIVIERA SERIES 4700 ENGINE
Specifications were the same as listed for the 1963 Electra 225 Series 4800.

CHASSIS FEATURES: Wheelbase: (Series 4000, 4100 and 4300) 112.1 inches; (Series 4400 and 4600) 123 inches; (Series 4800) 126 inches; (Series 4700) 117 inches. Overall length: (Series 4000, 4100 and 4300) 192.1 inches; (Series 4400 and 4600) 215.7 inches; (Series 4800) 221.7 inches; (Series 4700) 208 inches. Front tread: (Series 4000, 4100 and 4300) 56 inches; (Series 4400, 4600, 4800 and 4700) 62 inches. Rear tread: (Series 4000, 4100 and 4300) 56 inches; (Series 4400, 4600, 4800 and 4700) 61 inches. Tires: (Series 4000, 4100 and 4300) 6.50 x 13; (Series 4400 and 4600) 7.60 x 15; (Series 4800) 8.00 x 15; (Series 4700) 7.10 x 15.

POWERTRAIN OPTIONS: A three-speed manual transmission was standard on Series 4000, 4100, 4300, 4400 and 4600. Turbine drive was standard on Series 4800 and 4700 and optional on other Series at $231. A four-speed manual transmission was optional on Series 4300 , 4400 and 4600 models at $200-$263. The Series 4300 200-hp V-8 was optional on Series 4000 and 4100 models. A 9.0:1 compression 265 horsepower regular fuel engine was a no-cost option in all Series 4400 models. A 425 cubic inch, 340 brake horsepower V-8 was optional on Series 4700. Positive traction differental optional on all models.

CONVENIENCE OPTIONS: Power steering (standard on Series 4800, 4700). Power brakes (standard on Series 4700 and 4800). Air conditioning. Cruise control on Model 4747. Wire wheel covers. Cloth/vinyl or leather/vinyl trim on Model 4747. Seven-position tilt steering wheel on Series 4400, 4600, 4800. Electro-Cruise. Cornering lights. Power door locks. Auto trunk release. Seat belts. Sonomatic radio. Wonderbar radio. Rear seat speaker. Soft-Ray glass. Rear window defroster. Chrome door guards. Remote control outside rear view mirror. Whitewall tires. Power windows (standard on Electra 225 Convertible and Custom interior). Guide-Matic dimmer. Twilight Sentinel. Gas door guard. Compass. Litter basket. Tissue dispenser. Seat covers. Spotlite. Carpet covers. Carpet savers. Trunk mat. Ski rack. Heater/Defroster delete. Divided rear-seat, luggage rack and luggage locker for Station Wagons.

Historical footnotes: Models 4445, 4435 and 4635 are Estate Wagons.

1964 BUICK

SPECIAL SERIES 4000 V-6 AND V-8 — A new, larger and more flowing body was used for the 1964 Special, now classed as an 'intermediate' in the GM family. Except for the Special script on rear fenders and trio of ventiports on front fenders, the Special was devoid of bright ornamentation. Interiors were in 'Brigade' cloth. Standard features included electric windshield wipers, ash trays, directional signals, Step-On parking brake, dome lights and, on the Convertible only, carpeting.

SPECIAL SERIES 4000 I.D. NUMBERS: Serial numbers for cars equipped with the V-6 began with AK(   )001001. Serial numbers for cars equipped with the V-8 began with OK(   )001001. The first digit represents the series and engine. The second symbol, the letter K, indicates the 1964 model year. The third symbol, indicated by (   ) is a numeral representing the plant code. The last six symbols are the numerical sequence of assembly at the coded plant, with Series mixed in production.

SPECIAL SERIES 4000

Series Number	Model Number	Body Type & Seating	Factory Price	Shipping Weight	Production Total
4000	4069	4-dr Sedan-6P	2397	3000	17,983
4000	4027	2-dr Coupe-6P	2343	2983	15,030
4000	4067	Convertible-6P	2605	3099	6,308
4000	4035	4-dr Sta Wag-6P	2689	3258	6,270

NOTE: The V-8 line was considered a sub-series, not an option. Factory prices were $71 higher for V-8s than the prices listed above for the V-6. Shipping weights were 16 pounds heavier for the V-8 than those listed above for the V-6. Production figures include both V-6 and V-8.

SPECIAL SERIES 4000 FEATURES: V-6: Cast iron block. Displacement: 225 cubic inches. Bore and stroke: 3.75 x 3.4 inches. Compression ratio: 9.0:1. Brake horsepower: 155 at 4200 R.P.M. Four main bearings. Hydraulic lifters. Two-barrel carburetor.
V-8: Cast iron block. Displacement: 300 cubic inches. Bore and stroke: 3.75 x 3.4 inches. Compression ratio: 9.0:1. Brake horsepower: 210 at 4600 R.P.M. Five main bearings. Hydraulic lifters. Two-barrel carburetor.

1964 Buick, Special DeLuxe 4-dr sedan, V-8

SPECIAL DELUXE — SERIES 4100 — V-6 AND V-8 — A narrow bright bodyside molding swept the full length of the Special DeLuxe models, which were plusher inside. There was carpeting, cloth and vinyl combinations over foam-padded seats, and a padded instrument panel. Other line features were a DeLuxe steering wheel, dual armrests, dual horns and additional dome lights.

SPECIAL DELUXE SERIES 4100 I.D. NUMBERS: Serial numbers for cars equipped with the V-6 began with BK( )001001. Serial numbers for cars equipped with the V-8 began with 1K( )001001. The numbers were coded as explained under the 1964 Special Series 4000 listing.

SPECIAL DELXE SERIES 4100

Series Number	Model Number	Body Type & Seating	Factory Price	Shipping Weight	Production Total
4100	4169	4-dr Sedan-6P	2490	3018	31,742
4100	4127	2-dr Coupe-6P	2457	2998	11,962
4100	4135	4-dr Sta Wag-6P	2787	3277	9,467

NOTE: Cars equipped with V-8s listed for $71 more than the V-6 prices given above and they weighed 16 pounds more than the weights given for the V-6. Production totals include both V-6 and V-8s.

SPECIAL DELUXE SERIES 4100 ENGINES
Specifications were the same as those listed for the 1964 Special Series 4000.

SPORT WAGONS — SERIES 4200 AND 4300 — A new, long-wheelbase station wagon debuted for 1964. Offered in two stages of trim, the wagons were numbered in 4200 and 4300 (Skylark) series. Both Standard and Custom models had tinted transparent panels above the rear passenger compartment. The Custom models were trimmed like the Skylarks in the 4300 Series (see Skylark Series 4300). Interiors were all-vinyl.

SPORT WAGON I.D. NUMBERS: Serial numbers correspond to the numbers used for the Series 4100 and 4300 cars.

SERIES 4200/4300 SPORT WAGONS

Series Number	Model Number	Body Type & Seating	Factory Price	Shipping Weight	Production Total
4200	4265	4-dr Sta Wag-3S	3124	3689	2,586
4200	4255	4-dr Sta Wag-2S	2989	3557	2,709
4300	4365	4-dr Sta Wag-3S	3286	3727	4,446
4300	4355	4-dr Sta Wag-2S	3161	3595	3,913

SERIES 4200/4300 SPORT WAGON ENGINE
Specifications were the same as those listed for the 1964 Special Series 4000 V-8.

SKYLARK — SERIES 4300 — Buick's plushest version of their sporty intermediate had considerably more pizzaz this year with its new body and flashier trim. The Skylark emblem and signature was found on roof quarters (rear fenders on the convertible), while Skylark script was on the deck. A round Buick emblem dominated the grille. Another round emblem was housed in the deck cove, which was finished with a brushed metallic insert. Bright rocker moldings and a wider bright body side molding, with a brushed metallic insert, gave further distinction. Sport Coupes had twin bright strips on the roof. Standard features, in addition to those found on Special and Special DeLuxe models, include instrument panel safety padding, paddle-type armrests, Skylark steering wheel, Skylark wheel covers and full carpeting. An all-vinyl interior with bucket seats was standard for the Convertible and optional for the Sport Coupe. The sedan came in a cloth and vinyl combination with all-vinyl available as a substitution.

SKYLARK I.D. NUMBERS: Serial numbers began with CK( )001001 on cars equipped with the V-6. Serial numbers began with 3K( )001001 on cars equipped with the V-8. The number was coded as explained under the 1964 Special Series 4000 listing.

SKYLARK SERIES 4300

Series Number	Model Number	Body Type & Seating	Factory Price	Shipping Weight	Production Total
4300	4369	4-dr Sedan-6P	2669	3062	19,635
4300	4347	Sport Coupe-6P	2680	3049	42,356
4300	4367	Convertible-5P	2834	3169	10,255

NOTE: Cars equipped with V-8s listed for $71 more than the V-6 prices given above and they weighed 6 pounds more than the weights given for the V-6s. Production figures combine V-6 and V-8 production.

SKYLARK SERIES 4300 ENGINES
Specifications were the same as those listed for the 1964 Special Series 4000.

LASABRE — SERIES 4400 — Refined body sculpturing, with fresh frontal and rear treatments, set the 1964 LeSabre apart. A unique stamped grille was used. A narrow bright bodyside molding was found on the rear one-third of the body, with the Series signature residing near the fender end. Standard LeSabre features included electric windshield wipers; Step-On parking brake; padded instrument panel; directional signals; front and rear armrests; dual sunshades; smoking set; courtesy lights; dual horns and cloth upholstery. Cloth and vinyl trim was standard. The Convertible was trimmed in all-vinyl, with front bucket seats optional. A Custom trim package option included full-length bright body side moldings with a brushed metallic insert.

LESABRE SERIES 4400 I.D. NUMBERS: Serial numbers began with 4K( )001001. The numbers were coded as explained under the 1964 Special Series 4000 listing.

LESABRE SERIES 4400

Series Number	Model Number	Body Type & Seating	Factory Price	Shipping Weight	Production Total
4400	4469	4-dr Sedan-6P	2980	3693	56,729
4400	4439	4-dr H.T. Sed-6P	3122	3730	37,052
4400	4447	2-dr Spt Cpe-6P	3061	3629	24,177
4400	4467	Convertible-6P	3314	3787	6,685

LESABRE SERIES 4400 ENGINES
Specifications were the same as those listed for the Special Series 4000 V-8.

LESABRE — SERIES 4600 — Two hybrid station wagons made up this curious series. They were trimmed as LeSabres, but had Wildcat chassis and power. Leather grain vinyl or vinyl and cloth (two-seater only) were trim choices. A power tailgate window was standard.

LESABRE SERIES 4600 I.D. NUMBERS: Serial numbers began with 4KC( )001001. The numbers were coded as explained under the 1964 Special Series 4000 listing.

LESABRE SERIES 4600

Series Number	Model Number	Body Type & Seating	Factory Price	Shipping Weight	Production Total
4600	4645	4-dr Sta Wag-3S	3635	4362	4,003
4600	4635	4-dr Sta Wag-2S	3554	4352	6,517

LESABRE SERIES 4600 ENGINE
Specifications were the same as those listed for the Wildcat Series 4600.

WILDCAT — SERIES 4600 — Sportier and plusher, the 1964 Wildcat was liberally trimmed with bright work, including a ribbed, wide lower body molding; a trio of stacked, streamlined ventiports behind each front wheelhouse; a unique grille with heavy horizontal wing bars and a center emblem. There was Wildcat lettering on the deck lid and another emblem centered within the deck cove, which had a bright metallic insert with bright horizontal stripes. Wildcat badges appeared on roof quarters (except on the convertible, which had them on the fenders) and within the full wheel covers. Standard and Custom trim choices were available, including bucket seats and a console. Carpeting was standard, in addition to all the features found on the LeSabre.

WILDCAT SERIES 4600 I.D. NUMBERS: Serial numbers began with 6K( )001001. The number was coded as explained under the 1964 Special Series 4000 listing.

WILDCAT SERIES 4600

Series Number	Model Number	Body Type & Seating	Factory Price	Shipping Weight	Production Total
4600	4669	4-dr Sedan-6P	3164	4021	20,144
4600	4639	2-dr H.T.-6P	3327	4058	33,358
4600	4647	2-dr Spt Cpe-6P	3267	4003	22,893
4600	4667	Convertible-6P	3455	4076	7,850

WILDCAT SERIES 4600 ENGINE
V-8: Overhead valves. Cast iron block. Displacement: 401 cubic inches. Bore and stroke: 4.18 x 3.64. Compression ratio: 10.25:1. Brake horsepower: 325 at 4400 R.P.M. Five main bearings. Hydraulic lifters. Four-barrel carburetor.

1964 Buick, Electra 225 2-dr hardtop, V-8

ELECTRA 225 — SERIES 4800 — The large GM C-Body was used to create the Electra 225, Buick's richest full-size car. Vertical, narrow taillamps were found in the nearly straight-cut rear fender ends, and the E-225 came the fender skirts. Four traditional ventiports were found on the front fenders, with a heavy die-cast grille accenting the frontal aspect. Wide full length lower body moldings were used along with a bright deck cove insert. Electra 225 lettering was found on rear fenders and specific full wheel-covers were featured. Vinyl and brocade cloth interior trims were found in closed models, while leather upholstery was offered for seats in the Convertible. Among the Electra's exclusive standard equipment were power steering; power brakes; two-speed electric wipers with windshield washer; foam-padded seats; electric clock; license frame; trunk light; two-way power seat and power windows for the convertible; a Safety buzzer; and additional courtesy lights.

ELECTRA 225 SERIES 4800 I.D. NUMBERS: Serial numbers began with 8K( )001001. The numbers were coded as explained under the 1964 Special Series 4000 listing.

ELECTRA 225 SERIES 4800

Series Number	Model Number	Body Type & Seating	Factory Price	Shipping Weight	Production Total
4800	4819	4-dr Sedan-6P	4059	4212	15,968
4800	4829	Pillarless Sed	4261	4238	11,663
4800	4839	4-dr H.T. Sed-6P	4194	4229	24,935
4800	4847	2-dr Spt Cpe-6P	4070	4149	9,045
4800	4867	Convertible-6P	4374	4280	7,181

ELECTRA 225 SERIES 4800 ENGINE
Specifications were the same as those listed for the 1964 Wildcat Series 4600.

RIVIERA — SERIES 4700 — The 1963 Riviera was immediately recognized as a classic design and Buick saw little need for change in 1964. A new, stand-up hood ornament and revised Riviera scripts on the front fenders and right hand deck were the major changes. The simulated rear fender cooling vents were outlined in bright metal and a thin, bright highlight line continued to follow the body side crease, jumping over the wheelhouse in passing. The beautiful, twin grill with egg crate center grille frontal ensemble continued without alteration. The stylized letter 'R' appeared in wheel cover centers. Standard features were similar to those listed for the Electra 225, but also included deep-pile carpeting, foam-padded front and rear bucket seats and a center console with transmission selector lever. Interiors were trimmed in vinyl with wood accents.

1964 Buick, Riviera 2-dr hardtop sport coupe, V-8

RIVIERA SERIES 4700 I.D. NUMBERS: Serial numbers began with 7K( )001001. The numbers were coded as explained under the 1964 Special Series 4000 listing.

RIVIERA SERIES 4700

Series Number	Model Number	Body Type & Seating	Factory Price	Shipping Weight	Production Total
4700	4747	H.T. Coupe	4385	3951	37,958

RIVIERA ENGINE

V-8: Overhead valve. Cast iron block. Displacement: 425 cubic inches. Bore and stroke: 4.3125 x 3.64 inches. Compression ratio: 10.25 to 1. Brake horsepower: 340 at 4400 R.P.M. Five main bearings. Hydraulic lifters. Four-barrel carburetor.

CHASSIS FEATURES: Wheelbase (Series 4000, 4100, 4200, 4300) — 115 inches; (Series 4300 wagon) 120 inches; (Series 4400 and 4600) 123 inches; Series (4800) 126 inches; (Series 4700) 117 inches. Overall length: (Series 4000, 4100, 4200 and 4300) 203.5 inches; (Series 4400 and 4600) 218.5 inches; (Series 4800); (Series 4700) 208 inches. Front tread: (Series 4000, 4100, 4300, and 4200) 58 inches; (Series 4400, 4600 and 4800) 62.1 inches; (Series 4700) 60 inches. Rear tread: (Series 4000, 4100 and 4300) 58 inches; (Series 4400, 4600 and 4800) 61 inches; (Series 4700) 59 inches. Tires: (Series 4000, 41000 and 4300) 6.50 x 14; (Series 4200 wagon) 7.00 x 14; (Series 4300 wagons) 7.50 x 14; (Series 4400 and 4700) 7.10 x 15; (Series 4600) 7.60 x 15; (Series 4800) 8.00 x 15.

POWERTRAIN OPTIONS: A three-speed manual transmission was standard on Series 4000, 4100, 4200, 4300, 4400 and 4600. Turbine 300 automatic was optional on Series 4000, 4100, 4200, 4300, 4400 and 4600. Turbine 400 was optional on Series 4600, standard on Series 4700 and 4800. A four-speed manual transmission was optional for Series 4000, 4100, 4300, 4400 and 4600. A 250 brake horsepower 300 cubic inch V-8 was optional for Series 4000, 4100, 4200, 43 and 4400. The 340 brake horsepower, 425 cubic inch V-8 was optional for Series 4600, 4800 and 4600 Estate wagons. A 360 brake horsepower, 425 cubic inch V-8 was optional for Series 4600, 4700, and 3800.

CONVENIENCE OPTIONS: Power brakes (standard 4700 and 4800). Power steering (standard 4700 and 4800). Power windows (not available Special station wagon). Power seat control. Air conditioning. Seven-position tilt steering wheel. Carpeting (4000 Series). Bucket seats with console and storage bin on 4600. 'Formula Five' chromed steel wheel. Whitewall tires. Custom fabric roof cover. Bucket seats in Electra 225 convertible. AM radio on 4400, 4100 and 4300. Sonomatic radio. Wonder Bar radio. AM-FM radio on 4400, 4600, 4700 and 4800. Seat belts. Remote control inside rear view mirror. Electro-cruise. Cornering lights. Power door locks. Automatic trunk release. Rear seat speaker. Rear window defroster. Guide-Matic headlight dimmer. Compass. Litter basket. Tissue dispenser. Ski rack. Luggage rack for Estate Wagons. Heater-defroster deletion. Note: Power windows standard on Electra 225 convertible.

Historical footnotes: Models 4645 and 4635 are called Estate Wagons.

1965 BUICK

SPECIAL — SERIES 43300 (V-6) — A very slighty face-lifted car of intermediate size was marketed by Buick under the Special name for 1965. Still largely devoid of side trim, the Special did have its name in script on the rear flanks and had a trio of ventiports on each front fender. A Buick emblem was found at the rear, while the front horizontal grille bars were bare. Interiors were of cloth and vinyl. Standard equipment included electric windshield wipers, directional signals, dual sunshades, ash tray/lighter set, dual arm rests on sedans, courtesy lights, Step-On parking brake and carpeting in the convertible.

SPECIAL V-6 I.D. NUMBERS: Serial numbers began with 433005( )100001. The first five symbols were numerals representing the style. The sixth symbol was a numeral '5', representing the 1965 model year. The seventh symbol was a letter representing the plant code and the last six symbols were numerals representing the plant sequential production number, with series mixed in production.

SPECIAL SERIES 43300

Series Number	Model Number	Body Type & Seating	Factory Price	Shipping Weight	Production Total
43300	43369	4-dr Sedan-6P	2345	3010	12,945
43300	43327	2-dr Coupe-6P	2292	2977	13,828
43300	43367	Convertible-6P	2549	3087	3,357
43300	43335	4-dr Sta Wag-6P	2631	3258	2,868

SPECIAL V-6 ENGINE

V-6: Overhead valve. Cast-iron block. Displacement: 225 cubic inches. Bore and stroke: 3.75 by 3.4 inches. Compression ratio: 9.0:1. Brake horsepower: 155 at 4200 R.P.M. Four main bearings. Hydraulic valve lifters. Two-barrel carburetor.

SPECIAL SERIES 43400 (V-8) — Identical externally to the 1965 V-6 Special described above, the V-8 Specials were numbered as a separate series.

SPECIAL I.D. NUMBERS: Serial numbers began with 434005( )100001. The numbers were coded as explained under the 1965 Special Series 43300 listing.

SPECIAL SERIES 43400

Series Number	Model Number	Body Type & Seating	Factory Price	Shipping Weight	Production Total
43400	43469	4-dr Sedan-6P	2415	3117	5,309
43400	43427	2-dr Coupe-6P	2362	3080	8,121
43400	43467	Convertible-6P	2618	3197	3,365
43400	43435	4-dr Sta Wag-6P	2699	3365	3,676

SPECIAL V-8 ENGINE

V-8: Overhead valve. Cast-iron block. Displacement: 300 cubic inches. Bore and stroke: 3.75 x 3.4 inches. Compression ratio: 9.0:1. Brake horsepower: 210 at 4600 R.P.M. Five main bearings. Hydraulic valve lifters. Two-barrel carburetor.

SPECIAL DELUXE — SERIES 43500 (V-6) — A Special with a little more dressing, the Special DeLuxe had a bright body side moldings, bright window surrounds and a rear cove insert panel. Interiors were plusher vinyls with some cloth combinations. Floors were carpeted and the instrument panel was padded. Dual horns added to the standard equipment list.

SPECIAL DELUXE V-6 I.D. NUMBERS: Serial numbers began with 43500( )100001. The numbers were coded as explained under the 1965 Special Series 43300 listing.

SPECIAL DELUXE SERIES 43500 (V-6)

Series Number	Model Number	Body Type & Seating	Factory Price	Shipping Weight	Production Total
43500	43569	4-dr Sedan-6P	2436	3016	10,961
43500	43535	4-dr Sta Wag-6P	2727	3242	1,677

SPECIAL DELUXE V-6 ENGINE

Specifications were the same as those listed for the 1965 Special Series 43300.

SPECIAL DELUXE — SERIES 43600 (V-8) — Identical externally to the 1965 Special DeLuxe V-6 described above, the V-8 Special DeLuxes were numbered as a separate series.

SPECIAL DELUXE I.D. NUMBERS: Serial numbers began with 43600( )10001. The numbers were coded as explained under the 1965 Special Series 43300 listing.

SPECIAL DELUXE SERIES 43600 (V-8)

Series Number	Model Number	Body Type & Seating	Factory Price	Shipping Weight	Production Total
43600	43669	4-dr Sedan-6P	2506	3143	25,675
43600	43635	4-dr Sta Wag-6P	2796	3369	9,123

SPECIAL DELUXE V-8 ENGINE

Specifications were the same as those listed for the 1965 Special V-8 Series 43400.

SKYLARK — SERIES 44300 (V-6) — Buick's intermediate in its plushest form. Specific full wheel covers, bright rocker and wheelhouse moldings, a unique cove treatment with full-width taillamps and emblems centered front and rear signified Skylark-level trim on the outside. The Skylark badge appeared on front fenders, deck lid and roof quarters (rear fenders on convertible). Interiors were plusher cloth and vinyl, or leather-grain all-vinyl. Front buckets were optional. Standard equipment on Skylark in addition to that found on lesser series included: foam-padded seats, paddle-type arm rests, rear passenger courtesy lights on two doors, ash tray, glove compartment lights and full carpeting.

NOTE: A mid-1965 option was the Skylark Gran Sport, an option package offered on the two-door coupe, sport coupe and convertible. A 325 brake horsepower, 401 cubic inch V-8 was the heart of the option. Exterior identification was provided by red-filled Gran sport badges on the grille, deck and roof quarters (rear fenders on convertibles). Another badge was affixed to the instrument panel.

SKYLARK V-6 I.D. NUMBERS: Serial numbers began with 443005( )100001. The numbers were coded as explained under the 1965 Special Series 43300 listing.

SKYLARK SERIES 44300 (V-6)

Series Number	Model Number	Body Type & Seating	Factory Price	Shipping Weight	Production Total
44300	44369	4-dr Sedan-6P	2611	3086	3,385
44300	44327	2-dr Coupe-6P	2482	3035	4,195
44300	44337	2-dr Spt Cpe-6P	2622	3067	4,501
44300	44367	Convertible-6P	2773	3149	1,181

SKYLARK V-6 ENGINE

Specifications were the same as those listed for the 1965 Special Series 43300 V-6.

SKYLARK V-8 SERIES 44400 — Externally identical to the 1965 Skylark V-6 described above, the V-8 Skylarks were numbered as a separate series.

SKYLARK V-8 I.D. NUMBERS: Serial numbers began with 44405( )100001. Numbers were coded as explained under the 1965 Special Series 43300 listing.

SKYLARK SERIES 44400 (V-8)

Series Number	Model Number	Body Type & Seating	Factory Price	Shipping Weight	Production Total
44400	44469	4-dr Sedan-6P	2681	3194	22,239
44400	44427	2-dr Coupe-6P	2552	3146	11,877
44400	44437	2-dr Spt Cpe-6P	2692	3198	46,698
44400	44467	Convertible-6P	2842	3294	10,456

SKYLARK V-8 ENGINE

Specifications were the same as those listed for the 1965 Special V-8 Series 43400.

1965 Buick, Skylark 4-door Sport Wagon, V-8

SPORTWAGON: Buick's stretched wheelbase station wagon continued to feature the unusual Skyroof with shaded glass panels in a raised area above the rear compartment. The increased headroom allowed a three-seat version to be marketed. Cargo area was 95.6 cubic feet. Interiors were all-vinyl. Models 44465 and 44455 were Custom models and featured most Skylark equipment, but had only a full-length bright metal side molding. A tailgate lamp was also standard.

SPORT WAGON I.D. NUMBERS: Serial numbers began with the model number (sample: 44265(   )10001) and were coded as explained under the 1965 Special Series 43300 listing.

SPORT WAGON SERIES 44200/44400

Series Number	Model Number	Body Type & Seating	Factory Price	Shipping Weight	Production Total
44200	44265	4-dr Sta Wag-9P	3056	3750	4,664
44200	44255	4-dr Sta Wag-6P	2925	3642	4,226
44400	44465	4-dr Sta Wag-9P	3214	3802	11,166
44400	44455	4-dr Sta Wag-9P	3092	3690	8,300

SPORT WAGON ENGINE
Specifications were the same as those listed for the 1965 Special Series 43400 V-8.

LESABRE — SERIES 45200 — Buick's full-sized price leaders featured a new body with a wider appearance and softer, bulgy lines. A bright narrow lower body molding was used, along with a trio of ventiports on each front fender. The LeSabre signature appeared on rear body quarters. An extruded aluminum grille was used at the front. Standard equipment included electric windshield wipers; instrument panel safety pad directional signals; glove compartment light; dual arm rests front and rear; door-operated courtesy lights; full carpeting and a map light. Interiors were cloth or vinyl.

LESABRE I.D. NUMBERS: Serial numbers began with 452005(   )10001. Numbers were coded as explained under the 1965 Special Series 43300 listing.

LESABRE SERIES 45200

Series Number	Model Number	Body Type & Seating	Factory Price	Shipping Weight	Production Total
45200	45269	4-dr Sedan-6P	2888	3788	37,788
45200	45239	4-dr H.T. Sed-6P	3027	3809	18,384
45200	45237	2-dr Spt Cpe-6P	2968	3753	15,786

LESABRE ENGINES
Specifications were the same as those listed for the 1965 Special Series 43400 V-8.

LESABRE CUSTOM — SERIES 45400 — Custom interior fabrics of cloth and vinyl set the Custom Series apart. The convertible had a standard outside rear view mirror. Exterior trim was like the LeSabre Series 45200.

LESABRE CUSTOM — SERIES 45400 I.D. NUMBERS: Serial numbers began with 454005(   )10001. Numbers were coded as explained under the 1965 Special Series 43300 listing.

LESABRE CUSTOM SERIES 45400

Series Number	Model Number	Body Type & Seating	Factory Price	Shipping Weight	Production Total
45400	45469	4-dr Sedan-6P	2962	3777	20,052
45400	45439	4-dr H.T. Sed-6P	3101	3811	23,394
45400	45237	2-dr Spt Cpe-6P	3037	3742	21,049
45400		Convertible-5P	3257	3812	6,543

LESABRE CUSTOM ENGINES
Specifications were the the same as those listed for the 1965 Special Series 43300V-8.

WILDCAT — SERIES 46200 — Buick's medium-priced line, still equipped for superior performance, shared the LeSabre's new 1965 body, but was distinguished by a die-cast grille having a large center emblem, large simulated bright front fender vents and Wildcat script on the quarter panels and deck. Inside, Wildcat emblems appeared on door panels. The full wheel covers also used the Wildcat emblem. Standard equipment, in addition to that found on the LeSabre, included a smoking set and rear seat ash trays. Interiors were cloth or vinyl.

WILDCAT I.D. NUMBERS: Serial numbers began with 462005(   )10001. Numbers were coded. as explained under the 1965 Special Series 43300 listing.

WILDCAT SERIES 46200

Series Number	Model Number	Body Type & Seating	Factory Price	Shipping Weight	Production Total
46200	42269	4-dr Sedan-6P	3117	3788	10,184
46200	46239	4-dr H.T. Sed-6P	3278	3809	7,499
46200	46237	2-dr Spt Cpe-6P	3219	3753	6,031
46200	46267	Convertible-6P	3431	3812	4,616*

NOTE: The symbol (*) indicates that convertible production total also includes Wildcat DeLuxe convertibles.

WILDCAT ENGINE
V-8: Overhead valve. Cast iron block. Displacement: 401 cubic inches. Bore and stroke: 4.18x 3.64 inches. Compression ratio: 10.25:1. Brake horsepower: 325 at 4600 R.P.M. Five main bearings. Hydraulic lifters. Four-barrel carburetor.

WILDCAT DELUXE — SERIES 46400 — This was a trim variation on the Wildcat Series 46200, with slightly plusher interior combinations available.

WILDCAT DELUXE SERIES 46400 I.D. NUMBERS: Serial numbers began with 464005(   )10001. Numbers were coded as explained under the 1965 Special Series 43300 listing.

WILDCAT DELUXE SERIES 46400

Series Number	Model Number	Body Type & Seating	Factory Price	Shipping Weight	Production Total
46400	46469	4-dr Sedan-6P	3218	3777	9,765
46400	46439	4-dr H.T. Sed-6P	3338	3811	13,903
46400	46437	2-dr Spt Cpe-6P	3272	3724	11,617
46400	46467	Convertible-6P	3651	3988	4,616*

NOTE: Symbol (*) indicates that Wildcat DeLuxe convertible total also includes 46200 Wildcat convertibles.

WILDCAT DELUXE ENGINE
Specifications were the same as those listed for the 1965 Wildcat Series 46200.

WILDCAT CUSTOM — SERIES 46600 — This was the plushest of all Wildcats, with interiors featuring vinyl bucket seats or notch-back full-width seats in cloth. Offered only on two styles, this was essentially a trim option. Production figures are included with those given for corresponding Wildcat DeLuxe figures.

WILDCAT CUSTOM I.D. NUMBERS: Serial numbers began with 466005(   )1001. Numbers were coded as explained under the 1965 Special Series 43300 listing.

WILDCAT CUSTOM SERIES 46600

Series Number	Model Number	Body Type & Seating	Factory Price	Shipping Weight	Production Total
4660	46639	4-dr H.T. Sed-6P	3552	4058	—
46600	46637	2-dr Spt Cpe-6P	3493	4089	—

WILDCAT CUSTOM ENGINE
Specifications were the same as those listed for the 1965 Wildcat Series 45200.

ELECTRA — SERIES 48200 — The largest Buick was equipped with totally new styling for 1965, although the hallmark rear wheelhouse skirts and wide, ribbed lower body moldings were retained. A distinctive cross-hatch textured cast grille was used at the front. Interiors were fabrics or vinyls, with woodgrain dash accents. Standard Electra features, in addition to those found on less costly Buicks, included: Super Turbine transmission; power steering; power brakes; DeLuxe steering wheel; two-speed electric wipers with washer; electric clock; license frames; trip mileage indicator; cigar lighter in rear; Safety buzzer; backup lights, and power brake signal lamp. Convertibles had two-way power seat control and outside rear view mirror.

ELECTRA SERIES 48200

Series Number	Model Number	Body Type & Seating	Factory Price	Shipping Weight	Production Total
48200	48269	4-dr Sedan-6P	3989	4261	12,459
48200	48239	4-dr H.T. Sed-6P	4121	4284	12,842
48200	48237	2-dr Spt Cpe-6P	3999	4208	6,302

ELECTRA I.D. NUMBERS: Serial numbers with 482005(   )100001. Numbers were coded as explained under the 1965 Special Series 43300 listing.

ELECTRA ENGINE
Specifications were the same as those listed for the 1965 Wildcat Series 45200.

ELECTRA CUSTOM: A plusher car than the Electra, the Custom featured elegant interior appointment with fine vinyls and fabrics used for trimming.

ELECTRA CUSTOM I.D. NUMBERS: Serial numbers began with 484005(   )100001. Numbers were coded as explained under the 1965 Special Series 43300 listing.

ELECTRA CUSTOM SERIES 48400

Series Number	Model Number	Body Type & Seating	Factory Price	Shipping Weight	Production Total
48400	48469	4-dr Sedan-6P	4168	4292	7,197
48400	48439	4-dr H.T. Sed-6P	4300	4344	29,932
48400	48437	2-dr Spt Cpe-6P	4179	4228	9,570
48400	48467	Convertible-6P	4350	4325	8,508

ELECTRA CUSTOM ENGINE
Specifications were the same as those listed for the 1965 Wildcat Series 45200.

1965 Buick, Riviera 2-door hardtop sport coupe, V-8 (AA)

RIVIERA — SERIES 49447 — The last recycle of the original Riviera body was also the most distinctive. Headlamps were now stacked vertically behind the fender grilles, which opened when the lamps were turned on. Taillamps were housed in the bumper bar, giving a cleaner rear deck appearance. Riviera script appeared on the front fenders and deck lid. Standard Riviera features included: Super Turbine transmission; power steering; power brakes; two-speed electric wipers with washer; back-up lights; glare-proof rear view mirror; parking brake signal light; Safety buzzer; map light; electric clock; tilt steering wheel; automatic trunk light; license plate frames; upper and lower instrument panel safety pads; full carpeting; double door release handles; console-mounted gear selector; Walnut paneling on instrument panel and individual front bucket seats. Optional Custom interiors included carpeted lower doors.

RIVIERA I.D. NUMBERS: Serial numbers began at 494005(   )900001. Numbers were coded as explained under the 1965 Special Series 43300 listing.

RIVIERA SERIES 48400

Series Number	Model Number	Body Type & Seating	Factory Price	Shipping Weight	Production Total
49400	49447	Sport Coupe-4P	4318	4036	34,586

RIVIERA ENGINE
Specifications were the same as those listed for the 1965 Wildcat Series 45200.
NOTE: A Gran Sport option was available for the 1965 Riviera. It included a 360 brake horsepower Super Wildcat V-8 with dual four-barrel carburetors, large diameter dual exhausts, positive traction differential and bright metal engine accents including a large plated air cleaner and polished ribbed valve covers. Exterior identification was provided by the use of GS full wheel covers and Gran Sport lettering below the Riviera script on the deck lid and on the front fenders.

CHASSIS FEATURES: Wheelbase: (Series 43300, 43400, 44300, 44400) 115 inches; (Series 44200 and 44400 Sport Wagons) 120 inches; (Series 45200 and 45400) 123 inches; (Series 46200, 46400, 46600, 48200 and 48400) 126 inches; (Series 474447) 119 inches. Overall length: (Series 43300, 43400, 44300 and 44400) 203.2 inches; (Series 43300 Station Wagon) 203.4 inches; (Series 44200 and 44400 Sport Wagon) 208.2 inches; (Series 45200 and 45400) 123 inches; (Series 46200, 46400, 46600) 219.8 inches; (Series 48200 and 48400) 224.1 inches; (Series 47447) 209 inches. Front tread: (Series 43300, 43400, 44400 and 44200) 58 inches; (Series 45200 and 45400) 63 inches; (Series 46200, 46400, 46600, 48200 and 48400) 63 inches; (Series 47447) 60 inches. Rear tread: (Series 43300, 43400, 44400 and 44200) 58 inches; (Series 45200, 45400, 46200, 46400, 46600, 48200 and 48400) 62 inches; (Series 47447) 59 inches. Tire sizes: (Series 43300, 43400, 44300 and 44400) 6.95 x 14; (Series 44200 and 44400) 7.75 x 14; (Series 45200 and 45400) 8.15 x 5; (Series 46200, 46400 and 46600) 8.45 x 15; (Series 48200 and 48400) 8.75 x 15; and (Series 47447) 8.45 x 15.

POWERTRAIN OPTIONS: A three speed transmission was standard on Series 43300, 43400, 44300, 43400, 44200, 44400, 45200, 45400, 46200, 46400 and 46600. Super Turbine Drive was optional on the preceding Series and standard on Series 48200, 48400 and 47747. A 4-speed manual transmission was optional for Series 43300, 43400, 44300, 44200, 44400, 44400, 46200, 46400 and 46600. A 250 brake horsepower 300 cubic inch V-8 was optional for Series 43300, 43400, 44300, 44200, 44400, 45200 and 45400. The 340 brake horsepower, 425 cubic inch V-8 was optional for the Series 46200, 46400, 46600, 48200, 48400 and 47747. A 360 brake horsepower, 425 cubic inch V-8 equipped with dual carburetors was optional for Series 46200, 46400, 46600, 48200, 48400 and 47747. This 360 hp V-8 was included with Riviera Gran Sport option. The 325 hp 401 cubic inch V-8 was included with the Skylark Gran Sport option.

CONVENIENCE OPTIONS: Power steering (standard on 46000, 48000 and 47747 Series). Power brakes (standard on 46000, 48000 and 47747 Series). Power windows (standard on Electra Custom convertible, not offered for 4300 and 4400 Series). Power seat controls (4-way or 6-way; a 2-way power seat was standard on the Electra convertible). Air conditioning. AM radio. AM-FM radio (full-size only). 7-position tilt steering wheel (standard on 47747). Remote control outside rearview mirror. Tinted glass. Four-note horn. Tachometer. Automatic trunk release (full-size only). Electro cruise (full size only). Cornering lights (Full-size only). Consoles for Skylark bucket seats. Luggage rack for Sport Wagons. Front seat belt deletion. Heater/Defroster deletion.

Historical footnotes: 44200 and 44400 Series Station Wagons that had raised roof section, were called Sport Wagons.

1966 BUICK

SPECIAL — SERIES 43300 (V-6) — A new body, with more sheet metal sculpting, graced the 1966 Special. Each front fender had three ventiports. Rear fenders carried Special lettering. Otherwise, the car was almost completely devoid of bright metal trim on the sides. Small hubcaps were standard. Regular equipment included a heater and defroster; directional signals; ashtray; cigar lighter; key locking system; Step-On parking brake; front door-operated courtesy light; upper instrument panel pad; outside rear view mirror; two-speed wipers with washer; padded sun visors, front and rear seat belts and backup lamps. Interiors were vinyl and cloth, with an all-vinyl trim optional.

SPECIAL I.D. NUMBERS: Serial numbers began with 433006( )10001 and up. The first five symbols were numerals representing the style. The sixth symbol was a numeral '6' representing the 1966 model year. The seventh symbol was a letter representing the plant code and the last six symbols were numerals representing sequential plant production number, with series mixed in production.

Series Number	Model Number	Body Type & Seating	Factory Price	Shipping Weight	Production Total
43300	43369	4-dr Sedan-6P	2401	3046	8,797
43300	43307	2-dr Coupe-6P	2348	3009	9,322
43300	43367	Convertible-6P	2604	3092	1,357
43300	43335	4-dr Sta Wag-6P	2596	3296	1,451

SPECIAL ENGINE (V-6)
V-6: Overhead valve. Cast iron block. Displacement: 225 cubic inches. Bore and stroke 3.75 x 3.4 inches. Compression ratio 9.0:1. Brake horsepower: 160 at 4200 R.P.M. Four main bearings. Hydraulic lifters. Two-barrel carburetor.

SPECIAL — SERIES 43400 V-8 — Identical externally to the 1966 V-6 Special described above, the V-8 Specials were numbered as a separate series.

SPECIAL V-8 I.D. NUMBERS: Serial numbers began with 434006( )100001. Numbers were coded as explained under the Special Series 43300 listing.

SPECIAL SERIES 43400

Series Number	Model Number	Body Type & Seating	Factory Price	Shipping Weight	Production Total
43400	43469	4-dr Sedan-6P	2471	3148	9,355
43400	43407	2-dr Coupe-6P	2418	3091	5,719
43400	43467	Convertible-6P	2671	3223	2,036
43400	43435	4-dr Sta Wag-6P	2764	3399	3,038

SPECIAL V-8 ENGINE
V-8: Overhead valve. Cast-iron block. Displacement: 300 cubic inches. Bore and stroke: 3.75 x 3.4 inches. Compression ratio: 9.1:1. Brake horsepower: 210 at 4600 R.P.M. Five main bearings. Hydraulic lifters. Two-barrel carburetor.

SPECIAL DELUXE — SERIES 43500 V-6 — The Special Deluxe had the same body as the Special, but with slightly more bright work, including a rear quarter bright spear with Special lettering above it (over the wheelhouse) bright window reveals and a stand-up hood ornament. Special Deluxe models had additional standard features including: rear ashtray; DeLuxe steering wheel; dual arm rests; carpeting and dual horns. Sedan interiors were cloth and vinyl, while the other models were trimmed in all-vinyl material. A notch back all-vinyl front seat was optional for the coupe and sport coupe.

SPECIAL DELUXE I.D. NUMBERS: Serial numbers began with 435006( )10001. Numbers were coded as explained under the 1966 Special Series 43300.

SPECIAL DELUXE SERIES 43500

Series Number	Model Number	Body Type & Seating	Factory Price	Shipping Weight	Production Total
43500	43569	4-dr Sedan-6P	2485	3045	5,501
43500	43507	2-dr Coupe-6P	2432	3009	2,359
43500	43517	2-dr Spt Cpe-6P	2504	3038	25,071
43500	43535	4-dr Sta Wag-6P	2783	3290	824

SPECIAL DELUXE V-6 ENGINE
Specifications were the same as those listed for the 1966 Special Series 43300.

SPECIAL DELUXE V-8 — SERIES 43600 — Identical externally to the Special DeLuxe V-6 described above, the V-8 Special DeLuxes were numbered as a separate series.

SPECIAL DELUXE SERIES 43600

Series Number	Model Number	Body Type & Seating	Factory Price	Shipping Weight	Production Total
43600	43669	4-dr Sedan-6P	2555	3156	26,773
43600	43607	2-dr Coupe-6P	2502	3112	4,908
43600	43617	2-dr Spt Cpe-6P	2574	3130	10,350
43600	4635	2-dr Sta Wag-6P	2853	3427	7,592

SPECIAL DELUXE V-8 ENGINE
Specifications were the same as those listed for the 1966 Special Series 43400 V-8.

1966 Buick, Skylark 4-door hardtop sedan, V-8

SKYLARK — SERIES 44300 V-6 — Buick's plushest intermediate was the recipient of additional exterior bright moldings. They included a lower body molding that ran full-length with wheelhouse kickups, simulate vent grids on front fenders, Skylark script and emblems on rear fenders and a specific rear cove panel. A notch back front seat was standard on the four-door hardtop, optional on other models. Bucket seats, with a reclining passenger seat, were optional, as were headrests. Trim was all-vinyl or cloth and vinyl combinations. All Skylarks had the following additional standard equipment: Custom-padded seat cushions, DeLuxe specific wheel covers, ash tray and glove compartment lights and front interior courtesy lamps.

SKYLARK V-6 I.D. NUMBERS: Serial numbers began with 44300( )10001. Serial numbers were coded as explained under the 1965 Special Series 43300 listing.

SKYLARK SERIES 44300

Series Number	Model Number	Body Type & Seating	Factory Price	Shipping Weight	Production Total
44300	44339	4-dr H.T. Sed-6P	2846	3172	1,422
44300	44307	2-dr Coupe-6P	2624	3034	1,454
44300	44317	2-dr Spt Cpe-6P	2687	3087	2,456
44300	44367	Convertible-6P	2837	3158	608

SKYLARK V-6 ENGINE
Specifications were the same as those listed for the 1966 Special Series 43300 V-6.

SKYLARK — SERIES 44400 V-8 — Identical externally to the 1966 Skylark V-6 described above, the V-8 Skylarks were numbered as a separate series.

SKYLARK SERIES 44400

Series Number	Model Number	Body Type & Seating	Factory Price	Shipping Weight	Production Total
44400	44439	4-dr H.T. Sed-6P	2916	3285	18,729
44400	444307	2-dr Coupe-6P	2694	3145	6,427
44400	44417	2-dr Spt Cpe-6P	2757	3152	33,086
44400	44467	Convertible-6P	2904	3259	6,129

SKYLARK V-8 ENGINE
Specifications were the same as listed for the 1966 Special Series 43400 V-8.

SKYLARK GRAN SPORT — SERIES 44600 — Buick moved a step closer to a muscle car image with the 1966 Gran Sport. Equipped like the Skylark, the sporting image was pursued via a black matte finish rear cove panel, Skylark GS emblems on quarters and instrument panel, Gran Sport nameplates on the grille and deck, and whitewall or red line 7.75 x 14 tires. Bright simulated air scoops, side paint stripes and a blacked out grille gave further identity. There was no hood ornament. Interiors were all-vinyl, with a notch back front seat standard and bucket front seats optional.

SKYLARK GRAN SPORT I.D. NUMBERS: Vehicle Identification Numbers began with 446006( )100001. Numbers were coded as explained under the 1966 Special Series 43300 listing.

SKYLARK GRAN SPORT SERIES 44600

Series Number	Model Number	Body Type & Seating	Factory Price	Shipping Weight	Production Total
44600	44607	2-dr Coupe-6P	2956	3479	1,835
44600	44617	2-dr Spt Cpe-6P	3019	3428	9,934
44600	44667	Convertible-6P	3167	3532	2,047

SKYLARK GRAN SPORT ENGINE
V-8: Overhead valves. Cast-iron block. Displacement: 401 cubic inches (advertised as 400 cubic inches). Bore and stroke: 4.18 x 3.64 inches. Compression ratio: 10.25:1. Brake horsepower: 325 at 4600 R.P.M. Five main bearings. Hydraulic lifters. Four-barrel carburetor.

SPORT WAGON AND SPORT WAGON CUSTOM — SERIES 44200 AND 44400 V-8 — Buick's popular intermediate continued to feature a glass skyroof and two or three-seat configuration. The Sport Wagon had most Special DeLuxe features, plus rush-finished wiper arms, Sport Wagon quarter panel scripts and specific taillights. Interiors were all-vinyl. The Custom versions had satin finished lower body moldings, DeLuxe steering wheel and tailgate lamps. Custom padded seat cushions and Custom interior trim featuring plusher upholstery and carpeting extending to the lower doors was used.

SPORT WAGON AND SPORT WAGON CUSTOM I.D. NUMBERS: Serial numbers began with 442006( )100001 for the Sport Wagon and 444006( )100001 on the Sport Wagon Custom. Numbers were coded as described under the 1966 Special Series 43300 listing.

SPORT WAGONS SERIES 44200/44400

Series Number	Model Number	Body Type & Seating	Factory Price	Shipping Weight	Production Total
44200	44265	4-dr Sta Wag-3S	3173	3811	2,667
44200	44255	4-dr Sta Wag-2S	3025	3713	2,469
44400	44465	4-dr Sta Wag-3S	3293	3844	9,510
44400	44455	4-dr Sta Wag-2S	3155	3720	6,964

SPORT WAGON AND SPORT WAGON CUSTOM ENGINE

V-8: Overhead valve. Cast iron block. Displacement: 340 cubic inches. Bore and stroke: 3.75 x 3.85 inches. Compression ratio: 9.0:1. Brake horsepower: 220 at 4000 R.P.M. Five main bearings. Hydraulic lifters. Two-barrel carburetor.

LESABRE — SERIES 45200 — Slightly facelifted from 1965, the lowest-priced, full size Buick had three ventiports on each front fender and LeSabre scripts on the quarter panels. Narrow lower body moldings of bright metal were used. Interiors were vinyl and cloth. Standard equipment included front and rear seat belts, Step-On parking brake, door operated courtesy lamps, dual arm rests, dual horns and carpeting.

LESABRE I.D. NUMBERS: Vehicle Identification Numbers began with 45200( )10001. Numbers were coded as explained under the 1966 Buick Special Series 43300 listing.

LESABRE SERIES 45200

Series Number	Model Number	Body Type & Seating	Factory Price	Shipping Weight	Production Total
45200	45269	4-dr Sedan-6P	2942	3769	39,146
45200	45239	4-dr H.T. Sed-6P	3081	3828	17,740
45200	45237	2-dr H.T. Cpe-6P	3022	3751	13,843

LESABRE ENGINE

Specifications were the same as listed under 1966 Sport Wagon and Sport Wagon Custom engine data.

LESABRE CUSTOM — SERIES 45400 — Custom models had plusher interiors with DeLuxe steering wheel, two-speed wipers and washer equipment and backup lamps. Optional Custom trim included bucket seats with black accents.

LESABRE CUSTOM I.D. NUMBERS: Vehicle Identification Numbers began with 454006( )100001. Numbers were coded as explained under the 1966 Buick Special Series 43300 listing.

LESABRE CUSTOM SERIES 45400

Series Number	Model Number	Body Type & Seating	Factory Price	Shipping Weight	Production Total
45400	45469	4-dr Sedan-6P	3035	3788	25,932
45400	45439	4-dr H.T. Sed-6P	3174	3824	26,914
45400	45437	2-dr H.T. Cpe-6P	3109	3746	18,830
45400	45467	Convertible-6P	3326	3833	4,994

LESABRE CUSTOM ENGINE

Specifications were the same as those listed under 1966 Sport Wagon and Sport Wagon Custom engine data.

WILDCAT — SERIES 46400 — Buick's middle-priced, full-sized car again pursued a performance image. A specific grille with vertical texturing was used. There was a Wildcat hood ornament above it. Wildcat lettering appeared across the deck lid and on rear quarter panels. Simulated air intake grids appeared behind the front wheelhouses. Interiors were cloth and vinyl, or all-vinyl. Standard features included the LeSabre's accountrements plus a glove box light.

WILDCAT I.D. NUMBERS: Vehicle Identification Numbers began with 464006 ( ) 900001. Numbers were coded as explained under the 1966 Special Series 43300 listing.

WILDCAT SERIES 46400

Series Number	Model Number	Body Type & Seating	Factory Price	Shipping Weight	Production Total
46400	46469	4-dr Sedan-6P	3233	4070	14,389
46400	46439	4-dr H.T. Sed-6P	3391	4108	15,081
46400	46437	2-dr H.T. Cpe-6P	3326	4003	9,774
46400	46467	Convertible-6P	3480	4065	2,690

WILDCAT ENGINE

V-8: Overhead valve. Cast iron block. Displacement: 401 cubic inches. Bore and stroke: 4.18 x 3.64 inches. Compression ratio: 10.25:1. Brake horsepower: 325 at 4600 R.P.M. Five main bearings. Hydraulic lifters. Four-barrel carburetor.

WILDCAT CUSTOM — SERIES 46600 — A plusher Wildcat, with DeLuxe steering wheel, padded-type arm rests, outside rear view mirror and Custom headlining (except convertible). Plusher cloth and vinyl or all-vinyl trim was used, with notch back or Strato bucket front seat (reclining passenger seat with the latter) and headrests.

WILDCAT CUSTOM I.D. NUMBERS: Vehicle Identification Numbers began with 466006( )900001. Numbers were coded as explained under the 1966 Special Series 43300 listing.

WILDCAT CUSTOM SERIES 46600

Series Number	Model Number	Body Type & Seating	Factory Price	Shipping Weight	Production Total
46600	46639	4-dr H.T. Sed-6P	3606	4176	13,060
46600	46637	2-dr H.T. Cpe-6P	3547	4018	10,800
46600	46667	Convertible-6P	3701	4079	2,790

WILDCAT CUSTOM ENGINE

Specifications were the same as those listed under Wildcat Series 46400 engine data.

1966 Buick, Electra 225 4-door hardtop sedan, V-8 (AA)

ELECTRA 225 — SERIES 48200 — The largest Buick, with a larger, distinct body similar to 1965. Fender skirts were standard, with a full-length lower body molding that was wider than those of other Buicks. Electra 225 script appeared on the rear fenders and the car's prestige was further enhanced by the use of four ventiports per fender. Standard features, in addition to those of lower-priced Buicks, included Custom-padded seat cushions; Custom front seat belts with retractors; electric clock; parking brake signal lamp; glove box and map lights; Glareproof mirror; power steering; power brakes and Super Turbine automatic transmission. Interiors were cloth and vinyl combinations.

ELECTRA 225 I.D. NUMBERS: Vehicle Identification Numbers began with 482006 ( ) 100001. Numbers were coded as explained under the 1966 Special Series 43300 listing.

ELECTRA 225 SERIES 48200

Series Number	Model Number	Body Type & Seating	Factory Price	Shipping Weight	Production Total
48200	48269	4-dr Sedan-6P	4022	4255	11,692
48200	48239	4-dr H.T. Sed-6P	4153	4271	10,792
48200	42837	2-dr H.T. Cpe-6P	4032	4176	4,882

ELECTRA 225 ENGINE

Specifications were the same as listed under 1966 Wildcat Series 46400 engine data.

ELECTRA 225 CUSTOM — SERIES 48400 — An even plusher Electra 225, with Custom notch back front seat in cloth, or Strato buckets in vinyl for the Convertible. All Custom interiors had carpeted lower door panels. Although basically a trim option, Electra 225 Customs were numbered as a separate series.

ELECTRA 225 CUSTOM I.D. NUMBERS: Vehicle Identification Numbers with 484006( )100001. Numbers were coded as explained under the 1966 Buick Special Series 43300 listing.

ELECTRA 225 CUSTOM SERIES 48400

Series Number	Model Number	Body Type & Seating	Factory Price	Shipping Weight	Production Total
48400	48469	4-dr Sedan-6P	4201	4292	9,368
48400	48439	4-dr H.T. Sed-6P	4332	4323	34,149
48400	48437	2-dr H.T. Cpe-6P	4211	4230	10,119
48400	48467	Convertible-6P	4378	4298	7,175

ELECTRA 225 CUSTOM ENGINE

Specifications were the same as those listed under 1966 Wildcat Series 46400 engine data.

RIVIERA — SERIES 49487 — A sleek new body graced the first totally restyled Riviera since 1963. Headlamps were once again horizontally paired, unlike 1965. Now they retracted above the grille when not in use. The body's clean lines were enhanced by the lack of vent windows. Inside, a new instrument panel was found with a unique vertical, drum-type speedometer and a full complement of gauges. Standard equipment included power steering; power brakes; Super Turbine transmission; tilt steering wheel; dual exhausts; full carpeting; padded instrument panel; dual-speed wipers and washer; backup lamps; outside rear view mirror; shatter-resistant inside mirror and front and rear seat belts. Bucket or bench-style front seats were standard as the purchaser's choice. Strato-buckets with Custom all vinyl trim were availble, as were other Custom trim options.
NOTE: Gran Sport equipment was offered for the 1966 Riviera. This year it consisted of a chromed air cleaner and aluminum rocker covers for the standard 340 brake horsepower, 425 cubic inch V-8; plus heavy duty shocks front and rear, 8.45 x 15 red or white line tires, postitive traction differential and GS emblems on front fenders and instrument panel.

RIVIERA I.D. NUMBERS: Vehicle Identification Numbers began with 494876 ( ) 900001. Numbers were coded as explained under the 1966 Special Series 43300 listing.

RIVIERA SERIES 49400

Series Number	Model Number	Body Type & Seating	Factory Price	Shipping Weight	Production Total
49400	49487	2-dr Spt Cpe-4P	4424	4180	45,348

RIVIERA ENGINE

V-8: Overhead valve. Cast iron block. Displacement: 425 cubic inches. Bore and stroke: 4.3125 x 3.64 inches. Compression ratio: 10.25:1. Brake horsepower: 340 at 4400 R.P.M. Five main bearings. Hydraulic lifters. Four-barrel carburetor.

CHASSIS FEATURES: Wheelbase: (Series 43300, 43400, 43500, 43600, 44300, 44400, 44600) 115 inches; (Series 44200 and 44400 Sport Wagons) 120 inches; (Series 45200 and 45400) 123 inches; (Series 46400 and 46600) 126 inches; (Series 49487) 119 inches. Overall length: (Series 43300, 43400, 43500, 43600, 443000, 44400, 44600) 204 inches; (Series 44200 and 44400 Sport Wagons) 209 inches; (Series 45200 and 45400) 216.9 inches; (Series 46400 and 46600) 219.9 inches; (Series 48200 and 48400) 223.4 inches; (Series 49487) 211.2 inches. Tires: (Series 43300, 43500) 6.95 x 14; (Series 43400, 43600 and 44600) 7.35 x 14; (Series 44600) 7.75 x 14; (Series 44200 and 44400 Sport Wagons) 8.25 x 14; (Series 45200 and 45400) 8.45 x 15; (Series 46400 and 46600) 8.45 x 15; (Series 48200 and 48400) 8.85 x 15; (Series 49487) 8.45 x 15.

POWERTRAIN OPTIONS: A three-speed manual transmission was standard on Series 43300, 43400, 43500, 43600, 44300, 44400, 44200, 45200, 45400, 46400 and 46600. Super Turbine automatic transmission was standard on Series 48200 and 49487; and was optional on Series 46400 and 46400. Turbine transmission was optional for all other models. A four-speed manual transmission was optional for Series 44400 and 44600. A 260 brake horsepower, 340 cubic inch V-8 was optional for Series 43400, 44300, 44400, 44200, 45200 and 45400. The 340 horsepower, 425 cubic inch V-8 standard on Model 49487 and optional on Series 46400, 46600, 48200 and 48400.

CONVENIENCE OPTIONS: Power steering (standard on 48000 and 49487. Power brakes (standard on 48000 and 49487). Power windows. Four or Six-way power seat controls. Air conditioning. AM radio. AM/FM radio. Seven-position tilt steering wheel. Remote control outside rear view mirror. Tinted glass. Four-note horn. Automatic trunk release. Electro cruise. Cornering lights (full-size only). Simulated wire wheel covers. Five-spoke chromed wheels. Heater/Defroster deletion. Luggage rack for Sport Wagons.

Historical footnotes: None.

1967 BUICK

SPECIAL — SERIES 43300 V-6 — A rehash of the 1966 style distinguished by a new grille, the 1967 Special continued with rear quarter model name lettering and triple ventiports on front fenders. These lowest-priced buick were lacking in bright trim. Even the window surrounds were plain. Standard equipment included heater and defroster; ash tray; directional signals; cigar lighter; Step-On parking brake; front and rear seat belts; front door operated courtesy light; upper instrument panel safety pad; outside rear view mirror; dual speed wipers and washer; padded sun visors; backup lamps and other mandated safety items. Vinyl and cloth upholstery was standard, while an all-vinyl interior was optional.

SPECIAL I.D. NUMBERS: Vehicle Identification Numbers began with 433007 ( ) 600001. The first five symbols were numerals representing the series and model. The sixty symbol was a numeral '7' representing the 1967 model year. The seventh symbol ( ) was a letter respresenting the plant code and the last six symbols were numerals representing the sequential plant production number, with series mixed in production.

SPECIAL SERIES 43300

Series Number	Model Number	Body Type & Seating	Factory Price	Shipping Weight	Production Total
43300	43369	4-dr Sedan-6P	2462	3077	4,711
43300	43307	2-dr Coupe-6P	2411	3071	6,989
43300	43335	4-dr Sta Wag-6P	2742	2812	908

SPECIAL ENGINE
V-6: Overhead valve. Cast-iron block. Displacement: 225 cubic inches. Bore and stroke: 3.75 x 3.4 inches. Compression ratio: 9.0:1. Brake horsepower: 160 at 4200 R.P.M. Four main bearings. Hydraulic lifters. Two-barrel carburetor.

SPECIAL — SERIES 43400 V-8 — The Buick Special equipped with a V-8 engine was externally identical to the 1967 Special V-6 described above, except in regard to vehicle coding. The V-8 Specials were numbered as a separate series.

SPECIAL SERIES 43400 V-8 I.D. NUMBERS: Vehicle Identification Numbers began with 434007( )600001. Numbers were coded as explained under the 1967 Special V-6 Series 43300 listing.

SPECIAL SERIES 43400

Series Number	Model Number	Body Type & Seating	Factory Price	Shipping Weight	Production Total
43400	43469	4-dr Sedan-6P	2532	3196	5,793
43400	43407	2-dr Coupe-6P	2481	3173	8,937
43400	43435	4-dr Sta Wag-6P	2812	3425	1,688

SPECIAL V-8 ENGINE
V-8: Overhead valve. Cast iron block. Displacement: 300 cubic inches. Bore and stroke: 3.75 x 3.4 inches. Compression ratio: 9.0:1. Brake horsepower: 210 at 4600 R.P.M. Five main bearings. Hydraulic lifters. Two-barrel carburetor.

SPECIAL DELUXE V-6 — SERIES 43500 — A slightly plusher Special, with bright wheelhouse moldings, full-length body side bright moldings, black-accented rear cove panel and bright metal window surrounds. Special lettering appeared on the front fenders. Standard equipment was the same as the Special, plus a rear seat ash tray. DeLuxe steering wheel, dual side arm rests, full carpeting and dual horns. Interiors were cloth and vinyl or all-vinyl.

SPECIAL DELUXE SERIES 43500 V-6 I.D. NUMBERS: Vehicle Identification Numbers began with 435007( )600001. Numbers were coded as explained under the 1967 Special Series 43300 listing.

SPECIAL DELUXE SERIES 43500

Series Number	Model Number	Body Type & Seating	Factory Price	Shipping Weight	Production Total
43500	43569	4-dr Sedan-6P	2545	3142	3,602
43500	43517	2-dr H.T. Cpe-6P	2566	3127	2,333

SPECIAL DELUXE V-6 ENGINE
See 1967 Buick Special Series 43300 engine data.

SPECIAL DELUXE V-8 — SERIES 43600 — Externally identical to the V-6 powered Special DeLuxe described above, the V-8 Special DeLuxes were numbered as a separate series. The Station Wagon was available only as a V-8.

SPECIAL DELUXE SERIES 43600 I.D. NUMBERS: Vehicle identification numbers began with 436007( )100001 and up. Numbers were coded as explained under 1967 Special Series 43300 listing.

SPECIAL SERIES 43600 DELUXE V-8

Series Number	Model Number	Body Type & Seating	Factory Price	Shipping Weight	Production Total
43600	43669	4-dr Sedan-6P	2615	3205	25,361
43600	43617	2-dr H.T. Cpe-6P	2636	3202	14,408
43600	43635	4-dr Sta Wag-6P	2901	3317	6,851

SPECIAL DELUXE V-8 ENGINE
See 1967 Buick Special Series 43400 engine data.

SKYLARK — SERIES 44307 V-6 — Only one model, the coupe, offered with the V-6 for the 1967 Skylark. Standard equipment was the same as described for the 1967 Skylark V-8 Series 44400 below.

SKYLARK V-6 SERIES 44307 I.D. NUMBERS: Vehicle Identification Numbers began with 443077( )600001. Numbers were coded as explained under the 1967 Special Series 43300 listing.

SKYLARK SERIES 44307 V-6

Series Number	Model Number	Body Type & Seating	Factory Price	Shipping Weight	Production Total
44300	44307	2-dr Coupe-6P	2665	3137	894

SKYLARK SERIES V-6 ENGINE
See 1967 Buick Special Series 43300 engine data.

SKYLARK — SERIES 44400 V-8 — Exterior distinction was gained by the use of rear fender skirts, a full-length lower body bright molding, simulated front fender vents, a ribbed rear cove panel and a grille with more horizontal bars. Skylark script was used on the rear quarters and Skylarks had no ventiports. Cloth and vinyl trim with bench front seats were standard, except on the convertible, which was all-vinyl trimmed. All-vinyl was optional for other models and bucket seats with consoles were also offered as an option.

SKYLARK — SERIES 44400 V-8 I.D. NUMBERS: Vehicle Identification Numbers began with 44407( )600001. Numbers were coded as explained under the 1967 Special Series 43300 listing.

SKYLARK V-8 SERIES 44400

Series Number	Model Number	Body Type & Seating	Factory Price	Shipping Weight	Production Total
44400	44407	2-dr Coupe-6P	2735	3229	3,165
44400	44469	4-dr Sedan-6P	2767	3324	9,123
44400	44439	4-dr H.T. Sed-6P	2950	3373	13,673
44400	44417	2-dr H.T. Cpe-6P	2798	3199	40,940
44400	44467	Convertible-5P	2945	3335	6,319

SKYLARK V-8 ENGINE
Specifications for the Skylark Series 44400 models were the same as engine data listed for 1967 Buick Skylark Series 43300 models, except in the case of the four-door hardtop sedan. This car came standard with a 340 cubic inch V-8 having 3.75 x 3.85 inch bore and stroke measurements, 9.0:1 compression and 220 horsepower at 4200 R.P.M. with two-barrel induction.

SPORTWAGON — SERIES 44200 AND 44400 — Now spelled as one word, the series name, 'Sportwagon' appeared in script on station wagon rear fenders. These long-wheelbase wagons continued to feature the glass Skyroof raised roofline. They used the Skylark grille, but had ventiports and bright rocker and wheelhouse moldings. Specific taillights were used. Standard equipment was similar to that of the Special DeLuxe. Interiors were vinyl. Models in the 44400 series had Custom interiors with padded seat cushions and a tailgate lamp.

SPORTWAGON SERIES 44200/44400 I.D. NUMBERS: Vehicle Identification Numbers began with 44007( )600001 or 444007( )600001. Numbers were coded as explained under the 1967 Special Series 43300 listing.

SPORTWAGON SERIES 44200/44300

Series Number	Model Number	Body Type & Seating	Factory Price	Shipping Weight	Production Total
44200	44255	4-dr Sta Wag-6P	3025	3713	5,440
44200	44265	4-dr Sta Wag-9P	3173	3811	5,970
44400	44255	4-dr Cus Sta Wag-6P	3202	3772	3,114
44400	44265	4-dr Cus Sta Wag-9P	3340	3876	4,559

SPORTWAGON ENGINE
V-8: Overhead valve. Cast iron block. Displacement: 340 cubic inches. Bore and stroke: 3.75 x 3.85 inches. Compression ratio: 9.0:1. Brake horsepower: 220 at 4200 R.P.M. Five main bearings. Hydraulic valve lifters. Carburetor: Rochester two-barrel Model 2GC.

SKYLARK GS 340 — SERIES 43417 — A hybrid, the GS 340 was numbered in the Special V-8 series, but was trimmed as a low-cost GS. Broad Rally stripes and hood scoops were red, as was the lower deck molding. Two body colors, white or platinum mist, were offered. Specific front and rear shocks, springs and a large diameter stabilizer were included, as were 7.75 Rayon Cord tires on red 14 inch Rally-style wheels. Interiors were similar to the Skylark Series 43400 Series.

SKYLARK GS 340 SERIES 43417 I.D. NUMBERS: Vehicle Identification Numbers were the same as used on Skylark Series 44400 V-8 models.

SKYLARK G.S. 340 SERIES 43417

Series Number	Model Number	Body Type & Seating	Factory Price	Shipping Weight	Production Total
43400	43417	2-dr H.T. Cpe-6P	2845	3283	Note 1

Note 1: Research indicates that production of this model was included with the production of other Skylark series.

SKYLARK GS 340 V-8 ENGINE
The GS 340 used a 360 h.p. engine with four-barrel carburetor.

SKYLARK GS 400 — SERIES 44600 — The high-performance Skylark took its name from its 400 cubic inch V-8. Exterior appearance was strengthened by the use of twin hood scoops, Rally stripes and a Special grille. F70 x 14 Wide Oval red or white stripe tires were standard. Rear wheelhouses were open, unlike other Skylark models (except GS 340). Interiors were all-vinyl and standard equipment was the same as the Skylark 44400 Series.

SKYLARK GS 400 SERIES 44600 I.D. NUMBERS: Vehicle Identification Numbers began with 446007( )100001. Numbers were coded as explained under the 1967 Special Series 43300 listing.

SKYLARK GS 400 SERIES 44600

Series Number	Model Number	Body Type & Seating	Factory Price	Shipping Weight	Production Total
44600	44607	2-dr Coupe-6P	2956	3439	1,014
44600	44617	2-dr H.T. Cpe-6P	3019	3500	10,659
44600	44667	Convertible-6P	3167	3505	2,140

SKYLARK GS 400 SERIES ENGINE
V-8: Overhead valve. Cast iron block. Displacement: 400 cubic inches. Bore an stroke: 4.18 x 3.64 inches. Compression ratio: 10.25:1. Brake horsepower: 340 at 5000 R.P.M. Five main bearings. Hydraulic lifters. Four-barrel carburetor.

LESABRE — SERIES 45200 — A new body shell, with a revised sweepspear sculpted into the sheetmetal, was featured for 1967. A horizontal, multiple bar grille was used. Bright lower body moldings, with rear fender extensions on some models, were used. The traditional trio of ventiports was once again found on front fenders. LeSabre script appeared on the rear fenders and deck lid. Standard equipment included heater; defroster; front and rear seat belts; Step-On parking brake; front door operated courtesy lamps; smoking set; rear seat ash trays; dual front and rear arm rests; dual-key locking system and other mandated safety features.

LESABRE SERIES 45200 I.D. NUMBERS: Vehicle Identifiation Numbers began with 452007( )100001. Numbers were coded as explained under the 1967 Special Series 43300 listing.

LESABRE SERIES 45200

Series Number	Model Number	Body Type & Seating	Factory Price	Shipping Weight	Production Total
45200	45269	4-dr Sedan-6P	3002	3847	36,220
45200	45239	4-dr H.T. Sed-6P	3142	3878	17,464
45200	45287	2-dr H.T. Cpe-6P	3084	3819	13,760

LESABRE SERIES 45200 ENGINE

Specifications were the same as listed for the 1967 Skylark hardtop sedan model 44439.

LESABRE CUSTOM — SERIES 45400 —

A slightly plusher LeSabre, with Custom quality cloth and vinyl interior trim. The hardtop coupe was equipped with standard all-vinyl, front bucket seat interior. Standard equipment was the same as in the LeSabre, except for the addition of the DeLuxe steering wheel, outside rear view mirror, an upper instrument panel safety pad and a cross flow radiator.

LESABRE CUSTOM I.D. NUMBERS: Vehicle Identification Numbers began with 454007( )100001. Numbers were coded as explained under the 1967 Special Series 43300 listing.

LESABRE CUSTOM SERIES 45400

Series Number	Model Number	Body Type & Seating	Factory Price	Shipping Weight	Production Total
45400	45469	4-dr Sedan-6P	3096	3855	27,930
45400	45439	4-dr H.T. Sed-6P	3236	3873	32,526
45400	45487	2-dr H.T. Cpe-5P	3172	3853	11,871
45400	45467	Convertible-6P	3388	3890	2,913

LESABRE CUSTOM ENGINE

See 1967 Buick Sportwagon Series engine data.

WILDCAT — SERIES 46400 —

A specific, more open grille set the Wildcat apart from the LeSabre at the front. Side trim used a heavier bright lower body molding that continued across the standard rear fender skirts as a lip molding. The molding flowed out of the front fender's large simulated vent intakes. Wildcat lettering appeared on the rear quarters and deck. Interiors were vinyl and cloth, of a plusher grade than the LeSabre, which featured the same standard equipment.

WILDCAT I.D. NUMBERS: Vehicle Identification Numbers began with 464007 ( ) 100001. Numbers were coded as explained under the 1966 Special Series 43300 listing.

WILDCAT SERIES 46400

Series Number	Model Number	Body Type & Seating	Factory Price	Shipping Weight	Production Total
46400	46469	4-dr Sedan-6P	3277	4008	14,579
46400	46439	4-dr H.T. Sed-6P	3437	4069	15,510
46400	46487	2-dr H.T. Cpe-5P	3382	4021	10,585
46400	46467	Convertible-6P	3536	4064	2,276

WILDCAT ENGINE

V-8: Overhead valve. Cast iron block. Displacement: 430 cubic inches. Bore and stroke: 4.18 x 3.9 inches. Compression ratio: 10.5:1. Brakes horsepower: 360 at 5000 R.P.M. Five main bearings. Hydraulic lifters. Four-barrel carburetor.

WILDCAT CUSTOM — SERIES 46600 —

A Custom interior, with plusher materials, paddle-type arm rests and custom headlining (except convertible) set the Custom Wildcats apart. All-vinyl bucket seats or cloth notchback seats for front seat passengers were standard.

WILDCAT CUSTOM SERIES 46600 I.D. NUMBERS: Vehicle Identification Numbers began with 466007( )100001. Numbers were coded as explained under the 1967 Special Series 43300 listing.

WILDCAT CUSTOM SERIES 46600

Series Number	Model Number	Body Type & Seating	Factory Price	Shipping Weight	Production Total
46600	46639	4-dr H.T. Sed-6P	3652	4119	13,547
46600	46687	2-dr H.T. Cpe-5P	3603	4055	11,571
46600	46667	Convertible-5P	3757	4046	2,913

WILDCAT CUSTOM ENGINE

See 1967 Buick Wildcat Series 46400 engine data.

ELECTRA 225 — SERIES 48200 —

Buick's largest, most luxurious series was restyled for 1967, sharing with lesser full-sized Buick's a return to sweepspear bodyside motifs. The Electra used a larger body, however, with its own horizontally-barred grille, distinct squared-off rear fenders and four ventports on each front fender. The lower body was lined with bright metal bumper to bumper, continuing even across the lip of the fender skirts. Full-width taillights were used at the rear. Electra 225 script appeared on the rear fenders. Standard features included most items found on less costly Buicks plus, power steering; power brakes; custom padded seat cushions; front seat belt retractors; electric clock; trunk light; license frames and mandated safety features. Interiors were cloth and vinyl.

ELECTRA 225 SERIES 48200 I.D. NUMBERS: Vehicle Identification Numbers began with 482007 ( ) 100001. Numbers were coded as explained under the 1966 Special Series 43300 listing.

ELECTRA 225 SERIES 48200

Series Number	Model Number	Body Type & Seating	Factory Price	Shipping Weight	Production Total
48200	48269	4-dr Sedan-6P	4054	4246	10,787
48200	48239	4-dr H.T. Sed-6P	4184	4293	12,491
48200	48287	2-dr Spt Cpe-6P	4075	4197	6,845

ELECTRA 225 ENGINE

See 1967 Buick Wildcat Series 4600 engine data.

ELECTRA 225 CUSTOM — SERIES 48400 —

Plusher, Custom grade interiors in cloth and vinyl set the Custom models apart. Vinyl bucket seats were an option for the Custom convertible. Note: Custom 'Limited' equipment was available for the Style Number 48439 four-door hardtop sedan. Cars so equipped had Madrid grain or Bavere cloth and Madrid grain vinyl upholstery with etched Electra 225 emblems; walnut door and instrument panel inserts and dual storage compartments on the front seat backrest. Limited scripts were affixed to the roof sail panels. This package retailed for $149.27, but the number of cars so equipped was not individually recorded.

ELECTRA 225 CUSTOM I.D. NUMBERS: Vehicle Identification Numbers began with 484007( )100001. Numbers were coded as explained under the 1967 Special Series 43300 listing.

ELECTRA 225 CUSTOM SERIES 48400

Series Number	Model Number	Body Type & Seating	Factory Price	Shipping Weight	Production Total
48400	48469	4-dr Sedan-6P	4270	4312	10,106
48400	48439	4-dr H.T. Sed-6P	4363	4336	40,978
48400	48487	2-dr Spt Cpe-6P	4254	4242	12,156
48400	48467	Convertible-6P	4421	4304	6,941

ELECTRA 225 CUSTOM ENGINE

See 1967 Buick Wildcat Series 46400 engine data.

1967 Buick, Electra 225 4-door sedan, V-8 (TVB)

RIVIERA — SERIES 49487 —

A new grille was used with the basic 1966 body to very slightly face-lift the Riviera. Rocker moldings were altered and new taillamps were installed. Riviera script appeared on front fenders and the deck lid. Standard equipment included Super Turbine transmission; power steering; power brakes; tilt steering wheel; dual exhausts; heater/defroster; Custom padded seats; retractable seat belts; electric clock; trunk and glove box lights; Glareproof mirror; outside rear view mirror; license frames and carpeting. A bench or bucket seat all-vinyl interior was used.

NOTE: Gran Sport equipment was offered for the 1967 Riviera at $138. This consisted of heavy duty front and rear shocks, positive traction differential, Wide Oval red or white stripe tires and front fender and instrument panel GS monograms. The standard engine was used.

RIVIERA I.D. NUMBERS: Vehicle Idenfitication Numbers began with 494877( )90001. Numbers were coded as explained under the 1967 Special Series 43300 listing.

RIVIERA SERIES 49400

Series Number	Model Number	Body Type & Seating	Factory Price	Shipping Weight	Production Total
49400	49487	2-dr H.T. Cpe-5P	4469	4189	42,799

RIVIERA ENGINES

See 1967 Buick Wildcat 46400 Series engine data.

CHASSIS FEATURES: Wheelbase: (Series 43300, 43400, 43500, 43600, 44300, 44400, 44600) 115 inches; (Series 43200 and 43400 Sportwagons) 120 inches; (Series 45200 and 45400) 123 inches; (Series 46400, 46600, 48200 and 48400) 126 inches; (Series 49487) 119 inches. Overall length: (Series 43300, 43400, 43500, 43600, 44300, 44400 and 44600) 205 inches. (Station Wagons) 209.3 inches. (Series 44200 and 44400 Sportwagons) 214. inches; (Series 45200 and 45400) 217.5 inches; (Series 46400 and 46600) 220.5 inches; (Series 48200 and 48400) 223.9 inches; (Series 49487) 211.3 inches. Tread: (Series 44300, 43400, 43500, 43600, 44300, 44400, 44600 and 44200) 58 inches front, 59 inches rear. (Series 45200, 45400, 46400 and 46600) 63 inches front and rear. (Series 48200, 48400 and 49487) 63.4 inches front, 63 inches rear Tires: (Series 43300, 43400, 43500, 43600, 44300, 44400 and 44600) 7.75 x 14; (Series 44200 and 44400 Sportwagons) 8.25 x 14; (Series 45200, 45400, 46400 and 46600) 8.45 x 15; (Series 48200 and 48400) 8.85 x 15; (Series 49487) 8.45 x 15.

1967 Buick, Riviera 2-door hardtop sport coupe, V-8 (TVB)

POWERTRAIN OPTIONS: A three-speed manual transmission was standard on Series 43300, 43400, 43500, 43600, 44300, 44400, 44600, 44200, 45200, 45400, 46400 and 46600. Super Turbine automatic transmission was standard on Series 48200, 48400 and 49487 and was optional on Series 46400 and 46600. An automatic transmission was optional on all other Models. A four-speed manual transmission was optional on the GS 340 and GS 400 at $184. A '400' package, linking the 260 horsepower 340 cubic inch V-8 with four-barrel to a Super Turbine '400' transmission was offered for the Sportwagon and LeSabre models at a cost of $263.00. The 260 horsepower 340 cubic inch V-8 was also optional with other power teams in intermediates and LeSabres. No engine options were cataloged for Wildcat, Electra 225 or Riviera models.

CONVENIENCE FEATURES: Power steering (standard Electra 225, Riviera). Power brakes (standard Electra 225s, Riviera). Front power disc brakes (except Electra 225s). Automatic air conditioning (full-size only). Air conditioning. Five-spoke plated sport wheels. Wire wheel covers. DeLuxe wheel covers. Front seat headrests. Power door locks. Tilt steering wheel (standard on Riviera). Full-length console with bucket seats (automatic transmission equipped Skylark, GS 340, GS 400, Wildcat, Riviera). AM radio. AM/FM radio. Stereo radio (full size only). Reclining bucket seat. Reclining Strato bench seat (Riviera only). Power seat adjustment. Electro-cruise (automatic transmission only, not available on GS 400 or Sportwagon with 400 option). Power windows. Overhead courtesy lamps (LeSabre, Wildcat). Four-note horn. Remote control mirror. Automatic trunk release (except 115-120'' wheelbase). Rear window defroster (except convertibles and station wagons). Vinyl roof cover (specific models). Speed alert. Power tailgate for station wagons. Cornering lights (full-size models). Station wagon luggage rack.

1968 BUICK

SPECIAL DELUXE — SERIES 43300/43400 — The basic Buick was upgraded to DeLuxe status this year, as reflected by more brightwork on the restyled bodies, which now featured their own version of Buick's sculpted sweepspear. A trio of ventiports remained as a series hallmark, while more bright work appeared on the window surrounds and on the lower body and wheelhouse moldings. Special DeLuxe script was found on the rear fenders. Cloth and vinyl was used in the coupe and sedan. All-vinyl upholstery was used in the station wagon and was optional on the other models. Standard equipment included heater and defroster; cigar lighter; front and rear ash trays; energy-absorbing steering column; lane change feature in directional signals; shoulder and seat belts; inside day/night mirror; side marker lamps and other mandated safety equipment. Wipers were recessed below the hood line.

SPECIAL DELUXE SERIES 4300/43400 I.D. NUMBERS: On Special DeLuxes with V-6 power Vehicle Identification Numbers started with 433008( )600001. V-8 equipped car V.I.N.s started with 433008( )100001. The first five numerals represented the make and model. The sixth numeral '8' represented the 1968 model year. The seventh symbol was a letter representing the assembly plant. The last six digits represent the sequential assembly number at the plant with series mixed in production.

SPECIAL DELUXE SERIES 43300/43400

Series Number	Model Number	Body Type & Seating	Factory Price	Shipping Weight	Production Total
43300	43327	2-dr Coupe-6P	2988	3244	21,988
43300	43369	4-dr Sedan-6P	3039	3336	16,571
43400	43435	Sta Wag-6P	3371	3670	10,916

SPECIAL DELUXE ENGINES

V-6: Overhead valve. Cast iron block. Displacement: 250 cubic inches. bore and stroke: 3.875 x 3.53 inches. Compression ratio: 8.5:1. Brake horsepower: 155 at 4200 R.P.M. Hydraulic lifters. Two-barrel carburetor.

V-8: Overhead valve. Cast-iron block. Displacement: 350 cubic inches. Bore and stroke: 3.8 x 3.85 inches. Compression ratio: 9.0:1. Brake horsepower: 230 at 4400 R.P.M. Five main bearings. Hydraulic lifters. Two-barrel carburetor.

SKYLARK — SERIES 43500 — More similar to the Special DeLuxe than previous Skylarks, the 1968 version relied on a bright metal Sweepspear line, Skylark roof quarter panel emblems and Skylark script on the rear fenders for distinction. In place of the traditional ventiports there were triple-stacked horizontal bars mounted low on each fender. Inside was a DeLuxe steering wheel, lighted ash tray and glove box and full carpeting, in addition to Special DeLuxe features. Cloth and vinyl or all-vinyl upholstery was offered for the sedan. An all-vinyl front bench or notch back seat was offered for the two-door hardtop.

SKYLARK SERIES 43500 I.D. NUMBERS: On cars with V-6 power Vehicle Identification Numbers started with 435008( )600001. On V-8 equipped cars the V.I.N. started with 435008( )100001 up. An explanation of the V.I.N. code can be found under the 1968 Special DeLuxe Series 43300 listing.

SKYLARK SERIES 43500

Series Number	Model Number	Body Type & Seating	Factory Price	Shipping Weight	Production Total
43500	43569	4-dr Sedan-6P	3141	3374	27,384
43500	43537	2-dr H.T.-6P	3163	3286	32,795

SKYLARK ENGINES

V-6 and V-8 specifications were the same as those listed for the 1968 Special DeLuxe Series 43300.

SKYLARK CUSTOM — SERIES 44400 — More trim and fender skirts were added to the plushest Skylarks series. The Sweepspear molding continued onto the skirts and a Custom signature appeared below Skylark script on the rear fenders. Full wheel covers were featured. Interiors were refined with Custom padded seat cushions. The sedan was trimmed in plusher all-vinyl or vinyl and cloth and a notch back seat was available for the hardtop sedan. Convertibles came with all-vinyl trim and front bench seats with bucket seats optionally available. Custom seats had brushed metallic side braces, except on the buckets type. Standard equipment was otherwise similar to the Skylark.

SKYLARK CUSTOM SERIES 44400 I.D. NUMBERS: Vehicle Identification Numbers started at 44408( )100001. An explanation of the V.I.N. code may be found under the 1968 Special Series 43300 listing.

SKYLARK CUSTOM SERIES 44400

Series Number	Model Number	Body Type & Seating	Factory Price	Shipping Weight	Production Total
44400	44469	4-dr Sedan-6P	3294	3377	8,066
44400	44437	2-dr H.T. Cpe-6P	3326	3344	44,143
44400	44439	4-dr H.T. Sed-6P	3478	3413	12,984
44400	44467	Convertible-6P	3468	3394	8,188

SKYLARK CUSTOM ENGINES

Specifications were the same as those listed for the 1968 Special DeLuxe V-8.

GS 350 — SERIES 43400 — Trimmed like the Skylark Custom inside, the GS 350 had a more muscular outer appearance. Finned simulated air intakes were seen on the front fenders, while a lower body paint accent stripe replaced the bright molding. Bright wheel house moldings were used, but rear fender skirts were not. A GS 350 plaque was found on the center of the deck lid and further identification was seen on the grille and rear fenders with GS monogram appearing in such places and also on the door panels. All vinyl, foam-padded seats were standard equipment and bucket seats were optional. A specific grille with bright cross bar and textured background was used. An upper level instrument panel ventilation system was a new feature that eliminated the use of front ventipanes, or so Buick claimed. The hood had a scoop at the rear and concealed wipers.

NOTE: Another GS, the California GS, was actually numbered in the Special DeLuxe line (Style Number 43327). Standard California GS equipment included styled steel wheels, a vinyl roof covering, DeLuxe steering wheel, California script with GS emblems on the quarter panels and a GS emblem centered in the deck lid lip. Cloth and vinyl or horizontally pleated all-vinyl seating surfaces were offered. Standard features included DeLuxe steering wheel and crank-operated vent windows. Production figures and prices are not available.

GS 350 SERIES 43400

Series Number	Model Number	Body Type & Seating	Factory Price	Shipping Weight	Production Total
43400	43437	2-dr H.T. Cpe-6P	3295	3375	8,317

GS 350 ENGINE

Specifications were the same as listed for the 1968 Special Series 33300 V-8, except compression ratio was 10.25:1, brake horsepower was 280 at 4600 and a four-barrel carburetor was used.

GS 400 — SERIES 44600 — Yet another version of the new 1968 112-inch wheelbase intermediate coupe, the GS 400 was identified by a GS 400 plaque on each front fender, wide oval F70 x 14 white stripe tires, fake fender vents and functional hood scoops. Folding seat back latches were standard, with all-vinyl, bench front seating or optional front bucket seats.

GS 400 I.D. NUMBERS: Vehicle Identification Numbers began with 446008 ( ) 100001. An explanation of the V.I.N. code may be found under the 1968 Special DeLuxe Series 43300 listing.

GS 400 SERIES 44600

Series Number	Model Number	Body Type & Seating	Factory Price	Shipping Weight	Production Total
44600	44637	2-dr H.T. Cpe-6P	3528	3514	10,743
44600	44667	Convertible-6P	3672	3547	2,454

GS 400 ENGINE

V-8: Overhead valve. Cast iron block. Displacement: 400 cubic inches. Bore and stroke: 4.18 x 3.64 inches. Compression ratio: 10.25:1. Brake horsepower: 340 at 5000 R.P.M. Five main bearings. Hydraulic lifters. Four-barrel carburetor with chromed air cleaner top.

SPORTWAGON CUSTOM — SERIES 44400/44800 — Still on a stretched wheelbase and using the Skyroof treatment, the intermediate station wagons followed the sweepspear theme into 1968. All were Custom trimmed. Rear fender skirts were not used. Triple ventiports replaced the lower stacked fender bars that other models used. A full-length lower body highlight with wheel house moldings was seen. Sportwagon script decorated the rear quarters and tailgate. The all vinyl interior had full-carpeting and included 100 cubic feet of cargo space. Models with woodgrain body side transfers had their own style numbers.

SPORTWAGON SERIES 44400/44800

Series Number	Model Number	Body Type & Seating	Factory Price	Shipping Weight	Production Total
44400	44455	4-dr Sta Wag-2S	3341	3975	5,916
44400	44465	4-dr Sta Wag-3S	3499	4118	6,063
44800	44855	4-dr Sta Wag-2S	3711	3975	4,614
44800	44865	4-dr Sta Wag-3S	3869	4118	6,295

SPORTWAGON SERIES 44400/44800 I.D. NUMBERS: Vehicle Identification Numbers began with 444008( )100001. An explanation of the V.I.N. code may be found under the 1968 Special DeLuxe Series 43300 listing.

SPORTWAGON ENGINE

Specifications were the same as listed under 1968 Special DeLuxe Series 43300 V-8.

LESABRE — SERIES 45200 — Revised only slightly from 1967, the LeSabre was chiefly facelifted by the use of a new grille with more prominent center division and a textured background. The traditional trio of front fender ventiports was again a trademark. Bright rocker panel and wheelhouse moldings were used. Series designations were found on the rear fenders and instrument panel. Cloth and vinyl upholstery was standard. Regular features included shoulder belts (except convertible); glove box light; interior courtesy lights; smoking set; rear seat ash trays; two-speed wipers with washer and recessed arms; outside rear view mirror; energy absorbing steering column and other mandated safety features.

LESABRE SERIES 45200 I.D. NUMBERS: Vehicle Identification Numbers began with 452008( )100001. An explanation of V.I.N. codes may be found under the 1968 Special Series 4300 listing.

LESABRE SERIES 45200

Series Number	Model Number	Body Type & Seating	Factory Price	Shipping Weight	Production Total
45200	45269	4-dr Sedan-6P	4066	3956	37,433
45200	45287	2-dr H.T. Cpe-6P	4145	3923	14,922
45200	45239	4-dr H.T. Sed-6P	4203	3946	10,058

LESABRE ENGINE

Specifications were the same as those listed for the 1968 Special DeLuxe V-8.

LESABRE CUSTOM — SERIES 45400 — Custom interiors of plusher cloth and vinyl, with more ornate door panels, were used. All-vinyl was available and was standard in the convertible. Bucket seats were optional for the convertible and two-door hardtop. DeLuxe full wheel covers were included.

LESABRE CUSTOM SERIES 45400 I.D. NUMBERS: Vehicle Identification Numbers started with 454008( )100001. An explanation of V.I.N. codes appears in the 1968 Special DeLuxe Series 43300 listing.

LESABRE CUSTOM SERIES 45400

Series Number	Model Number	Body Type & Seating	Factory Price	Shipping Weight	Production Total
45400	45469	4-dr Sedan-6P	4157	3950	34,112
45400	45487	2-dr H.T.-6P	4233	3932	29,596
45400	45439	4-dr H.T.-6P	4297	4007	40,370
45400	45467	Convertible-6P	4426	3966	5,257

LESABRE CUSTOM ENGINE

Specifications were the same as listed for the 1968 Special DeLuxe V-8.

WILDCAT — SERIES 46400 — A new grille and revised body side moldings helped give the 1968 Wildcat a new look. Simulated air vents continued on front fenders. Narrow lower body side highlights and wheelhouse moldings were used to make a full-length bright lower strip. Wildcat lettering was found on the rear fenders, on the deck lid and on the instrument panel. An outside rear view mirror and back-up lamps were additional standard equipment inherited from lower-priced Buicks. Interiors were cloth and vinyl, with all-vinyl optional. Bucket seats upholstered in vinyl were a two-door hardtop option.

WILDCAT I.D. NUMBERS: Vehicle Identification Numbers began with 464008 ( ) 100001. An explanation of the V.I.N. code may be found under the 1968 Special DeLuxe Series 43300 listing.

WILDCAT SERIES 46400

Series Number	Model Number	Body Type & Seating	Factory Price	Shipping Weight	Production Total
46400	46469	4-dr Sedan-6P	4372	4107	15,201
46400	46487	2-dr H.T.-6P	4477	4125	10,708
46400	46439	4-dr H.T.-6P	4532	4171	15,173
46400	46667	Convertible-6P	4829	4122	3,572

WILDCAT ENGINE

V-8: Overhead valves. Cast iron block. Displacement: 430 cubic inches. Bore and stroke: 4.18 x 3.9 inches. Compression ratio: 10.5:1. Brake horsepower: 360 at 5000 R.P.M. Five main bearings. Hydraulic lifters. Four-barrel carburetor.

WILDCAT CUSTOM — SERIES 46600 — A plusher interior was the heart of the Custom Series. Brushed metallic door panel inserts were seen with cloth and vinyl trim combinations. A notch back seat with bright side braces was used, as were paddle-type arm rests and Custom headlining (except the convertible). All-vinyl trim was optional, except for the convertible, where it was standard. All-vinyl bucket seats were an option.

WILDCAT CUSTOM SERIES 46600 I.D. NUMBERS: Vehicle Identification Numbers began with 466008( )100001. An explanation of V.I.N. codes appears with the 1968 Special DeLuxe Series 43300 listing.

WILDCAT CUSTOM SERIES 46600

Series Number	Model Number	Body Type & Seating	Factory Price	Shipping Weight	Production Total
46600	46687	2-dr H.T. Cpe-6P	4698	4134	11,276
44600	44639	4-dr H.T. Sed-6P	4747	4253	14,059
46600	46667	Convertible-6P	4829	4122	3,572

WILDCAT CUSTOM ENGINE
Specifications were the same as listed for the 1968 Wildcat Series 46400.

1968 Buick, Electra 225 2-door hardtop, V-8 (TVB)

ELECTRA 225 — SERIES 48200 — The largest Buick was mildly restyled for 1968. New egg-crate textured grilles, divided by a color-accented panel, were up front. Squared rear fenders were tied together by a bumper housing the taillamps. Four ventiports continued to crown the largest of Buick fenders. Full length lower body moldings continued across the fender skirts. Specific full wheel covers were used. Electra 225 script was found on rear fenders and instrument panel, while the Series badge was found on the roof quarter panels (except the convertible). Standard features included power steering; power brakes; automatic transmission; custom padded seat cushions; electric clock; parking brake signal light; DeLuxe steering wheel and carpeted floors and lower doors.

ELECTRA 225 SERIES 48200 NUMBERS: Vehicle Identification Numbers began with 482008( )100001. An explanation of the V.I.N. code appears with the 1968 Special DeLuxe Series 43300 listing.

ELECTRA 225 SERIES 48200

Series Number	Model Number	Body Type & Seating	Factory Price	Shipping Weight	Production Total
48200	48269	4-dr Sedan-6P	4830	4253	12,723
48200	48257	2-dr H.T.-6P	4851	4180	10,705
48200	48239	4-dr H.T.-6P	4960	4270	15,376

ELECTRA 225 ENGINE
Specifications were the same as listed for the 1968 Wildcat Series 46400.

ELECTRA 225 CUSTOM — SERIES 48400 — Essentially a trim package, the Custom models were plusher inside. Cloth and vinyl combinations were used in the four-door hardtop, with an all-vinyl interior available. All-vinyl notch back seating was standard in the coupe and convertible, with all-vinyl buckets as option.

NOTE: Custom 'Limited' equipment was available for the Model 48439 four-door hardtop sedan and 48457 two-door hardtop cars so equipped had plusher cloth and vinyl upholstery with special accents. 'Limited' script appeared on the roof quarter panels. Production and price figures are not known.

ELECTRA 225 CUSTOM SERIES 48400

Series Number	Model Number	Body Type & Seating	Factory Price	Shipping Weight	Production Total
48400	48469	4-dr Sedan-6P	5045	4304	10,910
48400	48457	2-dr H.T. Cpe-6P	5030	4223	6,826
48400	48439	4-dr H.T. Sed-6P	5139	4314	50,846
48400	48467	Convertible-6P	5066	4285	7,976

ELECTRA 225 CUSTOM ENGINE
Specifications were the same as listed for the 1968 Wildcat Series 46400.

RIVIERA — SERIES 49487 — Once again using the same body shell, the Riviera had a new frontal appearance. Large parking lamps were housed within the bumper, which also framed the low, textured grille. Headlamps retracted above until needed. A wide, full-length lower body molding with bright wheel house moldings was used. Specific full wheel covers were seen. Riviera lettering appeared on front fenders and deck. Standard equipment included power steering; power brakes; tilt steering column; brake warning light; Custom-padded seat cushions; license frames and mandated safety features. Interior were bench or bucket seats in all-vinyl trim. Plusher Custom grade interiors were offered with fancier door panels incorporating the Riviera 'R' logo and all-vinyl Strato-bench or bucket seats, or cloth and vinyl Strato-bench front seats.

NOTE: Gran Sport equipment was offered for the 1968 Riviera. This consisted of heavy-duty front and rear suspension, positive traction differential, H70 x 15 red or white stripe tires and front fender GS monograms. The GS signature was also found on the instrument panel.

RIVIERA I.D. NUMBERS: Vehicle Identification Numbers began with 494878 ( ) 900001. An explanation of the V.I.N. code may be found under the 1968 Special DeLuxe Series 43300 listing.

RIVIERA SERIES 49487

Series Number	Model Number	Body Type & Seating	Factory Price	Shipping Weight	Production Total
49400	49487	2-dr H.T. Cpe-6P	5245	4222	49,284

RIVIERA ENGINE
Specifications were the same as listed for the 1968 Wildcat Series 46400.

CHASSIS FEATURES: Wheelbase: (Series 43300, 43500, 44400, 43400, and 44600 coupe and convertible) 112 inches: (Series 43300, 43500, 44400, 43400 and 44600 sedans and Special DeLuxe station wagon) 116 inches: (Sport wagons) 121 inches; (Series 45200 and 45400) 123 inches; (Series 46400 and 46600) 126 inches; (Series 49487) 119 inches. Overall length: (Series 43300, 43500, 44400, 43400 and 46600 coupe and convertible) 200.7 inches; (Series 43300, 43500, 44400, 43400 and 46600 sedan) 204.7 inches; (Sportwagon) 209.1 inches; (Series 45200 and 45400) 217.5 inches; (Series 46400 and 46600) 220.5 inches; (Series 48200 and 48400) 224.9 inches; (Series 49487) 215.2 inches. Tread: (Series 43300, 43500, 44400, 43400 and 44600) 59.35 inches front, 59.0 inches rear; (Series 45200 and 45400) 63 inches front and rear; (Series 46400, 46600, 48400 and 49487) 63.4 inches front, 63 inches rear. Tires: (Series 43300, 43500, 44400, 43400 and 44600) 7.75 x 14; (Sportwagon and Series 45200, 45400, 46400, 46600 and 49487) 8.45 x 15; (Series 48200 and 48400) 8.85 x 15.

CONVENIENCE FEATURES: Power steering (standard Series 48200, 48400 and 49487). Power brakes (standard on Series 48200, 48400 and 49487). Power windows (not offered for Special DeLuxe six-cyl.) Four-way power seat. Six-way power seat (full-size). Air conditioning. Vinyl top (special models). Seven-position tilt steering column. Limited trim on Electra Custom hardtops. AM/FM stereo radio. Tape deck. Strato seats (Series 49487) Chrome road wheels. AM radio. AM/FM radio. Whitewall tires. DeLuxe wheelcovers. Soft-Ray glass. Cruise Master. GS 350/GS 400 consolette, tachometer, for manual transmission. Full-length console (bucket seats and Super Turbine transmission required). Cornering lights (full-size only). Automatic Climate Control. Power front disc brakes. Automatic door locks. Trailer hitch. Rear window defroster. Remote control outside rear view mirror. Speed alert. Super DeLuxe wheelcovers. Radial ply tires. Power tailgate window on station wagons. Luggage rack for station wagons.

Historical footnotes: Styles 44455 and 44465 are Sportwagons; Styles 44855 and 44865 are Sportwagons with woodgrain sides. Style 43327 was the California GS.

1969 BUICK

SPECIAL DELUXE — SERIES 43300 — The basic Buick for 1969 appeared with a minimum of change form its 1968 counterpart. A trio of bright outlined ventiports and bright housings for the side marker lamps were part of the minimal bodyside bright work. Special DeLuxe script appeared on the rear fenders. Among the standard features, many being mandated by new federal safety standards, were backup lamps, a lefthand outside rear view mirror and seat belts.

SPECIAL DELUXE SERIES 43300/43400 I.D. NUMBERS: Cars with V-6 power had Vehicle Identification Numbers beginning with 433009( )600001 and V-8 equipped Vehicle Identification Numbers began with 433009( )100001. The first five numerals represent the make and model. The sixth numeral '9' represents the 1969 model year. The seventh symbol, a letter, represents the assembly plant. The last six digits represent the sequential assembly number at the plant with series mixed in production.

SPECIAL DELUXE SERIES 43300/43400

Series Number	Model Number	Body Type & Seating	Factory Price	Shipping Weight	Production Total
43300	43327	2-dr Coupe	2673	3245	15,268
43300	43369	4-dr Sedan	2724	3301	11,113
4400	43455	4-dr Sta Wag-2S	3446	3736	2,590
43400	43436	4-dr Sta-Wag-2S	3478	3783	6,677

SPECIAL DELUXE ENGINES
V-6: Overhead valves. Cast-iron block. Displacement: 250 cubic inches. Bore and stroke: 3.875 x 3.53 inches. Compression ratio: 8.5:1. Brake horsepower: 155 at 4200 R.P.M. Hydraulic valve lifters. Two-barrel carburetor.
V-8: Overhead valves. Cast iron block. Displacement: 350 cubic inches. Bore and stroke: 3.8 x 3.5 inches. Compression ratio: 9.0:1. Brake horsepower: 230 at 4400 R.P.M. Five main bearings. Hydraulic valve lifters. Two-barrel carburetor.

NOTE: Style 43327 was also built in California GS trim, with bright wheel house moldings, vinyl top with GS monograms on the roof quarters and a GS emblem on the deck lid. A functional hood scoop, with the opening near the windshield, was included as well. The word California was spelled out in script on the rear fenders. The California GS coupes had vent windows. Production numbers were included with the Special DeLuxe coupe.

SKYLARK — SERIES 43500 — Reduced to a two model line for 1969, the Skylark featured minimal side trim, with a trio of leaning vertical bright bars on each front fender. Skylark script appeared on the rear fenders. The grille had a horizontal division bar.

SKYLARK SERIES 43500 I.D. NUMBERS: Serial numbers began with 435009 ( ) 600001 on cars equipped with the V-6. Serial numbers began with 435009 ( ) 100001 on V-8 cars. An explanation of the V.I.N. code may be found under the 1968 Special DeLuxe Series 43300 listing.

SKYLARK SERIES 43500

Series Number	Model Number	Body Type & Seating	Factory Price	Shipping Weight	Production Total
43500	43537	2-dr Coupe-6P	2847	3298	38,658
43500	43569	4-dr Sedan-6P	2826	3328	22,349

SKYLARK ENGINES
Six-cylinder and V-8 specifications were the same as listed for the 1969 Special DeLuxe Series 43300.

SKYLARK CUSTOM — SERIES 44400 — The plushest intermediate Buick, had better quality vinyl and cloth or all-vinyl interiors, a bright lower body molding and wheel-house moldings. A chrome sweepspear molding was optional and, at the front, a Buick emblem was centered in the grille.

SKYLARK CUSTOM SERIES 44400 I.D. NUMBERS: Vehicle Identification Numbers began with 444009( )100001. V.I.N.s were coded as explained in the 1969 Special DeLuxe Series 43300 listing.

SKYLARK SERIES 43500

Series Number	Model Number	Body Type & Seating	Factory Price	Shipping Weight	Production Total
43500	43537	2-dr Coupe-6P	2847	3298	38,658
43500	43569	4-dr Sedan-6P	2826	3328	22,349

SKYLARK ENGINES
Six-cylinder and V-8 specifications were the same as listed for the 1969 Special DeLuxe Series 43300.

SKYLARK CUSTOM — SERIES 44400 — The plushest intermediate Buick, had better quality vinyl and cloth or all-vinyl interiors, a bright lower body molding and wheelhouse moldings. A chrome sweepspear molding was optional and, at the front, a Buick emblem was centered in the grille.

SKYLARK CUSTOM SERIES 44400 I.D. NUMBERS: Vehicle Identification Numbers began with 444009( )100001. V.I.N. s were coded as explained under the 1969 Special DeLuxe Series 43300 listing.

Series Number	Model Number	Body Type & Seating	Factory Price	Shipping Weight	Production Total
4440	44437	2-dr Spt Cpe-6P	3009	3341	35,639
44400	44439	4-dr H.T. Sed-6P	3151	3477	9,609
44400	44467	Convertible-6P	3152	3398	6,552
44400	44469	4-dr Sedan-6P	2978	3397	6,423

SKYLARK CUSTOM ENGINE: V-8 specifications were the same as listed for the 1969 Special DeLuxe Series 43300.

GS 350 — SERIES 43437 — A one-style series for 1969 was the GS 350. Once again this car combined the Skylark's Custom interior accoutrements with a sporting car's exterior. Front fenders carried neither ventiports or vents this year, while the wheelhouse, moldings were continued. A GS 350 plaque was used on the center of the deck lid, with monograms on the grille and door panels. All-vinyl, foam-padded seats were standard, with the bucket versions an option. Upper level ventilation, without vent windows, was a distinctive feature.

GS 350 SERIES 43437 I.D. NUMBERS: Vehicle Identification Numbers began with 434379( )100001. An explanation of V.I.N. codes appears in the 1969 Special DeLuxe listing.

GS 350 SERIES 43437

Series Number	Model Number	Body Type & Seating	Factory Price	Shipping Weight	Production Total
43400	43437	2-dr Spt Cpe-5P	2980	3406	4,933

GS 350 ENGINE
Specifications were the same as listed for the 1969 Special DeLuxe Series 43300 V-8 except the compression ratio was 10.25:1, brake horsepower was 280 at 4600 R.P.M. and a four-barrel carburetor was used.

1969 Buick, GS-400 2-dr hardtop sport coupe, V-8 (TVB)

GS 400 — SERIES 44600 — Similar to the GS 350, the most potent Buick had 400 numerals on the hood scoop and rear quarters. A DeLuxe steering wheel was standard, along with foam-padded seats, ash tray light, glove box light and upper interior light. Interiors were all-vinyl, with a bench front seat standard and buckets available optionally.

GS 400 SERIES 44600 I.D. NUMBERS: Vehicle Identification Numbers began with 446009( )100001. An explanation of the V.I.N. codes appears under the 1969 Special DeLuxe Series 43300 listing.

GS 400 SERIES 44600

Series Number	Model Number	Body Type & Seating	Factory Price	Shipping Weight	Production Total
44600	44637	2-dr H.T. Cpe-6P	3578	3549	6,356
44600	44667	Convertible-6P	3722	3594	1,176

GS 400 ENGINE
V-8: Overhead valve. Cast iron block. Displacement: 400 cubic inches. Bore and stroke: 4.18 x 3.64 inches. Compression ratio: 10.25:1. Brake horsepower: 340 at 5000 R.P.M. Hydraulic lifters: Four-barrel carburetor.

SPORTWAGON CUSTOM — SERIES 44400 — Numbered in the Skylark Custom series, but with varied trim, these wagons had bright wheelhouse and rocker panel moldings, woodgrain side trim and Sportwagon script on the rear fenders. They were fully carpeted, including the cargo areas and used expanded vinyl trimming. A DeLuxe steering wheel, Custom padded seat cushions and the features of the Custom Skylark were used.

SPORT WAGON CUSTOM SERIES 44400 I.D. NUMBERS: Vehicle Identification Numbers began with 444009H10001. V.I.N. numbers were coded as explained in the 1969 Special DeLuxe Series 43300 listing.

SPORTWAGON CUSTOM SERIES 44400

Series Number	Model Number	Body Type & Seating	Factory Price	Shipping Weight	Production Total
44400	44456	4-dr Sta Wag-2S	3819	4106	9,157
44400	44466	4-dr Sta Wag-3S	3975	4231	11,513

SPORTWAGON ENGINE
Specifications were the same as those listed for the Special DeLuxe V-8. Series 43300/43400.

1969 Buick, LeSabre 4-dr hardtop sedan, V-8 (TVB)

LESABRE — SERIES 45200 — A new body greeted LeSabre buyers for 1969. Styling was refined and lighter than in immediately preceding years. The LeSabre still wore its trios of front fenders ventiports and a narrow argent accent strip rocker panel was used. LeSabre script appeared on the rear fenders, with further series identification found on the instrument panel. Standard equipment included upper level ventilation system (instead of ventipanes); door-operated interior lights; glove compartment light; smoking set; rear seat ash tray; front and rear arm rests and full carpeting.

NOTE: The LeSabre '400' option, offered for LeSabre and LeSabre Custom models, included a 280 horsepower, 350 cubic inch V-8 and TurboHydramatic transmission. Cars so equipped had '400' emblems on the rear fenders, below the LeSabre script.

LESABRE SERIES 45200 I.D. NUMBERS: Vehicle Identification Numbers began with 452009( )100001. V.I.N. numbers were coded as explained under the 1969 Special DeLuxe Series 43300 listing.

LESABRE SERIES 45200

Series Number	Model Number	Body Type & Seating	Factory Price	Shipping Weight	Production Total
45200	45269	4-dr Sedan-6P	4126	3966	36,664
45200	45237	2-dr H.T.-6P	4208	3936	16,201
45200	45239	4-dr H.T.-6P	4266	3983	17,235

LESABRE ENGINE
Specifications were the same as listed for the 1969 Special DeLuxe V-8 Series 43300/43400.

LESABRE CUSTOM — SERIES 45400 This represented a plusher edition of the popular LeSabre. A broader metal rocker panel molding, with rear fender extension, was used with bright wheelhouse moldings to accent Custom level trim. Custom Script appeared on the rear fenders beneath the LeSabre signatures. Inside, plusher cloth and vinyl trim combinations were found, or an all-vinyl interior could be chosen. Bucket seats were optional for the Custom Sport Coupe.

LESABRE CUSTOM SERIES 45400 I.D. NUMBERS: Vehicle Identification Numbers began with 454009( )100001. V.I.N.s were coded as explained under the 1969 Special DeLuxe listing.

LESABRE CUSTOM SERIES 45400

Series Number	Model Number	Body Type & Seating	Factory Price	Shipping Weight	Production Total
45400	45469	4-dr Sedan-6P	4220	3941	37,136
45400	45437	2-dr H.T. Cpe-6P	4296	4018	38,887
45400	45439	4-dr H.T. Sed-6P	4360	4073	48,123
45400	45469	Convertible-6P	4489	3958	3,620

LESABRE CUSTOM ENGINE
Specifications are the same as listed for the Special DeLuxe V-8 Series 43300/43400.

WILDCAT — SERIES 46400 — Sharing the LeSabre's sheetmetal, but with styling touches suggesting a more powerful, sporting automobile, the Wildcat had a distinctive grille with vertical texturing. A bright, broad rocker molding with fender extensions and wheelhouse moldings was used. Wildcat script appeared above groups of five vertical bars on each front fender. Standard equipment was the same as the LeSabre except for the addition of a DeLuxe steering wheel. Interiors were cloth and vinyl or all-vinyl. Bucket seats, with all-vinyl seating surfaces, were offered for the Sport Coupe.

WILDCAT SERIES 46400 I.D. NUMBERS: Vehicle Identification Numbers began with 464009( )100001. V.I.N.s were coded as explained under the 1969 Special DeLuxe Series 43300 listing.

WILDCAT SERIES 46400

Series Number	Model Number	Body Type & Seating	Factory Price	Shipping Weight	Production Total
46400	46439	4-dr Sedan-6P	4448	4102	13,126
46400	46437	2-dr H.T. Cpe-6P	4553	3926	12,416
46400	46439	4-dr H.T. Sed-6P	4608	4204	13,805

WILDCAT ENGINE
V-8: Overhead valves. Cast iron block. Displacement: 430 cubic inches. Bore and stroke: 4.18 x 3.9 inches. Compression ratio: 10.5:1. Brake horsepower: 360 at 5000 R.P.M. Five main bearings. Hydraulic valve lifters. Four-barrel carburetor.

WILDCAT CUSTOM — SERIES 46600 — Custom quality cloth and vinyl or all-vinyl interiors were the hallmark of the custom series, with notch back front seats featured. Otherwise, the cars were the same as the Wildcat Series 45200 models.

WILDCAT CUSTOM SERIES 46600 I.D. NUMBERS: Vehicle Identification Numbers began with 466009( )100001. V.I.N.s were coded as explained under the 1969 Special DeLuxe listing.

WILDCAT CUSTOM SERIES 46600

Series Number	Model Number	Body Type & Seating	Factory Price	Shipping Weight	Production Total
46600	46637	2-dr H.T.-6P	4774	4134	12,136
46600	46639	4-dr H.T.-6P	4823	4220	13,596
46600	46667	Convertible-6P	4905	4152	2,374

WILDCAT CUSTOM ENGINE
Specifications were the same as listed for the 1969 Wildcat Series 46400.

ELECTRA 225 SERIES 48200 — A large, yet graceful, body was used for Buick's biggest models in 1969. A tapering sweepspear sculpture line and rear fender skirts contributed to the smooth-flowing Electra lines. A group of four ventiports were lined out on each front fender. The lower body was swathed in bright metal from the front bumper to the rear, with a kick-up over the front wheelhouse lip. A specifically designed grille texture was used. Rear taillamps were horizontal and were behind bright grids. Electra 225 emblems were on the rear fenders and deck. Round rear fender marker lights were exclusive to the Electra 225 styles. Standard features in addition to those found on the Wildcat, included power steering; power brakes; automatic transmission; Custom padded seat cushions; electric clock; carpeted floors and lower doors and side coat hooks. Interiors were cloth and vinyl or all-vinyl, with front bench seats.

ELECTRA 225 SERIES 48200 I.D. NUMBERS: Vehicle Identification Numbers began with 482009H100001. V.I.N.s were coded as explained under the 1969 Special DeLuxe Series 43300 listing.

ELECTRA 225 SERIES 48200

Series Number	Model Number	Body Type & Seating	Factory Price	Shipping Weight	Production Total
48200	42869	4-dr Sedan-6P	4932	4238	14,521
48200	48257	2-dr H.T. Cpe-6P	4953	4203	13,128
48200	48239	4-dr H.T. Sed-6P	5062	4294	15,983

ELECTRA 225 ENGINE
Specifications were the same as listed for the 1969 Wildcat Series 46400.

ELECTRA 225 CUSTOM — SERIES 48400 — A more refined interior was the basis of the Custom Electra. Expanded vinyl notch back front seats were used in the two-door hardtop and four-door hardtop, while vinyl and cloth bench or notch back type front seats were found in sedans. Expanded vinyl trim, with notch back front seat, power windows and two-way power seat adjustments were standard on the Custom Convertible.

NOTE: Custom Limited equipment was available for the two-door hardtop and four-door hardtop. Cars so-equipped had better quality vinyl and cloth or all-vinyl interior trims with a 60/40 front deck. Limited scripts appeared on the roof quarters.

ELECTRA 225 CUSTOM SERIES 48400 I.D. NUMBERS: Vehicle Identification Numbers began with 484009H100001. V.I.N.s were coded as explained under the 1969 Special DeLuxe Series 43300 listing.

ELECTRA 225 CUSTOM SERIES 48400

Series Number	Model Number	Body Type & Seating	Factory Price	Shipping Weight	Production Total
48400	48469	4-dr Sedan-6P	5147	4281	14,434
48400	48457	2-dr H.T. Cpe-6P	5132	4222	27,018
48400	48439	4-dr H.T. Sed-6P	5241	4328	65,240
48400	48467	Convertible-6P	5168	4309	8,294

ELECTRA 225 CUSTOM ENGINE
Specifications were the same as listed for the 1969 Wildcat Series 46400.

RIVIERA — SERIES 49487 — A slight facelift was seen for 1969 as the sleek Riviera continued to be offered only in sport coupe form. Retractable headlamps and an intregal front bumper/grille continued to distinguish the front of the Riviera. New body side trims using bright wheelhouse moldings and bright lower body moldings with argent accents were utilized. Expanded vinyl with front bench or bucket seats was standard Custom interiors with bench, buckets or notch back front seats in plusher vinyl or vinyl and cloth combinations was available. Standard Riviera features included all items found on other Buicks, plus wood grained dash accents and trunk lights.

NOTE: A new Riviera GS option package sold for $131.57 at retail. It included chrome covered air cleaner; front and rear heavy-duty suspension; performance axle with positive traction differential; and white sidewall tires. Cars with the package installed were outwardly distinguished by special narrow rocker panel covers, the lack of gravel deflectors, and a thin side trim molding.

RIVIERA I.D. NUMBERS: Vehicle Identification Numbers began with 494879H900001. V.I.N.s were coded as explained under the 1969 Special DeLuxe Series 43300 listing.

RIVIERA SERIES 49487

Series Number	Model Number	Body Type & Seating	Factory Price	Shipping Weight	Production Total
49400	49487	2-dr Spt Cpe-5P	5331	4199	52,872

RIVIERA ENGINE
Specifications were the same as listed for the 1969 Wildcat Series 46400.

CHASSIS FEATURES: Wheelbase: (Series 43300, 43500, 44400, 43400, 44600 two-door styles) 112 inches; (four-door styles) 116 inches; (Sportwagon) 121 inches; (Series 45200, 45400, 46400 and 46600) 123.2 inches; (Series 48200 and 48400) 126.2 inches; (Series 49487) 119 inches. Overall length: (Series 43300, 43500, 44400, 43400 and 44600 two-door styles) 200.7 inches; (four-door styles) 204.7 inches; (Station wagon) 209 inches; (Sportwagon) 214 inches; (Series 45200, 45400, 46400 and 46600) 218.2 inches. Tread: (Series 43300, 43500, 44400, and 43300 and 44600) 59 inches front and rear; (Series 42500, 45400, 46400 and 46600) 63.5 inches front and 63 inches rear; (Series 48200, 48400 and 49487) 63.4 inches front and 63 inches rear. Tires: (Series 43300, 43500, 44400, 43400 and 46600) 7.75 x 14; (Sportwagon) 8.55 x 14; (Series 45200, 45400, 46400, 46600, 48200, 48400 and 49487) 8.55 x 15.

POWERTRAIN OPTIONS: A three-speed manual transmission with column shift was standard on Special DeLuxe, Skylark, Skylark Custom, GS 350, LeSabre, and Wildcat models. A three-speed manual transmission with floor shift was standard on GS 400 models and optional on California GS and GS 350 models. A four-speed manual transmission was optional on California GS, GS 350 and GS 400 models. Super Turbine 300 automatic transmission was optional for Special DeLuxe, Skylark, Skylark Custom and LeSabre models. TurboHydramatic 350 automatic transmission was optional for Special DeLuxe, Skylark, Skylark Custom and GS 350 models. TurboHydramatic 400 automatic transmission was optional for GS 400 and Wildcat models and was standard on Electra 225, Electra Custom and Riviera models. A 280 brake horsepower, 350 cubic inch V-8 was optional for the Special DeLuxe, Skylark, Skylark Custom and LeSabre. A '400' option package for the LeSabre series included the 280 horsepower 350 V-8 an TurboHydramatic 400 transmission. Cars so equipped had '400' emblems below the rear fender LeSabre scripts. A 'Stage I' option was offered for the GS 400. It included a high-lift camshaft, special carburetor and large diameter dual exhausts, along with a 3.64 rear axle. Cars so equipped had 'Stage I' emblems on the front fenders.

CONVENIENCE OPTIONS included air conditioning ($376 on intermediate, $437 on full-size). Power windows. Vinyl top. Seven-position tilt wheel. AM radio. AM/FM radio. AM/FM radio with stereo tape. Five-spoke Sport Wheels (chrome). Strato buckt seats on specific models. Limited Trim option for Electra 225 Custom ($231). Map light on rear view mirror. 60/40 seat (Electra 225 styles). Electric window defogger (Riviera). Protective body side moldings (full-size). Power door locks. Power steering (standard Electra 225, Electra 225 Custom and Riviera). Power brakes (standard Electra 225, Electra 225 Custom and Riviera). Climate-control air (full-size). Center console with bucket seats on Skylark Custom, GS 350, GS 400 and Wildcat when equipped with TH-350 or TH-400 automatic transmission. Four-way power seat. Six-way power seat. (Electra 225s, Wildcat, LeSabre). Trailering packages. Dual action tailgate on station wagons.

Historical footnotes: Model 43536 was a station wagon with dual-action tailgate and plusher interior.

1970 BUICK

SKYLARK — SERIES 43300 — A new look was used for 1970, with crisper lines and more open wheelhouses. The sweepspear look was once again relagated to retirement, with horizontal sculpturing taking its place. The basic Buick had a vertically textured grille with a grid overlay. Narrow lower body moldings and wheelhouse bright moldings were used. Skylark emblems were on the roof sail panels and side marker lamps were rectangular. The Skylark signature appeared on rear fenders. Interiors were spartan with vinyl and cloth combinations on bench seats standard. All-vinyl was no-cost option for the Coupe and an extra cost option for the Sedan. Standard equipment included a host of mandated safety features, including lefthand outside rear view mirror and back-up lights.

SKYLARK SERIES 43300 I.D. NUMBERS: Vehicle Identification Numbers began with 433000( )600001 on V-6 cars. V.I.N.s began with 433000( )100001 on V-8 cars. The first five numerals represent the make and model. The sixth numeral, '0' represents the 1970 model year. The seventh symbol, a letter represents the assembly plant code. The last six digits are the sequential production number at the assembly plant with series mixed in production.

SKYLARK SERIES 43300

Series Number	Model Number	Body Type & Seating	Factory Price	Shipping Weight	Production Total
43300	43327	2-dr Coupe-6P	3177	3350	18,620
43300	43369	4-dr Sedan-6P	3228	3409	13,420

SKYLARK ENGINES
Six-cyl: Overhead valves. Cast-iron block. Displacement: 250 cubic inches. Bore and stroke: 3.875 x 3.53 inches. Compression ratio: 8.5:1. Brake horsepower: 155 at 4200 R.P.M. Five main bearings. Hydraulic valve lifters. Two-barrel carburetor.
V-8: Overhead valve. Cast iron block. Displacement: 350 cubic inches. Bore and stroke: 3.8 x 3.85 inches. Compression ratio: 9.0:1. Brake horsepower: 260 at 4600 R.P.M. Five main bearings. Hydraulic valve lifters. Two-barrel carburetor.

SKYLARK 350 — SERIES 43500 — Identical to the Skylark, except for the addition of 350 emblems to the body and a Buick emblem for the center grille.

SKYLARK 350 SERIES 43500 I.D. NUMBERS: Vehicle Identification Numbers began with 43500( )100001. V.I.N. codes are explained under the 1970 Skylark Series 43300 listing.

SKYLARK SERIES 43500

Series Number	Model Number	Body Type & Seating	Factory Price	Shipping Weight	Production Total
43500	43569	4-dr Sedan-6P	3350	3418	30,281
43500	43537	2-dr Coupe-6P	3351	3375	70,918

SKYLARK 350 ENGINE
Specifications were the same as listed for the 1970 Skylark Series 43300 V-8.

SKYLARK CUSTOM — SERIES 44400 — The plushest intermediate model had a Buick emblem centered in the grille, lower body and wheelhouse moldings and Skylark signatures on the hood, deck and rear fenders. The Custom badge appeared beneath the rear fender signatures. Interiors were done in all-vinyl or Kenora cloth and vinyl. A bench seat was standard, with bucket front seats available for the convertible and coupe.

SKYLARK CUSTOM SERIES 44400 I.D. NUMBERS: Vehicle Identification Numbers began with 44400( )100001. V.I.N. codes are explained under the 1970 Skylark Series 33300 listing.

SKYLARK CUSTOM SERIES 44400

Series Number	Model Number	Body Type & Seating	Factory Price	Shipping Weight	Production Total
44400	44469	4-dr Sedan-6P	3482	3499	7,113
44400	44437	2-dr H.T. Cpe-6P	3513	3435	36,367
44400	44439	4-dr H.T. Sed-6P	3601	3565	12,411
44400	44467	Convertible-6P	3656	3499	4,954

SKYLARK CUSTOM ENGINES
Six-cyl. and V-8 specifications were the same as listed for the 1970 Skylark Series 43300.

1970 Buick, GS-455 2-dr hardtop coupe, V-8 (TVB)

GRAN SPORT — SERIES 43437 — A one-model series constituted Buick's cosmetic muscle car for 1970. This was a mild-mannered intermediate with the trimmings of a rip-roaring charger. A textured black grille was used, with hood scoops on the panel above. GS signatures appeared on the left hand grille, front fenders and deck. All-vinyl bench seats in Sandalwood, blue or black were standard. An all-vinyl notch back seat was optional, as were individual front bucket seats. Standard equipment approximated that found on the Skylark Custom.

GRAN SPORT SERIES 43400 I.D. NUMBERS:
Vehicle Identification Numbers began with 434370( )100001. V.I.N.s were coded as explained under the 1970 Skylark Series 33300 listing.

GRAN SPORT SERIES 43400

Series Number	Model Number	Body Type & Seating	Factory Price	Shipping Weight	Production Total
43400	43437	2-dr H.T. Cpe-6P	3479	3434	9,948

GRAN SPORT ENGINE
V-8: Specifications were the same as the Skylark Series 33300 V-8 except the compression ratio was 10.25:1, brake horsepower was 315 at 4800 R.P.M. and dual exhausts were standard.

GRAN SPORT 445 — SERIES 44600 — This was the truly muscular Buick with a new big block V-8 and Hurst-shifted performance transmissions. Functional hood-scoops dumped cold air into the big V-8's intake. Chrome red-filled lower body and wheelhouse moldings were used with five-spoke 14 x 6 inch chrome wheels standard. A GS 455 emblem appeared on the lefthand blacked-out grille with others showing up on the front fenders and a GS monogram appearing on the deck lid. Standard interior appointments were the same as on the GS. A number of mandated safety features were standard.

GRAN SPORT SERIES 46600 I.D. NUMBERS:
Vehicle Identification Numbers began with 46000( )100001. V.I.N.s were coded as explained under the 1970 Skylark Series 43300 listing.

GRAN SPORT 455 SERIES 46600

Series Number	Model Number	Body Type & Seating	Factory Price	Shipping Weight	Production Total
44600	44637	2-dr H.T.-6P	3685	3562	8,732
44600	44667	Convertible-6P	3871	3619	1,416

GRAN SPORT 455 ENGINE
V-8: Overhead valves. Cast-iron block. Displacement: 455 cubic inches. Bore and stroke: 4.3 x 3.9 inches. Compression ratio: 10.0:1. Brake horsepower: 350 at 4600 R.P.M. Hydraulic valve lifters. Five main bearings. Four-barrel carburetor.

NOTE: Stage I equipment, consisting of a high-lift camshaft, special four-barrel carburetor and low-restriction dual exhaust increased brake horsepower to 360. Cars so equipped had Stage I badges in place of 455 emblems. There was also a Stage II dealer-installed package: hotter cam, 12 to 1 forged pistons, Edelbrock B4B manifold, Holley carb, Micky Thompson headers and 4.78 differential gears.

SPORTWAGON — SERIES 43400 — The traditional roof panel with glass inserts was missing from the 1970 Sportwagons which had a flat roof. Narrow lower body moldings were used with bright wheelhouse moldings. Sportwagon script appeared on the rear fenders. Interiors were similar to the corresponding Skylark models with all-vinyl trimming. Fiberglass belted tires were standard.

SPORTWAGON SERIES 43400 I.D. NUMBERS:
Vehicle Identification Numbers began with (434000( )100001. V.I.N.s were coded as explained under the 1970 Skylark Series 33300 listing.

SPORTWAGON SERIES 43400

Series Number	Model Number	Body Type & Seating	Factory Price	Shipping Weight	Production Total
43400	43435	4-dr Sta Wag-2S	3591	3775	2,239
43400	43436	4-dr Sta Wag-2S	3623	3998	10,002

NOTE: Prices and weights for V-8s are given. Deduct $11 for 6-cylinder models.

SPORTWAGON ENGINES
Specifications for 6-cyl and V-8 were the same as listed under 1970 Skylark Series 43300 engine date.

LESABRE — SERIES 45200 — The lowest-priced full-size Buick featured a very minor facelift for 1970. A new grille-bumper combination with horizontal textured grille was at the front, while at the rear the taillights dropped into the bumper assembly. A lower body molding was used, but there were no wheelhouse moldings. The LeSabre name appeared in script on the rear fenders an triple ventiports were found on the front. Cloth and vinyl seating surfaces were standard with a front bench. The LeSabre signature was on the righthand instrument panel. Standard equipment included Comfort-Flo ventilation; heater and defroster; front-door operated interior light; glove compartment; smoking set; rear seat ash tray and carpeting front and rear.

LESABRE SERIES 45200 I.D. NUMBERS:
Vehicle Identificaton Numbers began with 452000( )100001. V.I.N.s were coded as explained under the 1970 Skylark Series 43300 listing.

LESABRE SERIES 45200

Series Number	Model Number	Body Type & Seating	Factory Price	Shipping Weight	Production Total
45200	45269	4-dr Sedan-6P	4278	3970	35,404
45200	45237	2-dr H.T. Cpe-6P	4360	3866	14,163
45200	45239	4-dr H.T. Sed-6P	4418	4018	14,817

LESABRE ENGINE
Specifications were the same as listed for the 1970 Skylark Series 33300.

LESABRE CUSTOM — SERIES 45400 — A plusher LeSabre was seen this year. It had wheelhouse moldings in addition to bright lower body moldings, which now extended onto the rear fenders. Custom badges appeared below the rear fender LeSabre scripts. Richer cloth and vinyl or all-vinyl (convertible) interiors were standard.

LESABRE SERIES 45200 I.D. NUMBERS:
Vehicle Identification Numbers began with 45200( )100001. V.I.N.s were coded as explained under the 1970 Skylark Series 43300 listing.

LESABRE CUSTOM SERIES 45400

Series Number	Model Number	Body Type & Seating	Factory Price	Shipping Weight	Production Total
45400	45469	4-dr Sedan-6P	4372	3950	36,682
45400	45437	2-dr H.T. Cpe-6P	4448	3921	35,641
45400	45439	4-dr H.T. Cpe-6P	4512	3988	43,863
45400	45467	Convertible-6P	4641	3947	2,487

LESABRE CUSTOM ENGINE
Specifications were the same as listed for the 1970 Skylark Series 43300.

LESABRE CUSTOM — SERIES 45600 — Identical to the LeSabre Custom externally, this model had rear fender badges signifying use of the big 455 V-8 and was numbered as a separate series. The convertibles was not available in this series.

LESABRE CUSTOM 455 SERIES 45400 I.D. NUMBERS:
Vehicle Identification Numbers began with 456000( )100001. V.I.N.s were coded as explained under the 1970 Skylark Series 43300 listing.

LESABRE CUSTOM 455 SERIES 45600

Series Number	Model Number	Body Type & Seating	Factory Price	Shipping Weight	Production Total
45600	45669	4-dr Sedan-6P	4562	4107	5,555
45600	45637	2-dr H.T. Cpe-6P	4638	4066	5,469
45600	45639	4-d H.T. Sed-6P	4702	4143	6,541

LESABRE CUSTOM 455 ENGINE
V-8: Overhead valves. Cast-iron block. Displacement: 455 cubic inches. Bore and stroke: 4.3 x 3.9 inches. Compression ratio: 10.0:1. Brake horsepower: 370 at 4600 R.P.M. Five main bearings. Hydraulic valve lifters. Four-barrel carburetor.

1970 Buick, Estate Wagon 4-dr station wagon, V-8 (TVB)

ESTATE WAGONS — SERIES 46000 — A full-size Buick wagon was marketed for the first time since 1964. It had the basic LeSabre body, but wore four ventiports on the front fenders. The LeSabre Custom's bright rocker, wheelhouse and rear lower fender moldings were used. Woodgraining was an option for the body side. Interiors were all-vinyl in a Custom grade.

ESTATE WAGON SERIES 46000 I.D. NUMBERS:
Vehicle Identification Numbers began with 460000( )100001. V.I.N.s were coded as explained under the 1970 Skylark Series 43300 listing.

ESTATE WAGON SERIES 4600

Series Number	Model Number	Body Type & Seating	Factory Price	Shipping Weight	Production Total
46000	46036	4-dr Sta Wag-2S	4902	4691	11,427
46000	46046	4-dr Sta Wag-2S	5047	4779	16,879

ESTATE WAGON ENGINE
Specifications were the same as those listed for the 1970 LeSabre Custom 455.

WILDCAT CUSTOM — SERIES 46600 — The Wildcat came only with Custom trim for 1970. It shared the LeSabre body with its new intregal grille and front bumper assembly, but a grid-pattern bright overlay on the grille itself distinguished the Wildcat. There were no Ventiports, but there was a simulated bright air intake on each front fender. There was also a wide bright molding extending along the lower body, with connecting strips over the wheelhouse, from front to rear. The Wildcat signature appeared on the grille, deck and front fenders above the inlet grids. Vinyl notch back or bucket seats were standard, with a cloth and vinyl combination offered for the four-door hardtop. Standard equipment was the same as on the LeSabre except for DeLuxe steering wheel. The Wildcat signature appeared on the instrument panel.

WILDCAT CUSTOM SERIES 46600 I.D. NUMBERS:
Vehicle Identification Numbers began with 466000( )100001. V.I.N.s are coded as explained under the 1970 Skylark Series 43300 listing.

WILDCAT CUSTOM SERIES 4600

Series Number	Model Number	Body Type & Seating	Factory Price	Shipping Weight	Production Total
46600	46637	2-dr H.T. Cpe-6P	5096	4099	9,477
46600	46639	4-dr H.T. Sed-6P	5117	4187	12,924
46600	46667	Convertible-6P	5227	4214	1,244

WILDCAT CUSTOM ENGINE
Specifications were the same as those listed for the 1970 LeSabre Custom 455.

ELECTRA 225 — SERIES 48200 — The largest Buicks were also the least changed for 1970. A new grille with bright grid overlay represented the chief distinction from a 1969 edition. Once again four ventiports graced the front fenders, while a strip of bright trim ran along the lower body from front to rear and extended across the fender skirts. Standard Electra features included those found on less expensive Buicks plus Custom padded seat cushions; electric clock; trunk light; smoking set; rear seat ash trays; carpeting on floors and lower doors and front and rear arm rests. Cloth and vinyl bench seats were standard on the Electra.

ELECTRA 225 SERIES 48200 I.D. NUMBERS:
Vehicle Identification Numbers began with 48200( )100001. V.I.N.s were coded as explained under the 1970 Skylark Series 43300 listing.

ELECTRA 225 SERIES 48200

Series Number	Model Number	Body Type & Seating	Factory Price	Shipping Weight	Production Total
48200	48269	4-dr Sedan-6P	5096	4274	12,580
48200	48257	2-dr H.T. Cpe-6P	5117	4214	12,013
48200	48239	4-dr H.T. Sed-6P	5227	4296	14,338

ELECTRA 225 ENGINE
Specifications were the same as listed for the 1970 LeSabre Custom 455.

ELECTRA 225 CUSTOM — SERIES 48400 — Plusher interiors with side coat hooks and additional interior lighting made up the Custom series differences.

NOTE: 'Limited' Custom trim was available on Body Styles 48457 and 48439. The finest Buick interiors, with notch back or 60/40 notch back front seats were standard. Limited script appeared on the roof sail panels when this optional package was ordered.

ELECTRA 225 CUSTOM SERIES 48400 I.D. NUMBERS:
Vehicle Identification Numbers began with 484000( )100001. V.I.N.s were coded as explained under the 1970 Skylark Series 43300 listing.

ELECTRA 225 CUSTOM SERIES 48400

Series Number	Model Number	Body Type & Seating	Factory Price	Shipping Weight	Production Total
48400	48469	4-dr Sedan-6P	5312	4283	14,109
48400	48457	2-dr H.T. Cpe-6P	5296	4297	26,002
48400	48439	4-dr H.T. Sed-6P	5406	4385	65,114
48400	48467	Convertible-6P	5327	4341	6,045

ELECTRA 225 CUSTOM ENGINE
Specifications were the same as listed for the 1970 LeSabre Custom 455.

RIVIERA — SERIES 49487 — A new vertical textured grille within the front bumper ensemble updated the 1970 Riviera front end. At the sides, a new version of the famous Buick sweepspear was created with new body side moldings. Fender skirts were standard equipment for the first and only time on a Riviera. The headlamps were flanking the grille and did not retract. Bright metal outlined the lower body and fender skirt lip, continuing in a narrow line to the rear bumper. Riviera script appeared on the hood, deck, roof and said panels, while the 'R' trademark appeared within the round rear fender sidemarkers. Standard equipment included every feature found on less expensive Buicks plus padded seat cushions; full carpeting; smoking set; and an electric clock. Vinyl bench or bucket seating surfaces were standard. An optional Custom interior was available with Strato notch back seating in all-vinyl or a vinyl and cloth combination.

NOTE: A Gran Sport option was offered for the Riviera. Cars so equipped had heavy-duty suspension; positive traction differential; H78 x 15 fiberglass belted white sidewall tires and GS monograms on the front fenders and instrument panel.

RIVIERA SERIES 49400 I.D. NUMBERS: Vehicle Identification Numbers began with 494870( )100001. V.I.N.s were coded as explained under the 1970 Skylark Series 43300 listing.

RIVIERA SERIES 49487

Series Number	Model Number	Body Type & Seating	Factory Price	Shipping Weight	Production Total
49400	49487	2-dr H.T. Cpe-5P	5489	4216	37,366

RIVIERA ENGINE
Specifications were the same as listed for the 1970 LeSabre custom 455.

CHASSIS FEATURES: Wheelbase: (Series 43300, 43400, 44400, 44500 and 44600 two-door styles) 112 inches; (four-door styles) 116 inches; (Series 45300, 45400, 45600, 4600 and 46600) 124 inches; (Series 48200 and 48400) 127 inches; (Series 49487) 119 inches. Overall length: (Series 43300, 43400, 44400, 44500 and 46600 two-door styles) 202.2 inches; (four-door styles) 206.2 inches; (Series 45200, 45400, 45600, 4600 and 46600) 220.2 inches; (Series 48200 and 48400) 225.8 inches; (Series 49487) 215.5 inches. Tire size: (Series 43300, 43400, 44400, 45400, 44600) G78 x 14; (Series 45200, 45400, 45600 and 49487) H78 x 15; (Series 4600) L78 x 15; (Series 48200 and 48400) J78 x 15.

POWER OPTIONS: A three-speed manual transmission with column shift was standard on Skylark, Skylark 350, Skylark Custom, Gran Sport, LeSabre and Wildcat styles. A three-speed manual transmission with floor-mounted shifter was standard on GS 455. A four-speed manual transmission was optional on the GS and GS 455. TurboHydramatic 350 was available with Skylark series and the GS. TurboHydramatic 400 was optional for GS 455, LeSabre Custom 455 and Wildcat and was standard on Electra 225 Series and Riviera. A 285 brake horsepower, 350 cubic inch V-8 was optional for the Skylark Custom, as was a 315 horsepower version of the same engine when ordered with the "high performance group."

CONVENIENCE OPTIONS: GSX package for Gran Sport models including hood-mounted tachometer; Rally steering wheel; front and rear spoilers; outside sport mirrors; power front disc brakes; G60 x 15 tires; 15 x 7 inch chrome spoke wheels; black bucket seat interior; GSX ornament on instrument panel and grille; GSX decals and body stripes; black-finished hood panels; heavy-duty suspension; special 350 horse-power 455 cubic inch V-8 and Saturn Yellow or Apollo White exterior finish ($1196). Air conditioning. ($486 intermediate; $457 full-size). Power steering (standard on Electra 225s, Riviera). Power brakes (standard on Electra 225s, Riviera). Power windows. Vinyl top covering. AM radio. AM/FM radio. Stereo tape player. Tilt steering wheel. Limited trim for Electra 225 Custom ($318). Strato bench seats (Riviera). Five-spoke chromed wheels. Console with shifter (Riviera). Consoles (bucket seats on GS; GS 455). Automatic Climate Control (full-size). Rear view mirror map light. Cornering lights (full-size). Automatic level control (specific models). Protective body side moldings (except Riviera and GS-GS 455). Soft-ray tinted glass. Rim-mounted horn control. Remote control outside rear view mirror. Four-way or six-way power seat control. Electric door locks. Tow Master trailering package. Electric trunk release. Chrome luggage rack two-way door gate power rear window for Estate and Station Wagon styles.

Historical footnotes: Style 43436 is the Sportwagon with dual-action tailgate. Styles 46036 and 46046 are Estate Wagons.

1971 BUICK

1971 Buick, Skylark Custom 2-dr hardtop sport coupe, V-8

SKYLARK — SERIES 43300 — The basic 1970 styling was continued for another year. The Skylark had its own grille and used bright metal wheelhouse and lower body moldings of a very narrow width. Standard Skylark features included front and rear ash trays, heater and defroster, Step-On parking brake, padded head restraints and other features mandated by Federal safety standards. Interiors were cloth and vinyl, or all-vinyl.

SKYLARK SERIES 43300 I.D. NUMBERS: Vehicle Identification Numbers began with 433001( )100001. The first five numerals represented the make and model. The sixth numeral '1' represented the 1971 model year. The seventh symbol was a letter representing the assembly plant code. The last six digits were numerals representing the sequential assembly number at the coded plant with series mixed in production.

SKYLARK SERIES 43300

Series Number	Model Number	Body Type & Seating	Factory Price	Shipping Weight	Production Total
43300	43327	2-dr Coupe-6P	3208	3208	14,500
43300	43337	2-dr H.T. Cpe-6P	3421	3214	61,201
43300	43369	4-dr Sedan-6P	3400	3260	34,037

SKYLARK ENGINES
Six-cyl: Overhead valves. Cast iron block. Displacement: 250 cubic inches. Bore and stroke: 3.875 x 3.53 inches. Compression ratio: 8.5:1. Brake horsepower: 145 at 4200 R.P.M. Hydraulic valve lifters. Two-barrel carburetor.
V-8: Overhead valves. Cast iron block. Displacement: 350 cubic inches. Bore and stroke: 3.8 x 3.85 inches. Compression ratio: 8.5:1. Brake horsepower: 230 at 4200 R.P.M. Five main bearings. Hydraulic lifters. Two-barrel carburetor.

SKYLARK CUSTOM — SERIES 44400 — A plusher Skylark, with Comfort-Flo ventilation system, DeLuxe steering wheel, glove box light and plusher interiors with full carpeting. An additional rocker panel molding was used, along with a bright applique on the front fenders. Custom badges appeared below the Skylark rear fender scripts and on the grille. Skylark emblems were on the roof sail panels.

SKYLARK CUSTOM SERIES 44400 I.D. NUMBERS: Vehicle Identification Numbers began with 444001( )100001. V.I.N.s were coded as explained under the 1971 Skylark Series 43300 listing.

SKYLARK CUSTOM SERIES 44400

Series Number	Model Number	Body Type & Seating	Factory Price	Shipping Weight	Production Total
44400	44438	2-dr H.T. Cpe-6P	3698	3425	29,536
44400	44469	4-dr Sedan-6P	3670	3473	8,299
44400	44439	4-dr H.T. Sed-6P	3778	3557	20,418
44400	44467	Convertible-6P	3844	3482	3,993

SKYLARK CUSTOM ENGINE
Six-cyl. and V-8 specifications were the same as those listed for the 1971 Skylark Series 43300.

SPORTWAGON — SERIES 43436 — The Sportwagon shared the Skylark chassis and its improvements for 1971. The Sportwagon did not have bright wheelhouse moldings, using only a lower body bright molding for trim. Power front disc brakes were standard, as was an all-vinyl interior with front bench seat. The dual-action tailgate was now standard on this model only. Sportwagon script appeared on the rear fenders.

SPORTWAGON SERIES 43436 I.D. NUMBERS: Vehicle Identification Numbers began with 43461( )100001. V.I.N.s were coded as explained under the 1971 Skylark Series 43300 listing.

SPORTWAGON SERIES 43446

Series Number	Model Number	Body Type & Seating	Factory Price	Shipping Weight	Production Total
43400	43436	Sta Wag-2S	3896	3911	12,525

SPORTWAGON ENGINE
Specifications were the same as listed for the 1971 Skylark Series 43300 V-8.

GS AND GS 455 — SERIES 43400 — Buick combined these two series into one for 1971. These muscular Buicks had blacked-out grilles with bright trim, bright wheelhouse moldings and bright rocker panel moldings with red-filled accents. Dual, functional hood scoops were ahead of the windshield. GS monograms appeared on the front fenders, deck and hood. Cars equipped with the 455 or 455 Stage I option had additional emblems. Standard equipment was the same as the Skylark Custom, but bucket or notch back front seats in all vinyl trim were optional.

GS AND GS 455 SERIES 43400 I.D. NUMBERS: Vehicle Identification Numbers began with 434001( )100001. V.I.N.s were coded as explained under the 1971 Skylark Series 43300 listing.

GS/GS 455 SERIES 43400

Series Number	Model Number	Body Type & Seating	Factory Price	Shipping Weight	Production Total
43400	43437	2-dr H.T.	3666	3425	8,268
43400	43467	Convertible	3857	3479	902

NOTE: Prices and weights are for Grand Sports with 350 cubic inch engines. Production numbers include both GS and GS 455 cars.

GS AND GS 455 ENGINES
GS V-8: Specifications were the same as listed for the 1971 Skylark 350 Cubic inch V-8, except brake horsepower was 260 and a four-barrel carbureted V-8 with dual exhausts was used.
GS 455 V-8: Overhead valve. Cast iron block. Displacement: 455 cubic inches. Bore and stroke: 4.3 x 3.9 inches. Compression ratio: 8.5:1. Brake horsepower: 315 at 4600 R.P.M. Five main bearings. Hydraulic valve lifters. Four-barrel carburetor.

LESABRE — SERIES 45200 — A new, larger body was used on the 1971 LeSabre. Full-Flo ventilation with deck lid louvers was standard. The new body, with a sweeping side sculpture, used the customary Buick ventiports in groups of three on each front fender. Bright metal lower body and wheelhouse moldings were used. The LeSabre had its own grille. Interiors were fabric and vinyl. Standard equipment included arm rests; rear ash trays; glove box light; interior lights; front and rear carpeting; full-foam seat cushions; inside hood release; power front disc brakes, seat belts and other mandated Federal safety features. LeSabre script appeared on the front fenders.

LESABRE SERIES 45200 I.E. NUMBERS: Vehicle Identification Numbers began with 45200( )100001. V.I.N.s were coded as explained under the 1971 Skylark Series 43300 listing.

LESABRE SERIES 45200

Series Number	Model Number	Body Type & Seating	Factory Price	Shipping Weight	Production Total
45200	45269	4-dr Sedan-6P	4621	4051	26,348
45200	45257	2-dr H.T. Cpe-6P	4690	4014	13,385
45200	45239	4-dr H.T. Cpe-6P	4748	4069	41,098

LESABRE ENGINE
Specifications were the same as listed for the 1971 Skylark Series 43300 V-8.

LESABRE CUSTOM AND CUSTOM 455 — SERIES 45400 — A plusher Buick with more luxurious interiors. The convertible, offered only in this series, had a new top that folded inward on retracting. Custom models had a Custom badge beneath the LeSabre front fender script, unless they were equipped with the 455 cubic inch, V-8, in which case they had that engine's insignia instead.

LESABRE CUSTOM SERIES 45400 I.D. NUMBERS:
Vehicle Identification Numbers began with 454001( )100001. V.I.N.s were coded as explained under the 1971 Skylark Series 43300 listing.

LESABRE SERIES 45400

Series Number	Model Number	Body Type & Seating	Factory Price	Shipping Weight	Production Total
45400	45469	4-dr Sedan-6P	4715	4063	26,970
45400	45457	2-dr H.T. Cpe-6P	4778	4028	29,944
45400	45439	4-dr H.T. Sed-6P	4842	4069	41,098
45400	45467	Convertible-6P	4971	4092	1,856

LESABRE CUSTOM AND 455 ENGINES
350 V-8: Specifications were the same as listed for the 1971 Skylark Series 43300 V-8.
455 V-8: Specifications were the same as listed for the 1971 GS 455 Series 43400 V-8.

1971 Buick, Centurian 2-dr hardtop sport coupe, V-8 (TVB)

CENTURION — SERIES 46600 — A new line for Buick, replacing the Wildcat series. The Centurion was a masculine, performance image machine that went for the clean look. Side trim was minimal, with only a bright rocker panel molding and wheelhouse moldings. There were no ventports on the Centurion. The grille was of a special texture and the taillights had bright grids over them. Centurion lettering appeared on the front fenders and the round Centurion medallion was used on closed model roof sail panels. It also appeared on the deck and hood. The Formal Coupe (two-door hardtop) included a vinyl top covering. Standard equipment was the same as on the LeSabre, plus a DeLuxe steering wheel. Interiors were vinyl and fabric combinations, with bench or notch back front seats.

CENTURION SERIES I.D. 46600 NUMBERS: Vehicle Identification Numbers began with 466001( )100001. V.I.N.s were coded as explained under the 1971 Skylarks Series 43300 listing.

CENTURION SERIES 46600

Series Number	Model Number	Body Type & Seating	Factory Price	Shipping Weight	Production Total
46600	46647	2-dr H.T. Cpe-6P	5272	4181	11,892
46600	46639	4-dr H.T.-6P	5197	4263	15,345
46600	46667	Convertible-6P	5311	4181	2,161

CENTURION ENGINE
V-8: Specifications were the same as listed for the 1971 GS 455 Series 43400.

ELECTRA 225 — SERIES 48200 — The biggest Buicks were freshly styled for 1971 with a longer, wider look predominating. Four ventports again indicated the car's prestige in the Buick line. Series identification appeared on the deck lid and roof sail pillars. Standard equipment included Full-Flo ventilation with deck lid louvers; Custom foam seats; heater and defroster; DeLuxe steering wheel; plush pile carpeting; variable ratio power steering; power brakes; remote control outside rear view mirror; windshield radio antenna and a fully-padded instrument panel. A number of mandated safety features were also included.

ELECTRA 225 SERIES 48200 I.D. NUMBERS: Vehicle Identification Numbers began with 482001( )100001. V.I.N.s were coded as explained under the 1971 Skylark Series 43300 listing.

ELECTRA 225 SERIES 48200

Series Number	Model Number	Body Type & Seating	Factory Price	Shipping Weight	Production Total
48200	48237	2-dr H.T. Cpe-6P	5454	4302	8,662
48200	48239	4-dr H.T.-6P	5567	4355	17,589

ELECTRA 225 CUSTOM — SERIES 48400 — Custom models had a plusher interior than the regular Electra 225 with woodgrain inserts used liberally on door panels and the instrument panel. Exterior appearance was identical to the 48200 series.

ELECTRA 225 CUSTOM SERIES 48400 I.D. NUMBERS: Vehicle Identification Numbers began with 484001( )100001. Numbers were coded as explained under the 1971 Skylark Series 43300 listing.

ELECTRA 225 CUSTOM SERIES 48400

Series Number	Model Number	Body Type & Seating	Factory Price	Shipping Weight	Production Total
48400	48437	2-dr H.T.-6P	5633	4302	26,831
48400	48439	4-dr H.T.-6P	5746	4355	72,954

NOTE: 'Limited' interiors were offered for both Custom Electra 225 styles. Cars so equipped had even plusher interiors, with bench seats or 60/40 notch back front seats. 'Limited' badges were applied to the roof sail panels when this option was included.

ELECTRA 225 CUSTOM ENGINE
V-8: Specifications were the same as listed for the 1971 GS 455 Series 43400.

ESTATE WAGONS — SERIES 4600 — A new Estate Wagon was built on the 127-inch wheelbase Electra 225 chassis. Standard equipment was the same as the Electra 225, with Custom-grade all-vinyl interior trimming. Woodgrain sides were available. All wagons had the Glide-Away tailgate, Full-Flo ventilation with louvers in the tailgate, bright rocker panel and wheelhouse moldings and four ventports on each front fender.

ESTATE WAGON SERIES 46000 I.D. NUMBERS: Vehicle Identification Numbers began with 466001( )100001. V.I.N.s were coded as explained under the 1971 Skylarks Series 43300 listing.

ESTATE WAGON SERIES 46000

Series Number	Model Number	Body Type & Seating	Factory Price	Shipping Weight	Production Total
46000	46035	4-dr Sta Wag-2S	5268	4797	8,699
46000	40645	4-dr Sta Wag-3S	5414	4881	15,335

ESTATE WAGON ENGINE
V-8: Specifications were the same as listed for the 1971 GS 455 — Series 43400.

1971 Buick, Riviera 2-dr hardtop sport coupe, V-8 (TVB)

RIVIERA — SERIES 49487 — A sensational new Riviera debuted for 1971. A large car with a boattailed rear roof and window section and sweeping side sculpture greeted 1971's Riviera customers. Wheelhouses were wide open, after a year of skirted fenders. Riviera shared Full-Flo ventilation with other 1971 Buicks and had the louvers on the deck lid. Standard features were numerous and included heater and defroster; Custom padded contoured seats; deep pile carpeting; electric clock; smoking set; head restraints; new seat belt system; inside hood lock release; variable ratio power steering; TurboHydramatic; power front disc brakes and dual exhausts.

NOTE: A Gran Sport option was available for the Riviera. Cars so equipped had a 330 horsepower 445 cubic inch V-8 with chrome air cleaner top linked to a specially calibrated TurboHydramatic 400 transmission; heavy-duty suspension; positive traction differential; H78 x 15 Bias-belted whitewall tires and Riviera GS monogram on front fenders and instrument panel.

RIVIERA SERIES 49400 I.D. NUMBERS: Vehicle Identification Numbers began with 494871( )10001. Numbers were coded as explained under the 1971 Skylark Series 43300 listing.

RIVIERA SERIES 49400

Series Number	Model Number	Body Type & Seating	Factory Price	Shipping Weight	Production Total
49400	49487	2-dr Spt Cpe-5P	5903	4247	33,810

RIVIERA ENGINE
Specifications were the same as listed for the 1971 GS 455 Series 43400 models.

CHASSIS FEATURES: Wheelbase: (Series 43300, 44400 and 43400) two-door styles 112 inches; four-door styles 116 inches; (Series 45200, 45400, 46400) 124 inches; (Series 48200, 48400 and 46000) 127 inches; (Series 48487) 112 inches. Overall length: (Series 43300, 44400, 43400) two-door styles 203.3 inches; four-door styles 207.3 inches; (Sportwagons) 213.7 inches; (Series 45200, 45400 and 46400) 221.9 inches; (Series 48200, 48400) 227.9 inches; (Series 46000) 228.3 inches; (Series 48487) 218.3 inches. Tire size: (Skylark) F78 x 14; (Skylark Custom, Sportwagon, GS and GS 455) G78 x 14; (LeSabre Centurian and Riviera) H78 x 15; (Electra 225) J78 x 15; (Estate Wagons) L78 x 15.

POWERTRAIN OPTIONS: Three-speed manual transmission was standard in Series 43300, 44400, 43400, 45200, 45400 and 46600. Four-speed manual transmission was optional in Series 43400. TurboHydramatic-350 was optional for cars with six-cylinder or 350 cubic inch V-8 engines. TurboHydramatic-400 was optional for cars equipped with the 455 cubic inch V-8 and was also standard in Series 48200, 48400 and 49487. A 260 brake horsepower 350 cubic inch V-8 was optional for Series 43300, 44400, 43400, 45200 and 45400. A 330 brake horsepower 455 cubic inch V-8 with four-barrel induction was optional for Series 43400, 45200, 45400, 46600, 48200 and 48400. Max-Trac all-weather traction control rear axles were optional in Series 49487 models.

CONVENIENCE AND APPEARANCE FEATURES: Air conditioning. Power windows ($116). Vinyl top. Tilt steering wheel. Strato bucket seats (Riviera — $187). Chrome five spoke wheels ($95). Limited trim (Electra 225 Custom — $284). Custom Trim (Estate Wagon woodgrain — $199). AM radio. AM/FM radio. AM/FM stereo ($239). Speed alert control. Cornering lights (full size). Bumper guards (except Riviera and Estate Wagon). Protective body side moldings (except Riviera). Console (Riviera, GS, and Skylark Custom with bucket seats). Six-way power seats. GSX equipment for GS 455 including body side stripes; black hood panels; GSX grille emblem; body color headlamp bezels; black rocker moldings and rear spoiler. Sport mirrors (GS and GSX). Instrument panel gauges (GS and GSX). Hood-mounted tachometer (GS and GSX). Front spoiler (GS and GSX). Automatic Climate Control. Rear window defogger. Custom interior trim (Riviera). Electric trunk release. Special sport steering wheel. Ralley steering wheel (GS and GSX). DeLuxe steering wheel (LeSabre). Power door locks. Child safety seat. Chrome luggage rack (Estate Wagon). Power glide-away tailgate (Estate Wagon). Intermittent wippers. Auto Level Control. Remote outside rear view mirror (standard, Electra 225s).

Historical footnotes: Style 46647 was the Centurion Formal Coupe. Style 46035 was the two-seat Estate Wagon. Style 46045 was the three-seat Estate Wagon.

1972 BUICK

SKYLARK AND SKYLARK 350 — SERIES 43300 — A very mild facelift was done on the 1972 Skylark. The front bumper was redesigned with bumper guards now standard. At the rear, black vinyl surrounds were added to the taillamp/bumper assembly. The Skylark had a narrow lower body molding and bright wheelhouse molding. Skylark

script appeared on the rear fenders with a 350 badge added when equipment included the four-barrel 175 brake horsepower 350 cubic inch V-8. Standard Skylark features were front ash tray; heater and defroster; side terminal energizer battery; padded instrument panel and mandated safety features. Skylark 350 had DeLuxe cloth and vinyl seats, carpeting, rear ash trays, armrests, DeLuxe steering wheel and dual horns.

1972 Buick, Skylark 350 'Sun Coupe' 2-dr hardtop, V-8 (TVB)

SKYLARK AND SKYLARK 350 SERIES 43300 I.D. NUMBERS: Vehicle Identification Numbers began with 4D3002( )100001. V.I.N.s were coded as follows: The first symbol '4' indicated Buick. The second symbol, a letter, identified the series. The third and fourth symbols were numbers indicating the body style. The fifth symbol, a '2', represented the 1972 model year. The sixth symbol, a letter, was the plant code. The last six symbols are the sequential production number at the assembly plant with Series mixed in production.

SKYLARK/SKYLARK 350 SERIES 43300

Series Number	Model Number	Body Type & Seating	Factory Price	Shipping Weight	Production Total
43300	43327	2-dr Cpe-6P	3341	3348	14,552
43300	43337	2-dr H.T. Cpe-6P	3409	3403	84,868
43300	43369	4-dr Sedan-6P	3389	3408	42,206

SKYLARK AND SKYLARK 350 ENGINE
Skylark V-8: Overhead valve. Cast iron block. Displacement: 350 cubic inches. Bore and stroke: 3.8 x 3.85 inches. Compression ratio: 8.5:1. Net horsepower: 150 at 4200 R.P.M. Five main bearings. Hydraulic valve lifters. Two-barrel carburetor.
Skylark 350 V-8: Specifications were the same as above, except a four-barrel carburetor was used and net horsepower was 175.

SKYLARK CUSTOM — SERIES 44400 — A plusher Skylark, distinguished on the exterior by a grid-textured bright grille, wider bright rocker panel moldings with rear stone guard extensions and wheelhouse moldings. Plusher Custom interiors were of cloth and vinyl, or all-vinyl. The Sport Wagon featured a standard dual-action tailgate.

SKYLARK CUSTOM SERIES 44400 I.D. NUMBERS: Vehicle Identification Numbers began with 4H002( )100001 for Skylarks and 4F362( )100001 for Sport Wagons. V.I.N.s were coded as explained in the 1972 Skylark Series 43300 listing.

SKYLARK CUSTOM SERIES 44400

Series Number	Model Number	Body Type & Seating	Factory Price	Shipping Weight	Production Total
44400	44437	2-dr H.T. Cpe-6P	3671	3403	34,271
44400	44469	4-dr Sedan-6P	3644	3408	9,924
44400	44467	Convertible-6P	3809	3476	3,608
44400	44439	4-dr H.T. Sed-6P	3747	3546	12,925
44400	43436	4-dr Sta Wag-6P	3860	3936	14,417

SKYLARK CUSTOM ENGINES
Specifications were the same as those listed under 1972 Skylark and Skylark 350 engine data.

GS 350 AND GS 455 — SERIES 43400 — These sport coupe and convertible styles featured dual exhausts, functional dual hood scoops, heavy duty springs, shocks, and stabilizer bar in conjuction with a muscular look. Appearance was enhanced by wide bright rocker moldings, wheelhouse moldings and GS monograms on the front fenders and deck. When cars had the 455 cubic inch V-8 installed suitable emblems were attached. Vinyl bench seats were standard (black on the convertible). Bucket seats were available at extra cost.

GS 350 AND GS 455 SERIES 43400 I.D. NUMBERS: Vehicle Identification Numbers began with 46002( )100001. V.I.N.s were coded as explained in the 1972 Skylark Series 43300 listing.

GS 350/455 SERIES 43400

Series Number	Model Number	Body Type & Seating	Factory Price	Shipping Weight	Production Total
43400	43437	2-dr H.T. Cpe-6P	3641	3475	7,723
43400	43467	Convertible-6P	3822	3517	852

NOTE: Add $165 to above prices for 455 cubic inch V-8.

GS 350 AND GS 455 ENGINES
GS 350 V-8: Specifications were the same as listed under 1972 Skylark 350 cubic inch V-8 engine data.

GS 455 V-8: Overhead valve. Cast-iron block. Displacement: 455 cubic inches. Bore and stroke: 4.3 x 3.9 inches. Compression ratio: 8.5:1 Net horsepower: 225 at 4600 R.P.M. Five main bearings. Hydraulic valve lifters. Four-barrel carburetor. A GS 270 h.p. engine was an option.

LESABRE — SERIES 45200 — Little changed from 1971, the LeSabre had no deck louvers for the Full-Flo ventilation this year. A trio of ventiports did continue on the front fenders. Standard exterior trim included bright rocker panel moldings, but no wheelhouse moldings. LeSabre script appeared on front fenders. Interiors were of Kalmora cloth and Madrid vinyl. Standard equipment now included power front disc brakes and variable ratio power steering, plus numerous mandated Federal safety features.

LESABRE SERIES 45200 I.D. NUMBERS: Vehicle Identification Numbers began with 4L002( )100001. V.I.N.s were coded as explained in the Skylark Series 43300 listing.

LESABRE SERIES 45200

Series Number	Model Number	Body Type & Seating	Factory Price	Shipping Weight	Production Total
45200	45257	2-dr Spt Cpe-6P	4110	4132	14,001
45200	45269	4-dr Sedan-6P	4044	3958	29,505
45200	45239	4-dr H.T. Sed-6P	4165	4226	15,160

LESABRE ENGINE
Specifications were the same as listed under 1971 Skylark 350 cubic inch, two-barrel V-8 engine data.

LESABRE — CUSTOM — SERIES 45400 — The Custom featured a plusher interior of vinyl and fabric, or all vinyl. A broader lower body molding was used with bright wheelhouse moldings. Custom plaques were used beneath the LeSabre signatures on the front fenders.

LESABRE CUSTOM SERIES 45400 I.D. NUMBERS: Vehicle Identification Numbers began with 4N002( )100001. V.I.N.s were coded as explained in the 1972 Skylark Series 43300 listing.

LESABRE CUSTOM SERIES 45400

Series Number	Model Number	Body Type & Seating	Factory Price	Shipping Weight	Production Total
45400	45457	2-dr Spt Cpe-6P	4193	4149	36,510
45400	45469	4-dr Sedan-6P	4133	4158	35,295
45400	45469	4-dr H.T. Sed-6P	4254	4238	50,804
45400	45467	Convertible-6P	4377	4233	2,037

LESABRE CUSTOM ENGINES
Specifications were the same as listed under the 1972 Skylark 350 cubic inch, two-barrel V-8 engine data.

CENTURION — SERIES 46600 — A new vertical grille giving the hood more of a domed effect distinguished the 1972 Centurion. Side trim continued to be minimal with a bright metal lower body strip and wheelhouse moldings taking care of most superfluous touches. A Centurion medallion appeared on closed body roof sail panels and on all decks and hoods. Centurion lettering was used on the front fenders. There were no ventiports. Standard equipment duplicated that of the LeSabre, but interiors were of a more luxurious vinyl and fabric combination with notch back front seat standard.

CENTURION SERIES 46600 I.D. NUMBERS: Vehicle Identification Numbers began with 4P002( )100001. V.I.N.s were coded as explained under the 1972 Skylark Series 43300 listing.

CENTURION SERIES 46600

Series Number	Model Number	Body Type & Seating	Factory Price	Shipping Weight	Production Total
46600	46647	2-dr Spt Cpe-6P	4665	4331	14,187
46600	46639	4-dr H.T. Sed-6P	4594	4508	19,582
46600	46667	Convertible-6P	4702	4233	2,396

CENTURION ENGINE
Specifications were the same as listed under 1972 GS 455 V-8 engine data.

ESTATE WAGON — SERIES 46000 — These big wagons shared the Electra body and an Electra-like grille. All-vinyl interiors with a bench front seat were standard. A notch back front seat was optional on the nine-passenger, three-seat version. Standard equipment was the same as on the LeSabre, plus a four-jet windshield washer assembly.

ESTATE WAGON SERIES 46000 I.D. NUMBER: Vehicle Identification Numbers began with 4R002( )100001. V.I.N.s were coded as explained in the 1972 Skylark Series 43300 listing.

ESTATE WAGONS SERIES 46000

Series Number	Model Number	Body Type & Seating	Factory Price	Shipping Weight	Production Total
46000	46035	4-dr Sta Wag-2S	4675	4963	10,175
46000	46045	4-dr Sta Wag-3S	4814	5032	18,793

ESTATE WAGON ENGINE
Specifications were the same as listed under 1972 GS 455 V-8 engine data.

ELECTRA 225 — SERIES 48200 — A new grille was one of the facelift features of the 1972 Electra 225. Bumper guards front and rear promised better collision protection. The traditional four ventiports per fender remained. Fender skirts were again standard with their lower lip molding providing a link for the bright metal lower body strip that ran full-length. The Electra 225 emblem appeared on the grille and deck this year. Interiors were cloth and vinyl with bench front seat. Standard features included those of lower priced Buicks, plus such touches as variable ratio power steering, power front disc brakes and remote control outside rear view mirror.

ELECTRA 225 SERIES 48200 I.D. NUMBERS: Vehicle Identification Numbers began with 40002( )100001. V.I.N.s were coded as explained in the 1972 Skylark Series 43300.

ELECTRA 225 SERIES 48200

Series Number	Model Number	Body Type & Seating	Factory Price	Shipping Weight	Production Total
48200	48237	2-dr H.T. Cpe-6P	4868	4380	9,961
48200	48239	4-dr H.T. Sed-6P	4976	4484	19,433

ELECTRA 225 ENGINE
Specifications were the same as listed under 1972 GS 455 V-8 engine data.

ELECTRA 225 CUSTOM LIMITED — SERIES 48400 — A plusher interior of cloth and vinyl with fold down center arm rest for front seat passengers was standard. A notch back 60/40 seat was optional. Limited script appeared on the roof sail panels of this plushest of all Buicks. Exterior trim was otherwise identical to the Electra 225 Series 48200.

ELECTRA 225 CUSTOM LIMITED SERIES 48400 I.D. NUMBERS: Vehicle Identification Numbers began with 4V002( )100001. V.I.N.s were coded as explained in the Skylark Series 43300 listing.

ELECTRA 225 CUSTOM LIMITED SERIES 48400

Series Number	Model Number	Body Type & Seating	Factory Price	Shipping Weight	Production Total
48400	48437	2-dr H.T. Cpe-6P	5038	4411	37,974
48400	48439	4-dr H.T. Sed-6P	5146	4495	104,754

ELECTRA 225 CUSTOM LIMITED ENGINE
Specifications were the same as listed under 1972 GS 455 V-8 engine data.

1972 Buick, Riviera 2-dr hardtop sport coupe, V-8 (TVB)

RIVIERA — SERIES 49487 — A slightly restyled Riviera with the same boattailed body was marketed in 1972. A new egg crate grille thrust forward with the 'R' emblem on the left. A similar emblem was centered on the deck lid, which this year was clean, without the ill-fated Full-Flo ventilation louvers of 1971. Vinyl body side moldings were standard. Interiors were available with all-vinyl bench seats or in Custom trim with 60/40 notch back or bucket front seating. Standard features included all items found on the Electra 225.

NOTE: Riviera Gran Sport equipment was available at $200. Included was a 260 net horsepower 455 cubic inch V-8 with dual exhausts, positive traction differential and GS monograms for the front fenders. An engine turned instrument panel insert was featured.

RIVIERA SERIES 49400 I.D. NUMBERS: Vehicle Identification Numbers began with 4Y002( )100001. V.I.N.s were coded as explained in the Skylark Series 43300 listing.

RIVIERA SERIES 49400

Series Number	Model Number	Body Type & Seating	Factory Price	Shipping Weight	Production Total
49400	49487	2-dr Spt Cpe-6P	5666	4399	33,728

RIVIERA ENGINE
Specifications were the same as listed under 1972 GS 455 except net horsepower was 250.

CHASSIS FEATURES: Wheelbase: (Series 43300, 44400 and 43400) 112 inches; two-door styles; 116 inches, four-door styles. (Series 45200, 45400 and 46600) 124 inches; (Series 48200, 48400 and 46000) 127 inches; (Series 49487) 122 inches. Overall length: (Series 43300, 44400 and 43400) two-door styles 203.3 inches; four-door styles 207.3 inches; (Sportwagon) 213.7 inches; (Series 45200, 45400 and 46600) 221.9 inches; (Series 46000) 228.3 inches; (Series 48200 and 48400) 227.9 inches; (Series 48487) 218.3 inches. Tire Sizes: (Skylark, Skylark Custom, GS 350 and GS 455) G78 x 14; (LeSabre, Riviera and Centurion) H78 x 15; (Electra 225s) J78 x 15; (Estate Wagons) L78 x 15.

POWERTRAIN OPTIONS: A three-speed manual transmission was standard in Series 43300, 44400 and 43400. A four-speed manual transmission was optional for Series 43400. TurboHydramatic 350 was an automatic transmission option for Series 43300, 44400 and 43400 with 350 cubic inch V-8. TurboHydramatic 400 was optional for Series 43400 with 455 cubic inch V-8 and Series 45200 and 45400 with 455 cubic inch V-8 option; it was standard in Series 46600, 46000, 48200 and 49487. TurboHydramatic 375B was standard with LeSabre. Max-Trac differential was offered for all full-size Buicks. Maintenance-free battery was available for Series 48200, 48400 and 49487.

CONVENIENCE AND APPEARANCE OPTIONS: Customline hard boot cover (LeSabre and Centurion Convertible). Protective impact strips. Folding vinyl sun roof (Sun Coupe on Skylark 350 Sport Coupe with roof sail panel emblems) Steel panel sun roof, electrically operated (Riviera and Electra 225). Front light monitors (full-size). AM radio. AM/FM radio. AM/FM radio with stereo and tape player. Center console (Skylark, GS 350 and 455, Riviera with bucket seats). Climate Control. Automatic Climate Control (full-size). Power windows. Electric trunk release. Child safety seat. Remote control outside rear view mirror (standard on Electra 225 and Riviera). Custom seat and shoulder belts. Custom vinyl top with halo molding for Skylark Custom Sport Coupe; Sport Vinyl top for Skylark 350 Coupe and Riviera; full vinyl top for other specific styles. Soft-ray tinted glass. Rear window defroster. Mirror map light. Electric clock. Power tailgate window. Tilt steering wheel. (standard on Riviera). Cornering lights (full-size). Speed alert. Luggage rack for station wagons. Five-spoke chrome sport wheels. Trailer towing packages. Automatic Level Control.

Historical footnotes: Style 43436 was the Sportwagon. Styles 46035 and 46045 were Estate Wagons.

1973 BUICK

APOLLO SERIES — SIX AND V-8 — Introduced as a mid-year model, on April 12, 1973, the Apollo marked Buick's re-entry into the compact car market. The new car was based on the Chevrolet Nova X-body shell with Buick trim and styling motifs added. Features included unit construction on the cowl back, with a bolted-on front stub frame. Single round headlamps in large, square bezels flanked a low, rectangular grille insert of a vertical-dash type design. Single parking lamps were set into either side of the grille and a Buick medallion was placed at the center. Buick block lettering appeared on the hood; slit type cornering lamps on the front fender and three thin, rectangular ventiports on the upper rear side of front fenders. The base engine was a Chevrolet six and Apollos with the Buick 350 cubic inch V-8 were grouped as a separate series.

BUICK I.D. NUMBERS: Vehicle identification numbers began with 4 ( )( )( )( ) 3 ( ) 100001 up. The first symbol '4' indicated Buick. The second symbol, a letter, indicated the series. The third and fourth symbols indicated the body style and correspond to the numbers in column two of charts below. The fifth symbol designated type of engine. The sixth symbol, a '3' designated 1973 model year. The seventh symbol was the assembly plant code (with Apollo production quartered at Willow Run, Michigan (W) or Los Angeles, Van Nuys (L), which were GMAD factories, not Buick. The last group of six digits indicated the sequential production number.

1973 Buick, Apollo 2-dr hatch back coupe, 6-cyl (TVB)

APOLLO SERIES SIX/V-8

Model Number	Body/Style Number	Body Type & Seating	Factory Price	Shipping Weight	Production Total
4XB	B69	4-dr Sed-5P	2628/2746	3152/3326	8,450
4XB	B27	2-dr Notch-5P	2605/2723	3108/3282	14,475
4XB	B17	2-dr Hatch-5P	2754/2872	3210/3384	9,868

NOTE: Style B27 is a two-door notchback coupe; Style B17 a two-door hatchback coupe. Factory prices and shipping weights above slash are for Sixes; below slash for V-8s.

APOLLO ENGINES

Inline six. Overhead valves. Cast iron block. Displacement: 250 cubic inches. Bore and stroke: 3.87 x 3.50 inches. Compression ratio: 8.25:1. SAE net horsepower: 100 at 3600 R.P.M. Hydraulic valve lifters. Carburetor: one-barrel. (Chevrolet manufacture).

V-8. Overhead valves. Cast iron block. Displacement: 350 cubic inches. Bore and stroke: 3.8 x 3.85 inches. Compression ratio: 8.5:1. SAE net horsepower: 150 at 3800 R.P.M. Hydraulic valve lifters. Carburetor: two-barrel (Buick V-8).

1973 Buick, Century Regal 2-dr colonnade coupe, V-8 (TVB)

CENTURY/LUXUS/REGAL SERIES — (V-8) — The Buick Century lines represented a new intermediate range of offerings on the GM A-Body platform. The cars rode on a new chassis and had disc brakes up front as standard equipment. Styling features included GM's 'Colonnade' pillared hardtop look. There were single round headlights in square bezels flanking a thin crosshatch grille with three bright horizontal division bars. Inbetween the headlamps and grille were medium size round parking lamps. The Century 350 passenger cars were in the AD Series with comparable station wagons forming Series AF. These cars had '350' front fender tip nameplates. The Luxus line (Series AH passenger models and Series AK station wagons) had richer interior appointments and horizontal belt line moldings along the trailing edge of front fenders and on the front door. The Regal coupe (Series AJ) had a distinctive grille, with a vertically segmented design and special crest emblems on the front fender sides. A Grand Sport package, with special styling and suspension features, was available as a sports/performance option. It included electric clock; wheel opening moldings; instrument gages; glove box ash tray and courtesy lamps as standard extras.

CENTURY/LUXUS/REGAL SERIES

Model Number	Body/Style Number	Body Type & Seating	Factory Price	Shipping Weight	Production Total
CENTURY 350					
4AD	D29	4-dr HT Sed-6P	3057	3780	38,202
4AD	D37	4-dr HT Cpe-6P	3057	3713	56,154
4AF	F45	4-dr Sta Wag-9P	3601	4192	Note 1
4AF	F35	4-dr Sta Wag-6P	3486	4156	7,760
LUXUS					
4AH	H29	4-dr HT Sed-6P	3326	3797	22,438
4AH	H57	2-dr HT Cpe-6P	3331	3718	71,712
4AK	K45	4-dr Sta Wag-9P	3767	4227	Note 1
4AK	K35	4-dr Sta Wag-6P	3652	4190	10,645
REGAL					
4AJ	J57	2-dr HT Cpe-5P	3470	3743	91,557

NOTE 1: Production totals for six and nine-passenger station wagons are counted together, with no breakouts per seating configuration.

CENTURY/LUXUS/REGAL ENGINE
See 1973 Apollo Series V-8 engine data. Base engine for Century models was the optional Apollo 350 cubic inch V-8.

LESABRE CENTURION SERIES — (V-8) — LeSabres, LeSabre Customs and Centurions were built off the same 124 inch wheelbase platform with different levels of appointments and trims. Two Estate wagons were based on a 127 inch wheelbase version of the Electra chassis and grouped into their own separate series as well. Styling features for the entire group of cars included new energy absorbing front bumpers, dual headlamps set in square bezels, a low grille with short vertical bars and Buick medallions at the center of the hood. Standard equipment on all models included Turbo Hydramatic transmission, power steering and brakes. LeSabres had series identification scripts behind the front wheel cutouts. Custom LeSabres included standard extras such as Custom steering wheel, DeLuxe wheel covers, vinyl notch back seats

and a four-barrel carburetor. There were Custom nameplate badges placed under the LeSabre scripts on the one-step-up models. Centurions represented a slightly cleaner styled rendition of the LeSabre body, having the traditional Buick ventiports removed from the hoods. Centurion lettering was placed behind the front wheel cutout and a four-barrel V-8 was the base powerplant. An exclusive Centurion body style was the convertible. Estate wagons came with wood grain exterior body panelling and were trimmed comparable to Custom LeSabres, except that model identification took the form of Estate Wagons block lettering on the upper rear fender tips. They had lower rear bumper ends than other standard Buicks, with tail lamps notched into the blade-shaped body edges.

LESABRE CENTURION SERIES

Model Number	Body/Style Number	Body Type & Seating	Factory Price	Shipping Weight	Production Total
LESABRE					
4BL	L69	4-dr Sedan-6P	3998	4234	29,649
4BL	L39	4-dr HT Sed-6P	4125	4259	13,413
4BL	L57	2-dr HT Spt Cpe-6P	4067	4210	14,061
CUSTOM LESABRE					
4BN	N69	4-dr Sedan-6P	4091	4264	42,845
4BN	N39	4-dr HT Sed-6P	4217	4284	55,879
4BN	N57	2-dr HT Spt Cpe-6P	4154	4225	41,425
ESTATE WAGON					
4BR	R35	4-dr Sta Wag-6P	4645	4952	12,282
4BR	R45	4-dr Sta Wag-9P	4790	5021	23,513
CENTURION					
4BP	P39	4-dr HT Sed-6P	4390	4329	22,354
4BP	P57	2-dr HT Spt Cpe-5P	4336	4260	16,883
4BP	P67	2-dr Conv-5P	4534	4316	5,739

LESABRE ENGINE
See 1973 Apollo Series V-8 engine data. Base engine for LeSabre and LeSabre Custom models was the two-barrel 350 cubic inch V-8.

CENTURION ENGINE
Base engine for Centurions was the 350 cubic inch V-8 with four-barrel carburetion and 175 horsepower at 4000 R.P.M.

ESTATE WAGON ENGINE
V-8. Overhead valves. Cast iron block. Displacement: 455 cubic inches. Bore and stroke: 4.3 x 3.9 cubic inches. Compression ratio: 8.5:1. Brake horsepower: 225 at 4000 R.P.M. Hydraulic valve lifters. Carburetor: four-barrel.

1973 Buick, Electra 225 Limited 4-dr hardtop, V-8 (TVB)

ELECTRA 225/ELECTRA 225 CUSTOM SERIES — (V-8) —
The Electra series was a two model line, split into two sub-series, Electra 225 and Electra 225 Custom. A Limited trim package was available for the upper level. Standard equipment was the same as on Centurions plus electric clock; license frames; all courtesy and safety lights; foam seats; remote control OSRV mirror; Super DeLuxe wheel covers; Custom safety belts and some changes in technical features. Custom models had carpeted lower door panels and special trims. The Limited had wide, bright metal body underscores.

ELECTRA 225/ELECTRA CUSTOM SERIES

Model Number	Body/Style Number	Body Type & Seating	Factory Price	Shipping Weight	Production Total
ELECTRA 225					
4CT	T39	4-dr HT Sed-6P	4928	4581	17,189
4CT	T37	2-dr HT Spt Cpe-6P	4815	4488	9,224
ELECTRA 225 CUSTOM					
4CV	V39	4-dr HT Sed-6P	5105	4603	107,031
4CV	V37	2-dr HT Spt Cpe-6P	4993	4505	44,328

ELECTRA ENGINE
V-8. Overhead valves. Cast iron block. Displacement: 455 cubic inches. Bore and stroke: 4.313 x 3.900 inches. Compression ratio: 8.5:1. SAE net horsepower: 225 at 4000 R.P.M. Hydraulic valve lifters. Carburetor: four-barrel.

RIVIERA SERIES — (V-8) —
Along with the other regular-size cars from Buick Division, the Riviera had a new front and rear treatment with new hood, fenders, grille and lights. Standard equipment included new Accu Drive; variable-ratio power steering; power brakes with front discs; new, durable stamped steel rocker arms; computer selected springs; new windshield washer; radiator overflow coolant reservoirs; solenoid activated throttle stop and exhaust gas recirculation (EGR) emissions control system; integral voltage regulator and Delcotron and brake proportioning valve. The boat-tail body featured thicker rocker panel trim covers, which overlapped the lower door edge. New, notch style front cornering lamps were seen. Riviera scripts appeared on the lower front fenders, with Riviera emblems on the roof pillar.

RIVIERA SERIES

Model Number	Body/Style Number	Body Type & Seating	Factory Price	Shipping Weight	Production Total
4EY	Y87	2-dr HT Spt Cpe-5P	5221	4486	34,080

RIVIERA ENGINE
V-8. Overhead valves. Cast iron block. Displacement: 455 cubic inches. Bore and stroke: 4.313 x 3.900. Compression ratio: 8.5:1. SAE net horsepower: 250 at 4000 R.P.M. Carburetor: four-barrel.

CHASSIS FEATURES: Wheelbase: (Apollo) 111 inches; (Century, Luxus, Regal two-door) 112 inches; (Century, Luxus four-door) 116 inches; (LeSabre, Custom LeSabre, Centurion) 124 inches; (Estate Wagon) 127 inches; (Electra, Electra 225) 127 inches; (Riviera) 122 inches. Overall length: (Apollo) 197.5 inches; (Century, Luxus, Regal two-door) 210.7 inches; (Century, Luxus four-door) 212.4 inches; (LeSabre, Custom LeSabre, Centurion) 224.2 inches; (Estate wagon) 229.5 inches; (Electra, Electra 225) 229.8 inches; (Riviera) 223.4 inches. Tires: (Apollo) ET8 x 14; (Century) G78-14; (LeSabre) 8.78 x 14; (Centurion) L78 x 15; (Electra) J78-15; (Riviera) J78 x 15.

POWERTRAIN OPTONS: The 150 horsepower '350' V-8 was optional in Apollo. The 175 horsepower '350' V-8 was optional in all A-Body Buicks and in LeSabre/Customs. A 190 horsepower '350' V-8 was available in Century Grand Sport coupes. The 225 horsepower '455' V-8 was optional in Centurys / Luxus / Regal / LeSabre / Custom / Centurion / Electra 225 / 225 Custom. A 260 horsepower '455' V-8 was optional in Rivieras. A 270 horsepower '455' V-8 was optional in the Century Grand Sport Coupe.

CONVENIENCE OPTIONS: Vinyl top ($99). AM/FM stereo ($233). AM/FM stereo with tape ($363). Power seats ($103). Century Gran Sport package ($173). Power windows ($129). Vinyl top ($123). Riviera Stage I package ($139). Electra 225 Custom Limited trim ($174). 60/40 seats in Electra Custom ($77). Sun roof ($589). Riviera chrome styled wheels ($70). Apollo air-conditioning ($381). Century Stage I package ($546). Apollo Sport wagon disc brakes ($68). Disc brakes, other models ($46). Max trac ($89). Riviera Gran Sport package ($171).

Historical footnotes: Dealer introductions took place on September 21, 1972. Model year sales by U.S. dealers peaked at a record 726,191 cars. It was the second best season in Buick history. New 'Colonnade' styling was seen on Buick Century, Century Luxus and Regals in 1973. This type of design was essentially hardtop styling with a center pillar added to better satisfy federal roll over standards. G.R. Elges was general manager of Buick Motor Division this year. The Centurion nameplate disappeared at the end of the 1973 model run.

1974 BUICK

1974 Buick, Apollo 2-dr hatch back sedan, V-8 (TVB)

APOLLO SERIES — SIX AND V-8 —
Styling changes for the second year Apollo included a new, vertically segmented grille; a redesigned hood that dropped all the way to the upper grille header bar and the positioning of the front license plate bracket below the center of the bumper. A new, circular medallion was set into the center of the grille. Power for the base, six-cylinder series again came from an inline Chevrolet engine. Apollos with the 350 cubic inch Buick V-8 were considered a separate series. An Apollo GSX trim option was available for $96 extra.

BUICK I.D. NUMBERS: All Buicks continued to use the same type of serial numbers as in 1973. The sixth symbol was changed to a '4' to indicate 1974 model year.

APOLLO SERIES (SIX/V-8)

Model Number	Body/Style Number	Body Type & Seating	Factory Price	Shipping Weight	Production Total
4XB	B69	4-dr Sedan-5P	3060/3184	3256/3469	16,779
4XB	B27	2-dr Notch-5P	3037/3161	3216/3429	28,286
4XB	B17	2-dr Hatch-5P	3160/3284	3321/3534	11,644

NOTES: Style B27 is the two-door notch back coupe; Style B17 the two-door hatch back coupe. Factory prices and shipping weights above slash are for Sixes; below slash for V-8s.

APOLLO ENGINES
See 1973 Apollo Series engine data.

1974 Buick, Century Luxus 2-dr colonnade coupe, V-8 (TVB)

CENTURY/LUXUS/REGAL/SERIES — (V-8) — The 'Colonnade' styled A-Body Buicks were mildly facelifted. A larger grille with rectangular grid insert was seen. The front bumper guard arrangement of 1973 was replaced by a flat license plate holder. The guards became optional and, when used, were spaced wider apart. Century nameplates appeared behind the front wheel opening on Century 350 models. Luxus models had enriched trims and bright rocker moldings. Regals had a front fender crest, hood crest and more delicately cross hatched grille insert. The A-Body station wagons were again designated Sport Wagons. Four different Gran Sport packages were optionally available on the Century Sport Coupe. The base GS group ($108) included GS styling and suspension components; instrument gauge cluster; clock; wheel opening moldings; glove box; ash tray and courtesy lights. The GS 455 (code A5) package included all of the above plus a four-barrel 455 cubic inch V-8; dual exhausts and power front disc brakes for $292. The GS 455 (code A9) package included all of the above plus a dual snorkel air cleaner for $338. The ultimate option was the GS Stage I package ($558) including a performance modified 455 cubic inch V-8; all Gran Sport features; high energy ignition; dual snorkel air cleaner; positive traction axle; power front disc brakes and dual exhausts. The Turbo-Hydramatic 400 transmission was mandatory on Century GS Stage I models.

CENTURY/LUXUS/REGAL SERIES

Model Number	Body/Style Number	Body Type & Seating	Factory Price	Shipping Weight	Production Total
CENTURY 350					
4AD	D29	4-dr HT Sed-6P	3836	3890	22,856
4AD	D37	2-dr HT Cpe-6P	3790	3845	33,166
4AF	F45	4-dr Sta Wag-9P	4320	4305	Note 1
4AF	F35	4-dr Sta Wag-6P	4205	4272	4,860
LUXUS					
4AD	H29	4-dr HT Sed-6P	4109	3910	11,159
4AH	H57	2-dr HT Cpe-6P	4089	3835	44,930
4AK	K45	4-dr Sta Wag-9P	4486	4345	Note 1
4AK	K35	4-dr Sta Wag-6P	4371	4312	6,791
REGAL					
4AJ	J57	2-dr HT Cpe-6P	4201	3900	57,512
4AJ	J29	4-dr HT Sed-6P	4221	3930	9,333

NOTE 1: Production totals for six and nine-passenger station wagons are counted together, with no breakouts per seating configuration.

CENTURY/LUXUS/REGAL ENGINE
See 1973 Century/Luxus/Regal Series engine data.

LESABRE, LESABRE LUXUS SERIES — (V-8) — A very noticeable facelift marked the 1974 LeSabre. Round headlights were now set into individual square bezels which were separated by a body colored panel. The grille stretched across the car from end to end, but ran below and inbetween the headlamp bezels. The front, lower gravel pan was redesigned, having twin horizontal slots on either side of a center panel and horizontal parking lamps at the outboard ends. Cornering lamps were notched into the front fender tips. Buick lettering appeared on the upper grille shell header bar. LeSabre scripts were mounted at the trailing edge of the rear fenders. The rear end had a slanting, swept back look and side body sculpturing was of a crisper style. Standard LeSabre features included power brakes (front disc); power steering; Turbo-Hydramatic; Accu Drive; full-flow ventilation; semi-closed cooling system; time modulated choke; EGR system; air injection reactor; front and rear ash trays; inside hood release; full-foam seats; carpeting; DeLuxe steering wheel; recessed wipers; glove box light; automatic interior lamp; bumper guard strips and the two-barrel '350' V-8. The Luxus models also had Custom steering wheel: DeLuxe wheel covers; vinyl notch back seat (except convertible); Luxus trim and four-barrel '350' V-9s.

1974 Buick, LeSabre 4-dr sedan, V-8 (TVB)

LESABRE/LESABRE LUXUS SERIES

Model Number	Body/Style Number	Body Type & Seating	Factory Price	Shipping Weight	Production Total
LESABRE					
4BN	N69	4-dr Sedan-6P	4355	4337	18,572
4BN	N39	4-dr HT Sed-6P	4482	4387	11,879
4BN	N57	2-dr HT Cpe-6P	4424	4297	12,522
LESABRE LUXUS					
4BP	P69	4-dr Sedan-6P	4466	4352	16,039
4BP	P39	4-dr HT Sed-6P	4629	4397	23,910
4BP	P57	2-dr HT Cpe-6P	4575	4307	27,243
4BP	P67	2-dr Conv-6P	4696	4372	3,627
ESTATE WAGON					
4BR	R45	4-dr Sta Wag-9P	5163	5182	9,831
4BR	435	4-dr Sta Wag-6P	5019	5082	4,581

LESABRE ENGINE
See 1973 LeSabre Series engine data. A 210 horsepower 455 cubic inch V-8 was standard equipment for Estate wagons.

ELECTRA 225/ELECTRA 225 CUSTOM SERIES — (V-8) — Styling changes for the big Buicks paralleled those seen on LeSabres with individual head lamp bezels and slot style front gravel pans. A wide, chrome header bar was added to the grille and had the word Buick lettered at the center. Notch style cornering lamps were set into the front corners of the body. Standard equipment was the same as on LeSabre Luxus models, plus accessory lamp group (less sunshade light); foam padded seats; remote control OSRV mirror; Super DeLuxe wheel covers; seat belt restrainers; Custom safety belts; evaporative emissions control system; integral voltage regulator and Delcotron; Turbo-Hydramatic 400 transmission; J78-15 blackwall tires and the four-barrel '455' V-8. Custom trimmed Electra 225s had carpeted lower door panels and Custom exterior and interior trim. The Limited was now a separate series identified by wide rocker panel moldings, plus all other Custom features.

ELECTRA 222/ELECTRA 225 CUSTOM SERIES

Model Number	Body/Style Number	Body Type & Seating	Factory Price	Shipping Weight	Production Total
ELECTRA 225					
4CT	T39	4-dr HT Sed-6P	5373	4682	5,750
4CT	T37	2-dr HT Cpe-6P	5260	4607	3,339
ELECTRA 225 CUSTOM					
4CV	V39	4-dr HT Sed-6P	5550	4702	29,089
4CV	V37	2-dr HT Cpe-6P	5438	4682	15,099
ELECTRA LIMITED					
4CX	X39	4-dr HT Sed-6P	5921	4732	30,051
4CX	X37	2-dr HT Cpe-6P	5886	4682	16,086

ELECTRA ENGINE
V-8. Overhead valves. Cast iron block. Displacement: 455 cubic inches. Bore and stroke: 4.31 x 3.9. Compression ratio: 8.0:1. SAE net horsepower: 210. Hydraulic valve lifters. Carburetor: four-barrel.

1974 Buick, Riviera 2-dr hardtop sport coupe, V-8 (TVB)

RIVIERA SERIES — (V-8) — A new vertical grille with the Riviera name above it was seen as part of the 1974 restyling. An all-new notch back roofline appeared. A standup hood ornament was added. At the rear, the fender line sloped downward, dropping below the upper contour of the deck lid. Slanted, rectangular tail lamps were horizontally mounted and decorated with a grid work of bright metal strips. Equipment features started at the Electra 225 level, except that wire wheel hubcaps were standard and Custom safety belts were not. Standard extras included a tilt steering wheel; dual exhausts; foam contoured seats; digital clock; courtesy and glove box lights; dual front lighted ash trays and H78-15 blackwall bias belted tires. The Grand Sport ride and handling package ($108) included a rear stabilizer bar; J78-15 whitewall steel-belted tires; radial roadability suspension and specific body insulation and ornamentation. The Riviera Stage I option ($139) included a performance modified '455' V-8; positive traction axle and chrome plated air cleaner.

RIVIERA SERIES

Model Number	Body/Style Number	Body Type & Seating	Factory Price	Shipping Weight	Production Total
4EY	Y87	2-dr HT Spt Cpe-5P	5678	4572	20,129

RIVIERA ENGINE
V-8. Overhead valves. Cast iron block. Displacement: 455 cubic inches. Bore and stroke: 4.31 x 3.9. Compression ratio: 8.25:1. SAE net horsepower: 210. Carburetor: four-barrel.

CHASSIS FEATURES: Wheelbase: (Apollo) 111 inches; (Century four-door) 116 inches; (Century two-door) 112 inches; (LeSabre) 123.5 inches; (Estate Wagon and Electra) 127 inches; (Riviera) 122 inches. Overall lengths: (Apollo) 200.2 inches; (Century four-door) 212 inches; (Sport Wagons) 218.2 inches; (Century two-door) 209.5 inches; (LeSabre) 225.9 inches; (Estate Wagon) 231.1 inches; (Electra) 231.5 inches; (Riviera) 226.4 inches. Tires: (Apollo) E78-14; (Century) G78-14; (Sport Wagon) H78-14; (LeSabre) H78-15; (Estate Wagon) L78-14; (Electra) J78-15; (Riviera) J78-15.

POWERTRAIN OPTIONS: Heavy-duty air cleaner ($9). Heavy-duty Delco energizer ($15). Dual exhausts ($30). Emission test, required for California sale ($20). Apollo '350' two-barrel V-8 ($118). Apollo '350' four-barrel V-8 ($164). Four-barrel '350' V-8 in Century or LeSabre ($46). Two-barrel '455' V-8 in LeSabre and Century ($184). Performance-modified '455' V-8 in Electras ($96); in Estate Wagons ($152); in LeSabres ($322). Four-barrel '455' V-8 in Sport Wagons ($184); in other Centurys ($230); in LeSabres ($170). Engine block heater in Apollo ($10); in other models ($5); High-energy ignition in Apollo/Century ($77); in other models ($56). Instrument gauges and clock in Centurys, except Sport Wagons ($38). Positive traction axle ($43). Max track wheel spin control ($89). Turbo-Hydramatic 350 transmission in Apollo Six ($196); in Apollo '350' V-8 ($206). Turbo-Matic 400 transmission in Century ($21). Heavy-duty radiator in Apollo ($14); other models ($21). Heavy-duty 80-Amp Delcotron ($31-35).

CONVENIENCE OPTIONS: Air-conditioning ($396-446). Air cushion restraint system ($181-225). Station wagon air deflector ($21). Automatic climate control ($488-522). Custom safety belts ($11-37). Apollo bumper impact strips ($13). Riviera bumper reinforcement ($12). Electra rear bumper reinforcement ($6). Cargo area carpeting in Sport Wagons ($19); in Estate Wagons ($51). Trunk carpet in Electras and Riviera ($41). Electric clock, Apollo ($16); Century ($18). Full-length console for Century and Riviera two-doors ($61). Mini console in Century two-doors ($36). Convenience center console ($26). Customline convertible cover ($36). Cruise control in Century ($65). Rear window defogger ($33). Electric rear window defogger ($64). Tinted glass ($30-50). Tinted windshield ($30-35). Front and rear bumper guards ($31-35). Automatic level control ($77). Buick cornering lights ($36). Front monitors ($22). Front and rear monitors ($48). Station wagon luggage rack ($64-84). Sports mirrors, right and left ($22-44). Special order paint ($113). Apollo body striping ($21). Riviera body striping ($31). Wide rocker moldings for LeSabre Luxus and Electra 225s, except Limited ($28). Custom body side trim ($24-46). Custom door/window trim ($21-27). Two-tone paint ($27-43). Wide rocker panel group for LeSabre and Estate, including lower rear quarter, front and rear wheel well moldings ($69). Six-way right hand and left hand power seats of 60/40 design or 40/40 design ($211). Other six-way seat options ($80-106). Electric sunroof in Century ($325); in all Sports Coupes ($589). AM radio with stereo tape and dual rear speakers ($203-216). AM/FM stereo radio with stereo tape and front and rear dual speakers ($363). Rallye suspension ($30). Super lift shock absorbers ($41). Speed Alert ($11-17). Manual sunroof in Century ($275); in Sport Coupes ($539). Vinyl trim with Custom bucket seats ($124); with lumbar-support reclining bucket seats ($236); vinyl bucket seats ($119), all in Century two-doors only. Vinyl roofs, Custom Apollo ($82); Custom Century ($99); Custom Century short type ($84); Custom padded Electra ($385); Custom Landau Riviera ($385); Custom Landau Electra Sport Coupe ($525); Custom with moldings on Estate ($138); Custom Regal Landau ($310); Custom padded with moldings on Electra/LeSabre/Riviera ($123-138). DeLuxe wheel covers ($26); wire wheel covers ($56-82). Super DeLuxe wheel

covers ($34-56). DeLuxe wire wheel covers ($60-108). Chrome wheels ($66-118). Wood grain exterior station wagon panelling on Estate ($177); Luxus ($136); Century ($168). Code V4 accessory group ($26-36). Code V1 convenience group ($12-27). Ride and handling package ($15). LeSabre Luxus ride and performance package ($423-575). (Note: Prices for certain options and accessories varied by Series or body style. In such cases, the low-to-high range is reflected above).

Historical footnotes: Model year introductions took place on September 27, 1974. Calendar year production peaked at 400,262 cars or 5.49 percent of industry output. Model year production hit 495,063 units. Buick dealers also marketed Opels this year. George R. Elges remained Buick's general manager in 1974 and P.C. Bowser was chief engineer.

1975 BUICK

1975 Buick, Skyhawk 2-dr hatch back coupe, V-6 (TVB)

SKYHAWK SERIES — (V-6) — An all new car, the sub-compact Skyhawk was the smallest Buick in more than 60 years. It weighed below 3,000 pounds and stood less than four feet high. The Skyhawk shared the GM H-Body platform — featuring torque arm rear suspension and super sleek 2 + 2 styling — with the Chevrolet Monza. Under the hood, however, was a 231 cubic inch Buick V-6. This engine had started its life as a 225 cubic inch Buick powerplant for the Special Series in the early 1960s. In 1968, the tooling for the engine was sold to American Motors Corporation. Now, with a displacement increased, the motor was back in the Buick stable and many of its parts were interchangeable with a 260 cubic inch V-8. Mounted on a 97 inch wheelbase, the Skyhawk was 179.3 inches long (21 inches shorter than the Apollo) and came with all features of larger GM cars, including the Efficiency System and a full list of options.

BUICK I.D. NUMBERS: Vehicle identification numbers and number locations followed the previous system. The sixth symbol was changed to a '5' for 1975 model year.

SKYHAWK SERIES

Model Number	Body/Style Number	Body Type & Seating	Factory Price	Shipping Weight	Production Total
4H	HT07	2-dr 'S' Hatch-4P	3860	2851	Note 1
4H	HS07	2-dr Hatch-4P	4173	2891	Note 1

NOTE 1: Buick Skyhawks were manufactured exclusively in Canada this year. Buick reported U.S. dealer model year sales of 29,448 examples of the new 'H' car. No breakout was provided for the two trim levels.

SKYHAWK ENGINE

V-6. Overhead valves. Cast iron block. Displacement: 231 cubic inches. Bore and stroke: 3.80 x 3.40. Compression ratio: 8.0:1. SAE net horsepower: 110 at 4000 R.P.M. Overhead valves. Carburetor: two-barrel.

1975 Buick, Apollo 2-dr notch back sedan, V-6 (TVB)

APOLLO/SKYLARK SERIES — (L-6/V-6/V-8) — The Apollo lineup was the most extensively revised 1975 Buick series. Topped by the revived Skylark two-door coupe, other X-car models included a two-door hatchback coupe and a thin pillared four-door sedan. New styling gave the Apollo a European flair, with a low beltline, full-width grille, wraparound parking and directional lamps and large, horizontal taillamps. Both standard and luxury 'R/S' models were on a 111 inch wheelbase with Apollos offering the 250 cubic inch Chevrolet L-head Six as base powerplant. Cars with V-8 power were

considered to be in a separate series. The 260 cubic inch V-8 was the base V-8 and the 350 cubic inch job was optional. Base engine in the Skylark was the "new" V-6. Signature scripts below the rear fender belt moldings were helpful in identifying the various models.

APOLLO ENGINES

L-6. Overhead valves. Cast iron block. Displacement: 250 cubic inches. Bore and stroke: 3.87 x 3.5. Compression ratio: 8.0:1. Brake horsepower: 105 at 4000 R.P.M. Carburetor: one-barrel.

V-6. See 1975 Skyhawk Series engine data.

V-8: Overhead valves. Cast iron block. Displacement: 260 cubic inches. Bore and stroke: 3.5 x 3.385 inches. Compression ratio: 8.0:1. Brake horsepower: 110 at 4000 R.P.M. Carburetor: two-barrel.

APOLLO/SKYLARK SERIES

Model Number	Body/Style Number	Body Type & Seating	Factory Price	Shipping Weight	Production Total
(APOLLO SUB-SERIES)					
4BX	B69	4-dr Sedan-5P	3436/3514	3366/3511	21,138
(SKYLARK 'S' SUB-SERIES)					
4WX	W27	2-dr Notch-5P	3234/3260	3309/3502	Note 1
(SKYLARK SUB-SERIES)					
4BX	B27	2-dr Notch-5P	3463/3489	3341/3537	27,689
4BX	B17	2-dr Hatch-5P	3586/3612	3438/3587	6,814
(APOLLO 'SR' SUB-SERIES)					
4CX	C69	4-dr Sedan-5P	4092/4170	3383/3574	2,241
(SKYLARK 'SR' SUB-SERIES)					
4CX	C27	2-dr Notch-5P	4136/4162	3309/3498	3,746
4CX	C17	2-dr Notch-5P	4253/4279	3441/3586	1,505

NOTE 1: No breakout is provided for production of the Skylark 'S' notch back coupe. **ADDITIONAL NOTES:** A total of 504 Apollos were manufactured in Canada, late in the 1975 calendar year, to 1976 specifications. In the chart above Factory Prices and Shipping Weights above slash are for Sixes; below slash for V-8s. The L-6 was used in Apollos; the V-6 in Skylarks. The base V-8 was the 260 cubic-inch Buick motor.

1975 Buick, Century 2-dr colonnade coupe w/'Free Spirit' pkg, V-8

CENTURY/REGAL SERIES — (V-6/V-8) — The intermediate size Buick A-Body lineup offered the biggest selection of models for 1975. The Century was again the base level in terms of trim and appointments, with an equipment list comparable to similar 1974 models. A one-step up Century Custom was comparable to the 1974 Luxus, with the same type of features and extra decorative touches. The Gran Sport was no longer a separate sub-series, but 'GS' type equipment was available as a $171 options package. Basic styling changes from a year earlier included a wider grille that varied in design from line to line. On Century Specials it had a horizontal double-deck look, with vertical-dash type insert and vertically-mounted rectangular parking lamps housed, within the grille, at its outboard ends. On Centurys and Century Customs, the horizontal divider was deleted. On Regals, there was a shorter grille with vertical blades only and the same type of parking lamps were seen outside the grille, between the chrome surround and the headlamps. Regals had a model identification script on the lefthand side of the grille, while other models had Buick block lettering. The Century Special was marketed as a low-rung economy job with less basic equipment than other models, allowing it to be advertised at an attractive price. As in the past, the two-door A-Body cars were shorter, in wheelbase and overall length, than four-doors on this platform.

CENTURY/REGAL SERIES

Model Number	Body/Style Number	Body Type & Seating	Factory Price	Shipping Weight	Production Total
(CENTURY SPECIAL V-6)					
4AE	E37	2-dr Coupe-6P	3815	3613	Note 1
(CENTURY V-6/V-8)					
4AD	D29	4-dr Sedan-6P	3944/4022	3730/3906	22,075
4AD	D37	2-dr Coupe-6P	3894/3972	3674/3850	39,556
4AF	F45	4-dr Sta Wag-9P	4751	4370	Note 2
4AF	F35	4-dr Sta Wag-6P	4636	4320	4,416
(CENTURY CUSTOM V-6/V-8)					
4AH	H29	4-dr Sedan-6P	4211/4289	3763/3939	9,995
4AH	H57	2-dr Coupe-6P	4154/4232	3671/3847	32,966
4AK	K45	4-dr Sta Wag-9P	4917	4400	Note 2
4AK	K35	4-dr Sta Wag-6P	4802	4350	7,078
(REGAL V-6/V-8)					
4AJ	J29	4-dr Sedan-6P	4311/4389	3800/3976	10,726
4AJ	J57	2-dr Coupe-6P	4257/4335	3733/3909	56,646

NOTE 1: The Century Special came only with V-6 power and was technically an equipment-deleted model and *not* a distinct body style. Production of this car, Style Number E37, is counted with Style Number D37. **NOTE 2:** Station Wagons came only with V-8 power. Production of six and nine-passenger station wagons was counted as a single total. **ADDITIONAL NOTE:** Factory Prices and Shipping Weights above slash are for Sixes; below slash for V-8s. Cars with V-8 power were considered to be in a separate series.

CENTURY/REGAL ENGINES

V-6. See 1975 Skyhawk Series engine data.

V-8. Overhead valves. Cast iron block. Displacement: 350 cubic inches. Bore and stroke: 3.8 x 3.85 inches. Compression ratio: 8.0:1. Brake horsepower: 145 at 3800 R.P.M. Carburetor: two-barrel.

LESABRE/LESABRE CUSTOM/ESTATE WAGON SERIES — (V-8) — Both LeSabre and LeSabre Custom series offered B-Body two and four-door hardtops, plus four-door thin-pillar styles. A convertible was exclusive to the Custom level line. All LeSabres were on a 123.5 inch wheelbase with either a standard 350 cubic inch V-8 or optional '455'. The Estate Wagons shared the 127 inch Electra wheelbase and luxury appointments. As on all Buicks, the GM Efficiency System was standard and included High-Energy ignition a catalytic convertor and steel-belted radial tires. Styling updates included a new grid-style grille with under the headlamp extensions. The square headlamp housings returned to a side-by-side type mounting; ventiports were moved from the hood to the front fender sides and Buick block lettering was the only decoration on the lower lip of the hood. Equipment variations between the various sub-series were comparable to the previous year with Custom replaceing the Luxus designation.

1975 Buick, Riviera hardtop sport coupe, V-8 (TVB)

1975 Buick, LeSabre 4-dr hardtop sedan, V-8 (TVB)

LESABRE/LESABRE CUSTOM/ESTATE WAGON SERIES

Model Number	Body/Style Number	Body Type & Seating	Factory Price	Shipping Weight	Production Total
(LESABRE)					
4BN	N69	4-dr Sedan-6P	4771	4355	14,088
4BN	N39	4-dr HT Sedan-6P	4898	4411	9,119
4BN	N57	2-dr HT Cpe-6P	4840	4294	8,647
(LESABRE CUSTOM)					
4BP	P69	4-dr Sedan-6P	4936	4388	17,026
4BP	P39	4-dr HT Sed-6P	5061	4439	30,005
4BP	P57	2-dr HT Cpe-6P	5007	4316	25,016
4BP	P67	2-dr Conv-6P	5133	4392	5,300
(ESTATE WAGON)					
4BR	R45	4-dr Sta Wag-9P	5591	5135	9,612
4BR	R35	4-dr Sta Wag-6P	5447	5055	4,128

LESABRE/LESABRE CUSTOM
The 350 cubic inch V-8 was the standard engine in LeSabre and LeSabre Customs. General specifications were the same as for the Century '350' except that a four-barrel carburetor was used and the output was 165 horsepower at 4000 R.P.M.

ESTATE WAGON ENGINE
V-8. Overhead valves. Cast iron block. Displacement: 455 cubic inhces. Bore and stroke: 4.313 x 3.9 inches. Compression ratio: 7.9:1. Brake horsepower: 205 at 3800 R.P.M. Carburetor: Four-barrel.

ELECTRA 225 CUSTOM/ELECTRA 225 LIMITED SERIES — (V-8) — Buick's most prestigious series was reduced to four models, as full-sized cars continued to be de-emphasized by General Motors. These C-Body models were built off a 127 inch wheelbase platform. The 455 cubic inch V-8 was standard as were Efficiency System features. Rectangular headlamps were a styling change along with a Classic-looking egg crate grille that extended below the headlamps. Also new were monogrammed hood ornaments; large opera style rear quarter windows; shag carpeting and soft velour upholstery and headliners. An especially luxurious Park Avenue option package was available for the Limited hardtop sedan, as well as an even richer Park Avenue DeLuxe group.

ELECTRA 225 CUSTOM/ELECTRA 225 LIMITED

Model Number	Body/Style Number	Body Type & Seating	Factory Price	Shipping Weight	Production Total
(CUSTOM)					
4CV	V39	4-dr HT Sed-6P	6201	4706	27,357
4CV	V37	2-dr HT Cpe-6P	6041	4582	16,145
(LIMITED)					
4CX	X39	4-dr HT Sed-6P	6516	4762	33,778
4CX	X37	2-dr HT Cpe-6P	6352	4633	17,650

ELECTRA 225 CUSTOM/LIMITED ENGINE
See 1975 Estate Wagon engine data.

RIVIERA SERIES — (V-8) — The Riviera remained as Buick's personal luxury offering. A major redesign was seen up front. Changes to the bumper, grille and trim and new rectangular headlamps were seen. Overall length was 3-1/2 inches shorter. The ultra luxurious and sporty 'GS' option remained available and standard equipment was the same as the previous season, plus High-Energy ignition; Efficiency System features and steel-belted radial ply tires. Annual styling changes included closer together vertical blades in the Neo-Classic grille shell; clear cornering lamp lenses; a slotted-center bumper design and a Riviera script plate on the lefthand side of the grille.

RIVIERA SERIES

Model Number	Body/Style Number	Body Type & Seating	Factory Price	Shipping Weight	Production Total
4EZ	Z87	2-dr HT Spt Cpe-5P	6420	4539	17,306

RIVIERA ENGINE
See 1975 Estate Wagon engine data.

CHASSIS FEATURES: Wheelbase: (Skyhawk) 97 inches; (Apollo/Skylark) 111 inches; (Century two-door) 112 inches; (Century four-door) 116 inches; (LeSabre) 124 inches; (Electra and Estate) 127 inches; (Riviera) 122 inches. Overall length: (Skyhawk) 179.3 inches; (Apollo and Skylark) 200.3 inches; (Century two-door) 209.5 inches; (Century four-door) 213.5 inches; (Century station wagon) 218.2 inches; (Regal two-door) 212 inches; (Regal four-door) 216 inches; (LeSabre) 226.9 inches; (Estate Wagon) 233.4 inches; (Electra) 233.4 inches; (Riviera) 223 inches. Tires: (Skyhawk) BR78-13; (Skylark and Apollo) FR78-14; (Century) GR78-15; (Estate Wagon) LR78-15; (LeSabre) HR78-15; (Electra and Riviera) JR78-15.

POWERTRAIN OPTIONS: Optional engines for Apollos included the two and four-barrel versions of the 350 cubic inch V-8. Optional engines for Century/Regal models were the two and four-barrel versions of the 350 cubic inch V-8 (145 and 165 horsepower, respectively). The 350 cubic inch, four-barrel engine was standard in Century station wagons, with no other choices available. The four-barrel 455 cubic inch V-8 (205 horsepower) was optional in LeSabres. There were no engine options for Electras or Rivieras. A 400 cubic inch 185 horsepower engine was optional in LeSabres and was, most likely, released only for use in cars built for California sale. The horsepower rating indicates this is a Pontiac-built motor, although standard reference sources are unclear on this point.

CONVENIENCE OPTIONS: Skyhawk air conditioning ($398). Skyhawk AM/FM stereo ($214). Apollo air conditioning ($435). Apollo AM/FM stereo ($233); with tape player ($363). Century AM/FM stereo ($233); with tape player ($363). Century Six-Way power seat ($117). Century sun roof ($256). Gran Sport package ($171). Regal S/R package ($256). Station Wagon luggage rack ($68). Century Six-Way power seat ($117). LeSabre power windows ($149). Station wagon wood grain applique ($182). Estate Wagon luggage rack ($89). Riviera 'GS' ride and handling package ($73). Electra and Riviera sun roof ($644). Park Avenue option group ($495). Power brakes in Apollo ($55). Rear window defroster ($60). Electra rear window defroster ($73). Bucket seats ($75). Regal sun roof ($350). Custom trim ($165). Air bags ($275). Park Avenue DeLuxe package ($1,675). Electra and Riviera cornering lamps ($38). Heavy padded vinyl roof ($389).

Historical footnotes: Dealer introductions were held September 27, 1974. Calendar year production (U.S. built models only) peaked at 545,820 cars or 7.99 percent of the total industry output. Model year sales of domestically-built models peaked at 481,768 units. D.C. Collier was named general manager of Buick Division this year. A total of 49,226 Opels were also sold from Buick dealer showrooms this season. In late 1975, assemblies of Skyhawks built to 1976 specifications began at the GMAD plant in Southgate, California.

BUICK
1976-1986

Periodic flirtations with performance aside, Buick's reputation still relied most on its long history as a well-equipped, if slightly stodgy, family car. Not ordinarily a trend-setter, Buick regularly produced the kinds of reliable cars that millions of moderately well-off families wanted. By the mid-1970s, the sprightly GS and GSX editions had become memories. So had Buick ragtops, the last of which (a LeSabre) came off the line not long before the '76 model year began. Two years earlier, the pillarless two-door hardtop had given way to a "Colonnade" coupe design with large quarter windows. Those windows got smaller in subsequent years, but the "true" two-door hardtop was gone (though four-door pillarless hardtops hung on a bit longer).

1976 Regal Landau Coupe (B)

For 1975, the Skylark badge had returned on a compact Buick, and the Monza-based Skyhawk subcompact coupe arrived. Those two entered 1976 with little change, joining the mid- size Century and Regal, full-size LeSabre/Electra duo, and upscale Riviera--powered by a giant 455 cu. in., 205 horsepower V-8. Skylark was the only domestic V-6 powered compact, LeSabre the only V-6 full-size, both carrying Buick's own 231 cu. in. engine. Skyhawks could have a new Borg-Warner five-speed gearbox—a choice not common at this time. Century coupes sported a fastback roofline, and a Hurst twin-panel Hatch Roof made the option list. The fabled "ventiports" (portholes) that had made their initial appearance in 1949 still stood on full-size Buick fenders, albeit in different form. After two years of decline, Buick sales zoomed upward by over 52 percent, approaching the model-year record set in 1973. A Buick paced Indy for the second year in a row: this time a turbocharged Century, which prompted issuance of replica models with the pace car colors.

Both bodies and engines shrunk for 1977, in the first wave of Buick downsizing. This time the victims were LeSabre, Electra and Riviera (the latter temporarily becoming a variant of LeSabre). A 403 cu. in. V-8 took over the 455's spot as biggest Buick engine. Three different 350 cu. in. V-8s (including Chevrolet's) were available, and made standard on the shrunken Electra and Riviera. Those non-Buick engines soon would cause a lot of trouble for GM, as certain customers felt themselves cheated. Record-setting sales ended the year, though, led by popularity of the downsized full-size models.

1978 Electra Park Avenue Landau Coupe (B)

Century and Regal got their trimming-down for 1978. Buick displayed renewed interest in performance with the arrival of an optional turbocharged V-6 under Regal and LeSabre Sport Coupe hoods. In the other direction, the 231 cu. in. V-6 had its bore slimmed to become a 196, ready for the lighter-weight Century/Regal. Century coupes and sedans displayed a new "aeroback" profile that wouldn't attract as many customers as hoped for in the next couple of years. Among the more collectible Buicks is Riviera's silver/black 75th anniversary ('LXXV') model, of which 1,400 were produced.

Riviera not only shrunk in size for 1979; it switched to front-wheel drive, sharing mechanical components with Eldorado and Toronado. Named *Motor Trend* Car of the Year, the revised Riv was considered more closely related to the original '63 than to the boattail 1970s version. A sporty new S Type Riviera carried a turbo V-6. Century also added a Turbo Coupe package.

1979 LeSabre Sport Coupe (B)

First of the 1980 Buicks was the Skylark version of the new, but ill-fated X-car. Century continued its aero-style fastback coupe, but sedans switched to notchback bodies. That helped Century sales streak skyward. An aero restyle hit LeSabre/Electra. The 403 cu. in. V-8 disappeared, but Buicks might now have an enlarged (252 cu. in.) version of the familiar 231 V-6, a lightweight 265 V-8, or the troublesome Oldsmobile-built diesel V-8. Buick had installed its first V-8 back in 1953, but now produced no V-8 engines at all. Collectors might look for a limited-edition Regal Somerset, with tan/blue body and wire wheel covers, offered this year only. Skyhawk's Road Hawk option might also be tempting, and reasonably priced. This was the last year for Skyhawk, until it returned in front-drive form for 1982.

Regal took its turn at an aero restyle for 1981. All rear-drives now had a lockup converter clutch in their automatic transmissions. The sportiest Riviera was now called T Type, a designation that would find its way onto a whole line of sporty Buicks a few years later. Regal continued as Buick's best seller (and paced the Indy 500).

Either a four or V-6 powered the new '82 front-drive Skyhawk, while Century got an aerodynamic, wedge-shaped body. Regal, long offered only in coupe form, added a sedan and wagon. Turbocharged engines had lost popularity, and production fell to a small fraction of their former level. LeSabre's F/E limited-edition might be of modest interest, but Riviera's new convertible would probably attract more collector attention. So too might the revived Riv T Type, which now carried improved turbo power.

1983 Regal T Type coupe (AA)

All models except LeSabre/Electra came in T Type form for 1983. Only 1,750 Riv convertibles were built (and one paced Indy). Rarer yet is the 'XX Anniversary Edition' Riviera, painted two-tone beige with true wire wheels. Model year sales rose nicely, giving Buick a new record and a fourth-place ranking.

Late in the 1984 model year came what many view as the most wanted Buick of the era: the dramatic all-black turbo-powered Regal Grand National. Even while they were still in production, boosting Buick's image among younger motorists, some brought in startling amounts at auction. Car dealers who've managed to get their hands on one have sometimes put astronomical price tags on their windshields—or even implied that the car wasn't for sale at any price. Desirable, yes, but Grand Nationals aren't exactly Duesenbergs, so prices are likely to stabilize. On a more modest level, Century offered an Olympia Limited sedan to mark the Olympic Games. A turbocharged four became available under Skyhawk T Type hoods.

Front-drive moved all the way up the scale for 1985, reaching the Electra. A new Somerset Regal emerged as replacement for the Skylark X-car. Skylark actually sold fairly well through its 1980-85 lifespan, suffering less from the adverse publicity that its Citation cousin had endured as a result of recalls and lawsuits. Diesel engines finally left the lineup. Troublesome when new, they aren't likely to be much better under a collectible Buick's hood.

If Regal Grand Nationals were (and are) in strong demand, imagine the interest in LeSabre's version for 1986. Buick reports that only 117 of the special-edition coupes were built, receiving little publicity. Nearly as desirable, though, might be the performance-oriented, black-bodied Century Gran Sport. Just over a thousand of those came off the line. Turbochargers under Regal Grand National hoods added an intercooler this year, and 5,512 were produced. Anti-lock braking became a Buick option for the first time in 1986, and an all-new, V-6 powered front-drive LeSabre appeared. So did a revised Riviera, which no longer came in convertible form.

Turbocharged, all-black Buicks the most desirable? What happened to Buick's family-car image? It's been there all along, of course, and some of the luxury paint/trim options might be worth a close look today. Still, it's hard to resist the sight of a Grand National rolling by.

1976 BUICK

"Buick ownership," it was claimed, "is the knowledge that you have entered the House of Quality." And Buick for the Bicentennial year, according to the theme of the full- line catalog, was "Dedicated to the Free Spirit in just about everyone." No new models entered the lineup this year, but the Apollo name was dropped and replaced by Skylark. Convertibles were gone, the last LeSabre ragtop having been produced in July 1975. Depending on the Buick model ordered, though, air and sun fans could choose from four special roofs this year: an Astroroof, with sliding shade and heavily-tinted glass; electric sunroof; Hurst hatch roof; and on Skyhawk, a fixed- glass version with roof band. Rectangular headlamps that had been introduced previously on some models now appeared on Century, Regal and LeSabre. Buick's 231 cu. in. V-6, standard in Skyhawk, Skylark, Century and Regal Coupe, was the only V-6 designed and built in America. Its pistons, rings, wrist pins, rod bearings, timing gear and other parts were identical to those on the 350 V-8. But it weighed 200 pounds less and delivered a slightly better EPA rating than the inline six of 1975, due to improved fuel distribution. New carburetor calibrations for 1976 helped boost its performance. The V-6 could also squeeze into tighter engine compartments than an inline--a fact that would become more important as models were downsized. High-Energy Ignition, used on all engines, sent 35 percent more voltage to spark plugs and eliminated the old points and condenser. All Buicks needed unleaded fuel, carried a catalytic converter, and required less routine maintenance than predecessors of a few years earlier. The new "Freedom Battery," standard on Skyhawk and available on others, required no maintenance or addition of water, and had a built-in "state of charge" indicator. The Quadrajet carburetor was redesigned. Spark advance increased on the 350 and 455 cu. in. V-8 engines. A new camshaft on the 350 V-8 gave more power at low engine speeds. Riviera, LeSabre and Electra had a lower (2.56:1) rear axle ratio for improved economy. The familiar three-speed column shift remained standard on several economy-model Buicks (but not available in California). Three different Turbo Hydra-matic versions were offered. Computers were used to determine the optimum spring rates for each model, to give best height control, ride, and maneuvering characteristics. Front disc brakes were standard on all Buicks. Most models now have rubber protective strips on bumpers. All had Full-Flo ventilation and full-foam, contour-molded seats. Spray-on corrosion protection was used, along with galvanized metal and drainage panels, to improve rust-resistance. Bodies were coated with primer, sealer, and multiple applications of high-gloss acrylic lacquer. In keeping with the Bicentennial, standard Buick body colors for '76 were: Judicial Black (code A), Liberty White (C), Pewter Gray (D), Potomac Blue (G), Continental Blue (H), Concord Green (J), Constitution Green (L), Mount Vernon Cream (M), Buckskin Tan (Q), Musket Brown (R), Boston Red (V), and Independence Red (W). The list of special colors included Congressional Cream (P) and Revere Red (X), neither of which was available on Skyhawk or Skylark; plus Colonial Yellow (N) and Firecracker Orange (U) for Skyhawk/Skylark and offered at extra cost on other models. Buick's standard safety features included seat belts with pushbutton buckles; seat/shoulder belts in front (with reminder light and buzzer); energy-absorbing steering column, padded instrument panel and front seatback tops; passenger guard door locks; safety door latches and hinges; soft, low-profile window control knobs; smooth contoured door and window regulator handles; lane-change feature in turn signal control; vinyl-edged wide-view inside mirror; dual master cylinder brake system with warning light; and dual- action safety latches (on front-opening hoods). Buick also announced an optional Air Cushion Restraint System for LeSabre, Electra and Riviera.

1976 Skyhawk hatchback coupe (B)

SKYHAWK — SERIES 4H — V-6 — Buick's variant of the subcompact H-body Chevrolet Monza, descended from the Vega and directly related to Olds Starfire, was called the "smallest Buick in 60 years." As part of the attempt to capture the emerging youth market, it was also dubbed "The Free Spirit Hawk." In addition to the standard hatchback coupe, a low-budget 'S' version had been introduced halfway through the 1975 model year and continued for '76. New to the option list this year was a wide brushed aluminum band that wrapped over the roof, embossed with a Skyhawk emblem, coupled with a heavily-tinted (smoke-colored) glass Astroroof. Performance fans could also order their Skyhawk with a new Borg-Warner five-speed manual gearbox (overdrive top gear), instead of the standard fully synchronized four-speed. Three-speed Turbo Hydra-matic was also available. Sole powerplant was a V-6 engine with two- barrel carburetor that combined economy and spirited power. With the five-speed, Skyhawk turned in an impressive 30 MPG highway rating in economy tests. Skyhawk's rakish hatchback body had a "slippery, aerodynamic look" with fastback roofline and bulging hood. That hood sloped down in the middle toward the grille, but bulged upward to meet the headlamp housings. The front end carried quad rectangular headlamps. 'BUICK' letters stood above the upper corner of the minimalist rectangular grille, with a single dark horizontal bar across its small opening. Energy-absorbing bumpers had protective strips, plus front and rear guards. Large amber park/turn lamps sat below the front bumper. 'Skyhawk' and 'V6' emblems were on front fenders, ahead of the door. White, gold or black accent stripes were standard; so were side-window reveal moldings. Inside were high-backed, full-foam bucket seats in a 2 2 seating arrangement (cloth/vinyl or vinyl upholstery), a center console, small "comfortably-angled" steering wheel, European-style handbrake, and floor gearshift lever. Large, bold, easy-to- read instruments included a circular 7000-rpm tachometer and KM/H-MPH speedometer, ammeter, and electric clock. In the trunk sat a stowaway spare tire. Skyhawk offered almost 28 cubic feet of storage with the rear seatback folded down. Skyhawk used unibody construction. Its radial-tuned suspension included computer-selected springs, front and rear stabilizer bars (except 'S' model), plus special suspension geometry and radial tires. Front disc brakes had vented rotors to dissipate heat for fade-resistant braking. Each pad had a brake lining wear sensor that emitted an audible squeak when replacement was needed. An oil pressure switch connected to the fuel pump shut off the fuel supply whenever oil pressure fell below the normal operating limit.

1976 Skylark landau coupe (B)

SKYLARK — SERIES 4X — V-6/V-8 — Buick's European-inspired compact sedan—the only American compact powered by a V-6—came in seven models, from low-priced 'S' to sporty S/R. Body styles included a coupe, hatchback and four-door sedan. The new horizontal-design grille was made up of thin horizontal and vertical strips forming wide segments, with a 'BUICK' badge in the lower corner. It was divided into upper and lower sections by a wider horizontal bar, with widest bar across the top. Twin round headlamps in square housings were flanked by stacked outboard park/signal lamps that wrapped around the front fenders, with amber reflectors at the rear of each unit. Skylark interiors also were new, while a thickly-padded Landau top with small side windows, accented by a brushed aluminum band, was optional. Other options included a Fuel Usage Light, Cruise-Master speed control, power windows, electric door locks, automatic trunk release, and tilt steering wheel. Skylark carried a standard 3.8-liter V-6 with High- Energy Ignition, plus front disc brakes, computer-selected springs, hefty front stabilizer bar, and large full-foam seats. That V-6 weighed 200 pounds less than the optional 350 V-8 (two- or four-barrel carburetor). The base V-8 option, though, was an economical 260 cu. in. (4.3-liter) version. A fully synchronized three-speed manual column shift was standard on V-6 powered Skylarks (except in California). The .73:1 rear axle ratio offered excellent economy. Semi-unit construction had Skylark's engine and front suspension mounted on a separate sub-frame that helped isolate vibration and road shock. Hatchbacks carried a stowaway spare tire and had 28 cubic feet of storage space. Skylark 'S' came with a vinyl bench seat; standard Skylark offered a choice of vinyl or cloth bench seats; while the S/R carried special thick, ribbed velour cloth and vinyl bucket seats (reclining on the passenger side). Roof drip moldings were standard on Skylark and S/R. The S/R instrument panel had large black dials. Its turn signal lever doubled as a headlight dimmer switch, as on European touring cars. S/R also had a rallye steering wheel; large sports console with gearshift lever and stowage bins; carpeted door trim with map pocket and reflector; stand-up hood ornament; plus radial-tuned suspension.

1976 Century Custom colonnade coupe (B)

CENTURY — SERIES 4A — V-6/V-8 — Buick's A-bodied Century models didn't all look alike for 1976. GM-designed rectangular headlamps were new, but two-door coupes also got new lower body sheetmetal, a fastback roofline, flared wheel openings, and a canted aerodynamic nosepiece containing a new grille with many vertical bars. The new "formal" bodies eliminated the prior "sculptured" look that had been introduced in 1973. The coupe grille was a curious six-slot design (three large horizontal crosshatched sections on each side), set in body-colored framing. Quad rectangular headlamps stood atop quad rectangular clear park/turn lamps, with 'BUICK' emblem above the grille's upper corner. A hood ornament was standard. The 'Century' emblem sat at the trailing edge of front fenders. Small side lenses were at the front edge of front fenders, and rear of rear fenders. The Custom Coupe had the same formal roofline as Regal, but with the new, aerodynamic front end. Four-door sedans retained their old basic bodies, but front ends changed to hold their new vertically-stacked headlamps. Sedans had the formal Regal-style grille with 'BUICK' badge at the side, vertically-stacked headlamps, and clear vertical park/signal lamps. The Regal, which was considered a part of the Century series (see below) also had the formal-look grille. All told, the nine-model Century/Regal lineup included four different rooflines. Sedan and station wagon wheelbases were 4 in. longer than coupes. Century was described as "a leaner, smaller breed of Buick....a custom-tailored road car that rivals even the most opulent Buicks." It was the only domestic mid-size powered by a V-6. Century Special was the economy version. Custom Wagons, offering over 85 cubic feet of cargo space, came with two or three seats, standard variable-ratio power steering, power front disc brakes, Turbo Hydra-matic, and a 350 cu. in. (5.7- liter) V-8 with four-barrel carburetor. Other models had a standard 231 cu. in. (3.8-liter) V-6, with V-8 optional (except in Special). A three-speed manual transmission with column shift was standard on V-6 coupes and sedans. All models except the Special had protective bumper strips. Wagons had a "Tailgate Ajar" warning light. Base Century and Special models offered a choice of cloth or vinyl bench seat. Century Custom could have cloth or vinyl notchback seating; wagons, vinyl notchback seats. Like full-size Buicks, Century was built on a full- perimeter frame. The radial-tuned suspension used computer-selected springs, front stabilizer bar and special suspension geometry. Power front disc brakes were standard on Custom sedan and wagon; power steering on all. Disc brake pads emitted an audible squeak to warn that replacement was needed. Options included an all-metal electric sunroof, Landau vinyl roof, Cruise-Master speed control, power windows, six- way power seats, tilt steering wheel, electric door locks, automatic trunk release, and low-speed-delay wipers that could be set to operate periodically. A Hurst Hatch Roof with twin removable smoked (gray tinted) glass panels was offered on the Custom (and Regal) coupe only. Buyers could choose from two air conditioners: Climate-Control that cooled and dehumidified, or Custom-Aire (semi-automatic). There were also two economy options: a Fuel Usage Gauge that showed whether you were driving economically, and a Speed Alert that warned when you exceeded a preset speed.

1976 Regal Landau Coupe (B)

CENTURY — REGAL — SERIES 4A — V-6/V-8 — Regal was considered the "high-line Century" rather than a truly separate model, but with its own styling touches. Those included a formal roofline and classic vertical crosshatch grille with 'Regal' script at the side. Like their parent Century, Regal coupes had new lower body sheet metal and flared wheel openings, plus a new formal-look grille. They also had horizontally-placed rectangular headlamps with outboard vertical amber side lenses. Regal sedans looked different, with quad stacked rectangular headlamps flanking twin vertical clear park/signal lamps that sat between headlamps and grille. Regal's crest stood at the trailing edge of front fenders; the 'Regal' script just behind opera windows on the coupe. Inside, seats were upholstered in velour, and the simulated woodgrain instrument panel held deep-set dials. Except in California, the Regal sedan came with a standard 350 cu. in. (5.7-liter) V-8, while coupes had a standard 231 cu. in. (3.8-liter) V-6. Regal sedans had Turbo Hydra-matic as standard equipment, but V-6 coupes came with three-speed manual (column) shift. Coupes could be ordered with 350 V-8 and automatic transmission. Power steering was standard. Regal's S/R package included reclining front bucket seats upholstered in ribbed velour; a large center console with gearshift lever; rallye steering wheel; headlamp dimmer in the turn signal lever; and GM-spec steel-belted radial whitewall tires.

1976 LeSabre Custom hardtop coupe (B)

LESABRE — SERIES 4B — V-8 — LeSabre for '76 received the quad rectangular headlamps that had gone on Electra in 1975, set above clear horizontal quad park/signal lamps. The new classic-look horizontal crosshatch grille had Buick letters set into the wide upper crossbar. Clear horizontal cornering lamps (optional) at front of front fenders accompanied smaller amber lenses. Trailing ends of rear fenders displayed 'LeSabre' script. LeSabres had large three-hole horizontal "ventiport" trim strips on the upper portion of front fenders, just ahead of the door--descendants of the old Buick portholes. Front and rear bumpers carried protective strips. In a last-minute addition to the model year lineup, LeSabre added a base V-6 version--the only full-sized, six- passenger car in the world with a V-6 engine. LeSabre Custom models came with standard 350 cu. in. (5.7-liter) V-8, power steering, power front disc brakes, and Turbo Hydra-matic. Gas mileage of the optional 455 cu. in. V-8 engine improved to an 18 MPG rating. Teflon inside coatings improved shock absorber operation. Ample space for six was offered with either cloth/vinyl or vinyl notchback seats. Among the many options were low- speed-delay windshield wipers, a positive-traction differential, and firm suspension package.

1976 Electra Limited hardtop sedan (B)

ELECTRA — SERIES 4C — V-8 — Buick's posh full-size Electra 225 and Electra Limited came in coupe or hardtop sedan form. Electra's new grille had a heavy upper bar inset with large Buick block letters, 17 vertical bars with crosshatch pattern inside each section, and 'Electra' script at the side. Unlike the 1975 version, this grille didn't extend below the headlamps. Quad rectangular headlamps sat atop four clear park/signal lights, with clear cornering lamps (optional) at front of front fenders.

Horizontal "ventiport" trim strips were on upper section of front fenders, ahead of the door. They had four "holes" (actually gouge-like depressions) to distinguish Electras from the LeSabre's three. Rear fender bottoms held a small reflector lens, below the long bodyside trim molding. Front and rear bumpers had protective strips. Standard equipment included Turbo Hydra-matic, power steering, and power front disc brakes, along with power windows and a digital clock. Four-link rear suspension gave a smooth, quiet ride, improved by Teflon-coated shock absorbers. A vapor return system reduced the chance of vapor lock. An altitude compensator in the Turbo Hydra-matic provided smooth shifting in various elevation. The EPA highway rating of the 455 cu. in. (7.5-liter) V-8 engine improved by 3 MPG. Increased economy came as a result of improved carburetion, new crankshaft design, increased spark advance, better axle ratio, and reduced weight. Buyers had a choice of new full-foam seat designs: cloth bench or notchback seats (or vinyl notchback in Electra 225 sedan); cloth or vinyl notchback in the Electra 225 coupe. Limited models had cloth 60/40 notchback seating (two-way power) with a fold-down center armrest. Limiteds also had wide rocker appearance moldings, and the Limited sedan included a dome reading lamp. Top-of-the-line was the Park Avenue edition of the Electra Limited hardtop sedan. That package included a formal "halo" vinyl roof, thick cut-pile carpeting, and velour upholstery that even reached the executive center console and ceiling. Two Landau tops were available: traditional, or a new type with smaller opera windows and thickly-padded vinyl with French seams on the back portion. An optional Astroroof was available on the coupe. Drivers could enjoy a glass-topped driving compartment, roll the sunshade to closed position, or retract the glass for open-air driving. Coupes could also have an electric sunroof. Other options: variable-delay wipers, and an automatic door locking system that worked when the gear selector was put into and out of Park position. Optional Automatic Climate Control incorporated both heater and air conditioner.

ESTATE WAGON — SERIES 4BR — V-8 — Full-size station wagons came with two or three seats and 106 cubic foot cargo area. Standard powertrain was the 455 cu. in. (7.5-liter) V-8 engine and Turbo Hydra-matic transmission, plus variable-ratio power steering, power front disc brakes, and computer-selected front coil and rear leaf springs. Estates had vinyl bench seating, a hidden storage compartment, inside hood release, and a power tailgate window. The clever glide-away tailgate's lower section would glide away under the floor, while the window receded up into the roof area. Three-seat models had a forward-facing third seat and divided second seat. Front and rear bumpers had protective strips. Estate Wagon's simulated woodgrain instrument panel, steering wheel, carpeting and available notchback seat were identical to LeSabre.

1976 Riviera S/R coupe (B)

RIVIERA — SERIES 4E — V-8 — As it had since the first version came off the line for 1963, Riviera combined luxury with road car capabilities. As the catalog proclaimed, the personal-luxury coupe blended "performance, elegance and romance." This year it had new seat designs and interior trim, plus a more efficient engine, transmission and axle ratio combination. Riviera's 455 cu. in. (7.5-liter) V-8 offered improved gas mileage this year. Standard equipment included variable- ratio power steering and power front disc brakes; six- position tilt steering wheel; two-way power seats; electric windows; cut-pile carpeting; front bumper guards; front and rear bumper protective strips; computer-selected coil springs at all four wheels; Teflon-coated shock absorbers; JR78 steel-belted radial tires; and a digital clock. Wraparound three-section (clear/amber/clear) park/turn lamps flanked quad rectangular headlamps. Separate B-U-I-C-K letters stood above the horizontal crosshatch grille, with 'Riviera' script at the side. Similar 'Riviera' script was on the lower section of front fenders, to rear of wheel openings. A new two-tone color scheme was actually a vinyl applique bonded to bodysides. Silver plus a choice of four colors were available: dark red, dark blue, black, or dark gray. Options included a three-in-one Astroroof with heavily tinted glass and rollaway sunshade that permitted closed, open-air, or glass-topped motoring; Automatic Climate- Control; and an electric sunroof that came with or without a vinyl top. The popular Landau top returned for 1976.

I.D. DATA: The 13-symbol Vehicle Identification Number (VIN) was located on the upper left surface of the instrument panel, visible through the windshield. The first digit is '4', indicating the Buick division. The second symbol is a letter indicating series: 'S' Skyhawk; 'T' Skyhawk S; 'B' Skylark; 'C' Skylark S/R; 'W' Skylark S; 'D' Century; 'E' Century Special; 'H' Century Custom; 'J' Regal; 'K' Century Custom wagon; 'N' LeSabre; 'P' LeSabre Custom; 'R' Estate Wagon; 'V' Electra 225; 'X' Electra Limited; 'Z' Riviera. Next come two digits that denote body type: '07' Skyhawk hatchback coupe; '17' Skylark 2-dr. hatchback coupe; '27' Skylark 2-dr. thin-pillar coupe; '37' Century 2-dr. Colonnade coupe or Electra HT coupe; '57' Century/Regal 2-dr. Colonnade coupe or LeSabre HT coupe; '87' Riviera 2-dr. HT coupe; '29' 4-dr. Colonnade sedan; '39' 4-dr. HT sedan; '69' 4-dr. thin-pillar sedan; '35' 4-dr. 2-seat wagon; '45' 4-dr. 3-seat wagon. The fifth symbol is a letter indicating engine code: 'C' V6-231 2Bbl.; 'Y' V8-301 2Bbl.; 'U' V8-305 2Bbl.; 'H' V8-350 2Bbl.; 'L' V8-350 4Bbl. (LM1); 'R' V8-350 4Bbl. (L34); 'J' V8-350 4Bbl. (L77); 'K' V8-403 4Bbl. (L80). The sixth symbol denotes model year ('6' 1976). Next is a plant code: '2' Ste. Therese, Quebec (Canada); 'K' Leeds, Missouri; 'L' Van Nuys, Calif.; 'T' Tarrytown, NY; 'G' Framingham, Mass.; 'H' Flint, Mich.; 'Z' Fremont, Calif.; 'C' Southgate, Calif.; 'X' Fairfax, Kansas; 'E' Linden, New Jersey. The final six digits are the sequential serial number, which began with 100001 except for Skyhawks (700000 up); LeSabres, Estate Wagons, Electras and Rivieras built at Flint (400001 up). Engine numbers were stamped on the front of the block. A body number plate on the shroud identified model year, car division, series, style, body assembly plant, body number, trim combination, modular seat code, paint code, and date built code.

SKYHAWK (V-6)

Series Number	Body/Style Number	Body Type & Seating	Factory Price	Shipping Weight	Production Total
4H	T07	2-dr. 'S' Hatch-4P	3903	2857	Note 1
4H	S07	2-dr. Hatch-4P	4216	2889	Note 1

Note 1: Total model year production (U.S.), 15,769 Skyhawks.

SKYLARK 'S' (V-6/V-8)

4X	W27	2-dr Coupe-6P	3435/3470	3316/3515	Note 2

SKYLARK (V-6/V-8)

4X	B27	2-dr Coupe-6P	3549/3584	3327/3526	Note 2
4X	B17	2-dr Hatch-6P	3687/3722	3396/3591	6,703
4X	B69	4-dr Sedan-6P	3609/3644	3283/3484	48,157

Note 2: Total U.S. model year production, 51,260 Skylark base and 'S' coupes. Of the total 106,120 Skylarks produced, 87,881 had a V-6 engine, 18,239 a V-8.

SKYLARK S/R (V-6/V-8)

4X	C27	2-dr Coupe-5P	4281/4316	3319/3502	3,880
4X	C17	2-dr Hatch-5P	4398/4433	3338/3522	1,248
4X	C69	4-dr Sedan-5P	4324/4359	3312/3499	3,243

Note 3: Of the total 8371 S/R Skylarks produced for the model year, 4,818 had a V-6 engine and 3,553 a V-8. Prices shown are for the 260 cu. in. V-8; the 350 V-8 with 2Bbl. carburetor cost $50 more.

CENTURY SPECIAL (V-6)

4A	E37	2-dr Col cpe-6P	3935	3508	Note 4

CENTURY (V-6/V-8)

4A	D37	2-dr Col cpe-6P	4070/4155	3652/3844	Note 4
4A	D29	4-dr Col sed-6P	4105/4190	3741/3933	33,632

Note 4: Total Century and Century Special coupe production, 59,448. Of the 93,080 Century and Special models built, 66,440 had a V-6 engine and 26,640 a V-8.

CENTURY CUSTOM (V-6/V-8)

4A	H57	2-dr Col cpe-6P	4346/4431	3609/3801	34,036
4A	H29	4-dr Col sed-6P	4424/4509	3721/3913	19,728
4A	K35	4-dr Sta Wag-6P	-- /4987	-- /4363	Note 5
4A	K45	4-dr Sta Wag-8P	-- /5099	-- /4413	Note 5

Note 5: Total Century Custom wagon production, 16,625. Of the 70,389 Century Custom models built, 21,832 had a V-6 engine and 48,557 a V-8.

REGAL (V-6/V-8)

4A	J57	2-dr Col cpe-6P	4465/4910	3710/3902	124,498
4A	J29	4-dr Col sed-6P	-- /4825	-- /4104	17,118

Note 6: Total model year production, 141,616 Regals (31,907 with V-6 engine and 109,709 V-8).

LESABRE (V-6)

4B	N57	2-dr HT Cpe-6P	4815	4129	3,861
4B	N69	4-dr Sedan-6P	4747	4170	4,315
4B	N39	4-dr HT Sed-6P	4871	4056	2,312

LESABRE CUSTOM (V-8)

4B	P57	2-dr HT Cpe-6P	5114	4275	45,669
4B	P69	4-dr Sedan-6P	5046	4328	34,841
4B	P39	4-dr HT Sed-6P	5166	4386	46,109

ESTATE WAGON (V-8)

4B	R35	4-dr Sta Wag-6P	5591	5013	5,990
4B	R45	4-dr Sta Wag-8P	5731	5139	14,384

ELECTRA 225 (V-8)

4C	V37	2-dr Coupe-6P	6367	4502	18,442
4C	V39	4-dr HT Sed-6P	6527	4641	26,655

ELECTRA LIMITED (V-8)

4C	X37	2-dr Coupe-6P	6689	4521	28,395
4C	X39	4-dr HT Sed-6P	6852	4709	51,067

RIVIERA (V-8)

4E	Z87	2-dr Coupe-6P	6798	4531	20,082

FACTORY PRICE AND WEIGHT NOTE: Figure before the slash is for V-6 engine, after slash for V-8.

ENGINES: BASE EQUIPMENT V-6 (Skyhawk, Skylark, Century, Regal coupe, LeSabre): 90-degree, overhead-valve V-6. Cast iron alloy block and head. Displacement: 231 cu. in. (3.8 liters). Bore & stroke: 3.8 x 3.4 in. Compression ratio: 8.0:1. Brake horsepower: 105 at 3400 R.P.M. Torque: 185 lbs.-ft. at 2000 R.P.M. Four main bearings. Hydraulic valve lifters. Carburetor: 2Bbl. Rochester 2GC. VIN Code: C. OPTIONAL V-8 (Skylark): 90-degree overhead-valve V-8. Cast iron alloy block and head. Displacement: 260 cu. in. (4.3 liters). Bore & stroke: 3.50 x 3.385 in. Compression ratio: 8.5:1. Brake horsepower: 110 at 3400 R.P.M. Torque: 210 lbs.-ft. at 1600 R.P.M. Five main bearings. Hydraulic valve lifters. Carburetor: 2Bbl. Rochester. Built by Oldsmobile. VIN Code: F. BASE V-8 (Regal sedan); OPTIONAL (Skylark, Century/Custom, Regal cpe): 90-degree, overhead valve V-8. Cast iron alloy block and head. Displacement: 350 cu. in. (5.7 liters). Bore & stroke: 3.80 x 3.85 in. Compression ratio: 8.0:1. Brake horsepower: 140 at 3200 R.P.M. Torque: 280 lbs.-ft. at 1600 R.P.M. Five main bearings. Hydraulic valve lifters. Carburetor: 2Bbl. Roch. 2GC. VIN Code: H. BASE V-8 (Century wagon, LeSabre Custom); OPTIONAL (Skylark, Century/Custom, Regal): 90-degree, overhead valve V-8. Cast iron alloy block and head. Displacement: 350 cu. in. (5.7 liters). Bore & stroke: 3.80 x 3.85 in. Compression ratio: 8.0:1. Brake horsepower: 155 at 3400 R.P.M. Torque: 280 lbs.-ft. at 1800 R.P.M. Five main bearings. Hydraulic valve lifters. Carburetor: 4Bbl. Roch. M4MC. VIN Code: J. BASE V-8 (Electra, Estate Wagon, Riviera); OPTIONAL (LeSabre Custom): 90-degree, overhead valve V-8. Cast iron alloy block and head. Displacement: 455 cu. in. (7.5 liters). Bore & stroke: 4.3125 x 3.9 in. Compression ratio: 7.9:1. Brake horsepower: 205 at 3800 R.P.M. Torque: 345 lbs.-ft. at 2000 R.P.M. Five main bearings. Hydraulic valve lifters. Carburetor: 4Bbl. Roch. M4MC. VIN Code: T.

CHASSIS DATA: Wheelbase: (Skyhawk) 97.0 in.; (Skylark) 111.0 in.; (Century/Regal cpe) 112.0 in.; (Century/Regal sed/wag) 116.0 in.; (LeSabre) 124.0 in.; (Electra/Estate) 127.0 in.; (Riviera) 122.0 in. Overall length:- (Skyhawk) 179.3 in.; (Skylark) 200.3 in.; (Century/Regal cpe) 209.7 in.; (Century/Regal sed) 213.5 in.; (Century wag) 218.2 in.; LeSabre) 226.8 in.; (Electra) 233.3 in.; (Estate Wagon) 231.8 in.; (Riv) 218.6 in. Height:- (Skyhawk) 50.1 in.; (Skylark 2-dr.) 52.1 in.; (Skylark 4-dr.) 53.1 in.; (Century/Regal cpe) 52.6-52.8 in.; (Century/Regal sed) 53.6 in.; (Century wag) 55.3 in.; (LeSabre cpe) 53.2 in.; (LeSabre HT sed) 53.3 in.; (LeSabre 4-dr. sed) 54.0 in.; (Electra cpe) 54.0 in.; (Electra sed) 54.5 in.; (Estate 2S wag) 57.8 in.; (Estate 3S wag) 57.0 in.; (Riv) 53.0 in. Width:- (Skyhawk) 65.4 in.; (Skylark) 72.7 in.; (Century/Regal cpe) 77.0 in.; (Century/Regal sed/wag) 79.0 in.; (LeSabre/Electra/Estate/ Riv) 79.9 in. Front Tread:- (Skyhawk) 54.7 in.; (Skylark) 59.1 in.; (Century/Regal) 61.5 in.; (LeSabre/Electra/Estate/Riv) 63.4 in. Rear Tread:- (Skyhawk) 53.6 in.; (Skylark) 59.7 in.; (Century/Regal) 60.7 in.; (LeSabre/Electra/Estate/Riv) 64.0 in. Standard Tires:- (Skyhawk) BR78 x 13 SBR; (Skyawk 'S') B78 x 13; (Skylark) E78 x 14; (Skylark S/R) FR78 x 14 SBR WSW; (Century/Regal cpe) GR78 x 15 SBR; (Century Special cpe) FR78 x 15; (Century/Regal sed) FR78 x 15 SBR; (Century wagon) HR78 x 15; (LeSabre) HR78 x 15 SBR; (LeSabre w/455 V-8) JR78 x 15 SBR; (Electra/Riviera) JR78 x 15 SBR; (Estate) LR78 x 15 SBR.

TECHNICAL: Transmission:- Three-speed, fully synchronized manual gearbox (column shift) standard on Skylark, Century, and Regal cpe with V-6; Turbo Hydra-matic optional. Four-speed, fully synchronized floor shift standard on Skyhawk; five-speed optional. Turbo-Hydra-matic (three-speed) standard on Regal sedan, LeSabre, Electra, Estate and Riviera; also on other models with V-8 and Century sold in California. Three-speed manual transmission gear ratios: (1st) 3.11:1; (2nd) 1.84:1; (3rd) 1.00:1; (Rev) 3.22:1. Four-speed gear ratios: (1st) 3.11:1; (2nd) 2.20:1; (3rd) 1.47:1; (4th) 1.00:1; (Rev) 3.11:1. Five-speed gear ratios: (1st) 3.10:1; (2nd) 1.89:1; (3rd) 1.27:1; (4th) 1.00:1; (5th) 0.84:1; (Rev) 3.06:1. Automatic transmission gear ratios: (1st) 2.52:1; (2nd) 1.52:1; (3rd) 1.00:1; (Rev) 1.93:1 or 2.08:1. Standard axle ratio:- (Skyhawk) 2.56:1; (Skylark) 2.73:1; (Century/Regal) 3.08:1; (LeSabre/Electra/Riviera) 2.56:1. Hypoid bevel final drive. Steering:- recirculating ball; variable-ratio power steering standard on Century/Regal, LeSabre, Electra, Estate and Riviera. Suspension:- (Skyhawk) unequal-length front control arms w/anti-sway bar, rigid rear axle w/torque arm, Panhard rod and anti-sway bar; (Skylark) semi-elliptic rear leaf springs; (others) front/rear coil springs, independent front w/trailing links and anti-roll bar (exc. Special). Brakes:- front disc, rear drum; power brakes standard on LeSabre/Electra/Riviera plus Century custom sedan/wagon and Regal sedan. Body construction: (Skyhawk) unitized; (Skylark) separate front frame unit cushion-mounted to unitized body; (others) separate body and perimeter box frame. Fuel tank:- (Skyhawk) 18.5 gal.; (Skylark) 21 gal.; (Century/Regal/Estate) 22 gal.; (LeSabre/Electra/Riv) 26 gal. High-Energy electronic ignition (HEI) on all engines. Unleaded fuel only.

DRIVETRAIN OPTIONS: Engines:- 260 cu. in. V-8, 2Bbl.: Skylark ($35). 350 cu. in. V-8, 2Bbl.: Skylark, Century/Custom, Regal cpe ($85). 350 cu. in. V-8, 4Bbl.: Skylark, Century, Custom, Regal cpe ($140); Regal sed ($55). 455 cu. in. V-8, 4Bbl.: LeSabre Cust ($159). Transmission/Differential:- Five-speed manual floor shift: Skyhawk ($244). Turbo Hydra-matic.: Skyhawk ($244); Skylark, Century cpe/sed, Regal cpe ($262). Positive traction differential ($48-$54). Power Accessories:- Power brakes: Skyhawk ($55); Skylark/Century ($58) exc. Cust sed/wag. Power steering: Skyhawk ($120); Skylark ($136). Suspension:- H5 handling pkg.: Skyhawk 'S' ($104-$124). Firm ride/handling pkg. ($17-$21) exc. Skyhawk. Rallye ride/handling pkg.: Skylark ($39); Century, except Special wagon, Regal, Riviera ($34). Automatic level control: Century/Regal ($92); LeSabre/Electra/Riviera ($93). Other: Trailer towing flasher/harness: ($16-$27) except Skyhawk. Heavy-duty 80-amp alternator: Century/Regal/LeSabre/Electra/Riviera ($35-$39). Heavy-duty Energizer battery ($15-$17) except Electra, Riviera. Freedom battery ($28-$29) except Skyhawk/Electra. Heavy-duty cooling ($25-$52) except Skyhawk. Engine block heater ($12) except Skyhawk. Heavy-duty air cleaner ($11) except Skyhawk/Skylark. Chrome air cleaner: Riviera ($17). California emission system ($50).

SKYHAWK CONVENIENCE/APPEARANCE OPTIONS: Option Groups:- Shadow light Astroroof w/roof crown molding ($550). Appearance group: 'S' ($63). Convenience group ($20). Comfort/Convenience:- Air cond. ($424). Rear defogger, electric ($66). Soft Ray tinted glass ($44). Tinted windshield ($37). Rallye steering wheel: 'S' ($35). Tilt steering wheel ($48). Electric clock: 'S' ($16); clock and tach ($59). Right sport mirror ($12). Remote-control left sport mirror: 'S' ($15). Entertainment:- AM radio ($71). AM/FM radio ($134). AM/FM stereo radio ($219). Rear speaker ($19). Windshield antenna ($21). Exterior Trim:- Door edge guards ($8). Roof crown molding ($150). Protective bodyside moldings ($24-$39). Interior Trim/Upholstery:- Full-length console: 'S' ($73). Adjustable driver's seatback ($17). Front/rear floor mats ($14). Custom seatbelts ($13). Wheels:- Custom sport wheels ($74-$84). Deluxe wheel covers ($39); for radial tires only. Wheel trim rings ($33). Tires:- B78 x 13 WSW: 'S' ($26- $32). BR78 x 13 SBR blackwall: 'S' ($82-$103). BR78 x 13 SBR whitewall ($26-$135). BR70 x 13 SBR WLT ($35-$148).

SKYLARK CONVENIENCE/APPEARANCE OPTIONS: Option Packages:- Accessory pkg.: 'S' ($11). Convenience group ($29). Appearance group (wheel opening and roof drip moldings): 'S' ($31). Comfort/Convenience:- Air cond. ($452). Cruise Master ($73). Rear defogger, blower-type ($43). Power windows ($99-$140). Electric door locks ($62-$89). Rallye steering wheel ($35); std. on S/R. Tilt steering wheel ($52). Soft Ray tinted glass ($46). Dual horns ($7). Electric clock ($18). Headlamps-on indicator ($7). Fuel usage indicator ($16). Electric trunk release ($17). Three-speed wipers w/delay ($28). Remote-control left mirror ($14). Sport mirrors: left remote, right manual ($26); both remote ($40). Entertainment:- AM radio ($75). AM/FM radio ($137). AM/FM stereo radio ($233). AM radio and stereo tape player ($209). AM/FM stereo radio w/tape ($337). Rear speaker ($20). Windshield antenna ($22). Exterior Trim:- Custom vinyl roof ($91-$96). Landau top: cpe ($150-$155). Two-tone paint ($35). Special exterior paint ($107). Swing-out rear quarter vent window: two-doors ($48). Protective bodyside moldings ($37). Rocker panel moldings ($15). Wide rocker appearance group ($32). Decklid molding ($7). Custom door and window frame moldings ($23-$29). Door edge guards ($8-$12). Bodyside accent stripe ($23). Bumper guards, front ($17); front/rear ($34). Bumper strips, front/rear ($29). Interior Trim/Upholstery:- Full-length console ($71). Vinyl bucket seats: base ($79). Custom trim bench seats/cushion interior: base ($138). Custom seatbelts ($13-$15). Carpet savers ($8). Carpet savers and mats ($14). Carpeted door trim w/map pocket and reflector ($35); std. on S/R. Wheels:- Styled wheels ($77- $89). Chrome-plated wheels ($103-$122). Deluxe wheel covers ($31); for radial tires only. Deluxe wire wheel covers ($111); for radials only. Tires:- E78 x 14 whitewall ($26-$33) exc. S/R. ER78 x 14 SBR blackwall ($69-$86) exc. S/R. ER78 x 4 SBR whitewall ($95-$119) exc. S/R. FR78 x 14 SBR WLT ($119-$149) exc. S/R ($24-$30).

CENTURY/REGAL CONVENIENCE/APPEARANCE OPTIONS: Option Packages:- Regal S/R Coupe pkg. ($379). Sunroof: cpe ($370). Hurst hatch roof: Century Custom, Regal cpe ($550). Convenience group ($5-$29). Comfort/Convenience:- Air cond. ($476). Custom Aire semi-automatic air cond. ($513). Cruise Master ($73). Rear defogger: electric ($77); blower-type ($43). Soft Ray tinted glass ($50). Tinted windshield ($40). Six-way power seat ($124). Custom steering wheel ($18). Rallye steering wheel ($35). Tilt steering ($52). Power windows ($99-$140). Electric door locks ($62-$89). Electric trunk release ($17). Remote-control tailgate lock: Century wag ($20). Electric clock ($20). Headlamps-on indicator ($7). Instrument gauges and clock ($42) exc. wag. Fuel usage gauge ($25). Speed alert ($14). Dome reading lamp ($15). Three- speed wiper with delay ($28). Mirrors:- Remote control mirror ($14). Sport mirrors: left remote ($26). Lighted visor vanity mirror ($39). Entertainment:- AM radio ($79). AM/FM radio ($142). AM/FM stereo radio ($233). AM radio w/stereo tape player ($213). AM/FM stereo radio w/tape ($337). Rear speaker ($20). Front/rear speakers ($41). Windshield antenna ($22); incl. w/radios. Exterior Trim:- Landau vinyl top: Century Cust, Regal cpe ($110); Century/Spec. ($144). Custom vinyl top: Century cpe, Regal ($106). Short custom vinyl top: Century, Special cpe ($79). Custom vinyl top w/hood ornament: Century, Custom sed ($111). Swing-out rear quarter vent windows: Century 2S wag ($48). Two-tone paint ($30-$40). Special color paint ($125). Bumper guards, front/rear ($35); rear, Century wag ($17). Bumper strips: Century Special ($28). Protective bodyside and front fender moldings ($26). Lower bodyside molding and fender moldings ($34). Door edge guards ($8-$12). Wheel opening moldings: Century/Spec. ($18). Bodyside accent stripe ($49). Woodgrain applique: Century wag ($146). Luggage rack: Century wag ($71). Air deflector: Century wag ($24). Interior Trim/Upholstery:- Full-length console ($71). Custom notchback seat trim: Century, Special ($125-$151). Custom vinyl notchback seat trim: Century Cust cpe, Regal cpe ($99); cloth ($129). Custom vinyl 60/40 seat trim: Century Cust, Regal cpe ($185); cloth ($215). Custom reclining seat trim: Century Cust cpe ($226). Custom trim vinyl bucket seats: Century, Spec. ($132-$158). Vinyl bucket seats: Century Cust, Regal ($8). Custom seatbelts ($13-$20). Front/rear carpeting: Century Spec. ($23). Load floor mat: Century wag ($22). Carpet savers ($9); w/mats ($16). Litter pocket ($6). Wheels:- Chrome-plated wheels ($106-$149); N/A wagon. Styled wheels ($58-$89); N/A wag. Deluxe wire wheel covers: Century ($123); Regal ($91). Styled wheel covers: Century ($85); Regal ($53). Deluxe wheel covers: Century ($32). Super deluxe wheel covers: Regal ($62). Tires:- FR78 x 15 SBR WSW: Century ($28-$40). GR78 x 15 SBR BSW: Century/Cust sed ($20-$25); with V-8 (NC). GR78 x 15 SBR WSW $30-$62) exc. Century Special. White-letter tires ($22-$89) exc. Special. Space-saver spare tire (NC). Conventional spare tire: Century Spec. (NC).

LESABRE/ELECTRA/ESTATE WAGON/RIVIERA CONVENIENCE/APPEARANCE OPTIONS: Option Packages: Electra Limited Park Avenue pkg. ($419); w/deluxe console ($525). Riviera S/R pkg. ($276). Accessory group: LeSabre, Estate ($57-$72). Electric sunroof: Electra/Riviera cpe ($725). Astroroof: Electra/Riv cpe ($891). Comfort/Convenience:- Air cond. ($512). Automatic climate control air cond.: Electra/Riv ($594). Custom Aire air cond.: LeSabre/Estate ($549). Cruise Master ($79). Rear defogger, electric ($78); blower-type ($43). Soft Ray tinted glass ($64). Tinted windshield: LeSabre/Est ($41). Power windows: LeSabre/Est ($159). Electric door locks ($90). Power tailgate door: Estate ($52). Automatic door locks: Electra/Riv ($93-$120). Six-way power driver's seat ($98- $126) exc. base LeSabre. Six-way power bench seat ($126) exc. Electra Ltd. Dual six-way power seats ($220-$247) exc. base LeSabre. Custom steering wheel: LeSabre/Est ($16). Tilt steering wheel ($53); std. on Riv. Tilt/telescoping steering column ($95) exc. Riv ($42). Map light: Electra 225, Riv ($10). Low fuel indicator ($11). Fuel usage gauge ($25). Speed alert and trip odometer ($19). Electric trunk release ($17). Three-speed wipers w/delay ($28). Lighting, Horns and -Mirrors:- Cornering lamps ($40). Front light monitors: LeSabre/Est ($23). Front/rear monitors: Electra/Riv ($51). Door courtesy/warning lights: 2-dr ($30); 4-dr ($47). Headlamps-on indicator ($7). Dome/reading lamp ($15). Four- note horn ($17). Remote left mirror: LeSabre/Est ($14). Remote right mirror ($29). Dual remote sport mirrors ($36- $50). Remote left mirror w/thermometer ($19-$33). Lighted visor vanity mirror ($40). Entertainment:- AM radio ($92). AM/FM radio ($153). AM/FM stereo radio w/four speakers ($236). AM radio and stereo tape player ($228). AM/FM stereo radio and tape ($341). Rear speaker ($20). Front/rear speakers ($41); non-stereo radio req'd. Windshield antenna ($22); incl. w/radios. Power antenna ($40). Exterior Trim:- Landau top: Electra cpe ($549). Landau custom vinyl top: LeSabre/Electra cpe ($140-$159); Riviera ($399). Landau custom vinyl top w/roof crown molding: Riv ($499). Custom vinyl top: Electra Ltd sed ($62); heavy-padded ($399). Custom vinyl top and molding ($139-$150). Custom vinyl top w/halo molding: Electra cpe ($163). Two-tone paint ($35-$60); special Riviera two-tone ($135). Special color paint ($125). Protective bodyside moldings ($37-$52). Custom wide bodyside moldings: Electra ($72). Door edge guards ($8-$12). Wide rocker panel moldings: LeSabre Cust, Estate, Electra 225 ($32) Wide rocker moldings group: base LeSabre ($93); Estate ($77). Belt reveal molding: LeSabre, Estate ($30). Custom molding: base LeSabre ($61); Estate ($46). Custom door window frame molding: base LeSabre ($30). Bodyside accent stripes $33). Coach stripes: Electra ($52). Woodgrain applique: Estate ($193). Tailgate molding: Estate ($18). Bumper guards, front/rear ($37) exc. Riv; front, Riviera ($18). Front bumper reinforcement ($7-$14) exc. Riv. Luggage rack: Estate ($94). Locking luggage locker: Est ($14). Interior Trim/Upholstery:- Full-length console: Riv ($72). Custom notchback seat trim: Estate ($208); 60/40 ($295). Custom cloth notchback 60/40 seat trim: Riviera ($123); vinyl ($97); vinyl 40/40 seat ($97). Leather upholstery: Electra Ltd ($320). Leather upholstery group: Riv ($417). Custom seatbelts: LeSabre/Est ($17-$20). Carpet savers ($10); w/mats ($17). Litter container ($6). Deluxe trunk trim: LeSabre ($40). Load floor area carpet: Estate ($61). Wheels and Tires:- Chrome-plated wheels: LeSabre/Estate/Electra ($117-$151). Deluxe wheel covers: base LeSabre ($32). Super deluxe wheel covers: Riv ($40). Styled wheel covers ($32-$86). Deluxe wire wheel covers ($70-$124). Whitewall tires ($41-$47). Wide whitewalls: Electra/Riv ($60).

HISTORY: Introduced: September 25, 1975. Model year production (U.S.): 737,467 (238,298 sixes and 499,169 V-8s) for a 9.1 percent share of the industry total. Calendar year production (U.S.): 817,669. Calendar year sales by U.S. dealers: 738,385 for an 8.6 percent market share, up from 518,032 in 1975. Model year sales by U.S. dealers: 706,249 (plus 25,007 imported Opels), up from only 463,132 in 1975.

Historical Footnotes: Since the economy was rising, Buick forecast a 40 percent jump in sales for the Bicentennial model year. Year-end results exceeded even that optimistic prediction, with sales up 52.5 percent to 706,249. That total, in fact, almost reached the model-year record set in 1973—good news after two years of slippage. Calendar year production rose by 56 percent. Best sellers were the mid-size Century and compact Skylark, both up over 74 percent in sales. For 1976, Skylark production moved from Ste. Therese, Quebec, to Southgate, California. Skyhawk assembly continued in Canada. On the import front, a Japanese-built Opel Isuzu was introduced in mid-year. Sales amounted to less than half those of the former German-built Opel T-car, a result of dwindling import sales and a decline in the number of dealers carrying the car. Big cars, on the other hand, continued to sell strongly--a surprise to the industry. For the second year in a row, a Buick paced the Indianapolis 500 race. This year's pace car was a Century with turbocharged, highly modified 231 V-6. The turbo came from Rajay Industries, and the engine produced triple the normal horsepower. It was the first V-6 vehicle ever to handle the pace car duties. A total of 1,290 Century models wearing the pace car colors (orange, black and gray) and appropriate emblems were produced for the market.

1977 BUICK

This year saw a total restyle for the B- and C-bodied LeSabre, Electra and Riviera. All were downsized significantly, measuring closer to mid-size dimensions—but the trimmed-down designs didn't lose their traditional spacious comfort. LeSabre and Riviera coupes offered over 2-1/2 in. more rear leg room than in 1976, as well as increased head room. Trunk space also grew on some models. Most downsized GM cars, in fact, were 1-1/2 in. taller than before. Smaller Buick models had mainly cosmetic changes. The full-line catalog continued the previous year's theme, "dedicated to the Free Spirit in just about everyone." Buick called the slimmed-down designs "trim, functional, contemporary," adding that "Suspensions are taut. Handling and maneuverability, crisp and responsive." Heralding the move to smaller engines, the mighty 455 V-8 left the lineup, replaced by a 403 cu. in. (6.6-liter) V-8 as the biggest powerplant for full-size Buicks. New 301 and 305 cu. in. V-8 engines were offered as options on Skylark and LeSabre. The familiar 350 cu. in. (5.7-liter) four-barrel V-8, available on LeSabre, replaced the old 455 as standard equipment on the Electra, Riviera and Estate Wagon. Actually, three different 350 V-8s with four-barrel carburetor were offered, with two different bore/stroke dimensions, including one built by Chevrolet—a move that eventually led to serious criticism and lawsuits. The V-6 engine got redesigned cylinder heads with tapered-seat spark plugs, plus an added heat crossover hole in the head to speed warmups. Also new for 1977: an electric choke and back pressure exhaust gas recirculator. Diagnostic connections on full-size Buicks now allowed a mechanic to easily check the ignition switch, coil, starter and other critical areas by hooking up a diagnostic tester. All full-size Buicks had four-wheel coil-spring suspension, forward-mounted steering gear linkage, unequal- length front control arms, and four-link rear suspension. Corrosion protection was improved on big Buicks, including more use of galvanized steel and rust-resistant materials. Metric dimensions saw increased use. All Buicks could have a new Citizens Band radio option, including a CB transceiver built into the AM/FM stereo system. Full-size Buicks could have an all-metal electric sunroof, or the three-in-one Astroroof. Most Skylark, Century, Regal and LeSabre models could have the Highway Economy Package, including a specially-tuned V-6 engine with vacuum spark regulator, specially-calibrated Turbo Hydra- matic, lower (2.56:1) rear axle ratio, and a switch that shut off the air-conditioner compressor when the gas pedal was pushed to the floor. Various models could be ordered with special ride/handling suspension packages that included front and rear stabilizer bars, firmer springs, and stiffer shock-absorber valving. LeSabre Sport Coupe and Riviera carried this suspension as standard, along with quick-ratio power steering. Standard body colors for all 1977 models were: black; white; silver, light blue, dark blue or medium green metallic; light buckskin; buckskin, brown, firethorn or orange metallic. Dark blue gr. metallic, red and cream gold were offered as standard on all except Skyhawk and Skylark. Dark aqua metallic, bright yellow and bright red came only on Skyhawk and Skylark. Rivieras could also have blue, amber or red firemist.

SKYHAWK — SERIES 4H — V-6 — For its third model year, the subcompact Skyhawk got a new, completely different checkerboard grille: simply two rows of eight holes each, across the body-colored grille panel. Otherwise, there was little change in appearance. Built on an H-Special body, Skyhawk was a more luxurious, perhaps even sportier version of Chevrolet's Monza. Once again, the swept-back design came in standard or 'S' hatchback form. Large, easy-to-read instruments included an 7000-R.P.M. tachometer, ammeter, and electric clock. Though similar, the 'S' edition lacked such extras as the tach and clock. As before, Skyhawk was powered by a 231 cu. in. (3.8- liter) V-6 with standard four-speed manual shift. Five-speed overdrive gearbox and automatic transmisison were optional. The standard edition had front and rear stabilizer bars; the 'S' had front only. High-back bucket seats were upholstered in cloth or vinyl. The 'S' version also lacked the white, gold or black accent stripes. Skyhawks had side window reveal moldings, front and rear bumper guards, and bumper protection strips, plus a set-and-close door locking system. Options included a sliding glass sunroof, or fixed Astroroof with targa-type aluminum accent band that stretched over the car's roof.

SKYLARK — SERIES 4X — V-6/V-8 — Buick's compact derivative of the old Chevrolet Nova (also related to Olds Omega) again came in seven models: low-priced 'S', European-inspired S/R (Sports/Rallye), and standard Skylark. Coupe, hatchback and sedan bodies were again available. The 'S' coupe lacked some details, such as a cigarette lighter, roof and wheel-opening moldings, and inside day/night mirror. Though similar to before, the front end was changed. The new Skylark grille was composed entirely of vertical bars, peaked at the nose, with a wide horizontal bar across the top. Dual round headlamps were again flanked by clear park/signal lamps that wrapped around the fender into amber lenses. As in 1976, Skylark's three-hole "ventiport" fender trim piece sat just ahead of the wide bodyside molding that extended all the way to the tip of the rear quarter panels. A new instrument panel held large round gauges. Standard engine was the 231 cu. in. (3.8-liter) V-6, with two 5.0-liter V-8s available: 301 and 305 cu. in. Also optional was a 350 V-8 with four-barrel. All models had High- Energy ignition, front disc brakes, and front stabilizer bar. Skylark's S/R had standard Turbo Hydra-matic and full-length sports shifting console; others, three-speed manual (column shift). S/R also had a stand-up hood ornament, roof drip moldings, special cloth bucket seats with reclining right seatback, map pockets in doors, Rallye steering wheel, and console storage bins. Skylark's suspension consisted of wide- span front lower control arms with coil springs, and multiple-leaf rear springs. A new Acoustical Package to cut road noise consisted of special insulation in roof, floor and dashboard, as well as inside and under the doors, and between cowl and fenders. Also optional: a thickly-padded Landau top with small side windows, accented by brushed-aluminum band; and a V-6 Highway Economy Package.

CENTURY — SERIES 4A — V-6/V-8 — Century's body, lowered for 1976, received a new grille and header molding this year. As in 1976, coupes displayed a different front-end treatment, with canted-back grille, than the sedans. Century and Century Special coupe rooflines swept back and framed a large rear quarter window. The Custom coupe had a formal roofline like Regal's, plus the Regal rectangular opera windows. Century sedan's front-end looked similar to the Regal sedan, while coupes repeated the 1976 design, with crosshatching behind six large grille slots framed by body-colored segments. The model lineup included three coupes, two sedans, and a two- or three-seat wagon. Sedans and wagons were 4 in. longer in wheelbase than coupes. Station wagons had a 350 cu. in. (5.7-liter) V-8; other models, a 231 cu. in. V-6 or optional V-8. For 1977, the V-6 engine lost some weight. Power steering was standard. So were power brakes on the Custom Sedan and wagons. Three-speed manual (column) shift remained standard, except for wagons which had Turbo Hydra-matic. All models had front and rear ashtrays, and a wide-view day/night inside mirror. All except Special had front and rear bumper protection strips. Wipers had "mist control" that gave a single pass when you touched the switch. Custom coupes could have a Hurst hatch roof that consisted of twin rectangular panels of tinted glass, which could be removed and stored in the trunk (in a special "Hatch Hutch" case). Two air conditioners were optional: Climate- Control or Custom-Aire. Joining the option list: the V-6 Highway Economy Package, consisting of specially tuned engine, specially calibrated Turbo Hydra-matic, 2.56:1 axle ratio, and wide-open-throttle air-conditioning shutoff.

1977 Regal Landau Coupe (B)

REGAL — SERIES 4AJ — V-6/V-8 — Regal's coupe and sedan, like Century, received a new grille and header molding. A look more formal than Century came from the vertical, squarish grille and squared-off roofline with a small, formal opera window in the rear pillar. The coupe's grille was new but not drastically different from 1976 version. Its small vertical segments separated into six sections by two horizontal strips and a narrow vertical bar. Quad headlamps and park/signal lamps were also similar to the prior model. A 'V6' emblem sat at the front of front fenders. Regal's sedan again had its own front-end design featuring vertically stacked rectangular headlamps and vertical signal lamps, plus a mildly revised grille divided into four sections by dominant single horizontal and vertical bars. The subdued vertical strips sat farther apart, separating the grille into five segments on each side. 'Regal' script sat at the lower corner. Instruments were recessed in simulated woodgrain paneling, with two large dials directly ahead of the driver. Power front disc brakes were standard. Turbo Hydra-matic was standard on sedan; three-speed manual shift on coupe. Options included the Hurst hatch roof (like Century Custom coupe), plus Highway Economy Package with specially tuned V-6 engine. Regal's S/R package included reclining bucket seats with new black velour fabric; large center console with aircraft-grip shift lever; rallye steering wheel; headlamp dimmer in the turn-signal lever; and whitewall steel-belted radial tires.

1977 LeSabre Custom sedan (B)

LESABRE — SERIES 4B — V-6/V-8 — Downsized LeSabre was 10 in. shorter, 2.7 in. narrower, and 665 pounds lighter than before, described as "the American full-size car redefined." Wheelbase dropped from 123.4 to 115.9 in., while trunk space actually grew: from 16.8 cu. ft. in 1976 to 21.2 in the "shrunken" version. Inside, head and leg room managed to grow as well. LeSabre could still carry six adults and luggage in comfort. Aluminum reinforced bumpers cut 135 pounds from the car's weight, while a smaller frame saved 90 pounds. A 231 cu. in. V-6 was now standard. New styling included rear-canted headlamp bezels that sloped rearward from the upright grille, full-framed doors, and a pillared roof design. The airy four-door hardtop and thin-pillared variant were gone for good, replaced by sensible pillars and frames. The squared-off roof was designed to give maximum rear seat headroom. LeSabre's B-body was related to Chevrolet Caprice and Pontiac Bonneville/Parisienne, closer yet to Olds Delta 88, which received similar downsizing this year. Wraparound red/amber taillamps also served as side marker lights. Seven vertical bars divided the crosshatch grille into eight sections, slightly pointed at the front. Quad rectangular headlamps were directly above clear park/signal lamps; cornering lenses at the tip of front fenders. Farther back on the fender was the familiar three-hole "ventiport" LeSabre emblem. At the back of the rear fenders, a 'LeSabre' badge sat ahead of the wraparound taillamps. Bodyside moldings extended between front and rear wheel openings, but no farther onto the fenders. LeSabre was now powered by the 231 cu. in. (3.8-liter) V-6 or a choice of three optional V-8 engines: familiar 350 cu. in. (5.7-liter) four-barrel, new 403 cu. in. (6.6-liter) four-barrel, or new 301 cu. in. (5.0-liter) with two-barrel carburetor. Five models were offered this year: LeSabre and LeSabre Custom coupe or sedan, plus a new European-inspired LeSabre Sport Coupe. That one had a standard 301 cu. in. (5.0-liter) V-8, thin white-stripe radial tires, special steering linkage and suspension with higher-rate springs, Rallye steering wheel, chrome wheels, amber lights and, in Buick's words, "functional, downright mean-looking black accents." That meant black vertical grille bars; black anodized window frame, windshield and rear window moldings; wide black louvered rocker moldings; and wide black pillar appliques. Styling touches also included a stand-up tri-shield hood ornament, plus 'LeSabre Sport Coupe' nameplates on body and dash. Coupes had new inertia front seatback locks. Instrument panels were new, a maintenance-free Freedom battery and diagnostic connectors standard. Also standard: rear door (or rear quarter) armrests. Full-Flo ventilation, plus bumper protection strips front and rear. Crushed velour cloth or vinyl bench seats were standard on base LeSabre models; notchback seats on Custom and Sport Coupe. The turn signal lever doubled as a dimmer switch. An optional Highway Economy Package, intended for cruising rather than urban stop-and-go, included a specially-tuned V-6, specially calibrated automatic transmission, 2.56:1 axle ratio, and larger (24.5-gallon) gas tank.

ESTATE WAGON — SERIES 4BR — V-8 — The basic Estate Wagon's front-end appearance was just like LeSabre, but a Limited package transformed the wagon to Electra's front-end styling. Limited equipment included custom 60/40 notchback seats, power windows, power door and tailgate locks, tilt steering wheel, custom seat/shoulder belts, sunshade map light, quartz crystal clock (dial or digital), acoustic package, stand-up hood ornament, and woodgrain vinyl applique. The package also contained wheel opening, wide rocker panel, lower front fender and rear quarter,

window frame scalp, and belt reveal moldings; plus bumper guards, luggage rack and air deflector, remote-control left mirror, and chrome-plated wheels. Base and Limited editions were available with either two or three seats; 60/40 notchback seating (cloth or vinyl) standard on Limited, vinyl bench seats on base models. Tiny lamps at the dashboard underside "floodlit" the instrument dials for night visibility. Standard equipment included a Freedom battery, power steering and brakes, 350 cu. in. (5.7-liter) V-8 with four-barrel carburetor, and Turbo Hydra-matic. Estate Wagons also had diagnostic connectors, lockable storage compartments, and rocker panel moldings. The 403 cu. in. (6.6-liter) V-8 was optional. So were five different sound systems. The standard three-way tailgate could fold down or swing open like a door, with power window up or down. Cargo area measured 87 cubic feet.

1977 Electra Limited sedan (B)

ELECTRA — SERIES 4C — V-8 — Like the LeSabre, Electra lost 10 in. in overall length in its downsizing, but remained similar in form to the previous 225 model. Fender lines were the same as in 1976, with a more blunt front end and shorter overhangs, both front and rear. Buick called the fresh silhouette "lean, aerodynamic....a car of today, the future, instead of a tribute to the past." Electra's C-body was similar to Olds Ninety-Eight, slightly longer than LeSabre and riding the same platform as Cadillac DeVille. Turning diameter was 4 ft. tighter than in 1976. Models included a 225 coupe and sedan, Limited coupe and sedan, and top-line Park Avenue option package for the Limited sedan. All seated six with ease. Buyers now began with a standard 350 cu. in. (5.7-liter) engine, or could opt for the 403 cu. in. (6.6-liter) V-8. The big old 7.5-liter powerplant was gone. Power steering and brakes, Turbo Hydra-matic, diagnostic connectors, and Freedom battery were standard. New interior styling featured improved rear-seat access on coupes, a result of new inertia front seatback locks. The new crosshatch grille was divided into eight sections by two horizontal bars and three vertical bars. Quad rectangular headlamps sat atop clear quad rectangular park/signal lamps; amber lenses at front of fenders, just above the bumper. Electra's four-port trim piece was prominent at upper rear of front fenders, as in prior models. The 'Electra' nameplate stood at the back of the rear fenders, just below the long, slim bodyside molding. Wide taillamps were divided into upper and lower sections by a horizontal trim strip. Electras had bumper protective strips front and rear. Limiteds sported wide rocker panel moldings. The new instrument panel's controls and gauges set in brushed aluminum. Six sound systems were optional, including a digital-readout stereo radio that showed station frequency, time, date, and elapsed travel time. The Park Avenue package included a thickly-padded vinyl roof with coach lamps. Tiny lamps at the dashboard underside "floodlit" the instrument dials for night visibility. Cloth or vinyl notchback seats were standard on the 225; custom cloth or vinyl 60/40 notchback seating on Limited models; 50/50 cloth seats on the Park Avenue.

1977 Riviera coupe (BMD)

RIVIERA — SERIES 4BZ — V-8 — Buick's front-drive personal-luxury coupe received a total restyle, losing 5 in. of length and some 700 pounds. A new suspension was installed to improve roadholding and handling, while optional four-wheel disc brakes promised superior stopping power. Up front was a new vertical-bar grille. Body design included a pillared roof and full-frame door glass. Until a new downsized version emerged for 1979, Riviera was actually related to the B-body LeSabre. Its space-efficient six-passenger interior was more spacious and comfortable than before, with increased rear head/leg room. Trunk capacity grew too. Like its forerunners, the reduced Riviera was aimed at the buyer who would "like to surround him-self with quality. With things that are undeniably special." Riviera's "demeanor is that of a sporty road car," Buick insisted; "Its interior rivals the most opulent luxury cars." The new upright, formal appearing, vertical-bar grille-- a bit reminiscent of Rolls-Royce--curved outward at the base in a style that would soon become markedly Buick. Quad rectangular headlamps sat over quad clear park/signal lamps. Optional cornering lamps used a combination of clear, rectangular horizontal lens and smaller amber lens at the forward segment of each front fender. Standard fittings included a no-maintenance Freedom battery; lights for front ashtray, under-dash courtesy, glove compartment, trunk, and instrument flood; front and rear bumper protective strips; depressed-park windshield wipers; remote-control sport mirror on left side; custom wire wheel covers; and Rallye steering wheel. The new standard suspension included large-diameter front and rear anti-sway bars, plus special springs and shocks. New this year were inertia front seatback locks and a restyled instrument panel. Three special firemist exterior colors were available, as well as three new two-tone combinations. Buyers could have either the 350 cu. in. (5.7-liter) engine or new 403 cu. in. (6.6-liter) V-8. Standard 50/50 notchback seat with twin armrests were upholstered in plush velour cloth or vinyl. Custom wire wheel covers were standard. Options included a leather-covered steering wheel and CB transceiver. Lighted coach lamps came with the Landau vinyl top.

I.D. DATA: The 13-symbol Vehicle Identification Number (VIN) was located on the upper left surface of the instrument panel, visible through the windshield. The first digit is '4', indicating the Buick division. The second symbol is a letter indicating series: 'S' Skyhawk; 'T' Skyhawk S; 'B' Skylark; 'C' Skylark S/R; 'W' Skylark S; 'D' Century; 'E' Century Special; 'H' Century Custom; 'J' Regal; 'K' Century Custom wagon; 'F' LeSabre Sport Coupe; 'N' LeSabre; 'P' LeSabre Custom; 'R' Estate Wagon; 'Z' Riviera; 'V' Electra 225; 'X' Electra Limited. Next come two digits that denote body type: '07' Skyhawk hatchback coupe; '17' Skylark 2-dr. hatchback coupe; '27' Skylark 2-dr. coupe; '69' 4-dr. sedan; '29' 4-dr. Colonnade sedan; '37' Century/Regal 2-dr. Colonnade coupe or full- size 2-dr. coupe; '57' 2-dr. Colonnade coupe; '35' 4-dr. 2-seat wagon. The fifth symbol is a letter indicating engine code: 'C' V6-231 2Bbl.; 'Y' V8-301 2Bbl.; 'U' V8-305 2Bbl.; 'H' V8-350 2Bbl.; 'L' V8-350 4Bbl. (LM1); 'R' V8-350 4Bbl. (L34); 'J' V8-350 4Bbl. (L77); 'K' V8-403 4Bbl. (L80). The sixth symbol denotes model year ('7' 1977). Next is a plant code: '2' Ste. Therese (Canada); 'K' Leeds, MO; 'L' Van Nuys, CA; 'T' Tarrytown, NY; 'B' Baltimore, MD; 'G' Framingham, MA; 'H' Flint, MI; 'Z' Fremont, CA; 'C' Southgate, CA; 'X' Fairfax, KS; 'E' Linden, NJ. The final six digits are the sequential serial number, which began with 100001 except for Skyhawks (700001 up); LeSabres, Estate Wagons, Electras and Rivieras built at Flint (400001 up). Engine numbers were stamped on the front right of the block, except for L34 350 cu. in. V-8 and 403 cu. in. V-8, which were stamped on the front of the left side of the block. A body number plate on the shroud identified model year, car division, series, style, body assembly plant, body number, trim combination, modular seat code, paint code, and date built code.

SKYHAWK (V-6)

Series Number	Body/Style Number	Body Type & Seating	Factory Price	Shipping Weight	Production Total
4H	T07	2-dr 'S' Hatch-4P	3981	2805	Note 1
4H	S07	2-dr. Hatch-4P	4294	2817	Note 1

Note 1: Total model year production, 24,044 Skyhawks (built in Canada).

SKYLARK 'S' (V-6/V-8)

4X	W27	2-dr Coupe-6P	3642/3717	3258/3315	Note 2

SKYLARK (V-6/V-8)

4X	B27	2-dr Coupe-6P	3765/3830	3257/3314	49,858
4X	B17	2-dr Hatch-6P	3941/4006	3379/3436	5,316
4X	B69	4-dr Sedan-6P	3825/3890	3296/3353	48,121

SKYLARK S/R (V-6/V-8)

4X	C27	2-dr Coupe-5P	4527/4592	3277/3384	5,023
4X	C17	2-dr Hatch-5P	4695/4760	3304/3411	1,154
4X	C69	4-dr Sedan-5P	4587/4652	3271/3378	4,000

Note 2: Skylark 'S' is included in production total for base Skylark coupe. Of the 103,295 Skylarks built, 22,098 had a V-8 engine; of the total 10,177 Skylark S/R models, 5,040 had a V-8.

CENTURY SPECIAL (V-6)

4A	E37	2-dr Coupe-6P	4170	3590	Note 3

CENTURY (V-6/V-8)

4A	D37	2-dr Coupe-6P	4303/4470	3520/3643	52,864
4A	D29	4-dr Sedan-6P	4363/4530	3692/3815	29,065

Note 3: Century Special production is included in base Century coupe total. Of the 81,629 Century models built, 25,797 had a V-8 engine.

CENTURY CUSTOM (V-6/V-8)

4A	H57	2-dr Coupe-6P	4627/4794	3549/3672	20,834
4A	H29	4-dr Sedan-6P	4687/4854	3688/3811	13,645
4A	K35	4-dr Sta Wag-6P	-- /5218	-- /4260	19,282
4A	(AQ4)	4-dr Sta Wag-8P	-- /5371	-- / N/A	Note 4

Note 4: Three-seat wagon was an option package; production total included in K35 figure. Of the 53,761 Century Custom models built, only 12,142 had a V-6 engine.

REGAL (V-6/V-8)

4A	J57	2-dr Coupe-6P	4712/4915	3550/3673	174,560
4A	J29	4-dr Sedan-6P	-- /5243	-- /3928	17,946

Note 5: Only 36,125 Regal coupes carried a V-6 engine.

LESABRE (V-6/V-8)

4B	N37	2-dr Coupe-6P	5032/5142	3466/3578	8,455
4B	N69	4-dr Sedan-6P	5092/5202	3504/3616	19,827

LESABRE CUSTOM (V-6/V-8)

4B	F37	2-dr Spt Cpe-6P	-- /5818	-- /3634	Note 6
4B	P37	2-dr Coupe-6P	5321/5431	3474/3586	Note 6
4B	P69	4-dr Sedan-6P	5381/5491	3516/3628	103,855

Note 6: Total production, 58,589 Custom coupes (including Sport Coupe). Of all LeSabres built, just 19,744 were V-6 powered.

ESTATE WAGON (V-8)

4B	R35	4-dr Sta Wag-6P	5902	4015	25,075
4B	(AQ4)	4-dr Sta Wag-8P	6078	N/A	Note 7

Note 7: Three-seat Estate Wagon was an option package; production total is included in two-seat figure. Limited version was also an option package.

ELECTRA 225 (V-8)

4C	V37	2-dr Coupe-6P	6672	3761	15,762
4C	V69	4-dr Sedan-6P	6865	3814	25,633

ELECTRA LIMITED (V-8)

4C	X37	2-dr Coupe-6P	7032	3785	37,871
4C	X69	4-dr Sedan-6P	7225	3839	82,361

Note 8: Electra Park Avenue was a trim option, not a separate model.

RIVIERA (V-8)

4E	Z37	2-dr Coupe-6P	7357	3784	26,138

FACTORY PRICE AND WEIGHT NOTE: Figures before the slash are for V-6 engine, after the slash for V-8.

ENGINES: BUICK BASE EQUIPMENT V-6 (Skyhawk, Skylark, Century/Regal coupe, Century/Custom sedan, LeSabre): 90-degree, overhead-valve V-6. Cast iron alloy block and head. Displacement: 231 cu. in. (3.8 liters). Bore & stroke: 3.8 x 3.4 in. Compression ratio: 8.0:1. Brake horsepower: 105 at 3200 R.P.M. Torque: 185 lbs.-ft. at 2000 R.P.M. Four main bearings. Hydraulic valve lifters. Carburetor: 2Bbl. Rochester 2GC. VIN Code: C. BASE V-8 (Skylark, LeSabre Sport Coupe); OPTIONAL (other LeSabres): 90-degree overhead-valve V-8. Cast iron alloy block and head. Displacement: 301 cu. in. (5.0 liters). Bore & stroke: 4.0 x 3.0 in. Compression ratio: 8.2:1. Brake horsepower: 135 at 4000 R.P.M. Torque: 245 lbs.-ft. at 2000 R.P.M. Five main bearings. Hydraulic valve lifters. Carburetor: 2Bbl. Rochester M2MC. Built by Pontiac. VIN Code: Y. Ordering Code: L27. ALTERNATE 305 V-8; OPTIONAL (Skylark, Century wagon): 90-degree overhead-valve V-8. Cast iron alloy block and head. Displacement: 305 cu. in. (5.0 liters). Bore & stroke: 3.736 x 3.48 in. Compression ratio: 8.5:1. Brake horsepower: 145 at 3800 R.P.M. Torque: 245 lbs.-ft. at 2400 R.P.M. Five main bearings, Hydraulic valve lifters. Carburetor: 2Bbl. Roch. 2GC. VIN Code: U. BASE V-8 (Regal sedan); OPTIONAL (Century/Custom cpe/sed. Regal cpe): 90-degree, overhead valve V-8. Cast iron alloy block and head. Displacement: 350 cu. in. (5.7 liters). Bore & stroke: 3.80 x 3.85 in. Compression ratio: 8.1:1. Brake horsepower: 140 at 3200 R.P.M. Torque: 280 lbs.-ft. at 1400 R.P.M. Five main bearings. Hydraulic valve lifters. Carburetor: 2Bbl. Roch. 2GC. VIN Code: H. Ordering Code: L32. BASE V-8 (Century wagon, Electra, Estate, Riviera); OPTIONAL (Skylark, Century/Regal cpe/sed, LeSabre): 90-degree, overhead valve V-8. Cast iron alloy block and head. Displacement: 350 cu. in. (5.7 liters). Bore & stroke: 3.80 x 3.85 in. Compression ratio: 8.0:1. Brake horsepower: 155 at 3400 R.P.M. Torque: 275 lbs.-ft. at 1800 R.P.M. Five main bearings. Hydraulic valve lifters. Carburetor: 4Bbl. Rochester M4MC. VIN Code: J. ALTERNATE 350-4 V-8; OPTIONAL (Skylark, Century/Custom cpe/sed, Regal, LeSabre): 90-degree, overhead valve V-8. Cast iron alloy block and head. Displacement: 350 cu. in. (5.7 liters). Bore & stroke: 4.057 x 3.385 in. Compression ratio: 7.9:1. Brake horsepower: 170 at 3800 R.P.M. Torque: 275 lbs.-ft. at 2000 R.P.M. Five main bearings. Hydraulic valve lifters. Carburetor: 4Bbl. Roch. M4MC. Built by Oldsmobile. VIN Code: R. Ordering Code: L34. Not available in California. ALTERNATE 350-4 V-8 (Chevrolet-built): 90-degree, overhead valve V-8. Cast iron alloy block and head. Displacement: 350 cu. in. (5.7 liters). Bore & stroke: 4.00 x 3.48 in. Compression ratio: 8.5:1. Brake horsepower: 170 at 3800 R.P.M. Torque: 270 lbs.-ft. at 2400 R.P.M. Five main bearings. Hydraulic valve lifters. Carburetor: 4Bbl. Roch. M4MC. VIN Code: L. Ordering Code: LM1. OPTIONAL V-8 (Century wagon, LeSabre, Electra, Estate Wagon, Riviera): 90-degree, overhead valve V-8. Cast iron alloy block and head. Displacement: 403 cu. in. (6.6 liters). Bore & stroke: 4.351 x 3.385 in. Compression ratio: 8.5:1. Brake horsepower: 185 at 3600 R.P.M. Torque: 320 lbs.-ft. at 2200 R.P.M. Five main bearings. Hydraulic valve lifters. Carburetor: 4Bbl. Roch. M4MC. Built by Oldsmobile. VIN Code: K. Ordering Code: L80.

CHASSIS DATA: Wheelbase: (Skyhawk) 97.0 in.; (Skylark) 111.0 in.; (Century/Regal cpe) 112.0 in.; (Century/Regal sed/wag) 116.0 in.; (LeSabre/Estate/Riviera) 115.9 in; (Electra) 118.9 in. Overall length:- (Skyhawk) 179.3 in.; (Skylark) 200.2 in.; (Century/Regal cpe) 209.8 in.; (Century/Regal sedan) 213.6 in.; (Century wagon) 218.3 in.; (LeSabre/Riv) 218.2 in.; (Electra) 222.1 in.; (Estate) 216.7 in.. Height:- (Skyhawk) 50.1 in.; (Skylark 2-dr.) 52.2 in.; (Skylark 4-dr.) 53.1 in.; (Century/Regal cpe) 52.7 in.; (Century/Regal sed) 53.6 in.; (Century wag) 55.3 in.; (LeSabre cpe) 54.6 in.; (LeSabre sed) 55.3 in.; (Electra cpe) 54.8 in.; (Electra sed) 55.7 in.; (Estate) 57.0 in.; (Riviera) 54.6 in. Width:- (Skyhawk) 65.4 in.; (Skylark) 72.7 in.; (Century/Regal cpe) 76.5 in.; (Century/Regal sed/wag) 79.0 in.; (LeSabre/Electra/Estate/ Riviera) 77.2 in. Front Tread:- (Skyhawk) 54.7 in.; (Skylark) 59.1 in.; (Century/Regal) 61.5 in.; (LeSabre/Electra/Riviera) 61.8 in.; (Estate) 62.2 in. Rear Tread:- (Skyhawk) 53.6 in.; (Skylark) 59.7 in.; (Estate) 64.1 in.; (others) 60.7 in. Standard Tires:- (Skyhawk) BR78 x 13 SBR; (Skyawk 'S') B78 x 13; (Skylark) E78 x 14; (Skylark S/R) ER78 x 14 SBR WSW; (Century/Regal cpe) FR78 x 15 SBR exc. V-6, GBR; (Century/Regal sed) FR78 x 15 SBR; (Century wagon) HR78 x 15 SBR; (LeSabre) FR78 x 15 GBR; (Electra/Riviera) GR78 x 15; (Estate) HR78 x 15 SBR.

TECHNICAL: Transmission:- Three-speed, fully synchronized manual gearbox (column shift) standard on Skylark, Century cpe/sed, and Regal cpe; Turbo Hydra-matic optional. Four-speed, fully synchronized floor shift standard on Skyhawk; five-speed and automatic optional. Turbo Hydra-matic standard on Skylark S/R, Regal sedan, LeSabre, Electra, Estate and Riviera. Three-speed manual transmission gear ratios: (1st) 3.11:1; (2nd) 1.84:1; (3rd) 1.00:1; (Rev) 3.22:1. Four-speed gear ratios: (1st) 3.11:1; (2nd) 2.20:1; (3rd) 1.47:1; (4th) 1.00:1; (Rev) 3.11:1. Five-speed gear ratios: (1st) 3.40:1; (2nd) 2.08:1; (3rd) 1.39:1; (4th) 1.00:1; (5th) 0.80:1; (Rev) 3.36:1. Automatic trans. gear ratios: (1st) 2.52:1; (2nd) 1.52:1; (3rd) 1.00:1; (Rev) 2.08:1. Skyhawk auto. trans. gear ratios: (1st) 2.74:1; (2nd) 1.57:1; (3rd) 1.00:1; (Rev) 2.07:1. Standard axle ratio:- (Skyhawk) 2.56:1; (Skylark) 3.08:1 w/manual, 2.56:1 w/automatic, 2.41:1 w/V-8; (Century/Regal) 3.08:1 w/manual, 2.73:1 w/automatic, 2.41:1 w/350 V-8; (Century wagon) 2.73:1; (LeSabre V-6) 2.73:1; (LeSabre V-8) 2.41:1; (Electra/Riviera) 2.41:1; (Estate) 2.73:1 exc. 2.56:1 w/403 V-8. Steering:- recirculating ball; variable-ratio power steering standard on Century/Regal, LeSabre, Electra, Estate and Riviera. Suspension and Body Construction:- same as 1976. Brakes:- front disc, rear drum; power brakes standard on LeSabre/Electra/Riviera plus Century Custom sedan/wagon and Regal. Four-wheel power disc brakes optional on Riviera. High-Energy electronic ignition (HEI) on all engines. Unleaded fuel only.

DRIVETRAIN OPTIONS: Engines:- 301 cu. in. V-8, 2Bbl.: Skylark ($65); LeSabre ($110). 350 cu. in. V-8, 2Bbl.: Century/Cust, Regal cpe ($167). 350 cu. in. V-8, 4Bbl.: Skylark ($155); Century/Cust, Regal cpe ($222); Regal sed ($55); LeSabre ($200); LeSabre spt cpe ($90). 403 cu. in. V-8, 4Bbl.: LeSabre ($287); LeSabre spt cpe ($177); Century wag, Estate/Electra/Riviera ($65). V-6 economy pkg.: Skylark, 'S' ($302); Skylark S/R, LeSabre ($25). Transmission/Differential:- Five-speed manual floor shift: Skyhawk ($248). Turbo Hydra-matic trans.: Skyhawk ($248); Skylark, Century cpe/sed, Regal cpe ($282); Optional rear axle ratio: Century/Regal 3.08:1 or 3.23:1 (NC); LeSabre/Electra/Riviera 3.08:1 (NC); LeSabre 3.23:1 (NC). Positive traction differential ($51-$58). Power accessories: Power brakes, Skyhawk ($58); Skylark/Century ($61). Four-wheel disc brakes: Riviera ($186). Power steering: Skyhawk ($130); Skylark ($147). Suspension: WH5 handling package: Skyhawk ($11-$133). F40 Firm Ride handling package: Skylark ($22); Century/Regal/LeSabre/Electra/Riviera ($18). FE2 Rallye ride/handling package: Skylark ($42); Century, except Special wagon, Regal ($36); Riviera ($18). Automatic level control: Century/Regal/LeSabre/Electra/Riviera ($102). Other: Trailer towing flasher/harness ($20-32) except Skyhawk. Heavy-duty 80-amp alternator: Century/Regal/LeSabre/Electra/Riviera ($37-42). Heavy-duty Energizer battery ($16-$18). Freedom battery: Century/Regal ($30). Heavy-duty cooling ($27-$55) except Skyhawk. Heavy-duty radiator: Skylark ($19); Engine block heater ($13) except Skyhawk. High altitude emission system ($22). California emission system ($70-71).

SKYHAWK CONVENIENCE/APPEARANCE OPTIONS: Option Packages:- Free Spirit Skyhawk pkg. ($148). Appearance group: 'S' ($67). Convenience group ($21). Shadow light Astroroof w/roof crown molding ($591). Manual glass sunroof ($210). Comfort/Convenience:- Air cond. ($442). Rear defogger, electric ($71). Soft Ray tinted glass ($48). Tinted windshield ($40). Rallye steering wheel: 'S' ($37). Tilt steering ($50). Electric clock: 'S' ($18); clock and tach ($63). Right sport mirror ($13). Remote left sport mirror: 'S' ($16). Entertainment:- AM radio ($71). AM/FM radio ($134). AM/FM stereo radio ($219). AM radio and tape player ($197). AM/FM stereo radio and tape ($316). Rear speaker for non- stereo radios ($20). Radio accommodation pkg. ($22). Exterior Trim:- Door edge guards ($9). Roof crown molding ($162). Protective bodyside moldings ($25-$40). Hawk accent stripe ($33). Interior Trim/Upholstery:- Full-length console: 'S' ($77). Adjustable driver's seatback ($18). Front/rear mats ($15). Custom seatbelts ($14). Wheels:- Custom sport wheels $79-$90). Deluxe wheel covers ($42). Wheel trim rings ($35). Tires:- B78 x 13 WSW: 'S' ($30-$38). BR78 x 13 SBR blackwall: 'S' ($82-$103). BR78 x 13 SBR whitewall ($38-$141). White- letter tires ($51-$168). Conventional spare tire (NC).

SKYLARK CONVENIENCE/APPEARANCE OPTIONS: Option Packages:- Accessory pkg. (day/night mirror, lighter): 'S' ($12). Acoustic insulation pkg. ($24-$36). Convenience group ($29-$31). Appearance group: 'S' ($33). Comfort/Convenience:- Air cond. ($478). Cruise Master ($80). Three-speed wipers w/delay ($30). Rear defogger, blower-type ($48). Power windows ($108-$151). Electric door locks ($68- $96). Rallye steering wheel ($37) exc. S/R. Tilt steering ($57). Soft Ray tinted glass ($50). Tinted windshield ($42). Dual horns ($7). Electric clock ($21). Headlamps-on indicator ($7). Electric trunk release ($21). Remote-control mirror ($15). Sport mirrors: left remote, right manual ($28). Entertainment:- AM radio ($75). AM/FM radio ($137). AM/FM stereo radio ($233). AM radio and tape player ($337). CB Transceiver ($195). Rear speaker ($21). Exterior Trim:- Custom vinyl roof: S/R ($93). Custom vinyl roof w/hood ornament: base, 'S' ($98). Landau top ($162-$167). Two-tone paint ($42). Special exterior paint ($116). Swing-out rear quarter vent window: two-doors ($51). Protective bodyside moldings ($38). Rocker panel moldings ($16). Wide rocker appearance group ($34). Decklid molding ($8). Custom door and window rame moldings ($25-$31). Door edge guards ($9-$13). Bodyside accent stripes ($25). Bumper guards, front ($19); front/rear ($38). Bumper strips, front/rear ($29). Interior Trim/Upholstery:- Full-length console ($75). Vinyl bucket seats: base Skylark ($84). Custom trim bench seats/interior: base ($151). Custom seatbelts ($14-$16). Front carpet savers ($9). Carpet savers and handy mats ($15). Carpeted door trim with map pocket and reflector: Skylark ($37). Wheels:- Styled wheels ($82-$94). Chrome-plated wheels ($112-$132). Deluxe wheel covers ($33). Styled wheel covers ($91). Deluxe wire wheel covers ($121). Tires:- E78 x 14 WSW ($31-$39) exc. S/R. ER78 x 14 SBR BSW ($69-$86) exc. S/R. ER78 x 14 SBR WSW ($100-$125) exc. S/R. FR78 x 14 SBR WLT ($29-$156). Stowaway spare tire ($17); S/R cpe (NC).

CENTURY/REGAL CONVENIENCE/APPEARANCE OPTIONS: Option Packages:- Regal S/R Coupe pkg. ($432-$499). Electric sunroof: cpe ($394). Hurst hatch roof: Century Cust, Regal cpe ($587). Convenience group ($16-$31). Comfort/Convenience:- Air cond. ($499). Custom Aire ($538). Cruise Master ($80). Rear defogger: electric ($82); blower-type ($48). Soft Ray tinted glass ($54). Tinted windshield ($43). Six-way power driver's seat ($137). Custom steering wheel ($17). Rallye steering wheel ($37). Tilt steering ($57). Power windows ($108-$151). Electric door locks ($68-$96). Electric trunk release ($21). Remote-control tailgate lock: Century wag ($21). Electric clock ($21). Headlamps-on indicator ($7). Instrument gauges and electric clock ($45) exc. wag. Fuel usage gauge ($27). Speed alert ($15). Dome reading lamp ($16). Three-speed wiper with delay ($30). Lighting and Mirrors:- Remote control mirror ($15). Sport mirrors: left remote ($28). Lighted visor vanity mirror ($42). Trunk light: Century Cust, Regal cpe ($5). Entertainment:- AM radio ($79). AM/FM radio ($142). AM/FM stereo radio ($233). AM radio w/stereo tape player ($213). AM/FM stereo radio w/tape ($337). AM/FM stereo radio and CB ($453). CB Transceiver ($195). Rear speaker ($21). Front/rear speakers ($44). Exterior Trim:- Landau vinyl top: Century Cust, Regal cpe ($120); Century/Spec. ($156). Custom vinyl top: Century cpe, Regal ($111). Custom vinyl top w/hood ornament: Century/Cust cpe ($116). Swing-out rear quarter vent windows: Century wag ($51). Two-tone paint ($42) exc. wagon. Special color paint ($134). Bumper guards, front/rear ($38); rear, Century wag ($19). Bumper strips: Century Special ($30). Protective bodyside moldings ($27). Lower bodyside molding ($36). Door edge guards ($9-$13). Wheel opening moldings: Century, Special ($19). Bodyside accent stripes ($45). Woodgrain vinyl applique: Century wag ($185). Luggage rack: Century wag ($76). Air deflector: Century wag ($26). Interior Trim/Upholstery:- Full-length console ($75). Custom notchback seat trim: Century/Spec. ($136-$163). Custom vinyl notchback seat trim: Century Cust cpe, Regal ($108); cloth ($140). Custom vinyl 60/40 seat trim: Century Cust, Regal cpe ($199); loth ($231). Custom reclining seat trim: Century Cust cpe ($244). Custom vinyl bucket seats: Century/Spec. cpe ($143- $168). Custom seatbelts ($14-$18). Third seat: Century wag ($152). Front/rear carpeting: Century Special ($25). Load floor area carpet: Century wag ($24). Front carpet savers ($10). Carpet savers and handy mats ($17). Litter pocket ($7). Wheels:- Chrome-plated wheels ($114-$161). Styled wheels ($68-$94). Deluxe wire wheel covers: Century ($133); Regal ($99). Styled wheel covers: Century ($91); Regal ($57). Deluxe wheel covers: Century ($34). Moire wheel covers: Century ($102); Regal ($68). Tires:- FR78 x 15 GBR WSW ($33- $41) exc. Regal sed. FR78 x 15 SBR BSW ($36-$45) exc. Regal sed. FR78 x 15 SBR WSW ($69-$86) exc. Regal sed. GR78 x 15 SBR: Century/Cust, Regal cpe ($54-$67); with V-8 (NC). GR70 x 15 SBR WLT: Century/Cust, Regal cpe ($109-$136); with V-8 ($55-$69). GR78 x 15 SBR WSW: Century/Cust, Regal cpe ($88- $110); with V-8 ($34-$43). HR78 x 15 SBR WSW: Century wag ($47). Stowaway spare tire (NC). Conventional spare: Century Spec. (NC).

LESABRE/ELECTRA/ESTATE WAGON/RIVIERA CONVENIENCE/APPEARANCE OPTIONS: Option Packages: Estate Wagon Limited pkg. ($1442). Exterior molding pkg.: LeSabre/Estate/Electra 225 ($47-$152). Accessory group: LeSabre ($46-$84). Electric sunroof ($734). Astroroof ($898). Comfort/Convenience:- Air cond. ($539). Automatic climate control air cond.: Electra/Riv ($621). Custom Aire air cond.: LeSabre, Estate ($578). Cruise Master ($84). Rear defogger, electric ($83). Tinted glass ($69). Tinted windshield: LeSabre, Est ($44). Power windows: LeSabre, Est ($114-$171). Electric door locks ($70-$98). Automatic electric door locks: Electra/Riv ($124-$151). Nine- way power driver's seat ($109-$139). Six-way power seat: LeSabre, Electra 225 ($139). Six-way power passenger seat ($246-$276) exc. base LeSabre. Power passenger seatback recliner ($104); N/A on base LeSabre sedan. Custom steering wheel: LeSabre/Estate ($17). Leather steering wheel: Riviera ($36). Tilt steering ($58). Tilt/telescoping steering column ($44-$104) exc. LeSabre spt cpe. Digital clock (NC). Low fuel indicator ($12). Fuel usage light ($27). Speed alert and trip odometer ($20). Remote electric tailgate lock: Estate ($30). Electric trunk release ($21). Three-speed intermittent wipers ($30). Lighting, Horns and Mirrors:- Cornering lamps ($44). Front light monitors: LeSabre/Estate ($25). Front/rear monitors: Electra/Riv ($55). Door courtesy/warning lights ($32-$50). Rear courtesy lamps: Estate ($13). Headlamps-on indicator ($7). Dome reading lamp: LeSabre/Estate/Electra 225 ($16). Sunshade map light: Electra 225 ($11). Four-note horn ($18). Remote left mirror: LeSabre, Est ($15). Remote right mirror ($26-$31) exc. Riv. Remote right sport mirror: Riv ($19). Dual remote sport mirrors ($33-$53) exc. Riv. Remote left mirror w/thermometer ($20-$35) exc. Riv. Lighted visor vanity mirror ($43). Entertainment:- AM radio ($92). AM/FM radio ($153). AM/FM stereo radio w/four speakers ($236-$341). AM radio and stereo tape player ($228). AM/FM stereo radio and tape player ($341). AM/FM stereo radio and CB ($459). CB Transceiver ($197). Rear speaker ($21); front/rear ($44). Power antenna ($42). Exterior Trim:- Landau vinyl top: LeSabre ($146-$164). Custom padded landau vinyl top: Electra/Riv ($196). Padded landau vinyl top ($186-$417). Long vinyl top: base LeSabre, Electra ($135-$155). Two-tone paint: LeSabre/Electra ($51-$60); Riv ($185). Special color paint ($135) exc. Riviera Firemist ($152). Protective bodyside moldings ($38-$53). Hood ornament: base LeSabre, Estate ($22). Door edge guards ($9-$13). Wheel opening moldings: base LeSabre, Estate ($24). Bodyside accent stripes ($46). Woodgrain vinyl applique: Estate ($198). Bumper guards, front/rear ($38); front, Estate ($19). Luggage rack w/air deflector: Estate ($127). Interior Trim/Upholstery:- Custom notchback seat trim: Estate ($224); 60/40 ($318). Electra Park Ave. sedan seating ($385). Notchback 60/40 seating: LeSabre Cust/Spt Cpe, Electra 225 ($97). Third seat: Estate ($175). Custom seatbelts: LeSabre, Estate ($18-$21). Front carpet savers ($11-$12). Carpet savers and handy mats: ($18- $22). Litter pocket ($7) exc. Electra Ltd. Deluxe trunk trim: LeSabre ($43). Trunk carpeting: Electra/Riv ($53). Wheels:- Chrome-plated wheels: LeSabre/Estate/Electra ($116-$163); Riv ($51-$64). Styled wheels ($58-$92) exc. Riv. Deluxe wire wheels ($101-$135) exc. Riv. Custom wire wheels: Riviera (NC). Deluxe wheel covers: base LeSabre ($34). Super deluxe wheel covers: LeSabre/Electra ($24-$58). Moire wheel covers ($68-$102) exc. Riv. Tires:- FR78 x 15 SBR: LeSabre ($36-$45). FR78 x 15 SBR WSW: LeSabre ($33-$86). GR78 x 15 SBR WSW ($34- $43). GR78 x 15 SBR WSW ($47-$125). GR70 x 15 SBR WLT: LeSabre ($55-$136); LeSabre spt cpe ($7); Riviera ($55-$69). Stowaway spare tire (NC).

HISTORY: Introduced: September 30, 1976. Model year production (U.S.): 845,234, for 9.3 percent of the industry total. North American production for the U.S. market was 869,277 (234,520 V-6 and 634,757 V-8). Calendar year production (U.S.): 801,202. Model year sales by U.S. dealers: 773,313 (including 28,114 imported Opels). Calendar year sales (U.S.): 746,394 for an 8.2 percent market share.

Historical Footnotes: Sales set a record for the second year in a row, beating the 1955 mark by nearly 35,000 cars. Full-size Buick models accounted for a healthy 44 percent of sales, with each big Buick showing an impressive sales increase for the model year. Model year production gained 15 percent over 1976. Skylark production returned to Canada for 1977—but back again to Lordstown, Ohio in mid-year. An assembly line was added at Flint to build the popular V-6, which was also installed on other GM cars.

1978 BUICK

Following up on the 1977 slimming down of big Buicks, 1978 saw a trimming of the mid-size Century and Regal. Buick's full-line catalog featured many photos and descriptions of old Buicks, with a nod to the Buick Club of America. The catalog also admitted that Buicks were "equipped with GM-built engines produced by various divisions." That simple fact gained considerable publicity, as some buyers of a Buick or Olds that contained a "lesser" Chevrolet or Pontiac under the hood felt they'd been cheated. Five Buick series now offered the V-6 as standard equipment. For 1978, the V-6 added an "even-firing" feature. To improve smoothness, cylinder firing was changed from alternating 90- and 180-degree intervals of crankshaft rotation to even 120-degree intervals. Buick claimed that the revised V-6 idled like a V-8. A new smaller V-6, displacing just 196 cu. in. (3.2-liters), was available in the mid-size Century and Regal. This was essentially the 231 V-6 with bore reduced from 3.8 to 3.5 in. Four V-8 choices were offered: 301 cu. in. (4.9-liter), 305 (5.0-liter), 350 (5.7-liter) and 403 (6.6-liter) displacements. Of far greater interest to performance fans then and now was the new turbocharged V-6. Turbocharging wasn't a new idea, of course, having been used in the 1960s Corvair Spyder and Olds F85. But in line with its advertising slogan ("A little science. A little magic.") Buick was now pioneering the turbocharging of a small engine for a family car. The turbo arrived in both Regal and LeSabre Sport Coupes, with either two- or four-barrel carburetor. This engine was a production version of the 3.8-liter V-6 used in the Indianapolis 500 Pace Car of 1976. It was a demand-type turbocharger that didn't affect power output at normal highway speeds, but only when the accelerator was pressed. Horsepower was 150 with two-barrel, 165 with four-barrel, as opposed to the normal 105. Buick's goal: to achieve performance that matched a 350 V-8, but without losing the fuel economy of six cylinders. Turbo Buicks came with a specially calibrated automatic transmission and special rear axle ratio. Buick also introduced a new electronic spark control system on the turbo V-6 for 1978, a first in the industry. It monitored detonation (knocking) level in the engine and retarded spark to control detonation during turbo boost. To ensure reliability, each turbocharged Buick got a two-mile road test, a sensible practice that had virtually disappeared years before. Body colors available on all models were: white, silver metallic, black, medium blue metallic, light green metallic, tan, saffron metallic, dark gold metallic, brown metallic, and red metallic. Colors available only on Skyhawk/Skylark colors were bright blue metallic, dark green metallic, yellow, and bright red. Special Century/Regal, LeSabre, Estate Wagon, Electra and Riviera colors were: light blue, dark blue metallic, medium green metallic, and dark red metallic. For extra cost, Riviera buyers could have any of three Firemist metallic colors: blue, amber or red. Designers' accent colors this year were: gray accent (used with silver); or gold accent (used with tan). All Buicks had diagnostic connectors that enabled a mechanic to hook up a diagnostic test instrument to check operation of the ignition switch, coil, starter and other critical circuitry, much faster than traditional methods. All full-size Buicks (except Estate Wagon) might have a sunroof or Astroroof; cornering lights activated by the turn signal lever; or tri-color front light monitors. Other options included a new theft-deterrent system that included electric door, trunk and hood locks to trigger audible and visual alarms in the event of tampering, plus an outside mirror with built-in thermometer. Electra and Riviera could have a new frequency-synthesized radio with AM/FM stereo, 8-track tape, digital clock, and pushbutton scanner that automatically located and locked onto strong signals in remote areas. Also on their option list: an AM/FM stereo radio with built-in 40-channel CB transceiver and a Triband power antenna that disappeared into the car fender.

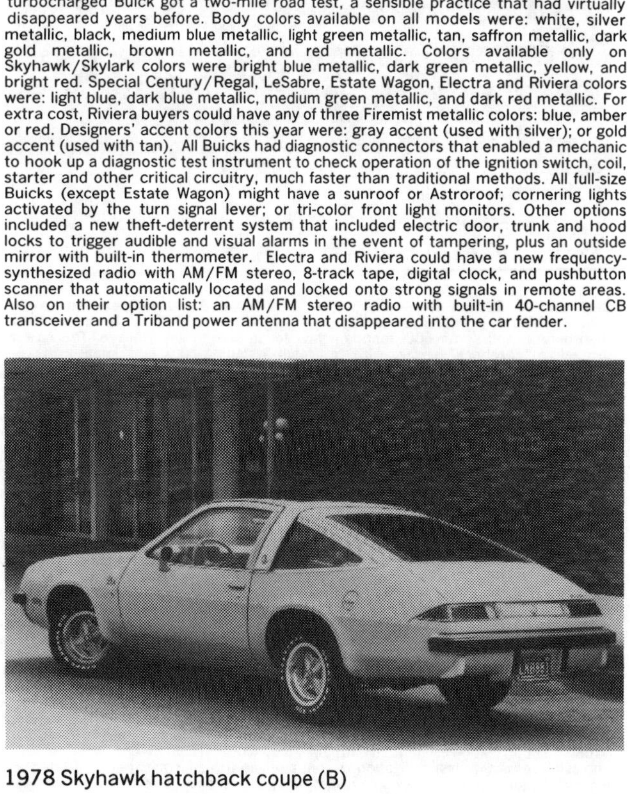

1978 Skyhawk hatchback coupe (B)

SKYHAWK — SERIES 4H — V-6 — Still riding a 97 in. wheelbase in one hatchback coupe body style, the subcompact Skyhawk returned for another season powered by the even-firing 231 cu. in. (3.8-liter) V-6. Standard gearbox was a four-speed manual floor shift, with automatic or five-speed overdrive manual available. Some California Skyhawks had a new Phase II three-way catalyst system that used an oxygen sensor to adjust the air/fuel mixture. Styling touches included rectangular headlamps, a domed hood, and louvered roof pillars. Interior trim was new this year. Low-cost 'S' Skyhawks wore standard rattan vinyl upholstery. Upper models could have vinyl or sporty hobnail velour and knit fabrics. Large gauges, including a voltmeter, were recessed in a simulated wood instrument panel. The 'S' model had a new two-spoke steering wheel. On the option list, both fixed-glass Astroroof (with Targa-type aluminum band) and manual sliding-glass sunroofs were offered, as was a Hawk accent stripe package. All Skyhawks had a cigarette lighter, heater/defroster, carpeting, front/rear bumper guards with protective strips, and front stabilizer bar. The base (S07) Skyhawk added a remote-controlled left-hand sport mirror, bodyside stripes (white, black or gold), wheel opening moldings, and steel-belted radial tires.

1978 Skylark Custom Landau Coupe (B)

SKYLARK — SERIES 4X — V-6/V-8 — A Custom Skylark replaced the former S/R version as the luxury edition. Standard and Custom Skylarks came in coupe, sedan and hatchback form, while the low-budget 'S' was again available only as a coupe. Powerplant choices were the standard 231 cu. in. (3.8-liter) "even-firing" V-6, or two optional V-8s. Standard transmission (except in California and high-altitude areas) was the three-speed manual shift. Apart from a similarly-shaped but restyled grille that added a pair of horizontal divider bands to the vertical-bar pattern, Skylark's styling changes were modest for 1978. The wraparound parking/signal lamps were divided into three sections rather than two. Taillamps were split into two horizontal sections instead of three, with full-height backup lamps at the inner ends. Interior trim was new. The Sport Package on base and Custom models included black paint accents on the front grille and around the headlamps, back window and side window frames. The package also featured ER78 x 14 blackwall steel-belted radials, a ride/handling suspension, black sport mirrors, and choice of four body colors: silver, dark gold, yellow, and bright red. All Skylarks except 'S' had front/rear ashtrays plus wheel opening and roof drip moldings. The Custom added a stand-up hood ornament, custom rocker panel moldings, and deluxe wheel covers.

1978 Century Sport Coupe (B)

CENTURY — SERIES 4A — V-6/V-8 — A redesigned and reduced mid-size "new generation" Century (and related Regal) emerged for 1978 about 10 inches shorter than before, and some 600 pounds lighter for improved gas mileage. The new and distinctive "aeroback" sedan, with "gracefully" sloping back end, measured 18 in. shorter and 7 in. narrower than its notchback predecessor. Yet passenger space stayed just about the same as in 1977. To keep inside space ample, designers reduced the Century and Regal bodyside curvature and pushed out the roof support pillars. Instrument panels were moved closer to the windshield to add leg room. Coupe wheelbases were cut by 4 in., sedans and wagons by 8 in. The shorter 108 in. wheelbase reduced the car's turning radius. Both coupes and sedans displayed a completely new side appearance: an aerodynamic, fastback "European look." The rear roof pillar and deck lid were on the same plane. Coupes and sedans came in three series: Special, Custom, and Limited (with same lavish interior as Regal's Limited). The Century Sport Coupe came equipped with Designers' wheels and P205/70R14 steel-belted radial tires, special paint treatment and striping, body-color bumpers, and ride/handling package. The new, wide-spaced grille had a horizontal-slat pattern separated by two horizontal bars and a vertical center bar, plus six subdued vertical bars, with 'BUICK' badge at the side. Quad headlamps were replaced by single rectangular headlamps this year, with wraparound park/signal lamps. Wraparound taillamps were divided into three horizontal sections, with clear backup lights at the inner ends of the lower segments. The new wider grille, coupled with single-headlight front end, made the car look broader, though it was actually 7 in. narrower than before. Century was closely related to Oldsmobile's Cutlass Salon and Cutlass Supreme. The new, "even-firing" 196 cu. in. (3.2-liter) V-6 with three-speed manual shift was standard, except in California and high-altitude areas which demanded the 3.8-liter V-6 and automatic transmission. A 305 cu. in. (5.0-liter) V-8 was optional. So was a floor-mounted four-speed manual gearshift, with larger 231 cu. in. V-6 engine. All Centurys carried a maintenance-free Delco Freedom battery. In addition to more extensive corrosion-resistant treatment, the front fender wells were made of corrosion-resistant plastic. Station wagons came in three forms: Special, Custom, and a Sport Wagon option that included Designers' Accent paint, Designers' Sport wheels,

Rallye suspension similar to Sport Coupe, body-color bumpers, and wide-oval (P205/70R14) steel-belted radial tires. Wagons in California and high-altitude areas required V-8 power rather than the standard 231 cu. in. V-6. A newly-designed fold-down rear deck and lift-up window made loading easier. Also, locking storage compartments were added behind the rear wheelhousings. The six-window sedans and wagons had fixed (not roll-down) windows in the back doors, and swing-out rear vent windows. All Century models now had a turn signal lever that doubled as a headlight dimmer, windshield wipers with single- wipe mist control, space-saving compact (temporary) spare tire, and coin holder in the glove box. Power-operated sunroof and Astroroof options were offered on coupes. Designers' Accent schemes used contrasting shades of similar colors to create a distinctive appearance, offered on all models except the Century Sport Coupe. Electronic leveling was another option. New standard compact spare tires, rated for 60 psi pressure, were meant for temporary use only.

1978 Regal Turbo Sport Coupe (B)

REGAL — SERIES 4A — V-6/V-8 — Regal became a separate Buick line this year, rather than a Century variant. The new version was 14 in. shorter than the '77 model, trimmed-down all around. Wheelbase cut from 112 to 108 in. permitted a smaller turning diameter. An entirely different, more formal look marked the restyled Regal. Gone were the skinny angled opera windows, replaced by upright rear windows that separated from the front windows by a bright vertical pillar. The new, slightly sloped grille, comprised of many vertical bars, angled outward at the base. Large single rectangular headlamps were recessed and flanked by wraparound park/signal lamps. As on Century, the instrument panel was moved closer to the windshield to add front knee/leg room. Gauges and warning lights set in a rectangular cluster, with radio, heater and air conditioner controls in a separate module. Notchback 55/45 seats (standard in Limited) were covered by crushed woven fabric, with standard folding center armrest. Door pull straps were standard. New thin-shell front seats allowed more leg room in back. Roof pillars were moved outward to add head room. Only the coupe body was offered, in three levels: base Regal, Regal Sport Coupe, and Regal Limited. Base and Limited models carried a new 196 cu. in. (3.2-liter) V-6 (except in California and high-altitude areas, where a 231 cu. in. V-6 was required). Standard equipment included a compact spare tire (except with positive-traction differential), Freedom battery, P195/75R14 tires, cigarette lighter, front/rear ashtrays, wide-view day/night mirror, bin-type glove box with coin holder, front and rear bumper protective strips, and deluxe wheel covers. Electronic leveling was optional. Regal's hot personal-luxury Sport Coupe came with a new 231 cu. in. (3.8-liter) turbocharged V-6 as standard. Along with LeSabre, these were the only two standard turbocharged production cars made in America. (Worldwide, only Porsche and Saab offered turbos at this time.) Buick's chief engineer Lloyd E. Reuss called Regal "the performance car of the future," since its blower cut in only when needed. Standard Sport Coupe equipment included automatic transmission, Rallye ride/handling suspension with front and rear stabilizer bars, firmer springs and shocks, distinctive domed hood with 'Turbo 3.8 Litre' insignia on the sides of the "bubble" dome, power brakes, and P205/70R145 radial tires. A dash light showed turbo "boost."

1978 LeSabre Sport Coupe (B)

LESABRE — SERIES 4B — V-6/V-8 — Design changes were fairly modest this year, after prior downsizing. LeSabre's grille was shaped like the 1977 version but was now wider-spaced, with a dominant vertical bar at the forward peak, plus two horizontal bars dividing the grille into six segments. Grille framing bars reached all the way outward, below the headlamps, to wrap around fenders. Interior trim was new; electronic leveling optional. Standard equipment included automatic transmission, power steering and brakes, heater/defroster, intermittent wipers, inside hood release, and front/rear protective bumper strips. LeSabre's Sport Coupe, similar to the Regal version, carried the new turbocharged 231 cu. in. V-6 engine and handling suspension. That engine replaced the 305 cu. in. V-8 in the 1977 LeSabre Sport Coupe. Instead of LeSabre's customary three-hole emblem on the front fenders, the Sport Coupe had a distinctive 'Turbo 3.8 Litre' badge at the forward end. Other distinctive touches included flat black trim around the windows and in the grille. Wide GR70 x 15 radial tires rode 7 in. chrome wheels. Other LeSabres came with a standard 231 cu. in. V-6 or optional V-8.

ESTATE WAGON — SERIES 4BR — V-8 — Though related most closely to LeSabre, the Estate Wagon wore an Electra grille and front-end look. Its three-way tailgate could fold down or swing open, with power window up or down. The three-seat version carried up to eight passengers, or 87 cubic feet of cargo with rear seat folded down. Estate Wagon Limited option included 55/45 notchback front seating, power windows, tilt steering wheel, luggage rack with air deflector, electric door locks, remote tailgate lock, remote-control left mirror, bumper guards, map light, dial clock, exterior molding package, woodgrain vinyl applique, acoustic package, special ornamentation, and chrome-plated road wheels.

1978 Electra Park Avenue Landau Coupe (B)

ELECTRA — SERIES 4C — V-8 — Electra's restyled checkerboard grille was similar to 1977 version, but with only a single horizontal bar across the center. Wide wraparound taillamps were new, but otherwise the big Buick's design didn't change much. Coupe and sedan were offered in 225, Limited, or Park Avenue form. With vertical roofline and side-mounted coach lights, the elegant Park Avenue took on a more formal appearance. The Park Avenue coupe was new this year. Upholstery choices ranged from textured vinyl to buttoned-and-tufted crushed velour. Standard powerplant was again the 350 cu. in. (5.7- liter) V-8 with four-barrel carburetor, as well as automatic transmission, power steering and brakes, and the customary coil springs all around. Also standard: power windows and driver's seat, wipers with mist control, quartz clock (dial or digital), and remote-control outside mirror. Limited and Park Avenue Electras added wide rocker appearance moldings.

1978 Riviera coupe (B)

RIVIERA — SERIES 4BZ — V-8 — Riviera retained its new downsized look from 1977 with few significant changes, other than modest revisions in grille and taillamps. Spoked-look road wheels were intended to remind observers of its "classic-car orientation." Optional was a new electrically-driven height control system, with sensor mounted on car frame. Powerplants included the standard 350 cu. in. V-8 with four-barrel carburetor, or an optional 403 cu. in. V-8. Standard equipment included power steering, padded three-spoke steering wheel, and power front disc brakes (four-wheel discs optionsl). Rich velour 50/50 seats with dual front armrests, padded Rallye steering wheel, cut-pile carpeting, and custom wire wheel covers were standard. Chrome wire wheels were optional. The padded Landau roof option included coach lamps on the roof pillars. Most interesting to collectors and enthusiasts would be the 75th anniversary Riviera, commemorating the founding of the Buick company. Introduced at the Chicago Auto Show in February 1978, only 1,400 of the LXXV Rivieras were built. Two-tone bodies were silver on the bottom, black on top. Hood, trunk lid and vinyl top were also black. 'LXXV Buick' nameplates were on front fenders and trunk lid. Inside was gray leather upholstery and dark brushed silver trim plates on the dash, plus a sport steering wheel with brushed silver accent.

I.D. DATA: The 13-symbol Vehicle Identification Number (VIN) was again on the upper left surface of the instrument panel, visible through the windshield. Coding was similar to 1977, with the first digit ('4') indicating the Buick division. The second symbol is a letter indicating series: 'S' Skyhawk; 'T' Skyhawk S; 'B' Skylark; 'C' Skylark Custom; 'W' Skylark S; 'E' Century Special; 'H' Century Custom; 'G' Century Sport Coupe; 'L' Century Ltd.; 'J' Regal; 'K' Regal Sport Coupe; 'M' Regal Ltd.; 'F' LeSabre Custom Sport Coupe; 'N' LeSabre; 'P' LeSabre Custom; 'R' Estate Wagon; 'V' Electra 225; 'X' Electra Limited; 'U' Electra Park Ave.; 'Z' Riviera. Next comes two digits that denote body type: '07' Skyhawk hatchback coupe; '17' Skylark 2-dr. hatchback coupe; '27' Skylark 2-dr. coupe; '69' 4-dr. sedan; '09' aero 4-dr. sedan; '37' LeSabre/Electra 2-dr. coupe; '47' Regal 2-dr. coupe; '87' aero 2-dr. coupe; '35' 4-dr. wagon. The fifth symbol is a letter indicating engine code: 'C' V6-196 2Bbl.; 'A' V6-231 2Bbl. (LD5); '2' V6-231 2Bbl. (LC6); 'G' V6-231 2Bbl. (LC5); '3' V6-231 4Bbl.; 'Y' V8-301 2Bbl.; 'U' V8-305 2Bbl.); 'H' V8-305 4Bbl.; 'L' V8-350 4Bbl. (LM1); 'R' V8-350 4Bbl. (L34); 'X' V8-350 4Bbl. (L77); 'K' V8-403 4Bbl. (L80). The sixth symbol denotes model year ('8' 1978). Next is a plant code: 'U' Lordstown, OH; 'W' Willow Run, MI; 'T' Tarrytown, NY; 'G' Framingham, MA; 'H' Flint, MI; 'Z' Fremont, CA; 'C' Southgate, CA; 'X' Fairfax, KS; 'E' Linden, NJ. The final six digits are the sequential serial number, which began with 100001 except for Skyhawks built at Lordstown and LeSabre/Electra models built at Flint, which started at 400001. Engine numbers were stamped on the front right of the block, except for L34 350 cu. in. V-8 and 403 cu. in. V-8, which were stamped on the front of the left side of the block. A body number plate on the shroud identified model year, car division, series, style, body assembly plant, body number, trim combination, modular seat code, paint code, and date built code.

SKYHAWK (V-6)

Series Number	Body/Style Number	Body Type & Seating	Factory Price	Shipping Weight	Production Total
4H	T07	2-dr 'S' Hatch-4P	4103	2678	Note 1
4H	S07	2-dr. Hatch-4P	4367	2707	Note 1

Note 1: Total production for the model year, 24,589 Skyhawks.

SKYLARK 'S' (V-6/V-8)

4X	W27	2-dr Coupe-6P	3872/4022	3201/3369	9,050

SKYLARK (V-6/V-8)

4X	B27	2-dr Coupe-6P	3999/4149	3203/3371	33,037
4X	B17	2-dr Hatch-6P	4181/4331	3313/3481	2,642
4X	B69	4-dr Sedan-6P	4074/4224	3234/3402	40,951

SKYLARK CUSTOM (V-6/V-8)

4X	C27	2-dr Coupe-5P	4242/4392	3186/3354	12,740
4X	C17	2-dr Hatch-5P	4424/4574	3285/3453	1,277
4X	C69	4-dr Sedan-6P	4317/4467	3219/3387	14,523

Note 2: Of the 114,220 Skylarks built, 17,116 carried a V-8 engine (only 287 'S' Skylarks had a V-8).

CENTURY SPECIAL (V-6/V-8)

4A	E87	2-dr Coupe-6P	4389/4599	3003/3149	10,818
4A	E09	4-dr Sedan-6P	4486/4696	3014/3160	12,533
4A	E35	4-dr Sta Wag-6P	4976/5126	3148/3314	9,586

CENTURY CUSTOM (V-6/V-8)

4A	H87	2-dr Coupe-6P	4633/4843	3011/3157	12,434
4A	H09	4-dr Sedan-6P	4733/4943	3038/3184	18,361
4A	H35	4-dr Sta Wag-6P	5276/5426	3181/3349	24,014

CENTURY SPORT (V-6/V-8)

4A	G87	2-dr Coupe-6P	5019/5228	3051/3197	Note 3

CENTURY LIMITED (V-6/V-8)

4A	L87	2-dr Coupe-6P	4991/5201	3048/3294	Note 3
4A	L09	4-dr Sedan-6P	5091/5301	3075/3221	Note 3

Note 3: Production of Century Sport and Limited models is included in figures above.

REGAL (V-6/V-8)

4A	J47	2-dr Coupe-6P	4852/5042	2992/3138	236,652

REGAL SPORT (V-6)

4A	K47	2-dr Coupe-6P	5853	3153	Note 4

REGAL LIMITED (V-6/V-8)

4A	M47	2-dr Coupe-6P	5233/5423	3041/3187	Note 4

Note 4: Production total listed under base Regal includes Sport and Limited models.

LESABRE (V-6/V-8)

4B	N37	2-dr Coupe-6P	5384/5582	3446/3613	8,265
4B	N69	4-dr Sedan-6P	5459/5657	3439/3606	23,354

LESABRE CUSTOM (V-6/V-8)

4B	P37	2-dr Coupe-6P	5657/5855	3413/3580	53,675
4B	P69	4-dr Sedan-6P	5757/5955	3450/3617	86,638

LESABRE SPORT (V-6)

4B	F37	2-dr Coupe-6P	6213	3559	Note 5

Note 5: Production of LeSabre Sport Coupe is included in standard LeSabre coupe total. Only 29,408 LeSabres came with a V-6.

ESTATE WAGON (V-8)

4B	R35	4-dr Sta Wag-6P	6301	4063	25,964

ELECTRA 225 (V-8)

4C	V37	2-dr Coupe-6P	7144	3682	8,259
4C	V69	4-dr Sedan-6P	7319	3730	14,590

ELECTRA LIMITED (V-8)

4C	X37	2-dr Coupe-6P	7526	3710	33,365
4C	X69	4-dr Sedan-6P	7701	3757	65,335

ELECTRA PARK AVENUE (V-8)

4C	U37	2-dr Coupe-6P	7837	3730	Note 6
4C	U69	4-dr Sedan-6P	8088	3777	Note 6

Note 6: Production totals listed under Electra Limited include the Park Avenue model. Total Limited production, 63,977.

RIVIERA (V-8)

4E	Z37	2-dr Coupe-6P	8082	3701	20,535

Note 7: Riviera had a hefty price increase during the model year, reaching $9224.

FACTORY PRICE AND WEIGHT NOTE: Figure before the slash is for V-6 engine, after the slash for smallest (lowest-priced) V-8 engine available.

ENGINES: BASE V-6 (Century, Regal): 90-degree, overhead-valve V-6. Cast iron alloy block and head. Displacement: 196 cu. in. (3.2 liters). Bore & stroke: 3.5 x 3.4 in. Compression ratio: 8.0:1. Brake horsepower: 90 at 3600 R.P.M. (95 at 3800 w/automatic). Torque: 165 lbs.-ft. at 2000 R.P.M. (155 at 2000 w/automatic). Four main bearings. Hydraulic valve lifters. Carburetor: 2Bbl. Rochester 2GE. VIN Code: C. Sales Code: LC9. BASE V-6 (Skyhawk, Skylark, Century wagon, LeSabre); OPTIONAL (Century sed/cpe, Regal): 90-degree, overhead-valve V-6. Cast iron alloy block and head. Displacement: 231 cu. in. (3.8 liters). Bore & stroke: 3.8 x 3.4 in. Compression ratio: 8.0:1. Brake horsepower: 105 at 3400 R.P.M. Torque: 185 lbs.-ft. at 2000 R.P.M. Four main bearings. Hydraulic valve lifters. Carburetor: 2Bbl. Rochester 2GE. VIN Code: A. Sales Code: LD5. Note: Alternate LC6 version had VIN code 2. TURBOCHARGED V-6 (Regal and LeSabre Sport Coupes): Same as 231 V-6 above, except as follows: Brake horsepower: 150 at 3800 R.P.M. Torque: 245 lbs.-ft. at 2400 R.P.M. VIN Code: G. Sales Code: LC5. TURBOCHARGED FOUR-BARREL V-6; OPTIONAL (Regal and LeSabre Sport Coupes): Same as turbocharged V-6 above, but with M4ME carburetor. Brake horsepower: 165 at 4000 R.P.M. Torque: 285 lbs.-ft. at 2800 R.P.M. VIN Code: 3. Sales Code: LC8. OPTIONAL V-8 (LeSabre) 90-degree overhead-valve V-8. Cast iron alloy block and head. Displacement: 301 cu. in. (4.9 liters). Bore & stroke: 4.0 x 3.0 in. Compression ratio: 8.2:1. Brake horsepower: 140 at 3600 R.P.M. Torque: 235 lbs.-ft. at 2000 R.P.M. Five main bearings. Hydraulic valve lifters. Carburetor: 2Bbl. Rochester M2MC. Built by Pontiac. VIN Code: Y. Sales Code: L27. OPTIONAL V-8 (Skylark, Century, Regal, LeSabre): 90-degree overhead-valve V-8. Cast iron alloy block and head. Displacement: 305 cu. in. (5.0 liters). Bore & stroke: 3.736 x 3.48 in. Compression ratio: 8.5:1. Brake horsepower: 145 at 3800 R.P.M. Torque: 245 lbs.-ft. at 2400 R.P.M. Five main bearings. Hydraulic valve lifters. Carburetor: 2Bbl. Rochester 2GC. Built by Chevrolet. VIN Code: U. Sales Code: LG3. OPTIONAL V-8 (Century/Regal): 90-degree, overhead valve V-8. Cast iron alloy block and head. Displacement: 305 cu. in. (5.0 liters). Bore & stroke: 3.736 x 3.48 in. Compression ratio: 8.5:1. Brake horsepower: 160 at 4000 R.P.M. Torque: 285 lbs.-ft. at 2400 R.P.M. Five main bearings. Hydraulic valve lifters. Carburetor: 4Bbl. Rochester 4GC. VIN Code: H. Sales Code: LG4. BASE V-8 (Electra, Estate, Riviera); OPTIONAL (Skylark, LeSabre): 90-degree, overhead valve V-8. Cast iron alloy block and head. Displacement: 350 cu. in. (5.7 liters). Bore & stroke: 3.80 x 3.85 in. Compression ratio: 8.0:1. Brake horsepower: 155 at 3400 R.P.M. Torque: 280 lbs.-ft. at 1800 R.P.M. Five main bearings. Hydraulic valve lifters. Carburetor: 4Bbl. Rochester M4MC. VIN Code: X. Sales Code: L77. ALTERNATE 350-4 V-8 (LeSabre, Electra, Estate, Riviera): 90-degree, overhead valve V-8. Cast iron alloy block and head. Displacement: 350 cu. in. (5.7 liters). Bore & stroke: 4.057 x 3.385 in. Compression ratio: 8.0:1. Brake horsepower: 170 at 3800 R.P.M. Torque: 275 lbs.-ft. at 2000 R.P.M. Five main bearings. Hydraulic valve lifters. Carburetor: 4Bbl. Rochester M4MC. VIN Code: R. Ordering Code: L34. OPTIONAL V-8 (Skylark, Century wagon): 90-degree, overhead valve V-8. Cast iron alloy block and head. Displacement: 350 cu. in. (5.7 liters). Bore & stroke: 4.00 x 3.48 in. Compression ratio: 8.2:1. Brake horsepower: 170 at 3800 R.P.M. Torque: 275 lbs.-ft. at 2000 R.P.M. Five main bearings. Hydraulic valve lifters. Carburetor: 4Bbl. Rochester M4MC. Chevrolet-built. VIN Code: L. Ordering Code: LM1. OPTIONAL V-8 (LeSabre, Electra, Estate, Riviera): 90-degree, overhead valve V-8. Cast iron alloy block and head. Displacement: 403 cu. in. (6.6 liters). Bore & stroke: 4.351 x 3.385 in. Compression ratio: 8.0:1. Brake horsepower: 185 at 3600 R.P.M. Torque: 320 lbs.-ft. at 2000 R.P.M. Five main bearings. Hydraulic valve lifters. Carburetor: 4Bbl. Rochester M4MC. Built by Oldsmobile. VIN Code: K. Ordering Code: L80.

CHASSIS DATA: Wheelbase: (Skyhawk) 97.0 in.; (Skylark) 111.0 in.; (Century/Regal) 108.1 in.; (LeSabre/Estate/Riviera) 115.9 in.; (Electra) 118.9 in. Overall length: (Skyhawk) 179.3 in.; (Skylark) 200.2 in.; (Century) 196.0 in.; (Regal) 200.0 in.; (LeSabre/Riviera) 218.2 in.; (Electra) 222.1 in.; (Estate Wagon) 216.7 in. Height: (Skyhawk) 50.2 in.; (Skylark 2-dr.) 52.2 in.; (Skylark 4-dr.) 53.1 in.; (Century cpe) 54.1 in.; (Century sed) 55.0 in.; (Century wagon) 55.7 in.; (Regal) 53.4 in.; (LeSabre/Electra/Riviera cpe) 55.0 in.; (LeSabre sed) 55.7 in.; (Electra sed) 55.9 in.; (Estate) 56.5 in. Width: (Skyhawk) 65.4 in.; (Skylark) 72.7 in.; (Century/Regal) 70.1 in.; (LeSabre/Electra/Riviera) 77.2 in.; (Estate) 79.9 in. Front Tread: (Skyhawk) 54.7 in.; (Skylark) 59.1 in.; (Century/Regal) 58.5 in.; (LeSabre/Electra/Riviera) 61.8 in.; (Estate) 62.2 in. Rear Tread: (Skyhawk) 53.6 in.; (Skylark) 59.7 in.; (Century/Regal) 57.8 in.; (LeSabre/Electra/Riviera) 60.7 in.; (Estate) 64.0 in. Standard Tires: (Skyhawk) BR78 x 13 SBR; (Skyhawk 'S') B78 x 13; (Skylark) E78 x 14; (Skylark Custom) ER78 x 14 SBR; (Century cpe/sed) P185/75R14 SBR; (Century wag/Regal) P195/75R14 SBR; (Century/Regal Spt Cpe) P205/70R14 SBR; (LeSabre) FR78 x 15 GBR; (LeSabre Spt Cpe) GR70 x 15 SBR; (Electra/Riviera) GR78 x 15; (Estate) HR78 x 15 SBR.

TECHNICAL: Transmission: Three-speed, fully synchronized manual gearbox (column shift) standard on Skylark, Century cpe/sed, and Regal cpe; Turbo-Hydra-Matic optional. Four-speed manual gearbox available on Century/Regal. Four-speed, fully synchronized floor shift standard on Skyhawk; five-speed and automatic optional. Turbo-Hydra-Matic standard on Regal sedan, LeSabre, Electra, Estate and Riviera. Three-speed manual transmission gear ratios: (1st) 3.50:1; (2nd) 1.81:1 or 1.90:1; (3rd) 1.00:1; (Rev) 3.62:1. Four-speed gear ratios: (1st) 3.50:1; (2nd) 2.48:1; (3rd) 1.66:1; (4th) 1.00:1; (Rev) 3.50:1. Five-speed gear ratios: (1st) 3.40:1; (2nd) 2.08:1; (3rd) 1.39:1; (4th) 1.00:1; (5th) 0.80:1; (Rev) 3.36:1. Automatic transmission gear ratios: (1st) 2.52:1; (2nd) 1.52:1; (3rd) 1.00:1; (Rev) 1.93:1. Standard axle ratios: (Skyhawk) 2.93:1 w/manual, 2.56:1 w/automatic; (Skylark) 3.08:1 w/manual, 2.56:1 w/automatic, 2.41:1 w/V-8; (Century/Regal) 2.93:1 w/manual, 2.56:1 w/automatic and 196 V-6, 2.73:1 w/231 V-6, 2.29:1 w/305 V-8; (Century wagon) 2.73:1 exc. 2.41:1 w/305 V-8; (Regal Sport Coupe) 2.73:1; (LeSabre V-6) 2.73:1; (LeSabre V-8) 2.41:1; LeSabre V-6 Sport Coupe) 2.58:1; (LeSabre V-8 Sport Coupe) 3.08:1; (Electra/Riviera) 2.41:1; (Estate) 2.73:1 exc. 2.56:1 w/403 V-8. Other axle ratios were standard in California and for high-altitude operation. Hypoid bevel final drive. Steering: recirculating ball; power assist standard on Century/Regal, LeSabre, Electra, Estate and Riviera. Suspension: front/rear coil springs, independent front except Skylark, semi-elliptic rear leaf springs. Front wishbones with lower trailing links and anti-roll bar; rigid rear axle with lower trailing radius arms, upper torque arms and transverse linkage bar. Brakes: front disc, rear drum; power brakes standard on LeSabre/Electra/Riviera plus Century wagon and Regal Sport Coupe. Four-wheel power disc brakes optional on Riviera. Body construction: (Skyhawk) unitized; (Skylark) separate front frame unit cushion-mounted to unitized body; (others) separate body and perimeter box frame. High-Energy electronic ignition (HEI) on all engines. Fuel tank: (Skyhawk) 18.5 gal.; (Skylark/LeSabre) 21 gal.; (Century/Regal) 18.1 gal.; (Electra/Estate/Riv) 22.5 gal. Unleaded fuel only.

DRIVETRAIN OPTIONS: Engines: 231 cu. in. V-6, 2Bbl.: Century cpe/sed, Regal ($40). Turbocharged 231 cu. in. V-6, 4Bbl.: Regal/LeSabre spt cpe ($50). 301 cu. in. V-8, 2Bbl.: LeSabre ($198). 305 cu. in. V-8, 2Bbl.: Skylark ($150); Century ($150-$210); Regal ($190); LeSabre ($198). 305 cu. in. V-8, 4Bbl.: Skylark ($265); Century ($200-$260); Regal ($240). 350 cu. in. V-8, 4Bbl.: Century wagon ($265); LeSabre ($313). 403 cu. in. V-8, 4Bbl.: LeSabre ($403). Transmission/Differential: Four-speed manual floor shift: Century cpe/sed, Regal w/231 2Bbl. V-6 ($125). Five-speed manual floor shift: Skyhawk ($175). Automatic trans.: Skyhawk ($270); Skylark, Century cpe/sed, Regal ($307). Optional rear axle ratio: Skyhawk 2.93:1 (NC); Skylark 3.08:1 or 3.23:1 (NC); Century/Regal 2.73:1 or 3.23:1 (NC); LeSabre/Electra/Riv 2.73:1, 3.08:1 or 3.23:1 (NC). Positive traction differential: Skyhawk ($56); Skylark/Century/Regal ($60); LeSabre/Electra/Riviera ($64). Power Accessories: Power brakes: Skyhawk ($66); Skylark, Century cpe/sed, Regal ($69). Four-wheel disc brakes: Riviera ($199). Power steering: Skyhawk ($134); Skylark/Century/Regal ($152). Suspension: WH5 handling pkg.: Skyhawk ($101-$122). F40 Firm ride/handling pkg.: Skylark ($24); Century / Regal / LeSabre / Electra / Riv ($20). FE2 Rallye ride/handling pkg.: Skylark ($46); Century exc. wag and spt cpe. Regal ($36); Riv ($20). Automatic level control; Century / Regal / LeSabre / Electra/ Riv ($116). Other: Trailer towing flasher/harness; Skylark ($21-$34) exc. Skyhawk. Heavy-duty 80-amp alternator: LeSabre / Electra / Riv ($44)/ H.D. battery ($17-$20). H.D. cooling; Skylark / Electra / LeSabre / Riv ($29-$56). H.D. radiator: Skylark ($21); Engine block heater ($14) exc. Skyhawk. H.D. engine/transmission cooling: Century/Regal ($29-$56). High altitude emission system ($33). California emission system ($75).

SKYHAWK CONVENIENCE/APPEARANCE OPTIONS: Option Packages: Appearance group: 'S' ($73). Convenience group ($23). Shadow light Astroroof w/roof crown molding ($615). Manual glass sunroof ($215). Comfort/Convenience: Air cond. ($470). Rear defogger, electric ($79). Soft Ray tinted glass ($54). Tinted windshield ($42). Rally steering wheel: 'S' ($41). Tilt steering ($62). Electric clock ($19); w/tach ($69). Right sport mirror ($13). Remote left sport mirror ($18). Entertainment: AM radio ($74). AM/FM radio ($139). AM/FM stereo radio ($222). AM radio and 8-track player ($216). AM/FM stereo radio and 8-track ($320). Rear speaker ($23). Windshield antenna ($25); incl. w/radios. Exterior Trim: Door edge guards ($11). Roof crown molding ($176). Protective bodyside moldings ($28-$44). Hawk accent stripe ($36). Interior Trim/Upholstery: Full-length console ($77). Adjustable driver's seatback ($19). Front/rear mats ($18). Custom seatbelts ($16). Wheels: Custom sport wheels ($97). Deluxe wheel covers ($42). Wheel trim rings ($38). Tires: B78 x 13 WSW: 'S' ($35-$43). BR78 x 13 SBR BSW: 'S' ($84-$105). BR78 x 13 SBR WSW ($35-$148). BR70 x 13 SBR WLT ($64-$184). Conventional spare tire (NC).

SKYLARK CONVENIENCE/APPEARANCE OPTIONS: Option Packages: Sport Coupe or Sport Sedan pkg.: FE2 Rallye ride/handling suspension, ER78 x 14 SBR tires, black styling accents, sport mirrors ($182-$200); N/A on hatchback. Accessory pkg. (day/night mirror, lighter): 'S' ($14). Acoustic pkg. ($27-$40). Convenience group ($31-$34). Comfort/Convenience: Air cond. ($508). Cruise Master ($90). Two-speed wipers w/delay ($32). Rear defogger, blower-type ($51). Power windows ($118-$164). Electric door locks ($74- $103). Rallye steering wheel ($41). Tilt steering wheel ($69). Soft Ray tinted glass ($56). Tinted windshield ($44). Dual horns ($10). Electric clock ($22). Headlamps-on indicator ($10). Electric trunk release ($22). Remote left mirror ($16). Sport mirrors: left remote, right manual ($32). Entertainment: AM radio ($79). AM/FM radio ($149). AM/FM stereo radio ($236). AM radio and 8-track player ($279). AM/FM stereo radio and 8-track or cassette player ($341). Rear speaker ($23). Windshield antenna ($26); incl. w/radios. Exterior Trim: Landau vinyl top ($179-$184). Full vinyl top ($97-$102). Two-tone paint ($46). Special paint ($126). Swing-out rear quarter vent window: two-doors ($54). Protective bodyside moldings ($42). Roof drip and wheel opening moldings: 'S' ($36). Rocker panel moldings ($17); std. on Custom. Wide rocker appearance group ($43). Decklid molding ($9). Custom door and window frame moldings ($27- $34). Door edge guards ($11-$18). Bodyside stripes ($33). Bumper guards, front/rear ($40); front only ($20). Bumper strips, front/rear ($33). Interior Trim/Upholstery: Full- length console ($80). Vinyl bucket seats: base ($89). Cloth bucket seats: Custom ($109). Custom seatbelts ($16-$18). Front carpet savers ($9). Carpet savers and mats ($18). Carpeted door trim w/map pocket and reflector: base ($41). Wheels: Styled wheels ($22-$92). Chrome-plated wheels ($112- $130). Deluxe wheel covers ($38). Styled wheel covers ($63- $101). Deluxe wire wheel covers ($112-$150). Tires: E78 x 14 WSW ($35-$44). ER78 x 14 SBR BSW ($74-$92). ER78 x 14 SBR WSW ($35-$136). FR78 x 14 SBR WLT ($64-$171). Stowaway spare tire ($17).

CENTURY/REGAL CONVENIENCE/APPEARANCE OPTIONS: Option Packages: Century Custom Sport Wagon pkg. ($430). Electric sunroof: cpe ($499). Silver electric Astroroof: cpe ($699). Hatch roof: coupe ($625). Exterior molding pkg.: Century Spec., Regal ($9-$141). Convenience group: Century Spec. ($6-$44); Regal ($6-$18). Comfort/Convenience: Air cond. ($544). Automatic climate control air cond. ($626). Cruise Master ($90). Rear defogger, electric ($92). Tinted glass ($62). Tinted windshield ($45). Six-way power driver's seat ($151). Manual seatback recliner ($59); N/A Century Spec. sed/wag. Custom steering wheel: Century ($10) exc. Ltd. Rallye steering wheel: Century ($41) exc. Ltd.; Regal ($31). Sport steering wheel: Regal spt cpe ($31). Tilt steering ($69). Power windows ($124-$172). Electric door locks ($80-$112). Electric trunk release ($22). Remote tailgate lock: Century wag ($23). Electric clock, dial-type ($22). Digital clock ($49). Headlamps-on indicator ($10). Trip odometer ($12). Instrument gauges: temp and voltmeter ($26). Fuel usage light and instrument gauges ($55). Dome reading lamp ($18). Two-speed wiper with delay ($32). Lighting and Mirrors: Front light monitors ($28). Remote left mirror ($16). Remote right mirror ($28-$33). Sport mirrors: left remote ($27-$32). Dual remote sport mirrors ($52-$57). Lighted right visor vanity mirror ($45). Entertainment: AM radio ($83). AM/FM radio ($154). AM/FM stereo radio ($236); w/digital readout ($392). AM radio w/8-track ($233). AM/FM stereo radio w/8-track or cassette ($341-$351); w/CB ($571). Rear speaker: each ($24). Windshield antenna ($26); incl. w/radios. Automatic power antenna ($45-$71). Triband power antenna ($83-$109). Exterior Trim: Landau vinyl top: Regal ($140-$155); heavy-padded ($168-$216). Long vinyl top ($116). Designers' accent paint ($155-$206). Solid special color paint ($146). Bumper guards, front/rear ($40). Protective bodyside moldings ($33). Rocker panel moldings: Century Spec. ($17). Door edge guards ($11-$18). Wheel opening moldings: Century Spec. wag ($21). Bodyside stripes ($72-$93). Woodgrain vinyl applique: Century wag ($235-$256). Luggage rack: Century wag ($85). Air deflector: Century wag ($29). Interior Trim/Upholstery: Full-length console ($90). Bucket seats: Century Custom/spt cpe, Regal ($40). 55/45 seating: Century Custom/spt cpe, Regal ($98). Custom seatbelts ($16- $20). Load floor area carpet: Century Spec. wag ($49). Front carpet savers ($10); w/mats ($18). Front/rear carpet savers with inserts ($42); front ($23). Litter pocket ($8). Trunk trim covering ($30). Lockable storage compartment: Century wag ($35-$40). Wheels: Chrome-plated wheels: Century exc. Spt ($159); Regal ($141). Designers' sport wheels: Century exc. Spt ($117); Regal ($99). Deluxe wheel covers: Century exc. Spt ($38). Styled wheel covers: Century exc. Spt ($101); Regal ($63). Designers' wheel covers: Century exc. Spt ($65); Regal ($27). Wire wheel covers: Century exc. Spt ($150); Regal ($112). Tires: P185/75R14 GBR WSW: Century V-6 cpe/sed ($37). P195/75R14 GBR BSW: Century cpe/sed ($20). P195/75R14 GBR WSW ($39-$59). P195/75R14 SBR BSW: Century ($39-$59). P195/75R14 SBR WSW: Century ($78-$97). P205/70R14 SBR wide- oval BSW: Regal ($30). P205/70R14 SBR WSW: Century Spt, Regal ($42-$72). P205/70R14 SBR WLT ($54-$143).

LESABRE/ELECTRA/ESTATE WAGON/RIVIERA CONVENIENCE/APPEARANCE OPTIONS: Option Packages: Riviera Anniversary pkg.: black/silver Designers' Accent paint, gray 50/50 leather seats, carpeting and seatbelts ($586). Estate Wagon Limited pkg. ($1568). Estate Wagon convenience group ($12-$62). Exterior molding pkg.: LeSabre/Estate/Electra 225 ($37-$167). Convenience group: LeSabre ($19-$92). Power sunroof ($695-$778). Sliding Astroroof ($895-$978). Comfort/Convenience: Air cond. ($581). Automatic climate control air cond. ($669). Cruise Master ($95). Rear defogger, electric ($94). Soft Ray tinted glass ($76). Tinted windshield: LeSabre/Est ($46). Power windows: LeSabre/Est ($130-$190). Electric door locks ($82-$114). Automatic door locks: Electra/Riviera ($139-$167). Six-way power driver's seat ($120-$151). Dual power seats ($271- $302); N/A on base LeSabre. Electric seatback recliner, passenger ($113); N/A on base LeSabre sedan. Custom steering wheel: base LeSabre ($10). Rally steering wheel: LeSabre ($31-$41). Tilt steering ($70). Tilt/telescoping steering column ($46-$126). Digital clock (NC). Low fuel indicator ($10). Fuel usage light ($16); N/A spt cpe. Speed alert and trip odometer ($22). Remote electric tailgate lock: Estate ($32). Electric trunk release ($22). Theft deterrent system ($130); N/A on Estate. Three-speed wiper w/delay ($32). Lighting, Horns and Mirrors: Front cornering monitors: LeSabre/Est ($28). Front/rear monitors: Electra/Riviera ($60). Door courtesy/warning lights ($35-$55). Rear courtesy lamps: Est ($15). Headlamps-on indicator ($10). Dome reading lamp: LeSabre/Estate/Electra 225 ($18). Sunshade map light: Electra 225 ($12). Four-note horn ($22). Remote left mirror: LeSabre/Est ($16). Remote right mirror ($28-$33) exc. Riv. Remote right sport mirror: Riviera ($33). Dual remote sport mirrors ($36-$57) exc. Riv. Remote left mirror w/thermometer ($21-$37) exc. Riv. Lighted visor vanity mirror ($46). Entertainment: AM radio ($96); N/A on Riv. AM/FM radio ($165); N/A on Riv. AM/FM stereo radio ($239). AM/FM stereo w/digital readout: LeSabre/Est ($342-$ 392). AM radio and 8- track ($250); N/A on Riv. AM/FM stereo radio and 8-track or cassette player ($345-$355) exc. Riv ($106-$116). AM/FM stereo radio and CB ($577) exc. Riv ($338). Signal-seeking AM/FM stereo with 8-track: Electra ($514); Riv ($275). Rear speaker ($24) exc. Riv. Windshield antenna ($26) exc. Riv. Automatic power antenna ($45-$71). Triband power antenna ($83-$109). Exterior Trim: Landau vinyl top: LeSabre ($151). Heavy-padded landau vinyl top ($194-$405). Long vinyl top: LeSabre, Electra sed ($142-$161). Long, heavy-padded vinyl top: Electra/Riviera ($196). Two-tone paint: LeSabre ($56). Designers' accent paint: LeSabre/Riviera ($175-$201). Solid special color paint ($147) exc. Riviera Firemist ($165). Protective bodyside moldings ($42-$65). Hood ornament and windsplit: LeSabre/Est ($24). Door edge guards ($11-$18). Window frame scalp molding: LeSabre/Est ($33). Wheel opening moldings: LeSabre/Est ($26). Bodyside stripes ($50). Woodgrain vinyl applique: Estate ($235). Bumper guards, front/rear ($40); front, Estate ($20). Luggage rack w/air deflector: Estate ($135). Interior Trim/Upholstery: Third seat: Estate ($186). Custom seatbelts: LeSabre/Est ($20-$23). Front carpet savers ($11) exc. Riv. Carpet savers and handy mats ($21) exc. Riv. Front/rear carpet savers w/inserts: Riviera ($42); front ($23). Trunk carpeting/covering ($46- $58). Wheels: Chrome-plated wheels ($62-$161). Deluxe wheel covers: LeSabre ($38). Custom wheel covers ($28-$66) exc. Riv. Styled wheel covers ($65) exc. Riv. Moire wheel covers ($75-$113) exc. Riv. Deluxe wire wheel covers ($112-$150) exc. Riv. Custom red wire wheel covers: Riv (NC). Tires: FR78 x 15 GBR WSW: LeSabre ($37-$46). FR78 x 15 SBR: LeSabre ($39- $48). FR78 x 15 SBR WSW: LeSabre ($37-$46). GR78 x 15 SBR WSW ($39-$121). GR78 x 15 SBR wide WSW: LeSabre ($51-$136).

HISTORY: Introduced: October 6, 1977 (Regal Sport Coupe, August 1977). Model year production (U.S.): 803,187, for 9.0 percent of the industry total. Calendar year production (U.S.): 810,350. Model year sales by U.S. dealers: 795,316 (including 18,801 imported Opels). Calendar year sales (U.S.): 781,364 for an 8.4 percent market share.

Historical Footnotes: Buick now looked toward the youth market for potential customers. Said J.D. Duffy Jr., the new general sales manager, in *Ward's Auto World*: "We can't live on traditional Buick buyers. They're getting older every year." A record 776,515 domestic Buicks sold through U.S. dealers, more than 30,000 over the 1977 mark. Though impressive, the figure fell short of early forecasts. Defying predictions, Skyhawk and Skylark sales rose (as did the imported Opel), while mid- and full-size Buicks didn't reach expected levels. Trimmed-down Regals grew popular, but buyers didn't take so kindly to the new fastback Century sedan styling. And Riviera sales weakened when prospective buyers heard about the new front-drive version expected for 1979. Part of the loss in full-size sales, in fact, came because production at the Linden, New Jersey plant was halted early to allow for changeover to the new E-body Riviera. This helped cause model year production to fall somewhat for the year. As part of the 75th anniversary festivities, an open house at Flint in June, coupled with a gathering of the Buick Club of America drew 36,000 visitors. Over 600 early Buicks paraded through town. Late in 1978, Donald H. McPherson became the new general manager of Buick division.

1979 BUICK

Riviera was downsized for 1979 and switched to front- wheel drive, while LeSabre and Electra were carried over except for trim changes. The free-breathing 90-degree V-6 engine, in 3.2- and 3.8-liter displacements, got a new carburetor, intake manifold, exhaust manifold, and camshaft this year. It also received an improved two-barrel carburetor (Dual Jet 210).

1979 Skyhawk "Road Hawk" hatchback coupe (B)

SKYHAWK — SERIES 4H — V-6 — All Skyhawks got a new hood and front-end treatment with single rectangular headlamps, meant to enhance the car's sporty image. The new body-color grille was comprised of many small openings, wider than they were high, split into 12 sections by five wider vertical bars and a single horizontal bar. A Hawk insignia sat above the grille, in the center. Buick block letters were off to the side, above the grille. Rounded-corner housings held Skyhawk's headlamps, with wide parking/signal lamps below the front bumper. The freshly styled hood had twin creases that tapered inward toward the front. Vertical louvers tapered back to the rear, from the quarter windows. Sport mirrors were standard. Sole powerplant remained the 231 cu. in. (3.8-liter) V-6, with the same choice of three transmissions as before: standard four-speed floor shift, five-speed overdrive, or automatic. Base Skyhawks (S07) had an AM radio, full-length console, sport steering wheel, twin sport mirrors (left remote-controlled), bodyside accent stripes, and bumper guards. The fewer-frills 'S' edition was again available, with rattan vinyl interior. Two special packages were offered this year, both stressing the "hawk" theme with air dam, spoiler, and hawk decal. The top level, limited-edition Road Hawk option included a Rallye ride-and-handling package with larger stabilizer bars and blackwall BR70 x 13 steel-belted radial tires. The package included 'Road Hawk' markings, Oyster White vinyl bucket seats with hawk emblem, altered interior trim, new steering wheel, black windshield wipers, black window reveal moldings and grille, plus a front air dam and sporty decklid spoiler integrated into the rear quarter panel. Body color was light silver above the beltline, darker silver below. Road Hawks also included fast-ratio power steering (when power steering was ordered). Skyhawk's "Designers' Accent Edition" came with a bright red or yellow exterior, flat black accent along and below the beltline, hawk decal on the hood, rear spoiler, deluxe wheel covers, and sporty-tone exhaust system.

SKYLARK — SERIES 4X — V-6/V-8 — Skylark entered 1979 with a totally redesigned front end, including new grille. The grille's crosshatch pattern split into four sections, peaked at the front. Single round headlamps combined with wraparound two-section park/signal lamps. Buick still promoted Skylark's tall "greenhouse" with its "generous glass." Fenders again sported triple-ventiport trim strips. Two-door, four-door and hatchback bodies were offered, in base or Custom trim. Custom Skylarks included a stand-up hood ornament, rocker panel moldings, carpeted door trim, map pockets, plus a visor vanity mirror and lights for underhood, glove box, trunk and ashtray. The low-budget Skylark 'S' lacked a day/night mirror, lighter, roof drip and wheel opening moldings. The new, improved, highly efficient "free breathing" 231 cu. in. (3.8-liter) 2Bbl. V-6 was standard, with smoother airflow adding 10 horsepower over the 1978 version. Standard powertrain was again the three-speed manual shift, with automatic transmission optional. Two V-8s were available. The Sport package (for coupe or sedan) included black paint accents on grille, around headlamps, windshield, back windows and side-window frames; plus ER78 x 14 steel-belted tires, ride/handling suspension and black sport mirrors. It came in four body colors: silver, dark gold, yellow, or bright red. Sport models could also have black painted wide rocker treatment and black protective side moldings. New individual options included sporty interiors, an AM/FM stereo radio with cassette player, and a wider range of colors and paint combinations that included a Designers' Accent treatment with darker accent color on the side body panels.

1979 Century Turbo coupe (B)

CENTURY — SERIES 4A — V-6/V-8 — Century continued its fastback styling, introduced for 1978, with a reworked front end. A new crosshatch grille had three rows of rectangular "holes." Three-section parking/signal lamps stood outboard of single headlamps, while tri-section taillamps wrapped around the rear fenders. Four models made up the lineup: coupe, sedan, sport coupe, and station wagon. Engine choices were revised slightly. Base engine was again the even-firing 196 cu. in. (3.2-liter) V-6; but 3.8 V-6 in California, and on wagons. Normal and turbocharged 3.8 V-6s were available. So was a 301 cu. in. (4.9-liter) V-8. California models had an electronic fuel control system. A new Turbo Coupe package was described as an enthusiast's car, powered by the free-breathing turbocharged 231 cu. in. (3.8-liter) V-6. The performance package included automatic transmission, power brakes and dual exhausts, plus a sport steering wheel, turbo hood ornament, 'Turbo Coupe' trunk decal in big and bold billboard letters on rear deck panels, and a turbo hood blister with 'Turbo 3.8 Litre' badge. In short, you couldn't help but think a turbo engine might lurk under the hood. It also included a front air dam and rear spoiler, flat black paint trim, and turbine-design polycast wheels with 7 in. rims. Many of the Turbo Coupe features were first seen on Buick's 1976 Indy 500 Pace Car, including the four-barrel turbocharged V-6, an improved-flow cylinder head, dual exhausts, front air dam, and rear spoiler. Turbo Coupes were offered in white, silver, medium blue, dark gold, and red. Century's basic Sport Coupe included flat black trim in the grille and around headlamps and moldings; black wipers; plus a hawk decal high on front fenders, ahead of the door. The package also featured Designers' Sport wheels, wide steel-belted tires, Rallye ride/handling suspension, fast- ratio power steering (optional), and a rear spoiler. Custom and Special sedans and wagons were also available, plus a Sport Wagon option with Rallye suspension, large (P205/70R14) tires on Designers' Sport wheels, hawk decal, sport mirrors, air deflector, and special paint with black accents on grille, headlamp trim, wipers, moldings and pillars. Sport Wagons had wide rocker panels and wheel opening moldings. All wagons had a split tailgate: the glass portion lifted up like a hatch, while the bottom section folded down. Limited sedans carried the same plush interior as the Regal Limited coupe, including crushed velour 55/45 seats, plus wide rocker panel and belt reveal moldings and a custom steering wheel. All three option packages were offered in a choice of five body colors. New options included different interior fabrics, reclining driver's seat, sport steering wheel, and visor vanity mirrors.

1979 Regal Limited Landau Coupe (B)

REGAL — SERIES 4A — V-6/V-8 — Regal had been set apart from the Century line for the first time in 1978. This year, the formal roofline and full-cut wheel openings were unchanged. Subdued horizontal bars were added to the basic Regal's strong vertical-patterned grille, which again sloped outward at the base. Taillamps were newly designed. So was the instrument panel. Cornering lamps were made available on all Regal models. Single rectangular headlamps were flanked by clear vertical park/signal lamps. The Buick name was inset in the top bar of the grille; 'Regal' script stood near the lower corner. Ahead of the door was an emblem denoting engine size in litres. Standard engine was the 196 cu. in. (3.2-liter) V-6, except in California. Options included the larger 231 V-6, or 301 and 305 V-8s. Standard transmission was three-speed manual (except in California, where automatic was required). California cars added a new C-4 (Computer Controlled Catalytic Converter) system to control emissions, which included an electronically-controlled carburetor and three-way catalytic converter. As noted on its fender insignia, Regal's Sport Coupe had the turbo 231 V-6 under the hood. Also standard was a Rallye ride/handling suspension with front/rear stabilizer bars; firmer springs and shocks; fast-ratio power steering; P205/70R14 tires; and turbo boost gauge on the dash. A special Sport Coupe Decor Package included blackout trim around windshield, on rocker moldings, wipers, door pillars, around taillamps and license plate molding; plus a blacked-out grille, twin sport mirrors, and Designers' Accent paint treatment on hood, top and deck lid. Four Turbine wheels, too. Regal interiors carried handy door-pull assist straps. A simulated woodgrain instrument panel with large instruments in squares sat far forward to allow extra leg room. Regal Limited added wide chrome rocker panel moldings plus 'Limited' insignia below the 'Regal' script on the roof pillar. Inside were soft velour 55/45 notchback seats, plus crushed velour door inserts and rear-seat side trim. New Regal options included cornering lamps, turbine-styled wheels, and visor vanity mirrors. Also available: a silver-tinted Astroroof, metal sunroof or Hatch roof; plus three vinyl top styles.

1979 LeSabre Sport Coupe (B)

LESABRE — SERIES 4B — V-6/V-8 — LeSabre's new grille had thin vertical elements separated into three sections by two horizontal bars. Quad rectangular headlamps sat over separate park/signal lamps. Buick block letters were atop the upper grille corner. Rear fenders held the LeSabre nameplates. Restyled taillamps split into two wide sections by a horizontal bar, with clear backup lamps toward the center and amber lenses wrapping around the rear quarter panels. Inside was plenty of space for six passengers. Under the hood, a standard 231 cu. in. (3.8- liter) V-6 or choice of optional V-8 engines. Standard were power steering and brakes. The new top-line LeSabre Limited coupe and sedan, replacing the former Custom model, had a special molding package. LeSabre Sport Coupe continued the turbocharged V-6 powerplant introduced for 1978, with four-barrel and automatic transmission. Grille, windows and moldings sported flat black trim, and wheels were chrome-plated. The special handling package included large front and rear stabilizer bars, firm springs and shocks, plus quick-ratio power steering and wide oval tires. Eight different sound systems were available to please audio fans. A four-page brochure announced LeSabre's Palm Beach limited edition, which featured Designers' Accent paint treatment with yellow beige accent color on door-handle inserts, center pillar applique (with logo), lower bodyside and fender moldings, grille bar sides, wheel covers, and bumper rub strips. Inside were 55/45 seats trimmed in yellow beige Palm Beach cloth; woodgrain door, dash and steering wheel appliques; and Palm Beach logo on the dash. Judging by its brochure picture, the Palm Beach with gold bodyside striping was a curious and colorful beast, reminiscent of some of the pastel models of the Fifties.

ESTATE WAGON — SERIES 4BR — V-8 — Buick's full-size station wagon front end looked similar to LeSabre. As before, it seated up to eight with optional third seat. Cargo area amounted to 88.6 cubic feet with rear seat folded down. This year, Estate fender trim strips carried only three "ventiports" instead of the previous four. The Limited option package included a special grille, power windows, tilt steering column, 55/45 notchback seats, luggage rack with air deflector, chrome wheels, and simulated woodgrain vinyl applique. Two engine choices were offered: 350 or 403 cu. in. V-8s, both with automatic transmission.

1979 Electra Park Avenue sedan (B)

ELECTRA — SERIES 4C — V-8 — The posh full-size Buick got a new front end look this year with new quad rectangular headlamps, plus new vertical- style wraparound taillamps and new body colors. The new grille ran the entire car width, encompassing the headlamps. Its tiny crosshatch pattern was divided into a dozen sections by two horizontal and five vertical bars, slightly peaked at the front. Quad rectangular headlamps stood above horizontal park/signal lamps. The slanted headlamp bezels that had become an integral part of the Buick "look" were there again for 1979. Electra still displayed the four-section "ventiport" trim strip on squared-off front fenders a vestige of the portholes famed on Buicks through the 1950s. Full-width wraparound taillamps were accented by the Electra crest. One bright bodyside molding sat low, not far above the rocker panels. In addition to the 14 standard Buick colors, there were three new Firemist colors (gold, gray and saffron) available on Electras. Inside was new simulated butterfly woodgrain trim on the instrument panel. A base engine was the 350 cu. in. (5.7-liter) V-8 with 4Bbl. carburetor; optional, the 403 (6.6-liter) V-8, which wouldn't be around much longer. Electra 225 and Limited models were offered again, plus the plush Park Avenue. That Park Avenue edition included elegantly buttoned-and-tucked velvet upholstery with an armrest for each 50/50 section—a total of seven armrests in the car. Two velvet pockets were sewn into the back of the front seat. High-intensity reading lamps illuminated from the headliner. Outside were unique new coach lamps, using electroluminiscent panels that had no bulbs to burn out. Options included a lighted vanity mirror on the underside of the driver's sun visor, and a selection of five wheel cover styles.

1979 Riviera S Type Turbo coupe (B)

RIVIERA — SERIES 4BZ — V-6/V-8 — In Buick's words, the all-new Riviera was meant to be "a statement of what we think is to come, rather than simply a well-turned expression of what is already here." Freshly downsized, the new fifth-generation Riv was re-engineered to front-drive, sharing mechanical details with Cadillac Eldorado and Oldsmobile Toronado, and reclassified as a (spacious) four-passenger. Once again, it sported full-cut wheel openings and sweeping quarter panels. Underneath was a new fully independent suspension (front and rear), using front torsion bars and rear leaf springs, to improve the ride and handling. It included a standard rear stabilizer bar. Construction remained the separate body-and-frame design. Riv's raked-back front end and squared-off roofline suggested luxury. But this edition was almost a foot shorter overall than the 1978 Riviera, and 2 inches shorter in wheelbase. The grille was made up of vertical bars that sloped outward slightly, divided into eight sections by slightly wider bars. 'Riviera' script was at the side of the grille. Quad headlamps sat above clear parking/signal lamps. Another 'Riviera' script stood just ahead of the door, not far above the rocker panel molding. Two models were now available: luxury and sport. Standard Rivieras were powered by the 350 cu. in. (5.7-liter) V-8, but the sporty new S Type carried a special version of the turbocharged 231 cu. in. (3.8-liter) V-6 with four-barrel carburetor. This was the only turbo V-6 front-drive car made in the U.S. Actually, either Riviera model could be ordered with the other engine as an option. Though hardly a lightweight, the turbocharged Riv could hit 60 MPH in about 12 seconds, while returning fairly thrifty gas mileage on the road. Riviera's lengthy standard equipment list included a Delco AM/FM stereo radio with power antenna, six-way power driver's seat, power windows, power brakes and steering, automatic transmission, digital clock, air conditioning, Soft-Ray tinted glass, side-window defrosters, cornering lights, and automatic level control. Four-wheel disc brakes were again available; front discs standard. A wide variety of fabrics and leather upholstery was available. Standard setup was 45/55 seating with velour or vinyl and a folding center armrest. S Type had new bucket seats in vinyl or cloth, with leather available. Riviera also had maintenance-free wheel bearings, front and rear. The S Type's instrument panel was trimmed in brushed black, while its chassis held ride/handling extras. Standard equipment was firmer-rate front torsion bars and rear springs; firmer shock absorbers; larger-diameter stabilizer bars (front and rear); fast-ratio power steering; bucket seats and center storage console; plus a sport steering wheel with T-shaped center section and padded rim. Outside, the S Type had flat black trim around windows, and on grille and rocker panels; streamlined sport mirrors; amber front parking lights; and Designers' Sport wheel covers. New electronically-tuned (ETR) radios were available, with digital readout and signal seeking. Other notable (if not new) options: padded Landau top with coach lamps in roof pillars; electric sunroof; and glass Astroroof. A new digital speedometer and fuel gauge—part of the optional computer-controlled Trip Monitor—was offered later in the model year. Touch the right buttons and you could learn estimated time of arrival, how far you could travel on remaining fuel, and miles remaining to destination. Plus digital readouts of engine temperature, R.P.M. and voltage; current time, average speed and elapsed trip time; and a trip odometer. This option was a harbinger of things to come in digital equipment; but the standard Riviera dash still carried a conventional speedometer and fuel gauge.

I.D. DATA: The 13-symbol Vehicle Identification Number (VIN) was again on the upper left surface of the instrument panel, visible through the windshield. Coding was similar to 1978; see that listing for details. One series was added ('Y' Riviera S Type), and LeSabre (code 'P') was now called Limited rather than Custom. Engine coding (symbol five) was as follows: 'C' V6-196 2Bbl. (LD5); 'A' V6-231 2Bbl. (LD5); '2' V6-231 2Bbl. (LC6); '3' Turbo V6-231 4Bbl. (LC8); 'Y' V8-301 2Bbl. (L27); 'W' V8-301 4Bbl. (L37); 'G' V8-305 2Bbl. (LG3); 'H' V8-305 4Bbl. (LG4); 'L' V8-350 4Bbl. (LM1); 'R' V8-350 4Bbl. (L34); 'X' V8-350 4Bbl. (L77); 'K' V8-403 4Bbl. (L80). The sixth symbol (model year) changed to '9' for 1979. The code for the Lordstown plant changed to '7'.

1979 Skyhawk ''Designer Accent Edition'' hatchback coupe (B)

SKYHAWK (V-6)

Series Number	Body/Style Number	Body Type & Seating	Factory Price	Shipping Weight	Production Total
4H	T07	2-dr 'S' Hatch-4P	4380	2724	4,766
4H	S07	2-dr. Hatch-4P	4598	2740	18,373

SKYLARK 'S' (V-6/V-8)

4X	W27	2-dr Coupe-6P	4082/4277	3105/3224	1,605

BASE SKYLARK (V-6/V-8)

4X	B27	2-dr Coupe-6P	4208/4403	3114/3233	8,596
4X	B17	2-dr Hatch-6P	4357/4552	3195/3314	608
4X	B69	4-dr Sedan-6P	4308/4503	3158/3277	10,849

SKYLARK CUSTOM (V-6/V-8)

4X	C27	2-dr Coupe-5P	4462/4657	3123/3242	3,546
4X	C69	4-dr Sedan-6P	4562/4757	3176/3295	3,822

Note 1: Of the 20,053 base Skylarks built, 2,963 had a V-8; of the 7,368 Skylark Customs, 2,497 had a V-8.

CENTURY SPECIAL (V-6/V-8)

4A	E87	2-dr Coupe-6P	4599/4855	3038/3142	3,152
4A	E09	4-dr Sedan-6P	4699/4955	3053/3157	7,364
4A	E35	4-dr Sta Wag-6P	5247/5442	3158/3286	10,413

CENTURY CUSTOM (V-6/V-8)

4A	H87	2-dr Coupe-6P	4843/5099	3051/3155	2,474
4A	H09	4-dr Sedan-6P	4968/5224	3071/3175	6,987
4A	H35	4-dr Sta Wag-6P	5561/5756	3194/3322	21,100

CENTURY SPORT (V-6/V-8)

4A	G87	2-dr Coupe-6P	5151/5386	3047/3151	1,653

CENTURY LIMITED (V-6/V-8)

4A	L09	4-dr Sedan-6P	5336/5592	3104/3208	2,694

Note 2: Of the total 20,929 Century Specials built, 5,053 had a V-8 engine; of the 30,561 Century Customs, 16,110 were V-8 powered.

REGAL (V-6/V-8)

4A	J47	2-dr Coupe-6P	5080/5315	3029/3133	157,228

REGAL SPORT COUPE (TURBO V-6)

4A	K47	2-dr Coupe-6P	6223	3190	21,389

REGAL LIMITED (V-6/V-8)

4A	M47	2-dr Coupe-6P	5477/5712	3071/3175	94,748

LESABRE (V-6/V-8)

4B	N37	2-dr Coupe-6P	5680/5926	3428/3556	7,542
4B	N69	4-dr Sedan-6P	5780/6026	3459/3587	25,431

LESABRE LIMITED (V-6/V-8)

4B	P37	2-dr Coupe-6P	6124/6370	3454/3582	38,290
4B	P69	4-dr Sedan-6P	6249/6495	3503/3631	75,939

LESABRE SPORT COUPE (TURBO V-6)

4B	F37	2-dr Coupe-6P	6621	3545	3,582

Note 3: Only 14,851 base and Limited LeSabres had a V-6 engine.

ESTATE WAGON (V-8)

4B	R35	4-dr Sta Wag-6P	6714	4021	21,312

ELECTRA 225 V-8

4C	V37	2-dr Coupe-6P	7581	3767	5,358
4C	V69	4-dr Sedan-6P	7756	3831	11,055

ELECTRA LIMITED V-8

4C	X37	2-dr Coupe-6P	7981	3789	28,878
4C	X69	4-dr Sedan-6P	8156	3853	76,340

ELECTRA PARK AVENUE V-8

4C	U37	2-dr Coupe-6P	8423	3794	Note 4
4C	U69	4-dr Sedan-6P	8598	3860	Note 4

Note 4: Production totals listed under Electra Limited include Park Avenue models. A total of 61,096 Limiteds and 44,122 Park Avenue versions were produced. Note 5: Electra had massive price increases during the model year, of more than $1100. By mid-year, the base 225 coupe sold for $8703 and the Park Avenue sedan for $9959.

RIVIERA (V-8)

4E	Z57	2-dr Coupe-4P	10112	3759	37,881

RIVIERA S TYPE TURBO (V-6)

4E	Y57	2-dr Coupe-4P	10388	3774	14,300

Note 6: Total Riviera production includes 2,067 standard models with optional turbo V-6 engine, while S Type production includes 5,900 with a non-turbo V-8, which was offered as a price credit.

FACTORY PRICE AND WEIGHT NOTE: Figure before the slash is for V-6 engine, after the slash for smallest (lowest-priced) V-8 engine available.

ENGINES: BASE V-6 (Century, Regal): 90-degree, overhead-valve V-6. Cast iron alloy block and head. Displacement: 196 cu. in. (3.2 liters). Bore & stroke: 3.5 x 3.4 in. Compression ratio: 8.0:1. Brake horsepower: 105 at 4000 R.P.M. Torque: 160 lbs.-ft. at 2000 R.P.M. Four main bearings. Hydraulic valve lifters. Carburetor: 2Bbl. Rochester M2ME. VIN Code: C. Sales Code: LC9. BASE V-6 (Skyhawk, Skylark, Century wagon, LeSabre); OPTIONAL (Century sed/cpe, Regal): 90-degree, overhead-valve V-6. Cast iron alloy block and head. Displacement: 231 cu. in. (3.8 liters). Bore & stroke: 3.8 x 3.4 in. Compression ratio: 8.0:1. Brake horsepower: 115 at 3800 R.P.M. Torque: 190 lbs.-ft. at 2000 R.P.M. Four main bearings. Hydraulic valve lifters. Carburetor: 2Bbl. Rochester M2ME. VIN Code: A. Sales Code: LD5. Note: Alternate LC6 version (VIN code 2) with Computer Controlled Catalytic Converter (C4) and E2ME carburetor was used on California Century and Regal models. TURBOCHARGED V-6 (Regal and LeSabre Sport Coupes, Riviera S); OPTIONAL (Century, Riviera): Same as 231 V-6 above, but with M4ME four-barrel carburetor. Brake horsepower: 170 at 4000 R.P.M. (Century, 175 at 4000; Riviera, 185 at 4200). Torque: 265 lbs.-ft. at 2800 R.P.M. (Century, 275 at 2600; Riviera, 280 at 2400). VIN Code: 3. Sales Code: LC8. OPTIONAL V-8 (Century, Regal, LeSabre): 90-degree overhead-valve V-8. Cast iron alloy block and head. Displacement: 301 cu. in. (4.9 liters). Bore & stroke: 4.0 x 3.0 in. Compression ratio: 8.1:1. Brake horsepower: 140 at 3600 R.P.M. Torque: 235 lbs.-ft. at 2000 R.P.M. Five main bearings. Hydraulic valve lifters. Carburetor: 2Bbl. Roch. M2MC. Built by Pontiac. VIN Code: Y. Sales Code: L27. OPTIONAL V-8 (Century, Regal): Same as above but with M4MC 4Bbl. carburetor. Brake horsepower: 150 at 4000 R.P.M. Torque: 240 lbs.-ft. at 2000 R.P.M. VIN Code: W. Sales Code: L37. OPTIONAL V-8 (Skylark): 90-degree overhead-valve V-8. Cast iron alloy block and head. Displacement: 305 cu. in. (5.0 liters). Bore & stroke: 3.736 x 3.48 in. Compression ratio: 8.4:1. Brake horsepower: 115 at 3800 R.P.M. Torque: 245 lbs.-ft. at 2000 R.P.M. Five main bearings. Hydraulic valve lifters. Carburetor: 2Bbl. Rochester M2MC. Built by Chevrolet. VIN Code: U. Sales Code: LG3. OPTIONAL V-8 (Century/Regal in California and for high-altitude operation): 90-degree, overhead valve V-8. Cast iron alloy block and head. Displacement: 305 cu. in. (5.0 liters). Bore & stroke: 3.736 x 3.48 in. Compression ratio: 8.4:1. Brake horsepower: 130 at 3200 R.P.M. Torque: 225 lbs.-ft. at 2400 R.P.M. Five main bearings. Hydraulic valve lifters. Carburetor: 4Bbl. Rochester M4MC. VIN Code: H. Sales Code: LG4. BASE V-8 (Electra, Estate); OPTIONAL (LeSabre): 90-degree, overhead valve V-8. Cast iron alloy block and head. Displacement: 350 cu. in. (5.7 liters). Bore & stroke: 3.80 x 3.85 in. Compression ratio: 8.0:1. Brake horsepower: 155 at 3400 R.P.M. Torque: 280 lbs.-ft. at 1800 R.P.M. Five main bearings. Hydraulic valve lifters. Carburetor: 4Bbl. Rochester M4MC. VIN Code: X. Sales Code: L77. ALTERNATE 350-4 V-8 (Estate in California, Riviera); OPTIONAL (Calif./high-altitude LeSabre/Electra; Riviera S): 90-degree overhead-valve V-8. Cast iron alloy block and head. Displacement: 350 cu. in. (5.7 liters). Bore & stroke: 4.057 x 3.385 in. Compression ratio: 8.0:1. Brake horsepower: 160 at 3800 R.P.M. Torque: 270 lbs.-ft. at 2000 R.P.M. Five main bearings. Hydraulic valve lifters. Carburetor: 4Bbl. Rochester M4MC. Built by Oldsmobile. VIN Code: R. Ordering Code: L34. OPTIONAL V-8 (Skylark, Century wagon): 90-degree, overhead

valve V-8. Cast iron alloy block and head. Displacement: 350 cu. in. (5.7 liters). Bore & stroke: 4.00 x 3.48 in. Compression ratio: 8.2:1. Brake horsepower: 165 at 3800 R.P.M. Torque: 260 lbs.-ft. at 2400 R.P.M. Five main bearings. Hydraulic valve lifters. Carburetor: 4Bbl. Rochester M4MC. Chevrolet-built. VIN Code: L. Ordering Code: LM1. OPTIONAL V-8 (Electra): 90-degree, overhead valve V-8. Cast iron alloy block and head. Displacement: 403 cu. in. (6.6 liters). Bore & stroke: 4.351 x 3.385 in. Compression ratio: 8.0:1. Brake horsepower: 175 at 3600 R.P.M. Torque: 310 lbs.-ft. at 2000 R.P.M. Five main bearings. Hydraulic valve lifters. Carburetor: 4Bbl. Roch. M4MC. Built by Oldsmobile. VIN Code: K. Ordering Code: L80.

CHASSIS DATA: Wheelbase: (Skyhawk) 97.0 in.; (Skylark) 111.0 in.; (Century/Regal) 108.1 in.; (LeSabre/Estate) 115.9 in.; (Electra) 118.9 in.; (Riviera) 114.0 in. Overall length: (Skyhawk) 179.3 in.; (Skylark) 200.2 in.; (Century) 196.0 in.; (Regal) 200.0 in.; (LeSabre) 218.2 in.; (Electra) 222.1 in.; (Estate) 216.7 in.; (Riv) 206.6 in. Height: (Skyhawk) 50.2 in.; (Skylark 2-dr.) 52.2 in.; (Skylark 4-dr.) 53.1 in.; (Century cpe) 54.1 in.; (Century sed) 55.0 in.; (Century wagon) 55.7 in.; (Regal) 53.4 in.; (LeSabre/Electra cpe) 55.0 in.; (LeSabre sed) 55.7 in.; (Electra sed) 55.9 in.; (Estate) 56.5 in.; (Riv) 54.3 in. Width: (Skyhawk) 65.4 in.; (Skylark) 72.7 in.; (Century/Regal cpe) 76.5 in.; (Century/Regal) 72.2 in.; (LeSabre/Electra) 77.2 in.; (Estate) 79.9 in.; (Riv) 70.4 in. Front Tread: (Skyhawk) 54.7 in.; (Skylark) 59.1 in.; (Century/Regal) 58.5 in.; (LeSabre/Electra) 61.8 in.; (Estate) 62.2 in.; (Riv) 59.3 in. Rear Tread: (Skyhawk) 53.6 in.; (Skylark) 59.7 in.; (Century/Regal) 57.8 in.; (LeSabre/Electra) 60.7 in.; (Estate) 64.0 in.; (Riv) 60.0 in. Standard Tires: (Skyhawk) BR78 x 13; (Skyhawk 'S') B78 x 13; (Skylark) E78 x 14; (Century cpe/sed) P185/75R14 GBR; (Century wag/Regal) P195/75R14 GBR; (Century/Regal Spt Cpe) P205/70R14 SBR; (LeSabre) FR78 x 15 GBR; (LeSabre Spt Cpe) GR70 x 15 SBR: (Electra) GR78 x 15; (Estate) HR78 x 15 SBR.

TECHNICAL: Transmission: Three-speed, fully synchronized manual gearbox standard on Skylark (column), Century cpe/sed (floor), and Regal cpe (floor); Turbo Hydra-matic optional. Four-speed manual gearbox available on Century/Regal. Four-speed, fully synchronized floor shift standard on Skyhawk; five-speed and automatic optional. Turbo-Hydra-Matic standard on Regal sedan, LeSabre, Electra, Estate and Riviera. Three-speed manual trans. gear ratios: (1st) 3.50:1; (2nd) 1.81:1; (3rd) 1.00:1; (Rev) 3.62:1. Four-speed gear ratios: (1st) 3.50:1; (2nd) 2.48:1; (3rd) 1.66:1; (4th) 1.00:1; (Rev) 3.50:1. Five-speed gear ratios: (1st) 3.40:1; (2nd) 2.08:1; (3rd) 1.39:1; (4th) 1.00:1; (5th) 0.80:1; (Rev) 3.36:1. Automatic trans. gear ratios: (1st) 2.52:1; (2nd) 1.52:1; (3rd) 1.00:1; (Rev) 1.93:1. Electra automatic: (1st) 2.48:1; (2nd) 1.48:1; (3rd) 1.00:1; (Rev) 2.08:1. Century V-8/Riviera automatic: (1st) 2.74:1; (2nd) 1.57:1; (3rd) 1.00:1; (Rev) 2.07:1 (Riviera 2.57:1). Standard axle ratios: (Skyhawk) 2.93:1; (Skylark V-6) 3.08:1; (Skylark V-8) 2.41:1; (Century V6196) 2.93:1; (Century V6231, V8350) 2.73:1; (Century V8301) 2.29:1; (Century V8305) 2.41:1; (Century Turbo cpe) 3.08:1; (Regal) 2.93:1 exc. V-8, 2.29:1; (Regal Sport Coupe) 2.41:1; (LeSabre V-6) 2.73:1; (LeSabre V8301) 2.29:1; (LeSabre V-8) 2.41:1; (LeSabre V-6 Sport Coupe) 2.73:1; (Electra/Riviera) 2.41:1; (Riviera turbo) 2.93:1; (Estate) 2.73:1 exc. V8403, 2.41:1. Steering: recirculating ball; power assist standard on Century/Regal, LeSabre, Electra, Estate and Riviera. Suspension: (Riviera) front wishbones, longitudinal torsion bars and anti-roll bar; independent rear with swinging longitudinal trailing arms, transverse linkage bar and automatic leveling; front-wheel drive. (others) same as 1977- 78. Brakes: front disc, rear drum; power brakes standard on LeSabre/Electra/Riviera plus Century wagon and Regal Sport Coupe. Four-wheel power disc brakes optional on Riviera. Body construction: (Skyhawk) unitized; (Skylark) separate front frame unit cushion-mounted to unitized body; (others) separate body and frame. Fuel tank: (Skyhawk) 18.5 gal.; (Skylark) 21 gal.; (Century/Regal) 18.1 gal.; (LeSabre/Electra) 25.3 gal.; (Estate) 22.5 gal.; (Riv) 20 gal. Unleaded fuel only. High-Energy electronic ignition (HEI) on all engines.

DRIVETRAIN OPTIONS: Engines: 231 cu. in. V-6, 2Bbl.: Century cpe/sed, Regal ($40); Turbocharged 231 cu. in. V-6, 4Bbl.: Century cpe/sed ($470); Riv ($110). 301 cu. in. V-8, 2Bbl.: Century/Regal ($195-$256); LeSabre ($246). 301 cu. in. V-8, 4Bbl.: Century/Regal ($255-$316); 305 cu. in. V-8, 2Bbl.: Skylark ($195); 305 cu. in. V-8, 4Bbl.: Century/Regal ($255-$316). 350 cu. in. V-8, 4Bbl.: Skylark ($320); Century wagon ($320); LeSabre ($371); Riviera S (credit $110). 403 cu. in. V-8, 4Bbl.: Electra/Estate ($70). Transmission/Differential: Four- speed manual floor shift: Century cpe/sed, Regal with 231 V-6 ($135); Five-speed manual floor shift: Skyhawk ($175); Automatic trans.: Skyhawk ($295); Skylark, Century cpe/sed, Regal ($335); Optional rear axle ratio: Skylark 2.9:1, 3.08:1 or 3.23:1 (NC). Limited slip differential ($60-$68) exc. Riviera. Power Accessories: Power brakes: Skyhawk ($71); Skylark/Century/Regal ($76). Four-wheel disc brakes: LeSabre spt cpe, Riv ($205). Power steering: Skyhawk ($146); Skylark/Century/Regal ($163). Suspension: F40 Firm ride/handling pkg.: all exc. Skyhawk ($21). FE2 Rallye ride/handling pkg.: Century/Regal ($38). FE2 Rallye ride/handling pkg. incl. rear stabilizer bar: Skylark ($48), included in Sport package. Automatic level control: Century / Regal / LeSabre / Electra ($121). Other: Trailer towing flasher / harness package: Skylark / Century / Regal / LeSabre / Electra ($22-$35). Heavy-duty alternator, 80-ampere: LeSabre / Electra / Riviera V-8 ($43-$46). Heavy-duty battery ($18-$21). Heavy-duty cooling: Skyhawk / Skylark ($30-$58). Heavy-duty radiator; Skylark V-8 ($22). Engine block heater ($15). Heavy-duty engine/transmission cooling: Century / Regal / LeSabre / Electra / Riviera ($30-$58). High altitude emission system ($35). California emission system ($83-$150).

SKYHAWK CONVENIENCE/APPEARANCE OPTIONS: Option Packages: Road Hawk pkg. (BR70 x 13 SBR wide-oval blackwall tires, specific suspension, blackout molding (N/A). Appearance group (wheel opening moldings and bodyside stripe): 'S' ($57). Acoustic pkg. ($25). Convenience group: day/night mirror, underhood light, glove box light, headlamp- on indicator ($24). Shadow light Astroroof ($641). Vista Vent roof ($180). Comfort/Convenience: Air cond. ($496). Rear defogger, electric ($87). Tinted glass ($60). Tinted windshield ($50). Tilt steering ($68). Instrument gauges, electric clock and tach ($73). Electric clock ($21). Visor vanity mirrors, pair ($10). Entertainment: AM/FM radio ($74). AM/FM stereo radio ($148). AM radio and 8-track player ($157). AM/FM stereo radio and 8-track ($250). Rear speaker ($23). Exterior Trim: Door edge guard moldings ($12). Roof crown moldings ($183). Protective bodyside moldings ($10-$45). Designer's accent paint ($175). Interior Trim/Upholstery: Adjustable driver's seatback ($20). front/rear mats ($21). Custom seatbelts ($18). Wheels and Tires: Custom sport wheels ($58). Styled aluminum wheels ($230). B78 x 13 WSW ($36-$45) BR78 x 13 SBR BSW ($89-$111). BR78 x 13 SBR WSW ($36-$158). BR70 x 13 SBR wide-oval WLT ($49-$194). Conventional spare tire (NC).

SKYLARK CONVENIENCE/APPEARANCE OPTIONS: Option Packages: Sport Coupe or Sport Sedan pkg.: FE2 Rallye ride/handling suspension, ER78 x 14 SBR tires, sport mirrors ($202-$221); N/A on Skylark 'S'. Accessory pkg. (day/night mirror, lighter): 'S' ($15). Acoustic pkg. ($28-$42). Convenience group ($32-$43). Comfort/Convenience: Air cond. ($529). Cruise Master ($103). Two-speed wipers w/low-speed delay ($38). Rear defogger, blower-type ($55). Power windows ($126-$178). Electric door locks ($80-$111). Sport steering wheel ($42). Tilt steering ($75). Tinted glass ($64). Tinted windshield ($50). Dual horns ($10). Electric clock ($24). Headlamps-on indicator ($11). Remote-control left mirror ($18). Sport mirrors: left remote, right manual ($45). Electric trunk release ($24). Entertainment: AM radio ($82). AM/FM radio ($158). AM/FM stereo radio ($236). AM radio and 8-track player ($244). AM/FM stereo radio and 8-track or cassette ($345). Rear speaker ($25). Windshield antenna ($29); incl. w/radios. Exterior Trim: Landau vinyl top ($190- $195). Long vinyl top ($99-$104). Two-tone painted top ($48). Designers' accent paint ($161). Swing-out rear quarter vent window: two-doors ($59). Protective bodyside moldings ($43). Roof drip and wheel opening moldings: 'S' ($38). Rocker panel moldings ($18); std. on Custom. Wide rocker appearance group ($45). Decklid molding ($10). Custom door and window frame moldings ($28-$35). Door edge guards ($13-$21). Bodyside stripes ($34). Bumper guards, front/rear ($45). Bumper strips, front/rear ($37). Interior Trim/Upholstery: Full- length console ($80). Vinyl bucket trim: base Skylark ($90). Custom seatbelts ($19-$21). Front carpet savers ($15). Carpet savers and handy mats ($25). Carpeted door trim with map pocket and reflector: base ($43). Wheels: Styled wheels ($80- $99). Chrome-plated wheels ($120-$139). Deluxe wheel covers ($42). Custom wire wheel covers ($118-$160). Tires: E78 x 14 WSW ($37-$46). ER78 x 14 SBR BSW ($78-$97). ER78 x 14 SBR WSW ($37-$143). FR78 x 14 SBR WLT ($67-$180). Stowaway spare tire ($19).

CENTURY/REGAL CONVENIENCE/APPEARANCE OPTIONS: Option Packages and Groups: Regal Sport Coupe Decor ($473). Century Special Sport Wagon pkg. ($473). Century Turbo Coupe pkg.: special suspension, sporty exhaust, turbine wheels, decklid identification ($40). Electric sunroof: coupe ($529). Silver electric Astroroof: coupe ($729). Hurst hatch roof: Regal ($655). Exterior molding pkg. ($10-$147). Convenience group ($6-$58). Comfort/Convenience: Air cond. ($562). Automatic air cond. ($653). Cruise Master ($103). Rear defogger, electric ($99). Tinted glass ($70). Tinted windshield ($50). Six-way power driver's seat ($163). Manual seatback recliner ($62). Custom steering wheel: Century ($10). Sport steering wheel ($32-$42). Tilt steering ($75). Power windows ($132-$187). Electric door locks ($86-$120). Electric trunk release ($24). Remote tailgate lock: Century wag ($25). Electric dial clock ($24). Digital clock ($55). Headlamps-on indicator ($11). Trip odometer ($13). Instrument gauges ($27). Fuel usage light and instrument gauges ($57). Dome reading lamp ($19). Windshield wiper w/delay ($38). Lighting and Mirrors: Cornering lamps: Regal ($49). Front light monitors ($29). Remote left mirror ($18); right ($34-$39). Sport mirrors: left remote ($40-$45). Dual remote sport mirrors (25-$70). Visor vanity mirrors, pair ($10). Lighted right visor vanity mirror ($46). Entertainment: AM radio ($86). AM/FM radio ($163). AM/FM stereo radio ($236). AM radio w/8-track ($248); w/digital readout ($402); w/CB ($574). AM/FM stereo radio w/8-track or cassette ($345-$351). Rear speaker ($25). Windshield antenna ($29); incl. with radios. Automatic antenna ($47-$76). Triband power antenna ($86-$115). Exterior Trim: Landau vinyl top: Regal ($146- $162); heavy-padded ($178-$228). Long vinyl top ($116). Designers' accent paint ($161-$213). Solid special color paint ($152). Bumper guards, front/rear ($45). Protective bodyside moldings ($48). Rocker panel moldings: Century Special ($18). Door edge guards ($13-$21). Belt reveal moldings ($34). Wheel opening moldings: Century Spec. wag ($22). Bodyside stripes ($34). Woodgrain vinyl applique: Century wag ($267-$289). Luggage rack: Century wag ($90). Air deflector: Century wag ($30). Interior Trim/Upholstery: Full- length console ($90). Bucket seats: Century Custom, Regal ($45); Century sport ($181). 55/45 seating: Century Custom, Regal ($102); Century spt ($238). Limited 55/45 seating: Regal spt cpe ($272). Notchback seating: Century spt ($136). Custom seatbelts ($19-$22). Load floor carpet area: Century Spec. wag ($51). Front carpet savers ($15-$25). Carpet savers and mats ($25). Front/rear carpet savers with inserts ($45). Litter pocket ($9). Trunk trim covering ($31). Loackable storage compartment: Century wag ($37-$42). Wheels: Chrome-plated wheels ($44-$169). Designer's sport wheels ($106-$125). Deluxe wheel covers: Century exc. spt ($42). Designer's wheel covers: Century exc. spt ($70); Regal ($28). Custom wire wheel covers: Century exc. spt ($160); Regal ($118). Tires: P185/75R14 GBR WSW: Century cpe/sed ($39). P195/75R14 GBR BSW: Century cpe/sed ($21). P195/75R14 GBR WSW ($40-$61). P195/75R14 SBR BSW: Century ($41-$61). P195/75R14 SBR WSW: Century ($81-$101). P205/70R14 SBR wide-oval BSW: Regal ($32). P205/70R14 SBR WSW: Century spt. Regal ($44-$76). P205/70R14 SBR WLT ($56-$149)

LESABRE/ELECTRA/ESTATE WAGON CONVENIENCE/APPEARANCE OPTIONS: Option Packages: LeSabre coupe Sport pkg.: cloth front bucket seats, remote sport mirror ($160); w/ full-length console ($254). Estate Wagon convenience group ($13-$68). Estate Wagon Limited pkg.: 55/45 front seating, tilt steering, custom belts, power windows, electric door locks, remote tailgate lock, remote left mirror, chromed wheels, luggage rack, bumper guards, map light, dial clock, exterior molding pkg., woodgrain vinyl applique, acoustic pkg., special ornamentation ($1853). Exterior molding pkg. ($53-$173). Convenience group: LeSabre ($19-$99). Electric sunroof ($725- $798). Sliding Astroroof ($925-$998). Comfort/Convenience: Air cond. ($605). Automatic air cond. ($688). Cruise Master ($108). Rear defogger, electric ($101). Tinted glass ($84). Tinted windshield: LeSabre, Estate ($51). Power windows: LeSabre, Estate ($138-$205). Electric door locks ($88-$122). Automatic door locks: Electra ($146-$175). Six-way power driver's seat ($135-$166). Dual power seats ($301-$332); N/A on base models. Manual seatback recliner, one side: LeSabre base or sport cpe ($62). Electric seatback recliner, one side ($118); N/A on base LeSabre sedan. Custom steering wheel: base LeSabre ($10). Sport steering wheel: LeSabre ($32-$42). Tilt steering ($77). Tilt/telescoping steering column ($44- $131). Digital clock: LeSabre, Estate (NC w/convenience group). Low fuel indicator ($17). Fuel usage light ($30). Speed alert and trip odometer ($23). Remote electric tailgate lock: Est ($34). Electric trunk release ($25). Electric fuel cap lock ($36). Theft deterrent system ($135); N/A on Estate. Three-speed wiper w/low-speed delay ($39). Lighting, Horns and Mirrors: Cornering lamps ($49). Front light monitors: LeSabre/Est ($29). Front/rear monitors: Electra ($62). Door courtesy/warning light ($36-$57). Rear courtesy lamps: Estate ($16). Headlamps-on indicator ($11). Dome reading lamp ($19). Sunshade map light: Electra 225 ($13). Four-note horn ($23). Remote left mirror: LeSabre/Est ($19). Remote right mirror ($34-$39). Dual remote sport mirrors ($49-$65). Dual electric remote mirrors: Electra ($97). Remote left mirror w/thermometer ($21-$38). Dual electric mirrors w/left thermometer: Electra ($118). Visor vanity mirrors, pair ($10). Lighted visor vanity mirror ($47). Entertainment: AM radio ($99); N/A on Electra. AM/FM radio ($174). AM/FM stereo radio ($239); w/CB ($581). AM/FM stereo radio w/digital readout: LeSabre, Estate ($347-$402). AM radio and 8-track ($265). AM/FM stereo radio and 8-track or cassette player ($349-$355). AM/FM stereo with 8-track and CB: Electra ($691). Signal-seeking AM/FM stereo radio with CB: Electra ($789); w/CB and 8-track ($899). Signal-seeking AM/FM stereo radio w/digital readout: Electra ($447); w/8-track ($557). Rear speaker ($26). Windshield antenna ($29); incl. w/radios. Automatic power antenna ($48-$77). Triband power antenna ($87-$116). Exterior Trim: Landau vinyl top: LeSabre ($155). Heavy-padded landau vinyl top: Electra ($200). Long vinyl top ($145-$164). Long, heavy-padded vinyl top: Electra ($206). Two-tone painted top: LeSabre ($58). Designers' accent paint: LeSabre, Estate ($182-$240). Solid special color paint ($153) exc. Firemist on Electra ($172). Protective bodyside moldings: LeSabre/Est ($43). Color-coordinated bodyside moldings: Electra ($66). Hood ornament and windsplit: LeSabre/Est ($25). Door edge guards ($14-$21). Window frame scalp molding: LeSabre/Est ($34). Wheel opening moldings: LeSabre/Est ($27). Belt reveal molding: LeSabre spt cpe ($34). Bodyside stripes ($52); N/A on Estate. Woodgrain vinyl applique: Estate ($293). Bumper guards, front/rear ($45). Luggage rack w/air deflector: Est ($140). Interior Trim/Upholstery: Custom seat trim: notchback, LeSabre spt cpe or Estate ($404); 55/45 ($506); 55/45, LeSabre Ltd or Electra ($102). Third seat: Estate ($194). Custom seatbelts: LeSabre/Est ($22-$25). Full-length console: LeSabre cpe w/sport pkg. ($94). Front carpet savers ($15-$25). Front/rear carpet savers w/inserts ($45). Litter pocket ($9). Trunk carpeting/covering ($48-$60). Wheels: Deluxe wheel covers: LeSabre ($42). Custom wheel covers ($29-$71). Wire wheel covers ($87-$161). Chrome-plated wheels ($120-$171). Wire spoke wheels ($473-$625). Stowaway spare tire (N/C).

RIVIERA CONVENIENCE/APPEARANCE OPTIONS: Roof Options: Electric sunroof ($798). Electric Astroroof ($998). Comfort/Convenience: Automatic air cond. ($88). Cruise Master ($108). Rear defogger, electric ($101). Automatic door locks ($58). Six-way power seat, passenger ($166). Electric seatback recliner, one side ($118). Manual seatback recliner, one side: S ($62). Sport steering wheel ($32). Tilt steering ($77). Tilt/telescope steering wheel ($121). Electric fuel cap lock ($36). Electric trunk release ($25). Electric trunk lock ($60). Low fuel indicator, V-8 ($17). Fuel usage light, V-8 ($30). Lighting, Horns and Mirrors: Coach lamps ($85); incl. w/vinyl top. Front/rear light monitors ($62). Courtesy/reading lamp ($42). Lighted door lock and interior light control ($57). Headlamps-on indicator ($11). Four-note horn ($23). Remote left mirror w/thermometer ($21). Dual electric remote mirrors ($58); w/left thermometer ($79). Lighted visor vanity mirrors, each ($47). Entertainment: AM/FM stereo w/8-track or cassette player ($110-$116). AM/FM stereo radio w/CB ($294); w/CB and 8-track ($404). Signal-seeking AM/FM stereo radio w/digital readout ($182); w/8-track ($292). Signal-seeking AM/CB/FM stereo radio w/digital clock ($524); w/8-track and clock ($634). Triband power antenna ($39). Exterior Trim:

Heavy- padded landau top ($285). Long vinyl top ($285). Designers' accent paint ($193). Solid color special paint ($153) exc. Firemist ($172). Rear bumper guards ($22). Protective bodyside moldings ($59). Door edge guards ($14). Bodyside stripes ($52). Interior Trim/Upholstery: 45/55 notchback front seat, leather/vinyl ($350). Leather/vinyl bucket seats: S ($350). Front/rear carpet savers w/inserts ($57). Trunk mat ($12).

HISTORY: Introduced: September 28, 1978. Model year production (U.S.): 727,275. Calendar year production (U.S.): 787,123. Model year sales by U.S. dealers: 754,619 (including 17,564 imported Opels). Calendar year sales (U.S.): 714,508 which, though down significantly, still gave Buick an increased market share of 8.6 percent.

Historical Footnotes: Buick expected to emphasize the mid-size Century lineup with the new Turbo Coupe, but buyers still liked the look of Regal better. Most models rose in price during the model year, but none so dramatically as Electra, which shot upward by over a thousand dollars. Many observers felt that the all-new Riviera, built in Linden, New Jersey, was more a descendant of the 1963 original than the 1970s boattail version. *Motor Trend* names it "Car of the Year," the first Buick granted that title since the 1962 Special with its V-6 powerplant.

1980 BUICK

First arrival for the 1980 model year was the new Skylark, continuing the old name but on an all-new front-wheel drive chassis, cousin to the soon-to-be-notorious Chevrolet Citation X-car. All the X-bodies debuted in April. Century kept the aero-style fastback coupe a little longer, but sedans took on a fresh notchback appearance for 1980. Full-size LeSabres and Electras were restyled with aerodynamics in mind. New higher-pressure tires offered less rolling resistance. Riviera, Electra and LeSabre now had match-mounted tires/wheels. Some automatic transmissions contained a torque converter clutch to reduce slippage loss. Buick fielded three new engines: a larger 252 cu. in. (4.1-liter) version of the familiar Buick 3.8-liter V-6; a lightweight 265 cu. in. (4.3-liter) 2Bbl. V-8 option for Century and Regal, intended as a middle ground between the 3.8 V-6 and 4.9 V-8; and a 5.7-liter diesel V-8 produced by Oldsmobile. Standard on Electras, the 4.1 had a larger bore than the 3.8, siamesed (no water jacket between the bores) to allow for the larger bores. It had a new aluminum intake manifold, steel head gaskets (rather than composition), intake manifold gaskets with smaller exhaust gas crossover holes, and retuned engine mounts. The new diesel, available in Electras and Estates (later on LeSabre), differed a bit from the 5.7 diesel previously used by other GM divisions. Its new fuel nozzle didn't require a return system to the fuel tank. For the first time, a V-6 was offered in every Buick series. The big 403 (6.6-liter) V-8 was finally gone. So were the small 3.2-liter V-6, and the 301 (4.9-liter) 2Bbl. V-8. Joining the option list was Twilight Sentinel, an automatic headlight control that would turn Electra or Riviera lights on when it grew dark, then off again as daylight emerged. The system, formerly available on Cadillacs, also kept headlights on for three minutes after you shut the engine off. Also new: tungsten-halogen high-beam headlamps that produced an intense white beam, standard on Regal/LeSabre Sport Coupes and Riviera S Type, optional elsewhere in the lineup. Electronic Touch Climate Control on Electra and LeSabre used a row of touch surfaces on a smooth panel in place of the usual protruding knobs and switches. Stereo entertainment stretched all the way up to a new six-speaker Concert Sound System available in the Electra Park Avenue sedan. Buick's Theft Deterrent System included door and trunk locks, plus a starter interrupt system to prevent the engine from firing.

1980 Skyhawk "Road Hawk" hatchback coupe (AA)

SKYHAWK — SERIES 4H — V-6 — For its final year in this form, Skyhawk received only modest interior changes. In addition to standard and 'S' models, the sporty "Road Hawk" was offered again. That package included Oyster White bucket seats with hawk accents; flat black wipers, grille, headlamp trim and moldings; plus a rear spoiler and special suspension. The body featured silver/gray accent paint and striping. The Designers' Accent Edition, also available again this year, included a hawk decal, rear spoiler and special paint. Buick's subcompact was dropped early in the model year, to permit increased production of other H-Special bodied GM models. The name would return on an all-new model for 1982. Skyhawk's standard equipment included a maintenance-free battery, AM radio, front/rear bumper guards, protective bumper strips, deluxe wheel covers, carpeting, cigarette lighter, full-length console, high-energy ignition, day/night inside mirror, outside sport mirrors (left remote), vinyl bucket seats, sport steering wheel, rear stabilizer bar, space-saver spare tire, and four-speed floor shift. The 'S' Skyhawk lacked wheel opening moldings and bodyside stripes.

SKYLARK — SERIES 4X — FOUR/V-6 — To tumultous fanfare and glowing reviews, the new front-drive unibodied Skylark, far different from its predecessor of that name, arrived in spring 1979 as an early 1980 model. Weighing much less (700-800 pounds) than prior Skylarks, it was part of the X-body family that also included Chevrolet Citation, Oldsmobile Omega, and Pontiac Phoenix. Fuel-efficient, with a roomy interior, transverse-mounted engine (four or V-6) and standard door and window frame moldings, the new Skylark came in standard, Limited or Sport trim. A compact spare tire replaced the old full-size version. The suspension used coil springs all around. The new Skylark was 19 inches shorter than its forerunner, and far more expensive (by some $1500). It carried five passengers (six with squeezing) and was

1980 Skylark Sport Coupe (AA)

powered by a standard "Iron Duke" 2.5-liter four-cylinder engine from Pontiac, or optional Chevrolet-built 2.8-liter V-6. The base Skylark and Limited had a slightly peaked checkerboard grille, single rectangular recessed headlamps, and vertical parking/signal lamps at the outer edge of the front-end. A Skylark nameplate was at the forward end of the front fenders; Buick lettering on the trunk lid. On the roof pillar was a round emblem. Skylark's standard AM radio could be deleted for credit. Other standard equipment included a four-speed manual transmission with floor shift lever, compact spare tire, glass-belted radial tires, rack-and-pinion steering, step-on parking brake, locking glove compartment, cigarette lighter, and cloth or vinyl notchback seating. The Limited had tan upholstery in brushed woven fabric, plus carpeted lower door panels and under-dash courtesy lamps. Other Limited extras were gas-assisted hood struts, acoustical insulation, stand-up hood ornament and windsplit molding, wheel opening moldings, wide rocker moldings that extended to front fenders and rear quarters, and deluxe wheel covers. Skylark's Sport Coupe and Sport Sedan options had an entirely different three-row, six-section blackout grille, with body-colored horizontal separators. They also had black body moldings, bright wheel opening moldings, bumper strips front and rear, smoked taillamp lenses, sport steering wheel, Designers' Sport road wheels, and amber parking/signal lamps up front. Sport Skylarks also carried a heftier Rallye suspension, larger rear stabilizer bar, black dash treatment with full instruments including a voltmeter, and P205/70R13 blackwall steel-belted radials. For extra accent, they could have wide lower body stripes with a hawk decal. One pleasant option: a flip-open glass sunroof. Before long, all the X-cars would be plagued by a long list of safety recalls and mechanical problems, which resulted in one of the worst reputations among modern American automobiles. Chevrolet's Citation got the worst publicity of the bunch, but the troubles affected all of the 980-85 X-bodied models, even though the most serious recalls applied only to the early editions.

1980 Century Sport Turbo Aerodynamic Coupe (AA)

CENTURY — SERIES 4A — V-6/V-8 After two years in slantback form, a new notchback sedan roofline replaced the fastback shape on two-door Century models. These new, dramatically styled sedans had a more formal appearance than before, resembling both Skylark and Regal. Styling features included wraparound taillamps, an angular-look decklid, and sloping fenders. A horizontal grille and new signal lamps emphasized the car's angular appearance. The four-row, eight-column crosshatch grille had a tiny crosshatch pattern within each segment. Vertical rectangular parking/signal lights sat between the single recessed rectangular headlamps and the grille, with amber lenses around the fender corners. Century coupes retained the fastback design for one final attempt at luring buyers. Custom and Special designations were dropped, with their equivalents now called, simply, Century. Thus, Century came in two trim levels: base and Limited. Optional models included a Turbo coupe and Sport coupe. This year saw a larger standard engine: the 231 cu. in. (3.8-liter) V-6. Options included new 4.3-liter and 4.9-liter V-8s (5.0-liter in California), plus the turbocharged V-6. Power brakes became standard this year. Century standard equipment included a dome light; Limited added lights for front ashtray, under-dash courtesy, and glove compartment. Seats were upholstered in supple vinyl or plush, crushed-knit cloth; 55/45 type in the Limited sedan. Standard Century equipment included three-speed manual transmission, fiberglass-belted radial tires, compact spare tire, wide-view day/night mirror, protective bumper strips, and stand-up hood ornament. The Limited also offered wheel opening moldings and bodyside stripes. On the station wagon front, Century fielded standard and Estate (formerly Custom) Wagons, plus a Sport Wagon option. Each sat six, or held 71.8 cubic feet of cargo with second seat folded down. The Sport Wagon package contained black headlamp and grille trim, wipers, window reveal moldings, center pillar, wide rocker treatment, wheel opening moldings, air deflector, and sport mirrors; plus a hawk decal, Rallye suspension, and P205/70R14 steel-belted radial tires on Designers' Sport wheels. Sport Coupe and Turbo Coupe options had a black treatment on grille, headlamp bezels, windshield wiper arms, pillars, moldings, decklid panel, and instrument panel trim; plus twin sport mirrors and a functional rear spoiler. A hawk decal was on the front fender, just ahead of the door. Black-trimmed instrument panel, too. They also had the ride-and-handling Rallye package with firmer springs and shocks, plus larger-diameter stabilizer bars, Designers' Sport wheels, and P205/70R14 steel-belted radials. The Turbo version included a special bulged hood with 'Turbo 3.8 Litre' nameplate, Turbo Coupe identification on body side and deck lid, turbine wheels, and exhaust system with what Buick described as a "rather authoritative voice." Styled aluminum wheels were available for the first time on the Sport versions.

239

1980 Regal Sport Turbo Coupe (AA)

REGAL — SERIES 4A — V-6/V-8 — Regal's new look included wider taillamps and quad rectangular headlamps. It came in Limited and Sport Coupe trim, as well as standard Regal. New taillamps split by horizontal lines, stretching from license plate to decklid edge, gave a wider look to the back end. A restyled grille had an undivided, tight checkerboard pattern that angled outward at the base in the Buick style. Park/signal lamps set in the base of the front bumper. Regal Limited had special wide chrome rocker panel moldings, as well as standard crushed velour cloth upholstery. The Sport Coupe, still powered by a turbocharged 231 cu. in. (3.8-liter) V-6 engine, could have an optional Designers' Accent paint treatment, blacked-out grille and headlamp trim, plus sport mirrors and turbine wheels. New tungsten-halogen high beams that produced intense white light were standard on Sport Coupe, optional on other Regals. "Once in a while," declared the brochure describing the Regal Somerset limited edition, "you have an opportunity to buy a first edition....So owning one will be a rare treat." Owning one today might be similarly pleasing. The two-tone body came only in Somerset Tan and Dark Blue Designers' Accent. The dark blue swept back over the hood and onto the top of the roof. The package (offered for the Limited coupe) included wire wheel covers, sleek sport mirrors, and special Somerset identification on front fenders. Inside, the tan and dark blue motif continued with special Somerset design plush knit velour 55/45 seat upholstery and dark blue carpeting. A color-keyed umbrella fit in a pouch on the back of the front seat. Brushed aluminum trim highlighted the instrument panel and doors. There was a roof-mounted passenger assist strap, plus Somerset identification on the glove box door. Regal's base powerplant was the 231 cu. in. (3.8-liter) two-barrel, with other engine possibilities the new 265 (4.3-liter) two-barrel V-8, or 301 (4.9-liter) four-barrel V-8. Power brakes and steering were standard. So were steel-belted radial tires, compact spare tire, day/night inside mirror, twin chrome outside mirrors, wipers with mist feature, an underhood light, and cigarette lighter. Regals had bumper guards and protective strips front and rear, a stand-up hood ornament, windshield and back window reveal moldings, and wheel opening moldings. Regal Limited added wide rocker moldings (extending to front fenders and rear quarter panels), belt reveal moldings, and bright pillar moldings.

1980 LeSabre Limited coupe (AA)

LESABRE — SERIES 4B — V-6/V-8 — New sheet metal arrived on both LeSabre and Electra to produce a lower, longer front end appearance. The reshaped rear end was higher, with a sharper forward thrust to the decklid. A rear deck spoiler treatment, sloping hood, and reduced front-end radius improved the car's aerodynamics, cutting air drag by a claimed 14 percent. New recessed quad rectangular headlamps, set in bezels with a vertical dividing wall, highlighted the angular look. A new checkerboard grille had large holes in four rows, and the bottom row extended outward all the way to fender edges. At the side of the grille was a Buick badge. Parking/signal lamps were now set into the bumper. The familiar LeSabre "ventiport" fender trim, descended from old Buick portholes, faded away with the new restyle. LeSabres now rode on high-pressure, low-rolling-resistance tires. Match-mounted tires and wheels, plus new shock absorbers, improved ride quality. Powerplant was again the standard 3.8-liter V-6, but a new and bigger 252 cu. in. (4.1-liter) V-6 was also offered (except in California). LeSabre could also have Oldsmobile's 350 cu. in. diesel V-8. The dashboard included a blacked-out panel that showed information on headlight beam, engine conditions, brake warning, and a seat belt reminder. A new side-frame jack was standard; wheel covers were new. Optional: a theft-deterrent system with starter interrupt. LeSabre's Sport Coupe featured a blacked-out grille, black window and side moldings, plus chrome wheels. Also a ride/handling package with large stabilizer bars, firm springs and shock valving, and fast-ratio power steering. Sport Coupes were again powered by the turbocharged 231 V-6 with four-barrel carburetor. The dash held a vacuum boost light. Standard equipment included bucket seats, full-length console, tungsten-halogen headlamps, sport mirrors and sport steering wheel. Four-wheel disc brakes were optional. Standard LeSabre equipment included wheel opening and roof drip scale moldings, bumper protective strips and guards, rear end panel molding, notchback seating (cloth or vinyl), and a compact spare tire. To the basic list, LeSabre Limited added such styling touches as deluxe wheel covers, rocker panel moldings and black pillar applique.

ESTATE WAGON — SERIES 4B — V-8 — Not much was new in the Estate Wagon arena, as was usually the case. The LeSabre Estate seated six, with a third seat available, and had 86.8 cubic foot cargo volume. Standard powerplant was a 4.9-liter (301 cu. in.) gasoline V-8 this year (except in California); but the familiar 350 (5.7-liter) V-8 was available too. Electra's new Estate Wagon differed little and had the same engine choices. For the extra price, Electra buyers got standard air conditioning, tilt steering column, digital clock, remote-control left outside mirror, 55/45 notchback seating (cloth or vinyl), power windows, and chrome wheels. All Estates had mist wipers, dual outside mirrors, front and rear bumper guards with protective strips, power steering and brakes, and automatic transmission.

1980 Electra Estate Wagon (AA)

ELECTRA — SERIES 4C — V-6/V-8 — Sporting a new vertical-style grille, sloping fenders and higher decklid, Electra presented a streamlined appearance--and lost over 200 pounds of curb weight. Standard engine, except in California, was the new 252 cu. in. (4.1-liter) V-6, with 350 (5.7-liter) V-8 optional. For the first time, a diesel was also available. The new grille was divided into sections by nine vertical bars, tapering outward at the base, with Buick badge at the side. Quad rectangular headlamps sat in recessed housings. Park/signal lamps were inset in the bumper bottom. Electra's hood had a slight downward rake. The Electra 225 designation was dropped, replaced by Limited and Park Avenue series (those were formerly models rather than series). An Electra Estate Wagon was added (see above). Suspensions now used Pliacell-R-shock absorbers, and a new compact spare tire rested in the trunk. Park Avenue coupe and sedan instrument panels and coach lamps were new electro-luminescent lighting. Park Avenue also had a new standard halo-effect padded-vinyl roof, plus knit velour fabric upholstery with a draped, sheared look (leather available). Both Limited and Park Avenue had new higher-pressure tires that offered less rolling resistance. New tungsten-halogen high-beam headlamps were available. So were 14 choices of entertainment systems, including a Concert Sound System for the Park Avenue with six speakers. Park Avenue also had exclusive Touch Climate Control with no levers, buttons or switches; just a smooth touch panel. Electra kept their four-section "ventiports," which formed part of the Park Avenue's wide full-length bodyside molding.

1980 Riviera coupe (AA)

RIVIERA — SERIES 4E — V-6/V-8 — The downsized Riviera body that had been introduced for 1979 received modest refinements this year, including revised body mounts. Rivs also got match-mounted tires and wheels, retuned shock absorbers, restyled mirrors that fit snugly against the car body for an integrated look, and a selection of new interior fabrics. Options included Twilight Sentinel, which gave automatic control of outside lights, controlled by a sensor atop the dashboard. As before, Riviera was front-drive, with fully independent suspension and 350 cu. in. (5.7-liter) V-8 engine. Pliacell-R- shock absorbers were new, as was an optional theft-deterrent system with starter interrupt system. Also optional: a digital Trip Monitor that displayed a selection of travel and engine functions. Riviera standard equipment included automatic transmission, power front disc brakes, cornering lights, six- way power driver's seat, power steering, digital clock, automatic level control, air conditioning, electric door locks, remote-controlled outside mirrors, and Delco AM/FM stereo radio with power antenna. One of the new interior colors, brown, was a Riviera exclusive. Four-wheel disc brakes were again available. Riviera's S Type had been chosen 1979 Car of the Year by *Motor Trend*. New flat black, styled outside mirrors complemented its flat black trim around windows, grille and rocker panels. Powerplant remained the turbocharged 231 cu. in. V-6 with four-barrel carb. Bucket seats were velour upholstered with ribbed inserts; the instrument panel was black-accented.

I.D. DATA: For one more year, a 13-symbol Vehicle Identification Number (VIN) was on the upper left surface of the instrument panel, visible through the windshield. Coding was similar to 1979, with the first digit ('4') indicating the Buick division. The next letter indicates series: 'S' Skyhawk; 'T' Skyhawk S; 'B' Skylark; 'C' Skylark Limited; 'E' Century wagon; 'H' Century cpe/sed and Estate wagon; 'G' Century Sport Coupe; 'L' Century Ltd.; 'J' Regal; 'K' Regal Sport Coupe; 'M' Regal Ltd.; 'F' LeSabre Sport Coupe; 'N' LeSabre; 'P' LeSabre Limited; 'R' LeSabre Estate Wagon; 'I' Electra Estate; 'X' Electra Limited; 'W' Electra Park Ave.; 'Z' Riviera; 'Y' Riviera S Type. The next two digits denote body type: '07' Skyhawk hatchback coupe; '09' aero 4-dr. sedan; '37' Skylark/LeSabre/Electra 2-dr. coupe; '47' Regal 2-dr. coupe; '57' Riviera 2-dr. coupe; '87' aero 2-dr. coupe; '69' 4-dr. sedan; '35' 4-dr. wagon. The fifth symbol indicated engine code: '5' 4-151 2Bbl.; '7' V6-173 2Bbl.; 'A' V6-231 2Bbl.; '3' Turbo V6-231 4Bbl.; 'S' V8-265 2Bbl.; 'W' V8-301 4Bbl.; 'R' V8-350 4Bbl. (L34); 'X' V8-350 4Bbl. (L77). The sixth symbol denotes model year ('A' 1980). Next a plant code: '7' Lordstown, OH; 'W' Willow Run, MI; '6' Oklahoma City, OK; 'G' Framingham, MA; 'H' Flint, MI; 'Z' Fremont, CA; 'X' Fairfax, KS; 'E' Linden, NJ. The final six digits are the sequential serial number, which began with 100001, except 400001 for Skyhawks and for LeSabre/Electra/Estate models built at Flint. Engine numbers were stamped on the front right of the block, except for L34 and LF9 350 cu. in. V-8s, which were stamped on the front of the left side of the block; LD5, LC8 and LC6 V-6s, on left rear of block; Skylark V-6, on rear (or front) of right rocker cover; and Skylark four, on pad at left front below cylinder head. The body number plate on the shroud was the same as before.

SKYHAWK (V-6)

Series Number	Body/Style Number	Body Type & Seating	Factory Price	Shipping Weight	Production Total
4H	T07	2-dr 'S' Hatch-4P	4993	2754	Note 1
4H	S07	2-dr. Hatch-4P	5211	2754	Note 1

Note 1: Total production for the model year, 8,322 Skyhawks.

SKYLARK (FOUR/V-6)

4X	B37	2-dr Coupe-5P	5160/5385	2410/2449	55,114
4X	B69	4-dr Sedan-5P	5306/5531	2438/2477	80,940

SKYLARK LIMITED (FOUR/V-6)

4X	C37	2-dr Coupe-5P	5579/5804	2438/2477	42,652
4X	C69	4-dr Sedan-5P	5726/5951	2478/2517	86,948

SKYLARK SPORT (FOUR/V-6)

4X	D37	2-dr Coupe-5P	5774/5999	2443/2482	Note 2
4X	D69	4-dr Sedan-5P	5920/6145	2471/2510	Note 2

Note 2: Production of Skylark Sport models is included in Limited totals above. Total Limited production: 100,396.

CENTURY (V-6/V-8)

4A	H87	2-dr Aero Cpe-6P	5546/5751	3086/3190	1,074
4A	H69	4-dr Sedan-6P	5646/5851	3106/3210	129,740
4A	E35	4-dr Sta Wag-6P	5922/6102	3236/3364	6,493
4A	H35	4-dr Est Wag-6P	6220/6400	3247/3375	11,122

CENTURY SPORT (V-6/V-8)

4A	G87	2-dr Aero Cpe-6P	6063/6243	3150/3254	Note 3

CENTURY LIMITED (V-6/V-8)

4A	L69	4-dr Sedan-6P	6132/6337	3150/3254	Note 3

Note 3: Production figures shown for Century include Sport and Limited models.

REGAL (V-6/V-8)

4A	J47	2-dr Coupe-6P	6305/6485	3115/3243	Note 4

REGAL SPORT COUPE (TURBO V-6)

4A	K47	2-dr Coupe-6P	6952	3194	Note 4

REGAL LIMITED (V-6/V-8)

4A	M47	2-dr Coupe-6P	6724/6904	3142/3370	Note 4

Note 4: Total model year production, 214,735 Regals. Note 5: Prices shown after slash for Century/Regal V-8 are for the smaller (265 cu. in.) version; larger V-8 cost $115 more.

LESABRE (V-6/V-8)

4B	N37	2-dr Coupe-6P	6674/6971	3320/3440	8,342
4B	N69	4-dr Sedan-6P	6769/7064	3369/3497	23,873

LESABRE LIMITED (V-6/V-8)

4B	P37	2-dr Coupe-6P	6929/7224	3327/3455	20,561
4B	P69	4-dr Sedan-6P	7071/7366	3375/3503	37,676

LESABRE SPORT (TURBO V-6)

4B	F37	2-dr Coupe-6P	7782	3430	Note 6

Note 6: Production of Sport Turbo Coupe is included in totals for standard LeSabre coupe.

LESABRE ESTATE WAGON (V-8)

4B	R35	4-dr Sta Wag-6P	7673	3898	9,318
4B	(AQ4)	4-dr 3S Wag-8P	7866	3928	Note 7

Note 7: Three-seat Estate Wagon was actually an option package (AQ4); production of all Estate Wagons is included in above figure.

ELECTRA LIMITED (V-6/V-8)

4C	X37	2-dr Coupe-6P	9132/9467	3571/3756	14,058
4C	X69	4-dr Sedan-6P	9287/9622	3578/3763	54,422

ELECTRA PARK AVENUE (V-6/V-8)

4C	W37	2-dr Coupe-6P	10244/10579	3600/3785	Note 8
4C	W69	4-dr Sedan-6P	10383/10718	3607/3792	Note 8

Note 8: Production figures shown for Electra Limited include Park Avenue.

ELECTRA ESTATE WAGON (V-8)

4C	V35	4-dr Sta Wag-6P	10513	4105	N/A
4C	(AQ4)	4-dr 3S Wag-8P	10706	4135	N/A

RIVIERA (V-8)

4E	Z57	2-dr Coupe-4P	11492	3741	41,404

RIVIERA S TYPE TURBO (V-6)

4E	Y57	2-dr Coupe-4P	11823	3633	7,217

FACTORY PRICE AND WEIGHT NOTE: Figure before the slash is for V-6 engine, after the slash for smallest (lowest-priced) V-8 engine available. For Skylark, figure before the slash is for four-cylinder engine, after the slash for V-6.

ENGINES: BASE FOUR (Skylark): Inline, ohv, four-cylinder. Cast iron block and head. Displacement: 151 cu. in. (2.5 liters). Bore & stroke: 4.0 x 3.0 in. Compression ratio: 8.2:1. Brake horsepower: 90 at 4000 R.P.M. Torque: 134 lbs.-ft. at 2400 R.P.M. Five main bearings. Hydraulic valve lifters. Carburetor: 2Bbl. Rochester 2SE (Varajet II). VIN Code: 5. Sales Code: LW9. OPTIONAL V-6 (Skylark): 60-degree, overhead-valve V-6. Cast iron alloy block and head. Displacement: 173 cu. in. (2.8 liters). Bore & stroke: 3.5 x 3.0 in. Compression ratio: 8.5:1. Brake horsepower: 115 at 4800 R.P.M. Torque: 145 lbs.-ft. at 2400 R.P.M. Four main bearings. Hydraulic valve lifters. Carburetor: 2Bbl. Rochester 2SE. VIN Code: 7. Sales Code: LE2. BASE V-6 (Skyhawk, Century, Regal, LeSabre): 90-degree, overhead-valve V-6. Cast iron alloy block and head. Displacement: 231 cu. in. (3.8 liters). Bore & stroke: 3.8 x 3.4 in. Compression ratio: 8.0:1. Brake horsepower: 110 at 3800 R.P.M. Torque: 190 lbs.-ft. at 1600 R.P.M. Four main bearings. Hydraulic valve lifters. Carburetor: 2Bbl. Rochester M2ME. Even-firing. VIN Code: A. Sales Code: LD5. TURBOCHARGED V-6 (Regal and LeSabre Sport Coupes, Riviera S): Same as 231 V-6 above, but with M4ME four-barrel carburetor. Brake horsepower: 170 at 4000 R.P.M. Torque: 265 lbs.-ft. at 2400 R.P.M. VIN Code: 3. Sales Code: LC8. BASE V-6 (Electra); OPTIONAL (LeSabre): 90-degree, overhead-valve V-6. Cast iron alloy block and head. Displacement: 252 cu. in. (4.1 liters). Bore & stroke: 3.965 x 3.4 in. Compression ratio: 8.0:1. Brake horsepower: 125 at 4000 R.P.M. Torque: 205 lbs.-ft. at 2000 R.P.M. Four main bearings. Hydraulic valve lifters. Carburetor: 4Bbl. Rochester M4ME. VIN Code: 4. Sales Code: LC4. OPTIONAL V-8 (Century/Regal): 90-degree, overhead-valve V-8. Cast iron alloy block and head. Displacement: 265 cu. in. (4.3 liters). Bore & stroke: 3.75 x 3.00 in. Compression ratio: 8.0:1. Brake horsepower: 120 at 3600 R.P.M. Torque: 210 lbs.-ft. at 1800 R.P.M. Four main bearings. Hydraulic valve lifters. Carburetor: 2Bbl. Rochester M2ME. VIN Code: S. BASE V-8 (Estate); OPTIONAL (Century, Regal, LeSabre): 90-degree overhead-valve V-8. Cast iron alloy block and head. Displacement: 301 cu. in. (4.9 liters). Bore & stroke: 4.0 x .00 in. Compression ratio: 8.2:1. Brake horsepower: 140 at 4000 R.P.M. Torque: 240 lbs.-ft. at 1800 R.P.M. Five main bearings. Hydraulic valve lifters. Carburetor: 4Bbl. Rochester M4ME. Built by Pontiac. VIN Code: W. Sales Code: L37. OPTIONAL V-8 (Century/Regal): 90-degree, overhead valve V-8. Cast iron alloy block and head. Displacement: 305 cu. in. (5.0 liters). Bore & stroke: 3.736 x 3.48 in. Compression ratio: 8.6:1. Brake horsepower: 155 at 4000 R.P.M. Torque: 240 lbs.-ft. at 1600 R.P.M. Five main bearings. Hydraulic valve lifters. Carburetor: 4Bbl. Rochester M4MC. VIN Code: H. Sales Code: LG4. BASE V-8 (Riviera); OPTIONAL (LeSabre, Estate, Electra, Riviera S): 90-degree, overhead valve V-8. Cast iron alloy block and head. Displacement: 350 cu. in. (5.7 liters). Bore & stroke: 3.80 x 3.85 in. Compression ratio: 8.0:1. Brake horsepower: 155 at 3400 R.P.M. Torque: 280 lbs.-ft. at 1600 R.P.M. Five main bearings. Hydraulic valve lifters. Carburetor: 4Bbl. Rochester M4MC. VIN Code: X. Sales Code: L77. ALTERNATE 350-4 V-8: 90-degree, overhead valve V-8. Cast iron alloy block and head. Displacement: 350 cu. in. (5.7 liters). Bore & stroke: 4.057 x 3.385 in. Compression ratio: 8.3:1. Brake horsepower: 60 at 3600 R.P.M. Torque: 270 lbs.-ft. at 1600 R.P.M. Five main bearings. Hydraulic valve lifters. Carburetor: 4Bbl. Rochester M4MC. Built by Oldsmobile. VIN Code: R. Sales Code: L34. OPTIONAL DIESEL V-8 (Electra, Estate): 90-degree, overhead valve V-8. Cast iron alloy block and head. Displacement: 350 cu. in. (5.7 liters). Bore & stroke: 4.057 x 3.385 in. Compression ratio: 22.5:1. Brake horsepower: 105 at 3200 R.P.M. Torque: 205 lbs.-ft. at 1600 R.P.M. Five main bearings. Hydraulic valve lifters. Fuel injection. Oldsmobile-built. VIN Code: N. Sales Code: LF9.

CHASSIS DATA: Wheelbase: (Skyhawk) 97.0 in.; (Skylark) 104.9 in.; (Century/Regal) 108.1 in.; (LeSabre) 116.0 in.; (Estate) 115.9 in.; (Electra) 118.9 in.; (Riviera) 114.0 in. Overall length:- (Skyhawk) 179.3 in.; (Skylark) 181.9 in.; (Century) 196.0 in.; (Regal) 200.3 in.; (LeSabre) 217.4 in.; (Electra) 220.9 in.; (Estate) 218.8 in.; (Riv) 206.6 in. Height:- (Skyhawk) 50.8 in.; (Skylark) 53.5 in.; (Century cpe) 54.6 in.; (Century sed/wag) 55.5 in.; (Regal) 54.6 in.; (LeSabre) 55.0 in.; (Electra cpe) 54.2 in.; (Electra sed) 55.6 in.; (Estate) 57.1 in.; (Riv) 54.3 in. Width:- (Skyhawk) 65.4 in.; (Skylark) 67.7 in.; (Century/Regal) 71.1 in.; (LeSabre/Electra) 78.0 in.; (Estate) 80.1 in.; (Riv) 72.7 in. Front Tread:- (Skyhawk) 54.7 in.; (Skylark) 58.7 in.; (Century/Regal) 58.5 in.; (LeSabre/Electra) 61.8 in.; (Estate) 62.2 in.; (Riv) 59.3 in. Rear Tread:- (Skyhawk) 53.6 in.; (Skylark) 57.0 in.; (Century/Regal) 57.8 in.; (LeSabre) 60.7 in.; (Electra) 61.0 in.; (Estate) 64.1 in.; (Riv) 60.0 in. Standard Tires:- (Skyhawk) BR78 x 13 SBR; (Skyhawk 'S') B78 x 13; (Skylark) P185/80R13 GBR; (Skylark Sport) P205/70R13 SBR; (Century cpe/sed) P185/75R14 GBR; (Century wag/Regal) P195/75R14; (Regal Spt Cpe) P205/70R14 SBR; (LeSabre) P205/75R15 SBR; (LeSabre Spt Cpe) P225/70R15 SBR: (Electra) P215/75R15 SBR; (Estate) P225/75R15 SBR; (Riviera) P205/75R15 SBR WSW; (Riviera S) GR70 x 15.

TECHNICAL: Transmission:- Three-speed, fully synchronized manual gearbox standard on Century cpe/sed; Turbo Hydra-matic optional. Four-speed, fully synchronized floor shift standard on Skyhawk/Skylark; automatic optional. Turbo Hydra-matic standard on Regal, LeSabre, Electra, Estate and Riviera. Three-speed manual transmission gear ratios: (1st) 3.50:1; (2nd) 1.81:1; (3rd) 1.00:1; (Rev) 3.62:1. Skyhawk four-speed gear ratios: (1st) 3.50:1; (2nd) 2.48:1; (3rd) 1.66:1; (4th) 1.00:1; (Rev) 3.50:1. Skylark four-speed gear ratios: (1st) 3.53:1; (2nd) 1.95:1; (3rd) 1.24:1; (4th) 0.81:1; (Rev) 3.42:1. Auto. trans. gear ratios: (1st) 2.52:1; (2nd) 1.52:1; (3rd) 1.00:1; (Rev) 1.93:1. Skylark automatic: (1st) 2.84:1; (2nd) 2.60:1; (3rd) 1.00:1; (Rev) 2.07:1. Automatic on Century V-8, Electra diesel and Riviera: (1st) 2.74:1; (2nd) 1.57:1; (3rd) 1.00:1; (Rev) 2.07:1. Standard axle ratio:- (Skyhawk) 2.93:1; (Skylark) 3.34:1; (Century V6-231) 3.08:1; (Century/Regal V8-265) 2.41:1; (Century/Regal V8-301) 2.14:1 or 2.41:1; (Century/Regal V8-305) 2.29:1 or 2.73:1; (Century/Regal/LeSabre turbo/spt cpe) 2.73:1 or 3.08:1; (Century wag) 2.29:1, 2.41:1, 2.56:1 or 2.73:1; (LeSabre V6-231) 2.73:1 or 3.23:1; (LeSabre V6-252) 2.93:1; (LeSabre V8) 2.41:1 or 3.23:1; (Electra V-6) 2.93:1; (Electra V8-301) 2.56:1 or 3.23:1; (Electra V8-350) 2.41:1 or 3.23:1; (Electra diesel) 2.73:1; (Estate) 2.56:1, 2.73:1 or 3.08:1; (Riv) 2.41:1 exc. turbo V-6, 2.93:1. Steering:- (Skylark) rack and pinion; power assist standard on Regal, LeSabre, Electra, Estate and Riviera. Suspension:- front/rear coil springs; (Skylark) MacPherson strut front suspension, trailing arm rear with track bar; (Riviera) same as 1979; (others) same as 1976-79. Brakes:- front disc, rear drum; power brakes standard on all except Skyhawk/Skylark. Four-wheel power disc brakes optional on Riviera. Body construction:- (Skyhawk/Skylark) unitized; (others) separate body and frame. Fuel tank: (Skyhawk) 18.5 gal.; (Skylark) 14 gal.; (Century/Regal) 18.2 gal.; (LeSabre/Electra) 25 gal.; (Riviera) 21 gal. Unleaded fuel only.

DRIVETRAIN OPTIONS: Engines:- 173 cu. in. (2.8-liter) V-6, 2Bbl.: Skylark ($225). Turbocharged 231 cu. in. V-6, 4Bbl.: Century cpe/sed ($500); Riviera ($160). 252 cu. in. (4.1-liter) V-6, 4Bbl.: LeSabre ($90). 265 cu. in. (4.3-liter) V-8, 2Bbl.: Century/Regal ($180-$205). 301 cu. in. (4.9-liter) V-8, 2Bbl.: LeSabre ($295). 301 cu. in. V-8, 4Bbl.: Century/Regal ($295-$320). 305 cu. in. V-8, 4Bbl.: Century/Regal ($295-$320). 350 cu. in. (5.7-liter) V-8, 4Bbl.: LeSabre ($425); Estate ($130); Electra ($335); Riviera S (credit $160). 350 cu. in. diesel V-8: Estate ($860); Electra ($930). Transmission/Differential:- Automatic trans., floor shift: Skyhawk ($320). Automatic trans., column shift: Skylark ($337); Century cpe/sed ($358). Optional rear axle ratio (NC). Limited slip differential: Skyhawk ($65); Century/Regal ($70); LeSabre/Electra ($74). Power Accessories:- Power brakes: Skyhawk/Skylark ($76). Four-wheel disc brakes: LeSabre spt cpe, Riv ($222). Power steering: Skyhawk ($158); Skylark ($164); Century ($174). Suspension:- F40 Firm ride/handling pkg.: all exc. Skyhawk ($21-$22). F41 Rallye ride/handling pkg.: Skylark ($129); incl. in Sport. FE2 Rallye ride/handling pkg.: Century/Regal ($41); Riv ($22). Automatic level control: Century/Regal/LeSabre/Electra ($145). Superlift rear shocks: Skylark ($55). Other:- Trailer towing flasher/harness ($24-$38) exc. Skyhawk. Heavy-duty alternator, 80-amp: LeSabre/Electra ($24-$61); 70-amp ($15- 52) exc. Skyhawk. H.D. battery ($19-$22); diesel ($44). H.D. cooling: Skyhawk/Skylark/Century/Regal ($32-$63). Engine block heater ($16). H.D. engine/transmission cooling: LeSabre/Electra/Riv ($32-$63). California emission system ($83-$250).

SKYHAWK CONVENIENCE/APPEARANCE OPTIONS: Option Packages:- Road Hawk pkg.: Oyster white vinyl bucket seats; black wipers, grille, headlamp trim, moldings, front air dam; body-color spoiler and sport mirrors; BR70 x 13 SBR wide-oval blackwall tires; special handling suspension; silver/gray paint ($696). Appearance group (wheel opening moldings and bodyside stripes): 'S' ($62). Acoustic insulation pkg. ($27). Convenience group: underhood light, glove box light, headlamp-on indicator ($22). Shadow light Astroroof ($693). Vista Vent roof ($193). Comfort/Convenience:- Air cond. ($531). Rear defogger, electric ($95). Tinted glass ($65). Tinted windshield ($54). Tilt steering ($73). Instrument gauges, electric clock and tach ($79). Electric clock ($23). Front/rear mats ($23). Tungsten-halogen high-beam headlamps ($27). Visor vanity mirrors, pair ($11). Entertainment:- AM/FM radio ($64). AM/FM stereo radio ($101). AM/FM radio and cassette player ($188). AM/FM stereo radio and 8-track ($176). Rear speaker for non-stereo radios ($18). Delete AM radio ($52 credit). Exterior Trim: Bodyside stripes (NC). Door edge guards ($13). Roof crown moldings ($198). Protective bodyside moldings ($32- $49). Designer's accent paint ($189). Interior Trim/Upholstery:- Adjustable driver's seatback ($21). Custom seatbelts ($19). Wheels and Tires:- Custom sport wheels ($63). Styled aluminum wheels ($249). B78 x 13 WSW ($42-$52). BR78 x 13 SBR BSW ($104-$129). BR78 x 13 SBR WSW ($41-$181). BR70 x 13 SBR wide-oval WLT ($57-$226). Conventional spare tire (NC).

SKYLARK CONVENIENCE/APPEARANCE OPTIONS: Option Packages:- Acoustic pkg. ($43). Lamp group: underhood, glove box, ashtray, courtesy, trunk, headlamps-on ($41-$50). Vista Vent flip-open glass sunroof ($240). Comfort/Convenience:- Air cond. ($564). Cruise Master ($105). Two-speed w/delay ($39). Rear defogger, electric ($101). Power windows ($133-$189). Electric door locks ($87-$123). Six-way power driver's seat ($165). Manual seatback recliner: each ($42). Sport steering wheel ($42). Tilt steering ($75). Tinted glass ($70). Dual horns ($11). Electric clock ($25). Digital clock ($56). Trip odometer ($13). Gauge pkg. incl. trip odometer ($40). Electric trunk release ($25). Lights and Mirrors:- Tungsten-halogen high-beam headlamps ($27). Headlamps-on indicator ($11). Dome reading light ($19). Door courtesy/warning light ($39-$62). Sunshade map light ($13). Remote left mirror ($18); sport-type ($28). Sport mirrors: left remote, right manual ($43); dual ($28-$71). Visor vanity mirrors ($11). Lighted passenger visor mirror ($39). Entertainment:- AM radio delete ($52 credit). AM/FM radio ($64). AM/FM stereo radio ($101); w/8-track or cassette player ($176-$188). AM/FM stereo and CB radio ($413); w/8- track or cassette ($479-$491). Rear speaker ($18); pair, for non-stereo radio ($28). Power antenna ($48); triband ($88). Exterior Trim:- Landau vinyl top ($175). Long vinyl top ($116). Designers' accent paint ($174). Protective bodyside moldings ($43). Belt reveal moldings ($25). Wide rocker panel group ($54). Door edge guards ($13-$20). Hood ornament and windsplit ($25). Pillar applique molding ($22). Wheel opening moldings ($22). Bodyside stripes ($40). Bumper guards, front/rear ($32). Bumper strips, front/rear ($40). Roof rack ($87). Interior Trim/Upholstery:- Full-length console ($80). Bucket seats ($48). Notchback bench seat: Spt ($146). Color- keyed seatbelts ($23). Front carpet savers ($15). Carpet savers and mats ($25). Trunk trim carpeting ($31). Wheels:- Designers' sport wheels ($82-$101); incl. on Spt. Chrome- plated wheels ($40-$141). Deluxe wheel covers ($43). Custom wire wheel covers ($151-$194). Sport wheel covers ($11-$54). Tires:- P185/80R13 GBR ($45). P185/80R13 SBR ($49). P185/80R13 SBR WSW ($93). P205/70R13 SBR WSW ($51). P205/70R13 SBR WLT ($66).

CENTURY/REGAL CONVENIENCE/APPEARANCE OPTIONS: Option Packages:- Regal Somerset pkg.: blue/tan interior trim, umbrella pouch, roof assist strap, decor pkg., custom belts, brushed aluminum instrument panel, sport mirrors, wire wheel covers ($695). Regal Sport Coupe Decor pkg.: designers' accent paint, turbine wheels, sport mirrors and steering wheel, black paint accents ($511). Century Sport Wagon pkg. ($511). Century Turbo Coupe pkg.: special suspension and exhaust, 3.08:1 axle, turbine wheels ($43). Electric sunroof: cpe ($561). Silver electric sliding Astroroof: cpe ($773). Hatch roof: Regal cpe ($695). Exterior molding pkg. ($64- $178). Convenience group ($18-$67). Comfort/Convenience:- Air cond. ($601). Automatic air cond. ($700). Cruise control ($112). Rear defogger, electric ($107). Tinted glass ($75). Tinted windshield ($54). Six-way power driver's seat ($175); both ($350). Manual seatback recliner ($67). Custom steering wheel: Century ($11). Sport steering wheel ($35-$46). Tilt steering ($81). Power windows ($143-$202). Electric door locks ($93-$132). Electric trunk release ($26). Remote tailgate lock: wag ($27). Electric clock ($26). Digital clock ($59). Headlamps-on indicator ($12). Trip odometer ($14). Instrument gauges: temp, volt, trip odometer ($29-$43). Two- speed wiper w/delay ($41). Lighting and Mirrors:- Cornering lamps: Regal ($53). Tungsten-halogen high-beams ($27). Coach lamps ($92). Front light monitors ($31). Dome reading lamp $20). Door/courtesy/warning lights: Ltd sed ($39-$62). Underhood light ($5). Remote left mirror ($19); right ($37- $42). Sport mirrors: left remote ($44-$49). Dual remote sport mirrors ($27-$76). Visor vanity mirrors, pair ($11). Lighted right visor vanity mirror ($50). Entertainment:- AM radio ($97). AM/FM radio ($153). AM/FM stereo radio ($192); w/8- track or cassette ($272-$285). AM/FM stereo radio and CB ($525). Rear speaker ($20); pair ($30). Automatic power antenna ($51-$80). Triband power antenna ($93-$122). Exterior Trim:- Landau vinyl top: Regal ($158-$175). Heavy-padded landau vinyl top: Regal ($188-$238). Long vinyl top ($124). Long padded vinyl top: Century sed ($207). Designers' accent paint ($174-$230). Solid special color paint ($165). Bumper guards, front: Century ($25). Protective bodyside moldings ($52). Rocker panel moldings: Century ($19). Door edge guards ($14-$22). Belt reveal moldings ($37). Wheel opening moldings: Century ($24). Body accent stripes ($37). Woodgrain vinyl applique: Century wag ($292-$316). Luggage rack: wag ($98). Air deflector: wag ($32). Tailgate hinge cover ($13). Interior Trim/Upholstery:- Full-length console ($96). Bucket seats: cpe/wag ($38-$197). 55/45 bench seating: cpe/wag ($112-$159). Limited 55/45 seating: Regal spt cpe ($294). Notchback seating: Century spt ($147). Custom seatbelts ($20- $24). Load floor carpet area: Century wag ($55). Front carpet savers ($16). Carpet savers and mats ($27). Front carpet savers w/inserts ($27); rear ($49). Litter pocket ($10). Trunk trim covering ($33). Lockable storage compartment: wag $40-$45). Wheels:- Chrome-plated wheels ($48-$183). Designers' sport wheels ($116-$135). Styled aluminum wheels ($152-$335). Turbine wheels: Regal spt cpe ($116). Deluxe wheel covers: Century exc. spt ($45). Designers' wheel covers: Century exc. spt ($76); Regal ($31). Wire wheel covers: Century exc. spt ($208); Regal ($48-$164). Tires:- P185/75R14 GBR WSW: Century cpe/sed ($45). P195/75R14 GBR BSW: Century six cpe/sed ($25); V-8 (NC). P195/75R14 GBR WSW ($46-$171). P195/75R14 SBR BSW: Century ($46-$73). P195/75R14 SBR WSW: Century ($95-$119); Regal ($46). P205/70R14 SBR wide-oval BSW: Regal ($37). P205/70R14 SBR WSW: Century spt, Regal ($51-$88). P205/70R14 SBR WLT ($66-$176).

LESABRE/ELECTRA/ESTATE WAGON CONVENIENCE/APPEARANCE OPTIONS: Option packages: LeSabre coupe Sport package: front bucket seats, dual remote sport mirrors ($106-$126). Exterior molding pkg.: LeSabre ($95-$114). Lamp/indicator group: LeSabre ($48-$66). Sliding Astroroof: LeSabre ($981); Electra ($1058). Accessory group (color-coordinated seatbelts, left remote mirror, rocker panel moldings, trip odometer, visor mirrors): LeSabre ($35-$95). Accessory group (trip odometer; headlamps-on, low fuel and washer fluid indicators): Electra ($25-$55). Comfort/Convenience:- Air cond.: LeSabre ($647). Automatic air cond.: LeSabre ($738); Electra ($91). Touch climate control air cond.: LeSabre ($834); Electra ($187). Cruise control ($118). Rear defogger, electric ($109). Tinted glass ($90). Tinted windshield: LeSabre/Est ($55). Power windows: LeSabre/Est ($149-$221). Electric door locks ($95-$135). Automatic door locks: Electra ($158-$189). Six-way power driver's seat ($148-$179); passenger ($179). Manual seatback recliner, one side: LeSabre cpe ($67). Electric seatback recliner, each side ($128). Sport steering wheel: LeSabre ($35). Tilt steering ($83). Tilt/telescoping steering column ($121-$131). Dial clock: LeSabre ($60). Remote tailgate lock: LeSabre Est ($37). Electric trunk release ($27). Electric trunk lock: Electra ($65). Electric fuel cap lock ($39). Theft deterrent system ($146); N/A on Estate. Three-speed wiper w/delay ($42). Lighting, Horns and Mirrors:- Tungsten- halogen high-beam headlamps ($27). Cornering lamps ($53). Twilight Sentinel: Electra ($51). Front light monitors: LeSabre/Est ($31). Front/rear monitors: Electra ($67). Door courtesy/warning lights ($39-$62). Lighted door lock and interior ($62). Four-note horn ($25). Remote left mirror: LeSabre/Est ($20). Remote right mirror ($22-$42). Dual remote sport mirrors ($36-$76). Remote electric right mirror: Park Ave. ($54-$74). Dual electric remote mirrors ($85-$125). Remote left mirror w/thermometer ($33-$53). Remote electric left mirror w/thermometer: Park Ave. ($33). Dual electric mirrors w/left thermometer ($118-$158). Lighted visor vanity mirror, each ($40-$51). Entertainment: AM radio: LeSabre ($99). AM/FM radio: LeSabre ($156). AM/FM stereo radio ($195); w/8-track or cassette player ($276-$289) exc. Park Ave. ($81-$94). Full-feature AM/FM stereo radio: Electra $208-$403); w/8-track or cassette ($289-$497). AM/FM stereo radio and CB: LeSabre ($533); Electra ($338-$533). AM/FM stereo with 8-track and CB: LeSabre ($603); Electra ($408- $603). Signal-seeking AM/FM stereo radio with CB: Electra ($521-$716); w/CB and 8-track or cassette ($635-$856). Signal-seeking AM/FM stereo radio w/digital readout: Electra ($185-$380); w/8-track ($298-$493); w/cassette ($325-$520). Rear speaker: LeSabre ($21); dual ($31). Windshield antenna ($29); incl. w/radios. Automatic power antenna ($52-$81). Tri-band power antenna ($94-$123); w/CB (NC). Delete radio: Park Ave. ($164 credit). Exterior Trim:- Heavy-padded landau vinyl top: LeSabre, Electra Ltd cpe ($213). Long vinyl top ($155-$174). Long, heavy-padded vinyl top: Electra Ltd ($216). Designers' accent paint: LeSabre ($197). Solid special color paint: LeSabre ($166) exc. Firemist on Electra ($186). Protective bodyside moldings: LeSabre/Est ($47). Color-coordinated bodyside moldings: Electra Ltd ($72). Door edge guards ($15-$22). Belt reveal molding: LeSabre spt cpe ($37). Bodyside accent stripes ($56); N/A on Estate. Luggage rack w/air deflector: LeSabre Estate ($152). Interior Trim/Upholstery:- Custom seat trim: notchback, LeSabre spt cpe ($152 credit); 55/45, LeSabre spt cpe ($40 credit); 55/45, LeSabre ($112). Limited notchback seating: LeSabre spt cpe ($8). Limited 55/45 seating: LeSabre spt cpe ($120); LeSabre Ltd ($112). Leather/vinyl 50/50 seating: Park Ave. ($466). Third seat: Estate ($193). Full-length console: LeSabre cpe w/spt pkg. ($102). Front carpet savers ($27). Front/rear carpet savers w/inserts ($49). Carpet savers and mats ($27). Litter pocket: LeSabre ($10). Trunk trim carpet ($52-$65). heels:- Chrome-plated wheels ($154-$188). Custom wheel covers: Electra ($31). Wire wheel covers ($130-$164). Tires:- P205/75R15 SBR WSW: LeSabre ($50). P215/75R15 SBR BSW: LeSabre ($31). P215/75R15 SBR WSW: LeSabre ($84); Electra ($53). P225/70R15 SBR WSW: LeSabre spt cpe ($56). P225/70R25 SBR WLT: LeSabre spt cpe ($72). P225/75R15 SBR WSW: Estate ($56); Electra ($87).

RIVIERA CONVENIENCE/APPEARANCE OPTIONS: Roof Options:- Electric sunroof ($848). Electric sliding Astroroof ($1058). Comfort/Convenience:- Trip monitor ($859). Automatic air cond. ($95). Cruise Master ($118). Rear defogger, electric ($109). Automatic door locks ($69). Six-way power seat, passenger ($179). Electric seatback recliner, one side ($128). Manual seatback recliner, one side: S ($67). Sport steering wheel ($35). Tilt steering ($83). Tilt/telescope steering wheel ($131). Electric fuel cap lock ($39). Electric trunk release ($27). Electric trunk lock ($65). Low fuel indicator ($18). Fuel usage light, V-8 ($32). Windshield washer fluid indicator ($11). Three-speed wipers w/delay ($42). Theft deterrent system ($146). Lighting, Horns and Mirrors:- Tungsten-halogen high beams ($27). Coach lamps ($92); incl. w/vinyl top. Front/rear light monitors ($67). Twilight Sentinel ($51). Courtesy/reading lamps ($45). Lighted door locks and interior light control ($62). Four- note horn ($25). Dual electric remote mirrors ($63). Lighted visor vanity mirrors, each ($51). Entertainment:- AM/FM stereo w/8-track or cassette tape player ($81-$94). AM/FM stereo radio w/CB ($290); w/CB and 8-track ($360). Full-feature AM/FM stereo radio ($208); w/8-track or cassette ($289-$302). Signal-seeking AM/FM stereo radio w/digital readout ($185); w/8-track or cassette ($298-$325). Signal-seeking AM/CB/FM stereo radio w/digital clock ($461); w/8-track or cassette ($587-$661). Triband power antenna ($42); w/CB radio (NC). Delete radio ($164 credit). Exterior Trim:- Heavy-padded landau top ($298). Long vinyl top w/coach lamps ($305). Designers' accent paint ($209). Solid color special Firemist paint ($186). Protective bodyside moldings ($64). Door edge guards ($15). Bodyside stripes ($56). Interior Trim/Upholstery:- 45/55 notchback front seat, leather/vinyl ($360). Leather/vinyl bucket seats: S ($360). Front/rear carpet savers w/inserts ($62). Trunk trim carpet ($27). Trunk mat ($13). Wheels and Tires:- Chrome-plated wheels ($130). Wire wheel covers ($166). GR70 x 15 SBR WSW tires ($33). P205/75R15 SBR WSW tires: S ($33 credit).

HISTORY: Introduced: October 11, 1979 (Skylark, April 19, 1979). Model year production (U.S.): 854,011 (including early '80 Skylarks). Calendar year production (U.S.): 783,575. Model year sales by U.S. dealers: 700,083 (including just 950 imported Opels). Calendar year sales (U.S.): 720,368, which gave Buick a healthy 11.0 percent share of the market.

Historical Footnotes: Although other automakers endured weak sales for the 1980 model year, Buick did comparatively well, ending the year in third place among the GM quintet. Sales that totaled 7 percent less than 1979 still proved better than the average industry loss of 22 percent. Part of the reason may have been an upsurge of interest in the new notchback Century four-door, which proved much more popular than its Aeroback predecessor. Century sales zoomed upward by 137 percent, and the aero coupe was abandoned in February 1980. Regal continued as Buick's best seller, even though sales fell by 28 percent. Full-size Buick sales dropped by similar levels. Skyhawk never had attracted many buyers, and was dropped from the lineup in December 1979. The last imported Opels were also sold during 1980. As of April 1980, Buick no longer manufactured a V-8 engine, thus ending a long series of popular V-8s that began in 1953. The Olds-built diesel V-8 offered beginning this year on Buicks created plenty of trouble, and eventually resulted in lawsuits against GM (and settlements) because of its mechanical problems. Rather than an all-new design, it was simply a modification of the standard gasoline-powered 350 cu. in. V-8 that had been popular in the 1970s, and couldn't withstand the pressures of diesel operation. Diesel popularity was short-lived, in any case, and it would be dropped after 1985. Skylarks were first built at Buick's Willow Run (Michigan) plant. Overall development of the GM X-car quartet had cost $1.5 billion. Initially priced at $4769 and up, Skylark endured a series of increses during its first half-season and beyond. Though priced higher than the Chevrolet, Olds and Pontiac versions, Skylark enjoyed strong demand.

1981 BUICK

One model was missing from the 1981 Buick lineup: the subcompact Skyhawk. The name would return the following year on an all-new model. Meanwhile, fuel economy was the focus for 1981. That included widened availability of the Olds-built 5.7-liter diesel V-8. Most Buicks had Computer Command Control, which responded to sensors around the engine and exhaust system to keep gas mileage up while meeting federal emissions regulations. All Buicks (and other GM vehicles) carried a new "Freedom II" maintenance-free battery, whose label included more test ratings and service information. Century, Regal and Skylark wore new high-pressure tires, introduced on 1980 B-bodies. All '81 Buicks had low rolling resistance radial tires, introduced a year earlier on Skylark, LeSabre and Electra. All tires except Skylark's were now match-mounted. Self-sealing tires were now available on most Buicks. A new "fluidic" windshield washer system sprayed two fans of fluid, but had no moving parts. Buick's turbocharged V-6 got changes for cold-engine driveability this year, including an aluminum intake manifold, thermal vacuum choke valve, and Early Fuel Evaporation system to help vaporize the air/fuel mixture. New "low-drag" brake calipers arrived on Skylark, LeSabre and Electra models, with a special piston seal to pull brake pads away from the rotor. B- and C-bodied models had new quick-takeup master cylinders with a large-bore third piston for faster initial flow of brake fluid. This was especially useful for the new calipers. Cruise-Master speed controls had a new resume-speed feature. Century, Regal, LeSabre and Electra with V-6 engines could have trailer-towing packages capable of hauling a 4000-pound load. The Turbo Hydra-matic 200-4R transmission, offered on full-size models with 5.0-liter V-8, had a new overdrive fourth-speed range to improve highway gas mileage, coupled to a higher axle ratio. It came on Electras and LeSabre Estate Wagons, and was available in LeSabre coupes and sedans. The new transmission was also standard in C-body GM cars with 4.1-liter V-6 engine. Its overdrive (0.67:1) fourth gear engaged at about 45 MPH. The converter clutch added to the standard automatic transmission on some 1980 models was now included on all rear-drive Buicks.

1981 Skylark Limited sedan (AA)

SKYLARK — SERIES 4X — FOUR/V-6 — Apart from a new grille and taillamps, Skylark didn't change much for 1981. The new grille, made up of vertical bars, offered a rather formal look not unlike the 1980 Electra. Buick block letters were inset across the bar at top of grille. Vertical rectangular signal lamps sat outboard of single rectangular headlamps. Skylark's nameplate was at the forward end of fenders. Revised full-width wraparound taillamps split into two horizontal segments, eliminating the amber turn signal lenses. Inside was new cloth upholstery. Limited models had new woven velour cloth. The standard Delco AM radio came with a new fixed-mast antenna to improve fringe-area reception. A center console with storage bin was added, and the instrument panel now had black-face gauges (as did full-size Buicks). Controls for turn signals, dimmer, wiper/washer (and optional cruise control with resume) were now on the multifunction stalk lever. Four-speed manual transmission remained standard, with automatic available. Base powerplant was again the transverse-mounted Pontiac 2.5-liter four-cylinder engine, or optional Chevrolet 2.8-liter V-6. Both engines had Computer Command Control. Rear suspension isolating/damping improved ride feel. Skylark also added higher-pressure tires with low resistance. Buick's mist wiper system continued. Skylark's Sport coupe and sedan had a new sport steering wheel to join the black-accented interior and body. Again, its grille was totally different from other Skylarks: a black-accented six-slot design. Sport models also had amber park/signal lamps, smoked taillamp lenses, bumper strips, Rallye suspension, and P205/70R13 steel-belted radial tires. Optional Sport lower body stripes included a Hawk decal. Electro-luminescent coach lamps were optional on the Limited.

1981 Century Limited sedan (AA)

CENTURY — SERIES 4A — V-6/V-8 — The Aeroback two-door was finally dropped, leaving only a notchback four-door to replace the prior fastback of 1978-80 (a design that wasn't universally loved). Century was described in the full-line catalog as Buick's "little limousine" for its "elegant, even formal, styling." It did indeed display a formal notchback roofline. The restyled grille contained a tiny checkerboard pattern in five rows, separated by a single vertical divider. Vertical rectangular parking lights sat between the grille and the single recessed rectangular headlamps. Amber lenses were at fender tips. Designers' Accent paint combinations were available. At the rear were new wraparound taillamps: red upper lenses, amber below. Just ahead of the taillamps was 'Century' lettering, with a 'BUICK' badge on the decklid. Base engine remained the 231 cu. in. (3.8-liter) V-6, with a 265 cu. in. V-8 the sole option. Century was the last Buick to carry a three-speed manual transmission (on the base model). Century Limited had standard automatic transmission with converter clutch. All Century models had standard power steering and brakes. Two station wagons were offered: base and Estate Wagon. A fixed mast antenna improved radio reception range and interference level. A new side-lift frame jack replaced the former bumper jack. Interiors had new fabrics. Century Limited had new soft knit velour cloth upholstery in 55/45 seating. Low-rolling-resistance tires were standard; new self-sealing tires were available. Optional wraparound moldings ran the full length of the car. Also optional: electro-luminescent coach lamps, and a theft-deterrent system with starter interrupt.

1981 Regal coupe (AA)

REGAL — SERIES 4A — V-6/V-8 — After three years of life as a downsized coupe, Regal got a serious aerodynamic restyle for 1981, including a raked front end and taller back end, with spoiler-type cutoff. A new grille and downward-sloping hood helped to reduce Regal's drag coefficient by 18 percent over the 1980 model. The new vertical-bar grille angled outward sharply from a point near the top. Buick block letters were inset in the upper horizontal bar, with 'Regal' script at the lower corner. Bumper tips flush with fender edges added to the clean look. Wide horizontal turn/parking lamps were built into the bumper. At the rear sat full-width, squarish wraparound taillamps. A new rear deck was topped by an "aerodynamically correct" wedge-styled spoiler lip. Flush-set front and rear bumpers enhanced the smooth aero look. Regal Limited had a full-length, wide rocker panel molding that extended ahead of the front wheels and back of the rears for an unbroken front-to-back line. A new blue crest for '81, in stylized contemporary design, appeared on the hood, new wheel covers, and optional cornering lamps. In addition to solid colors or Designers' Accent schemes, Regals were available with a Decor Package in four colors, each with a silver lower section. The package also included sport mirrors, turbine wheels, and a sport steering wheel. The standard 231 cu. in. (3.8-liter) V-6 engine came with automatic transmission that carried a converter clutch. Options above the standard V-6 were a turbo edition and a 4.3-liter V-8. New standards included low-rolling-resistance tires and a new, lighter battery. Regal had a redesigned fiber-reinforced plastic wheelhouse panel that incorporated a battery tray, plus a new side-lift frame jack. An electronically-tuned radio with Extended Range speakers was offered for the first time on Regals. Self-sealing tires were available. Regal's Sport Coupe was easy to spot. A bulge at rear of hood displayed a 'Turbo 3.8 Litre' chrome emblem at its side. Sport Coupes kept their fast-ratio power steering, sport mirrors and other goodies, but added a new Gran Touring suspension for handling equivalent to LeSabre and Riviera T Type. That suspension (also available on other Century and LeSabre models) was intended to deliver a tempting combination of road feel and smooth ride. The two-tone Decor Package included a black-trimmed grille, headlamps and taillamps; wide bright center rocker molding; turbine-style wheels; sport steering wheel; and choice of four body colors over a silver lower section. Limited interiors used new soft knit velour fabric, even on the upper doors. New fur-like carpeting extended to lower door sections. Limiteds also had the option of new 45/45 seating, or standard 55/45 with fold-down center armrest.

1981 LeSabre coupe (AA)

LESABRE — SERIES 4B — V-6/V-8 — Restyled for 1980, the base and Limited LeSabres enjoyed some detail changes in their second year. The rectangular grille, though similar to 1980 version, gained an extra row of holes and a more refined look. Color-coordinated, protective bodyside moldings were now standard. Taillamps were also modified to all-red design. Base engine remained the 231 cu. in. (3.8-liter) V-6. Both the 252 cu. in. (4.1-liter) V-6 and 5.0-liter V-8 now came with new overdrive automatic transmission; the larger diesel V-8 kept the prior three-speed automatic. All gas engines had Computer Command Control. LeSabres had bumper guards and protective strips, cut-pile carpeting, mist wipers, compact spare tire and a side-frame jack, as well as power brakes and steering. Interiors sported woven velour fabrics. Black dial faces for easier reading were set off by woodgrain vinyl trim. Optional Cruise-Master speed control had a new resume-speed feature. Also optional: an illuminated entry system for nighttime convenience, newly-styled aluminum wheels with exposed chrome lug nuts, electro-luminescent coach lamps (for Limited), and automatic door locks. An option package for the new T Type included bucket seats, console, sport steering wheel, custom seatbelts, sport mirrors, black accented pillar, and Gran Touring suspension.

ESTATE WAGON — SERIES 4B/C — V-8 — Estate Wagons came in two versions: LeSabre and Electra. Dimensions were identical, with 87.9 cubic foot cargo area; but the lower-priced edition sported LeSabre's front end. Both carried the 307 cu. in. (5.0-liter) V-8 engine with overdrive automatic transmission, or optional 5.7-liter diesel. Standard equipment included whitewall steel-belted tires, air conditioning, power steering and brakes, tilt steering column, electric door locks, load floor carpeting, two-way tailgate, and roof rack with air deflector. A wide selection of interiors included five all-cloth front-seat colors on the 55/45 notchback seats, plus two vinyl trim possibilities, and two choices of cloth up front and vinyl in back. Estates sported new colonial oak exterior vinyl woodgrain trim. A dozen Delco radio choices were available.

1981 Electra Estate Wagon (AA)

ELECTRA — SERIES 4C — V-6/V-8 — Electra received few exterior changes except for its grille, which got a different paint treatment to set Electra apart from other Buick series. The basic Electra grille, a bold rectangular design, contained six separate crosshatch sections. Park Avenue's grille relied on vertical strips alone within each section, for a formal look. The new grille was created to blend with the downward-sloping hood, and with Park Avenue's brushed-finish bodyside molding. Fender "ventiports" disappeared from the Limited but remained on the Park Avenue, incorporated into the bodyside molding. Thus, Park Avenue was the only Buick left with vestigial portholes. The standard 252 cu. in. (4.1-liter) V-6 and optional 5.0-liter V-8 were coupled to a new overdrive automatic transmission, with a fourth gear that engaged at about 45 MPH. Diesel V-8 Electras retained the old automatic. Gas engines had Computer Command Control. Low-rolling-resistance whitewall tires were standard; self-sealing tires available. Match-mounted tires were offered. Electro-luminescent coach lamps, formerly only on the Park Avenue, were now offered on the Limited. Park Avenue's standard padded halo top revealed a sliver of body color above the windows. Park Avenue models had fur-like carpet as well as velour or leather seats. Aluminum wheels were newly styled. Electra also had new standard color-coordinated, protective bodyside moldings. As always, Electra carried plenty of standard equipment, including air conditioning, power brakes and steering, single-wipe feature on the windshield wipers, remote-controlled left outside mirror, analog clock, dome reading lamp, and lights for front ashtray, trunk, underdash and glove compartment. Park Avenue added wide rocker appearance moldings, an electric left mirror, and Delco AM/FM stereo radio.

1981 Riviera coupe (AA)

RIVIERA — SERIES 4E — V-6/V-8 — Buick's full-line catalog stressed the claim that some experts had declared Riviera to be on the "leading edge of Detroit technology" by combining "Interesting weight-saving materials and engineering approaches...in a way that's synergistic: the sum becomes greater than its parts." New touches this year included a revised, bolder, more distinctly detailed grille and gray bumper protective strips. The grille consisted of tiny crosshatch elements, split into eight sections by narrow vertical bars, with a 'Riviera' script at the side. Horizontal parking and signal lamps sat directly beneath the quad rectangular headlamps. The oval stand-up hood ornament carried an 'R' insignia. Rivieras rode new low-rolling-resistance radial tires, except for the T Type which carried GR70 x 15 tires. Self-sealing tires were offered as options. A new 'fluidic' windshield washer used no moving parts to spray droplets in a fan pattern. Standard equipment included air conditioning, automatic transmission, six-way power driver's seat, quartz clock, electric door locks, and Delco AM/FM stereo radio with power antenna. New shocks and chassis tuning allowed higher tire pressures while retaining smooth ride. Two new engines were offered: the base 252 cu. in. (4.1- liter) V-6 plus an optional 350 diesel V-8. That diesel, offered through 1985, would eventually cause more trouble than pleasure to both its owners and the company. T Type was the new designation for the sporty Riviera, replacing the S Type of 1980. Special touches included black accents and black side mirrors, plus the familiar amber turn signal lamps. The Gran Touring suspension was intended to give quicker steering and increased road feedback, without a harsh ride. Standard T Type engine continued to be the 231 cu. in. (3.8-liter) turbocharged V-6; but the 4.1-liter V-6 or 5.0-liter V-8 could also be ordered, as well as the diesel. The T Type's instrument panel was now simulated woodgrain. Seats were new, in cloth or leather. A new 45/45 seating arrangement up front featured a fold-down center armrest on the driver's side. Cloth bucket seats and a storage console were standard on the T Type. New option for stereo fans: a Concert Sound six-speaker system. Electronic climate control was also available.

I.D. DATA: All Buicks had a new 17-symbol Vehicle Identification Number (VIN), stamped on a metal tag attached to the upper left surface of the cowl, visible through the windshield. The number begins with a '1' to indicate the manufacturing country (U.S.A.), followed by 'G' for General Motors and '4' for Buick Division. The next letter indicates restraint system. The fifth symbol is a letter denoting series: 'B' Skylark; 'C' Skylark Limited; 'D' Skylark Sport; 'E' Century; 'H' Century Estate Wagon; 'L' Century Limited; 'J' Regal; 'K' Regal Sport Coupe; 'M' Regal Limited; 'N' LeSabre; 'P' LeSabre Limited; 'R' LeSabre Estate Wagon; 'V' Electra Estate Wagon; 'X' Electra Limited; 'W' Electra Park Avenue; 'Y' Riviera T Type; 'Z' Riviera. Digits six and seven indicate body type: '37' 2-dr. coupe; '47' 2-dr. coupe; '57' 2-dr. notchback coupe; '35' 4- dr. wagon; '69' 4-dr. sedan. Next is the engine code: '5' L4-151 2Bbl.; 'X' V6-173 2Bbl.; 'A' V6-231 2Bbl.; '3' V6-231 Turbo; '4' V6-252 4Bbl.; 'S' V8-265 2Bbl.; 'Y' V8-307 4Bbl.; 'N' V8-350 diesel. Symbol nine is a check digit ('8'). Symbol ten denotes model year ('B' 1981). Symbol eleven is the plant code: 'W' Willow Run, MI; '6' Oklahoma City, OK; 'G' Framingham, MA; 'H' Flint, MI; 'Z' Fremont, CA; 'K' Leeds, MO; 'X' Fairfax, KS; 'E' Linden, NJ. The final six digits are the sequential serial number, starting with 100001 except for full-size models built in Flint and Linden, which begin with 400001. A Body Style Identification Plate on the upper horizontal surface of the shroud showed the model year, series, style number, body number, body assembly plant, trim code, paint code, modular seat code, and roof option. Skylarks had their body plate on the front tie bar just behind right headlamp. The five-symbol series and body style number was identical to the combination of series and model number shown in the tables below. Example: 4XB37 indicates a Skylark two-door coupe ('4' indicates Buick; 'X' the X-body; 'B' for base Skylark; and '37' for coupe body style).

SKYLARK (FOUR/V-6)

Series Number	Body/Style Number	Body Type & Seating	Factory Price	Shipping Weight	Production Total
4X	B37	2-dr Coupe-5P	6405/6530	2424/2481	46,515
4X	B69	4-dr Sedan-5P	6551/6676	2453/2510	104,091

SKYLARK LIMITED (FOUR/V-6)

4X	C37	2-dr Coupe-5P	6860/6985	2453/2510	30,080
4X	C69	4-dr Sedan-5P	7007/7132	2484/2541	81,642

SKYLARK SPORT (FOUR/V-6)

4X	D37	2-dr Coupe-5P	7040/7165	2453/2520	Note 1
4X	D69	4-dr Sedan-5P	7186/7311	2484/2541	Note 1

Note 1: Production totals shown for Skylark include Sport models.

CENTURY (V-6/V-8)

4A	H69	4-dr Sedan-6P	7094/7170	3179/3269	127,119
4A	E35	4-dr Sta Wag-6P	7391/7441	3269/3384	5,489

CENTURY LIMITED (V-6/V-8)

4A	L69	4-dr Sedan-6P	7999/8075	3191/3306	Note 2

CENTURY ESTATE WAGON (V-6/V-8)

4A	H35	4-dr Sta Wag-6P	7735/7785	3311/3426	11,659

Note 2: Century sedan production figure included Limited model. Century models had a significant price increase during the model year. The base sedan reached $7924, though rises for other models were less dramatic.

REGAL (V-6/V-8)

4A	J47	2-dr Coupe-6P	7555/7605	3188/3303	Note 3

REGAL SPORT COUPE (TURBO V-6)

4A	K47	2-dr Coupe-6P	8528	3261	Note 3

Note 3: Total Regal coupe production for the model year, 123,848.

REGAL LIMITED (V-6/V-8)

4A	M47	2-dr Coupe-6P	8024/8074	3224/3339	116,352

LESABRE (V-6/V-8)

4B	N37	2-dr Coupe-6P	7715/7715	3464/3623	4,909
4B	N69	4-dr Sedan-6P	7805/7805	3493/3652	19,166

LESABRE LIMITED (V-6/V-8)

4B	P37	2-dr Coupe-6P	7966/7966	3482/3641	14,862
4B	P69	4-dr Sedan-6P	8101/8101	3515/3674	39,006

Note 4: A V-8 engine cost $203 extra on LeSabres; but no charge for the Computer Command version. Like other Buicks, LeSabres rose in price during the model year. The base V-6 coupe reached $8187. LeSabre Estate wagon rose even higher, reaching $9926.

LESABRE ESTATE WAGON (V-8)

4B	R35	4-dr Sta Wag-6P	8722	4002	4,934

ELECTRA LIMITED (V-6/V-8)

4C	X37	2-dr Coupe-6P	10237/10237	3656/3817	10,151
4C	X69	4-dr Sedan-6P	10368/10368	3722/3883	58,832

ELECTRA PARK AVENUE (V-6/V-8)

4C	W37	2-dr Coupe-6P	11267/11267	3728/3889	Note 5
4C	W69	4-dr Sedan-6P	11396/11396	3788/3949	Note 5

Note 5: Production figures for Electra Limited also include Park Avenue models. Total model year production of Limited, 27,826; Park Avenue, 41,157. Only 13,922 Electras carried a V-6 engine. Prices for Electras rose $728 to $962 during the model year, while the Electra Estate Wagon reached $12,092.

ELECTRA ESTATE WAGON (V-8)

4C	V35	4-dr Sta Wag-6P	11291	4174	6,334

RIVIERA (V-6/V-8)

4E	Z57	2-dr Coupe-5P	12147/12147	3563/3724	Note 6

RIVIERA T TYPE TURBO (V-6)

4E	Y57	2-dr Coupe-5P	13091	3651	Note 6

Note 6: Total Riviera production, 52,007 (11,793 with V-6). For the model year, 3,990 turbocharged V-6 engines were produced.

FACTORY PRICE AND WEIGHT NOTE: Figure before the slash is for V-6 engine, after the slash for smallest (lowest-priced) V-8 engine available. For Skylark, figure before the slash is for four-cylinder engine, after the slash for V-6.

ENGINES: BASE FOUR (Skylark): Inline, ohv four-cylinder. Cast iron block and head. Displacement: 151 cu. in. (2.5 liters). Bore & stroke: 4.0 x 3.0 in. Compression ratio: 8.2:1. Brake horsepower: 84 at 3600 R.P.M. Torque: 125 lbs.-ft. at 2400 R.P.M. Five main bearings. Hydraulic valve lifters. Carburetor: 2Bbl. Rochester. Built by Pontiac. VIN Code: 5. Sales Code: LW9. OPTIONAL V-6 (Skylark): 60-degree, overhead-valve V-6. Cast iron block and head. Displacement: 173 cu. in. (2.8 liters). Bore & stroke: 3.5 x 3.0 in. Compression ratio: 8.5:1. Brake horsepower: 110 at 4800 R.P.M. Torque: 145 lbs.-ft. at 2400 R.P.M. Four main bearings. Hydraulic valve lifters. Carburetor: 2Bbl. Roch. 2SE. Built by Chevrolet. VIN Code: X. Sales Code: LE2. BASE V-6 (Century, Regal, LeSabre): 90-degree, overhead-valve V-6. Cast iron block and head. Displacement: 231 cu. in. (3.8 liters). Bore & stroke: 3.8 x 3.4 in. Compression ratio: 8.0:1. Brake horsepower: 110 at 3800 R.P.M. Torque: 190 lbs.-ft. at 1600 R.P.M. Four main bearings. Hydraulic valve lifters. Carburetor: 2Bbl. Rochester M2ME. VIN Code: A. Sales Code: LD5. TURBOCHARGED V-6 (Regal Sport Coupe, Riviera T Type); OPTIONAL (Riviera): Same as 231 V-6 above, but with E4ME four-barrel carburetor. Brake horsepower: 170 at 4000 R.P.M. (Riviera, 180 H.P.) Torque: 275 lbs.-ft. at 2400 R.P.M. (Riviera, 270 lbs.-ft.) VIN Code: 3. Sales Code: LC8. BASE V-6 (Electra, Riviera); OPTIONAL (LeSabre, Riviera T Type): 90-degree, overhead-valve V-6. Cast iron block and head. Displacement: 252 cu. in. (4.1 liters). Bore & stroke: 3.965 x 3.4 in. Compression ratio: 8.0:1. Brake horsepower: 125 at 4000 R.P.M. Torque: 205 lbs.-ft. at 2000 R.P.M. Four main bearings. Hydraulic valve lifters. Carburetor: 4Bbl. Rochester E4ME. VIN Code: 4. Sales Code: LC4. OPTIONAL V-8 (Century/Regal): 90-degree, overhead-valve V-8. Cast iron block and head. Displacement: 265 cu. in. (4.3 liters). Bore & stroke: 3.75 x 3.00 in. Compression ratio: 8.0:1. Brake horsepower: 119 at 4000 R.P.M. Torque: 203 lbs.-ft. at 2000 R.P.M. Five main bearings. Hydraulic valve lifters. Carburetor: 2Bbl. Roch. M2ME. Built by Pontiac. VIN Code: S. Sales Code: LS5. BASE V-8 (Estate); OPTIONAL (LeSabre, Electra, Riviera): 90-degree, overhead valve V-8. Cast iron block and head. Displacement: 307 cu. in. (5.0 liters). Bore & stroke: 3.80 x 3.385 in. Compression ratio: 8.0:1. Brake horsepower: 140 at 3600 R.P.M. Torque: 240 lbs.-ft. at 1600 R.P.M. Five main bearings. Hydraulic valve lifters. Carburetor: 4Bbl. Roch. M4MC. Built by Oldsmobile. VIN Code: Y. Sales Code: LV2. OPTIONAL DIESEL V-8 (Century, LeSabre, Electra, Estate, Riviera): 90-degree, overhead valve V-8. Cast iron block and head. Displacement: 350 cu. in. (5.7 liters). Bore & stroke: 4.057 x 3.385 in. Compression ratio: 22.5:1. Brake horsepower: 105 at 3200 R.P.M. Torque: 200 lbs.-ft. at 1600 R.P.M. Five main bearings. Hydraulic valve lifters. Fuel injection. Oldsmobile-built. VIN Code: N. Sales Code: LF9.

CHASSIS DATA: Wheelbase: (Skylark) 104.9 in.; (Century/Regal) 108.1 in.; (LeSabre/Estate) 115.9 in.; (Electra) 118.9 in.; (Riviera) 114.0 in. Overall length:- (Skylark) 181.1 in.; (Century) 196.0 in.; (Regal) 200.6 in.; (LeSabre) 218.4 in.; (Electra) 221.2 in.; (Estate Wagon) 220.5 in.; (Riviera) 206.6 in. Height:- (Skylark) 53.5 in.; (Century cpe/sed) 55.5 in.; (Century wag) 55.7 in.; (Regal) 54.1 in.; (LeSabre/Electra) 55.0 in.; (Estate) 57.1 in.; (Riviera) 54.3 in. Width:- (Skylark cpe) 69.1 in.; (Skylark sed) 68.9 in.; (Century/Regal) 71.5 in.; (Century wag) 71.2 in.; (LeSabre/Electra) 75.9 in.; (Estate) 79.3 in.; (Riviera) 71.5 in. Front Tread:- (Skylark) 58.7 in.; (Century/Regal) 58.5 in.; (LeSabre/Electra) 61.8 in.; (Estate) 62.2 in.; (Riviera) 59.3 in. Rear Tread:- (Skylark) 56.9 in.; (Century/Regal) 57.8 in.; (LeSabre/Electra) 60.7 in.; (Estate) 64.0 in.; (Riviera) 60.0 in. Standard Tires:- (Skylark) P185/80R13 GBR; (Skylark Sport) P205/70R13 SBR; (Century sed) P185/75R14 GBR; (Century wag) P195/75R14 GBR; (Regal) P195/75R14 SBR; (Regal Spt Cpe) P205/70R14 SBR; (LeSabre) P205/75R15 SBR; (Electra) P215/75R15 SBR WSW; (Estate) P225/75R15 SBR; (Riviera) P205/75R15 SBR WSW; (Riviera T) GR70 x 15 SBR WSW.

TECHNICAL: Transmission:- Three-speed, fully synchronized manual gearbox standard on Century; Turbo Hydra-matic optional. Four-speed, fully synchronized floor shift standard on Skylark; automatic optional. Turbo Hydra-matic standard on all other models. Century three-speed manual transmission gear ratios: (1st) 3.50:1; (2nd) 1.81:1; (3rd) 1.00:1; (Rev) 3.62:1. Skylark four-speed gear ratios: (1st) 3.53:1; (2nd) 1.95:1; (3rd) 1.24:1; (4th) 0.81:1; (Rev) 3.42:1. Automatic trans. gear ratios: (1st) 2.52:1; (2nd) 1.52:1; (3rd) 1.00:1; (Rev) 1.93:1. Skylark automatic gear ratios: (1st) 2.84:1; (2nd) 1.60:1; (3rd) 1.00:1; (Rev) 2.07:1. Riviera auto. gear ratios: (1st) 2.74:1; (2nd) 1.57:1; (3rd) 1.00:1; (Rev) 2.07:1. Overdrive automatic gear ratios: (1st) 2.74:1; (2nd) 1.57:1; (3rd) 1.00:1; (4th) 0.67:1; (Rev) 2.07:1. Standard axle ratio:- (Skylark) 3.32:1; (Century/Regal V-6) 3.08:1; (Century V-8) 2.41:1; (Regal V-8) 2.29:1; (Century wagon) 2.73:1; (Regal Sport Coupe) 2.73:1 or 3.08:1; (LeSabre) 2.41:1, 2.73:1, or 3.23:1; (Electra) 3.08:1 or 3.23:1; (Electra diesel) 2.41:1; (Riviera) 2.93:1 or 2.41:1. Other axle ratios were standard in California. Final drive: (Skylark) spiral bevel; (others) hypoid bevel. Steering:- (Skylark) rack and pinion; (others) recirculating ball; power assist standard on all except Skylark. Suspension:- same as 1980. Brakes:- front disc, rear drum; power brakes standard on all except Skylark. Four-wheel power disc brakes optional on Riviera. Body construction:- (Skylark) unitized; (others) separate body and frame. Fuel tank:- (Skylark) 14 gal.; (Century/Regal) 18.2 gal.; (LeSabre/Electra) 25 gal.; (Riv) 23 gal. Unleaded fuel only.

DRIVETRAIN OPTIONS: Engines:- 173 cu. in. (2.8-liter) V-6, 2Bbl.: Skylark ($125) Turbocharged 231 cu. in. (3.8-liter) V-6, 4Bbl.: Riviera ($750). 252 cu. in. (4.1-liter) V-6, 4Bbl.: LeSabre ($238); Riviera T Type ($750 credit). 265 cu. in. (4.3-liter) V-8: Century/Regal ($50-$76). 307 cu. in. (5.0-liter) V-8, 4Bbl.: LeSabre cpe/sed ($203) but (NC) with computer command control; Electra cpe/sed, Riviera (NC); Riviera T ($750 credit). 350 cu. in. (5.7-liter) diesel V-8: Century ($695- $721); LeSabre/Riviera ($695); Electra/Estate ($542). Transmission/Differential:- Three-speed automatic trans.: Skylark ($349); LeSabre cpe/sed with 4.1 or 5.0-liter ($153 credit). Optional rear axle ratio: Century/Regal/LeSabre/ Electra (NC). Limited slip differential: Century/Regal/ LeSabre/Electra ($69). Suspension, Steering and Brakes:- F40 Firm ride/handling pkg. ($21-$22). FE2 Gran Touring suspension: Century/Regal/LeSabre ($40); Riviera ($21). F41 Rallye ride/handling suspension incl. P205/70R13 SBR tires: Skylark ($134). Superlift rear shock absorbers: Skylark ($57). Automatic level control: Century/Regal/LeSabre/Electra ($142). Power steering: Skylark ($27). Power brakes: Skylark ($79). Four-wheel disc brakes: Riv ($215). Other:- Trailer towing flasher/harness ($23-$40). Trailer towing pkg.: Century/Regal ($148-$226); LeSabre ($434); Electra exc. wag ($141). H.D. alternator, 85-amp ($27-$75). H.D. battery ($21- $22) exc. diesel ($42). H.D. cooling: Skylark ($34-$63). Engine block heater ($16). Diesel fuel heater ($42). Heavy- duty engine/transmission cooling ($32-$61) exc. Skylark. California emission system ($46); diesel ($82).

SKYLARK CONVENIENCE/APPEARANCE OPTIONS: Option Packages:- Acoustic pkg. ($45). Flip-open Vista Vent glass sunroof ($246). Lamp group ($43-$52). Comfort/Convenience:- Air cond. ($385). Cruise Master w/resume ($132). Rear defogger, electric ($107). Power windows ($140- $195). Electric door locks ($93-$132). Six-way power driver's seat ($173). Manual seatback recliners, passenger ($43); both ($87). Sport steering wheel ($43); N/A on Sport. Tilt steering ($81). Tinted glass ($75). Instrument gauges incl. trip odometer ($42). Trip odometer ($14). Electric dial clock ($23). Digital clock ($55). Electric trunk release ($27). Two-speed wipers w/low-speed delay ($41). Lights, Horns and Mirrors:- Tungsten-halogen high beams ($27). Coach lamps: Ltd ($90). Headlamps-on indicator ($12). Dome reading light ($20). Dual horns ($12). Remote-control left mirror ($19); N/A on sport. Sport mirrors: left remote, right manual ($47). Dual remote sport mirrors ($28-$75). Visor vanity mirror, passenger ($12). Lighted visor vanity mirror, either side ($41). Entertainment:- AM/FM radio ($64). AM/FM stereo radio ($100); w/8-track or cassette player ($174-$186). AM/FM stereo radio with CB ($398); with CB and 8-track or cassette ($463-$475). Graphic equalizer ($146). Dual rear speakers $23-$28). Windshield antenna ($10). Power antenna ($47). Triband power antenna ($77). Delete AM radio ($51 credit). Exterior Trim:- Landau vinyl top: cpe ($173). Long vinyl top ($115). Designers' accent paint ($182); N/A on Sport. Protective bodyside moldings ($44). Wide rocker panel moldings ($56). Belt reveal moldings ($27). Wheel opening moldings ($25). Door edge guards ($13-$21). Pillar applique: sed exc. Spt ($23). Hood ornament and windsplit ($27); N/A on Sport. Bodyside or Sport stripes ($42). Bumper guards, front/rear ($34). Bumper strips, front/rear ($42). Interior Trim/Upholstery:- Full-length console ($86). Bucket seats, base ($48); limited cloth/vinyl ($48-$227); limited leather/vinyl ($308-$485). Notchback bench seating: Sport ($177). Color-keyed seatbelts ($24). Front carpet savers ($15). Carpet savers and mats ($25). Trunk trim carpeting ($33). Wheels:- Chrome-plated wheels ($21-$148). Designers' sport wheels ($107-$127). Sport wheel covers ($11-$56). Deluxe wheel covers ($45). Locking wire wheel covers ($157- $202). Tires:- P185/80R13 GBR WSW ($51); N/A on Sport. P185/80R13 SBR BSW ($47); N/A on Spt. P185/80R13 SBR wide WSW ($105); N/A on Spt. P205/70R13 SBR WSW ($58). P205/70R13 SBR WLT ($75). Self-sealing tires ($99).

CENTURY/REGAL CONVENIENCE/APPEARANCE OPTIONS: Option Packages:- Regal Limited Somerset II pkg.: designers' paint (dark sandstone and camel), turbine wheels with camel accents, doeskin 55/45 seats with dark brown buttons/laces ($459). Regal Turbo performance pkg.: dual exhausts and 3.08:1 axle ratio ($75). Regal Sport Coupe Decor pkg. ($427). Regal Coupe Decor pkg. ($385). Sliding electric Astroroof: Regal ($773). Electric sunroof: Regal ($561). Hatch roof: Regal ($695). Convenience group ($12-$78). Exterior molding pkg. ($94-$175). Comfort/Convenience:- Air cond. ($585); automatic ($677). Cruise Master with resume ($132). Rear defogger, electric ($107). Tinted glass ($75). Tinted windshield ($53). Six-way power seat, each side ($173). Manual passenger seatback recliner ($66). Custom steering wheel ($11). Sport steering wheel ($35-$46). Tilt steering ($81). Power windows ($140-$195). Electric door locks ($93- $132). Automatic door locks ($154-$183). Electric trunk release ($27). Remote electric tailgate lock: wag ($29). Electric dial clock ($23). Digital clock ($55). Headlamps-on indicator ($12). Trip odometer ($14). Instrument gauges: temp, voltage, trip odometer ($42). Two-speed wiper w/delay ($41). Theft deterrent system ($142). Lighting and Mirrors:- Tungsten-halogen high-beam headlamps ($27). Cornering lamps: Regal ($52). Coach lamps: Ltd ($90). Front lamp monitors ($31). Door courtesy/warning lights: Ltd ($38-$60). Dome reading lamp ($20). Underhood light ($5). Remote left mirror ($19); right ($35-$41). Dual sport mirrors, left remote ($41- $47). Dual remote sport mirrors ($28-$75). Visor vanity mirrors ($11). Lighted visor vanity mirror ($49). Entertainment:- AM radio ($90). AM/FM radio ($142). AM/FM stereo radio ($178); w/8-track or cassette ($252-$264). Signal-seeking AM/FM stereo radio ($379-$402). Electronic- tuning AM/FM stereo radio w/8-track or cassette ($483-$555). AM/FM stereo radio with CB ($487). Dual rear speakers ($23- $28). Fixed-mast antenna: w/radio ($10). Windshield antenna ($27); incl. w/radio. Automatic power antenna ($47-$74). Triband power antenna ($86-$113). Exterior Trim:- Landau vinyl top: Regal ($146). Heavy-padded landau vinyl top: Regal ($186). Long vinyl top ($115). Long padded vinyl top: Century ($192). Designers' accent paint ($130-$202). Solid special color paint ($162). Protective bodyside moldings ($48). Wraparound bodyside moldings: Century, Ltd ($62-$96). Rocker panel moldings: Century sed ($19). Wheel opening moldings: Century ($25). Door edge guards ($13-$21). Belt reveal moldings: Regal spt cpe w/decor pkg. ($36). Bodyside stripes ($36). Front bumper guards: Century ($24). Woodgrain vinyl applique: wag ($286-$311). Luggage rack: wag ($96). Air deflector: wag ($32). Tailgate follower board: wag ($13). Interior Trim/Upholstery:- Full-length console ($95). Non-shifting console: Regal ($69). Bucket seats ($72). Bench seat: Century sed ($144 credit). 55/45 seating: cloth bench ($134); leather/vinyl, Regal Ltd ($324). Limited 55/45 cloth seating: Regal spt cpe ($358); leather/vinyl ($682). 45/45 seating, Regal Ltd: cloth (NC); leather/vinyl ($324). Limited 45/45 Spt Cpe seating: cloth ($358); leather/vinyl ($682). Custom seat/shoulder belts ($23). Front carpet savers ($15). Carpet savers and mats ($25). Front/rear carpet savers with inserts ($45). Trunk trim covering ($44). Lockable storage compartment: wag ($45). Load floor carpet: wag ($54). Wheels:- Chrome-plated wheels ($47-$180). Styled aluminum wheels ($197-$329). Turbine wheels ($114-$158). Locking wire wheel covers: Century ($205); Regal ($47-$161). Deluxe wheel covers: Century ($45). Tires:- P185/75R14 GBR WSW: Century V-6 ($49). P195/75R14 GBR: Century V-6 ($26). P195/75R14 SBR BSW: Century ($53-$78). P195/75R14 GBR WSW: Century ($49-$76). P195/75R14 SBR WSW: Century ($101-$126); Regal ($49). P205/70R14 SBR wide-oval BSW: Regal ($39). P205/70R14 SBR whitewall: Regal ($54-$94). P205/70R14 SBR WLT: Century ($162-$187); Regal ($70-$109). Self-sealing tires ($99).

LESABRE/ELECTRA/ESTATE WAGON CONVENIENCE/APPEARANCE OPTIONS: **Option Packages:** LeSabre T Type pkg.: bucket seats, console, sport mirrors, sport steering wheel, Gran Touring suspension ($271-$295). LeSabre Coupe Sport pkg.: front bucket seats, remote sport mirrors ($103-$122). Accessory group: LeSabre ($24-$43); Electra ($30-$77). Lamp/indicator group: LeSabre ($47-$64). Comfort/Convenience:- Sliding electric Astroroof ($981-$995). Air cond.: LeSabre ($625). Automatic air cond.: LeSabre ($708); Electra ($83). Air cond. with touch-climate control: LeSabre ($796); Electra ($171). Cruise Master w/resume: LeSabre ($135). Rear defogger, electric ($107). Tinted glass ($107). Power windows: LeSabre ($143-$211). Electric door locks ($93-$132). Automatic door locks ($154-$183). Six-way power seat, driver's or passenger's ($146- $173); both ($319-$346). Electric seatback recliner, one side ($124). Manual seatback recliner, one side: LeSabre ($65). Sport steering wheel: LeSabre ($34). Tilt steering ($81). Tilt/telescoping steering column ($119-$128). Dial clock: LeSabre ($55). Trip

odometer: LeSabre ($14). Remote electric tailgate lock: LeSabre Estate ($43). Electric trunk lock: Electra ($63). Electric trunk release ($27). Electric fuel cap lock ($38). Theft deterrent system ($142); N/A on Estate. Three-speed wiper w/delay ($41). Lighting, Horns and Mirrors:- Tungsten-halogen high-beam headlamps ($27). Twilight Sentinel headlamp control: Electra ($50). Cornering lamps ($51). Coach lamps: Electra Ltd ($90). Light monitors, front: LeSabre, Electra Estate ($31); front/rear, Electra ($65). Door courtesy/warning lamps ($38-$60). Lighted door lock and interior light control ($60). Four-note horn ($24). Remote left mirror: LeSabre ($19). Remote right mirror: LeSabre ($40); Electra Ltd ($21-$40). Remote electric right mirror: Park Ave. ($52-$72). Dual remote sport mirrors: LeSabre ($56- $75); Electra Ltd, Estate ($37-$55). Dual electric remote mirrors: LeSabre ($102-$121); Electra Ltd, Estate ($83-$102). Remote left mirror w/thermometer: LeSabre ($32-$52); Electra Ltd, Estate ($19-$32). Electric left mirror w/thermometer: Electra Park Ave. ($32). Dual electric mirrors w/left thermometer: LeSabre ($134-$153); Electra ($115-$134). Visor vanity mirrors: LeSabre ($11). Lighted visor vanity mirror, driver or passenger ($115-$153). Entertainment:- AM radio: LeSabre ($90). AM/FM radio: LeSabre ($142). AM/FM stereo radio: LeSabre, Electra Ltd/Estate ($178). AM/FM stereo radio and 8-track or cassette player: LeSabre ($252-$264); Electra ($74-$264). Full-feature AM/FM stereo radio: LeSabre ($369); Electra ($346-$369); Park Ave. cpe ($191). Full-feature AM/FM stereo radio w/ 8-track or cassette: LeSabre ($420-$455); Electra ($265-$455). Signal-seeking AM/FM stereo radio: LeSabre ($379-$402); Electra ($170-$348). Signal-seeking radio and 8-track or cassette: LeSabre ($483-$555); Electra ($273-$500). AM/FM stereo radio with CB: LeSabre ($488). Signal-seeking AM/FM stereo radio with CB and 8-track or cassette player: Electra ($581-$783). Delete AM/FM stereo radio: Park Ave. ($150 credit). Concert Sound speaker system: Electra exc. wag ($91); ETR or full-feature radio req'd. Dual rear speakers ($23-$28) when ordered with radio. Windshield antenna ($27); incl. w/radio. Automatic power antenna ($48- $75). Triband power antenna ($86-$113); w/CB radio (NC). Exterior Trim:- Exterior molding pkg.: LeSabre ($92). Landau vinyl top: LeSabre, Electra Ltd cpe ($195). Long vinyl top: LeSabre, Electra Ltd sed ($142-$159). Heavy-padded long vinyl top: Electra Ltd sedan ($198). Designers' accent paint: LeSabre ($191). Special single-color paint: ($161); Firemist, Electra ($180). Protective bodyside moldings: Estate ($48). Wide rocker panel moldings: Electra Ltd/Estate ($56). Door edge guards ($14-$21). Bodyside stripes ($54). Woodgrain vinyl applique: LeSabre Estate ($279). Roof rack: LeSabre Estate ($139). Interior Trim/Upholstery:- Full console: LeSabre cpe ($100). 55/45 seating: LeSabre ($108). Leather/vinyl 50/50 seating: Electra ($452). Custom seatbelts: LeSabre ($23). Third seat: Estate ($108). Front carpet savers: Electra ($25). Carpet savers and handy mats ($25). Front/rear carpet savers w/inserts ($45). Trunk trim carpet ($51-$63). Trunk mat ($13). Wheels:- Chrome-plated wheels ($152-$182). Styled aluminum wheels ($253-$283). Custom wheel covers: Electra Ltd ($30). Custom locking wire wheel covers ($129-$159). Tires:- P205/75R15 SBR WSW: LeSabre ($53). P215/75R15 SBR WSW: LeSabre ($88). P225/75R15 SBR wide WSW: Electra ($36). P225/70R15 SBR wide WSW: LeSabre cpe ($139). Self-sealing tires ($99-$122).

RIVIERA CONVENIENCE/APPEARANCE OPTIONS: Comfort/Convenience:- Electric sliding Astroroof ($995). Electric sunroof ($848). Automatic touch climate control air cond. ($175). Cruise control w/resume ($135). Rear defogger, electric ($107). Automatic electric door locks ($62). Six-way power seat, passenger ($173). Electric seatback recliner, one side ($124). Sport steering wheel ($34). Tilt steering ($81). Tilt/telescope steering wheel ($128). Electric fuel cap lock $38). Electric trunk release ($27). Electric trunk lock ($63). Low fuel indicator ($17). Fuel usage light ($31). Trip monitor ($833). Three-speed wipers w/delay ($41). Windshield washer fluid indicator ($11). Theft deterrent system ($142). Lighting, Horns and Mirrors:- Tungsten-halogen high-beam headlamps ($27). Twilight Sentinel ($50). Coach lamps ($90); incl. w/vinyl top. Front/rear light monitors ($65). Rear quarter courtesy/reading lamp ($43). Lighted door lock and interior light control ($60). Four-note horn ($24). Dual electric remote mirrors ($61). Lighted visor vanity mirrors, each ($50). Entertainment:- Full-feature AM/FM stereo radio ($190); w/8-track or cassette ($264-$276). AM/FM stereo radio w/8-track or cassette tape player ($74)-$86); with CB and 8-track or cassette ($537-$561). Signal-seeking AM/FM stereo radio ($169); w/8-track ($273); w/cassette ($322). Delete radio ($150 credit). Rear speakers ($23). Concert Sound system ($91); N/A with base radio. Triband power antenna ($42). Exterior Trim:- Heavy-padded landau vinyl top w/coach lamps ($273). Designers' accent paint ($202). Special color Firemist paint ($180). Protective bodyside moldings ($59). Door edge guards ($14). Bodyside stripes ($54). Interior Trim/Upholstery:- 45/55 leather/vinyl front seat ($349). Storage console ($67). Front/rear carpet savers w/inserts ($55). Trunk trim carpeting ($27). Trunk mat ($13). Wheels and Tires:- Chrome-plated wheels ($126). Custom locking wire wheel covers ($161). GR70 x 15 SBR whitewalls ($33). Self- sealing tires ($122).

HISTORY: Introduced: September 25, 1980. Model year production (U.S.): 856,996 for a 12.8 percent share of the industry total. That number included 138,058 four-cylinder Buicks, 521,837 sixes, and 197,101 V-8s--quite a drop from the days when the V-8 was king among Buick buyers. Calendar year production (U.S.): 839,960. Model year sales by U.S. dealers: 756,186 (led by Regal and Skylark). Calendar year sales (U.S.): 722,617 for a market slice of 11.6 percent.

Historical Footnotes: Buick assembled its 23 millionth car in 1981 and enjoyed a good sales year as well, beating the 1980 mark by over 56,000 cars. Such good performance came as a surprise, as other U.S. automakers endured a slump. Skylark sales rose by over 25 percent, but Regal hung on as Buick's best seller. Sales of full-size Buicks dwindled. For the fifth time, a Buick served as pace car for the Indy 500. This time it was a Regal with special 4.1-liter V-6 engine, developed by Buick along with Baker Engineering. The souped-up 4.1 produced 281 horsepower, compared with 125 for the stock version used in full-size Buicks (not yet in Regals). The same car also paced the July 4 Pike's Peak hill climb.

1982 BUICK

After a year's absence, the Skylark name returned--but on an all-new front-wheel drive subcompact Buick. The new version debuted in March 1982 as a mid-year entry. Also new was a front-drive (and shrunken) Century, no longer closely related to the rear-drive Regal. Two new gas engines were offered: a high-output 2.8- liter V-6 for Skylarks (delivering 20 percent more horsepower), and a 181 cu. in. (3.0-liter) V-6 for Century, with shorter stroke than the 3.8 version from which it evolved. Flat-top pistons boosted the new 3.0's compression ratio to 8.45:1. It developed just as much horsepower as the 3.8, but at higher engine speed. The high-output 2.8 also gained compression, from standard 8.0:1 in the base version to 8.94:1 in the high-output variant, as a result of larger intake and exhaust valves and increased valve duration and lift. A new diesel 4.3-liter V-6 became available during the model year. On existing powerplants, the biggest news was fuel injection added to the Skylark (and new Century) four. Turbo performance in the Regal Sport Coupe and Riviera T Type got a boost for 1982. The turbocharged V-6 gained a low- restriction dual exhaust sytem as standard on the Regal Sport Coupe, along with upgraded electronics and a larger (five-quart) oil-pan capacity. Turbo response time was reduced, and incoming air was warmed in an exhaust-heated plenum chamber. Oldsmobile's big (5.7-liter) diesel V-8 was now available on Regal, LeSabre, Electra, Riviera, and Estate Wagons. More models added the overdrive automatic transmission that had been offered on selected 1981 Buicks. Producing a claimed 10-20 percent economy boost, overdrive was standard in Electra and Riviera, optional under LeSabre hoods. Pliacell-R- shock absorbers, formerly used only on big Buicks, were added to the rear of all 1982 models. They used a sealed fluid chamber and special gas rather than air. "Memory Seat" was offered as an option on Electra and Riviera, returning automatically to either of two selected positions at the touch of a button. 1982 Buick body colors were light gray, black and white, plus a selection of metallics: silver, dark gray Firemist, charcoal, light sandstone, medium sandstone, dark brown Firemist, medium blue, dark blue, light or dark jadestone, light or dark redwood, and red Firemist. Not all colors were available in all models.

1982 Skyhawk Limited sedan (JG)

SKYHAWK — SERIES 4J — FOUR — Styled along Century lines on GM's J-car platform, the new Skyhawk rode a front-wheel drive chassis. According to Buick, it displayed the "aerodynamic wedge shape of the fuel-efficient future." The fresh subcompact debuted at the Chicago Auto Show in February 1982. The contemporary five-passenger design featured a low hood and high rear deck to reduce drag, along with a unified front end and grille and integrated headlamp system. Backup lights sat in a black panel between the wraparound taillamps. Deluxe wheel covers carried the Buick tri-shield emblem. Buyers could eventually choose from three transverse-mounted engines. First came the base 112 cu. in. (1.8-liter) OHV four. Late arrivals were a fuel-injected 1.8-liter overhead-cam four from GM of Brazil, and a 121 cu. in. (2.0- liter) carbureted four. The 88-horsepower base engine had a cross-flow cylinder head design with intake valves on one side, exhaust on the other. GM's computer command control module controlled spark timing, and it used a fast-burn combustion chamber. The 2.0 engine was essentially the same, but with longer stroke, developing two more horsepower. Skyhawk's chassis now had MacPherson independent front suspension and semi-independent crank arm rear suspension, plus rack-and-pinion steering and Pliacell-R-rear shock absorbers. Skyhawk came in Custom or Limited trim level, on coupe and sedan bodies. Limiteds carried standard soft knit velour upholstery, while Customs could have a woven cloth or vinyl interior. Coupes had swing-out rear quarter windows; sedans, roll-down rear windows. Coupes also had a standard "easy entry" passenger door. Standard Skyhawk equipment included a Delco 2000 series AM radio (which could be deleted), full console, reclining bucket seats, front and rear ashtrays, roof-mounted assist handles, Freedom II battery, two-speed wiper/washer, cigarette lighter, power brakes, power rack-and-pinion steering, side-window front defoggers, compact spare tire, front stabilizer bar, and black left-hand mirror. The Limited added a front-seat armrest, gauge package, trip odometer, custom steering wheel, and acoustic insulation package. Skyhawk options included electronic-tuning radios, six-way power driver's seat, remote trunk release, Vista-Vent flip-open removable glass sunroof, and styled aluminum wheels. A four-speed (overdrive) manual gearbox was standard, but five-speed became available later in the model year.

1982 Skylark coupe (AA)

SKYLARK — SERIES 4X — FOUR/V-6 — Six models made the Skylark lineup: coupe and sedan in base, Limited or Sport trim. Not much changed except for minor revisions in grille and front-end sheetmetal. Skylark now had a "fluidic" windshield washer with single spray nozzle, plus new Pliacell-R- shock absorbers in back. Major changes came under the hood and in the suspension. The base 151 cu. in. (2.5-liter) four switched from a carburetor to single-point electronic fuel injection, intended to improve cold-weather operation as well as gas mileage, and eliminate engine run-on. Two optional engines were offered: a standard 173 cu. in. (2.8-liter) V-6, or a high-output 2.8 V-6 with 20 percent more horsepower. That one had revised carburetion, larger valves, and an altered camshaft. Higher axle ratio boosted Skylark performance with the potent V-6 even more. Four-speed manual shift (floor lever) remained standard; automatic available. A refined interior replaced the vinyl bolsters with cloth fabric on Skylark and Sport notchback front seats. Limited and Sport again offered optional leather. There was a new steering wheel. Special lighting in glove box, under dash, in ashtray and elsewhere that was formerly optional now became standard. A Graphic Equalizer was now available with cassette tape players, offering tone control in five bands. Optional speakers delivered better frequency response. For the first time, Limiteds could have back-seat reading lamps. Also optional: the Vista-Vent flip-open glass sunroof.

CENTURY — SERIES 4A — FOUR/V-6 — Introduced after the model year began, Century underwent a total restyle for a contemporary, wedge-shaped aerodynamic appearance. Bumpers and outside mirrors integrated into the basic body form added to the slick, even "slippery" look. With a transverse-mounted four-cylinder engine under the hood and a front-drive chassis, the new Century hardly seemed related to the old rear-drive that wore that name for so many years. Gas and diesel V-6 engines were available, but it was still a much different car. The modern version had MacPherson strut independent front suspension, plus trailing axle rear suspension with

1982 Century Limited sedan (B)

Pliacell-R- shocks. Though almost 8 inches shorter than before, it retained similar interior dimensions and trunk capacity. An integrated grille with center crest had two bright horizontal bars and a single vertical bar. Half of the lower segment extended all the way outward and around the fender tips, below the wraparound lights. Wide wraparound taillamps were split into two sections by a body-color strip. A Century script badge was at the back of the rear quarter panels, and an engine identifier at the forward end of front fenders. The rear roof pillar held a crest. Grille, front end and hood were said to "flow in an unbroken line past the windshield and side windows." Those windows were flush-mounted to cut wind resistance, giving the new Century the lowest drag coefficient of any Buick. Standard engine was the 151 cu. in. (2.5-liter) four; optional, either a new 181 cu. in. (3.0-liter) V-6 or 4.3- liter diesel V-6. Standard three-speed automatic transmission included a converter clutch for added efficiency. Power rack-and-pinion steering was standard; so were power brakes and deluxe wheel covers. Custom and Limited models were offered. A new Delco AM2000 radio was standard. So were wide belt reveal moldings, color-coordinated bodyside moldings, front/rear bumper guards, wheel opening moldings, black rocker panels, front and side-window defoggers, black outside mirrors, cigarette lighter, and maintenance-free battery. Limiteds also carried dual horns, a stand-up hood ornament, 45/45 pillow seats (soft velour cloth or vinyl) with armrest, a custom steering wheel, and wide lower bodyside moldings. Rocker switches and thumbwheels controlled lights and other functions at the instrument panel.

1982 Regal Sport Turbo coupe (AA)

REGAL — SERIES 4G — V-6/V-8 — After several years of success in coupe form as a top Buick seller, Regal added a four-door sedan and Estate Wagon. Now that Century had turned to front-drive, Regal remained alone as a rear-drive mid-size. Regal's formal-look grille, made up of narrow vertical bars split into eight sections and angled outward at the base, went on both coupes and new models. Both the grille and taillamp displayed Regal identification. The new sedan offered dual outside mirrors plus color-coordinated bodyside moldings, with seating for six. The Regal Estate Wagon could carry up to 71.8 cubic feet of cargo with rear seat folded down. Standard fittings included deluxe wheel covers and whitewall tires, plus bodyside moldings and bumper guards. Standard engine was the familiar 231 cu. in. (3.8-liter) V-6, hooked to automatic transmission. All but the Regal Sport Coupe could have a 252 (4.1-liter) V-6, or choice of a V-6 or V-8 diesel. Coil spring suspensions used Pliacell-R- shock absorbers at the rear. Regal's Limited could be ordered with 45/45 front seating in a choice of two-tone combinations: sandstone and brown, or gray and dark charcoal. Limiteds also sported a new deluxe steering wheel. The optional resume-speed cruise control now included a tiny memory light. Other new options: Delco electronically-tuned AM/FM stereo radio with tape player; quartz analog clock; rear-seat reading lamps; Twilight Sentinel headlamp control; and Electronic Touch Climate Control air conditioning (offered on other Buicks since 1980). A trailering package was available for the 3.8 engine. Regal Limiteds could also have electro-luminiscent coach lamps, automatic door locks, and Gran Touring suspension. The turbocharged Regal coupe continued, with improved performance. The Sport Coupe featured a special hood, black accents, styled aluminum wheels, and Gran Touring suspension. Axle ratio switched to 3.08:1, and the turbo 3.8-liter V-6 now included a low-restriction dual exhaust system.

1982 LeSabre Custom coupe (AA)

LESABRE — SERIES 4B — V-6/V-8 — Still (relatively) full-size and rear-drive, the six-passenger LeSabre entered 1982 with a new grille and more trim, including convenience lights and new color on the woodgrain-trimmed instrument panel. The vertical-slat grille was divided into three rows and four columns, with Buick badge on the side of the center row. Quad headlamps were deeply recessed; parking/signal lamps set into the bumper. Taillamps were wide, but not full-width. The former base LeSabre was now called LeSabre Custom. Buyers could take the standard 231 cu. in. (3.8-liter) V-6 engine for economy, or elect a 252 cu. in. (4.1-liter) V-6 for power. Other options: a 5.0-liter gas V-8 and 5.7 diesel V-8. The 4.1 V-6 had the same electronic idle speed control as the smaller version, plus electronic spark control that adjusted the spark timing when it sensed that the engine was just about to begin knocking. More carpeting was on the floor up front. Standard equipment included whitewalls, wheel opening moldings, deluxe wheel covers, and color-coordinated bodyside moldings. LeSabres also had power brakes and steering, a maintenance-free battery, front/rear bumper guards and protective strips, a compact spare tire, instrument panel courtesy lights, and lights for dome, glove compartment, trunk, front ashtray and engine compartment. The Limited carried the new woodgrain color on doors as well as dash, and also included tinted glass. New options: sail panel reading lights and programmable headlamps. Arriving later in the model year was a limited-edition LeSabre F/E ("formal edition"), offered in two-tone blue and gray. The body was blue all across the top and down to the beltline molding on doors, rear quarter and front fender. Below that point, it was solid gray. Inside were gray cloth seats in a dark blue interior. F/E had light gray bodyside moldings, special 'F/E' exterior identification, a Park Avenue type steering wheel, custom locking wire wheel covers, whitewall steel-belted radials, and remote sport mirrors.

ESTATE WAGON — SERIES 4B/C — V-8 — Estate Wagons available in LeSabre and Electra dress (plus the new Regal described above). LeSabre and Electra offered the same 87.9 cubic foot cargo area and powerteams: standard 5.0-liter gas V-8 or 5.7 diesel V-8, with automatic overdrive transmission. Electra included a standard power tailgate window with remote-controlled tailgate lock plus electric door locks, power windows, chrome-plated road wheels, and woodgrain vinyl applique.

1982 Electra Park Avenue sedan (AA)

ELECTRA — SERIES 4C — V-6/V-8 — Not much changed in the look of Electra, with its formal-style grille. Limited and Park Avenue editions were offered, in coupe or sedan form. New convenience features included optional electronic memory seats and standard Soft-Ray tinted glass. Automatic four-speed overdrive transmission, introduced the prior year, was refined. Electras's ample equipment list included standard right and left mirrors, whitewall tires, bumper guards and protective strips, digital clock, instrument panel floodlighting, two-way power driver's seat, power windows, and air conditioning. Base engine was the 252 cu. in. (4.1-liter) V-6; optional, a 307 cu. in. (5.0-liter) gasoline V-8 or the Oldsmobile 5.7- liter diesel V-8. Park Avenue again incorporated the traditional ventiport design into a bodyside molding, rather than separate as in past years. That model also featured wide, bright chrome rocker moldings and a padded halo vinyl top, plus standard Delco AM/FM stereo radio. Other Park Avenue extras; a six-way power driver's seat, remote-control trunk release, door courtesy and warning lights, and dome reading lamp. The Concert Sound Speaker introduced two years earlier was available again. The optional "Memory Seat" returned to either of two preferred positions automatically.

1982 Riviera coupe (AA)

RIVIERA — SERIES 4E — V/6-V-8 — Though the basic Riviera was basically a carryover for 1982, the biggest news came in mid-year with the arrival of the limited-production convertible--the first ragtop Buick since 1975. It came in Firemist red or white with white convertible top, red leather seats, four-wheel disc brakes, and locking wire wheel covers. According to the one-page flyer, only 500 Limited Edition convertibles were planned for the year. Buick wasn't the first domestic automaker to return to the ragtop fold in the 1980s, but its arrival was a welcome sign for open-air fans. The conversion was done by American Sunroof Corp. to Buick specifications, and sold with a Buick warranty. Riviera's T Type also reappeared later in the model year, after a six-month absence from the lineup. Now it carried the new-generation turbo V-6, four-wheel power disc brakes, tungsten-halogen high-beam headlamps, Gran Touring suspension, and special aluminum wheels. T Type's exterior was gray Firemist with custom blacked-out grille, twin styled remote mirrors, amber turn signal lamps, and matching gray interior with cloth bucket seats. New insignias on front fenders and deck lid highlighted the turbo V-6. Axle ratio changed to 3.36:1. Base Riviera engine remained the 252 cu. in. (4.1-liter) -6 with 4Bbl. carburetor. Options included the 305 cu. in. (5.0-liter) gas V-8 and 350 cu. in. (5.7-liter) diesel V-8. Additional standard

equipment included overdrive automatic transmission and resume-speed cruise control. The optional Gran Touring suspension offered quicker steering feel and increased road feedback. Also on Riviera's standard equipment list were cornering lights, automatic level control, power brakes and steering, and automatic overdrive transmission. A new deluxe steering wheel had a padded center. Bumpers had black protective strips. On the steering column, a new multi-function lever commanded turn signal, headlamps, wiper/washer, and resume-speed cruise control. The standard electronically-tuned AM/FM stereo radio with automatic power antenna could be deleted for credit.

I.D. DATA: All Buicks again had a 17-symbol Vehicle Identification Number (VIN), introduced in 1981, stamped on a metal tag attached to the upper left surface of the cowl, visible through the windshield. The number begins with a '1' to indicate U.S.A., followed by 'G' for General Motors and '4' for Buick Division. The next letter indicates restraint system. The fifth symbol shows series: 'S' Skyhawk; 'T' Skyhawk Limited; 'B' Skylark; 'C' Skylark Limited; 'D' Skylark Sport; 'H' Century Custom; 'L' Century Limited; 'J' Regal; 'K' Regal Sport Coupe; 'M' Regal Limited; 'N' LeSabre; 'P' LeSabre Limited; 'R' LeSabre Estate Wagon; 'V' Electra Estate Wagon; 'X' Electra Limited; 'W' Electra Park Avenue; 'Y' Riviera T Type; 'Z' Riviera. Digits six and seven indicate body type: '27' 2-dr. coupe; '37' 2-dr. coupe; '47' Regal 2-dr. coupe; '57' Riviera 2-dr. coupe; '67' 2-dr. convertible coupe; '35' 4-dr. wagon; '19' Century 4-dr. sedan; '69' 4-dr. sedan. Next is the engine code: 'G' L4-112 2Bbl.; 'O' L4-112 TBI; 'B' L4-121 2Bbl.; 'R' L4-151 TBI; 'X' V6-173 2Bbl.; 'Z' H.O. V6-173 2Bbl.; 'E' V6-181 2Bbl.; 'A' V6-231 2Bbl.; '3' V6-231 Turbo; '4' V6-252 4Bbl.; 'V' V6-263 diesel; 'Y' V8-307 4Bbl.; 'N' V8-350 diesel. Symbol nine is a check digit ('8'). Symbol ten denotes model year ('C' 982). Symbol eleven is the plant code. The final six digits are the sequential serial number. An additional identifying number can be found on the engine, showing codes for GM division, model year, assembly plant, and vehicle sequence number. A body number plate shows model year, car division, series, style, body assembly plant, body number, trim combination, modular seat code, paint code, and date build code.

SKYHAWK CUSTOM (FOUR)

Series Number	Body/Style Number	Body Type & Seating	Factory Price	Shipping Weight	Production Total
4J	S27	2-dr Coupe-5P	7297	2327	25,378
4J	S69	4-dr Sedan-5P	7489	2385	22,540

SKYHAWK LIMITED (FOUR)

4J	T27	2-dr Coupe-5P	7739	2349	Note 1
4J	T69	4-dr Sedan-5P	7931	2411	Note 1

Note 1: Production totals listed under Skyhawk Custom also include Limited models. A total of 32,027 Customs and 15,891 Limiteds were produced for the model year.

SKYLARK (FOUR/V-6)

4X	B37	2-dr Coupe-5P	7477/7602	2462/2519	21,017
4X	B69	4-dr Sedan-5P	7647/7772	2493/2550	65,541

SKYLARK LIMITED (FOUR/V-6)

4X	C37	2-dr Coupe-5P	7917/8042	2489/2546	13,712
4X	C69	4-dr Sedan-5P	8079/8204	2519/2576	44,290

SKYLARK SPORT (FOUR/V-6)

4X	D37	2-dr Coupe-5P	8048/8173	2494/2551	Note 2
4X	D69	4-dr Sedan-5P	8219/8344	2524/2581	Note 2

Note 2: Production figures listed under base Skylark also include equivalent Sport models. Total production for the model year came to 85,263 base Skylarks, 1,295 Skylark Sports, and 58,002 Limiteds.

CENTURY CUSTOM (FOUR/V-6)

4A	H27	2-dr Coupe-5P	8980/9105	2603/2684	19,715
4A	H19	4-dr Sedan-5P	9141/9266	2631/2712	83,250

CENTURY LIMITED (FOUR/V-6)

4A	L27	2-dr Coupe-5P	9417/9542	2614/2695	Note 3
4A	L19	4-dr Sedan-5P	9581/9706	2643/2724	Note 3

Note 3: Production figures for Century Custom coupe and sedan also include Century Limited models. Total production for the model year amounted to 45,036 Customs and 57,929 Limiteds.

REGAL (V-6)

4G	J47	2-dr Coupe-6P	8712	3152	134,237
4G	J69	4-dr Sedan-6P	8862	3167	74,428
4G	J35	4-dr Sta Wag-6P	9058	3317	14,732

REGAL LIMITED (V-6)

4G	M47	2-dr Coupe-6P	9266	3192	Note 4
4G	M69	4-dr Sedan-6P	9364	3205	Note 4

Note 4: Coupe/sedan production figures listed under base Regal also include Regal Limited. A total of 105,812 base Regals and 102,850 Regal Limiteds were made; only 8,276 of those had a V-8 engine.

REGAL SPORT COUPE (TURBO V-6)

4G	K47	2-dr Coupe-6P	9738	3225	2,022

LESABRE CUSTOM (V-6/V-8)

4B	N37	2-dr Coupe-6P	8774/9016	3474/3656	5,165
4B	N69	4-dr Sedan-6P	8876/9118	3503/3685	23,220

LESABRE LIMITED (V-6/V-8)

4B	P37	2-dr Coupe-6P	9177/9419	3492/3674	16,062
4B	P69	4-dr Sedan-6P	9331/9573	3625/3707	47,224

LESABRE ESTATE WAGON (V-8)

4B	R35	4-dr Sta Wag-6P	10668	4171	7,149

ELECTRA LIMITED (V-6/V-8)

4C	X37	2-dr Coupe-6P	11713/11713	3657/3836	8,449
4C	X69	4-dr Sedan-6P	11884/11884	3717/3896	59,601

ELECTRA PARK AVENUE (V-6/V-8)

4C	W37	2-dr Coupe-6P	13408/13408	3734/3913	Note 5
4C	W69	4-dr Sedan-6P	13559/13559	3798/3977	Note 5

Note 5: Production figures listed under Electra Limited also include Park Avenue coupes and sedans. A total of 22,709 Limited and 45,346 Park Avenue editions were produced, 9,748 with a V-6 engine.

ELECTRA ESTATE WAGON (V-8)

4C	V35	4-dr Sta Wag-6P	12911	4175	8,182

RIVIERA (V-6/V-8)

4E	Z57	2-dr Coupe-5P	14272/14272	3600/3760	42,823
4E	Z67	2-dr Conv-5P	23994/24064	N/A	1,248

RIVIERA T TYPE (TURBO V-6)

4E	Y57	2-dr Coupe-5P	14940	N/A	Note 6

Note 6: T Type production is included in basic Riviera figure.

FACTORY PRICE AND WEIGHT NOTE: Figure before the slash is for four-cylinder engine, after the slash for V-6. For full-size models, figure before the slash is for V-6 engine, after slash for V-8.

ENGINES: BASE FOUR (Skyhawk): Inline, overhead-valve four-cylinder. Cast iron block and head. Displacement: 112 cu. in. (1.8 liters). Bore & stroke: 3.50 x 2.91 in. Compression ratio: 9.0:1. Brake horsepower: 88 at 5100 R.P.M. Torque: 100 lbs.-ft. at 2800 R.P.M. Five main bearings. Hydraulic valve lifters. Carburetor: 2Bbl. Rochester E2SE. VIN Code: G. OPTIONAL FOUR (Skyhawk): Inline, overhead-cam four-cylinder. Cast iron block and head. Displacement: 112 cu. in. (1.8 liters). Bore & stroke: 3.33 x 3.12 in. Compression ratio: 9.0:1. Brake horsepower: 80 at 5200 R.P.M. Torque: 115 lbs.-ft. at 2800 R.P.M. Five main bearings. Hydraulic valve lifters. Throttle-body fuel injection. VIN Code: O. OPTIONAL FOUR (Skyhawk): Inline, overhead-cam four-cylinder. Cast iron block and head. Displacement: 121 cu. in. (2.0 liters). Bore & stroke: 3.50 x 3.14 in. Compression ratio: 9.0:1. Brake horsepower: 90 at 5100 R.P.M. Torque: 111 lbs.-ft. at 2700 R.P.M. Five main bearings. Hydraulic valve lifters. Carburetor: 2Bbl. Rochester E2SE. VIN Code: B. BASE FOUR (Skylark, Century): Inline, overhead-valve four-cylinder. Cast iron block and head. Displacement: 151 cu. in. (2.5 liters). Bore & stroke: 4.0 x 3.0 in. Compression ratio: 8.2:1. Brake horsepower: 90 at 4000 R.P.M. Torque: 134 lbs.-ft. at 4000 R.P.M. Five main bearings. Hydraulic valve lifters. Throttle-body fuel injection. Built by Pontiac. VIN Code: R. Sales Code: LW9. OPTIONAL V-6 (Skylark): 60-degree, overhead-valve V-6. Cast iron block and head. Displacement: 173 cu. in. (2.8 liters). Bore & stroke: 3.5 x 3.0 in. Compression ratio: 8.4:1. Brake horsepower: 112 at 5100 R.P.M. Torque: 148 lbs.-ft. at 2400 R.P.M. Four main bearings. Hydraulic valve lifters. Carburetor: 2Bbl. Rochester E2SE. Built by Chevrolet. VIN Code: X. Sales Code: LE2. HIGH-OUTPUT 173 V-6; OPTIONAL (Skylark): Same as 173 cu. in. V-6 above except as follows: Compression ratio: 8.9:1. Brake horsepower: 135 at 5400 R.P.M. Torque: 142 lbs.-ft. at 2400 R.P.M. VIN Code: Z. OPTIONAL V-6 (Century): 90-degree, overhead-valve V-6. Cast iron block and head. Displacement: 181 cu. in. (3.0 liters). Bore & stroke: 3.8 x 2.66 in. Compression ratio: 8.45:1. Brake horsepower: 110 at 800 R.P.M. Torque: 145 lbs.-ft. at 2600 R.P.M. Four main bearings. Hydraulic valve lifters. Carburetor: 2Bbl. Rochester E2ME. VIN Code: E. BASE V-6 (Regal, LeSabre): 90-degree, overhead-valve V-6. Cast iron alloy block and head. Displacement: 231 cu. in. (3.8 liters). Bore & stroke: 3.8 x 3.4 in. Compression ratio: 8.0:1. Brake horsepower: 110 at 3800 R.P.M. Torque: 190 lbs.-ft. at 1600 R.P.M. Four main bearings. Hydraulic valve lifters. Carburetor: 2Bbl. Rochester M2ME. VIN Code: A. Sales Code: LD5. TURBOCHARGED V-6 (Regal Sport Coupe, Riviera T Type): Same as 231 V-6 above, but with E4ME four-barrel carburetor. Brake horsepower: 170 at 3800 R.P.M. (Riviera, 180 at 4000) Torque: 275 lbs.-ft. at 2400 R.P.M. (Riviera, 200 at 2400). VIN Code: 3. Sales Code: LC8. BASE V-6 (Electra, Riviera); OPTIONAL (Regal, LeSabre): 90-degree, overhead-valve V-6. Cast iron block and head. Displacement: 252 cu. in. (4.1 liters). Bore & stroke: 3.965 x 3.4 in. Compression ratio: 8.0:1. Brake horsepower: 125 at 4000 R.P.M. Torque: 205 lbs.-ft. at 2000 R.P.M. Four main bearings. Hydraulic valve lifters. Carburetor: 4Bbl. Rochester. VIN Code: 4. Sales Code: LC4. DIESEL V-6; OPTIONAL (Century, Regal cpe/sed): 90-degree, overhead-valve V-6. Cast iron block and head. Displacement: 262.5 cu. in. (4.3 liters). Bore & stroke: 4.057 x 3.385 in. Compression ratio: 21.6:1. Brake horsepower: 85 at 3600 R.P.M. Torque: 165 lbs.-ft. at 1600 R.P.M. Four main bearings. Hydraulic valve lifters. Fuel injection. VIN Code: V. BASE V-8 (Estate); OPTIONAL (LeSabre, Electra, Riviera): 90-degree, overhead-valve V-8. Cast iron block and head. Displacement: 307 cu. in. (5.0 liters). Bore & stroke: 3.80 x 3.385 in. Compression ratio: 8.0:1. Brake horsepower: 140 at 3600 R.P.M. Torque: 240 lbs.-ft. at 1600 R.P.M. Five main bearings. Hydraulic valve lifters. Carburetor: 4Bbl. Roch. M4MC. Built by Oldsmobile. VIN Code: Y. Sales Code: LV2. OPTIONAL DIESEL V-8 (Regal, LeSabre, Electra, Estate, Riviera): 90-degree, overhead valve V-8. Cast iron block and head. Displacement: 350 cu. in. (5.7 liters). Bore & stroke: 4.057 x 3.385 in. Compression ratio: 21.6:1. Brake horsepower: 105 at 3200 R.P.M. Torque: 200 lbs.-ft. at 1600 R.P.M. Five main bearings. Hydraulic valve lifters. Fuel injection. Oldsmobile-built. VIN Code: N. Sales Code: LF9.

CHASSIS DATA: Wheelbase: (Skyhawk) 101.2 in.; (Skylark/Century) 104.9 in.; (Regal) 108.1 in.; (LeSabre/Estate) 115.9 in.; (Electra) 118.9 in.; (Riviera) 114.0 in. Overall length:- (Skyhawk) 175.3 in.; (Skylark) 181.1 in.; (Century) 189.1 in.; (Regal cpe) 200.6 in.; (Regal sed) 196.0 in.; (Regal wag) 196.7 in.; (LeSabre) 218.4 in.; (Electra) 221.3 in.; (Estate Wagon) 220.5 in.; (Riviera) 206.6 in. Height:- (Skyhawk) 54.0 in.; (Skylark) 53.7 in.; (Century) 53.6 in.; (Regal cpe) 54.5 in.; (Regal sed) 55.4 in.; (Regal wag) 56.5 in.; (LeSabre) 56.0- 56.7 in.; (Electra) 56.8-56.9 in.; (Estate) 59.1-59.4 in.; (Riviera) 54.3 in. Width:- (Skyhawk) 62.0 in.; (Skylark) 69.1 in.; (Century) 66.8 in.; (Regal cpe) 71.6 in.; (Regal sed) 71.1 in.; (Regal wag) 71.2 in.; (LeSabre) 78.0 in.; (Electra cpe) 76.2 in.; (Estate) 79.3 in.; (Riviera) 72.8 in. Front Tread:- (Skyhawk) 55.4 in.; (Skylark/Century) 58.7 in.; (Regal) 58.5 in.; (LeSabre/Electra) 61.8 in.; (Estate) 62.2 in.; (Riviera) 59.3 in. Rear Tread:- (Skyhawk) 55.2 in.; (Skylark/Century) 57.0 in.; (Regal) 57.7 in.; (LeSabre/Electra) 60.7 in.; (Estate) 64.0 in.; (Riviera) 60.0 in. Standard Tires:- (Skyhawk) (Skylark/Century) P185/80R13 GBR; (Skylark Sport) P205/70R13 SBR; (Regal) P195/75R14 SBR WSW; (Regal Spt Cpe) P205/70R14 SBR; (LeSabre) P205/75R15 SBR WSW; (Electra) P215/75R15 SBR WSW; (Estate) P225/75R15 SBR WSW; (Riviera) P205/75R15 SBR WSW.

TECHNICAL: Transmission: Four-speed, fully synchronized floor shift standard on Skyhawk/Skylark; automatic optional. Turbo Hydra-matic standard on all other models. Skyhawk four-speed gear ratios: (1st) 3.53:1; (2nd) 1.95:1; (3rd) 1.24:1; (4th) 0.81:1; (Rev) 3.42:1. Four-speed gear ratios: (1st) 3.53:1; (2nd) 1.95:1; (3rd) 1.24:1; (4th) 0.73:1; (Rev) 3.92:1. Skylark/Century auto. trans. gear ratios: (1st) 2.84:1; (2nd) 1.60:1; (3rd) 1.00:1; (Rev) 2.07:1. Three-speed auto. trans. gear ratios: (1st) 2.52:1; (2nd) 1.52:1; (3rd) 1.00:1; (Rev) 1.94:1. Four-speed automatic gear ratios: (1st) 2.74:1; (2nd) 1.57:1; (3rd) 1.00:1; (4th) 0.67:1; (Rev) 2.07:1. Steering:- (Skyhawk/Skylark/Century) rack and pinion; (others) recirculating ball; power assist standard on all except Skyhawk. Suspension:- front/rear coil springs; (Skyhawk/Skylark/Century) MacPherson strut front suspension; trailing axle rear; front/rear stabilizer bars. (Riviera) fully independent suspension with front torsion bar, front/rear stabilizers. Brakes:- power front disc, rear drum. Four-wheel power disc brakes available on Riviera. Body construction:- (Skyhawk/Skylark/Century) unitized; (others) separate body and frame. Wheel size:- (Skyhawk/Century) 13 x 5.5 in.; (Regal) 14 x 6 in.; (LeSabre/Riviera) 15 x 6 in.; (Estate) 15 x 7 in.

DRIVETRAIN OPTIONS: Engines:- 112 cu. in. (1.8-liter) EFI four: Skyhawk ($75). 121 cu. in. (2.0-liter) four, 2Bbl.: Skyhawk ($50). 173 cu. in. (2.8-liter) V-6, 2Bbl.: Skylark ($125); High-output 173 cu. in. (2.8-liter) V-6, 2Bbl.: Skylark ($250); 181 cu. in. (3.0-liter) V-6, 2Bbl.: Century ($125); 252 cu. in. (4.1- liter) V-6, 4Bbl.: Regal ($95); LeSabre exc. wag ($267) incl. overdrive automatic transmission. 263 cu. in. (4.3-liter) diesel V-6: Century ($859); Regal exc. spt cpe or wag ($874); 307 cu. in. (5.0-liter) V-8, 4Bbl.: LeSabre cpe/sed ($242) incl. overdrive automatic trans.; Electra cpe/sed (NC); Riviera (NC). 350 cu. in. (5.7-liter) diesel V-8: Regal exc. spt cpe ($924); LeSabre/Riviera ($924); LeSabre Estate, Electra ($752). Transmission/Differential:- Five-speed manual trans.: Skyhawk ($196). Three-speed auto. trans.: Skyhawk ($370); Skylark ($396); LeSabre cpe/sed with 4.1 or 5.0-liter ($172 credit); Optional rear axle ratio: Century 2.97:1 (NC); Regal 3.23:1 (NC); Regal cpe/sed 3.08:1 (NC); LeSabre 3.08:1 or 3.23:1 (NC). Limited slip differential: Regal/LeSabre/Electra ($80). Suspension, Steering and Brakes:- F40 Firm ride/handling pkg. ($27) exc. Skyhawk. F41 Gran Touring suspension: Skyhawk ($158); Century four, Riviera ($27); Regal exc. wag, LeSabre ($49). F41 Rallye ride/handling suspension incl. P205/70R13 SBR tires: Skylark ($206). Superlift rear shock absorbers: Skylark ($68). Automatic level control: Century/Regal/LeSabre/Electra ($165). Power steering: Skyhawk ($180). Four-wheel disc brakes: Riviera ($235). Other:- Trailer towing flasher/harness ($28-$43) exc. Skyhawk. Trailer towing pkg.: Regal exc. spt cpe ($182); LeSabre exc. wagon ($459); Electra exc. wagon ($167). Heavy-duty alternator, 85-amp ($32-$85). H.D.: ($22- $50). H.D. radiator: Skyhawk ($37-$67). H.D.: Skylark/Century ($38-$73); Engine block heater ($17-$18). H.D. engine/transmission cooling: Regal/LeSabre/Electra/Riviera ($38-$73). California emission system: Skyhawk ($46); Skylark ($65); Century ($65-$205). Diesel cold climate pkg. delete: Regal/LeSabre/Electra/Riviera ($99 credit).

SKYHAWK CONVENIENCE/APPEARANCE OPTIONS: Option Packages:- Vista Vent flip-open sunroof ($261). Acoustic pkg. ($36). Instrument gauge pkg.: temp, oil pressure, volts, trip odometer ($60). Gauges and tachometer ($78-$138). Comfort/Convenience:- Air cond. ($625). Rear defogger, electric ($115). Cruise control w/resume ($145- $155). Power windows ($152-$216). Power door locks ($99- $142). Six-way power driver's seat ($183). Tinted glass ($82). Tinted windshield ($57). Sport steering wheel ($45). Tilt steering ($88). Trip odometer ($15). Electric trunk release ($29). Two-speed wipers w/delay ($44). Lights, Horns and Mirrors:- Halogen high-beam headlamps ($29). Headlamps-on indicator ($15). Dome reading lamp ($21). Rear seat reading lamps ($30). Styled left remote mirror ($21). Dual styled mirrors: left remote ($51). Dual electric styled mirrors ($130). Visor vanity mirror, passenger ($7). Lighted visor vanity mirror, either side ($45). Entertainment:- AM radio w/digital clock ($55). AM/FM radio ($119). AM/FM stereo radio ($155); w/digital clock and 8-track tape player ($234); w/cassette ($272). Electronic-tuning AM/FM stereo radio ($385); w/8-track ($464); w/cassette ($497). AM radio delete ($56 credit). Power antenna ($50). Dual rear speakers ($25- $30). Exterior Trim:- Door edge guards ($14-$22). Bodyside stripes ($40). Designers' accent paint ($195). Decklid luggage rack ($98). Interior Trim/Upholstery:- Front carpet savers ($20); rear ($15). Trunk trim ($33). Wheels and Tires:- Styled aluminum wheels ($229). Styled wheel covers ($38). Custom locking wire wheel covers ($165). P175/80R13 GBR WSW ($55). P195/70R13 SBR BSW ($133). P195/70R13 SBR WSW ($55- $188). P195/70R13 SBR WLT ($72-$205). P195/70R13 SBR wide WSW ($55-$188). Self-sealing tires ($94).

SKYLARK CONVENIENCE/APPEARANCE OPTIONS: Option Packages:- Acoustic pkg. ($60). Flip-open Vista Vent glass sunroof ($275). Comfort/Convenience:- Air cond. ($675). Cruise Master w/resume ($155-$165). Rear defogger, electric ($125). Power windows ($165-$235). Electric door locks ($106- 152). Six-way power driver's seat ($197). Manual seatback recliners, passenger ($50); both ($100). Sport steering wheel ($50); N/A on Sport. Tilt steering ($95). Tinted glass ($88). Instrument gauges incl. trip odometer ($48). Trip odometer ($16). Electric dial clock ($30). Digital clock ($60). Electric trunk release ($32). Two-speed wipers w/delay ($47). Lights, Horns and Mirrors:- Coach lamps: Ltd ($102). Headlamps-on indicator ($16). Dome reading light ($24). Rear seat reading lamp: Ltd ($30). Dual horns ($15). Remote- control left mirror ($24); N/A on sport. Sport mirrors: left remote, right manual ($55); dual remote ($31-$86). Visor vanity mirror, passenger ($8). Lighted visor vanity mirror, either side ($50). Entertainment:- AM/FM radio ($75). AM/FM stereo radio ($106); w/8-track or cassette player ($192- $193). AM/FM stereo radio with CB ($419); with CB and 8-track or cassette ($494-$495). Graphic equalizer ($150). Rear speakers ($25-$30). Power antenna ($55). Triband power antenna ($100). Delete AM radio ($56 credit). Exterior Trim:- Landau vinyl top: cpe ($195). Long vinyl top ($140). Designers' accent paint ($210); N/A on Sport. Protective bodyside moldings ($47). Wide rocker panel moldings ($65). Belt reveal molding ($35). Wheel opening moldings ($28). Door edge guards ($15-$25). Pillar applique moldings: sed exc. Spt ($27). Hood ornament and windsplit ($32); N/A on Spt. Bodyside or Sport stripes ($48). Bumper guards, front/rear ($45). Bumper strips, front/rear ($49). Interior Trim/Upholstery: Full-length console ($100). 45/45 seating, cloth or vinyl ($57-$252). Leather/vinyl 45/45 limited seating ($358-$553). Notchback bench seating: Spt ($195). Front carpet savers ($16); rear ($11). Carpet savers w/inserts: front ($25); rear ($20). Trunk trim carpeting ($35). Wheels:- Chrome-plated wheels ($155-$175). Sport wheel covers ($20). Locking wire wheel covers ($165-$185). Tires:- P185/80R13 GBR WSW ($58); N/A on Sport. P185/80R13 SBR BSW ($64); N/A on Sport. P185/80R13 SBR wide whitewall ($122); N/A on Sport. P205/70R13 SBR WSW ($66). P205/70R13 SBR WLT ($88). Self-sealing GBR whitewall tires ($106).

CENTURY/REGAL CONVENIENCE/APPEARANCE OPTIONS: Option Packages:- Regal Sport Coupe Decor pkg.: designers' accent paint, wide rocker moldings, sport steering wheel, black paint treatment ($125). Regal Coupe Decor pkg. w/turbine wheels ($428). Sliding electric Astroroof: Regal cpe ($885). Flip-open Vista Vent glass sunroof: Century ($275). Hatch roof: Regal cpe ($790). Comfort/Convenience:- Air cond. ($675). Automatic touch climate control air cond.: Regal ($825). Cruise Master w/resume ($155). Rear defogger, electric ($125). Tinted glass ($88). Tinted windshield: Regal ($65). Six-way power seat, each side ($197); both ($394); passenger's side N/A on Century. Manual passenger seatback recliner ($50-$75); both seats, Century only ($100). Sport steering wheel ($40). Tilt steering ($95). Power windows ($165-$235). Electric door locks ($106-$152). Automatic door locks ($180-$215). Electric trunk release ($32). Remote electric tailgate lock: Regal wag ($38). Electric dial clock ($30). Digital clock ($60). Headlamps-on indicator ($16). Trip odometer: Regal ($16). Instrument gauges: temp, voltage, trip odometer ($48). Windshield wiper w/low-speed delay ($47). Theft deterrent system ($159). Lighting and Mirrors:- Tungsten-halogen high-beam headlamps ($10). Twilight Sentinel headlamp control ($57). Cornering lamps: Regal ($57). Coach lamps: Ltd ($102). Front lamp monitors ($37). Door courtesy/warning lights: Ltd ($44-$70). Rear seat reading light: Regal ($30). Dome reading lamps ($24). Remote left mirror ($24). Remote right mirror: Regal exc. spt cpe ($48). Dual mirrors, left remote ($48-$55). Dual electric remote mirrors: Century ($137). Dual remote sport mirrors: Regal ($31-$79). Visor vanity mirror ($8). Lighted visor vanity mirror ($58); driver's N/A on Regal. Dual horns: Century ($15). Entertainment:- AM radio: Regal ($99). AM/FM radio ($82-$153). AM/FM stereo radio ($118-$184). AM/FM stereo radio w/digital clock: Century ($178); w/8-track or cassette player ($277-$282). AM/FM stereo radio w/8-track or cassette: Regal ($270-$271). Electronic-tuning AM/FM stereo radio ($377-$402); w/8-track or cassette ($481-$555). AM/FM radio with CB: Regal ($497). CB radio: Century ($263). Dual rear speakers ($25-$30). Fixed-mast antenna: Regal ($39); w/radio $12). Automatic power antenna ($55-$90). Triband power antenna ($100-$135). Exterior Trim:- Landau vinyl top: cpe ($166). Heavy-padded landau vinyl top: Regal cpe ($220). Long vinyl top ($140). Long padded vinyl top: Regal sed ($220). Designers' accent paint ($195-$235). Solid special color paint ($200). Exterior molding pkg.: Regal exc. Ltd ($110). Protective bodyside moldings: Century, Regal spt cpe ($47- $51). Wraparound bodyside moldings: Regal sed ($104). Lower bodyside moldings: Century ($65). Hood ornament and windplit: Century ($32); std. on Ltd. Door edge guards ($15-$25). Belt reveal moldings: Regal spt cpe w/decor pkg. ($40). Bodyside stripe ($42). Woodgrain vinyl appliqué: Regal wag ($330). Roof rack: Regal wag ($115). Air deflector: Regal wag ($37). Interior Trim/Upholstery:- Full-length console ($100). Non-shifting console ($82). Bucket seats: Regal ($56). 55/45 seating: Regal ($133). Limited 55/45 seating: Regal spt cpe ($385). 45/45 seating: Century Cust ($133); Regal Ltd (NC). Front carpet savers ($16); rear ($11). Front carpet savers with inserts ($25); rear ($20). Litter pocket ($9). Trunk trim covering ($47). Lockable storage compartment: Regal wag ($55). Wheels:- Chrome-plated wheels ($40-$175); Regal spt cpe ($110 credit). Styled aluminum wheels: Regal exc. spt cpe ($150-$285). Turbine wheels: Regal exc. spt cpe ($135). Locking wire wheel covers: Century ($185); Regal ($50-$185); Regal spt cpe ($100 credit). Tires:- P185/80R13 GBR WSW: Century four ($58). P185/80R13 SBR BSW: Century four ($64). P185/80R13 SBR WSW: Century four ($122). P185/75R14 GBR and SBR: Century V-6 ($37-$159). P195/75R14 SBR BSW: Regal exc. spt cpe (NC). P205/70R13 SBR BSW: Century four w/F41 suspension ($179). P205/70R13 SBR WSW: Century four w/F41 suspension ($245). P205/70R13 SBR WLT: Century four w/F41 ($267). P205/70R14 SBR wide-oval BSW: Regal (N/A). P205/70R14 SBR WSW: Regal spt cpe ($66). P205/70R14 SBR WLT: Regal ($84- $88). Self-sealing tires ($106).

LESABRE/ELECTRA/ESTATE WAGON CONVENIENCE/APPEARANCE OPTIONS: Comfort/Convenience:- Sliding electric Astroroof ($1125). Air cond.: LeSabre ($695). Air cond. w/touch-climate control: LeSabre ($845); LeSabre Est, Electra ($150). Cruise Master with resume ($155); std. on Park Ave. Rear defogger, electric ($125). Tinted glass: LeSabre Cust ($102). Power windows: LeSabre ($165-$240). Electric door locks ($106-$152). Automatic door locks ($63-$215). Six-way power seat, driver's or passenger's ($167-$197); both ($364-$394). Memory driver's power seat: Electra ($178-$345). Electric seatback recliner, one side ($139). Sport steering wheel: LeSabre ($40). Tilt steering: LeSabre, Electra Ltd ($95). Tilt/telescoping steering column ($55-$150). Dial clock: LeSabre ($60). Digital clock: LeSabre, Estate (NC w/convenience group). Lamp and indicator group: LeSabre ($52-$70). Trip odometer: LeSabre ($16). Remote tailgate lock: LeSabre Estate ($49). Electric trunk lock: Electra Ltd ($72). Electric trunk release ($32). Electric fuel cap lock ($44). Theft deterrent system ($159); N/A on Estate. Two-speed wiper w/delay ($47). Accessory group (trip odometer, dome reading lamp, headlamps-on indicator, low fuel indicator, washer fluid indicator): Electra ($28-$86). Lighting, Horns and Mirrors: Tungsten halogen high-beam headlamps ($10). Twilight Sentinel ($57). Cornering lamps ($57). Coach lamps: LeSabre/Electra Ltd ($102). Light monitors, front: LeSabre, Electra Est ($37); front/rear, Electra ($74). Door courtesy/warning lamps ($44- $70). Rear seat reading lamp: LeSabre Ltd, Electra ($30). Lighted door lock and interior light control ($72). Four-note horn ($28). Remote left mirror: LeSabre ($24). Remote right mirror: LeSabre ($48); Electra Ltd, Est ($24). Remote electric right mirror: Electra Park Ave. ($57). Dual remote sport mirrors: LeSabre ($85); Electra Ltd, Estate ($38). Dual electric remote mirrors: LeSabre ($137); Electra Ltd, Estate ($90). Remote left mirror w/thermometer: LeSabre ($62); Electra Ltd, Estate ($38). Electric left mirror w/thermometer: Electra Park Ave. ($39). Dual electric mirrors w/left thermometer: LeSabre ($170); Electra Ltd, Estate ($123). Lighted visor vanity mirror, driver or passenger ($58). Entertainment:- AM radio: LeSabre ($99). AM/FM radio: LeSabre ($153). AM/FM stereo radio: LeSabre, Electra Ltd/Estate ($184). AM/FM stereo radio and 8-track or cassette player ($86-$271). Electronic-tuning AM/FM stereo radio: LeSabre ($377-$402); Electra ($170-$348). Electronic-tuning AM/FM stereo radio and 8-track or cassette ($273-$555). AM/FM stereo radio with CB ($314-$498). Electronic-tuning radio with CB and 8-track or cassette ($585-$841). Delete AM/FM stereo radio: Electra Park Ave. (credit ($153). Concert Sound speaker system: Electra exc. wagon ($95); ETR radio req'd. Dual rear speakers ($25-$30) when ordered with radio. Automatic power antenna ($55-$90). Tri-band power antenna ($100-$135). Exterior Trim:- Exterior molding pkg.: LeSabre ($110). Landau vinyl top: LeSabre, Electra Ltd cpe ($225). Long vinyl top: LeSabre, Electra Ltd sed ($165-$180). Heavy-padded long vinyl top: Electra Ltd sedan ($225). Designers' accent paint: LeSabre ($215). Special single-color paint: ($200); Firemist, Electra exc. Est ($210). Protective bodyside moldings: Est ($51). Color-coordinated bodyside moldings: LeSabre Est ($51). Wide rocker panel moldings: Electra Ltd/Estate ($65). Door edge guards ($15-$25). Belt reveal molding: LeSabre ($40). Bodyside stripes ($63). Woodgrain vinyl applique: LeSabre Est ($320). Roof rack: LeSabre Est ($140). Interior Trim/Upholstery:- 55/45 seating: LeSabre ($125). Leather-vinyl 50/50 seating: Park Ave. ($525). Third seat: Estate ($215). Front carpet savers ($16); rear ($11). Front carpet savers w/inserts ($25); rear ($20). Trunk carpeting trim ($53-$65). Trunk mat ($13). Wheels:- Chrome-plated wheels ($180-$215). Styled aluminum wheels ($40-$255). Custom wheel covers: Electra Ltd ($35). Locking wire wheel covers ($150-$185); Electra Estate ($30 credit). Tires:- P215/75R15 SBR wide WSW: LeSabre cpe/sed ($39). P225/75R15 SBR wide WSW: LeSabre ($106); Electra ($39). Self- sealing tires ($106-$131).

RIVIERA CONVENIENCE/APPEARANCE OPTIONS: Comfort/Convenience:- Electric sliding Astroroof ($1125). Automatic touch climate control air cond. ($150). Rear defogger, electric ($125). Automatic electric door locks ($74). Six-way power seat, passenger ($197). Two-position memory power driver's seat ($178). Electric seatback recliner, one side ($139). Sport steering wheel ($40). Tilt steering ($95). Tilt/telescope steering wheel ($150). Electric fuel cap lock ($44). Electric trunk release ($32). Electric trunk lock ($72). Low fuel indicator ($18). Fuel usage light, gas engine ($35). Two-speed wipers w/delay ($47). Windshield washer fluid indicator ($12). Theft deterrent system ($159). Lighting, Horns and Mirrors: Tungsten-halogen high-beam headlamps ($10). Twilight Sentinel ($57). Coach lamps ($102); incl. w/vinyl top. Front/rear light monitors ($74). Rear quarter courtesy/reading lamp ($48). Lighted door lock and interior light control ($72). Four-note horn ($28). Dual

electric remote mirrors ($65). Lighted visor vanity mirrors, each ($58). Entertainment:- Full-feature electronic-tuning AM/FM stereo radio ($90). Electronic-tuning AM/FM stereo radio w/8-track or cassette tape player ($193-$242); w/CB and 8-track or cassette ($455- $479). Delete radio ($230 credit). Rear speakers ($25-$30). Concert Sound system ($95); N/A with base radio. Triband power antenna ($45). Exterior Trim:- Heavy-padded landau vinyl top w/coach lamps ($305). Designers' accent paint ($235). Special color Firemist paint ($210). Protective bodyside moldings ($61). Door edge guards ($15). Bodyside stripes ($63). Interior Trim/Upholstery:- 45/55 leather/vinyl front seat ($405). Front carpet savers w/inserts ($35); rear ($20). Trunk trim carpeting ($30). Trunk mat ($15). Wheels and Tires:- Chrome-plated wheels ($145). Custom locking wire wheel covers ($185). P225/70R15 SBR BSW: conv/T ($40). P225/70R15 SBR WSW: conv/T ($106). GR70 x 15 SBR WSW ($85). Self-sealing tires ($131).

HISTORY: Introduced: September 24, 1981 except Skylark, December 12, 1981; Century, November 30, 1981; Skyhawk, March 4, 1982; and Riviera convertible, mid-April 1982. Skyhawk and Riviera convertible debuted at the Chicago Auto Show on Feb. 25, 1982. Model year production (U.S.): 739,984 for a 14.3 percent share of the industry total. That number included 157,668 four-cylinder Buicks, 409,857 sixes, and 172,463 V-8s. The total also included 35,062 diesel engines and 2,551 turbos. Calendar year production (U.S.): 751,338. Model year sales by U.S. dealers: 694,742. Calendar year sales (U.S.): 723,011 for a market share of 12.6 percent.

Historical Footnotes: A series of mid-year introductions drew customers' attention to Buick offerings. Several Buick plants turned to employee involvement programs in an attempt to cut absenteeism and improve quality. Officials at one plant reported an impressive improvement in both areas. Turbo V-6 production fell sharply, from 25,500 in the 1979 model year to just 3,990 in 1981, in response to sluggish demand for turbocharged engines. In February 1982, a limited-edition Grand National Regal ran at Daytona. A forerunner of one of the most sought-after 1980s Buicks, it sported silver-gray and charcoal-gray paint with red accent stripes, a T-top roof, blackout grille and trim, air dam and rear spoiler. Grand National's powerplant was the 4.1-liter V-6 with four-barrel carb.

1983 BUICK

Buick now offered four front-drive car lines, stretching from the subcompact Skyhawk to the big Riviera. The company's full-line color catalog focused on small town America this year, including small tales and lore on locales to which one might travel by Buick. Sporty T Types, with performance packages that included sport trim, special wheels and bucket seats, were offered on every line except LeSabre and Electra. Though different, they shared a family resemblance. All except Regal's featured blacked-out sections for a striking visual appearance. And all but Regal and Riviera had charcoal accents on the car's lower body. Regal's version, powered by the 180-horsepower turbo 3.8-liter V-6, was recorded as delivering 0-50 MPH acceleration time of 7.6 seconds. Riviera used the same turbo V-6, while Skyhawk T Type's 1.8-liter engine produced 84 horsepower at 5200 R.P.M. Each T Type carried a Gran Touring suspension except for Skylark, which had a Sport suspension. On all but Riviera, quick-ratio power steering replaced the standard version. The "T" in T Type, incidentally, didn't stand for anything in particular. An electrically-heated grid in the 3.8-liter V-6 now preheated the fuel/air mixture for better response with a cold engine. On 3.0- and 3.8-liter V-6 engines, the Exhaust Gas Recirculation system was refined to regulate both timing and rate of exhaust gas flow back into the air/fuel mixture. Turbocharged engines had a new piezo sensor in the Electronic Spark Control system, plus computer-controlled EGR. Optional on some models was a new digital readout instrument cluster, which displayed numbers for miles-per-hour, trip odometer, and fuel level in English or metric form. Instead of the previous buzzer, a new electronic tone warned that seatbelts were not buckled or the key remained in the ignition. Riviera coupes could get ultimate sound with the new Delco GM/Bose Music System that delivered 50 watts of audio output per stereo channel.

1983 Skyhawk Limited wagon (AA)

SKYHAWK — SERIES 4J — FOUR — Buick's front-drive, J-bodied subcompact looked about the same as in 1982. Eight new body colors and two carryover colors were offered. Skylark Limited had standard deluxe full wheel covers and wide rocker moldings. Both Custom and Limited had a wide wraparound bodyside molding that gave the impression of running all around the car. Standard engine this year was a fuel-injected 2.0-liter four, hooked to four-speed manual gearbox and low (4.10:1) final drive (transaxle) ratio. That engine was essentially a stroked version of the carbureted 1.8-liter four that served as base engine the year before. Powertrain options included a fuel-injected 1.8-liter overhead-cam engine and five-speed manual shift, or three-speed automatic transmission with either engine. The 1.8 used a crossflow aluminum cylinder head, with intake and exhaust ports on opposite sides. Skyhawk offered a new station wagon for 1983, in both Custom and Limited trim--the first Buick front-drive wagons. Cargo volume was 64.5 cubic feet, with split-folding rear seat. Engine and transmission choices were the same as other Skyhawks, except the 1.8-liter engine wasn't available with air conditioning. Limited wagons had front armrests and reclining driver and passenger seats. The new subcompact T Type was "rather authoritative looking," according to Buick's catalog. Smallest of the T Types, it was powered by the overhead-cam 1.8-liter four, producing 84 horsepower, coupled to the five-speed manual overdrive gearbox. Axle ratio of 3.83:1 helped standing-start

performance. So did the engine's claimed quick throttle response and strong low-end torque. When hitting the gas hard, the air conditioner compressor shut off automatically so it wouldn't drain away needed power. T Types had the usual blacked-out grille--though in Skyhawk's case, even the standard grille was barely visible, consisting of a set of wide body-colored strips set below the headlamps and skinny minimal bumper. Other black accents were found on the T Type's headlamp housings, door handles, locks, and twin outside mirrors (the left one remote-controlled). Park/signal lamps and foglamps were included. Lower bodies displayed charcoal accents. A Gran Touring suspension helped handling, while styled aluminum wheels held P195/70R13 blackwall tires. Skyhawk T's dash carried a voltmeter, oil pressure and temperature gauges, resettable trip odometer, and electronic tachometer. Skyhawks had standard reclining bucket seats. Both Limited and T Type had easy-entry front passenger seats. Limiteds used the same luxurious fabric as in Electras. T Types held charcoal cloth bucket seats with adjustable headrests.

1983 Century T Type sedan (AA)

SKYLARK — SERIES 4X — FOUR/V-6 — Buick continued to downplay Skylark's economy image, promoting it more as a car that "looks and feels like a Buick," which just happened to be compact in size. Styling was essentially unchanged this year, except for a new aerodynamically-designed lip above new taillamps. The left- hand mirror was also restyled. Five new interior colors were offered, plus new cloth trim on the Limited. Custom Skylarks had a new seat design with adjustable headrests. Skylark's chassis continued in the same form: MacPherson struts up front, trailing axle coil springs in the rear, with standard power rack-and-pinion steering and low-drag power front disc brakes. All Skylarks carried a new Delco Freedom II Plus battery. Base engine remained the Pontiac 2.5-liter four with electronic fuel injection; optional, two forms of Chevrolet's 2.8-liter V-6. One new Skylark appeared, however: the T Type, wearing a blacked-out grille as well as black accents at headlamp housings, door handles and locks, taillamp bezels, and styled outside mirror. Four body colors were offered (white, silver, dark red, or light sand gray), each with special charcoal lower accent paint that reached almost halfway up the doors. Taillamp lenses were smoked, parking/signal lenses amber, and 14 in. wheels of aggressive-looking styled aluminum held blackwall P215/60R14 steel-belted radials (the widest tires of any Buick T Type). Under the T's hood was the high-output (135 horsepower) 2.8-liter V-6 with specially tuned exhaust, manual four-speed gearbox, and 3.65:1 final drive ratio. Sport suspension consisted of stiffer rate springs and shocks, a stiffer front stabilizer bar, and a rear stabilizer bar. On the dash, T Types included a voltmeter and temperature gauge. Front and rear bumper rub strips and a front passenger assist strap were included, and the left-hand mirror was remote-controlled.

1983 Skylark T Type coupe (AA)

CENTURY — SERIES 4A — FOUR/V-6 — Buick's A-bodied five-passenger front-drive model, introduced for 1982, offered the lowest drag coefficient in the lineup. Appearance was similar to before, but Skyhawks could have ten new body colors and five new interior colors. Bodies had Plastisol-R- protection in critical spots. A new electronic tone reminded drivers to fasten seat belts and remove the ignition key. The Delco 2000 AM radio included dual front speakers. A digital readout instrument cluster was also offered. Buyers could choose from the standard 2.5- liter four-cylinder engine, a 3.0-liter gasoline V-6, or 4.3- liter diesel V-6. An on-board computer added EGR monitoring to the gas V-6. Century had standard automatic transmission, power steering and brakes. At mid-year came a new overdrive automatic transmission. Limited models had integrated bumpers and a bright wide lower molding. Joining the Custom and Limited models this year was a new T Type Century sedan and coupe. Styling touches included subtle black accents on grille and moldings, around headlamps and on taillamp bezels, plus twin black mirrors (left-hand remote controlled), antenna and door handles. The 'Buick' badge went to the lower corner of the grille rather than the side, and front fenders held 'Century T Type' nameplates. Painted silver over charcoal, T Types also had special bumper detailing plus black accent stripes on the body, and rode 14 in. styled aluminum wheels with P195/75R14 blackwall steel-belted radial tires. Their Gran Touring suspension included high-rate springs, revalved shocks, and front/rear stablizer bars. The 110-horsepower 3.0-liter V-6 drove an automatic transmission and 2.97:1 final drive ratio. A leather-covered sport steering wheel, full-length storage console and 45/45 front seats filled out the T Type goodie list. Lear Siegler cloth bucket seats with leather trim were optional.

1983 Regal T Type coupe (AA)

REGAL — SERIES 4G — V-6 — Rear-drive Regals, little changed since their 1978 restyle, came with two personalities. Coupes were billed as having an "aerodynamic, sleek look" while sedans offered "crisp, limousine-like styling." All Regals had a new grille, with Buick block letters in the center of the upper horizontal bar. Strong vertical bars angled outward from a point above the halfway mark. Regal's script sat at the side of the grille. Wide parking/signal lamps were inset in the bumper. Quad rectangular headlamps were deeply recessed. Standard wheel covers got a restyle this year, and Regals came in a revised selection of body (four new choices) and interior colors. Regal's Estate Wagon was also powered by the 3.8-liter V-6 with automatic. Customers could choose a base Regal, Limited, or sporty turbo T Type. Limiteds could be ordered with leather- and vinyl-trimmed seats and cloth-trimmed doors. Standard engine was again the 231 cu. in. (3.8-liter) V-6, with automatic transmission. Larger V-6s (4.1-liter gas or 4.3-liter diesel) and a diesel V-8 were optional. A "discreet" tone told of unbuckled seatbelt, with the option of a chime that warned headlamps were still turned on. T Type coupes were easily identifiable by the bulge at the rear of the hood, as well T Type identification. They wore wide-oval P205/70R14 steel-belted radials on distinctively styled aluminum wheels. Under the hood, the turbocharged 3.8- liter V-6 fed into low-restriction dual exhausts for a "gutty exhaust growl," feeding power to a four-speed automatic overdrive transmission (with torque-converter clutching) and 3.42:1 performance axle ratio. T Type's handling was assisted by the Gran Touring suspension and fast-ratio power steering. At the dash, gauges showed turbo boost and engine temperature. A T Type Decor Package added Designers' Accent paint, blacked-out grille, black headlamp and taillamp trim, black wiper arms and blades, bright center rocker panel moldings, and a sport steering wheel. Regal T could have a hood ornament that said 'Turbo 3.8 Litre' below the Buick tri-shield emblem--words that also appeared on the hood bulge.

1983 LeSabre Limited sedan (AA)

LESABRE — SERIES 4B — V-6/V-8 — Once again, the 231 cu. in. (3.8-liter) V-6 was standard on LeSabre. This year, it received an electric preheater grid below the carburetor to warm up the fuel/air mixture when the engine was cold. On the powerplant option list: a 4.1-liter V-6 and 5.0-liter V-8, as well as the 5.7 diesel V-8. Automatic transmission was standard with all engines, and included overdrive (0.67:1 gearing) when coupled to any engine other than the base V-6. Converter clutches in third gear and overdrive, which engaged and disengaged at preset speeds, helped to eliminate slippage within the transmission. Of the dozen body colors, all but one was new for 1983. Designers' Accent paint treatments were also available, and interior colors were new. Custom seats were covered with rich velour, Limited seats with knit fabric. Electric seatback recliners were optional. A multi-function control lever handled turn signals, high/low beams, and wiper/washer. All LeSabres had front and rear armrests and a woodtone dash. LeSabre Custom included standard whitewall tires, deluxe wheel covers, bumper guards and protective strips, cigarette lighter, left-hand outside mirror, compact spare tire, and color-coordinated bodyside moldings. Limiteds added such extras as a headlamps-on indicator/chime, tinted glass, simulated woodgrain door trim, 55/45 notchback seats, and custom steering wheel.

ESTATE WAGON — SERIES 4B/C — V-8 — As before, both Electra and LeSabre Estate wagons were offered (as well as a Regal version). Electra's was the most luxurious, with standard roof rack and air deflector, vinyl woodgrain trim, 55/45 seating up front with two-way power driver's seat, remote-control left-hand mirror, electric door and tailgate locks, power windows, and digital clock. The standard 307 cu. in. (5.0-liter) V-8 engine came with four-speed overdrive automatic transmission, and could be held in third-gear range when hauling a heavy load. LeSabre Estate Wagons offered the same cargo capacity but a little less luxury. They included a power tailgate window, two-way tailgate with "ajar" indicator, air conditioning, and Soft-Ray tinted glass, and the same standard V-8 engine. A diesel V-8 was also offered.

ELECTRA — SERIES 4C — V-6/V-8 — Apart from a dozen new body colors, the full-size Buick line didn't change much this year, either mechanically or in appearance. Measuring over 221 inches, it was still the longest regular production car made in America. A combination of slim bodyside moldings and wide rocker panel moldings accentuated Electra's long, formal lines. The upscale Park Avenue again displayed brushed aluminum bodyside moldings that contained the familiar ventiport identity

1983 Electra Park Avenue sedan (AA)

badge. A padded halo vinyl top was standard again, revealing a bit of body color at the edges. Wide rocker panel moldings continued onto front and rear fenders. Soft-Ray tinted glass was standard. Electras also included a headlamps-on indicator, digital clock, bumper guards and protective strips, 25-gallon fuel tank, compact spare tire, and power windows. In addition to wide color-keyed protective bodyside moldings, both models carried moldings for back and side window reveal, roof drip, window frame scalp, belt reveal, windshield, and wheel openings. Park Avenue added resume-speed Cruise Control and a tilt steering column, plus AM/FM stereo radio, six-way power driver's seat, electric door locks, and power remote left-hand mirror. Standard powertrain was the 252 cu. in. (4.1-liter V-6) and automatic transmission with overdrive (including torque converter clutch). Options included a 5.0-liter gas V-8 or the big diesel V-8, which offered excellent mileage but proved troublesome to many owners.

1983 Riviera convertible (AA)

RIVIERA — SERIES 4E — V-6/V-8 — To mark Riviera's 20th birthday, Buick produced 502 copies of an "XX Anniversary Edition." To the normally ample list of Riviera equipment was added a tempting selection of extras, including true wire wheels. The body was painted two-tone beige, with Anniversary grille and front-end panel. Bumper strips, front and rear, were brown with gold inserts. Rocker, belt and roof drip moldings were dark brown. Fender, decklid and grille emblems were plated in 24 carat gold. Special identification appeared on hood and wheel centers. The medium beech Anniversary interior featured English walnut wood veneer trim plates and 26-ounce wool-like carpeting. Suede inserts highlighted the glove leather seat upholstery. There was also a leather-wrapped wood steering wheel, wood horn cap, leather upper door trim, 140 MPH speedometer, and gold-plated Anniversary identification. Also standard: a rear window defogger, Gran Touring suspension and dual electric mirrors, plus Uniroyal goldwall stripe steel-belted radial tires. Even the trunk trim was distinctive. Standard engine was the 4.1-liter V-6, with 5.0-liter V-8 optional. Apart from that special edition there were three "ordinary" Rivieras: a basic but luxurious Coupe, sporty T Type, and recently-introduced convertible. Riviera's T Type had a blacked-out grille (with fewer vertical bars), amber park/signal lenses, tungsten-halogen high/low beam headlamps, accent stripes on the body, sport steering wheel, and special T Type identification inside and out. Styled aluminum wheels held wide, self-sealing, all-season whitewall radial tires. Under the hood once again was the turbocharged 3.8-liter V-6, coupled to overdrive automatic transmission and 3.36:I final drive axle ratio. T Type's Gran Touring suspension blended higher-rate springs with recalibrated shock absorbers and special front/rear stabilizer bars. T Types were available in any Riviera color except light green and light brown. The hood ornament carried the letter 'R'. As usual, all Rivieras were loaded with power assists and conveniences, including air conditioning and an electronically-tuned Delco 2000 AM/FM stereo radio (which could be deleted for credit). Stereo buffs could go all the way up to a premium Delco GM/Bose Music System, acoustically tailored to the Riviera interior, with 50-watt power output. Interiors had new door pull straps, and the range of colors included a tan that was a Riviera exclusive. Standard equipment included a six-way power seat. A new optional digital instrument panel cluster showed miles-per-hour, remaining fuel, and a trip mileage in either English or metric values. Trailer towing equipment was available for loads up to 3,000 pounds. Convertibles were produced in somewhat limited number (only 1,750 this year) in choice of white or Firemist red with white top and contrasting bodyside stripes. Interiors were upholstered in soft red Sierra grain leather and vinyl. Four-wheel disc brakes were standard. Convertibles also had custom locking wire wheel covers and heavy-duty suspension. Standard Riviera powerplant was the 4.1-liter V-6 with overdrive automatic transmission, with option of a 5.0-liter gas V-8 or 5.7-liter diesel V-8. Convertibles could not have the diesel.

I.D. DATA: Buicks again had a 17-symbol Vehicle Identification Number (VIN), introduced in 1981, stamped on a metal tag attached to the upper left surface of the cowl, visible through the windshield. The number begins with '1' to indicate U.S.A., followed by 'G' for General Motors and '4' for Buick Division. The next letter indicates restraint system. Symbol five denotes series: 'S' Skyhawk; 'T' Skyhawk Limited; 'E' Skyhawk T Type; 'B' Skylark Custom; 'C' Skylark Limited; 'D' Skylark T Type; 'H' Century Custom; 'L' Century Limited; 'G' Century T Type; 'J' Regal; 'K' Regal T Type; 'M' Regal Limited; 'N' LeSabre Custom; 'P' LeSabre Limited; 'R' LeSabre Estate Wagon; 'V' Electra Estate Wagon; 'X' Electra Limited; 'W' Electra Park Avenue; 'Y' Riviera T Type; 'Z' Riviera. Digits six and seven indicate body type: '27' 2-dr. coupe; '37' Skylark 2-dr. coupe; '47' Regal 2-dr. coupe; '57' Riviera 2-dr. coupe; '35' 4-dr. wagon; '19' 4-dr. sedan; '69' 4-dr. sedan. Next is the engine code: 'O' L4-112 TBI; 'P' L4-121 TBI; 'R' L4-151 TBI; 'X' V6-173 2Bbl.; 'Z' H.O. V6-173 2Bbl.;

V6-181 2Bbl.; 'A' V6-231 2Bbl.; '8' V6-231 Turbo; '4' V6-252 4Bbl.; 'V' V6-263 diesel; 'Y' V8-307 4Bbl.; 'N' V8-350 diesel. Symbol nine is a check digit. Symbol ten denotes model year ('D' 1983). Symbol eleven is the plant code. The final six digits are the sequential serial number. An additional identifying number can be found on the engine, showing codes for GM division, model year, assembly plant, and vehicle sequence number. A body number plate shows model year, car division, series, style, body assembly plant, body number, trim combination, modular seat code, paint code, and date build code.

SKYHAWK CUSTOM (FOUR)

Series Number	Body/Style Number	Body Type & Seating	Factory Price	Shipping Weight	Production Total
4J	S27	2-dr Coupe-5P	6958	2316	27,557
4J	S69	4-dr Sedan-5P	7166	2369	19,847
4J	S35	4-dr Sta Wag-5P	7492	2439	10,653

SKYHAWK LIMITED (FOUR)

4J	T27	2-dr Coupe-5P	7457	2333	Note 1
4J	T69	4-dr Sedan-5P	7649	2411	Note 1
4J	T35	4-dr Sta Wag-5P	7934	2462	Note 1

Note 1: Production figures listed under Skyhawk Custom also include equivalent Skyhawk Limited models. For the model year, a total of 45,105 Customs and 12,952 Limiteds were manufactured.

SKYHAWK T TYPE (FOUR)

4J	E27	2-dr Coupe-5P	7961	2336	5,095

SKYLARK CUSTOM (FOUR/V-6)

4X	B37	2-dr Coupe-5P	7548/7698	2462/2523	11,671
4X	B69	4-dr Sedan-5P	7718/7868	2493/2554	51,950

SKYLARK LIMITED (FOUR/V-6)

4X	C37	2-dr Coupe-5P	7988/8138	2489/2550	7,863
4X	C69	4-dr Sedan-5P	8150/8300	2519/2580	30,674

SKYLARK T TYPE (V-6)

4X	D37	2-dr Coupe-5P	9337	2608	2,489

CENTURY CUSTOM (FOUR/V-6)

4A	H27	2-dr Coupe-5P	8841/8991	2614/2719	13,483
4A	H19	4-dr Sedan-5P	9002/9152	2662/2767	114,443

CENTURY LIMITED (FOUR/V-6)

4A	L27	2-dr Coupe-5P	9261/9411	2632/2737	Note 2
4A	L19	4-dr Sedan-5P	9425/9575	2675/2780	Note 2

CENTURY T TYPE (V-6)

4A	G27	2-dr Coupe-5P	10017	2749	Note 2
4A	G19	4-dr Sedan-5P	10178	2801	Note 2

Note 2: Production figures listed under Century Custom also include Limited and T Type models. Total production for the model year came to 50,296 Customs, 73,030 Limiteds, and 4,600 Century T Types.

REGAL (V-6)

4G	J47	2-dr Coupe-6P	9100	3123	147,935
4G	J69	4-dr Sedan-6P	9279	3139	61,285
4G	J35	4-dr Sta Wag-6P	9550	3289	15,287

REGAL LIMITED (V-6)

4G	M47	2-dr Coupe-6P	9722	3164	Note 3
4G	M69	4-dr Sedan-6P	9856	3177	Note 3

Note 3: Production figures listed under base Regal coupe and sedan also include Regal Limited models. Total coupe/sedan production was 108,458 base Regals and 100,762 Limiteds. Only 4,340 Regals had the optional diesel V-8 engine.

REGAL T TYPE (V-6)

4G	K47	2-dr Coupe-6P	10366	3194	3,732

LESABRE CUSTOM (V-6/V-8)

4B	N37	2-dr Coupe-6P	9292/9517	3459/3631	6,974
4B	N69	4-dr Sedan-6P	9394/9619	3488/3660	31,196

LESABRE LIMITED (V-6/V-8)

4B	P37	2-dr Coupe-6P	9836/10061	3494/3666	22,029
4B	P69	4-dr Sedan-6P	9990/10215	3527/3699	66,547

LESABRE ESTATE WAGON (V-8)

4B	R35	4-dr Sta Wag-6P	11187	4105	9,306

ELECTRA LIMITED (V-6/V-8)

4C	X37	2-dr Coupe-6P	12415/12490	3644/3823	8,885
4C	X69	4-dr Sedan-6P	12586/12661	3704/3883	79,700

ELECTRA PARK AVENUE (V-6/V-8)

4C	W37	2-dr Coupe-6P	14094/14169	3716/3895	Note 4
4C	W69	4-dr Sedan-6P	14245/14320	3781/3960	Note 4

Note 4: Production figures listed under Electra Limited also include equivalent Park Avenue models. All told, 24,542 Limiteds and 64,043 Park Avenue Electras were built, only 4,878 with V-8 engine.

ELECTRA ESTATE WAGON (V-8)

4C	V35	4-dr Sta Wag-6P	13638	4175	9,581

RIVIERA (V-6/V-8)

4E	Z57	2-dr Coupe-5P	15238/15313	3609/3769	47,153
4E	Z67	2-dr Conv-5P	24960/24960	3795/3955	1,750

Note 5: Only 128 Riviera convertibles and 2,993 standard coupes had a V-6 engine.

RIVIERA T TYPE (V-6)

4E	Y57	2-dr Coupe-5P	15906	3593	1,331

FACTORY PRICE AND WEIGHT NOTE: Figure before the slash is for four-cylinder engine, after the slash for V-6. For full-size models, figure before the slash is for V-6 engine, after the slash for V-8.

BUICK ENGINES: BASE FOUR (Skyhawk): Inline, overhead valve four-cylinder. Cast iron cylinder block and head. Displacement: 121 cu. in. (2.0 liters). Bore & stroke: 3.50 x 3.14 in. Compression ratio: 9.0:1. Brake horsepower: 90 at 5100 R.P.M. Torque: 111 lbs.-ft. at 2700 R.P.M. Five main bearings. Hydraulic valve lifters. Throttle-body fuel injection. VIN Code: P. OPTIONAL FOUR (Skyhawk): Inline, overhead-cam four-cylinder. Cast iron block and head. Displacement: 112 cu. in. (1.8 liters). Bore & stroke: 3.34 x 3.13 in. Compression ratio: 9.0:1. Brake horsepower: 84 at 5200 R.P.M. Torque: 102 lbs.-ft. at 2800 R.P.M. Five main bearings. Hydraulic valve lifters. Throttle-body fuel injection. VIN Code: O. BASE FOUR (Skylark, Century): Inline, overhead-valve four-cylinder. Cast iron block and head. Displacement: 151 cu. in. (2.5 liters). Bore & stroke: 4.0 x 3.0 in. Compression ratio: 8.2:1. Brake horsepower: 90 at 4000 R.P.M. Torque: 134 lbs.-ft. at 2400 R.P.M. Five main bearings. Hydraulic valve lifters. Throttle-body fuel injection. Built by Pontiac. VIN Code: R. OPTIONAL V-6 (Skylark): 60-degree, overhead-valve V-6. Cast iron alloy block and head. Displacement: 173 cu. in. (2.8 liters). Bore & stroke: 3.5 x 3.0 in. Compression ratio 8.4:1. Brake horsepower: 112 at 5100 R.P.M. Torque: 148 lbs.-ft. at 2400 R.P.M. Four main bearings. Hydraulic valve lifters. Carburetor: 2Bbl. Rochester E2SE. Built by Chevrolet. VIN Code: X. HIGH-OUTPUT 173 V-6: (Skylark T Type) OPTIONAL (Skylark): Same as 173 cu. in V-6 above except as follows: Compression ratio: 8.94:1. Brake horsepower: 135 at 5400 R.P.M. Torque: 145 lbs.-ft. at 2400 R.P.M. VIN Code: Z. OPTIONAL V-6 (Century): 90-degree, overhead-valve V-6. Cast iron block and head. Displacement: 181 cu. in. (3.0 liters). Bore & stroke: 3.8 x 2.66 in. Compression ratio: 8.45:1. Brake horsepower 110 at 4800 R.P.M. Torque: 145 lbs.-ft. at 2400 R.P.M. Four main bearings. Hydraulic valve lifters. Carburetor: 2Bbl. Rochester E2ME. VIN Code: E. BASE V-6 (Regal, LeSabre): 90-degree, overhead-valve V-6. Cast iron alloy block and head. Displacement: 231 cu. in. (3.8 liters). Bore & stroke: 3.8 x 3.4 in. Compression ratio: 8.0:1. Brake horsepower: 110 at 800 R.P.M. Torque: 190 lbs.-ft. at 1600 R.P.M. Four main bearings. Hydraulic valve lifters. Carburetor: 2Bbl. Rochester. VIN Code: A. TURBOCHARGED V-6 (Regal T Type, Riviera T Type): Same as 231 V-6 above, but with E4ME four-barrel carburetor. Brake horsepower: 180 at 4000 R.P.M. Torque: 280 lbs.-ft. at 2400 R.P.M. (Riviera, 290 lbs.-ft.) VIN Code: 8. BASE V-6 (Electra, Riviera); OPTIONAL (Regal, LeSabre): 90-degree, overhead-valve V-6. Cast iron alloy block and head. Displacement: 252 cu. in. (4.1 liters). Bore & stroke: 3.965 x 3.4 in. Compression ratio: 8.0:1. Brake horsepower: 125 at 4000 R.P.M. Torque: 205 lbs.-ft. at 2000 R.P.M. Four main bearings. Hydraulic valve lifters. Carburetor: 4Bbl. Rochester. VIN Code: 4. DIESEL V-6; OPTIONAL (Century, Regal); 90-degree, overhead-valve V-6. Cast iron block; cast iron or aluminum head. Displacement: 262.5 cu. in. (4.3 liters). Bore & stroke: 4.057 x 3.385 in. Compression ratio: 21.6:1. Brake horsepower: 85 at 3600 R.P.M. Torque: 165 lbs.-ft. at 1600 R.P.M. Four main bearings. Hydraulic valve lifters. Fuel injection. VIN Code: V. BASE V-8 (Estate); OPTIONAL (LeSabre, Electra, Riviera): 90-degree, overhead valve V-8. Cast iron block and head. Displacement: 307 cu. in. (5.0 liters). Bore & stroke: 3.80 x 3.385 in. Compression ratio: 8.0:1. Brake horsepower: 140 at 3600 R.P.M. Torque: 240 lbs.-ft. at 1600 R.P.M. Five main bearings. Hydraulic valve lifters. Carburetor: 4Bbl. Rochester. Built by Oldsmobile. VIN Code: Y. OPTIONAL DIESEL V-8 (Regal, LeSabre, Electra, Estate, Riviera): 90-degree, overhead valve V-8. Cast iron block and head. Displacement: 350 cu. in. (5.7 liters). Bore & stroke: 4.057 x 3.385 in. Compression ratio: 21.6:1. Brake horsepower: 105 at 3200 R.P.M. Torque: 200 lbs-ft. at 1600 R.P.M. Five main bearings. Hydraulic valve lifters. Oldsmobile-built. VIN Code: N.

CHASSIS DATA: Wheelbase: (Skyhawk) 101.2 in.; (Skylark/Century) 104.9 in.; (Regal) 108.1 in.; (LeSabre/Estate) 115.9 in.; (Electra) 118.9 in.; (Riviera) 114.0 in. Overall length:- (Skyhawk) 175.3 in.; (Skyhawk wag) 177.1 in.; (Skylark) 181.0 in.; (Century) 189.1 in.; (Regal cpe) 200.6 in.; (Regal sed) 196.0 in.; (Regal wag) 196.7 in.; (LeSabre) 218.4 in.; (Electra) 221.3 in.; (Estate Wagon) 220.5 in.; (Riviera) 206.6 in. Height:- (Skyhawk) 54.0 in.; (Skylark/Century) 53.6 in.; (Regal cpe) 54.5 in.; (Regal sed) 55.4 in.; (Regal wag) 57.1 in.; (LeSabre cpe) 56.0 in.; (Electra cpe) 56.8 in.; (LeSabre/Electra sed) 56.7-56.9 in.; (Estate) 59.1 in.; (Riv) 54.3 in. Width:- (Skyhawk) 62.0 in.; (Skylark/Century) 69.1 in.; (Century) 66.8 in.; (Regal cpe) 71.6 in.; (Regal sed/wag) 71.1-71.2 in.; (LeSabre) 78.0 in.; (Electra) 76.2 in.; (Estate) 79.3 in.; (Riv) 72.8 in. Front Tread:- (Skyhawk) 55.4 in.; (Skylark/Century) 58.7 in.; (Regal) 58.5 in.; (LeSabre/ Electra) 61.8 in.; (Estate) 62.2 in.; (Riviera) 59.3 in. Rear

Tread:- (Skyhawk) 55.2 in.; (Skylark/Century) 57.0 in.; (Regal) 57.7 in.; (LeSabre/Electra) 60.7 in.; (Estate) 64.0 in.; (Riviera) 60.0 in. Standard Tires:- (Skyhawk) P175/80R13 GBR; (Skylark/Century) P185/80R13 GBR; (Skylark T Type) P205/70R13 SBR; (Regal) P195/75R14 SBR WSW; (Regal T Type) P205/70R14 SBR; (LeSabre) P205/75R15 SBR WSW; (Electra) P215/75R15 SBR WSW; (Estate) P225/75R15 SBR WSW; (Riviera) P205/75R15 SBR WSW.

TECHNICAL: Transmission:- Four-speed, fully synchronized floor shift standard on Skyhawk/Skylark; automatic optional (standard on all other models). Five-speed standard on Skyhawk T Type. Four-speed gear ratios: (1st) 3.53:1; (2nd) 1.95:1; (3rd) 1.24:1; (4th) 0.81:1 or 0.73:1; (Rev) 3.42:1. Five-speed gear ratios: (1st) 3.91:1; (2nd) 2.15:1; (3rd) 1.45:1; (4th) 1.03:1; (5th) 0.74:1; (Rev) 3.50:1. Three-speed auto. trans. gear ratios: (1st) 2.74:1; (2nd) 1.57:1; (3rd) 1.00:1; (Rev) 1.93:1 or 2.07:1. Skyhawk/Skylark/Century auto. trans. gear ratios: (1st) 2.84:1; (2nd) 1.60:1; (3rd) 1.00:1; (Rev) 2.07:1. Four-speed overdrive automatic gear ratios: (1st) 2.74:1; (2nd) 1.57:1; (3rd) 1.00:1; (4th) 0.67:1; (Rev) 2.07:1. T Type Final Drive Ratios:- (Skyhawk) 3.83:1; (Skylark) 3.65:1; (Century) 2.97:1; (Regal) 3.42:1; (Riviera) 3.36:1. Steering:- Same as 1982. Suspension:- Same as 1982. Brakes:- Same as 1982. Body construction:- Same as 1982. Wheel size:- (Skyhawk/Century) 13 x 5.5 in.; (Regal) 14 x 6 in.; (LeSabre/Riviera) 15 x 6 in.; (Estate) 15 x 7 in. Fuel tank:- (Skyhawk) 13.6 gal.; (Skylark) 15.1 gal.; (Century) 15.7 gal.; (Regal) 18.1 gal.; (LeSabre/Electra) 25.0 gal.; (Estate) 22.0 gal.; (Riviera) 21.1 gal. Unleaded fuel only.

DRIVETRAIN OPTIONS: Engines:- 112 cu. in. (1.8-liter) EFI four: Skyhawk ($50). 173 cu. in. (2.8-liter) V-6, 2Bbl.: Skylark ($150). High-output 173 cu. in. (2.8-liter) V-6, 2Bbl.: Skylark ($300); std. on T Type. 181 cu. in. (3.0-liter) V-6, 2Bbl.: Century ($150). 252 cu. in. (4.1-liter) V-6, 4Bbl.: Regal ($150; LeSabre exc. wagon ($150). 263 cu. in. (4.3-liter) diesel V-6: Century Cust/Ltd ($599); Regal exc. T Type or wag ($599). 307 cu. in. (5.0-liter) V-8, 4Bbl.: LeSabre cpe/sed ($225); Electra cpe/sed, Riviera ($75). 350 cu. in. (5.7-liter) diesel V-8: Regal/LeSabre/Estate/Electra/Riviera ($799). Transmission/Differential:- Five-speed manual trans.: Skyhawk ($75). Automatic trans.: Skyhawk ($395); Skyhawk T Type ($320); Skylark ($425). Automatic overdrive trans.: LeSabre cpe/sed ($175); std. automatic on LeSabre (NC). Optional rear axle ratio: Regal exc. T Type 2.73:1 or 3.23:1 (NC); Regal, Ltd 3.08:1 (NC); LeSabre 2.73:1, 3.08:1 or 3.23:1 (NC); Electra 3.08:1 or 3.23:1 (NC). Limited slip differential: Regal/LeSabre/Electra ($95). Suspension, Steering and Brakes:- F40 Firm ride/handling pkg.: Skylark/Century Cust/Ltd ($27); Regal exc. T Type ($27); LeSabre/Electra ($27). F41 Gran Touring suspension: Skyhawk ($196); Century Cust/Ltd ($27); Regal/Ltd, LeSabre ($49); Riviera ($27). F41 Gran Touring ride/handling suspension incl. P205/70R13 SBR WSW tires: Skylark Cust/Ltd ($272). Superlift rear shock absorbers: Skylark Cust/Ltd ($68). Automatic level control: Century/Regal/LeSabre/Electra ($175). Power steering: Skyhawk ($199). Four-wheel disc brakes: Riviera ($235); std. on conv. Other:- Trailer towing pkg.: LeSabre exc. wag ($127). Heavy- duty alternator, 85-amp ($35-$85). H.D. battery: ($25); w/diesel ($50). H.D. radiator: Skyhawk ($40-$70). H.D. cooling: Skylark ($40-$70); Cold climate pkg.: Regal exc. T (NC). Engine block heater ($18). H.D. engine/transmission cooling: Century/Regal/LeSabre/Electra ($40-$70). High altitude emission pkg. (NC) except w/diesel cold climate pkg. delete ($49). California emission system ($75) exc. diesel ($215). Diesel cold climate pkg. delete ($99 credit).

SKYHAWK CONVENIENCE/APPEARANCE OPTIONS: Option Packages:- Vista Vent flip-open removable glass sunroof ($295). Acoustic pkg. ($36). Instrument gauge pkg.: temp, oil pressure, volts, trip odometer: Cust ($60). Gauges and tach: Cust ($138); Ltd ($78). Comfort/Convenience:- Air cond. ($625). Touch climate control air cond. ($775). Rear defogger, electric ($125). Cruise Master w/resume ($170). Power windows ($180-$255). Electric door locks ($120-$170). Six-way power driver's seat ($210). Easy-entry passenger seat adjuster: Cust cpe ($16). Tinted glass ($90). Sport steering wheel ($50). Tilt steering ($99). Trip odometer: Cust ($15). Electric clock ($35). Electric trunk release ($40). Remote tailgate lock: wag ($35). Tailgate wiper/washer: wag ($120). Two-speed wipers w/delay ($49). Lights, Horns and Mirrors:- Tungsten-halogen headlamps ($22). Headlamps-on indicator ($15). Dome reading lamp ($30). Dual horns: Cust cpe/sed ($15). Left remote mirror ($21). Dual mirrors: left remote ($51). Dual electric remote mirrors ($137); T Type ($86). Visor vanity mirror, passenger ($7). Lighted visor vanity mirror, either side ($45). Entertainment:- Basic electronic- tuning AM/FM stereo radio ($138); w/clock ($177); w/cassette ($277). Electronic-tuning AM/FM stereo radio ($302); w/cassette and graphic equalizer ($505). Radio delete ($56 credit). Power antenna ($60). Dual rear speakers ($25-$30). Exterior Trim:- Door edge guards ($15-$25). Rocker panel moldings: Cust cpe/sed ($26). Bodyside stripes ($42). Designers' accent paint ($195). Decklid luggage rack ($105). Roof rack: wag ($105). Interior Trim/Upholstery:- Suede bucket seats: Ltd cpe/sed ($295). Front carpet savers ($17); rear ($12). Front carpet savers w/inserts ($18); rear ($15). Deluxe trunk trim ($33). Wheels and Tires:- Styled aluminum wheels ($229). Styled wheel covers w/trim rings ($38). Custom locking wire wheel covers ($165). P175/80R13 GBR WSW ($54). P195/70R13 SBR BSW ($169). P195/70R13 SBR WSW ($62-$231). P195/70R13 SBR WLT ($84-$253). P195/70R13 SBR wide WSW ($62- $231). Self-sealing tires ($106).

SKYLARK/CENTURY CONVENIENCE/APPEARANCE OPTIONS: Option Packages:- Acoustic pkg.: Skylark Cust ($60). Flip-open Vista Vent glass sunroof ($295). Standard option delete (rocker panel moldings and front armrest): Century Cust ($67 credit). Comfort/Convenience:- Air cond. ($725). Cruise Master w/resume ($170). Rear defogger, electric ($135). Power windows: cpe ($180); Skylark sed ($255). Electric door locks ($120-$170). Six-way power driver's seat ($210). Manual seatback recliners, passenger: Cust/Ltd ($45); both ($90). Sport steering wheel ($50). Tilt steering ($105). Tinted glass ($105). Instrument gauges incl. trip odometer ($48). Trip odometer: Skylark Cust/Ltd ($16). Digital electronic instrument cluster: Century ($299). Dial clock ($35). Electric trunk release ($40). Two-speed wipers w/delay ($49). Theft deterrent system: Century ($159). Lights, Horns and Mirrors:- Tungsten-halogen headlamps: Century ($22). Twilight Sentinel: Century ($57). Front light monitors: Century ($37). Coach lamps: Ltd ($102-$129). Headlamps-on indicator ($16). Door courtesy/warning light: Century Ltd ($44). Dome reading light ($24). Rear seat reading lamp: Skylark Ltd, Century ($30). Remote left mirror: Cust/Ltd ($24). Sport mirrors (left remote): Cust/Ltd ($59). Dual electric remote mirrors: Cust/Ltd ($137); T Type ($78). Visor vanity mirror, passenger ($7). Lighted visor vanity mirror, passenger: Skylark ($50); either side, Century ($58). Entertainment:- Same as Skyhawk above). Exterior Trim:- Landau vinyl top: Cust/Ltd cpe ($181-$215). Long vinyl top: Cust/Ltd ($155). Designers' accent paint: Cust/Ltd ($205-$210). Special solid color paint: Century Cust/Ltd ($200). Protective bodyside moldings ($55). Lower wide bodyside moldings: Century Cust ($65). Wide rocker panel/rear quarter moldings: Skylark Cust ($65). Belt reveal molding: Skylark Cust, T ($40). Wheel opening moldings: Skylark Cust ($30). Door edge guards ($15-$25). Pillar applique moldings: Skylark Cust sed ($27). Hood ornament and windsplit: Cust ($22-$32). Bodyside stripe: Cust/Ltd ($42). Bumper guards, front/rear: Skylark ($45). Bumper strips, front/rear: Skylark Cust ($49). Front license plate mounting: Skylark (NC). Interior Trim/Upholstery:- Full-length console: Skylark ($100); Century ($57). Full-length operating console: Century ($75); T Type ($18). Bucket seats: Skylark ($95). Lear Siegler bucket seats: Century T Type ($600). 45/45 seating: cloth, Century Cust ($158); leather, Century Ltd ($295). Front carpet savers ($17); rear ($12). Carpet savers w/inserts: front ($25); rear ($20). Trunk trim ($35-$47). heels:- Styled aluminum wheels: Century Cust/Ltd ($195). Chrome-plated wheels: Skylark Cust/Ltd ($175). Locking wire wheel covers: Cust/Ltd ($185). Skylark Tires:- P185/80R13 GBR WSW: Cust/Ltd ($58). P185/80R13 SBR WSW: Cust/Ltd ($123). P205/70R13 SBR WSW: Cust/Ltd ($255). P215/60R14 SBR WLT: T Type ($92). Self-sealing tires: Cust/Ltd ($106). Century Cust/Ltd Tires:- P185/75R14 GBR WSW ($58). P185/75R14 SBR BSW $64). P185/75R14 SBR WSW ($122). P195/75R14 SBR BSW ($95). P195/75R14 SBR WSW ($157). Self-sealing tires ($106).

REGAL CONVENIENCE/APPEARANCE OPTIONS: Option Packages:- Regal T Type Decor pkg.: designers' accent paint, wide rocker molding, black paint treatment, sport steering wheel ($365). Sliding electric Astroroof: cpe ($895). Hatch roof: cpe ($825). Standard option delete: Regal sedan w/o narrow rocker moldings, bright steering wheel bezel, passenger mirror, underhood light, bodyside moldings, brushed deck lid molding, wheel opening and window reveal moldings; with P185/75R14 GBR WSW tires ($278 credit). Comfort/Convenience:- Air cond. ($725); climate control ($875). Cruise Master w/resume ($170). Rear defogger, electric ($135). Tinted glass ($105). Tinted windshield ($80). Six-way power seat, each side ($210); both ($420). Manual passenger seatback recliner ($75). Sport steering wheel ($50). Tilt steering ($105). Power windows ($180-$255). Electric door locks ($120-$170). Electric trunk release ($40). Remote electric tailgate lock: wag ($40). Electric clock ($35). Headlamps-on indicator ($16). Trip odometer ($16) exc. T. Instrument gauges: temp, voltage, trip odometer ($48). Two-speed wiper w/low-speed delay ($49). Theft deterrent system ($159); N/A on wag. Lighting and Mirrors:- Tungsten-halogen headlamps ($22). Twilight Sentinel headlamp control ($57). Cornering lamps ($57). Coach lamps: Ltd ($102). Door courtesy/warning lights: Ltd ($44-$70). Rear seat reading light ($30). Dome reading lamps ($24). Remote left mirror ($24) exc. T Type; right ($42). Dual sport mirrors, left remote ($51). Dual remote sport mirrors ($81); T ($30). Visor vanity mirror, passenger ($7). Lighted visor vanity mirror, passenger ($58). Entertainment:- AM radio ($112). AM/FM stereo radio ($198); w/cassette ($298). Electronic-tuning AM/FM stereo radio ($402); w/cassette ($555). Dual rear speakers ($25-$30). Automatic power antenna ($95); w/radio ($60). Exterior Trim:- Landau vinyl top: cpe ($181). Heavy-padded landau vinyl top: cpe ($240). Long vinyl top: sed ($155). Long padded vinyl top: sed ($240). Designers' accent paint ($200-$235). Solid special color paint ($200). Exterior molding pkg. ($110); std. on Ltd. Protective bodyside moldings: T Type ($55). Wraparound bodyside moldings: Ltd sedan ($104). Hood ornament and windsplit: Century ($22); std. on Ltd. Door edge guards ($15-$25). Belt reveal moldings: T Type w/decor pkg. ($40). Bodyside stripe ($42). Woodgrain vinyl applique: wag ($355). Roof rack: wag ($125). Air deflector: wag ($37). Interior Trim/Upholstery:- Full-length console ($82) exc. wag; operating console for bucket seats (NC). Bucket seats: cpe/sed ($195). 55/45 seating ($133). Limited 55/45 seating: T Type ($385). Limited 45/45 leather/vinyl seating: T ($680). Leather/vinyl 45/45 seating: Ltd ($295). Front carpet savers $17); rear ($12). Front carpet savers w/inserts ($25); rear ($20). Trunk trim covering ($47). Lockable storage compartment: wag ($55). Wheels:- Chrome-plated wheels ($195); T Type ($90 credit). Styled aluminum wheels ($285); std. on T. Locking wire wheel covers ($185); T ($100 credit). Body- color wheels ($85) exc. T. Tires:- P205/70R14 SBR WSW ($62-$66). P205/70R14 SBR WLT ($88). Self-sealing tires ($106) exc. T Type.

LESABRE/ELECTRA/ESTATE WAGON CONVENIENCE/APPEARANCE OPTIONS: Comfort/Convenience:- Sliding electric Astroroof: silver, gray or gold ($1195). Air cond.: LeSabre ($725). Air cond. w/touch-climate control ($875); LeSabre Estate, Electra ($150). Cruise Master w/resume ($170); std. on Park Ave. Rear defogger, electric ($135). Tinted glass: LeSabre Cust ($105). Power windows: LeSabre ($180-$255). Electric door locks ($120-$170). Automatic door locks ($200-$250); exc. Park Ave. ($80). Six-way power seat, driver's or passenger's ($180- $210); both ($390-$420). Memory driver's seat: Electra Ltd ($358); Park Ave. ($178). Electric seatback recliner, one side ($139). Sport steering wheel: LeSabre ($50). Tilt steering: LeSabre, Electra Ltd ($105). Tilt/telescoping steering column ($160) exc. Electra Park Ave./Estate ($55). Dial clock: LeSabre ($60). Trip odometer: LeSabre ($16). Remote tailgate lock: LeSabre Est ($50). Electric trunk lock: Electra ($80). Electric trunk release ($40). Electric fuel cap lock ($44) exc. wag. Theft deterrent system ($159); N/A on Estate. Two-speed wiper w/delay ($49). Accessory group (trip odometer, dome reading lamp, low fuel indicator, washer fluid indicator): Electra ($30-$70). Lighting, Horns and Mirrors:- Tungsten-halogen high-beam headlamps ($22). Twilight Sentinel ($57). Cornering lamps ($57). Coach lamps: LeSabre/Electra Ltd ($102). Light monitors, front: LeSabre, Electra Est ($37); front/rear, Electra ($74). Lamp and indicator group: LeSabre ($38-$70). Door courtesy/warning lamps ($44-$70). Lighted door lock and interior light control ($72). Four-note horn ($28). Remote left mirror: LeSabre ($24). Remote right mirror: LeSabre ($48); Electra Ltd, Est ($24). Remote electric right mirror: Electra Park Ave. ($57). Dual remote sport mirrors: LeSabre ($88); Electra Ltd, Est ($40). Dual electric remote mirrors: LeSabre ($137); Electra Ltd, Est ($89). Remote left mirror w/thermometer: LeSabre ($62); Electra Ltd, Est ($38). Electric left mirror w/thermometer: Park Ave. ($38). Dual electric mirrors w/left thermometer: LeSabre ($175); Electra Ltd, Est ($127). Lighted visor vanity mirror, driver or passenger ($58). Entertainment:- AM radio: LeSabre ($112). AM/FM stereo radio: LeSabre, Electra Ltd/Estate ($198); w/8- track or cassette ($298) exc. Park Ave. ($100). AM/FM stereo radio with CB: Estate ($473). Electronic-tuning AM/FM stereo radio: LeSabre ($377-$402); Electra ($165-$363). Electronic- tuning radio and 8-track or cassette ($491-$555) exc. Park Ave. ($319). Electronic-tuning radio with CB and cassette player: Estate ($766-$805). Delete AM/FM stereo radio: Electra Park Ave. ($153 credit). Concert Sound speaker system: Electra exc. wag ($95); ETR radio req'd. Dual rear speakers ($25-$30). Automatic power antenna ($95); w/radio ($60). Triband power antenna: Estate ($140); w/radio ($105). Exterior Trim:- Exterior molding pkg. (wide rocker panel, front/rear fender lower and belt reveal moldings): LeSabre ($110). Landau vinyl top: LeSabre, Electra Ltd cpe ($240). Long vinyl top: LeSabre, Electra Ltd sed ($180-$185). Heavy- padded long vinyl top: Electra Ltd sed ($240). Designers' accent paint: LeSabre ($215) exc. Estate. Special single- color paint: ($200); Firemist, Electra exc. Estate ($210). Protective bodyside moldings: Est ($55). Wide rocker panel moldings: Electra Ltd/Est ($65). Door edge guards ($15-$25). Belt reveal molding: LeSabre ($40). Bodyside stripes ($42). Woodgrain vinyl applique: LeSabre Est ($345). Roof rack w/air deflector: LeSabre Est ($150). Interior Trim/Upholstery:- 55/45 seating: LeSabre Custom/Est ($125). Leather/vinyl 50/50 seating: Park Ave. ($525). Third seat: Estate ($215). Front carpet savers ($17); rear ($12). Front carpet savers w/inserts ($25); rear ($20). Trunk carpeting trim ($53-$65). Trunk mat ($14). Wheels:- Chrome-plated wheels ($180-$215). Styled aluminum wheels ($220-$255) exc. Electra Est ($40). Custom wheel covers: Electra Ltd ($35). Locking wire wheel covers ($150-$185); Electra Est ($30 credit). Tires:- P215/75R15 SBR wide whitewall: LeSabre cpe/sed ($38). P225/75R15 SBR wide whitewall: Electra cpe/sed ($39). Self- sealing tires ($132).

RIVIERA CONVENIENCE/APPEARANCE OPTIONS: Comfort/Convenience:- Electric sliding Astroroof: silver, gray or gold ($210). Automatic touch climate-control air cond. ($150). Digital electronic instrument cluster ($238). Six-way power seat, passenger ($210). Two-position memory driver's seat ($178). Electric seatback recliner, one side ($139). Sport steering wheel ($40) exc. T Type. Tilt/telescope steering wheel ($55) exc. T Type. Electric fuel cap lock ($44). Electric trunk release ($40); lock ($80). Low fuel indicator ($16). Two-speed wipers w/delay ($49). Windshield washer fluid indicator ($16). Theft deterrent system ($159). Lighting, Horns and Mirrors:- Tungsten-halogen high-beam headlamps ($22); std. on T Type. Twilight Sentinel headlamp control ($57). Coach lamps ($102); incl. w/vinyl top. Front/rear light monitors: T Type ($74). Rear quarter courtesy/reading lamp ($48). Lighted door lock and interior light control ($72). Four-note horn ($28). Dual electric remote mirrors ($65). Lighted visor vanity mirrors, each ($58). Entertainment:- Full-feature electronic-tuning AM/FM stereo radio ($125); w/8-track tape player ($278). Basic electronic-tuning AM/FM stereo radio w/cassette player ($100). Electronic-tuning AM/FM stereo radio with cassette and graphic equalizer ($328); w/cassette, Dolby and Bose speaker system ($895) exc. conv. CB radio ($220). Delete radio ($230 credit). Rear speakers for base radio ($25). Concert Sound system ($95) exc. conv. Triband power antenna ($45); incl. w/CB. Exterior Trim:- Heavy-padded landau vinyl top w/coach lamps ($325). Designers' accent paint ($235). Special color Firemist paint ($210); std. on conv. Color-coordinated protective bodyside moldings ($55). Door edge guards ($15). Bodyside stripe ($42). Interior Trim/Upholstery:- 45/45 leather/vinyl front seat ($405) exc. conv. Front carpet savers w/inserts ($35); rear ($20). Trunk trim carpeting ($30). Trunk mat ($15). Wheels and Tires:- Chrome-plated wheels ($145); on conv. ($40 credit). Custom locking wire wheel covers ($185). P225/70R15 SBR wide oval tires: BSW or WSW (NC).

HISTORY: Introduced: September 23, 1982. Model year production (U.S.): 808,415 for a 14.2 percent share of the industry total. That number included 143,725 four-cylinder Buicks, 416,810 sixes, and 247,880 V-8s—an intriguing jump in V-8 production, accounted for only in part by rising overall production. A total of 10,680 diesels and 5,065 turbocharged engines were installed. Calendar year production (all U.S.): 905,608 Buicks. Model year sales by U.S. dealers: 810,435. Calendar year sales (U.S.): 845,083, beating the record set in 1978.

Historical Footnotes: Sales rose markedly for the 1983 model year, edging past the record set in 1979 and giving Buick a fourth-place ranking among U.S. automakers. Skyhawk sales more than doubled but the compact Skylark didn't fare quite so well. Buick couldn't quite secure a tight grip on the sought-after youth market. Well over three-fourths of Buicks sold were mid- or full-size, and the average buyer was determined to be 52 years old. Topping the chart was the Regal coupe, which outsold the Regal sedan 2-to-1. Century upped sales by some 90 percent over 1982. Corporate plans centered around a massive $300 million project, known as Buick City, to be built at Flint, Michigan. A complex of random existing plants, now 60 years old, would be turned into a streamlined operation, consolidating the activity of a trio of separate organizations. In January 1983 came an announcement that two rear-drive assembly plants would be consolidated into one, to build front-drive Buicks for 1986. This caused 3,600 workers to be permanently laid off. Once again, a Buick paced the Indy 500. This time is was a Riviera convertible with twin-turbo 4.1-liter V-6 under the hood. Churning out 450 horsepower, it used many standard Buick heavy-duty parts. A new concept car called Questor was displayed at shows. Among its futuristic features were laser key entry, a map/navigation system, video rear-view mirror, and road surface traction monitor. On a more mundane level, Buick was pilot testing a high-technology videotex marketing system called Electronic Product Information Center at six dealerships. A video terminal and keyboard were linked by phone to Buick's own computer. The terminal displayed information in color and graphic form, and could be used to answer specific customer or salesman inquiries. With this sytem, dealerships could have constant access to the Buick central computer for up-to-date information.

1984 BUICK

As in the industry generally, high-tech engines got the emphasis for 1984, along with modern electronics and aero styling. T Types were now offered on five Buick models, which gained a performance boost. Two new 3.8-liter V-6s were introduced: one with multi-port fuel injection (optional on Century), the other with sequential fuel injection (standard on Regal/Riviera T Types). With multi-port injection (MFI), a computer analyzed air/fuel requirements and sent a charge to all six cylinders during each engine revolution. Sequential injection gave each cylinder a precisely-metered charge, just before firing, for best performance all the way from idle to full load. Both V-6 versions had been developed at Buick Special Products Engineering. An acceleration/deceleration feature on the new electronic cruise control allowed speed change in 1 MPH increments by touching a button on the lever. Cellular phones were offered for the first time, factory-approved but installed by dealers. 1984 Buick body colors were: beige, light sand gray, bright red, white and black, plus a selection of metallics: light brown, brown, light green, green, light blue, blue, red Firemist, red, dark red, sand gray Firemist, gold Firemist, and silver. Firemists cost extra.

1984 Skyhawk T Type coupe (B)

SKYHAWK — SERIES 4J — FOUR — New front-end panels with bigger cooling slots went on all Skyhawks this year, along with new bumper rub strips and modified turn signal lamps. The aerodynamic design used a low hood and high deck for wedge-shaped profile. Skyhawk came in Custom and Limited trim as well as the sporty T Type, which expanded its color selection to include silver, light maple and white bodies, with charcoal accents. Newly optional: an electronic radio with five-band graphic equalizer and four speakers. All Skyhawks had an AM radio and power brakes. T Types turned to P195/70R13 tires on styled aluminum wheels and had dual mirrors (left remote-controlled), Gran Touring suspension, and a sport steering wheel. Apart from the T Type, the Chevrolet-built 121 cu. in. (2.0-liter) four remained standard, with four-speed gearbox; a 1.8 four from Brazil was again optional. Shortly after production began, a turbocharged version of the 1.8-liter overhead-cam four became available (at extra cost) on the Skyhawk T Type, with multi-port fuel injection. Horsepower shot up to 150; torque to 150 lb.-ft. Included with that turbo engine was a Level III suspension system, with 205/60 series Eagle GT tires on 14 in. forged aluminum wheels. Standard T type powerplant remained the normally- aspirated 1.8 four, with five-speed manual gearbox. Turbos came with four-speed manual. All three engines could have three-speed automatic transmission instead.

SKYLARK — SERIES 4X — FOUR/V-6 — Aside from a distinctive new (notably Buick) grille, the X-bodied Buick didn't change much for '84. One new option on either coupe or sedan: a decklid luggage rack. Electronic cruise control also available. T Type coupes now had an electronic LED tachometer. As before, the 151 cu. in. (2.5-liter) four was standard; a 173 cu. in. (2.8-liter) V-6 optional, with a more powerful version standard in the T Type and optional on other models. Overdrive automatic transmissions were now available in the similar-size A-cars, but not in X models. Standard equipment included an AM radio, power steering, four-speed manual gearbox, notchback bench seat with adjustable headrests, roof drip and window moldings, glovebox lock, cigarette lighter, compact spare, and P185/80R13 steel-belted radial tires. Skylark Limited also came with belt reveal and wheel-opening moldings, a hood ornament, wide rocker panel and rear quarter moldings, protective bumper rub strips, and a pillar applique on sedans. T Types added a tachometer, gauges, halogen headlamps, Rallye ride/handling suspension, specially styled sport aluminum wheels with P215/60R14 steel-belted radials, black sport mirrors, and a sport steering wheel. The sporty Skylarks also had a blacked-out grille; black anodized aluminum bumpers; smoked taillamp lenses; and styled black mirrors. T bodies came in silver, light maple or white, with charcoal accent.

1984 Skylark T Type coupe (B)

1984 Century Estate Wagon (B)

CENTURY — SERIES 4A — FOUR/V-6 — All Century models displayed a new grille, headlamp bezels, bumper rub strips and standard wheel covers, along with new graphics at front and rear. Coupes and sedans added a new rear end and taillamps, plus a modified back bumper. A new new three-passenger front seat gave the Custom space for six. Century offered two new wagons for 1984: Custom and Estate, each with a unique one-piece top-hinged tailgate. Both had a split-folding back seat and separate lift-up rear window with available washer/wiper. They replaced the old Regal rear-drive wagon, which dropped out this season. Carrying six passengers in normal trim, they could have a rear-facing third seat that held two more. Wagons could hold over 74 cubic feet of cargo. Century Customs came with a standard AM radio, power brakes and steering, three-speed automatic transmission, bumper guards and rub strips, dual horns, locking glove box, side-window defogger, storage console, and full carpeting. The Limited added 55/45 cloth seating, a hood ornament, and wide lower bodyside moldings. Among other sporty extras, T Types included dual exhausts, temp/volt gauges, a blacked-out grille, styled black mirrors, black moldings, charcoal lower accent paint and striping, Gran Touring suspension, cloth bucket seats, and styled aluminum wheels. T Type dashes carried a new ribbon-type LED tachometer, and could be equipped with a special Lear Siegler bucket interior. Base Century engine remained the 2.5-liter four with throttle-body fuel injection, rated 90 horsepower. Options included a carbureted 3.0-liter V-6 and a diesel V-6. Most notable, though, was the new fuel-injected 231 cu. in. (3.8-liter) V-6, standard in T Type and optional elsewhere, available with four-speed overdrive automatic transmission. On the special-edition roster, to complement Buick's role as official car and sponsor of the games of the 23rd Olympiad in Los Angeles, there was a Century Olympia Limited sedan. Offered in white with "subtly classic" U.S. Olympic identification on front fender, decklid and hood ornament, the sedan was accented with gold body stripe and gold aluminum wheels. It had a decklid luggage rack, and the headrest on the tan cloth interior was embroidered with the official U.S. Olympic logo in dark brown.

1984 Regal coupe (JG)

REGAL — SERIES 4G — V-6 — Continuing for another season in rear-drive form, Regal dropped its station wagon this year. The diesel V-8 also disappeared, but a 4.3-liter V-6 diesel remained as an option. Regals showed a new grille and front end design, along with new graphics and taillamps, and a modified instrument panel. Coupes added new headlamp bezels and park/signal lamps. Joining the option list: a digital instrument cluster similar to Riviera's, with flourescent displays that showed speed, distance and fuel level. Standard equipment included dual mirrors and horns,

254

automatic transmission, power brakes and steering, bumper guards and rub strips, and whitewall P195/75R14 steel-belted tires. T Type tires were P215/65R15 blackwalls, on styled aluminum wheels. Limiteds carried a 55/45 notchback seat, along with wide rocker panel and rear quarter moldings. All engines except the base 231 cu. in. (3.8-liter) V-6 could have four-speed overdrive automatic transmission (standard in T Type) for $175 more. Regal's high-performance T Type had the new 3.8-liter V-6 with turbocharger and sequential port fuel injection, which produced 200 horsepower and 300 pound-feet of torque. Distributorless ignition on the turbo used three computer-controlled ignition coils to send current to the spark plugs. T Types came with a 3.42:1 performance axle ratio, overdrive automatic transmission, Gran Touring suspension, leather-wrapped steering wheel, turbo boost gauge, trip odometer, tachometer, and air conditioning. Buick's display of turbo technology at auto shows during 1984 was highlighted later in the model year by emergence of the '84 Regal Grand National, "produced in limited numbers for those who demand a high level of performance." Its purpose: to give much of the feeling of a NASCAR race car. Though officially on the option list, carrying a relatively moderate $1282 price tag, not too many Regal customers managed to get their hands on the Grand National package. Grand Nationals carried the turbo 3.8 engine, P215/60R blackwalls, sport steering wheel, tachometer and boost gauge, and 94-amp Delcotron. Distinctive bodies came only in black, with black bumpers, rub strips and guards; black front air dam and decklid spoiler; black headlamp bezels; turbo aluminum wheels with black paint; and Grand National identification on front fender. A Lear Siegler interior held front seats embroidered with the Grand National logo. Though officially on the option list, carrying a relatively modest $1282 price tag, not many Grand National packages found their way onto T Type Regals in 1984.

1984 LeSabre Custom sedan (B)

LESABRE — SERIES 4B — V-6/V-8 — Not much of substance changed this year on the rear-drive LeSabre, but a different grille and front-end panel gave a fresh look. Rear-end styling was also reworked, including new taillamps. New standard equipment included remote left (manual right) mirrors on all models and a redesigned steering wheel. Optional automatic touch climate control system was revised to give more precise temperature settings and control of fan speed. Standard under the hood was the familiar 231 cu. in. (3.8-liter) V-6, with 4.1-liter V-6 or 5.0-liter V-8 optional. So was the 5.7-liter diesel V-8, but not in California where it couldn't meet emissions standards. All LeSabres had color-keyed bodyside moldings, front and rear protective bumper strips, and bumper guards. Standard equipment also included dual horns, deluxe wheel covers, cut-pile carpeting, three-speed automatic transmission, power steering and brakes. LeSabre Limited added a two-way adjustable power driver's seat, headlamps-on indicator and warning chime, tinted glass, custom steering wheel, and woodgrain door trim. Limited instrument panels offered electro-luminescent floodlighting. LeSabre Custom had standard notchback seats in cloth velour with woven fabric trim; Limited cloth seats were in 55/45 arrangement.

ELECTRA ESTATE WAGON — SERIES 4D — V-8 — For '84 the LeSabre Estate Wagon was dropped, so Electra's became the last remaining Buick full-size wagon. Base engine was again the 307 cu. in. (5.0-liter) V-8, with only the 350 diesel V-8 optional. Standard 55/45 notchback seating had two-way power for the driver's side. In back, buyers could have the same cloth-covered seating as in front, or easy-to-clean vinyl. Standard equipment also included a tilt steering column, digital clock, electric door locks, power windows, remote tailgate lock, air conditioning, Soft Ray tinted glass, door edge guards, light oak woodgrain vinyl applique, and a luggage rack.

ELECTRA — SERIES 4D — V-6/V-8 — Since a totally new front-drive Electra was expected soon (and arrived in the spring as an early '85), the old rear-drive carried on unchanged. The new compact Electra was scheduled to arrive earlier, but mechanical and assembly difficulties held back its debut. When it finally appeared, it cut sharply into sales of its larger predecessor--even though the rear-drive had earned some popularity lately. Base engine was the 252 cu. in. (4.1-liter) V-6, with 5.0-liter gas V-8 and 5.7 diesel available. Electra Limited carried standard equipment similar to LeSabre, including a remote-controlled left outside mirror, along with 55/45 cloth notchback seating, air conditioning, digital clock, power windows, and P215/75R15 whitewalls. Park Avenue buyers got 50/50 seats (power on driver's side), a tilt steering wheel, power door locks, electronic-tuning stereo radio, reading light, remote trunk release, and power remote left mirror.

1984 Riviera coupe (JG)

RIVIERA — SERIES 4E — V-6/V-8 — Accompanying the new turbocharged 231 cu. in. (3.8-liter) V-6 engine on Riviera's T Type for '84 were a new standard turbo boost gauge and LED tachometer, leather-wrapped sport steering wheel, styled black mirrors, and new accent stripes. All Rivs got a new grille and front end panel, plus modified taillamp styling. Coupes (including T Type) now carried a front bench seat that held three people, while the convertible kept its bucket seats up front. Convertible tops held a new cloth headliner, while an electric defogger for the glass back window was optional. As before, the convertible was specially modified by American Sunroof Corporation. Standard Riv powertrain was the 252 cu. in. (4.1-liter) four-barrel V-6 with four-speed overdrive automatic; or optional 5.0-liter carbureted

1984 Riviera T Type coupe (JG)

V-8. GM's 5.7-liter diesel V-8 was now offered as a Riviera option for the first time (except in California). Base Rivs had whitewall tires, power brakes and steering, a notchback 55/45 front seat, power windows, tinted glass, an AM/FM eletronically-tuned stereo with automatic power antenna and clock, electric door locks, power six-way driver's seat, cruise control, automatic level control, air conditioning, and P205/75R15 steel-belted radial tires. Tungsten-halogen headlamps, styled aluminum wheels, blacked-out grille and Gran Touring suspension were T Type standards. Riviera convertibles had Firemist paint and four-wheel disc brakes, plus custom locking wire wheel covers and trunk carpeting. On the option list (except for convertibles): a high-end Delco/Bose music system.

I.D. DATA: Buicks again had a 17-symbol Vehicle Identification Number (VIN), stamped on a metal tag attached to the upper left surface of the cowl, visible through the windshield. Coding was similar to 1983. LeSabre Estate (series code 'R') was dropped, and the code for Electra Park Ave. changed from 'W' to 'U'. Two engine codes were added: 'J' turbo L4-110 MFI and '3' V6-231 MFI. The code for turbocharged V6-231 (now with SFI) changed to '9'. Model year symbol changed to 'E' for 1984. Symbol eleven (plant code) was as follows: 'W' Willow Run, MI; '6' Oklahoma City, OK; 'H' Flint, MI; 'K' Leeds, MO; 'X' Fairfax, KS; 'E' Linden, NJ; and 'D' Doraville. The final six digits are the sequential serial number, starting with 400001 except for LeSabres built in Flint, which began with 800001.

SKYHAWK CUSTOM (FOUR)

Series Number	Body/Style Number	Body Type & Seating	Factory Price	Shipping Weight	Production Total
4J	S27	2-dr Coupe-5P	7133	2316	74,760
4J	S69	4-dr Sedan-5P	7345	2369	45,648
4J	S35	4-dr Sta Wag-5P	7677	2439	13,668

SKYHAWK LIMITED (FOUR)

4J	T27	2-dr Coupe-5P	7641	2356	Note 1
4J	T69	4-dr Sedan-5P	7837	2404	Note 1
4J	T35	4-dr Sta Wag-5P	8127	2469	Note 1

Note 1: Skyhawk Custom production figures also include equivalent Limited models. Coupe/sedan production came to 97,962 Customs and 22,446 Limiteds.

SKYHAWK T TYPE (FOUR)

4J	E27	2-dr Coupe-5P	8152	2332	11,317

SKYLARK CUSTOM (FOUR/V-6)

4X	B37	2-dr Coupe-5P	7545/7795	2458/2519	12,377
4X	B69	4-dr Sedan-5P	7707/7957	2489/2550	56,495

SKYLARK LIMITED (FOUR/V-6)

4X	C37	2-dr Coupe-5P	8119/8369	2484/2545	7,621
4X	C69	4-dr Sedan-5P	8283/8533	2515/2576	33,795

SKYLARK T TYPE (V-6)

4X	D37	2-dr Coupe-5P	9557	2606	923

CENTURY CUSTOM (FOUR/V-6)

4A	H27	2-dr Coupe-6P	9110/9360	2609/2714	15,429
4A	H19	4-dr Sedan-6P	9274/9524	2658/2763	178,454
4A	H35	4-dr Sta Wag-6P	9660/9910	2825/2930	25,975

CENTURY LIMITED (FOUR/V-6)

4A	L27	2-dr Coupe-6P	9562/9812	2631/2736	Note 2
4A	L19	4-dr Sedan-6P	9729/9979	2679/2784	Note 2
4A	L35	4-dr Sta Wag-6P	10087/10337	2843/2948	Note 2

CENTURY T TYPE (V-6)

4A	G27	2-dr Coupe-5P	10510	2775	Note 2
4A	G19	4-dr Sedan-5P	10674	2823	Note 2

Note 2: Production figures listed under Century Custom include totals for Century Limited and T Type models. In all, 71,160 Customs, 119,246 Limiteds and 3,477 Century T Types were manufactured.

1984 Regal Grand National coupe (B)

REGAL (V-6)

4G	J47	2-dr Coupe-6P	9487	3079	160,638
4G	J69	4-dr Sedan-6P	9671	3125	58,715

REGAL LIMITED (V-6)

4G	M47	2-dr Coupe-6P	10125	3106	Note 3
4G	M69	4-dr Sedan-6P	10263	3125	Note 3

Note 3: Base Regal production totals also include Limited models. Total model year production, 106,306 base Regals and 113,047 Limiteds.

REGAL T TYPE (V-6)

4G	K47	2-dr Coupe-6P	12118	3249	5,401

LESABRE CUSTOM (V-6/V-8)

4B	N37	2-dr Coupe-6P	9984/10534	3472/3663	3,890
4B	N69	4-dr Sedan-6P	10129/10679	3484/3675	36,072

LESABRE LIMITED (V-6/V-8)

4B	P37	2-dr Coupe-6P	10780/11330	3497/3688	28,332
4B	P69	4-dr Sedan-6P	10940/11490	3530/3721	86,418

ELECTRA LIMITED (V-6/V-8)

4D	R37	2-dr Coupe-6P	13155/13380	3656/3835	4,075
4D	R69	4-dr Sedan-6P	13332/13557	3716/3895	52,551

ELECTRA PARK AVENUE (V-6/V-8)

4D	U37	2-dr Coupe-6P	14888/15113	3700/3879	Note 4
4D	U69	4-dr Sedan-6P	15044/15269	3766/3945	Note 4

Note 4: Park Avenue production totals are included in Electra Limited figures.

ELECTRA ESTATE WAGON (V-8)

4B	V35	4-dr Sta Wag-6P	14483	4160	17,563

RIVIERA (V-6/V-8)

4E	Z57	2-dr Coupe-5P	15967/16192	3574/3748	56,210
4E	Z67	2-dr Conv-5P	25832/26057	3680/3854	500

Note 5: Only 1,424 standard Riviera coupes and 58 convertibles had a V-6 engine this year.

RIVIERA T TYPE (V-6)

4E	Y57	2-dr Coupe-5P	17050	3660	1,153

FACTORY PRICE AND WEIGHT NOTE: Figure before the slash is for four-cylinder engine, after the slash for V-6. For full-size models, figure before slash is for V-6 engine, after slash for V-8.

ENGINES: BASE FOUR-CYLINDER (Skyhawk): Inline, overhead-valve four-cylinder. Cast iron block and head. Displacement; 121 cu. in. (2.0 liters). Bore & stroke: 3.50 x 3.15 in. Compression ratio: 9.3:1. Brake horsepower: 86 at 4900 R.P.M. Torque: 100 lbs.- ft. at 3000 R.P.M. Five main bearings. Hydraulic valve lifters. Throttle-body fuel injection. VIN Code: P. OPTIONAL FOUR (Skyhawk); STANDARD (Skyhawk T Type): Inline, overhead-cam four-cylinder. Cast iron block; aluminum cylinder head. Displacement: 110 cu. in. (1.8 liters). Bore & stroke: 3.34 x 3.13 in. Compression ratio: 9.0:1. Brake horsepower: 84 at 5200 R.P.M. Torque: 102 lbs.-ft. at 2800 R.P.M. Five main bearings. Hydraulic valve lifters. Throttle- body fuel injection. VIN Code: O. TURBOCHARGED FOUR (Skyhawk T Type): Same as 1.8-liter OHC four above, except-- Compression ratio: 8.0:1. Brake H.P.: 150 at 5600 R.P.M. Torque: 150 lbs.-ft. at 2800 R.P.M. Multi-point fuel injection. VIN Code: J. BASE FOUR (Skylark, Century): Inline, overhead-valve four-cylinder. Cast iron block and head. Displacement: 151 cu. in. (2.5 liters), Bore & stroke: 4.0 x 3.0 in. Compression ratio: 9.0:1. Brake horsepower: 92 at 4400 R.P.M. Torque: 132 lbs-ft. at 2800 R.P.M. Five main bearings. Hydraulic valve lifters. Throttle-body fuel injection. Built by Pontiac. VIN Code: R. OPTIONAL V-6 (Skylark): 60-degree, overhead-valve V-6. Cast iron block and head. Displacement: 173 cu. in. (2.8 liters). Bore & stroke: 3.50 x 2.99 in. Compression: 8.4:1. Brake horsepower: 112 at 5100 R.P.M. Torque: 148 lbs.-ft. at 2400 R.P.M. Four main bearings. Hydraulic valve lifters. Carburetor: 2Bbl. Rochester. Built by Chevrolet, VIN Code: X. HIGH-OUTPUT V-6; (Skylark T Type); OPTIONAL (Skylark); STANDARD (Skylark T): Same as 173 cu. in V-6 above except as follows: Compression ratio: 8.94:1. Brake horsepower: 135 at 5400 R.P.M. Torque: 145 lbs.-ft. at 2400 R.P.M. VIN Code: Z. OPTIONAL V-6 (Century); 90-degree, overhead-valve V-6. Cast iron block and head. Displacement: 181 cu. in (3.0 liters). Bore & stroke: 3.8 x 2.66 in. Compression ratio: 8.45:1. Brake horsepower: 110 at 4800 R.P.M. Torque: 145 lbs.-ft. at 2600 R.P.M. Four main bearings. Hydraulic valve lifters. Carburetor: 2Bbl. Rochester E2SE. VIN Code: E. BASE V-6 (Regal, LeSabre): 90-degree, overhead-valve V-6. Cast iron alloy block and head. Displacement: 231 cu. in. (3.8 liters). Bore & stroke: 3.8 x 3.4 in. Compression ratio: 8.0:1. Brake horsepower: 110 at 3800 R.P.M. Torque: 190 lbs-ft. at 1600 R.P.M. Four main bearings. Hydraulic valve lifters. Carburetor: 2Bbl. Rochester 2ME, VIN Code A. Base V-6 (Century T Type); OPTIONAL (Century): Same as 231 V-6 above, but with multi-point fuel injection. Compression ratio: 8.0:1. Brake H.P.: 125 at 4400 R.P.M. Torque: 195 lbs.-ft. at 2000 R.P.M. VIN Code: 3. TURBOCHARGED V-6 (Regal T Type); Same as 231 V-6 above, with turbocharger; switched from four-barrel carburetor to sequential fuel injection. Brake H.P.: 200 at 4000 R.P.M. Torque: 300 lbs.-ft. at 2400 R.P.M. TURBOCHARGED V-6 (Riviera T Type): Same as turbo 231 V-6 above, with sequential fuel injection. Brake H.P.: 190 at 4000 R.P.M. VIN Code: 9. BASE V-6 (Electra, Riviera); OPTIONAL (Regal, LeSabre); 90-degree, overhead-valve V-6. Cast iron alloy block and head. Displacement: 252 cu. in (4.1 liters). Bore & stroke: 3.965 x 3.4 in. Compression ratio: 8.0:1. Brake horsepower: 125 at 4000 R.P.M. Torque: 205 lbs.-ft. at 2000 R.P.M. Four main bearings. Hydraulic valve lifters. Carburetor: 4Bbl. Rochester. VIN Code: 4. DIESEL V-6; OPTIONAL (Century, Regal): 90-degree, overhead-valve V-6. Cast iron block; cast iron or aluminum head. Displacement: 262.5 cu. in. (4.3 liters). Bore & stroke: 4.057 x 3.385 in. Compression ratio: 21.6:1. Brake horsepower: 85 at 3600 R.P.M. Torque: 165 lbs-ft. at 1600 R.P.M. Four main bearings. Hydraulic valve lifters. Fuel injection. VIN Code: V. BASE V-8 (Estate); OPTIONAL (LeSabre, Electra, Riviera): 90-degree, overhead valve V-8. Cast iron block and head. Displacement: 307 cu. in. (5.0 liters). Bore & stroke: 3.80 x 3.385 in. Compression ratio: 8.0:1. Brake horsepower: 140 at 3600 R.P.M. Torque: 240 lbs.-ft. at 1600 R.P.M. Five main bearings. Hydraulic valve lifters. Carburetor: 4Bbl. Rochester M4ME. Built by Oldsmobile. VIN Code: Y. OPTIONAL DIESEL V-8 (LeSabre, Estate, Riviera): 90-degree, overhead valve V-8. Cast iron block and head. Displacement: 350 cu. in (5.7 liters). Bore & stroke: 4.057 x 3.385 in. Compression ratio: 21.6:1. Brake horsepower: 105 at 3200 R.P.M. Torque: 200 lbs-ft. at 1600 R.P.M. Five main bearings. Hydraulic valve lifters. Fuel injection. Oldsmobile-built. VIN Code: N.

CHASSIS DATA: Wheelbase: (Skyhawk) 101.2 in.; (Skylark/Century) 104.9 in.; (Regal) 108.1 in.; (LeSabre/Estate) 115.9 in.; (Electra) 118.9 in.; (Riviera) 114.0 in. Overall length:- (Skyhawk cpe) 171.3 in.; (Skyhawk wag) 173.3 in.; (Skylark) 181.1 in.; (Century) 189.1 in.; (Century wag) 190.9 in.; (Regal cpe) 200.6 in.; (Regal sed) 196.0 in.; (LeSabre) 218.4 in.; (Electra/Estate) 221.3 in.; (Riviera) 206.6 in. Height:- (Skyhawk) 53.4-53.6 in.; (Skylark/Century) 53.6 in.; (Century wag) 54.1 in.; (Regal cpe) 54.6 in.; (Regal sed) 55.5 in.; (LeSabre/Electra cpe) 56.0 in.; (LeSabre/Electra sed) 56.7-56.9 in.; (Estate) 59.1 in.; (Riv) 54.3 in. Width:- (Skyhawk) 65.0 in.; (Skylark) 69.1 in.; (Century) 66.8 in.; (Century wag) 69.4 in.; (Regal cpe) 71.6 in.; (Regal sed) 71.1 in.; (LeSabre) 78.0 in.; (Electra/Estate) 76.2 in.; (Riv) 72.8 in. Front Tread:- (Skyhawk) 55.3 in.; (Skylark/Century) 58.7 in.; (Regal) 58.5 in.; (LeSabre/Electra/Est) 61.8 in.; (Riv) 59.3 in. Rear Tread:- (Skyhawk) 55.1 in.; (Skylark) 57.0 in.; (Century) 56.7 in.; (Regal) 57.7-57.8 in.; (LeSabre/Electra/Est) 60.7 in.; (Riviera) 60.0 in. Standard Tires:- (Skyhawk) P175/80R13 GBR; (Skylark/Century) P185/80R13 GBR; (Skylark T Type) P205/70R13 SBR; (Regal) P195/75R14 SBR WSW; (Regal T Type) P205/70R14 SBR; (LeSabre) P205/75R15 SBR WSW; (Electra) P215/75R15 SBR WSW; (Estate) P225/75R15 SBR WSW; (Riviera) P205/75R15 SBR WSW.

TECHNICAL: Transmission:- Four-speed, fully synchronized floor shift standard on Skyhawk/Skylark; automatic optional (standard on all other models). Five-speed standard on Skyhawk T Type. Four-speed gear ratios: (1st) 3.53:1; (2nd) 1.95:1; (3rd) 1.24:1; (4th) 0.81:1 or 0.73:1; (Rev) 3.42:1. Skylark H.O. four-speed: (1st) 3.31:1; (2nd) 1.95:1; (3rd) 1.24:1; (4th) 0.81:1; (Rev) 3.42:1. Five-speed gear ratios: (1st) 3.91:1; (2nd) 2.15:1; (3rd) 1.45:1; (4th) 1.03:1; (5th) 0.74:1; (Rev) 3.50:1. Three-speed auto. trans. gear ratios: (1st) 2.74:1; (2nd) 1.57:1; (3rd) 1.00:1; (Rev) 2.07:1. Skyhawk/Skylark auto. trans. gear ratios: (1st) 2.84:1; (2nd) 1.60:1; (3rd) 1.00:1; (Rev) 2.07:1. Four-speed overdrive automatic gear ratios: (1st) 2.74:1; (2nd) 1.57:1; (3rd) 1.00:1; (4th) 0.67:1; (Rev) 2.07:1. Century four-speed automatic: (1st) 2.92:1; (2nd) 1.57:1; (3rd) 1.00:1; (4th) 0.70:1; (Rev) 2.38:1. Standard axle ratio:- (Skyhawk) 2.84:1 or 3.06:1 w/4- spd, 3.45:1 w/5-spd, 3.18:1 w/auto.; (Skyhawk turbo) 3.65:1 w/4-spd, 3.33:1 w/auto.; (Skylark) 3.32:1 or 3.65:1 w/4-spd, 2.39:1 or 2.53:1 w/auto., 3.23:1 w/H.O. V-6 and auto.; (Century) 2.39:1 or 2.53:1 w/3-spd, 2.84:1 or 3.06:1 w/4-spd; (Century wag) 2.84:1, 2.97:1 or 3.06:1; (Regal) 2.41:1 w/3-spd, 3.08:1 w/4-spd exc. diesel 2.93:1; (Regal T Type) 3.42:1; (LeSabre/Electra) 2.73:1 w/3-spd; 2.73:1, 2.93:1 or 3.23:1 w/4-spd; (Riviera) 2.73:1, 2.93:1 or 3.36:1; (Riv turbo) .36:1. Steering:- (Skyhawk/Skylark/Century) rack and pinion; (others) recirculating ball; power assist standard on all except Skyhawk. Suspension:- front/rear coil springs. (Skyhawk) MacPherson strut front; semi-independent beam rear axle w/trailing arms; stabilizer bar on T Type. (Skylark/Century) MacPherson strut front suspension; beam twist rear axle w/trailing arms and Panhard rod; front/rear stabilizer bars. (Riviera) fully independent suspension with front torsion bars, semi-trailing arms at rear, front/rear stabilizers and automatic level control. (Rear-drive models) front stabilizer bar; rear stabilizer bar on T Type; rigid four-link rear axle. Brakes:- power front disc, rear drum. Four-wheel power disc brakes available on Riviera (std. on conv.). Body construction:- (Skyhawk/Skylark/Century) unitized; (others) separate body and frame. Fuel tank:- (Skyhawk) 13.6 gal.; (Skylark 2-dr) 14.6 gal.; (Skylark 4-dr) 15.1 gal.; (Century) 15.7 gal.; (Regal) 18.1 gal.; (LeSabre/Electra) 26.0 gal.; (Estate) 22.0 gal.; (Riviera) 21.1 gal. Unleaded fuel only.

DRIVETRAIN OPTIONS: Engines:- 110 cu. in. (1.8-liter) EFI four: Skyhawk ($50). Turbocharged 110 cu. in. (1.8-liter) MFI four: Skyhawk T Type ($800). 173 cu. in. (2.8-liter) V-6, 2Bbl.: Skylark ($250). High-output 173 cu. in. (2.8-liter) V-6, 2Bbl.: Skylark ($400); std. on T Type. 181 cu. in. (3.0-liter) V-6, 2Bbl.: Century ($250). Turbocharged 231 cu. in. (3.8-liter) V-6: Riviera conv. ($900). 252 cu. in. (4.1-liter) V-6, 4Bbl.: Regal/LeSabre ($225). 263 cu. in. (4.3-liter) diesel V-6: Century/Regal Cust/Ltd ($599). 307 cu. in. (5.0-liter) V-8, 4Bbl.: LeSabre ($375); Electra cpe/sed, Riviera ($225). 350 cu. in. (5.7-liter) diesel V-8: LeSabre/Estate/Riviera ($799). Transmission/Differential:- Four-speed manual trans.: Skyhawk T ($75 credit). Five-speed manual trans.: Skyhawk ($75). Automatic trans.: Skyhawk ($395); Skyhawk T Type ($320); Skylark ($425). Automatic overdrive trans.: Century (N/A); Regal/LeSabre ($175). Optional rear axle ratio: Skyhawk 3.43:1 (NC); Skylark 2.84:1 or 3.65:1; Century 2.84:1 or 2.97:1; Regal/LeSabre/Electra 3.08:1 or 3.23:1 (NC). Limited slip differential: Regal/LeSabre/Electra ($95). Suspension, Steering and Brakes:- F40 Firm ride/handling pkg. ($27). F41 Gran Touring suspension: Skyhawk ($196); Skylark ($207); Century Cust/Ltd cpe/sed, LeSabre, Riviera ($27); Regal/Ltd, LeSabre ($49). Superlift rear shock absorbers: Skylark Cust/Ltd ($68). Automatic level control: Century/Regal/LeSabre/Electra ($175). Power steering: Skyhawk ($204). Four-wheel disc brakes: Riviera ($235). Other:- Trailer towing pkg.: LeSabre ($128). Heavy-duty alternator: Skyhawk/Regal/LeSabre/Electra 85-amp ($35 or $85); 94-amp ($35 or $85) exc. Skylark; Skylark 99-amp ($35 or $85); Century/Riv 108-amp ($40). H.D. battery: ($26); diesel ($52). H.D. radiator: Skyhawk ($40-$70). H.D. cooling: Skylark ($40- $70); Engine block heater ($18). H.D. engine/transmission cooling: Century/Regal/LeSabre/Electra/Riviera ($40-$70). California emission system ($99).

SKYHAWK CONVENIENCE/APPEARANCE OPTIONS: Option Packages:- Vista Vent flip-open removable glass sunroof ($300). Instrument gauge pkg.: temp, oil pressure, volts, trip odometer: Cust ($60). Gauges and tach: Cust ($138); Ltd ($78). Acoustic pkg. ($36); std. on Ltd. Comfort/Convenience:- Air cond. ($630). Touch climate control air cond. ($780). Rear defogger, electric ($130). Electronic cruise control w/resume ($175). Power windows ($185-$260). Electric door locks ($125-$175). Six-way power driver's seat ($215). Easy-entry passenger seat adjuster: Cust cpe ($16). Tinted glass ($95). Sport steering wheel: cust/Ltd ($50). Leather-wrapped steering wheel: T Type ($40). Tilt steering ($104). Trip odometer: Cust ($15). Electric clock ($35). Electric trunk release ($40). Remote tailgate lock: wag ($40). Tailgate wiper/washer: wag ($120). Two-speed wipers w/delay ($50). Lights, Horns and Mirrors:- Tungsten-halogen headlamps ($22). Headlamps-on indicator ($15). Dome reading lamp ($30). Dual horns: Cust cpe/sed ($15). Left remote mirror: Cust/Ltd ($22). Dual mirrors: left remote ($53). Dual electric remote mirrors ($139); T ($86). Visor vanity mirror, passenger ($7). Lighted visor vanity mirror, either side ($45). Entertainment:- Basic electronic-tuning AM/FM stereo radio ($138); w/clock ($177); w/cassette ($277). Electronic-tuning AM/FM stereo radio ($302); w/cassette and graphic equalizer ($505). Radio delete ($56 credit). Power antenna ($60). Dual rear speakers ($25-$30); incl. w/radios. Exterior Trim:- Door edge guards ($15-$25). Rocker panel moldings: Cust cpe/sed ($26). Bodyside stripes ($42). Designers' accent paint ($195). Decklid luggage rack ($100). Roof rack: wag ($105). Interior Trim/Upholstery:- Suede bucket seats: Ltd cpe/sed ($295). Front carpet savers ($17); rear ($12). Front carpet savers w/inserts ($18); rear ($15). Deluxe trunk trim ($33). Security cover: wag ($69). Wheels and Tires:- Styled aluminum wheels ($229). Styled wheel covers w/trim rings ($38). Locking wire wheel covers ($170). P175/80R13 GBR WSW ($54). P195/70R13 SBR BSW ($169). P195/70R13 SBR WSW or wide WSW ($62-$231). P195/70R13 SBR WLT ($84-$253). P205/60R14 SBR WLT: T Type ($94-$182). Self-sealing tires ($106).

SKYLARK/CENTURY CONVENIENCE/APPEARANCE OPTIONS: Option Packages:- Century Olympia Sedan pkg. (white body w/gold bodyside stripe, gold-accented aluminum wheels, decklid luggage rack, brown cloth seats with Olympic logo on headrests): Ltd sed ($406). Acoustic pkg.: Skylark Cust ($60). Flip-open Vista Vent glass sunroof ($300). Lamp group: Skylark Cust ($32-$42). Comfort/Convenience:- Air cond. ($730). Cruise control ($175). Rear defogger, electric ($135- $140). Power windows ($185-$260). Electric door locks ($125- $175). Six-way power driver's seat ($215). Manual seatback recliners, passenger ($45); both ($90). Sport steering wheel ($50). Leather-wrapped steering wheel: Skylark T ($40). Tilt steering ($110). Tinted glass ($110). Instrument gauges incl. trip odometer ($48). Tachometer: Skylark Cust/Ltd ($78). Trip odometer: Skylark Cust/Ltd ($16). Digital electronic instrument cluster: Century ($205-$299). Dial clock ($35). Electric trunk release ($40). Remote tailgate lock: Century wag ($40). Tailgate washer/wiper: Century wag ($120). Two-speed wipers with delay ($49-$50). Theft deterrent system: Century ($159). Lights, Horns and Mirrors:- Tungsten-halogen headlamps: Skylark Cust ($10); Century ($22). Twilight Sentinel: Century ($57). Front light monitors: Century ($37). Coach lamps: Ltd ($102-$129). Headlamps-on indicator ($16). Door courtesy/warning light: Century Ltd wag ($44). Dome reading light ($24). Rear seat reading lamp: Skylark Ltd, Century Cust ($30). Dual horns: Skylark Cust ($15). Remote-control left mirror: Cust/Ltd ($25). Sport mirrors (left remote, right manual): Cust/Ltd ($61). Dual electric remote mirrors: Cust/Ltd ($139); T Type ($78). Visor vanity mirror, passenger ($7). Lighted visor vanity mirror, passenger: Skylark ($58); either side, Century ($58). Entertainment:- Same as Skyhawk (above). Exterior Trim:- Landau vinyl top for Cust/Ltd cpe: Skylark ($220); Century ($186). Long vinyl top: Cust/Ltd ($160). Designers' accent paint: Cust/Ltd ($205- $210). Special solid color paint: Century Cust/Ltd ($200). Protective bodyside moldings ($55); color-coordinated on Century. Lower wide bodyside moldings: Century Cust ($65). Rocker panel moldings: Skylark Cust ($26). Wide rocker panel/rear quarter moldings: Skylark Cust ($91). Belt reveal molding: Skylark Cust, T Type ($40). Wheel opening moldings: Skylark Cust ($30). Door edge guards ($15-$25). Pillar applique moldings: Skylark Cust sed ($27). Hood ornament and windsplit: Cust ($22-$32). Bodyside stripe: Cust/Ltd ($45). Bumper guards, front/rear: Skylark ($45). Bumper strips, front/rear: Skylark Cust ($49). Front license plate mounting: Skylark (NC). Decklid luggage rack: Century ($100). Roof rack: Century wag ($105). Swing-out rear quarter vent windows: Century wag ($75). Woodgrain vinyl applique: Century wag ($350). Tailgate air deflector: Century wag ($37). Interior Trim/Upholstery:- Full-length console: Century ($57). Full-length operating console: Century ($80); T Type ($23). Bucket seats: Skylark Cust ($140); Skylark Ltd ($95); Century Cust ($97). 55/45 cloth seat trim: Century Cust ($133). Notchback bench seating w/armrest, cloth or vinyl: Skylark Cust ($45). Lear Siegler bucket seats: Century T type ($600). 45/45 seating: cloth, Century Ltd/Estate (NC); leather/vinyl ($295). Third seat: Century wag ($215). Front carpet savers ($17); rear ($12). Carpet savers w/inserts: front ($25); rear ($20). Trunk trim ($25-$47). Wheels:- Styled aluminum wheels: Century ($195); std. on T Type. Chrome-plated wheels: Skylark Cust/Ltd ($175). Locking wire wheel covers: Cust/Ltd ($175- $190). Skylark Tires:- P185/80R13 SBR WSW: Cust/Ltd ($58). P205/70R13 SBR WSW: Cust/Ltd ($180). P215/60R14 SBR WLT: T Type ($92). Self-sealing tires: Cust/Ltd ($106). Century Tires:- P185/75R14 SBR WSW: Cust/Ltd ($58). P195/75R14 SBR BSW: Cust/Ltd ($31). P195/75R14 SBR WSW: Cust/Ltd ($93). P195/70R14 SBR WLT: T Type ($84). P215/60R14 SBR BSW: T ($123). P215/60R14 SBR WLT: T ($215). Self-sealing tires: Cust/Ltd ($106).

REGAL CONVENIENCE/APPEARANCE OPTIONS: Option Packages:- Regal Grand National pkg. (black bumpers, lamps, moldings, spoilers, special interior trim w/console, special alum. wheels: T Type ($1282). Regal T Type Designer pkg.: designers' accent paint and rear spoiler ($403). Sliding electric silver Astroroof: cpe ($895). Hatch roof: cpe ($825). Comfort/Convenience:- Air cond. ($730); std. T Type. Touch climate control air cond. ($880); T Type ($150). Electronic cruise control w/resume ($175). Rear defogger, electric ($140). Tinted glass ($110). Tinted windshield ($90). Six-way power seat, each side ($215). Manual passenger seatback recliner ($75). Sport steering wheel ($50). Tilt steering ($110). Power windows ($185-$260). Electric door locks ($125-$175). Headlamps-on indicator ($16). Trip odometer ($16) exc. T Type. Electronic instrumentation ($299) exc. T Type ($173). Two-speed wiper w/low-speed delay ($50). Theft deterrent system ($159). Lighting and Mirrors:- Tungsten-halogen headlamps ($22). Twilight Sentinel ($57). Cornering lamps ($57). Coach lamps: Ltd ($102). Door courtesy/warning lights: Ltd ($44-$70). Rear seat reading light ($30). Dome reading lamp ($24). Remote left mirror ($25) exc. T Type. Dual sport mirrors, left remote ($53) exc. T. Dual remote sport mirrors ($83); T ($30). Visor vanity mirror, passenger ($7). Lighted visor vanity mirror, passenger ($58). Entertainment:- AM radio ($112). AM/FM stereo radio ($238). Electronic-tuning AM/FM stereo radio ($402); w/cassette and graphic equalizer ($605). Concert sound speaker system ($95). Dual rear speakers ($25-$30); incl. w/stereo radio. Automatic power antenna ($95); w/radio ($60). Exterior Trim:- Landau vinyl top: cpe ($186) exc. T Type; heavily-padded ($245). Long vinyl top: sed ($160); padded ($245). Designers' accent paint ($200-$205). Solid special color paint ($200). Exterior molding pkg.: wide rocker panel and belt reveal ($110); std. on Ltd. Protective bodyside moldings: T Type ($55); choice of six colors. Wraparound bodyside moldings: sed ($104). Door edge guards ($15-$25). Bodyside stripe ($42); choice of nine colors. Interior Trim/Upholstery:- Full-length console ($82). Bucket seats ($195) exc. Ltd. Lear Siegler bucket seats: T Type ($600). 55/45 seating ($133) exc. Ltd. 45/45 leather/vinyl seating: Ltd ($295). Front carpet savers ($17); rear ($12). Front carpet savers w/inserts ($25); rear ($20). Wheels:- Chrome- plated wheels ($195) T Type ($90 credit). Styled aluminum wheels ($285); std. T Type. Locking wire wheel covers ($190) exc. T. Body-color wheels ($85) exc. T. Tires:- P205/70R14 SBR WSW ($62) exc. T Type. P215/65R15 SBR WLT : T Type ($92). Self-sealing tires ($106) exc. T.

LESABRE/ELECTRA/ESTATE WAGON CONVENIENCE/APPEARANCE OPTIONS: Comfort/Convenience:- Sliding electric Astroroof: silver, gray or gold ($1195). Air cond.: LeSabre ($730). Air cond. w/touch-climate control: LeSabre ($880); Electra ($150). Cruise control w/resume ($175); std. Park Ave. Rear defogger, electric ($140). Tinted glass: LeSabre Cust ($110). Power windows: LeSabre ($185-$260). Electric door locks ($125- $175). Automatic door locks ($205-$255); exc. Park Ave. ($80). Six-way power seat, driver's or passenger's ($185- $215); both ($400-$430). Memory driver's seat: Electra Ltd ($363); Park Ave. ($178). Electric seatback recliner, either side ($139). Manual passenger seatback recliner: LeSabre/Estate ($75). Tilt steering: LeSabre, Electra Ltd ($110). Tilt/telescoping steering column: Electra Ltd ($165); Park Ave. ($55). Dial clock: LeSabre ($60). Digital clock: LeSabre Ltd ($60). Trip odometer ($16). Electric trunk lock: Electra ($80). Electric trunk release ($40). Electric fuel cap lock: Electra ($44) exc. wag. Theft deterrent system ($159); N/A on Estate. Two-speed wiper w/delay ($49-$50). Accessory group (trip odometer, dome reading lamp, low fuel indicator, washer fluid indicator): Electra ($46-$70). Lighting, Horns and Mirrors:- Tungsten-halogen high-beam headlamps ($22). Twilight Sentinel ($60). Cornering lamps ($60). Coach lamps: LeSabre/Electra Ltd ($102). Light monitors, front: LeSabre/Est ($37); front/rear, Electra $74). Lamp and indicator group ($38-$70). Door courtesy/warning lamps ($44-$70). Lighted door lock and interior light control ($75). Four-note horn ($28). Remote right mirror: LeSabre ($49); Electra ($25) exc. Park Ave. Remote electric right mirror: Park Ave. ($58). Dual electric remote mirrors ($91) exc. Park Ave. Dual electric mirrors w/left thermometer: Electra Ltd ($129). Lighted visor vanity mirror, driver or passenger ($58). Entertainment:- AM radio: LeSabre ($112). AM/FM stereo radio: Electra ($198); std. on Park Ave. Basic ETR AM/FM stereo radio: LeSabre/Estate ($238); w/clock ($277) but. std. on Park Ave.; w/cassette ($338-$402) exc. Park Ave. ($125). Electronic-tuning AM/FM stereo radio ($338-$402) exc. Park Ave. ($125). Electronic-tuning AM/FM stereo radio w/cassette and equalizer ($541- $605) exc. Park Ave. ($328). CB radio: Estate ($275). Delete AM/FM stereo radio: Park Ave. ($230 credit). Concert Sound speaker system: Electra exc. wagon ($95); ETR radio req'd. Dual rear speakers ($25-$30). Automatic power antenna ($95); w/radio ($60). Triband power antenna ($140); w/radio ($105). Exterior Trim:- Exterior molding pkg. (wide rocker panel, front/rear fender lower and belt reveal moldings): LeSabre ($110). Landau vinyl top: LeSabre, Electra Ltd cpe ($245). Long vinyl top: LeSabre, Electra Ltd sed ($185-$190). Heavy-padded long vinyl top: Electra Ltd sedan ($245). Designers' accent paint: LeSabre ($215). Special single-color paint: ($200); Firemist, Electra exc. Estate ($210). Protective bodyside moldings: Estate ($55). Wide rocker panel moldings: Electra Ltd/Est ($65). Door edge guards ($15-$25). Belt reveal molding: LeSabre ($40). Bodyside stripes ($42-$45); choice of nine colors. Interior Trim/Upholstery:- 55/45 seating: LeSabre Custom ($133). Leather/vinyl 50/50 seating: Park Ave. ($525). Third seat: Estate ($220). Front carpet savers ($17); rear ($12). Front carpet savers w/inserts ($25); rear ($20). Trunk carpeting trim ($53-$65). Trunk mat ($15). Wheels:- Chrome-plated wheels ($180-$215) exc. Estate ($40 credit). Styled aluminum wheels ($220-$255). Custom wheel covers: Electra Ltd ($35). Locking wire wheel covers ($155-$190) exc. Estate ($65 credit). Tires:- P215/75R15 SBR wide WSW: LeSabre ($38). P225/75R15 SBR wide WSW: Electra cpe/sed ($39). Self-sealing tires ($107-$132).

1984 Riviera convertible (B)

RIVIERA CONVENIENCE/APPEARANCE OPTIONS: Comfort/Convenience:- Electric sliding Astroroof: silver, gray or gold ($1195). Touch climate control air cond. ($150). Electric rear defogger ($140). Digital electronic instrument cluster ($238). Six-way power seat, passenger ($215). Two-position memory driver's seat ($178). Electric seatback recliner, either side ($139). Automatic door locks ($80). Leather-wrapped steering wheel ($96); std. on T Type. Tilt/telescope steering wheel ($55) exc. T Type. Electric fuel cap lock ($44). Electric trunk release ($40); lock ($80). Low fuel indicator ($16). Two-speed wipers w/delay ($49). Windshield washer fluid indicator ($16). Theft deterrent system ($159). Lighting, Horns and Mirrors:- Tungsten-halogen high-beam headlamps ($22); std. on T Type. Twilight Sentinel ($60). Coach lamps ($102); incl. w/vinyl top. Front/rear light monitors: T Type ($77). Rear quarter courtesy/reading lamp ($50). Lighted door lock and interior light control ($75). Four-note horn ($28). Dual electric remote mirrors ($66). Lighted visor vanity mirrors, each ($58). Entertainment:- Full-feature electronic-tuning AM/FM stereo radio ($125). Basic electronic-tuning AM/FM stereo radio w/cassette tape player ($125). Electronic-tuning AM/FM stereo radio with cassette and equalizer ($328); w/cassette, Dolby and Bose speaker system ($895) exc. conv. CB radio ($215). Delete radio ($230 credit). Rear speakers for base radio ($25). Concert Sound system ($95) exc. conv. Triband power antenna ($45); incl. w/CB radio. Exterior Trim: Heavy-padded landau vinyl top w/coach lamps: base ($330). Designers' accent paint: base ($235). Special color Firemist paint ($210); std. on conv. Color-coordinated protective bodyside moldings ($55); choice of eight colors but only white and dark red on conv. Door edge guards ($15). Bodyside striping ($45). Interior Trim/Upholstery:- 45/45 leather/vinyl front seat ($487); std. on conv. 45/45 leather/suede seating w/storage console ($537) exc. conv. Front carpet savers w/inserts ($35); rear ($20). Trunk trim carpeting ($30); std. on conv. Trunk mat ($15). Wheels and Tires:- Chrome-plated wheels ($145); exc. conv. ($45 credit). Styled aluminum wheels: conv. w/turbo V-6 ($65). Locking wire wheel covers ($190); std. on conv. P225/70R15 SBR wide oval tires: BSW or WSW (NC).

HISTORY: Introduced: October 2, 1983. Model year production (U.S.): 987,980. The yearly total included 229,934 four-cylinder Buicks and 258,422 V-8s, demonstrating that the venerable V-8 was still hanging on. Of the total production, 4,428 Buicks had a diesel engine and 15,556 a turbo. Calendar year production (U.S.): 987,833. Model year sales by U.S. dealers: 906,626 (not including front-drive Electras built during the 1984 model year). Calendar year sales (U.S.): 941,611 for a market share of 11.8 percent. When Canadian totals were added in, calendar year sales topped a million for the first time in Buick history.

Historical Footnotes: Century became Buick's best seller this year, nudging aside the Regal which had held that title since Century sedan/wagon and Regal coupe merged under the Regal banner in 1982. Skylark sales, like those of the other GM X-cars, were slipping as a result of the lengthy recall list—including a well-publicized and inconclusive recall for replacement of rear brake linings—even though those problems mainly affected 1980-81 models. Regardless, Skylark now sold almost as well as Chevrolet's Citation, which was the X-car that suffered most from bad publicity. To boost Skyhawk sales, dealers were encouraged to offer the subcompacts with extras that might appeal to young, sporty-minded buyers: electronic radios, aluminum wheels, tachometers, luggage racks and the like. LeSabre and Electra gained renewed

popularity in 1982-83, with an impressive sales rise this year. Riviera was especially Popular among doctors, merchants and executives. As part of the preliminaries for the summer Olympics in Los Angeles, the cross-country torch passed through Flint in May, carried for a time by several Buick employees. A fleet of Rivieras and other Buick vehicles, modified for low-speed endurance running, accompanied torch-bearers on their way to L.A. For off-road racing, Buick added a Stage I piston and Stage II intake manifold to the long list of heavy-duty 4.1-liter V-6 components available at dealers. Several Buick-powered vehicles had proven successful on race courses, including a record set at Bonneville this year. Bobby Allison had also driven a Regal to win the 1983 NASCAR driver's prize. At more mundane levels, a portable Diagnostic Data Analyzer could hook the electronic control module of any 1981-84 Buick into the dealer's diagnostic display--or to the computer at Flint. From there, an engineer could even alter the faraway engine's speed for evaluating problems. Buick's objective, according to retiring general manager Lloyd Reuss, was to be "Best in Class" and rank No. 3 in sales. General Motors was divided into small-car and large-car groups in January 1984, with Buick falling into the latter category. Robert C. Stempel was named head of the B-O-C (Buick-Oldsmobile-Cadillac) group, while Donald E. Hackworth took over as GM vice-president and Buick's general manager.

1985 BUICK

This year marked both the beginning and end of several eras. The last rear-drive Electra had been built in April 1984, replaced by a totally different front-drive version. Though the name was the same, the contemporary Electra stood far apart from its traditional full-size predecessors. Regal's dramatic black Grand National coupe, though marketed in modest numbers, was altering Buick's image among youthful motorists. Diesels went under Buick hoods for the last time this year. The final X-bodied Skylark was produced, ending Buick's connection with that sad episode in GM history. Rear- drive days were numbered. This would be LeSabre's final season in that form, but the name reappeared on an Estate Wagon for 1985, after a year's absence. A new name joined the Buick lineup: Somerset Regal.

1985 Skyhawk Custom coupe (B)

SKYHAWK — SERIES 4J — FOUR — After setting a sales record in 1984, Buick's J-car subcompact entered 1985 with no significant change beyond new body colors and interior trim. The lineup continued as before: Custom and Limited versions of coupe and sedan, plus a station wagon. The T Type also continued, powered by a normally-aspirated or turbocharged 1.8-liter overhead-cam four that came from GM of Brazil. Turbos added a boost gauge on the dash this year, and produced 150 horsepower as opposed to only 84 with the non-turbo 1.8 engine. That much power in a lightweight brought 0-60 acceleration times down to less than 9 seconds. All-season (fourth-generation) radials were now standard on all Skyhawks. Chevrolet and Olds offered a 2.8-liter V-6 on their versions of the J-body, but Buick stuck with the fours. Standard powertrain was again the Chevrolet-made 121 cu. in. (2.0-liter) four with four-speed manual gearbox and 3.65:1 final drive ratio (three-speed automatic available). Non-turbo T Types had a five-speed gearbox; turbos the four-speed. T Types had a blacked-out grille and headlamp housings, black door handles and locks and blackout side mirrors. Upper bodies came in silver, red or white; lower body was charcoal. Styled aluminum wheels held P195/70R13 blackwall radial tires; fatter 60-series tires were available, either blackwall or white-lettered. T Types had a leather-wrapped sport steering wheel, reclining bucket seats, foglamps, Gran Touring suspension, and full instruments. Powerplant was the 1.8-liter fuel-injected overhead-cam four. The optional turbo 1.8 with multi-port fuel injection rated 150 horsepower. On the Buick proving grounds, the turbo version reached 60 MPH in 8.5 seconds.

SKYLARK — SERIES 4X — FOUR/V-6 — Only the four-door sedan remained in Skylark's final year. The new Somerset Regal would offer buyers a coupe without the taint of the X-car's unpleasant recall and reliability history. Skylarks received a new grille that angled outward near the base, new wide taillamps split into upper/lower sections, and altered interior trim. Vertical rectangular parking lights sat between grille and single headlamps. Accentuating the revised rear-end look was a new center applique, and the license plate moved from the trunk lid to the bumper. The standard 2.5-liter four-cylinder engine, now dubbed "Tech-4," gained new roller bearings. The 2.8-liter carbureted V-6 was again optional, but a new addition this year was a high-output version with port fuel injection. That 2.8 used injectors mounted on a fuel rail, a design from Bosch that fed fuel from a high-pressure electric pump in the gas tank. It also had a cast aluminum intake manifold. All engines had new hydraulic engine mounts to cut vibration.

1985 Skylark Limited sedan (B)

1985 Century Limited sedan (B)

CENTURY — SERIES 4A — FOUR/V-6 — Once again, Century offered coupe, sedan and station wagon models, in Custom or Limited trim, along with the performance T Type. All showed a new grille and hood ornament this year, along with a new selection of body colors. Front ends held quad headlamps; rear ends, full-width taillamps. Sedans had a narrow window behind the rear door. European-look T Types now carried the advanced 3.8-liter V-6 with multi-port fuel injection, which had become available late in the 1984 model year. That engine was also offered on other Century models. Base engine, however, remained the 2.5-liter four with throttle-body fuel injection. This year, it gained roller valve lifters. Buyers could also choose a Chevrolet-built 2.8-liter V-6, Buick's own 3.0-liter V-6, or the 4.3-liter diesel V-6. The 2.8 was offered in case Buick couldn't meet production demands of its own 3.0 V-6. Many buyers chose a gas V-6 over the low-powered 2.5 base engine. Century Customs came with three-speed automatic transmission, power brakes and steering, AM radio, notchback seating (cloth or vinyl), dual horns, bumper guards and protective strips, side-window defoggers, full carpeting, and P185/75R14 tires. Limiteds didn't add too much beyond wide lower bodyside moldings, a hood ornament and wind split moldings. In addition to the 3.8-liter engine and dual exhausts, T Types included four-speed overdrive automatic transmission, a left-hand remote-control mirror, blacked-out grille, temp/volt gauges, cloth bucket seats, Gran Touring suspension, leather-wrapped sport steering wheel, and styled aluminum road wheels with P195/70R14 tires. The F41 Gran Touring suspension, with firmer springs, recalibrated shocks and hefty stabilizer bars, was also available on other coupes and sedans.

1985 Somerset Regal coupe (B)

SOMERSET REGAL — SERIES 4N — FOUR/V-6 — Buick's totally new, formally styled personal-luxury sport coupe, meant to replace the X-bodied Skylark, targeted the affluent "yuppies" and baby boomers who might otherwise buy upscale imports. Oldsmobile's Calais and Pontiac's Grand Am were its close N-body front-drive relatives. Base engine was a "Tech-4" 2.5-liter four-cylinder with throttle-body fuel injection, plus new roller bearings. Standard transaxle was a five-speed manual, but three-speed automatic was optional. The optional 181 cu. in. (3.0-liter) V-6 engine with multi-port fuel injection, putting out 125 horsepower, was smaller and lighter than the same-size (lower-powered) V-6 in Buick's Century. Styled in a dramatic wedge shape, the compact coupe was accentuated by a sloping nose and raked-back windshield, plus a high roofline, large quarter windows, and vertical rear window. Somerset had body-colored bumpers with rub strips, a standard electronic-tuning AM radio, cloth or vinyl bucket seats, tachometer, trip odometer, tinted glass, full-length console, and a digital clock. The Limited added chrome bumpers, front/rear armrests, dual horns, woodgrain instrument panel, wheel opening moldings, and narrow rocker panel

moldings. Options included body-color side moldings. Somersets had standard electronic digital instrumentation, including a multi-gage which gave, at driver's command, readouts for voltage, oil pressure, engine temperature, and R.P.M. Radio controls were atop a pod remote from the radio itself. The right front seat slid forward when its seatback was tipped forward, for easy entry into the back. Controls sat in pods at each side of the steering column, and instruments were electronic. Somersets could be ordered with a high-mounted brake light (which would be required on '86 models). Somerset's chassis used a MacPherson strut front suspension, and at the rear a special trailing axle suspension patterned after the type used in the sporty Skyhawk.

1985 Regal T Type Grand National coupe (B)

REGAL — SERIES 4G — V-6 — Only the Regal coupe remained this year, as the four-door sedan left the lineup. In addition to base and Limited trim levels, buyers had a choice of two performance editions: the familiar T Type and a dramatic step-up Grand National. Regal's forward-slanted front end carried a new slanted grille. Wheel covers were restyled, new body colors were offered, and interiors came in an altered selection of colors. T Types had a new power brake system, with boost provided by an electric pump rather than the power steering pump. A carbureted 231 cu. in. (3.8-liter) V-6 was standard, with three-speed automatic transmission. A diesel V-6 was optional. Both performance Regals came with a turbocharged version of the 3.8, with sequential port fuel injection and four-speed overdrive automatic transmission. Base Regal equipment included bumper guards and protective strips, power brakes and steering, AM radio, cigarette lighter, dual horns, dual chrome mirrors, color-keyed bodyside moldings, notchback seats (cloth or vinyl), and P195/75R14 steel-belted radial whitewalls. Regal Limited added an exterior molding package and 55/45 notchback seating. T Types included air conditioning, a performance axle ratio, temp and turbo boost gauges, 94-amp alternator, leather-wrapped steering wheel, tachometer, trip odometer, and 15 in. styled aluminum wheels with wide 65-series tires. Grand National (actually a $675 T Type option package) was offered again for 1985 with its aggressive all-black exterior (even the windshield wipers), special black aluminum wheels, firm-ride Gran Touring suspension, and new two-tone cloth bucket seats. Grand Nationals carried a 200-horsepower turbo 3.8-liter V-6 with sequential fuel injection. On the test track it had hit 60 MPH in 8 seconds. Equipment also included black bumpers, rub strips and guards; black front air dam and decklid spoiler; and Grand National identification on body and instrument panel.

1985 LeSabre Limited Collector Edition sedan (B)

LESABRE — SERIES 4B — V-6/V-8 — For its final year as a rear-drive Buick, LeSabre received a new grille and a few new colors (inside and out), but few other changes. The new grille was made up of thin vertical bars and stood more vertically than the sloped-back quad-headlamp section. Coupes and sedans again came in Custom or Limited dress, but to make the final season the Limited was called a Collector's Edition. Standard engine remained the 231 cu. in. (3.8-liter) V-6, but buyers could also choose the familiar four-barrel 307 (5.0-liter) V-8, or the diesel V-8. Standard Custom equipment included an AM radio, power brakes and steering, three-speed automatic transmission (four-speed overdrive required with V-8 engines), woodtone dash applique, dual horns, compact spare tire, bumper guards and protective strips, and front armrest. LeSabre's Collector's Edition had plush velour upholstery on loose pillow seats. It also had a standard six-way power driver's seat, seatbelt and ignition key warning chime, headlamps-on indicator and chime, and Soft Ray tinted glass, plus wide rocker panel moldings and accent strips. Doors carried woodgrain trim; bodies showed special identification and hood ornament. Buyers even received a booklet on Buick history and special set of keys.

ESTATE WAGON — SERIES 4B/C — V-8 — LeSabre's Estate Wagon returned to the fold for 1985, after a year's absence. As usual, Electra's version was the posher of the pair. Even though the new Electra coupe and sedan were shrunken in size with front-drive, the wagons hung on with rear-drive. Two- and three-seat versions were offered. LeSabre included air conditioning, tinted glass, dual horns, AM radio, power steering and brakes, heavy-duty suspension, styled aluminum wheels, and narrow rocker panel moldings among its many standard items. Electra's wagon added front/rear armrests, a digital clock, AM/FM seek/scan stereo ratio, woodgrain vinyl applique, remote electric tailgate lock, power windows all around, and a roof luggage rack.

1985 Electra Estate Wagon (B)

ELECTRA — SERIES 4C — V-6 — An entirely new Electra debuted in early spring 1984, along with the similarly downsized Cadillac DeVille/Fleetwood and Oldsmobile Ninety-Eight. Dramatic cuts in exterior size and weight did not affect interior dimensions much (except for narrower width and smaller trunk volume), though Electra's six-passenger capacity tightened somewhat. The modern Electra weighed 600-900 pounds less than before, measured 2 feet shorter and 4 in. narrower, and rode a 110.8 in. wheelbase (8 in. shorter than in 1984). Electra's hood now opened from the rear. The new edition turned to contemporary front-wheel drive with a transverse-mounted engine: standard 181 cu. in. (3.0- liter) V-6, optional 231 cu. in. (3.8-liter) V-6 with multi-port fuel injection, or the 4.3-liter diesel. A coupe and four-door sedan came in base or plush Park Avenue form, or the enthusiast's T Type.

1985 Electra sedan (B)

The 3.8 V-6 was standard on both Park Avenue and T. (The very existence of a "sporty" T Type carrying the renowned Electra nameplate startled a good many traditional buyers.) Though far smaller than before, Electra hardly lacked poshness. Standard equipment on base Electras included four-speed overdrive automatic transmission, electronic climate and level controls, six-way power driver's seat. AM/FM stereo radio with seek/scan electronic tuning, power windows, side window defoggers, remote fuel filler door release, courtesy lights, headlamps-on reminder, trip odometer, velour upholstery, and P205/75R14 all-season radials. Stepping up to Park Avenue brought buyers the bigger (3.8-liter) V-6 along with power door locks, tilt steering, power decklid release, rear reading lamps, cruise control, wide bodyside moldings, accent paint striping, and luxury upholstery in cloth or leather.

1985 Riviera convertible (B)

RIVIERA — SERIES 4E — V-6/V-8 — Since a dramatically different Riviera was expected for 1986, not much changed this year for the coupe, T Type or convertible. Late in the 1984 model year, the 5.0-liter V-8 had become the standard Riv powerplant, and that continued in 1985. The coupe could also have a 5.7-liter diesel

259

for one more year, but T Types kept the 231 cu. in. (3.8-liter) turbocharged V-6 with sequential port fuel injection. Joining the option list was a cellular telephone--a factory-approved dealer option rather than a factory installation. A hundred or so test Rivieras carried a new optional Graphic Control Center, which had originally been planned as a regular production option. Drivers could select radio, climate control and trip functions by simply touching appropriate portions of the video screen. The convertible's hefty price tag kept sales down to a modest level, and this would be its final season. A limited-edition Riviera for 1985 featured genuine wood in the form a burled walnut veneer on dash and door panels, wood/leather steering wheel, and beige leather/suede interior trim.

I.D. DATA: All Buicks again had a 17-symbol Vehicle Identification Number (VIN), stamped on a metal tag attached to the upper left surface of the cowl, visible through the windshield. Coding was similar to 1984, starting with '1' to indicate the manufacturing country (U.S.A.), followed by 'G' for General Motors and '4' for Buick Division. The next letter indicates restraint system. Symbol five denotes series: 'S' Skyhawk Custom; 'T' Skyhawk Ltd.; 'E' Skyhawk T Type; 'B' Skylark Custom; 'C' Skylark Ltd.; 'J' Somerset Regal; 'M' Somerset Regal Ltd.; 'H' Century Custom; 'L' Century Ltd.; 'G' Century T Type (or Estate); 'J' Regal; 'K' Regal T Type; 'M' Regal Ltd.; 'N' LeSabre Custom; 'P' LeSabre Ltd.; 'R' LeSabre Estate Wagon; 'X' Electra; 'W' Electra Park Ave.; 'F' Electra T Type; 'V' Electra Estate Wagon; 'Z' Riviera; 'Y' Riviera T Type. Digits six and seven indicate body type: '27' 2-dr. coupe; '37' LeSabre 2-dr. coupe; '47' Regal 2-dr. coupe; '57' Riviera 2-dr. coupe; '11' Electra 2-dr. sedan; '19' Electra 4-dr. sedan; '69' 4-dr. sedan. '35' 4-dr. wagon; '67' 2-dr. convertible coupe. Next symbol is the engine code: 'O' L4-110 TBI; 'J' turbo L4-110 MFI; 'P' L4-121 TBI; 'U' L4-151 TBI; 'R' L4-151 TBI; 'X' V6-173 2Bbl.; 'W' V6-173 MFI; 'E' V6-181 2Bbl.; 'L' V6-181 MFI; 'A' V6-231 2Bbl.; '3' V6-231 MFI; '9' turbo V6-231 SFI; 'T' diesel V6-263; 'Y' V8-307 4Bbl.; 'N' diesel V8-350. Symbol nine is a check digit. Symbol ten denotes model year ('F' 1985). Symbol eleven is the plant code: 'M' Lansing, MI; 'T' Tarrytown, NY; 'D' Doraville, GA; 'W' Willow Run, MI; '6' Oklahoma City, OK; 'H' Flint, MI; 'K' Leeds, MO; 'X' Fairfax, KS; 'E' Linden, NJ; '1' Wentzville, MO; '2' St. Therese, Quebec. The final six digits are the sequential serial number, starting with 400001. An additional identifying number may be found on the engine. A body number plate on upper shroud or radiator support assembly reveals model year, car division, series, style, body assembly plant, body number, trim combination, modular seat code, paint code, and date build code.

SKYHAWK CUSTOM (FOUR)

Series Number	Body/Style Number	Body Type & Seating	Factory Price	Shipping Weight	Production Total
4J	S27	2-dr Coupe-5P	7365	2276	44,804
4J	S69	4-dr Sedan-5P	7581	2325	27,906
4J	S35	4-dr Sta Wag-5P	7919	2401	5,285

SKYHAWK LIMITED (FOUR)

4J	T27	2-dr Coupe-5P	7883	2312	Note 1
4J	T69	4-dr Sedan-5P	8083	2429	Note 1
4J	T35	4-dr Sta Wag-5P	8379	2356	Note 1

Note 1: Skyhawk Custom production totals include equivalent Skyhawk Limited models. For the model year, 63,148 Custom and 9,562 Limited coupes and sedans were built.

SKYHAWK T TYPE (FOUR)

4J	E27	2-dr Coupe-5P	8437	2295	4,521

SKYLARK CUSTOM (FOUR/V-6)

4X	B69	4-dr Sedan-5P	7707/7967	2478/2539	65,667

SKYLARK LIMITED (FOUR/V-6)

4X	C69	4-dr Sedan-5P	8283/8543	2515/2576	27,490

CENTURY CUSTOM (FOUR/V-6)

4A	H27	2-dr Coupe-6P	9377/9637	2609/2714	13,043
4A	H19	4-dr Sedan-6P	9545/9805	2658/2763	215,928
4A	H35	4-dr Sta Wag-6P	9941/10201	2825/2930	28,221

CENTURY LIMITED (FOUR/V-6)

4A	L27	2-dr Coupe-6P	9841/10101	2632/2737	Note 2
4A	L19	4-dr Sedan-6P	10012/10272	2681/2786	Note 2
4A	L35	4-dr Sta Wag-6P	10379/10639	2845/2950	Note 2

CENTURY T TYPE (V-6)

4A	G27	2-dr Coupe-5P	11249	2802	Note 2
4A	G19	4-dr Sedan-5P	11418	2850	Note 2

Note 2: Century Custom production totals include equivalent Century Limited and T Type models. Total model year production came to 99,751 Customs, 125,177 Limiteds and 4,043 Century T Type coupes and sedans.

SOMERSET REGAL (FOUR/V-6)

4N	J27	2-dr Coupe-5P	8857/9417	2472/2523	48,470

SOMERSET REGAL LIMITED (FOUR/V-6)

4N	M27	2-dr Coupe-5P	9466/10026	2478/2529	37,601

REGAL (V-6)

4G	J47	2-dr Coupe-6P	9928	3066	60,597

REGAL LIMITED (V-6)

4G	M47	2-dr Coupe-6P	10585	3107	59,780

REGAL T TYPE (V-6)

4G	K47	2-dr Coupe-6P	12640	3256	4,169

Note 3: Regal T Type total includes 2,102 Grand Nationals.

LESABRE CUSTOM (V-6/V-8)

4B	N37	2-dr Coupe-6P	10453/11018	3438/3629	5,156
4B	N69	4-dr Sedan-6P	10603/10568	3447/3638	32,091

LESABRE LIMITED COLLECTOR'S EDITION (V-6/V-8)

4B	P37	2-dr Coupe-6P	11751/12316	3462/3653	22,211
4B	P69	4-dr Sedan-6P	11916/12481	3495/3686	84,432

LESABRE ESTATE WAGON (V-8)

4B	R35	4-dr Sta Wag-6P	12704	4085	5,597

ELECTRA (V-6)

4C	X11	2-dr Coupe-6P	14149	3114	5,852
4C	X69	4-dr Sedan-6P	14331	3158	131,011

1985 Electra Park Avenue sedan (B)

ELECTRA PARK AVENUE (V-6)

4C	W11	2-dr Coupe-6P	16080	3144	Note 4
4C	W69	4-dr Sedan-6P	16240	3190	Note 4

ELECTRA T TYPE (V-6)

4C	F11	2-dr Coupe-5P	15386	3138	Note 4
4C	F69	4-dr Sedan-5P	15568	3183	Note 4

Note 4: Production figures for base Electra coupe and sedan include totals for Park Avenue and T Type models. Total T Type production, 4,644.

ELECTRA ESTATE WAGON (V-8)

4C	V35	4-dr Sta Wag-6P	15323	4148	7,769

RIVIERA (V-6/V-8)

4E	Z57	2-dr Coupe-5P	-- /16710	-- /3748	63,836
4E	Z67	2-dr Conv-5P	27457/26797	3700/3873	400

Note 5: Only 49 Riviera convertibles had a turbo V-6 engine installed.

RIVIERA T TYPE (V-6)

4E	Y57	2-dr Coupe-5P	17654	3564	1,069

FACTORY PRICE AND WEIGHT NOTE: Figure before the slash is for four-cylinder engine, after the slash for V-6. For LeSabre and Riviera, figure before slash is for V-6 engine, after slash for V-8. **FACTORY PRICE NOTE:** Buick announced several price increases during the model run, including some for optional engines.

ENGINES: BASE FOUR (Skyhawk): Inline, ohv, four-cylinder. Cast iron block and head. Displacement: 121 cu. in. (2.0 liters). Bore & stroke: 3.50x3.15. Compression ratio: 9.3:1. Brake horsepower: 86 at 4900 R.P.M. Torque: 100 lbs.-ft. at 3000 R.P.M. Five main bearings. Hydraulic valve lifters. Throttle-body fuel injection. VIN Code: P. OPTIONAL FOUR (Skyhawk); STANDARD (Skyhawk T Type): Inline, overhead-cam four-cylinder. Cast iron block; aluminum cylinder head. Displacement: 110 cu. in. (1.8 liters). Bore & stroke: 3.34 x 3.13 in. Compression ratio: 8.8:1. Brake horsepower: 84 at 5200 R.P.M. Torque: 102 lbs.-ft. at 2800 R.P.M. Five main bearings. Hydraulic valve lifters. Throttle- body fuel injection. VIN Code: O. TURBOCHARGED FOUR (Skyhawk T Type): Same as 1.8-liter OHC four above, except--Compression ratio: 8.0:1. Brake H.P.: 150 at 5600 R.P.M. Torque: 150 lbs.-ft. at 2800 R.P.M. Multi-point fuel injection. VIN Code: J. BASE FOUR (Skylark, Century, Somerset Regal): Inline, overhead-valve four-cylinder. Cast iron block and head. Displacement: 151 cu. in. (2.5 liters). Bore & stroke: .0 x 3.0 in. Compression ratio: 9.0:1. Brake horsepower: 92 at 4400 R.P.M. Torque: 134 lbs.-ft. at 2800 R.P.M. Five main bearings. Hydraulic valve lifters. Throttle-body fuel injection. Built by Pontiac. VIN Code: R. OPTIONAL V-6 (Skylark, Century): 60-degree, overhead-valve V-6. Cast iron block and head. Displacement: 173 cu. in. (2.8 liters). Bore & stroke: 3.50 x 2.99 in. Compression ratio: 8.5:1. Brake horsepower: 112 at 4800 R.P.M. Torque: 145 lbs.-ft. at 2100 R.P.M. Four main bearings. Hydraulic valve lifters. Carburetor: 2Bbl. Built by Chevrolet. VIN Code: X. HIGH-OUTPUT V-6; OPTIONAL (Skylark): Same as 173 cu. in. V-6 above except--Compression ratio: 8.9:1. Brake horsepower: 125 at 5400 R.P.M. Torque: 165 lbs.- ft. at 3600 R.P.M. VIN Code: W. BASE V-6 (Electra); OPTIONAL (Century): 90-degree, overhead-valve V-6. Cast iron block and head. Displacement: 181 cu. in. (3.0 liters). Bore & stroke: 3.8 x 2.66 in. Compression ratio: 8.45:1. Brake horsepower: 110 at 3600 R.P.M. Torque: 145 lbs.-ft. at 2600 R.P.M. Four main bearings. Hydraulic valve lifters. Carb.: 2Bbl. VIN Code: E. OPTIONAL V-6 (Somerset Regal): Same as 181 cu. in. V-6 above, with multi-point fuel injection. C.R.: 9.0:1. B.H.P.: 125 at 4900 R.P.M. Torque: 150 lbs.-ft. at 2400 R.P.M. VIN Code: L. BASE V-6 (Regal, LeSabre): 90-degree, overhead-valve V-6. Cast iron alloy block and head. Displacement: 231 cu. in. (3.8 liters). Bore & stroke: 3.8 x 3.4 in. Compression ratio: 8.0:1. Brake horsepower: 110 at 3800 R.P.M. Torque: 190 lbs.-ft. at 1600 R.P.M. Four main bearings. Hydraulic valve lifters. Carb.: 2Bbl. VIN Code: A. BASE V-6 (Century T Type, Electra T/Park Ave.); OPTIONAL (Century, Electra): Same as 231 V-6 above, but with multi-point fuel injection. Brake H.P.: 125 at 4400 R.P.M. Torque: 195 lbs.-ft. at 2000 R.P.M. VIN Code: 3. TURBOCHARGED V-6 (Regal/Riviera T Type): Same as 231 V-6 above, but with turbocharger and sequential fuel injection. Brake horsepower: 200 at 4000 R.P.M. (Riviera, 190 H.P.). Torque: 300 lbs.-ft. at 2400 R.P.M. VIN Code: 9. DIESEL V-6; OPTIONAL (Century, Regal, Electra): 90-degree, overhead-valve V-6. Cast iron block. Displacement: 262.5 cu. in. (4.3 liters). Bore & stroke: 4.057 x 3.385 in. Compression ratio: 21.6:1. Brake horsepower: 85 at 3600 R.P.M. Torque: 165 lbs.-ft. at 1600 R.P.M. Four main bearings. Hydraulic valve lifters. Fuel injection. VIN Code: V or T. BASE V-8 (Estate, Riviera); OPTIONAL (LeSabre): 90-degree, overhead valve V-8. Cast iron block and head. Displacement: 307 cu. in. (5.0 liters). Bore & stroke: 3.80 x 3.385 in. Compression ratio: 8.0:1. Brake horsepower: 140 at 3200 R.P.M. (LeSabre, 140 at 3600). Torque: 255 lbs.-ft. at 2000 R.P.M. (LeSabre, 240 at 1600). Five main bearings. Hydraulic valve lifters. Carburetor: 4Bbl. Built by Oldsmobile. VIN Code: Y or H. OPTIONAL DIESEL V-8 (LeSabre, Estate, Riviera): 90-degree, overhead valve V-8. Cast iron block and head. Displacement: 350 cu. in. (5.7 liters). Bore & stroke: 4.057 x 3.385 in. Compression ratio: 21.6:1. Brake horsepower: 105 at 3200 R.P.M. Torque: 200 lbs-ft. at 1600 R.P.M. Five main bearings. Hydraulic valve lifters. Fuel injection. Oldsmobile-built. VIN Code: N.

CHASSIS DATA: Wheelbase: (Skyhawk) 101.2 in.; (Skylark) 104.9 in.; (Somerset Regal) 103.4 in.; (Century) 104.8 in.; (Century wag) 104.9 in.; (Regal) 108.1 in.; (LeSabre/Estate) 115.9 in.; (Electra) 110.8 in.; (Riviera) 114.0 in. Overall length:- (Skyhawk cpe) 175.3 in.; (Skyhawk sed/wag) 177.3 in.; (Skylark) 181.1 in.; (Somerset Regal) 180.0 in.; (Century) 189.1 in.; (Century wag) 190.9 in.; (Regal) 200.6 in.; (LeSabre) 218.4 in.; (Electra) 197.0 in.; (Estate) 221.3 in.; (Riviera) 206.6 in. Height:- (Skyhawk) 54.0 in.; (Skyhawk wag) 54.4 in.; (Skylark/Century) 53.6-53.7 in. (Century wag) 54.2 in.; (Somerset Regal) 52.1 in.; (Regal) 54.6 in.; (LeSabre cpe) 56.0 in.; (LeSabre sed) 56.7 in.; (Estate) 59.3 in.; (Electra/Riv) 54.3 in. Width:- (Skyhawk) 65.0 in.; (Skylark) 69.1 in.; (Somerset Regal/Century) 67.7 in.; (Regal) 71.6 in.; (LeSabre) 78.0 in.; (Estate) 79.3 in.; (Electra) 72.4 in.; (Riv) 72.8 in. Front Tread:- (Skyhawk) 55.3 in.; (Skylark/Century) 58.7 in.; (Somerset Regal) 55.5 in.; (Regal) 58.5 in.; (LeSabre) 61.8 in.; (Electra) 60.3 in.; (Estate) 62.2 in.; (Riv) 59.3 in. Rear Tread:- (Skyhawk) 55.1 in.; (Skylark) 57.0 in.; (Somerset Regal) 55.2 in.; (Century) 56.7 in.; (Regal) 57.7 in.; (LeSabre) 60.7 in.; (Electra) 59.8 in.; (Estate) 64.0 in.; (Riviera) 60.0 in. Standard Tires:- (Skyhawk) P175/80R13 SBR; (Skyhawk T Type) P195/70R13 SBR; (Skylark/Somerset Regal) P185/80R13 SBR; (Century) P185/75R14 SBR; (Century T Type) P195/70R14 SBR; (Regal) P195/75R14 SBR WSW; (Regal T Type) P215/65R15 SBR; (LeSabre) P205/75R15 SBR WSW; (Electra) P205/75R14 SBR BSW; (Estate) P225/75R15 SBR WSW; (Riviera) P205/75R15 SBR WSW.

TECHNICAL: Transmission:- Four-speed, fully synchronized floor shift standard on Skyhawk/Skylark. Five-speed manual standard on Somerset Regal, available on Skyhawk. Four-speed overdrive automatic standard on Electra/Riviera, available on Century/Regal/LeSabre; three-speed automatic on other models. Four-speed gear ratios: (1st) 3.53:1; (2nd) 1.95:1; (3rd) 1.24:1; (4th) 0.81:1 or 0.73:1; (Rev) 3.42:1. Skylark V-6 four-speed: (1st) 3.51:1; (2nd) 1.95:1; (3rd) 1.24:1; (4th) 0.90:1; (Rev) 3.42:1. Skyhawk five-speed gear ratios: (1st) 3.91:1; (2nd) 2.15:1; (3rd) 1.45:1; (4th) 1.03:1; (5th) 0.74:1; (Rev) 3.50:1. Somerset Regal five-speed: (1st) 3.73:1; (2nd) 2.04:1; (3rd) 1.45:1; (4th) 1.03:1; (5th) 0.74:1; (Rev) 3.50:1. Three-speed auto. trans. gear ratios: (1st) 2.74:1; (2nd) 1.57:1; (3rd) 1.00:1; (Rev) 2.07:1. Skyhawk/Skylark auto. trans. gear ratios: (1st) 2.84:1; (2nd) 1.60:1; (3rd) 1.00:1; (Rev) 2.07:1. Four-speed overdrive automatic gear ratios: (1st) 2.74:1; (2nd) 1.57:1; (3rd) 1.00:1; (4th) 0.67:1; (Rev) 2.07:1. Century/Electra four-speed automatic: 1st) 2.92:1; (2nd) 1.57:1; (3rd) 1.00:1; (4th) 0.70:1; (Rev) 2.38:1. Standard axle ratio:- (Skyhawk) 3.65:1 w/4-spd, 3.45:1 w/5-spd, 3.18:1 w/auto.; (Skyhawk turbo) 4.10:1 w/4-spd, 3.33:1 w/auto.; (Skylark) 3.32:1 or 3.65:1 w/4-spd, 2.39:1 or 2.53:1 w/auto., 2.84:1 w/H.O. V-6 and auto.; (Somerset Regal): 3.35:1 w/5-speed, 2.84:1 w/auto.; (Century) 2.84:1 or 2.97:1 w/3-spd, 2.84:1 or 3.06:1 w/4-spd; 2.39:1 w/diesel. (Regal) 2.41:1; (Regal T Type) 3.42:1; (LeSabre) 2.73:1 exc. diesel, 2.93:1; (Electra) 3.08:1 exc. V6-231, 2.84:1; (Riviera) 2.73:1; (Riv diesel); (Riv turbo) 3.15:1. Steering:- (Skyhawk/Skylark/Century/Somerset Regal) rack and pinion; (others) recirculating ball; power assist standard on all except Skyhawk. Suspension:- front/rear coil springs. (Skyhawk/Somerset Regal) MacPherson strut front w/stabilizer; semi-independent beam rear axle w/trailing arms; rear stabilizer bar optional, std. on T Type. (Skylark/Century) MacPherson strut front suspension; beam twist rear axle w/trailing arms and Panhard rod; front/rear stabilizer bars. (Electra) MacPherson front struts, barrel springs and stabilizer bar; rear struts w/stabilizer bar and electronic level control. (Riviera) fully independent suspension with front torsion bars, semi-trailing arms at rear, front/rear stabilizers and automatic level control. (Rear-drive models) front stabilizer bar; rear stabilizer bar on T Type; rigid four-link rear axle. Brakes:- power front disc, rear drum. Four-wheel power disc brakes available on Riviera (std. on conv.). Body construction:- (front-drive models) unitized; (others) separate body and frame. Fuel tank:- (Skyhawk/Somerset Regal) 13.6 gal.; (Skylark) 15.1 gal.; (Century) 15.7 gal.; (Regal) 18.1 gal.; (LeSabre) 25.0 gal.; (Electra) 18.0 gal.; (Estate) 22.0 gal.; (Riviera) 21.1 gal.

DRIVETRAIN OPTIONS: Engines:- 110 cu. in. (1.8-liter) EFI four: Skyhawk Cust/Ltd ($50). Turbocharged 110 cu. in. (1.8-liter) MFI four: Skyhawk T Type ($800). 173 cu. in. (2.8-liter) V-6, 2Bbl.: Skylark ($260); Century (N/A). High-output 173 cu. in. (2.8-liter) V-6, 2Bbl.: Skylark ($435). 181 cu. in. (3.0-liter) V-6, 2Bbl.: Century ($260); Somerset ($560). 231 cu. in. (3.8- liter) V-6, MFI.: Century ($520); std. T Type; early base Electra ($260). Turbocharged 231 cu. in. (3.8-liter) V-6, SFI: Riviera ($660); std. on T Type. 263 cu. in. (4.3-liter) diesel V-6: Century/Regal/Electra ($359) exc. T Type; Park Ave. ($99). 307 cu. in. (5.0-liter) V-8, 4Bbl.: LeSabre ($390). 350 cu. in. (5.7-liter) diesel V-8: Regal ($589); LeSabre ($489); Estate/Electra/Riviera ($99) exc. T Type or conv. Transmission/Differential:- Four-speed manual trans.: Skyhawk T Type ($75 credit). Five-speed manual trans.: Skyhawk Cust/Ltd ($75). Auto. trans.: Skyhawk/Skylark/ Somerset ($425); Skyhawk T Type ($350). Automatic overdrive trans.: Century Cust/Ltd/Est, LeSabre ($175); Regal (N/A). Optional rear axle ratio: Skyhawk 3.43:1; Skylark; Century 2.84:1 or 2.97:1; Regal; LeSabre; base Electra 3.33:1; Estate; Riviera 3.15:1 (all NC). Limited slip differential: Regal/LeSabre/Est ($95). Suspension, Steering and Brakes:- F40 Firm ride/handling pkg. ($27). F41 Gran Touring suspension: Skyhawk/Skylark/Somerset ($27); Century Cust/Ltd cpe/sed ($27); Regal/LeSabre ($49); Electra/Riviera ($27). Special G.T. suspension: Skyhawk T Type (NC). Electronic control suspension: Electra (N/A); std. T Type. Superlift rear shock absorbers: Skylark ($68). Automatic level control: Century/Regal/LeSabre/Estate ($175). Power steering: Skyhawk ($215). Four-wheel disc brakes; Riviera ($235). Other: Heavy-duty alternator: Skyhawk/Regal/LeSabre/Electra 85-amp ($35 or $85); 94-amp ($35 or $85); Century/Somerset/Electra 108-amp ($25-$40). Heavy-duty battery ($26); diesel ($52). Power reserve Freedom battery: Electra ($145) Heavy-duty radiator: Skyhawk ($40-$70). Heavy-duty cooling: Skylark ($40-$70). Engine block heater ($18). Heavy-duty engine/transmission cooling: Century/Regal/LeSabre/Electra/Riviera ($40-$70). High altitude emission package (NC). California emission system ($99).

SKYHAWK CONVENIENCE/APPEARANCE OPTIONS: Option packages: Decor pkg.: T Type ($195). Vista Vent flip-open removable glass sunroof ($310). Instrument gauge pkg.: temp, oil pressure, volts, trip odometer: Cust ($60). Gauges and tach: Cust ($138); Ltd ($78). Acoustic pkg. ($36); std. on Ltd. Comfort/Convenience:- Air cond. ($645); touch climate control ($795). Rear defogger, electric ($135). Cruise control w/resume ($175). Power windows ($195-$270). Electric door locks ($130-$180). Six-way power driver's seat ($225). Easy-entry passenger seat adjuster: Cust cpe ($16). Tinted glass ($25). Sport steering wheel: cust/Ltd ($50). Leather-wrapped steering wheel: T Type ($40). Tilt steering ($115). Trip odometer: Cust ($15). Electric trunk or tailgate release ($40). Tailgate wiper/washer: wag ($125). Two-speed wipers w/delay ($50). Lights, Horns and Mirrors:- Tungsten-halogen headlamps ($18). Headlamps-on indicator ($15). Front seat reading light ($30). Dual horns: Cust cpe/sed ($15). Left remote black mirror: Cust/Ltd ($22). Dual black mirrors: left remote ($53). Dual black electric remote mirrors ($139); T Type ($86). Visor vanity mirror, passenger ($7). Lighted visor vanity mirror, either side ($45). Entertainment:- Electronic-tuning AM/FM stereo radio ($138); w/clock ($177). Seek/scan AM/FM stereo ET radio w/clock ($222); w/cassette ($344). Seek/scan AM stereo/FM ET stereo radio w/clock ($242); w/cassette and equalizer ($494). Radio delete ($56 credit). Automatic power antenna ($65). Dual rear speakers ($25). Exterior Trim:- Door edge guard moldings ($15-$25). Wide rocker moldings: Cust cpe/sed ($26). Bodyside stripes ($45). Designers' accent paint ($195). Decklid luggage rack ($100). Roof rack: wag ($105). Interior Trim/Upholstery:- Front console armrest: T Type ($45). Front carpet mats ($17); rear ($12). Front carpet mats w/inserts ($18); rear ($15). Front/rear fiber floor mats: T Type ($65). Deluxe trunk trim ($33). Security cover: wag ($69). Wheels and Tires:- Styled aluminum wheels ($229); std. T Type. Styled wheel covers w/trim rings ($38); N/A T Type. Locking wire wheel covers ($180); N/A T Type. P175/80R13 SBR WSW ($54). P195/70R13 SBR BSW ($104). P195/70R13 SBR WSW ($166). P195/70R13 SBR WLT ($188); T Type ($84). P205/60R14 SBR BSW: T Type ($94). P205/60R14 SBR WLT: T Type ($182). Self-sealing tires ($115).

SKYLARK/CENTURY CONVENIENCE/APPEARANCE OPTIONS: Comfort/Convenience: Flip-open Vista Vent glass sunroof ($300). Acoustic pkg.: Skylark Cust ($60). Lamp groups: Skylark Cust ($42). Air cond. ($730). Elect. cruise control ($175). Rear defogger, electric ($140). Power windows ($185- $260). Electric door locks ($125-$175). Six-way power driver's seat ($215). Manual seatback recliners, passenger ($45); both ($90). Sport steering wheel ($50). Tilt steering ($110). Tinted glass ($110). Instrument gauges incl. trip odometer ($48); w/tachometer, Century ($126). Tachometer: Skylark ($78). Trip odometer: Skylark ($16). Digital electronic instrument cluster: Century ($225); T Type ($131). Dial clock ($35). Electric trunk release ($40). Remote tailgate lock: Century wag ($40). Tailgate washer/wiper: Century wag ($120). Two-speed wipers w/delay ($50). Theft deterrent system: Century ($159). Lights, Horns and Mirrors:- Tungsten-halogen headlamps: Skylark Cust ($10); Century ($22). Twilight Sentinel: Century ($57). Front light monitors: Century ($37). Coach lamps: Ltd ($102-$129). Center-mounted high stoplight: Century ($25). Headlamps-on indicator ($16). Door courtesy/warning light: Century Ltd/wag ($44). Front seat reading lamp ($24). Rear seat reading lamp: Skylark Ltd, Century Cust/Ltd ($30). Dual horns: Skylark Cust ($15). Remote-control color-keyed left mirror: Cust/Ltd/Est ($25). Sport mirrors (left remote, right manual): Cust/Ltd/Est ($61). Dual electric remote mirrors ($139) exc. Century T Type ($78). Visor vanity mirror, passenger ($7). Lighted visor vanity mirror, passenger: Skylark ($50); either side, Century ($58). Entertainment:- Same as Skyhawk (above). Exterior Trim:- Landau vinyl top: Century Cust/Ltd cpe ($186); heavily-padded ($623). Long vinyl top: Cust/Ltd ($160). Designers' accent paint ($205-$210); N/A T Type. Special solid color paint: Century ($200) exc. T Type. Protective bodyside moldings ($55); color-coordinated on Century. Lower wide bodyside moldings: Century Cust ($65). Rocker panel moldings: Skylark Cust ($26). Wide rocker panel/rear quarter moldings: Skylark Cust ($91). Belt reveal molding: Skylark Cust ($40). Wheel opening moldings: Skylark Cust ($30). Door edge guards ($15-$25). Pillar applique moldings: Skylark Cust ($27). Hood ornament and windsplit: Skylark Cust ($32). Windsplit molding: Century Cust ($22). Bodyside stripe: Cust/Ltd/Est ($45). Bumper guards, front/rear: Skylark ($45). Bumper strips, front/rear: Skylark Cust ($49). Decklid luggage rack: Century ($100). Roof rack: Century wag ($105). Cargo area vent windows: Century wag ($75). Woodgrain vinyl applique: Century wag ($350). Tailgate air deflector: Century wag ($37). Front license bracket (NC). Interior Trim/Upholstery:- Front center armrest: Skylark Cust ($45). Full-length console: Century ($57). Full-length operating console: Skylark ($105); Century ($80); T Type ($23). Bench seat: Skylark Cust ($55 credit). Cloth bucket seats: Skylark Cust ($140); Ltd ($95); Century Cust ($97). 55/45 notchback cloth seating: Century Cust ($133). Lear Siegler bucket seats: Century T Type ($600). Cloth 45/45 seating: Century Ltd/Est (NC). Leather/vinyl 45/45 seating: Century Ltd ($295); T ($425). Third seat: Century wag ($215). Locking storage compartment: Century wag ($44). Front carpet mats ($17); rear ($12). Carpet mats w/inserts: front ($25); rear ($20). Trunk trim ($25-$47). Wheels:- Styled aluminum wheels: Century ($195); std. on T Type. Chrome wheels: Skylark ($175). Locking wire wheel covers ($190) exc. T Type. Skylark Tires:- P185/80R13 SBR WSW ($58). P205/70R13 SBR WSW ($180). Self-sealing tires ($105). Century Tires:- P185/75R14 SBR WSW: Cust/Ltd/Est ($58). P195/75R14 SBR BSW: Cust/Ltd/Est ($30). P195/75R14 SBR WSW: Cust/Ltd/Est ($92). P195/70R14 SBR WLT: T Type ($84). P215/60R14 SBR BSW: T ($122). P215/60R14 SBR WLT: T ($214). Self-sealing tires ($105).

SOMERSET REGAL CONVENIENCE/APPEARANCE OPTIONS: Comfort/Convenience:- Vista Vent flip-open removable glass sunroof ($310-$329). Air cond. ($645). Electronic cruise control ($175). Rear defogger, electric ($135). Six-way power driver's seat ($225). Sport steering wheel ($50) exc. Ltd. Tilt steering ($115). Power windows ($195). Electric door locks ($130); automatic ($220). Electric trunk release ($40). Two-speed wipers w/delay ($50). Lights and Mirrors:- Center high-mounted stoplight ($25). Front door courtesy/warning light: Ltd ($44). Front-rear seat reading/courtesy lights ($40-$54). Dual mirrors, left remote ($53); std. on Ltd. Dual electric remote mirrors ($86-$139). Lighted right visor vanity mirror ($38). Entertainment:- Seek/scan AM/FM stereo radio w/clock ($157); w/cassette and equalizer ($424); w/Delco GM/Bose music system and Dolby ($995). Cassette player ($142). Concert sound speakers ($100-$125). Dual extended-range speakers ($25). Automatic power antenna ($65). Exterior Trim:- Designers' accent paint ($195). Bodyside stripes ($45). Rocker panel moldings ($26); std. Ltd. Wide rocker panel moldings ($50-$76). Color-keyed protective bodyside moldings ($45). Wheel opening moldings ($30); std. Ltd. Decklid luggage rack ($100). Door edge guards ($15). Interior Trim/Upholstery:-

Leather bucket seats: Ltd ($275). Floor mats w/inserts: front ($18); rear ($15). Wheels and Tires:- Styled aluminum wheels ($229). P185/80R13 SBR WSW $58). P205/70R13 SBR BSW ($114). P205/70R13 SBR WSW ($180). P205/70R13 SBR WLT ($202). Self-sealing tires ($115).

REGAL CONVENIENCE/APPEARANCE OPTIONS: Option Packages:- Regal Grand National pkg.: black exterior, front air dam, decklid spoiler, rub strips/guards, Gran Touring suspension, front bucket seats, aluminum wheels ($675). Regal T Type Designer pkg.: black/dark gray designers' accent paint and rear spoiler ($403). Base Regal exterior molding pkg.: wide rocker panel and belt reveal moldings ($110). Sliding electric silver Astroroof ($895). Hatch roof ($825). Comfort/Convenience:- Air cond. ($730); std. T Type. Touch climate control air cond. ($880); T Type ($150). Cruise control w/resume ($175). Rear defogger, electric ($140). Tinted glass ($110). Tinted windshield ($90). Six-way power seat, each side ($215). Manual passenger seatback recliner ($75). Sport steering wheel ($50); N/A T Type. Tilt steering ($110). Power windows ($185). Electric door locks ($125). Electric trunk release ($40). Digital electronic instrument cluster ($299); T Type ($173). Headlamps-on indicator ($16). Trip odometer ($16) exc. T. Two-speed wiper w/delay ($50). Theft deterrent system ($159). Lighting and Mirrors:- Tungsten-halogen headlamps ($22). Twilight Sentinel ($57). Cornering lamps ($57); N/A T Type. Coach lamps: Ltd ($102). Door courtesy/warning lights: Ltd $44). Front seat reading light ($24); rear ($30). Dual sport mirrors, left remote ($53); std. T Type. Dual remote sport mirrors ($83); T Type ($30). Dual chrome mirrors, left remote ($25); N/A T Type. Visor vanity mirror, passenger ($7); lighted ($58). Entertainment:- Same as Skyhawk (above) plus: Concert sound speakers ($95). Exterior Trim:- Landau vinyl top ($186) exc. T Type; heavily-padded ($245). Designers' accent paint ($205); N/A T Type. Solid special color paint ($200). Black protective bodyside moldings: T Type ($55). Door edge guards ($15). Bodyside stripe ($45). Interior Trim/Upholstery:- Storage console: Ltd ($82). Bucket seats ($195) exc. Ltd. Lear Siegler bucket seats: T Type ($600). 55/45 seating ($133) exc. Ltd. 45/45 leather/vinyl seating: Ltd ($295); T Type ($595). Front carpet mats ($17); rear ($12). Front carpet mats w/inserts ($25); rear ($20). Trunk trim ($44). Wheels:- Chrome-plated wheels ($195); N/A T Type. Styled aluminum wheels ($285); std. T Type. Locking wire wheel covers ($190) exc. T. Color-keyed wheels ($85) exc. T. Tires:- P205/70R14 SBR WSW ($62) exc. T Type. P215/65R15 SBR WLT: T Type ($92). Self-sealing tires ($105) exc. T.

LESABRE/ELECTRA/ESTATE WAGON CONVENIENCE/APPEARANCE OPTIONS: Comfort/Convenience: Sliding electric Astroroof ($1195. Air cond: LeSabre ($730); Est ($150). air cond. with touch-climate control: LeSabre ($880); Electra ($165) Cruise control w/resume ($175); std. on Park Ave. Rear defogger, electric ($140). Tinted glass: LeSabre Custom ($110). Power windows: LeSabre ($185-$260). Keyless entry system: Electra ($185). Electric door locks ($125-$175). Automatic door locks ($205-$255) exc. Electra Est/Park Ave. ($80). Six-way power passenger seat ($215); driver's: LeSabre Cust, Est ($185- $215). Memory driver's seat: Electra ($178). Two-way power driver's seat: LeSabre Est ($60). Electric seatback recliner, either side ($139) exc. Electra Est passenger ($220). Manual passenger seatback recliner: LeSabre, Estate ($75). Tilt steering ($110); std. Park Ave. Tilt/telescoping steering column: Electra ($165); Park Ave. ($55). Dial clock: LeSabre Cust ($60). Digital clock: LeSabre Ltd ($60). Accessory group (low fuel indicator, trip odometer, reading lights, washer fluid indicator): Electra Est ($54-$86). Trip odometer: LeSabre ($16). Remote tailgate lock: LeSabre Estate ($50). Electric trunk lock: Electra ($80). Electric trunk release ($40). Theft deterrent system ($159); N/A on Estate. Two-speed wiper w/delay ($50); std. Park Ave. Lighting, Horns and Mirrors: Tungsten-halogen headlamps ($22). Twilight Sentinel ($60). Cornering lamps: LeSabre, Electra Cust ($60). Coach lamps: LeSabre Ltd ($102). Light monitors, front: LeSabre ($37); front/rear, Electra ($77). Lamp and indicator group: LeSabre ($38-$70). Door courtesy/warning lamps ($44-$70). Lighted door lock and interior light control ($75). Four-note horn ($28). Dual remote chrome mirrors: LeSabre ($49). Dual electric remote mirrors ($91); std. Park Ave. Dual electric remote mirrors, left heated: Electra ($126); Park Ave. ($35). Lighted visor vanity mirror, driver or passenger ($58). Entertainment:- LeSabre--same selection as Skyhawk (above). Electra as follows--Seek/scan electronic-tuning AM stereo/FM stereo radio w/clock ($20); w/cassette and equalizer ($272). Seek/scan AM/FM stereo radio w/cassette ($122); w/cassette, Dolby and Delco GM/Bose music system ($895) but N/A on Estate. Delete radio ($275 credit). Concert Sound system ($95). CB radio: Estate ($275). Automatic power antenna: LeSabre/Electra/Est ($60). Triband power antenna: LeSabre, Est ($105). Exterior Trim:- Exterior molding pkg. (wide rocker panel, front/rear fender lower and belt reveal moldings): LeSabre ($110). Landau padded vinyl top: LeSabre cpe ($245). Long vinyl top: LeSabre ($185). Heavy-padded long vinyl top: Electra sed ($245). Designers' accent paint: LeSabre ($215). Special single-color paint: ($200); Firemist, Electra ($200). Protective bodyside moldings: Est ($55). Wide rocker panel moldings: Electra Est ($65). Door edge guards ($15-$25). Belt reveal molding: LeSabre Cust/Est ($40). Bodyside stripes ($45); std. Ltd/Park Ave. Rear air deflector: Est ($40). Woodgrain vinyl applique: LeSabre Estate ($345); delete from Electra Est ($320 credit). Luggage rack: LeSabre Estate ($150). Front license bracket (NC). Interior Trim/Upholstery:- Cloth 55/45 seating: LeSabre Cust ($133). Leather/vinyl 50/50 seating: LeSabre Ltd ($525). Leather/vinyl 55/45 seating: Park Ave. ($425). Leather/vinyl 45/45 seating: Electra T Type ($175). Third seat: Estate ($220). Front carpet mats: LeSabre ($17); rear ($12). Front carpet mats w/inserts ($25); rear ($20). Trunk carpeting/trim ($53). Trunk mat ($15). Wheels:- Chrome-plated wheels: LeSabre ($215); Estate ($40 credit). Styled aluminum wheels ($220-$255); Electra T Type (N/A). Locking wire wheel covers ($155-$190) exc. Estate ($65 credit). Tires:- P215/75R15 SBR WSW: LeSabre ($42). P205/75R14 SBR WSW: Electra ($66); BSW, Park Ave. ($66 credit). Self- sealing tires ($105-$130).

RIVIERA CONVENIENCE/APPEARANCE OPTIONS: Comfort/Convenience:- Electric sliding Astroroof: silver, gray or gold ($1195). Touch climate control air cond. ($150). Electric rear defogger ($140). Digital electronic instrument cluster ($238); T Type ($160). Six-way power seat, passenger ($215). Two-position memory power driver's seat ($178). Electric seatback recliner, either side ($139). Automatic door locks ($80). Leather-wrapped steering wheel ($96);std. on T Type. Tilt/telescope steering wheel ($55) exc. T Type. Electric trunk release ($40); pulldown ($80). Low fuel indicator ($16). Two-speed wipers w/delay ($50). Windshield washer fluid indicator ($16). Theft deterrent system ($159). Lighting, Horns and Mirrors:- Tungsten-halogen high/low beam headlamps ($22); std. on T Type. Twilight Sentinel ($60). Coach lamps: base ($102); incl. w/vinyl top. Front/rear light monitors ($77) exc. conv. Rear reading lamps ($50) exc. conv. Lighted door lock and interior light control ($75). Four-note horn ($28). Automatic day/night mirror ($80). Dual electric remote mirrors ($66). Lighted visor vanity mirrors, each ($58); N/A conv. Entertainment:- Seek/scan electronic-tuning AM stereo/FM stereo radio w/clock ($20); w/cassette and equalizer ($272). Seek/scan AM/FM stereo radio w/cassette ($122); w/cassette, Dolby and Delco GM/Bose music system ($895). CB radio ($215). Delete radio ($275 credit). Concert Sound system ($95). Triband power antenna ($45); incl. w/CB radio. Exterior Trim:- Heavy-padded landau vinyl top w/coach lamps: base ($330). Designers' accent paint: base ($235). Special color Firemist paint ($210); std. on conv. Color- keyed protective bodyside moldings ($55). Door edge guards ($15). Bodyside stripe: base ($45). Interior Trim/Upholstery:- 45/45 leather/vinyl front seat ($487); std. on conv. Front floor mats w/inserts ($35); rear ($20). Trunk trim carpeting ($30); std. on conv. Trunk mat ($15); N/A conv. Wheels and Tires:- Chrome-plated wheels: base ($145); conv. ($45 credit). Styled aluminum wheels: conv. w/turbo V-6 ($65). Locking wire wheel covers: base ($190). Credit given for BSW tires on conv.; and for P225/70R15 SBR non-self-sealing on base and conv. P225/70R15 SBR WSW: T Type ($48); BSW ($26 credit).

HISTORY: General introduction was October 2, 1984; but Electras had been introduced on April 5, 1984 and the Skyhawk didn't appear until November 8, 1984. Model year production (U.S.): 1,002,906 (including early '85 Electras); that was the first time Buick passed the one million barrier. The total included 271,423 four-cylinder Buicks, 515,995 sixes, and 215,488 V-8s. Only 1,178 diesels and 6,137 turbos were installed this year. Calendar year production (U.S.): 1,001,461 (first time for breaking the million mark). Model year sales by U.S. dealers: 915,336, which amounted to 10.9 percent of the industry total. Calendar year sales (U.S.): 845,579 for a market share of 10.3 percent.

Historical Footnotes: The last rear-drive Electra had come off the line on April 25, 1984, a month after its rear-drive replacement emerged. It was the last of over 2.6 million old-style Electras, and would be joined by LeSabre for 1986. Clearly, front-drive and aero styling was the wave of the future, and Buick hoped to attract a new breed of buyer. Both the new Electra and the coming front-drive LeSabre were developed by the C/H Product Team ('C" for C-bodies, 'H' for the H-bodied LeSabre). Part of Buick's youth-oriented promotion for the Regal Grand National included a TV commercial with a song called "Bad to the Bone," performed by the Destroyers. Quite a change from the advertising aimed at gray-flannel-suited executives in the 1950s, or even the performance promotions during the muscle-car era. Looking farther back in history, the Classic Car Club announced acceptance of all 1931-42 Series 90 Buicks into classic status. Even a few custom- bodied Series 80 models might be deemed worthy on an individual basis.

1986 BUICK

1986 Skyhawk T Type hatchback coupe (B)

Eleven new models joined Buick's list for '86, making a total of 39 (including a couple of special editions). Every line except Skylark and LeSabre fielded a T Type version. New choices included the Skyhawk Sport and T Type hatchback; Skylark Custom and Limited sedan; and Somerset T Type coupe. Most notable, though, were the all-new V-6 front-drive LeSabre (Custom and Limited coupe/sedan) and Riviera coupe and T Type. Leaving the lineup this year were Electra's T Type coupe and the Riviera convertible. On the 3.0-liter V-6 with multi-port fuel injection, introduced for 1985, a single belt drove all accessories. It also got a redesigned water pump, hardened valve seats, new air cleaner and inlet. A redesigned combustion chamber allowed more efficient combustion. This engine was 50 pounds lighter (and 5.5 inches narrower) than the carbureted 3.0 from which it evolved. Two versions of the 3.8-liter V-6 were offered: with or without roller valve lifters. A revised intake manifold improved breathing and gave more hood clearance. Spark plugs were placed in the center of the combustion chamber for added efficiency. Turbocharged 3.8s got a new intercooler between the compressor and intake manifold, to supply a denser air/fuel charge and boost horsepower output. New leading/trailing rear drum brakes on LeSabres were said to improve braking consistency and automatic adjustment. Hinged taillamps on Electra, LeSabre and Riviera allowed easier servicing of bulbs and lenses. More galvanized steel panels for rust protection were used on 1986 Buicks than on any previous models. LeSabre became the first to offer double-sided galvanized sheet metal on both sides of hood and fenders. Going a giant step further, the whole Riviera body (except the roof) would now be double-side, hot-dipped galvanized. Riviera's new Graphic Control Center, similar to the preliminary version introduced in 1984, drew considerable attention at the Chicago Auto Show. Also standard on Riviera was the Retained Accessory Power feature, which kept certain components operating after the ignition was shut off: radio, electric windows, wipers, fuel door, decklid, and glove compartment release. Most noteworthy among the new options was the anti-lock braking system (ABS), developed jointly with the West German firm of Alfred Teves GmbH, now offered on Electra. Sensors at each wheel could determine when a wheel was about to lock and relax braking pressure as needed, to prevent skidding on slippery surfaces. Pressure might be applied and released as many as 15 times per second, helping the driver to remain in control and stop in the shortest possible distance.

SKYHAWK — SERIES 4J — FOUR — Buick gained a full line of subcompact models with the mid-year addition of a new Sport/Hatch and T Type hatchback. Both hatchbacks and Limited/T Type coupes had a new front-end design that featured concealed tungsten-halogen headlamps behind electrically-operated doors. They also had smoked glass taillamps. Otherwise, styling was similar to prior models. As before, the wide body-colored grille sat low on the front end, below the narrow protective strip. The sharply slanted nose held a center crest. Wide taillamps wrapped slightly around the side. In all, the modern Skyhawk offered clean, wedge-shape styling with an "aggressive" profile, highlighted by flush-mounted glass, integrated bumpers, and styled mirrors. All Skyhawks were available in white, silver metallic, black, or red. All except the T Type could have bodies in metallic light blue, bright blue, dark red, gray, dark blue, light brown, or brown; or in regular cream beige. T Types could have gray metallic as the lower accent color. Hatchbacks featured a blackout treatment, and a rear spoiler was optional. Custom and Limited Skyhawks had new standard wheel covers, while hatchbacks came with turbine-design wheel covers. Hatchbacks could have an optionsl retractable security cover to keep valuables out of sight. Base engine remained the fuel-injected 2.0-liter four with four-speed manual gearbox. five-speed (overdrive) manual and three-speed automatic transmissions were available. So was a 1.8-liter powerplant. Skyhawk's T Type was powered by the 1.8-liter four with overhead camshaft, either normally aspirated or (at extra cost) turbocharged. Turbos produced 150 horsepower and had multi-port fuel injection. That version delivered a claimed 0-60 MPH test time of under 9 seconds. They came with a four- speed gearbox rather than the usual five. T Types also had cloth front bucket seats with console, gauges (including tachometer), sport steering wheel with T Type insignia, Gran Touring suspension, aluminum wheels, a front passenger assist strap, black antenna, foglamps, amber park/signal lamps, black door handles and locks, plus black moldings and mirrors. For looks without added performance, a low-cost SCS Coupe package came with the regular 2.0-liter engine and four-speed, riding P175/80R13 all-season blackwalls. The extras: custom cloth bucket seats and door panels, three-tone interior trim, custom steering wheel, black moldings, and styled steel wheels.

1986 Skylark Limited sedan (B)

SKYLARK — SERIES 4N — FOUR/V-6 — Now that the X-bodied Skylark was gone, Buick offered a four-door replacement to match the Somerset coupe. Even through the bad publicity about X-cars, Buick's version had sold well and the company didn't want to lose the power of the Skylark name, which began with the limited-edition convertible way back in 1953. The new five-passenger sedan came in Custom and Limited trim, with rakish windshield, flush-mounted glass, and rounded rear body corners. Front-end styling was just like Somerset's. The grille was comprised of tight vertical bars, flowing smoothly down from the sloping hood. Parking/signal lamps were inset low, below the bumper protective strip that wrapped around fender tips. The required high-mount stop lamp was placed on the rear shelf, flush with the back window. Bumpers were body-colored on the Custom, bright on the Limited. Standard body colors were white and tan, plus 10 metallics: silver, dark gray, black, light brown, brown, flame red, light blue, medium blue, light sage, and dark sage. Both Skylark and Somerset carried a new 'S' logo. Inside, brushed aluminum trim panels contained standard electronic digital instruments with vacuum-fluorescent displays that offered metric readings at the touch of a button. Readouts included voltage, engine speed, coolant temperature, oil pressure, and a trip odometer. Soft-touch, low-travel controls for lights, wiper/washers and other frequently-used functions were positioned on a pod near the steering wheel. Skylark's chassis layout consisted of a transverse-mounted engine, MacPherson struts, low-drag front disc brakes, and trailing-link rear suspension. Base engine was the 2.5-liter four, with electronic fuel injection and five-speed manual gearbox. Hydraulic clutch adjustment provided easier engagement and smooth shifting. A 3.0-liter V-6 was optional, with multi-port fuel injection and three-speed automatic transmission. The 125-horsepower V-6 had a high-efficiency combustion chamber and a gerotor oil pump.

1986 Buick Somerset T Type coupe (B)

SOMERSET — SERIES 4N — FOUR/V-6 — Introduced for 1985, the Somerset Regal coupe lost the "Regal" from its name this year. Now it served as a mate to the similar N-body Skylark sedan. One difference: Somerset now offered a T Type, while Skylark did not. Manual transmission Somersets had a new hydraulic clutch. All had a new brushed-finish instrument panel. The aerodynamically-styled, rounded wedge-look coupe came with a choice of four-cylinder or V-6 power and front- wheel drive, in Custom or Limited trim (or new T Type). Styling highlights included flush windshield and backlight glass. The smooth front end carried a grille with narrow vertical strips and Buick badge on the side, with wide parking/signal lamps down in the bumper below the rub strip. A Somerset script went at the forward end of the front fenders, above the amber lenses inset into the protective bumper strip. Somerset's chassis used MacPherson struts up front, with semi-independent coil spring suspension in the back. All Somersets had power rack-and-pinion steering, plus low-drag power front disc brakes. Limiteds carried new velour cloth upholstery. Reclining bucket seats were standard, with a front center armrest. Standard digital instruments included readouts for voltage, oil pressure, temperature, engine R.P.M. and trip odometer. Radio controls were housed in a pod separate from the radio, easy to reach. Standard powertrain was the 2.5-liter four-cylinder engine with electronic fuel injection, driving a close-ratio five-speed manual gearbox. Optional: an automatic transmission and 3.0-liter V-6 with multi-port fuel injection. T Types carried the 3.0-liter V-6 engine, with computer-controlled coil ignition. That meant no more distributor under the hood. A Gran Touring suspension (Level III) and low-profile P215/60R14 Eagle GT blackwall tires on new cast aluminum alloy wheels delivered a firmer ride than the standard Somerset. The minimally-trimmed body sported charcoal lower body accents all around the car, plus a new front air dam and blacked-out grille and trim items. The performance-oriented axle ratio was 3.18:1. Other T Type touches: gray instrument panel, console and door trim plates, leather-wrapped steering wheel, black pillar applique, wide charcoal rocker panel moldings, amber parking/signal lamp lenses, red/amber taillamps, gray protective bodyside moldings, and twin rear-view mirrors (the left one remote- controlled). T Type upper body colors were silver, black, white or red, all with dark gray lower accent. Tan and seven metallic finishes were offered on other Somersets: dark gray, light brown, brown, light blue, medium blue, light sage, and dark sage.

CENTURY — SERIES 4A — FOUR/V-6 — A distinctive new front-end look for Century focused on the slanted vertical-element grille that extended below the low-profile quad headlamps, all the way around the edges of front fenders. A horizontal/vertical

1986 Century Custom sedan (B)

crossbar pattern divided the grille into four sections, with Buick block letters off to the side, below the center. Parking/signal lamps were inset into the bumper protective strip, and amber wraparound cornering lenses stood outboard of the headlamps. A flush-mounted hood ornament completed the modern look. The T Type coupe was dropped this year, but the T sedan remained. Century's lineup also included custom and Limited sedans and oupes, plus Custom or Estate Wagons. The contemporary Century was intended to compete with European sedans and coupes. Base powertrain was the 2.5-liter, 92-horsepower four with three-speed automatic transaxle. The formerly optional 3.0-liter V-6 was gone, replaced by a carbureted Chevrolet 2.8 V-6 (except in California). Also available: the 3.8-liter V-6, which gained 25 horsepower (now rated 150) by adding sequential port fuel injection and Computer Controlled Coil Ignition, along with low-friction roller valve lifters. T Type sedans ran with the 3.8-liter V-6, hooked to four-speed overdrive automatic. T Types also carried the Gran Touring suspension and low-profile (P215/60R14) steel-belted radial tires on cast aluminum wheels, and wore blackout trim. Instrument panels were gray, with LED tachometer, and the steering wheel was wrapped in leather. Blackout accents went on headlamp and taillamp bezels, radio antenna, door handles, moldings, grille, and accent stripes. Optional Lear Siegler bucket seats provided improved lateral and lumbar support. Wagons had standard side-window defoggers, split-folding rear seat, plus load area light and floor carpeting. Electronic cruise control and six-way power seats were optional this year. A Vista-Vent sunroof was available on all models. T Type body colors were gray, white, silver and black, with gray lower accent paint available. Other Century models came in cream beige or seven metallic shades: light brown, brown, light sage, light blue, dark blue, rosewood, or dark red. Vinyl tops came in white, black, light sage, dark red, dark gray, dark blue, or tan. Century's Gran Sport was described as "a car to be reckoned with," and as "the hottest Buick this side of a race course." Just 1,029 were produced, all painted black and devoid of brightwork. The Gran Sport package for the Custom coupe included the 3.8-liter V-6 SFI engine, tough suspension, tachometer, black/gray cloth reclining bucket seats with power-6 logo, console with shift lever boot, front/rear floor mats (GS insignia up front), seek/scan AM/FM stereo radio with cassette player and clock, temp/volt gauges, and black leather-wrapped sport steering wheel. The Gran Sport body had a front air dam and spoiler plus blackout grille, black moldings and headlamp bezels, and wide aero rocker panel moldings. Black front floor mats displayed a special Gran Sport insignia. Aluminum wheels with GS identification held P205/60R15 steel-belted radial Eagle GT tires. 'Buick' decals for door and spoiler were in the trunk, for installation by the dealer, and additional GS ornamentation was all over the car. To draw even more attention, the sporty exhaust emitted a "very authoritative growl," according to Buick. All told, a tempting selection of extras, but with a price tag approaching $4000.

1986 Regal T Type Turbo Coupe (B)

REGAL — SERIES 4G — V-6/V-8 — While most of Buick's lineup had switched to contemporary front-wheel drive, Regal hung on with rear-drive and little evident change. Under T Type turbo hoods, though, lay a major change: a new intercooler for the turbocharged 3.8-liter V-6. That fuel-injected engine now churned out 235 horsepower and 330 pound-feet of torque. The intercooler not only added power, but reduced the likelihood of detonation. Regal's T Type sported a blackout-trimmed grille, windows, wipers and headlamp bezels, plus a revised taillamp treatment with black moldings. It rode low-profile P215/65R15 tires on aluminum wheels, as opposed to the P195/75R14 whitewalls on regular Regals. The Gran Touring suspension included a rear stabilizer, larger-diameter front stabilizer bar, higher-rate springs and shocks. Performance rear axle ratio was 3.42:1. Engine identification appeared on the side of the hood bulge. T Types also had body-color sport mirrors, a trip odometer, turbo boost gauge, LED tachometer, leather-wrapped steering wheel, and air conditioning. An optional T Type Designer's Package added a front air dam, rear deck spoiler, and special black and dark gray accent paint on the body. Optional, firmer Lear Siegler bucket seats had an adjustable back. Regal's Grand National, the modern-day "muscle car," strode a lengthy step beyond the "ordinary" T Type. Its all-black body, complete with air dam and spoiler, held virtually no chrome or brightwork of any kind. Rolling on four stylish chrome-plated wheels, with handling provided by a firm, performance-tuned Gran Touring suspension, the driver enjoyed the comfort of gray cloth bucket seats. The turbocharged V-6 with intercooler and sequential port fuel injection was claimed to be "the most advanced high-performance engine offered in a Buick." Rated at more than twice the horsepower of the normally-aspirated version, it fed that power to a standard four-speed overdrive automatic transmission. Grand Nationals soon brought some hefty prices at auctions, a result of their striking and stark appearance and relatively low production figures. A total of 5,512 were produced this year. Customers could also choose a base or Limited Regal, and V-8 fanciers could order their Regals fitted with a 307 cu. in. (5.0-liter) engine, supplied by Oldsmobile. Standard powertrain was a carbureted version of the 3.8-liter V-6, with three-speed automatic transmission. Optional: four-speed overdrive automatic. The diesel V-6 was gone. Regals were sold in an even dozen colors: white, black and cream beige, plus nine metallics: silver, gray, light brown, brown, light blue, dark blue, rosewood, dark red, and light sage (not available on T Types).

1986 LeSabre Limited coupe (B)

LESABRE — SERIES 4H — V-6 — Buick continued the trend toward aerodynamic design with a fully restyled LeSabre, still six-passenger but with a transverse-mounted engine and front-wheel drive. The new H-body version, sharing the same platform as Oldsmobile's Delta 88, was 400 pounds lighter and 22 inches shorter (on 5 in. shorter wheelbase), yet didn't lose much interior space. LeSabres came in fastback coupe or notchback sedan form, Custom or Limited trim, with front-hinged hood. The new grille had a wide five-row crosshatch pattern, with familiar Buick badge near the lower corner. As on earlier LeSabres, the bottom row of the grille extended outward to the outer tip of the fenders, below deeply recessed quad headlamps. Wide, clear parking/signal lamps were inset in the bumper, directly below the protective rub strip. Outside mirrors were sleek and modern looking. Bodyside moldings stretched the full length of the car, wrapping around into the front and back bumpers. Taillamps were hinged, with a slide-in license plate holder. LeSabre used new body/frame integral construction with a separate front frame to support the powertrain. The chassis used a modified MacPherson strut front suspension with barrel springs, and fully independent rear suspension with inboard coil springs. Standard engine (except in California) was a transverse- mounted 181 cu. in. (3.0-liter) V-6 with multi-port fuel injection, coupled to four-speed automatic transmission with overdrive top gear. Capable of 125 horsepower, the 3.0 had Computer Controlled Coil Ignition, Bosch injectors, a mass air flow sensor, high-output camshaft, plus cast aluminum intake manifold and rocker covers. Performance-minded buyers could choose the optional, proven 231 cu. in. (3.8-liter) V-6, with sequential port fuel injection and roller valve lifters, rated 150 horsepower. Power rack-and-pinion steering was standard. Tires were all-season P205/75R14 blackwalls. An optional "performance package" included the Gran Touring suspension, P215/65R15 Eagle GT tires, specific transmission calibration, faster steering response, and a leather-wrapped sport steering wheel. Custom models had notchback seats covered in velour cloth with woven fabric trim. Limiteds turned to plush, reclining loose-pillow velour seats in 55/45 arrangement. LeSabre's generous standard equipment list included air conditioning and tinted glass. Body colors were: white, black and tan; plus silver, dark gray, light brown, brown, dark teal, light blue, dark blue, flame red or dark red metallic. Sedan vinyl tops came in white, black, tan, dark red, dark gray, dark blue and dark teal. Electronic instrumentation was available. Ranking among the rarest of modern Buicks is the LeSabre Grand National. "We're looking for a few good drivers," proclaimed Buick's specialty brochure; drivers who are "serious about performance." Only 117 of the special-edition coupes were built. Powered by the turbocharged 3.8 V-6 with sequential fuel injection and roller lifters, and riding fat P215/65R15 Eagle GT tires on aluminum alloy wheels. Grand national's chassis carried a muscular, fully independent sport suspension. Bodies were finished in black or white, and the car was packed with extras including blackout moldings, a black 'B' pillar, ribbed quarter-window closeouts, leather-wrapped sport steering wheel, lay-down hood ornament, and dual-outlet exhaust. Grand National ornamentation was on front fenders; a power-6 logo on the front floor mats; interior upholstered in gray cloth.

ESTATE WAGON — SERIES 4B/C — V-8 As before, the old rear-drive Estate Wagons came in both LeSabre and Electra editions. Styling and capacity remained as in prior models. Sole powertrain was the old familiar 307 cu. in. (5.0-liter) V-8, producing 140 horsepower, with four-barrel carburetor and four-speed overdrive automatic transmission. Wagon colors were white, black and cream beige; plus metallic silver. gray, light brown, brown, light sage, light blue, dark blue, rosewood, or dark red.

1986 Electra Park Avenue sedan (B)

ELECTRA — SERIES 4C — V-6 — Switched to front-drive a year earlier, Electra changed little for 1986. Coupe and sedan came in base or Park Avenue trim. The T coupe was abandoned, but the T sedan stayed in the lineup. The 3.0-liter V-6 offered in 1985 was no longer available. Sole powerplant was the 231 cu. in. (3.8-liter) V-6, producing 15 more horsepower with sequential fuel injection, driving a four-speed overdrive automatic transaxle. All Electras had power rack-and-pinion steering, a modified MacPherson strut front suspension with barrel springs, and independent rear suspension with automatic level control. Added to the option list was an anti-lock braking system (ABS) that sensed wheel speed and traction, adjusting pressure to prevent lockup during a quick stop or on slippery surfaces. Other new options: an electronic instrument cluster and automatic day/night rear view mirror. A Keyless Entry System option required that a five-number sequence be entered correctly on a little keyboard before the door would open. Electra's standard AM/FM stereo radio had seek-and-scan tuning. Other standard equipment included Soft-Ray tinted glass, an electric fuel filler door release, six-way power driver's seat, power windows, front-seat reading lamps, power windows, air conditioning, and the required high-mounted stop lamp. Park Avenue interiors featured rich velour upholstery in choice of five colors. Extra fittings included Electronic Cruise Control, tilt steering column, electric door locks, remote-control trunk lid, Soft-Ray back seat reading lamps, and lighted vanity mirror on the passenger's visor. Powered by the same 3.8 V-6, the T Type sedan carried a Gran Touring suspension and standard 15 in. aluminum wheels with P215/65R15 Goodyear Eagle GT tires. Also included were a leather-wrapped sport steering wheel, 45/45 seats in gray or red cloth, storage console, brushed gray instrument panel and door trim, front carpet savers with T Type logo, twin-outlet exhaust, and special taillamp treatment. T Types came in five body colors: silver, white, black, flame red, or dark gray. Other Electras could be in painted standard light or dark blue metallic, dark teal metallic, tan, or medium brown metallic. Dark brown, blue and red firemist metallic paint cost extra. Vinyl tops were offered in white, dark gray, black, dark blue, dark teal, beige, flame red, and red.

1986 Riviera T Type coupe (B)

RIVIERA — SERIES 4E — V-6 — In an attempt to lure both new and traditional Buick buyers, Riviera turned to a total restyle this year--the first since 1979. Still front-drive with fully independent suspension, Riv was otherwise all-new: over 19 inches shorter, with wheelbase cut by 6 inches (to 108). Curb weight shrunk to a mere 3,309 pounds, over 500 pounds less than before. Yet passenger space stayed close to previous dimensions. The modern version's silhouette was described as a "gentle wedge shape." Improved aerodynamically, it carried new high-intensity quad headlamps and wide taillamps. The sail panel area offered greater visibility. A new independent strut front suspension used barrel-type coil springs and a link-type control arm. Rear suspension was also a new design, using a transverse fiberglass leaf spring. Standard fittings included a front stabilizer bar, electronic level control, and four-wheel disc brakes. The new Riv was powered by the old favorite 231 cu. in. (3.8-liter) V-6, now producing 140 horsepower with sequential port fuel injection, a mass air flow sensor, and Computer Controlled Coil Ignition. Transmission was the four- speed automatic, with overdrive top gear. Rivieras contained from 7 to 10 microprocessors, depending on their option list. All of them worked with the exclusive Graphic Control Center (GCC), standard on all Rivieras. GCC, using a touch-sensitive cathode ray tube (video screen) in the center of the dash, served as the car's control center and information display. It replaced 91 controls that would otherwise be needed. When the ignition key was switched on, the display showed a summary page from the access areas: climate control, trip monitor, gauges, radio, and diagnostic data. Most of the time, no further effort was needed. But a touch of the screen at the appropriate spot pulled in further information. Certain electrical equipment could remain in use after the ignition was switched off. Standard equipment included electronic instrumentation and Electronic Touch Climate Control. Instrument panel, doors, glove box and pillars were cloth-covered. A console held controls for the glove box and deck lid release, fuel filler door, and cassette player. Also standard: side window defoggers (in doors), assist straps, sliding sun screen visor extensions, header console with dome and reading lamps, and electro-luminescent backlight control switches. A tool kit and new scissors jack fit under the trunk floor. Two new Riviera options: keyless entry and a heated outside driver's mirror. Riviera's new T Type included a Gran Touring (Level III) suspension, aluminum wheels with P215/60R15 Eagle GT blackwall tires, power comfort seats that even adjusted headrest height, reversible (leather/velour) front seat cushions and backs, leather-wrapped steering wheel and shift selector, plus gauges for washer fluid level, oil pressure, and external lamp monitors. T Types came in four two-tone body color combinations, with sporty graphics. Buick reported acceleration times of the T Type Riviera at 8.3 seconds to 50 MPH, or 11.3 seconds to 60.

I.D. DATA: Buicks continued the standardized 17-symbol Vehicle Identification Number (VIN), stamped on a metal tag attached to the upper left surface of the cowl, visible through the windshield. Coding was similar to 1985, starting with '1' to indicate U.S.A., followed by 'G' for General Motors, '4' for Buick Division, and a letter to indicate restraint system. Symbol five denotes series: 'S' Skyhawk; 'T' Skyhawk Ltd.; 'E' Skyhawk T Type; 'J' Skylark/Somerset Custom; 'M' Skylark/Somerset Ltd.; 'K' Somerset T Type; 'H' Century Custom; 'L' Century Ltd.; 'G' Century T Type; 'J' Regal; 'K' Regal T Type; 'M' Regal Ltd.; 'H' LeSabre; 'P' LeSabre Custom; 'R' LeSabre Ltd.; 'L' LeSabre T Type; 'X' Electra; 'W' Electra Park Ave.; 'F' Electra T Type; 'V' Electra Estate Wagon; 'Z' Riviera; 'Y' Riviera T Type. Digits six and seven indicate body type: '27' 2-dr. coupe; '37' LeSabre 2-dr. coupe; '47' Regal 2-dr. coupe; '57' Riviera 2-dr. coupe; '11' Electra 2-dr. sedan; '19' Electra 4-dr. sedan; '69' 4-dr. (4-window) sedan. '35' 4-dr. wagon. Next is the engine code: 'O' L4-110 TBI; 'J' turbo L4-110 MFI; 'P' L4-121 TBI; 'U' L4-151 TBI; 'R' L4-151 TBI; 'X' V6-173 2Bbl.; 'L' V6-181 MFI; 'A' V6-231 2Bbl.; '3' V6-231 SFI; 'B' V6-231 SFI; '7' turbo V6-231 SFI; 'T' diesel V6-263; 'Y' V8-307 4Bbl. Symbol nine is a check digit. Symbol ten denotes model year ('G' 1986). Symbol eleven is the plant code: 'M' Lansing, MI; 'T' Tarrytown, NY; 'D' Doraville, GA; '6' Oklahoma City, OK; 'H' Flint, MI; 'K' Leeds, MO; 'X' Fairfax, KS; '1' Wentzville, MO. The final six digits are the sequential serial number. An additional identifying number may be found on the engine. A body number plate on upper shroud or radiator support assembly reveals model year, car division, series, style, body assembly plant, body number, trim combination, modular seat code, paint code, and date build code.

SKYHAWK CUSTOM (FOUR)

Series Number	Body/Style Number	Body Type & Seating	Factory Price	Shipping Weight	Production Total
4J	S27	2-dr Coupe-5P	7844	2277	45,884
4J	S69	4-dr Sedan-5P	8073	2325	29,959
4J	S35	4-dr Sta Wag-5P	8426	2402	6,079

SKYHAWK LIMITED (FOUR)

4J	T27	2-dr Coupe-5P	8388	2314	Note 1
4J	T69	4-dr Sedan-5P	8598	2356	Note 1
4J	T35	4-dr Sta Wag-5P	8910	2429	Note 1

SKYHAWK SPORT (FOUR)

4J	S77	2-dr Hatch-5P	8184	2336	Note 2

SKYHAWK T TYPE (FOUR)

4J	E77	2-dr Hatch-5P	9414	2360	Note 2
4J	E27	2-dr Coupe-5P	8971	2301	Note 1

Note 1: Production figures listed under Skyhawk Custom coupe, sedan and station wagon include totals for Limited and T Type models. For the model year, 72,687 Custom, 6,584 Limited and 6,071 T Type coupes and sedans were built. Note 2: Total hatchback production, 9,499 units.

SKYLARK CUSTOM (FOUR/V-6)

4N	J69	4-dr Sedan-5P	9620/10230	2502/2611	Note 3

SKYLARK LIMITED (FOUR/V-6)

4N	M69	4-dr Sedan-5P	10290/10900	2519/2576	Note 3

Note 3: Total Skylark production, 62,235.

SOMERSET CUSTOM (FOUR/V-6)

4N	J27	2-dr Coupe-5P	9425/10035	2456/2561	Note 4
4N	M27	2-dr Coupe-5P	10095/10705	2473/2578	Note 4

SOMERSET T TYPE (V-6)

4N	K27	2-dr Coupe-5P	11390	2608	3,558

Note 4: Total Somerset production, 75,620. A total of 98,641 Skylark/Somerset Customs and 35,658 Limiteds were produced.

CENTURY CUSTOM (FOUR/V-6)

4A	H27	2-dr Coupe-6P	10052/10487	2616/2677	14,781
4A	H19	4-dr Sedan-6P	10228/10663	2663/2724	229,066
4A	H35	4-dr Sta Wag-6P	10648/11083	2828/2889	25,374

CENTURY LIMITED (FOUR/V-6)

4A	L27	2-dr Coupe-6P	10544/10979	2639/2700	Note 5
4A	L19	4-dr Sedan-6P	10729/11164	2685/2746	Note 5
4A	L35	4-dr Sta Wag-6P	11109/11544	2847/2908	Note 5

Note 5: Century Custom production totals include Limited models. Total model year coupe/sedan production, 116,862 Customs and 126,985 Limiteds. Coupe total includes 1,029 Gran Sport models.

CENTURY T TYPE (V-6)

4A	G19	4-dr Sedan-6P	12223	2863	5,286

REGAL (V-6/V-8)

4G	J47	2-dr Coupe-6P	10654/11194	3106/3345	39,734

REGAL LIMITED (V-6/V-8)

4G	M47	2-dr Coupe-6P	11347/11887	3132/3371	43,599

REGAL T TYPE (V-6)

4G	K47	2-dr Coupe-6P	13714	3285	7,896

Note 6: Regal production total includes 5,512 Grand Nationals.

LESABRE CUSTOM (V-6)

4H	P37	2-dr Coupe-6P	12511	3042	7,191
4H	P69	4-dr Sedan-6P	12511	3081	30,235

LESABRE LIMITED (V-6)

4H	R37	2-dr Coupe-6P	13633	3070	14,331
4H	R69	4-dr Sedan-6P	13633	3112	43,215

Note 7: Only 117 LeSabre Grand National coupes were built.

LESABRE ESTATE WAGON (V-8)

4B	R35	4-dr Sta Wag-6P	13622	4093	7,755

ELECTRA (V-6))

4C	X11	2-dr Coupe-6P	15396	3147	4,996
4C	X69	4-dr Sedan-6P	15588	3189	109,042

ELECTRA PARK AVENUE (V-6)

4C	W11	2-dr Coupe-6P	17158	3181	Note 8
4C	W69	4-dr Sedan-6P	17338	3223	Note 8

Note 8: Electra production figures include Park Avenue models. Total model year production, 23,017 base Electras and 91,021 Park Avenues.

ELECTRA T TYPE (V-6)

4C	F69	4-dr Sedan-6P	16826	3234	5,816

ELECTRA ESTATE WAGON (V-8)

4C	V35	4-dr Sta Wag-6P	16402	4172	10,371

RIVIERA (V-6)

4E	Z57	2-dr Coupe-5P	19831	3203	20,096

RIVIERA T TYPE (V-6)

4E	Y57	2-dr Coupe-5P	21577	3263	2,042

FACTORY PRICE AND WEIGHT NOTE: Figure before the slash is for four-cylinder engine, after the slash for V-6. For Regal, figure before the slash is for V-6 engine, after slash for V-8.

ENGINES: BASE FOUR (Skyhawk): Inline, overhead-valve four-cylinder. Cast iron block and head. Displacement: 121 cu. in. (2.0 liters). Bore & stroke: 3.50 x 3.15 in. Compression ratio: 9.0:1. Brake horsepower: 88 at 4800 R.P.M. Torque: 110 lbs.-ft. at 2400 R.P.M. Five main bearings. Hydraulic valve lifters. Throttle-body fuel injection. VIN Code: P. OPTIONAL FOUR (Skyhawk); STANDARD (Skyhawk T Type): Inline, overhead-cam four-cylinder. Cast iron block; aluminum cylinder head. Displacement: 110 cu. in. (1.8 liters). Bore & stroke: 3.34 x 3.13 in. Compression ratio: 8.8:1. Brake horsepower: 88 at 4800 R.P.M. Torque: 98 lbs.-ft. at 2800 R.P.M. Five main bearings. Hydraulic valve lifters. Throttle-body fuel injection. VIN code: O. TURBOCHARGED FOUR; OPTIONAL (Skyhawk): Same as 1.8-liter OHC four above, except--Compression ratio: 8.0:1. Brake H.P.: 150 at 5600 R.P.M. Torque: 150 lbs.-ft. at 2800 R.P.M. Multi-point fuel injection. VIN Code: J. BASE FOUR (Skylark, Century, Somerset): Inline, overhead-valve four-cylinder. Cast iron block and head. Displacement: 151 cu. in. (2.5 liters). Bore & stroke: 4.0 x 3.0 in. Compression ratio: 9.0:1. Brake horsepower: 92 at 4400 R.P.M. Torque: 134 lbs.-ft. at 2800 R.P.M. Five main bearings. Hydraulic valve lifters. Throttle-body fuel injection. VIN Code: R. OPTIONAL V-6 (Century): 60-degree, overhead-valve V-6. Cast iron block and head. Displacement: 173 cu. in. (2.8 liters). Bore & stroke: 3.50 x 2.99 in. Compression ratio: 8.5:1. Brake horsepower: 112 at 4800 R.P.M. Torque: 145 lbs.-ft. at 2100 R.P.M. Four main bearings. Hydraulic valve lifters. Carburetor: 2Bbl. Built by Chevrolet. VIN Code: X. BASE V-6 (Somerset Type, LeSabre); OPTIONAL (Somerset/Skylark): 90-degree, overhead-valve V-6. Cast iron block and head. Displacement: 181 cu. in. (3.0 liters). Bore & stroke: 3.80 x 2.66 in. Compression ratio: 9.0:1. Brake horsepower: 125 at 4900 R.P.M. Torque: 150 lbs.-ft. at 2400 R.P.M. Four main bearings. Hydraulic valve lifters. Multi-point fuel injection. VIN Code: L. BASE V-6 (Regal): 90-degree, overhead-valve V-6. Cast iron alloy block and head. Displacement: 231 cu. in. (3.8 liters). Bore & stroke: 3.8 x 3.4 in. Compression ratio: 8.0:1. Brake horsepower: 110 at 3800 R.P.M. Torque: 190 lbs.-ft. at 1600 R.P.M. Four main bearings. Hydraulic valve lifters. Carb.: 2Bbl. VIN Code: A. BASE V-6 (Century T Type); OPTIONAL (Century, LeSabre): Same as 231 V-6 above, but with sequential fuel injection. Brake H.P.: 150 at 4400 R.P.M. Torque: 200 lbs.-ft. at 2000 R.P.M. VIN Code: 3. BASE V-6 (Electra, Riviera): Same as 231 V-6 above, with sequential fuel injection. Compression ratio: 8.5:1. Brake H.P.: 140 at 4400 R.P.M. Torque: 200 lbs.-ft. at 2000 R.P.M. VIN Code: B. TURBOCHARGED V-6 (Regal T Type): Same as 231 V-6 above, with turbocharger, intercooler and sequential fuel injection. Brake horsepower: 235 at 4400 R.P.M. Torque: 330 lbs.-ft. at 2800 R.P.M. VIN Code: 7. BASE V-8 (Estate); OPTIONAL (Regal): 90-degree, overhead valve V-8. Cast iron block and head. Displacement: 307 cu. in. (5.0 liters). Bore & stroke: 3.80 x 3.385 in. Compression ratio: 8.0:1. Brake horsepower: 140 at 3200 R.P.M. Torque: 255 lbs.-ft. at 2000 R.P.M. Five main bearings. Hydraulic valve lifters. Carburetor: 4Bbl. Built by Oldsmobile. VIN Code: Y or H.

CHASSIS DATA: Wheelbase: (Skyhawk) 101.2 in.; (Skylark/Somerset) 103.4 in.; (Century) 104.8 in.; (Century wag) 104.9 in.; (Regal) 108.1 in.; (LeSabre) 115.9 in.; (LeSabre/Electra) 110.8 in.; (Riviera) 108.0 in. Overall length:- (Skyhawk cpe) 175.3 in.; (Skyhawk sed/wag) 177.3 in.; (Skylark) 181.1 in.; (Somerset Regal) 180.0 in.; (Century) 189.1 in.; (Century wag) 190.9 in.; (Regal) 200.6 in.; (LeSabre) 196.4 in.; (Electra) 197.0 in.; (Estate) 221.3 in.; (Riviera) 187.8 in. Height:- (Skyhawk) 54.0 in.; (Skyhawk hatch) 51.9 in.; (Skyhawk wag) 54.4 in.; (Skylark) 52.2 in.; (Somerset) 52.1 in.; (Century cpe) 53.7 in.; (Century sed/wag) 54.2 in.; (Regal) 54.6 in.; (LeSabre cpe) 54.7 in.; (LeSabre sed) 55.4 in.; (Estate) 59.3 in.; (Electra) 54.3 in.; (Riv) 53.5 in. Width:- (Skyhawk) 65.0 in.; (Skylark) 66.6 in.; (Somerset/Century) 67.7 in.; (Regal) 71.6 in.; (Estate) 79.3 in.; (LeSabre/Electra) 72.4 in.; (Riv) 71.3 in. Front Tread:- (Skyhawk cpe) 55.3 in.; (Skyhawk sed/wag) 55.4 in.; (Century) 58.7 in.; (Skylark/Somerset) 55.5 in.; (Regal) 58.5 in.; (LeSabre/Electra) 60.3 in.; (Estate) 62.2 in.; (Riv) 59.9 in. Rear Tread:- (Skyhawk) 55.1-55.2 in.; (Skylark/Somerset) 55.2 in.; (Century) 56.7 in.; (Regal) 57.7 in.; (LeSabre/Electra) 59.8 in.; (Estate) 64.0 in.; (Riviera) 59.9 in. Standard Tires:- (Skyhawk) P175/80R13 SBR; (Skyhawk T Type) P195/70R13 SBR; (Skylark) P185/80R13 SBR; (Century) P185/75R14 SBR; (Somerset/Century T Type) P215/60R14 Eagle GT SBR; (Regal) P195/75R15 SBR WSW; (Regal T Type) P215/65R15 SBR; (LeSabre/Electra) P205/75R14 SBR WSW; (Electra T) P215/65R15 SBR Eagle GT; (Park Ave.) P205/75R14 SBR WSW; (Estate) P225/75R15 SBR WSW; (Riviera) P205/70R14 SBR WSW; (Riviera T) P215/60R15 Eagle GT SBR.

TECHNICAL: Transmission:- Four-speed, fully synchronized floor shift standard on Skyhawk. Five-speed manual standard on Skylark/Somerset, available on Skyhawk. Four-speed overdrive automatic standard on LeSabre/Electra/Estate/Riviera, available on Century/Regal, which have standard three-speed automatic. Three-speed auto. trans. gear ratios: (1st) 2.74:1; (2nd) 1.57:1; (3rd) 1.00:1; (Rev) 2.07:1. Skyhawk/Skylark/Somerset Century auto. trans. gear ratios: (1st) 2.84:1; (2nd) 1.60:1; (3rd) 1.00:1; (Rev) 2.07:1. Regal four-speed overdrive automatic gear ratios: (1st) 2.74:1; (2nd) 1.57:1; (3rd) 1.00:1; (4th) 0.67:1; (Rev) 2.07:1. Century/Electra four-speed automatic: (1st) 2.92:1; (2nd) 1.57:1; (3rd) 1.00:1; (4th) 0.70:1; (Rev) 2.38:1. Standard axle ratio:- (Skyhawk) 3.65:1 w/4-spd, 3.45:1 w/5-spd, 3.18:1 w/auto.; (Skyhawk turbo) 3.65:1 w/4-spd, 3.33:1 w/auto.; (Skylark/Somerset): 2.84:1; (Century) 2.84:1 w/3-spd, 2.84:1 or 3.06:1 w/4-spd. (Regal) 2.41:1 exc. w/V-8, 2.56:1; (Regal T Type) 3.41:1; (LeSabre) 2.73:1 or 3.06:1; (Electra/Riv) .84:1; (Estate) 2.73:1. Steering:- (Regal/Estate) recirculating ball; (others) rack and pinion; power assist standard on all except Skyhawk. Suspension:- (Skyhawk/Somerset/Skylark) MacPherson strut front w/stabilizer; semi-independent beam rear axle w/trailing arms; rear stabilizer bar optional, std. on T Type. (Century) MacPherson strut front suspension; beam twist rear axle w/trailing arms and Panhard rod; front/rear stabilizer bars. (Leabre/Electra) MacPherson front struts, barrel springs and stabilizer bar; fully independent rear suspension using struts w/stabilizer bar and electronic level control. (Riviera) four-wheel independent suspension with front struts, barrel springs, link control arms and stabilizer bar; transverse leaf rear springs w/control arms and electronic level control. (Regal/Estate) front/rear coil springs; stabilizer bars; rigid four-link rear axle. Brakes:- power front disc, rear drum. Four-wheel disc brakes on Riviera. Anti-lock braking system available on Electra. Body construction:- (front-drive models) unitized; (Regal/Estate) separate body and frame. Fuel tank:- (Skyhawk/Somerset/ Skylark) 13.6 gal.; (Century) 15.7 gal.; (Regal) 18.1 gal.; (LeSabre/Electra/Riv) 18.0 gal.; (Estate) 22.0 gal.

DRIVETRAIN OPTIONS: Engines:- 110 cu. in. (1.8-liter) EFI four: Skyhawk ($50); std. on T Type. Turbocharged 110 cu. in. (1.8-liter) EFI four: Skyhawk T Type ($800) incl. boost gauge, engine block heater and Shelby aluminum wheels. 173 cu. in. (2.8-liter) V-6, 2Bbl.: Century ($435). 181 cu. in. (3.0-liter) V-6, 2Bbl.: Skylark/Somerset ($610). 231 cu. in. (3.8-liter) V-6, SFI: Century ($695), std. on T Type; LeSabre ($370), std. w/Grand National pkg. 307 cu. in. (5.0-liter) V-8, 4Bbl.: Regal ($540). Transmission/Differential:- Four-speed manual trans.: Skyhawk T Type ($75 credit). Five-speed manual trans.: Skyhawk ($75); std. on T. Three-speed auto. trans.: Skyhawk ($465); Skyhawk T Type ($390); Skylark/Somerset ($465), std. on T Type. Four-speed automatic overdrive trans.: Century/Regal ($175); std. on T Type. Optional rear axle ratio: Skyhawk 3.19:1 or 3.43:1; Century 2.84:1; Regal; LeSabre 2.84:1; Electra 2.73:1 or 2.97:1 (all NC). Limited slip differential: Regal/Estate ($95). Suspension, Steering and Brakes:- F40 heavy-duty suspension ($27). F41 Gran Touring suspension ($27) exc. Regal ($49); N/A on Estate. Special G.T. suspension: Skyhawk T Type (NC). Automatic level control: Estate ($175). Power steering: Skyhawk ($125). Anti-lock brakes: Electra ($825). other: Heavy-duty alternator: 85, 94, 100, 108 and 120-amp ($20-$90). H.D. battery ($25-$26). H.D. radiator: Skyhawk ($40-$70); Century ($30). Engine block heater ($18). H.D. engine/trans. cooling: Century/Regal/LeSabre/Electra/Riviera ($40-$70). Trailer towing harness: Riviera ($30).

SKYHAWK CONVENIENCE/APPEARANCE OPTIONS: Option Packages:- Performance pkg.: GT suspension, aluminum wheels, P205/60R14 SBR BSW, leather-wrapped steering wheel ($574) exc. T type/wag. SCS pkg. (P185/70R13 SBR BSW, custom seats and door trim, custom steering wheel, black moldings): Cust cpe ($51). Vista Vent flip-open removable glass sunroof ($310). Acoustic pkg. ($36). Instrument gauge pkg.: temp, oil pressure, volts, trip odometer: Cust, Spt ($60). Instrument gauges and tachometer: Cust, Spt ($138); Ltd ($78). Comfort/Convenience:- Air cond. ($645). Rear defogger, electric ($135). Louvered rear window sun shield: hatch ($199). Cruise control w/resume ($175). Power windows ($195- $270). Power door locks ($130-$180). Six-way power driver's seat ($225). Easy-entry passenger seat adjuster: Cust cpe, Spt ($16). Tinted glass ($99). Sport steering wheel ($50). Leather-wrapped steering wheel: T Type ($40). Tilt steering ($115). Trip odometer: Cust, Spt ($15). Electric trunk release ($40). Remote tailgate release: wag ($40). Tailgate wiper/washer: wag, hatch ($125). Two-speed wipers w/delay ($50). Lights, Horns and Mirrors:- Tungsten-halogen headlamps ($25). Headlamps-on indicator ($15). Front seat reading lamp $30). Dual horns: Cust cpe/sed, Spt ($15). Left black remote mirror ($22) exc. T Type. Dual black mirrors: left remote ($53); std. T Type. Visor vanity mirror, passenger ($7). Lighted visor vanity mirror ($45). Entertainment:- Basic seek/scan electronic-tuning AM/FM stereo radio ($158); w/clock ($222); w/cassette ($344). Electronic-tuning AM/FM stereo radio ($242); w/cassette and graphic equalizer ($494). Radio delete ($56 credit). Power antenna ($65). Dual rear speakers ($25). Exterior Trim:- Rear spoiler: Sport ($70). Door edge guards ($15-$25). Wide chrome rocker panel moldings: Cust cpe/sed ($26). Black rocker panel moldings: Spt ($76). Black wheel opening moldings: Spt ($30). Bodyside stripes ($45). Sport stripes: Cust cpe ($95). Designers' accent paint ($195). Lower gray accent paint: T Type ($195). Decklid luggage rack ($100). Roof rack: wag ($105). Front license bracket (NC). Interior Trim/Upholstery:- Seat trim for SCS pkg.: Cust cpe ($291). Front armrest: Cust, T cpe ($45). Front/rear fiber floormats: Cust, T Type cpe ($66). Front carpet savers ($17); rear ($12). Front carpet savers w/inserts ($18); rear ($15). Deluxe trunk trim ($33). Rear compartment security cover ($69). Wheels and Tires:- Styled aluminum wheels ($229); std. T Type. Styled alum. wheels (14 in.): Sport ($259). Locking wire wheel covers ($180). Hubcaps and trim rings: Cust/Ltd ($38). P175/80R13 SBR WSW ($54). P195/70R13 SBR BSW ($104). P195/70R13 SBR WSW ($166). P195/70R13 SBR WLT ($188); T Type ($84). P205/60R14 SBR BSW: Spt ($198); T ($94). P205/60R14 SBR WLT: Spt ($286); T ($182).

SKYLARK/SOMERSET/CENTURY CONVENIENCE/APPEARANCE OPTIONS: Option Packages:- Century Gran Sport pkg.: 3.8-liter V-6, sporty exhaust, P205/60R15 SBR GT tires on alum. wheels, tach, black leather-wrapped steering wheel, AM/FM stereo w/cassette, air dam, spoiler, gauges, black trim, wide rocker moldings: Cust cpe ($3895). Skylark/Somerset performance pkg.: Gran Touring suspension, P215/60R14 BSW tires, alum. wheels, leather-wrapped steering wheel ($592). Flip-open Vista Vent removable glass sunroof ($310-$339). Skylark/Somerset value option pkg.: tilt steering, cruise control, electric door locks, delay wiper, wire wheel covers or alum. wheels ($200 credit from list price). Century value option pkg.: tilt, cruise, lighted vanity mirror, delay wiper and AM/FM ET radio ($200 credit). Comfort/Convenience:- Air cond. ($645); Century ($750). Cruise control ($175). Rear defogger, electric ($135-$145). Power windows: 2-dr. ($195); 4-dr. ($270). Electric door locks ($130-$180). Automatic door locks ($220-$270). Six-way power driver's seat ($225). Manual seatback recliner, passenger: Century ($45); both ($90). Sport steering wheel: Skylark/Somerset Cust, Century ($50). Tilt steering ($115). Tinted glass: Century ($115). Instrument gauges incl. trip odometer: Century ($48); w/tach $126). Trip odometer: Century ($16). Digital electronic instrument cluster: Century ($225); T Type ($131). Electric trunk release ($40-$45). Remote tailgate lock: Century wag ($40). Remote fuel filler door release: Skylark/Somerset Cust, T ($11). Two-speed wipers w/delay ($50). Rear wiper/washer: Century wag ($125). Low washer fluid indicator: Skylark/Somerset ($16). Theft deterrent system: Century ($159). Lights, Horns and Mirrors:- Tungsten-halogen headlamps: Century ($25). Twilight Sentinel: Century ($57). Coach lamps: Century Ltd ($129). Headlamps-on chime: Century ($16). Door courtesy/warning light: Ltd/wag ($44). Front/rear reading/courtesy lights: Skylark/Somerset ($40-$54). Rear seat reading lamp: Skylark/Somerset Ltd, Century ($30); front, Century ($24). Remote-control left mirror: Century Cust/Ltd ($25). Dual mirrors (left remote, right manual): Skylark/Somerset Cust ($53); Century ($61). Dual power remote mirrors: Cust, Century ($139); Ltd, T Type ($86). Dual black electric remote mirrors: Century ($139); T ($78). Visor vanity mirror, passenger: Century ($7). Lighted visor vanity mirror, passenger: Skylark/Somerset ($38); Century ($58). Entertainment:- Electronic-tuning seek/scan AM/FM stereo radio ($157); w/cassette and equalizer ($424-$494). Somerset/Skylark AM/FM stereo w/cassette and Delco-GM/Bose music system ($995). Century ET radio w/clock ($222-$242); w/cassette ($344). Cassette tape player: Somerset/Skylark ($142); stereo radio req'd. Concert sound six-speaker system ($70-$125). Premium speakers: Century wag ($35-$60). Rear speakers ($25). Power antenna ($65). Delete radio ($56-$96 credit). Exterior Trim:- Landau vinyl top: Century cpe ($186); heavy-padded ($623). Long vinyl top: Century sed ($160). Designers' accent paint: Skylark/Somerset Cust/Ltd ($195); Century ($205). Charcoal lower accent: Century T ($205). Special solid color paint: Century Cust/Ltd/Estate ($200). Color-keyed bodyside moldings: Skylark/Somerset ($45); Century T ($55). Rocker panel moldings: Skylark/Somerset Cust ($26). Wide rocker panel/rear quarter moldings: Skylark/Somerset Cust ($76); Ltd ($50); Century Cust ($65). Wheel opening moldings: Skylark/Somerset Cust ($30). Windsplit molding: Century Cust ($22). Door edge guards ($15- $25). Bodyside stripes ($45). Woodgrain applique: Century wag ($350). Decklid luggage rack ($100). Tailgate air deflector: Century wag ($37). Roof rack: Century wag ($105). Swing-out rear quarter vent windows: Century wag ($75). Front license bracket (NC). Interior Trim/Upholstery:- Cloth 55/45 notchback seating: Century ($133). Cloth bucket seats: Century Cust ($97). Leather/vinyl 45/45 seats: Century Ltd ($295); T ($425). Cloth 45/45 seats: Century Ltd/Estate (NC). Full-length console: Century ($57). Operating console: Century ($85); T Type($28). Leather/vinyl bucket seats: Skylark/Somerset Ltd ($275). Lear Siegler bucket seats: Somerset, Century T Type ($600). Front floor mats w/inserts: Skylark/Somerset ($18); rear ($15). Front mats: Century $17); rear ($12). Floor mats w/inserts: Century front ($25); rear ($20). Trunk trim: Century ($25-$47). Locking storage compartment: Century wag ($44). Wheels:- Cast aluminum wheels: Century ($199); std. on T. Styled aluminum wheels: Skylark/Somerset Cust/Ltd ($229). Locking wire wheel covers ($199). Skylark/Somerset All-Season Tires:- P185/80R13 SBR WSW ($58). P205/70R13 SBR BSW ($114). P205/70R13 SBR WSW ($180). P215/60R14 SBR WLT ($202). P215/60R14 SBR Eagle GT WLT: Somerset T ($92). Century All-Season Tires:- P185/75R14 SBR WSW ($58). P195/75R14 SBR BSW ($30). P195/75R14 SBR WSW ($92). P215/60R14 SBR WLT: T Type ($92).

REGAL CONVENIENCE/APPEARANCE OPTIONS: Option Packages:- Regal Grand National pkg. (black body, front/rear bumpers, front air dam, rub strips/guards; cloth bucket seats, operating console, spoiler, performance-tuned suspension, chromed wheels): T Type ($635). Regal T Type Designer pkg.: black front air dam, rear spoilers and special black/dark gray accent paint ($403). Sliding silver electric Astroroof ($925). Hatch roof ($850). Value option pkg.: 5.0- liter V-8, cruise control, lighted visor mirror, delay wiper, tilt steering, stereo radio w/cassette, automatic power antenna ($425 credit from list prices). Comfort/Convenience:- Air cond. ($750). Automatic touch climate control air cond. ($900); T ($150). Cruise control w/resume ($175). Rear defogger, electric ($145). Tinted glass ($115). Tinted windshield ($99). Six-way power driver's seat ($225). Manual passenger seatback recliner ($75). Digital electronic instrument cluster ($299); T Type ($173). Sport steering wheel ($50); N/A T Type. Tilt steering ($115). Power windows ($195). Electric door locks ($130). Electric trunk release ($40). Headlamps-on indicator ($16). Trip odometer ($16); std. T Type. Two-speed wiper w/delay ($50). Theft deterrent system ($159). Lighting and Mirrors:- Tungsten-halogen headlamps ($25). Twilight Sentinel ($57). Cornering lamps ($57) exc. T Type. Coach lamps: Ltd ($102). Door courtesy/warning lights: Ltd ($44). Rear seat reading light ($30); rear ($24). Dual sport mirrors, left remote ($53); std. T Type. Dual chrome mirrors, left remote ($25) exc. T. Dual remote color-keyed mirrors ($83); T ($30). Visor vanity mirror, passenger ($7). Lighted visor vanity mirror, passenger ($58). Entertainment:- Seek/scan electronic-tuning AM/FM stereo radio ($158); w/clock ($222); w/cassette ($344). Electronic-tuning AM/FM stereo radio ($242); w/cassette and equalizer ($494). Concert sound speakers ($95). Dual rear speakers ($25). Automatic power antenna ($65). Radio delete ($56 credit). Exterior Trim:- Landau vinyl top ($186) exc. T Type. Heavy-padded landau vinyl top ($245) exc. T Type. Designers' accent paint ($205). Solid special color paint ($200). Exterior molding pkg. (wide rocker panel and belt reveal moldings): base ($110). Black protective bodyside moldings: T Type ($55). Door edge guards ($15). Bodyside stripes ($45). Front license bracket (NC). Interior Trim/Upholstery:- Full-length console: Ltd/T ($82). Lear Siegler bucket seats: T Type ($600). Cloth bucket seats: base/T ($195). Cloth 55/45 seating ($133); std. on Ltd. Leather/vinyl 45/45 seating: Ltd ($295); T Type ($595). Front mats ($17); rear ($12). Front mats w/inserts ($25); rear ($20). Trunk trim covering ($47). Wheels:- Chrome-plated wheels ($195); N/A T Type. Cast aluminum wheels ($285); std. T Type. Color-keyed wheels ($85) exc. T Type. Locking wire wheel covers ($199); N/A T Type. All-Season Tires:- P205/70R14 SBR WSW ($62). P215/65R15 SBR WLT: T Type ($92).

LESABRE/ELECTRA/ESTATE WAGON CONVENIENCE & APPEARANCE OPTIONS: Option Packages: LeSabre Grand National pkg. (3.8-liter V-6, dual exhausts, white or black paint, 2.84:1 rear axle, P215/65R15 Eagle GT tires on alum. wheels, Gran Touring suspension, leather-wrapped sport steering wheel, front floor mats, side window and belt moldings, and quarter-window close-out): Cust cpe ($1237). LeSabre performance pkg.: G.T. suspension, 2.84:1 axle, P215/65R15 Eagle GT tires on alum. wheels, leather-wrapped steering wheel ($878); 3.8-liter engine incl. later. Electra performance pkg.: G.T. suspension, P215/65R15 tires on alum. wheels, leather-wrapped steering wheel ($508); Park Ave. ($407). Sliding electric Astroroof: Electra ($1230). Vista Vent flip-open sunroof: LeSabre ($310). Comfort/Convenience:- Air cond.: LeSabre ($150). Automatic air cond.: Electra ($165). Air cond. w/touch-climate control: Estate ($150). Cruise control ($175); std. on Park Ave. Rear defogger, electric ($145). Power windows: LeSabre ($195-$270). Power door locks ($130- $180). Automatic door locks: Electra ($220-$270); exc. Park Ave. ($90). Six-way power seat, passenger's: Electra ($225); either side, LeSabre ($225). Two-position memory driver's seat: Electra ($178). Power seatback recliner, one side: Electra ($145); passenger only, LeSabre Cust ($145); Ltd ($70). Manual seatback recliner, passenger: LeSabre Cust ($75). Sport steering wheel: LeSabre ($50). Tilt steering ($115); std. Park Ave. Tilt/telescoping steering column: Electra ($175) exc. Park Ave. ($60). Trip odometer: LeSabre ($16). Windshield washer fluid indicator ($16). Low fuel indicator ($16). Digital electronic instrumentation ($315). Keyless entry system: Electra ($185) exc. T Type. Electric trunk pulldown: Electra ($80). Electric trunk release ($40); std. on Park Ave.. Theft deterrent system: Electra ($159); N/A on Estate. Two-speed wiper w/delay ($50); std. on Park Ave. Lighting, Horns and Mirrors:- Lamp and indicator group: Estate ($70-$86). Tungsten-halogen headlamps ($25). Twilight Sentinel: Electra ($60). Cornering lamps ($60). Light monitors, front/rear: Electra ($77). Door courtesy/warning lamps ($44-$70). Lighted door lock and interior light control: Electra ($75). Four-note horn: Electra ($28). Dual chrome remote mirrors: Estate ($49). Dual electric remote mirrors: LeSabre ($91); Electra Ltd/T ($91). Dual electric remote mirrors (left heated): Electra ($126); Park Ave. ($35). Lighted visor vanity mirror ($58). Automatic day/night mirror: Electra ($80). Entertainment:- Seek/scan electronic- tuning AM/FM stereo radio w/clock: LeSabre ($222). AM/FM stereo ET seek/scan radio w/clock and casssette: LeSabre ($344); Electra ($122). AM stereo/FM stereo ET seek/scan radio w/clock: LeSabre ($242); Electra ($20). AM stereo/FM stereo radio w/cassette and equalizer: LeSabre ($494); Electra ($272). AM stereo/FM stereo ET radio w/Dolby cassette and Delco GM/Bose sound system: LeSabre ($1117); Electra ($895). Radio delete: LeSabre ($56 credit); Electra ($275 credit). Concert sound speakers ($70-$100). Power antenna: Electra ($65). Exterior Trim:- Exterior molding pkg. (wide rocker panel, rear fender lower and belt reveal moldings): LeSabre/Estate ($110). Landau vinyl top: LeSabre cpe ($185). Heavy-padded vinyl top: Electra ($245) exc. T Type. Special paint: Electra ($200) exc. Firemist ($210). Black lower bodyside moldings: LeSabre Cust ($55). Door edge guards ($15- $25). Bodyside stripes ($45). Woodgrain vinyl applique: LeSabre Estate ($345); delete from Electra Est ($320 credit). Roof rack w/air deflector: LeSabre Estate ($110). Rear air deflector: Est ($40). Decklid luggage rack ($100). Rear bumper guards: LeSabre ($24). Front license bracket (NC). -Interior Trim/Upholstery:- Cloth 55/45 seating: LeSabre Cust ($133). Leather/vinyl 55/45 seating: Park Ave. ($425). Leather/vinyl 45/45 seating: Electra T Type ($325). Third seat: Estate ($220). Front carpet mats w/inserts ($25); rear ($20). Trunk carpeting trim: Electra ($53). Trunk mat: Electra ($15). Wheels and Tires:- Chrome-plated wheels: Estate ($40 credit). Styled aluminum wheels ($220-$285). Custom locking wire wheel covers ($164-$199); Estate ($56 credit). P205/75R14 SBR WSW ($66). P215/65R15 SBR BSW: LeSabre ($100). Self-sealing tires ($140).

RIVIERA CONVENIENCE/APPEARANCE OPTIONS: Comfort/Convenience:- Performance pkg.: G.T. suspension, P215/60R15 tires on alum. wheels, leather-wrapped steering wheel ($454). Electric sliding Astroroof ($1230). Rear defogger, electric ($145). Keyless entry system ($185). Six- way power seat, passenger ($225). Electric seatback recliner, one side ($75). Automatic door locks ($90). Leather-wrapped sport steering wheel ($96); std. T Type. Electric trunk pulldown ($80). Theft deterrent system ($159). Lighting, Horns and Mirrors:- Lamp and indicator group ($93). Twilight Sentinel ($60). Lighted door lock and interior light control ($75). Four-note horn ($28). Heated left mirror ($35). Lighted visor vanity mirrors, each ($58). Entertainment:- Electronic-tuning AM/FM stereo radio w/cassette and clock $342). Cassette player ($122); std. radio req'd. Electronic- tuning AM/FM stereo radio w/Dolby cassette tape player ($895). Concert Sound II speaker system ($70). Exterior Trim:- Designers' accent paint ($235). Special color Firemist paint ($210). Color-coordinated protective bodyside moldings ($55). Door edge guards ($15). Bodyside stripes ($45). Front license bracket (NC). Interior Trim/Upholstery:- Cloth bucket seats ($460). Leather/suede power reclining bucket seats ($487). Leather/suede bucket seats w/lumbar support ($947). Front mats w/inserts ($35); rear ($20). Trunk mat ($50). Wheels and Tires:- 14 in. aluminum wheels ($199); std. T Type. Locking wire wheel covers ($199) exc. T Type. P215/60R15 SBR WLT tires: w/performance pkg. ($70). P205/70R14 SBR BSW tires ($66 credit). Self-sealing tires ($140).

HISTORY: Buick's general introduction was October 3, 1985, but the new Somerset had debuted on August 28, 1985; and LeSabre and Riviera didn't emerge until November 14, 1985. Model year production (U.S.): 850,103 for a 10.7 percent share of the industry total. That number included 333,281 four-cylinder Buicks (up sharply from previous total), 442,699 with six cylinders, and only 74,124 V-8s—first time the V-8 total fell below 100,000. A total of 10,171 Buick engines were turbocharged this year. Calendar year production (U.S.): 775,966. Model year sales by U.S. dealers: 757,001 for a 9.4 percent share of the industry total. Calendar year sales (U.S.): 769,434 for a market share of 9.4 percent.

Historical Footnotes: Buick's sales slipped in 1986, down more than 17 percent — the lowest total since 1982. A V-6 shortage must have contributed to the slack figure. Century was the best seller by far. Starting in late September 1985, Riviera were built at the new plant in Hamtramck, Michigan. The downsized Rivieras didn't fare as well as expected, however, as big rear-drive cars began to enjoy a comeback. LeSabre production began on September 16, 1985 at the refurbished 1.5 million square-foot Buick City assembly plant in Flint, Michigan. Far fewer LeSabres than predicted were turned out. (Sales figures include the rear-drive B-body LeSabre station wagons.) The Buick City operation had a number of high-tech innovations. Instead of the usual receiving dock, 22 separate docking locations put incoming materials near the areas where they would be used. "Just-in-time" scheduling meant there was no provision for storage of inventory. Robots were to be used to unload engines, seats and transaxles. Nearly 200 robots were planned for use in body assembly. At the separate Dimensional Verification Center, a car could be placed on a huge granite block, then automatically measured to make sure all fixtures and tooling were sufficiently precise. Front-drive cars with V-6 engines—especially the 3.8- liter with sequential fuel injection—were gaining in popularity. So the Buick-Oldsmobile-Cadillac (BOC) Group boosted output at the Flint plant, and initiated V-6 production at the Lansing, Michigan facility as well. Some of the 2.8-liter V-6 engines were built in Mexico, while 1.8-liter Skyhawk fours came from Brazil. In a much different use of technology, new Consumer Information Centers were tested at shopping malls in Miami and suburban Dallas. They offered shoppers a variety of information on cars, driving, safety—and of course on the new Buicks. A futuristic Computerized Automotive Maintenance System could now let a dealer hook into a car's electronic control module to send data directly to Buick headquarters for analysis. At the design/evaluation stage, an OSCAR (On-Site Computer-Aided Research) system used sensors in a test car to send signals to a computer inside a nearby van.

BUICK

1987-1990

Buick constructed its 26 millionth vehicle in 1986 and, for 1987, proclaimed that "traditionally Buicks have offered quality." Playing off the old "When better cars are built, Buick will build them," Buick also notes that "it is easy for someone to utter the words, 'We will build better cars.'" But if those words are spoken by the automotive descendants of pioneers whose first cars appeared four years after the turn of the century, they take on an added meaning.

By Robert Ackerson

In that historical context the latest Riviera could be regarded as an "Automotive Legend." In its second year of production the down-sized Riviera was available in both coupe and T-Type form. Both were powered by the 3.8-liter V-6 but the T-type differed from the coupe by having among its features the firmer Gran Touring suspension. The T-Type's "power comfort" seats were the result of a four-year long joint project between Buick and a major university to develop orthopoedically correct seats that prevented fatique while providing comfort.

The six-passenger, front-wheel drive Electra, Electra T-Type and Park Avenue models were depicted as epitomizing "the attention to luxury values that have, for more than 80 years, set the Buick name—and the car that proudly bears it—apart." All four Electras were powered by 3.8-liter V-6 engines updated for 1987 for quieter and more efficient operation. The Electra and Park Avenue were available with a T Package based upon the T-Type's Gran Touring suspension.

The LeSabre was again offered as a coupe or sedan in three series: LeSabre, LeSabre Custom and LeSabre Limited. A new specialty version—the LeSabre T-Type coupe—was new for 1987. Also new for 1987 was the LeSabre T Package, directed toward the driver who preferred a firm suspension package.

The rear drive Regal, reaching the end of its long production run, was still a popular Buick. Available in Regal, Regal Limited and Regal Grand National, this Buick was regarded as offering "time-tested mechanical components that rank with the best: rear-wheel drive, with the smoothness of available V-8 power up front."

Both the Century Custom and Limited were available in coupe or sedan body styles. Buyers could also select a Century four-door Custom or Estate Wagon. The Century standard 2.5-liter Tech IV four-cylinder engine was equipped with electronic fuel injection and mated to a three-speed automatic transmission. Optional engines included a 2.8-liter V-6 with multi-port fuel injection and a 3.5-liter V-6 with sequential-port fuel injection.

The Buick Somerset was again available only as a coupe in either Custom or Limited form. A T Package, as well as a 3.0-liter V-6, was optional. The standard 2.5-liter Tech IV engine was paired with a close-ratio five-speed manual transmission.

The Skylark continued to be directed to the market located just below the Century in size. Two sedans were offered, the Skylark Custom and the Skylark Limited. Buick promised that "the T Package, coupled with the available 3.0-liter V-6 will transform the standard Skylark Limited or Custom Sedan into a road-ready cruiser."

Buick's J-Car, the Skyhawk, was available as a Custom coupe and sedan, a Sport Hatchback, a Limited coupe and sedan, and as a Custom and Limited station wagon. The major Skyhawk development for sporting drivers was a new turbocharged engine/manual transmission combination and four new touring option packages. By selecting these touring options separately or in combination, the Skyhawk owner could create a highly individualistic automobile.

The full-size Electra and LeSabre Estate Wagons were continued into 1987 for customers needing the capacity to carry up to eight passengers.

Buick's 1988 model year lineup was highlighted by the all-new Royal coupe, two new engines and improvements throughout the line. Noting that Buick was in tune with current market demands, General Manager Edward Mertz noted that "Buick is covering the market with distinctive products, high quality workmanship, backed by what we are convinced is the finest group of dealers in the industry." Mertz also emphasized that with the 1988 models special attention had been given to ride and handling, durability, and ease of maintenance and service."

All car lines had changes in their equipment level. New standard suspension packages improved ride and handling. Optional Gran Touring packages were continued.

Buick's new front-wheel drive Regal did not share any of its exterior sheet metal with any other car.

"The entire exterior body," said Mertz, "is exclusive to Buick. We think the design is youthful, and it has the elegance—the implied self-confidence—of a Buick." Although the new Regal was 8.4 inches shorter than the previous model (192.2 inches compared with 200.6 inches), front-seat room was within one inch of the other model's, and total interior dimensions were within two inches of the '87 Regal. The new Regal was produced in a totally renovated Plant 2 of General Motors of Canada in Oshawa, Ontario.

Mertz notes that "the small, thoughtful features designed into the Regal to enhance customer satisfaction are examples of the kind of planning of the design team." Examples of these features included a "lubed for life" suspension in place of the rear-drive Regal's clever lubrication fittings, and a remote jumpstart terminal as a convenient hookup for emergency battery jumping, to keep sparks away from battery vapors.

In regard to the new 2.3-liter Quad 4 and the updated 3800 V-6 engines, David S. Sharpe, Buick's general engineering and planning manager, noted, "Buick has a tradition of offering advanced engine and drivetrain technology, and these two new engines certainly are in keeping with Buick's traditional engine excellence." The Quad 4 met current emission requirements without the use of an exhaust gas recirculation system. The 3800 V-8 block was redesigned to bring all components on center. The cylinder heads were revised to fit the new block. A new one-piece intake manifold was also used.

The Skyhawk line was expanded to four models with the addition of the S/E Coupe. The new Skylark coupes had a distinctive composite front end treatment as well as new

exterior colors and interior fabrics. The Skylark was available in both Custom and Limited trim levels. The Century was also offered in Custom and Limited models. Now included as standard equipment on the Century were such items as AM/FM radio with seek and scan and a clock, extended range speakers, tinted glass and whitewall tires.

All LeSabre models—the LeSabre coupe, Custom sedan, Limited coupe and sedan, and the LeSabre T Type coupe had new exterior colors as well as numerous interior refinements. Similarly, the rear-wheel drive LeSabre and Electra Estate Wagons were offered in six new exterior colors as well as a number of interior refinements.

The four-door sedan Electra series again consisted of the Electra Limited, Park Avenue and T Type. The T-Type's appearance was refined by the additional use of chrome trim for such exterior items as door frames and rear lamp bezels. The 3.8-liter 3800 V-6 was standard for the Electra as well as the Riviera which continued to be offered in coupe and T-Type coupe form.

Buick celebrated its 85th anniversary year in 1989 by enhancing its position in the GM automotive strata of offering "premium American motorcars" via the introduction of extensively restyled Riviera and Century models. At mid-year Buick took another major step in this direction with the introduction of its most luxurious sedan, the Park Avenue Ultra. With these new models highlighting the 1989 model year, Buick also enhanced the appeal of its entire line by adopting more powerful engines, improving Dynaride suspension and increasing the availability of anti-lock braking. Among the new equipment offered for 1989 was a compact disc player on Regal and a remote keyless entry system, standard on Reatta and optional on Riviera, Electra/Park Avenue sedans and Regal.

"Buick is committed to offering distinctive, substantial, powerful and mature automobiles specifically tailored for the American market," said Buick General Manager Edward Mertz. "We emphasized that," Mertz continued, "when we introduced the all-new front-wheel drive Regal for 1988, and our luxury two-seater, the Reatta, in January of '88."

Dynaride, introduced on some models in 1988, was standard on all 1989 Buicks except station wagons and those cars equipped with Gran Touring suspension.

Buick's prestige luxury coupe, the Riviera, was eleven inches longer than the 1988 model. It had a "stronger" vertical grille, a new chrome bumper design, wider roof pillars and more curvaceous rear quarter panels.

The mid-size Century's new styling was joined by a new, optional V-6 engine.

All models of Buick's luxury Electra/Park Avenue sedan series were given appearance and content refinements. The series continued to consist of the Electra Limited, Electra T-Type, Park Avenue, and, at mid-year, the Park Avenue Ultra. Mr. Mertz paved the way for the Ultra by explaining, "the Ultra will provide superior comfort and personal accomodation, as well as ease of operation. It is a contemporary expression of states for an individual who wants even more style and comfort than is offered in the rest of the Electra/Park Avenue lineup."

New features for the subcompact Skyhawk besides Dynaride suspension on most models, included an acoustical insulation package. Its styling and model lineup were unchanged from 1988.

The compact Skylark had a new, more powerful optional V-6 engine, major acoustical insulation improvements and a number of front and rear appearance revisions. The Skylark Special Edition coupe and sedan, which were marketed only in California in 1988, was offered across the country in 1989. During the 1989 model year a Skylark Luxury Edition was also introduced.

The Regal, LeSabre and Reatta received numerous refinements for 1989. The Regal's appeal was enhanced by a new Dynaride suspension and the replacement of its 2.8-liter V-6 by a larger, 3.1-liter version during the model year. The LeSabre, Buick's best-selling car during the 1988 model year, had new interior trim. Its exterior styling was unchanged. Except for a larger hood medallion, the Reatta's exterior styling was also unchanged.

The LeSabre/Electra Estate Wagons were refined for 1989 with a new trailer towing package and several new options.

The 1990 Buick line-up was highlighted by the elmination of the Skyhawk models and the introduction of the Reatta convertible and the Regal sedan.

1987 BUICK

Buick selected Hal Holbrook to be its spokesperson for its 1987 models. Holbrook, perhaps best known for his portrayal of Mark Twain, was depicted as "the only star of a super-status proportions to represent Buick in its advertising in nearly two decades."

Buick used such terms as "substantial," "value" and "reliability" in promoting its new models. The Riviera was described as the "solid alternative to spending more for a luxurious performance automobile than you really need to." The 1987 Skylark was regarded as an automobile that "has Buick quality written all over it." The Electra, said Buick, was "the car that fits your lifestyle." The LeSabre was "the Buick that's so good at the things that really count." Buick called the Century the car that "today, as yesterday...stands for value that endures," while it considered the Regal a car with "traditional Buick comfort and ride, but decidedly performance-minded." The Somerset earned a description as "an exciting blend of sport and luxury in a personal size car." The Skylark was not left out of the receiving end of pleasing superlatives as Buick suggested: "If pure driving pleasure is the name of the game, Skyhawk is the name of the car."

Throughout its product line, Buick made a strong effort to combine the virtues of a time-tested approach to building automobiles with an ample infusion of contemporary technology and performance. Its 3.8-liter SFI V-6 was standing in the Riviera, Electra and LeSabre and optional for the Century. All four Buicks were also available with a T Package for the driver oriented toward an automobile with a firm suspension and quicker steering.

The Regal, Buick's rear-drive mid-size car, was available with any of the three new Touring options, as well as the Turbo Package.

The Skyhawk Custom, Limited and Sport hatchbacks were also available with a T Package that complemented their sporty wedge profile. Similarly, the Somerset's T Package, in conjunction with the Exterior Sport Package, made for an appealing automobile.

1987 Buick Skyhawk Sport hatchback.

SKYHAWK—SERIES 4J—FOUR—The big news for the 1987 Skyhawk was its new turbocharged 2.0-liter engine. Buick also offered four performance-oriented Touring options for the Skyhawk.

1987 Buick Somerset Limited two-door.

SOMERSET—SERIES 4N—FOUR/V-6—The Somerset was offered with a T Package that included a Gran Touring suspension, Eagle GT tires, cast-aluminum wheels and a leather-wrapped steering wheel. The Somerset grille was redesigned for 1987. Both the Somerset Custom and Limited models had new seat and cloth trim designs. Both were also fitted with new shale gray trim plates on the dash, console and doors. Somerset coupes built after January 1987 had new automatic seat belt systems.

1987 Buick Skylark Custom four-door sedan.

SKYLARK—SERIES 4N—FOUR/V-6—The 1987 Skylark could be equipped with a variety of new equipment intended to improve its road performance. The T package consisted of a firmer Gran Touring suspension, leather-wrapped steering wheel, cast aluminum wheels and Eagle GT steel-belted radial tires. Beginning in January 1987, all Skylark sedans were equipped with an automatic safety belt system.

1987 Buick Century Limited four-door sedan.

CENTURY—SERIES 4A—FOUR/V-6—The Century was virtually unchanged for 1987. Both the Century Custom and Limited were again offered as either coupe or sedan models. Also available was the T Package, which included the Gran Touring suspension with firmer springs, larger diameter front and rear stabilizer bars and a quicker steering ratio. Low profile Eagle GT blackwall tires were also specified. The Century was also offered with the Exterior Sport package, which consisted of a blackout treatment for the grille, bumpers, moldings and wheel opening. As alternatives to the standard 2.5-liter Tech IV engine, either a 2.8-liter V-6 with multi-port fuel injection or a 3.8-liter V-6 with sequential fuel injection were available.

The Custom interior consisted of a cloth fabric. The Limited model had 55/45 notched seats finished in velour. Optional 45/45 seats were upholstered in either cloth or leather. A new shale gray dash was used on Century coupes. The sedans had a new brushed pewter trim.

1987 Buick Regal Grand National two-door coupe.

270

REGAL SERIES 4G—V-6/V-8—The Regal retained its rear wheel drivetrain for 1987. Three versions were offered: the Regal, Regal Limited and Regal Grand National. Three performance packages were available. The Regal Grand National with its turbocharged and intercooled engine equipped with sequential-port fuel injection (SFI) was one of the fastest accelerating cars built in the United States. It was easily identified by its blacked-out exterior. Standard on the Grand National was a firm Gran Touring suspension. The other Regal coupes could be ordered with the T Package as well as an Exterior Sport Package consisting of aluminum alloy wheels and Eagle GT blackwall tires. It was also possible to order the Turbo Package for any Regal coupe. The Turbo engine's SFI was developed by Buick and the Bosch firm of Germany. It injected a precisely timed and metered amount of fuel directly into the cylinders. The intercooler cooled the pressurized air charge from the turbocharger to the engine. The turbocharger increased engine output by 122 percent over the normally aspirated engine. The SFI engine's 245 horsepower was linked to a four-speed automatic transmission with overdrive. The Turbo Package also included a 3.42:1 axle ratio and a turbo hood treatment.

The Regal was also available with a 5.0-liter V-8 and automatic overdrive transmission. All Regals were equipped with power steering and power-assisted low-drag front disc and rear drum brakes.

1987 Buick LeSabre Limited two-door coupe.

LESABRE—SERIES 4H—V-6—A new model of the LeSabre, the LeSabre T Type coupe, was introduced for 1987. It featured a blackout trim treatment, Gran Touring suspension, 3.8-liter V-6, leather-wrapped steering wheel, operating console, 45/45 seating, Eagle GT blackwall tires and aluminum alloy wheels. The T Package was also available as a separate option. Other new options included an instrument gauge package and electronic anti-lock brakes. All LeSabre coupes had a new automatic safety belt system. After December 1986, this system was also installed on LeSabre sedans.

ESTATE WAGON—SERIES 4B/C—V-8—The LeSabre and Electra Estate Wagons were carried over in virtually unchanged form from 1986.

1987 Buick Electra T Type four-door sedan.

ELECTRA—SERIES 4C—V-6—The Electra's V-6 engine was improved for 1987 by the use of roller valve lifters. The Electra continued to be offered in a T Type version with the Gran Touring suspension, leather-wrapped steering wheel, operating console, 45/45 seats, aluminum wheels and Eagle GT tires. Both the Electra and Park Avenue were also available with a T Package based upon the Gran Touring suspension.

1987 Buick Riviera T Type two-door coupe.

RIVIERA—SERIES 4E—V-6—Although an all-new model in 1986, the 1987 Riviera was set apart from its 1986 version by many refinements and improvements. The Riviera's 3.8-liter SPI V-6 now had roller lifters. A hydraulic engine mount was also standard equipment. The Riviera's Graphic Control Center (GCC) was revised. Low travel touch switches replaced the membrane function switches on the perimeter of the screen. The GCC software was revised to include a standard oil pressure gauge and an optional windshield washer fluid level sensor.

An ambient light sensor was now standard, allowing the GCC to stay on full brightness when the headlights were switched on during the day.

A front seat in knit velour or leather was a new option. A standard passenger assist strap above the door was another new feature. A new, reversible, non-slip floor mat was optional.

The Riviera T Type had a unique two-tone paint theme, with a silver lower body and a selected color above. It also had Level III suspension and exclusive Power Comfort seats. In addition to six-way power adjustments, they included inflatable lumbar supports, reversible cushions, and four-way manual articulating head rests.

The T Package included Gran Touring suspension, 2.97:1 final drive ratio, Eagle GT blackwall tires on 15-inch aluminum wheels, leather-wrapped steering wheel and shift handle and exterior T emblems. Several new exterior metallic colors were offered for the Riviera.

1987 Buick Skyhawk Custom four-door sedan.

I.D. DATA: Buick continued use of the previous year's system. The symbol 'H' designated the 1987 model year.

Model Number	Body Style Number	Body Type & Seating	Factory Price	Shipping Weight	Production Total
Skyhawk Custom (Four)					
S27	JS1	2-dr. Cpe.—5P	$8522	2336	19814
S69	JS5	4-dr. Sed.—5P	$8559	2285	15778
S35	JS8	4-dr. Sta. Wag.—5P	$9249	2463	3061
Skyhawk Limited (Four)					
T27	JT1	2-dr. Cpe.—5P	$9445	2345	1556
T69	JT5	4-dr. Sed.—5P	$9503	2423	2200
T35	JT8	4-dr. Sta. Wag.—5P	$9841	2498	498
Skyhawk Sport (Four)					
S77	JS2	2-dr. Hatch—5P	$8965	2396	3757
Somerset Custom (Four/V-6)					
J27	NJ1	2-dr. Cpe.—5P	$9957/10617	2456/2522	34916
Somerset Limited (Four/V-6)					
M27	NM1	2-dr. Cpe.—5P	$11003/11663	2473/2700	11585
Skylark Custom (Four/V-6)					
C69	NC5	4-dr. Sed.—5P	$9915/10575	2502/2568	26173
Skylark Limited (Four/V-6)					
D69	ND5	4-dr. Sed.—5P	$11033/11663	2519/2700	7532
Century Custom (Four/V-6)					
H27	AH1	2-dr. Cpe.—6P	$10844/11454	2696/2777	2878
H19	AH5	4-dr. Sed.—6P	$10989/11599	2743/2824	88445
H35	AH8	4-dr. Sta. Wag.—6P	$11478/12088	2824/2908	10414
Century Limited (Four/V-6)					
L27	AL1	2-dr. Cpe.—6P	$11297/12007	2824/2806	4384
L19	AL5	4-dr. Sed.—6P	$11593/12203	2771/2852	71340

1987 Buick Century Estate Wagon.

Model Number	Body/Style Number	Body Type & Seating	Factory Price	Shipping Weight	Production Total
Century Estate Station Wagon (Four/V-6)					
L35	AL8	4-dr. Sta. Wag.—6P	$11998/12608	2847/2928	6990
Regal (V-6)					
J47	GJ1	2-dr. Cpe.—6P	$11562	3196	44844
Regal (V-6 Turbocharged)					
J47	GJ1	2-dr. Cpe.—6P	$14857	-----	
J47	GJ1	Grand National	$15136	-----	
Regal Limited (V-6/V-8)					
M47	GM1	2-dr. Cpe.—6P	$12303/12893	3225/3405	20441
LeSabre (V-6)					
H37	HH1	2-dr. Cpe.—6P	$13438	3105	
H69	HH5	4-dr. Sed.—6P	$13438	3141	
LeSabre Custom (V-6)					
P69	HP1	2-dr. Cpe.—6P	$13616	3104	5035
P37	HP5	4-dr. Sed.—6P	$13616	3140	60392
LeSabre Limited (V-6)					
R37	HR1	2-dr. Cpe.—6P	$14918	3137	7741
R69	HR5	4-dr. Sed.—6P	$14918	3171	70797
LeSabre Estate Station Wagon (V-8)					
R35	BR8	4-dr. Sta. Wag.—6P	$14724	4160	5251

1987 Buick Electra Limited four-door sedan.

Model Number	Body/Style Number	Body Type & Seating	Factory Price	Shipping Weight	Production Total
Electra Limited (V-6)					
X69	CX5	4-dr. Sed.—6P	$16902	3269	7787
Electra Park Avenue (V-6)					
W11	CW1	2-dr. Cpe.—6P	$18577	3338	4084
W69	CW5	4-dr. Sed.—6P	$18577	3236	75600
Electra T-Type					
F69	CF5	4-dr. Sed.—6P	$18224	3278	2570
Electra Estate Station Wagon					
R35	BV8	4-dr. Sta. Wag.	$17697	4239	7508
Riviera (V-6)					
Z57	EZ1	2-dr. Cpe.—6P	$20337	3320	15223

ENGINE DATA: BASE FOUR (Skyhawk) Inline, overhead valve, four-cylinder, cast-iron block and aluminum head. Displacement: 121 cu. in. (2.0 liters). Bore & stroke: 3.50 in. x 3.15 in. Compression ratio: 9.0:1. Brake horsepower: 90 @ 5600 rpm. Torque: 108 lb.-ft. @ 3200 rpm. Five main bearings. Hydraulic valve lifters. Throttle-body electronic fuel injection. BASE FOUR (Somerset and Skylark) Inline, overhead valve, four-cylinder, cast iron block and head. Displacement: 151 cu. in. (2.5 liters). Bore & stroke: 4.00 in. x 3.00 in. Compression ratio: 9.0:1. Brake horsepower: 92 @ 4400 rpm. Torque: 134 lb.-ft. @ 3400 rpm. Five main bearings. Hydraulic lifters. Throttle-body fuel injection. BASE FOUR (Century) Inline, overhead valve, four-cylinder, cast iron block and head. Displacement: 151 cu. in. (2.5 liters). Bore & stroke: 4.00 in. x 3.00 in. Compression ratio: 9.0:1. Brake horsepower: 98 @ 4800 rpm. Torque: 135 lb.-ft. @ 3200 rpm. Five main bearings. Hydraulic lifters. Throttle-body electric fuel injection. BASE V-6 (Regal) 90-degree overhead valve V-6. Cast iron block and head. Displacement: 231 cu. in. (3.8 liters). Bore & stroke: 3.80 in. x 3.40 in. Compression ratio: 8.0:1. Brake horsepower: 110 @ 3800 rpm. Torque: 190 lb.-ft. @ 1800 rpm. Four main bearings. Hydraulic lifters. 2-bbl. BASE V-6 (LeSabre) 90-degree overhead valve V-6. Cast iron block and head. Displacement: 231 cu. in. (3.8 liters). Bore & stroke: 3.80 in. x 3.40 in. Compression ratio: 8.5:1. Brake horsepower: 150 @ 4400 rpm. Torque: 200 lb.-ft. @ 2000 rpm. Four main bearings. Hydraulic lifters. Sequential fuel injection. BASE V-8 (LeSabre Estate station wagon) 90-degree overhead valve V-8. Cast iron block and head. Displacement: 307 cu. in. (5.0 liters). Bore & stroke: 3.8 in. x 3.39 in. Compression ratio: 8.0:1. Brake horsepower: 140 @ 3200 rpm. Torque: 255 lb.-ft. @ 2000 rpm. Five main bearings. Hydraulic lifters. 4-bbl. carb. BASE V-6 (Electra) 90-degree overhead valve V-6. Cast iron block and head. Displacement: 231 cu. in. (3.8 liters). Bore & stroke: 3.80 in. x 3.40 in. Compression ratio: 8.5:1. Brake horsepower: 150 @ 4400 rpm. Torque: 200 lb.-ft. @ 2000 rpm. Four main bearings. Hydraulic lifters. Sequential fuel injection. BASE V-8 (Electra Estate Station wagon) 90-degree overhead valve V-8. Cast iron block and head. Displacement: 307 cu. in. (5.0 liters). Bore & stroke: 3.8 in. x 3.39 in. Compression ratio: 8.0:1. Brake horsepower: 140 @ 3200 rpm. Torque: 255 lb.-ft. @ 2000 rpm. Five main bearings. Hydraulic lifters. 4-bbl. carb. BASE V-6 (Riviera) 90-degree overhead valve V-6. Cast iron block and head. Displacement: 231 cu. in. (3.8 liters). Bore & stroke: 3.80 in. x 3.40 in. Compression ratio: 8.5:1. Brake horsepower: 150 @ 4400 rpm. Torque: 200 lb.-ft. @ 2000 rpm. Four main bearings. Hyrdaulic lifters. Sequential fuel injection. OPTIONAL (Skyhawk) Inline, overhead valve, overhead cam, four-cylinder, cast iron block and aluminum head. Displacement: 121 cu. in. (2.0 liters). Bore & stroke: 3.50 in. x 3.14 in. Compression ratio: 8.8:1. Brake horsepower: 96 @ 4800 rpm. Torque: 118 lb.-ft. @ 3600 rpm. Five main bearings. Hydraulic valve lifters. Multi-port fuel injection. OPTIONAL (Skyhawk) Inline, overhead valve, overhead cam, four-cylinder, cast iron block and aluminum head. Displacement: 121 cu. in. (2.0 liters). Bore & stroke: 3.50 in. x 3.14 in. Compression ratio: 8.0:1. Brake horsepower: 165 @ 5600 rpm. Torque: 175 lb.-ft. @ 4000 rpm. Five main bearings. Hydraulic valve lifters. Multi-port fuel injection, turbocharged. OPTIONAL (Skylark, Somerset) 90-degree, overhead valve, V-6. Displacement: 181 cu. in. (3.0 liters). Bore & stroke: 3.8 in. x 2.66 in. Compression ratio: 9.0:1. Brake horsepower: 125 @ 4900 rpm. Torque: 150 @ 2400 rpm. Hydraulic valve lifters. OPTIONAL (Century, Century Estate Wagon) 60-degree V-6. Cast iron block and cylinder head. Displacement: 173 cu. in. (2.8 liters). Bore & stroke: 3.50 in. x 2.99 in. Compression ratio: 8.9:1. Brake horsepower: 125 @ 4800 rpm. Torque: 160 lb.-ft. @ 3600 rpm. Five main bearings. Hydraulic lifters. Multi-port fuel injection. 90-degree overhead valve V-6. Cast iron block and head. Displacement: 231 cu. in. (3.8 liters). Bore & stroke: 3.80 in. x 3.40 in. Compression ratio: 8.5:1. Brake horsepower: 150 @ 4400 rpm. Torque: 200 lb.-ft. @ 2000 rpm. Four main bearings. Hydraulic lifters. Sequential fuel injection. OPTIONAL (Regal) 90-degree overhead valve V-6. Cast iron block and head. Displacement: 231 cu. in. (3.8 liters). Bore & stroke: 3.80 in. x 3.40 in. Compression ratio: 8.0:1. Brake horsepower: 245 @ 4400 rpm. Torque: 355 lb.-ft. @ 2000 rpm. Four main bearings. Hydraulic lifters. Sequential fuel injection. 90-degree overhead valve V-8. Cast iron block and head. Displacement: 307 cu. in. (5.0 liters). Bore & stroke: 3.8 in. x 3.39 in. Compression ratio: 8.0:1. Brake horsepower: 140 @ 3200 rpm. Torque: 255 lb.-ft. @ 2000 rpm. Five main bearings. Hydraulic lifters. 4-bbl. carb.

CHASSIS DATA: Wheelbase: (Skyhawk) 101.2 in.; (Skylark, Somerset) 103.4 in.; (Century) 104.9 in.; (Regal) 108.1 in.; (LeSabre) 110.8 in.; (LeSabre Estate Wagon) 115.9 in.; (Electra) 110.8 in.; (Riviera) 108.0 in. **Overall length:** (Skyhawk) 175.3 in.; (Skylark) 180.1 in.; (Somerset) 180.0 in.; (Century) 189.1 in.; (Century Custom/Estate station wagon) 191.0 in.; (Regal) 200.6 in.; (LeSabre) 196.2 in.; (LeSabre Estate station wagon) 220.5 in.; (Electra) 197.4 in.; (Electra Estate station wagon) 220.5 in.; (Riviera) 187.2 in. **Height:** (Skyhawk) 54.0 in.; (Skylark, Somerset) 52.1 in.; (Century) 53.6 in.; (Century Custom/Estate station wagon) 54.2 in.; (Regal) 54.5 in.; (LeSabre coupe) 54.7 in.; (LeSabre sedan) 55.5 in.; (LeSabre Estate station wagon) 59.3 in.; (Electra) 54.2 in.; (Riviera) 53.5 in. **Width:** (Skyhawk) 62.0 in.; (Skylark) 66.6 in.; (Somerset) 67.7 in.; (Century) 69.4 in.; (Century Custom/Estate station wagon) 69.4 in.; (Regal) 71.6 in.; (LeSabre sedan/coupe) 72.1 in.; (LeSabre Estate station wagon) 79.3 in.; (Electra) 72.1 in.; (Riviera) 71.7 in. **Front Tread:** (Skyhawk) 55.4 in.; (Skylark) 55.6 in.; (Somerset) 55.5 in.; (Century) 58.7 in.; (Century Custom/Estate station wagon) 59.7 in.; (Regal) 58.5 in.; (LeSabre coupe/sedan) 60.3 in.; (LeSabre Estate station wagon) 62.2 in.; (Electra) 60.3 in.; (Riviera) 59.9 in. **Rear Tread:** (Skyhawk) 55.2 in.; (Skylark) 55.2 in.; (Somerset) 55.2 in.; (Century) 56.8 in.; (Century Custom/Estate station wagon) 56.8 in.; (Regal) 57.8 in.; (LeSabre coupe/sedan) 59.8 in.; (LeSabre Estate station wagon) 64.0 in.; (Electra) 59.7 in.; (Riviera) 59.9 in. **Standard Tires:** (Skyhawk) P175/80R13; (Skylark) P185/80R13; (Somerset) P185/80R13; (Century) P185/75R14; (Century Custom/Estate station wagon) P185/75R14; (Regal) P195/75R14; (LeSabre coupe/sedan) P205/75R14; (LeSabre Estate station wagon) P225/75R15; (Electra) P20575/R14 (blackwall on Limited, whitewall on Park Avenue); (Electra T-Type) P215/65R15; (Riviera) P205/75R14.

TECHNICAL: Transmission: (Skyhawk) Four-speed manual; (Skylark) Five-speed manual; (Somerset) Five-speed manual; (Century) Three-speed automatic; (Century Custom/Estate station wagon) Three-speed automatic; (Regal) Three-speed automatic; (LeSabre coupe/sedan) Four-speed overdrive automatic; (LeSabre Estate station wagon) Four-speed overdrive automatic; (Electra) Three-speed automatic (four-speed overdrive automatic on Electra T-Type); (Riviera) Four-speed overdrive automatic. **Steering:** (Skyhawk) Manual rack and pinion; (Skylark) Power rack and pinion; (Somerset) Power rack and pinion; (Century) Power rack and pinion; (Century Custom/Estate station wagon) Power rack and pinion; (Regal) Power recirculating ball; (LeSabre coupe/sedan) Power rack and pinion; (LeSabre Estate station wagon) Power recirculating ball; (Electra) Power rack and pinion; (Riviera) Power rack and pinion. **Front Suspension:** (Skyhawk, Skylark, Somerset, Century, Century Custom/Estate station wagon, LeSabre coupe/sedan, Electra, Electra T-type, Riviera) MacPherson struts with coil springs, lower control arms and stabilizer bar; (Regal, LeSabre Estate station wagon) Coil springs, unequal length control arms, stabilizer bar. **Rear Suspension:** (Skyhawk) Semi-independent with beam axle, trailing arms, coil springs, stabilizer bar available; (Skylark, Somerset) Trailing crank bar, coil springs and stabilizer bar; (Century) Beam twist axle with integral stabilizer bar, trailing arms, Panhard arm and coil springs; (LeSabre coupe/sedan) MacPherson struts, coil springs, stabilizer bar; (LeSabre Estate station wagon) Solid axle with four links, coil springs; (Electra, Electra T-Type) Independent MacPherson struts, inboard coil springs, stabilizer bar; (Riviera) Independent tri-link, transverse fiberglass leaf spring, stabilizer bar. **Brakes:** (Skyhawk, Skylark, Somerset, Century, Century Custom/Estate station wagon, Regal, LeSabre coupe/sedan, LeSabre Estate station wagon, Electra, Electra T-type) Power front discs, rear drum; (Riviera) Power disc front and rear. **Body Construction:** Unibody except for Regal, Electra and LeSabre Estate station wagons. **Fuel Tank:** (Skyhawk) 13.6 gal.; (Skylark) 13.6 gal.; (Somerset) 13.6 gal.; (Century) 15.7 gal.; (Century Custom/Estate station wagon) 16.6 gal.; (Regal) 18.1 gal.; (LeSabre coupe/sedan) 18.0 gal.; (LeSabre and Electra Estate station wagon) 22.0 gal.; (Electra and Electra T-type) 18.0 gal.; (Riviera) 18.0 gal.

DRIVETRAIN OPTIONS: Engines: (Skyhawk) 2.0 liter, overhead cam with electronic fuel injection; 2.0 liter, overhead cam with electronic fuel injection and turbocharger; (Skylark and Somerset) 3.0 liter V-6 with multi-port fuel injection; (Century, Century Custom/Estate station wagon) 2.8 liter V-6 with multi-port fuel injection; 3.8 liter V-6 with sequential-port fuel injection; (Regal) 5.0 liter V-8 with 4 bbl. carb., 3.8 liter V-6 with turbocharger, intercooler and sequential-port fuel injection. (LeSabre coupe/sedan and LeSabre Estate station wagon, Electra, Electra T-Type and Riviera) None offered. **Transmission/Differential:** (Skyhawk) Five-speed manual overdriver, three-speed automatic; (Skylark) Three-speed automatic; (Century, Century Custom/Estate station wagon) Automatic transmission with overdrive; (Regal) Automatic with overdrive; (LeSabre coupe/sedan) None offered; (LeSabre and Electra Estate station wagon) None offered; (Electra and Electra T-Type) None offered; (Riviera) None offered. **Power Accessories:** (Skyhawk) Automatic power antenna, also with black mount, six-way power driver seat, power steering, power windows; (Skylark) Automatic power antenna, six-way power driver seat, power windows; (Somerset) Automatic power antenna, six-way power base driver seat, power windows; (Century) Automatic power antenna, also with black base, six-way power driver seat, power windows; (Century Custom/Estate station wagon) Automatic power antenna, six-way power driver seat, power windows; (Regal) Automatic power antenna, also with black mount, six-way power driver seat, power windows; (LeSabre and Electra Estate station wagon) Automatic power antenna, two-way power driver seat [requires 55/45 seats—Electra only], six-way power driver seat [requires 55/45 seats], power windows [standard on Electra]; (Electra) Automatic power antenna, six-way power passenger seat; (Riviera) Six-way power passenger seat. **Suspension:** (Skyhawk, Skylark, Somerset) Gran Touring suspension; (Century) Gran Touring suspension, heavy-duty suspension; (Century Custom/Estate station wagon) Heavy-duty suspension; (Regal) Gran Touring suspension, heavy-duty suspension; (LeSabre coupe/sedan) P205/75R14; (LeSabre and Electra Estate station wagon) Automatic level control; (Electra) Gran Touring suspension, heavy-duty suspension; (Riviera) Gran Touring suspension.

SERIES NAME CONVENIENCE/APPEARANCE OPTIONS:
Skyhawk: Air conditioning, 3.43:1 axle ratio, heavy-duty battery, electronic cruise control, electric rear window defogger, California assembly line emission equipment and testing, engine block heater, engine block heater cord delete, front carpet savers with inserts, rear carpet savers with inserts, soft-ray tinted glass, "headlamps on" warning chime, dual horns (standard on Limited), instrument gauges (includes temperature, voltmeter, oil trip odometer—standard on Limited), instrument gauges (includes temperature, voltmeter, oil, tachometer and trip-odometer, Trip-odometer—standard on Limited), front-seat reading lamps, concealed headlamps (Custom models and Limited

1987 Buick Skyhawk Custom wagon.

sedans, includes smoked tail lamp lens), electric door locks, remote electric trunk/hatch lock release, styled black remote-control, outside mirrors (left remote, right manual), lighted passenger visor vanity mirror, black rocker panel molding (Sport), black wheel opening molding (Sport), narrow, bright rocker panel molding (Custom), black door edge guards (Sport), bright door-edge guards (Custom, Limited), designers' accent paint, lower accent paint—gray (coupes/sport), ETR AM-FM stereo radio with seek and scan, ETR AM-FM stereo with seek and scan and clock, ETR AM-FM stereo with seek and scan, cassette tape, auto reverse and clock, graphic equalizer, cassette tape, ETR AM stereo-FM stereo with seek and scan with search/repeat and clock, radio delete (front speakers not deleted), rear extended-range speakers, Concert Sound II speaker system, easy-entry seat (Custom coupe/sport), four-way manual driver seat adjuster, front console-mounted armrest (standard on Limited), acoustic insulation package (standard on Limited), hatch window washer and wiper (Sport), luggage rack (black), luggage rack (bright), rear compartment security cover (Sport), rear-window louvered sunshield (Sport), front license plate mounting, tilt steering wheel, sport steering wheel, leather-wrapped sport steering wheel, body-side stripes, flip-open, Vista-Vent removable glass sunroof, styled hubcap with trim ring (not available on Sport), 13 in. aluminum wheels, custom locking wire wheel covers. Tires: Steel-belted, radial-ply, all-season: P175/80R13, whitewall, P195/70R13 blackwall, P195/70R13 whitewall, P195/70R13 white letter, P205/60R14 white letter. *Touring options:* Interior Sport Package (coupes and sport) Includes easy-entry front seats, custom instrument panel with red backlighting and trip odometer, front and rear custom seat cushions, black and white interior with red striping and sport steering wheel. Exterior Sport Package (coupes and Sport): includes Turbo hood, blackout treatment on door handle and locks, headlamps, roof drip molding, rocker panels, wheel opening molding, belt reveal, body-side and side window reveal molding mirrors, fixed-mast antenna and bumper guards, amber park and trunk lamps; fog lamps. Available in five exterior colors. "T" Package: Inclues Gran Touring suspension, 14 in. aluminum wheels, steel-belted, radial-ply Eagle GT blackwall P205/60R14 tires, leather-wrapped sport steering wheel and "T" ornamentation. Turbo package: includes 2.0 liter MFI turbo engine five-speed manual transmission, Gran Touring suspension, P205/60R14 Eagle GT tires, 14 in. aluminum wheels, 3.61:1 transaxle ratio, turbo hood with turbo emblem, instrument cluster with custom instrumentation and red backlighting, leather-wrapped sport steering wheel.

Skylark: Air conditioning, 2.84:1 axle ratio, electronic cruise control, electric rear window defogger, California assembly line emission equipment and testing, engine block heater, front carpet savers with inserts, rear carpet savers with inserts, front and rear seat reading lamps, front door courtesy and warning lights (Limited), electric door locks, remote electric trunk lock release, styled black remote-control, outside mirrors (left remote, right manual—standard in Limited), lighted passenger side visor vanity mirror, electric mirrors, body color (left and right remote), wide rocker panel moldings, narrow bright rocker panel moldings (standard on Limited), color-coordinated, protective body-side moldings, wide body-side molding, bright wheel opening moldings (Custom), lower designers' accent paint, lower accent paint—available with all exterior colors, ETR AM-FM stereo radio with seek and scan, ETR AM-FM stereo with seek and scan, cassette tape, auto reverse and clock, graphic equalizer, cassette tape, ETR AM stereo-FM stereo with seek and scan with search/repeat and clock, Delco Bose Music System including Dolby, cassette and ETR AM stereo-FM stereo with seek and scan and clock, radio delete (front speakers not deleted), rear extended-range speakers, Concert Sound II speaker system, flip-open, Vista-Vent removable glass sunroof with wind reflector, four-way manual driver seat adjuster, front seat center armrest (Custom), reclining front seat backs (Custom), remote fuel-filler door release (standard on Limited), bright deck lid luggage rack, front license plate mounting, title steering column, body side stripes, custom locking wire wheel covers, aluminum wheels, styled hubcap with trim ring, two-speed windshield wiper with low-speed delay feature. Tires: steel-belted, radial-ply, all-season: P185/80R13, whitewall, P205/70R13 blackwall, P205/70R13 whitewall, P205/70R13 white letter, P215/60R14 white letter.

1987 Buick Somerset Sport Edition two-door.

Somerset: Air conditioning, 2.84:1 axle ratio, electronic cruise control, electric rear window defogger, California assembly line emission equipment and testing, engine block heater, front carpet savers with inserts, rear carpet savers with inserts, electric door locks, remote electric trunk lock release, styled black remote-control, outside mirrors (left remote, right manual—standard on Limited), electric black mirrors (left and right remote), lighted passenger visor vanity mirror, wide rocker panel moldings, narrow, bright rocker panel moldings (standard on Limited), color-coordinated protective body-side moldings, bright door-edge guards, bright wheel opening moldings (Custom), lower designers' accent paint, ETR AM-FM stereo radio with seek and scan, ETR AM-FM stereo with seek and scan and clock, ETR AM-FM stereo with seek and scan, cassette tape, auto reverse and clock, graphic equalizer, cassette tape, ETR AM stereo-FM stereo with seek and scan with search/repeat and clock. radio delete (front speakers not deleted), rear dual extended-range speakers, Delco-Bose Music System including Dolby, cassette and ETR AM stereo-FM stereo with seek and scan and clock, Concert Sound II speaker system, flip-open Vista-Vent removable glass sunroof with wind reflector, four-way manual driver seat adjuster, remote fuel-filler door release (standard on Limited), bright luggage rack, black luggage rack, front license plate-mounting, tilt steering wheel, sport steering wheel, body-side stripes, 13 in. aluminum wheels, custom locking wire wheel cover. Tires: steel-belted, radial-ply, all-season: P185/80R13, whitewall, P205/70R13 blackwall, P205/70R13 whitewall, P20/70R13 white letter, P215/60R14 white letter. *Touring options:* "T" Package: includes Gran Touring suspension, 14 in. aluminum wheels, steel-belted radial-ply P215/60R14 Eagle GT blackwall tires, leather-wrapped sport steering wheel and "T" ornamentation. Exterior Sport Package: includes blackout treatment on door handle and locks, headlamp bezels, roof drip molding, wheel opening molding, grille, radio antenna, tail lamp bezels and trim, front and rear bumper rub strip, front air dam, hood ornament deleted, aero rocker panel molding, amber parking and tail lamps. Available in five exterior colors.

1987 Buick Century Limited two-door coupe.

Century: Air conditioning, 3.18:1 axle ratio, electronic cruise control, electric rear defogger, California assembly line emission equipment and testing, engine block heater, 100, 105, 120-amp Delcotrons, heavy-duty radiator, heavy-duty engine and transmission cooling, front carpet savers, rear carpet savers, front carpet savers with inserts, rear carpet savers with inserts, deluxe trunk trim, electric door locks, remote electric trunk lock release, styled black remote-control outside mirror (left), styled black remote-control outside mirrors (left remote, right manual), lighted passenger visor vanity mirror, Soft-Ray tinted glass, Twilight Sentinel headlamp control, trip odometer, electronic digital instrumentation, instrument gauges (includes temperature, voltmeter and tachometer), front-door courtesy and warning lights (Limited), front-seat reading lamps, electric door locks, remote electric trunk lock release, wide rocker panel moldings (standard on Limited), color-coordinated protective body-side moldings, bright door-edge guards, windsplit molding and stand-up hood ornament (standard on Limited), designers' accent paint, ETR AM-FM stereo radio with seek and scan, ETR AM-FM stereo with seek and scan and clock, ETR AM-FM stereo with seek and scan, cassette tape, auto reverse and clock, graphic equalizer, cassette tape, ETR AM stereo-FM stereo with seek and scan with search/repeat and clock, radio and front speakers delete, premium speaker system, flip-open Vista-Vent removable glass sunroof, Landau vinyl top (coupes), Landau heavily padded vinyl top (coupes), full vinyl top (sedans), manual seat back recliners (driver and passenger), manual seat back recliner (passenger), six-way power driver seat, remote fuel-filler door release, bright luggage rack, black luggage rack, front license-plate mounting, tilt steering wheel, sport steering wheel, body-side stripes, custom locking wire wheel covers, styled hubcap and trim ring, 14 in. aluminum wheels, two-speed windshield wiper system with low-speed delay feature. Tires, steel-belted, radial-ply, all-season: P185/75R14, whitewall, P195/75R14 blackwall, P195/75R14 whitewall. *Touring options:* "T" Package (coupes/sedans): Includes Gran Touring suspension, 14 in. aluminum wheels, steel-belted radial-ply P215/60R14 Eagle GT blackwall tires, leather-wrapped sport steering wheel and "T" emblem on front fender. Exterior Sport Package (sedans): Includes blackout treatment on door handle and locks, headlamp/taillamp bezels, bumpers and rub stripes, roof drip molding, belt reveal and wheel opening moldings (rocker panel moldings deleted). Available in four exterior colors. (Century Custom/Estate station wagon): Air conditioning, heavy-duty battery, full-length operating console, electronic cruise control, electric rear window defogger, California assembly line emission equipment and testing, engine block heater, 100, 105, 120-amp Delcotrons, heavy-duty radiator, heavy-duty engine and transmission cooling, front carpet savers with inserts, swing-out rear-quarter vent window, electric door locks, remote-control electric tailgate lock, lockable storage compartment, styled black remote-control outside mirror (left), styled black remote-control, outside mirrors (left remote, right manual), electric black outside rearview mirrors (left and right remote), lighted passenger visor vanity mirror, Soft-Ray tinted glass, Twilight Sentinel headlamp control, trip odometer, electronic digital instrumentation, instrument gauges (includes temperature, voltmeter and trip odometer), instrument gauges (includes temperature, voltmeter, and tachometer), front-door courtesy and warning lights (Estate only), front-seat reading lamps, electric door locks, remote electric trunk lock release, wide rocker panel moldings (standard on Estate), color-coordinated protective body-side moldings, bright door-edge guards, windsplit molding (standard on Estate), designers' accent paint, ETR AM-FM stereo radio with seek and scan, ETR AM-FM stereo with seek and scan and clock, ETR AM-FM stereo with seek and scan, cassette tape, auto reverse and clock, graphic equalizer, cassette tape, ETR AM stereo-FM stereo with seek and scan with search/repeat and clock, radio and front speakers delete, premium speaker system (not available with standard radio), flip-open Vista-Vent removable glass sunroof, manual seatback recliners (driver and passenger), manual seatback recliner (passenger), six-way power driver seat, roof rack, front license plate mounting, tailgate air deflector, tilt steering wheel, sport steering wheel, third seat (vinyl), body-side stripes, 14 in. aluminum wheels, custom locking wire wheel covers, styled hubcap and trim ring, two-speed windshield wiper system with low-speed delay feature, tailgate window wiper and washer. Tires: steel-belted, radial-ply, all-season: P185/75R14, whitewall.

1987 Buick Regal Limited two-door coupe.

Regal: Air conditioning, 2.56, 3.08, 3.23:1 axle ratios, electronic cruise control, electric rear window defogger, California assembly line emission equipment and testing, engine block heater, 85-amp, 94-amp Delcotrons, heavy-duty battery, heavy-duty engine and transmission cooling, front carpet savers, rear carpet savers, front carpet savers with inserts, rear carpet savers with inserts, trunk trim covering, Soft-Ray tinted glass, Soft-Ray tinted windshield, electric door locks, remote electric trunk lock release, "Headlights On" warning chime, theft-deterrent system with starter interrupt, trip odometer, styled black remote-control outside mirror (left), body-colored sport remote-control outside mirrors (left and right remote), coach lamps (Limited), vanity visor mirror (passenger), lighted passenger visor vanity mirror, Twilight Sentinel headlamp control, trip odometer, electronic digital instrumentation, front-door courtesy and warning lights (Limited), front-seat reading lamps, tungsten-halogen headlamps, cornering lamps, electric door locks, remote electric trunk lock release, exterior molding package includes wide rocker panel moldings and belt reveal (standard on Limited), bright door-edge guards, black door edge guards, designers' accent paint, ETR AM-FM stereo with seek and scan, ETR AM-FM stereo with seek and scan and clock, ETR AM-FM stereo with seek and scan, cassette tape, auto reverse and clock, graphic equalizer, cassette tape, ETR AM stereo-FM stereo with seek and scan with search/repeat and clock, radio and front speakers delete, rear dual extended-range speakers, Concert Sound speaker system, Silver Astroroof (electric sliding), lockable hatch roof, Landau vinyl top, Landau heavily padded vinyl top, manual seatback recliner (passenger), six-way power driver seat, remote electric trunk lock release, front license plate mounting, limited slip differential, tilt steering wheel, sport steering wheel, body-side stripes, chrome-plated wheels, color-keyed wheels with trim rings, 14 in. aluminum wheels, custom locking wire wheel covers, two-speed windshield wiper system with low-speed delay feature. Tires: steel-belted, radial-ply, all-season: P205/70R14 whitewall, P215/65R15 white letter, P195/75R14 blackwall. *Touring Options:* "T" Package: Includes Gran Touring suspension, fast ratio power steering, gas shock absorbers, 15 in. aluminum wheels, steel-belted radial-ply P215/65R15 Eagle GT blackwall tires, leather-wrapped sport steering wheel and "T" ornamentation. Exterior Sport Package: Includes blackout treatment on door handle and locks, grille, headlamp/tail lamp bezels, antenna and door edge guards, bumpers and rub stripes, roof drip and window trim, side window reveal, belt reveal and rear window (rocker panel and body-side moldings are deleted). Regal Grand National Package: 3.8 EFI turbocharged engine with intercooler, automatic transmission with overdrive, 3.42:1 axle ratio, Gran Touring suspension, fast-ratio power steering, sport mirrors, turbo boost gauge and tachometer, trip odometer, leather-wrapped steering wheel, air conditioning, P215/85R15 Eagle GT blackwall tires, chrome-plated steel wheels, black bumpers, molding, grille, and exterior trim, deck lid spoiler, full-length operating console and reclining front bucket seats. Turbo Package: Includes 3.8 liter turbocharged SFI engine with intercooler, instrumentation panel cluster with tachometer, turbo boost gauge and trip odometer, turbo hood and ornamentation, acoustical insulation package and 3.42:1 axle ratio.

1987 Buick LeSabre four-door sedan.

LeSabre coupe/sedan: electronic touch climate control air conditioner, electronic cruise control, electric rear window defogger, California assembly line emission equipment and testing, engine block heater, heavy-duty battery, heavy-duty engine and transmission cooling, front carpet savers with inserts, rear carpet savers with inserts, deluxe trunk trim (Custom/Limited), electric door locks, remote electric trunk lock release, trip odometer, quartz analog gauge cluster (trip odometer, tachometer, voltmeter, oil and temperature gauge), quartz analog gauge cluster (tachometer, voltmeter, oil and temparature gauge), low fuel indicator, electronic digital instrumentation, electric body-color, outside, rearview mirrors (left and right remote), lighted passenger visor vanity mirror, front and rear seat reading and courtesy lights, front-door courtesy and warning lamps, electric door locks, remote electric trunk lock release, black protective lower body-side (standard on Limited), bright door-edge guards, rear bumper guards and bright bumper bead, designers' accent paint, ETR AM-

FM stereo with seek and scan and clock, ETR AM-FM stereo with seek and scan, cassette tape, auto reverse and clock, graphic equalizer, cassette tape, ETR AM stereo-FM stereo with seek and scan with search/repeat and clock, Delco Bose music system with ETR AM-FM stereo Dolby seek and scan, cassette tape with auto reverse, search/repeat and clock, radio delete (front speakers not deleted), Concert Sound speaker system, black power antenna base, flip-open, Vista-Vent removable glass sunroof, full vinyl top (sedans), manual passenger seatback recliner (standard on Limited), manual driver seatback recliner, electric passenger seatback recliner, six-way power driver seat, six-way power passenger seat, electric door locks, remote electric trunk lock release, front license plate mounting, bright luggage rack, anti-lock brake system, tilt steering wheel, sport steering wheel, body-side stripes, 14 in. aluminum wheels, 15 in. aluminum wheels, styled hubcap and trim ring, custom locking wire wheel covers, low windshield washer fluid indicator, two-speed windshield wiper system with low-speed delay feature. Tires: steel-belted, radial-ply, all-season: P205/70R14, whitewall, P215/65R15 Eagle GT white stripe, P215/65R15 blackwall, self-sealing tires. *Special Option Packages:* LeSabre T Type: Includes special 15 in. aluminum wheels, P215/65R15 Eagle GT blackwall tires, Gran Touring suspension, 2.97:1 ratio transaxle, leather-wrapped sport steering wheel and shift handle, red and amber tail lamps, dual exhaust outlets, black body-side molding treatment, lay-down hood ornament, gray-black 45/45 seats (required), front floor mats with "Power 6" logo, T-type identification blackout trim, tail lamp, door handles and lock cylinder and grille, rear deck spoiler, front air dam, ETR AM-FM stereo radio with graphic equalizer, cassette tape and red backlighting, operating console with red backlighting, blacked-out instrument panel controls, special gauge package with red backlighting. Available in four exterior colors. T Package: Includes special 15 in. aluminum wheels, P215/65R15 Eagle GT blackwall tires, Gran Touring suspension, 2.97:1 ratio transaxle, leather-wrapped sport steering wheel, "T" ornamentation.

1987 Buick LeSabre Estate Wagon.

LeSabre and Electra Estate station wagon: electronic touch climate control air conditioner, 3.08, 3.23:1 axle ratios, electronic cruise control, electric rear window defogger, California assembly line emission equipment and testing, engine block heater, heavy-duty battery, heavy-duty engine and transmission cooling, front carpet savers with inserts, rear carpet savers with inserts, four-note horn, electric door locks (LeSabre), automatic electric door locks, remote-control electric tailgate lock (LeSabre), trip odometer (LeSabre), chrome electric outside, rearview mirrors (left and right remote), chrome remote-control outside mirrors (left and right), lighted passenger visor vanity mirror, driver side lighted visor vanity mirror, door courtesy and warning lamps, illuminated driver door lock and interior light control, Twilight Sentinel headlamp control, cornering lamps, tungsten-halogen headlamp, front light monitors, lamp and indicator group (LeSabre—consists of "Headlamps on" low fuel and low windshield washer fluid indicators and front reading lamps), lamp and indicator group (Electra—consists of trip odometer, front seat reading lamp, low fuel and low windshield washer fluid), electric door locks (LeSabre), remote-control electric tailgate lock (LeSabre), color-coordinated protective body-side molding, belt reveal molding, bright door-edge guards (LeSabre), wide rocker, front and rear lower panel moldings (Electra), woodgrain vinyl applique (LeSabre), exterior molding package (consists of wide rocker panel, front and rear fender and belt reveal moldings (LeSabre), ETR AM-FM stereo with seek and scan and clock (LeSabre), ETR AM-FM stereo with seek and scan, cassette tape, auto reverse and clock, graphic equalizer, cassette tape, ETR AM stereo-FM stereo with seek and scan with search/repeat and clock, CB radio, radio delete (front speakers not deleted), manual passenger seatback recliner (requires 55/45 seat), electric passenger seatback recliner, two-way power driver seat (Electra —55/45 seat required), six-way passenger and driver power seats (55/45 seats required), six-way driver power seat with 55/45 seat (vinyl), third seat (vinyl), electric door locks (LeSabre), front license plate mounting, roof luggage rack (LeSabre), tilt steering column (LeSabre), automatic ride control, limited slip differential, chrome-plated wheels, custom locking wire wheel covers, two-speed windshield wiper system with low-speed delay feature, self-sealing tires.

1987 Buick Park Avenue four-door sedan.

Electra/Park Avenue: Electronic touch climate control air conditioner, 2.53:1 axle ratio, electronic cruise control (standard on Park Avenue), electric rear window defogger, California assembly line emission equipment and testing, engine block heater, heavy-duty battery, heavy-duty engine and transmission cooling, front carpet savers with inserts (standard on Park Avenue), rear carpet savers with inserts (standard on Park Avenue), trunk compartment mat, deluxe trunk trim, electric door locks (standard on Park Avenue), remote electric trunk lock release (standard on Park Avenue), electric trunk pull-down, keyless entry system, automatic electric locks, theft-deterrent system with starter interrupt, four-note horn, quartz analog gauge cluster (trip odometer, tachometer, voltmeter, oil and temperature gauge), quartz analog gauge cluster (tachometer, voltmeter, oil and temperature gauge), low fuel indicator, front and rear light monitors, electronic digital instrumentation, automatic day/light monitor, electric body-color, outside rearview mirrors (left and right remote), lighted passenger visor vanity mirror (standard on Park Avenue), lighted driver side visor vanity mirror, rear seat reading lights, door courtesy and warning lamps (standard on Park Avenue), illuminated driver door lock and interior light control, Twilight Sentinel headlamp control, cornering lamps, electric door locks, remote electronic trunk lock release (standard on Park Avenue), bright door-edge guards, ETR AM-FM stereo with seek and scan auto reverse and clock, graphic equalizer, cassette tape, ETR AM stereo-FM stereo with seek and scan with search/repeat and clock, Delco Bose Music System with ETR AM-FM stereo Dolby seek and scan, cassette tape with auto reverse, search/repeat and clock, radio delete (front speakers not deleted), Concert Sound speaker system, automatic power antenna, graphic power antenna base, Astroroof, electric sliding roof, full heavily padded vinyl top, electric driver seatback recliner, electric passenger seatback recliner, two-position memory, six-way power driver seat, six-way power passenger seat, front license plate mounting, black luggage rack (T-type), bright luggage rack (Limited and Park Avenue), anti-lock brake system, tilt and telescoping steering column, tilt steering column (standard on Park Avenue), cellular telephone accommodation package, body-side stripes (standard on Park Avenue), 14 in. aluminum wheels, custom locking wire wheel covers, low windshield washer fluid indicator and two-speed windshield wiper system with low-speed delay feature (standard on Park Avenue). Tires: steel-belted, radial-ply, all-season: P205/70R14, whitewall (standard on Park Avenue), P215/75R14 blackwall (standard on Electra), P215/65R15 blackwall, self-sealing tires. *Touring Options:* Electra T-Type sedan: includes 3.8 liter SFI V-6, automatic transmission with overdrive, steel-belted, radial-ply, Eagle GT blackwall P215/65R15 tires, 15 in. aluminum wheels, leather-wrapped sport steering wheel, gray, red or beige cloth 45/45 seats, rear seat head rests, operating console with leather shift handle, quartz analog gauge cluster, brushed gray instrument panel and door trim, specific front carpet savers with embroidered TR Type logo, dual-outlet exhaust, special tail lamp treatment and Gran Touring suspension. Available in five exterior colors. T Package: Includes Gran Touring suspension, 2.97:1 transaxle ratio, 15 in. aluminum wheels, steel-belted, radial-ply P215/675R15, blackwall Eagle GT tires, "T" ornamentation, leather-wrapped sport steering wheel.

1987 Buick Riviera two-door coupe.

Riviera: Electric rear window defogger, California assembly line emission equipment and testing, engine block heater, heavy-duty engine and transmission cooling, reversible anti-slip front carpet savers with insert, reversible anti-slip rear carpet savers with inserts, trunk compartment mat, automatic electric door locks, electric trunk pull-down, automatic Twilight Sentinel headlamp control, theft-deterrent system with starter interrupt, day/night rearview mirror, black electric outside, rearview mirrors, heated left, lighted passenger visor vanity mirror, lighted driver visor vanity mirror, rear seat reading lights, illuminated driver door lock and interior light control, door-edge guards, color-coordinated protective body-side molding, designers' accent paint (not available on Riviera T-Type), ETR AM-FM stereo with seek and scan and clock, ETR AM-FM stereo with seek and scan, cassette tape, auto reverse and clock, graphic equalizer, cassette tape, ETR AM stereo-FM stereo with seek and scan with search/repeat and clock, Delco Bose music system with ETR AM-FM stereo Dolby seek and scan, cassette tape with auto reverse, search/repeat and clock, Concert Sound speaker system, black power antenna base, Astroroof, electric sliding, electric driver seatback recliner, electric passenger seatback recliner, six-way power passenger seat, front license plate mountng, trailer towing harness, cellular telephone accommodation package (tri-band power antenna, wiring harness and hand-held storage), leather-wrapped sport steering wheel and shift handle, 14 in. aluminum wheels, custom locking wire wheel covers, low windshield washer fluid indicator. Tires: steel-belted, radial-ply, P205/75R14, whitewall. *Special Option Packages:* Riviera T-Type coupe: Includes 3.8 liter V-6 SFI engine, automatic transmission with overdrive, 2.97:1 performance transaxle ratio, Gran Touring suspension, amber park and turn signal lenses, 15 in. aluminum wheels, steel-belted, radial-ply P215/60R15 Eagle GT blackwall tires, fast-ratio power steering, "T"-Type ornamentation, silver lower body-side molding, black rocker panel molding, reversible leather/sheepskin power control seats in red or gray, leather-wrapped shift handle, specific paint in five colors with silver lower accent treatment. T Package: Included "T" ornamentation, leather-wrapped sport steering wheel and shift handle, 2.97:1 performance transaxle ratio, Gran Touring suspension, 15 in. aluminum wheels, steel-belted, radial-ply P215/60R15 Eagle GT blackwall tires, fast-ratio power steering.

HISTORY: Buick's Somerset and Skylark models ranked 11th among compact cars in model year output with a combined total of 80,206 units. The Century ranked fourth in the intermediate class with a volume of 184,178. The LeSabre also held fourth place in the standard size class with a production of 154,331 cars. Riviera production totalled 15,223 cars.

1988 BUICK

Buick's 1988 lineup for 1988 was highlighted by the all-new Regal coupe, the introduction of the Reatta at mid-year, two new engines and improvements in virtually all its models. Special attention was given to improvements in ride, handling, durability and easier maintenance and service. Changes also took place in equipment levels in all lines. New suspension packages provided improved road performance. Numerous interior features that were either new or improved were introduced. Buick General Manager Edward H. Mertz noted that "Buick is covering the market with distinctive products, high quality workmanship, backed by what we are convinced is the finest group of dealers in the industry."

1988 Buick Skyhawk coupe.

SKYHAWK—SERIES 4J—FOUR—A new S/E coupe was added to the Skyhawk line. Among the features of the S/E were: a gauge package with tachometer, carpeted front and rear floor mats, leather-wrapped sport steering wheel, concealed headlights, blacked-out exterior trim and Gran Touring suspension. A new paint, beechwood brown, was added to the Skyhawk's color list, making a total of six exterior colors.

1988 Buick Skylark Custom coupe.

SKYLARK—SERIES 4N—FOUR/V-6—The latest Skylark coupes had a composite headlamp front-end treatment, along with new exterior colors and new interior fabrics. The most noticeable interior change was a new standard analog gauge cluster, which included a trip odometer. The Limited coupe had a new combination of woven and knit fabrics, and a new door trim design. The base 2.5 liter engine was given many improvements for 1988. They included the addition of a balance shaft and lighter pistons. The 2.3-liter Quad 4 was a new Skylark option.

CENTURY—SERIES 4Q—FOUR/V-6—The Century line continued to offer coupe, sedan and station wagon models. There were six new exterior colors for 1988, along with new interior colors, fabrics and other improvements. Custom models had a new seat and door design in a new knit fabric. The Limited coupe also had a new door design. All Century models had a new steering wheel. A new storage armrest was standard on Limited models, and optional for the Custom. A number of items were added to the Century's standard equipment. They included an AM/FM radio with seek and scan, rear extended range speakers, tinted glass, remote-controlled driver's mirror and whitewall tires. The base 2.5 liter engine had numerous refinements. The optional 2.8 liter V-6 was improved through more precise manufacturing methods.

1988 Buick Regal Limited with Exterior Appearance and Gran Touring packages.

1988 Buick Regal Gran Sport.

REGAL—SERIES 4W—V-6—The all-new Regal featured front-wheel drive and the most aerodynamic design of any Buick in history. Its aerodynamics were 33 percent improved over the previous model's. The advance was made possible by the use of flush glass and "door-into-roof" construction. The Regal's front appearance, with vertical ribs in the grille, maintained a family resemblance with the old Regal. High priority considerations in the Regal's design were performance, ride and handling. A "lubed for life" suspension was featured. All inside body metal was galvanized on both sides, and a base coat process with Plastisol was used. A stainless exhaust system was also installed. The Regal's powertrain included the 2.8-liter MFI V-6 with computer-controlled coil ignition and a self-tensioning single accessory belt. Power assisted four-wheel disc brakes were standard, as well as power rack and pinion steering. The Regal was the first General Motors car to be influenced by what Buick called the "Mona Lisa" process. This involved the identification by engineers of the best features on the best cars in the world and a systematic process to decide which ones should be incorporated into the Regal.

1988 Buick LeSabre four-door sedan.

LESABRE—SERIES 4H—V-6—The LeSabre lineup for 1988 was carried over from 1987. All models were available in new exterior colors and numerous interior refinements. The T Type was offered in four colors: black, white, red and silver. It was fitted with a rear deck spoiler. A new seat design and door trim was found on the base coupe. The Limited coupe had a new seat design in a combination woven velour and knit cloth. Also standard were new rear seat lap and shoulder belts. A new, optional leather in red, gray or tan was available for the Limited coupe. The new 3.8 liter 3800 V-6 was standard for the T Type and optional for all other LeSabre models. It had a redesigned cylinder block with a balanced shaft chain driven by the crankshaft. A revised standard suspension eliminated the need for heavy-duty suspension components.

276

1988 Buick LeSabre Estate Wagon.

ESTATE WAGON—SERIES 4B—V-8—The full-size rear-wheel drive LeSabre and Electra station wagons were offered in six new exterior colors. The door design in both versions was revised to include a new armrest with the power seat controls located in a pod. A new standard steering wheel was shared by both wagons and two new interior colors, blue and saddle, were offered. New standard features included an upscale AM/FM stereo radio with dual front and rear speakers, manual reclining passenger seats, a six-way power driver's seat in the Electra, low windshield washer fluid and low fuel indicators, trip odometer, front seat reading lamps, and a third seat.

1988 Buick Electra Park Avenue four-door sedan.

ELECTRA—SERIES 4C—V-6—The 1988 Electra was available in Limited, Park Avenue and T Type form. Five new exterior colors were introduced. Interior color choices now included rosewood and taupe. A new front seat storage armrest was available for the Limited and Park Avenue. The appearance of the T Type was refined by the use of chrome door frames, belt and wheel opening moldings, rear lamp bezels and license plate frame. The T Type could be ordered in an exclusive ruby red finish. The T Type package also included interior consoles, leather-wrapped steering wheel and anti-lock brakes.

1988 Buick Riviera T-Type coupe.

RIVIERA—SERIES 4E—V-6—The silver anniversary Riviera had a special hood ornament and instrument panel trim plate. Other appearance changes included a front-end design with composite headlamps. Three new exterior colors were introduced along with a landau top option available in 10 colors. A new optional chrome accent stripe was also introduced. The power seat controls were changed from rocker switches to a paddle type. The Electronic Control Center featured a new 70-degree deflection CRT screen with improved visibility. Other improvements included a personal reminder feature allowing the driver to enter specific calendar events, which would later appear at a selected date. Two new functions were added to the ECC as optional items. They were an electronic compass and the integration of a cellular telephone directory into the system. Other changes for 1988 involved improved serviceability, a theft-deterrent door lock mechanism and identification on major body panels.

REATTA—SERIES 4E—V-6—The Reatta, Buick's luxury two-passenger car, was introduced in January 1988. It combined a sporty appearance, aerodynamic styling, a .34 drag coefficient, and a traditional Buick ride. The Reatta was intended to carve out a market niche that involved a combination of luxury car and sports car elements at a price well below that of cars at the upper end of both markets. Initially offered as a coupe, the Reatta had front-wheel drive, the V-6 3800 engine, independent suspension and fast ratio power steering. A long list of features was standard for the Reatta. A partial listing includes air conditioning, fog lamps, stereo radio with cassette player, power leather bucket seats, power windows and door locks, stainless steel exhaust and ECC. The only options were a power-operated sunroof and a 16-way power seat.

I.D. DATA: The 1988 Buick vehicle identification number (V.I.N.) contained 17 characters. The first was the producing country; "1"—United States. The second character was "G"—General Motors. The third was "4" for the Buick division. The fourth character identified the car line: "A"—Century, "B"—LeSabre and Electra Estate wagon, "C"—Electra, "D"—incomplete LeSabre wagon, "E"—Riviera and Reatta, "H"—LeSabre, "J"—Skyhawk, "N"—Skylark, "W"—Regal. The fifth character designated the series: "B"—Regal Custom/incomplete wagon, "C"—Skylark Custom/Reatta, "D"—Skylark Limited/Regal Limited, "F"—Electra T-Type, "H"—Century Custom, "J"—Skylark Custom, "L"—Century Limited/Estate wagon, "M"—Skylark Limited, "P"—LeSabre/LeSabre Custom, "R"—LeSabre Limited/Estate wagon, "S"—Skyhawk, "U"—Electra Ultra, "V"—Electra Estate Wagon, "W"—Electra Park Avenue, "Z"—Riviera. The sixth digit represented the body style code as follows: "1"—two-door coupe, "5"—four-door sedan, "8"—four-door station wagon, "9"—four-door station wagon (incomplete). The seventh character identified the restraint system: "1"—manual belts, "4"—automatic belts, "0"—incomplete vehicle. The eighth character represented the engine code: "1"—2.0 liter L4-121, "U"—2.5 liter Tech IV L4-151, "D"—2.3 liter DOHC Quad L4-140, "N"—3.3 liter 3300 V-6-204, "R"—2.5 liter Tech IV-L4-151 (98 hp), "WE"—2.8 liter V-6-173, "C"—3.8 liter 3800 V-6-231, "Y"-5.0 liter V-8-307. The ninth unit is a check digit that verifies the accuracy of the VIN. The next letter, "J," represents the 1988 model year. The 10th entry identifies the assembly plant: "A"—Lakewood, Ga., "B"—Lansing, Mich., "G"—Framingham, Mass., "H"—Flint, Mich., "J"—Janesville, Wis., "M"—Lansing, Mich., "T"—Tarrytown, N.Y., "U"—Hamtramck, Mich., "I"—Wentzville, Mo., "1"—Oshawa, Ontario, Canada, "6"—Oklahoma City, Okla. The characters from 12-17 are the sequence production number.

Model Number	Body Style Number	Body Type & Seating	Factory Price	Shipping Weight	Production Total
Skyhawk (Four)					
S27	JS1	2-dr. Cpe.—5P	$8884	2336	13156
S69	JS5	4-dr. Sed.—5P	$8884	2336	14271
S35	JS8	4-dr. Sta. Wag.—5P	$9797	2474	1707
Skyhawk S/E (Four)					
S27	JS1	2-dr. Cpe.—5P	$9979	-----	
					29134*
*—All models					
Skylark Custom (Four/V-6)*					
J27	NJ1	2-dr. Cpe.—5P	$10684	2522	19590
C69	NC5	4-dr. Sed.—5P	$10399	2568	24940
Skylark Limited (Four/V-6)					
M27	NM1	2-dr. Cpe.—5P	$11791	2543	4946
D69	ND5	4-dr. Sed.—5P	$11721	2589	5316
					54792[a]
a—includes all Skylark models					
*Add $660 for V-6 engines.					
Century Custom (Four/V-6)					
H37	AH1	2-dr. Cpe.—6P	$11643/12253	2691/2760	1322
H69	AH5	4-dr. Sed.—6P	$11793/12403	2762/2831	62214
H35	AH8	4-dr. Sta. Wag.—6P	$12345/12955	2911/2980	5312
Century Limited(Four/V-6)					
L69	AL5	4-dr. Sed.—6P	$12613/13223	2769/2838	39137
L37	AL1	2-dr. Cpe.—6P	$12410/13020	2698/2767	1127
Century Estate Station Wagon (Four/V-6)					
L35	AL8	4-dr. Sta. Wag.—6P	$13077/13687	2915/2984*	4146
*Total Century production—113,258.					
Regal Custom (V-6)					
B57	WB1	2-dr. Cpe.—6P	$12449	2953	64773
Regal Limited (V-6)					
D57	WD1	2-dr. Cpe.—6P	$12782	2972*	65224
*Total Regal production—10,635.					
LeSabre (V-6)					
P37	HP1	2-dr. Cpe.—6P	$14560	3192	8829
LeSabre Custom (V-6)					
P69	HP5	4-dr. Sed.—6P	$14405	3239	67213
LeSabre Limited (V-6)					
R37	HR1	2-dr. Cpe.—6P	$16350	3242	2474
R69	HP5	4-dr. Sed.—6P	$15745	3291	57524
LeSabre Estate Station Wagon (V-8)					
R35	BR8	4-dr. Sta Wag—6P	$16040	4156*	3723
*Total LeSabre production—1136,044—Fwd; 9659—rwd.					
Electra Limited (V-6)					
X69	CX5	4-dr. Sed.—6P	$17479	3288	5191
Electra T Type (V-6)					
F69	CF5	4-dr. Sed.—6P	$19464	3326	1869
Electra Park Avenue (V-6)					
W69	CW5	4-dr. Sed.—6P	$20229	3329	84853
Electra Estate Station Wagon					
V35	BV8	4-dr. Sta Wag.	$18954	4217*	5901
*Total Electra production—91,913.					
Riviera (V-6)					
Z57	EZ1	2-dr. Cpe.—6P	$21615[a]	3364	8625
a—Add $1765 for T Type option.					
Reatta (V-6)					
C97	EC1	2-dr. Cpe.—2P	$25000	3500	4708

ENGINE DATA: BASE FOUR (Skyhawk) inline, overhead valve, four-cylinder, cast iron block and aluminum head. Displacement: 121 cu. in (2.0 liters). Bore & Stroke: 3.39 in. x 3.39 in. Compression ratio: 8.8:1. Brake horsepower: 96 @ 4800 rpm. Torque: 118 lb.-ft. @ 3600 rpm. Five main bearings. Hydraulic valve lifters. Throttle-body electronic fuel injection. BASE FOUR (Skylark) inline, overhead valve, four-cylinder, cast iron block and head. Displacement: 151 cu. in. (2.5 liters). Bore & Stroke: 4.00 in. x 3.00 in. Compression ratio: 9.0:1. Brake horsepower: 135 @ 5200 rpm. Torque: 135 lb.-ft. @ 3200 rpm. Five main bearings. Hydraulic lifters. Electronic fuel injection. BASE FOUR (Century) inline, overhead valve, four-cylinder, cast alloy iron block and head. Displacement: 151 cu. in. (2.5 liters) Bore & Stroke: 4.00 in. x 3.00 in. Compression ratio: 9.0:1. Brake horsepower: 98 @ 4800 rpm. Torque: 135 lb.-ft. @ 3200 rpm. Five main bearings. Hydraulic lifters. Throttle-body electric fuel injection. BASE V-6 (Regal) 60-degree overhead value V-6. Cast iron block and aluminum heads. Displacement: 173 cu. in. (3.8 liters). Bore & Stroke: 3.50 in. x 2.99 in. Compression ratio: 8.9:1. Brake horsepower: 130 @ 4500 rpm. Torque: 160 lb.-ft. @ 3600 rpm. Hydraulic lifters. Multi-port fuel injection. BASE V-6 (LeSabre) 90-degree overhead valve V-6 with balance shaft. Cast iron alloy block and head. Displacement: 231 cu. in. (3.8 liters). Bore & Stroke: 3.80 in. x 3.40 in. Compression ratio: 8.5:1. Brake horsepower: 150 @ 4400 rpm. Torque: 200 lb.-ft. @ 2000 rpm. Four main bearings. Hydraulic lifters. Sequential fuel injection. BASE V-8 (LeSabre Estate Station Wagon) 90-degree overhead valve V-8. Cast iron block and head. Displacement: 307 cu. in. (5.0 liters). Bore & Stroke: 3.8 in. x 3.39 in. Compression ratio: 8.0:1. Brake horsepower: 140 @ 3200 rpm. Torque: 255 lb.-ft. @ 2000 rpm. Five main bearings. Hydraulic lifters. 4-bbl. carb. BASE V-6 (Electra) 90-degree overhead valve V-6 with balance shaft. Cast iron alloy block and head. Displacement: 231 cu. in. (3.8 liters). Bore & Stroke: 3.80 in. x 3.40 in. Compression ratio: 8.5:1. Brake horsepower: 165 @ 5200 rpm. Torque: 210 lb.-ft. @ 2000 rpm. Four main bearings. Hydraulic lifters. Sequential fuel injection. BASE V-8 (Electra Estate Station Wagon) 90-degree overhead valve V-8. Cast iron block and head. Displacement: 307 cu. in. (5.0 liters). Bore & Stroke: 3.8 in. x 3.39 in. Compression ratio: 8.0:1. Brake horsepower: 140 @ 3200 rpm. Torque: 255 lb.-ft. @ 2000 rpm. Five main bearings. Hydraulic lifters. 4-bbl. carb. BASE V-6 (Riviera) 90-degree overhead valve V-6. Cast iron alloy block and head. Displacement: 231 cu. in. (3.8 liters). Bore & Stroke: 3.80 in. x 3.40 in. Compression ratio: 8.5:1. Brake horsepower: 165 @ 5200 rpm. Torque: 210 lb.-ft. @ 2000 rpm. Four main bearings. Hydraulic lifters. Sequential fuel injection. Base V-6 (Reatta) 90-degree overhead valve V-6. Cast iron alloy block and head. Displacement: 231 cu. in. (3.8 liters). Bore & Stroke: 3.80 in. x 3.40 in. Compression ratio: 8.5:1. Brake horsepower: 165 @ 4800 rpm. Torque: 210 lb.-ft. @ 2000 rpm. Four main bearings. Hydraulic lifters. Sequential fuel injection. OPTIONAL (Skyhawk) None. OPTIONAL (Skylark) inline, DOHC, overhead valve, four-cylinder cast alloy iron block, cast aluminum head. Displacement 138 cu. in. (2.3 liters). Bore & Stroke: 3.62 in. x 3.346 in. Compression ratio: 9.5:1. Brake horsepower: 150 @ 5200 rpm. Torque: 160 @ 4000 rpm. Hydraulic valve lifters. Multi port fuel injection. OPTIONAL (Skylark) 90-degree V-6. Cast iron block and cylinder heads. Displacement: 204 cu. in. (3.3 liters). Bore & Stroke: 3.73 in. x 3.16 in. Compression ratio: 9.0:1. Brake horsepower: 160 @ 5200 rpm. Torque: 185 @ 2000 rpm. Main bearings. Hydraulic valve lifters. Multi port fuel injection. OPTIONAL (Century, Century Estate Wagon) 60-degree V-6. Cast iron block and cylinder head. Displacement: 204 cu. in. (3.3 liters) Bore & Stroke: 3.70 in. x 3.16 in. Compression ratio: 9.00:1. Brake horsepower: 160 @ 5200 rpm. Torque: 185 lb.-ft. @ 2000 rpm. Four main bearings. Hydraulic lifters. Multi-port fuel injection. 90-degree overhead valve V-6, Cast iron block and head. OPTIONAL (Regal): None. (LeSabre): None. OPTIONAL (Electra): None. OPTIONAL: (Reatta): None.

CHASSIS DATA: Wheelbase: (all models in succession), (Skyhawk) 101.2 in.; (Skylark): 103.4 in.; (Century): 104.8 in.; (Regal): 107.5 in.; (LeSabre): 110.8 in.; (LeSabre Estate Wagon): 115.9 in.; (Electra): 110.8 in.; (Riviera): 108.0 in.; (Reatta): 98.5 in. **Overall Length:** (all models in succession) (Skyhawk): Coupe: 179.3 in.; sedan and station wagon: 181.7 in.; (Skylark): 180.1 in.; (Century): 189.1 in.; (Century Custom/Estate station wagon): 190.9 in.; (Regal): 192.2 in.; (LeSabre): 196.5 in.; (LeSabre Estate station wagon): 220.5 in.; (Electra): 197.0 in.; (Electra Estate station wagon): 220.5 in.; (Riviera): 198.3 in. (Reatta): 183.7 in. **Height:** (all models in succession) (Skyhawk): coupe and sedan: 54.0 in.; station wagon: 54.4 in.; (Skylark): 52.1 in.; (Century): coupe: 53.7 in.; sedan and Century Custom/Estate station wagon: 54.2 in.; (Regal): 53.0 in.; (LeSabre coupe): 54.7 in.; (LeSabre sedan): 55.4 inc.; (LeSabre Estate station wagon): 59.3 in.; (Electra): 54.3 in.; (Riviera): 53.6 in.; (Reatta) 51.2 in. **Width:** (all models in succession) (Skyhawk): coupe: 65.0 in.; (Skylark): 66.6 in.; (Century): 69.4 in.; (Century Custom/Estate station wagon): 69.4 in., (Regal): 72.5 in.; (LeSabre Sedan/Coupe): 72.4 in.; (LeSabre Estate station wagon): 79.3 in.; (Electra): 72.4 in.; (Riviera): 71.7 in.; (Reatta): 73.0 in. **Front Tread:** (all models in succession) (Skyhawk): coupe and sedan: 55.6, station wagon: 55.4 in.; (Skylark): 55.6 in.; (Century): 58.7 in.; (Century Custom/Estate station wagon): 58.7 in.; (Regal): 59.3 in.; (LeSabre coupe/sedan): 60.3 in.; (LeSabre Estate station wagon): 62.2 in.; (Electra): 60.3 in.; (Riviera): 59.9 in.; (Reatta): 60.3 in. **Rear Tread:** (all models in succession) (Skyhawk): 55.2 in.; (Skylark): 55.2 in.; (Century): 56.7 in.; (Century Custom/Estate station wagon): 56.7 in.; (Regal): 58.0 in.; (LeSabre coupe/sedan): 59.8 in.; (LeSabre Estate station wagon): 64.0 in.; (Electra): 59.8 in.; (Riviera): 59.9 in.; (Reatta): 60.3 in. **Standard Tires:** (all models in succession) (Skyhawk): P175/80R13; (Skylark): P185/80R13; (Century): P185/75R14; (Century Custom/Estate station wagon): P185/75R14; (Regal): P205/75R14; (LeSabre coupe/sedan): P205/75R14; (LeSabre Estate station wagon): P225/75R15; (Electra): P20575/R14, (blackwall on Limited, whitewall on Park Avenue), Electra T-Type: P215/64R15; Park Avenue Ultra: P205/70R15 whitewall; (Riviera): P205/75R15; (Reatta): P215/65R15 blackwall.

1988 Buick LeSabre T-Type coupe.

TECHNICAL: Transmission: (Skyhawk) Five-speed manual; (Skylark): Three-speed automatic; (Century): Three-speed automatic; (Century Custom/Estate station wagon): Three-speed automatic; (Regal): four-speed automatic with overdrive; (LeSabre coupe/sedan): Four-speed overdrive automatic; (LeSabre Estate station wagon): Four-speed overdrive automatic; (Electra): Four-seed automatic with overdrive; (Riviera): Four-speed overdrive automatic; (Reatta): MXO four-speed automatic. **Steering:** (Skyhawk): Power rack and pinion; (Skylark): Power rack and pinion; (Century): Power rack and pinion; (Century Custom/Estate station wagon): Power rack and pinion; (LeSabre Estate station wagon): Power recirculating ball; (Electra): Power rack and pinion; (Riviera): Power rack and pinion. (Reatta): Fast-Ratio power. **Front Suspension:** (Skyhawk, Skylark, Century, Century Custom/Estate station wagon, LeSabre coupe/sedan, Electra, Electra T-type, Riviera): MacPherson struts with coil springs, lower control arms and stabilizer bar; (Regal): MacPherson strut with lower control arms and unitized coil springs; (LeSabre Estate station wagon): Coil springs, unequal

length control arms, stabilizer bar; (Reatta): Fully independent with MacPherson struts and roll bar. **Rear Suspension:** (Skyhawk): Semi-independent with beam axle, trailing arms, coil springs, stabilizer bar available; (Skylark): Trailing crank bar, coil springs and stabilizer bar; (Century): Beam twist axle with integral stabilizer bar, trailing arms, Panhard arm and coil springs; (LeSabre coupe/sedan): MacPherson struts, coil springs, stabilizer bar; (LeSabre Estate station wagon): Solid axle with four links, coil springs; (Electra, Electra T-type): Independent MacPherson struts, inboard coil springs, stabilizer bar; (Riviera): Independent tri-link, transverse fiberglass leaf spring, stabilizer bar; (Reatta): Independent modular assembly with single traverse leaf springs. **Brakes:** (Skyhawk, Skylark, Century, Century Custom/Estate station wagon, Regal, LeSabre coupe/sedan, LeSabre Estate station wagon, Electra, Electra T-type): Power front discs, rear drum; (Riviera): Power disc front and rear; (Reatta): Power disc front and rear. **Body Construction:** (Skyhawk, Skylark): Unibody, (Century/Century station wagons): Integral body/frame; (Regal): Integral body/frame with bolted-on power-train cradle; (LeSabre): Unitized body/frame integral with isolated engine cradle; (Electra and LeSabre Estate station wagons): Welded body with full perimeter frame; (Electra): unitized body/frame construction with isolated engine cradle; (Riviera): Unitized body with isolated front frame and rear sub-frame; (Reatta): Unitized body with isolated front and rear sub-frames. **Fuel Tank:** (Skyhawk): 13.6 gal.; (Skylark): 13.6 gal.; (Century): 15.7 gal.; (Century Custom/Estate station wagon): 16.6 gal.; (Regal): 16.5 gal.; (LeSabre coupe/sedan): 18.0 gal.; (LeSabre and Electra Estate station wagon): 22.0 gal.; (Electra and Electra T-type): 18.0 gal.; (Riviera): 18.2 gal.; (Reatta): 18.2 gal. **DRIVETRAIN OPTIONS: Engines:** (Skyhawk): None; (Skylark): 2.3 liter Quad-4, MFI, $660; 3.3 liter V-6, MFI, $710; (Century, Century Custom/Estate station wagon): 3.3 liter V-6, MFI, $710; (Regal): None; (LeSabre coupe/sedan and LeSabre Estate station wagon, Electra, Electra T-type and Riviera): None. **Transmission/Differential:** (Skyhawk): Three-speed automatic, $440; (Skylark): None; (Century, Century Custom/Estate station wagon): Automatic transmission with overdrive, with 3.3 liter engine only, $200; (Regal): None; (LeSabre coupe/sedan): None; (LeSabre and Electra Estate station wagon): None; (Electra and Electra T-type): None; (Riviera): None; (Reatta): None. **Optional rear axle ratios: Suspension, steering and brakes:** (Skylark): Gran Touring Package (14 in. aluminum wheels, P215/60R14 Eagle GT+4 blackwall tires, Gran Touring suspension, leather wrapped steering wheel): $603; engine block heater: $18; (Century): Heavy-duty engine and transmission cooling: $70 (without air conditioning); $40 with A/C; heavy duty suspension (required with 3.3 liter engine): $27; Gran Touring Package, not available for station wagons (aluminum wheels, P15/60R Eagle GT tires, leather-wrapped steering wheel and Gran Touring suspension): $515; (Regal): Gran Touring Package consisting of Gran Touring suspension, 16 in. aluminum wheels, P215/60R16 tires and leather-wrapped steering wheel; anti-lock brake system: $925; (LeSabre coupe and sedan); 2.97:1 axle (included in Y56-Gran Touring Package and WE2-T-Type; required with V-8-heavy-duty engine and transmission cooling): No additional charge; heavy-duty engine and transmission cooling (included in WE2 and Y56): $40; Gran Touring Package consisting of Gran Touring Suspension, 15 in. aluminum wheels, P215/65R15 blackwall tires, 2.97:1 axle ratio, heavy-duty cooling and leather-wrapped steering wheel; (LeSabre/Electra Estate Wagon): Trailer Towing Package consisting of 3.23:1 axle ratio, V-8-heavy-duty engine and transmission cooling, automatic level control: $215; Limited slip differential: $100; (Electra): heavy-duty battery, required with electronic air conditioning: $26; heavy-duty engine and transmission cooling (standard with T-type), included in Y56-Gran Touring Package: $40; 2.97:1 axle ratio (requires V-8, included in Y56-Gran Touring Package and T-type: No additional charge); Electronic anti-lock brake system: $925 (standard on T-type and Ultra); Gran Touring Suspension (standard on T-type, not available for Ultra or with fully padded vinyl top), consists of Gran Touring Suspension, 15 in. styled aluminum wheels, P215/65R15 Eagle GT blackwall tires, 2.97:1 axle ratio, heavy-duty cooling and leather wrapped steering wheel; (Riviera): Gran Touring Package consisting of Gran Touring Suspension, 2.97:1 axle ratio, 15 in. aluminum wheels, leather-wrapped sport steering wheel and shift handle, fast ratio power steering and P215/65R15 steel belted radial ply Eagle GT+4 tires: $104.

SERIES NAME CONVENIENCE/APPEARANCE OPTIONS: Prices following option identification represent the cost of that option when purchased separately.

Skyhawk: automatic transmission, $440; tilt steering column, $125; two-speed windshield wipers with low speed delay, $55; electronic cruise control, $185; AM/FM ETR stereo radio with cassette tape, seek and scan, auto reverse and clock, $122; four-way manual driver seat adjuster, front console mounted arm rest, electric rear window defogger, $150; electric door locks, $1162 (coupe), $1212 (sedan), $1262 (station wagon), air conditioner, $695; emission equipment and testing, $100.

Skyhawk S/E Package consist of front and rear carpet savers, Gran Touring Package (Gran Touring suspension, P215/60R14 Eagle GT+4 blackwall tires, 14 in. Shelby aluminum wheels, leather-wrapped steering wheel), instrument gauges and tachometer, exterior trim package (blackout moldings, concealed headlamps and fog lamps), $1095. Various Popular, Premium and Luxury Packages—$1157-1412. **Skylark:** Air conditioning, $695; tilt steering column, $125; P185/80R13 whitewall tires, $68; mirrors-remote control, left, right manual, $53; electric rear window defogger, $150; protective wide body side molding, $80; wheel opening molding, $30; plus electronic cruise control with resume, $185; two-speed windshield wipers with resume feature, $55; front and rear carpet savers, $45; AM/FM ETR stereo radio with cassette tape, seek and scan, auto reverse with search and repeat and clock, $152; custom locking wheel covers, $215; four-way manual driver seat adjuster, $35; power windows, $220-coupe; $295-sedan; electric door locks, $155-coupe, $295-sedan; six-way power driver seat adjuster, $250; power antenna, $70; passenger side lighted visor vanity mirror, $38; electric trunk lock release, $50; front and rear courtesy lights, $14; chrome deck lid luggage rack (not available with S/E package and exterior sport package), $115; lower body accent paint, $195; body side stripes, $145; Custom and Limited cloth bucket seats with full length operating console $180; styled 13 in. aluminum wheels, $245; styled hubcaps and trim rings, $38; custom locking wire wheel covers, $215. Special packages: Gran Touring Package, $603. Includes 14 in. aluminum wheels, P215/60R14 Eagle GT blackwall tires, Gran Touring suspension, leather wrapped steering wheel. Exterior Sport Package, $374-Custom coupe; $318-Limited coupe. Includes blackout moldings, front air dam, aero rocker moldings, wide body side moldings.

1988 Buick Century four-door sedan.

Century: Air conditioning, $795; tilt steering column, $150; electric rear window defogger, $150; electronic cruise control with resume, $185; two-speed windshield wipers with resume feature, $55; front carpet savers, $25; rear carpet savers, $20; AM/FM ETR stereo radio with cassette seek and scan, auto reverse and clock, $122; custom locking wire wheel covers, $215; styled steel wheels, $115; aluminum wheels, $270; body stripes, $45; six-way power driver seat adjuster, $70; power windows, $220-coupe; $295-sedan; electric door locks, $155-coupe; $295-sedan; six-way power driver seat adjuster, $250; power antenna, $70; passenger side lighted visor vanity mirror, $50; electric trunk lock release, $50; door edge guards, $15-coupe; $25-sedan; passenger manual seat back recliner, $45; driver manual seat back recliner, $45; dual electric remote control mirrors, $70; automatic power antenna, $70; Custom only: 55/45 cloth seat with armrest, $183; Limited cloth 55/45 seat with storage armrest, $233-$416. Century Limited only: Front seat reading lights, $24. Century Estate wagon only: Vinyl third seat, $215; air deflector, $47; vinyl applique wood grain trim, $350; rear window windshield wiper, $125. Special Packages. Gran Touring Package. Includes aluminum wheels and P215/60R14 Eagle GT tires, leather wrapped steering wheel and Gran Touring suspension, $515.

1988 Buick Regal Custom.

Regal: Electric rear window defogger, $150; electronic cruise control with resume, $185; two-speed windshield wipers with resume feature, $55; front carpet savers, $25; rear carpet savers, $20; AM/FM ETR stereo radio with cassette tape, seek and scan, auto reverse and clock, $122; graphic equalizer cassette tape with auto reverse, and search/repeat and AM stereo, $150-$272; compact disc player with ETR AM/FM radio with seek/scan and clock, $274; electric glass sunroof (includes dual reading lamps and rear courtesy lamps, $650-$680; custom locking wire wheel covers, $215; styled aluminum wheels, $270; styled steel wheels, $115; 15 in. aluminum wheels with P205/70 blackwall tires, $320; six-way power driver seat adjuster, $250; power windows with express down feature, $230; electric door locks, $155; six-way power driver seat adjuster, $250; automatic power antenna, $70; passenger side lighted visor vanity mirror, $50; electric trunk lock release, $50; door edge guards, $15; dual electric remote control mirrors, $91; automatic power antenna, $70; concert sound speakers, $85; redundant accessory controls-steering wheel mounted, $125; remote keyless entry (Limited and Gran Sport only), $125; electronic digital/graphic instrumentation, $299; luggage rack, $115; wide black with red striping body molding, $55-$70; lower accent paint, $205; body side stripes, $45; cloth 55/45 seat with storage armrest (Custom only), $183; cloth reclining buckets with console (Custom only), $185; leather/vinyl 55/45 with recliners (Limited only), $450.

1988 Buick LeSabre coupe.

LeSabre: Electric rear window defogger, $150; electronic cruise control with resume, $185; two-speed windshield wipers with low speed delay feature, $55; black protective body side molding, $60; front carpet savers, $25; rear carpet savers, $20; 55/45 split front seat with storage armrest, $183; rear bumper guards and body side molding extensions, $24; AM/FM ETR stereo radio with cassette tape, seek and scan, auto reverse and clock, $132; graphic equalizer cassette tape with auto reverse, and search/repeat and AM/FM stereo and Concert Sound speaker system, $367; Concert Sound speaker system, $85; locking wire wheel covers, $215; styled aluminum wheels, $270; styled steel wheels, $115; six-way power driver seat adjuster, $250; electric passenger seat back recliner, $70; deluxe trunk trim, $53; electronic touch climate control air conditioner, $165; power windows, coupe-$220; sedan-$295; electric door locks, coupe-$155; sedan-$205; six-way power drive seat adjuster, $250; six-way passenger seat adjuster, $250; front and rear courtesy and warning lights, $44; automatic power antenna, $70; passenger side lighted visor vanity mirror, $50; electric trunk lock release, $50; door edge guards, coupe-$15; sedan-$25; dual electric remote control mirrors, $91; automatic power antenna, $70; Concert Sound speakers, $85; chrome luggage rack, $115; wide rocker panel molding package, $110. Instru-

mentation — tachometer, temperature, oil and volt gauges, $110; body side stripes, $45; cloth 55/45 seat with storage armrest (Custom only), $183; leather vinyl 55/45 with recliners (Limited only), $450. Special Estate Wagon options - Roof rack, $115; air deflector, $40; remote control electric tailgate lock, $60; tungsten halogen headlamps, $25; Twilight Sentinal headlamp control, $60; illuminated driver door lock and interior light control, $75; cornering lights, $60; front lights monitor, $37. Special Packages - Gran Touring Package. Includes Gran Touring suspension, 15 in. aluminum wheels, P215/65R15 Eagle GT+4 blackwall tires, 2.97:1 axle ratio, heavy duty cooling, leather wrapped steering wheel, $563. T-Type Package. Includes Gran Touring package (with different wheels) plus specific interior and exterior trim, cruise, gauges, 55/45 front seats and operating console, AM/FM stereo radio with cassette and graphic equalizer, rear deck spoiler and front air dam, dual exhaust outlets, blackout trim, $1958.

1988 Buick Electra T-Type four-door sedan.

Electra: Electric rear window defogger, $150; P205/75R14 whitewall tires, $76; electronic cruise control with resume, $185; two-speed windshield wipers with low speed delay feature, $55; black protective body side molding, $60; front carpet savers, $25; rear carpet savers, $20; 55/45 split front seat with storage armrest, $183; rear bumper guards and body side molding extensions, $24; AM/FM ETR stereo radio with cassette tape, seek and scan, auto reverse and clock, $132; graphic equalizer cassette tape with auto reverse, and search/repeat and AM/FM stereo and Concert Sound speaker system, $367; Concert Sound speaker system, $85; locking wire wheel covers, $215; styled aluminum wheels, $270; styled steel wheels, $115; electric passenger seat back recliner, $70; deluxe trunk trim, $53; electronic touch climate control air conditioner, $165; power windows, coupe-$220; sedan-$295; electric door locks, $205; six-way power driver seat adjuster[$250; six-way passenger seat adjuster, $250; front and rear courtesy and warning lights, $44; automatic power antenna $70; passenger side lighted visor vanity mirror, $50; Twilight Sentinel headlamp control, $60; four note horn, $28; low windshield washer fluid indicator, $16; cornering lights, $60; front and rear light monitor, $77; low fuel indicator, $16; electric trunk pull-down, $80; automatic day/night mirror, $80; dual electric remote control mirrors with heated left, $35; two-position memory driver belt adjuster, $150; deluxe trunk trim with mat, $68; rear reading lamps, $50; quartz analog gauge cluster $26; electronic instrumentation, $299; electric trunk lock release, $50; door edge guards, $25; dual electric remote control mirrors, $91; automatic power antenna, $70; remote keyless entry system, $175; Concert sound speakers, $70; chrome luggage rack, $115; firemist paint, $210; Bose music system, $553-$905; body side stripes, $45; leather/vinyl 55/45 (Park Avenue), $450; (T Type), $395; full heavily padded top, $260-$695; electric sliding Astroroof (not available with padded roof), $1230; 14 in. styled aluminum wheels, $235-$270.

Special Packages: Gran Touring Package. Includes Gran Touring Suspension, 15 in. styled aluminum wheels, P215/65R15 eagle GT blackwall tires, 2.97:1 axle ratio, heavy-duty cooling, leather wrapped steering wheel, $462-563.

1988 Buick Riviera coupe.

Riviera: Graphic equalizer cassette tape with auto reverse, and search/repeat and ETR AM/FM stereo and digital clock, $120; Delco Bose music system with cassette, ETR AM/FM stereo with Dolby, seek and scan, auto reverse with search/repeat, and clock, $583-$703; six-way power passenger seat with power recliner, $325; electric trunk pull-down, $250; remote keyless entry system with automatic power door locks, $265; Twilight headlamp control, $60; theft deterrent system, $159; left and right remote mirrors with heated left, $35; automatic rearview mirror, $80; electric compass, $75; firemist paint, $210; lower accent paint, $190; electric Astroroof sliding

roof, $1230; heavily padded roof, $695; leather and suede bucket seats, $550; 16-way adjustable driver leather and suede bucket seats, $1230; styled aluminum wheels, $55; cellular telephone, $1975.

Special Packages: Gran Touring Package. Includes Gran Touring Package, 2.97:1 axle ratio, 15 in. aluminum wheels, leather wrapped steering wheel and shift handle, fast ratio power steering and P215/65R15 blackwall Eagle GT+4 tires, $104.

Riviera Appearance Package: Includes platinum beige firemist lower accent paint, body side stripe and painted aluminum wheels, $205.

Reatta: Sliding electric steel sunroof, $895; articulated driver's seat.

HISTORY: Buick produced 484,764 vehicles in the 1988 calendar year. Its 1988 model year output was 458,768m a drop of 189,921 cars. Buick's Skylark and Skyhawk models ranked 14th and 15th in output of compact cars. The Riviera was listed last in production among 30 intermediates built in the United State. The front-wheel-drive LeSabre held fifth position among domestic standard-size cars. The Reatta outproduced Cadillac's Allante by a margin of 2139 vehicles.

1989 BUICK

Buick celebrated its 86th anniversary by offering automobiles that it regarded as a combination of "exhilirating driving luxury without ostentation." As part of General Motors' overall strategy to regain lost market share, the Buick was depicted as the "premium American motorcar." A key aspect of this philosophy was to join the best of Buick's heritage with plenty of contemporary design features and advanced technology. As a result, the 1989 Buick's Dynaride suspension was engineered to provide crisp handling without a loss of riding comfort.

Similarly, the Reatta, promoted as the "premium American two-seater," was seen as a car that fused the fun of owning a two-seater sports car with the luxury surroundings typical of a Buick. The new-styled Riviera was, in Buick's view, "a classic all over again." For those Riviera owners who had been unhappy with the truncated look of the previous model, the latest Riviera was enthusiastically received. "You recognize it immediately," said Buick. "It could only be the Riviera."

Perhaps the most graphic example of Buick's resurgence came in the form of the LeSabre's ranking as the highest-placed domestic vehicle in the J.D. Powers and Associates Initial Quality Survey. As a result, LeSabre sales more than doubled.

1989 Buick Skyhawk SE coupe.

SKYHAWK—SERIES 4J—FOUR—The Buick Skyhawk had a number of new standard features for 1989 including the 2.0-liter EFI L-4 engine, an upgraded acoustical insulation package and a rear-seat lap/shoulder belt system. The door and window frames on the station wagon were now body color. A new all-leather sport steering wheel was available on the SE model.

1989 Buick Skylark Limited sedan.

SKYLARK—SERIES 4N—FOUR/V-6—Numerous features, both standard and optional, were introduced on the 1989 Skylarks. The LE sedan was available in a Formal Appearance Luxury Edition with the following features: a formal vinyl roof with a reduced size rear window and rear side windows, tri-shield emblems on the rear deck and rear side door panel, wire wheel covers, bright ''B'' pillar applique, wide rocker panel moldings, wide lower body-side moldings, black windshield trim, wheel opening molding and grille header applique. The 3.0 liter V-6 of 1988 was replaced by the 3.8 liter 3300 V-6 engine. As in 1988 the coupes were fitted with composite headlights. These were now also installed on the sedans. A revised tail lamp design was adopted. The lower body facia was changed from black to body color. A new stand-up hood ornament with a tri-shield design was installed on all models. New standard equipment consisted of a rear-seat lap/shoulder belt system, split bench reclining seat with storage tray, champagne burl woodgrain trim plates, extended-range speakers and foot-operated parking brake. The Convenience Group Package consisting of front-seat armrest, seat recliner, trunk trim, passenger vanity mirror and remote fuel filler door release was also standard on all Skylarks. A new sew trim pattern was found in Custom and Limited models. New or revised options included restyled 13 in. aluminum wheels, an all-leather sport steering wheel and bucket seats of a new design. The Skylark package was offered for both the coupe and sedan models.

1989 Buick LeSabre Custom coupe.

LESABRE—SERIES 4H—V-6—The appearance of the LeSabre models was virtually unchanged for 1989. The most apparent visual alteration was due to the elimination of the standard vinyl top previously installed on the LeSabre Limited coupe. Revisions applicable to all LeSabres consisted of a new outside rearview mirror control, a modified horn pad and the inclusion of a tilt steering column, trip odometer and a leather-wrapped sport steering wheel as standard LeSabre equipment. A replaceable-mast power antenna was now available as was a modified Concert Sound speaker system. The quartz analog gauge cluster was revised to read 10-100 mph. A new champagne burl woodgran trim was standard on both Custom and Limited models. A front-seat storage armrest was standard on Limited models and optional for the Custom LeSabre when fitted with 55/45 seats. The LeSabre T Type continued to be available. Although retailed as a separate model, it remained technically a special option package.

ESTATE WAGON—SERIES 4B—V-8—The LeSabre and Electra station wagons were, except for some very minor refinements and revisions, carryover models from 1988. Both versions now had standard rear-seat lap/shoulder belt systems and a front license plate mounting. A trailer-towing package was now available, and the Electra model could be ordered with leather interior trim. The previously offered gray cloth interior for the Electra was cancelled for 1989.

1989 Buick Century Custom sedan.

CENTURY—SERIES 4Q—FOUR/V-6—The 1989 Century models had an all-new front and rear appearance highlighted by composite headlights and wraparound park and turn signal lamps. Both coupe and sedan models had standard black wide body side moldings and dual, black, outside rearview mirrors (left remote, right manual). Additional new or revised standard equipment included a stand-up tri-shield hood ornament, rear-seat lap/shoulder belt system, analog gauge cluster graphics, champagne burl woodgrain trimplates and a new horn pad design. The Limited sedan had the UJ5 instrument panel gauge option as standard equipment. The Limited coupe model was cancelled. If 55/45 seats were ordered, a front seat storage armrest was installed. New 14 in. aluminum wheels were available.

1989 Buick Park Avenue Ultra four-door sedan.

ELECTRA—SERIES 4C—V-6—Beyond any doubt, the most significant development in the 1989 Electra lineup was the introduction of the Park Avenue Ultra sedan. This automobile was depicted as ''the ultimate in Buick luxury'' and was specifically targeted toward upscale sales prospects. Buick advised its sales personnel that ''the Ultra appeals to many current Park Avenue owners who are ready for an upgrade.'' It was, continued Buick, ''a most substantial motorcar, offering more of what makes a Buick a Buick.'' Sales strategy for the Ultras also viewed it as an automobile that enabled Buick to compete in what it described as the ''premium luxury sedan market,'' which it said was occupied by individuals ''accustomed to paying $28,000 to $30,000 for high-content luxury sedans.'' Its ''distinctive styling,'' said Buick, plus a ''powerful performance and premium ride are Buick Motor Division's signature characteristics carried to their highest expression.'' Included in its standard features were all-leather seating and trim, a 20-way power seat, anti-lock brake system, specific dark elm burl woodgrain trim, specific grille texture and tail lamp array, a choice of six two-tone color treatments, smoked tail lamps, specific 15 in. aluminum wheels and chrome side pillars. The Ultra was also identified by its sterling silver lower accent paint treatment and silver accent body stripe.

The 1989 Electra/Park Avenue models were distinguished from the 1988 versions by their stand-up hood ornament (except for the T Type), new outside rearview mirror control, automatic front safety belt system, analog gauge cluster modified to read from 10-100 mph, flash-to-pass signal, a new seat design for the Park Avenue and, except for the T Type, a front-seat storage armrest. New optional equipment consisted of a replaceable-mast antenna, full vinyl top for the Park Avenue Ultra, a blue leather interior for the Park Avenue, and a remote radio Keyless Entry System. A leather-wrapped sport steering wheel for the T Type and Gran Touring Package (Y56) was also offered.

1989 Buick Regal Custom coupe.

REGAL—SERIES 4W—V-6—The front-wheel drive Regal was refined both in terms of appearance and equipment for 1989. Joining the Custom and Limited model was a new Gran Sport version. The Gran Sport was marketed as a separate model but technically it was option Z13 consisting of blackout molding for the windshield, reveal moldings, grille, and antenna; a front air dam, black tail lamp bezels, black front and rear bumpers, wide lower body side molding with red stripe, full areo rocker panels, fog lamps, 16 in. aluminum wheels, bucket seats with operating controls and the Y56 Gran Touring package. Standard equipment on all models now included air conditioning, a stand-up tri-shield hood ornament, rear seat lap/shoulder belt system, flash-to-pass signal, ETR AM-FM stereo radio and a tilt steering column. The Custom Regal now had standard driver and passenger seat back recliners as well as extendable sunvisors. Both the Custom and Limited models were available with 15 in. aluminum wheels. A wide, ribbed body side molding was standard on the Limited model. The instrument panel HVAC outlets were now chrome. New 16 in. wheels were included in the Y56, Gran Touring Package. An ''express down'' feature was added on the driver's power window option. Anti-lock brakes were now available as was a new electric sunroof and a ETR AM-FM stereo radio with a compact disc player. All Regals could be ordered with a steering wheel that included radio controls.

1989 Buick Riviera two-door coupe.

RIVIERA—SERIES 4E—V-6—The Riviera's appearance was significantly altered for 1989 to bring it more closely in line with the format established by previous models. A new roofline with a wider C or sail panel, plus handsomely contoured tail lamps, were major contributors to the Riviera's return to the basics that had made the pre-1986 models sales successes. Also playing an important role in this Riviera Renaissance was the longer length of the 1989 model. The wheelbase remained at 108 inches but 11 inches were added to the Riviera's rear overhang. Additional changes for 1989 involved the following standard items: body side moldings, larger 15 in. wheels and tires, revised front end and rocker panel molding styling, two-piece body color outside mirrors, chrome windshield and backlight moldings, coach lamps and body color door-edge guards, wire wheelcovers, black rub strips, domed wheel-opening moldings, leather-wrapped sport steering wheel and shift handle, vinyl trim for the door and instrument panel, dark elm burl woodgrain trim plates and flash-to-pass signal. A heavy-duty engine and transmission system was also standard as was a new engine mount system with hydraulics. A new diamond white exterior color was offered. Features added to the Riviera's option list consisted of the remote keyless entry system with automatic door locks, a new-design landau roof and an electrochromic automatic day/night mirror. The T type model and the 16-way optional cloth bucket seats were cancelled for 1989. The trunk and fuel access buttons were moved to the glove box.

1989 Buick Reatta.

REATTA—SERIES 4E—V-6—A number of small changes were found in the 1989 Reatta. Like those on the Riviera, the Reatta's trunk and fuel access buttons were now located in the glove box. Similarly, the 1989 Reatta had a new hydraulic engine mount system. Additional new features included hood and steering wheel ornamentation, all-leather interior trim and a standard remote keyless entry system. An electric sunroof was now optional.

I.D. DATA: The 1988 Buick vehicle identification number (V.I.N.) contained 17 characters. The first was the producing country; "1"—United States. The second character was "G"—General Motors. The third was "4" for the Buick Division. The fourth character identified the car line: "A"—Century, "B"—LeSabre and Electra Estate wagon, "C"—Electra, "D"—incomplete LeSabre wagon, "E"—Riviera and Reatta, "H"—LeSabre, "J"—Skyhawk, "N"—Skylark, "W"—Regal. The fifth character designated the series: "B"—Regal Custom/incomplete wagon, "C"—Skylark Custom/Reatta, "D"—Skylark Limited/Regal Limited, "F"—Electra T-Type, "H"—Century Custom, "J"—Skylark Custom, "L"—Century Limited/Estate wagon, "M"—Skylark Limited, "P"—LeSabre/LeSabre Custom, "R"—LeSabre Limited/Estate wagon, "S"—Skyhawk, "U"—Electra Ultra, "V"—Electra Estate Wagon, "W"—Electra Park Avenue, "Z"—Riviera. The sixth digit represented the body style code as follows: "1"—two-door coupe, "5"—four-door sedan, "8"—four-door station wagon, "9"—four-door station wagon (incomplete). The seventh character identified the restraint system: "1"—manual belts, "4"—automatic belts, "0"—incomplete vehicle. The eighth character represented the engine code: "1"—2.0 liter L4-121, "U"—2.5 liter Tech IV L4-151, "D"—2.3 liter DOHC Quad L4-140, "N"—3.3 liter 3300 V-6-204, "R"—2.5 liter Tech IV-L4-151 (98 hp), "WE"—2.8 liter V-6-173, "C"—3.8 liter 3800 V-6-231, "Y"-5.0 liter V-8-307. The ninth unit is a check digit that verifies the accuracy of the VIN. The next letter, "K," represents the 1989 model year. The 10th entry identifies the assembly plant: "A"—Lakewood, Ga., "B"—Lansing, Mich., "G"—Framingham, Mass., "H"—Flint, Mich., "J"—Janesville, Wis., "M"—Lansing, Mich., "T"—Tarrytown, N.Y., "U"—Hamtramck, Mich., "I"—Wentzville, Mo., "1"—Oshawa, Ontario, Canada, "6"—Oklahoma City, Okla. The characters from 12-17 are the sequence production number.

Model Number	Body Style Number	Body Type & Seating	Factory Price	Shipping Weight	Production Total
Skyhawk Custom (Four)					
S27	JS1	2-dr. Cpe.-5P	$9285	2420	7837
S69	JS5	4-dr. Sed.-5P	$9285	2469	13841
S35	JS8	4-dr. Sta. Wag.-5P	$10230	2551	1688
Skyhawk Limited (Four)					
T27	JT1	2-dr. Cpe.-5P	$9445	2345	
T69	JT5	4-dr. Sed.-5P	$9503	2423	
T35	JT8	4-dr. Sta. Wag.-5P	$9841	2498	
					20658*
*—All models					
Skylark Custom (Four/V-6)*					
J27	NJ1	2-dr. Cpe.-5P	$11115	2583	12714
C69	NC5	4-dr. Sed.-5P	$11115	2640	42636
Skylark Limited (Four/V-6)					
M27	NM1	2-dr. Cpe.-5P	$12345	2600	1416
D69	ND5	4-dr. Sed.-5P	$12345	2657	4774
Add $660 for 2.4 liter Quad 4 and $710 for 3.3 liter V-6 engines.					
Century Custom (Four/V-6)					
H37	AH1	2-dr. Cpe.-6P	$12199/12909	2725/2835	6953
H69	AH5	4-dr. Sed.-6P	$12429/12909	2769/2879	89281
H35	AH8	4-dr. Sta. Wag.-6P	$13156/13866	2905/3012	5479
Century Limited (Four/V-6)					
L69	AL5	4-dr. Sed.-6P	$13356/14066	2785/2895	49839
Century Estate Station Wagon (Four/V-6)					
L35	AL8	4-dr. Sta. Wag.-6P	$13956/14666	2924/3031	3940
Regal Custom (V-6)					
B57	WB1	2-dr. Cpe.-6P	$14614	3144	41554
Regal Limited (V-6)					
D57	WB1	2-dr.Cpe.-6P	$15139	3163	47203*
*This includes 14,503 Gran sports.					
LeSabre (V-6)					
P37	HP1	2-dr. Cpe.-6P	$15425	3227	1830
LeSabre Custom (V-6)					
P69	HP5	4-dr. Sed.-6P	$15330	3267	78738
LeSabre Limited (V-6)					
R37	HR1	2-dr. Cpe.-6P	$16630	3262	2287
R69	HP5	4-dr. Sed.-6P	$16730	3299	61328
LeSabre Estate Station Wagon (V-8)					
R35	BR8	4-dr. Sta. Wag.-6P	$16770	4209	2971
Electra Limited (V-6)					
X69	CX5	4-dr. Sed.-6P	$18525	3289	5814
Electra T Type (V-6)					
F69	CF5	4-dr. Sed.-6P	$21325	3384	1151
Electra Park Avenue (V-6)					
W69	CW5	4-dr. Sed.-6P	$20460	3329	71786
Electra Park Avenue Ultra (V-6)					
U69	CU5	4-dr. Sed.-6P	$26218	3426	4815
Electra Estate Station Wagon					
V35	BV8	4-dr. Sta. Wag.	$19860	4273	4560
Riviera (V-6)					
Z57	EZ1	2-dr. Cpe.-6P	$22540	3436	21189
Reatta (V-6)					
C97	EC1	2-dr. Cpe.-2P	$26700	3394	7,009

ENGINE DATA: BASE FOUR (Skyhawk): Inline, overhead valve, four-cylinder, cast iron block and aluminum head. Displacement: 121 cu. in. (2.0 liters). Bore & stroke: 3.50 in. x 3.15 in. Compression ratio: 9.0:1. Brake horsepower: 90 @ 5600 rpm. Torque: 108 lb.-ft. @ 3200 rpm. Five main bearings. Hydraulic valve lifters. Throttle-body electronic fuel injection. BASE FOUR (Skylark): Inline, overhead valve, four-cylinder, cast iron block and head. Displacement: 151 cu. in. (2.5 liters). Bore & stroke: 4.00 in. x 3.00 in. Compression ratio: 9.0:1. Brake horsepower: 110 @ 5200 rpm. Torque: 135 lb.-ft. @ 3200 rpm. Five main bearings. Hydraulic lifters. Throttle-body fuel injection. BASE FOUR (Century): Inline, overhead valve, four-cylinder, cast alloy iron block and head. Displacement: 151 cu. in. (2.5 liters). Bore & stroke: 4.00 in. x 3.00 in. Compression ratio: 9.0:1. Brake horsepower: 98 @ 4800 rpm. Torque: 135 lb.-ft. @ 3200 rpm. Five main bearings. Hydraulic lifters. Throttle-body electric fuel injection. BASE V-6 (Regal): 60-degree overhead valve V-6. Cast iron block and aluminum heads. Displacement: 173 cu. in. (3.8 liters). Bore & stroke: 3.50 in. x 2.99 in. Compression ratio: 8.9:1. Brake horsepower: 130 @ 4500 rpm. Torque: 170 lb.-ft. @ 3600 rpm. Hydraulic lifters. Multi-port fuel injection. BASE V-6 (LeSabre): 90-degree overhead valve V-6 with balance shaft Cast iron alloy block and head. Displacement: 231 cu. in. (3.8 liters). Bore & stroke: 3.80 in. x 3.40 in. Compression ratio: 8.5:1. Brake horsepower: 165 @ 4800 rpm. Torque: 210 lb.-ft. @ 2000 rpm. Four main bearings. Hydraulic lifters. Sequential fuel injection. BASE V-8 (LeSabre Estate station wagon): 90-degree overhead valve V-8. Cast iron block and head. Displacement: 307 cu. in. (5.0 liters). Bore & stroke: 3.8 in. x 3.39 in. Compression ratio: 8.0:1. Brake horsepower: 140 @ 3200 rpm. Torque: 255 lb.-ft. @ 2000 rpm. Five main bearings. Hydraulic lifters. 4-bbl. carb. BASE V-6 (Electra): 90-degree overhead valve V-6 with balance shaft. Cast iron alloy block and head. Displacement: 231 cu. in. (3.8 liters). Bore & stroke: 3.80 in. x 3.40 in. Compression ratio: 8.5:1. Brake horsepower: 165 @ 4800 rpm. Torque: 210 lb.-ft. @ 2000 rpm. Four main bearings. Hydraulic lifters. Sequential fuel injection. BASE V-8 (Electra Estate station wagon): 90-degree overhead valve V-8. Cast iron block and head. Displacement: 307 cu. in. (5.0 liters). Bore & stroke: 3.8 in. x 3.39 in. Compression ratio: 8.0:1. Brake horsepower: 140 @ 3200 rpm. Torque: 255 lb.-ft. @ 2000 rpm. Five main bearings. Hydraulic lifters. 4-bbl. carb. BASE V-6 (Riviera): 90-degree overhead valve V-6. Cast iron alloy block and head. Displacement: 231 cu. in. (3.8 liters). Bore & stroke: 3.80 in. x 3.40 in. Compression ratio: 8.5:1. Brake horsepower: 165 @ 4800 rpm. Torque: 210 lb.-ft. @ 2000 rpm. Four main bearings. Hydraulic lifters. Sequential fuel injection. BASE V-6 (Reatta): 90-degree overhead valve V-6. Cast iron alloy block and head. Displacement: 231 cu. in. (3.8 liters). Bore & stroke: 3.80 in. x 3.40 in. Compression ratio: 8.5:1. Brake horsepower: 165 @ 4800 rpm. Torque: 210 lb.-ft. @ 2000 rpm. Four main bearings. Hydraulic lifters. Sequential fuel injection. OPTIONAL (Skyhawk): None. OPTIONAL (Skylark): Inline, DOHC, overhead valve, four-cylinder. Cast alloy iron block, cast aluminum head. Displacement: 138 cu. in. (2.3 liters). Bore & stroke: 3.62 in. x 3.346 in. Compression ratio: 9.5:1. Brake horsepower: 150 @ 5200 rpm. Torque: 160 @ 4000 rpm. Hydraulic valve lifters. Multi-port fuel injection. OPTIONAL (Skylark): 90-degree V-6, cast iron block and cylinder heads. Displacement: 204 cu. in. (3.3 liters). Bore & stroke: 3.73 in. x 3.16 in. Compression ratio: 9.0:1. Brake horsepower: 160 @ 5200 rpm. Torque: 185 @ 2000 rpm. Main bearings. Hydraulic valve lifters. Multi-port fuel injection. OPTIONAL (Century, Century Estate wagon): 60-degree V-6. Cast iron block and cylinder head. Displacement: 204 cu. in. (3.3 liters). Bore & stroke: 3.70 in. x 3.16 in. Compression ratio: 9.00:1. Brake horsepower: 160 @ 5200 rpm. Torque: 185 lb.-ft. @ 2000 rpm. Four main bearings. Hydraulic lifters. Multi-port fuel injection. 90-degree overhead valve V-6. Cast iron block and head. OPTIONAL (Regal): None. OPTIONAL (LeSabre): None. OPTIONAL (Electra): None. OPTIONAL (Reatta): None.

CHASSIS DATA: Wheelbase: (Skyhawk) 101.2 in.; (Skylark) 103.4 in.; (Century) 104.8 in.; (Regal) 107.5 in.; (LeSabre) 110.8 in.; (LeSabre Estate Wagon) 115.9 in.; (Electra) 110.8 in.; (Riviera) 108.0 in. **Overall Length:** (Skyhawk) coupe: 179.3 in., sedan and station wagon: 181.7 in.; (Skylark) 180.1 in.; (Century) 189.1 in.; (Century Custom/Estate station wagon) 190.9 in.; (Regal) 192.2 in.; (LeSabre) 196.5 in.; (LeSabre Estate station wagon) 220.5 in.; (Electra) 197.0 in.; (Electra Estate station wagon) 220.5 in.; (Riviera) 198.3 in. **Height:** (Skyhawk) coupe and sedan: 54.0 in., station wagon: 54.4 in.; (Skylark) 52.1 in.; (Century) coupe: 53.7 in., sedan and Century Custom/Estate station wagon: 54.2 in.; (Regal) 53.0 in.; (LeSabre coupe) 54.7 in.; (LeSabre sedan) 55.4 in.; (LeSabre Estate station wagon) 59.3 in.; (Electra) 54.3 in.; (Riviera) 53.6 in. **Width:** (Skyhawk) coupe: 65.0 in.; (Skylark): 66.6 in.; (Century): 69.4 in.; (Century Custom/Estate station wagon) 69.4 in.; (Regal) 72.5 in.; (LeSabre sedan/coupe) 72.4 in.; (LeSabre Estate station wagon) 79.3 in.; (Electra) 72.4 in.; (Riviera) 71.7 in. **Front Tread:** (Skyhawk) coupe and sedan: 55.6, station wagon: 55.4 in.; (Skylark) 55.6 in.; (Century) 58.7 in.; (Century) 58.7 in.; (Century Custom/Estate station wagon) 58.7 in.; (Regal) 59.3 in.; (LeSabre coupe/sedan) 60.3 in.; (LeSabre Estate station wagon) 62.2 in.; (Electra) 60.3 in.; (Riviera) 59.9 in. **Rear Tread:** (Skyhawk) 55.2 in.; (Skylark) 55.2 in.; (Century) 56.7 in.; (Century Custom/Estate station wagon) 56.7 in.; (Regal) 58.0 in.; (LeSabre coupe/sedan) 59.8 in.; (LeSabre Estate station wagon) 64.0 in.; (Electra) 59.8 in.; (Riviera) 59.9 in. **Standard Tires:** (Skyhawk) P175/80R13; (Skylark) P185/80R13; (Century) P185/75R14; (Century Custom/Estate station wagon) P185/75R14; (Regal) P205/75R14; (LeSabre coupe/sedan) P205/75R14; (LeSabre Estate station wagon) P225/75R15; (Electra) P20575/R14 (blackwall on Limited, whitewall on Park Avenue); (Electra T-Type) P215/65R15; (Park Avenue Ultra) P205/70R15 whitewall; (Riviera) P205/75R15.

TECHNICAL: Transmission: (Skyhawk) Five-speed manual; (Skylark) Three-speed automatic; (Century) Three-speed automatic; (Century Custom/Estate station wagon) Three-speed automatic; (Regal) Four-speed automatic with overdrive; (LeSabre coupe/sedan) Four-speed automatic overdrive; (LeSabre Estate station wagon) Four-speed overdrive automatic; (Electra) Four-speed automatic with overdrive; (Riviera) Four-speed overdrive automatic. **Steering:** (Skyhawk) Power rack and pinion; (Skylark) Power rack and pinion; (Century) Power rack and pinion; (Century Custom/Estate station wagon) Power rack and pinion; (Regal) Power rack and pinion; (LeSabre coupe/sedan) Power rack and pinion; (LeSabre Estate station wagon) Power recircu-

lating ball; (Electra) Power rack and pinion; (Riviera) Power rack and pinion. **Front suspension:** (Skyhawk, Skylark, Century, Century Custom/Estate station wagon, LeSabre coupe/sedan, Electra, Electra T-Type, Riviera) MacPherson struts with coil springs, lower control arms and stabilizer bar; (Regal) MacPherson strut with lower control arms and unitized coil springs; (LeSabre Estate station wagon) Coil springs, unequal length control arms, stabilizer bar. **Rear suspension:** (Skyhawk) Semi-independent with beam axle, trailing arms, coil springs, stabilizer bar available; (Skylark) Trailing crank bar, coil springs and stabilizer bar; (Century) Beam twist axle with integral stabilizer bar, trailing arms, Panhard arm and coil srpings; (LeSabre coupe/sedan) MacPherson struts, coil springs, stabilizer bar; (LeSabre Estate station wagon) Solid axle with four links, coil springs; (Electra, Electra T-Type) Independent MacPherson struts, inboard coil springs, stabilizer bar; (Riviera) Independent tri-link, transverse fiberglass leaf spring, stabilizer bar; (Reatta) Independent modular assembly with single traverse leaf springs. **Brakes:** (Skyhawk, Skylark, Somerset, Century, Century Custom/Estate station wagon, Regal, LeSabre coupe/sedan, LeSabre Estate station wagon, Electra, Electra T-Type) Power front discs, rear drum; (Riviera) Power disc front and rear; (Reatta) Power disc front and rear. **Body construction:** (Skyhawk, Skylark) Unibody; (Century/Century station wagon) Integral body/frame; (Regal) Integral body/frame with bolted-on powertrain cradle; (LeSabre) Unitized body/frame integral with isolated engine cradle; (Electra and LeSabre Estate station wagons) Welded body with full perimeter frame; (Electra) Unitized body/frame construction with isolated engine cradle; (Riviera) Unitized body with isolated front frame and rear sub-frame; (Reatta) Unitized body with isolated front and rear sub-frames. **Fuel tank:** (Skyhawk) 13.6 gal.; (Skylark) 13.6 gal.; (Somerset) 13.6 gal.; (Century) 15.7 gal.; (Century Custom/Estate station wagon) 16.6 gal.; (Regal) 16.5 gal.; (LeSabre coupe/sedan) 18.0 gal.; (LeSabre and Electra Estate station wagon) 22.0 gal.; (Electra and Electra T-Type) 18.0 gal.; (Riviera) 18.2 gal.; (Reatta) 18.2 gal.

DRIVETRAIN OPTIONS: Engines: (Skyhawk) None; (Skylark) 2.3 liter Quad-4, MFI, $660; 3.3 liter V-6, MFI, $710; (Century, Century Custom/Estate station wagon) 3.3 liter V-6, MFI, $710; (Regal) None; (LeSabre coupe/sedan and LeSabre Estate station wagon, Electra, Electra T-Type and Riviera) None. **Transmission/Differential:** (Skyhawk) Three-speed automatic, $440; (Skylark) None; (Century, Century Custom/Estate station wagon) Automatic transmission with overdrive, with 3.3 liter engine only, $200; (Regal) None; (LeSabre coupe/sedan) None; (LeSabre and Electra Estate station wagon) None; (Electra and Electra T-Type) None; (Riviera) None; (Reatta) None. **Optional rear axle ratios: Suspension, steering and brakes:** (Skylark) Gran Touring Package (14 in. aluminum wheels, P215/60R14 Eagle GT4 blackwall tires, Gran Touring suspension, leather wrapped steering wheel) $603; engine block heater, $18; (Century) Heavy-duty engine and transmission cooling: $70 (without air conditioning); $40 with air conditioning; heavy duty suspension (required with 3.3 liter engine): $27; Gran Touring Package, not available for station wagons (aluminum wheels, P15/60R Eagle GT tires, leather-wrapped steering wheel and Gran Touring suspension): $515; (Regal) Gran Touring Package consisting of Gran Touring suspension, 16 in. aluminum wheels, P215/60R16 tires and leather-wrapped steering wheel: $531-$607, depending on model; anti-lock brake system: $925; (LeSabre coupe and sedan) 2.91:1 axle (included in Y56—Gran Touring package and WE2—T-Type; required with V-8-heavy-duty engine and transmission cooling): No additional charge; heavy-duty engine and transmission cooling (included in WE2 and Y56): $40; Gran Touring Package consisting of Gran Touring suspension, 15 in. aluminum wheels, P215/65R15 blackwall tires, 2.97:1 axle ratio, heavy-duty cooling and leather-wrapped steering wheel; (LeSabre/Electra Estate wagon) trailer towing package consisting of 3.23:1 axle ratio, V-8-heavy-duty engine and transmission cooling, automatic level control: $215; Limited slip differential: $100; (Electra) heavy-duty battery, required with electronic air conditioning: $26; heavy-duty engine and transmission cooling (standard with T-Type, included in Y56—Gran Touring Package): $40; 2.97:1 axle ratio (requires V-8, included in Y56—Gran Touring Package and T-Type): No additional charge; Electronic anti-lock brake system: $925 (standard on T-Type and Ultra); Gran Touring Package (standard on T-Type, not available for Ultra or with fully padded vinyl top), consists of Gran Touring suspension, 15 in. styled aluminum wheels, P215/65R15 Eagle GT blackwall tires, 2.97:1 axle ratio, heavy-duty cooling and leather-wrapped steering wheel, $563 for Limited, $462 for Park Avenue; (Riviera) Gran Touring Package consisting of Gran Touring Suspension, 2.97:1 axle ratio, 15 in. aluminum wheels, leather-wrapped sport steering wheel and shift handle, fast ratio power steering and P215/65R15 steel belted radial ply Eagle GT+4 tires: $104.

SERIES NAME CONVENIENCE/APPEARANCE OPTIONS: Prices following option identification represent the cost of that option when purchased separately.

Skyhawk: Automatic transmission, $440; tilt steering column, $125; two-speed windshield wipers with low speed delay, $55; electronic cruise control, $185; AM/FM ETR stereo radio with cassette tape, seek and scan, auto reverse and clock, $122; four-way manual driver seat adjuster, front console-mounted armrest, electric rear window defogger, $150; electric door locks: $1162 (coupe), $1212 (sedan), $1262 (station wagon). Air conditioner, $695; emission equipment and testing, $100. Skyhawk S/E Package: consists of front and rear carpet savers, Gran Touring Package (Gran Touring suspension, P215/60R14 Eagle GT+4 blackwall tires, 14 in. Shelby aluminum wheels, leather-wrapped steering wheel; instrument gauges and tachometer, exterior trim package (blackout moldings, concealed headlamps and fog lamps): $1095. Various Popular, Premium and Luxury packages—$1157-$1412.

Skylark: Air conditioning, $695; tilt steering column, $125; P185/80R13 whitewall tires, $68; mirrors—remote control left, right manual, $53; electric rear window defogger, $150; protective wide body side molding, $80; wheel opening molding, $30; plus electronic cruise control with resume, $185; two-speed windshield wipers with resume feature, $55; front and rear carpet savers, $45; AM/FM ETR stereo radio with cassette tape, seek and scan, auto reverse with search and repeat and clock, $152; custom locking wheel covers, $215; four-way manual driver seat adjuster, $35; power windows, $220-coupe, $295-sedan; electric door locks, $155-coupe, $295-sedan; six-way power driver seat adjuster, $250; power antenna, $70; passenger side lighted visor vanity mirror, $38; electric trunk lock release, $50; front and rear courtesy lights, $14; chrome deck lid luggage rack (not available with S/E package and exterior sport package), $115; lower body accent paint, $195; body side stripes, $45; Custom and Limited cloth bucket seats with full length operating console, $180, styled 13 in. aluminum wheels, $245; styled hubcaps and trim rings, $38; custom locking wire wheel covers, $215. Special packages: Gran Touring Package, $603; includes 14 in. aluminum wheels, P215/60R14 Eagle GT blackwall tires, Gran Touring suspension, leather-wrapped steering wheel. Exterior Sport Package, $374-Custom coupe, $318-Limited coupe; includes blackout moldings, front air dam, aero rocker moldings, wide body side moldings. Skylark S/E Package, $1134. Available for Custom models only. Includes bucket seat and console, dual mirrors with left remote, body side moldings, rocker moldings, wheel opening moldings, cassette tape radio, and Gran Touring Package. Skylark L/E Formal Appearance Luxury Edition, $1050-$1495). Includes full formal vinyl roof, wire wheel covers, wide rocker molding, body side molding, wheel opening molding, dual mirrors with left remote, and lower accent paint. Various Popular, Premium, Luxury and Prestige packages. Tires (all-steel belted radial ply): P205/70R13 blackwall, $124; P205/70/R13 whitewall, $190.

Century: Air conditioning, $795; tilt steering column, $150; electric rear window defogger, $150; electronic cruise control with resume, $185; two-speed windshield wipers with resume feature, $55; front carpet savers, $25; rear carpet savers, $20; AM/FM ETR stereo radio with cassette tape, seek and scan, auto reverse and clock, $122; custom locking wire wheel covers, $215; styled steel wheels, $115; aluminum wheels, $270; body stripes, $45; six-way power driver seat adjuster, $70; power windows, $220-coupe, $295-sedan; electric door locks, $155-coupe, $295-sedan; six-way power driver seat adjuster, $250; power antenna, $70; passenger side lighted visor vanity mirror, $50; electric trunk lock release, $50; door edge guards, $15-coupe, $25-sedan; passenger manual seat back recliner, $45; dual electric remote control mirrors, $70; automatic power antenna, $70; (Custom only) 55/45 cloth seat with armrest, $183). Limited cloth 55/45 seat with storage armrest, $233-$416. (Century Limited only)

1989 Buick Century Estate Wagon.

Front seat reading lights, $24; premium rear speakers, $70). (Century Estate wagon only) Vinyl third seat, $215; air deflector, $37; vinyl applique wood grain trim, $350; rear window windshield wiper, $125. Special Packages: Gran Touring Package. Includes aluminum wheels and P215/60R14 Eagle GT tires, leather-wrapped steering wheel and Gran Touring suspension, $515).

1989 Buick Regal Limited coupe.

Regal: Electric rear window defogger, $150; electronic cruise control with resume, $185; two-speed windshield wipers with resume feature, $55; front carpet savers, $25; rear carpet savers, $20; AM/FM ETR stereo radio with cassette tape, seek and scan, auto reverse and clock, $122; graphic equalizer cassette tape with auto reverse, and search/repeat and AM stereo, $150-$272; compact disc player with ETR AM/FM radio with seek/scan and clock, $274; electric glass sunroof (includes dual reading lamps and rear courtesy lamps; $650-$680; custom locking wire wheel covers, $215; styled aluminum wheels, $270; styled steel wheels, $115; 15 in. aluminum wheel with P205/70 blackwall tires, $320; six-way power driver seat adjuster, $250; power windows with express down feature, $230; electric door locks, $155; six-way power driver seat adjuster, $250; automatic power antenna, $70; passenger side lighted visor vanity mirror, $50; electric trunk lock release, $50; door edge guards, $15; dual electric remote control mirrors, $91; automatic power antenna, $70; concert Sound speakers, $85; redundant accessory controls—steering wheel mounted, $125; remote keyless entry (Limited and Gran Sport only), $125; electronic digital/graphics instrumentation, $299; luggage rack, $115; wide black with red striping body molding, $55-$70; lower accent paint, $205; body side stripes, $45; cloth 55/45 seat with storage armrest (Custom only), $183; cloth reclining buckets with console (Custom only), $185; leather/vinyl 55/45 with recliners (Limited only), $450. Special Packages: Four Seater Package, includes front and rear bucket seats with special armrests and storgage console with cassette storage, leather-wrapped steering wheel, rear headrests, $409. Gran Sport, includes Gran Touring Package, bucket seats and console, specific exterior appearance with blackout, fog lamps, aero rocker panels, wide body side molding and front spoiler, $1212.

LeSabre: Electric rear window defogger, $150; electronic cruise control with resume, $185; two-speed windshield wipers with low speed delay feature, $55; black protective body side molding, $60; front carpet savers, $25; rear carpet savers, $20; 55/45 split front seat with storage armrest, $183; rear bumper guards and bodyside molding extensions, $24; AM/FM ETR stereo radio with cassette tape, seek and scan, auto reverse and clock, $132; graphic equalizer cassette tape with auto reverse, and search/repeat and AM/FM stereo and Concert Sound speaker system, $367; Concert Sound speaker system, $85; locking wire wheel covers, $215; styled aluminum wheels, $270; styled steel wheels, $115; six-way power driver seat adjuster, $250; electric passenger seat back recliner, $70; deluxe trunk trim, $53; electronic touch climate control air conditioner, $165; power windows, coupe-$220, sedan-$295; electric door locks, coupe-$155, sedan-$205; six-way power driver seat adjuster, $250; electric passenger seat back recliner, $70; deluxe trunk trim, $53; electronic touch climate control air conditioner, $165; power windows, coupe-$220, sedan-$295; electric door locks, coupe-$155, sedan-$205; six-way power driver seat adjuster, $250; six-way passenger seat adjuster, $250; front and rear courtesy and warning lights, $44; automatic power antenna, $70; passenger side lighted visor vanity mirror, $50; electric trunk lock release, $50; door edge guards, coupe-$15, sedan-$25; dual electric remote control mirrors, $91; automatic power antenna, $70; Concert Sound speakers, $85; chrome luggage rack, $115; wide rocker panel molding package, $110; instrumentaion—tachometer, temperature, oil and volt gauges, $110; body side stripes, $45; cloth 55/45 seat with storage armrest (Custom only), $183; leather/vinyl 55/45 with recliners (Limited only), $450. Special Estate wagon options—Roof rack, $115; air deflector, $40; remote control electric tailgate lock, $60; tungsten halogen headlamps, $25; twilight sentinel headlamp control, $60; illuminated driver door lock and interior light control, $75; cornering lights, $60; front lights monitor, $37. Special

Packages—Gran Touring Package, includes Gran Touring suspension, 15 in. aluminum wheels, P215/65R15 Eagle GT+4 blackwall tires, 2.97:1 axle ratio, heavy-duty cooling, leather-wrapped steering wheel, $563. T-Type Package, includes Gran Touring package (with different wheels) plus specific interior and exterior trim, cruise, gauges, 55/45 front seats and operating console, AM/FM stereo radio with cassette and graphic equalizer, rear deck spoiler and front air dam, dual exhaust outlets, blackout trim, $1927.

Electra: Electric rear window defogger, $150; P205/75R14 whitewall tires, $76; electronic cruise control with resume, $185; two-speed windshield wipers with low speed delay feature, $55; black protective body side molding, $60; front carpet savers, $25; rear carpet savers, $20; 55/45 split front seat with storage armrest, $183; rear bumper guards and body side molding extensions, $24; AM/FM ETR stereo radio with cassette tape, seek and scan, auto reverse and clock, $132; graphic equalizer cassette tape with auto reverse, and search/repeat and AM/FM stereo and Concert Sound speaker system, $367; Concert Sound speaker system, $85; locking wire wheel covers, $215; styled aluminum wheels, $270; styled steel wheels, $115; six-way power driver seat adjuster, $250; electric passenger seat back recliner, $70; deluxe trunk trim, $53; electronic touch climate control air conditioner, $165; power windows, coupe-$220, sedan-$295; electric door locks, $205; six-way power driver seat adjuster, $250; six-way passenger seat adjuster, $250; front and rear courtesy and warning lights, $44; automatic power antenna, $70; passenger side light visor vanity mirror, $50; Twilight Sentinel headlamp control, $60; four note horn, $28; low windshield washer fluid indicator, $16; cornering lights, $60; front and rear light monitor, $77; low fuel indicator, $16; electric trunk pull-down, $80; automatic day/night mirror, $80; dual electric remote control mirrors with heated left, $35; two-position memory driver belt adjuster, $150; deluxe trunk trim with mat, $68; rear reading lamps, $24; quartz analog gauge cluster, $126; electronic instrumentation, $299; electric trunk lock release, $50; door edge guards, $25; dual electric remote control mirrors, $91; automatic power antenna, $70; remote keyless entry system, $175; concert sound speakers, $70; chrome luggage rack, $115; firemist paint, $210; Bose music system, $553-$905; body side stripes, $45; leather/vinyl 55/45 (Park Avenue), $450; (T Type), $395; theft deterrent system, $159; full heavily padded top, $260-$895; electric sliding Astroroof (not available with padded roof), $1230; 14 in. styled aluminum wheels, $235-$270. Special Packages: Gran Touring Package, includes Gran Touring suspension, 15 in. styled aluminum wheels, P215/65R15 Eagle GT blackwall tires, 2.97:1 axle ratio, heavy-duty cooling, leather-wrapped steering wheel, $462-$563.

Riviera: Graphic equalizer cassette tape with auto reverse, and search/repeat and ETR AM/FM stereo and digital clock, $120; Delco Bose music system with cassette, ETR AM/FM stereo with Dolby, seek and scan, auto reverse with search/repeat, and clock, $583-$703; six-way power passenger seat with power recliner, $325; electric trunk pull-down, $250; remote keyless entry system with automatic power door locks, $265; Twilight Sentinel headlamp control, $60; theft deterrent system, $159; left and right remote mirrors with heated left, $35; automatic rearview mirrors, $80; electronic compass, $75; firemist paint, $210; lower accent paint, $190; electric Astroroof sliding roof, $1230; heavily padded roof, $695; leather and suede bucket seats, $550; 16-way adjustable driver leather and suede bucket seats, $1230; styled aluminum wheels, $55; cellular telephone, $1975. Special packages: Gran Touring Package, includes Gran Touring suspension, 2.97:1 axle ratio, 15 in. aluminum wheels, leather-wrapped steering wheel and shift handle, fast ratio power steering and P215/65R15 blackwall Eagle GT+4 tires, $104). Riviera Appearance Package, includes platinum beige firemist lower accent paint, body side stripe and painted aluminum wheels, $205.

Reatta: Sliding electric steel sunroof, $895; 16-way adjustable driver side leather bucket seats, $680.

HISTORY: Buick's general manager was Edward H. Mertz. Buick's total 1989 calendar sales totalled 542,917 vehicles. Buick's market share rose slightly to 5.5% from 5.49% in 1988. Its Century series ranked fourth among all intermediate-sized automobiles sold in the United States. The LeSabre was the third-best selling standard-sized automobile.

1990 BUICK

Buick's first models of the 1990s emphasized new features, new designs, new standard and optional equipment and new technology. Buick sales material highlighted the form of Buicks of the near future by featuring the Buick Essence and Lucerne show cars. Viewed from that perspective, the 1990 Buicks were perceived as automobiles that were, in Buick's words, "powerful and mature, substantial and distinctive."

After its extensive restyling in 1989, the Century received important new safety features for 1990. Numerous models, including the Electra and LeSabre, benefitted from structural and engineering revisions that improved their ride and handling. The new generation 3800 V-6 engine with tuned-port fuel injection was regarded as "the smoothest, most sophisticated production V-6 ever used in a Buick."

1990 Buick Skylark four-door sedan.

SKYLARK—SERIES 4N—FOUR/V-6—The Skylark model lineup was revised for 1990. The Skylark SE Package of 1989 became the Gran Sport model while the Formal Appearance Luxury Edition Package was now listed as a Skylark model. The Limited model designation of 1989 was discontinued. Coupe and sedan base models were added. Numerous styling/design changes were apparent for 1990. They included a new vertical grille, a new gunmetal gray exterior color, and a slate color interior trim. The Custom, Gran Sport and Luxury Edition Skylarks had a standard split folding rear seat as standard equipment. Among the new or revised interior features and appointments was a bright bead added to the power window switch trim plate and the relocation of the windshield wiper controls to the multi-function lever. A new instrument panel pod was introduced for 1990 that included an intergral radio and temperature controls. A new backlit cluster was also featured as was a new console with a storage bin and armrest. Both the shift and tilt levers were now chrome with black handles. Standard on the Custom coupe and sedan were 14 in. P185/7R14 tires and styled hubcaps with trim rings. The Skylark coupe and sedan had standard 13 in. P185/80R13 tires and deluxe wheel covers. The optional driver/passenger reading lamps were integral with the interior mirror. Fourteen in. Shelby aluminum wheels were included in the Gran Touring Package and also offered as a separate, "free-flow" option. A higher level of interior illumination was standard as was a new 2000 Series radio and a turn signal "on" chime.

CENTURY—SERIES 4Q—FOUR/V-6—After the extensive revisions of 1989, changes for the 1990 model year were relatively limited. Four new exterior colors were announced and a smaller jack was found in the coupe and sedan models. Buick also reported that the ride quality of the Century's Dynaride suspension was improved. Also enhanced was the acoustical insulation package. Interior alterations included a new dark red interior, a new automatic front safety belt system and new door trim. The armrests now had reflectors and a new door-mounted map pocket was installed. New power window and door lock switches were used, and optional power seat recliners replaced the manual recliners. Air conditioning was now standard equipment. Limited models had standard four-door courtesy lights. A new seat design was found in the Limited sedan. The steering column was revised for improved theft deterrence. The Estate Wagon was now redesignated the "Limited" wagon. All station wagons were available with four new options.

1990 Buick Regal Limited four-door sedan.

REGAL—SERIES 4W—V-6—Befitting the Regal's position in Buick's marketing strategy were the extensive changes, new models and revisions introduced with the 1990 Regal. Three new sedan models, Custom, Limited, and Gran Sport, were added at mid-year. Also becoming available at mid year was the 3800 V-6 engine and a four-speed automatic transmission. A new gunmetal gray exterior color was offered. New "Regal" fender lettering was used for 1990. The following specific exterior features were found on the sedan exterior: new major body panels, black "B" and "C" pillar appliques, clear park and turn lenses, back-up lights integrated into the rear bumper, see-through hood ornament (except Gran Sport), vertical grille with tri-shield, bright door handles and body-color mirrors. The Limited and Gran Sport versions had bright and black upper door moldings, standard bumper guards, bright finish on the front and rear bumper face bar, wraparound rear tail lamp lenses and body-color flared rocker panels. The wheel opening moldings on the Custom sedan were bright and black; those on the Limited and Gran Sport were black. The Custom sedan also had body-color lower front and rear facia with bright rub stripes. Black rub stripes were fitted to the Limited and Gran Sport sedans. The Limited and Gran Sport versions had chrome bumpers with bumper guards. Body-color bumpers were standard for the Custom sedan. Two-tone paint was restricted to the coupes and the Gran Sport sedan. A four-passenger package was exclusive to the Limited sedan. A new chrome luggage rack was available for the sedan with the black version continued as an option for the coupes. Other changes for 1990 consisted of the addition of a UXI radio to the SE Package on Limited models, the availability of anti-lock brakes with the SE Package on Limited models and the SF Package on the Gran Sport, two-tone paint available only on coupes (standard on the Gran Sport sedan), the replacement of 14 in. with 15 in. wire wheel covers, the addition of a new interior illumination option, three new free-flow options, electric door locks, cruise control, and power windows, new P215/60R16 blackwall touring tires and a driver lockout feature for power windows on sedans.

1990 Buick LeSabre Limited four-door sedan.

LESABRE—SERIES 4H—V-6—Buick cancelled the T Type LeSabre model for 1990. The remaining models' styling was highlighted by a new front-end appearance, a new tail lamp assembly that included integral back-up lights and license plate pocket and a new rear-end filler panel. Custom models featured a standard lower body-side molding and a body-color "B" pillar applique. Limited models also had a new standard lower body-side molding. All models shared a new body structure package that improved ride quality. The Gran Touring Package now included electronic level control. Additional revisions included a new gunmetal gray exterior color and a matching medium slate vinyl top, a new slate gray interior and a revamped interior seat design on the Limited sedan with Primavera cloth.

1990 Buick Estate Wagon.

ESTATE WAGON—SERIES 4B—V-8—Only one model, an Estate wagon with LeSabre content, was offered for 1990. The LeSabre/Electra designations were dropped. This marketing change was accompanied by a number of interesting revisions and new features. Two new colors, light maple red and dark maple red, were introduced along with a new dark red interior color. Three new standard equipment features—delay windshield wipers, tilt steering column and tungsten-halogen headlamps—were also introduced. A new automatic front safety belt system was also included in the Estate Wagon's standard equipment. The Estate Wagon's seats, in cloth or optional leather, were carried over from the 1989 Electra wagon. Added option package content was also available. External changes were limited to the new tri-shield hood ornament and a new "Estate Wagon" emblem on the front fender. A third seat delete option was also offered.

1990 Buick Park Avenue Ultra four-door sedan.

ELECTRA—SERIES 4C—V-6—Key developments in the Electra and Park Avenue models were primarily oriented towards refinement of the existing format rather than startling design or styling changes. Four new exterior colors were available: dove gray, palomino brown, chestnut brown and gunmetal gray. In association with these colors were new color choices for the optional vinyl top: taupe, dark brown, dark red and medium slate. In addition, two new interior colors were offered: brown and slate. The Limited and Park Avenue now had standard 14 in. wire wheelcovers. Standard on the Limited were P205/75R14 tires. Both the limited and T-Type were fitted with a two-speed wiper system with a delay feature as well as cruise control as standard equipment. A rear-window defogger was standard on all models along with a modified windshield wiper system. A compact disc player was offered at extra cost.

1990 Buick Riviera coupe.

RIVIERA—SERIES 4E—V-6—After the successful "up-sizing" of the "down-sized" Riviera in 1989, Buick was content to refine what was clearly a Riviera tailored to the desires of its clients. An improved body structure resulted in significantly improved ride quality. A closer look at the latest Riviera resulted in the discovery of some small external alterations. The license plate bezel was now chrome and the tail lamps had a chrome bead around their perimeters. Three new exterior colors were introduced: palomino brown, chestnut brown and gunmetal gray. The Riviera's vinyl roof could be selected in six additional colors for 1990: medium slate, dark brown, light brown, black, medium blue and slate. The 1990 Riviera's lengthy list of interior revisions consisted of a new instrument panel design with analog gauges, headlamps and light control switches, push-button climate control and high-gloss woodgrain trim plates. A console with armrest, cassette storage, coin holder, ashtray and PRNDL backlighting was now standard. Additional features included as standard equipment on the 1990 Riviera were door-mounted window/mirror controls with theater lighting, door armrest with courtesy light and wraparound warning light, a steering wheel with Supplemental Inflatable Restraint System (SIRS), a 200 series cassette and ETR® AM-FM stereo radio and the "pass-key"® anti-theft system. A new door design with a pull-strap was also introduced along with new seat trim design. The cruise control/windshield wiper controls were now located on a multi-function control lever. If a new CD player (two versions were offered: a unit with cassette and graphic equalizer or a unit with cassette and a Delco/Bose Gold series radio) was ordered, a covered storage compartment was also installed. Replacing the older 16-way optional seat was a 14-way power seat. Two new interior colors were also offered: brown and slate.

1990 Buick Reatta convertible.

REATTA—SERIES 4E—V-6—The spring 1990 introduction of the convertible model was the major development concerning the Reatta. The convertible featured a manual-operated top with a glass backlight plus a standard defogger. The hard tonneau cover was power released with a power top pull-down. The convertible top was available in two fabrics: vinyl and Sta-fast cloth. Both Reatta models were delivered with the following new items: auxiliary transmission cooler, instrument panel design with dark finish trim plates, analog gauges, integral radio and push-button climate controls, door-mounted window/mirror controls with theater lighting, console with armrest, coin holder, cassette storage and ashtray, push-button headlamp switch, steering wheel with SIRS, multi-function lever with cruise control and wiper/washer controls and "pass-key" anti-theft system. Improved rear speakers were adopted for 1990 along with the 2000 series AM/FM radio with cassette and graphic equalizer. A compact disc player was also available.

I.D. DATA: The V.I.N. identification process was unchanged from 1989 except for the use of an "L" designation for the 1990 model year.

Model Number	Body Style Number	Body Type & Seating	Factory Price	Shipping Weight	Production Total
Skylark Custom					
V27	NV1	2-dr. Cpe.-5P	$10565	2558	4248
V69	NV5	4-dr. Sed.-5P	$10465	2625	46705
Skylark Limited (Four/V-6)					
J27	NJ1	2-dr. Cpe.-5P*	$11460	2570	5490
C69	NC5	4-dr. Sed.-5P	$11460	2638	24469
Skylark Gran Sport (Four/V-6)					
M27	NM1	2-dr. Cpe.-5P	$12935	2603	1637
Skylark Luxury Edition (Four/V-6)					
D69	ND5	4-dr. Sed.-5P	$13855	2647	3019
*Add $660 for 2.4 liter Quad 4 and $710 for 3.3 liter V-6 engines to the price of all models.					
Century Custom (Four/V-6)					
H37	AH1	2-dr. Cpe.-6P	$13250/13960	2839/2950	1944
H69	AH5	4-dr. Sed.-6P	$13150/13860	2869/2980	88309
H35	AH8	4-dr. Sta. Wag.-6P	$14570/15280	3048/3159	4383
Century Limited (Four/V-6)					
L69	AL5	4-dr. Sed.-6P	$14075/14785	2870/2981	35248
L35	AL8	4-dr. Sta. Wag.-6P	$15455/16165	2870/3164	2837
Regal Custom (V-6)					
B57	WB1	2-dr. Cpe.-6P	$15200	3237	26071
B19	WB1	4-dr. Sed.-6P	$15400		
Regal Limited (V-6)					
D57	WD1	2-dr. Cpe.-6P	$15860	3243	31751*
D19	WD1	4-dr. Sed.-6P	$16120		
*This includes 12965 Gran Sports.					
LeSabre (V-6)					
P37	HP1	2-dr. Cpe.-6P	$16145	3234	2406
LeSabre Custom (V-6)					
P69	HP5	4-dr. Sed.-6P	$16050	3270	96616
LeSabre Limited (V-6)					
R37	HR1	2-dr. Cpe.-6P	$17300	3281	1855
R69	HP5	4-dr. Sed.-6P	$17400	3312	62,504
Estate Wagon (V-8)					
R35	BR8	4-dr. Sta. Wag.-6P	$17940	4339	7999
Electra Limited (V-6)					
X69	CX5	4-dr. Sed.-6P	$20225	3307	2261
Electra T Type (V-6)					
F69	CF5	4-dr. Sed.-6P	$23025	3390	478

1990 Buick Park Avenue four-door sedan.

Model Number	Body/Style Number	Body Type & Seating	Factory Price	Shipping Weight	Production Total
Electra Park Avenue (V-6)					
W69	CW5	4-dr. Sed.-6P	$21750	3390	44072
Electra Park Avenue Ultra (V-6)					
U69	CU5	4-dr. Sed.-6P	$27825	3437	1967
Riviera (V-6)					
Z57	EZ1	2-dr. Cpe.-6P	$23040	3464	22526
Reatta					
C97	EC1	2-dr. Cpe.-2P	$28335	3373	6383
C67	EC3	2-dr. Conv.-2P	$34995	3570	2132

ENGINE DATA: BASE FOUR (Skylark) Inline, overhead valve, four-cylinder, cast iron block and head. Displacement: 151 cu in. (2.5 liters). Bore & stroke: 4.00 in. x 3.00 in. Compression ratio: 9.0:1. Brake horsepower: 110 @ 5200 rpm. Torque: 135 lb.-ft. @ 3200 rpm. Five main bearings. Hydraulic lifters. Throttle-body fuel injection. BASE FOUR (Century) Inline, overhead valve, four-cylinder, cast alloy iron block and head. Displacement: 151 cu. in. (2.5 liters). Bore & stroke: 4.00 in. x 3.00 in. Compression ratio: 9.0:1. Brake horsepower: 110 @ 5200 rpm. Torque: 135 lb.-ft. @ 3200 rpm. Five main bearings. Hydraulic lifters. Throttle-body electric fuel injection. BASE V-6 (Regal) 60-degree overhead valve V-6. Cast iron block and aluminum heads. Displacement: 3.1 liters. Bore & stroke: 3.60 in. x 3.31 in. Compression ratio: 8.8:1. Brake horsepower: 135 @ 4400 rpm. Torque: 180 lb.-ft. @ 3600 rpm. Hydraulic lifters. Multi-port fuel injection. BASE V-6 (LeSabre) 90-degree overhead valve V-6 with balance shaft. Cast iron alloy block and head. Displacement: 231 cu. in. (3.8 liters). Bore & stroke: 3.80 in. x 3.40 in. Compression ratio: 8.5:1. Brake horsepower: 165 @ 4800 rpm. Torque: 210 lb.-ft. @ 2000 rpm. Four main bearings. Hydraulic lifters. Sequential fuel injection. BASE V-8 (LeSabre Estate station wagon) 90-degree overhead valve V-8. Cast iron block and head. Displacement: 307 cu. in. (5.0 liters). Bore & stroke: 3.8 in. x 3.39 in. Compression ratio: 8.0:1. Brake horsepower: 140 @ 3200 rpm. Torque: 255 lb.-ft. @ 2000 rpm. Five main bearings. Hydraulic lifters. 4-bbl. carb. BASE V-6 (Electra) 90-degree overhead valve V-6 with balance shaft. Cast iron alloy block and head. Displacement: 231 cu. in. (3.8 liters). Bore & stroke: 3.80 in. x 3.40 in. Compression ratio: 8.5:1. Brake horsepower: 165 @ 4800 rpm. Torque: 210 lb.-ft. @ 2000 rpm. Four main bearings. Hydraulic lifters. Sequential fuel injection. BASE V-8 (Electra Estate station wagon) 90-degree overhead valve V-8. Cast iron block and head. Displacement: 307 cu. in. (5.0 liters). Bore & stroke: 3.8 in. x 3.39 in. Compression ratio: 8.0:1. Brake horsepower: 140 @ 3200 rpm. Torque: 255 lb.-ft. @ 2000 rpm. Five main bearings. Hydraulic lifters. 4-bbl. carb. BASE V-6 (Riviera) 90-degree overhead valve V-6. Cast iron alloy block and head. Displacement: 231 cu. in. (3.8 liters). Bore & stroke: 3.80 in x 3.40 in. Compression ratio: 8.5:1. Brake horsepower: 165 @ 4800 rpm. Torque: 210 lb.-ft. @ 2000 rpm. Four main bearings. Hydraulic lifters. Sequential fuel injection. BASE V-6 (Reatta) 90-degree overhead valve V-6. Cast iron alloy block and head. Displacement: 231 cu. in. (3.8 liters). Bore & stroke: 3.80 in. x 3.40 in. Compression ratio: 8.5:1. Brake horsepower: 165 @ 4800 rpm. Torque: 210 lb.-ft. @ 2000 rpm. Four main bearings. Hydraulic lifters. Sequential fuel injection. OPTIONAL (Skylark) Inline, DOHC, overhead valve, four-cylinder. Cast iron alloy block, cast aluminum head. Displacement: 138 cu. in. (2.3 liters). Bore & stroke: 3.62 in. x 3.346 in. Compression ratio: 9.5:1. Brake horsepower: 150 @ 5200 rpm. Torque: 160 @ 4000 rpm. Hydraulic valve lifters. Multi-port fuel injection. OPTIONAL (Skylark) 90-degree V-6. Cast iron block and cylinder heads. Displacement: 204 cu. in. (3.3 liters). Bore & stroke: 3.73 in. x 3.16 in. Compression ratio: 9.0:1. Brake horsepower: 160 @ 5200 rpm. Torque: 185 @ 2000 rpm. Hydraulic valve lifters. Multi-port fuel injection. OPTIONAL (Century, Century Estate Wagon) 60-degree V-6. Cast iron block and cylinder head. Displacement: 204 cu. in. (3.3 liters). Bore & stroke: 3.70 in. x 3.16 in. Compression ratio: 9.00:1. Brake horsepower: 160 @ 5200 rpm. Torque: 185 lb.-ft. @ 2000 rpm. Four main bearings. Hydraulic lifters. Multi-port fuel injection. 90-degree overhead valve V-6. Cast iron block and head. OPTIONAL (Regal) 90-degree overhead valve V-6 with balance shaft. Cast iron alloy block and head. Displacement: 231 cu. in. (3.8 liters). Bore & stroke: 3.80 in. x 3.40 in. Compression ratio: 8.5:1. Brake horsepower: 170 @ 4800 rpm. Torque: 220 lb.-ft. @ 3200 rpm. Four main bearings. Hydraulic lifters. Sequential fuel injection. V-6. LeSabre: None. Electra: None. Reatta: None.

CHASSIS DATA: Wheelbase: (Skylark) 103.4 in.; (Century) 104.8 in.; (Regal) 107.5 in.; (LeSabre) 110.8 in.; (LeSabre Estate Wagon) 115.9 in.; (Electra) 110.8 in.; (Riviera) 108.0 in. **Overall length:** (Skylark) 180.1 in.; (Century) 189.1 in.; (Century Custom/Estate station wagon) 190.9 in.; (Regal) 192.2 in.; (LeSabre) 196.5 in.; (LeSabre Estate station wagon) 220.5 in.; (Electra) 197.0 in.; (Electra Estate station wagon) 220.5 in.; (Riviera) 198.3 in. **Height:** (Skylark) 52.1 in.; (Century) coupe: 53.7 in.; sedan and Century Custom/Estate station wagon: 54.2 in.; (Regal) 53.0 in.; (LeSabre coupe) 54.7 in.; (LeSabre sedan) 55.4 in.; (Estate station wagon) 59.3 in.; (Electra) 54.3 in.; (Riviera) 53.6 in. **Width:** (Skylark) 66.6 in.; (Century) 69.4 in.; (Century Custom/Estate station wagon) 69.4 in.; (Regal) 72.5 in.; (LeSabre coupe/sedan) 72.5 in.; (Estate station wagon) 79.3 in.; (Electra) 72.4 in.; (Riviera) 71.7 in. **Front Tread:** (all models in succession) (Skylark) 55.6 in.; (Century) 58.7 in.; (Century Custom/Estate station wagon) 58.7 in.; (Regal) 59.3 in.; (LeSabre coupe/sedan): 60.3 in.; (Estate station wagon) 62.2 in.; (Electra) 60.3 in.; (Riviera) 59.9 in. **Rear Tread:** (all models in succession) (Skylark) 55.2 in.; (Century) 56.7 in.; (Century Custom/Estate station wagon) 56.7 in.; (Regal) 58.0 in.; (LeSabre coupe/sedan) 59.8 in.; (Estate station wagon) 64.0 in.; (Electra) 59.8 in.; (Riviera) 59.9 in. **Standard Tires:** (all models in succession) (Skylark) P185/80R13; (Century) P185/75R14; (Century Custom/Estate station wagon) P185/75R14; (Regal) P205/75R14; (LeSabre coupe/sedan) P205/75R14; (Estate station wagon) P225/75R15; (Electra) P20575/R14 (blackwall on Limited, whitewall on Park Avenue); (Electra T-Type) P215/65R15; (Park Avenue Ultra) P205/70R15 whitewall; (Riviera) P205/75R15.

TECHNICAL: Transmission: (Skylark) Three-speed automatic; (Century) Three-speed automatic; (Century Custom/Estate station wagon) Three-speed automatic; (Regal) Four-speed automatic with overdrive; (LeSabre coupe/sedan) Four-speed overdrive automatic; (Estate station wagon) Four-speed overdrive automatic; (Electra) Four-speed automatic with overdrive; (Riviera) Four-speed overdrive automatic. **Steering:** (Skylark) Power rack and pinion; (Century) Power rack and pinion; (Century Custom/Estate station wagon) Power rack and pinion; (Regal) Power rack and pinion; (LeSabre coupe/sedan) Power rack and pinion; (Estate station wagon) Power recirculating ball; (Electra) Power rack and pinion; (Riviera) Power rack and pinion. **Front Suspension:** (Skylark, Century, Century Custom/Estate station wagon, LeSabre coupe/sedan, Electra, Electra T-Type, Riviera) MacPherson struts with coil springs, lower control arms and stabilizer bar; (Regal) MacPherson struts with lower control arms and unitized coil springs; (Estate station wagon) Coil springs, unequal length control arms, stabilizer bar. **Rear Suspension:** (Skylark) Trailing crank bar, coil springs and stabilizer bar; (Century) beam twist axle with integral stabilizer bar, trailing arms, Panhard arm and coil springs; (LeSabre coupe/sedan) MacPherson struts, coil springs, stabilizer bar; (Estate station wagon) Solid axle with four links, coil springs; (Electra, Electra T-Type) Independent MacPherson struts, inboard coil springs, stabilizer bar; (Riviera) Independent tri-link, transverse fiberglass leaf spring, stabilizer bar; (Reatta) Independent modular assembly with single transverse leaf springs. **Brakes:** (Skylark, Century, Century Custom/Estate station wagon, Regal, LeSabre coupe/sedan, Estate station wagon, Electra, Electra T-Type) Power front discs, rear drum; (Riviera) Power disc front and rear; (Reatta) Power disc front and rear. **Body Construction:** (Skylark) Unibody; (Century/Century station wagons) Integral body/frame; (Regal) Integral body/frame with bolted-on powertrain cradle; (LeSabre) Unitized body/frame integral with isolated engine cradle; (Estate station wagon) Welded body with full perimeter frame; (Electra) Unitized body/frame construction with isolated engine cradle; (Riviera) Unitized body with isolated front frame and rear sub-frame; (Reatta) Unitized body with isolated front and rear sub-frames. **Fuel Tank:** (Skylark) 13.6 gal.; (Somerset) 13.6 gal.; (Century) 15.7 gal.; (Century Custom/Estate station wagon) 16.6 gal.; (Regal) 16.5 gal.; (LeSabre coupe/sedan) 18.0 gal.; (Estate station wagon) 22.0 gal.; (Electra and Electra T-Type) 18.0 gal.; (Riviera) 18.2 gal.; (Reatta) 18.2 gal.

DRIVETRAIN OPTIONS: Engines: (Skylark) 2.3 liter Quad-4, MFI, $660; 3.3 liter V-6, MFI, $710; (Century, Century Custom/Estate station wagon) 3.3 liter V-6, MFI, $710; (Regal) None; (LeSabre coupe/sedan and Estate station wagon, Electra, Electra T-Type and Riviera) None. **Transmission/Differential:** (Skylark) None; (Century, Century Custom/Estate station wagon) Automatic transmission with overdrive, with 3.3 liter engine only, $200; (Regal) None; (LeSabre coupe/sedan) None; (Estate station wagon) None; (Electra and Electra T-Type) None; (Riviera) None; (Reatta) None. **Optional rear axle ratios: Suspension, steering and brakes:** (Skylark) Gran Touring Package (14 in. aluminum wheels, P215/60R14 Eagle GT+4 blackwall tires, Gran Touring suspension, leather-wrapped steering wheel): $603; engine block heater: $18; (Century) heavy-duty engine and transmission cooling: $70 without air conditioning, $40 with A/C; heavy-duty suspension (required with 3.3 liter engine): $27; Gran Touring Package, not available for station wagons (aluminum wheels, P15/60R Eagle GT tires, leather-wrapped steering wheel and Gran Touring suspension): $515; (Regal): Gran Touring Package consisting of Gran Touring suspension, 16 in. aluminum wheels, P215/60R16 tires and leather-wrapped steering wheel; anti-lock brake system: $925; (LeSabre coupe and sedan) 2.97:1 axle (included in Y56-Gran Touring Package and WE2-T-Type; required with V-8-heavy-duty engine and transmission cooling): no additional charge; heavy-duty engine and transmission cooling (included in WE2 and Y56): $40; Gran Touring Package consisting of Gran Touring Suspension, 15 in. aluminum wheels, P215/65R15 blackwall tires, 2.97:1 axle ratio, heavy-duty cooling and leather-wrapped steering wheel; (Estate wagon) trailer towing package consisting of 3.23:1 axle ratio, V-8-heavy-duty engine and transmission cooling, automatic level control: $215; limited slip differential: $100; (Electra) heavy-duty battery, required with electronic air conditioning: $26; heavy-duty engine and transmission cooling (standard with T-Type, included in Y56-Gran Touring Package): $40; 2.97:1 axle ratio (requires V-8, included in Y56-Gran Touring Package and T-Type): No additional charge; electronic anti-lock brake system; $925 (standard on T-Type and Ultra); Gran Touring suspension (standard on T-Type, not available for Ultra or with fully padded vinyl top), consists of Gran Touring suspension, 15 in. styled aluminum wheels, P215/65R15 Eagle GT blackwall tires, 2.97:1 axle ratio, heavy-duty cooling and leather-wrapped steering wheel; (Riviera) Gran Touring Package consisting of Gran Touring Suspension, 2.97:1 axle ratio, 15 in. aluminum wheels, leather-wrapped sport steering wheel and shift handle, fast ratio power steering and P215/65R15 steel-belted radial ply Eagle GT+4 tires: $104.

SERIES NAME CONVENIENCE/APPEARANCE OPTIONS: Skylark: Air conditioning, $695; tilt steering column, $125; P185/80R13 whitewall tires, $68; mirrors—remote control left, right manual, $53; electric rear window defogger, $150; protective wide body side molding, $80; wheel opening molding, $30; plus electronic cruise control with resume, $185; two-speed windshield wipers with resume feature, $55; front and rear carpet savers, $45; AM/FM ETR stereo radio with cassette tape, seek and scan, auto reverse with search and repeat and clock, $152; custom locking wheel covers, $215; four-way manual driver seat adjuster, $35; power windows, $220-coupe, $295-sedan; electric door locks, $155-coupe, $295-sedan; six-way power driver seat adjuster, $250; power antenna, $70; passenger side lighted visor vanity mirror, $38; electric trunk lock release, $50; front and rear courtesy lights, $14; chrome deck lid luggage rack (not available with S/E and exterior sport package), $115; lower body accent paint, $195; body side stripes, $45; Custom and Limited cloth bucket seats with full length operation console, $180; styled 13 in. aluminum wheels, $245; styled hubcaps and trim rings, $38, custom locking wire wheel covers, $215. Special packages: Gran Touring Package, $603, includes 14 in. aluminum wheels, P215/60R14 Eagle GT blackwall tires, Gran Touring suspension, leather-wrapped steering wheel. Exterior Sport Package, $374-Custom coupe; $318-Limited coupe, includes blackout moldings, front air dam, aero rocker moldings, wide body side moldings. Skylark S/E Package, $1134; available for Custom models only, includes bucket seats and console, dual mirrors with left remote, body side moldings, rocker moldings, wheel opening moldings, cassette tape radio, and Gran Touring Package. Skylark L/E Formal Appearance Luxury Edition, $1050-$1495, includes full formal vinyl roof, wire wheel covers, wide rocker molding, body side molding, wheel opening molding, dual mirrors with left remote, and lower accent paint. Various Popular, Premium, Luxury and Prestige Packages. Tires, all steel-belted radial ply): P205/70R13 blacwall, $124; P205/70/R13 whitewall, $190.

Century: Air conditioning, $795; tilt steering column, $150; electric rear window defogger, $150; electronic cruise control with resume, $185; two-speed windshield wipers with resume feature, $55; front carpet savers, $25; rear carpet savers, $20; AM/FM ETR stereo radio with cassette tape, seek and scan, auto reverse and clock, $122; custom locking wire wheel covers, $215; styled steel wheels, $115; aluminum wheels, $270; body stripes, $45; six-way power driver seat adjuster, $70; power windows, $220-coupe; $295-sedan; electric door locks, $155-coupe; $295-sedan; six-way power driver seat adjuster, $250; power antenna, $70; passenger side lighted visor vanity mirror, $50; electric trunk lock release, $50; door edge guards, $15-coupe;$25-sedan; passenger manual seat back recliner, $45; driver manual seat back recliner, $45; dual electric remote control mirrors, $70; automatic power antenna, $70; (Custom only) 55/45 cloth seat with armrest, $183; Limited cloth 55/45 seat with storage armrest, $233-$416; (Century Limited only) front seat reading lights, $24; Premium rear speakers, $70; (Century Estate wagon only) vinyl third seat, $215; air deflector, $37; vinyl applique woodgrain trim, $350; rear window windshield wiper, $125. Special packages. Gran Touring Package, includes aluminum wheels and P215/60R14 Eagle GT tires, leather-wrapped steering wheel and Gran Touring suspension, $515.

Regal: Electric rear window defogger, $150; electronic cruise control with resume, $185; two-speed windshield wipers with resume feature, $55; front carpet savers, $25; rear carpet savers, $20; AM/FM ETR stereo radio with cassette tape, seek and scan, auto reverse and clock, $122; graphic equalizer cassette tape with auto reverse, and search/repeat and AM stereo, $150-$272; compact disc player with ETR AM/FM radio with seek/scan and clock, $274; electric glass sunroof (includes dual reading lamps and rear courtesy lamps), $650-$680; custom locking wire wheel covers, $215; styled aluminum wheels, $270; styled steel wheels, $115; 15 in. aluminum wheels with P205/70 blackwall tires, $320; six-way power driver seat adjuster, $250; power windows with express down feature, $230; electric door locks, $155; six-way power driver seat adjuster, $250; automatic power antenna, $70; passenger side lighted visor vanity mirror, $50; electric trunk lock release, $50; door edge guards, $15; dual electric remote control mirrors, $91; automatic power antenna, $70; Concert Sound speakers, $85; redundant accessory controls—steering wheel mounted, $125; remote keyless entry (Limited and Gran Sport only), $125; electronic digital/graphic instrumentation, $299; luggage rack, $115; wide black with red striping body molding, $55-$70; lower accent paint, $205; body side stripes, $45; cloth 55/45 seat with storage armrest (Custom only), $183; cloth reclining buckets with console (Custom only), $185; leather/vinyl 55/45 with recliners, (Limited only) $450. Special packages: Four-Seater Package, includes front and rear bucket seats with rear armrests and storage console with cassette storage, leather-wrapped steering wheel, rear headrests $409. Gran Sport. Includes Gran Touring Package, bucket seats and console, specific exterior appearance with blackout, fog lamps, aero rocker panels, wide body side molding and front spoiler, $1212.

1990 Buick LeSabre coupe.

LeSabre: Electric rear window defogger, $150; electronic cruise control with resume, $185; two-speed windshield wipers with low speed delay feature, $55; black protective bodyside molding, $60; front carpet savers, $25; rear carpet savers, $20; 55/45 split front seat with storage armrest, $183; rear bumper guards and bodyside molding extensions, $24; AM/FM ETR stereo radio with cassette tape, seek and scan, auto reverse and clock, $132; graphic equalizer cassette tape with auto reverse, and search/repeat and AM/FM stereo and Concert Sound speaker system, $367; Concert Sound speaker system, $85; locking wire wheel covers, $215; styled aluminum wheels, $270; styled steel wheels, $115; six-way power driver seat adjuster, $250; electric passenger seat back recliner, $70; deluxe trunk trim, $53; electronic touch climate control air conditioner, $165; power windows, coupe-$220, sedan-$295; electric door locks, coupe-$155, sedan-$205; six-way power driver seat adjuster, $250; six-way passenger seat adjuster, $250; front and rear courtesy and warning lights, $44; automatic power antenna, $70; passenger side lighted visor vanity mirror, $50; door edge guards, coupe-$15, sedan-$25; dual electric remote control mirrors, $91; automatic power antenna, $70; concert sound speakers, $85; chrome luggage rack, $115; wide rocker panel molding package, $110; instrumentation—tachometer, temperature, oil and volt gauges, $110; body side stripes, $45; cloth 55/45 seat with storage armrest (Custom only), $183; leather/vinyl 55/45 with recliners (limited only), $450. Special Estate wagon options—roof rack, $115; air deflector, $40; remote control electric tailgate lock, $60; tungsten halogen headlamps, $25; Twilight Sentinel headlamp control, $60; illuminated driver door lock and interior light control, $75; cornering lights, $60; front lights monitor, $37. Special packages—Gran Touring Package, includes Gran Touring suspension, 15 in. aluminum wheels, P215/65R15 Eagle GT+4 blackwall tires, 2.97:1 axle ratio, heavy-duty cooling, leather-wrapped steering wheel, $563. T-Type Package, includes Gran Touring package (with different wheels) plus specific interior and exterior trim, cruise, gauges, 55/45 front seats and operating console, AM/FM stereo radio with cassette and graphic equalizer, rear deck spoiler and front air dam, dual exhaust outlets, blackout trim, $1927.

Electra: Electric rear window defogger, $150; P205/75R14 whitewall tires, $76; electronic cruise control with resume, $185; two-speed windshield wipers with low speed delay feature, $55; black protective bodyside molding, $60; front carpet savers, $25; rear carpet savers, $20; 55/45 split front seat with storage armrest, $183; rear bumper guards and bodyside molding extensions, $183; rear bumper guards and bodyside molding extensions, $24; AM/FM ETR stereo radio with cassette tape, seek and scan, auto reverse and clock, $132; graphic equalizer cassette tape with auto reverse, and search/repeat and AM/FM stereo and Concert Sound speaker system, $367; Concert Sound speaker system, $85; locking wire wheel covers, $215; styled aluminum wheels, $270; styled steel wheels, $115; six-way power driver seat adjuster, $250; electric passenger seat back recliner, $70; deluxe trunk trim, $53; electronic touch climate control air conditioner, $165; power windows, coupe-$220, sedan-$295; electric door locks, $205; six-way power driver seat adjuster, $250; six-way passenger seat adjuster, $250; front and rear courtesy and warning lights, $44; automatic power antenna, $70; passenger side lighted visor vanity mirror, $50; Twilight Sentinel headlamp control, $60; four note horn, $28; low windshield washer fluid indicator, $16; cornering lights, $60; front and rear light monitor, $77; low fuel indicator, $16; electric

1990 Buick Electra T-Type four-door sedan.

trunk pull-down, $80; automatic day/night mirror, $80; dual electric remote control mirrors with heated left, $35; two-position memory driver belt adjuster, $150; deluxe trunk trim with mat, $68; rear reading lamps, $50; quartz analog gauge cluster, $126; electronic instrumentation, $299; electric trunk release, $50; door edge guards, $25; dual electric remote control mirrors, $91; automatic power antenna, $70; remote keyless entry system, $175; Concert Sound speakers, $70; chrome luggage rack, $115; firemist paint, $210; Bose music sysem, $553-$905; body side stripes, $45; leather/vinyl 55/45 (Park Avenue), $450; (T-Type), $395; theft deterrent system, $159; full heavily padded top, $260-$895; electric sliding Astroroof (not available with padded roof), $1230; 14 in. styled aluminum wheels, $235-$270. Special Packages: Gran Touring Package, Gran Touring suspension, 15 in. styled aluminum wheels, P215/65R15 Eagle GT blackwall tires, 2.97:1 axle ratio, heavy-duty cooling, leather-wrapped steering wheel, $462-$563.

Riviera: Graphic equalizer cassette tape with auto reverse, and search/repeat and ETR AM/FM stereo and digital clock, $120; Delco Bose music system with cassette, ETR AM/FM stereo with Dolby, seek and scan, auto reverse with search/repeat, and clock, $583-$703; six-way power passenger seat with power recliner, $325; electric trunk pull-down, $250; remote keyless entry system with automatic power door locks, $265; twilight headlamp control, $60; theft deterrent system, $159; left and right remote mirrors with heated left, $35; automatic rearview mirror, $80; electronic compass, $75; firemist paint, $210; lower accent paint, $190; electric Astroroof sliding roof, $1230; heavily padded roof, $695; leather and suede bucket seats, $550; 16-way adjustable driver leather and suede bucket seats, $1230; styled aluminum wheels, $55; cellular telephone, $1975. Special packages: Gran Touring Package, includes Gran Touring suspension, 2.97:1 axle ratio, 15 in. aluminum wheels, leather-wrapped steering wheel and shift handle, fast ratio power steering and P215/65R15 blackwall Eagle GT+4 tires, $104. Riviera Appearance Package, includes platinum beige firemist lower accent paint, body side stripe and painted aluminum wheels, $205.

1990 Buick Reatta coupe.

Reatta: Sliding electric steel sunroof, $895; 16-way adjustable driver side leather bucket seats, $680.

HISTORY: Buick's efforts to strengthen its competitive position were evident by two mid-year developments. The Reatta convertible arrived at mid-year along with a Regal four-door sedan. The Reatta convertible was the first Buick soft top model since the 1982-1985 Riviera model. The Buick Skyhawk was no longer offered in 1990.

A WORD ABOUT OLD BUICKS...

The market for cars more than 10 years old is strong. Some buyers of pre-1981 cars are collectors who invest in vehicles likely to increase in value the older they get. Other buyers prefer the looks, size, performance and reliability of yesterday's better-built automobiles.

With a typical 1991 model selling for $13,000 or more, some Americans find themselves priced out of the new-car market. Late-model used cars are pricy, too, although short on distinctive looks and roominess. The old cars may use a little more gas, but they cost a lot less.

New cars and late-model used cars rapidly depreciate in value. Many can't tow large trailers or mobile homes. Their high-tech engineering is expensive to maintain or repair. In contrast, well-kept old cars are mechanically simpler, but very powerful. They appreciate in value as they grow more scarce and collectible. Insuring them is cheaper, too.

Selecting a car and paying the right price for it are two considerations old car buyers face. What models did Buick offer in 1958? Which '63 Buick is worth the most today? What should one pay for a 1968 Wildcat Custom convertible?

The Standard Catalog of Buick 1903-1990 answers such questions. The "Price Guide" section shows most models made between 1903 and 1984. It helps to gauge what they sell for in six different graded conditions. Models built since 1984 are generally considered "used cars" of which few, as yet, have achieved collectible status.

The price estimates contained in this book are current as of the publication date, August 1991. After that date, more current prices may be obtained by referring to *Old Cars Price Guide*, which is available from Krause Publications, 700 E. State St., Iola, WI 54990, telephone (715) 445-2214.

HOW TO USE THE BUICK PRICE GUIDE

On the following pages is a **BUICK PRICE GUIDE.** The worth of an old car is a "ballpark" estimate at best. The estimates contained in this book are based upon national and regional data compiled by the editors of *Old Cars News & Marketplace* and *Old Cars Price Guide.* These data include actual bids and prices at collector car auctions and sales, classified and display advertising of such vehicles, verified reports of private sales and input from experts.

Price estimates are listed for cars in six different states of condition. These conditions (1-6) are illustrated and explained in the **VEHICLE CONDITION SCALE** on the following pages. Values are for complete vehicles — not parts cars — except as noted. Modified car values are not included, but can be estimated by figuring the cost of restoring the subject vehicle to original condition and adjusting the figures shown here accordingly.

Appearing below is a section of chart taken from the **BUICK PRICE GUIDE** to illustrate the following elements:

A. MAKE The make of car, or marque name, appears in large, boldface type at the beginning of each value section.

B. DESCRIPTION The extreme left-hand column indicates vehicle year, model name, body type, engine configuration and, in some cases, wheelbase.

C. CONDITION CODE The six columns to the right are headed by the numbers one through six (1-6) which correspond to the conditions described in the **VEHICLE CONDITION SCALE** on the following page.

D. PRICE. The price estimates, in dollars, appear below their respective condition code headings and across from the vehicle descriptions.

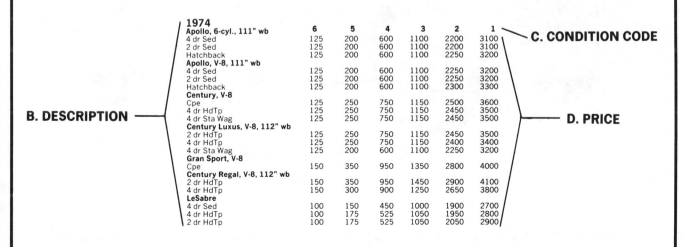

A. MAKE —————— **BUICK**

1974	6	5	4	3	2	1
Apollo, 6-cyl., 111" wb						
4 dr Sed	125	200	600	1100	2200	3100
2 dr Sed	125	200	600	1100	2200	3100
Hatchback	125	200	600	1100	2250	3200
Apollo, V-8, 111" wb						
4 dr Sed	125	200	600	1100	2250	3200
2 dr Sed	125	200	600	1100	2250	3200
Hatchback	125	200	600	1100	2300	3300
Century, V-8						
Cpe	125	250	750	1150	2500	3600
4 dr HdTp	125	250	750	1150	2450	3500
4 dr Sta Wag	125	250	750	1150	2450	3500
Century Luxus, V-8, 112" wb						
2 dr HdTp	125	250	750	1150	2450	3500
4 dr HdTp	125	250	750	1150	2400	3400
4 dr Sta Wag	125	200	600	1100	2250	3200
Gran Sport, V-8						
Cpe	150	350	950	1350	2800	4000
Century Regal, V-8, 112" wb						
2 dr HdTp	150	350	950	1450	2900	4100
4 dr HdTp	150	300	900	1250	2650	3800
LeSabre						
4 dr Sed	100	150	450	1000	1900	2700
4 dr HdTp	100	175	525	1050	1950	2800
2 dr HdTp	100	175	525	1050	2050	2900

B. DESCRIPTION ——————

C. CONDITION CODE

D. PRICE

VEHICLE CONDITION SCALE

Excellent

1) EXCELLENT: Restored to current maxiumum professional standards of quality in every area, or perfect original with components operating and appearing as new. A 95-plus point show vehicle that is not driven.

Fine

2) FINE: Well-restored, or a combination of superior restoration and excellent original. Also, an *extremely* well-maintained original showing very minimal wear.

Very Good

3) VERY GOOD: Completely operable original or "older restoration" showing wear. Also, a good amateur restoration, all presentable and serviceable inside and out. Plus, combinations of well-done restoration and good operable components or a partially restored vehicle with all parts necessary to complete and/or valuable NOS parts.

Good

4) GOOD: A driveable vehicle needing no or only minor work to be functional. Also, a deteriorated restoration or a very poor amateur restoration. All components may need restoration to be "excellent," but the vehicle is mostly useable "as is."

Restorable

5) RESTORABLE: Needs *complete* restoration of body, chassis and interior. May or may not be running, but isn't weathered, wrecked or stripped to the point of being useful only for parts.

Parts Car

6) PARTS VEHICLE: May or may not be running, but is weathered, wrecked and/or stripped to the point of being useful primarily for parts.

	6	5	4	3	2	1
1904						
Model B, 2-cyl.						
Tr					value not estimable	
1905						
Model C, 2-cyl.						
Tr	1500	4800	8000	16,000	28,000	40,000
1906						
Model F & G, 2-cyl.						
Tr	1450	4700	7800	15,600	27,300	39,000
Rds	1450	4550	7600	15,200	26,600	38,000
1907						
Model F & G, 2-cyl.						
Tr	1450	4700	7800	15,600	27,300	39,000
Rds	1450	4550	7600	15,200	26,600	38,000
Model D, S, K & H, 4-cyl.						
Tr	1500	4800	8000	16,000	28,000	40,000
Rds	1450	4700	7800	15,600	27,300	39,000
1908						
Model F & G, 2-cyl.						
Tr	1700	5400	9000	18,000	31,500	45,000
Rds	1650	5300	8800	17,600	30,800	44,000
Model D & S, 4-cyl.						
Tr	1550	4900	8200	16,400	28,700	41,000
Rds	1600	5050	8400	16,800	29,400	42,000
Model 10, 4-cyl.						
Tr	1500	4800	8000	16,000	28,000	40,000
Model 5, 4-cyl.						
Tr	1700	5400	9000	18,000	31,500	45,000
1909						
Model G, (only 6 built in 1909).						
Rds	1750	5500	9200	18,400	32,200	46,000
Model F & G						
Tr	1650	5300	8800	17,600	30,800	44,000
Rds	1700	5400	9000	18,000	31,500	45,000
Model 10, 4-cyl.						
Tr	1600	5150	8600	17,200	30,100	43,000
Rds	1650	5300	8800	17,600	30,800	44,000
Model 16 & 17, 4-cyl.						
Rds	1700	5400	9000	18,000	31,500	45,000
Tr	1650	5300	8800	17,600	30,800	44,000
1910						
Model 6, 2-cyl.						
Tr	1500	4800	8000	16,000	28,000	40,000
Model F, 2-cyl.						
Tr	1450	4550	7600	15,200	26,600	38,000
Model 14, 2-cyl.						
Rds	1400	4450	7400	14,800	25,900	37,000
Model 10, 4-cyl.						
Tr	1300	4200	7000	14,000	24,500	35,000
Rds	1300	4200	7000	14,000	24,500	35,000
Model 19, 4-cyl.						
Tr	1550	4900	8200	16,400	28,700	41,000
Model 16 & 17, 4-cyl.						
Rds	1500	4800	8000	16,000	28,000	40,000
Tr	1450	4700	7800	15,600	27,300	39,000
Model 7, 4-cyl.						
Tr	1650	5300	8800	17,600	30,800	44,000
Model 41, 4-cyl.						
Limo	1450	4700	7800	15,600	27,300	39,000
1911						
Model 14, 2-cyl.						
Rds	1300	4100	6800	13,600	23,800	34,000
Model 21, 4-cyl.						
Tr	1300	4200	7000	14,000	24,500	35,000
Model 26 & 27, 4-cyl.						
Rds	1350	4300	7200	14,400	25,200	36,000
Tr	1300	4100	6800	13,600	23,800	34,000
Model 32 & 33						
Rds	1300	4200	7000	14,000	24,500	35,000
Tr	1300	4100	6800	13,600	23,800	34,000
Model 38 & 39, 4-cyl.						
Rds	1450	4550	7600	15,200	26,600	38,000
Tr	1450	4700	7800	15,600	27,300	39,000
Limo	2050	6600	11,000	22,000	38,500	55,000
1912						
Model 34, 35 & 36, 4-cyl.						
Rds	1250	3950	6600	13,200	23,100	33,000
Tr	1300	4100	6800	13,600	23,800	34,000
Model 28 & 29, 4-cyl.						
Rds	1300	4100	6800	13,600	23,800	34,000
Tr	1300	4200	7000	14,000	24,500	35,000
Model 43, 4-cyl.						
Tr	1350	4300	7200	14,400	25,200	36,000
1913						
Model 30 & 31, 4-cyl.						
Rds	1200	3850	6400	12,800	22,400	32,000
Tr	1250	3950	6600	13,200	23,100	33,000
Model 40, 4-cyl.						
Tr	1300	4200	7000	14,000	24,500	35,000
Model 24 & 25, 4-cyl.						
Rds	1300	4200	7000	14,000	24,500	35,000
Tr	1350	4300	7200	14,400	25,200	36,000
1914						
Model B-24 & B-25, 4-cyl.						
Rds	1250	3950	6600	13,200	23,100	33,000
Tr	1300	4100	6800	13,600	23,800	34,000

	6	5	4	3	2	1
Model B-36, B-37 & B-38, 4-cyl.						
Rds	1300	4100	6800	13,600	23,800	34,000
Tr	1300	4200	7000	14,000	24,500	35,000
Cpe	1200	3850	6400	12,800	22,400	32,000
Model B-55, 6-cyl.						
7P Tr	1350	4300	7200	14,400	25,200	36,000
1915						
Model C-24 & C-25, 4-cyl.						
Rds	1300	4100	6800	13,600	23,800	34,000
Tr	1300	4200	7000	14,000	24,500	35,000
Model C-36 & C-37, 4-cyl.						
Rds	1300	4200	7000	14,000	24,500	35,000
Tr	1350	4300	7200	14,400	25,200	36,000
Model C-54 & C-55, 6-cyl.						
Rds	1350	4300	7200	14,400	25,200	36,000
Tr	1400	4450	7400	14,800	25,900	37,000
1916						
Model D-54 & D-55, 6-cyl.						
Rds	1300	4100	6800	13,600	23,800	34,000
Tr	1300	4200	7000	14,000	24,500	35,000
1916-1917						
Model D-34 & D-35, 4-cyl.						
Rds	1200	3850	6400	12,800	22,400	32,000
Tr	1250	3950	6600	13,200	23,100	33,000
Model D-44 & D-45, 6-cyl.						
Rds	1250	3950	6600	13,200	23,100	33,000
Tr	1300	4100	6800	13,600	23,800	34,000
Model D-46 & D-47, 6-cyl.						
Conv Cpe	1150	3600	6000	12,000	21,000	30,000
Sed	850	2750	4600	9200	16,100	23,000
1918						
Model E-34 & E-35, 4-cyl.						
Rds	1100	3500	5800	11,600	20,300	29,000
Tr	1150	3600	6000	12,000	21,000	30,000
Model E-37, 4-cyl.						
Sed	850	2650	4400	8800	15,400	22,000
Model E-44, E-45 & E-49, 6-cyl.						
Rds	1150	3600	6000	12,000	21,000	30,000
Tr	1150	3700	6200	12,400	21,700	31,000
7P Tr	1200	3850	6400	12,800	22,400	32,000
Model E-46, E-47 & E-50, 6-cyl.						
Conv Cpe	1050	3350	5600	11,200	19,600	28,000
Sed	850	2750	4600	9200	16,100	23,000
7P Sed	900	2800	4700	9400	16,500	23,500
1919						
Model H-44, H-45 & H-49, 6-cyl.						
2d Rds	1100	3500	5800	11,600	20,300	29,000
4d Tr	1150	3600	6000	12,000	21,000	30,000
4d 7P Tr	1150	3700	6200	12,400	21,700	31,000
Model H-46, H-47 & H-50, 6-cyl.						
2d Cpe	900	2900	4800	9600	16,800	24,000
4d Sed	750	2400	4000	8000	14,000	20,000
4d 7P Sed	800	2500	4200	8400	14,700	21,000
1920						
Model K, 6-cyl.						
2d Cpe K-46	850	2650	4400	8800	15,400	22,000
4d Sed K-47	700	2150	3600	7200	12,600	18,000
2d Rds K-44	1100	3500	5800	11,600	20,300	29,000
4d Tr K-49	1050	3350	5600	11,200	19,600	28,000
4d Tr K-45	1000	3250	5400	10,800	18,900	27,000
4d 7P Sed K-50	700	2300	3800	7600	13,300	19,000
1921						
Series 40, 6-cyl.						
2d Rds	1100	3500	5800	11,600	20,300	29,000
4d Tr	1050	3350	5600	11,200	19,600	28,000
4d 7P Tr	1100	3500	5800	11,600	20,300	29,000
2d Cpe	600	1900	3200	6400	11,200	16,000
4d Sed	550	1800	3000	6000	10,500	15,000
2d Ewb Cpe	650	2050	3400	6800	11,900	17,000
4d 7P Sed	600	1900	3200	6400	11,200	16,000
1921-1922						
Series 30, 4-cyl.						
2d Rds	1000	3250	5400	10,800	18,900	27,000
4d Tr	1000	3100	5200	10,400	18,200	26,000
2d Cpe OS	550	1800	3000	6000	10,500	15,000
4d Sed	500	1550	2600	5200	9100	13,000
Series 40, 6-cyl.						
2d Rds	1100	3500	5800	11,600	20,300	29,000
4d Tr	1050	3350	5600	11,200	19,600	28,000
4d 7P Tr	1100	3500	5800	11,600	20,300	29,000
2d Cpe	600	1900	3200	6400	11,200	16,000
4d Sed	550	1700	2800	5600	9800	14,000
2d Cpe	700	2150	3600	7200	12,600	18,000
4d 7P Sed	650	2050	3400	6800	11,900	17,000
4d 50 7P Limo	700	2300	3800	7600	13,300	19,000
1923						
Series 30, 4-cyl.						
2d Rds	900	2900	4800	9600	16,800	24,000
2d Spt Rds	950	3000	5000	10,000	17,500	25,000
4d Tr	900	2900	4800	9600	16,800	24,000
2d Cpe	600	1900	3200	6400	11,200	16,000
4d Sed	550	1700	2800	5600	9800	14,000
4d Tr Sed	550	1800	3000	6000	10,500	15,000
Series 40, 6-cyl.						
2d Rds	1000	3100	5200	10,400	18,200	26,000
4d Tr	950	3000	5000	10,000	17,500	25,000
4d 7P Tr	1000	3100	5200	10,400	18,200	26,000

	6	5	4	3	2	1
2d Cpe	700	2150	3600	7200	12,600	18,000
4d Sed	600	1900	3200	6400	11,200	16,000
Master Series 50, 6-cyl.						
2d Spt Rds	1000	3250	5400	10,800	18,900	27,000
4d Spt Tr	1050	3350	5600	11,200	19,600	28,000
4d 7P Sed	700	2150	3600	7200	12,600	18,000
1924						
Standard Series 30, 4-cyl.						
2d Rds	1000	3100	5200	10,400	18,200	26,000
4d Tr	1000	3250	5400	10,800	18,900	27,000
2d Cpe	650	2050	3400	6800	11,900	17,000
4d Sed	550	1800	3000	6000	10,500	15,000
Master Series 40, 6-cyl.						
2d Rds	1000	3250	5400	10,800	18,900	27,000
4d Tr	1050	3350	5600	11,200	19,600	28,000
4d 7P Tr	1100	3500	5800	11,600	20,300	29,000
2d Cpe	700	2150	3600	7200	12,600	18,000
4d Sed	600	1900	3200	6400	11,200	16,000
4d Demi Sed	600	2000	3300	6600	11,600	16,500
Master Series 50, 6-cyl.						
2d Spt Rds	1050	3350	5600	11,200	19,600	28,000
4d Spt Tr	1100	3500	5800	11,600	20,300	29,000
2d Cabr Cpe	1000	3250	5400	10,800	18,900	27,000
4d Town Car	800	2500	4200	8400	14,700	21,000
4d 7P Sed	700	2300	3800	7600	13,300	19,000
4d Brgm Sed	750	2400	4000	8000	14,000	20,000
4d Limo	850	2650	4400	8800	15,400	22,000
1925						
Standard Series 20, 6-cyl.						
2d Rds	950	3000	5000	10,000	17,500	25,000
2d Spt Rds	1000	3100	5200	10,400	18,200	26,000
2d Encl Rds	1000	3250	5400	10,800	18,900	27,000
4d Tr	950	3000	5000	10,000	17,500	25,000
4d Encl Tr	1000	3100	5200	10,400	18,200	26,000
2d Bus Cpe	750	2400	4000	8000	14,000	20,000
2d Cpe	750	2450	4100	8200	14,400	20,500
4d Sed	700	2150	3600	7200	12,600	18,000
4d Demi Sed	700	2200	3700	7400	13,000	18,500
Master Series 40, 6-cyl.						
2d Rds	1000	3250	5400	10,800	18,900	27,000
2d Encl Rds	1050	3350	5600	11,200	19,600	28,000
4d Tr	1050	3350	5600	11,200	19,600	28,000
4d Encl Tr	1100	3500	5800	11,600	20,300	29,000
2d Cpe	800	2500	4200	8400	14,700	21,000
2d Sed	700	2150	3600	7200	12,600	18,000
4d Sed	700	2300	3800	7600	13,300	19,000
Master Series 50, 6-cyl.						
2d Spt Rds	1050	3350	5600	11,200	19,600	28,000
4d Spt Tr	1100	3500	5800	11,600	20,300	29,000
2d Cabr Cpe	1100	3500	5800	11,600	20,300	29,000
4d 7P Sed	800	2500	4200	8400	14,700	21,000
4d Limo	850	2650	4400	8800	15,400	22,000
4d Brgm Sed	850	2750	4600	9200	16,100	23,000
4d Town Car	950	3000	5000	10,000	17,500	25,000
1926						
Standard Series, 6-cyl.						
2d Rds	1000	3100	5200	10,400	18,200	26,000
4d Tr	1000	3250	5400	10,800	18,900	27,000
2d 2P Cpe	850	2750	4600	9200	16,100	23,000
2d 4P Cpe	850	2650	4400	8800	15,400	22,000
2d Sed	700	2300	3800	7600	13,300	19,000
4d Sed	750	2400	4000	8000	14,000	20,000
Master Series, 6-cyl.						
2d Rds	1000	3250	5400	10,800	18,900	27,000
4d Tr	1050	3350	5600	11,200	19,600	28,000
2d Spt Rds	1050	3350	5600	11,200	19,600	28,000
4d Spt Tr	1100	3500	5800	11,600	20,300	29,000
2d 4P Cpe	900	2900	4800	9600	16,800	24,000
2d Spt Cpe	950	3000	5000	10,000	17,500	25,000
2d Sed	850	2650	4400	8800	15,400	22,000
4d Sed	850	2750	4600	9200	16,100	23,000
4d Brgm	900	2900	4800	9600	16,800	24,000
4d 7P Sed	950	3000	5000	10,000	17,500	25,000
1927						
Series 115, 6-cyl.						
2d Rds	1000	3100	5200	10,400	18,200	26,000
4d Tr	1000	3250	5400	10,800	18,900	27,000
2d 2P Cpe	850	2650	4400	8800	15,400	22,000
2d 4P RS Cpe	850	2750	4600	9200	16,100	23,000
2d Spt Cpe	850	2650	4400	8800	15,400	22,000
2d Sed	700	2300	3800	7600	13,300	19,000
4d Sed	750	2400	4000	8000	14,000	20,000
4d Brgm	800	2500	4200	8400	14,700	21,000
Series 120, 6-cyl.						
2d 4P Cpe	850	2750	4600	9200	16,100	23,000
2d Sed	750	2400	4000	8000	14,000	20,000
4d Sed	800	2500	4200	8400	14,700	21,000
Series 128, 6-cyl.						
2d Spt Rds	1100	3500	5800	11,600	20,300	29,000
4d Spt Tr	1150	3600	6000	12,000	21,000	30,000
2d Conv	1000	3250	5400	10,800	18,900	27,000
2d 5P Cpe	900	2900	4800	9600	16,800	24,000
2d Spt Cpe RS	950	3000	5000	10,000	17,500	25,000
4d 7P Sed	850	2650	4400	8800	15,400	22,000
4d Brgm	850	2750	4600	9200	16,100	23,000
1928						
Series 115, 6-cyl.						
2d Rds	1000	3100	5200	10,400	18,200	26,000
4d Tr	1000	3250	5400	10,800	18,900	27,000
2d 2P Cpe	750	2400	4000	8000	14,000	20,000
2d Spt Cpe	800	2500	4200	8400	14,700	21,000
2d Sed	700	2150	3600	7200	12,600	18,000
4d Sed	700	2300	3800	7600	13,300	19,000
4d Brgm	750	2400	4000	8000	14,000	20,000
Series 120, 6-cyl.						
2d Cpe	800	2500	4200	8400	14,700	21,000
4d Sed	700	2300	3800	7600	13,300	19,000
4d Brgm	750	2400	4000	8000	14,000	20,000
Series 128, 6-cyl.						
2d Spt Rds	1150	3600	6000	12,000	21,000	30,000
4d Spt Tr	1150	3700	6200	12,400	21,700	31,000
2d 5P Cpe	800	2500	4200	8400	14,700	21,000
2d Spt Cpe	850	2650	4400	8800	15,400	22,000
4d 7P Sed	750	2400	4000	8000	14,000	20,000
4d Brgm	800	2500	4200	8400	14,700	21,000
1929						
Series 116, 6-cyl.						

	6	5	4	3	2	1
4d Spt Tr	1150	3600	6000	12,000	21,000	30,000
2d Bus Cpe	700	2150	3600	7200	12,600	18,000
2d RS Cpe	750	2400	4000	8000	14,000	20,000
2d Sed	550	1800	3000	6000	10,500	15,000
4d Sed	600	1900	3200	6400	11,200	16,000
Series 121, 6-cyl.						
2d Spt Rds	1150	3700	6200	12,400	21,700	31,000
2d Bus Cpe	700	2300	3800	7600	13,300	19,000
2d RS Cpe	800	2500	4200	8400	14,700	21,000
2d 4P Cpe	750	2400	4000	8000	14,000	20,000
4d Sed	650	2050	3400	6800	11,900	17,000
4d CC Sed	650	2100	3500	7000	12,300	17,500
Series 129, 6-cyl.						
2d Conv	1200	3850	6400	12,800	22,400	32,000
4d Spt Tr	1250	3950	6600	13,200	23,100	33,000
4d 7P Tr	1150	3600	6000	12,000	21,000	30,000
2d 5P Cpe	850	2650	4400	8800	15,400	22,000
4d CC Sed	750	2400	4000	8000	14,000	20,000
4d 7P Sed	800	2500	4200	8400	14,700	21,000
4d Limo	850	2650	4400	8800	15,400	22,000
1930						
Series 40, 6-cyl.						
2d Rds	1250	3950	6600	13,200	23,100	33,000
4d Phae	1300	4100	6800	13,600	23,800	34,000
2d Bus Cpe	700	2150	3600	7200	12,600	18,000
2d RS Cpe	800	2500	4200	8400	14,700	21,000
2d Sed	650	2100	3500	7000	12,300	17,500
4d Sed	700	2150	3600	7200	12,600	18,000
Series 50, 6-cyl.						
2d 4P Cpe	700	2300	3800	7600	13,300	19,000
4d Sed	700	2150	3600	7200	12,600	18,000
Series 60, 6-cyl.						
2d RS Rds	1300	4200	7000	14,000	24,500	35,000
4d 7P Tr	1350	4300	7200	14,400	25,200	36,000
2d RS Spt Cpe	850	2750	4600	9200	16,100	23,000
2d 5P Cpe	800	2500	4200	8400	14,700	21,000
4d Sed	700	2300	3800	7600	13,300	19,000
4d 7P Sed	750	2400	4000	8000	14,000	20,000
4d Limo	800	2500	4200	8400	14,700	21,000
Marquette - Series 30, 6-cyl.						
2d Spt Rds	1050	3350	5600	11,200	19,600	28,000
4d Phae	1100	3500	5800	11,600	20,300	29,000
2d Bus Cpe	600	1900	3200	6400	11,200	16,000
2d RS Cpe	700	2150	3600	7200	12,600	18,000
2d Sed	550	1800	3000	6000	10,500	15,000
4d Sed	600	1850	3100	6200	10,900	15,500
1931						
Series 50, 8-cyl.						
2d Spt Rds	1300	4200	7000	14,000	24,500	35,000
4d Phae	1350	4300	7200	14,400	25,200	36,000
2d Bus Cpe	750	2400	4000	8000	14,000	20,000
2d RS Cpe	800	2500	4200	8400	14,700	21,000
2d Sed	700	2150	3600	7200	12,600	18,000
4d Sed	700	2300	3800	7600	13,300	19,000
2d Conv	1350	4300	7200	14,400	25,200	36,000
Series 60, 8-cyl.						
2d Spt Rds	1400	4450	7400	14,800	25,900	37,000
4d Phae	1450	4550	7600	15,200	26,600	38,000
2d Bus Cpe	800	2500	4200	8400	14,700	21,000
2d RS Cpe	850	2650	4400	8800	15,400	22,000
4d Sed	750	2400	4000	8000	14,000	20,000
Series 80, 8-cyl.						
2d Cpe	950	3000	5000	10,000	17,500	25,000
4d Sed	850	2650	4400	8800	15,400	22,000
4d 7P Sed	850	2750	4600	9200	16,100	23,000
Series 90, 8-cyl.						
2d Spt Rds	1700	5400	9000	18,000	31,500	45,000
4d 7P Tr	1650	5300	8800	17,600	30,800	44,000
2d 5P Cpe	1150	3700	6200	12,400	21,700	31,000
2d RS Cpe	1150	3600	6000	12,000	21,000	30,000
2d Conv	1600	5150	8600	17,200	30,100	43,000
4d 5P Sed	950	3000	5000	10,000	17,500	25,000
4d 7P Sed	1000	3100	5200	10,400	18,200	26,000
4d Limo	1000	3250	5400	10,800	18,900	27,000
1932						
Series 50, 8-cyl						
4d Spt Phae	1450	4550	7600	15,200	26,600	38,000
2d Conv	1450	4700	7800	15,600	27,300	39,000
2d Phae	1500	4800	8000	16,000	28,000	40,000
2d Bus Cpe	850	2650	4400	8800	15,400	22,000
2d RS Cpe	850	2750	4600	9200	16,100	23,000
2d Vic Cpe	900	2900	4800	9600	16,800	24,000
4d Sed	700	2300	3800	7600	13,300	19,000
4d Spt Sed	750	2400	4000	8000	14,000	20,000
Series 60, 8-cyl.						
4d Spt Phae	1550	4900	8200	16,400	28,700	41,000
2d Conv	1600	5050	8400	16,800	29,400	42,000
2d Phae	1600	5150	8600	17,200	30,100	43,000
2d Bus Cpe	850	2750	4600	9200	16,100	23,000
2d RS Cpe	900	2900	4800	9600	16,800	24,000
2d Vic Cpe	950	3000	5000	10,000	17,500	25,000
4d Sed	800	2500	4200	8400	14,700	21,000
Series 80, 8-cyl.						
2d Vic Cpe	900	2900	4800	9600	16,800	24,000
4d Sed	850	2650	4400	8800	15,400	22,000
Series 90, 8-cyl.						
4d 7P Sed	1150	3600	6000	12,000	21,000	30,000
4d Limo	1200	3850	6400	12,800	22,400	32,000
4d Clb Sed	1150	3700	6200	12,400	21,700	31,000
4d Spt Phae	1850	5900	9800	19,600	34,300	49,000
2d Phae	1800	5750	9600	19,200	33,600	48,000
2d Conv Cpe	1900	6000	10,000	20,000	35,000	50,000
2d RS Cpe	1250	3950	6600	13,200	23,100	33,000
2d Vic Cpe	1300	4100	6800	13,600	23,800	34,000
4d 5P Sed	1150	3600	6000	12,000	21,000	30,000
1933						
Series 50, 8-cyl.						
2d Conv	1200	3850	6400	12,800	22,400	32,000
2d Bus Cpe	750	2400	4000	8000	14,000	20,000
2d RS Spt Cpe	800	2500	4200	8400	14,700	21,000
2d Vic Cpe	850	2750	4600	9200	16,100	23,000
4d Sed	700	2300	3800	7600	13,300	19,000
Series 60, 8-cyl.						
2d Conv Cpe	1200	3850	6400	12,800	22,400	32,000
4d Phae	1250	3950	6600	13,200	23,100	33,000
2d Spt Cpe	850	2750	4600	9200	16,100	23,000
2d Vic Cpe	1000	3250	5400	10,800	18,900	27,000

	6	5	4	3	2	1
4d Sed	850	2650	4400	8800	15,400	22,000
Series 80, 8-cyl.						
2d Conv	1400	4450	7400	14,800	25,900	37,000
4d Phae	1450	4700	7800	15,600	27,300	39,000
2d Spt Cpe	1100	3500	5800	11,600	20,300	29,000
2d Vic	1150	3600	6000	12,000	21,000	30,000
4d Sed	900	2900	4800	9600	16,800	24,000
Series 90, 8-cyl.						
2d Vic	1300	4100	6800	13,600	23,800	34,000
4d 5P Sed	1050	3350	5600	11,200	19,600	28,000
4d 7P Sed	1100	3500	5800	11,600	20,300	29,000
4d Clb Sed	1150	3600	6000	12,000	21,000	30,000
4d Limo	1250	3950	6600	13,200	23,100	33,000
1934						
Special Series 40, 8-cyl.						
2d Bus Cpe	800	2500	4200	8400	14,700	21,000
2d RS Cpe	850	2650	4400	8800	15,400	22,000
2d Tr Sed	700	2300	3800	7600	13,300	19,000
4d Tr Sed	800	2500	4200	8400	14,700	21,000
4d Sed	750	2400	4000	8000	14,000	20,000
Series 50, 8-cyl.						
2d Conv	1400	4450	7400	14,800	25,900	37,000
2d Bus Cpe	900	2900	4800	9600	16,800	24,000
2d Spt Cpe	1000	3100	5200	10,400	18,200	26,000
2d Vic Cpe	1000	3250	5400	10,800	18,900	27,000
4d Sed	800	2500	4200	8400	14,700	21,000
Series 60, 8-cyl.						
2d Conv	1450	4550	7600	15,200	26,600	38,000
4d Phae	1400	4450	7400	14,800	25,900	37,000
2d Spt Cpe	1000	3100	5200	10,400	18,200	26,000
2d Vic	1000	3250	5400	10,800	18,900	27,000
4d Sed	850	2650	4400	8800	15,400	22,000
4d Clb Sed	850	2750	4600	9200	16,100	23,000
Series 90, 8-cyl.						
2d Conv	1500	4800	8000	16,000	28,000	40,000
4d Phae	1450	4700	7800	15,600	27,300	39,000
4d Spt Cpe	1000	3250	5400	10,800	18,900	27,000
4d 5P Sed	950	3000	5000	10,000	17,500	25,000
4d 7P Sed	1000	3100	5200	10,400	18,200	26,000
4d Clb Sed	1000	3250	5400	10,800	18,900	27,000
4d Limo	1050	3350	5600	11,200	19,600	28,000
2d Vic	1150	3600	6000	12,000	21,000	30,000
1935						
Special Series 40, 8-cyl.						
2d Conv	1300	4100	6800	13,600	23,800	34,000
2d Bus Cpe	850	2650	4400	8800	15,400	22,000
2d RS Spt Cpe	900	2900	4800	9600	16,800	24,000
2d Sed	700	2300	3800	7600	13,300	19,000
2d Tr Sed	750	2400	4000	8000	14,000	20,000
4d Sed	750	2400	4000	8000	14,000	20,000
4d Tr Sed	800	2500	4200	8400	14,700	21,000
Series 50, 8-cyl.						
2d Conv	1300	4200	7000	14,000	24,500	35,000
2d Bus Cpe	850	2750	4600	9200	16,100	23,000
2d Spt Cpe	900	2900	4800	9600	16,800	24,000
2d Vic	950	3000	5000	10,000	17,500	25,000
4d Sed	800	2500	4200	8400	14,700	21,000
Series 60, 8-cyl.						
2d Conv	1300	4100	6800	13,600	23,800	34,000
4d Phae	1250	3950	6600	13,200	23,100	33,000
2d Vic	1050	3350	5600	11,200	19,600	28,000
4d Sed	850	2650	4400	8800	15,400	22,000
4d Clb Sed	850	2750	4600	9200	16,100	23,000
2d Spt Cpe	1000	3250	5400	10,800	18,900	27,000
Series 90, 8-cyl.						
2d Conv	1350	4300	7200	14,400	25,200	36,000
4d Phae	1300	4200	7000	14,000	24,500	35,000
2d Spt Cpe	1050	3350	5600	11,200	19,600	28,000
2d Vic	1100	3500	5800	11,600	20,300	29,000
4d 5P Sed	950	3000	5000	10,000	17,500	25,000
4d 7P Sed	1000	3100	5200	10,400	18,200	26,000
4d Limo	1050	3350	5600	11,200	19,600	28,000
4d Clb Sed	1000	3250	5400	10,800	18,900	27,000
1936						
Special Series 40, 8-cyl.						
2d Conv	1300	4100	6800	13,600	23,800	34,000
2d Bus Cpe	850	2650	4400	8800	15,400	22,000
2d RS Cpe	850	2750	4600	9200	16,100	23,000
2d Sed	750	2400	4000	8000	14,000	20,000
4d Sed	750	2400	4000	8000	14,000	20,000
Century Series 60, 8-cyl.						
2d Conv	1350	4300	7200	14,400	25,200	36,000
2d RS Cpe	1000	3100	5200	10,400	18,200	26,000
2d Sed	850	2650	4400	8800	15,400	22,000
4d Sed	900	2900	4800	9600	16,800	24,000
Roadmaster Series 80, 8-cyl.						
4d Phae	1300	4100	6800	13,600	23,800	34,000
4d Sed	950	3000	5000	10,000	17,500	25,000
Limited Series 90, 8-cyl.						
4d Sed	1000	3100	5200	10,400	18,200	26,000
4d 7P Sed	1000	3250	5400	10,800	18,900	27,000
4d Fml Sed	1050	3350	5600	11,200	19,600	28,000
4d 7P Limo	1150	3600	6000	12,000	21,000	30,000
1937						
Special Series 40, 8-cyl.						
2d Conv	1500	4800	8000	16,000	28,000	40,000
4d Phae	1450	4550	7600	15,200	26,600	38,000
2d Bus Cpe	800	2500	4200	8400	14,700	21,000
2d Spt Cpe	850	2650	4400	8800	15,400	22,000
2d FBk	750	2400	4000	8000	14,000	20,000
2d Sed	700	2300	3800	7600	13,300	19,000
4d FBk Sed	750	2400	4000	8000	14,000	20,000
4d Sed	750	2400	4000	8000	14,000	20,000
Century Series 60, 8-cyl.						
2d Conv	1600	5150	8600	17,200	30,100	43,000
4d Phae	1550	4900	8200	16,400	28,700	41,000
2d Spt Cpe	900	2900	4800	9600	16,800	24,000
2d FBk	800	2500	4200	8400	14,700	21,000
2d Sed	800	2500	4200	8400	14,700	21,000
4d FBk Sed	850	2650	4400	8800	15,400	22,000
4d Sed	850	2650	4400	8800	15,400	22,000
Roadmaster Series 80, 8-cyl.						
4d Sed	850	2750	4600	9200	16,100	23,000
4d Fml Sed	900	2900	4800	9600	16,800	24,000
4d Phae	1550	4900	8200	16,400	28,700	41,000
Limited Series 90, 8-cyl.						
4d Sed	900	2900	4800	9600	16,800	24,000
4d 7P Sed	950	3000	5000	10,000	17,500	25,000
4d Fml Sed	1000	3100	5200	10,400	18,200	26,000
4d Limo	1100	3500	5800	11,600	20,300	29,000
1938						
Special Series 40, 8-cyl.						
2d Conv	1600	5050	8400	16,800	29,400	42,000
4d Phae	1500	4800	8000	16,000	28,000	40,000
2d Bus Cpe	800	2500	4200	8400	14,700	21,000
2d Spt Cpe	850	2650	4400	8800	15,400	22,000
2d FBk	750	2400	4000	8000	14,000	20,000
2d Sed	750	2400	4000	8000	14,000	20,000
4d FBk Sed	800	2500	4200	8400	14,700	21,000
4d Sed	800	2500	4200	8400	14,700	21,000
Century Series 60, 8-cyl.						
2d Conv	1700	5400	9000	18,000	31,500	45,000
4d Phae	1600	5150	8600	17,200	30,100	43,000
2d Spt Cpe	900	2900	4800	9600	16,800	24,000
2d Sed	850	2650	4400	8800	15,400	22,000
4d FBk Sed	850	2650	4400	8800	15,400	22,000
4d Sed	850	2750	4600	9200	16,100	23,000
Roadmaster Series 80, 8-cyl.						
4d Phae	1700	5400	9000	18,000	31,500	45,000
4d FBk Sed	950	3000	5000	10,000	17,500	25,000
4d Sed	1000	3100	5200	10,400	18,200	26,000
4d Fml Sed	1000	3250	5400	10,800	18,900	27,000
Limited Series 90, 8-cyl.						
4d Sed	1050	3350	5600	11,200	19,600	28,000
4d 7P Sed	1100	3500	5800	11,600	20,300	29,000
4d Limo	1200	3850	6400	12,800	22,400	32,000
1939						
Special Series 40, 8-cyl.						
2d Conv	1650	5300	8800	17,600	30,800	44,000
4d Phae	1600	5050	8400	16,800	29,400	42,000
2d Bus Cpe	850	2750	4600	9200	16,100	23,000
2d Spt Cpe	900	2900	4800	9600	16,800	24,000
2d Sed	800	2500	4200	8400	14,700	21,000
4d Sed	800	2500	4200	8400	14,700	21,000
Century Series 60, 8-cyl.						
2d Conv	1750	5650	9400	18,800	32,900	47,000
4d Phae	1700	5400	9000	18,000	31,500	45,000
2d Spt Cpe	1000	3100	5200	10,400	18,200	26,000
2d Sed	850	2750	4600	9200	16,100	23,000
4d Sed	850	2750	4600	9200	16,100	23,000
Roadmaster Series 80, 8-cyl.						
4d Phae FBk	1800	5750	9600	19,200	33,600	48,000
4d Phae	1850	5900	9800	19,600	34,300	49,000
4d FBk Sed	1000	3100	5200	10,400	18,200	26,000
4d Sed	1000	3100	5200	10,400	18,200	26,000
4d Fml Sed	1050	3350	5600	11,200	19,600	28,000
Limited Series 90, 8-cyl.						
4d 8P Sed	1050	3350	5600	11,200	19,600	28,000
4d 4d Sed	1150	3600	6000	12,000	21,000	30,000
4d Limo	1000	3250	5400	10,800	18,900	27,000
1940						
Special Series 40, 8-cyl.						
2d Conv	1750	5500	9200	18,400	32,200	46,000
4d Phae	1650	5300	8800	17,600	30,800	44,000
2d Bus Cpe	850	2650	4400	8800	15,400	22,000
2d Spt Cpe	900	2900	4800	9600	16,800	24,000
2d Sed	800	2500	4200	8400	14,700	21,000
4d Sed	800	2500	4200	8400	14,700	21,000
Super Series 50, 8-cyl.						
2d Conv	1650	5300	8800	17,600	30,800	44,000
4d Phae	1600	5150	8600	17,200	30,100	43,000
2d Cpe	950	3000	5000	10,000	17,500	25,000
4d Sed	800	2500	4200	8400	14,700	21,000
4d Sta Wag	1200	3850	6400	12,800	22,400	32,000
Century Series 60, 8-cyl.						
2d Conv	1750	5650	9400	18,800	32,900	47,000
4d Phae	1700	5400	9000	18,000	31,500	45,000
2d Bus Cpe	1000	3100	5200	10,400	18,200	26,000
2d Spt Cpe	1000	3250	5400	10,800	18,900	27,000
4d Sed	850	2750	4600	9200	16,100	23,000
Roadmaster Series 70, 8-cyl.						
2d Conv	1800	5750	9600	19,200	33,600	48,000
4d Phae	1750	5500	9200	18,400	32,200	46,000
2d 2d Cpe	1050	3350	5600	11,200	19,600	28,000
4d Sed	950	3000	5000	10,000	17,500	25,000
Limited Series 80, 8-cyl.						
4d FBk Phae	1800	5750	9600	19,200	33,600	48,000
4d Phae	1850	5900	9800	19,600	34,300	49,000
4d FBk Sed	1050	3350	5600	11,200	19,600	28,000
4d Sed	1150	3600	6000	12,000	21,000	30,000
4d Fml Sed	1150	3700	6200	12,400	21,700	31,000
4d Fml FBk	1200	3850	6400	12,800	22,400	32,000
Limited Series 90, 8-cyl.						
4d 7P Sed	1150	3700	6200	12,400	21,700	31,000
4d Fml Sed	1200	3850	6400	12,800	22,400	32,000
4d Limo	1200	3850	6400	12,800	22,400	32,000
1941						
Special Series 40-A, 8-cyl.						
2d Conv	1600	5050	8400	16,800	29,400	42,000
2d Bus Cpe	800	2500	4200	8400	14,700	21,000
2d Spt Cpe	850	2650	4400	8800	15,400	22,000
4d Sed	750	2400	4000	8000	14,000	20,000
Special Series 40-B, 8-cyl.						
2d Bus Cpe	850	2750	4600	9200	16,100	23,000
2d S'net	900	2900	4800	9600	16,800	24,000
4d Sed	800	2500	4200	8400	14,700	21,000
4d Sta Wag	1200	3850	6400	12,800	22,400	32,000
NOTE: Add 5 percent for SSE.						
Super Series 50, 8-cyl.						
2d Conv	1750	5650	9400	18,800	32,900	47,000
4d Phae	1900	6100	10,200	20,400	35,700	51,000
2d Cpe	900	2950	4900	9800	17,200	24,500
4d Sed	850	2650	4400	8800	15,400	22,000
Century Series 60, 8-cyl.						
2d Bus Cpe	950	3000	5000	10,000	17,500	25,000
2d S'net	1000	3100	5200	10,400	18,200	26,000
4d Sed	900	2900	4800	9600	16,800	24,000
Roadmaster Series 70, 8-cyl.						
2d Conv	2000	6350	10,600	21,200	37,100	53,000
4d Phae	2050	6600	11,000	22,000	38,500	55,000
2d Cpe	1000	3250	5400	10,800	18,900	27,000
4d Sed	950	3000	5000	10,000	17,500	25,000
Limited Series 90, 8-cyl.						
4d 7P Sed	1300	4100	6800	13,600	23,800	34,000
4d Sed	1050	3350	5600	11,200	19,600	28,000

	6	5	4	3	2	1
4d Fml Sed	1150	3700	6200	12,400	21,700	31,000
4d Limo	1300	4100	6800	13,600	23,800	34,000
1942						
Special Series 40-A, 8-cyl.						
2d Bus Cpe	700	2150	3600	7200	12,600	18,000
2d S'net	750	2350	3900	7800	13,700	19,500
2d 3P S'net	700	2200	3700	7400	13,000	18,500
2d Conv	1200	3850	6400	12,800	22,400	32,000
4d Sed	700	2150	3600	7200	12,600	18,000
Special Series 40-B, 8-cyl.						
2d 3P S'net	750	2400	4000	8000	14,000	20,000
2d S'net	800	2500	4200	8400	14,700	21,000
4d Sed	700	2150	3600	7200	12,600	18,000
4d Sta Wag	1150	3700	6200	12,400	21,700	31,000
Super Series 50, 8-cyl.						
2d Conv	1300	4100	6800	13,600	23,800	34,000
2d S'net	850	2650	4400	8800	15,400	22,000
4d Sed	700	2200	3700	7400	13,000	18,500
Century Series 60, 8-cyl.						
2d S'net	850	2750	4600	9200	16,100	23,000
4d Sed	750	2350	3900	7800	13,700	19,500
Roadmaster Series 70, 8-cyl.						
2d Conv	1550	4900	8200	16,400	28,700	41,000
2d S'net	900	2900	4800	9600	16,800	24,000
4d Sed	850	2650	4400	8800	15,400	22,000
Limited Series 90, 8-cyl.						
4d 8P Sed	850	2750	4600	9200	16,100	23,000
4d Sed	850	2650	4400	8800	15,400	22,000
4d Fml Sed	900	2900	4800	9600	16,800	24,000
4d Limo	950	3000	5000	10,000	17,500	25,000
1946-1948						
Special Series 40, 8-cyl.						
2d S'net	650	2100	3500	7000	12,300	17,500
4d Sed	650	2050	3400	6800	11,900	17,000
Super Series 50, 8-cyl.						
2d Conv	1500	4800	8000	16,000	28,000	40,000
2d S'net	800	2500	4200	8400	14,700	21,000
4d Sed	700	2200	3700	7400	13,000	18,500
4d Sta Wag	1200	3850	6400	12,800	22,400	32,000
Roadmaster Series 70, 8-cyl.						
2d Conv	1750	5500	9200	18,400	32,200	46,000
2d S'net	900	2900	4800	9600	16,800	24,000
4d Sed	850	2650	4400	8800	15,400	22,000
4d Sta Wag	1300	4200	7000	14,000	24,500	35,000
1949						
Special Series 40, 8-cyl.						
2d S'net	700	2300	3800	7600	13,300	19,000
4d Sed	700	2150	3600	7200	12,600	18,000
Super Series 50, 8-cyl.						
2d Conv	1450	4700	7800	15,600	27,300	39,000
2d S'net	800	2500	4200	8400	14,700	21,000
4d Sed	750	2400	4000	8000	14,000	20,000
4d Sta Wag	1150	3700	6200	12,400	21,700	31,000
Roadmaster Series 70, 8-cyl.						
2d Conv	1700	5400	9000	18,000	31,500	45,000
2d Riv HT	1150	3600	6000	12,000	21,000	30,000
2d S'net	900	2900	4800	9600	16,800	24,000
4d Sed	850	2750	4600	9200	16,100	23,000
4d Sta Wag	1300	4100	6800	13,600	23,800	34,000

NOTE: Add 10 percent for sweap spear side trim on late 1949 Road master models.

	6	5	4	3	2	1
1950						
Special Series 40, 8-cyl., 121 1/2" wb						
2d Bus Cpe	550	1700	2800	5600	9800	14,000
2d S'net	600	1900	3200	6400	11,200	16,000
4d S'net	550	1800	3000	6000	10,500	15,000
4d Tr Sed	550	1700	2800	5600	9800	14,000
Special DeLuxe Series 40, 8-cyl., 121 1/2" wb						
2d S'net	650	2050	3400	6800	11,900	17,000
4d S'net	600	1900	3200	6400	11,200	16,000
4d Tr Sed	550	1800	3000	6000	10,500	15,000
Super Series 50, 8-cyl.						
2d Conv	1100	3500	5800	11,600	20,300	29,000
2d Riv HT	800	2500	4200	8400	14,700	21,000
2d S'net	700	2150	3600	7200	12,600	18,000
4d Sed	600	1900	3200	6400	11,200	16,000
4d Sta Wag	1150	3700	6200	12,400	21,700	31,000
Roadmaster Series 70, 8-cyl.						
2d Conv	1300	4200	7000	14,000	24,500	35,000
2d Riv HT	1050	3350	5600	11,200	19,600	28,000
2d S'net	800	2500	4200	8400	14,700	21,000
4d Sed 71	650	2050	3400	6800	11,900	17,000
4d Sed 72	700	2150	3600	7200	12,600	18,000
4d Sta Wag	1250	3950	6600	13,200	23,100	33,000
4d Riv Sed DeL	700	2150	3600	7200	12,600	18,000
1951-1952						
Special Series 40, 8-cyl., 121 1/2" wb						
2d Bus Cpe (1951 only)	550	1700	2800	5600	9800	14,000
2d Sed (1951 only)	500	1550	2600	5200	9100	13,000
4d Sed	500	1550	2600	5200	9100	13,000
2d Spt Cpe	550	1700	2800	5600	9800	14,000
Special DeLuxe Series 40, 8-cyl., 121 1/2" wb						
4d Sed	550	1700	2800	5600	9800	14,000
2d Sed	550	1700	2800	5600	9800	14,000
2d Riv HT	800	2500	4200	8400	14,700	21,000
2d Conv	1000	3250	5400	10,800	18,900	27,000
Super Series 50, 8-cyl.						
2d Conv	1050	3350	5600	11,200	19,600	28,000
2d Riv HT	850	2750	4600	9200	16,100	23,000
4d Sta Wag	1150	3700	6200	12,400	21,700	31,000
2d S'net (1951 only)	700	2150	3600	7200	12,600	18,000
4d Sed	600	1900	3200	6400	11,200	16,000
Roadmaster Series 70, 8-cyl.						
2d Conv	1150	3600	6000	12,000	21,000	30,000
2d Riv HT	1000	3250	5400	10,800	18,900	27,000
4d Sta Wag	1200	3850	6400	12,800	22,400	32,000
4d Riv Sed	700	2150	3600	7200	12,600	18,000
1953						
Special Series 40, 8-cyl.						
4d Sed	550	1800	3000	6000	10,500	15,000
2d Sed	550	1800	3050	6100	10,600	15,200
2d Riv HT	800	2500	4200	8400	14,700	21,000
2d Conv	1150	3700	6200	12,400	21,700	31,000
Super Series 50, V-8						
2d Riv HT	850	2650	4400	8800	15,400	22,000
2d Conv	1200	3850	6400	12,800	22,400	32,000

	6	5	4	3	2	1
4d Sta Wag	1200	3850	6400	12,800	22,400	32,000
4d Riv Sed	600	1900	3200	6400	11,200	16,000
Roadmaster Series 70, V-8						
2d Riv HT	1000	3100	5200	10,400	18,200	26,000
2d Skylark	2150	6850	11,400	22,800	39,900	57,000
2d Conv	1300	4100	6800	13,600	23,800	34,000
4d DeL Sta Wag	1250	3950	6600	13,200	23,100	33,000
4d Riv Sed	700	2150	3600	7200	12,600	18,000
1954						
Special Series 40, V-8						
4d Sed	500	1550	2600	5200	9100	13,000
2d Sed	500	1550	2600	5200	9100	13,000
2d Riv HT	750	2400	4000	8000	14,000	20,000
2d Conv	1200	3850	6400	12,800	22,400	32,000
4d Sta Wag	550	1800	3000	6000	10,500	15,000
Century Series 60, V-8						
4d DeL	550	1700	2800	5600	9800	14,000
2d Riv HT	850	2750	4600	9200	16,100	23,000
2d Conv	1450	4550	7600	15,200	26,600	38,000
4d Sta Wag	600	1900	3200	6400	11,200	16,000
Super Series 50, V-8						
4d Sed	500	1550	2600	5200	9100	13,000
2d Riv HT	800	2500	4200	8400	14,700	21,000
2d Conv	1250	3950	6600	13,200	23,100	33,000
Roadmaster Series 70, V-8						
4d Sed	550	1700	2800	5600	9800	14,000
2d Riv HT	1000	3100	5200	10,400	18,200	26,000
2d Conv	1450	4550	7600	15,200	26,600	38,000
Skylark Series, V-8						
2d Spt Conv	2050	6500	10,800	21,600	37,800	54,000
1955						
Special Series 40, V-8						
4d Sed	500	1550	2600	5200	9100	13,000
4d Riv HT	600	1900	3200	6400	11,200	16,000
2d Sed	500	1550	2600	5200	9100	13,000
2d Riv HT	900	2900	4800	9600	16,800	24,000
2d Conv	1450	4700	7800.	15,600	27,300	39,000
4d Sta Wag	600	1900	3200	6400	11,200	16,000
Century Series 60, V-8						
4d Sed	550	1700	2800	5600	9800	14,000
4d Riv HT	650	2050	3400	6800	11,900	17,000
2d Riv HT	950	3000	5000	10,000	17,500	25,000
2d Conv	1550	4900	8200	16,400	28,700	41,000
4d Sta Wag	650	2050	3400	6800	11,900	17,000
Super Series 50, V-8						
4d Sed	550	1700	2800	5600	9800	14,000
2d Riv HT	950	3000	5000	10,000	17,500	25,000
2d Conv	1450	4700	7800	15,600	27,300	39,000
Roadmaster Series 70, V-8						
4d Sed	600	1900	3200	6400	11,200	16,000
2d Riv HT	1050	3350	5600	11,200	19,600	28,000
2d Conv	1650	5300	8800	17,600	30,800	44,000
1956						
Special Series 40, V-8						
4d Sed	500	1550	2600	5200	9100	13,000
4d Riv HT	650	2050	3400	6800	11,900	17,000
2d Sed	500	1550	2600	5200	9100	13,000
2d Riv HT	950	3000	5000	10,000	17,500	25,000
2d Conv	1500	4800	8000	16,000	28,000	40,000
4d Sta Wag	600	1900	3200	6400	11,200	16,000
Century Series 60, V-8						
4d Sed	550	1700	2800	5600	9800	14,000
4d Riv HT	700	2300	3800	7600	13,300	19,000
2d Riv HT	1000	3100	5200	10,400	18,200	26,000
2d Conv	1600	5050	8400	16,800	29,400	42,000
4d Sta Wag	650	2050	3400	6800	11,900	17,000
Super Series 50						
4d Sed	550	1700	2800	5600	9800	14,000
4d Riv HT	800	2500	4200	8400	14,700	21,000
2d Riv HT	950	3000	5000	10,000	17,500	25,000
2d Conv	1450	4700	7800	15,600	27,300	39,000
Roadmaster Series 70, V-8						
4d Sed	550	1800	3000	6000	10,500	15,000
4d Riv HT	850	2750	4600	9200	16,100	23,000
2d Riv HT	1000	3250	5400	10,800	18,900	27,000
2d Conv	1600	5150	8600	17,200	30,100	43,000
1957						
Special Series 40, V-8						
4d Sed	450	1450	2400	4800	8400	12,000
4d Riv HT	650	2050	3400	6800	11,900	17,000
2d Sed	450	1450	2400	4800	8400	12,000
2d Riv HT	900	2900	4800	9600	16,800	24,000
2d Conv	1400	4450	7400	14,800	25,900	37,000
4d Sta Wag	700	2150	3600	7200	12,600	18,000
4d HT Wag	850	2750	4600	9200	16,100	23,000
Century Series 60, V-8						
4d Sed	500	1550	2600	5200	9100	13,000
4d Riv HT	700	2150	3600	7200	12,600	18,000
2d Riv HT	1000	3250	5400	10,800	18,900	27,000
2d Conv	1450	4700	7800	15,600	27,300	39,000
4d HT Wag	950	3000	5000	10,000	17,500	25,000
Super Series 50, V-8						
4d Riv HT	700	2300	3800	7600	13,300	19,000
2d Riv HT	1000	3250	5400	10,800	18,900	27,000
2d Conv	1450	4550	7600	15,200	26,600	38,000
Roadmaster Series 70, V-8						
4d Riv HT	750	2400	4000	8000	14,000	20,000
2d Riv HT	1050	3350	5600	11,200	19,600	28,000
2d Conv	1500	4800	8000	16,000	28,000	40,000

NOTE: Add 5 percent for 75 Series.

	6	5	4	3	2	1
1958						
Special Series 40, V-8						
4d Sed	400	1300	2200	4400	7700	11,000
4d Riv HT	550	1700	2800	5600	9800	14,000
2d Sed	400	1300	2200	4400	7700	11,000
2d Riv HT	700	2300	3800	7600	13,300	19,000
2d Conv	950	3000	5000	10,000	17,500	25,000
4d Sta Wag	450	1450	2400	4800	8400	12,000
4d HT Wag	650	2050	3400	6800	11,900	17,000
Century Series 60, V-8						
4d Sed	450	1450	2400	4800	8400	12,000
4d Riv HT	550	1800	3000	6000	10,500	15,000
2d Riv HT	850	2650	4400	8800	15,400	22,000
2d Conv	1000	3250	5400	10,800	18,900	27,000
4d HT Wag	700	2300	3800	7600	13,300	19,000
Super Series 50, V-8						

	6	5	4	3	2	1
4d Riv HT	600	1900	3200	6400	11,200	16,000
2d Riv HT	700	2300	3800	7600	13,300	19,000
Roadmaster Series 75, V-8						
4d Riv HT	650	2050	3400	6800	11,900	17,000
2d Riv HT	850	2650	4400	8800	15,400	22,000
2d Conv	1150	3700	6200	12,400	21,700	31,000
Limited Series 700, V-8						
4d Riv HT	700	2300	3800	7600	13,300	19,000
2d Riv HT	850	2750	4600	9200	16,100	23,000
2d Conv	1600	5050	8400	16,800	29,400	42,000

1959

	6	5	4	3	2	1
LeSabre Series 4400, V-8						
4d Sed	400	1300	2200	4400	7700	11,000
4d HT	500	1550	2600	5200	9100	13,000
2d Sed	400	1350	2250	4500	7800	11,200
2d HT	600	1900	3200	6400	11,200	16,000
2d Conv	950	3000	5000	10,000	17,500	25,000
4d Sta Wag	500	1550	2600	5200	9100	13,000
Invicta Series 4600, V-8						
4d Sed	450	1450	2400	4800	8400	12,000
4d HT	550	1700	2800	5600	9800	14,000
2d HT	650	2050	3400	6800	11,900	17,000
2d Conv	1050	3350	5600	11,200	19,600	28,000
4d Sta Wag	550	1700	2800	5600	9800	14,000
Electra Series 4700, V-8						
4d Sed	500	1550	2600	5200	9100	13,000
4d HT	550	1800	3000	6000	10,500	15,000
2d HT	650	2050	3400	6800	11,900	17,000
Electra 225 Series 4800, V-8						
4d Riv HT 6W	550	1700	2800	5600	9800	14,000
4d HT 4W	550	1800	3000	6000	10,500	15,000
2d Conv	1150	3700	6200	12,400	21,700	31,000

1960

	6	5	4	3	2	1
LeSabre Series 4400, V-8						
4d Sed	400	1300	2200	4400	7700	11,000
4d HT	500	1550	2600	5200	9100	13,000
2d Sed	400	1350	2250	4500	7800	11,200
2d HT	600	1900	3200	6400	11,200	16,000
2d Conv	1000	3100	5200	10,400	18,200	26,000
4d Sta Wag	450	1450	2400	4800	8400	12,000
Invicta Series 4600, V-8						
4d Sed	450	1450	2400	4800	8400	12,000
4d HT	550	1700	2800	5600	9800	14,000
2d HT	650	2050	3400	6800	11,900	17,000
2d Conv	1100	3500	5800	11,600	20,300	29,000
4d Sta Wag	500	1550	2600	5200	9100	13,000
Electra Series 4700, V-8						
4d Riv HT 6W	550	1800	3000	6000	10,500	15,000
4d HT 4W	600	1900	3200	6400	11,200	16,000
2d HT	700	2150	3600	7200	12,600	18,000
Electra 225 Series 4800, V-8						
4d Riv HT 6W	600	1900	3200	6400	11,200	16,000
4d HT 4W	650	2050	3400	6800	11,900	17,000
2d Conv	1150	3700	6200	12,400	21,700	31,000

NOTE: Add 5 percent for bucket seat option.

1961

	6	5	4	3	2	1
Special Series 4000, V-8, 112" wb						
4d Sed	400	1200	2000	4000	7000	10,000
2d Cpe	400	1300	2200	4400	7700	11,000
4d Sta Wag	400	1300	2200	4400	7700	11,000
Special DeLuxe Series 4100, V-8, 112" wb						
4d Sed	400	1250	2100	4200	7400	10,500
2d Skylark Cpe	450	1450	2400	4800	8400	12,000
4d Sta Wag	450	1450	2400	4800	8400	12,000

NOTE: Deduct 5 percent for V-6.

	6	5	4	3	2	1
LeSabre Series 4400, V-8						
4d Sed	400	1300	2200	4400	7700	11,000
4d HT	450	1450	2400	4800	8400	12,000
2d Sed	400	1300	2200	4400	7700	11,000
2d HT	500	1550	2600	5200	9100	13,000
2d Conv	850	2650	4400	8800	15,400	22,000
4d Sta Wag	450	1450	2400	4800	8400	12,000
Invicta Series 4600, V-8						
4d HT	450	1450	2400	4800	8400	12,000
2d HT	550	1700	2800	5600	9800	14,000
2d Conv	900	2900	4800	9600	16,800	24,000
Electra Series 4700, V-8						
4d Sed	450	1400	2300	4600	8100	11,500
4d HT	450	1450	2400	4800	8400	12,000
2d HT	500	1550	2600	5200	9100	13,000
Electra 225 Series 4800, V-8						
4d Riv HT 6W	450	1450	2400	4800	8400	12,000
4d Riv HT 4W	450	1500	2500	5000	8800	12,500
2d Conv	1050	3350	5600	11,200	19,600	28,000

1962

	6	5	4	3	2	1
Special Series 4000, V-6, 112.1" wb						
4d Sed	400	1250	2100	4200	7400	10,600
2d Cpe	450	1400	2300	4600	8100	11,500
2d Conv	650	2050	3400	6800	11,900	17,000
4d Sta Wag	400	1300	2200	4400	7700	11,000
Special DeLuxe Series 4100, V-8, 112.1" wb						
4d Sed	400	1300	2200	4400	7700	11,000
2d Conv	700	2300	3800	7600	13,300	19,000
4d Sta Wag	450	1450	2400	4800	8400	12,000
Special Skylark Series 4300, V-8, 112.1" wb						
2d HT	450	1400	2300	4600	8100	11,500
2d Conv	750	2400	4000	8000	14,000	20,000
LeSabre Series 4400, V-8						
4d Sed	400	1300	2200	4400	7700	11,000
4d HT	450	1450	2400	4800	8400	12,000
2d Sed	400	1300	2200	4400	7700	11,000
2d HT	500	1550	2600	5200	9100	13,000
Invicta Series 4600, V-8						
4d HT	450	1450	2400	4800	8400	12,000
2d HT	550	1700	2800	5600	9800	14,000
2d HT Wildcat	550	1800	3000	6000	10,500	15,000
2d Conv	900	2900	4800	9600	16,800	24,000
4d Sta Wag*	450	1450	2400	4800	8400	12,000

NOTE: Add 10 percent for bucket seat option where offered.

	6	5	4	3	2	1
Electra 225 Series 4800, V-8						
4d Sed	400	1300	2200	4400	7700	11,000
4d Riv HT 6W	500	1550	2600	5200	9100	13,000
4d HT 4W	550	1700	2800	5600	9800	14,000
2d HT	600	1900	3200	6400	11,200	16,000
2d Conv	1050	3350	5600	11,200	19,600	28,000

1963

	6	5	4	3	2	1
Special Series 4000, V-6, 112" wb						
4d Sed	400	1250	2100	4200	7400	10,600
2d Cpe	400	1300	2150	4300	7500	10,700
2d Conv	550	1800	3000	6000	10,500	15,000
4d Sta Wag	400	1300	2200	4400	7700	11,000
Special DeLuxe Series 4100, V-6, 112" wb						
4d Sed	400	1300	2150	4300	7500	10,700
4d Sta Wag	450	1400	2300	4600	8100	11,500
Special DeLuxe Series 4100, V-8, 112" wb						
4d Sed	400	1300	2150	4300	7600	10,800
4d Sta Wag	450	1400	2350	4700	8300	11,800
Special Skylark Series 4300, V-8, 112" wb						
2d HT	450	1500	2500	5000	8800	12,500
2d Conv	600	1900	3200	6400	11,200	16,000
LeSabre Series 4400, V-8						
4d Sed	400	1300	2150	4300	7500	10,700
4d HT	450	1450	2400	4800	8400	12,000
2d Sed	400	1250	2100	4200	7400	10,500
2d HT	500	1550	2600	5200	9100	13,000
4d Sta Wag	400	1300	2200	4400	7700	11,000
2d Conv	700	2300	3800	7600	13,300	19,000
Invicta Series 4600, V-8						
4d Sta Wag	450	1500	2500	5000	8800	12,500
Wildcat Series 4600, V-8						
4d HT	450	1500	2500	5000	8800	12,500
2d HT	500	1600	2700	5400	9500	13,500
2d Conv	850	2650	4400	8800	15,400	22,000
Electra 225 Series 4800, V-8						
4d Sed	400	1250	2100	4200	7400	10,500
4d HT 6W	450	1450	2400	4800	8400	12,000
4d HT 4W	450	1500	2500	5000	8800	12,500
2d HT	500	1600	2700	5400	9500	13,500
2d Conv	900	2900	4800	9600	16,800	24,000
Riviera Series 4700, V-8						
2d HT	650	2050	3400	6800	11,900	17,000

1964

	6	5	4	3	2	1
Special Series 4000, V-6, 115" wb						
4d Sed	450	1080	1800	3600	6300	9000
2d Cpe	950	1100	1850	3700	6450	9200
2d Conv	550	1800	3000	6000	10,500	15,000
4d Sta Wag	450	1140	1900	3800	6650	9500
Special Deluxe Series 4100, V-6, 115" wb						
4d Sed	450	1120	1875	3750	6500	9300
2d Cpe	450	1140	1900	3800	6650	9500
4d Sta Wag	400	1200	2000	4000	7000	10,000
Special Skylark Series 4300, V-6, 115" wb						
4d Sed	450	1140	1900	3800	6650	9500
2d HT	400	1200	2000	4000	7000	10,000
2d Conv	650	2050	3400	6800	11,900	17,000
Special Series 4000, V-8, 115" wb						
4d Sed	450	1140	1900	3800	6650	9500
2d Cpe	450	1150	1900	3850	6700	9600
2d Conv	650	2050	3400	6800	11,900	17,000
4d Sta Wag	400	1200	2050	4100	7100	10,200
Special DeLuxe Series 4100, V-8, 115" wb						
4d Sed	450	1160	1950	3900	6800	9700
2d Cpe	450	1170	1975	3900	6850	9800
4d Sta Wag	400	1250	2100	4200	7400	10,500
Skylark Series 4300, V-8, 115" wb						
4d Sed	400	1200	2000	4000	7000	10,000
2d HT	400	1300	2200	4400	7700	11,000
2d Conv	750	2400	4000	8000	14,000	20,000
Skylark Series 4200, V-8, 120" wb						
4d Spt Wag	400	1200	2000	4000	7000	10,000
4d Cus Spt Wag	400	1200	2050	4100	7100	10,200
LeSabre Series 4400, V-8						
4d Sed	400	1200	2050	4100	7100	10,200
4d HT	400	1250	2100	4200	7400	10,500
2d HT	450	1500	2500	5000	8800	12,500
2d Conv	750	2400	4000	8000	14,000	20,000
4d Spt Wag	400	1350	2250	4500	7900	11,300
Wildcat Series 4600, V-8						
4d Sed	400	1250	2050	4100	7200	10,300
4d HT	450	1500	2500	5000	8800	12,500
2d HT	500	1600	2700	5400	9500	13,500
2d Conv	800	2500	4200	8400	14,700	21,000
Electra 225 Series 4800, V-8						
4d Sed	400	1250	2100	4200	7300	10,400
4d HT 6W	450	1400	2300	4600	8100	11,500
4d HT 4W	450	1450	2400	4800	8400	12,000
2d HT	550	1700	2800	5600	9800	14,000
2d Conv	850	2650	4400	8800	15,400	22,000
Riviera Series 4700, V-8						
2d HT	650	2050	3400	6800	11,900	17,000

1965

	6	5	4	3	2	1
Special, V-6, 115" wb						
4d Sed	350	900	1500	3000	5250	7500
2d Cpe	350	950	1500	3050	5300	7600
2d Conv	550	1700	2800	5600	9800	14,000
4d Sta Wag	350	1020	1700	3400	5950	8500
Special DeLuxe, V-6, 115" wb						
4d Sed	350	1040	1750	3500	6100	8700
4d Sta Wag	450	1050	1800	3600	6200	8900
Skylark, V-6, 115" wb						
4d Sed	450	1080	1800	3600	6300	9000
2d Cpe	450	1120	1875	3750	6500	9300
2d HT	400	1250	2050	4100	7200	10,300
2d Conv	650	2050	3400	6800	11,900	17,000
Special, V-8, 115" wb						
4d Sed	350	1040	1750	3500	6100	8700
2d Cpe	450	1050	1750	3550	6150	8800
2d Conv	700	2150	3600	7200	12,600	18,000
4d Sta Wag	350	1040	1750	3500	6100	8700
Special DeLuxe, V-8, 115" wb						
4d Sed	450	1050	1800	3600	6200	8900
4d Sta Wag	450	1080	1800	3600	6300	9000
Skylark, V-8, 115" wb						
4d Sed	450	1120	1875	3750	6500	9300
2d Cpe	450	1140	1900	3800	6650	9500
2d HT	400	1300	2150	4300	7600	10,800
2d Conv	700	2300	3800	7600	13,300	19,000

NOTE: Add 20 percent for Skylark Gran Sport Series (400 CID/325hp V-8). Deduct 5 percent for V-6.

	6	5	4	3	2	1
Sport Wagon, V-8, 120" wb						
4d 2S Sta Wag	450	1150	1900	3850	6700	9600
4d 3S Sta Wag	450	1160	1950	3900	6800	9700
Custom Sport Wagon, V-8, 120" wb						

	6	5	4	3	2	1
4d 2S Sta Wag	450	1170	1975	3900	6850	9800
4d 3S Sta Wag	450	1190	2000	3950	6900	9900
LeSabre, V-8, 123" wb						
4d Sed	350	975	1600	3250	5700	8100
4d HT	350	1000	1650	3350	5800	8300
2d HT	450	1120	1875	3750	6500	9300
LeSabre Custom, V-8, 123" wb						
4d Sed	350	1000	1650	3350	5800	8300
4d HT	450	1050	1800	3600	6200	8900
2d HT	450	1170	1975	3900	6850	9800
2d Conv	550	1800	3000	6000	10,500	15,000
Wildcat, V-8, 126" wb						
4d Sed	450	1050	1750	3550	6150	8800
4d HT	450	1120	1875	3750	6500	9300
2d HT	400	1250	2050	4100	7200	10,300
Wildcat DeLuxe, V-8, 126" wb						
4d Sed	450	1080	1800	3600	6300	9000
4d HT	450	1140	1900	3800	6650	9500
2d HT	400	1250	2100	4200	7400	10,600
2d Conv	600	1900	3200	6400	11,200	16,000
Wildcat Custom, V-8, 126" wb						
4d HT	450	1170	1975	3900	6850	9800
2d HT	400	1300	2150	4300	7600	10,800
2d Conv	650	2050	3400	6800	11,900	17,000
Electra 225, V-8, 126" wb						
4d Sed	450	1120	1875	3750	6500	9300
4d HT	400	1250	2050	4100	7200	10,300
2d HT	400	1350	2250	4500	7900	11,300
Electra 225 Custom, V-8, 126" wb						
4d Sed	450	1140	1900	3800	6650	9500
4d HT	400	1250	2100	4200	7400	10,600
2d HT	450	1400	2350	4700	8200	11,700
2d Conv	650	2050	3400	6800	11,900	17,000
Riviera, V-8, 117" wb						
2d HT	550	1800	3000	6000	10,500	15,000
2d HT GS	600	1900	3200	6400	11,200	16,000

NOTE: Add 20 percent for 400.

1966

	6	5	4	3	2	1
Special, V-6, 115" wb						
4d Sed	350	840	1400	2800	4900	7000
2d Cpe	350	850	1450	2850	4970	7100
2d Conv	550	1800	3000	6000	10,500	15,000
4d Sta Wag	350	840	1400	2800	4900	7000
Special DeLuxe, V-6, 115" wb						
4d Sed	350	850	1450	2850	4970	7100
2d Cpe	350	860	1450	2900	5050	7200
2d HT	350	1000	1650	3350	5800	8300
4d Sta Wag	350	850	1450	2850	4970	7100
Skylark, V-6, 115" wb						
4d HT	350	880	1500	2950	5180	7400
2d Cpe	350	900	1500	3000	5250	7500
2d HT	450	1050	1750	3550	6150	8800
2d Conv	600	1900	3200	6400	11,200	16,000
Special, V-8, 115" wb						
4d Sed	350	870	1450	2900	5100	7300
2d Cpe	350	880	1500	2950	5180	7400
2d Conv	550	1800	3000	6000	10,500	15,000
4d Sta Wag	350	870	1450	2900	5100	7300
Special DeLuxe, V-8						
4d Sed	350	900	1500	3000	5250	7500
2d Cpe	350	950	1550	3150	5450	7800
2d HT	450	1050	1750	3550	6150	8800
4d Sta Wag	350	900	1500	3000	5250	7500
Skylark, V-8						
4d HT	350	975	1600	3200	5600	8000
2d Cpe	350	975	1600	3250	5700	8100
2d HT	450	1120	1875	3750	6500	9300
2d Conv	650	2050	3400	6800	11,900	17,000
Skylark Gran Sport, V-8, 115" wb						
2d Cpe	700	2150	3600	7200	12,600	18,000
2d HT	450	1450	2400	4800	8400	12,000
2d Conv	700	2300	3800	7600	13,300	19,000
Sport Wagon, V-8, 120" wb						
4d 2S Sta Wag	350	1020	1700	3400	5900	8400
4d 3S Sta Wag	350	1020	1700	3400	5950	8500
4d 2S Cus Sta Wag	350	1040	1700	3450	6000	8600
4d 3S Cus Sta Wag	450	1050	1750	3550	6150	8800
LeSabre, V-8, 123" wb						
4d Sed	350	870	1450	2900	5100	7300
4d HT	350	1000	1650	3350	5800	8300
2d HT	450	1120	1875	3750	6500	9300
LeSabre Custom, V-8, 123" wb						
4d Sed	350	950	1550	3100	5400	7700
4d HT	350	1000	1650	3350	5800	8300
2d H p	450	1150	1900	3850	6700	9600
2d Conv	650	2050	3400	6800	11,900	17,000
Wildcat, V-8, 126" wb						
4d Sed	350	950	1550	3150	5450	7800
4d HT	450	1050	1750	3550	6150	8800
2d HT	450	1170	1975	3900	6850	9800
2d Conv	700	2150	3600	7200	12,600	18,000
Wildcat Custom, V-8, 126" wb						
4d Sed	350	975	1600	3200	5500	7900
4d HT	350	1000	1650	3300	5750	8200
2d HT	450	1120	1875	3750	6500	9300
2d Conv	700	2300	3800	7600	13,300	19,000

NOTE: Add 20 percent for Wildcat Gran Sport Series.

	6	5	4	3	2	1
Electra 225, V-8, 126" wb						
4d Sed	450	1050	1750	3550	6150	8800
4d HT	450	1120	1875	3750	6500	9300
2d HT	400	1250	2050	4100	7200	10,300
Electra 225 Custom, V-8						
4d Sed	450	1050	1750	3550	6150	8800
4d HT	450	1170	1975	3900	6850	9800
2d HT	400	1300	2150	4300	7600	10,800
2d Conv	750	2400	4000	8000	14,000	20,000
Riviera, V-8						
2d HT GS	450	1450	2400	4800	8400	12,000
2d HT	400	1300	2200	4400	7700	11,000

NOTE: Add 20 percent for 400. Not available in Riviera.

1967

	6	5	4	3	2	1
Special, V-6, 115" wb						
4d Sed	350	830	1400	2950	4830	6900
2d Cpe	350	840	1400	2800	4900	7000
4d Sta Wag	350	820	1400	2700	4760	6800
Special DeLuxe, V-6, 115" wb						
4d Sed	350	840	1400	2800	4900	7000
2d HT	350	975	1600	3200	5600	8000
Skylark, V-6, 115" wb						
2d Cpe	350	950	1550	3150	5450	7800
Special, V-8, 115" wb						
4d Sed	350	850	1450	2850	4970	7100
2d Cpe	350	900	1500	3000	5250	7500
4d Sta Wag	350	860	1450	2900	5050	7200
Special DeLuxe, V-8, 115" wb						
4d Sed	350	860	1450	2900	5050	7200
2d HT	350	1020	1700	3400	5950	8500
4d Sta Wag	350	870	1450	2900	5100	7300
Skylark, V-8, 115" wb						
4d Sed	350	870	1450	2900	5100	7300
4d HT	350	900	1500	3000	5250	7500
2d Cpe	350	975	1600	3200	5600	8000
2d HT	450	1080	1800	3600	6300	9000
2d Conv	600	1900	3200	6400	11,200	16,000
Sport Wagon, V-8, 120" wb						
4d 2S Sta Wag	350	850	1450	2850	4970	7100
4d 3S Sta Wag	350	860	1450	2900	5050	7200
Gran Sport 340, V-8, 115" wb						
2d HT	450	1450	2400	4800	8400	12,000
Gran Sport 400, V-8, 115" wb						
2d Cpe	400	1200	2000	4000	7000	10,000
2d HT	450	1500	2500	5000	8800	12,500
2d Conv	650	2050	3400	6800	11,900	17,000
LeSabre, V-8, 123" wb						
4d Sed	350	880	1500	2950	5180	7400
4d HT	350	950	1500	3050	5300	7600
2d HT	350	975	1600	3200	5600	8000
LeSabre Custom, V-8, 123" wb						
4d Sed	350	950	1500	3050	5300	7600
4d HT	350	950	1550	3150	5450	7800
2d HT	350	1020	1700	3400	5950	8500
2d Conv	550	1800	3000	6000	10,500	15,000
Wildcat, V-8, 126" wb						
4d Sed	350	950	1550	3150	5450	7800
4d HT	350	975	1600	3200	5600	8000
2d HT	450	1140	1900	3800	6650	9500
2d Conv	600	1900	3200	6400	11,200	16,000
Wildcat Custom, V-8, 126" wb						
4d HT	350	950	1550	3150	5450	7800
2d HT	450	1080	1800	3600	6300	9000
2d Conv	700	2150	3600	7200	12,600	18,000
Electra 225, V-8, 126" wb						
4d Sed	350	950	1550	3100	5400	7700
4d HT	350	975	1600	3200	5500	7900
2d HT	400	1200	2000	4000	7000	10,000
Electra 225 Custom, V-8, 126" wb						
4d Sed	350	975	1600	3250	5700	8100
4d HT	350	1020	1700	3400	5900	8400
2d HT	400	1250	2100	4200	7400	10,500
2d Conv	750	2400	4000	8000	14,000	20,000
Riviera Series, V-8						
2d HT GS	400	1250	2100	4200	7400	10,500
2d HT	400	1300	2200	4400	7700	11,000

NOTE: Add 20 percent for 400. Not available in Riviera.

1968

	6	5	4	3	2	1
Special DeLuxe, V-6, 116" wb, 2 dr 112" wb						
4d Sed	350	800	1350	2700	4700	6700
2d Sed	350	820	1400	2700	4760	6800
Skylark, V-6, 116" wb, 2 dr 112" wb						
4d Sed	350	820	1400	2700	4760	6800
2d HT	350	900	1500	3000	5250	7500
Special DeLuxe, V-8, 116" wb, 2 dr 112" wb						
4d Sed	350	820	1400	2700	4760	6800
2d Sed	350	830	1400	2950	4830	6900
4d Sta Wag	350	830	1400	2950	4830	6900
Skylark, V-8, 116" wb, 2 dr 112" wb						
4d Sed	350	830	1400	2950	4830	6900
4d HT	350	840	1400	2800	4900	7000
Skylark Custom, V-8, 116" wb, 2 dr 112" wb						
4d Sed	350	840	1400	2800	4900	7000
4d HT	350	870	1450	2900	5100	7300
2d HT	350	975	1600	3200	5600	8000
2d Conv	550	1800	3000	6000	10,500	15,000
Sport Wagon, V-8, 121" wb						
4d 2S Sta Wag	350	870	1450	2900	5100	7300
4d 3S Sta Wag	350	880	1500	2950	5180	7400
Gran Sport GS 350, V-8, 112" wb						
2d HT	450	1500	2500	5000	8800	12,500
Gran Sport GS 400, V-8, 112" wb						
2d HT	500	1550	2600	5200	9100	13,000
2d Conv	600	1900	3200	6400	11,200	16,000

NOTE: Add 15 percent for Skylark GS Calif. Spl.

	6	5	4	3	2	1
LeSabre, V-8, 123" wb						
4d Sed	350	870	1450	2900	5100	7300
4d HT	350	950	1500	3050	5300	7600
2d HT	350	1020	1700	3400	5950	8500
LeSabre Custom, V-8, 123" wb						
4d Sed	350	880	1500	2950	5180	7400
4d HT	350	950	1550	3100	5400	7700
2d HT	450	1080	1800	3600	6300	9000
2d Conv	600	1900	3200	6400	11,200	16,000
Wildcat, V-8, 126" wb						
4d Sed	350	900	1500	3000	5250	7500
4d HT	350	950	1550	3150	5450	7800
2d HT	450	1140	1900	3800	6650	9500
Wildcat Custom, V-8, 126" wb						
4d HT	350	975	1600	3250	5700	8100
2d HT	400	1200	2000	4000	7000	10,000
2d Conv	700	2150	3600	7200	12,600	18,000
Electra 225, V-8, 126" wb						
4d Sed	350	975	1600	3200	5600	8000
4d HT	350	1020	1700	3400	5900	8400
2d HT	400	1250	2100	4200	7400	10,500
Electra 225 Custom, V-8, 126" wb						
4d Sed	350	975	1600	3250	5700	8100
4d HT	350	1020	1700	3400	5950	8500
2d HT	400	1300	2200	4400	7700	11,000
2d Conv	750	2400	4000	8000	14,000	20,000
Riviera Series, V-8						
2d HT GS	450	1400	2300	4600	8100	11,500
2d HT	400	1300	2200	4400	7700	11,000

NOTE: Add 20 percent for 400. Not available in Riviera.

1969

Special DeLuxe, V-6, 116" wb, 2 dr 112" wb

	6	5	4	3	2	1
4d Sed	350	800	1350	2700	4700	6700
2d Sed	350	790	1350	2650	4620	6600
Skylark, V-6, 116" wb, 2 dr 112" wb						
4d Sed	350	820	1400	2700	4760	6800
2d HT	350	840	1400	2800	4900	7000
Special DeLuxe, V-8, 116" wb, 2 dr 112" wb						
4d Sed	350	820	1400	2700	4760	6800
2d Sed	350	800	1350	2700	4700	6700
4d Sta Wag	350	820	1400	2700	4760	6800
Skylark, V-8, 116" wb, 2 dr 112" wb						
4d Sed	350	830	1400	2950	4830	6900
2d HT	350	975	1600	3200	5600	8000
Skylark Custom, V-8, 116" wb, 2 dr 112" wb						
4d Sed	350	840	1400	2800	4900	7000
4d HT	350	850	1450	2850	4970	7100
2d HT	450	1080	1800	3600	6300	9000
2d Conv	550	1700	2800	5600	9800	14,000
Gran Sport GS 350, V-8, 112" wb						
2d Calif GS	450	1450	2400	4800	8400	12,000
2d HT	500	1550	2600	5200	9100	13,000
Gran Sport GS 400, V-8, 112" wb						
2d HT	550	1700	2800	5600	9800	14,000
2d Conv	700	2150	3600	7200	12,600	18,000

NOTE: Add 30 percent for Stage I option.

	6	5	4	3	2	1
Sport Wagon, V-8, 121" wb						
4d 2S Sta Wag	350	850	1450	2850	4970	7100
4d 3S Sta Wag	350	860	1450	2900	5050	7200
LeSabre, V-8, 123.2" wb						
4d Sed	350	860	1450	2900	5050	7200
4d HT	350	870	1450	2900	5100	7300
2d HT	350	950	1550	3150	5450	7800
LeSabre Custom, V-8, 123.2" wb						
4d Sed	350	870	1450	2900	5100	7300
4d HT	350	880	1500	2950	5180	7400
2d HT	350	975	1600	3200	5600	8000
2d Conv	550	1700	2800	5600	9800	14,000
Wildcat, V-8, 123.2" wb						
4d Sed	350	900	1500	3000	5250	7500
4d HT	350	950	1550	3100	5400	7700
2d HT	350	1020	1700	3400	5950	8500
Wildcat Custom, V-8, 123.2" wb						
4d HT	350	975	1600	3200	5500	7900
2d HT	450	1080	1800	3600	6300	9000
2d Conv	550	1800	3000	6000	10,500	15,000
Electra 225, V-8, 126.2" wb						
4d Sed	350	950	1500	3050	5300	7600
4d HT	350	950	1550	3100	5400	7700
2d HT	450	1140	1900	3800	6650	9500
Electra 225 Custom, V-8, 126.2" wb						
4d Sed	350	950	1550	3150	5450	7800
4d HT	350	975	1600	3250	5700	8100
2d HT	400	1200	2000	4000	7000	10,000
2d Conv	700	2150	3600	7200	12,600	18,000
Riviera Series, V-8						
2d GS HT	450	1400	2300	4600	8100	11,500
2d HT	400	1300	2200	4400	7700	11,000

NOTE: Add 20 percent for 400. Not available in Riviera.

1970

	6	5	4	3	2	1
Skylark, V-6, 116" wb, 2 dr 112" wb						
4d Sed	350	820	1400	2700	4760	6800
2d Sed	350	800	1350	2700	4700	6700
Skylark 350, V-6, 116" wb, 2 dr 112" wb						
4d Sed	350	830	1400	2950	4830	6900
2d HT	350	900	1500	3000	5250	7500
Skylark, V-8, 116" wb, 2 dr 112" wb						
4d Sed	350	830	1400	2950	4830	6900
2d Sed	350	820	1400	2700	4760	6800
Skylark 350, V-8, 116" wb, 2 dr 112.2" wb						
4d Sed	350	840	1400	2800	4900	7000
2d HT	350	1020	1700	3400	5950	8500
Skylark Custom, V-8, 116" wb, 2 dr 112" wb						
4d Sed	350	850	1450	2850	4970	7100
4d HT	350	860	1450	2900	5050	7200
2d HT	450	1140	1900	3800	6650	9500
2d Conv	700	2150	3600	7200	12,600	18,000
Gran Sport GS, V-8, 112" wb						
2d HT	500	1550	2600	5200	9100	13,000
Gran Sport GS 455, V-8, 112" wb						
2d HT	550	1700	2800	5600	9800	14,000
2d Conv	700	2300	3800	7600	13,300	19,000

NOTE: Add 40 percent for Stage I 455.

	6	5	4	3	2	1
GSX, V-8, 455, 112" wb						
2d HT	750	2400	4000	8000	14,000	20,000
Sport Wagon, V-8, 116" wb						
2S Sta Wag	350	860	1450	2900	5050	7200
LeSabre, V-8, 124" wb						
4d Sed	350	880	1500	2950	5180	7400
4d HT	350	950	1500	3050	5300	7600
2d HT	350	1020	1700	3400	5950	8500
LeSabre Custom, V-8, 124" wb						
4d Sed	350	900	1500	3000	5250	7500
4d HT	350	950	1550	3100	5400	7700
2d HT	450	1080	1800	3600	6300	9000
2d Conv	550	1700	2800	5600	9800	14,000
LeSabre Custom 455, V-8, 124" wb						
4d Sed	350	950	1550	3100	5400	7700
4d HT	350	975	1600	3200	5600	8000
2d HT	450	1120	1875	3750	6500	9300
Estate Wagon, V-8, 124" wb						
4d 2S Sta Wag	350	900	1500	3000	5250	7500
4d 3S Sta Wag	350	950	1550	3150	5450	7800
Wildcat Custom, V-8, 124" wb						
4d HT	350	975	1600	3200	5500	7900
2d HT	450	1140	1900	3800	6650	9500
2d Conv	550	1800	3000	6000	10,500	15,000
Electra 225, V-8, 127" wb						
4d Sed	350	950	1550	3150	5450	7800
4d HT	350	1000	1650	3300	5750	8200
2d HT	450	1140	1900	3800	6650	9500
Electra Custom 225, V-8, 127" wb						
4d Sed	350	975	1600	3200	5500	7900
4d HT	350	1020	1700	3400	5900	8400
2d HT	400	1200	2000	4000	7000	10,000
2d Conv	700	2300	3800	7600	13,300	19,000
Riviera Series, V-8						
2d GS Cpe	400	1250	2100	4200	7400	10,500
2d HT Cpe	400	1300	2200	4400	7700	11,000

NOTE: Add 40 percent for 455, except in Riviera.

1971-1972

	6	5	4	3	2	1
Skylark, V-8, 116" wb, 2 dr 112" wb						
4d Sed	200	745	1250	2500	4340	6200
2d Sed	200	730	1250	2450	4270	6100
2d HT	350	840	1400	2800	4900	7000
Skylark 350, V-8, 116" wb, 2 dr 112" wb						
4d Sed	350	770	1300	2550	4480	6400
2d HT	350	975	1600	3200	5600	8000
Skylark Custom, V-8						
4d Sed	200	750	1275	2500	4400	6300
4d HT	350	780	1300	2600	4550	6500
2d HT	450	1080	1800	3600	6300	9000
2d Conv	550	1700	2800	5600	9800	14,000
Gran Sport, 350, V-8						
2d HT	500	1550	2600	5200	9100	13,000
2d Conv	700	2150	3600	7200	12,600	18,000
2d HT GSX	750	2400	4000	8000	14,000	20,000

NOTE: Add 40 percent for Stage I & 20 percent for GS-455 options.
Add 15 percent for folding sun roof.

	6	5	4	3	2	1
Sport Wagon, V-8, 116" wb						
4d 2S Sta Wag	200	650	1100	2150	3780	5400
LeSabre						
4d Sed	200	670	1200	2300	4060	5800
4d HT	200	720	1200	2400	4200	6000
2d HT	200	745	1250	2500	4340	6200
LeSabre Custom, V-8						
4d Sed	200	700	1200	2350	4130	5900
4d HT	200	730	1250	2450	4270	6100
2d HT	350	770	1300	2550	4480	6400
2d Conv	500	1550	2600	5200	9100	13,000
Centurion, V-8						
4d HT	200	750	1275	2500	4400	6300
2d HT	350	790	1350	2650	4620	6600
2d Conv	550	1700	2800	5600	9800	14,000
Estate Wagon, V-8, 124" wb						
4d 2S Sta Wag	200	720	1200	2400	4200	6000
4d 3S Sta Wag	200	730	1250	2450	4270	6100
Electra 225, V-8, 127" wb						
4d HT	350	770	1300	2550	4480	6400
2d HT	350	800	1350	2700	4700	6700
Electra Custom 225, V-8						
4d HT	350	780	1300	2600	4550	6500
2d HT	350	840	1400	2800	4900	7000
Riviera, V-8						
2d HT GS	350	1020	1700	3400	5950	8500
2d HT	350	900	1500	3000	5250	7500
Wagons						
4d 2S Wag	200	750	1275	2500	4400	6300
4d 4S Wag	350	770	1300	2550	4480	6400

NOTE: Add 40 percent for 455.

1973

	6	5	4	3	2	1
Apollo, 6-cyl., 111" wb						
4d Sed	200	700	1050	2100	3650	5200
2d Sed	200	650	1100	2150	3780	5400
2d HBk	200	670	1150	2250	3920	5600
Apollo, V-8						
4d Sed	200	700	1075	2150	3700	5300
2d Sed	200	660	1100	2200	3850	5500
2d HBk	200	685	1150	2300	3990	5700
Century, V-8, 116" wb, 2 dr 112" wb						
2d Cpe	200	670	1150	2250	3920	5600
4d Sed	200	660	1100	2200	3850	5500
4d 3S Sta Wag	200	650	1100	2150	3780	5400
Century Luxus, V-8						
4d HT	200	670	1150	2250	3920	5600
2d Cpe	200	685	1150	2300	3990	5700
4d 3S Wag	200	660	1100	2200	3850	5500
Century Regal, V-8						
2d HT	350	780	1300	2600	4550	6500

NOTE: Add 30 percent for Gran Sport pkg. Add 70 percent for GS Stage I, 455 option.

	6	5	4	3	2	1
LeSabre, V-8, 124" wb						
4d Sed	200	700	1050	2050	3600	5100
4d HT	200	700	1050	2100	3650	5200
2d HT	200	660	1100	2200	3850	5500
LeSabre Custom, V-8						
4d Sed	200	685	1150	2300	3990	5700
4d HT	200	670	1200	2300	4060	5800
2d HT	200	750	1275	2500	4400	6300
4d 3S Est Wag	200	685	1150	2300	3990	5700
Centurion, V-8						
4d HT	200	700	1200	2350	4130	5900
2d HT	350	770	1300	2550	4480	6400
2d Conv	400	1250	2100	4200	7400	10,500
Electra 225, V-8, 127" wb						
4d HT	200	720	1200	2400	4200	6000
2d HT	350	800	1350	2700	4700	6700
Electra Custom 225, V-8						
4d HT	200	730	1250	2450	4270	6100
2d HT	350	820	1400	2700	4760	6800
Riviera, V-8						
2d HT GS	350	975	1600	3200	5600	8000
2d HT	350	840	1400	2800	4900	7000

1974

	6	5	4	3	2	1
Apollo, 6-cyl., 111" wb						
4d Sed	200	700	1050	2050	3600	5100
2d Sed	200	700	1050	2050	3600	5100
2d HBk	200	700	1050	2100	3650	5200
Apollo, V-8, 111" wb						
4d Sed	200	745	1250	2500	4340	6200
2d Sed	200	745	1250	2500	4340	6200
2d HBk	200	750	1275	2500	4400	6300
Century, V-8						
2d Cpe	200	670	1150	2250	3920	5600
4d HT	200	660	1100	2200	3850	5500
4d Sta Wag	200	660	1100	2200	3850	5500
Century Luxus, V-8, 112" wb						
2d HT	200	660	1100	2200	3850	5500
4d HT	200	650	1100	2150	3780	5400
4d Sta Wag	200	650	1100	2150	3780	5400
Gran Sport, V-8						
2d Cpe	200	720	1200	2400	4200	6000
Century Regal, V-8, 112" wb						
2d HT	200	730	1250	2450	4270	6100
4d HT	200	670	1200	2300	4060	5800
LeSabre						
4d Sed	200	685	1150	2300	3990	5700

	6	5	4	3	2	1
4d HT	200	670	1200	2300	4060	5800
2d HT	200	700	1200	2350	4130	5900
LeSabre, V-8, 123" wb						
4d Sed	350	790	1350	2650	4620	6600
4d HT	350	800	1350	2700	4700	6700
2d HT	350	830	1400	2950	4830	6900
LeSabre Luxus, V-8, 123" wb						
4d Sed	350	800	1350	2700	4700	6700
4d HT	350	820	1400	2700	4760	6800
2d HT	350	840	1400	2800	4900	7000
2d Conv	400	1200	2000	4000	7000	10,000
Estate Wagon, V-8						
4d Sta Wag	350	820	1400	2700	4760	6800
Electra 225, V-8						
2d HT	350	860	1450	2900	5050	7200
4d HT	350	800	1350	2700	4700	6700
Electra 225 Custom, V-8						
2d HT	350	880	1500	2950	5180	7400
4d HT	350	830	1400	2950	4830	6900
Electra Limited, V-8						
2d HT	350	950	1500	3050	5300	7600
4d HT	350	850	1450	2850	4970	7100
Riviera, V-8						
2d HT	350	900	1500	3000	5250	7500

NOTES: Add 10 percent for Apollo GSX.
Add 10 percent for Century Grand Sport.
Add 15 percent for Century GS-455.
Add 20 percent for GS-455 Stage I.
Add 5 percent for sunroof.
Add 15 percent for Riviera GS or Stage I.

1975

Skyhawk, V-6	6	5	4	3	2	1
2d 'S'HBk	200	700	1075	2150	3700	5300
2d HBk	200	700	1075	2150	3700	5300
Apollo, V-8						
4d Sed	200	700	1050	2100	3650	5200
4d 'SR' Sed	200	700	1075	2150	3700	5300
Skylark, V-8						
2d Cpe	200	650	1100	2150	3780	5400
2d HBk	200	660	1100	2200	3850	5500
2d 'SR' Cpe	200	660	1100	2200	3850	5500
2d 'SR' HBk	200	670	1150	2250	3920	5600
Century, V-8						
4d Sed	200	700	1050	2050	3600	5100
2d Cpe	200	700	1050	2050	3600	5100
4d Cus Sed	200	650	1100	2150	3780	5400
2d Cus Cpe	200	660	1100	2200	3850	5500
4d 2S Sta Wag	200	700	1050	2050	3600	5100
4d 3S Sta Wag	200	700	1050	2100	3650	5200
Regal, V-8						
4d Sed	200	700	1075	2150	3700	5300
2d Cpe	200	700	1075	2150	3700	5300
LeSabre, V-8						
4d Sed	200	650	1100	2150	3780	5400
4d HT	200	670	1150	2250	3920	5600
2d Cpe	200	660	1100	2200	3850	5500
LeSabre Custom, V-8						
4d Sed	200	670	1150	2250	3920	5600
4d HT	200	700	1200	2350	4130	5900
2d Cpe	200	700	1200	2350	4130	5900
2d Conv	400	1200	2000	4000	7000	10,000
Estate Wagon, V-8						
4d 2S Sta Wag	200	685	1150	2300	3990	5700
4d 3S Sta Wag	200	700	1200	2350	4130	5900
Electra 225 Custom, V-8						
4d HT	200	720	1200	2400	4200	6000
2d Cpe	200	745	1250	2500	4340	6200
Electra 225 Limited, V-8						
4d HT	200	730	1250	2450	4270	6100
2d Cpe	350	770	1300	2550	4480	6400
Riviera, V-8						
2d HT	350	780	1300	2600	4550	6500

NOTE: Add 15 percent for Park Avenue DeLuxe.
Add 5 percent for Park Avenue, Century, GS or Riviera GS options.

1976

Skyhawk, V-6	6	5	4	3	2	1
2d HBk	150	575	900	1750	3100	4400
Skylark S, V-8						
2d Cpe	150	600	950	1850	3200	4600
Skylark, V-8						
4d Sed	150	600	950	1850	3200	4600
2d Cpe	150	650	950	1900	3300	4700
2d HBk	150	650	975	1950	3350	4800
Skylark SR, V-8						
4d Sed	150	650	950	1900	3300	4700
2d Cpe	150	650	975	1950	3350	4800
2d HBk	200	675	1000	1950	3400	4900
Century Special, V-6						
2d Cpe	150	600	900	1800	3150	4500
Century, V-8						
4d Sed	200	675	1000	2000	3500	5000
2d Cpe	150	650	950	1900	3300	4700
Century Custom, V-8						
4d Sed	200	700	1050	2100	3650	5200
2d Cpe	150	650	975	1950	3350	4800
4d 2S Sta Wag	150	600	950	1850	3200	4600
4d 3S Sta Wag	150	650	950	1900	3300	4700
Regal, V-8						
4d Sed	200	700	1075	2150	3700	5300
2d Cpe	200	675	1000	1950	3400	4900
LeSabre, V-6						
4d Sed	200	650	1100	2150	3780	5400
4d HT	200	675	1000	2000	3500	5000
2d Cpe	200	700	1050	2050	3600	5100
LeSabre Custom, V-8						
4d Sed	200	660	1100	2200	3850	5500
4d HT	200	700	1050	2100	3650	5200
2d Cpe	200	700	1075	2150	3700	5300
Estate, V-8						
4d 2S Sta Wag	200	660	1100	2200	3850	5500
4d 3S Sta Wag	200	670	1150	2250	3920	5600
Electra 225, V-8						
4d HT	200	685	1150	2300	3990	5700
2d Cpe	200	660	1100	2200	3850	5500
Electra 225 Custom, V-8						
4d HT	200	700	1200	2350	4130	5900
2d Cpe	200	685	1150	2300	3990	5700

298

	6	5	4	3	2	1
Riviera, V-8						
2d Spt Cpe	200	720	1200	2400	4200	6000

NOTE: Deduct 5 percent for 6 cylinder.

1977

Skyhawk, V-6	6	5	4	3	2	1
2d HBk	100	360	600	1200	2100	3000
Skylark S, V-8						
2d Cpe	125	380	650	1300	2250	3200
Skylark, V-8						
4d Sed	125	380	650	1300	2250	3200
2d Cpe	125	400	675	1350	2300	3300
2d HBk	125	400	700	1375	2400	3400
Skylark SR, V-8						
4d Sed	125	400	675	1350	2300	3300
2d Cpe	125	400	700	1375	2400	3400
2d HBk	125	450	700	1400	2450	3500
Century, V-8						
4d Sed	150	500	800	1600	2800	4000
2d Cpe	150	550	850	1650	2900	4100
Century Special, V-6						
2d Cpe	150	550	850	1675	2950	4200
Century Custom, V-8						
4d Sed	150	550	850	1650	2900	4100
2d Cpe	150	550	850	1675	2950	4200
4d 2S Sta Wag	150	500	800	1550	2700	3900
4d 3S Sta Wag	150	500	800	1600	2800	4000
Regal, V-8						
4d Sed	150	575	875	1700	3000	4300
2d Cpe	150	575	900	1750	3100	4400
LeSabre, V-8						
4d Sed	150	550	850	1650	2900	4100
2d Cpe	150	550	850	1675	2950	4200
LeSabre Custom, V-8						
4d Sed	150	550	850	1675	2950	4200
2d Cpe	150	575	875	1700	3000	4300
2d Spt Cpe	150	575	900	1750	3100	4400
Electra 225, V-8						
4d Sed	150	575	900	1750	3100	4400
2d Cpe	150	600	900	1800	3150	4500
Electra 225 Limited, V-8						
4d Sed	150	600	950	1850	3200	4600
2d Cpe	150	650	975	1950	3350	4800
Riviera, V-8						
2d Cpe	200	675	1000	1950	3400	4900

NOTE: Deduct 5 percent for V-6.

1978

Skyhawk	6	5	4	3	2	1
2d 'S' HBk	125	380	650	1300	2250	3200
2d HBk	125	400	700	1375	2400	3400
Skylark						
2d 'S' Cpe	125	400	675	1350	2300	3300
4d Sed	125	400	700	1375	2400	3400
2d Cpe	125	400	700	1375	2400	3400
2d HBk	125	450	700	1400	2450	3500
Skylark Custom						
4d Sed	125	400	700	1375	2400	3400
2d Cpe	125	450	700	1400	2450	3500
2d HBk	125	450	750	1450	2500	3600
Century Special						
4d Sed	125	450	700	1400	2450	3500
2d Cpe	125	450	750	1450	2500	3600
Sta Wag	125	400	700	1375	2400	3400
Century Custom						
4d Sed	125	450	750	1450	2500	3600
2d Cpe	150	475	750	1475	2600	3700
Sta Wag	125	450	700	1400	2450	3500
Century Sport						
2d Cpe	150	500	800	1550	2700	3900
Century Limited						
4d Sed	150	475	775	1500	2650	3800
2d Cpe	150	500	800	1550	2700	3900
Regal						
2d Cpe	150	475	750	1475	2600	3700
Spt Cpe	150	475	775	1500	2650	3800
Regal Limited						
2d Cpe	150	500	800	1600	2800	4000
LeSabre						
4d Sed	150	475	750	1475	2600	3700
2d Cpe	150	475	775	1500	2650	3800
2d Spt Turbo Cpe	150	550	850	1650	2900	4100
LeSabre Custom						
4d Sed	150	475	775	1500	2650	3800
2d Cpe	150	500	800	1550	2700	3900
Estate Wagon						
4d Sta Wag	150	475	750	1475	2600	3700
Electra 225						
4d Sed	150	500	800	1550	2700	3900
2d Cpe	150	550	850	1675	2950	4200
Electra Limited						
4d Sed	150	500	800	1600	2800	4000
2d Cpe	150	600	900	1800	3150	4500
Electra Park Avenue						
4d Sed	150	550	850	1675	2950	4200
2d Cpe	150	650	975	1950	3350	4800
Riviera						
2d Cpe	200	660	1100	2200	3850	5500

NOTE: Deduct 5 percent for 6 cyl.

1979

Skyhawk, V-6	6	5	4	3	2	1
2d HBk	125	450	700	1400	2450	3500
2d 'S' HBk	125	400	700	1375	2400	3400
Skylark 'S', V-8						
2d 'S' Cpe	125	400	675	1350	2300	3300
Skylark, V-8						
4d Sed	125	450	700	1400	2450	3500
2d Cpe	125	450	700	1400	2450	3500
2d HBk	125	450	750	1450	2500	3600
Skylark Custom, V-8						
4d Sed	125	450	750	1450	2500	3600
2d Cpe	125	450	750	1450	2500	3600
Century Special, V-8						
4d Sed	125	450	750	1450	2500	3600
2d Cpe	125	450	700	1400	2450	3500
2d Sta Wag	125	450	750	1450	2500	3600
Century Custom, V-8						
4d Sed	150	475	750	1475	2600	3700

	6	5	4	3	2	1
2d Cpe	125	450	750	1450	2500	3600
4d Sta Wag	150	475	750	1475	2600	3700
Century Sport, V-8						
2d Cpe	150	500	800	1600	2800	4000
Century Limited, V-8						
4d Sed	150	500	800	1550	2700	3900
NOTE: Deduct 7 percent for 6-cyl.						
Regal, V-6						
2d Cpe	150	500	800	1550	2700	3900
Regal Sport Turbo, V-6						
2d Cpe	150	575	900	1750	3100	4400
Regal, V-8						
2d Cpe	150	500	800	1600	2800	4000
Regal Limited, V-8 & V-6						
2d Cpe V-6	150	500	800	1550	2700	3900
2d Cpe V-8	150	550	850	1675	2950	4200
LeSabre, V-8						
4d Sed	150	500	800	1550	2700	3900
2d Cpe	150	475	775	1500	2650	3800
LeSabre Limited, V-8						
4d Sed	150	500	800	1600	2800	4000
2d Cpe	150	500	800	1550	2700	3900
NOTE: Deduct 7 percent for V-6.						
LeSabre Sport Turbo, V-6						
2d Cpe	150	600	900	1800	3150	4500
LeSabre Estate Wagon						
4d Sta Wag	150	500	800	1600	2800	4000
Electra 225, V-8						
4d Sed	150	550	850	1650	2900	4100
2d Cpe	150	575	875	1700	3000	4300
Electra Limited, V-8						
4d Sed	150	575	875	1700	3000	4300
2d Cpe	150	600	950	1850	3200	4600
Electra Park Avenue, V-8						
4d Sed	150	600	950	1850	3200	4600
2d Cpe	200	675	1000	1950	3400	4900
Riviera, V-8						
2d 'S'Cpe	350	975	1600	3200	5600	8000
NOTE: Deduct 10 percent for V-6.						

1980

	6	5	4	3	2	1
Skyhawk, V-6						
2d HBk S	150	475	750	1475	2600	3700
2d HBk	150	475	775	1500	2650	3800
Skylark, V-6						
4d Sed	150	475	775	1500	2650	3800
2d Cpe	150	500	800	1550	2700	3900
4d Sed Ltd	150	500	800	1550	2700	3900
2d Cpe Ltd	150	500	800	1600	2800	4000
4d Sed Spt	150	550	850	1650	2900	4100
2d Cpe Spt	150	550	850	1675	2950	4200
NOTE: Deduct 10 percent for 4-cyl.						
Century, V-8						
4d Sed	125	450	750	1450	2500	3600
2d Cpe	150	475	775	1500	2650	3800
4d Sta Wag Est	150	475	750	1475	2600	3700
2d Cpe Spt	150	500	800	1550	2700	3900
NOTE: Deduct 12 percent for V-6.						
Regal, V-8						
2d Cpe	150	500	800	1550	2700	3900
2d Cpe Ltd	150	500	800	1600	2800	4000
NOTE: Deduct 12 percent for V-6.						
Regal Turbo, V-6						
2d Cpe	200	660	1100	2200	3850	5500
LeSabre, V-8						
4d Sed	150	550	850	1650	2900	4100
2d Cpe	150	550	850	1675	2950	4200
4d Sed Ltd	150	575	875	1700	3000	4300
2d Cpe Ltd	150	575	900	1750	3100	4400
4d Sta Wag Est	150	575	875	1700	3000	4300
LeSabre Turbo, V-6						
2d Cpe Spt	200	675	1000	1950	3400	4900
Electra, V-8						
4d Sed Ltd	150	600	950	1850	3200	4600
2d Cpe Ltd	150	650	950	1900	3300	4700
4d Sed Park Ave	150	650	950	1900	3300	4700
2d Cpe Park Ave	150	650	975	1950	3350	4800
4d Sta Wag Est	200	675	1000	1950	3400	4900
Riviera S Turbo, V-6						
2d Cpe	200	745	1250	2500	4340	6200
Riviera, V-8						
2d Cpe	350	975	1600	3200	5600	8000

1981

	6	5	4	3	2	1
Skylark, V-6						
4d Sed Spt	150	550	850	1675	2950	4200
2d Cpe Spt	150	575	875	1700	3000	4300
NOTE: Deduct 10 percent for 4-cyl. Deduct 5 percent for lesser model.						
Century, V-8						
4d Sed Ltd	150	475	775	1500	2650	3800
4d Sta Wag Est	150	500	800	1550	2700	3900
NOTE: Deduct 12 percent for V-6. Deduct 5 percent for lesser model.						
Regal, V-8						
2d Cpe	150	500	800	1550	2700	3900
2d Cpe Ltd	150	500	800	1600	2800	4000
NOTE: Deduct 12 percent for V-6.						
Regal Turbo, V-6						
2d Cpe Spt	200	670	1150	2250	3920	5600
LeSabre, V-8						
4d Sed Ltd	150	575	875	1700	3000	4300
2d Cpe Ltd	150	575	900	1750	3100	4400
4d Sta Wag Est	150	600	900	1800	3150	4500
NOTE: Deduct 12 percent for V-6 except Estate Wag. Deduct 5 percent for lesser models.						
Electra, V-8						
4d Sed Ltd	150	575	900	1750	3100	4400
2d Cpe Ltd	150	600	900	1800	3150	4500
4d Sed Park Ave	150	600	950	1850	3200	4600
2d Cpe Park Ave	150	650	950	1900	3300	4700
4d Sta Wag Est	150	650	950	1900	3300	4700
NOTE: Deduct 15 percent for V-6 except Estate Wag.						
Riviera, V-8						
2d Cpe	350	975	1600	3200	5600	8000
Riviera, V-6						
2d Cpe	350	900	1500	3000	5250	7500
2d Cpe Turbo T Type	350	950	1550	3100	5400	7700

1982

	6	5	4	3	2	1
Skyhawk, 4-cyl.						
4d Sed Ltd	150	500	800	1550	2700	3900
2d Cpe Ltd	150	500	800	1600	2800	4000
NOTE: Deduct 5 percent for lesser models.						
Skylark, V-6						
4d Sed Spt	150	575	900	1750	3100	4400
2d Cpe Spt	150	600	900	1800	3150	4500
NOTE: Deduct 10 percent for 4-cyl. Deduct 5 percent for lesser models.						
Regal, V-6						
4d Sed	150	575	900	1750	3100	4400
2d Cpe	150	600	900	1800	3150	4500
2d Cpe Turbo	200	660	1100	2200	3850	5500
2d Grand National	850	2650	4400	8800	15,400	22,000
4d Sed Ltd	150	650	950	1900	3300	4700
2d Cpe Ltd	150	650	975	1950	3350	4800
4d Sta Wag	150	650	975	1950	3350	4800
NOTE: Add 10 percent for T-top option.						
Century, V-6						
4d Sed Ltd	200	675	1000	1950	3400	4900
2d Cpe Ltd	200	675	1000	2000	3500	5000
NOTE: Deduct 10 percent for 4-cyl. Deduct 5 percent for lesser models.						
LeSabre, V-8						
4d Sed Ltd	200	675	1000	1950	3400	4900
2d Cpe Ltd	200	675	1000	2000	3500	5000
4d Sta Wag Est	200	675	1000	2000	3500	5000
NOTE: Deduct 12 percent for V-6 except Estate Wag. Deduct 5 percent for lesser models.						
Electra, V-8						
4d Sed Ltd	200	675	1000	1950	3400	4900
2d Cpe Ltd	200	700	1050	2050	3600	5100
4d Sed Park Ave	200	700	1050	2100	3650	5200
2d Cpe Park Ave	200	650	1100	2150	3780	5400
4d Sta Wag Est	200	650	1100	2150	3780	5400
NOTE: Deduct 15 percent for V-6 except Estate Wag.						
Riviera, V-6						
2d Cpe	350	900	1500	3000	5250	7500
2d Cpe T Type	350	950	1550	3150	5450	7800
2d Conv	650	2050	3400	6800	11,900	17,000
Riviera, V-8						
2d Cpe	350	975	1600	3200	5600	8000
2d Conv	700	2150	3600	7200	12,600	18,000

1983

	6	5	4	3	2	1
Skyhawk, 4-cyl.						
4d Sed Ltd	150	550	850	1675	2950	4200
2d Cpe Ltd	150	575	875	1700	3000	4300
4d Sta Wag Ltd	150	575	875	1700	3000	4300
2d Cpe T Type	200	675	1000	1950	3400	4900
NOTE: Deduct 5 percent for lesser models.						
Skylark, V-6						
4d Sed Ltd	150	550	850	1675	2950	4200
2d Cpe Ltd	150	575	875	1700	3000	4300
2d Cpe T Type	200	700	1050	2050	3600	5100
NOTE: Deduct 10 percent for 4-cyl. except T Type. Deduct 5 percent for lesser models.						
Century, V-6						
4d Sed T Type	200	675	1000	2000	3500	5000
2d Cpe T Type	200	660	1100	2200	3850	5500
NOTE: Deduct 12 percent for 4-cyl. except T Type. Deduct 5 percent for lesser models.						
Regal, V-6						
4d Sed T Type	200	670	1200	2300	4060	5800
2d Cpe T Type	200	745	1250	2500	4340	6200
4d Sta Wag	150	650	950	1900	3300	4700
NOTE: Add 10 percent for T-top option. Deduct 5 percent for lesser models.						
LeSabre, V-8						
4d Sed Ltd	200	700	1050	2100	3650	5200
2d Cpe Ltd	200	700	1075	2150	3700	5300
4d Sta Wag	200	700	1075	2150	3700	5300
NOTE: Deduct 12 percent for V-6 except Estate. Deduct 5 percent for lesser models.						
Electra, V-8						
4d Sed Ltd	200	700	1050	2100	3650	5200
2d Cpe Ltd	200	700	1075	2150	3700	5300
4d Sed Park Ave	200	650	1100	2150	3780	5400
2d Cpe Park Ave	200	660	1100	2200	3850	5500
4d Sta Wag Est	200	660	1100	2200	3850	5500
NOTE: Deduct 15 percent for V-6.						
Riviera, V-6						
2d Cpe	350	900	1500	3000	5250	7500
2d Conv	650	2050	3400	6800	11,900	17,000
2d T Type	350	1020	1700	3400	5950	8500
NOTE: Add 20 percent for XX option.						
Riviera, V-8						
2d Cpe	350	1040	1700	3450	6000	8600
2d Conv	700	2150	3600	7200	12,600	18,000

1984

	6	5	4	3	2	1
Skyhawk Limited, 4-cyl.						
4d Sed	150	575	875	1700	3000	4300
2d Sed	150	575	875	1700	3000	4300
4d Sta Wag	150	575	875	1700	3000	4300
NOTE: Deduct 5 percent for lesser models.						
Skyhawk T Type, 4-cyl.						
2d Sed	200	675	1000	2000	3500	5000
Skylark Limited, V-6						
4d Sed	150	575	900	1750	3100	4400
2d Sed	150	600	900	1800	3150	4500
NOTE: Deduct 5 percent for lesser models. Deduct 8 percent for 4-cyl.						
Skylark T Type, V-6						
2d Sed	200	700	1050	2100	3650	5200
Century Limited, 4-cyl.						
NOTE: Deduct 5 percent for lesser models. Deduct 8 percent for 4-cyl.						
Century Limited, V-6						
4d Sed	150	600	900	1800	3150	4500
2d Sed	150	600	950	1850	3200	4600
4d Sta Wag Est	150	600	950	1850	3200	4600
Century T Type, V-6						
4d Sed	200	700	1050	2050	3600	5100
2d Sed	200	670	1150	2250	3920	5600
Regal, V-6						
4d Sed	150	575	900	1750	3100	4400
2d Sed	150	600	900	1800	3150	4500
2d Grand Natl	550	1700	2800	5600	9800	14,000

	6	5	4	3	2	1
Regal Limited, V-6						
4d Sed	150	600	900	1800	3150	4500
2d Sed	150	600	950	1850	3200	4600
Regal T Type, V-6						
2d Sed	200	720	1200	2400	4200	6000
LeSabre Custom, V-8						
4d Sed	200	700	1050	2100	3650	5200
2d Sed	200	700	1050	2100	3650	5200
LeSabre Limited, V-8						
4d Sed	200	700	1075	2150	3700	5300
2d Sed	200	700	1075	2150	3700	5300
NOTE: Deduct 10 percent for V-6 cyl.						
Electra Limited, V-8						
4d Sed	200	670	1150	2250	3920	5600
2d Sed	200	685	1150	2300	3990	5700
4d Est Wag	200	685	1150	2300	3990	5700
Electra Park Avenue, V-8						
4d Sed	200	670	1150	2250	3920	5600
2d Sed	200	685	1150	2300	3990	5700
NOTE: Deduct 10 percent for V-6 cyl.						
Riviera, V-6						
2d Cpe	350	950	1500	3050	5300	7600
2d Conv	650	2100	3500	7000	12,300	17,500
Riviera, V-8						
2d Cpe	350	975	1600	3200	5600	8000
2d Conv	700	2200	3700	7400	13,000	18,500
Riviera T Type, V-6 Turbo						
2d Cpe	350	975	1600	3200	5500	7900
1985						
Skyhawk, 4-cyl.						
4d Sed Ltd	150	575	900	1750	3100	4400
2d Ltd	150	575	900	1750	3100	4400
4d Sta Wag Ltd	150	575	900	1750	3100	4400
2d T Type	200	700	1050	2050	3600	5100
NOTE: Deduct 5 percent for lesser models.						
Skylark, V-6						
4d Cus Sed	150	575	900	1750	3100	4400
4d Sed Ltd	150	600	900	1800	3150	4500
NOTE: Deduct 10 percent for 4-cyl.						
Century, V-6						
4d Sed Ltd	150	600	950	1850	3200	4600
2d Ltd	150	600	950	1850	3200	4600
4d Sta Wag Est	150	650	975	1950	3350	4800
4d Sed T Type	200	660	1100	2200	3850	5500
2d T Type	200	685	1150	2300	3990	5700
NOTE: Deduct 10 percent for 4-cyl. where available.						
Deduct 5 percent for lesser models.						
Somerset Regal, V-6						
2d Cus	150	650	950	1900	3300	4700
2d Ltd	150	650	975	1950	3350	4800
NOTE: Deduct 10 percent for 4-cyl.						
Regal, V-6						
2d	150	600	950	1850	3200	4600
2d Ltd	150	650	950	1900	3300	4700
2d T Type	200	720	1200	2400	4200	6000
2d T Type Grand Natl	450	1450	2400	4800	8400	12,000
LeSabre, V-8						
4d Sed Ltd	200	650	1100	2150	3780	5400
2d Ltd	200	650	1100	2150	3780	5400
4d Sta Wag Est	200	685	1150	2300	3990	5700
4d Electra Sta Wag Est	200	670	1200	2300	4060	5800
NOTE: Deduct 20 percent for V-6.						
Deduct 5 percent for lesser models.						
Electra, V-6						
4d Sed	200	660	1100	2200	3850	5500
2d	200	670	1150	2250	3920	5600
Electra Park Avenue, V-6						
4d Sed	200	670	1150	2250	3920	5600
2d Sed	200	685	1150	2300	3990	5700
Electra T Type, V-6						
4d Sed	200	670	1200	2300	4060	5800
2d	200	700	1200	2350	4130	5900
Riviera T Type, V-6						
2d Turbo	350	975	1600	3200	5500	7900
Riviera, V-8						
2d	350	975	1600	3200	5600	8000
Conv	700	2300	3800	7600	13,300	19,000
NOTE: Deduct 30 percent for diesel where available.						
1986						
Skyhawk, 4-cyl.						
4d Cus Sed	150	575	900	1750	3100	4400
2d Cus Cpe	150	575	875	1700	3000	4300
4d Cus Sta Wag	150	600	900	1800	3150	4500
4d Ltd Sed	150	600	900	1800	3150	4500
2d Cpe Ltd	150	575	900	1750	3100	4400
4d Sta Wag Ltd	150	600	950	1850	3200	4600
2d Spt HBk	150	650	950	1900	3300	4700
2d T-Type HBk	150	650	975	1950	3350	4800
2d T-Type Cpe	150	650	950	1900	3300	4700
Skylark, V-6						
2d Cus Cpe	150	575	900	1750	3100	4400
4d Sed Ltd	150	600	900	1800	3150	4500
Somerset, V-6						
2d Cus Cpe	150	650	975	1950	3350	4800
2d Cpe T Type	200	700	1050	2100	3650	5200
Century Custom						
2d Cpe	200	675	1000	1950	3400	4900
4d Sed	150	650	975	1950	3350	4800
4d Sta Wag	200	675	1000	2000	3500	5000
Century Limited, V-6						
2d Cpe	200	675	1000	2000	3500	5000
4d Sed	200	675	1000	1950	3400	4900
4d Sta Wag	200	700	1050	2050	3600	5100
4d Sed T Type	200	650	1100	2150	3780	5400
Regal, V-6						
2d Cpe, V-8	150	650	950	1900	3300	4700
2d Cpe Ltd, V-8	200	675	1000	1950	3400	4900
2d Cpe T Type	350	975	1600	3200	5600	8000
2d T Type Grand Natl	550	1800	3000	6000	10,500	15,000
LeSabre Custom, V-6						
2d Cpe	200	660	1100	2200	3850	5500
4d Sed	200	650	1100	2150	3780	5400
LeSabre Limited						
2d Cpe Grand Natl	450	1450	2400	4800	8400	12,000
2d Cpe	200	670	1150	2250	3920	5600
4d Sed	200	660	1100	2200	3850	5500
4d Sta Wag Est, V-8	200	720	1200	2400	4200	6000

	6	5	4	3	2	1
Electra, V-6						
2d Cpe	200	670	1150	2250	3920	5600
4d Sed	200	670	1150	2250	3920	5600
Electra Park Avenue, V-6						
2d Cpe	200	685	1150	2300	3990	5700
4d Sed	200	685	1150	2300	3990	5700
4d Sed T Type	200	700	1200	2350	4130	5900
4d Sta Wag Est	200	745	1250	2500	4340	6200
Riviera, V-6						
2d Cpe	350	950	1550	3150	5450	7800
2d Cpe T Type	350	975	1600	3200	5600	8000
NOTES: Add 10 percent for deluxe models.						
Deduct 5 percent for smaller engines where available.						
1987						
Skyhawk, 4-cyl.						
4d Sed	150	575	900	1750	3100	4400
2d Cus Cpe	150	575	875	1700	3000	4300
4d Cus Sta Wag	150	600	900	1800	3150	4500
4d Sed Ltd	150	600	900	1800	3150	4500
4d Sta Wag Ltd	150	600	950	1850	3200	4600
Spt HBk	150	650	950	1900	3300	4700
NOTE: Add 5 percent for Turbo.						
Somerset, 4-cyl.						
2d Cus Cpe	200	675	1000	1950	3400	4900
2d Cpe Ltd	200	675	1000	2000	3500	5000
NOTE: Add 10 percent for V-6.						
Skylark						
4d Cus Sed	150	650	950	1900	3300	4700
4d Sed Ltd	150	650	975	1950	3350	4800
NOTE: Add 10 percent for V-6.						
Century, 4-cyl.						
4d Cus Sed	200	675	1000	1950	3400	4900
2d Cus Cpe	150	650	975	1950	3350	4800
4d Cus Sta Wag	200	675	1000	2000	3500	5000
4d Sed Ltd	200	675	1000	2000	3500	5000
2d Cpe Ltd	200	675	1000	1950	3400	4900
4d Sta Wag Est	200	700	1050	2050	3600	5100
NOTE: Add 10 percent for V-6.						
Regal, V-6						
2d Cpe	200	675	1000	2000	3500	5000
2d Cpe Ltd	200	700	1050	2050	3600	5100
2d Cpe Turbo T	550	1800	3000	6000	10,500	15,000
2d Cpe Turbo T Ltd	600	1900	3200	6400	11,200	16,000
2d Cpe Turbo Grand Natl	750	2400	4000	8000	14,000	20,000
2d Cpe GNX	1250	3950	6600	13,200	23,100	33,000
Regal, V-8						
2d Cpe	200	670	1200	2300	4060	5800
2d Cpe Ltd	200	700	1200	2350	4130	5900
LeSabre, V-6						
4d Sed	200	660	1100	2200	3850	5500
4d Cus Sed	200	670	1150	2250	3920	5600
2d Cus Cpe	200	660	1100	2200	3850	5500
2d Cpe T Type	200	685	1150	2300	3990	5700
LeSabre, V-8						
4d Sta Wag	200	730	1250	2450	4270	6100
Electra, V-6						
4d Sed Ltd	200	670	1200	2300	4060	5800
4d Sed Park Ave	200	720	1200	2400	4200	6000
2d Cpe Park Ave	200	700	1200	2350	4130	5900
4d Sed T Type	200	720	1200	2400	4200	6000
Electra, V-8						
4d Sta Wag Est	200	745	1250	2500	4340	6200
Riviera, V-6						
2d Cpe	350	975	1600	3200	5600	8000
2d Cpe T Type	350	1000	1650	3300	5750	8200
1988						
Skyhawk, 4-cyl.						
4d Sed	150	600	950	1850	3200	4600
2d Cpe	150	600	900	1800	3150	4500
2d Cpe SE	150	650	975	1950	3350	4800
4d Sta Wag	150	650	950	1900	3300	4700
Skylark, 4-cyl.						
4d Cus Sed	150	650	950	1900	3300	4700
2d Cus Cpe	150	650	975	1950	3350	4800
4d Sed Ltd	150	650	975	1950	3350	4800
2d Cpe Ltd	200	675	1000	1950	3400	4900
NOTE: Add 10 percent for V-6.						
Century, 4-cyl.						
4d Cus Sed	150	650	950	1900	3300	4700
2d Cus Cpe	150	650	975	1950	3350	4800
4d Cus Sta Wag	200	675	1000	1950	3400	4900
4d Sed Ltd	150	650	975	1950	3350	4800
2d Cpe Ltd	200	675	1000	1950	3400	4900
4d Sta Wag Ltd	200	675	1000	2000	3500	5000
NOTE: Add 10 percent for V-6.						
Regal, V-6						
2d Cus Cpe	200	720	1200	2400	4200	6000
2d Cpe Ltd	350	780	1300	2600	4550	6500
LeSabre, V-6						
2d Cpe	200	660	1100	2200	3850	5500
4d Cus Sed	200	720	1200	2400	4200	6000
2d Cpe Ltd	200	750	1275	2500	4400	6300
4d Sed Ltd	200	745	1250	2500	4340	6200
2d Cpe T Type	350	770	1300	2550	4480	6400
4d Sta Wag, V-8	350	790	1350	2650	4620	6600
Electra, V-6						
4d Sed Ltd	350	780	1300	2600	4550	6500
4d Sed Park Ave	350	860	1450	2900	5050	7200
4d Sed T Type	350	840	1400	2800	4900	7000
4d Sta Wag, V-8	350	950	1550	3100	5400	7700
Riviera, V-6						
2d Cpe	350	880	1500	2950	5180	7400
2d Cpe T Type	350	1000	1650	3300	5750	8200
Reatta, V-6						
2d Cpe	400	1300	2200	4400	7700	11,000
1989						
Skyhawk, 4-cyl.						
4d Sed	150	650	975	1950	3350	4800
2d Cpe	150	650	950	1900	3300	4700
2d SE Cpe	200	700	1050	2100	3650	5200
4d Sta Wag	200	675	1000	2000	3500	5000
Skylark, 4-cyl.						
2d Cus Cpe	200	675	1000	2000	3500	5000
2d Cpe Ltd	200	700	1050	2100	3650	5200
4d Cus Sed	200	650	1100	2150	3780	5400
4d Sed Ltd	200	670	1150	2250	3920	5600

	6	5	4	3	2	1
Skylark, V-6						
2d Cus Cpe	200	700	1050	2050	3600	5100
2d Cpe Ltd	200	700	1075	2150	3700	5300
4d Cus Sed	200	660	1100	2200	3850	5500
4d Sed Ltd	200	685	1150	2300	3990	5700
Century, 4-cyl.						
4d Cus Sed	200	700	1050	2100	3650	5200
4d Sed Ltd	200	650	1100	2150	3780	5400
2d Cus	200	700	1075	2150	3700	5300
4d Cus Sta Wag	200	670	1150	2250	3920	5600
4d Sta Wag Ltd	200	685	1150	2300	3990	5700
Century, V-6						
4d Cus Sed	200	700	1075	2150	3700	5300
4d Sed Ltd	200	660	1100	2200	3850	5500
2d Cus	200	650	1100	2150	3780	5400
4d Cus Sta Wag	200	685	1150	2300	3990	5700
4d Sta Wag Ltd	200	670	1200	2300	4060	5800
Regal, V-6						
2d Cus	350	820	1400	2700	4760	6800
2d Ltd	350	830	1400	2950	4830	6900
LeSabre, V-6						
2d	350	820	1400	2700	4760	6800
2d Ltd	350	830	1400	2950	4830	6900
2d T Type	350	900	1500	3000	5250	7500
4d Cus	350	800	1350	2700	4700	6700
4d Ltd	350	820	1400	2700	4760	6800
4d Sta Wag, V-8	350	860	1450	2900	5050	7200
Electra, V-6						
4d Sed Ltd	350	975	1600	3200	5500	7900
4d Park Ave	450	1050	1800	3600	6200	8900
4d Park Ave Ultra	400	1300	2200	4400	7700	11,000
4d T Type	350	1020	1700	3400	5950	8500
4d Sta Wag, V-8	450	1140	1900	3800	6650	9500
Riviera, V-6						
2d Cpe	450	1080	1800	3600	6300	9000
Reatta, V-6						
2d Cpe	400	1300	2200	4400	7700	11,000

1990

	6	5	4	3	2	1
Skylark, 4-cyl.						
2d Cpe	200	660	1100	2200	3850	5500
4d Sed	200	670	1150	2250	3920	5600
2d Cus Cpe	200	685	1150	2300	3990	5700
4d Cus Sed	200	670	1200	2300	4060	5800
2d Gran Spt Cpe	200	720	1200	2400	4200	6000
4d LE Sed	200	720	1200	2400	4200	6000

NOTE: Add 10 percent for V-6 where available.

	6	5	4	3	2	1
Century, 4-cyl.						
2d Cus	350	780	1300	2600	4550	6500
4d Cus	350	790	1350	2650	4620	6600
4d Cus Sta Wag	350	820	1400	2700	4760	6800
4d Ltd Sed	350	820	1400	2700	4760	6800
4d Ltd Sta Wag	350	840	1400	2800	4900	7000

NOTE: Add 10 percent for V-6 where available.

	6	5	4	3	2	1
Regal, V-6						
2d Cus Cpe	350	900	1500	3000	5250	7500
2d Ltd Cpe	350	975	1600	3200	5600	8000
LeSabre, V-6						
2d Cpe	350	975	1600	3200	5600	8000
4d Cus Sed	350	975	1600	3250	5700	8100
2d Ltd Cpe	350	1020	1700	3400	5950	8500
4d Ltd Sed	350	1040	1700	3450	6000	8600
Estate, V-8						
4d Sta Wag	450	1080	1800	3600	6300	9000
Electra, V-6						
4d Ltd Sed	450	1080	1800	3600	6300	9000
4d Park Ave	450	1140	1900	3800	6650	9500
4d Ultra Sed	450	1450	2400	4800	8400	12,000
4d T Type Sed	450	1140	1900	3800	6650	9500
Riviera, V-6						
2d Cpe	450	1140	1900	3800	6650	9500
Reatta, V-6						
2d Cpe	400	1300	2200	4400	7700	11,000
2d Conv	600	1900	3200	6400	11,200	16,000

1991

	6	5	4	3	2	1
Skylark, 4-cyl.						
2d Cpe	200	675	1000	2000	3500	5000
4d Sed	200	700	1050	2050	3600	5100
2d Cus Cpe	200	700	1050	2050	3600	5100
4d Cus Sed	200	700	1050	2100	3650	5200
2d Gran Spt Cpe	200	660	1100	2200	3850	5500
4d LE Sed	200	670	1150	2250	3920	5600

NOTE: Add 10 percent for V-6 where available.

	6	5	4	3	2	1
Century, 4-cyl.						
4d Spl Sed	200	700	1050	2050	3600	5100
4d Cus Sed	200	700	1050	2100	3650	5200
2d Cus Cpe	200	700	1050	2050	3600	5100
4d Cus Sta Wag	200	650	1100	2150	3780	5400
4d Ltd Sed	200	700	1075	2150	3700	5300
4d Ltd Sta Wag	200	670	1150	2250	3920	5600

NOTE: Add 10 percent for V-6 where available.

	6	5	4	3	2	1
Regal, V-6						
4d Cus Sed	350	770	1300	2550	4480	6400
2d Cus Cpe	200	750	1275	2500	4400	6300
4d Ltd Sed	350	790	1350	2650	4620	6600
2d Ltd Cpe	350	780	1300	2600	4550	6500
LeSabre, V-6						
2d Cpe	350	820	1400	2700	4760	6800
4d Cus Sed	350	830	1400	2950	4830	6900
4d Ltd Sed	350	880	1500	2950	5180	7400
2d Ltd Cpe	350	870	1450	2900	5100	7300
Roadmaster, V-8						
4d Est Sta Wag	450	1140	1900	3800	6650	9500
Park Avenue, V-6						
4d Sed	350	1020	1700	3400	5950	8500
4d Ultra Sed	450	1080	1800	3600	6300	9000
Riviera, V-6						
2d Cpe	450	1140	1900	3800	6650	9500
Reatta, V-6						
2d Cpe	500	1550	2600	5200	9100	13,000
2d Conv	650	2050	3400	6800	11,900	17,000

ILLINOIS

Chicagoland Chapter
PO Box 863
Arlington Heights, IL 60006

Gateway Buick Club
423 W. Legion
Columbia, IL 62236

INDIANA

Central Indiana Chapter
4082 Rocking Chair Rd.
Greenwood, IN 46142

IOWA

Hawkeye Chapter
RD 2
Searsboro, IA 50242

KANSAS

Mid America Chapter
216 S. Chestnut
Olathe, KS 66061

KENTUCKY

Bluegrass Chapter
8019 Huntsman Trail
Louisville, KY 40291

MARYLAND

B.O.O.M. Chapter
226 Sudbrook Ln.
Baltimore, MD 21208

MASSACHUSETTS

Central New England Chapter
26 Riverview Terrace
Springfield, MA 01108

Minute Man Chapter
92 Deerfield Rd.
Sharon, MA 02067

MICHIGAN

Buicktown Chapter
4287 Underhill Dr.
Flint, MI 48506

Central Michigan Chapter
196 Hidden Forest
Battle Creek, MI 49017

Southeast Michigan Chapter
6945 Hubbard Hill
Clarkston, MI 48016

West Michigan Chapter
6070 10 Mile Rd. NE
Rockford, MI 49341

Water Wonderland Chapter
7910 Sprinkle Rd.
Kalamazoo, MI 49002

MINNESOTA

Fireball Chapter
PO Box 24776
Edina, MN 55424

Gopher State Chapter
976 W. Minnehaha
St. Paul, MN 55104

MISSOURI

St. Louis Gateway Chapter
1770 Patterson Rd.
Florissant, MO 63031

NEBRASKA

Crossroads Chapter
9346 Monroe St.
Omaha, NE 68127

NEW JERSEY

Jersey Shore Chapter
2425 Cedar St.
Manasquan, NJ 08736

North Jersey Chapter
67 Myrtle Ave.
Butler, NJ 07405

NEW YORK

Central New York Chapter
114 Byrne Place
Syracuse, NY 13205

Empire State Chapter
PO Box 337
Pound Ridge, NY 10576

Finger Lakes Chapter
70 Eileen Dr.
Rochester, NY 14616

Long Island Chapter
21 Dorothy Dr.
Syosset, NY 11791

Niagara Frontier
7264 Townline Rd.
North Tonawanda, NY 14120

OHIO

Akron-Canton Chapter
357 Mark Dr.
Tallmadge, OH 44278

Central Ohio Chapter
842 Mission Hills Ln.
Columbus, OH 43235

Glass City Chapter
Rt. 2, 15-375-127-39
Bryan, OH 43506

Northeastern Ohio Chapter
18337 Fairville Ave.
Cleveland, OH 44135

Southwestern Ohio Chapter
8529 Clough Pk.
Cincinnati, OH 45244

Youngstown Buicks of Yesteryear Chapter
529 E. Judson Ave.
Youngstown, OH 44502

OREGON

Portland Area Chapter
8920 SE 73rd Ave.
Portland, OR 97206-9349

PENNSYLVANIA

Appalachian Chapter
233½ W. Brady St.
Butler, PA 16001

Free Spirit Chapter
1424 Elliott Ave.
Bethlehem, PA 18018

Mason Dixon Chapter
74 Ensminger Ln.
Jacobus, PA 17407

Northwest Pennsylvania Chapter
990 Boyer Rd.
Erie, PA 16511

National Pike Chapter
385 Leonard Ave.
Washington, PA 15301

Philadelphia '76 Chapter
8116 Burholme Ave.
Philadelphia, PA 19111

SOUTH CAROLINA

Dixie Chapter
PO Box 614
Clemson, SC 29633

TENNESSEE

Music City Chapter
5829 Beauregard Dr.
Nashville, TN 37215

TEXAS

Lone Star Chapter
14021 Stoneshire
Houston, TX 77060

North Texas Chapter
322 Canyon Ridge Dr.
Richardson, TX 75080

VIRGINIA

Northern Virginia Chapter
728 Hope Rd.
Stafford, VA 23520

Old Dominion Chapter
8311 Trabue Rd.
Richmond, VA 23235

WASHINGTON

Inland Northwest Chapter
E1814 S. Riverton, Apt. B-104
Spokane, WA 99207

North Cascade Chapter
18824 84th W.
Edmonds, WA 98026

Puget Sound Chapter
2725 SW 347th St.
Federal Way, WA 98023

WASHINGTON, D.C.

Metro Chapter
6204 Lone Oak Dr.
Bethesda, MD 20817

WISCONSIN

Cream City Chapter
PO Box 27372
West Allis, WI 53227

Dairyland Chapter
Rt. 4, 1755 Kavanaugh Rd.
Kaukauna, WI 54130

Rock Valley Chapter
Rt. 1, Box 200
Evansville, WI 53536

FOREIGN

Buick Club of America, England Chapter
47 Higham Rd.
Woodford Green, Essex, England

Buick Club of America, Niagara Frontier Chapter
PO Box 220
Crystal Beach, Ontario, LOS 1BO Canada

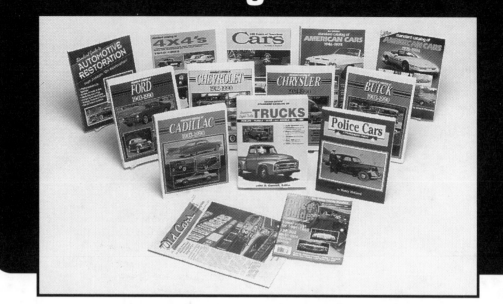